סידור קורן אני תפילה לשבת • נוסח אשכנז

The Koren Ani Tefilla Shabbat Siddur • Nusaḥ Ashkenaz

קורן ירושלים

THE LOBEL EDITION

סידור קורן
אני תפילה לשבת

THE KOREN
ANI TEFILLA SHABBAT SIDDUR

טוב
להודות
לד׳
ולזמר
לשמך
עליון

WITH TRANSLATION BY

Rabbi Lord Jonathan Sacks שליט״א

AND COMMENTARY BY

Rabbi Dr. Jay Goldmintz

•

KOREN PUBLISHERS JERUSALEM

The Koren Ani Tefilla Shabbat Siddur
The Lobel Edition
First North American Hebrew/English Edition, 2016

Koren Publishers Jerusalem Ltd.
POB 4044, Jerusalem 9104001, ISRAEL
POB 8531, New Milford, CT 06776, USA

www.korenpub.com

The English translation and commentary in this edition are based on the English translation and commentary first published in Great Britain in 2006 in the Authorised Daily Prayer Book of the United Hebrew Congregations of the Commonwealth: New Translation and Commentary by Chief Rabbi Jonathan Sacks, (Fourth Edition, Compilation © United Synagogue) by Collins, a division of HarperCollins Publishers, London.

The Koren Siddur Alef-Beit Chart with its distinct font, is an adaptation of NJOP's Alef-Beit Chart that was created by Florence Wiener, NJOP's Hebrew Reading Specialist, and dedicated in loving memory of her parents, Isak and Esther Bauman, Yitzchak Ben Yaakov Simcha and Esther Bat Yitzchak Isaac, ז״ל. The Alef-Beit Chart with its clever mnemonic devices has been the foundation for NJOP's highly successful Hebrew Reading Crash Courses that have been offered throughout North America and in forty additional countries throughout the world, free of charge. Contact NJOP at 800-44 HEBRE(W) or info@njop.org to find a Hebrew Reading Crash Course near you.

Standard Size, Hardcover, Nusaḥ Ashkenaz, ISBN 978 965 301 685 9
Compact Size, Softcover, Nusaḥ Ashkenaz, ISBN 978 965 301 866 2

ATSACOM02

The Lobel Edition
of this
Koren Siddur
is dedicated to all those who seek,
through prayer, to understand and connect
to the special gift that is Shabbat.

May your prayers be speedily answered
and be a source of blessing
for each of you, your families,
and Klal Yisrael.

The Lobel Family
New York, USA

CONTENTS

PREFACE

"One generation will praise Your works to the next…"

We are pleased to introduce the *Koren Ani Tefilla Shabbat Siddur*, a dedicated Shabbat Siddur that combines the sublime English translation of Rabbi Lord Jonathan Sacks, with extensive elucidating commentary by Rabbi Jay Goldmintz.

This is a unique Siddur that aims to open the gates of Jewish prayer for the newcomer, and simultaneously reveal the depths of *tefilla* for the more experienced. The need for this became apparent following discussions with leaders of beginners' *Shabbat Minyanim*, who sought not only instructions for participants – many siddurim achieve this, including our own Koren Sacks Siddur – but also to bring an understanding of practice, Halakha, the reasons behind the words, and how prayer relates directly to the individual. In response to this need, we found that a new approach to *tefilla*, from the perspective of the unhabituated, opened fresh vistas over the ancient landscape of the liturgy, views that were just as novel to the seasoned worshiper.

It is always a privilege to collaborate on a project with those who share our commitment and enthusiasm for bringing out the beauty of *tefilla*. We are grateful to Judith and David Lobel for their support and proud to have their name grace this edition. On behalf of the scholars, editors and designers of this volume, we thank you; on behalf of the users of this Siddur, we are forever in your debt.

We must thank Rabbi Ephraim Buchwald of Lincoln Square Synagogue, for his counsel. Rabbi Buchwald is one of the leaders in the movement of Jewish return in America today, and has, since 1975, led the now renowned "Beginners Service," a special Shabbat service for people with little or no synagogue experience. We thank also Rabbi Elie Weinstock and Mr. George Rohr of Kehillat Jeshurun. All were especially helpful with practical and useful advice in bringing this Siddur to fruition. And we are, of course, indebted to Rabbi Lord Sacks for his continual inspiration in thought, word, and deed.

Rabbi Jay Goldmintz draws upon a distinguished career as an educator and leader, with special talents for making prayer – one of the hardest subjects to teach – universally relevant to all. We thank him for this monumental achievement.

We thank the highly professional team at Koren Publishers Jerusalem, including Rabbi Dr. Daniel Rose – who oversaw the project – Esther Be'er, and Rachel Meghnagi, whose work in designing and editing this volume continues to advance the aim of Koren's founder, Eliyahu Koren, "to present to worshipers a means to draw and connect them not only to the words of the prayers, but also to the contents and meaning that were before our sages when engraving the phrases of the prayers, and our rabbis throughout the ages when compiling versions of the prayers."

We hope this new edition of a Koren classic will enhance the experience of Shabbat for Jews everywhere.

Matthew Miller, Publisher
Jerusalem 5775 (2014)

FOREWORD

Philosophers speculate about God. Scientists argue about God. Theologians theorize about God. We as Jews do something simpler and ultimately more profound. We talk to God. We bring Him our thanks and our hopes, our fears and our dreams. That conversation is what we call prayer, and Jews have engaged in it ever since the days of Abraham. The Siddur, the book you have in your hand, grew out of those conversations. Every time we pray we become part of the long dialogue between earth and heaven that has lasted now for almost four thousand years. Prayer was our ancestors' source of strength, and when we learn to pray it becomes ours also.

This new Siddur was designed for those of you who wonder why we pray as we do, why in these words not those, how the various elements that make up a service relate to each other, and how these ancient texts relate to us in the present, in the immediacy of our lives. I hope you will enjoy this new Koren edition with its multiple commentaries and beautiful design. I wish it had existed when I started my journey, but in those days we tended to take prayer for granted. We prayed because Jews pray. Our parents did. So did our grandparents. So did countless generations before them. We didn't ask questions. We didn't read commentaries. We just prayed, often not really understanding what we were doing. I think that the new approach is better, because the more we understand what we say, the more deeply we enter into the act of prayer, and the more profoundly it changes us.

If I were to try to summarize briefly what prayer is, I would call it a journey in three stages. The first stage is *opening our eyes to wonder*. We are here, but we might not have been. The universe exists in almost infinite dimensions, as does the earth in all its sublime beauty. Scientists are just beginning to understand how finely tuned the universe had to be for stars, planets and life to emerge. Biologists, having mapped the human genome, are just beginning to understand how complex the human body

◂ is. There

is. There is wonder here, and the opening sequences of prayer give expression to that wonder in the majestic poetry we call *Pesukei DeZimra,* "the verses of praise." In these poems, mostly taken from the last chapters of *Sefer Tehillim,* we move from creation to the Creator, from the universe to God, Architect of the universe. It is almost as if we were taking a rocket journey into space, seeing the earth in all its beauty while traveling beyond it.

The second stage, beginning with *Barekhu* and ending with *Kaddish Titkabal* after the *Amida,* is *approaching the presence of God.* This is a difficult idea and each of us has to find our own way of thinking about it. Imagine this, for example. You have been invited to meet the President (or King or Queen) of your country. It is a huge honor, and as the day approaches, you find yourself full of excitement. You prepare yourself. You dress in your best clothes. You rehearse exactly how you are going to conduct yourself and what you are going to say. The day comes. You enter the building. You are taken through many rooms and corridors until you finally find yourself face to face with the most powerful person in the country. You have to pinch yourself to make sure that this is really happening; it is not just a dream. Whatever is said and whatever is left unsaid, the memory of that encounter will stay with you for a lifetime.

That, multiplied a billion times over, is what it means to be in the presence of God. Only the fact that we do it several times a day, every day, takes away some of the wonder. Yet that is what is happening when, for example, we say the *Amida.* We are having a direct, personal encounter with the Creator of the universe. God, who has seven billion people to worry about, three million other life forms, and a hundred billion galaxies, *cares about us,* personally and individually. That may just be the most remarkable, empowering idea in the entire history of human thought. We matter. We count. God created us in love, and in love He listens to us as we declare our needs and ask for His help. In that moment we are rescued from insignificance and powerlessness. We are here because we are loved by God Himself. If we are fully open to it – and this may take years of practice and concentration – that encounter is life-changing.

Finally, from the second *Ashrei* to *Aleinu,* we come back down to earth, a little different than we were before we began the journey. We have seen

◂ the beauty

the beauty of the created world. We have had a personal meeting with the Creator Himself. And now we know there is work to do, because there is much in the world around us that is not as it should be. There is poverty, sickness, loneliness and injustice. People are cruel to one another. There is too much conflict and too little love. God wants us to bring a little of His light into other people's lives. He wants us to become "His partners in the work of creation." He has given us a sacred mission, to show by the way we live that God exists and that His existence makes a difference. Meeting God helps us become, in some small way, a little more like God, by doing acts of *tzedek umishpat, ḥesed veraḥamim*, righteousness and justice, kindness and compassion. We are small; God is great. But by opening ourselves to One so much greater than us, we become greater than we would have been if all we cared about was ourselves.

Those are the three phases of *Shaḥarit*, the Morning Prayer, and they correspond to the three ways in which we come to know God: through *creation* (the universe and its wonders), *revelation* (direct experience of the Divine Presence), and *redemption* (God's work in making the world more loving and just). *Minḥa* and *Ma'ariv*, the Afternoon and Evening prayers, have a somewhat different and more abridged structure.

Prayer matters. It changes the world because it changes us. It brings the Divine Presence into our lives and gives us strength we didn't know we had. It is to the soul (the mind, the self, our inner life) what exercise is to the body. Like exercise, it is important that we do it daily at set times, and like exercise, it makes us healthier (though in a different way) and more highly charged with positive energy. Prayer aligns us with the creative energies that run through the universe, the energies we call life and love, the supreme gifts of God.

So I hope you use this Siddur not just to pray but also to reflect on what we are doing when we pray. May God hear and answer all your prayers, and may we be worthy of the great challenge He has set us: of being His children, His ambassadors, His partners in creating a world worthy of His Presence. May He bless us, helping us to become a blessing to those whose lives we touch.

Rabbi Lord Jonathan Sacks
Tammuz 5774 (July 2014)

INTRODUCTION

It was when I was in my late teenage years when I first read a description of Shabbat that helped change the way that I felt about it and ultimately celebrated it. Until that point, Shabbat had seemed like a series of prohibitions, things that one was not permitted to do because God rested on that day. And because He rested, I was not allowed to watch TV or go see a movie, or play music, or turn on lights so I could read or relax. In short, His rest, as it were, seemed to get in the way of my notion of rest, and there were times when it felt like anything but relaxation.

The essay I read, however, suggested that the prohibitions were only one part of the story. In fact, they were there as a supporting prop to the essence of what Shabbat is all about, namely, relationships.

One relationship was between myself and others. In an age when work seems to consume us, when we spend disproportionately large amounts of our time at school or on the job, there seems to be less and less time for the most important people in our lives. Try to add up the amount of time that husbands and wives or parents and children speak to one another during the week, about things having nothing to do with routines and household chores and the like, but rather about bigger things that matter: issues or ideas or feelings or hopes or beliefs. Years ago, that number was small indeed and today one can find surveys that measure not only how much time families speak to one another but how much time they spend just being with one another during the work week – a little more than a half hour in total. One doesn't need studies, however, to know what many of us already intuit; there just isn't enough quality time to spend with the people we care about, be they family or friends. Shabbat is an antidote to that as one day a week no one can run away to watch a show, make some calls, use computers, go to the office or to one's desk to finish up some work. Rather, with its emphasis on long meals filled with conversation and song, with its focus on community worship and celebration, Shabbat is a guarantor of never losing touch.

◂ A second

A second relationship that Shabbat highlighted was between me and myself. Precisely because we are such driven and creative beings, our focus in life can always seem like it is predominantly outer-directed. We are forever barraged by messages from those who want our attention, we are always alert to the opportunities and challenges that lie before us, we are often sensitive to the ways in which we are perceived or want to be perceived by others. All the more so when technology itself has made greater and greater demands on our time and attention. Indeed, there is evidence to suggest that the more engrossed we become with contact with the world outside ourselves, the less comfortable we become with our own internal world. People who are deprived of their computers or mobile devices, for example, can become agitated and disoriented. Being alone with oneself can be harder and harder to do. But being alone with oneself is an important ingredient to growth and to relieving stress in one's life. It is certainly an opportunity to catch up on one's sleep, an important factor not to be underestimated or undervalued. But it is also an opportunity to sit back, to stop time as it were, and to ask myself what's it all for, what do I like about the way my life is going, the way my last week went, and how I would like next week to shape up differently. Shabbat is that opportunity, an antidote to not having the time to reflect and take care of oneself. It is that one day a week when we take the time out to draw on our own inner resources, to become more inner-directed, to take stock, so that we may live the rest of the week with greater perspective and balance.

Finally, in addition to the relationship between myself and others, and between me and myself, there is also the relationship between me and God. What, after all, is your relationship with God? Are you comfortable with it? Do you think about it at all? Have you grown lately? Have you nurtured it? Even if you attend synagogue services or pray the requisite three times a day during the week, chances are that you are hurried or harried, that you don't always have the time to spend in conversation with God as you should or as you could. Some of us never really felt comfortable talking to God directly and to some it has even been a barrier to observance. Others among us live a religiously observant lifestyle but working on a personal connection with God can be divorced from the day-to-day rituals and practices that we have adopted; we are observant

◂ but not as

but not as religious or spiritual as we would like to be. Some of us have a hard time giving the relationship the time it deserves during the week, we pray but we do not always live such a prayerful life.

While prayer is not the only medium through which to nurture one's relationship with the Creator, it is surely one of the most obvious and it is no wonder, then, that Shabbat is a time when services are longer than during the rest of the week. There is more time to help us clear our heads of distractions, more opportunity to help us dig deeper into our experiences and our perceptions of the world, and into the role that God plays in our individual and collective lives.

In that context, the siddur plays a critical role. For it was never intended as a formulaic standardized text to be recited blindly and automatically, as if the words were a magic incantation that would bring instantaneous results. Rather, it is filled with signposts and trail markers, reminders to recall what we should hold dear and what we believe to be true. It is a book that is meant to educate as well as remind us about fundamental beliefs of Judaism and about God and our relationship with Him. Its very name, *siddur*, from the Hebrew word for "order," points to its being a roadmap, taking us on a step-by-step journey to the palace, to a rendezvous with the Creator in a most intimate and personal way. In the process, we hopefully walk away with a renewed sense of the presence of God in our lives and we are transformed.

Along the way, the siddur also provides opportunities for insights into ourselves. If we peer into it carefully and deliberately we can see reflections of our true selves, the way we are and the way we hope to be. It enables us to judge ourselves. It also enables us to reorder our priorities and to come to a better understanding of our needs as opposed to our wants. Formulating all of these in the presence of the Creator, we have no choice but to be anything but honest. In the search for God, then, we can also find ourselves.

Similarly, in its constant use of the plural as opposed to the singular, the siddur reminds us that we are not alone but are members of a larger community of souls who are on the same journey as we are, who also seek a relationship with God. There is hardly a generation in Jewish history that has not left its imprint upon the siddur's composition, and, mindful of that, we connect ourselves to Jews across the millennia. At the same time, it reminds us of our fellow travelers in the here and now and of our ability to support one another, how we should treat one another, and how we can respond to one another. In the search for God, then, we can also find the companionship of fellow men.

What thus began as a focus on our relationship with God, also turns out to further develop the cause of improving, deepening and expanding our relationship with ourselves and with others. The siddur becomes a microcosm of the Shabbat experience as a whole.

The road signs that greet us on this journey, however, are not always easily intelligible to the uninitiated reader, for the language and intention can be difficult to understand, even in translation. And so I devised this commentary not as a comprehensive explanation of the siddur but merely as a guide to enable one to find one's own way to the palace. While the words of the prayers are usually to be taken literally, that is not necessarily their only meaning. They are but cloaks for the true intention which can only come from the heart. As the Jewish philosopher Rabbeinu Baḥye ibn Pakuda wrote in the eleventh century: "Know that the words one is forming with his tongue are like the shell and the meditation on the words is like the fruit, [or] that the uttering of the prayer is like the body, and the meditation is like the soul." The goal, then, is to use the words as a portal to the outpouring of the heart.

In this endeavor I cannot say that I have exhausted all of the possibilities, for there are probably almost as many possibilities as there are people. I can only share some of the paths that I have taken and the ones that have become meaningful for me. Hopefully, this will serve as a stepping stone for your own journey. In this context, the story told in the name of the Hasidic leader Rabbi Ḥayyim of Sanz may be instructive. Once a man lost his way in a great forest. He searched for a way out, but each path he took only led him deeper into the woods. Eventually he heard the sound of someone approaching. His heart lifted. He waited till the other approached and asked him to show him the way out. "I do not know," said the other, "for I too am lost. But this I can tell you. Do not take the way I have been taking for it will lead you astray. And now let us search for a new way together." The rabbi lifted up his eyes to his followers, and they understood.

* * *

◂ The commentary

The commentary is actually divided into four sections, each with its own emphasis. In addition, there are a number of features that have been added to the siddur, each of which is explained below.

BIUR TEFILLA – ביאור תפילה

The *Biur Tefilla* helps in gaining a thorough understanding of the text and context of the prayers. It examines the micro-understanding of a specific word or phrase in the text of the *Tefilla,* as well as presenting a wider understanding of the historical background of the *Tefilla,* and its place in the context of the overall structure of the service. Such comments are noted in the text with a [B] or [ב].

IYUN TEFILLA – עיון תפילה

Iyun Tefilla explores the deeper meaning behind the *tefillot,* taking a broader approach to the text. It presents a macro-understanding of the prayers, including philosophical and theological approaches to *Tefilla* in general and the text in particular. Such comments are noted in the text with the letter [I] or [ע].

HILKHOT TEFILLA – הלכות תפילה

This section ensures that one is aware of the ritual requirements surrounding the mitzva to pray. These comments are interspersed throughout the Siddur as well as concentrated in an appendix at the back which focuses on the laws of daily prayer and changes that need to be made during the course of the year. Such comments are noted int he text with the letter [H] or [ה].

ANI TEFILLA – אני תפילה

The expressed aim of the *Ani Tefilla* sections is to encourage connection to the *tefillot* in a direct and personal way. It is hoped this will be achieved through encouraging the reader to consider the prayers in an experiential way through inspiring and thought-provoking quotes and narratives, as well as through a process of personal creative thinking.

The name for this section derives from a statement made by King David in *Tehillim* 109:4 which says: וַאֲנִי תְפִלָּה (*ve'ani tefilla*). This could be translated as "I pray"; but it could also mean "I am prayer." At its best, prayer is an extension of the person who says it. It is shaped by who you are and what thoughts, emotions, memories, moods, feelings and expression you bring to it. The words of the Siddur, then, are not only

◂ to be taken

to be taken literally, they are also signposts to help generate the range of thoughts and emotions and associations that reside within you on any given day. Think and feel beyond the words. These comments are noted in the text with an [A] or [א].

KEVOD VE'ONEG SHABBAT

There are two categories of the laws of Shabbat that relate to the positive commandments (as opposed to the negative commandments or prohibitions, so called because they are expressed in terms of things which one may not do). These positive commandments relate to the honor (*kavod*) one gives Shabbat (and God) by preparing for it in advance, and the pleasure (*oneg*) with which one is supposed to enjoy the day itself. Since prayer is often an outgrowth of the passionate relationship one has with Shabbat itself, we have included an appendix which consists of a brief explanation of these commandments through a contemporary lens.

We recognize that not everyone who opens the Siddur will have the same level of comfort interacting with the text. Toward that end, we have included some other features which are intended to enhance and eventually deepen one's prayer experience.

TRANSLATION

In a similar vein, I am honored to include the accessible and elegant translation of Rabbi Lord Jonathan Sacks, which improves upon its predecessors in so many ways. Even so, it should be recalled that translations, of necessity, are often interpretations as well and so the more one learns Hebrew, the more one can provide one's own alternatives.

GLOSSARY

Rather than use English terms throughout the commentary, we have used the original names of classic books and terms in transliteration and have appended a glossary of the meanings of these terms at the back of the Siddur. It is our hope that this will help the novice to more quickly and easily become familiar with these terms which are the building blocks of a literate Jewish life.

ALEF BEIT

For those who are just beginning the task of learning Hebrew, we have appended a Hebrew alphabet reading chart designed and shared by the

National Jewish Outreach Project. Hebrew is referred to as *lashon kodesh*, the holy tongue, for with it the Torah was given. It is quite different from many other languages in that it is made up of cognates, root words upon which other words are built. Thus, for example, the Hebrew word for blessing (*berakha* – an acknowledgment of expansion) shares similarities with the word for knee (*berekh* – as when one prostrates oneself) and perhaps too the word for a spring (*bereikha*), an expanding source of water. Knowledge of Hebrew thus expands the possibilities of meaning which in turn provides the heart with greater means of expression. Learning to read and eventually understand Hebrew are the building blocks not only of a literate life but a more meaningful one as well.

KERIAT SHEMA TRANSLITERATION

Given the central importance of the Shema to Jewish life as explained in the commentary, we thought it important that the novice who had little familiarity with Hebrew could still read those passages in the original, perhaps as a way too of starting on the path toward greater Hebrew literacy. That transliteration appears in an appendix at the back of the book.

AUTHORS CITED

The commentary draws on numerous sources, some traditional, some not. Brief biographies of the authors cited are appended in order to give one a sense of the person in his or her historical context. Every effort has been made to provide proper attribution. If there have been omissions or errors, please let us know.

Acknowledgments

Projects of this scope cannot be written in a vacuum and I am grateful to some old friends and new ones for their help in shaping my thinking about a commentary that would speak to different audiences. Rabbis Elie Weinstock and Daniel Kraus all gave generously of their time and insight born of experience. Particular thanks are due to Rabbi Effie Buchwald, one of the pioneers of Jewish outreach in America, an educator par excellence whose passion and sensitivity about all things Jewish are infectious.

Rabbi Dr. Daniel Rose, the Director of Educational Projects at Koren, is the primary person with whom I began this journey. He specifically contributed the summary of the Torah readings for *Minḥa* and the transliteration of the *Shema* which appear in the appendix but more generally he served as a constant sounding board when there were decisions to be made at various turns in the road. Rabbi David Fuchs reviewed the material for content with a care, precision and wit that saved me from myself more than once and I am forever thankful for the serious scholarship and insight he brought to the task. Rachel Meghnagi reviewed the manuscript as she has in the past with what I have come to learn is an extraordinarily keen eye and felicitous touch, skills she brought to bear not only on the text but often on its substance as well. Esther Be'er is the one who is responsible for the many compliments that have come my way for the design of the work thereby providing a pleasing aesthetic experience which complements the spiritual. Matthew Miller, Publisher of Koren, continues to provide an exciting catalyst and home for innovative and important works which might otherwise not have seen the light of day.

The work is dedicated to the memory of my father-in-law Werner Rosenbaum, Aharon Meir ben Menaḥem ז״ל, a gentleman and a scholar, a survivor of the Shoah who never saw himself as such, a man of profound humility who cast a giant shadow. His appreciation for the need to preserve one's *minhag* or family tradition, especially but not exclusively in prayer, was an inspiration to both those who did not have such a tradition and those who did not always appreciate what they had. His deep love of books can be found in many of the sources from my shelves cited in this work. His deep love of God and his ability to see the hand of God in current events found expression in prayer and the way he lived his life. His love of science and his curiosity about the world of ideas found a religious voice in the words in this book that he uttered with such devotion. His sense of integrity and honesty were a beacon to which all were attracted to seek his sagacious counsel. And, above all else, he was a man of peace; like his namesake Aharon the High Priest, he was an *ohev shalom verodef shalom*, a lover and pursuer of peace, a man who not only prayed but lived a prayerful life. *Yehi zikhro barukh* – May his memory be for a blessing, for my mother-in-law, for their children, their grandchildren, their great-grandchildren and all those who use this Siddur in the search for a personal relationship with the Divine.

Rabbi Jay Goldmintz
Teaneck, NJ
Tammuz 5774 (July 2014)

THE STRUCTURE OF THE SHABBAT MORNING PRAYERS

SHAḤARIT

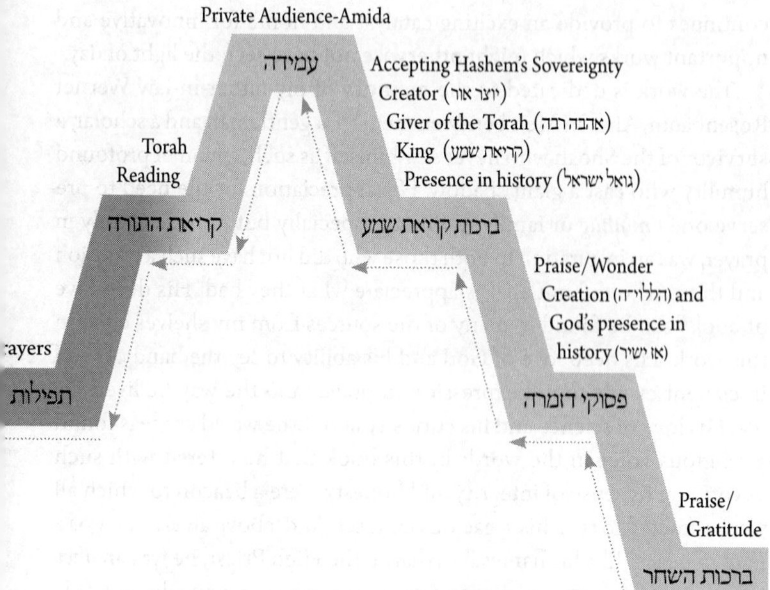

The name of the prayerbook, *siddur*, comes from the Hebrew word *seder* which means order or sequence. The implication is that despite what might seem to the uninitiated like a disconnected collection of liturgical compositions, is in fact an intricate arrangement designed to not only help direct one's thoughts and feelings but to help generate them as well. The diagram above gives an overview of that progression in the Shabbat morning service.

◂ In truth

MUSAF

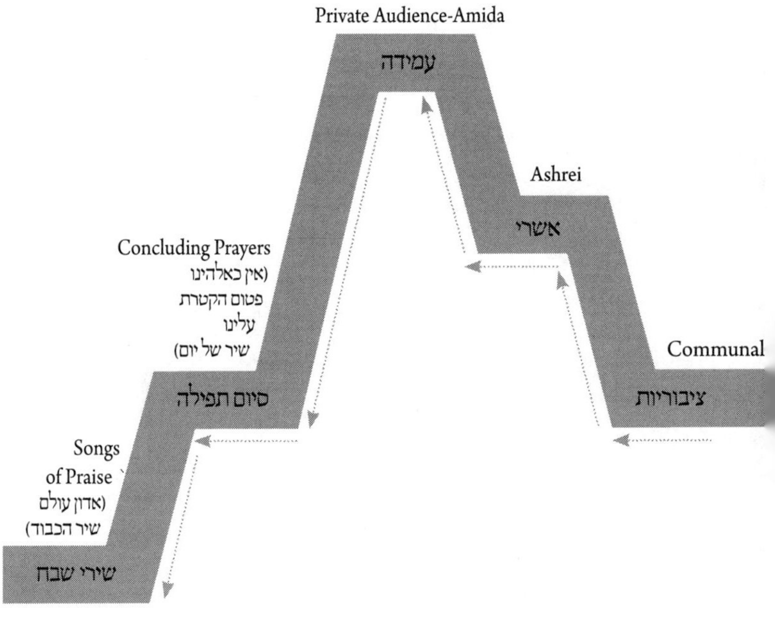

In truth, there are really two services that take place, the Shabbat morning *Shaḥarit* and the special additional service called *Musaf*. As we shall see, there were times when the two were separate but today they have generally been combined into one, thus accounting for the ups and downs of the overall theme of a rendezvous with the Divine.

אני תפילה לשבת

ANI TEFILLA FOR SHABBAT

Minḥa for Erev Shabbat

אַשְׁרֵי Happy[B] are those who dwell in Your House; Ps. 84
they shall continue to praise You, Selah!
Happy are the people for whom this is so; Ps. 144
happy are the people whose God is the Lord.
A song of praise by David. Ps. 145

א I will elevate You, my God, the King, and bless Your name for ever and all time. ב Every day I will bless You, and praise Your name for ever and all time. ג Great is the Lord and greatly to be praised; His greatness is unfathomable. ד One generation will praise Your works to the next, and tell of Your mighty deeds. ה On the glorious splendor of Your majesty I will meditate, and on the acts of Your wonders. ו They shall talk of the power of Your awesome deeds, and I will tell of Your greatness. ז They shall recite the record of Your great goodness, and sing with joy of Your righteousness. ח The Lord is generous and compassionate, slow to anger and great in loving-kindness. ט The Lord is good to all, and His compassion extends to all His works. י All Your works shall thank You, Lord, and Your devoted ones shall bless You. כ They shall talk of the glory of Your kingship, and speak of Your might. ל To make known to

---

close together is to bring the same or even greater devotion and intent to both of them. After all, to the extent that some prayers are repeated in both services, there may be a sense that "I just said these same words a few minutes ago." On Friday afternoon and evening, however, there is no such concern. For the core of the central prayer of *Minḥa* is filled with requests, the kind that occupy our thoughts and worries throughout the week, concerns for health and material success, for our present and for our future. On Shabbat, however, as we shall see, our focus shifts and our perspective changes. Seen in this light, *Minḥa* becomes an opportunity to purge ourselves, as it were, of our weekly concerns and apprehensions. Give voice to them one more time, have faith that you have been heard and although come Saturday night they may be there still, your view of them may be very different. Hang in there, Shabbat is coming.

BIUR TEFILLA • ביאור תפילה

אַשְׁרֵי – *Happy are those.* The prayer itself is essentially *Tehillim* (Psalms) 145 yet the Rabbis curiously added a couple of lines at the beginning which come from other

This **BIUR TEFILLA** *continues on page 4.*

מנחה לערב שבת

אַשְׁרֵי יוֹשְׁבֵי בֵיתֶךָ, עוֹד יְהַלְלְוּךָ סֶּלָה: תהלים פד
אַשְׁרֵי הָעָם שֶׁכָּכָה לּוֹ, אַשְׁרֵי הָעָם שֶׁיהוה אֱלֹהָיו: תהלים קמד
תְּהִלָּה לְדָוִד תהלים קמה

א אֲרוֹמִמְךָ אֱלוֹהַי הַמֶּלֶךְ, וַאֲבָרְכָה שִׁמְךָ לְעוֹלָם וָעֶד:
ב בְּכָל־יוֹם אֲבָרְכֶךָּ, וַאֲהַלְלָה שִׁמְךָ לְעוֹלָם וָעֶד:
ג גָּדוֹל יהוה וּמְהֻלָּל מְאֹד, וְלִגְדֻלָּתוֹ אֵין חֵקֶר:
ד דּוֹר לְדוֹר יְשַׁבַּח מַעֲשֶׂיךָ, וּגְבוּרֹתֶיךָ יַגִּידוּ:
ה הֲדַר כְּבוֹד הוֹדֶךָ, וְדִבְרֵי נִפְלְאֹתֶיךָ אָשִׂיחָה:
ו וֶעֱזוּז נוֹרְאֹתֶיךָ יֹאמֵרוּ, וּגְדוּלָּתְךָ אֲסַפְּרֶנָּה:
ז זֵכֶר רַב־טוּבְךָ יַבִּיעוּ, וְצִדְקָתְךָ יְרַנֵּנוּ:
ח חַנּוּן וְרַחוּם יהוה, אֶרֶךְ אַפַּיִם וּגְדָל־חָסֶד:
ט טוֹב־יהוה לַכֹּל, וְרַחֲמָיו עַל־כָּל־מַעֲשָׂיו:
י יוֹדְוּךָ יהוה כָּל־מַעֲשֶׂיךָ, וַחֲסִידֶיךָ יְבָרְכוּכָה:
כ כְּבוֹד מַלְכוּתְךָ יֹאמֵרוּ, וּגְבוּרָתְךָ יְדַבֵּרוּ:
ל לְהוֹדִיעַ לִבְנֵי הָאָדָם גְּבוּרֹתָיו, וּכְבוֹד הֲדַר מַלְכוּתוֹ:

INTRODUCTION TO MINḤA

The Rabbis decreed that we should pray three times a day, evening, morning and afternoon. Each of these prayers originated with the Patriarchs but each also finds its parallel in an aspect of the sacrificial service from the times of the *Beit HaMikdash* (the Temple). The afternoon prayer is thus called *Minḥa,* an offering, from the biblical word for a "gift" which was brought daily at dusk (*Berakhot* 26b). At the same time, this particular prayer is also identified with the Patriarch Yitzḥak, who went out to meditate in the field (*Bereshit* 24:63) during the daytime. Interestingly, it is Yitzḥak who also offered himself as a sacrifice during the so-called Binding of Isaac (*Bereshit* 22), a metaphor that might be helpful in terms of entering the correct mindset for prayer.

While the correct time to pray *Minḥa* is earlier in the day, the custom of convenience in many communities is to wait until just before the earliest time that one can pray *Ma'ariv* (the evening service) thereby saving an extra trip to the synagogue and ensuring that one can always pray with the requisite quorum. But the challenge in praying two different but similar services so

mankind His mighty deeds and the glorious majesty of His kingship. מ Your kingdom is an everlasting kingdom, and Your reign is for all generations. ס The Lord supports all who fall, and raises all who are bowed down. ע All raise their eyes to You in hope, and You give them their food in due season. פ You open Your hand, and satisfy every living thing with favor. צ The Lord is righteous in all His ways, and kind in all He does. ק The Lord is close to all who call on Him, to all who call on Him in truth. ר He fulfills the will of those who fear Him; He hears their cry and saves them. ש The Lord guards all who love Him, but all the wicked He will destroy. ת ▸ My mouth shall speak the praise of the Lord, and all creatures shall bless His holy name for ever and all time.

We will bless the Lord now and for ever. Halleluya! *Ps. 115*

In Ashkenazi communities many have the custom to stand for Kaddish because of the holiness associated with the sanctification of Hashem's name in the prayer in general and in the central response by the congregation in particular. (In Sephardic communities the custom is to sit, while others have the custom to remain standing if they are already doing so.)

HALF KADDISH

Leader: יִתְגַּדַּל Magnified and sanctified may His great name be,
in the world He created by His will.
May He establish His kingdom
in your lifetime and in your days,
and in the lifetime of all the house of Israel,
swiftly and soon – and say: Amen.

All: May His great name be blessed for ever and all time.

Leader: Blessed and praised, glorified and exalted,
raised and honored, uplifted and lauded
be the name of the Holy One, blessed be He,
beyond any blessing, song, praise and consolation
uttered in the world – and say: Amen.

---

tehillim. Why the addition? Rav Soloveitchik suggested that if one looks, for example, at the context of the first line one will see that it was spoken by those who had made a pilgrimage to the *Beit HaMikdash*. Amidst the pageantry and the holiness of the place, they felt a closeness to God that was difficult to recreate in any other place. Sensing what they were about to lose by going home, they uttered words of longing to be among

This **BIUR TEFILLA** *continues on page 7.*

מ מַלְכוּתְךָ מַלְכוּת כָּל־עֹלָמִים, וּמֶמְשַׁלְתְּךָ בְּכָל־דּוֹר וָדֹר:

ס סוֹמֵךְ יהוה לְכָל־הַנֹּפְלִים, וְזוֹקֵף לְכָל־הַכְּפוּפִים:

ע עֵינֵי־כֹל אֵלֶיךָ יְשַׂבֵּרוּ, וְאַתָּה נוֹתֵן־לָהֶם אֶת־אָכְלָם בְּעִתּוֹ:

פ פּוֹתֵחַ אֶת־יָדֶךָ, וּמַשְׂבִּיעַ לְכָל־חַי רָצוֹן:

צ צַדִּיק יהוה בְּכָל־דְּרָכָיו, וְחָסִיד בְּכָל־מַעֲשָׂיו:

ק קָרוֹב יהוה לְכָל־קֹרְאָיו, לְכֹל אֲשֶׁר יִקְרָאֻהוּ בֶאֱמֶת:

ר רְצוֹן־יְרֵאָיו יַעֲשֶׂה, וְאֶת־שַׁוְעָתָם יִשְׁמַע, וְיוֹשִׁיעֵם:

ש שׁוֹמֵר יהוה אֶת־כָּל־אֹהֲבָיו, וְאֵת כָּל־הָרְשָׁעִים יַשְׁמִיד:

◂ ת תְּהִלַּת יהוה יְדַבֶּר פִּי, וִיבָרֵךְ כָּל־בָּשָׂר שֵׁם קָדְשׁוֹ לְעוֹלָם וָעֶד:

וַאֲנַחְנוּ נְבָרֵךְ יָהּ מֵעַתָּה וְעַד־עוֹלָם, הַלְלוּיָהּ: תהלים קטו

In Ashkenazi communities many have the custom to stand for קדיש *because of the holiness associated with the sanctification of Hashem's name in the prayer in general and in the central response by the congregation in particular. (In Sephardic communities the custom is to sit, while others have the custom to remain standing if they are already doing so.)*

חצי קדיש

ש״ץ: יִתְגַּדַּל וְיִתְקַדַּשׁ שְׁמֵהּ רַבָּא (קהל: אָמֵן)

בְּעָלְמָא דִּי בְרָא כִרְעוּתֵהּ וְיַמְלִיךְ מַלְכוּתֵהּ

בְּחַיֵּיכוֹן וּבְיוֹמֵיכוֹן וּבְחַיֵּי דְכָל בֵּית יִשְׂרָאֵל

בַּעֲגָלָא וּבִזְמַן קָרִיב, וְאִמְרוּ אָמֵן. (קהל: אָמֵן)

קהל וש״ץ: יְהֵא שְׁמֵהּ רַבָּא מְבָרַךְ לְעָלַם וּלְעָלְמֵי עָלְמַיָּא.

ש״ץ: יִתְבָּרַךְ וְיִשְׁתַּבַּח וְיִתְפָּאַר וְיִתְרוֹמַם וְיִתְנַשֵּׂא

וְיִתְהַדָּר וְיִתְעַלֶּה וְיִתְהַלָּל

שְׁמֵהּ דְּקֻדְשָׁא בְּרִיךְ הוּא (קהל: בְּרִיךְ הוּא)

לְעֵלָּא מִן כָּל בִּרְכָתָא / בעשרת ימי תשובה: לְעֵלָּא לְעֵלָּא מִכָּל בִּרְכָתָא/

וְשִׁירָתָא, תֻּשְׁבְּחָתָא וְנֶחֱמָתָא

דַּאֲמִירָן בְּעָלְמָא, וְאִמְרוּ אָמֵן. (קהל: אָמֵן)

THE AMIDA

The following prayer, until "in former years" on page 24, is said silently, standing with feet together.

Take three steps forward.

When I proclaim the LORD's name, give glory to our God. Deut. 32

O LORD, open my lips, so that my mouth may declare Your praise. Ps. 51

PATRIARCHS

▼ *Bend the knees:* Blessed *Bow:* are You, *Stand straight:* LORD
our God and God of our fathers,
God of Abraham, God of Isaac and God of Jacob;
the great, mighty and awesome God, God Most High,
who bestows acts of loving-kindness and creates all,
who remembers the loving-kindness of the fathers
and will bring a Redeemer to their children's children
for the sake of His name, in love.

These words are added between Rosh HaShana & Yom Kippur: Remember us for life, O King who desires life,
and write us in the book of life –
for Your sake, O God of life.

King, Helper, Savior, Shield:
▼ *Bend the knees:* Blessed *Bow:* are You, *Stand straight:* LORD,
Shield of Abraham.

DIVINE MIGHT

אַתָּה גִּבּוֹר You are eternally mighty, LORD.
You give life to the dead and have great power to save.

The phrase "He makes the wind blow and the rain fall" is added from Simḥat Torah until Pesaḥ. In Israel the phrase "He causes the dew to fall" is added from Pesaḥ until Shemini Atzeret.

In fall & winter: He makes the wind blow and the rain fall.

In Israel, in spring & summer: He causes the dew to fall.

---

to have that kind of intimate relationship with Him. It is, in effect, a way of psyching ourselves, if you will, for prayer is not always an easy thing to do. It requires preparing ourselves for the encounter for which we long. It is, then, a prayer that we be able to pray.

עמידה

The following prayer, until קַדְמֹנִיּוֹת *on page 25, is said silently, standing with feet together. If there is a* מנין, *the* עמידה *is repeated aloud by the* שליח ציבור.

Take three steps forward.

כִּי שֵׁם יהוה אֶקְרָא, הָבוּ גֹדֶל לֵאלֹהֵינוּ: דברים לב
אֲדֹנָי, שְׂפָתַי תִּפְתָּח, וּפִי יַגִּיד תְּהִלָּתֶךָ: תהלים נא

אבות

▼ *Bend the knees* בָּרוּךְ *Bow* אַתָּה *Stand straight* יהוה
אֱלֹהֵינוּ וֵאלֹהֵי אֲבוֹתֵינוּ
אֱלֹהֵי אַבְרָהָם, אֱלֹהֵי יִצְחָק, וֵאלֹהֵי יַעֲקֹב
הָאֵל הַגָּדוֹל הַגִּבּוֹר וְהַנּוֹרָא, אֵל עֶלְיוֹן
גּוֹמֵל חֲסָדִים טוֹבִים, וְקוֹנֵה הַכֹּל
וְזוֹכֵר חַסְדֵי אָבוֹת
וּמֵבִיא גוֹאֵל לִבְנֵי בְנֵיהֶם לְמַעַן שְׁמוֹ בְּאַהֲבָה.

בעשרת ימי תשובה: זָכְרֵנוּ לְחַיִּים, מֶלֶךְ חָפֵץ בַּחַיִּים
וְכָתְבֵנוּ בְּסֵפֶר הַחַיִּים, לְמַעַנְךָ אֱלֹהִים חַיִּים.

מֶלֶךְ עוֹזֵר וּמוֹשִׁיעַ וּמָגֵן.
▼ *Bend the knees* בָּרוּךְ *Bow* אַתָּה *Stand straight* יהוה, מָגֵן אַבְרָהָם.

גבורות

אַתָּה גִּבּוֹר לְעוֹלָם, אֲדֹנָי
מְחַיֵּה מֵתִים אַתָּה, רַב לְהוֹשִׁיעַ

The phrase מַשִּׁיב הָרְוּחַ *is added from* שמחת תורה *until* פסח.
In ארץ ישראל *the phrase* מוֹרִיד הַטָּל *is added from* פסח *until* שמיני עצרת.

בחורף: מַשִּׁיב הָרְוּחַ וּמוֹרִיד הַגֶּשֶׁם / בארץ ישראל בקיץ: מוֹרִיד הַטָּל

---

those who could reside in God's House forever. The line from that psalm was added to our prayer, said the Rav, to reflect our own longing to be in the presence of the Divine,

He sustains the living with loving-kindness,
and with great compassion revives the dead.
He supports the fallen, heals the sick, sets captives free,
and keeps His faith with those who sleep in the dust.
Who is like You, Master of might,
and who can compare to You,
O King who brings death and gives life,
and makes salvation grow?

These words are added between Rosh HaShana & Yom Kippur: Who is like You, compassionate Father,
who remembers His creatures
in compassion, for life?

Faithful are You to revive the dead.
Blessed are You, LORD, who revives the dead.

When saying the Amida silently, continue with "You are holy" on the next page.

KEDUSHA

During the Leader's Repetition, the following is said standing with feet together, rising on the toes at the words indicated by ˄.

Cong. then Leader: נְקַדֵּשׁ We will sanctify Your name on earth,
as they sanctify it in the highest heavens,
as is written by Your prophet,
"And they [the angels] call to one another saying: *Is. 6*

Cong. then Leader: ˄Holy, ˄holy, ˄holy is the LORD of hosts
the whole world is filled with His glory."
Those facing them say "Blessed – "

Cong. then Leader: ˄"Blessed is the LORD's glory from His place." *Ezek. 3*
And in Your holy Writings it is written thus:

Cong. then Leader: ˄"The LORD shall reign for ever. He is your God, Zion, *Ps. 146*
from generation to generation, Halleluya!"

Leader: From generation to generation we will declare Your greatness,
and we will proclaim Your holiness for evermore.
Your praise, our God, shall not leave our mouth forever,
for You, God, are a great and holy King. Blessed are You, LORD,
the holy God. / *Between Rosh HaShana & Yom Kippur:* the holy King./

The Leader continues with "You grace humanity" on the next page.

מְכַלְכֵּל חַיִּים בְּחֶסֶד, מְחַיֵּה מֵתִים בְּרַחֲמִים רַבִּים
סוֹמֵךְ נוֹפְלִים, וְרוֹפֵא חוֹלִים, וּמַתִּיר אֲסוּרִים
וּמְקַיֵּם אֱמוּנָתוֹ לִישֵׁנֵי עָפָר.
מִי כָמְוֹךָ, בַּעַל גְּבוּרוֹת
וּמִי דּוֹמֶה לָּךְ
מֶלֶךְ, מֵמִית וּמְחַיֶּה וּמַצְמִיחַ יְשׁוּעָה.

בעשרת ימי תשובה: מִי כָמְוֹךָ אַב הָרַחֲמִים
זוֹכֵר יְצוּרָיו לְחַיִּים בְּרַחֲמִים.

וְנֶאֱמָן אַתָּה לְהַחֲיוֹת מֵתִים.
בָּרוּךְ אַתָּה יהוה, מְחַיֵּה הַמֵּתִים.

When saying the עמידה *silently, continue with* אַתָּה קָדוֹשׁ *on the next page.*

קדושה

During the חזרת הש״ץ, *the following is said standing with feet together, rising on the toes at the words indicated by* ˄.

then קהל ש״ץ: נְקַדֵּשׁ אֶת שִׁמְךָ בָּעוֹלָם, כְּשֵׁם שֶׁמַּקְדִּישִׁים אוֹתוֹ בִּשְׁמֵי מָרוֹם
כַּכָּתוּב עַל יַד נְבִיאֶךָ: וְקָרָא זֶה אֶל־זֶה וְאָמַר ישעיה ו

then קהל ש״ץ: ˄קָדוֹשׁ, ˄קָדוֹשׁ, ˄קָדוֹשׁ, יהוה צְבָאוֹת, מְלֹא כָל־הָאָרֶץ כְּבוֹדוֹ:
לְעֻמָּתָם בָּרוּךְ יֹאמֵרוּ

then קהל ש״ץ: ˄בָּרוּךְ כְּבוֹד־יהוה מִמְּקוֹמוֹ: יחזקאל ג
וּבְדִבְרֵי קָדְשְׁךָ כָּתוּב לֵאמֹר

then קהל ש״ץ: ˄יִמְלֹךְ יהוה לְעוֹלָם, אֱלֹהַיִךְ צִיּוֹן לְדֹר וָדֹר, הַלְלוּיָהּ: תהלים קמו

ש״ץ: לְדוֹר וָדוֹר נַגִּיד גָּדְלֶךָ, וּלְנֵצַח נְצָחִים קְדֻשָּׁתְךָ נַקְדִּישׁ
וְשִׁבְחֲךָ אֱלֹהֵינוּ מִפִּינוּ לֹא יָמוּשׁ לְעוֹלָם וָעֶד
כִּי אֵל מֶלֶךְ גָּדוֹל וְקָדוֹשׁ אָתָּה.
בָּרוּךְ אַתָּה יהוה, הָאֵל הַקָּדוֹשׁ./ בעשרת ימי תשובה: הַמֶּלֶךְ הַקָּדוֹשׁ./

The שליח ציבור *continues with* אַתָּה חוֹנֵן *on the next page.*

HOLINESS

אַתָּה קָדוֹשׁ You are holy and Your name is holy,
and holy ones praise You daily, Selah!
Blessed are You, LORD,
the holy God. / *Between Rosh HaShana & Yom Kippur:* the holy King./
(*If forgotten, repeat the Amida.*)

KNOWLEDGE

אַתָּה חוֹנֵן You grace humanity with knowledge
and teach mortals understanding.
Grace us with the knowledge, understanding
and discernment that come from You.
Blessed are You, LORD,
who graciously grants knowledge.

REPENTANCE

הֲשִׁיבֵנוּ Bring us back, our Father, to Your Torah.
Draw us near, our King, to Your service.
Lead us back to You in perfect repentance.
Blessed are You, LORD,
who desires repentance.

FORGIVENESS

Strike the left side of the chest at °.

סְלַח לָנוּ Forgive us, our Father, for we have °sinned.
Pardon us, our King, for we have °transgressed;
for You pardon and forgive.
Blessed are You, LORD,
the gracious One who repeatedly forgives.

REDEMPTION

רְאֵה Look on our affliction, plead our cause,
and redeem us soon for Your name's sake,
for You are a powerful Redeemer.
Blessed are You, LORD,
the Redeemer of Israel.

קדושת השם

אַתָּה קָדוֹשׁ וְשִׁמְךָ קָדוֹשׁ
וּקְדוֹשִׁים בְּכָל יוֹם יְהַלְלוּךָ סֶּלָה.
בָּרוּךְ אַתָּה יהוה, הָאֵל הַקָּדוֹשׁ./ בעשרת ימי תשובה: הַמֶּלֶךְ הַקָּדוֹשׁ./
(*If forgotten, repeat the* עמידה.)

דעת

אַתָּה חוֹנֵן לְאָדָם דַּעַת, וּמְלַמֵּד לֶאֱנוֹשׁ בִּינָה.
חָנֵּנוּ מֵאִתְּךָ דֵּעָה בִּינָה וְהַשְׂכֵּל.
בָּרוּךְ אַתָּה יהוה, חוֹנֵן הַדָּעַת.

תשובה

הֲשִׁיבֵנוּ אָבִינוּ לְתוֹרָתֶךָ, וְקָרְבֵנוּ מַלְכֵּנוּ לַעֲבוֹדָתֶךָ
וְהַחֲזִירֵנוּ בִּתְשׁוּבָה שְׁלֵמָה לְפָנֶיךָ.
בָּרוּךְ אַתָּה יהוה, הָרוֹצֶה בִּתְשׁוּבָה.

סליחה

Strike the left side of the chest at °.

סְלַח לָנוּ אָבִינוּ כִּי °חָטָאנוּ
מְחַל לָנוּ מַלְכֵּנוּ כִּי °פָשָׁעְנוּ
כִּי מוֹחֵל וְסוֹלֵחַ אָתָּה.
בָּרוּךְ אַתָּה יהוה, חַנּוּן הַמַּרְבֶּה לִסְלֹחַ.

גאולה

רְאֵה בְעָנְיֵנוּ, וְרִיבָה רִיבֵנוּ
וּגְאָלֵנוּ מְהֵרָה לְמַעַן שְׁמֶךָ
כִּי גּוֹאֵל חָזָק אָתָּה.
בָּרוּךְ אַתָּה יהוה, גּוֹאֵל יִשְׂרָאֵל.

HEALING

רְפָאֵנוּ Heal us, LORD, and we shall be healed.
Save us and we shall be saved,
for You are our praise.
Bring complete recovery for all our ailments,

The following prayer for a sick person may be said here:
May it be Your will, O LORD my God and God of my ancestors, that You speedily send a complete recovery from heaven, a healing of both soul and body, to the patient (*name*), son/daughter of (*mother's name*) among the other afflicted of Israel.

for You, God, King, are a faithful and compassionate Healer.
Blessed are You, LORD, Healer of the sick of His people Israel.

PROSPERITY

The phrase "Grant dew and rain as a blessing" is said from December 5th (in the year before a civil leap year, December 6th) until Pesaḥ. In Israel, it is said from the 7th of Marḥeshvan. The phrase "Grant blessing" is said from Ḥol HaMo'ed Pesaḥ until December 4th (in the year before a civil leap year, December 5th). In Israel it is said through the 6th of Marḥeshvan.

בָּרֵךְ Bless this year for us, LORD our God,
and all its types of produce for good.

In winter: Grant dew and rain as a blessing
In other seasons: Grant blessing
on the face of the earth, and from its goodness satisfy us,
blessing our year as the best of years.
Blessed are You, LORD, who blesses the years.

INGATHERING OF EXILES

תְּקַע Sound the great shofar for our freedom,
raise high the banner to gather our exiles,
and gather us together
from the four quarters of the earth.
Blessed are You, LORD,
who gathers the dispersed of His people Israel.

רפואה

רְפָאֵנוּ יהוה וְנֵרָפֵא, הוֹשִׁיעֵנוּ וְנִוָּשֵׁעָה, כִּי תְהִלָּתֵנוּ אָתָּה
וְהַעֲלֵה רְפוּאָה שְׁלֵמָה לְכָל מַכּוֹתֵינוּ

The following prayer for a sick person may be said here:

יְהִי רָצוֹן מִלְּפָנֶיךָ יהוה אֱלֹהַי וֵאלֹהֵי אֲבוֹתַי, שֶׁתִּשְׁלַח מְהֵרָה רְפוּאָה שְׁלֵמָה
מִן הַשָּׁמַיִם רְפוּאַת הַנֶּפֶשׁ וּרְפוּאַת הַגּוּף לַחוֹלֶה/לַחוֹלָה *name of patient*
בֶּן/בַּת *mother's name* בְּתוֹךְ שְׁאָר חוֹלֵי יִשְׂרָאֵל.

כִּי אֵל מֶלֶךְ רוֹפֵא נֶאֱמָן וְרַחֲמָן אָתָּה.
בָּרוּךְ אַתָּה יהוה, רוֹפֵא חוֹלֵי עַמּוֹ יִשְׂרָאֵל.

ברכת השנים

The phrase וְתֵן טַל וּמָטָר לִבְרָכָה *is said from December 5th (in the year before a civil leap year, December 6th) until* פסח. *In* ארץ ישראל, *it is said from* ז׳ מרחשון.
The phrase וְתֵן בְּרָכָה *is said from* חול המועד פסח *until December 4th (in the year before a civil leap year, December 5th). In* ארץ ישראל *it is said through* ו׳ מרחשון.

בָּרֵךְ עָלֵינוּ יהוה אֱלֹהֵינוּ אֶת הַשָּׁנָה הַזֹּאת
וְאֶת כָּל מִינֵי תְבוּאָתָהּ, לְטוֹבָה

בחורף: **וְתֵן טַל וּמָטָר לִבְרָכָה** / בקיץ: **וְתֵן בְּרָכָה**

עַל פְּנֵי הָאֲדָמָה, וְשַׂבְּעֵנוּ מִטּוּבָהּ
וּבָרֵךְ שְׁנָתֵנוּ כַּשָּׁנִים הַטּוֹבוֹת.
בָּרוּךְ אַתָּה יהוה, מְבָרֵךְ הַשָּׁנִים.

קבוץ גלויות

תְּקַע בְּשׁוֹפָר גָּדוֹל לְחֵרוּתֵנוּ
וְשָׂא נֵס לְקַבֵּץ גָּלֻיּוֹתֵינוּ
וְקַבְּצֵנוּ יַחַד מֵאַרְבַּע כַּנְפוֹת הָאָרֶץ.
בָּרוּךְ אַתָּה יהוה, מְקַבֵּץ נִדְחֵי עַמּוֹ יִשְׂרָאֵל.

JUSTICE

הָשִׁיבָה Restore our judges as at first,
and our counselors as at the beginning,
and remove from us sorrow and sighing.
May You alone, LORD,
reign over us with loving-kindness and compassion,
and vindicate us in justice.
Blessed are You, LORD,
the King who loves righteousness and justice.
/ *Between Rosh HaShana & Yom Kippur, end the blessing:* the King of justice./

AGAINST INFORMERS

וְלַמַּלְשִׁינִים For the slanderers let there be no hope,
and may all wickedness perish in an instant.
May all Your people's enemies swiftly be cut down.
May You swiftly uproot, crush, cast down
and humble the arrogant swiftly in our days.
Blessed are You, LORD,
who destroys enemies and humbles the arrogant.

THE RIGHTEOUS

עַל הַצַּדִּיקִים To the righteous, the pious,
the elders of Your people the house of Israel,
the remnant of their scholars,
the righteous converts, and to us,
may Your compassion be aroused, LORD our God.
Grant a good reward to all who sincerely trust in Your name.
Set our lot with them,
so that we may never be ashamed,
for in You we trust.
Blessed are You, LORD,
who is the support and trust of the righteous.

השבת המשפט

הָשִׁיבָה שׁוֹפְטֵינוּ כְּבָרִאשׁוֹנָה וְיוֹעֲצֵינוּ כְּבַתְּחִלָּה
וְהָסֵר מִמֶּנּוּ יָגוֹן וַאֲנָחָה
וּמְלֹךְ עָלֵינוּ אַתָּה יהוה לְבַדְּךָ בְּחֶסֶד וּבְרַחֲמִים
וְצַדְּקֵנוּ בַּמִּשְׁפָּט.
בָּרוּךְ אַתָּה יהוה
מֶלֶךְ אוֹהֵב צְדָקָה וּמִשְׁפָּט. / בעשרת ימי תשובה: הַמֶּלֶךְ הַמִּשְׁפָּט./

ברכת המינים

וְלַמַּלְשִׁינִים אַל תְּהִי תִקְוָה
וְכָל הָרִשְׁעָה כְּרֶגַע תֹּאבֵד
וְכָל אוֹיְבֵי עַמְּךָ מְהֵרָה יִכָּרֵתוּ
וְהַזֵּדִים מְהֵרָה תְעַקֵּר וּתְשַׁבֵּר וּתְמַגֵּר וְתַכְנִיעַ בִּמְהֵרָה בְיָמֵינוּ.
בָּרוּךְ אַתָּה יהוה, שׁוֹבֵר אוֹיְבִים וּמַכְנִיעַ זֵדִים.

על הצדיקים

עַל הַצַּדִּיקִים וְעַל הַחֲסִידִים
וְעַל זִקְנֵי עַמְּךָ בֵּית יִשְׂרָאֵל
וְעַל פְּלֵיטַת סוֹפְרֵיהֶם
וְעַל גֵּרֵי הַצֶּדֶק, וְעָלֵינוּ
יֶהֱמוּ רַחֲמֶיךָ יהוה אֱלֹהֵינוּ
וְתֵן שָׂכָר טוֹב לְכָל הַבּוֹטְחִים בְּשִׁמְךָ בֶּאֱמֶת
וְשִׂים חֶלְקֵנוּ עִמָּהֶם
וּלְעוֹלָם לֹא נֵבוֹשׁ כִּי בְךָ בָטָחְנוּ.
בָּרוּךְ אַתָּה יהוה, מִשְׁעָן וּמִבְטָח לַצַּדִּיקִים.

REBUILDING JERUSALEM

וְלִירוּשָׁלַיִם To Jerusalem, Your city, may You return in compassion,
and may You dwell in it as You promised.
May You rebuild it rapidly in our days as an everlasting structure,
and install within it soon the throne of David.
Blessed are You, LORD, who builds Jerusalem.

KINGDOM OF DAVID

אֶת צֶמַח May the offshoot of Your servant David soon flower,
and may his pride be raised high by Your salvation,
for we wait for Your salvation all day.
Blessed are You, LORD, who makes the glory of salvation flourish.

RESPONSE TO PRAYER

שְׁמַע קוֹלֵנוּ Listen to our voice, LORD our God.
Spare us and have compassion on us,
and in compassion and favor accept our prayer,
for You, God, listen to prayers and pleas.
Do not turn us away, O our King,
empty-handed from Your presence,*
for You listen with compassion to the prayer of Your people Israel.
Blessed are You, LORD, who listens to prayer.

At this point, in times of drought in Israel, say "And answer us" on page 732.

TEMPLE SERVICE

רְצֵה Find favor, LORD our God,
in Your people Israel and their prayer.
Restore the service to Your most holy House,
and accept in love and favor
the fire-offerings of Israel and their prayer.
May the service of Your people Israel always find favor with You.

On Rosh Ḥodesh and Ḥol HaMo'ed, say:

אֱלֹהֵינוּ Our God and God of our ancestors, may there rise, come, reach, appear, be favored, heard, regarded and remembered before You, our recollection and remembrance, as well as the remembrance of our ancestors, and of the Messiah son of David Your servant, and of Jerusalem Your holy city,

בניין ירושלים

וְלִירוּשָׁלַיִם עִירְךָ בְּרַחֲמִים תָּשׁוּב, וְתִשְׁכֹּן בְּתוֹכָהּ כַּאֲשֶׁר דִּבַּרְתָּ
וּבְנֵה אוֹתָהּ בְּקָרוֹב בְּיָמֵינוּ בִּנְיַן עוֹלָם
וְכִסֵּא דָוִד מְהֵרָה לְתוֹכָהּ תָּכִין.
בָּרוּךְ אַתָּה יהוה, בּוֹנֵה יְרוּשָׁלָיִם.

משיח בן דוד

אֶת צֶמַח דָּוִד עַבְדְּךָ מְהֵרָה תַצְמִיחַ
וְקַרְנוֹ תָּרוּם בִּישׁוּעָתֶךָ, כִּי לִישׁוּעָתְךָ קִוִּינוּ כָּל הַיּוֹם.
בָּרוּךְ אַתָּה יהוה, מַצְמִיחַ קֶרֶן יְשׁוּעָה.

שומע תפילה

שְׁמַע קוֹלֵנוּ יהוה אֱלֹהֵינוּ, חוּס וְרַחֵם עָלֵינוּ
וְקַבֵּל בְּרַחֲמִים וּבְרָצוֹן אֶת תְּפִלָּתֵנוּ
כִּי אֵל שׁוֹמֵעַ תְּפִלּוֹת וְתַחֲנוּנִים אָתָּה
וּמִלְּפָנֶיךָ מַלְכֵּנוּ רֵיקָם אַל תְּשִׁיבֵנוּ*
כִּי אַתָּה שׁוֹמֵעַ תְּפִלַּת עַמְּךָ יִשְׂרָאֵל בְּרַחֲמִים.
בָּרוּךְ אַתָּה יהוה, שׁוֹמֵעַ תְּפִלָּה.

**At this point, in times of drought in* ארץ ישראל*, say* וַעֲנֵנוּ *on page 733.*

עבודה

רְצֵה יהוה אֱלֹהֵינוּ בְּעַמְּךָ יִשְׂרָאֵל וּבִתְפִלָּתָם
וְהָשֵׁב אֶת הָעֲבוֹדָה לִדְבִיר בֵּיתֶךָ
וְאִשֵּׁי יִשְׂרָאֵל וּתְפִלָּתָם בְּאַהֲבָה תְקַבֵּל בְּרָצוֹן
וּתְהִי לְרָצוֹן תָּמִיד עֲבוֹדַת יִשְׂרָאֵל עַמֶּךָ.

On ראש חודש *and* חול המועד*, say:*

אֱלֹהֵינוּ וֵאלֹהֵי אֲבוֹתֵינוּ, יַעֲלֶה וְיָבוֹא וְיַגִּיעַ, וְיֵרָאֶה וְיֵרָצֶה וְיִשָּׁמַע,
וְיִפָּקֵד וְיִזָּכֵר זִכְרוֹנֵנוּ וּפִקְדוֹנֵנוּ וְזִכְרוֹן אֲבוֹתֵינוּ, וְזִכְרוֹן מָשִׁיחַ בֶּן דָּוִד

and of all Your people the house of Israel – for deliverance and well-being, grace, loving-kindness and compassion, life and peace, on this day of:

On Rosh Ḥodesh: Rosh Ḥodesh.
On Pesaḥ: the Festival of Matzot.
On Sukkot: the Festival of Sukkot.

On it remember us, Lord our God, for good; recollect us for blessing, and deliver us for life. In accord with Your promise of salvation and compassion, spare us and be gracious to us; have compassion on us and deliver us, for our eyes are turned to You because You, God, are a gracious and compassionate King.

וְתֶחֱזֶינָה And may our eyes witness Your return to Zion in compassion. Blessed are You, Lord, who restores His Presence to Zion.

THANKSGIVING

▾*Bow:* We give thanks to You, for You are *Stand straight* the Lord our God and God of our ancestors for ever and all time. You are the Rock of our lives, Shield of our salvation from generation to generation. We will thank You and declare Your praise for our lives,[A] which are entrusted into Your hand; for our souls, which are placed in Your charge; for Your miracles which are with us every day; and for Your wonders[1] and favors at all times, evening, morning and midday. You are good – for Your compassion never fails. You are compassionate – for Your loving-kindnesses never cease. We have always placed our hope in You.

During the Leader's Repetition, the congregation says quietly:
▾*Bow:* We give thanks to You, for You are *Stand straight* the Lord our God and God of our ancestors, God of all flesh, who formed us and formed the universe. Blessings and thanks are due to Your great and holy name for giving us life and sustaining us. May You continue to give us life and sustain us; and may You gather our exiles to Your holy courts, to keep Your decrees, do Your will and serve You with a perfect heart, for it is for us to give You thanks. Blessed be God to whom thanksgiving is due.

עַבְדֶּךָ, וְזִכְרוֹן יְרוּשָׁלַיִם עִיר קָדְשֶׁךָ, וְזִכְרוֹן כָּל עַמְּךָ בֵּית יִשְׂרָאֵל, לְפָנֶיךָ, לִפְלֵיטָה לְטוֹבָה, לְחֵן וּלְחֶסֶד וּלְרַחֲמִים, לְחַיִּים וּלְשָׁלוֹם בְּיוֹם בראש חודש: **רֹאשׁ הַחֹדֶשׁ** / בפסח: **חַג הַמַּצּוֹת** / בסוכות: **חַג הַסֻּכּוֹת** הַזֶּה. זָכְרֵנוּ יהוה אֱלֹהֵינוּ בּוֹ לְטוֹבָה, וּפָקְדֵנוּ בוֹ לִבְרָכָה, וְהוֹשִׁיעֵנוּ בוֹ לְחַיִּים. וּבִדְבַר יְשׁוּעָה וְרַחֲמִים, חוּס וְחָנֵּנוּ וְרַחֵם עָלֵינוּ וְהוֹשִׁיעֵנוּ, כִּי אֵלֶיךָ עֵינֵינוּ, כִּי אֵל מֶלֶךְ חַנּוּן וְרַחוּם אָתָּה.

וְתֶחֱזֶינָה עֵינֵינוּ בְּשׁוּבְךָ לְצִיּוֹן בְּרַחֲמִים.
בָּרוּךְ אַתָּה יהוה, הַמַּחֲזִיר שְׁכִינָתוֹ לְצִיּוֹן.

הודאה

▾ *Bow* מוֹדִים אֲנַחְנוּ לָךְ
Stand straight שָׁאַתָּה הוּא
יהוה אֱלֹהֵינוּ וֵאלֹהֵי אֲבוֹתֵינוּ
לְעוֹלָם וָעֶד.
צוּר חַיֵּינוּ, מָגֵן יִשְׁעֵנוּ
אַתָּה הוּא לְדוֹר וָדוֹר.
נוֹדֶה לְּךָ וּנְסַפֵּר תְּהִלָּתֶךָ
עַל חַיֵּינוּ[א] הַמְּסוּרִים בְּיָדֶךָ
וְעַל נִשְׁמוֹתֵינוּ הַפְּקוּדוֹת לָךְ
וְעַל נִסֶּיךָ שֶׁבְּכָל יוֹם עִמָּנוּ
וְעַל נִפְלְאוֹתֶיךָ[ע] וְטוֹבוֹתֶיךָ
שֶׁבְּכָל עֵת, עֶרֶב וָבֹקֶר וְצָהֳרָיִם.
הַטּוֹב, כִּי לֹא כָלוּ רַחֲמֶיךָ
וְהַמְרַחֵם, כִּי לֹא תַמּוּ חֲסָדֶיךָ
מֵעוֹלָם קִוִּינוּ לָךְ.

During the חזרת הש״ץ, *the* קהל *says quietly:*

▾ *Bow* מוֹדִים אֲנַחְנוּ לָךְ
Stand straight שָׁאַתָּה הוּא
יהוה אֱלֹהֵינוּ וֵאלֹהֵי אֲבוֹתֵינוּ
אֱלֹהֵי כָל בָּשָׂר
יוֹצְרֵנוּ, יוֹצֵר בְּרֵאשִׁית.
בְּרָכוֹת וְהוֹדָאוֹת
לְשִׁמְךָ הַגָּדוֹל וְהַקָּדוֹשׁ
עַל שֶׁהֶחֱיִיתָנוּ וְקִיַּמְתָּנוּ.
כֵּן תְּחַיֵּנוּ וּתְקַיְּמֵנוּ
וְתֶאֱסֹף גָּלֻיּוֹתֵינוּ
לְחַצְרוֹת קָדְשֶׁךָ
לִשְׁמֹר חֻקֶּיךָ
וְלַעֲשׂוֹת רְצוֹנֶךָ וּלְעָבְדְּךָ
בְּלֵבָב שָׁלֵם
עַל שֶׁאֲנַחְנוּ מוֹדִים לָךְ.
בָּרוּךְ אֵל הַהוֹדָאוֹת.

On Ḥanukka:

עַל הַנִּסִּים [We thank You also] for the miracles, the redemption, the mighty deeds, the salvations, and the victories in battle which You performed for our ancestors in those days, at this time.

בִּימֵי מַתִּתְיָהוּ In the days of Mattityahu, son of Yoḥanan, the High Priest, the Hasmonean, and his sons, the wicked Greek kingdom rose up against Your people Israel to make them forget Your Torah and to force them to transgress the statutes of Your will. It was then that You in Your great compassion stood by them in the time of their distress. You championed their cause, judged their claim, and avenged their wrong. You delivered the strong into the hands of the weak, the many into the hands of the few, the impure into the hands of the pure, the wicked into the hands of the righteous, and the arrogant into the hands of those who were engaged in the study of Your Torah. You made for Yourself great and holy renown in Your world, and for Your people Israel You performed a great salvation and redemption as of this very day. Your children then entered the holiest part of Your House, cleansed Your Temple, purified Your Sanctuary, kindled lights in Your holy courts, and designated these eight days of Ḥanukka for giving thanks and praise to Your great name.

Continue with "For all these things."

On Purim:

עַל הַנִּסִּים [We thank You also] for the miracles, the redemption, the mighty deeds, the salvations, and the victories in battle which You performed for our ancestors in those days, at this time.

בִּימֵי מָרְדְּכַי In the days of Mordekhai and Esther, in Shushan the capital, the
wicked Haman rose up against them and sought to destroy, slay and exterminate *Esther 3*
all the Jews, young and old, children and women, on one day, the thirteenth day of the twelfth month, which is the month of Adar, and to plunder their possessions. Then You in Your great compassion thwarted his counsel, frustrated his plans, and caused his scheme to recoil on his own head, so that they hanged him and his sons on the gallows.

Continue with "For all these things."

וְעַל כֻּלָּם For all these things may Your name be blessed
and exalted, our King, continually, for ever and all time.

These words are added between Rosh HaShana & Yom Kippur: And write, for a good life,
all the children of Your covenant.

Let all that lives thank You, Selah!
and praise Your name in truth,
God, our Savior and Help, Selah!

▾ *Bend the knees:* Blessed *Bow:* are You, *Stand straight:* LORD,
whose name is "the Good" and to whom thanks are due.

בחנוכה:

עַל הַנִּסִּים וְעַל הַפֻּרְקָן וְעַל הַגְּבוּרוֹת וְעַל הַתְּשׁוּעוֹת וְעַל הַמִּלְחָמוֹת שֶׁעָשִׂיתָ לַאֲבוֹתֵינוּ בַּיָּמִים הָהֵם בִּזְּמַן הַזֶּה.

בִּימֵי מַתִּתְיָהוּ בֶּן יוֹחָנָן כֹּהֵן גָּדוֹל חַשְׁמוֹנַאי וּבָנָיו, כְּשֶׁעָמְדָה מַלְכוּת יָוָן הָרְשָׁעָה עַל עַמְּךָ יִשְׂרָאֵל לְהַשְׁכִּיחָם תּוֹרָתֶךָ וּלְהַעֲבִירָם מֵחֻקֵּי רְצוֹנֶךָ, וְאַתָּה בְּרַחֲמֶיךָ הָרַבִּים עָמַדְתָּ לָהֶם בְּעֵת צָרָתָם, רַבְתָּ אֶת רִיבָם, דַּנְתָּ אֶת דִּינָם, נָקַמְתָּ אֶת נִקְמָתָם, מָסַרְתָּ גִבּוֹרִים בְּיַד חַלָּשִׁים, וְרַבִּים בְּיַד מְעַטִּים, וּטְמֵאִים בְּיַד טְהוֹרִים, וּרְשָׁעִים בְּיַד צַדִּיקִים, וְזֵדִים בְּיַד עוֹסְקֵי תוֹרָתֶךָ, וּלְךָ עָשִׂיתָ שֵׁם גָּדוֹל וְקָדוֹשׁ בְּעוֹלָמֶךָ, וּלְעַמְּךָ יִשְׂרָאֵל עָשִׂיתָ תְּשׁוּעָה גְדוֹלָה וּפֻרְקָן כְּהַיּוֹם הַזֶּה. וְאַחַר כֵּן בָּאוּ בָנֶיךָ לִדְבִיר בֵּיתֶךָ, וּפִנּוּ אֶת הֵיכָלֶךָ, וְטִהֲרוּ אֶת מִקְדָּשֶׁךָ, וְהִדְלִיקוּ נֵרוֹת בְּחַצְרוֹת קָדְשֶׁךָ, וְקָבְעוּ שְׁמוֹנַת יְמֵי חֲנֻכָּה אֵלּוּ, לְהוֹדוֹת וּלְהַלֵּל לְשִׁמְךָ הַגָּדוֹל.

Continue with וְעַל כֻּלָּם.

בפורים:

עַל הַנִּסִּים וְעַל הַפֻּרְקָן וְעַל הַגְּבוּרוֹת וְעַל הַתְּשׁוּעוֹת וְעַל הַמִּלְחָמוֹת שֶׁעָשִׂיתָ לַאֲבוֹתֵינוּ בַּיָּמִים הָהֵם בִּזְּמַן הַזֶּה.

בִּימֵי מָרְדְּכַי וְאֶסְתֵּר בְּשׁוּשַׁן הַבִּירָה, כְּשֶׁעָמַד עֲלֵיהֶם הָמָן הָרָשָׁע, בִּקֵּשׁ לְהַשְׁמִיד לַהֲרֹג וּלְאַבֵּד אֶת־כָּל־הַיְּהוּדִים מִנַּעַר וְעַד־זָקֵן טַף וְנָשִׁים בְּיוֹם אֶחָד, בִּשְׁלוֹשָׁה עָשָׂר לְחֹדֶשׁ שְׁנֵים־עָשָׂר, הוּא־חֹדֶשׁ אֲדָר, וּשְׁלָלָם לָבוֹז: וְאַתָּה בְּרַחֲמֶיךָ הָרַבִּים הֵפַרְתָּ אֶת עֲצָתוֹ, וְקִלְקַלְתָּ אֶת מַחֲשַׁבְתּוֹ, וַהֲשֵׁבוֹתָ לּוֹ גְּמוּלוֹ בְּרֹאשׁוֹ, וְתָלוּ אוֹתוֹ וְאֶת בָּנָיו עַל הָעֵץ. אסתר ג

Continue with וְעַל כֻּלָּם.

וְעַל כֻּלָּם יִתְבָּרַךְ וְיִתְרוֹמַם שִׁמְךָ מַלְכֵּנוּ תָּמִיד לְעוֹלָם וָעֶד.

בעשרת ימי תשובה: וּכְתֹב לְחַיִּים טוֹבִים כָּל בְּנֵי בְרִיתֶךָ.

וְכֹל הַחַיִּים יוֹדוּךָ סֶּלָה, וִיהַלְלוּ אֶת שִׁמְךָ בֶּאֱמֶת הָאֵל יְשׁוּעָתֵנוּ וְעֶזְרָתֵנוּ סֶלָה.

▾ *Bend the knees* בָּרוּךְ *Bow* אַתָּה *Stand straight* יהוה הַטּוֹב שִׁמְךָ וּלְךָ נָאֶה לְהוֹדוֹת.

PEACE

שָׁלוֹם רָב Grant great peace to Your people Israel for ever,
for You are the sovereign LORD of all peace;
and may it be good in Your eyes
to bless Your people Israel
at every time, at every hour, with Your peace.

These words are added between Rosh HaShana & Yom Kippur: In the book of life, blessing, peace and prosperity,
may we and all Your people the house of Israel
be remembered and written before You
for a good life, and for peace.*

Blessed are You, LORD, who blesses His people Israel with peace.

**Between Rosh HaShana and Yom Kippur outside Israel, many have the custom to end the blessing:*
Blessed are You, LORD, who makes peace.

The following verse concludes the Leader's Repetition of the Amida. Some also say it here as part of the silent Amida.

May the words of my mouth and the meditation of my heart *Ps. 19*
find favor before You, LORD, my Rock and Redeemer.

אֱלֹהַי My God, *Berakhot 17a*
guard my tongue from evil and my lips from deceitful speech.
To those who curse me, let my soul be silent;
may my soul be to all like the dust.
Open my heart to Your Torah and let my soul
pursue Your commandments. As for all who plan evil against me,
swiftly thwart their counsel and frustrate their plans.
Act for the sake of Your name; act for the sake of Your right hand;
act for the sake of Your holiness; act for the sake of Your Torah.
That Your beloved ones may be delivered, *Ps. 60*
save with Your right hand and answer me.
May the words of my mouth and the meditation of my heart *Ps. 19*
find favor before You, LORD, my Rock and Redeemer.

Bow and take three steps back as if taking leave of the Divine Presence.

Bow left: May He who makes peace in His high places,
Bow right: make peace *Bow forward:* for us and all Israel –
and say: Amen.

ברכת שלום

שָׁלוֹם רָב עַל יִשְׂרָאֵל עַמְּךָ תָּשִׂים לְעוֹלָם
כִּי אַתָּה הוּא מֶלֶךְ אָדוֹן לְכָל הַשָּׁלוֹם.
וְטוֹב בְּעֵינֶיךָ לְבָרֵךְ אֶת עַמְּךָ יִשְׂרָאֵל
בְּכָל עֵת וּבְכָל שָׁעָה בִּשְׁלוֹמֶךָ.

בעשרת ימי תשובה: בְּסֵפֶר חַיִּים, בְּרָכָה וְשָׁלוֹם, וּפַרְנָסָה טוֹבָה
נִזָּכֵר וְנִכָּתֵב לְפָנֶיךָ, אֲנַחְנוּ וְכָל עַמְּךָ בֵּית יִשְׂרָאֵל
לְחַיִּים טוֹבִים וּלְשָׁלוֹם.*

בָּרוּךְ אַתָּה יהוה, הַמְבָרֵךְ אֶת עַמּוֹ יִשְׂרָאֵל בַּשָּׁלוֹם.

*During the עשרת ימי תשובה in חוץ לארץ,
many have the custom to end the blessing:

בָּרוּךְ אַתָּה יהוה, עוֹשֵׂה הַשָּׁלוֹם.

The following verse concludes the חזרת הש״ץ. *Some also say it here as part of the silent* עמידה.

יִהְיוּ לְרָצוֹן אִמְרֵי־פִי וְהֶגְיוֹן לִבִּי לְפָנֶיךָ, יהוה צוּרִי וְגֹאֲלִי: תהלים יט

אֱלֹהַי ברכות יז.
נְצֹר לְשׁוֹנִי מֵרָע וּשְׂפָתַי מִדַּבֵּר מִרְמָה
וְלִמְקַלְלַי נַפְשִׁי תִדֹּם, וְנַפְשִׁי כֶּעָפָר לַכֹּל תִּהְיֶה.
פְּתַח לִבִּי בְּתוֹרָתֶךָ, וּבְמִצְוֹתֶיךָ תִּרְדֹּף נַפְשִׁי.
וְכָל הַחוֹשְׁבִים עָלַי רָעָה, מְהֵרָה הָפֵר עֲצָתָם וְקַלְקֵל מַחֲשַׁבְתָּם.
עֲשֵׂה לְמַעַן שְׁמֶךָ, עֲשֵׂה לְמַעַן יְמִינֶךָ
עֲשֵׂה לְמַעַן קְדֻשָּׁתֶךָ, עֲשֵׂה לְמַעַן תּוֹרָתֶךָ.
לְמַעַן יֵחָלְצוּן יְדִידֶיךָ, הוֹשִׁיעָה יְמִינְךָ וַעֲנֵנִי: תהלים ס
יִהְיוּ לְרָצוֹן אִמְרֵי־פִי וְהֶגְיוֹן לִבִּי לְפָנֶיךָ, יהוה צוּרִי וְגֹאֲלִי: תהלים יט

Bow and take three steps back as if taking leave of the Divine Presence.

Bow left עֹשֶׂה שָׁלוֹם/ בעשרת ימי תשובה: הַשָּׁלוֹם/ בִּמְרוֹמָיו
Bow right הוּא יַעֲשֶׂה שָׁלוֹם *Bow forward* עָלֵינוּ וְעַל כָּל יִשְׂרָאֵל
וְאִמְרוּ אָמֵן.

יְהִי רָצוֹן May it be Your will, Lord our God and God of our ancestors,
that the Temple be rebuilt speedily in our days,
and grant us a share in Your Torah.
And there we will serve You with reverence,
as in the days of old and as in former years.
Then the offering of Judah and Jerusalem will be pleasing to the Lord *Mal. 3*
as in the days of old and as in former years.

The Leader says Full Kaddish below.

FULL KADDISH

Leader: יִתְגַּדַּל Magnified and sanctified may His great name be,
in the world He created by His will.
May He establish His kingdom
in your lifetime and in your days,
and in the lifetime of all the house of Israel,
swiftly and soon –
and say: Amen.

All: May His great name be blessed for ever and all time.

Leader: Blessed and praised, glorified and exalted,
raised and honored, uplifted and lauded be
the name of the Holy One, blessed be He,
beyond any blessing,
song, praise and consolation uttered in the world –
and say: Amen.

May the prayers and pleas of all Israel
be accepted by their Father in heaven –
and say: Amen.

May there be great peace from heaven,
and life for us and all Israel –
and say: Amen.

Bow, take three steps back, as if taking leave of the Divine Presence, then bow, first left, then right, then center, while saying:

May He who makes peace in His high places,
make peace for us and all Israel –
and say: Amen.

יְהִי רָצוֹן מִלְּפָנֶיךָ יהוה אֱלֹהֵינוּ וֵאלֹהֵי אֲבוֹתֵינוּ
שֶׁיִּבָּנֶה בֵּית הַמִּקְדָּשׁ בִּמְהֵרָה בְיָמֵינוּ, וְתֵן חֶלְקֵנוּ בְּתוֹרָתֶךָ
וְשָׁם נַעֲבָדְךָ בְּיִרְאָה כִּימֵי עוֹלָם וּכְשָׁנִים קַדְמֹנִיּוֹת.
וְעָרְבָה לַיהוה מִנְחַת יְהוּדָה וִירוּשָׁלָםִ כִּימֵי עוֹלָם וּכְשָׁנִים קַדְמֹנִיּוֹת: מלאכי ג

The שליח ציבור *says* קדיש שלם *below.*

קדיש שלם

ש״ץ: יִתְגַּדַּל וְיִתְקַדַּשׁ שְׁמֵהּ רַבָּא (קהל: אָמֵן)
בְּעָלְמָא דִּי בְרָא כִרְעוּתֵהּ
וְיַמְלִיךְ מַלְכוּתֵהּ
בְּחַיֵּיכוֹן וּבְיוֹמֵיכוֹן וּבְחַיֵּי דְכָל בֵּית יִשְׂרָאֵל
בַּעֲגָלָא וּבִזְמַן קָרִיב, וְאִמְרוּ אָמֵן. (קהל: אָמֵן)

קהל וש״ץ: יְהֵא שְׁמֵהּ רַבָּא מְבָרַךְ לְעָלַם וּלְעָלְמֵי עָלְמַיָּא.

ש״ץ: יִתְבָּרַךְ וְיִשְׁתַּבַּח וְיִתְפָּאַר
וְיִתְרוֹמַם וְיִתְנַשֵּׂא וְיִתְהַדָּר וְיִתְעַלֶּה וְיִתְהַלָּל
שְׁמֵהּ דְּקֻדְשָׁא בְּרִיךְ הוּא (קהל: בְּרִיךְ הוּא)
לְעֵלָּא מִן כָּל בִּרְכָתָא / בעשרת ימי תשובה: לְעֵלָּא לְעֵלָּא מִכָּל בִּרְכָתָא/
וְשִׁירָתָא, תֻּשְׁבְּחָתָא וְנֶחֱמָתָא
דַּאֲמִירָן בְּעָלְמָא, וְאִמְרוּ אָמֵן. (קהל: אָמֵן)

תִּתְקַבַּל צְלוֹתְהוֹן וּבָעוּתְהוֹן דְּכָל יִשְׂרָאֵל
קֳדָם אֲבוּהוֹן דִּי בִשְׁמַיָּא, וְאִמְרוּ אָמֵן. (קהל: אָמֵן)

יְהֵא שְׁלָמָא רַבָּא מִן שְׁמַיָּא
וְחַיִּים, עָלֵינוּ וְעַל כָּל יִשְׂרָאֵל, וְאִמְרוּ אָמֵן. (קהל: אָמֵן)

Bow, take three steps back, as if taking leave of the Divine Presence, then bow, first left, then right, then center, while saying:

עֹשֶׂה שָׁלוֹם/ בעשרת ימי תשובה: הַשָּׁלוֹם/ בִּמְרוֹמָיו
הוּא יַעֲשֶׂה שָׁלוֹם עָלֵינוּ וְעַל כָּל יִשְׂרָאֵל, וְאִמְרוּ אָמֵן. (קהל: אָמֵן)

Stand while saying Aleinu.

עָלֵינוּ It is our duty to praise the Master of all,
and ascribe greatness to the Author of creation,
who has not made us like the nations of the lands
nor placed us like the families of the earth;
who has not made our portion like theirs,
nor our destiny like all their multitudes.
(For they worship vanity and emptiness,
and pray to a god who cannot save.)
▾ *Bow:* But we bow in worship and thank the Supreme King of kings,
the Holy One, blessed be He,
who extends the heavens and establishes the earth,
whose throne of glory is in the heavens above,
and whose power's Presence is in the highest of heights.
He is our God; there is no other.
Truly He is our King, there is none else,
as it is written in His Torah:
"You shall know and take to heart this day that the LORD is God, *Deut. 4*
in heaven above and on earth below.
There is no other."

Therefore, we place our hope in You, LORD our God,
that we may soon see the glory of Your power,
when You will remove abominations from the earth,
and idols will be utterly destroyed,
when the world will be perfected under the sovereignty of the Almighty,
when all humanity will call on Your name,
to turn all the earth's wicked toward You.
All the world's inhabitants will realize and know
that to You every knee must bow and every tongue swear loyalty.
Before You, LORD our God, they will kneel and bow down
and give honor to Your glorious name.
They will all accept the yoke of Your kingdom,
and You will reign over them soon and for ever.
For the kingdom is Yours, and to all eternity You will reign in glory,
as it is written in Your Torah: "The LORD will reign for ever and ever." *Ex. 15*

Stand while saying עָלֵינוּ.

עָלֵינוּ לְשַׁבֵּחַ לַאֲדוֹן הַכֹּל, לָתֵת גְּדֻלָּה לְיוֹצֵר בְּרֵאשִׁית
שֶׁלֹּא עָשָׂנוּ כְּגוֹיֵי הָאֲרָצוֹת, וְלֹא שָׂמָנוּ כְּמִשְׁפְּחוֹת הָאֲדָמָה
שֶׁלֹּא שָׂם חֶלְקֵנוּ כָּהֶם וְגוֹרָלֵנוּ כְּכָל הֲמוֹנָם.
(שֶׁהֵם מִשְׁתַּחֲוִים לְהֶבֶל וָרִיק וּמִתְפַּלְּלִים אֶל אֵל לֹא יוֹשִׁיעַ.)
▾ *Bow* וַאֲנַחְנוּ כּוֹרְעִים וּמִשְׁתַּחֲוִים וּמוֹדִים
לִפְנֵי מֶלֶךְ מַלְכֵי הַמְּלָכִים, הַקָּדוֹשׁ בָּרוּךְ הוּא
שֶׁהוּא נוֹטֶה שָׁמַיִם וְיוֹסֵד אָרֶץ, וּמוֹשַׁב יְקָרוֹ בַּשָּׁמַיִם מִמַּעַל
וּשְׁכִינַת עֻזּוֹ בְּגָבְהֵי מְרוֹמִים.
הוּא אֱלֹהֵינוּ, אֵין עוֹד.
אֱמֶת מַלְכֵּנוּ, אֶפֶס זוּלָתוֹ
דברים ד כַּכָּתוּב בְּתוֹרָתוֹ, וְיָדַעְתָּ הַיּוֹם וַהֲשֵׁבֹתָ אֶל־לְבָבֶךָ
כִּי יהוה הוּא הָאֱלֹהִים בַּשָּׁמַיִם מִמַּעַל וְעַל־הָאָרֶץ מִתָּחַת
אֵין עוֹד:

עַל כֵּן נְקַוֶּה לְּךָ יהוה אֱלֹהֵינוּ, לִרְאוֹת מְהֵרָה בְּתִפְאֶרֶת עֻזֶּךָ
לְהַעֲבִיר גִּלּוּלִים מִן הָאָרֶץ, וְהָאֱלִילִים כָּרוֹת יִכָּרֵתוּן
לְתַקֵּן עוֹלָם בְּמַלְכוּת שַׁדַּי.
וְכָל בְּנֵי בָשָׂר יִקְרְאוּ בִשְׁמֶךָ לְהַפְנוֹת אֵלֶיךָ כָּל רִשְׁעֵי אָרֶץ.
יַכִּירוּ וְיֵדְעוּ כָּל יוֹשְׁבֵי תֵבֵל
כִּי לְךָ תִּכְרַע כָּל בֶּרֶךְ, תִּשָּׁבַע כָּל לָשׁוֹן.
לְפָנֶיךָ יהוה אֱלֹהֵינוּ יִכְרְעוּ וְיִפֹּלוּ, וְלִכְבוֹד שִׁמְךָ יְקָר יִתֵּנוּ
וִיקַבְּלוּ כֻלָּם אֶת עֹל מַלְכוּתֶךָ
וְתִמְלֹךְ עֲלֵיהֶם מְהֵרָה לְעוֹלָם וָעֶד.
כִּי הַמַּלְכוּת שֶׁלְּךָ הִיא וּלְעוֹלְמֵי עַד תִּמְלֹךְ בְּכָבוֹד
שמות טו כַּכָּתוּב בְּתוֹרָתֶךָ, יהוה יִמְלֹךְ לְעֹלָם וָעֶד:

▸ And it is said: "Then the LORD shall be King over all the earth; *Zech. 14*
on that day the LORD shall be One and His name One."

Some add:
Have no fear of sudden terror or of the ruin when it overtakes the wicked. *Prov. 3*
Devise your strategy, but it will be thwarted; *Is. 8*
propose your plan, but it will not stand, for God is with us.
When you grow old, I will still be the same. *Is. 46*
When your hair turns gray, I will still carry you.
I made you, I will bear you, I will carry you, and I will rescue you.

MOURNER'S KADDISH

The following prayer, said by mourners, requires the presence of a minyan. A transliteration can be found on page 892.

Mourner: יִתְגַּדַּל Magnified and sanctified may His great name be,
in the world He created by His will.
May He establish His kingdom
in your lifetime and in your days,
and in the lifetime of all the house of Israel,
swiftly and soon –
and say: Amen.

All: May His great name be blessed for ever and all time.

Mourner: Blessed and praised, glorified and exalted,
raised and honored, uplifted and lauded
be the name of the Holy One, blessed be He,
beyond any blessing, song, praise and consolation
uttered in the world –
and say: Amen.

May there be great peace from heaven,
and life for us and all Israel –
and say: Amen.

Bow and take three steps back as if taking leave of the Divine Presence.

Bow left: May He who makes peace in His high places,
Bow right: make peace *Bow forward:* for us and all Israel –
and say: Amen.

◂ וְנֶאֱמַר, וְהָיָה יהוה לְמֶלֶךְ עַל־כָּל־הָאָרֶץ
בַּיּוֹם הַהוּא יִהְיֶה יהוה אֶחָד וּשְׁמוֹ אֶחָד: זכריה יד

Some add:

אַל־תִּירָא מִפַּחַד פִּתְאֹם וּמִשֹּׁאַת רְשָׁעִים כִּי תָבֹא: משלי ג
עֻצוּ עֵצָה וְתֻפָר, דַּבְּרוּ דָבָר וְלֹא יָקוּם, כִּי עִמָּנוּ אֵל: ישעיה ח
וְעַד־זִקְנָה אֲנִי הוּא, וְעַד־שֵׂיבָה אֲנִי אֶסְבֹּל אֲנִי עָשִׂיתִי וַאֲנִי אֶשָּׂא וַאֲנִי אֶסְבֹּל וַאֲמַלֵּט: ישעיה מו

קדיש יתום

The following prayer, said by mourners, requires the presence of a מנין.
A transliteration can be found on page 892.

אבל: יִתְגַּדַּל וְיִתְקַדַּשׁ שְׁמֵהּ רַבָּא (קהל: אָמֵן)
בְּעָלְמָא דִּי בְרָא כִרְעוּתֵהּ, וְיַמְלִיךְ מַלְכוּתֵהּ
בְּחַיֵּיכוֹן וּבְיוֹמֵיכוֹן וּבְחַיֵּי דְכָל בֵּית יִשְׂרָאֵל
בַּעֲגָלָא וּבִזְמַן קָרִיב, וְאִמְרוּ אָמֵן. (קהל: אָמֵן)

קהל ואבל: יְהֵא שְׁמֵהּ רַבָּא מְבָרַךְ לְעָלַם וּלְעָלְמֵי עָלְמַיָּא.

אבל: יִתְבָּרַךְ וְיִשְׁתַּבַּח וְיִתְפָּאַר
וְיִתְרוֹמַם וְיִתְנַשֵּׂא וְיִתְהַדָּר וְיִתְעַלֶּה וְיִתְהַלָּל
שְׁמֵהּ דְּקֻדְשָׁא בְּרִיךְ הוּא (קהל: בְּרִיךְ הוּא)
לְעֵלָּא מִן כָּל בִּרְכָתָא / בעשרת ימי תשובה: לְעֵלָּא לְעֵלָּא מִכָּל בִּרְכָתָא/
וְשִׁירָתָא, תֻּשְׁבְּחָתָא וְנֶחֱמָתָא
דַּאֲמִירָן בְּעָלְמָא, וְאִמְרוּ אָמֵן. (קהל: אָמֵן)

יְהֵא שְׁלָמָא רַבָּא מִן שְׁמַיָּא
וְחַיִּים, עָלֵינוּ וְעַל כָּל יִשְׂרָאֵל, וְאִמְרוּ אָמֵן. (קהל: אָמֵן)

Bow and take three steps back as if taking leave of the Divine Presence.

Bow left עֹשֶׂה שָׁלוֹם/ בעשרת ימי תשובה: הַשָּׁלוֹם/ בִּמְרוֹמָיו
Bow right הוּא יַעֲשֶׂה שָׁלוֹם *Bow forward* עָלֵינוּ
וְעַל כָּל יִשְׂרָאֵל, וְאִמְרוּ אָמֵן.

Erev Shabbat

EIRUV TEḤUMIN

On Shabbat and Yom Tov it is forbidden to walk more than 2000 cubits (about 3000 feet) beyond the boundary (teḥum) of the town where you live or are staying when the day begins. By placing food sufficient for two meals, before nightfall, at a point within 2000 cubits from the town limits, you confer on that place the status of a dwelling for the next day, and are then permitted to walk 2000 cubits from there.

בָּרוּךְ Blessed are You, Lord our God, King of the Universe, who has made us holy through His commandments, and has commanded us about the mitzva of Eiruv.

By this Eiruv may we be permitted to walk from this place, two thousand cubits in any direction.

EIRUV ḤATZEROT

On Shabbat it is forbidden to carry objects from one private domain to another, or from a private domain into space shared by others, such as a communal staircase, corridor or courtyard. An Eiruv Ḥatzerot is created when each of the Jewish households in a court or apartment block, before Shabbat, places a loaf of bread or matza in one of the homes. The entire court or block then becomes a single private domain within which it is permitted to carry.

בָּרוּךְ Blessed are You, Lord our God, King of the Universe, who has made us holy through His commandments, and has commanded us about the mitzva of Eiruv.

By this Eiruv may we be permitted to move, carry out and carry in from the houses to the courtyard, or from the courtyard to the houses, or from house to house, for all the houses within the courtyard.

ערב שבת

עירוב תחומין

On שבת *and* יום טוב *it is forbidden to walk more than 2000 cubits (about 3000 feet) beyond the boundary* (תחום) *of the town where you live or are staying when the day begins. By placing food sufficient for two meals, before nightfall, at a point within 2000 cubits from the town limits, you confer on that place the status of a dwelling for the next day, and are then permitted to walk 2000 cubits from there.*

בָּרוּךְ אַתָּה יהוה אֱלֹהֵינוּ מֶלֶךְ הָעוֹלָם
אֲשֶׁר קִדְּשָׁנוּ בְּמִצְוֹתָיו וְצִוָּנוּ עַל מִצְוַת עֵרוּב.

בְּדֵין עֵרוּבָא יְהֵא שְׁרֵא לִי לְמֵיזַל מֵאַתְרָא הָדֵין
תְּרֵין אַלְפִּין אַמִּין לְכָל רוּחָא.

עירוב חצרות

On שבת *it is forbidden to carry objects from one private domain to another, or from a private domain into space shared by others, such as a communal staircase, corridor or courtyard. An* עירוב חצרות *is created when each of the Jewish households in a court or apartment block, before* שבת*, places a loaf of bread or matza in one of the homes. The entire court or block then becomes a single private domain within which it is permitted to carry.*

בָּרוּךְ אַתָּה יהוה אֱלֹהֵינוּ מֶלֶךְ הָעוֹלָם
אֲשֶׁר קִדְּשָׁנוּ בְּמִצְוֹתָיו וְצִוָּנוּ עַל מִצְוַת עֵרוּב.

בְּדֵין עֵרוּבָא יְהֵא שְׁרֵא לַנָא לְטַלְטוּלֵי
וּלְאַפּוּקֵי וּלְעַיּוּלֵי מִן הַבָּתִּים לֶחָצֵר וּמִן הֶחָצֵר לַבָּתִּים
וּמִבַּיִת לְבַיִת לְכָל הַבָּתִּים שֶׁבֶּחָצֵר.

CANDLE LIGHTING

On Ḥanukka, light the Ḥanukkia (see page 724) before lighting the Shabbat candles.
On Erev Shabbat cover the eyes with the hands after lighting the candles, and say:

בָּרוּךְ Blessed are You, LORD our God, King of the Universe,
who has made us holy through His commandments,
and has commanded us to light the Sabbath light.

Prayer after candle lighting (add the words in parentheses as appropriate):

יְהִי May it be Your will, LORD my God and God of my forebears,
that You give me grace –
me (and my husband/and my father/and my mother/
and my sons and my daughters) and all those close to me,
and give us and all Israel good and long lives.
And remember us with a memory that brings goodness and blessing;
come to us with compassion
and bless us with great blessings.
Build our homes until they are complete,
and allow Your Presence to live among us.
And may I merit to raise children and grandchildren,
each one wise and understanding,
loving the LORD and in awe of God,
people of truth, holy children,
who will cling on to the LORD
and light up the world with Torah
and with good actions,
and with all the kinds of work that serve the Creator.
Please, hear my pleading at this time,
by the merit of Sarah and Rebecca, Rachel and Leah our mothers,
and light our candle that it should never go out,
and light up Your face,
so that we shall be saved, Amen.

הדלקת נרות

On חנוכה*, light the* חנוכיה *(see page 725) before lighting the* שבת *candles.*
On ערב שבת *cover the eyes with the hands after lighting the candles, and say:*

בָּרוּךְ אַתָּה יהוה אֱלֹהֵינוּ מֶלֶךְ הָעוֹלָם
אֲשֶׁר קִדְּשָׁנוּ בְּמִצְוֹתָיו וְצִוָּנוּ לְהַדְלִיק נֵר שֶׁל שַׁבָּת.

Prayer after candle lighting (add the words in parentheses as appropriate):

יְהִי רָצוֹן מִלְּפָנֶיךָ יהוה אֱלֹהַי וֵאלֹהֵי אֲבוֹתַי
שֶׁתְּחוֹנֵן אוֹתִי (וְאֶת אִישִׁי/ וְאֶת אָבִי/ וְאֶת אִמִּי/
וְאֶת בָּנַי וְאֶת בְּנוֹתַי) וְאֶת כָּל קְרוֹבַי
וְתִתֶּן לָנוּ וּלְכָל יִשְׂרָאֵל חַיִּים טוֹבִים וַאֲרֻכִּים
וְתִזְכְּרֵנוּ בְּזִכְרוֹן טוֹבָה וּבְרָכָה
וְתִפְקְדֵנוּ בִּפְקֻדַּת יְשׁוּעָה וְרַחֲמִים
וּתְבָרְכֵנוּ בְּרָכוֹת גְּדוֹלוֹת
וְתַשְׁלִים בָּתֵּינוּ וְתַשְׁכֵּן שְׁכִינָתְךָ בֵּינֵינוּ.
וְזַכֵּנִי לְגַדֵּל בָּנִים וּבְנֵי בָנִים חֲכָמִים וּנְבוֹנִים
אוֹהֲבֵי יהוה יִרְאֵי אֱלֹהִים
אַנְשֵׁי אֱמֶת זֶרַע קֹדֶשׁ
בַּיהוה דְּבֵקִים
וּמְאִירִים אֶת הָעוֹלָם בַּתּוֹרָה וּבְמַעֲשִׂים טוֹבִים
וּבְכָל מְלֶאכֶת עֲבוֹדַת הַבּוֹרֵא.
אָנָּא שְׁמַע אֶת תְּחִנָּתִי בָּעֵת הַזֹּאת
בִּזְכוּת שָׂרָה וְרִבְקָה וְרָחֵל וְלֵאָה אִמּוֹתֵינוּ
וְהָאֵר נֵרֵנוּ שֶׁלֹּא יִכְבֶּה לְעוֹלָם וָעֶד
וְהָאֵר פָּנֶיךָ וְנִוָּשֵׁעָה. אָמֵן.

Most congregations sing "Beloved of the soul" before the Kabbalat Shabbat service. On Motza'ei Yom Tov falling on Shabbat (when Shabbat begins the evening immediately after a Yom Tov), the service begins with Psalm 92 on page 66.

יְדִיד Beloved of the soul, Father of compassion,
draw Your servant close to Your will.
Like a deer will Your servant run
and fall prostrate before Your beauty.
To him Your love is sweeter
than honey from the comb, than any taste.

הָדוּר Glorious, beautiful, radiance of the world,
my soul is sick with love for You.
Please, God, heal her now
by showing her Your tender radiance.
Then she will recover her strength and be healed,
Be Your servant for eternity.

One must allow body and mind to let down their defenses, to peel back the facades and concerns of our weekday lives, in order to get in touch with things that matter most. For those who have incorporated Shabbat observance into their lives, the transition is easier and more natural, for the body and the soul come to expect this reprieve. Even so, preparation is still required.

For millennia it has been known that one must embrace this day in order to be embraced by it. To be sure, it will come whether we prepare for it or not, but our experience of it will be enhanced the more we seek to be conscious of its presence. Like any activity in life, the more we anticipate, the more we prepare and ready ourselves, the more meaningful will the encounter be. And so there developed customs designed to put us into the correct frame of mind, to enable us to make the switch that our body and soul so badly crave. That is much of the purpose of this special service known as *Kabbalat Shabbat*, or "receiving the Sabbath."

Almost two thousand years ago the Talmud made reference to greeting the Sabbath as an important guest or as a bride whom the groom goes out to greet in order to escort her to the bridal canopy. But the standardized service that we now use is actually a relatively late composition, attributed to the Kabbalists, the mystics who lived in Tzefat (Safed) in northern Israel in the sixteenth century who created their own ceremonies to welcome the Sabbath into their midst. Led by the influential Rabbi Isaac Luria, known as the Ari (the Lion), or the Ari *zal* (the Ari, may his memory be for a blessing), many would gather in the courtyard of the synagogue or actually go out into the fields reciting psalms and songs to greet the Sabbath, as it were, as she entered one's life. Over the course of time, the ceremony moved indoors – sometimes into a different room of the synagogue since this was not a part of the regular service – and

This **INTRODUCTION** *continues on page 37.*

Most congregations sing יְדִיד נֶפֶשׁ *at this point before* קבלת שבת.
On מוצאי יום טוב *falling on* שבת (*when* שבת *begins the evening immediately after a* יום טוב), *the service begins with* מִזְמוֹר שִׁיר *on page 67.*

יְדִיד נֶפֶשׁ, אָב הָרַחֲמָן, מְשֹׁךְ עַבְדָּךְ אֶל רְצוֹנָךְ.
יָרוּץ עַבְדָּךְ כְּמוֹ אַיָּל, יִשְׁתַּחֲוֶה מוּל הֲדָרָךְ.
כִּי יֶעֱרַב לוֹ יְדִידוּתָךְ, מִנֹּפֶת צוּף וְכָל טָֽעַם.

הָדוּר, נָאֶה, זִיו הָעוֹלָם, נַפְשִׁי חוֹלַת אַהֲבָתָךְ.
אָנָּא, אֵל נָא, רְפָא נָא לָהּ, בְּהַרְאוֹת לָהּ נֹֽעַם זִיוָךְ.
אָז תִּתְחַזֵּק וְתִתְרַפֵּא, וְהָיְתָה לָךְ שִׁפְחַת עוֹלָם.

INTRODUCTION TO YEDID NEFESH

This poem was written by Rabbi Elazar Azikri around 1584. Its language is reminiscent of the love poetry of the Song of Songs, an ode to the love between God and Israel. First published as part of the author's own work, it then appeared in a collection of midnight prayers (*Tikkun Ḥatzot*) associated in Kabbalistic circles with the end of the exile and the coming of the Messiah. It subsequently came to be printed as a concluding prayer to Torah study, and then appeared in a number of different but related contexts where one wanted to focus on the love of God and the prayer for redemption. These are precisely the themes one finds in *Kabbalat Shabbat* and so the poem, actually a song, came to be included there by many congregations. Others include it in the songs sung in the afternoon as Shabbat ebbs away.

The present rendition is taken from a manuscript in the author's own hand and thus differs in some ways from those subsequently printed. Consider, for example, the difference in meaning rendered in the second last word in the second stanza which is **שִׁפְחָה**, a maidservant, as opposed to the common version which uses the word **שִׂמְחָה** or happiness.

Read carefully and you will see that this is one of the boldest expressions of the intimate relationship between man and God that is expressed in the siddur. Moreover, unlike so much of the rest of the siddur, this prayer is almost entirely in the singular rather than the plural expressing a particularly personal expression of longing. Most important is the expression it is meant to give to our desire, our passion, our need to be close to the Divine, and if we are not feeling it at the moment, then hopefully we can do so by the end.

INTRODUCTION TO KABBALAT SHABBAT

The transition from a life of the mundane to a life of holiness usually does not happen in a fleeting moment or two. It takes time and a mental shift to another plane.

וָתִיק Ancient of Days, let Your mercy be aroused;
please have pity on Your beloved child.
How long have I yearned
to see the glory of Your strength.
Please, my God, my heart's desire –
hasten; do not hide Yourself.

הִגָּלֵה Reveal Yourself, beloved, and spread over me
the tabernacle of Your peace.
Let the earth shine with Your glory,
let us be overjoyed and rejoice in You.
Hurry, beloved, for the appointed time has come,
and be gracious to me as in the times of old.

Much has been written about the first group of psalms and about the ways in which their themes and language connect with one another and with the service. Suffice it to say here that the overarching theme is praise and thanks to God for creation. We acknowledge His kingship and power which can be both terrifying and awe inspiring, both for us and for the nations of the world. Because the Sabbath marks the climax of creation, we gain perspective on it by looking backwards at the rest of creation and evaluating our place within it, both as individuals and as a nation.

These themes are symbolically alluded to by the very choice of the number of psalms recited; there are six of them corresponding to the six days of the week. The climax will be the realization that comes with the presence of God on Shabbat that is the subject of the song *Lekha Dodi*, the seventh component. It might therefore be helpful to see these psalms as a journey, a recap, as it were, of our week. With each psalm we can move one step closer to the present, the presence that is Shabbat.

For those who are interested in delving further, the first group of psalms are actually quite complex and intriguing from both a literary and theological point of view. The language is highly reminiscent of the language used on Rosh HaShana and Yom Kippur, particularly about God's sovereignty. But there also seems to be some internal structure in which chapters 95 and 96 form a single unit as do chapters 97 and 98. Rav Moshe Lichtenstein describes it thus: "In each group, the first psalm relates to creation itself and the response to it, while the second chapter deals with God's kingship in the world and His judgment of the world. The second psalm of both units focuses not on nature itself, but rather the control and authority over it. If you will, the first of the pair deals with the past, the period of creation itself and that which came into existence at the time, while the second relates to the Almighty's ongoing involvement in the natural world as King and Magistrate. It speaks of the continuing reality resulting from creation, as opposed to the actual moment of creation." (Yet one must also explain

This **OVERVIEW** *continues on page 39.*

וָתִיק, יֶהֱמוּ רַחֲמֶיךָ, וְחוּס נָא עַל בֵּן אוֹהֲבָךְ
כִּי זֶה כַּמֶּה נִכְסֹף נִכְסַף לִרְאוֹת בְּתִפְאֶרֶת עֻזָּךְ
אָנָּא, אֵלִי, מַחְמַד לִבִּי, חוּשָׁה נָּא, וְאַל תִּתְעַלָּם.

הִגָּלֶה נָא וּפְרֹשׂ, חָבִיב, עָלַי אֶת סֻכַּת שְׁלוֹמָךְ
תָּאִיר אֶרֶץ מִכְּבוֹדָךְ, נָגִילָה וְנִשְׂמְחָה בָךְ.
מַהֵר, אָהוּב, כִּי בָא מוֹעֵד, וְחָנֵּנִי כִּימֵי עוֹלָם.

then eventually into the main sanctuary itself (*Noheg KeTzon Yosef*, *Magen Avraham*). Since the Shabbat itself has not yet arrived at this point, there were communities that used musical instruments in the service in keeping with the Talmudic dictum (*Shabbat* 30b) that the Divine Presence only descends in a place where there is joy, as it says of the prophet Elisha "And it came to pass when the minstrel played, that the hand of God came upon him" (*Melakhim* II 3:15). Instruments in a synagogue are now eschewed, but an atmosphere of joy still remains the goal.

HILKHOT TEFILLA • הלכות תפילה

Since the standardized *Kabbalat Shabbat* service as we know it is a relatively recent phenomenon (400 years old in a tradition of millennia), there is a custom in many communities that the person leading the service stands in a different place than he would for most other occasions in order to convey that this is not one of the services that is part of a biblical or rabbinic tradition. In some congregations, in order to highlight the difference, he will go back to the usual place at the podium where the leader (*ḥazan*) normally stands for the evening service (*Ma'ariv*) which follows this one.

The beginning of *Kabbalat Shabbat* through the singing of the song *Lekha Dodi* is omitted in many communities in whole or in part when Yom Tov "clashes" with Shabbat. So, for example, when Yom Tov begins on a Friday night, some felt that it would be a slap in the face to Yom Tov, as it were, to have a service which welcomed the Shabbat but ignored the Yom Tov (*Arukh HaShulḥan* 270:3). Some felt that some of the themes of the *Kabbalat Shabbat* service were less in keeping with the themes of Shabbat (e.g. *Alef le'Magen* in *Mateh Efraim* 625). As such, much of *Kabbalat Shabbat* is omitted.

AN OVERVIEW OF THE KABBALAT SHABBAT SERVICE

The structure of the service consists of three parts:

1. Chapters from the book of *Tehillim* (Psalms): 95, 96, 97, 98, 99, 29
2. The poetic song called *Lekha Dodi* (Come, My Beloved)
3. More chapters of *Tehillim*: 92 and 93

Kabbalat Shabbat

Mourners during the week of Shiva leave the synagogue at this point, returning after "Come, my Beloved" on page 66.

לְכוּ נְרַנְּנָה Come, let us sing for joy to the LORD, *Ps. 95*
let us shout aloud[B] to the Rock of our salvation.
Let us greet Him with thanksgiving,
shout aloud to Him with songs of praise.
For the LORD is the great God, the King great above all powers.
In His hand are the depths of the earth,
and the mountain peaks are His.
The sea is His, for He made it;
the dry land too, for His hands formed it.
Come, let us bow in worship
and bend the knee before the LORD our Maker.
For He is our God, and we are the people of His pasture,
the flock He tends[I] – today, if you would heed His voice.[I]

---

to the Temple (Ibn Ezra). Or, rather than a call to physical movement, it could be an expression of encouragement to the reader (Radak) to participate spiritually. Alternatively, it could be a call to believe in God and His providence (Meiri). Or, finally, it could be a combination of all of these: to join physically, spiritually, theologically in the community of celebration that is Shabbat.

Allow yourself to relax and join in with those around you.

נְקַדְּמָה פָנָיו – *Let us greet Him.* The word פָּנָיו (*panav*) literally means His face or countenance. In the Torah it is used as an expression when one encountered God in the Tabernacle (*Shemot* 27:21), or before the Holy Ark there (*Shemot* 16:33 and Rashi) or, alternatively, when one stands before the Divine Presence (*Shemot* 33:14). Shabbat too can be such an encounter. One can stand in the presence of the Divine not only in place but also in time.

Imagine yourself there now.

IYUN TEFILLA • עיון תפילה

כִּי הוּא אֱלֹהֵינוּ, וַאֲנַחְנוּ עַם מַרְעִיתוֹ וְצֹאן יָדוֹ – *For He is our God, and we are the people of His pasture, the flock He tends.* This verse parallels the third verse above in that they both give reasons why one should praise Hashem. In the verse above, it was because He is "great...above all powers," that is, He is a universal God. But here it is because we have a special relationship with Him. We can be both universalistic and

This IYUN TEFILLA *continues on page 41.*

קבלת שבת

Mourners during the week of שבעה *leave the* בית כנסת *at this point, returning after* לְכָה דוֹדִי *on page 67.*

תהלים צה

לְכוּ נְרַנְּנָה לַיהוה, נָרִיעָה לְצוּר יִשְׁעֵנוּ:
נְקַדְּמָה פָנָיו בְּתוֹדָה, בִּזְמִרוֹת נָרִיעַ לוֹ:
כִּי אֵל גָּדוֹל יהוה, וּמֶלֶךְ גָּדוֹל עַל־כָּל־אֱלֹהִים:
אֲשֶׁר בְּיָדוֹ מֶחְקְרֵי־אָרֶץ, וְתוֹעֲפוֹת הָרִים לוֹ:
אֲשֶׁר־לוֹ הַיָּם וְהוּא עָשָׂהוּ, וְיַבֶּשֶׁת יָדָיו יָצָרוּ:
בֹּאוּ נִשְׁתַּחֲוֶה וְנִכְרָעָה, נִבְרְכָה לִפְנֵי־יהוה עֹשֵׂנוּ:
כִּי הוּא אֱלֹהֵינוּ, וַאֲנַחְנוּ עַם מַרְעִיתוֹ וְצֹאן יָדוֹ
הַיּוֹם אִם־בְּקֹלוֹ תִשְׁמָעוּ:

why the need for both units. Try to find a difference between them.)

In short, what we are supposed to be thinking about and what we may be feeling, are guided not only by what words we say but how they are said as well. Look for common words and expressions, be sensitive to the nuances of difference, but never lose sight of the destination, the holiness of time that is Shabbat.

BIUR TEFILLA • ביאור תפילה

לְכוּ נְרַנְּנָה לַיהוה, נָרִיעָה – *Come, let us sing for joy to the* Lord, *let us shout aloud.* The psalm begins with a joyful celebratory tone, calling on everyone to join together to sing and shout. From the outset, the goal is to move us away from our work week and recognize that we are about to enter into a different state of mind. That happens not by itself, but by a change in our perspective.

Think joyfulness.

The word **לְכוּ** (*lekhu*) can literally mean to walk, which in this context could mean urging people to walk

ANI TEFILLA • אני תפילה

Imagine a building with a soundproof room in which takes place a party where the music is blaring and people are dancing wildly with reckless abandon. Someone from another planet arrives at that moment and is positioned outside the building. He sees what is going on but cannot hear the sounds nor can he understand what these people are doing. Their actions can look strangely incomprehensible, people gesturing wildly and moving quickly with no apparent purpose. That is the way I sometimes look back upon my week. At the moment, it all seemed to make sense; now, in retrospect, at least some of my actions look foreign and misplaced and I resolve to make next week look different.

Do not harden your hearts as you did at Meribah,
as you did that day at Massah in the desert,[B]
when your ancestors tested and tried Me
though they had seen My deeds.
▸ For forty years I strove with that generation.
I said, "They are a people whose hearts go astray,
who have not understood My ways."
So I swore in My anger,
"They shall not enter My place of rest."

שִׁירוּ Sing to the LORD a new song;[B] *Ps. 96*
sing to the LORD all the earth.
Sing to the LORD,[A] bless His name;
proclaim his deliverance day after day.

BIUR TEFILLA • ביאור תפילה

Psalm 96. These verses are reminiscent of those that appear with some variations in the book of Chronicles (*Divrei Hayamim* I 16), recited as part of the celebration by David when the Holy Ark was brought to Jerusalem (*Avoda Zara* 24b). Its celebratory tone is in keeping with the spirit of welcoming the Shabbat into one's midst for, like being in the presence of the Ark, or immersed in the unique atmosphere of Jerusalem and the Temple, so, too, we find ourselves now on the verge of an encounter with holiness.

שִׁירוּ לַיהוה שִׁיר חָדָשׁ – *Sing to the LORD a new song.* The phrase "a new song" appears in a few of these psalms. Its purpose is to convey that we believe that God was not like a watchmaker who created the world, wound it up so that it would operate by itself and then walked away. Rather, He is forever involved in creation, each day is a new day of re-creation. As such, each day requires a new song (Malbim). In Judaism, we take nothing for granted. **How can you see your today as a new day? Think of the small things. Sometimes the special can be found in the everyday.**

ANI TEFILLA • אני תפילה

שִׁירוּ לַיהוה שִׁיר חָדָשׁ, שִׁירוּ לַיהוה כָּל־הָאָרֶץ שִׁירוּ לַיהוה – ***Sing*** *to the LORD a new song;* ***sing*** *to the LORD all the earth,* ***Sing*** *to the LORD.* Sing! Sing! Sing! That is the message of the first verses of this psalm. Sometimes we sing because we are happy; at other times we are happy because we sing.

אַל־תַּקְשׁוּ לְבַבְכֶם כִּמְרִיבָה, כְּיוֹם מַסָּה בַּמִּדְבָּר: ב

אֲשֶׁר נִסּוּנִי אֲבוֹתֵיכֶם, בְּחָנוּנִי גַּם רָאוּ פָעֳלִי:

◂ אַרְבָּעִים שָׁנָה אָקוּט בְּדוֹר, וָאֹמַר עַם תֹּעֵי לֵבָב הֵם

וְהֵם לֹא־יָדְעוּ דְרָכָי:

אֲשֶׁר־נִשְׁבַּעְתִּי בְאַפִּי, אִם־יְבֹאוּן אֶל מְנוּחָתִי:

תהלים צו

שִׁירוּ לַיהוה שִׁיר חָדָשׁ, ב שִׁירוּ לַיהוה כָּל־הָאָרֶץ:

שִׁירוּ לַיהוה, א בָּרְכוּ שְׁמוֹ, בַּשְּׂרוּ מִיּוֹם־לְיוֹם יְשׁוּעָתוֹ:

---

particularistic at the same time. To be Jewish means to see yourself as special and unique even as you see yourself as part of humanity at large.

BIUR TEFILLA • ביאור תפילה

אַל־תַּקְשׁוּ לְבַבְכֶם כִּמְרִיבָה, כְּיוֹם מַסָּה בַּמִּדְבָּר – *Do not harden your hearts as you did at Meribah, as you did that day at Massah in the desert.* In a dramatic turn, the psalm shifts from the third person to God Himself speaking, as it were, in the first person, directly to the Jewish people. He admonishes us not to make the same mistakes our ancestors did in the desert: they saw the plagues, the splitting of the sea, the revelation at Sinai. Nevertheless, they lost their faith (cf. *Shemot* 17:7). Supernatural miracles are no guarantor of ongoing belief.

IYUN TEFILLA • עיון תפילה

הַיּוֹם אִם־בְּקֹלוֹ תִשְׁמָעוּ – *Today, if you would heed His voice.* (previous page) The *Midrash Shoḥer Tov* homiletically interprets the word "today" as a reference to the Shabbat day. And so "Rabbi Levi said, 'If the entire Jewish people were to observe even one Shabbat appropriately, then they would be redeemed immediately' (*Yerushalmi Ta'anit* 1:1)." Of course, this isn't a statement just about the nation, but about each of us, today, right now.

ANI TEFILLA • אני תפילה

"Hardening of the heart" is both an intellectual and spiritual malady. It is what prevented Pharaoh from letting the Hebrews leave Egypt. And it is what prevented the Jews from entering the Promised Land. This, despite the fact that the generation of the desert was the first to feel the Divine Presence in its midst. It is as if the psalmist is saying, "You have that opportunity again right now, this evening. Don't make the same mistake. Suspend your intellectual and spiritual doubts. Immerse yourself in My Sabbath, "My place of rest."

Try to do that now. Let go.

Declare His glory among the nations,
His marvels among all peoples.
For great is the LORD and greatly to be praised;
He is awesome beyond all heavenly powers.
For all the gods of the peoples are mere idols:
it was the LORD who made the heavens.
Before Him are majesty and splendor;
there are strength and beauty in His holy place.
Render to the LORD, O families of the peoples;|
render to the LORD glory and might.
Render to the LORD| the glory due to His name;
bring an offering and come into His courts.
Bow down| to the LORD in the splendor of holiness.
Tremble before Him, all the earth.
Say among the nations, "The LORD is King."
The world stands firm, it will not be shaken.
He will judge the peoples with equity.

וּבֹאוּ לְחַצְרוֹתָיו: הִשְׁתַּחֲווּ – *Come into His courts, Bow down.* Like a servant who cannot gain entry to the inner chambers of the palace, one might mistakenly think that one cannot approach God; He is too hidden, too distant. Not so. If one is prepared to simply acknowledge Hashem as Creator of the world, then one's entry to the courtyard is guaranteed. This is because one will perforce "bow" and be humbled by the realization of one's place in the universe.

Think of being somewhere in nature that made you "bow."

ANI TEFILLA • אני תפילה

"The Egyptian, the Babylonian, and the Persian rose, filled the planet with sound and splendor, then faded to dream-stuff and passed away; the Greek and the Roman followed, and made a vast noise, and they are gone; other peoples have sprung up and held their torch high for a time, but it burned out, and they sit in twilight now, or have vanished. The Jew saw them all, beat them all, and is now what he always was, exhibiting no decadence, no infirmities of age, no weakening of his parts, no slowing of his energies, no dulling of his alert and aggressive mind.

All things are mortal but the Jew; all other forces pass, but he remains. What is the secret of his immortality?" (Mark Twain)

Welcome to Shabbat. Welcome to immortality.

סַפְּרוּ בַגּוֹיִם כְּבוֹדוֹ, בְּכָל־הָעַמִּים נִפְלְאוֹתָיו:
כִּי גָדוֹל יהוה וּמְהֻלָּל מְאֹד, נוֹרָא הוּא עַל־כָּל־אֱלֹהִים:
כִּי כָּל־אֱלֹהֵי הָעַמִּים אֱלִילִים, וַיהוה שָׁמַיִם עָשָׂה:
הוֹד־וְהָדָר לְפָנָיו, עֹז וְתִפְאֶרֶת בְּמִקְדָּשׁוֹ:
הָבוּ לַיהוה מִשְׁפְּחוֹת עַמִּים, הָבוּ לַיהוה כָּבוֹד וָעֹז:
הָבוּ לַיהוה כְּבוֹד שְׁמוֹ, שְׂאוּ־מִנְחָה וּבֹאוּ לְחַצְרוֹתָיו:
הִשְׁתַּחֲווּ לַיהוה בְּהַדְרַת־קֹדֶשׁ, חִילוּ מִפָּנָיו כָּל־הָאָרֶץ:
אִמְרוּ בַגּוֹיִם יהוה מָלָךְ, אַף־תִּכּוֹן תֵּבֵל בַּל־תִּמּוֹט
יָדִין עַמִּים בְּמֵישָׁרִים:

BIUR TEFILLA • ביאור תפילה

סַפְּרוּ בַגּוֹיִם כְּבוֹדוֹ – *Declare His glory among the nations.* His glory could be a description of God Himself and the miracles He has performed. Alternatively, it could be a reference to the Jewish people: Our very survival against all odds through the millennia is a subject of incredulousness by the nations of the world. In their eyes, we are His glory (Radak).

How might this still be true in our own time?

IYUN TEFILLA • עיון תפילה

הָבוּ לַיהוה מִשְׁפְּחוֹת עַמִּים, הָבוּ לַיהוה כָּבוֹד וָעֹז: הָבוּ לַיהוה – ***Render** to the Lord, O families of the peoples, **render** to the Lord glory and might, **Render** to the Lord.* The threefold invitation to "sing…sing… sing" at the beginning of the psalm is paralleled by the threefold call to the nations of the world to "render to Hashem," to come together in unity to recognize that there is but one God, a belief that is one of Judaism's most significant contributions to civilization. One of the byproducts of being filled with happiness is the desire to share it with others. We do so not by trying to impose our will but by sharing our joy. We can share that joy by being joyful. We can also become joyful by allowing ourselves to be drawn in by the joy of others.

Look around you. Whom can you influence?

Who can be made joyful by you? Who can help you be more joyful?

הָבוּ לַיהוה מִשְׁפְּחוֹת עַמִּים – *literally: Bring to the Lord the families of the nations.* The midrash homiletically suggests that unlike so many nations of the world, our shared lineage goes back to a time well before the giving of the Torah at Sinai (*Yalkut Shimoni* 684). Our history and our beliefs have been uninterrupted and unparalleled.

▸ Let the heavens rejoice and the earth be glad.
Let the sea roar, and all that is in it;
let the fields be jubilant, and all they contain.
Then the trees of the forest will sing for joy before the LORD,
for He is coming to judge the earth.[1]
He will judge the world with justice,
and the peoples with His faithfulness.

יהוה מָלָךְ The LORD reigns, let the earth be glad.[B] *Ps. 97*
Let the many islands rejoice.
Clouds and thick darkness surround Him;
righteousness and justice are the foundation of His throne.[B]
Fire goes ahead of Him,
consuming His enemies on every side.
His lightning lights up the world;
the earth sees and trembles.
Mountains melt like wax before the LORD,
before the LORD of all the earth.
The heavens proclaim His righteousness,
and all the peoples see His glory.

יהוה מָלָךְ תָּגֵל הָאָרֶץ – *The LORD reigns, let the earth be glad.* This is an imperative directed to us. Sometimes one must be commanded to be positive and optimistic even if one is not feeling it (*Da'at Sofrim*).

עָנָן וַעֲרָפֶל סְבִיבָיו, צֶדֶק וּמִשְׁפָּט מְכוֹן כִּסְאוֹ – *Clouds and thick darkness surround Him; righteousness and justice are the foundation of His throne.* The initial image is one of darkness and foreboding (*Metzuda*). Alternatively, perhaps it is an allusion to the fact that God can be hidden and unfathomable, especially in a world where evil and injustice can seem to get the upper hand so often. Responds the psalmist: If you want to see God, look at acts of kindness and fairness, righteousness and justice (Radak). Therein lies the light that allows one to keep the faith. Think back to one's week.

Where did you see such an act this week? How can you be the agent of such an act this coming week?

◂ יִשְׂמְחוּ הַשָּׁמַיִם וְתָגֵל הָאָרֶץ, יִרְעַם הַיָּם וּמְלֹאוֹ:
יַעֲלֹז שָׂדַי וְכָל־אֲשֶׁר־בּוֹ, אָז יְרַנְּנוּ כָּל־עֲצֵי־יָעַר:
לִפְנֵי יהוה כִּי בָא, כִּי בָא לִשְׁפֹּט הָאָרֶץ
יִשְׁפֹּט־תֵּבֵל בְּצֶדֶק, וְעַמִּים בֶּאֱמוּנָתוֹ:

תהלים צז
יהוה מָלָךְ תָּגֵל הָאָרֶץ, יִשְׂמְחוּ אִיִּים רַבִּים:
עָנָן וַעֲרָפֶל סְבִיבָיו, צֶדֶק וּמִשְׁפָּט מְכוֹן כִּסְאוֹ:
אֵשׁ לְפָנָיו תֵּלֵךְ, וּתְלַהֵט סָבִיב צָרָיו:
הֵאִירוּ בְרָקָיו תֵּבֵל, רָאֲתָה וַתָּחֵל הָאָרֶץ:
הָרִים כַּדּוֹנַג נָמַסּוּ מִלִּפְנֵי יהוה, מִלִּפְנֵי אֲדוֹן כָּל־הָאָרֶץ:
הִגִּידוּ הַשָּׁמַיִם צִדְקוֹ, וְרָאוּ כָל־הָעַמִּים כְּבוֹדוֹ:

IYUN TEFILLA • עיון תפילה

כִּי בָא לִשְׁפֹּט הָאָרֶץ – *He is coming to judge the earth.* Perhaps this is another reference to the return of the Ark, which contained the laws of the Torah, to Jerusalem as mentioned at the outset. It symbolizes a return of justice to the world, a code of morality that all can share, the guarantee of a measure of universal integrity. For our mission as Jews is not to proselytize but to act as a light unto the nations by the way we live our lives, being the most moral we can be, living Shabbat as it should be.

BIUR TEFILLA • ביאור תפילה

Psalm 97. It has been suggested that this psalm is a continuation of the previous one but in what way is the subject of dispute. Perhaps it is merely a continuation of the description of the kinds of events which must precede God's revelation and the ideal society (Rabbi S. Hirsch). Alternatively, if the previous one was about singing a new song announcing God's reign, here God comes to reveal Himself. There is a description of the reaction of the entire world, the heavens and the earth, the idol worshipers and the righteous, resulting in a world that is more moral and upright. Certainly Shabbat may be seen to be a foretaste and foreshadowing of that world.

All who worship images and boast in idols are put to shame.[AI]
Bow down to Him, all you heavenly powers.
Zion hears and rejoices, and the towns of Judah are glad
because of your judgments, LORD.
For You, LORD, are supreme over all the earth;
You are exalted far above all heavenly powers.
▸ Let those who love the LORD hate evil,[I]
for He protects the lives of his devoted ones,
delivering them from the hand of the wicked.
Light is sown for the righteous,[I] and joy for the upright in heart.
Rejoice in the LORD, you who are righteous,
and give thanks to His holy name.

---

of loving God is the desire to be like God, to imitate His ways, just as a young child wants to be like his parents out of a deep abiding connection with them. The commandment to be like Him is not translated into abstract theological concepts but into concrete practical ones.

> R. Ḥama son of R. Ḥanina further said: What means the text: You shall walk after the LORD your God? (*Devarim* 13:5) Is it, then, possible for a human being to literally walk after the Divine Presence; for has it not been said: "For the LORD your God is a devouring fire" (*Devarim* 4:24)? But [the meaning is] to walk after the *attributes* of the Holy One, blessed be He. As He clothes the naked, for it is written: "And the LORD God made for Adam and for his wife coats of skin, and clothed them," (*Bereshit* 3:21), so should you also clothe the naked. The Holy One, blessed be He, visited the sick, for it is written: "And the LORD appeared to him by the oaks of Mamre" (*Bereshit* 18:1), so should you also visit the sick. The Holy One, blessed be He, comforted mourners, for it is written: "And it came to pass after the death of Abraham, that God blessed Isaac his son," (*Bereshit* 25:11), so should you also comfort mourners. The Holy one, blessed be He, buried the dead, for it is written: "And He buried him in the valley," (*Devarim* 34:6), so should you also bury the dead. (*Sotah* 14a)

To love Hashem means to be sensitive to one another's needs.

How can you imitate God this Shabbat?

Alternatively, the "lovers of Hashem" are the non-Jews who return to monotheism (Meiri). Our dream is join forces with all peoples who can share our core values even if they do not share our lifestyle.

אוֹר זָרֻעַ לַצַּדִּיק – *Light is sown for the righteous.* Righteous behavior can be a light which illuminates the world for those around you. Earlier, fire and lightning were mentioned but these are temporary sources of light that can quickly dissipate. Good deeds, however, have the potential to light up small dark corners of the world, one act at time, like seeds that are sown that ultimately bear fruit (*Da'at Sofrim*).

This **IYUN TEFILLA** *continues on page 49.*

יֵבֹשׁוּ כׇּל־עֹבְדֵי פֶסֶל הַמִּתְהַלְלִים בָּאֱלִילִים[אע]
הִשְׁתַּחֲווּ־לוֹ כׇּל־אֱלֹהִים:
שָׁמְעָה וַתִּשְׂמַח צִיּוֹן, וַתָּגֵלְנָה בְּנוֹת יְהוּדָה
לְמַעַן מִשְׁפָּטֶיךָ יהוה:
כִּי־אַתָּה יהוה עֶלְיוֹן עַל־כׇּל־הָאָרֶץ
מְאֹד נַעֲלֵיתָ עַל־כׇּל־אֱלֹהִים:
◂ אֹהֲבֵי יהוה שִׂנְאוּ רָע,[ע] שֹׁמֵר נַפְשׁוֹת חֲסִידָיו
מִיַּד רְשָׁעִים יַצִּילֵם:
אוֹר זָרֻעַ לַצַּדִּיק,[ע] וּלְיִשְׁרֵי־לֵב שִׂמְחָה:
שִׂמְחוּ צַדִּיקִים בַּיהוה, וְהוֹדוּ לְזֵכֶר קׇדְשׁוֹ:

ANI TEFILLA • אני תפילה

יֵבֹשׁוּ כׇּל־עֹבְדֵי פֶסֶל הַמִּתְהַלְלִים בָּאֱלִילִים – *All who worship images and boast in idols are put to shame.* A young man came to his grandfather wanting to understand the dangers of materialism. His grandfather asked him to look outside the window which overlooked the street and asked him what he saw. "I see people of all kinds, walking past the building," he replied. "And now," said the grandfather, "look into this mirror and tell me what you see." The boy was perplexed but did as he was told and responded, "Well, I see myself." "Now you will understand," said the grandfather. "For, in truth, the window pane and the mirror are both made of glass, the only difference being that one of them is covered in silver. But that is the impact of silver, that it has a tendency to make people lose sight of others, and only see themselves."

Shabbat in general, and prayer in particular, are an opportunity to look beyond the self and ask oneself what one sees.

IYUN TEFILLA • עיון תפילה

יֵבֹשׁוּ כׇּל־עֹבְדֵי פֶסֶל הַמִּתְהַלְלִים בָּאֱלִילִים – *All who worship images and boast in idols are put to shame.* Alternatively, "they are praised through idols." People rejoice in their gods – idols, money, materialism, career success – fame, but in our heart of hearts we know that what really counts is to be a good person. Shabbat can be about regaining that perspective, and taking it into the following week.

Resolve to do something different next week.

אֹהֲבֵי יהוה שִׂנְאוּ רָע – *Let those who love the Lord hate evil.* In Jewish life, a major aspect

מִזְמוֹר A Psalm. Sing a new song to the LORD,[I] Ps. 98
for He has done wondrous things;
He has saved by His right hand and His holy arm.
The LORD has made His salvation known;
He has displayed His righteousness in the sight of the nations.[B]
He remembered His loving-kindness
and faithfulness to the house of Israel;[I]
all the ends of the earth have seen the victory of our LORD.[I]

because we are different today than we were yesterday and, hopefully, we are also renewed.

Shake off the old you for a moment or two and feel new again.

זָכַר חַסְדּוֹ וֶאֱמוּנָתוֹ לְבֵית יִשְׂרָאֵל – *He remembered His loving-kindness and faithfulness to the house of Israel.* The words could also homiletically be understood to mean "He remembered the faith of the house of Israel." The Jewish people believed in God at the time of the exodus but the Egyptians did not, yet they saw the same miracles before their very eyes (*Kedushat Levi*). Two people can see the same event and come to very different conclusions. Truth can be difficult to see or it can be staring you in the face.

רָאוּ כָל־אַפְסֵי־אָרֶץ אֵת יְשׁוּעַת אֱלֹהֵינוּ – *All the ends of the earth have seen the victory of our LORD.* Even before the age of telecommunications, the world was aware of the Jewish people. At times there was anti-Semitism in countries where there were not even any Jews. Instead, we pray for the day when Jews are known in the far corners of the globe only for their morality and religiosity. In what way can I make a difference in that mission?

The harp, the trumpets, the songs, the shofar, the shouts for joy are all reminiscent of the coronation of a king. Indeed, much of the language here is reminiscent of that used in the Rosh HaShana services where the theme of God's sovereignty is emphasized most. The clapping of the thunder and the seas, the breaking surf of the ocean, the grandeur of the mountains evoke a world that is in sync with man's own recognition of a force that is greater than the self.

Was there ever a time when you experienced the thunder or the ocean or the view from atop a mountain and felt that there was something bigger than yourself?

ANI TEFILLA • אני תפילה

A young man who thought he did not need a life of Torah and mitzvot once recounted to Rav Noach Weinberg that he was riding along mountain road on his motorcycle, when a big truck came barreling at him. He swerved and went off the road and instinctively he called out to God to save him. "I landed in a bush and was unscathed," said the young man. "So you see, God and I are the best of friends [even without Judaism]." Rav Noach responded: "And who do you think it was who sent the truck?"

תהלים צח

מִזְמוֹר, שִׁירוּ לַיהוה שִׁיר חָדָשׁ כִּי־נִפְלָאוֹת עָשָׂה
הוֹשִׁיעָה־לּוֹ יְמִינוֹ וּזְרוֹעַ קָדְשׁוֹ:
הוֹדִיעַ יהוה יְשׁוּעָתוֹ, לְעֵינֵי הַגּוֹיִם גִּלָּה צִדְקָתוֹ:
זָכַר חַסְדּוֹ וֶאֱמוּנָתוֹ לְבֵית יִשְׂרָאֵל
רָאוּ כָל־אַפְסֵי־אָרֶץ אֵת יְשׁוּעַת אֱלֹהֵינוּ:

What small act of light can you plant today?

In addition, righteous behavior can lead you out of the darkness, for it has a way of changing your perspective.

This could also be interpreted to mean that light is planted within the righteous. Each of us has that spark of light within us that can be uncovered further by our simply making changes in our lives.

How can I enable my inner light to shine brighter today?

This psalm and the next one are often part of the service held on Israel Independence Day, Yom Ha'Atzma'ut.

What themes do you think they that made them an appropriate choice for that day?

BIUR TEFILLA • ביאור תפילה

Psalm 98. If in the previous psalm God was revealed to the world, here there is a celebration of His having been revealed specifically through the restoration of the Jewish people in the eyes of the nations of the world. This, in turn, will have two consequences: it will lead man to a greater knowledge of God and it will enable the Jewish people to fulfill its mission to convey to the rest of the world how God should be worshiped. The glimpse of that future brings joy not only to humankind but to all of creation as the forces of nature all make themselves felt in celebratory terms. In the eyes of the religious personality, the world is one organic whole that lives together and celebrates together.

הוֹדִיעַ יהוה יְשׁוּעָתוֹ, לְעֵינֵי הַגּוֹיִם גִּלָּה צִדְקָתוֹ – *The Lord has made His salvation known; He has displayed His righteousness in the sight of the nations.* He has made His salvation known through his restoration of the Jewish people.

What evidence can you see of this today? In what ways do you think it is acknowledged by the people of the world?

IYUN TEFILLA • עיון תפילה

שִׁירוּ לַיהוה שִׁיר חָדָשׁ – *Sing a new song to the Lord.* We have seen this expression already in Psalm 96. Each fresh insight into life dictates the need for a new song, sometimes for others, sometimes for ourselves. The siddur wants us to take nothing for granted. And even if the words of this new song become familiar and worn, we ourselves change, our realizations grow with each passing minute and week. Our song is new

Shout for joy to the LORD, all the earth;
burst into song,[A] sing with joy, play music.
Play music to the LORD on the harp –
on the harp with the sound of singing.
With trumpets and the sound of the shofar,
shout for joy before the LORD, the King.
▸ Let the sea and all that is in it thunder,
the world and all who live in it.
Let the rivers clap their hands,
the mountains sing together for joy –
before the LORD, for He is coming to judge the earth.
He will judge the world with justice, and the peoples with equity.

יהוה מָלָךְ The LORD reigns, let the peoples tremble. *Ps. 99*
He sits enthroned on the Cherubim, let the earth quake.
Great is the LORD in Zion, He is exalted[B] over all the peoples.
Let them praise Your name, O great and awesome One: He is holy!

BIUR TEFILLA • ביאור תפילה

Psalm 99. The psalm may be divided into three sections. He is the God of all of the nations. He represents justice and righteousness. He answers all who are close to Him. Each section contains the word "exalted" (*ram/romemu*). Each contains some reference to the Temple. And each speaks about His holiness. For holiness and exaltedness can mean set apart, seemingly distant and remote from the everyday. Nevertheless, the theme is exactly the opposite.

וְרָם הוּא – *He is exalted.* The word "exalted" or "on high" (*ram*), which appears three times in this psalm, is a reference to that which is high but disconnected from any foundation, such as the sky, whereas the synonymous "great" (*gadol*) is a reference to that which is high but is rooted in the ground and grows upwards. There are those who say that God is on high, removed from this world, whereas the Jewish people have always seen Him as very much connected to our daily lives here on earth. We may view Him as being beyond our grasp but He is nevertheless very close (Rabbi Mordekhai Benet). For Judaism, religion is not only something otherworldly; it must be in the here and now, of this earth and this life.

הָרִיעוּ לַיהוה כָּל־הָאָרֶץ, פִּצְחוּ[א] וְרַנְּנוּ וְזַמֵּרוּ:
זַמְּרוּ לַיהוה בְּכִנּוֹר, בְּכִנּוֹר וְקוֹל זִמְרָה:
בַּחֲצֹצְרוֹת וְקוֹל שׁוֹפָר, הָרִיעוּ לִפְנֵי הַמֶּלֶךְ יהוה:
◂ יִרְעַם הַיָּם וּמְלֹאוֹ, תֵּבֵל וְיֹשְׁבֵי בָהּ:
נְהָרוֹת יִמְחֲאוּ־כָף, יַחַד הָרִים יְרַנֵּנוּ:
לִפְנֵי יהוה כִּי בָא לִשְׁפֹּט הָאָרֶץ
יִשְׁפֹּט־תֵּבֵל בְּצֶדֶק, וְעַמִּים בְּמֵישָׁרִים:

תהלים צט
יהוה מָלָךְ יִרְגְּזוּ עַמִּים, יֹשֵׁב כְּרוּבִים תָּנוּט הָאָרֶץ:
יהוה בְּצִיּוֹן גָּדוֹל, וְרָם[ב] הוּא עַל־כָּל־הָעַמִּים:
יוֹדוּ שִׁמְךָ גָּדוֹל וְנוֹרָא קָדוֹשׁ הוּא:

ANI TEFILLA • אני תפילה

פִּצְחוּ – *Burst into song.* The word **פצח** can mean to burst or to crack open. Sometimes one must crack open one's heart to sing. It does not come so easily to everyone or when one is not necessarily in the mood. The siddur encourages us to open ourselves up, to crack our outer layer like the earth's crust so that our inner voice may be heard. **Take a deep breath. Give your soul permission to be heard.**

Once when I was in Auschwitz, I found myself in the presence of the Rebbe of Sanz, Rabbi Yekutiel Halberstam, and I heard him provide some teaching on the verse "Sing a new song to Hashem, for He has done wondrous things; He has saved by His right hand and His holy arm." The Rebbe said whatever he said, first translating each word into Yiddish so all would understand. I couldn't understand at that time exactly what he was saying, but the verse alone awakened such fury within me: What am I hearing from this man?! Where [in Auschwitz] are the "wonders"?! Where is "His arm"?!

Even so, as the years passed and many experiences later, I recalled that event once again and suddenly it occurred to me: was that scene itself not a "wonder"? Is it not an incredible thing that in the midst of the hell of Auschwitz there is a Jew who believes in God and has faith in Him and is heartened by the miracles that He will yet perform? It was this understanding that caused me, albeit very belatedly, to return to Judaism. (Lapid HaEsh, p. 211)

The King in His might loves justice.|
You have established equity.|
The justice and righteousness in Jacob is Your doing.|
Exalt the LORD our God, and bow at His footstool: He is holy!
Moses and Aaron were among His priests;
Samuel was among those who called on His name.[B]
They called on the LORD and He answered them.
▸ He spoke to them in a pillar of cloud;
they observed His testimonies and the statute He gave them.
LORD our God, You answered them.
You were for them a forgiving God,
though You punished their misdeeds.[B]
Exalt the LORD our God and bow at His holy mountain,
for the LORD our God is holy.

---

personalities these three were picked for special mention. It could be because they were priests (*kohanim*) and Levites and thus responsible for the functioning of the Temple which is soon to be mentioned. Or, on a related note, they all heard the voice of God calling out to them from atop the Ark where the cherubim, mentioned in the opening verse of this psalm, were located.

Alternatively, it could be because they represent the three roles of prophecy, priesthood and kingship (Shmuel was the one who anointed Israel's first kings, Shaul and David) (Rabbi Jonathan Sacks).

Furthermore, it could be for their teaching roles; Moshe was responsible for the first Jewish legal system while Aharon was the leader of ritual and, in a later generation, Shmuel traveled around the country doing both. The law has a home in the Temple, but it cannot reside only there.

It could also be because despite their higher status, they too called out in prayer, or because their prayers were answered. Despite the fact that all is decreed from Heaven, there is always room for man's requests to be fulfilled. Change is always possible.

וְנֹקֵם עַל־עֲלִילוֹתָם – *Though You punished their misdeeds.* If this is a reference to Moshe and Aharon and Shmuel, then the implication is clear. Judaism has always recognized that our most illustrious leaders were also human beings replete with their own failings for which they were held accountable (*Bemidbar* 20:12; *Shmuel* I 8:3). They nevertheless provide inspiration in that they were able to become the great people that they were, despite their shortcomings. Could we not do the same?

The more we raise our biblical role models to the status of angels, the more we reduce their stature as great men (Rav Aharon Lichtenstein). We too can overcome our own inclinations.

וְעֹז מֶלֶךְ מִשְׁפָּט אָהֵב, אַתָּה כּוֹנַנְתָּ מֵישָׁרִים
מִשְׁפָּט וּצְדָקָה בְּיַעֲקֹב אַתָּה עָשִׂיתָ:
רוֹמְמוּ יהוה אֱלֹהֵינוּ, וְהִשְׁתַּחֲווּ לַהֲדֹם רַגְלָיו, קָדוֹשׁ הוּא:
מֹשֶׁה וְאַהֲרֹן בְּכֹהֲנָיו, וּשְׁמוּאֵל בְּקֹרְאֵי שְׁמוֹ
קֹרְאִים אֶל־יהוה וְהוּא יַעֲנֵם:
◂ בְּעַמּוּד עָנָן יְדַבֵּר אֲלֵיהֶם, שָׁמְרוּ עֵדֹתָיו וְחֹק נָתַן־לָמוֹ:
יהוה אֱלֹהֵינוּ אַתָּה עֲנִיתָם
אֵל נֹשֵׂא הָיִיתָ לָהֶם, וְנֹקֵם עַל־עֲלִילוֹתָם:
רוֹמְמוּ יהוה אֱלֹהֵינוּ, וְהִשְׁתַּחֲווּ לְהַר קָדְשׁוֹ
כִּי־קָדוֹשׁ יהוה אֱלֹהֵינוּ:

IYUN TEFILLA • עיון תפילה

וְעֹז מֶלֶךְ מִשְׁפָּט אָהֵב – *The King in His might loves justice.* Most sovereigns rule by physical force and power. The God of Israel rules through justice.
How do you use your power with your friends, your family, your employees?

אַתָּה כּוֹנַנְתָּ מֵישָׁרִים – *You have established equity.* A person sees his enemy's donkey suffering under a burden. He goes to help him in keeping with the biblical commandment (*Shemot* 23:5): "And if you see your enemy's donkey crouching under his burden...you shall surely help him." His enemy is overwhelmed by the gesture and they become steadfast friends (*Midrash Shoḥer Tov* 99:5). The word equity can also be understood as *yashrut*, doing the right thing. Following the laws of the Torah leads to doing the right thing, even if it may go against our natural inclination, and peace is the inevitable result.
What acts of justice could I have done this week?

מִשְׁפָּט וּצְדָקָה בְּיַעֲקֹב אַתָּה עָשִׂיתָ – *The justice and righteousness in Jacob is Your doing.* Morality has always been at the center of the Jewish mission to be a light unto the nations. Despite our belief that our system of laws is the most far-reaching and the most ethical, we know that does not make us better than other peoples; it simply gives us more responsibility.
What can I do next week to better live up to that responsibility?
How can I start today?

BIUR TEFILLA • ביאור תפילה

מֹשֶׁה וְאַהֲרֹן בְּכֹהֲנָיו, וּשְׁמוּאֵל בְּקֹרְאֵי שְׁמוֹ – *Moses and Aaron were among His priests; Samuel was among those who called on His name.* It is not clear why of all the biblical

The following psalm is said standing:

מִזְמוֹר לְדָוִד A psalm of David. *Ps. 29*
Render to the LORD, you angelic powers,
render to the LORD glory and might.
Render to the LORD the glory due to His name.
Bow to the LORD in the beauty of holiness.
The LORD's voice echoes over the waters;
the God of glory thunders;
the LORD is over the mighty waters.
The LORD's voice in power,[I]
the LORD's voice in beauty,[A]
the LORD's voice breaks cedars,[I]
the LORD shatters the cedars of Lebanon.

---

the force of that voice equally. Instead, it says, when standing at Sinai each person heard the voice of revelation according to his or her own ability to be attuned to the sound (*Shemot Raba* 5:9). Spirituality is not a one-size-fits-all phenomenon. Each of us can hear the sound, but each in our own way.

What is your way?

קוֹל יהוה שֹׁבֵר אֲרָזִים – *The LORD's voice breaks cedars.* The cedars of Lebanon are the biblical symbols for great strength and power. Like nuclear energy, God's presence can be felt in the destructive forces that man can harness for the purposes of war and oppression, no less than they can be found in the positive ways in which we use such forces of nature for our benefit. Shabbat is about maintaining our sense of balance between the two.

ANI TEFILLA • אני תפילה

קוֹל יהוה בֶּהָדָר – *The LORD's voice in beauty.* Imagine the voice of beauty in nature. Think about a place where you once heard that voice, the rustling of the leaves, the wind whistling through your hair, the deafening sound of silence. The voice that speaks to you through the beauty of nature is that same voice that speaks to you through the beauty of the Torah, for their origins are the same. As nature is there to sensitize you to your place, so too the voice of the Torah is there to guide you in shaping and developing your human personality (Rabbi S. Hirsch).

What can you do to better hear those voices?

The Ba'al Shem Tov said that no two people have the same abilities. Each person must worship Hashem using his own strengths. If he tries to imitate another person he will not only lose out on his own merit but will not be able to accomplish anything using someone else's talents.

What are your strengths that you can utilize to worship Hashem?

The following psalm is said standing:

תהלים כט

מִזְמוֹר לְדָוִד, הָבוּ לַיהוה בְּנֵי אֵלִים, הָבוּ לַיהוה כָּבוֹד וָעֹז:
הָבוּ לַיהוה כְּבוֹד שְׁמוֹ, הִשְׁתַּחֲווּ לַיהוה בְּהַדְרַת־קֹדֶשׁ:
קוֹל יהוה עַל הַמָּיִם, אֵל־הַכָּבוֹד הִרְעִים, יהוה עַל־מַיִם רַבִּים:
קוֹל־יהוה בַּכֹּחַ,[ע] קוֹל יהוה בֶּהָדָר:[א]
קוֹל יהוה שֹׁבֵר אֲרָזִים,[ע] וַיְשַׁבֵּר יהוה אֶת־אַרְזֵי הַלְּבָנוֹן:

BIUR TEFILLA • ביאור תפילה

Psalm 29. This psalm breaks the sequence of the preceding Psalms 95-99. Various reasons have been given as to why this particular one was chosen. At its core, it seems to emphasize the presence of Hashem in all of His majesty and power. Too overwhelming to be experienced firsthand, His presence is symbolized by the many references to His voice, both thunderous and beautiful. The word voice (*kol*) appears seven times, which the Talmud (*Berakhot* 29a) says is reminiscent of the seven blessings of the *Amida* prayer we are yet to say where we rendezvous with God most personally. Others note that it has no fewer than eighteen references to God's name, an allusion to the eighteen blessings we say in the weekday *Amida* (*Berakhot* 28b) and, indeed, the midrash goes to great lengths to show how each line corresponds to each one of those blessings (*Shoḥer Tov*).

Still others suggest that the imagery is very reminiscent of the scene at the revelation of Sinai when the Torah was given (*Shemot* 19:16-19; 20:15), described in terms of thunder and lightning and the sounds or voice of God (*Zevaḥim* 116a; *Mekhilta Yitro*). Further, there is a tradition that the giving of the Torah itself took place on Shabbat (*Shabbat* 86b). This explains why the psalm will be recited again in the morning when we remove the Torah from the Ark for public reading.

Any or all of these reasons would account for the prevalent custom that there is to stand when reciting this psalm. The previous psalms have been leading us to this point, preparing us for an encounter with the Divine as we are to welcome the Shabbat. As with the arrival of any important guests, our first impulse is to stand with excitement to greet them. If we have been unable to muster the right intentions until now, our physical act helps guide our thoughts and feelings. Stand to welcome the Shabbat.

IYUN TEFILLA • עיון תפילה

קוֹל־יהוה בַּכֹּחַ – *The Lord's voice in power.* The midrash homiletically opines that the verse should have said in "its" or "His" power which would have suggested that all felt

He makes Lebanon skip like a calf, Sirion like a young wild ox.
The LORD's voice cleaves flames of fire.
The LORD's voice makes the desert quake,
the LORD shakes the desert of Kadesh.
▸ The LORD's voice makes hinds calve and strips the forests bare,
and in His temple all say: "Glory!"
The LORD sat enthroned at the Flood,
the LORD sits enthroned as King for ever.
The LORD will give strength to His people;
the LORD will bless His people with peace.[1]

The following is said in some congregations:

Please, by the power[B] of Your great right hand, set the captive nation free.
Accept Your people's prayer. Strengthen us, purify us, You who are revered.
Please, Mighty One, guard like the pupil of the eye those who seek Your unity.
Bless them, cleanse them, have compassion on them,
grant them Your righteousness always.
Mighty One, Holy One, in Your great goodness guide Your congregation.
Only One, Exalted One, turn to Your people, who proclaim Your holiness.
Accept our plea and heed our cry, You who know all secret thoughts.[1]
Blessed be the name of His glorious kingdom for ever and all time.

---

forbidden to pronounce. The first letter of each word is said to form that name and so these verses were substituted in their place, although there were differing traditions as to how they should be read (*Responsa Rashba* 1:220). Some suggest that the seven verses parallel the seven references to the voice (*kol*) of God mentioned in the previous psalm (*Tikkunei Zohar, tikkun* 21); others suggest that the 42-letter name of God is particularly associated with the mystery of Creation (*Tosafot Ḥagiga* 11b). In any event, its association with these mystical traditions is what also led some congregations to omit the prayer altogether. For others, it is a most sublime introduction to the experience of the prayer which immediately follows.

IYUN TEFILLA • עיון תפילה

וְשְׁמַע צַעֲקָתֵנוּ, יוֹדֵעַ תַּעֲלוּמוֹת – *Heed our cry, You who know all secret thoughts.* Just as our thoughts are internal, so too can be our cry. Just as our thoughts can express our will without our speaking so can the longing of our heart and soul express themselves in a cry even if it cannot be heard (*Sefat Emet*). That is the meaning of the verse, "I will hear them before they speak" (*Yeshayahu* 65:24). Hashem "knows all secret thoughts." We need only open our hearts to speak, or to cry. **Try to open your heart now.**

וַיַּרְקִידֵם כְּמוֹ־עֵגֶל, לְבָנוֹן וְשִׂרְיוֹן כְּמוֹ בֶן־רְאֵמִים:
קוֹל־יהוה חֹצֵב לַהֲבוֹת אֵשׁ:
קוֹל יהוה יָחִיל מִדְבָּר, יָחִיל יהוה מִדְבַּר קָדֵשׁ:
› קוֹל יהוה יְחוֹלֵל אַיָּלוֹת וַיֶּחֱשֹׂף יְעָרוֹת
וּבְהֵיכָלוֹ, כֻּלּוֹ אֹמֵר כָּבוֹד:
יהוה לַמַּבּוּל יָשָׁב, וַיֵּשֶׁב יהוה מֶלֶךְ לְעוֹלָם:
יהוה עֹז לְעַמּוֹ יִתֵּן, יהוה יְבָרֵךְ אֶת־עַמּוֹ בַשָּׁלוֹם:ע

The following is said in some congregations:

אָנָּא, בְּכֹחַ גְּדֻלַּת יְמִינְךָ, תַּתִּיר צְרוּרָה.
קַבֵּל רִנַּת עַמְּךָ, שַׂגְּבֵנוּ, טַהֲרֵנוּ, נוֹרָא.
נָא גִבּוֹר, דּוֹרְשֵׁי יִחוּדְךָ כְּבָבַת שָׁמְרֵם.
בָּרְכֵם, טַהֲרֵם, רַחֲמֵם, צִדְקָתְךָ תָּמִיד גָּמְלֵם.
חֲסִין קָדוֹשׁ, בְּרֹב טוּבְךָ נַהֵל עֲדָתֶךָ.
יָחִיד גֵּאֶה, לְעַמְּךָ פְּנֵה, זוֹכְרֵי קְדֻשָּׁתֶךָ.
שַׁוְעָתֵנוּ קַבֵּל וּשְׁמַע צַעֲקָתֵנוּ, יוֹדֵעַ תַּעֲלוּמוֹת.ע
בָּרוּךְ שֵׁם כְּבוֹד מַלְכוּתוֹ לְעוֹלָם וָעֶד.

BIUR TEFILLA • ביאור תפילה

אָנָּא, בְּכֹחַ – *Please, by the power.* This short prayer seems to interrupt the sequence of six psalms that culminate with the saying of *Lekha Dodi* in the next section. Indeed, that is one reason why some congregations do not recite it at all. The prayer is said to date back to the first century CE and it has a long history in the mystical tradition, appearing in different parts of different services in addition to Friday night. There are essentially seven verses (the eighth has a history of its own) wherein each verse consists of six words, thus totaling 42 words, the same number of letters in one of God's mystical names that we are

IYUN TEFILLA • עיון תפילה

יהוה יְבָרֵךְ אֶת־עַמּוֹ בַשָּׁלוֹם – *The Lord will bless His people with peace.* It is possible that the peace (*shalom*) referred to here is the state where there is no strife among men. But it could also be a reference to the inner peace that comes to the one who has a sense of place in the world, a calmness and security that come with the faith and perspective that lie at the heart of the greeting we give one another this day: *Shabbat Shalom.*

לְכָה דוֹדִי Come, my Beloved,[BH] to greet the bride;
let us welcome the Sabbath.
Come, my Beloved, to greet the bride;
let us welcome the Sabbath.

שָׁמוֹר "Observe" and "Remember" in one act of speech,[B]
The One and Only God made us hear.
The LORD is One and His name is One,
For renown, for splendor, and for praise.
Come, my Beloved, to greet the bride;
let us welcome the Sabbath.

---

go out to greet the "Sabbath Queen" then, we also seek to greet the King and welcome Him into our midst in a way that we do not and usually cannot during the week. As the individual's weekday pain or sorrow recedes so too does that of the nation as a whole and the focus becomes one of optimism for both – the individual and the national entity hoping to be restored (Rabbi S. Hirsch).

The poem is an acrostic wherein the first letter of each stanza forms the name of the author – ShLoMoH HaLeVI **שלמה הלוי**. It is almost always sung aloud in unison, sometimes accompanied by dancing in the aisles, a far cry from going out into the fields but still a physical act designed to go out to greet one's guest rather than sitting back and waiting passively for the guest to come to you. In some congregations it is said responsively instead.

HILKHOT TEFILLA • הלכות תפילה

לְכָה דוֹדִי – *Come, my Beloved.* Although there is no obligation to stand for this prayer, some have the custom to do so, just as one would when greeting a guest. Others stand only for the last stanza when the guest arrives as it were. In many congregations, one can see both customs going on at the same time for either is appropriate. Do whichever enables you to bring greater meaning.

ANI TEFILLA • אני תפילה

It is told that the Ari, who lived in Tzefat at the same time as Rabbi Alkabetz, said that one should go out into the field, ideally to a mountain top, face the west where the sun was setting and, at the moment it sets, close your eyes, put one hand atop another on your chest and have in mind with great awe and trembling that you are standing before Hashem ready to accept the Shabbat, and sing in a pleasant voice (*Petura DeAbba ot* 17).

Think of yourself atop that mountain. Close your eyes. Sing your heart out.

BIUR TEFILLA • ביאור תפילה

שָׁמוֹר וְזָכוֹר בְּדִבּוּר אֶחָד – *"Observe" and "Remember" in one act of speech.* This is a reference to the two versions of the Ten Commandments found in the Torah. In one (*Shemot* 20:8), it says that we should "Remember the Shabbat day to keep it holy." In the other (*Devarim* 5:12), the

This **BIUR TEFILLA** *continues on page 61.*

לְכָה דוֹדִי[כב] לִקְרַאת כַּלָּה, פְּנֵי שַׁבָּת נְקַבְּלָה.
לְכָה דוֹדִי לִקְרַאת כַּלָּה, פְּנֵי שַׁבָּת נְקַבְּלָה.

שָׁמוֹר וְזָכוֹר בְּדִבּוּר אֶחָד[ב]
הִשְׁמִיעָנוּ אֵל הַמְיֻחָד
יהוה אֶחָד וּשְׁמוֹ אֶחָד
לְשֵׁם וּלְתִפְאֶרֶת וְלִתְהִלָּה.
לְכָה דוֹדִי לִקְרַאת כַּלָּה, פְּנֵי שַׁבָּת נְקַבְּלָה.

BIUR TEFILLA • ביאור תפילה

לְכָה דוֹדִי – *Come, my beloved.* The Talmud relates that "R. Ḥanina robed himself and stood at sunset of Sabbath eve [and] exclaimed, 'Come and let us go forth to welcome the queen Sabbath.' R. Yannai donned his robes on Sabbath eve and exclaimed, 'Come, O bride, Come, O bride!'" (*Shabbat* 119a). Rashi explains that the Shabbat is so called because of the profound sense of love that Israel has for her.

The language of R. Ḥanina "Come let us go forth" and the suggestion of R. Yannai that our relationship to the Shabbat is like that of two lovers, form the basis for this central poem of the Shabbat service. Written by Rabbi Shlomo HaLevi Alkabetz in the sixteenth century in Tzefat (Safed), who was a member of that influential group of mystics mentioned earlier, the song took its language from the biblical *Shir HaShirim* (Song of Songs), the allegorical love song about the relationship between God and the Jewish people:

> I am my beloved's (*dodi*); and his longing is for me. Come, my beloved (*lekha dodi*), let us go to the field...we will get up early and go to the vineyards, to see if the vine has flowered, whether its blossoms have opened out, if the pomegranate buds have burst; and there shall I give you my love. (*Shir HaShirim* 7:11–14)

Already in ancient times, this unique relationship was expressed thus: "As creation unfolded, it became clear that each day had a partner: Sunday had Monday, Tuesday had Wednesday, Thursday had Friday. The Shabbat came to God and said, 'Master of the Universe! Each day has a partner, yet I have none!' God replied: 'The Jewish People (*Knesset Yisrael*) will be your partner'" (*Bereshit Raba* 11:8). As if to say, from the first days of creation itself, the two were wedded to one another, and their destinies were intertwined forever. Every week, that commitment is renewed.

The truth is that of the nine stanzas of the song, only three speak about Shabbat; the others speak about the yearning for redemption, the rebuilding of the *Beit HaMikdash* (Temple) and the longing for the *Shekhina* or Divine Presence, themes which are part and parcel of the Shabbat experience which is described as a taste of the World to Come (*Berakhot* 56b). When we

לִקְרַאת To greet the Sabbath, come let us go,
For of blessing, she is the source.[ׁ]
From the outset, as of old, ordained:
Last in deed, first in thought.[ׁ]

Come, my Beloved, to greet the bride;
let us welcome the Sabbath.

מִקְדַּשׁ Sanctuary of the King, royal city,[ׁ]
Arise, go forth from your ruined state.
Too long have you dwelt in the valley of tears.
He will shower compassion on you.

Come, my Beloved, to greet the bride;
let us welcome the Sabbath.

---

that was created according to the Torah during the six days of Creation and yet man is often considered the ultimate goal of that Creation. Why, then, was Shabbat created last? Perhaps it is because history has proven that man can then come to mistakenly see himself as the ultimate creator and to conduct himself as if he has absolute power. As such, Shabbat was given in order to help us maintain perspective that we too are but creations despite our power to create. Shabbat reminds us to use that power positively and, in that sense, it was the intended goal of creation even if it was not created first.

מִקְדַּשׁ מֶלֶךְ עִיר מְלוּכָה – *Sanctuary of the King, royal city.* The reference is to Jerusalem, and herein begins the focus on her restoration as the symbol of the redemption when Israel and God will be reconnected , so to speak, in the holy city. "R. Yoḥanan said in the name of R. Shimon bar Yoḥai: 'If Israel were to keep two Sabbaths [in succession] according to its laws, then Israel would be redeemed immediately'" (*Shabbat* 118b). In keeping Shabbat we fulfill our national destiny too.

How?

ANI TEFILLA • אני תפילה

"The Talmud (*Shabbat* 118b) says that if the Jews were to observe Shabbat twice in a row, the *Geula* [redemption] would come immediately. If we could observe Shabbat as it should be, the *Geula* would come because there would be no need for *Geula*. That would be *Geula*. That would be redemption. That would be the messianic time" (Elie Wiesel).

לִקְרַאת שַׁבָּת לְכוּ וְנֵלְכָה
כִּי הִיא מְקוֹר הַבְּרָכָה[ע]
מֵרֹאשׁ מִקֶּדֶם נְסוּכָה
סוֹף מַעֲשֶׂה בְּמַחֲשָׁבָה תְּחִלָּה.[ע]
לְכָה דוֹדִי לִקְרַאת כַּלָּה, פְּנֵי שַׁבָּת נְקַבְּלָה.

מִקְדַּשׁ מֶלֶךְ עִיר מְלוּכָה[ע]
קוּמִי צְאִי מִתּוֹךְ הַהֲפֵכָה
רַב לָךְ שֶׁבֶת בְּעֵמֶק הַבָּכָא
וְהוּא יַחֲמֹל עָלַיִךְ חֶמְלָה.
לְכָה דוֹדִי לִקְרַאת כַּלָּה, פְּנֵי שַׁבָּת נְקַבְּלָה.

---

commandment is expressed as "Observe the Shabbat day to keep it holy." The Rabbis explained that the two were expressed by God in a single breath, in a way that the human mouth cannot utter and the ear cannot hear (*Shevuot* 20b). In practical terms it was understood that "observe" (*shamor*) is a reference to the negative commandments regarding Shabbat, the things we are not permitted to do. "Remember" (*zakhor*) on the other hand, encompasses those positive commandments which guide us to making the day special (cf. Ramban on *Shemot* 20:8). Both go hand in hand: the prohibitions make room for us to create the physical and emotional space that are the hallmarks of Shabbat. One without the other is only a shadow of the Shabbat experience, a body without a soul.

Allow yourself to observe and remember.

IYUN TEFILLA • עיון תפילה

כִּי הִיא מְקוֹר הַבְּרָכָה – *For of blessing, she is the source.* Of all of the days of creation, only of the seventh day does it say that God blessed it (*Bereshit* 2:3). Shabbat, then, is a day of blessing. What exactly does that mean? The text does not say. Perhaps it is riches for the one who observes it, or added insight, or added calm, or added food or rest or... (see *Bereshit Raba* 11). The blessing is for each of us to find for ourselves.

Stop for a moment and ask yourself, what blessing do I seek this Shabbat?

סוֹף מַעֲשֶׂה בְּמַחֲשָׁבָה תְּחִלָּה – *Last in deed, first in thought.* Shabbat was the last thing

הִתְנַעֲרִי Shake yourself off, arise from the dust!
Put on your clothes of glory, My people.[B]
Through the son of Jesse the Bethlehemite,
Draw near to my soul and redeem it.

Come, my Beloved, to greet the bride;
let us welcome the Sabbath.

הִתְעוֹרְרִי Wake up, wake up,[H]
For your light has come: rise, shine!
Awake, awake, break out in song,
For the LORD's glory is revealed on you.

Come, my Beloved, to greet the bride;
let us welcome the Sabbath.

לֹא תֵבֹשִׁי Do not be ashamed, do not be confounded.
Why be downcast? Why do you mourn?
In you the needy of My people find shelter,
And the city shall be rebuilt on its hill.

Come, my Beloved, to greet the bride;
let us welcome the Sabbath.

HILKHOT TEFILLA • הלכות תפילה

הִתְעוֹרְרִי הִתְעוֹרְרִי – *Wake up, wake up.* There is an old tradition in many communities to change the melody at some point near the middle of the song. A custom from Frankfurt, Germany, for example, changes it at this stanza where the acrostic of the second part of the author's name begins. They then revert to the first melody for the last stanza which returns to the theme of Shabbat with which the song began (*Divrei Kehillot*). Less complicated is a more widespread custom to change the melody with the sixth stanza (Lo tevoshi – "Do not be ashamed") and, in some communities, that melody is often more upbeat than the one used at the beginning. While numerous reasons have been given for these changes, none is considered authoritative . Nevertheless the custom, like so many others, has taken on a life of its own.

הִתְנַעֲרִי, מֵעָפָר קוּמִי
לִבְשִׁי בִּגְדֵי תִפְאַרְתֵּךְ עַמִּי[ב]
עַל יַד בֶּן יִשַׁי בֵּית הַלַּחְמִי
קָרְבָה אֶל נַפְשִׁי, גְּאָלָהּ.
לְכָה דוֹדִי לִקְרַאת כַּלָּה, פְּנֵי שַׁבָּת נְקַבְּלָה.

הִתְעוֹרְרִי הִתְעוֹרְרִי[ה]
כִּי בָא אוֹרֵךְ קוּמִי אוֹרִי
עוּרִי עוּרִי, שִׁיר דַּבֵּרִי
כְּבוֹד יהוה עָלַיִךְ נִגְלָה.
לְכָה דוֹדִי לִקְרַאת כַּלָּה, פְּנֵי שַׁבָּת נְקַבְּלָה.

לֹא תֵבֹשִׁי וְלֹא תִכָּלְמִי
מַה תִּשְׁתּוֹחֲחִי וּמַה תֶּהֱמִי
בָּךְ יֶחֱסוּ עֲנִיֵּי עַמִּי
וְנִבְנְתָה עִיר עַל תִּלָּהּ.
לְכָה דוֹדִי לִקְרַאת כַּלָּה, פְּנֵי שַׁבָּת נְקַבְּלָה.

BIUR TEFILLA • ביאור תפילה

לִבְשִׁי בִּגְדֵי תִפְאַרְתֵּךְ עַמִּי – *Put on your clothes of glory, My people.* There are those who say that the subject of the sentence is Jerusalem herself (*Iyun Tefilla*, *Barukh She'amar*) because the verb and noun are in the feminine form yet the word "people" is masculine. As such, the phrase "My people" describes the clothes, that is, My people are the clothes of Jerusalem. When they do not act appropriately, then Jerusalem is naked. It is up to us, then, to adorn ourselves with deeds and attitudes that can adorn her.

What can you do a little differently this Shabbat to make "Jerusalem" more beautiful?

וְהָיוּ Those who despoiled you shall be despoiled,
And all who devoured you shall be far away.
Your God will rejoice over you
As a bridegroom rejoices over his bride.

Come, my Beloved, to greet the bride;
let us welcome the Sabbath.

יָמִין Right and left you shall spread out,
And God you will revere.
Through the descendant of Peretz,
We shall rejoice and we shall be glad.

Come, my Beloved, to greet the bride;
let us welcome the Sabbath.

Stand and turn to face the door or the rear (usually western side) of the synagogue, as if to greet the incoming bride, bowing at the words "Enter, O bride!," then turn back to face the front.

בּוֹאִי Come in peace, O crown of her husband;
Come with joy and jubilation,
Among the faithful of the treasured people.
Enter, O bride! Enter, O bride![H]

Come, my Beloved, to greet the bride;
let us welcome the Sabbath.

---

from the west (*Bava Batra* 25a), while others insist that one face the door regardless of where it is, because a guest always comes via the door. Some turn clockwise to do so, others counterclockwise, some bow once at the mention of these final words of the stanza, as one would when royalty appears, while others bow two or three times. All are deeply rooted customs. It is fairly common however, that at the very end one turns back toward the Ark again, and bows slightly once again, this time to indicate having shown no disrespect to the Ark from which one normally does not turn away.

ANI TEFILLA • אני תפילה

The Talmud (*Shabbat* 10a) relates that God said to Moshe, "I have a gift in My treasury that I have been storing in order to give to Israel. Go and tell them." Rabbi Menaḥem Mendel of Kosov reminds us that the true value of a gift is not the gift itself but rather the love that it represents.

וְהָיוּ לִמְשִׁסָּה שֹׁאסָיִךְ
וְרָחֲקוּ כָּל מְבַלְּעָיִךְ
יָשִׂישׂ עָלַיִךְ אֱלֹהָיִךְ
כִּמְשׂוֹשׂ חָתָן עַל כַּלָּה.
לְכָה דוֹדִי לִקְרַאת כַּלָּה, פְּנֵי שַׁבָּת נְקַבְּלָה.

יָמִין וּשְׂמֹאל תִּפְרֹצִי
וְאֶת יהוה תַּעֲרִיצִי
עַל יַד אִישׁ בֶּן פַּרְצִי
וְנִשְׂמְחָה וְנָגִילָה.
לְכָה דוֹדִי לִקְרַאת כַּלָּה, פְּנֵי שַׁבָּת נְקַבְּלָה.

Stand and turn to face the door or the rear (usually western side) of the בית כנסת*, as if to greet the incoming bride, bowing at the words* בּוֹאִי כַלָּה*, then turn back to face the front.*

בּוֹאִי בְשָׁלוֹם עֲטֶרֶת בַּעְלָהּ
גַּם בְּשִׂמְחָה וּבְצָהֳלָה
תּוֹךְ אֱמוּנֵי עַם סְגֻלָּה
בּוֹאִי כַלָּה, בּוֹאִי כַלָּה.[ה]
לְכָה דוֹדִי לִקְרַאת כַּלָּה, פְּנֵי שַׁבָּת נְקַבְּלָה.

HILKHOT TEFILLA • הלכות תפילה

בּוֹאִי כַלָּה, בּוֹאִי כַלָּה - *Enter, O bride! Enter, O bride!* As we are finally welcoming the Shabbat bride or the Divine Presence into our midst, there is a custom to actually stand up and turn to face the door. As in so many other customs, there are differences in tradition. Since the door is usually in the back of the synagogue, some turn there, the direction of the setting sun. If the door is located elsewhere, then some will still turn to the west, in keeping with a tradition that the *Shekhina* (Divine Presence) comes

Mourners during the week of Shiva return to the synagogue at this point. They are greeted with the following words of consolation:

הַמָּקוֹם May the Almighty comfort you
among the other mourners of Zion and Jerusalem.

When Shabbat begins the evening immediately after a Yom Tov, Kabbalat Shabbat begins here.

מִזְמוֹר A psalm. A song for the Sabbath day.[B] *Ps. 92*
It is good to thank the LORD[B] and sing psalms to Your name,
Most High[B] –

So significant was this psalm considered, that for many it represented that singular moment when the Shabbat actually is accepted by the person praying and the point at which the prohibitions of Shabbat take effect (*Beit Yosef* 261). That is why the mourner was welcomed before this point. It is also the reason why, on a day when all of the preceding paragraphs of *Kabbalat Shabbat* are omitted (e.g. when a Yom Tov ends or its onset or intermediate days coincide with Shabbat), the service still begins here, for this, according to many, marks the official liturgical acceptance of Shabbat.

The midrash relates that Adam was born and sinned on the sixth day of the week toward the very end of the day. And when Shabbat was created and Adam was about to be punished, the Shabbat protested and said, "Master of the Universe, of all of the days of the week, are You going to pick me as the one on which man is to be sentenced to die for the very first time?! You blessed me and decreed that I should be a day of respite and this is it?" And Adam was thereby saved from expulsion. As a result Adam created "A song for the Sabbath day." Whereupon the Shabbat said, don't sing to me, sing instead "It is good to thank Hashem and sing psalms to Your name" (*Midrash Shoḥer Tov* 92).

Why was the argument of Shabbat effective? What does it say about the unique character of the day?

Why is this story said in the name of Adam and not some later personality from the Torah?

What underlying mistaken belief did Adam have singing the song to Shabbat?

What is the correction that Shabbat made?

What are the ideas or lessons that the midrash seeks to convey?

שִׁיר לְיוֹם הַשַּׁבָּת – *A song for the Sabbath day.* A song to be sung on the day of Shabbat (Ibn Ezra).

Alternatively, a song to be sung to the Shabbat day for the benefit I derive from her (Alsheikh).

טוֹב לְהֹדוֹת לַיהוה – *It is good to thank the LORD.* The Shabbat day is particularly suited for thanking God because it is a day when one's body is less encumbered by the demands of the week, thereby freeing up the soul to be heard (Radak).

What does Shabbat make you thankful for?

Alternatively, the word *lehodot* can also mean to acknowledge.

What would you like to acknowledge to God today?

וּלְזַמֵּר לְשִׁמְךָ עֶלְיוֹן – *And sing psalms to Your name, Most High.* Shabbat is particularly conducive to song. Sing.

Mourners during the week of שבעה *return to the* בית כנסת *at this point. They are greeted with the following words of consolation:*

הַמָּקוֹם יְנַחֵם אֶתְכֶם בְּתוֹךְ שְׁאָר אֲבֵלֵי צִיּוֹן וִירוּשָׁלָיִם.

When שבת *begins the evening immediately after a* יום טוב*,* קבלת שבת *begins here.*

תהלים צב

מִזְמוֹר שִׁיר לְיוֹם הַשַּׁבָּת:ב
טוֹב לְהֹדוֹת לַיהוה,ב וּלְזַמֵּר לְשִׁמְךָ עֶלְיוֹן:ב

HILKHOT TEFILLA • הלכות תפילה

The *Kabbalat Shabbat* service is considered so happy and celebratory, that it is deemed to be at odds with the mood of a mourner whose presence at a public event is normally not allowed during the seven days (*shiva*) of mourning. As such, one who is still in that mourning period does not join the congregation for this service. Since Shabbat has not yet actually begun, we take the opportunity to wish him the traditional blessing given in the house of mourning, something which is not permitted on Shabbat itself because its somber message is not in keeping with the atmosphere we seek to create on that day. At this moment, then, now that his public display of mourning is temporarily ending (for public *shiva* is suspended on Shabbat), he is welcomed back into the community and we stand ready to enter into Shabbat together.

ANI TEFILLA • אני תפילה

The name of Hashem here is HaMakom, which literally means the Place. This is because God is both immanent and transcendent; "He is the place of the world, but the world is not His place" (Bereshit Raba 68:12). It is a name that is used most often when it is difficult to sense Hashem's Presence, when He seems to be hiding. We thus wish for the mourner that despite his pain and sorrow, his feeling of abandonment and aloneness, that he find the One who can seem distant but is really very close. May Hashem, the Place, comfort him. (Rabbi Joseph B. Soloveitchik)

BIUR TEFILLA • ביאור תפילה

Psalm 92: This psalm is said no less than three different times over the course of Shabbat, once this evening and twice tomorrow morning. And yet, surprisingly, despite its opening title as "A song for the Sabbath day," there is little mention of the Shabbat within. Rather, it begins by speaking about how great Hashem is, clearly in terms of everything He does, a realization that engenders feelings of happiness, song and music. One might think that such happiness should be tempered by the fact that there is evil in the world and that bad people seem to succeed. Nevertheless, one should know that such success is ephemeral in the larger scheme of things. It thus concludes on a positive and optimistic note. Its future-oriented perspective led the Rabbis to conclude that it refers to an ideal point in the distant future, "which would be entirely Shabbat," a messianic or eschatological point in time (*Rosh HaShana* 31a). Shabbat is a taste of the World to Come.

to tell of Your loving-kindness in the morning
and Your faithfulness at night,
to the music of the ten-stringed lyre and the melody of the harp.
For You have made me rejoice by Your work, O LORD;
I sing for joy at the deeds of Your hands.
How great are Your deeds, LORD,
and how very deep Your thoughts.
A boor cannot know, nor can a fool understand,[I]
that though the wicked spring up like grass
and all evildoers flourish,
it is only that they may be destroyed for ever.
But You, LORD, are eternally exalted.
For behold Your enemies, LORD, behold Your enemies will perish;
all evildoers will be scattered.
You have raised my pride like that of a wild ox;
I am anointed with fresh oil.
My eyes shall look in triumph on my adversaries,
my ears shall hear the downfall of the wicked who rise against me.[A]
▸ The righteous will flourish like a palm tree
and grow tall like a cedar in Lebanon.
Planted in the LORD's House, blossoming in our God's courtyards,
they will still bear fruit in old age, and stay vigorous and fresh,
proclaiming that the LORD is upright:
He is my Rock, in whom there is no wrong.

ANI TEFILLA • אני תפילה

בְּקָמִים עָלַי מְרֵעִים תִּשְׁמַעְנָה אׇזְנָי – *My ears shall hear the downfall of the wicked who rise against me.* In Hebrew we generally refer to "love of Hashem" but "fear of Heaven." Why do we not say "fear of Hashem" or "love of Heaven"? The answer may be that love is a reflection of our feeling of closeness, the kind of intimacy that allows one to address the other by name. Fear, however, conveys a sense of distance in a relationship, like the gap which separates man from the heavens (Rabbi J.B. Soloveitchik). In human affairs, love is probably more favored than fear. But in a relationship with the Divine, both are natural and both are to be embraced.

Do you love more than you fear? Do you fear more than you love? How might you reach a greater level of each?

לְהַגִּיד בַּבֹּקֶר חַסְדֶּךָ, וֶאֱמוּנָתְךָ בַּלֵּילוֹת:
עֲלֵי־עָשׂוֹר וַעֲלֵי־נָבֶל, עֲלֵי הִגָּיוֹן בְּכִנּוֹר:
כִּי שִׂמַּחְתַּנִי יהוה בְּפָעֳלֶךָ, בְּמַעֲשֵׂי יָדֶיךָ אֲרַנֵּן:
מַה־גָּדְלוּ מַעֲשֶׂיךָ יהוה, מְאֹד עָמְקוּ מַחְשְׁבֹתֶיךָ:
אִישׁ־בַּעַר לֹא יֵדָע, וּכְסִיל לֹא־יָבִין אֶת־זֹאת:[ע]
בִּפְרֹחַ רְשָׁעִים כְּמוֹ עֵשֶׂב, וַיָּצִיצוּ כָּל־פֹּעֲלֵי אָוֶן
לְהִשָּׁמְדָם עֲדֵי־עַד:
וְאַתָּה מָרוֹם לְעֹלָם יהוה:
כִּי הִנֵּה אֹיְבֶיךָ יהוה, כִּי־הִנֵּה אֹיְבֶיךָ יֹאבֵדוּ
יִתְפָּרְדוּ כָּל־פֹּעֲלֵי אָוֶן:
וַתָּרֶם כִּרְאֵים קַרְנִי, בַּלֹּתִי בְּשֶׁמֶן רַעֲנָן:
וַתַּבֵּט עֵינִי בְּשׁוּרָי
בַּקָּמִים עָלַי מְרֵעִים תִּשְׁמַעְנָה אָזְנָי:[א]
◂ צַדִּיק כַּתָּמָר יִפְרָח, כְּאֶרֶז בַּלְּבָנוֹן יִשְׂגֶּה:
שְׁתוּלִים בְּבֵית יהוה, בְּחַצְרוֹת אֱלֹהֵינוּ יַפְרִיחוּ:
עוֹד יְנוּבוּן בְּשֵׂיבָה, דְּשֵׁנִים וְרַעֲנַנִּים יִהְיוּ:
לְהַגִּיד כִּי־יָשָׁר יהוה, צוּרִי, וְלֹא־עַוְלָתָה בּוֹ:

IYUN TEFILLA • עיון תפילה

אִישׁ־בַּעַר לֹא יֵדָע, וּכְסִיל לֹא־יָבִין אֶת־זֹאת – *A boor cannot know, nor can a fool understand.* A boor is a like a brute beast who only comprehends what lies before him. The conceited fool is the one who tenaciously adheres to his views even if they are utterly unjustifiable. The institution of Shabbat presupposes that we are neither, for if either were the case, the lessons that Shabbat is designed to teach would be lost upon us.

How might I use reason to learn those lessons today?

Whoever doesn't know what he doesn't know, knows nothing (Rashba).

יהוה מָלָךְ The LORD reigns. He is robed in majesty. Ps. 93
The LORD is robed, girded with strength.
The world is firmly established; it cannot be moved.
Your throne stands firm as of old; You are eternal.
Rivers lift up, LORD, rivers lift up their voice,[B]
rivers lift up their crashing waves.
▸ Mightier than the noise of many waters,
than the mighty waves of the sea is the LORD on high.
Your testimonies are very sure;[I]
holiness adorns Your House, LORD, for evermore.

In Ashkenazi communities many have the custom to stand for Kaddish because of the holiness associated with the sanctification of Hashem's name in the prayer in general and in the central response by the congregation in particular. (In Sephardic communities the custom is to sit, while others have the custom to remain standing if they are already doing so.)

MOURNER'S KADDISH

The following prayer, said by mourners, requires the presence of a minyan.
A transliteration can be found on page 892.

Mourner: יִתְגַּדַּל Magnified and sanctified may His great name be,
in the world He created by His will.
May He establish His kingdom
in your lifetime and in your days,
and in the lifetime of all the house of Israel,
swiftly and soon – and say: Amen.

IYUN TEFILLA • עיון תפילה

עֵדֹתֶיךָ נֶאֶמְנוּ מְאֹד – *Your testimonies are very sure.* Your laws, among which the Shabbat stands out first and foremost, are constants. They accompany the individual throughout one's life, through all of the changes that life may bring (Rabbi S. Hirsch). They are the anchor that gives one the stability with which to negotiate the turbulent waters and they are the subtle force that imposes calm. Shabbat, and all of the rest of the Torah's laws, are what have kept the Jewish people alive and vibrant for millennia and so it will always be, "for evermore."

ANI TEFILLA • אני תפילה

"Anyone who feels a true bond in his heart, with the life of the nation over many generations, simply will not be able – even if he believes neither in the World to Come nor the Jewish State – to imagine the Jewish People without *Shabbat Malketa* (the Sabbath Queen). It may be said without exaggeration that more than the Jews kept the Sabbath, it was the Sabbath that kept them" (Aḥad HaAm).

The **INTRODUCTION TO KADDISH** *is on page 73.*

תהלים צג

יהוה מָלָךְ, גֵּאוּת לָבֵשׁ, לָבֵשׁ יהוה עֹז הִתְאַזָּר
אַף־תִּכּוֹן תֵּבֵל בַּל־תִּמּוֹט:
נָכוֹן כִּסְאֲךָ מֵאָז, מֵעוֹלָם אָתָּה:
נָשְׂאוּ נְהָרוֹת יהוה, נָשְׂאוּ נְהָרוֹת קוֹלָם,ב יִשְׂאוּ נְהָרוֹת דָּכְיָם:
◂ מִקֹּלוֹת מַיִם רַבִּים, אַדִּירִים מִשְׁבְּרֵי־יָם, אַדִּיר בַּמָּרוֹם יהוה:
עֵדֹתֶיךָ נֶאֶמְנוּ מְאֹד,ע לְבֵיתְךָ נַאֲוָה־קֹדֶשׁ, יהוה לְאֹרֶךְ יָמִים:

In Ashkenazi communities many have the custom to stand for קדיש *because of the holiness associated with the sanctification of Hashem's name in the prayer in general and in the central response by the congregation in particular. (In Sephardic communities the custom is to sit, while others have the custom to remain standing if they are already doing so.)*

קדיש יתום

The following prayer, said by mourners, requires the presence of a מנין*.* *A transliteration can be found on page 892.*

אבל: **יִתְגַּדַּל וְיִתְקַדַּשׁ שְׁמֵהּ רַבָּא** (קהל: אָמֵן)
בְּעָלְמָא דִּי בְרָא כִרְעוּתֵהּ וְיַמְלִיךְ מַלְכוּתֵהּ
בְּחַיֵּיכוֹן וּבְיוֹמֵיכוֹן וּבְחַיֵּי דְכָל בֵּית יִשְׂרָאֵל
בַּעֲגָלָא וּבִזְמַן קָרִיב, וְאִמְרוּ אָמֵן. (קהל: אָמֵן)

BIUR TEFILLA • ביאור תפילה

נָשְׂאוּ נְהָרוֹת יהוה, נָשְׂאוּ נְהָרוֹת קוֹלָם... – *Rivers lift up, Lord, rivers lift up their voice...* The floods may symbolize the rising and falling of nations, each desirous of imposing its will on others or on the world or on God (Radak, Rabbi S. Hirsch). Alternatively, they may be symbols for Hashem's mastery over nature, both the fact that the oceans do not overtake the world, and the fact that they can be harnessed for man's benefit for drinking and irrigation (Malbim). What would our lives be like without the oceans and rivers, lakes and streams that help comprise more than 70 percent of the Earth's surface?

Psalm 93: This short psalm is said to be an extension of the previous one and the pair will be seen again during the *Pesukei DeZimra* section of the service in the morning. In its tight structure it summarizes a number of the themes seen thus far: a God who is eternal, a force in nature and the history of man, the God recognized by all mankind who has a special relationship with Israel, symbolized by the Temple and the laws that govern our lives as Jews.

All: May His great name[A] be blessed for ever and all time.

Mourner: Blessed and praised, glorified and exalted,
raised and honored, uplifted and lauded
be the name of the Holy One,
blessed be He,
beyond any blessing,
song, praise and consolation
uttered in the world –
and say: Amen.

May there be great peace from heaven,
and life for us and all Israel –
and say: Amen.

Bow and take three steps back as if taking leave of the Divine Presence.
Bow left: May He who makes peace in His high places,
Bow right: make peace *Bow forward:* for us and all Israel –
and say: Amen.

---

has passed away. The text is similar to *Kaddish Shalem* except that it is missing the primary line of *Titkabal,* which asks for the acceptance of our prayers, since that is reserved for a *Ḥazan* on behalf of the congregation whereas this version of the prayer is said by an individual.

Kaddish DeRabbanan (Rabbis') includes a prayer for scholars and is recited at the conclusion of a section of public learning of rabbinic literature – Halakha, Aggada, Gemara.

Its ancient origins are attested to by the unusual language which is a combination of Hebrew and a form of Aramaic used millennia ago.

So important was the prayer considered, so especially inspiring is the one line at its center, that it is one of those that can only be said with a *minyan* or quorum (and is thus technically called a *davar shebikedusha* literally, something having to do with holiness, namely, a prayer which sanctifies the name of God).

ANI TEFILLA • אני תפילה

יְהֵא שְׁמֵהּ רַבָּא – *May His great name.* *Whoever says "yeheh shemeh raba..." with all his strength, the Heavenly Court rips up any negative decree against him.* (*Shabbat* 119b)

קהל ואבל: יְהֵא שְׁמֵהּ רַבָּא[א] מְבָרַךְ לְעָלַם וּלְעָלְמֵי עָלְמַיָּא.

אבל: יִתְבָּרַךְ וְיִשְׁתַּבַּח וְיִתְפָּאַר
וְיִתְרוֹמַם וְיִתְנַשֵּׂא וְיִתְהַדָּר וְיִתְעַלֶּה וְיִתְהַלָּל
שְׁמֵהּ דְּקֻדְשָׁא בְּרִיךְ הוּא (קהל: בְּרִיךְ הוּא)
לְעֵלָּא מִן כָּל בִּרְכָתָא
/ בשבת שובה: לְעֵלָּא לְעֵלָּא מִכָּל בִּרְכָתָא/
וְשִׁירָתָא, תֻּשְׁבְּחָתָא וְנֶחֱמָתָא
דַּאֲמִירָן בְּעָלְמָא
וְאִמְרוּ אָמֵן. (קהל: אָמֵן)

יְהֵא שְׁלָמָא רַבָּא מִן שְׁמַיָּא
וְחַיִּים, עָלֵינוּ וְעַל כָּל יִשְׂרָאֵל
וְאִמְרוּ אָמֵן. (קהל: אָמֵן)

Bow and take three steps back as if taking leave of the Divine Presence.

Bow left עֹשֶׂה שָׁלוֹם/ בשבת שובה: הַשָּׁלוֹם/ בִּמְרוֹמָיו
Bow right הוּא יַעֲשֶׂה שָׁלוֹם *Bow forward* עָלֵינוּ וְעַל כָּל יִשְׂרָאֵל
וְאִמְרוּ אָמֵן.

INTRODUCTION TO KADDISH

There are four variations of this prayer in the siddur.

The shorter one, called *Ḥatzi* (Half) *Kaddish*, serves to separate between sections of the service; it acts as a transition. Despite its name, this is the oldest and original version.

Kaddish Titkabal or *Shalem* (Full) has three extra lines at the end, added during the times of the Geonim, which speak of the acceptance of our prayers. It is usually recited to mark a conclusion of a service, defined here as one involving *Seliḥot* or the *Amida*.

Kaddish Yatom ("of the Orphan," Mourner's) is recited on behalf of someone who

The following is not said when Shabbat begins the evening immediately after a Yom Tov.

1. בַּמֶּה מַדְלִיקִין With what wicks may we light[1] the Sabbath lamp and with what may we not light? We may not use a wick of cedar bast, or

1. ***Ner with kik oil.*** *Samuel said:*

I asked all the seafarers about it, and they told me that there is a certain bird in the towns of the sea called kik. Rabbi

---

INTRODUCTION TO BAMEH MADLIKIN

The following passages are from the second chapter of the Mishna tractate *Shabbat* and consist of technical discussions about the different kinds of oils and wicks that were acceptable for use in Talmudic times. The reasons for its presence in the service is the subject of dispute leading to some reciting it here, others later on and still others not at all.

Those reasons are fascinating in themselves for, like so many other parts of the Siddur, they lend insight into the history of the Jewish communities through the centuries. One opinion, for example, contends that it was placed here as a kind of filler for the congregation to say so that latecomers could catch up and not be left alone at the end of the service to face perceived perils at the time (*Sefer Haltim*). Another opinion suggests that it was placed here for those who did not want to start eating the Shabbat meal until night fell and so they chose to fill the time in learning Torah in the broadest sense, in this case learning the laws that governed the light in the house (*Baḥ*). Another opinion points to the need to teach the ignorant what oils and wicks can be used (*Roke'aḥ*), although another says that is precisely the reason not to say it at all since we do not use forbidden materials today (*Magen Avraham*). Still another says that this particular mitzva was selected because one of the reasons for lighting candles is to enhance the atmosphere of peace in one's home and this was a theme to be emphasized before returning home to be with one's family (Abudarham). Finally, there is an historical reason that has been suggested; namely, the Sadducees, and later the Karaites, were sects who rejected the validity of the Oral Law, including the interpretation of the biblical verse which said that one may not light a candle in one's home on Shabbat "Do not light a fire in any of your dwellings on the Sabbath day" (*Shemot* 35:3). They interpreted this to mean that no artificial light whatsoever was permitted in one's home on Shabbat, whereas the Rabbis had ruled that one may not actually kindle a flame on Shabbat but there was nothing wrong with having a preexisting flame that lasted into Shabbat. Hence the study of this particular section of the Mishna, part of the Oral Law, that deals with Shabbat lights was selected for study as a reminder of the validity of the Oral Law which goes hand in hand with the Written Law of Torah (*Sefer Haltim*).

The following is not said when שבת begins the evening immediately after a יום טוב.

א בַּמֶּה מַדְלִיקִין[1] וּבַמָּה אֵין מַדְלִיקִין. אֵין מַדְלִיקִין לֹא בְלֶכֶשׁ, וְלֹא בְחֹסֶן, וְלֹא בְכַלָּךְ, וְלֹא בִּפְתִילַת הָאִידָן, וְלֹא בִּפְתִילַת הַמִּדְבָּר, וְלֹא בִירוֹקָה שֶׁעַל פְּנֵי הַמַּיִם. וְלֹא בְזֶפֶת וְלֹא בְשַׁעֲוָה וְלֹא בְּשֶׁמֶן קִיק וְלֹא בְּשֶׁמֶן שְׂרֵפָה וְלֹא בְאַלְיָה וְלֹא בְחֵלֶב. נַחוּם הַמָּדִי אוֹמֵר: מַדְלִיקִין בְּחֵלֶב מְבֻשָּׁל, וַחֲכָמִים אוֹמְרִים: אֶחָד מְבֻשָּׁל וְאֶחָד שֶׁאֵינוֹ מְבֻשָּׁל, אֵין מַדְלִיקִין בּוֹ.

With what may we light [the Sabbath lamp] and with what may we not light? We may not light with cedar fibre, uncombed flax, or raw silk, or a wick made of willow bast or desert weed, or seaweed. [For oil] we may not use pitch, or wax, or cottonseed oil or [contaminated consecrated] oil that must be destroyed by burning, or fat from sheeps' tails, or tallow. Naḥum the Mede says: We may use boiled tallow. But the sages say: Whether boiled or not boiled, we may not use it.

Yitzḥak son of Rav Yehuda said: It is cotton-seed oil; Resh Lakish said: Oil from Yona's kikayon (Shabbat 21a).

In Bameh Madlikin, Rav Kook sees a parallel between oil and success, and between the wick and an individual. The loftier kind of success we seek is one which fills a person with inner happiness and raises one's life to a higher plane.

This success is akin to the oil which is drawn through the extent of the wick, fully saturating it. Each Talmudic explanation of the term "kik" hints to a success which remains external to the individual.

First, the towns of the sea, though reputably prosperous, were known for their moral corruption. Anyone who pursues success there could be guaranteed that it would not penetrate their inner being nor bring them serenity. True happiness is not found on a distant island, but in the home of every Jew, in a life of modesty, humility and pure-heartedness. The love of family and the Torah awaken the holiest emotions of the heart by the light of the candles in one's home on Shabbat eve.

Second, the cotton plant resembles a grapevine in its form. The grapevine represents happiness, which appears to be internal, but in truth remains external to a person. Ultimately, the heart is empty.

Third, the kikayon of Yona was here today and gone tomorrow. It highlights an ephemeral happiness, which dissipates all too soon. Because there is no inherent connection between material success and an individual, nothing can be harvested in the long term.

1. משנה שבת, פרק שני – *Mishna Shabbat, chapter 2.*

2. [Contaminated consecrated] oil that must be destroyed by burning may not be used for a festival lamp. Rabbi Yishmael says: We may not use tar out of respect for the honor due to the Sabbath. But the sages permit all these oils: sesame oil, nut oil, radish oil, fish oil, gourd oil, tar or naphtha. Rabbi Tarfon, however, says: We may use only olive oil.

3. No product from a tree may be used as a wick for the Sabbath lamp, except flax. Also no product of a tree can contract "tent" uncleanness, except flax. If a wick was made from a cloth that has been twisted but not singed, Rabbi Eliezer declares, it is susceptible to contamination and may not be used for a Sabbath lamp; but Rabbi Akiva says, it is not susceptible to contamination, and may be used for the Sabbath lamp.

4. One may not pierce an eggshell, fill it with oil, and put it over the mouth of a lamp so that the oil may drip from it into the lamp, even if the vessel is of earth-

ב אֵין מַדְלִיקִין בְּשֶׁמֶן שְׂרֵפָה בְּיוֹם טוֹב. רַבִּי יִשְׁמָעֵאל אוֹמֵר: אֵין מַדְלִיקִין בְּעִטְרָן מִפְּנֵי כְּבוֹד הַשַּׁבָּת. וַחֲכָמִים מַתִּירִין בְּכָל הַשְּׁמָנִים, בְּשֶׁמֶן שֻׁמְשְׁמִין, בְּשֶׁמֶן אֱגוֹזִים, בְּשֶׁמֶן צְנוֹנוֹת, בְּשֶׁמֶן דָּגִים, בְּשֶׁמֶן פַּקּוּעוֹת, בְּעִטְרָן וּבְנֵפְט. רַבִּי טַרְפוֹן אוֹמֵר: אֵין מַדְלִיקִין אֶלָּא בְּשֶׁמֶן זַיִת בִּלְבָד.

ג כָּל הַיּוֹצֵא מִן הָעֵץ אֵין מַדְלִיקִין בּוֹ, אֶלָּא פִשְׁתָּן. וְכָל הַיּוֹצֵא מִן הָעֵץ אֵינוֹ מִטַּמֵּא טֻמְאַת אֹהָלִים, אֶלָּא פִשְׁתָּן. פְּתִילַת הַבֶּגֶד שֶׁקִּפְּלָהּ וְלֹא הִבְהֲבָהּ, רַבִּי אֱלִיעֶזֶר אוֹמֵר: טְמֵאָה הִיא, וְאֵין מַדְלִיקִין בָּהּ. רַבִּי עֲקִיבָא אוֹמֵר: טְהוֹרָה הִיא, וּמַדְלִיקִין בָּהּ.

ד לֹא יִקֹּב אָדָם שְׁפוֹפֶרֶת שֶׁל בֵּיצָה וִימַלְּאֶנָּה שֶׁמֶן וְיִתְּנֶנָּה עַל פִּי הַנֵּר,

Rather, what our souls yearn for in earnest from Shabbat can only be acquired through hard work and a pure heart. This inherent happiness spreads naturally to the downhearted. This is the success we seek, and this is the oil we light.

2. Rabbi Tarfon says: We only light with olive oil. *The Shabbat lights allude to the enlightenment of the mind, which comes with the holiness of the day of rest. There are many kinds of oil, and there are many kinds of wisdom. Human wisdom can lead to character refinement and can prepare an individual to bring much good to the world. But the purest olive oil, the enlightenment of the Torah, is reserved for Shabbat. It is impervious to confusion and evil intention. The*

enware, but Rabbi Yehuda permits it. If, however, the potter had originally attached it to the lamp, it is permitted because it constitutes a single vessel. One may not fill a bowl with oil, put it beside a lamp, and put the end of the wick in it so that it draws oil from the bowl; but Rabbi Yehuda permits this.

5. One who extinguishes a lamp because he is afraid of heathens, robbers, or depression, or to enable a sick person to sleep, is not liable [for violating the Sabbath]. If he did it to spare the lamp, or the oil, or the wick, he is liable. Rabbi Yose absolves him in all these cases except that of sparing the wick, because he thereby turns it into charcoal.

6. For three transgressions women may die in childbirth: for being careless in observing the laws of menstruation, separating ḥalla [dough-offering], and lighting the Sabbath light.

בִּשְׁבִיל שֶׁתְּהֵא מְנַטֶּפֶת, וַאֲפִילוּ הִיא שֶׁל חֶרֶס. וְרַבִּי יְהוּדָה מַתִּיר. אֲבָל אִם חִבְּרָהּ הַיּוֹצֵר מִתְּחִלָּה מֻתָּר, מִפְּנֵי שֶׁהוּא כְּלִי אֶחָד. לֹא יְמַלֵּא אָדָם אֶת הַקְּעָרָה שֶׁמֶן וְיִתְּנֶנָּה בְּצַד הַנֵּר וְיִתֵּן רֹאשׁ הַפְּתִילָה בְּתוֹכָהּ, בִּשְׁבִיל שֶׁתְּהֵא שׁוֹאֶבֶת. וְרַבִּי יְהוּדָה מַתִּיר.

ה הַמְכַבֶּה אֶת הַנֵּר מִפְּנֵי שֶׁהוּא מִתְיָרֵא מִפְּנֵי גוֹיִם, מִפְּנֵי לִסְטִים, מִפְּנֵי רְוּחַ רָעָה, אוֹ בִּשְׁבִיל הַחוֹלֶה שֶׁיִּישַׁן, פָּטוּר. כְּחָס עַל הַנֵּר, כְּחָס עַל הַשֶּׁמֶן, כְּחָס עַל הַפְּתִילָה, חַיָּב. רַבִּי יוֹסֵי פּוֹטֵר בְּכֻלָּן חוּץ מִן הַפְּתִילָה, מִפְּנֵי שֶׁהוּא עוֹשָׂהּ פֶּחָם.

ו עַל שָׁלֹשׁ עֲבֵרוֹת נָשִׁים מֵתוֹת בִּשְׁעַת לֵדָתָן, עַל שֶׁאֵינָן זְהִירוֹת בְּנִדָּה, בְּחַלָּה וּבְהַדְלָקַת הַנֵּר.

holiest day is dedicated to the pursuit of the wisdom of the Torah.

6. ***For three transgressions women may die in childbirth.*** *Rav Kook explains that the moment of childbirth signifies the influx of divine energy into a person's home. To bring a new soul into this world, women must first prepare spiritually. The observance of Nidda represents the disruption of a natural animal pattern of sexual engagement in favor of a relationship built on ideals and lofty aspirations. Ḥalla, a portion of dough reserved for the Kohen, shows that a family accepts their interdependence with unique and holy individuals whom they hope will influence their home. The Shabbat lights demonstrate the inner light that a family seeks to reveal in its home through calm interactions. Every heart rests from sadness and anxiety; every simple delight is sanctified and raised up. With these practices, a family is ready to receive the divine light and a new soul.*

7. One should say three things at home on the eve of the Sabbath just before dark: Have you tithed? Have you prepared the Eiruv? Light the Sabbath lamp. If there is doubt whether or not darkness has fallen, we may not tithe definitely untithed produce, nor immerse [unclean] vessels, nor light the Sabbath lamp. We may tithe produce about which there is a doubt whether it has been tithed or not, we may prepare an Eiruv, and insulate hot food.

ז שְׁלֹשָׁה דְבָרִים צָרִיךְ אָדָם לוֹמַר בְּתוֹךְ בֵּיתוֹ עֶרֶב שַׁבָּת עִם חֲשֵׁכָה: עִשַּׂרְתֶּם, עֵרַבְתֶּם, הַדְלִיקוּ אֶת הַנֵּר. סָפֵק חֲשֵׁכָה סָפֵק אֵינָהּ חֲשֵׁכָה, אֵין מְעַשְּׂרִין אֶת הַוַּדַּאי, וְאֵין מַטְבִּילִין אֶת הַכֵּלִים, וְאֵין מַדְלִיקִין אֶת הַנֵּרוֹת. אֲבָל מְעַשְּׂרִין אֶת הַדְּמַאי, וּמְעָרְבִין וְטוֹמְנִין אֶת הַחַמִּין.

It was taught,[2] Rabbi Hanina said: One should examine his clothing on the eve of the Sabbath before nightfall [to ensure that one is not carrying anything], for one may forget and go out. Rabbi Yosef said: This is an important law about the Sabbath [for it is easy to forget, and thus inadvertently violate the holiness of the day].

תַּנְיָא,[2] אָמַר רַבִּי חֲנִינָא: חַיָּב אָדָם לְמַשְׁמֵשׁ בְּגָדָיו בְּעֶרֶב שַׁבָּת עִם חֲשֵׁכָה, שֶׁמָּא יִשְׁכַּח וְיֵצֵא. אָמַר רַב יוֹסֵף: הִלְכְתָא רַבְּתָא לְשַׁבְּתָא.

7. ***One should say three things at home on the eve of Sabbath.*** *Rav Kook emphasizes the importance of attaining certainty that the most important tasks in one's home have been fulfilled. As Shabbat enters and the holiness of Israel shines brightest, the soul which attains certainty that one's home is completely ready shall be engraved with its light.*

Rabbi Ḥanina said: One should examine his clothing. *According to Rav Kook, one of the fundamentals of Shabbat is comparing one's external life with one's inner life. The greater the distance is between the two, the greater the alienation one feels from one's true nature. In our external lives, we are*

2. שבת יב. – *Shabbat 12a.*

אָמַר רַבִּי אֶלְעָזָר,³ אָמַר רַבִּי חֲנִינָא: תַּלְמִידֵי חֲכָמִים מַרְבִּים שָׁלוֹם בָּעוֹלָם, שֶׁנֶּאֱמַר: וְכָל־בָּנַיִךְ לִמּוּדֵי יהוה, וְרַב שְׁלוֹם בָּנָיִךְ:⁴ אַל תִּקְרֵי בָּנָיִךְ, אֶלָּא בּוֹנָיִךְ. שָׁלוֹם רָב לְאֹהֲבֵי תוֹרָתֶךָ, וְאֵין־לָמוֹ מִכְשׁוֹל: יְהִי־שָׁלוֹם בְּחֵילֵךְ, שַׁלְוָה בְּאַרְמְנוֹתָיִךְ. לְמַעַן אַחַי וְרֵעָי אֲדַבְּרָה־נָּא שָׁלוֹם בָּךְ:⁵ לְמַעַן בֵּית־יהוה אֱלֹהֵינוּ אֲבַקְשָׁה טוֹב לָךְ:⁶ ◂ יהוה עֹז לְעַמּוֹ יִתֵּן, יהוה יְבָרֵךְ אֶת־עַמּוֹ בַשָּׁלוֹם:⁷

Rabbi Elazar said[3] in the name of Rabbi Ḥanina: The disciples of the sages increase peace in the world, as it is said, "And all your children shall be taught of the LORD, and great shall be the peace of your children [*banayikh*]."[4] Read not *banayikh*, "your children," but *bonayikh*, "your builders." Those who love Your Torah have great peace; there is no stumbling block for them. May there be peace within your ramparts, prosperity in your palaces. For the sake of my brothers and friends, I shall say, "Peace be within you."[5] For the sake of the House of the LORD our God, I will seek your good.[6] ▸ May the LORD grant strength to His people; may the LORD bless His people with peace.[7]

constantly pulled by others in many different directions. Shabbat is a process not only of accentuating one's inner life, but also of bringing one's two lives in step with each other. Though one would not violate the spiritual dimension of Shabbat if his clothing is not examined, one would not have achieved a refocusing of one's external life, represented by one's clothing. Therefore, in addition to examining one's clothing, special Shabbat clothing is worn to demonstrate the realignment of one's external life.

Adapted by Rabbi Sarna from Rav Kook, *Olat Re'iyya*. Rabbi Avraham Yitzchak Kook, a renowned Halakhist, Kabbalist, and Jewish thinker was the first Chief Rabbi of Israel.

3. ברכות סד. – *Berakhot 64a*
4. ישעיה נד – *Yeshayahu 54*
5. תהלים קיט – *Tehillim 119*
6. תהלים קכב – *Tehillim 122*
7. תהלים כט – *Tehillim 29*

THE RABBIS' KADDISH

The following prayer, said by mourners, requires the presence of a minyan.
A transliteration can be found on page 891.

Mourner: יִתְגַּדַּל Magnified and sanctified[B] may His great name be,
in the world He created by His will.
May He establish His kingdom in your lifetime
and in your days,
and in the lifetime of all the house of Israel,
swiftly and soon – and say: Amen.

All: May His great name be blessed for ever and all time.

Mourner: Blessed and praised, glorified and exalted,
raised and honored, uplifted and lauded
be the name of the Holy One, blessed be He,
beyond any blessing, song, praise and consolation
uttered in the world – and say: Amen.

To Israel, to the teachers,
their disciples and their disciples' disciples,
and to all who engage in the study of Torah,
in this (*In Israel add:* holy) place or elsewhere,
may there come to them
and you great peace, grace, kindness and compassion,
long life, ample sustenance and deliverance,
from their Father in Heaven – and say: Amen.

BIUR TEFILLA • ביאור תפילה

יִתְגַּדַּל וְיִתְקַדַּשׁ – *Magnified and sanctified. Kaddish* was originally recited after communal learning of homiletic portions of the Oral Law. Since there were many people who did not understand Hebrew, the prayer was composed in Aramaic, the language of the Talmud and the vernacular at the time, so that everyone could understand and participate in the sanctification of God's name (*Tosafot Berakhot* 3b). The original text is preserved even though Aramaic has not really survived as a spoken language of the Jews. I have often wondered what lessons the creators of the prayerbook sought to convey by remaining faithful to the original. **What do you think an answer might be?**

קדיש דרבנן

The following prayer, said by mourners, requires the presence of a מנין.
A transliteration can be found on page 891.

אבל: **יִתְגַּדַּל וְיִתְקַדַּשׁ** שְׁמֵהּ רַבָּא (קהל: אָמֵן)
בְּעָלְמָא דִּי בְרָא כִרְעוּתֵהּ
וְיַמְלִיךְ מַלְכוּתֵהּ
בְּחַיֵּיכוֹן וּבְיוֹמֵיכוֹן וּבְחַיֵּי דְכָל בֵּית יִשְׂרָאֵל
בַּעֲגָלָא וּבִזְמַן קָרִיב
וְאִמְרוּ אָמֵן. (קהל: אָמֵן)

קהל ואבל: **יְהֵא שְׁמֵהּ רַבָּא מְבָרַךְ לְעָלַם וּלְעָלְמֵי עָלְמַיָּא.**

אבל: **יִתְבָּרַךְ וְיִשְׁתַּבַּח וְיִתְפָּאַר וְיִתְרוֹמַם וְיִתְנַשֵּׂא**
וְיִתְהַדָּר וְיִתְעַלֶּה וְיִתְהַלָּל
שְׁמֵהּ דְּקֻדְשָׁא בְּרִיךְ הוּא (קהל: בְּרִיךְ הוּא)
לְעֵלָּא מִן כָּל בִּרְכָתָא / בשבת שובה: **לְעֵלָּא לְעֵלָּא מִכָּל בִּרְכָתָא**/
וְשִׁירָתָא, תֻּשְׁבְּחָתָא וְנֶחֱמָתָא, דַּאֲמִירָן בְּעָלְמָא
וְאִמְרוּ אָמֵן. (קהל: אָמֵן)

עַל יִשְׂרָאֵל וְעַל רַבָּנָן
וְעַל תַּלְמִידֵיהוֹן וְעַל כָּל תַּלְמִידֵי תַלְמִידֵיהוֹן
וְעַל כָּל מָאן דְּעָסְקִין בְּאוֹרַיְתָא
דִּי בְּאַתְרָא (בארץ ישראל: **קַדִּישָׁא**) **הָדֵין, וְדִי בְּכָל אֲתַר וַאֲתַר**
יְהֵא לְהוֹן וּלְכוֹן שְׁלָמָא רַבָּא
חִנָּא וְחִסְדָּא, וְרַחֲמֵי, וְחַיֵּי אֲרִיכֵי, וּמְזוֹנֵי רְוִיחֵי
וּפֻרְקָנָא מִן קֳדָם אֲבוּהוֹן דִּי בִשְׁמַיָּא
וְאִמְרוּ אָמֵן. (קהל: אָמֵן)

May there be great peace from heaven,
and (good) life for us and all Israel –
and say: Amen.

Bow and take three steps back as if taking leave of the Divine Presence.
Bow left: May He who makes peace in His high places,
Bow right: in His compassion make peace *Bow forward:* for us and all Israel – and say: Amen.

---

the services. Before that lies the prayer popularly known simply as *Shema*, one of the most important in all of Jewish liturgy and life. It is bounded by two blessings on each side, thus forming one large unit consisting of two blessings, *Shema*, two more blessings, and then the *Amida*. The service ends with a number of brief concluding declarations. As in every service, each of the constituent parts is interconnected and related to the overall theme of the service. In short, there is an order or sequence, translated in Hebrew as *seder*, from which the name of this book, *Siddur*, derives.

1.	Introduction	בָּרְכוּ אֶת יהוה	*Bless the Lord*	Calling the community together
2.	First blessing	הַמַּעֲרִיב עֲרָבִים	*Who brings on evenings*	Hashem as Creator and His love for humanity
3.	Second blessing	אַהֲבַת עוֹלָם	*With everlasting love*	Hashem's love of Israel in particular
4.	*Shema*	שְׁמַע יִשְׂרָאֵל	*Listen, Israel*	1. Acceptance of His sovereignty 2. Acceptance of His commandments 3. The exodus from Egypt
5.	Third blessing	אֱמֶת וֶאֱמוּנָה... גָּאַל יִשְׂרָאֵל	*True and faithful… who redeemed Israel*	Hashem as Redeemer
6.	Fourth blessing	הַשְׁכִּיבֵנוּ... הַפּוֹרֵשׂ סֻכַּת שָׁלוֹם...	*Help us lie down…* *Who spreads a canopy of peace…*	Peace
7.	*Amida*			

יְהֵא שְׁלָמָא רַבָּא מִן שְׁמַיָּא
וְחַיִּים (טוֹבִים) עָלֵינוּ וְעַל כָּל יִשְׂרָאֵל
וְאִמְרוּ אָמֵן. (קהל: אָמֵן)

Bow and take three steps back as if taking leave of the Divine Presence.

Bow left עֹשֶׂה שָׁלוֹם/ בשבת שובה: הַשָּׁלוֹם/ בִּמְרוֹמָיו
Bow right הוּא יַעֲשֶׂה בְרַחֲמָיו שָׁלוֹם *Bow forward* עָלֵינוּ וְעַל
כָּל יִשְׂרָאֵל, וְאִמְרוּ אָמֵן.

INTRODUCTION TO MA'ARIV

Ma'ariv is one of the three prayer times in the Jewish day. The times correspond to certain sacrificial rites that took place during the time of the *Beit HaMikdash* but their origins are said to date back to the times of the three Patriarchs, Avraham, Yitzḥak and Yaakov (*Berakhot* 26b). It has been suggested that the timing of each service also relates to the character and life experience of the Patriarch who established it. Avraham, the bold and assertive pioneer, is associated with the morning, and thus *Shaḥarit*. Yitzḥak, the one who never left Israel, but stayed and worked the Land, is associated with the afternoon and *Minḥa*. Yaakov's life, on the other hand, was filled with trials and tribulations, with uncertainty and clouds of darkness. Yaakov is the one who established *Ma'ariv*.

The phrase the Torah uses is "*vayifga baMakom*" (*Bereshit* 28:11), which in Rabbinic Hebrew could be read to mean, "He bumped into God." There are spiritual experiences we have when we are least expecting them – when we are alone, afraid, thinking of something else altogether. This was Yaakov's vision of prayer. Not everything in the life of the spirit is under our control. The great transformative experiences – love, a sudden sense of beauty, an upsurge of happiness – happen unpredictably and leave us, in Wordsworth's famous words, "surprised by joy." The glory of Yaakov's epiphany is that it happened at night, in the midst of fear and flight (Rabbi J. Sacks).

The nighttime hours are often a time of uncertainty, when the insecurities of our lives rear their heads the most. What better time to search out an encounter with the One who knows us best? Preoccupied with the successes or disappointments of our day, we enter into an intimate conversation with Hashem, finding friendship and support, and, perhaps, a transformative experience.

In terms of structure, the *Amida* lies at the core and climax of *Ma'ariv* as it does in all of

Ma'ariv for Shabbat

BLESSINGS OF THE SHEMA

Leader: *Bow* **BLESS**[B]
Stand straight the LORD, the blessed One.

Congregation: *Bow* Bless *Stand straight* the LORD, the blessed One, for ever and all time.

Leader: *Bow* Bless *Stand straight* the LORD, the blessed One, for ever and all time.

בָּרוּךְ Blessed are You, LORD our God, King of the Universe,
who by His word brings on evenings,
by His wisdom opens the gates of heaven,
with understanding makes time change
and the seasons rotate,
and by His will
orders the stars in their constellations in the sky.

---

revelation in Torah. God can be found in both, although in different ways.

בָּרוּךְ – *Blessed.* This opening formula ("Blessed are You...") marks the first of the two blessings before the *Shema* and it concludes at the end of the paragraph with the same formula ("Blessed are You who brings on evenings.") Although the formula appears twice, the prayer itself is actually considered one long blessing with an introduction and conclusion.

ANI TEFILLA • אני תפילה

"The sun descending in the west, / The evening star does shine; / The birds are silent in their nest, / And I must seek for mine." (William Blake)

מעריב לשבת

קריאת שמע וברכותיה

ש״ץ: *Bow* בָּרְכוּ
Stand straight אֶת יהוה הַמְבֹרָךְ.

קהל: *Bow* בָּרוּךְ *Stand straight* יהוה הַמְבֹרָךְ לְעוֹלָם וָעֶד.

ש״ץ: *Bow* בָּרוּךְ *Stand straight* יהוה הַמְבֹרָךְ לְעוֹלָם וָעֶד.

בָּרוּךְ אַתָּה יהוה אֱלֹהֵינוּ מֶלֶךְ הָעוֹלָם
אֲשֶׁר בִּדְבָרוֹ מַעֲרִיב עֲרָבִים
בְּחָכְמָה פּוֹתֵחַ שְׁעָרִים
וּבִתְבוּנָה מְשַׁנֶּה עִתִּים וּמַחֲלִיף אֶת הַזְּמַנִּים
וּמְסַדֵּר אֶת הַכּוֹכָבִים בְּמִשְׁמְרוֹתֵיהֶם בָּרָקִיעַ כִּרְצוֹנוֹ.

BIUR TEFILLA • ביאור תפילה

בָּרְכוּ – *Bless.* Just as in the morning, as a prelude to the *Shema*, the *Ḥazan* invites us to join together as a single entity to declare our most basic beliefs and allegiance. Let's support one another. We will declare Him One, as one.

בָּרוּךְ – *Bless.* Like in *Shaḥarit*, *Keriat Shema* has two introductory blessings, and as in the morning, the theme of the first is Hashem's revelation in nature, and the theme of the second is Hashem's

He creates day and night,
rolling away the light before the darkness,
and darkness before the light.
▸ He makes the day pass and brings on night,
distinguishing day from night:
the LORD of hosts is His name.
May the living and forever enduring God rule over us for all time.
Blessed are You, LORD, who brings on evenings.[1]

אַהֲבַת עוֹלָם With everlasting love[B]
have You loved Your people, the house of Israel.
You have taught us Torah and commandments,
decrees and laws of justice.
Therefore, LORD our God, when we lie down and when we rise up[B]
we will speak of Your decrees,
rejoicing in the words of Your Torah
and Your commandments for ever.
▸ For they are our life and the length of our days;
on them will we meditate day and night.[B]
May You never take away Your love from us.
Blessed are You, LORD, who loves His people Israel.

BIUR TEFILLA • ביאור תפילה

אַהֲבַת עוֹלָם – *With everlasting love.* The previous blessing was universalistic in its focus on God's presence in nature; this blessing moves toward God's relationship with the Jewish people, in particular with the gift of Torah.

בְּשָׁכְבֵנוּ וּבְקוּמֵנוּ – *When we lie down and when we rise up.* These two Hebrew words anticipate the words of the *Shema* and the reason that we recite it twice a day: "when you go to sleep and when you rise up."

וּבָהֶם נֶהְגֶּה יוֹמָם וָלָיְלָה – *On them will we meditate day and night.* The source of this line is a verse from *Yehoshua*. As *Benei Yisrael* were about to enter the Promised Land, the very first message to the people was the centrality of Torah in their lives and the need to "*meditate upon them day and night*... do not fear and do not lose resolve, for Hashem is with you wherever you will go" (*Yehoshua* 1:8–9). By reciting the *Shema* a second time today, we fulfill that mandate. And in doing so, we pray that Hashem will be with us wherever we will go, physically and emotionally.

בּוֹרֵא יוֹם וָלָיְלָה, גּוֹלֵל אוֹר מִפְּנֵי חֹשֶׁךְ וְחֹשֶׁךְ מִפְּנֵי אוֹר
◂ וּמַעֲבִיר יוֹם וּמֵבִיא לָיְלָה, וּמַבְדִּיל בֵּין יוֹם וּבֵין לָיְלָה
יהוה צְבָאוֹת שְׁמוֹ.
אֵל חַי וְקַיָּם תָּמִיד, יִמְלֹךְ עָלֵינוּ לְעוֹלָם וָעֶד.
בָּרוּךְ אַתָּה יהוה, הַמַּעֲרִיב עֲרָבִים.[ע]

אַהֲבַת עוֹלָם[הב] בֵּית יִשְׂרָאֵל עַמְּךָ אָהָבְתָּ
תּוֹרָה וּמִצְוֹת, חֻקִּים וּמִשְׁפָּטִים, אוֹתָנוּ לִמַּדְתָּ
עַל כֵּן יהוה אֱלֹהֵינוּ בְּשָׁכְבֵנוּ וּבְקוּמֵנוּ[ב] נָשִׂיחַ בְּחֻקֶּיךָ
וְנִשְׂמַח בְּדִבְרֵי תוֹרָתֶךָ וּבְמִצְוֹתֶיךָ לְעוֹלָם וָעֶד
◂ כִּי הֵם חַיֵּינוּ וְאֹרֶךְ יָמֵינוּ, וּבָהֶם נֶהְגֶּה יוֹמָם וָלָיְלָה.[ב]
וְאַהֲבָתְךָ אַל תָּסִיר מִמֶּנּוּ לְעוֹלָמִים.
בָּרוּךְ אַתָּה יהוה, אוֹהֵב עַמּוֹ יִשְׂרָאֵל.

IYUN TEFILLA • עיון תפילה

הַמַּעֲרִיב עֲרָבִים – *Who brings on evenings.* If in the morning we were conscious of the sun and the beginning of the day, here we are aware of the ending of the day and the descent of darkness which envelops us. The Gemara (*Berakhot* 11b) says that we must recall the attributes of day and night together, for both reflect the miracle of creation and its single source, Hashem, whose unity we will declare momentarily. Night and day; sun and stars; past, present, and future are all part of one continuum. The world is whole and there is a pattern and there is a plan. We need only find our place in it.

HILKHOT TEFILLA • הלכות תפילה

אַהֲבַת עוֹלָם – *With everlasting love.* This marks the beginning of the second blessing prior to the *Shema*. Unlike the first one, here the standard formula (*Barukh ata…*/ Blessed are You…) is only to be found at the very end of the blessing and not at the beginning. This is a common formulation in the Siddur where the concluding formula from the previous blessing is deemed sufficient to also act as the opening for the next. It is known in halakhic (legal) terminology as *berakha hasemukha leḥaverta*, a blessing [without the opening formula] that is appended to its neighbor [which has the formula at its end].

A transliteration can be found on page 890.
The Shema must be said with intense concentration. In the first paragraph one should accept, with love, the sovereignty of God; in the second, the mitzvot as the will of God. The end of the third paragraph constitutes fulfillment of the mitzva to remember, morning and evening, the exodus from Egypt.
For introduction and further commentary on Shema see pages 316–323 in Shaḥarit.

When not with a minyan, say:
God, faithful King!

The following verse should be said aloud, while covering the eyes with the right hand:

Listen, Israel:[1] **the LORD is our God, the LORD is One.** *Deut. 6*

Quietly: Blessed be the name of His glorious kingdom for ever and all time.

וְאָהַבְתָּ Love the LORD[A] your God with all your heart, with all *Deut. 6*
your soul, and with all your might. These words which I command you today shall be on your heart. Teach them repeatedly to

---

ANI TEFILLA • אני תפילה

Father explained that the reason it is customary to cover one's eyes is a symbolic gesture to indicate that although our sense perceptions may tell that what we are experiencing is bad, we are willing to let our faith supersede and overrule our perception. There are times when we may look at the world and wonder about God or about His mercy or justice in the world, and so we cover our eyes as if to declare that we recognize that our perceptions are not always correct and we rely instead on God's judgment and wisdom. (Rabbi Abraham Twerski)

וְאָהַבְתָּ אֵת יהוה – *Love the LORD.*
Rabbi Moshe Leib of Sassov announced to his disciples that he had learned what it meant to love another from a conversation he overheard between two villagers. One said to the other: "Tell me, dear Ivan, do you love me?" Ivan replied, "I love you very much." The first one responded: "Do you know what causes me pain?" Ivan replied: "How can I know what gives you pain?" The first one responded: "If you do not know what gives me pain, then how can you say that you truly love me?"

"Understand, then," said Rabbi Moshe Leib, "to love, to truly love someone, means to know what brings them pain."

A transliteration can be found on page 890.
The שמע *must be said with intense concentration. In the first paragraph one should accept, with love, the sovereignty of God; in the second, the mitzvot as the will of God. The end of the third paragraph constitutes fulfillment of the mitzva to remember, morning and evening, the exodus from Egypt.*
For introduction and further commentary on שמע *see pages 316–323 in* שחרית.

When not with a מנין*, say:*

אֵל מֶלֶךְ נֶאֱמָן

The following verse should be said aloud, while covering the eyes with the right hand:

שְׁמַע יִשְׂרָאֵל, יהוה אֱלֹהֵינוּ, יהוה | אֶחָד׃ דברים ו

Quietly בָּרוּךְ שֵׁם כְּבוֹד מַלְכוּתוֹ לְעוֹלָם וָעֶד.

וְאָהַבְתָּ אֵת יהוה אֱלֹהֶיךָ, בְּכָל־לְבָבְךָ וּבְכָל־נַפְשְׁךָ וּבְכָל־ דברים ו
מְאֹדֶךָ׃ וְהָיוּ הַדְּבָרִים הָאֵלֶּה, אֲשֶׁר אָנֹכִי מְצַוְּךָ הַיּוֹם, עַל־לְבָבֶךָ׃

IYUN TEFILLA • עיון תפילה

שְׁמַע יִשְׂרָאֵל – *Listen, Israel.* This statement and paragraph are generally said to comprise *kabbalat ol malkhut shamayim*, accepting upon oneself the yoke of the sovereignty of Heaven. The "yoke of heaven" sounds like such a scary term, but the truth is that yokes are put on animals not for the purpose of hurting them, but for the purpose of enabling them to stay on a path and to achieve a purpose. Similarly, when we declare that we accept the "yoke of heaven," we are not accepting some sort of master that is going to work us to death, we are accepting upon ourselves a King who will lead us to spiritual freedom, give us strength to conquer our weaknesses, and guide us to a common, higher, purpose (Rabbi N. Mindel).

ANI TEFILLA • אני תפילה

Prayer in general is about a dialogue where man and Hashem speak to one another. The fact that one of the parties cannot be "heard" does not mean that the He is not involved in the conversation. Knowing someone is at the other end of the line even if they do not speak, doesn't mean that one is talking to oneself. In Shema, however, that element of dialogue is missing. "It expresses itself more in the form of declaration, confession, profession of faith. Whether this takes the form of soliloquy, in which man declares and challenges himself, or a colloquy – in which he addresses himself to a Thou – is irrelevant. What is important is the fact that if there is a thou in Shema, the thou is not God but a finite being like myself." (Rabbi Joseph B. Soloveitchik)

your children, speaking of them when you sit at home and when you travel on the way, when you lie down and when you rise. Bind them as a sign on your hand, and they shall be an emblem between your eyes. Write them on the doorposts of your house and gates.

וְהָיָה If you indeed heed My commandments with which I charge you today, to love the LORD your God and worship Him with all your heart and with all your soul, I will give rain in your land in its season, the early and late rain; and you shall gather in your grain, wine and oil. I will give grass in your field for your cattle, and you shall eat and be satisfied. Be careful lest your heart be tempted and you go astray and worship other gods, bowing down to them. Then the LORD's anger will flare against you and He will close the heavens so that there will be no rain. The land will not yield its crops, and you will perish swiftly from the good land that the LORD is giving you. Therefore, set these, My words, on your heart and soul. Bind them as a sign on your hand, and they shall be an emblem between your eyes. Teach them to your children, speaking of them when you sit at home and when you travel on the way, when you lie down and when you rise. Write them on the doorposts of your house and gates, so that you and your children may live long in the land that the LORD swore to your ancestors to give them, for as long as the heavens are above the earth. *Deut. 11*

וַיֹּאמֶר The LORD spoke[H] to Moses, saying: Speak to the Israelites and tell them to make tassels on the corners of their garments *Num. 15*

HILKHOT TEFILLA • הלכות תפילה

וַיֹּאמֶר יהוה – *The LORD spoke.* The primary halakhic function of the third paragraph of the *Shema* at this time is to recall the exodus from Egypt. The exodus is the rationale

This **HILKHOT TEFILLA** *continues on page 93.*

וְשִׁנַּנְתָּם לְבָנֶיךָ וְדִבַּרְתָּ בָּם, בְּשִׁבְתְּךָ בְּבֵיתֶךָ וּבְלֶכְתְּךָ בַדֶּרֶךְ,
וּבְשָׁכְבְּךָ וּבְקוּמֶךָ: וּקְשַׁרְתָּם לְאוֹת עַל־יָדֶךָ וְהָיוּ לְטֹטָפֹת בֵּין
עֵינֶיךָ: וּכְתַבְתָּם עַל־מְזֻזוֹת בֵּיתֶךָ וּבִשְׁעָרֶיךָ:

וְהָיָה אִם־שָׁמֹעַ תִּשְׁמְעוּ אֶל־מִצְוֺתַי אֲשֶׁר אָנֹכִי מְצַוֶּה אֶתְכֶם דברים יא
הַיּוֹם, לְאַהֲבָה אֶת־יהוה אֱלֹהֵיכֶם וּלְעָבְדוֹ, בְּכָל־לְבַבְכֶם וּבְכָל־
נַפְשְׁכֶם: וְנָתַתִּי מְטַר־אַרְצְכֶם בְּעִתּוֹ, יוֹרֶה וּמַלְקוֹשׁ, וְאָסַפְתָּ
דְגָנֶךָ וְתִירֹשְׁךָ וְיִצְהָרֶךָ: וְנָתַתִּי עֵשֶׂב בְּשָׂדְךָ לִבְהֶמְתֶּךָ, וְאָכַלְתָּ
וְשָׂבָעְתָּ: הִשָּׁמְרוּ לָכֶם פֶּן־יִפְתֶּה לְבַבְכֶם, וְסַרְתֶּם וַעֲבַדְתֶּם
אֱלֹהִים אֲחֵרִים וְהִשְׁתַּחֲוִיתֶם לָהֶם: וְחָרָה אַף־יהוה בָּכֶם, וְעָצַר
אֶת־הַשָּׁמַיִם וְלֹא־יִהְיֶה מָטָר, וְהָאֲדָמָה לֹא תִתֵּן אֶת־יְבוּלָהּ,
וַאֲבַדְתֶּם מְהֵרָה מֵעַל הָאָרֶץ הַטֹּבָה אֲשֶׁר יהוה נֹתֵן לָכֶם:
וְשַׂמְתֶּם אֶת־דְּבָרַי אֵלֶּה עַל־לְבַבְכֶם וְעַל־נַפְשְׁכֶם, וּקְשַׁרְתֶּם
אֹתָם לְאוֹת עַל־יֶדְכֶם, וְהָיוּ לְטוֹטָפֹת בֵּין עֵינֵיכֶם: וְלִמַּדְתֶּם
אֹתָם אֶת־בְּנֵיכֶם לְדַבֵּר בָּם, בְּשִׁבְתְּךָ בְּבֵיתֶךָ וּבְלֶכְתְּךָ בַדֶּרֶךְ,
וּבְשָׁכְבְּךָ וּבְקוּמֶךָ: וּכְתַבְתָּם עַל־מְזוּזוֹת בֵּיתֶךָ וּבִשְׁעָרֶיךָ: לְמַעַן
יִרְבּוּ יְמֵיכֶם וִימֵי בְנֵיכֶם עַל הָאֲדָמָה אֲשֶׁר נִשְׁבַּע יהוה לַאֲבֹתֵיכֶם
לָתֵת לָהֶם, כִּימֵי הַשָּׁמַיִם עַל־הָאָרֶץ:

וַיֹּאמֶר יהוה אֶל־מֹשֶׁה לֵּאמֹר: דַּבֵּר אֶל־בְּנֵי יִשְׂרָאֵל וְאָמַרְתָּ במדבר טו
אֲלֵהֶם, וְעָשׂוּ לָהֶם צִיצִת עַל־כַּנְפֵי בִגְדֵיהֶם לְדֹרֹתָם, וְנָתְנוּ

ANI TEFILLA • אני תפילה

Faith is not the absence of reason, it is a skill in its own right which, when cultivated, allows us to experience the ultimate. *(Rabbi Menaḥem Mendel Schneerson. Cited in Toward a Meaningful Life by Rabbi Simon Jacobson)*

for all generations. They shall attach to the tassel at each corner a thread of blue. This shall be your tassel, and you shall see it and remember all of the LORD's commandments and keep them, not straying after your heart and after your eyes, following your own sinful desires. Thus you will be reminded to keep all My commandments, and be holy to your God. I am the LORD your God, who brought you out of the land of Egypt to be your God. I am the LORD your God.

True[B] –

The Leader repeats:

▸ The LORD your God is true –

וֶאֱמוּנָה – and faithful is all this,[BIH]
and firmly established for us
that He is the LORD our God,
and there is none besides Him,
and that we, Israel, are His people.

IYUN TEFILLA • עיון תפילה

וֶאֱמוּנָה – *Faithful.* After a long day of work and pressures, there is no person whose soul does not ache. When the person goes to sleep, the soul rises to heaven and although Hashem orders her to return to the body, she does not wish to do so. Hashem responds: "Man placed his faith in Me at night by placing his soul in My hands for safekeeping." Hashem therefore remains faithful to man, protects his soul overnight, and a miracle takes place in the morning when the soul is restored and he awakes feeling refreshed and invigorated, ready to begin a new day. (Rashi)

HILKHOT TEFILLA • הלכות תפילה

וֶאֱמוּנָה – *Faithful.* Rav says (*Berakhot* 12a) that whoever does not include the theme of *Emet Ve-Emuna* in the evening prayer does not fulfill his obligation. The assertion is based upon the verse in *Tehillim* (92:3), "I will tell of Your *ḥesed* in the morning and Your *emuna* (faithfulness) at night. The nighttime is all about Hashem's faithfulness...and our faith.

עַל־צִיצִת הַכָּנָף פְּתִיל תְּכֵלֶת: וְהָיָה לָכֶם לְצִיצִת, וּרְאִיתֶם אֹתוֹ וּזְכַרְתֶּם אֶת־כָּל־מִצְוֹת יהוה וַעֲשִׂיתֶם אֹתָם, וְלֹא תָתוּרוּ אַחֲרֵי לְבַבְכֶם וְאַחֲרֵי עֵינֵיכֶם, אֲשֶׁר־אַתֶּם זֹנִים אַחֲרֵיהֶם: לְמַעַן תִּזְכְּרוּ וַעֲשִׂיתֶם אֶת־כָּל־מִצְוֹתָי, וִהְיִיתֶם קְדֹשִׁים לֵאלֹהֵיכֶם: אֲנִי יהוה אֱלֹהֵיכֶם, אֲשֶׁר הוֹצֵאתִי אֶתְכֶם מֵאֶרֶץ מִצְרַיִם, לִהְיוֹת לָכֶם לֵאלֹהִים, אֲנִי יהוה אֱלֹהֵיכֶם:

אֱמֶת[ב]

The שליח ציבור *repeats:*

◂ יהוה אֱלֹהֵיכֶם אֱמֶת

וֶאֱמוּנָה[בעה] כָּל זֹאת וְקַיָּם עָלֵינוּ
כִּי הוּא יהוה אֱלֹהֵינוּ וְאֵין זוּלָתוֹ
וַאֲנַחְנוּ יִשְׂרָאֵל עַמּוֹ.

---

provided for many mitzvot in the Torah. It lies at the heart of our chosenness, and at the heart of our need to be empathetic toward others less fortunate.

BIUR TEFILLA • ביאור תפילה

אֱמֶת – *True.* This word, while technically not part of the biblical passage just recited, is nevertheless appended to the final line of the *Shema* so that the sentence reads "The Lord your God is true."

וֶאֱמוּנָה – *And faithful.* This marks the beginning of the third blessing. If the first blessing was about creation and the second about revelation, the third is about redemption, in this case God's presence in the history of the Jewish people. To be a Jew standing before God means to be cognizant of being a part of an unending continuum of Jewish history, to see oneself as the link in a chain that goes back thousands of years if not beyond. To be a Jew means to belong.

He is our King,
who redeems us from the hand of kings
and delivers us from the grasp of all tyrants.
He is our God, who on our behalf repays our foes
and brings just retribution on our mortal enemies;
who performs great deeds beyond understanding
and wonders beyond number;
who kept us alive, *Ps. 66*
not letting our foot slip;
who led us on the high places of our enemies,
raising our pride above all our foes;
who did miracles for us
and brought vengeance against Pharaoh;
who performed signs and wonders
in the land of Ham's children;
who smote in His wrath all the firstborn of Egypt,
and brought out His people Israel from their midst
into everlasting freedom;
who led His children through the divided Reed Sea,
plunging their pursuers and enemies into the depths.

When His children saw His might,
they gave praise
and thanks to His name,
▸ and willingly accepted His Sovereignty.
Moses and the children of Israel
then sang a song to You with great joy,
and they all exclaimed:

It is customary to wait for the Leader to reach this point, whereupon the congregation recites this verse aloud, followed by the Leader:

"Who is like You, LORD, among the mighty? *Ex. 15*
Who is like You, majestic in holiness,
awesome in praises, doing wonders?"

הַפּוֹדֵנוּ מִיַּד מְלָכִים
מַלְכֵּנוּ הַגּוֹאֲלֵנוּ מִכַּף כָּל הֶעָרִיצִים.
הָאֵל הַנִּפְרָע לָנוּ מִצָּרֵינוּ
וְהַמְשַׁלֵּם גְּמוּל לְכָל אוֹיְבֵי נַפְשֵׁנוּ.
הָעוֹשֶׂה גְדוֹלוֹת עַד אֵין חֵקֶר, וְנִפְלָאוֹת עַד אֵין מִסְפָּר
תהלים סו הַשָּׂם נַפְשֵׁנוּ בַּחַיִּים, וְלֹא־נָתַן לַמּוֹט רַגְלֵנוּ:
הַמַּדְרִיכֵנוּ עַל בָּמוֹת אוֹיְבֵינוּ
וַיָּרֶם קַרְנֵנוּ עַל כָּל שׂוֹנְאֵינוּ.
הָעוֹשֶׂה לָּנוּ נִסִּים וּנְקָמָה בְּפַרְעֹה
אוֹתוֹת וּמוֹפְתִים בְּאַדְמַת בְּנֵי חָם.
הַמַּכֶּה בְעֶבְרָתוֹ כָּל בְּכוֹרֵי מִצְרָיִם
וַיּוֹצֵא אֶת עַמּוֹ יִשְׂרָאֵל מִתּוֹכָם לְחֵרוּת עוֹלָם.
הַמַּעֲבִיר בָּנָיו בֵּין גִּזְרֵי יַם סוּף
אֶת רוֹדְפֵיהֶם וְאֶת שׂוֹנְאֵיהֶם בִּתְהוֹמוֹת טִבַּע

וְרָאוּ בָנָיו גְּבוּרָתוֹ, שִׁבְּחוּ וְהוֹדוּ לִשְׁמוֹ
◂ וּמַלְכוּתוֹ בְּרָצוֹן קִבְּלוּ עֲלֵיהֶם.
מֹשֶׁה וּבְנֵי יִשְׂרָאֵל, לְךָ עָנוּ שִׁירָה בְּשִׂמְחָה רַבָּה
וְאָמְרוּ כֻלָּם

It is customary to wait for the שליח ציבור *to reach this point, whereupon the* קהל *recites this verse aloud, followed by the* שליח ציבור*:*

שמות טו מִי־כָמֹכָה בָּאֵלִם יהוה
מִי כָּמֹכָה נֶאְדָּר בַּקֹּדֶשׁ
נוֹרָא תְהִלֹּת עֹשֵׂה פֶלֶא:

▸ Your children beheld Your majesty
as You parted the sea before Moses.
"This is my God!" they responded, and then said:

Wait for the Leader, then say the following verse aloud, which is then repeated by the Leader.

"The LORD shall reign for ever and ever." *Ex. 15*

▸ And it is said,
"For the LORD has redeemed Jacob *Jer. 31*
and rescued him from a power
stronger than his own."
Blessed are You, LORD, who redeemed Israel.

הַשְׁכִּיבֵנוּ Help us lie down,[B] O LORD our God, in peace,
and rise up, O our King, to life.
Spread over us Your canopy of peace.
Direct us with Your good counsel,[A]
and save us for the sake of Your name.
Shield us and remove from us every enemy,
plague, sword, famine and sorrow.
Remove the adversary from before and behind us.[B]
Shelter us in the shadow of Your wings,[A]
for You, God, are our Guardian and Deliverer;
You, God, are a gracious and compassionate King.

ANI TEFILLA • אני תפילה

וְתַקְּנֵנוּ בְּעֵצָה טוֹבָה – *Direct us with Your good counsel.* At night, we are more open to possibilities, more open to divine inspiration. I pray that I will be open to Your direction and advice. (*Iyun Tefilla*, Rabbi Yaakov Tzvi Mecklenburg)

וּבְצֵל כְּנָפֶיךָ תַּסְתִּירֵנוּ – *Shelter us in the shadow of Your wings.* Like a mother bird who protects her chicks by gathering them under her wing. The warm embrace of a parent, the feeling of comfort and security that comes with being enveloped, protected and secure. That is what we all long for, no matter how old we are. That is what Hashem provides. Feel enveloped.

◂ מַלְכוּתְךָ רָאוּ בָנֶיךָ, בּוֹקֵעַ יָם לִפְנֵי מֹשֶׁה
זֶה אֵלִי עָנוּ, וְאָמְרוּ

Wait for the שליח ציבור, then say the following verse aloud, which is then repeated by the Leader.

שמות טו יהוה יִמְלֹךְ לְעֹלָם וָעֶד:

◂ וְנֶאֱמַר

ירמיהו לא כִּי־פָדָה יהוה אֶת־יַעֲקֹב, וּגְאָלוֹ מִיַּד חָזָק מִמֶּנּוּ:
בָּרוּךְ אַתָּה יהוה, גָּאַל יִשְׂרָאֵל.

הַשְׁכִּיבֵנוּ[ב] יהוה אֱלֹהֵינוּ לְשָׁלוֹם, וְהַעֲמִידֵנוּ מַלְכֵּנוּ לְחַיִּים
וּפְרֹשׂ עָלֵינוּ סֻכַּת שְׁלוֹמֶךָ, וְתַקְּנֵנוּ בְּעֵצָה טוֹבָה[א] מִלְּפָנֶיךָ
וְהוֹשִׁיעֵנוּ לְמַעַן שְׁמֶךָ.
וְהָגֵן בַּעֲדֵנוּ, וְהָסֵר מֵעָלֵינוּ אוֹיֵב, דֶּבֶר וְחֶרֶב וְרָעָב וְיָגוֹן
וְהָסֵר שָׂטָן מִלְּפָנֵינוּ וּמֵאַחֲרֵינוּ,[ב] וּבְצֵל כְּנָפֶיךָ תַּסְתִּירֵנוּ[א]
כִּי אֵל שׁוֹמְרֵנוּ וּמַצִּילֵנוּ אָתָּה
כִּי אֵל מֶלֶךְ חַנּוּן וְרַחוּם אָתָּה.

BIUR TEFILLA • ביאור תפילה

הַשְׁכִּיבֵנוּ – *Help us lie down.* This marks the beginning of the second blessing following the *Shema*. It is considered an extension of the previous one (*Berakhot* 4b) though here the redemption which is requested sounds personal as much as communal. For night-time can be a period of great uncertainty and insecurity. And so, just as the *tallit* or prayer shawl which is worn in the morning can be seen as a protective cloak, here we ask Hashem Himself to shelter us from the dangers that lurk from our enemies and, perhaps even more daunting, from the negative forces that lie within ourselves. **From what insecurities do you wish for protection this evening?**

וְהָסֵר שָׂטָן מִלְּפָנֵינוּ וּמֵאַחֲרֵינוּ – *Remove the adversary from before and behind us.* The *Satan* is the evil inclination (*Bava Batra* 16a), the disposition that we sometimes have to do what we know in our heart of hearts we should not do. We therefore ask here for help with our own inclinations which, especially at night, can seem to overwhelm us.

Guard our going out and our coming in,
for life and peace, from now and for ever.
Spread over us Your canopy of peace.
Blessed are You, LORD,
who spreads a canopy of peace[B] over us,
over all His people Israel, and over Jerusalem.

In anticipation of the Amida which is recited while standing, the custom is to stand for this passage, which is said aloud together with the Leader.

וְשָׁמְרוּ The children of Israel must keep the Sabbath,[I] Ex. 31
observing the Sabbath[I] in every generation
as an everlasting covenant.
It is a sign between Me and the children of Israel for ever,
for in six days God made the heavens and the earth,
but on the seventh day He ceased work
and refreshed Himself.

---

service, we stop to remind ourselves of the theme of the day. For all of the emphasis that there has just been on Hashem's protection of us, we must recall that it is contingent upon our doing our share; in the present case, that means that Hashem will protect us only if we protect the specialness of Shabbat (Abudarham). Perhaps that is a reason for the emphasis on "observing the Sabbath" (literally, "to make the Sabbath"); it is dependent on us.

לַעֲשׂוֹת אֶת־הַשַּׁבָּת – *Observing the Sabbath.* Literally the phrase means "to make the Shabbat." The Midrash therefore suggests that whoever keeps the Shabbat, it is as if he actually created the Shabbat (*Mekhilta*). One explanation is because unlike other ritual objects such as a *tallit* or *tefillin*, or the like, Shabbat has no external visible distinguishing characteristics. It can be a day like any other day of the week. The difference lies in what we "make" of it (*Torah Temima*).

ANI TEFILLA • אני תפילה

A man is walking down the road with his young son and they come across a large rock. Says the boy, "Father, do you think that I can move that rock?" The father answers, "If you use all of your strength, I'm sure that you can do it." The boy walks up to the rock and begins to push. He strains and struggles and tries desperately to dislodge it, only to give up in frustration and disappointment. "You were wrong," he said to his father, "I couldn't do it." His father put his arm around him and said, "You didn't use all of your strength – you didn't ask me for help."

◂ וּשְׁמֹר צֵאתֵֽנוּ וּבוֹאֵֽנוּ לְחַיִּים וּלְשָׁלוֹם מֵעַתָּה וְעַד עוֹלָם.
וּפְרֹשׂ עָלֵֽינוּ סֻכַּת שְׁלוֹמֶֽךָ.
בָּרוּךְ אַתָּה יהוה
הַפּוֹרֵשׂ סֻכַּת שָׁלוֹם[ב] עָלֵֽינוּ
וְעַל כָּל עַמּוֹ יִשְׂרָאֵל וְעַל יְרוּשָׁלָֽיִם.

In anticipation of the עמידה *which is recited while standing, the custom is to stand for this passage, which is said aloud together with the* שליח ציבור*.*

שמות לא
וְשָׁמְרוּ בְנֵי־יִשְׂרָאֵל אֶת־הַשַּׁבָּת[ע]
לַעֲשׂוֹת אֶת־הַשַּׁבָּת[ע] לְדֹרֹתָם בְּרִית עוֹלָם:
בֵּינִי וּבֵין בְּנֵי יִשְׂרָאֵל, אוֹת הִוא לְעֹלָם
כִּי־שֵׁשֶׁת יָמִים עָשָׂה יהוה אֶת־הַשָּׁמַיִם וְאֶת־הָאָֽרֶץ
וּבַיּוֹם הַשְּׁבִיעִי שָׁבַת וַיִּנָּפַשׁ:

BIUR TEFILLA • ביאור תפילה

הַפּוֹרֵשׂ סֻכַּת שָׁלוֹם – *Who spreads a canopy of peace.* The conclusion of this final blessing is different than its parallel in the weekday service. For while we ask for protection from external and internal forces, the truth is that on Shabbat the feeling is that one is already protected to some extent. To what might this be compared? It is similar to a king who has a shepherd who watches his flock. Each day the shepherd remains in the field and stays awake at night to guard his flock. But one night a week, the shepherd brings the flock back home and thus he is able to get a good night's sleep. Similarly, on weekdays, the Guardian of Israel does not sleep because He must guard the Jewish people who go about their business, some by going out in the fields and some by going to work. But on Shabbat, with everyone at home, the Jewish people do not need to be guarded but instead God spreads His blanket of peace over us (Roke'aḥ).

IYUN TEFILLA • עיון תפילה

וְשָׁמְרוּ בְנֵי־יִשְׂרָאֵל אֶת־הַשַּׁבָּת – *The children of Israel must keep the Sabbath.* As we get closer to the *Amida* prayer which is our most intimate encounter with the Divine in the

HALF KADDISH

Leader: יִתְגַּדַּל Magnified and sanctified may His great name be,
in the world He created by His will.
May He establish His kingdom
in your lifetime and in your days,
and in the lifetime of all the house of Israel,
swiftly and soon – and say: Amen.

All: May His great name[A] be blessed for ever and all time.

Leader: Blessed and praised, glorified and exalted,
raised and honored, uplifted and lauded
be the name of the Holy One, blessed be He,
beyond any blessing, song, praise and consolation
uttered in the world – and say: Amen.

INTRODUCTION TO THE AMIDA

This prayer which is the key component of any service, is known by a number of names and has a number of variations. It is known in Rabbinic literature simply as *Tefilla* or "prayer" because it is the ultimate prayer, a most intimate moment between man and his Creator. It is also called the *Amida*, which means "standing," because it is essentially a prayer said like a servant standing before one's master. (The version that is said during the week is also called *Shemoneh Esreh* or "Eighteen" as a reference to the number of blessings it contains. Some popularly also refer to the version said on Shabbat as *Shemoneh Esreh* even though that is technically a misnomer since the number of blessings on Shabbat is reduced to seven. Nevertheless, the one during the week can still be called the *Amida* since one's posture at that time remains the same.)

On Shabbat, the *Amida* is recited on four different occasions. In each case, there are a total of seven blessings and in each case the first three and last three blessings are identical. However, in contrast to all of the weekday services where the middle section is also exactly the same, on Shabbat, the text and theme of the middle section is different for each one of the four versions. There is no one authoritative reason for this so each person may find his or her own meaning. One suggestion comes from the fourteenth-century commentator Abudarham, who suggests that the theme of this evening parallels the wedding ceremony. On Friday night, the middle blessing begins with the words *ata kidashta* (You sanctified), a word reminiscent of the betrothal ceremony (*kiddushin*); in the morning, the initial focus is on happiness (*Yismaḥ Moshe*); the third *Amida* focuses on the extra sacrificial offerings, reminiscent of a celebratory feast; and the middle blessing of the afternoon *Amida* begins with words *ata eḥad*,

This **INTRODUCTION TO THE AMIDA** *continues on page 103.*

חצי קדיש

ש״ץ: יִתְגַּדַּל וְיִתְקַדַּשׁ שְׁמֵהּ רַבָּא (קהל: אָמֵן)
בְּעָלְמָא דִּי בְרָא כִרְעוּתֵהּ
וְיַמְלִיךְ מַלְכוּתֵהּ
בְּחַיֵּיכוֹן וּבְיוֹמֵיכוֹן וּבְחַיֵּי דְכָל בֵּית יִשְׂרָאֵל
בַּעֲגָלָא וּבִזְמַן קָרִיב, וְאִמְרוּ אָמֵן. (קהל: אָמֵן)

קהל וש״ץ: יְהֵא שְׁמֵהּ רַבָּא[א] מְבָרַךְ לְעָלַם וּלְעָלְמֵי עָלְמַיָּא.

ש״ץ: יִתְבָּרַךְ וְיִשְׁתַּבַּח וְיִתְפָּאַר וְיִתְרוֹמַם וְיִתְנַשֵּׂא
וְיִתְהַדָּר וְיִתְעַלֶּה וְיִתְהַלָּל
שְׁמֵהּ דְּקֻדְשָׁא בְּרִיךְ הוּא (קהל: בְּרִיךְ הוּא)
לְעֵלָּא מִן כָּל בִּרְכָתָא
/ בשבת שובה: לְעֵלָּא לְעֵלָּא מִכָּל בִּרְכָתָא/
וְשִׁירָתָא, תֻּשְׁבְּחָתָא וְנֶחֱמָתָא
דַּאֲמִירָן בְּעָלְמָא, וְאִמְרוּ אָמֵן. (קהל: אָמֵן)

ANI TEFILLA • אני תפילה

יְהֵא שְׁמֵהּ רַבָּא – *May His great name.*
Rav Yose said: I was once traveling on the road and I entered one of the ruins of Jerusalem in order to pray.

Eliyahu, of blessed memory, came and guarded the door/waited for me until I completed my *Amida* prayer…

He said, "My son, what sound did you hear in this ruin?" I replied, "I heard a divine voice cooing like a dove and saying: 'Woe to the children, on account of whose sins I destroyed My House and burnt My Temple and exiled them among the nations of the world.'"

And he said to me, "By your life and by your head! Not in this moment alone does it so exclaim, but three times each day does it exclaim thus. And more than that, whenever Israel fulfills the will of the *Makom* and goes into the synagogues and schoolhouses and responds: 'May His great name be blessed!' the Holy One, blessed be He, shakes His head and says: 'Happy is the King who is thus praised in this House! Woe to the Father who had to banish His children' – and woe to the children who had to be banished from the table of their father." (*Berakhot* 3a)

THE AMIDA

The following prayer, until "in former years" on page 118, is said silently, standing with feet together.

Take three steps forward.

O Lord, open my lips,
so that my mouth may declare Your praise. Ps. 51

PATRIARCHS

▾ *Bend the knees:* Blessed[B] *Bow:* are You, *Stand straight:* Lord
our God and God of our fathers,[I]
God of Abraham, God of Isaac and God of Jacob;
the great, mighty and awesome God, God Most High,
who bestows acts of loving-kindness and creates all,
who remembers the loving-kindness of the fathers
and will bring a Redeemer to their children's children
for the sake of His name, in love.

These words are added on Shabbat Shuva: Remember us for life, O King who desires life,
and write us in the book of life –
for Your sake, O God of life.

King, Helper, Savior, Shield:
▾ *Bend the knees:* Blessed *Bow:* are You, *Stand straight:* Lord,
Shield of Abraham.

---

us during the week. The siddur, then, not only is a response to our moods but is also designed to help shape our experience of the day.

BIUR TEFILLA • ביאור תפילה

בָּרוּךְ – *Blessed.* The Hebrew word for blessing, *berakha,* shares a linguistic root with the word *bereikha* which refers to an underground spring of water (*Responsa, Rashba*).

What might be the connection between the two? How might this help direct your intentions or mindset (*kavana*) for the remainder of the prayer?

IYUN TEFILLA • עיון תפילה

אֱלֹהֵינוּ וֵאלֹהֵי אֲבוֹתֵינוּ – *Our God and God of our fathers.* There are two ways to achieve faith: through tradition, the information and experience handed down to us by our parents and ancestors; and the faith that we acquire on our own. It is not enough to base one's commitment

This IYUN TEFILLA *continues on page 105.*

עמידה

The following prayer, until קַדְמֹנִיּוֹת *on page 119, is said silently, standing with feet together. Take three steps forward.*

אֲדֹנָי, שְׂפָתַי תִּפְתָּח, וּפִי יַגִּיד תְּהִלָּתֶךָ: תהלים נא

אבות

▾ *Bend the knees* בָּרוּךְ[ב] *Bow* אַתָּה *Stand straight* יהוה
אֱלֹהֵינוּ וֵאלֹהֵי אֲבוֹתֵינוּ[ע]
אֱלֹהֵי אַבְרָהָם, אֱלֹהֵי יִצְחָק, וֵאלֹהֵי יַעֲקֹב
הָאֵל הַגָּדוֹל הַגִּבּוֹר וְהַנּוֹרָא, אֵל עֶלְיוֹן
גּוֹמֵל חֲסָדִים טוֹבִים, וְקוֹנֵה הַכֹּל, וְזוֹכֵר חַסְדֵי אָבוֹת
וּמֵבִיא גוֹאֵל לִבְנֵי בְנֵיהֶם לְמַעַן שְׁמוֹ בְּאַהֲבָה.

בשבת שובה: זָכְרֵנוּ לְחַיִּים, מֶלֶךְ חָפֵץ בַּחַיִּים
וְכָתְבֵנוּ בְּסֵפֶר הַחַיִּים, לְמַעַנְךָ אֱלֹהִים חַיִּים.

מֶלֶךְ עוֹזֵר וּמוֹשִׁיעַ וּמָגֵן.
▾ *Bend the knees* בָּרוּךְ *Bow* אַתָּה *Stand straight* יהוה, מָגֵן אַבְרָהָם.

Another critical difference between the middle blessings of the *Amida* on Shabbat and the weekday is that those during the week are filled almost entirely with personal requests: petitions for health, wealth, forgiveness and the like. The Talmud Yerushalmi (15:3), however, tells us that on Shabbat all personal requests are forbidden for they are at odds with the spirit of the day (*Shabbat* 21a). Focusing on someone's illness, for example, could lead one to a feeling of sadness (*Tanḥuma*, *Vayera*). Instead, our focus on Shabbat is more about communal and spiritual concerns than about the things which preoccupy

reminiscent of the word *yiḥud*, the most intimate moment when bride and groom are alone (Abudarham and Shela). All of this, of course, is in keeping with the theme of marriage between Israel and the Shabbat and the Creator as mentioned earlier.

Regardless of what reason one devises, the changing themes of the *Amida* potentially tell us something about the shifting moods of the day. Shabbat is not just one long continuum of sameness but rather a dynamic day with its own rhythms. One needs to help create them, just as much as one needs to be drawn in by them. The siddur is designed to help do that.

DIVINE MIGHT

אַתָּה גִּבּוֹר You are eternally mighty, LORD.
You give life to the dead and have great power to save.

The phrase "He makes the wind blow and the rain fall" is added from Simḥat Torah until Pesaḥ. In Israel, the phrase "He causes the dew to fall" is added from Pesaḥ until Shemini Atzeret.

In fall & winter: He makes the wind blow and the rain fall.
In Israel, in spring & summer: He causes the dew to fall.

He sustains the living with loving-kindness,
and with great compassion revives the dead.
He supports the fallen, heals the sick, sets captives free,
and keeps His faith with those who sleep in the dust.
Who is like You, Master of might,
and who can compare to You,
O King who brings death and gives life,
and makes salvation grow?

These words are added on Shabbat Shuva: Who is like You, compassionate Father,
who remembers His creatures in
compassion, for life?

Faithful are You to revive the dead.
Blessed are You, LORD, who revives the dead.

HOLINESS

אַתָּה קָדוֹשׁ You are holy and Your name is holy,
and holy ones praise You daily, Selah!
Blessed are You, LORD,
the holy God. / *On Shabbat Shuva:* the holy King./
(*If forgotten, repeat the Amida.*)

ANI TEFILLA • אני תפילה

Someone once complained to Rav Simḥa Bunim that he had headaches after he prayed. Said Rav Bunim, "What does the head have to do with prayer? Prayer is a service of the heart not a labor of the head."

גבורות

אַתָּה גִּבּוֹר לְעוֹלָם, אֲדֹנָי
מְחַיֵּה מֵתִים אַתָּה, רַב לְהוֹשִׁיעַ

The phrase מַשִּׁיב הָרוּחַ *is added from* שמחת תורה *until* פסח.
In ארץ ישראל *the phrase* מוֹרִיד הַטָּל *is added from* פסח *until* שמיני עצרת.

בחורף: מַשִּׁיב הָרוּחַ וּמוֹרִיד הַגֶּשֶׁם / בארץ ישראל בקיץ: מוֹרִיד הַטָּל

מְכַלְכֵּל חַיִּים בְּחֶסֶד, מְחַיֵּה מֵתִים בְּרַחֲמִים רַבִּים
סוֹמֵךְ נוֹפְלִים, וְרוֹפֵא חוֹלִים, וּמַתִּיר אֲסוּרִים
וּמְקַיֵּם אֱמוּנָתוֹ לִישֵׁנֵי עָפָר.
מִי כָמוֹךָ, בַּעַל גְּבוּרוֹת, וּמִי דּוֹמֶה לָּךְ
מֶלֶךְ, מֵמִית וּמְחַיֶּה וּמַצְמִיחַ יְשׁוּעָה.

בשבת שובה: מִי כָמוֹךָ אַב הָרַחֲמִים
זוֹכֵר יְצוּרָיו לְחַיִּים בְּרַחֲמִים.

וְנֶאֱמָן אַתָּה לְהַחֲיוֹת מֵתִים.
בָּרוּךְ אַתָּה יהוה, מְחַיֵּה הַמֵּתִים.

קדושת השם

אַתָּה קָדוֹשׁ וְשִׁמְךָ קָדוֹשׁ
וּקְדוֹשִׁים בְּכָל יוֹם יְהַלְלוּךָ סֶּלָה.
בָּרוּךְ אַתָּה יהוה, הָאֵל הַקָּדוֹשׁ. / בשבת שובה: הַמֶּלֶךְ הַקָּדוֹשׁ./
(*If forgotten, repeat the* עמידה.)

---

solely on tradition but, rather, one has to make it one's own. And, though people may not talk about it much, one must continue to do so. We change and develop over time, even once we become adults, and so too, therefore, our relationship with Hashem can also change. But then, like all relationships, it is something we need to work on. Let today's prayer be a next step to a more personal relationship.

HOLINESS OF THE DAY

אַתָּה קִדַּשְׁתָּ You sanctified the seventh day
for Your name's sake,[I]
as the culmination of the creation of heaven and earth.
Of all days, You blessed it;[I]
of all seasons You sanctified it[I] –
and so it is written in Your Torah:[B]

---

exclusively on Shabbat, while another sees it in the light that fills his home on Shabbat, while still another expresses it in terms of the added light that shines from a person's face on Shabbat which is different than the rest of the week (*Bereshit Raba* 11:2). Food, clothing, external light, internal light; these are just some of the options.

What blessing do you wish for yourself this Shabbat?

וְקִדַּשְׁתּוֹ – *You sanctified it.* What does it mean to sanctify something? What does it mean to bless a day? Sanctification means to set something aside for a holy purpose; to use it for something mundane is to deprive it of its special status. We are trained to understand this concept as it relates to objects or rituals, but the Torah here conveys a revolutionary idea, namely, that one can also make time itself holy. Holiness is the space that we make for God in our lives.

How can you use this day to give Him more space?

BIUR TEFILLA • ביאור תפילה

וְכֵן כָּתוּב בְּתוֹרָתֶךָ – *And so it is written in Your Torah.* The following verses come from *Bereshit* 2:1-3. The numeration of chapters and verses in the Bible are a non-Jewish invention from the medieval period. Jews, however, had a different way of dividing the text, namely, according to the seven *aliyot* or chapters used for the weekly public recitation of the Torah (*Keriat HaTorah*). It is interesting to note that the verses about Shabbat are numbered in the Bible as the beginning of Chapter 2, whereas according to the Rabbis, in the Torah they are a part of the previous chapter about creation.

What might this signify?

קדושת היום

אַתָּה קִדַּשְׁתָּ אֶת יוֹם הַשְּׁבִיעִי לִשְׁמֶךָ[ע]
תַּכְלִית מַעֲשֵׂה שָׁמַיִם וָאָרֶץ
וּבֵרַכְתּוֹ[ע] מִכָּל הַיָּמִים
וְקִדַּשְׁתּוֹ[ע] מִכָּל הַזְּמַנִּים
וְכֵן כָּתוּב בְּתוֹרָתֶךָ[ב]

IYUN TEFILLA • עיון תפילה

אַתָּה קִדַּשְׁתָּ אֶת יוֹם הַשְּׁבִיעִי לִשְׁמֶךָ – *You sanctified the seventh day for Your name's sake.* A holy person is one who has opened himself up to holiness. A holy place is a place which draws people looking for holiness. A holy time is a time that awakens or invites us to holiness (Rabbi Ḥayyim Vidal). Prayer is about opening one's heart to holiness. The synagogue is a place that draws others like us looking for holiness. Shabbat is a holy time that invites us to do so.

אַתָּה קִדַּשְׁתָּ אֶת יוֹם הַשְּׁבִיעִי לִשְׁמֶךָ – *You sanctified the seventh day for Your name's sake.* Shabbat is a day not only for rest and relaxation, a day to get back to oneself and one's family and friends and community. For if one does not use it as an opportunity to also recognize the role of God then one has missed the essence of the day. From the perspective of Hashem, Shabbat would theoretically remain holy regardless of man's presence. But from the perspective of man, Shabbat is an opportunity not a foregone conclusion. Whether we take advantage of the gift of time to focus on these relationships is dependent upon us.

וּבֵרַכְתּוֹ – *You blessed it.* As the text goes on to prove, this concept comes from the description of Shabbat at the time of its creation. "And God blessed the seventh day and He sanctified it." What does it mean that God blessed the day? The word blessing generally denotes being bestowed with something extra. The Midrash cites the example of the manna in the desert which came in double portions for Shabbat so that the Israelites would not have to collect it on Shabbat itself. Alternatively, says the Midrash, there are those who see the blessing in the special clothes that they wear

וַיְכֻלּוּ Then the heavens and the earth were completed, Gen. 2
and all their array.
With the seventh day, God[B] completed the work He had done.[AB]
He ceased on the seventh day from all the work He had done.
God blessed the seventh day and declared it holy,
because on it He ceased from all His work He had created to do.[B]

אֱלֹהֵינוּ Our God and God of our ancestors,
may You find favor in our rest.[B]
Make us holy through Your commandments
and grant us our share in Your Torah.
Satisfy us with Your goodness, grant us joy in Your salvation,
and purify our hearts to serve You in truth.[I]

What might be the difference between the two?

אֲשֶׁר־בָּרָא אֱלֹהִים לַעֲשׂוֹת – *He had created to do.* The wording is a little awkward and redundant. What does the last phrase mean? It could be that with the Shabbat, He set everything to work on its own, to continue to function in the way it was conceived (Ibn Ezra). Whatever creation was about, with the completion of Shabbat, time as we know it began. This could mean that there was a system of time, a life to our planet, before the one we are familiar with. In any event, the world was set in motion, though the Creator did not walk away.

Alternatively, it is a reference not to the world but to Shabbat. He created the Shabbat day in such a way that it would continue to do the work for which it was intended: the moral and spiritual betterment of mankind (Rabbi S. Hirsch).

How might I permit Shabbat to do its work with me?

רְצֵה בִמְנוּחָתֵנוּ – *Find favor in our rest...* In another example of the relationship between form and content, what follows are seven expressions of our hopes for this Shabbat day that is upon us.

What different meaning do you want to bring to each one of these expressions?

IYUN TEFILLA · עיון תפילה

וְטַהֵר לִבֵּנוּ לְעָבְדְּךָ בֶּאֱמֶת – *Purify our hearts to serve You in truth.* How can we ask God for this? Isn't it up to us what goes on in our hearts? The Gemara explains "Whoever comes to be purified gets assistance from above (*Yoma* 38b). In other words, the first steps must come from us and only then can we expect to get help. Perhaps the same is true for all of the other expressions which precede this one; one needs to invest in Shabbat in order to reap its rewards.

For more commentary on these final three blessings, see *Shaharit* (pages 349–362), *Musaf* (pages 431–440) and *Minha* (pages 519–526).

בראשית ב

וַיְכֻלּוּ הַשָּׁמַיִם וְהָאָרֶץ וְכָל־צְבָאָם:
וַיְכַל אֱלֹהִים בַּיּוֹם הַשְּׁבִיעִי מְלַאכְתּוֹ אֲשֶׁר עָשָׂה
וַיִּשְׁבֹּת בַּיּוֹם הַשְּׁבִיעִי מִכָּל־מְלַאכְתּוֹ אֲשֶׁר עָשָׂה:
וַיְבָרֶךְ אֱלֹהִים אֶת־יוֹם הַשְּׁבִיעִי, וַיְקַדֵּשׁ אֹתוֹ
כִּי בוֹ שָׁבַת מִכָּל־מְלַאכְתּוֹ, אֲשֶׁר־בָּרָא אֱלֹהִים לַעֲשׂוֹת:

אֱלֹהֵינוּ וֵאלֹהֵי אֲבוֹתֵינוּ, רְצֵה בִמְנוּחָתֵנוּ.
קַדְּשֵׁנוּ בְּמִצְוֹתֶיךָ, וְתֵן חֶלְקֵנוּ בְּתוֹרָתֶךָ
שַׂבְּעֵנוּ מִטּוּבֶךָ, וְשַׂמְּחֵנוּ בִּישׁוּעָתֶךָ
וְטַהֵר לִבֵּנוּ לְעָבְדְּךָ בֶּאֱמֶת.

BIUR TEFILLA • ביאור תפילה

וַיְכַל אֱלֹהִים בַּיּוֹם הַשְּׁבִיעִי – *With the seventh day, God completed.* Here is but one of many examples where the form of the text reflects its substance – if only we can discern its clues. These next three statements from the Torah contain 35 (5x7) Hebrew words. And the entire creation narrative (*Bereshit* 1–2:3) speaks of seven and its multiples. The word "good" appears seven times, the word "God" 35 times, the word "earth" 21 times, and the words "firmament"/"heavens" 21 times. The opening verse contains seven words, and the complete text 469 (7x67) words. From the very outset, seven dominates, as if to signal from the beginning that the seventh day was the culmination and purpose of creation (Rabbi Jonathan Sacks).

וַיְכַל אֱלֹהִים בַּיּוֹם הַשְּׁבִיעִי מְלַאכְתּוֹ אֲשֶׁר עָשָׂה – *With the seventh day, God completed the work He had done.* The verse seems to imply that the work was actually completed on the seventh day, and yet wasn't the seventh day a day of rest? The answer is that counter-intuitively rest, too, was something that needed to be proactively created (Rashi). This rest was apparently different than just a state of non-exertion which cannot really be said to be a creation.

ANI TEFILLA • אני תפילה

וַיְכַל אֱלֹהִים בַּיּוֹם הַשְּׁבִיעִי מְלַאכְתּוֹ אֲשֶׁר עָשָׂה – *With the seventh day God completed the work He had done.*

Asks the Midrash: "To what may this be compared? To a *ḥuppa*, a wedding canopy. One decorates it and adorns it so that it is most beautiful. What is missing? The bride. So, too, Hashem created the world. What was it missing? Shabbat.

Rabbanan say: To what may this be compared? To a king's beautiful signet ring that was missing his seal. So, too, Hashem created the world. What was it missing? Shabbat" (*Bereshit Raba* 10:10).

What might be the differences in perspective about Shabbat between these two parables?

In love and favor, O LORD our God,
grant us as our heritage Your holy Shabbat,
so that Israel, who sanctify Your name, may find rest on it.
Blessed are You, LORD, who sanctifies the Sabbath.

TEMPLE SERVICE

רְצֵה Find favor, LORD our God, in Your people Israel and their prayer.
Restore the service[1] to Your most holy House,
and accept in love and favor
the fire-offerings of Israel and their prayer.
May the service of Your people Israel always find favor with You.

On Rosh Ḥodesh and Ḥol HaMo'ed, say:

אֱלֹהֵינוּ Our God and God of our ancestors, may there rise, come,[B] reach, appear, be favored, heard, regarded and remembered before You, our recollection and remembrance, as well as the remembrance of our ancestors, and of the Messiah son of David Your servant, and of Jerusalem Your holy city, and of all Your people the house of Israel – for deliverance and well-being, grace, loving-kindness and compassion, life and peace, on this day of:

On Rosh Ḥodesh: Rosh Ḥodesh.
On Pesaḥ: the Festival of Matzot.
On Sukkot: the Festival of Sukkot.

On it remember us, LORD our God, for good; recollect us for blessing, and deliver us for life. In accord with Your promise of salvation and compassion, spare us and be gracious to us; have compassion on us and deliver us, for our eyes are turned to You because You, God, are a gracious and compassionate King.

וְתֶחֱזֶינָה And may our eyes witness Your return to Zion in compassion.
Blessed are You, LORD, who restores His Presence to Zion.

BIUR TEFILLA • ביאור תפילה

יַעֲלֶה וְיָבוֹא – *May there rise, come.* On Rosh Ḥodesh and on Ḥol HaMo'ed (the intermediate days of a festival), this prayer is added "as a supplication of Israel and Jerusalem for the reinstitution of the Temple service and of the sacrifices of the day" (Rashi, *Shabbat* 24a). In truth, however, the passage does not explicitly mention these themes. The Torah ordains that "on your days of rejoicing and your holy days and on your Rosh Ḥodesh, you will blow the trumpets over your offerings that they may to you a

This **BIUR TEFILLA** *continues on page 113.*

וְהַנְחִילֵנוּ, יהוה אֱלֹהֵינוּ, בְּאַהֲבָה וּבְרָצוֹן שַׁבַּת קָדְשֶׁךָ
וְיָנוּחוּ בָהּ יִשְׂרָאֵל מְקַדְּשֵׁי שְׁמֶךָ.
בָּרוּךְ אַתָּה יהוה, מְקַדֵּשׁ הַשַּׁבָּת.

עבודה

רְצֵה יהוה אֱלֹהֵינוּ בְּעַמְּךָ יִשְׂרָאֵל וּבִתְפִלָּתָם
וְהָשֵׁב אֶת הָעֲבוֹדָה[ע] לִדְבִיר בֵּיתֶךָ
וְאִשֵּׁי יִשְׂרָאֵל וּתְפִלָּתָם בְּאַהֲבָה תְקַבֵּל בְּרָצוֹן
וּתְהִי לְרָצוֹן תָּמִיד עֲבוֹדַת יִשְׂרָאֵל עַמֶּךָ.

On ראש חודש *and* חול המועד, *say:*

אֱלֹהֵינוּ וֵאלֹהֵי אֲבוֹתֵינוּ, יַעֲלֶה וְיָבוֹא[ב] וְיַגִּיעַ, וְיֵרָאֶה וְיֵרָצֶה וְיִשָּׁמַע, וְיִפָּקֵד וְיִזָּכֵר זִכְרוֹנֵנוּ וּפִקְדוֹנֵנוּ וְזִכְרוֹן אֲבוֹתֵינוּ, וְזִכְרוֹן מָשִׁיחַ בֶּן דָּוִד עַבְדֶּךָ, וְזִכְרוֹן יְרוּשָׁלַיִם עִיר קָדְשֶׁךָ, וְזִכְרוֹן כָּל עַמְּךָ בֵּית יִשְׂרָאֵל, לְפָנֶיךָ, לִפְלֵיטָה לְטוֹבָה, לְחֵן וּלְחֶסֶד וּלְרַחֲמִים, לְחַיִּים וּלְשָׁלוֹם בְּיוֹם
בראש חודש: רֹאשׁ הַחֹדֶשׁ / בפסח: חַג הַמַּצּוֹת / בסוכות: חַג הַסֻּכּוֹת
הַזֶּה. זָכְרֵנוּ יהוה אֱלֹהֵינוּ בּוֹ לְטוֹבָה, וּפָקְדֵנוּ בוֹ לִבְרָכָה, וְהוֹשִׁיעֵנוּ בוֹ לְחַיִּים. וּבִדְבַר יְשׁוּעָה וְרַחֲמִים, חוּס וְחָנֵּנוּ וְרַחֵם עָלֵינוּ וְהוֹשִׁיעֵנוּ, כִּי אֵלֶיךָ עֵינֵינוּ, כִּי אֵל מֶלֶךְ חַנּוּן וְרַחוּם אָתָּה.

וְתֶחֱזֶינָה עֵינֵינוּ בְּשׁוּבְךָ לְצִיּוֹן בְּרַחֲמִים.
בָּרוּךְ אַתָּה יהוה, הַמַּחֲזִיר שְׁכִינָתוֹ לְצִיּוֹן.

IYUN TEFILLA • עיון תפילה

וְהָשֵׁב אֶת הָעֲבוֹדָה – *Restore the service.* Why do we long for the restoration of the *Beit HaMikdash* and its sacrifices? Why not just be satisfied with prayers? Imagine being separated from a loved one for years, communicating only through some technological device that can help span the distance. Now imagine that person is in the next room. That feeling of being close to someone you love, someone who loves you, is irreplaceable.

THANKSGIVING

▾*Bow:* We give thanks[1] to You,
for You are *Stand straight*
the Lord our God and God of our ancestors
for ever and all time.
You are the Rock of our lives,
Shield of our salvation from generation to generation.
We will thank You and declare Your praise for our lives,
which are entrusted into Your hand;
for our souls, which are placed in Your charge;
for Your miracles which are with us every day;
and for Your wonders and favors
at all times, evening, morning and midday.
You are good – for Your compassion never fails.
You are compassionate – for Your loving-kindnesses never cease.
We have always placed our hope in You.

On Ḥanukka:

עַל הַנִּסִּים [We thank You also] for the miracles, the redemption, the mighty deeds, the salvations, and the victories in battle which You performed for our ancestors in those days, at this time.[B]

בִּימֵי מַתִּתְיָהוּ In the days of Mattityahu, son of Yoḥanan, the High Priest, the Hasmonean, and his sons, the wicked Greek kingdom rose up against Your

---

a thousand years to prove; recent studies show that gratitude can be an antidote for materialism. Grateful people, it turns out, are more satisfied with their lives. When Yaakov's wife Leah gives birth to a fourth son, she is overwhelmed with gratitude (*Bereshit* 29:35): "She conceived again, and bore a son and said 'This time let me ***thank*** (*odeh*) God' and she named the child Yehuda." Yehuda or Judah, thus derives from the word for gratitude and Yehuda/Judah is of course the derivation of the name *Yehudi* or Jew. In other words, to be a Jew means to give thanks.

BIUR TEFILLA • ביאור תפילה

עַל הַנִּסִּים – *For the miracles.*

שֶׁעָשִׂיתָ לַאֲבוֹתֵינוּ בַּיָּמִים הָהֵם בַּזְּמַן הַזֶּה – *Which You performed for our ancestors in those days, at this time.* "At this time" means on the 25th of Kislev, the date of Ḥanukka.

Alternatively, there are those who

This **BIUR TEFILLA** *continues on page 115.*

הודאה

▾ *Bow* מוֹדִים ע אֲנַחְנוּ לָךְ

שָׁאַתָּה הוּא *Stand straight*

יהוה אֱלֹהֵינוּ וֵאלֹהֵי אֲבוֹתֵינוּ לְעוֹלָם וָעֶד.
צוּר חַיֵּינוּ, מָגֵן יִשְׁעֵנוּ, אַתָּה הוּא לְדוֹר וָדוֹר.
נוֹדֶה לְּךָ וּנְסַפֵּר תְּהִלָּתֶךָ, עַל חַיֵּינוּ הַמְּסוּרִים בְּיָדֶךָ
וְעַל נִשְׁמוֹתֵינוּ הַפְּקוּדוֹת לָךְ, וְעַל נִסֶּיךָ שֶׁבְּכָל יוֹם עִמָּנוּ
וְעַל נִפְלְאוֹתֶיךָ וְטוֹבוֹתֶיךָ שֶׁבְּכָל עֵת, עֶרֶב וָבֹקֶר וְצָהֳרָיִם.
הַטּוֹב, כִּי לֹא כָלוּ רַחֲמֶיךָ, וְהַמְרַחֵם, כִּי לֹא תַמּוּ חֲסָדֶיךָ
מֵעוֹלָם קִוִּינוּ לָךְ.

בחנוכה:

עַל הַנִּסִּים וְעַל הַפֻּרְקָן וְעַל הַגְּבוּרוֹת וְעַל הַתְּשׁוּעוֹת וְעַל הַמִּלְחָמוֹת שֶׁעָשִׂיתָ לַאֲבוֹתֵינוּ בַּיָּמִים הָהֵם בַּזְּמַן הַזֶּה.[ב]

בִּימֵי מַתִּתְיָהוּ בֶּן יוֹחָנָן כֹּהֵן גָּדוֹל חַשְׁמוֹנַאי וּבָנָיו, כְּשֶׁעָמְדָה מַלְכוּת יָוָן הָרְשָׁעָה עַל עַמְּךָ יִשְׂרָאֵל לְהַשְׁכִּיחָם תּוֹרָתֶךָ וּלְהַעֲבִירָם מֵחֻקֵּי

---

memorial before your God" (*Bemidbar* 10:10). Perhaps, then, this prayer is a substitute for the trumpet sound, in *tefilla*, the substitute for the offerings (Rabbi E. Munk).

Alternatively, the prayer is an antidote to forgetting. We ask Hashem to remember but we need to do the same. I remember my poor behavior. I remember the good things I have done and commandments to which I try to adhere. I recall my past and my future, my place in the context of my people and ask myself if I have lived up to my potential. And I ask Hashem to do the same and to find my remembering and my commitment to this day worthy of His ongoing support.

IYUN TEFILLA • עיון תפילה

מוֹדִים – *We give thanks.* The eleventh-century text *Ḥovot HaLevavot* suggests some reasons why ingratitude is so bad. First of all, the constant striving to acquire more material things, especially those which he may never attain, prevents a person from being satisfied with what he has. If you can be grateful to God for what you have, then you will be less likely to get as caught up in the obsessions of the material world. What they knew intuitively in the eleventh century took social scientists

people Israel to make them forget Your Torah and to force them to transgress the statutes of Your will. It was then that You in Your great compassion stood by them in the time of their distress. You championed their cause, judged their claim, and avenged their wrong. You delivered the strong into the hands of the weak, the many into the hands of the few, the impure into the hands of the pure, the wicked into the hands of the righteous, and the arrogant into the hands of those who were engaged in the study of Your Torah. You made for Yourself great and holy renown in Your world, and for Your people Israel You performed a great salvation and redemption as of this very day. Your children then entered the holiest part of Your House, cleansed Your Temple, purified Your Sanctuary, kindled lights in Your holy courts, and designated these eight days of Ḥanukka for giving thanks and praise to Your great name.

Continue with "For all these things."

On Shushan Purim in Jerusalem:

עַל הַנִּסִּים [We thank You also] for the miracles, the redemption, the mighty deeds, the salvations, and the victories in battle which You performed for our ancestors in those days, at this time.

בִּימֵי מָרְדְּכַי In the days of Mordekhai and Esther, in Shushan the capital,
the wicked Haman rose up against them and sought to destroy, slay and exterminate all the Jews, young and old, children and women, on one day, the thirteenth day of the twelfth month, which is the month of Adar, and to plunder their possessions. Then You in Your great compassion thwarted his counsel, frustrated his plans, and caused his scheme to recoil on his own head, so that they hanged him and his sons on the gallows. *Esther 3*

Continue with "For all these things."

וְעַל כֻּלָּם For all these things
may Your name be blessed and exalted,
our King, continually, for ever and all time.

These words are added on Shabbat Shuva: And write, for a good life,
all the children of Your covenant.

Let all that lives thank You, Selah!
and praise Your name in truth,
God, our Savior and Help, Selah!
▾ *Bend the knees:* Blessed *Bow:* are You, *Stand straight:* LORD,
whose name is "the Good" and to whom thanks are due.

רְצוֹנֶךָ, וְאַתָּה בְּרַחֲמֶיךָ הָרַבִּים עָמַדְתָּ לָהֶם בְּעֵת צָרָתָם, רַבְתָּ אֶת רִיבָם, דַּנְתָּ אֶת דִּינָם, נָקַמְתָּ אֶת נִקְמָתָם, מָסַרְתָּ גִבּוֹרִים בְּיַד חַלָּשִׁים, וְרַבִּים בְּיַד מְעַטִּים, וּטְמֵאִים בְּיַד טְהוֹרִים, וּרְשָׁעִים בְּיַד צַדִּיקִים, וְזֵדִים בְּיַד עוֹסְקֵי תוֹרָתֶךָ, וּלְךָ עָשִׂיתָ שֵׁם גָּדוֹל וְקָדוֹשׁ בְּעוֹלָמֶךָ, וּלְעַמְּךָ יִשְׂרָאֵל עָשִׂיתָ תְּשׁוּעָה גְדוֹלָה וּפֻרְקָן כְּהַיּוֹם הַזֶּה. וְאַחַר כֵּן בָּאוּ בָנֶיךָ לִדְבִיר בֵּיתֶךָ, וּפִנּוּ אֶת הֵיכָלֶךָ, וְטִהֲרוּ אֶת מִקְדָּשֶׁךָ, וְהִדְלִיקוּ נֵרוֹת בְּחַצְרוֹת קָדְשֶׁךָ, וְקָבְעוּ שְׁמוֹנַת יְמֵי חֲנֻכָּה אֵלּוּ, לְהוֹדוֹת וּלְהַלֵּל לְשִׁמְךָ הַגָּדוֹל.

Continue with וְעַל כֻּלָּם.

בשושן פורים בירושלים:

עַל הַנִּסִּים וְעַל הַפֻּרְקָן וְעַל הַגְּבוּרוֹת וְעַל הַתְּשׁוּעוֹת וְעַל הַמִּלְחָמוֹת שֶׁעָשִׂיתָ לַאֲבוֹתֵינוּ בַּיָּמִים הָהֵם בַּזְּמַן הַזֶּה.

בִּימֵי מָרְדְּכַי וְאֶסְתֵּר בְּשׁוּשַׁן הַבִּירָה, כְּשֶׁעָמַד עֲלֵיהֶם הָמָן הָרָשָׁע, בִּקֵּשׁ לְהַשְׁמִיד לַהֲרֹג וּלְאַבֵּד אֶת־כָּל־הַיְּהוּדִים מִנַּעַר וְעַד־זָקֵן טַף וְנָשִׁים בְּיוֹם אֶחָד, בִּשְׁלוֹשָׁה עָשָׂר לְחֹדֶשׁ שְׁנֵים־עָשָׂר, הוּא־חֹדֶשׁ אֲדָר, וּשְׁלָלָם לָבוֹז: וְאַתָּה בְּרַחֲמֶיךָ הָרַבִּים הֵפַרְתָּ אֶת עֲצָתוֹ, וְקִלְקַלְתָּ אֶת מַחֲשַׁבְתּוֹ, וַהֲשֵׁבוֹתָ לּוֹ גְּמוּלוֹ בְּרֹאשׁוֹ, וְתָלוּ אוֹתוֹ וְאֶת בָּנָיו עַל הָעֵץ. (אסתר ג)

Continue with וְעַל כֻּלָּם.

וְעַל כֻּלָּם יִתְבָּרַךְ וְיִתְרוֹמַם שִׁמְךָ מַלְכֵּנוּ תָּמִיד לְעוֹלָם וָעֶד.

בשבת שובה: וּכְתֹב לְחַיִּים טוֹבִים כָּל בְּנֵי בְרִיתֶךָ.

וְכֹל הַחַיִּים יוֹדוּךָ סֶּלָה, וִיהַלְלוּ אֶת שִׁמְךָ בֶּאֱמֶת הָאֵל יְשׁוּעָתֵנוּ וְעֶזְרָתֵנוּ סֶלָה.

▼ *Bend the knees* בָּרוּךְ *Bow* אַתָּה *Stand straight* יהוה הַטּוֹב שִׁמְךָ וּלְךָ נָאֶה לְהוֹדוֹת.

---

interpret it as in those days *and* in this time (*Levush*).

What might this be referring to? Give thanks for it.

PEACE

שָׁלוֹם רָב Grant great peace[B] to Your people Israel for ever,
for You are the sovereign LORD of all peace;
and may it be good in Your eyes
to bless Your people Israel
at every time, at every hour, with Your peace.

These words are added on Shabbat Shuva: In the book of life, blessing, peace and prosperity,
may we and all Your people the house of Israel
be remembered and written before You
for a good life, and for peace.*

Blessed are You, LORD, who blesses His people Israel with peace.[|]

**On Shabbat Shuva outside Israel, many have the custom to end the blessing:*
Blessed are You, LORD, who makes peace.

Some say the following verse:
May the words of my mouth and the meditation of my heart *Ps. 19*
find favor before You, LORD, my Rock and Redeemer.

אֱלֹהַי My God, *Berakhot 17a*
guard my tongue from evil[A] and my lips from deceitful speech.
To those who curse me, let my soul be silent;
may my soul be to all like the dust.

ANI TEFILLA • אני תפילה

נְצֹר לְשׁוֹנִי מֵרָע – *Guard my tongue from [speaking] evil. A man came to his rabbi to confess that he had spent many years gossiping about other people and that he had told many stories, some true, some false, about others but he now regretted his behavior in all sincerity. "Tell me," he pleaded, "how can I atone for this once and for all?" The rabbi told him to go home, find a feather pillow, take it to the middle of the town square and cut it open. The man dutifully followed the advice, went home, got a pillow, took it to the town square, cut it open and watched as the feathers were carried in all different directions by the wind. He went back to his rabbi and asked, "Now, Rabbi, what should I do?" Answered the rabbi, "Now, go collect the feathers."*

ברכת שלום

שָׁלוֹם רָב[ב] עַל יִשְׂרָאֵל עַמְּךָ תָּשִׂים לְעוֹלָם
כִּי אַתָּה הוּא מֶלֶךְ אָדוֹן לְכָל הַשָּׁלוֹם.
וְטוֹב בְּעֵינֶיךָ לְבָרֵךְ אֶת עַמְּךָ יִשְׂרָאֵל
בְּכָל עֵת וּבְכָל שָׁעָה בִּשְׁלוֹמֶךָ.

בשבת שובה: בְּסֵפֶר חַיִּים, בְּרָכָה וְשָׁלוֹם, וּפַרְנָסָה טוֹבָה
נִזָּכֵר וְנִכָּתֵב לְפָנֶיךָ, אֲנַחְנוּ וְכָל עַמְּךָ בֵּית יִשְׂרָאֵל
לְחַיִּים טוֹבִים וּלְשָׁלוֹם.*

בָּרוּךְ אַתָּה יהוה, הַמְבָרֵךְ אֶת עַמּוֹ יִשְׂרָאֵל בַּשָּׁלוֹם.[ע]

**On שבת שובה in חוץ לארץ, many have the custom to end the blessing:*
בָּרוּךְ אַתָּה יהוה, עוֹשֵׂה הַשָּׁלוֹם.

Some say the following verse:

יִהְיוּ לְרָצוֹן אִמְרֵי־פִי וְהֶגְיוֹן לִבִּי לְפָנֶיךָ, יהוה צוּרִי וְגֹאֲלִי: תהלים יט

אֱלֹהַי ברכות יז.
נְצֹר לְשׁוֹנִי מֵרָע[א] וּשְׂפָתַי מִדַּבֵּר מִרְמָה
וְלִמְקַלְלַי נַפְשִׁי תִדֹּם, וְנַפְשִׁי כֶּעָפָר לַכֹּל תִּהְיֶה.

IYUN TEFILLA • עיון תפילה

הַמְבָרֵךְ אֶת עַמּוֹ יִשְׂרָאֵל בַּשָּׁלוֹם – *Who blesses His people Israel with peace.* One of God's names is "Peace" (*Shabbat* 10b). That is one meaning of the greeting *Shalom Aleikhem* – May peace be upon you, that is, May Hashem's name be upon you. Perhaps, too, that is the meaning of the phrase *Shabbat Shalom*. May the peace of Shabbat be upon you; May Hashem be upon you. Without Peace, there is nothing.

BIUR TEFILLA • ביאור תפילה

שָׁלוֹם רָב – *Grant great peace.* The theme of this particular blessing is different than the parallel one in *Shaḥarit* and *Musaf* because the themes there are tied to the Priestly Blessing (*Birkat Kohanim*) which is generally only recited in the morning.

As night approaches, our fears and insecurities can become larger than life. Perhaps that's one reason that the emphasis here is on "great" peace, for we need more of it during this part of the day.

Open my heart to Your Torah[B]
and let my soul pursue Your commandments.
As for all who plan evil against me,
swiftly thwart their counsel and frustrate their plans.
Act for the sake of Your name;
act for the sake of Your right hand;
act for the sake of Your holiness;
act for the sake of Your Torah.
That Your beloved ones may be delivered, *Ps. 60*
save with Your right hand and answer me.
May the words of my mouth *Ps. 19*
and the meditation of my heart find favor before You,
LORD, my Rock and Redeemer.

Bow and take three steps back as if taking leave of the Divine Presence.
Bow left: May He who makes peace in His high places,
Bow right: make peace *Bow forward:* for us and all Israel –
and say: Amen.

יְהִי רָצוֹן May it be Your will, LORD our God and God of our ancestors,
that the Temple be rebuilt speedily in our days,
and grant us a share in Your Torah.
And there we will serve You with reverence,
as in the days of old and as in former years.
Then the offering of Judah and Jerusalem *Mal. 3*
will be pleasing to the LORD as in the days of old and as in former years.

---

into a reader. The statement in this prayer is about "Torah readiness."

What is the state of your Torah readiness?

Alternatively, perhaps the phrase could be translated "Open my heart with Your Torah" in which case readiness will only come about when you take the plunge.

Are you ready?

פְּתַח לִבִּי בְּתוֹרָתֶךָ, וּבְמִצְוֹתֶיךָ תִּרְדֹּף נַפְשִׁי.
וְכָל הַחוֹשְׁבִים עָלַי רָעָה
מְהֵרָה הָפֵר עֲצָתָם וְקַלְקֵל מַחֲשַׁבְתָּם.
עֲשֵׂה לְמַעַן שְׁמֶךָ
עֲשֵׂה לְמַעַן יְמִינֶךָ
עֲשֵׂה לְמַעַן קְדֻשָּׁתֶךָ
עֲשֵׂה לְמַעַן תּוֹרָתֶךָ.
לְמַעַן יֵחָלְצוּן יְדִידֶיךָ, הוֹשִׁיעָה יְמִינְךָ וַעֲנֵנִי: תהלים ס
יִהְיוּ לְרָצוֹן אִמְרֵי־פִי וְהֶגְיוֹן לִבִּי לְפָנֶיךָ, יהוה צוּרִי וְגוֹאֲלִי: תהלים יט

Bow and take three steps back as if taking leave of the Divine Presence.

Bow left עֹשֶׂה שָׁלוֹם/ בשבת שובה: הַשָּׁלוֹם/ בִּמְרוֹמָיו
Bow right הוּא יַעֲשֶׂה שָׁלוֹם *Bow forward* עָלֵינוּ וְעַל כָּל יִשְׂרָאֵל
וְאִמְרוּ אָמֵן.

יְהִי רָצוֹן מִלְּפָנֶיךָ יהוה אֱלֹהֵינוּ וֵאלֹהֵי אֲבוֹתֵינוּ
שֶׁיִּבָּנֶה בֵּית הַמִּקְדָּשׁ בִּמְהֵרָה בְיָמֵינוּ
וְתֵן חֶלְקֵנוּ בְּתוֹרָתֶךָ
וְשָׁם נַעֲבָדְךָ בְּיִרְאָה כִּימֵי עוֹלָם וּכְשָׁנִים קַדְמֹנִיּוֹת.
וְעָרְבָה לַיהוה מִנְחַת יְהוּדָה וִירוּשָׁלָםִ כִּימֵי עוֹלָם וּכְשָׁנִים קַדְמֹנִיּוֹת: מלאכי ג

BIUR TEFILLA • ביאור תפילה

פְּתַח לִבִּי בְּתוֹרָתֶךָ – *Open my heart to Your Torah.* In education there is such a thing as "reading readiness" which has been defined as the point at which a person is ready to learn to read and the time during which a person transitions from being a non-reader

All stand and say:

וַיְכֻלּוּ Then the heavens and the earth were completed,[BH] Gen. 2
and all their array.
With the seventh day, God completed the work He had done.
He ceased on the seventh day from all the work He had done.
God blessed the seventh day
and declared it holy,
because on it He ceased from all His work
He had created to do.

ME'EIN SHEVA

The following until "who sanctifies the Sabbath" on page 124, is omitted when praying with an occasional minyan or alone.

The Leader continues:

בָּרוּךְ Blessed are You, LORD our God and God of our fathers,
God of Abraham, God of Isaac and God of Jacob,
the great, mighty and awesome God,
God Most High, Creator of heaven and earth.

---

testimony in a Jewish court of law. Indeed, there is another law which says that two witnesses are required for the testimony to be valid. Hence, there arose another custom that one might see from time to time: if someone failed to say this paragraph with the congregation because his own *Amida* was prolonged, then once he has finished he joins with some other person to recite this paragraph together, two witnesses bearing testimony to an eternal truth.

ANI TEFILLA • אני תפילה

What makes these verses so significant? The Gemara suggests that "Whoever recites this paragraph, it is as if he is a partner with God in the creation of the world" (*Shabbat* 119b).

What do you think this might mean?

Rav Ḥisda said in Mar Ukba's name: He who prays on the eve of the Sabbath and recites, "and the the heaven and the earth were finished," the two ministering angels who accompany each man place their hands on his head and say to him: Your iniquity is taken away and your sin purged. (*Shabbat* 119b)

All stand and say:

בראשית ב

וַיְכֻלּוּ הַשָּׁמַיִם וְהָאָרֶץ וְכָל־צְבָאָם: וַיְכַל אֱלֹהִים בַּיּוֹם הַשְּׁבִיעִי מְלַאכְתּוֹ אֲשֶׁר עָשָׂה
וַיִּשְׁבֹּת בַּיּוֹם הַשְּׁבִיעִי מִכָּל־מְלַאכְתּוֹ אֲשֶׁר עָשָׂה:
וַיְבָרֶךְ אֱלֹהִים אֶת־יוֹם הַשְּׁבִיעִי, וַיְקַדֵּשׁ אֹתוֹ
כִּי בוֹ שָׁבַת מִכָּל־מְלַאכְתּוֹ, אֲשֶׁר־בָּרָא אֱלֹהִים, לַעֲשׂוֹת:

ברכה מעין שבע

The following until מְקַדֵּשׁ הַשַּׁבָּת *on page 121,*
is omitted when praying with an occasional מנין *or alone.*

The שליח ציבור *continues:*

בָּרוּךְ אַתָּה יהוה, אֱלֹהֵינוּ וֵאלֹהֵי אֲבוֹתֵינוּ
אֱלֹהֵי אַבְרָהָם, אֱלֹהֵי יִצְחָק, וֵאלֹהֵי יַעֲקֹב
הָאֵל הַגָּדוֹל הַגִּבּוֹר וְהַנּוֹרָא, אֵל עֶלְיוֹן, קוֹנֵה שָׁמַיִם וָאָרֶץ.

BIUR TEFILLA • ביאור תפילה

וַיְכֻלּוּ הַשָּׁמַיִם וְהָאָרֶץ – *Then the heavens and the earth were completed.* This paragraph, which was just recited in the *Amida,* is now recited again by the entire community together and, so important is it, that it will be repeated once again a little later on in *Kiddush.* From historical perspective, this paragraph is not found in the festival *Amida* since the theme here is Shabbat and so, when a festival fell on a Friday night, the paragraph was added after the *Amida* was over so that its message would not be lost (*Tosafot Pesaḥim* 106a). In order not to distinguish from one Shabbat to another, the prayer was added every Friday night. Origins aside, there is much power to a communal declaration of God as Creator (*HaManhig, Shabbat* 6). **Feel its power.**

HILKHOT TEFILLA • הלכות תפילה

וַיְכֻלּוּ הַשָּׁמַיִם וְהָאָרֶץ – *Then the heavens and the earth were completed.* The custom is to recite these verses while standing, just as is required of witnesses who give

The congregation then the Leader:

מָגֵן אָבוֹת By His word, He was the Shield of our ancestors.[B]
By His promise, He will revive the dead.
There is none like the holy God/*On Shabbat Shuva:* the holy King/
who gives rest to His people on His holy Sabbath day,
for He found them worthy of His favor to give them rest.
Before Him we will come in worship with reverence and awe,
giving thanks to His name daily, continually, with due blessings.
He is God to whom thanks are due, the LORD of peace
who sanctifies the Sabbath and blesses the seventh day,
and in holiness gives rest to a people filled with delight,
in remembrance of the work of creation.

The Leader continues:

אֱלֹהֵינוּ Our God and God of our ancestors,
may You find favor in our rest.
Make us holy through Your commandments
and grant us our share in Your Torah.

---

aloud in order to make sure that everyone could fulfill the mitzva of *Kiddush* (*Talmud Yerushalmi Berakhot* 8:1, *Sefer Ḥaredim*).

What both reasons have in common is the concern for community on this night. To ensure that we act together, on behalf of one another, we share our knowledge and our companionship.

מָגֵן אָבוֹת – *Shield of our ancestors.* This whole section is sometimes referred to as the "abridged seven," a reference to the fact that, as described above, it contains words or phrases which are reminiscent of the words or phrases in each of the seven blessings in the *Amida*. Thus, this particular phrase, "shield of our ancestors," would correspond to the phrase *magen Avraham* or "shield of Abraham" in the *Amida*. Can you find the other six correspondences?

HILKHOT TEFILLA • הלכות תפילה

Because the reasons for the recitation of this prayer are so community driven, it is not recited when praying alone. Similarly, it is not said when services are held in a temporary location or correspondingly, where there is no Torah scroll present. Because of the association between the recitation of this prayer and the protection from danger, there is a custom not to recite it when the first night of Pesaḥ occurs on a Friday night, since that night (often called *Leil Shimurim*) is known to be a particularly auspicious time in its own right for protection by the Guardian of Israel.

The קהל *then the* שליח ציבור:

מָגֵן אָבוֹת בִּדְבָרוֹ, מְחַיֵּה מֵתִים בְּמַאֲמָרוֹ
הָאֵל / בשבת שובה: הַמֶּלֶךְ / הַקָּדוֹשׁ שֶׁאֵין כָּמוֹהוּ
הַמֵּנִיחַ לְעַמּוֹ בְּיוֹם שַׁבַּת קָדְשׁוֹ
כִּי בָם רָצָה לְהָנִיחַ לָהֶם
לְפָנָיו נַעֲבֹד בְּיִרְאָה וָפַחַד
וְנוֹדֶה לִשְׁמוֹ בְּכָל יוֹם תָּמִיד, מֵעֵין הַבְּרָכוֹת
אֵל הַהוֹדָאוֹת, אֲדוֹן הַשָּׁלוֹם
מְקַדֵּשׁ הַשַּׁבָּת וּמְבָרֵךְ שְׁבִיעִי
וּמֵנִיחַ בִּקְדֻשָּׁה לְעַם מְדֻשְּׁנֵי עֹנֶג
זֵכֶר לְמַעֲשֵׂה בְרֵאשִׁית.

The שליח ציבור *continues:*

אֱלֹהֵינוּ וֵאלֹהֵי אֲבוֹתֵינוּ, רְצֵה בִמְנוּחָתֵנוּ.
קַדְּשֵׁנוּ בְּמִצְוֹתֶיךָ וְתֵן חֶלְקֵנוּ בְּתוֹרָתֶךָ

BIUR TEFILLA • ביאור תפילה

מָגֵן אָבוֹת – *Shield of our ancestors.* This prayer is very unusual in that if you look carefully, you will see a number of elements of the *Amida* that was just recited, both in themes and in the language used. (Compare and contrast the two. What similarities and differences can you find?) It would thus make it appear that this prayer is a kind of repetition of the *Amida*, a practice which, while mandated for morning and afternoon services, is not at all the practice for the regular *Ma'ariv* service. And so, like many prayers with ancient roots, this one's origins are not entirely clear. One view from the Talmud Bavli suggests that it was placed here in order to accommodate those who came to the synagogue late from outlying areas. They would need extra time to catch up and there was a concern that if they did not, being left alone could leave one in potential peril, and so the service was prolonged with this prayer so that everyone could leave together (*Shabbat* 24b, Rashi). Alternatively, the Talmud Yerushalmi suggests that when there was no wine available, the recitation of the *Amida* could also serve as a substitute for making *Kiddush*, since both share the same themes and language. For illiterate Jews who could not read the *Amida* or *Kiddush*, this blessing was recited

Satisfy us with Your goodness, grant us joy in Your salvation,
and purify our hearts to serve You in truth.
In love and favor, LORD our God,
grant us as our heritage Your holy Sabbath,
so that Israel who sanctify Your name may find rest on it.
Blessed are You, LORD, who sanctifies the Sabbath.

FULL KADDISH

Leader: יִתְגַּדַּל Magnified and sanctified may His great name be,
in the world He created by His will.
May He establish His kingdom
in your lifetime and in your days,
and in the lifetime of all the house of Israel,
swiftly and soon –
and say: Amen.

All: May His great name be blessed for ever and all time.

Leader: Blessed and praised, glorified and exalted,
raised and honored,
uplifted and lauded be
the name of the Holy One,
blessed be He, beyond any blessing,
song, praise and consolation
uttered in the world –
and say: Amen.

May the prayers and pleas of all Israel
be accepted by their Father in heaven –
and say: Amen.

May there be great peace from heaven,
and life for us and all Israel –
and say: Amen.

שַׂבְּעֵנוּ מִטּוּבֶךָ וְשַׂמְּחֵנוּ בִּישׁוּעָתֶךָ
וְטַהֵר לִבֵּנוּ לְעָבְדְּךָ בֶּאֱמֶת.
וְהַנְחִילֵנוּ יהוה אֱלֹהֵינוּ בְּאַהֲבָה וּבְרָצוֹן שַׁבַּת קָדְשֶׁךָ
וְיָנוּחוּ בָהּ יִשְׂרָאֵל מְקַדְּשֵׁי שְׁמֶךָ.
בָּרוּךְ אַתָּה יהוה, מְקַדֵּשׁ הַשַּׁבָּת.

קדיש שלם

ש״ץ: יִתְגַּדַּל וְיִתְקַדַּשׁ שְׁמֵהּ רַבָּא (קהל: אָמֵן)
בְּעָלְמָא דִּי בְרָא כִרְעוּתֵהּ
וְיַמְלִיךְ מַלְכוּתֵהּ
בְּחַיֵּיכוֹן וּבְיוֹמֵיכוֹן וּבְחַיֵּי דְכָל בֵּית יִשְׂרָאֵל
בַּעֲגָלָא וּבִזְמַן קָרִיב, וְאִמְרוּ אָמֵן. (קהל: אָמֵן)

קהל וש״ץ: יְהֵא שְׁמֵהּ רַבָּא מְבָרַךְ לְעָלַם וּלְעָלְמֵי עָלְמַיָּא.

ש״ץ: יִתְבָּרַךְ וְיִשְׁתַּבַּח וְיִתְפָּאַר
וְיִתְרוֹמַם וְיִתְנַשֵּׂא וְיִתְהַדָּר וְיִתְעַלֶּה וְיִתְהַלָּל
שְׁמֵהּ דְּקֻדְשָׁא בְּרִיךְ הוּא (קהל: בְּרִיךְ הוּא)
לְעֵלָּא מִן כָּל בִּרְכָתָא
/בשבת שובה: לְעֵלָּא לְעֵלָּא מִכָּל בִּרְכָתָא/
וְשִׁירָתָא, תֻּשְׁבְּחָתָא וְנֶחֱמָתָא
דַּאֲמִירָן בְּעָלְמָא, וְאִמְרוּ אָמֵן. (קהל: אָמֵן)

תִּתְקַבַּל צְלוֹתְהוֹן וּבָעוּתְהוֹן דְּכָל יִשְׂרָאֵל
קֳדָם אֲבוּהוֹן דִּי בִשְׁמַיָּא, וְאִמְרוּ אָמֵן. (קהל: אָמֵן)

יְהֵא שְׁלָמָא רַבָּא מִן שְׁמַיָּא
וְחַיִּים, עָלֵינוּ וְעַל כָּל יִשְׂרָאֵל, וְאִמְרוּ אָמֵן. (קהל: אָמֵן)

Bow, take three steps back, as if taking leave of the Divine Presence, then bow, first left, then right, then center, while saying:

May He who makes peace in His high places,[1]
make peace for us and all Israel – and say: Amen.

KIDDUSH IN THE SYNAGOGUE

The Leader raises a cup of wine and says:

Please pay attention, my masters.

בָּרוּךְ Blessed are You, Lord our God, King of the Universe,
who creates the fruit of the vine.

בָּרוּךְ Blessed are You, Lord our God, King of the Universe,
who has made us holy with His commandments, has favored us,
and in love and favor given us His holy Sabbath as a heritage,
a remembrance of the work of creation.
It is the first among the holy days of assembly,
a remembrance of the exodus from Egypt.
For You chose us and sanctified us from all the peoples,
and in love and favor gave us Your holy Sabbath as a heritage.
Blessed are You, Lord, who sanctifies the Sabbath.

The wine should be drunk by children under the age of Bar/Bat Mitzva or, if there are none, by the Leader.

From the second night of Pesaḥ until the night before Shavuot, the Omer is counted here (*page 660*).

INTRODUCTION TO KIDDUSH IN THE SYNAGOGUE

The custom to say *Kiddush* in the synagogue is another vestige of an ancient practice of communal solidarity, though which one in particular may not be clear. There was a time when guests who had no place else to go would stay in the synagogue or nearby for a communal meal. *Kiddush* was recited at this point in the service for all of those who would not be able to have wine in the place they were eating, either because they could not afford it or because it was unavailable (*Pesaḥim* 101, Rashi). Alternatively, or concomitantly, it was considered a kind of folk remedy for the community restoring one's eyesight, physical or spiritual (*Berakhot* 43b, *Seder R. Amram Gaon*).

While there are some communities, especially in Israel, that have abandoned the custom because it is no longer necessary since synagogues are no longer used as hostels, other communities continue the practice in deference to tradition and to the values that it symbolizes. There is, however, one technical complication.

This **INTRODUCTION TO KIDDUSH IN THE SYNAGOGUE** *continues on page 143.*

Bow, take three steps back, as if taking leave of the Divine Presence, then bow, first left, then right, then center, while saying:

עֹשֶׂה שָׁלוֹם/ בשבת שובה: הַשָּׁלוֹם/ בִּמְרוֹמָיו
הוּא יַעֲשֶׂה שָׁלוֹם עָלֵינוּ וְעַל כָּל יִשְׂרָאֵל, וְאִמְרוּ אָמֵן. (קהל: אָמֵן)

קידוש בבית הכנסת

The שליח ציבור *raises a cup of wine and says:*

סַבְרִי מָרָנָן

בָּרוּךְ אַתָּה יהוה אֱלֹהֵינוּ מֶלֶךְ הָעוֹלָם בּוֹרֵא פְּרִי הַגָּפֶן.

בָּרוּךְ אַתָּה יהוה אֱלֹהֵינוּ מֶלֶךְ הָעוֹלָם
אֲשֶׁר קִדְּשָׁנוּ בְּמִצְוֹתָיו, וְרָצָה בָנוּ
וְשַׁבַּת קָדְשׁוֹ בְּאַהֲבָה וּבְרָצוֹן הִנְחִילָנוּ, זִכָּרוֹן לְמַעֲשֵׂה בְרֵאשִׁית
כִּי הוּא יוֹם תְּחִלָּה לְמִקְרָאֵי קֹדֶשׁ, זֵכֶר לִיצִיאַת מִצְרָיִם
כִּי בָנוּ בָחַרְתָּ וְאוֹתָנוּ קִדַּשְׁתָּ מִכָּל הָעַמִּים
וְשַׁבַּת קָדְשְׁךָ בְּאַהֲבָה וּבְרָצוֹן הִנְחַלְתָּנוּ.
בָּרוּךְ אַתָּה יהוה, מְקַדֵּשׁ הַשַּׁבָּת.

The wine should be drunk by children under the age of בר מצווה *or* בת מצווה *or, if there are none, by the* שליח ציבור.

From the second night of פסח *until the night before* שבועות*, the* עומר *is counted here* (*page 661*).

IYUN TEFILLA • עיון תפילה

עֹשֶׂה שָׁלוֹם בִּמְרוֹמָיו – *May He who makes peace in His high places*. What peace is referred to here? One opinion refers to an ancient view that angels do not serve multiple purposes but rather each has its own single mission "no one angel can have more than one charge" (*Bereshit Raba* 50:2). As such, one might easily imagine them coming into conflict with one another, as each tries to accomplish his one goal even if it were to mean negating the task of another. Nevertheless, such conflicts do not take place for what they have in common is their unswerving devotion to Hashem; they thus recognize the value of the other and avoid any conflict (*Rinat Ḥayyim*). So, too, should it be with man. Perhaps that is a reason that all of our prayer services end with the emphasis on peace. As we are about to take leave the synagogue with a greater appreciation for the role of God in our lives, we commit ourselves to living a more prayerful and peaceful life with our fellow man.

How can I add more peace to my relationships this evening?

Stand while saying Aleinu.

עָלֵינוּ It is our duty to praise the Master of all,
and ascribe greatness to the Author of creation,
who has not made us like the nations of the lands
nor placed us like the families of the earth;
who has not made our portion like theirs,
nor our destiny like all their multitudes.
(For they worship vanity and emptiness,
and pray to a god who cannot save.)
▾ *Bow:* But we bow in worship and thank the Supreme King of kings,
the Holy One, blessed be He,
who extends the heavens and establishes the earth,
whose throne of glory is in the heavens above,
and whose power's Presence is in the highest of heights.
He is our God; there is no other.
Truly He is our King, there is none else,
as it is written in His Torah:
"You shall know and take to heart this day that the LORD is God, *Deut. 4*
in heaven above and on earth below. There is no other."

---

home" message at the end of every prayer service.

A conflicting tradition suggests that the prayer is even older, having been composed by Moshe's successor, Yehoshua. The initial paragraph of the prayer, which among other things, expresses disgust at the existence and fallacy of idolatry is said to be a reference to Yehoshua's reaction to the paganism he witnessed during the conquest of Canaan. To reconcile those traditions, there are those who say it was written by Rav but he did so from the perspective of Yehoshua as he conquered the Land.

There are two distinct but interrelated themes here. The first paragraph is all about our chosenness in the eyes of Hashem. The second is about why we were chosen: to perfect or repair the world, known in Hebrew as *tikkun olam*. It is a phrase that has commonly been adopted for every cause of social justice, yet those who do so mistakenly omit the rest of the original which reads "to perfect the world under the sovereignty of the Almighty." The American poet and essayist Ralph Waldo Emerson once said, "One man's justice is another's injustice." Only an immutable absolute morality that is based on an unchanging God has a chance of truly repairing the world, else we are left to a world of relativism.

As you prepare to leave the synagogue this evening and reenter the world of human interaction, what can you do to repair the world under the sovereignty of the Almighty?

Stand while saying עָלֵינוּ.

עָלֵינוּ לְשַׁבֵּחַ לַאֲדוֹן הַכֹּל, לָתֵת גְּדֻלָּה לְיוֹצֵר בְּרֵאשִׁית
שֶׁלֹּא עָשָׂנוּ כְּגוֹיֵי הָאֲרָצוֹת, וְלֹא שָׂמָנוּ כְּמִשְׁפְּחוֹת הָאֲדָמָה
שֶׁלֹּא שָׂם חֶלְקֵנוּ כָּהֶם וְגוֹרָלֵנוּ כְּכָל הֲמוֹנָם.
(שֶׁהֵם מִשְׁתַּחֲוִים לְהֶבֶל וָרִיק וּמִתְפַּלְלִים אֶל אֵל לֹא יוֹשִׁיעַ.)
▾ *Bow* וַאֲנַחְנוּ כּוֹרְעִים וּמִשְׁתַּחֲוִים וּמוֹדִים
לִפְנֵי מֶלֶךְ מַלְכֵי הַמְּלָכִים, הַקָּדוֹשׁ בָּרוּךְ הוּא
שֶׁהוּא נוֹטֶה שָׁמַיִם וְיוֹסֵד אָרֶץ, וּמוֹשַׁב יְקָרוֹ בַּשָּׁמַיִם מִמַּעַל
וּשְׁכִינַת עֻזּוֹ בְּגָבְהֵי מְרוֹמִים.
הוּא אֱלֹהֵינוּ, אֵין עוֹד.
אֱמֶת מַלְכֵּנוּ, אֶפֶס זוּלָתוֹ
דברים ד כַּכָּתוּב בְּתוֹרָתוֹ, וְיָדַעְתָּ הַיּוֹם וַהֲשֵׁבֹתָ אֶל־לְבָבֶךָ
כִּי יהוה הוּא הָאֱלֹהִים בַּשָּׁמַיִם מִמַּעַל וְעַל־הָאָרֶץ מִתָּחַת
אֵין עוֹד:

Kiddush is legally required to be said at the place where one eats a meal (*ein Kiddush ela bemakom seuda*), and parenthetically, that is the reason that one does not fulfill one's obligation with this recitation and must repeat it at one's meal. Also, one is not permitted to eat or drink before saying *Kiddush* at that meal, thus putting the person reciting this *Kiddush* in a technical suspended state where on the one hand, he must say *Kiddush* but on the other not drink from the wine, but if he does not drink from the wine then his blessing is in vain! As a result another custom developed for young children, who would otherwise not be reciting *Kiddush* on their own, to derive the benefit by being the ones to drink the wine.

INTRODUCTION TO ALEINU

Aleinu is one of the oldest prayers in the siddur having been attributed to Rav, the head of one of the largest *yeshivot* in Babylonia (third century). Interestingly, it originally appeared not in the daily service but in the Rosh HaShana *Maḥzor* where it served as an introduction to *malkhiyot*. *Malkhiyot* is that first section of *Shemoneh Esreh* of *Musaf* on Rosh HaShana which declares Hashem's sovereignty in the world above all else. The prayer's ideas were considered so beautifully expressed and so central to the mission of the Jewish People, that it was eventually adopted as the "take

Therefore, we place our hope in You, LORD our God,
that we may soon see the glory of Your power,
when You will remove abominations from the earth,
and idols will be utterly destroyed,
when the world will be perfected under the sovereignty of the Almighty,
when all humanity will call on Your name,
to turn all the earth's wicked toward You.
All the world's inhabitants will realize and know
that to You every knee must bow and every tongue swear loyalty.
Before You, LORD our God, they will kneel and bow down
and give honor to Your glorious name.
They will all accept the yoke of Your kingdom,
and You will reign over them soon and for ever.
For the kingdom is Yours,
and to all eternity You will reign in glory,
as it is written in Your Torah: "The LORD will reign for ever and ever." *Ex. 15*
▸ And it is said: "Then the LORD shall be King over all the earth; *Zech. 14*
on that day the LORD shall be One and His name One."

Some add:

Have no fear of sudden terror or of the ruin when it overtakes the wicked. *Prov. 3*
Devise your strategy, but it will be thwarted; *Is. 8*
propose your plan, but it will not stand, for God is with us.
When you grow old, I will still be the same. *Is. 46*
When your hair turns gray, I will still carry you.
I made you, I will bear you, I will carry you, and I will rescue you.

MOURNER'S KADDISH

The following prayer, said by mourners, requires the presence of a minyan.
A transliteration can be found on page 892.

Mourner: יִתְגַּדַּל Magnified and sanctified may His great name be,
in the world He created by His will.
May He establish His kingdom
in your lifetime and in your days,
and in the lifetime of all the house of Israel,
swiftly and soon – and say: Amen.

All: May His great name be blessed for ever and all time.

עַל כֵּן נְקַוֶּה לְּךָ יהוה אֱלֹהֵינוּ, לִרְאוֹת מְהֵרָה בְּתִפְאֶרֶת עֻזֶּךָ
לְהַעֲבִיר גִּלּוּלִים מִן הָאָרֶץ, וְהָאֱלִילִים כָּרוֹת יִכָּרֵתוּן
לְתַקֵּן עוֹלָם בְּמַלְכוּת שַׁדַּי.
וְכָל בְּנֵי בָשָׂר יִקְרְאוּ בִשְׁמֶךָ לְהַפְנוֹת אֵלֶיךָ כָּל רִשְׁעֵי אָרֶץ.
יַכִּירוּ וְיֵדְעוּ כָּל יוֹשְׁבֵי תֵבֵל
כִּי לְךָ תִּכְרַע כָּל בֶּרֶךְ, תִּשָּׁבַע כָּל לָשׁוֹן.
לְפָנֶיךָ יהוה אֱלֹהֵינוּ יִכְרְעוּ וְיִפֹּלוּ, וְלִכְבוֹד שִׁמְךָ יְקָר יִתֵּנוּ
וִיקַבְּלוּ כֻלָּם אֶת עֹל מַלְכוּתֶךָ
וְתִמְלֹךְ עֲלֵיהֶם מְהֵרָה לְעוֹלָם וָעֶד.
כִּי הַמַּלְכוּת שֶׁלְּךָ הִיא וּלְעוֹלְמֵי עַד תִּמְלֹךְ בְּכָבוֹד
כַּכָּתוּב בְּתוֹרָתֶךָ, יהוה יִמְלֹךְ לְעֹלָם וָעֶד: שמות טו
◄ וְנֶאֱמַר, וְהָיָה יהוה לְמֶלֶךְ עַל־כָּל־הָאָרֶץ זכריה יד
בַּיּוֹם הַהוּא יִהְיֶה יהוה אֶחָד וּשְׁמוֹ אֶחָד:

Some add:

אַל־תִּירָא מִפַּחַד פִּתְאֹם וּמִשֹּׁאַת רְשָׁעִים כִּי תָבֹא: משלי ג
עֻצוּ עֵצָה וְתֻפָר, דַּבְּרוּ דָבָר וְלֹא יָקוּם, כִּי עִמָּנוּ אֵל: ישעיה ח
וְעַד־זִקְנָה אֲנִי הוּא, וְעַד־שֵׂיבָה אֲנִי אֶסְבֹּל, אֲנִי עָשִׂיתִי וַאֲנִי אֶשָּׂא וַאֲנִי אֶסְבֹּל וַאֲמַלֵּט: ישעיה מו

קדיש יתום

The following prayer, said by mourners, requires the presence of a מנין*.*
A transliteration can be found on page 892.

אבל: יִתְגַּדַּל וְיִתְקַדַּשׁ שְׁמֵהּ רַבָּא (קהל: אָמֵן)
בְּעָלְמָא דִּי בְרָא כִרְעוּתֵהּ
וְיַמְלִיךְ מַלְכוּתֵהּ
בְּחַיֵּיכוֹן וּבְיוֹמֵיכוֹן וּבְחַיֵּי דְכָל בֵּית יִשְׂרָאֵל
בַּעֲגָלָא וּבִזְמַן קָרִיב, וְאִמְרוּ אָמֵן. (קהל: אָמֵן)

קהל ואבל: יְהֵא שְׁמֵהּ רַבָּא מְבָרַךְ לְעָלַם וּלְעָלְמֵי עָלְמַיָּא.

Mourner: Blessed and praised, glorified and exalted,
raised and honored, uplifted and lauded
be the name of the Holy One,
blessed be He,
beyond any blessing,
song, praise and consolation
uttered in the world – and say: Amen.

May there be great peace from heaven,
and life for us and all Israel – and say: Amen.

Bow and take three steps back as if taking leave of the Divine Presence.

Bow left: May He who makes peace in His high places,
Bow right: make peace *Bow forward:* for us and all Israel –
and say: Amen.

From the second day of Rosh Hodesh Elul until and including Shemini Atzeret, the following psalm is said:

לְדָוִד A psalm of David. The Lord is my light and my salvation – whom then shall I fear? The Lord is the stronghold of my life – of whom shall I be afraid? When evil men close in on me to devour my flesh, it is they, my enemies and foes, who stumble and fall. Should an army besiege me, my heart would not fear. Should war break out against me, still I would be confident. One thing I ask of the Lord, only this do I seek: to live in the House of the Lord all the days of my life, to gaze on the beauty of the Lord and worship in His Temple. For He will keep me safe in His pavilion on the day of trouble. He will hide me under the cover of His tent. He will set me high upon a rock. Now my head is high above my enemies who surround me. I will sacrifice in His tent with shouts of joy. I will sing and chant praises to the Lord. Lord, hear my voice when I call. Be gracious to me and answer me. On Your behalf my heart says, "Seek My face." Your face, Lord, will I seek. Do not hide Your face from me. Do not turn Your servant away in anger. You have been my help. Do not reject or forsake me, God, my Savior. Were my father and my mother to forsake me, the Lord would take me in. Teach me Your way, Lord, and lead me on a level path, because of my oppressors. Do not abandon me to the will of my foes, for false witnesses have risen against me, breathing violence. ▸ Were it not for my faith that I shall see the Lord's goodness in the land of the living. Hope in the Lord. Be strong and of good courage, and hope in the Lord! *Ps. 27*

Mourner's Kaddish (on previous page)

אבל: יִתְבָּרַךְ וְיִשְׁתַּבַּח וְיִתְפָּאַר
וְיִתְרוֹמַם וְיִתְנַשֵּׂא וְיִתְהַדָּר וְיִתְעַלֶּה וְיִתְהַלָּל
שְׁמֵהּ דְּקֻדְשָׁא בְּרִיךְ הוּא (קהל: בְּרִיךְ הוּא)
לְעֵלָּא מִן כָּל בִּרְכָתָא / בשבת שובה: לְעֵלָּא לְעֵלָּא מִכָּל בִּרְכָתָא/
וְשִׁירָתָא, תֻּשְׁבְּחָתָא וְנֶחֱמָתָא
דַּאֲמִירָן בְּעָלְמָא, וְאִמְרוּ אָמֵן. (קהל: אָמֵן)

יְהֵא שְׁלָמָא רַבָּא מִן שְׁמַיָּא
וְחַיִּים, עָלֵינוּ וְעַל כָּל יִשְׂרָאֵל, וְאִמְרוּ אָמֵן. (קהל: אָמֵן)

Bow and take three steps back as if taking leave of the Divine Presence.

Bow left עֹשֶׂה שָׁלוֹם/ בשבת שובה: הַשָּׁלוֹם/ בִּמְרוֹמָיו
Bow right הוּא יַעֲשֶׂה שָׁלוֹם *Bow forward* עָלֵינוּ
וְעַל כָּל יִשְׂרָאֵל, וְאִמְרוּ אָמֵן.

From the second day of ראש חודש אלול *until and including* שמיני עצרת*,*
the following psalm is said:

תהלים כז
לְדָוִד, יהוה אוֹרִי וְיִשְׁעִי, מִמִּי אִירָא, יהוה מָעוֹז־חַיַּי, מִמִּי אֶפְחָד: בִּקְרֹב
עָלַי מְרֵעִים לֶאֱכֹל אֶת־בְּשָׂרִי, צָרַי וְאֹיְבַי לִי, הֵמָּה כָשְׁלוּ וְנָפָלוּ: אִם־תַּחֲנֶה
עָלַי מַחֲנֶה, לֹא־יִירָא לִבִּי, אִם־תָּקוּם עָלַי מִלְחָמָה, בְּזֹאת אֲנִי בוֹטֵחַ: אַחַת
שָׁאַלְתִּי מֵאֵת־יהוה, אוֹתָהּ אֲבַקֵּשׁ, שִׁבְתִּי בְּבֵית־יהוה כָּל־יְמֵי חַיַּי, לַחֲזוֹת
בְּנֹעַם־יהוה, וּלְבַקֵּר בְּהֵיכָלוֹ: כִּי יִצְפְּנֵנִי בְּסֻכֹּה בְּיוֹם רָעָה, יַסְתִּרֵנִי בְּסֵתֶר
אָהֳלוֹ, בְּצוּר יְרוֹמְמֵנִי: וְעַתָּה יָרוּם רֹאשִׁי עַל אֹיְבַי סְבִיבוֹתַי, וְאֶזְבְּחָה
בְאָהֳלוֹ זִבְחֵי תְרוּעָה, אָשִׁירָה וַאֲזַמְּרָה לַיהוה: שְׁמַע־יהוה קוֹלִי אֶקְרָא,
וְחָנֵּנִי וַעֲנֵנִי: לְךָ אָמַר לִבִּי בַּקְּשׁוּ פָנָי, אֶת־פָּנֶיךָ יהוה אֲבַקֵּשׁ: אַל־תַּסְתֵּר
פָּנֶיךָ מִמֶּנִּי, אַל תַּט־בְּאַף עַבְדֶּךָ, עֶזְרָתִי הָיִיתָ, אַל־תִּטְּשֵׁנִי וְאַל־תַּעַזְבֵנִי,
אֱלֹהֵי יִשְׁעִי: כִּי־אָבִי וְאִמִּי עֲזָבוּנִי, וַיהוה יַאַסְפֵנִי: הוֹרֵנִי יהוה דַּרְכֶּךָ, וּנְחֵנִי
בְּאֹרַח מִישׁוֹר, לְמַעַן שׁוֹרְרָי: אַל־תִּתְּנֵנִי בְּנֶפֶשׁ צָרָי, כִּי קָמוּ־בִי עֵדֵי־שֶׁקֶר,
וִיפֵחַ חָמָס: ◄ לוּלֵא הֶאֱמַנְתִּי לִרְאוֹת בְּטוּב־יהוה בְּאֶרֶץ חַיִּים: קַוֵּה אֶל־
יהוה, חֲזַק וְיַאֲמֵץ לִבֶּךָ, וְקַוֵּה אֶל־יהוה: קדיש יתום (*on previous page*)

Most congregations sing Yigdal at this point.
In Israel, most congregations sing Adon Olam (*page 176*).

GREAT
is the living God and praised.
He exists, and His existence is beyond time.

He is One, and there is no unity like His.
Unfathomable, His oneness is infinite.

He has neither bodily form nor substance;
His holiness is beyond compare.

He preceded all that was created.
He was first: there was no beginning to His beginning.

Behold He is Master of the Universe; every creature
shows His greatness and majesty.

The rich flow of His prophecy He gave
to His treasured people in whom He gloried.

Never in Israel has there arisen another like Moses,
a prophet who beheld God's image.

God gave His people a Torah of truth
by the hand of His prophet, most faithful of His House.

God will not alter or change His law
for any other, for eternity.

He sees and knows our secret thoughts;
as soon as something is begun, He foresees its end.

He rewards people with loving-kindness according to their deeds;
He punishes the wicked according to his wickedness.

At the end of days He will send our Messiah,
to redeem those who await His final salvation.

God will revive the dead in His great loving-kindness.
Blessed for evermore is His glorious name!

Most congregations sing יגדל *at this point.*
In ארץ ישראל*, most congregations sing* אדון עולם (*page 177*).

יִגְדַּל

אֱלֹהִים חַי וְיִשְׁתַּבַּח, נִמְצָא וְאֵין עֵת אֶל מְצִיאוּתוֹ.

אֶחָד וְאֵין יָחִיד כְּיִחוּדוֹ, נֶעְלָם וְגַם אֵין סוֹף לְאַחְדוּתוֹ.

אֵין לוֹ דְּמוּת הַגּוּף וְאֵינוֹ גוּף, לֹא נַעֲרֹךְ אֵלָיו קְדֻשָּׁתוֹ.

קַדְמוֹן לְכָל דָּבָר אֲשֶׁר נִבְרָא, רִאשׁוֹן וְאֵין רֵאשִׁית לְרֵאשִׁיתוֹ.

הִנּוֹ אֲדוֹן עוֹלָם, וְכָל נוֹצָר יוֹרֶה גְדֻלָּתוֹ וּמַלְכוּתוֹ.

שֶׁפַע נְבוּאָתוֹ נְתָנוֹ אֶל־אַנְשֵׁי סְגֻלָּתוֹ וְתִפְאַרְתּוֹ.

לֹא קָם בְּיִשְׂרָאֵל כְּמֹשֶׁה עוֹד נָבִיא וּמַבִּיט אֶת תְּמוּנָתוֹ.

תּוֹרַת אֱמֶת נָתַן לְעַמּוֹ אֵל עַל יַד נְבִיאוֹ נֶאֱמַן בֵּיתוֹ.

לֹא יַחֲלִיף הָאֵל וְלֹא יָמִיר דָּתוֹ לְעוֹלָמִים לְזוּלָתוֹ.

צוֹפֶה וְיוֹדֵעַ סְתָרֵינוּ, מַבִּיט לְסוֹף דָּבָר בְּקַדְמָתוֹ.

גּוֹמֵל לְאִישׁ חֶסֶד כְּמִפְעָלוֹ, נוֹתֵן לְרָשָׁע רָע כְּרִשְׁעָתוֹ.

יִשְׁלַח לְקֵץ יָמִין מְשִׁיחֵנוּ לִפְדּוֹת מְחַכֵּי קֵץ יְשׁוּעָתוֹ.

מֵתִים יְחַיֶּה אֵל בְּרֹב חַסְדּוֹ, בָּרוּךְ עֲדֵי עַד שֵׁם תְּהִלָּתוֹ.

Kiddush and Zemirot for Shabbat Evening

BLESSING THE CHILDREN

On the evenings of Shabbat many have the custom to bless their children.

To sons, say:
יְשִׂמְךָ May God
make you like Ephraim
and Manasseh.

To daughters, say:
יְשִׂימֵךְ May God
make you like Sarah, Rebecca,
Rachel and Leah.

Gen. 48

יְבָרֶכְךָ May the LORD bless you and protect you.
May the LORD make His face shine on you
and be gracious to you.
May the LORD turn His face toward you
and grant you peace.

Num. 6

---

again ends in the prayer for peace. How is such peace achieved? Perhaps in part through the blessing itself. Rabbi Yaakov Tzvi Mecklenburg noted that during the week parents may come to curse (!) children because of the strife that can occur between them. The blessing is a way for them to reconnect. A somewhat gentler version of this can be found in a contemporary explanation by former Vice-Presidential nominee, Senator Joe Lieberman. "Of all the things that observant Jews do on the Sabbath," he writes, "...I would put blessing your family high on the list. It is a priceless moment of connection that no matter what has happened during the week, the parent feels blessed to have that child... As a parent you know that weeks can go by when you think of your children less as blessings and more as problems to be solved... Stopping to bless your children once a week makes us pause to appreciate how blessed we are to have them in the first place and reminds them of the love we feel for them."

קידוש וזמירות לליל שבת

ברכת הבנים

On ליל שבת many have the custom to bless their children.

To sons, say:

יְשִׂמְךָ אֱלֹהִים
כְּאֶפְרַיִם וְכִמְנַשֶּׁה:

To daughters, say:

בראשית מח
יְשִׂימֵךְ אֱלֹהִים
כְּשָׂרָה רִבְקָה רָחֵל וְלֵאָה.

במדבר ו
יְבָרֶכְךָ יהוה וְיִשְׁמְרֶךָ:
יָאֵר יהוה פָּנָיו אֵלֶיךָ וִיחֻנֶּךָּ:
יִשָּׂא יהוה פָּנָיו אֵלֶיךָ וְיָשֵׂם לְךָ שָׁלוֹם:

INTRODUCTION TO BIRKAT HABANIM

The blessing of one's children can be one of the most moving rituals of Shabbat night. The parent puts one hand or two upon the head of one's child and first invokes the blessing that the boys be like Efraim and Menashe while the girls be like the Matriarchs. Why aren't the boys similarly blessed that they should be like the Patriarchs? Perhaps it is because if one looks at all of the sons of the Patriarchs, one will notice that there was always strife between them, always a battle over who would be the bearer of the future. Efraim and Menashe, blessed by their grandfather Yaakov (*Bereshit* 48:14), are the first siblings between whom there is no such rivalry; indeed, the first where the birthright is not contested. What better way to bless one's children, then, than with the blessing of peace (Rabbi Shlomo Riskin)?

This blessing is followed by the tripartite blessing of the *kohanim* (priests) which

Many people sing each of the four verses of the following song three times:

שָׁלוֹם עֲלֵיכֶם Welcome,
ministering angels, angels of the Most High,
from the Supreme King of kings,
the Holy One, blessed be He.

Enter in peace,
angels of peace, angels of the Most High,
from the Supreme King of kings,
the Holy One, blessed be He.

Bless me with peace,
angels of peace, angels of the Most High,
from the Supreme King of kings,
the Holy One, blessed be He.

Go in peace,
angels of peace, angels of the Most High,
from the Supreme King of kings,
the Holy One, blessed be He.

כִּי מַלְאָכָיו He will command His angels about you, *Ps. 91*
to guard you in all your ways.
May the LORD guard your going out and your return, *Ps. 121*
from now and for all time.

---

for Judaism generally rejects any notion of intermediaries between man and God, the song nevertheless spread quickly since its creation around the seventeenth century in Kabbalistic circles. It has thus become a common way to transition from welcoming the Shabbat in the synagogue to welcoming her into one's home.

The motif of the song is clearly peace. It is a hallmark of Shabbat and if one is not yet feeling it then now is the time to let it wash over you. The warm glow of the candles, the camaraderie of friends or family or newly found acquaintances, the festive air of a good meal should individually or all contribute to a different kind of awareness. As one allows the pressures or routines of the week to slip away, peace and a sense of wholeness begin to take their place.

Many people sing each of the four verses of the following song three times:

שָׁלוֹם עֲלֵיכֶם
מַלְאֲכֵי הַשָּׁרֵת, מַלְאֲכֵי עֶלְיוֹן
מִמֶּלֶךְ מַלְכֵי הַמְּלָכִים, הַקָּדוֹשׁ בָּרוּךְ הוּא.

בּוֹאֲכֶם לְשָׁלוֹם
מַלְאֲכֵי הַשָּׁלוֹם, מַלְאֲכֵי עֶלְיוֹן
מִמֶּלֶךְ מַלְכֵי הַמְּלָכִים, הַקָּדוֹשׁ בָּרוּךְ הוּא.

בָּרְכוּנִי לְשָׁלוֹם
מַלְאֲכֵי הַשָּׁלוֹם, מַלְאֲכֵי עֶלְיוֹן
מִמֶּלֶךְ מַלְכֵי הַמְּלָכִים, הַקָּדוֹשׁ בָּרוּךְ הוּא.

צֵאתְכֶם לְשָׁלוֹם
מַלְאֲכֵי הַשָּׁלוֹם, מַלְאֲכֵי עֶלְיוֹן
מִמֶּלֶךְ מַלְכֵי הַמְּלָכִים, הַקָּדוֹשׁ בָּרוּךְ הוּא.

כִּי מַלְאָכָיו יְצַוֶּה־לָּךְ, לִשְׁמָרְךָ בְּכָל־דְּרָכֶיךָ: תהלים צא
יהוה יִשְׁמָר־צֵאתְךָ וּבוֹאֶךָ, מֵעַתָּה וְעַד־עוֹלָם: תהלים קכא

INTRODUCTION TO SHALOM ALEIKHEM

The roots of this song can be found in the Gemara (*Shabbat* 119b). "It was taught by the *tanna* Rabbi Yose son of Yehuda: Two ministering angels accompany a person on Friday night on his way home from the synagogue, one good and one evil. When he arrives at home and finds a lit candle, a set table, and his bed made, the good angel says, "May you have another Shabbat like this one,' and the evil angel is forced to respond 'Amen' against his will. If he does not find the house in this state the evil angel says, 'May you have another Shabbat like this one,' and the good angel is forced to answer 'Amen' against his will."

While there were those who objected to the potentially problematic notion of appealing directly to angels (Vilna Gaon),

אֵשֶׁת־חַיִל A woman of strength, who can find? Her worth is far beyond pearls. *Prov. 31*

Her husband's heart trusts in her, and he has no lack of gain.
She brings him good, not harm, all the days of her life.
She seeks wool and linen, and works with willing hands.
She is like a ship laden with merchandise, bringing her food from afar.
She rises while it is still night, providing food for her household,
    portions for her maids.
She considers a field and buys it; from her earnings she plants a vineyard.
She girds herself with strength, and braces her arms for her tasks.
She sees that her business goes well; her lamp does not go out at night.
She holds the distaff in her hand, and grasps the spindle with her palms.
She reaches out her palm to the poor, and extends her hand to the needy.
She has no fear for her family when it snows, for all her household is
    clothed in crimson wool.
She makes elegant coverings; her clothing is fine linen and purple wool.
Her husband is well known in the gates,
    where he sits with the elders of the land.
She makes linen garments and sells them, and supplies merchants
    with sashes.
She is clothed with strength and dignity; she can laugh at the days to come.
She opens her mouth with wisdom,
    and the law of kindness is on her tongue.
She watches over the ways of her household,
    and never eats the bread of idleness.
Her children rise and call her happy; her husband also praises her:
"Many women have excelled, but you surpass them all."
Charm is deceptive and beauty vain:
    it is the God-fearing woman who deserves praise.
Give her the reward she has earned;
    let her deeds bring her praise in the gates.

---

which a husband sings to his wife, thus reinforcing the message of the harmony and respect that are supposed to be the hallmark of the home on Shabbat.

At the same time, commentators have understood there to be mystical or allegorical overtones, wherein the subject of the poem is thought to be the human soul, or the Torah or the Matriarchs of the Jewish people, or the *Shekhina* (Divine Presence), or the nation of Israel, or the Shabbat. Pick one and see how it can change the meaning of the poem…and your appreciation for this moment of Shabbat.

אֵשֶׁת־חַיִל מִי יִמְצָא, וְרָחֹק מִפְּנִינִים מִכְרָהּ: משלי לא
בָּטַח בָּהּ לֵב בַּעְלָהּ, וְשָׁלָל לֹא יֶחְסָר:
גְּמָלַתְהוּ טוֹב וְלֹא־רָע, כֹּל יְמֵי חַיֶּיהָ:
דָּרְשָׁה צֶמֶר וּפִשְׁתִּים, וַתַּעַשׂ בְּחֵפֶץ כַּפֶּיהָ:
הָיְתָה כָּאֳנִיּוֹת סוֹחֵר, מִמֶּרְחָק תָּבִיא לַחְמָהּ:
וַתָּקָם בְּעוֹד לַיְלָה, וַתִּתֵּן טֶרֶף לְבֵיתָהּ, וְחֹק לְנַעֲרֹתֶיהָ:
זָמְמָה שָׂדֶה וַתִּקָּחֵהוּ, מִפְּרִי כַפֶּיהָ נָטַע כָּרֶם:
חָגְרָה בְעוֹז מָתְנֶיהָ, וַתְּאַמֵּץ זְרוֹעֹתֶיהָ:
טָעֲמָה כִּי־טוֹב סַחְרָהּ, לֹא־יִכְבֶּה בַלַּיִל נֵרָהּ:
יָדֶיהָ שִׁלְּחָה בַכִּישׁוֹר, וְכַפֶּיהָ תָּמְכוּ פָלֶךְ:
כַּפָּהּ פָּרְשָׂה לֶעָנִי, וְיָדֶיהָ שִׁלְּחָה לָאֶבְיוֹן:
לֹא־תִירָא לְבֵיתָהּ מִשָּׁלֶג, כִּי כָל־בֵּיתָהּ לָבֻשׁ שָׁנִים:
מַרְבַדִּים עָשְׂתָה־לָּהּ, שֵׁשׁ וְאַרְגָּמָן לְבוּשָׁהּ:
נוֹדָע בַּשְּׁעָרִים בַּעְלָהּ, בְּשִׁבְתּוֹ עִם־זִקְנֵי־אָרֶץ:
סָדִין עָשְׂתָה וַתִּמְכֹּר, וַחֲגוֹר נָתְנָה לַכְּנַעֲנִי:
עוֹז־וְהָדָר לְבוּשָׁהּ, וַתִּשְׂחַק לְיוֹם אַחֲרוֹן:
פִּיהָ פָּתְחָה בְחָכְמָה, וְתוֹרַת־חֶסֶד עַל־לְשׁוֹנָהּ:
צוֹפִיָּה הֲלִיכוֹת בֵּיתָהּ, וְלֶחֶם עַצְלוּת לֹא תֹאכֵל:
קָמוּ בָנֶיהָ וַיְאַשְּׁרוּהָ, בַּעְלָהּ וַיְהַלְלָהּ:
רַבּוֹת בָּנוֹת עָשׂוּ חָיִל, וְאַתְּ עָלִית עַל־כֻּלָּנָה:
שֶׁקֶר הַחֵן וְהֶבֶל הַיֹּפִי, אִשָּׁה יִרְאַת־יהוה הִיא תִתְהַלָּל:
תְּנוּ־לָהּ מִפְּרִי יָדֶיהָ, וִיהַלְלוּהָ בַשְּׁעָרִים מַעֲשֶׂיהָ:

INTRODUCTION TO EISHET ḤAYYIL

Another custom established by the Ari *zal* and his circle was the singing of this final chapter of the book of Proverbs (*Mishlei* 31:10-31), a 22-verse alphabetic acrostic. On its surface, it is a song of praise to the woman of the house in her capacity as homemaker, businesswoman, benefactor, mother and above all, a person whose beliefs permeate and carry her household. As such, it is often interpreted as something

KIDDUSH FOR SHABBAT EVENING

The Shabbat meal begins with the reciting of Kiddush, and is followed by the ritual washing of the hands in preparation for eating the Shabbat loaves.

Quietly: And it was evening, and it was morning – Gen. 1

יוֹם הַשִּׁשִּׁי the sixth day.

Then the heavens and the earth were completed, and all their array. Gen. 2
With the seventh day, God completed the work He had done.
He ceased on the seventh day from all the work He had done.
God blessed the seventh day and declared it holy,
because on it He ceased from all His work He had created to do.

When saying Kiddush for others, add:

Please pay attention, my masters.

Blessed are You, Lord our God, King of the Universe,
who creates the fruit of the vine.

HILKHOT TEFILLA • הלכות תפילה

There is a principle which states that *Kiddush* needs to be recited in the place where the meal is eaten (*ein Kiddush ela bemakom seuda*). As such, there is a custom to incorporate the *Kiddush* into the meal, as it were, by reciting the entire text while seated at the table as a prelude to the meal. Others maintain that the first paragraph is the equivalent of giving testimony to God's creation of the world and so one should stand for the entire *Kiddush*. Still others have the custom to stand for the first paragraph and then sit for the remainder of the *Kiddush*.

Participants are not required to drink from the wine, answering "Amen" to the blessing is sufficient, although there is a custom for the one reciting the *Kiddush* to share the wine from his cup with others (See *Shulḥan Arukh* 271:14).

ANI TEFILLA • אני תפילה

It was the custom of Rabbi David HaLevi, author of the *Turei Zahav* [on *Shulḥan Arukh*] that he would always recite *Kiddush* on Shabbat from a siddur. The reason, he said, apart from the holiness of the letters themselves, was because from time to time there would be a person at the table who did not know the *Kiddush* by heart and that person would be embarrassed to have to use a siddur to recite the words. Rabbi HaLevi himself would therefore use the siddur so that the guest would do so as well without fear of being embarrassed. He would sometimes say to the guest, "Follow along in the siddur just as I do, for to do so is really a very old custom." (*Sha'ar HaHakhana*).

קידוש לליל שבת

The שבת *meal begins with the reciting of* קידוש*, and is followed by the ritual washing of the hands in preparation for eating the* חלות.

Quietly וַיְהִי־עֶרֶב וַיְהִי־בֹקֶר בראשית א

יוֹם הַשִּׁשִּׁי:

וַיְכֻלּוּ הַשָּׁמַיִם וְהָאָרֶץ וְכָל־צְבָאָם: בראשית ב

וַיְכַל אֱלֹהִים בַּיּוֹם הַשְּׁבִיעִי מְלַאכְתּוֹ אֲשֶׁר עָשָׂה

וַיִּשְׁבֹּת בַּיּוֹם הַשְּׁבִיעִי מִכָּל־מְלַאכְתּוֹ אֲשֶׁר עָשָׂה:

וַיְבָרֶךְ אֱלֹהִים אֶת־יוֹם הַשְּׁבִיעִי, וַיְקַדֵּשׁ אֹתוֹ

כִּי בוֹ שָׁבַת מִכָּל־מְלַאכְתּוֹ, אֲשֶׁר־בָּרָא אֱלֹהִים, לַעֲשׂוֹת:

When saying קידוש *for others, add:*

סַבְרִי מָרָנָן

בָּרוּךְ אַתָּה יהוה אֱלֹהֵינוּ מֶלֶךְ הָעוֹלָם, בּוֹרֵא פְּרִי הַגָּפֶן.

INTRODUCTION TO KIDDUSH

The Ten Commandments (*Shemot* 20:7) mandate that we "remember the Shabbat day to keep it holy." Rather than leaving this as a general and somewhat ambiguous command, tradition informs us that one should "remember it over wine," that is, we should formally remember the Shabbat's presence and holiness by making a ritual declaration to that effect over a cup of wine. We use wine, says one authority, because it enlivens one's heart and the more positive feelings one has toward an act, the more lasting it will be; this is another case where the heart follows one's actions. (*Sefer HaḤinukh*).

The text is made up of three parts: testifying to the rationale for the day as expressed in the first version of the Ten Commandments – the theme of creation; the blessing usually recited before partaking of wine; and the sanctification of the day, which contains the added rationale of the exodus from Egypt which is found in the second version of the Ten Commandments (*Devarim* 5:14). Both aspects, creation and the exodus, are related. The one speaks of the God of creation; the other, the God of redemption. The one reminds man that he is not God; the other describes what can happen in a society where rulers come to see themselves as gods. In that sense, Shabbat is not only a religious institution but a political and moral one as well.

Blessed are You, LORD our God, King of the Universe,
who has made us holy through His commandments,
who has favored us,
and in love and favor gave us His holy Sabbath as a heritage,
a remembrance of the work of creation.
It is the first among the holy days of assembly,
a remembrance of the exodus from Egypt.
For You chose us and sanctified us from all the peoples,
and in love and favor gave us Your holy Sabbath as a heritage.
Blessed are You, LORD,
who sanctifies the Sabbath.

It is customary for all present to drink of the wine.

---

how the Sabbath preserves time and space for the family against the pressures of the world outside. As we walked away from the school, Penelope turned to me and said, "That Sabbath of yours is saving the parents' marriages." (Rabbi Jonathan Sacks)

ANI TEFILLA • אני תפילה

It was during the last of the Shabbat meals, Seuda Shelishit, that the founder of Ḥabad Hasidism, Rabbi Shneur Zalman of Liadi, asked his assistant to bring in the young Lithuanian peasant who had been standing outside the synagogue door. In answer to the assistant's questioning look, the Rebbe said, "I feel his Jewish soul; he is one of us."

The young man came in and after being asked by the Rebbe about his parentage, explained that he was a foundling, left at the doorstep of a kind Christian couple with no children. But he always felt an affinity toward Jews and Judaism. "You were left by your parents escaping a pogrom and certain death. You are a Jew," said the Rebbe.

The Rebbe went on to give a learned discourse and asked the young man "Do you understand?" "Nyet," he replied. The Rebbe then gave a brilliant analogy, interweaving a moving story with mystical symbolism. Again he asked the young man, "Do you understand?" to which he again replied "Nyet." And then the Rebbe started a melody, a wordless song, filled with heartfelt yearning for the Messiah, suffused with love of Torah and desire to joyously hold on to the departing Shabbat. The disciples danced, and the Russian peasant danced. With tears streaming down his cheeks, the youth turned to the Rebbe and cried out, "Now I understand." (Rabbi Shlomo Riskin)

בָּרוּךְ אַתָּה יהוה אֱלֹהֵינוּ מֶלֶךְ הָעוֹלָם
אֲשֶׁר קִדְּשָׁנוּ בְּמִצְוֹתָיו, וְרָצָה בָנוּ
וְשַׁבַּת קָדְשׁוֹ בְּאַהֲבָה וּבְרָצוֹן הִנְחִילָנוּ
זִכָּרוֹן לְמַעֲשֵׂה בְרֵאשִׁית
כִּי הוּא יוֹם תְּחִלָּה לְמִקְרָאֵי קֹדֶשׁ
זֵכֶר לִיצִיאַת מִצְרָיִם
כִּי בָנוּ בָחַרְתָּ וְאוֹתָנוּ קִדַּשְׁתָּ מִכָּל הָעַמִּים
וְשַׁבַּת קָדְשְׁךָ בְּאַהֲבָה וּבְרָצוֹן הִנְחַלְתָּנוּ.
בָּרוּךְ אַתָּה יהוה, מְקַדֵּשׁ הַשַּׁבָּת.

It is customary for all present to drink of the wine.

INTRODUCTION TO ZEMIROT

Recall that Psalm 92, the song for the Shabbat day, recited toward the end of *Kabbalat Shabbat*, and again during *Pesukei DeZimra*, and again at the end of *Musaf*, begins with the words "A song for the Sabbath day. It is good to thank Hashem and sing songs (*lezamer*) to Your name." Singing is an expression of one's happiness and, instead, sometimes it is a way to achieve a feeling of happiness. That is why singing *zemirot* or hymns are such an indelible part of the Shabbat meal experience.

The *Or Zarua* (*Shabbat* 42:4) points to a midrash (see the *Biur Tefilla* comment on *Kedusha* of *Shaḥarit* on page 336) which implies that there is a spiritual dimension of the songs that puts us in the category of angels. That is possible because on Shabbat we are so divorced from our daily concerns that we can dedicate ourselves to spirituality in a way simply not possible during the week.

The *zemirot* were written by both the famous and the anonymous over the centuries, each focusing on a different theme or aspect of Shabbat.

ANI TEFILLA • אני תפילה

Once, while making a television documentary about the state of the family in Britain, I took Penelope Leach, Britain's leading childcare expert, to see what happened in a Jewish school on Friday morning. The children, as usual, were performing their "mock Shabbat," role-playing what would happen that night at home. Penelope watched fascinated. The five-year-old parents blessed the five-year-old children and welcomed the five-year-old guests. When it was over, she asked one five-year-old boy what he liked most about the Sabbath. "I like it," he said, "because it's the only time Daddy doesn't have to rush off." It was a revealing insight into

ZEMIROT FOR SHABBAT EVENING

כָּל מְקַדֵּשׁ All who fittingly sanctify[B] the seventh day, / All who protect the Sabbath properly from desecration, / Will have great reward in accord with their deed. / "Each in his own camp, each under his own banner." *Num. 1*

Lovers of the Lord, who await the building of the Temple, / Be glad and joyful on the Sabbath as if receiving the gift of God's inheritance, / Raise your hands in holiness and say to God: / "Blessed is the Lord who has given rest to His people Israel." *1 Kings 8*

Seekers of the Lord, offspring of His beloved Abraham,[I] / Who are slow to leave the Sabbath but hasten to enter it, / Who rejoice to keep it and make its *eiruv* – / "This is the day the Lord has made, let us rejoice and be glad in it." *Ps. 118*

Remember Moses' Torah, from which the laws of Sabbath are learned,[B] / Engraved is the seventh day like a bedecked bride between her companions,[I] / The pure inherit it and sanctify it with the words: "All that He had made… / With the seventh day God completed the work He had done." *Gen. 2*

It is a sacred day from beginning to end, / All Jacob's offspring will honor it as the King's word and decree, / Resting on it and rejoicing with delights of food and drink. / "All the congregation of Israel will observe it." *Ex. 12*

Extend Your loving-kindness to those who know You, zealous and retributive God, / Those who keep the seventh day, fulfilling "Remember" and "Observe," / Grant them the joy of Jerusalem rebuilt, make them shine with the light of Your face. / "Fill them with the rich plenty of Your House, give them drink from Your river of delights." *Ps. 36*

Help those who, on the seventh day, rest from plow and harvest, / Who walk slowly, and eat three meals to bless You. / May their righteousness shine like the light of the seven days, / Lord God of Israel, grant completion. *1 Sam. 14*

חֲרוּתָה... כְּכַלָּה בֵּין רֵעוֹתֶיהָ מְשֻׁבָּצָה – *Engraved… like a bedecked bride between her companions.* Shabbat stands out among the other days of the week and its observance is a touchstone of Jewish identity. A Jew who is observant in general is nevertheless popularly known as someone who is *"shomer Shabbat"* (a Shabbat observer), for a commitment to Shabbat is symbolic of a more intimate relationship with God, like a bride and her groom.

BIUR TEFILLA • ביאור תפילה

זִכְרוּ תּוֹרַת מֹשֶׁה בְּמִצְוַת שַׁבָּת גְּרוּסָה – *Remember Moses' Torah, from which the laws of Sabbath are learned.* This could be understood as a reference to the Oral Law which is the source of a wealth of laws and information about Shabbat observance. Both the Oral and the Written Law were given at the same time.

זמירות לליל שבת

כָּל מְקַדֵּשׁ[ב] שְׁבִיעִי כָּרָאוּי לוֹ / כָּל שׁוֹמֵר שַׁבָּת כַּדָּת, מֵחַלְּלוֹ / שְׂכָרוֹ הַרְבֵּה מְאֹד
עַל פִּי פָעֳלוֹ / אִישׁ עַל־מַחֲנֵהוּ וְאִישׁ עַל־דִּגְלוֹ: במדבר א

אוֹהֲבֵי יהוה הַמְחַכִּים לְבִנְיַן אֲרִיאֵל / בְּיוֹם הַשַּׁבָּת שִׂישׂוּ וְשִׂמְחוּ כִּמְקַבְּלֵי מַתַּן
נַחֲלִיאֵל / גַּם שְׂאוּ יְדֵיכֶם קֹדֶשׁ וְאִמְרוּ לָאֵל / בָּרוּךְ יהוה אֲשֶׁר נָתַן מְנוּחָה מלכים א, ח
לְעַמּוֹ יִשְׂרָאֵל:

דּוֹרְשֵׁי יהוה זֶרַע אַבְרָהָם אוֹהֲבוֹ[ע] / הַמְאַחֲרִים לָצֵאת מִן הַשַּׁבָּת וּמְמַהֲרִים
לָבוֹא / וּשְׂמֵחִים לְשָׁמְרוֹ וּלְעָרֵב עֵרוּבוֹ / זֶה־הַיּוֹם עָשָׂה יהוה, נָגִילָה וְנִשְׂמְחָה בוֹ: תהלים קיח

זִכְרוּ תּוֹרַת מֹשֶׁה בְּמִצְוַת שַׁבָּת גְּרוּסָה[ב] / חֲרוּתָה לַיּוֹם הַשְּׁבִיעִי, כְּכַלָּה בֵּין רֵעוֹתֶיהָ
מְשֻׁבָּצָה[ע] / טְהוֹרִים יִירָשׁוּהָ, וִיקַדְּשׁוּהָ בְּמַאֲמַר כָּל אֲשֶׁר עָשָׂה / וַיְכַל אֱלֹהִים בראשית ב
בַּיּוֹם הַשְּׁבִיעִי מְלַאכְתּוֹ אֲשֶׁר עָשָׂה:

יוֹם קָדוֹשׁ הוּא, מִבּוֹאוֹ וְעַד צֵאתוֹ / כָּל זֶרַע יַעֲקֹב יְכַבְּדוּהוּ, כִּדְבַר הַמֶּלֶךְ וְדָתוֹ /
לָנוּחַ בּוֹ וְלִשְׂמֹחַ בְּתַעֲנוּג אָכוֹל וְשָׁתֹה / כָּל־עֲדַת יִשְׂרָאֵל יַעֲשׂוּ אֹתוֹ: שמות יב

מְשֹׁךְ חַסְדְּךָ לְיוֹדְעֶיךָ, אֵל קַנּוֹא וְנוֹקֵם / נוֹטְרֵי יוֹם הַשְּׁבִיעִי זָכוֹר וְשָׁמוֹר לְהָקֵם /
שַׂמְּחֵם בְּבִנְיַן שָׁלֵם, בְּאוֹר פָּנֶיךָ תַּבְהִיקֵם / יִרְוְיֻן מִדֶּשֶׁן בֵּיתֶךָ, וְנַחַל עֲדָנֶיךָ תַשְׁקֵם: תהלים לו

עֲזֹר לַשּׁוֹבְתִים בַּשְּׁבִיעִי, בֶּחָרִישׁ וּבַקָּצִיר עוֹלָמִים / פּוֹסְעִים בּוֹ פְּסִיעָה קְטַנָּה,
סוֹעֲדִים בּוֹ, לְבָרֵךְ שָׁלֹשׁ פְּעָמִים / צִדְקָתָם תַּצְהִיר כְּאוֹר שִׁבְעַת הַיָּמִים / יהוה שמואל א, יד
אֱלֹהֵי יִשְׂרָאֵל, הָבָה תָמִים:

BIUR TEFILLA • ביאור תפילה

כָּל מְקַדֵּשׁ – *All who fittingly sanctify.* This piyut or liturgical poem focuses on keeping the Shabbat, particularly the positive mitzvot associated with it and their reward.

IYUN TEFILLA • עיון תפילה

דּוֹרְשֵׁי יהוה זֶרַע אַבְרָהָם אוֹהֲבוֹ – *Seekers of the Lord, offspring of His beloved Abraham.* All of us long to be touched, most of us long for an encounter with the Divine. As the children of Avraham, we are all "seekers of Hashem" for he himself came to believe in God on his own by searching. We at least have the benefit of thousands of years of tradition.

How will you use that history for your own search?

מְנוּחָה וְשִׂמְחָה Rest and joy,[B] light for all Jews,
Is the Sabbath day, day of delights;
Those who keep and recall it bear witness
That in six days all creation was made.

The highest heavens, land and seas,
The hosts of heaven, high and sublime;
Sea monsters, humans and all wild beasts,
Were created by God, the LORD, who formed all worlds.[1]

It was He who spoke to His treasured people:
"Keep it to make it holy from beginning to end."
The holy Sabbath is His day of delight,
For on it God rested from all His work.

Through the Sabbath commandment
God will give you strength,
Rise, pray to Him, and He will invigorate you.
Recite the Nishmat prayer, and the Kedusha,
Then eat with joy, for He is pleased with you.

With twin loaves,[B] and wine for the Kiddush,
With many delicacies and a willing spirit;
Those who delight in it shall merit great reward:
The coming of the redeemer, and life in the World to Come.

God's creation of this world. The bottom of the letter is open, says the Gemara, to indicate that man is given free will; the world of choices in this world is open to him, so that if he wishes to choose not to conform, he may easily do so. The opening at the side of the *heh*, however, indicates that Heaven always recognizes the possibility of return, to go back under the protective dome and comfort of Heaven if one would only choose to do so.

BIUR TEFILLA • ביאור תפילה

בְּמִשְׁנֶה לֶחֶם – *With twin loaves.* A reference to the two loaves of bread on which the blessing of *HaMotzi* is said before the meal on Shabbat. This is a reminder of the double portion of manna which was collected on Fridays by the Israelites in the desert so that they would not need to perform the labor of collecting it on Shabbat.

Some suggest that this song was intended to be sung on Friday night while others contend it was to be sung on Shabbat after lunch. What "proofs" might one bring for each opinion from the words of the song?

מְנוּחָה וְשִׂמְחָה אוֹר לַיְּהוּדִים
יוֹם שַׁבָּתוֹן, יוֹם מַחֲמַדִּים
שׁוֹמְרָיו וְזוֹכְרָיו הֵמָּה מְעִידִים
כִּי לְשִׁשָּׁה כֹּל בְּרוּאִים וְעוֹמְדִים.

שְׁמֵי שָׁמַיִם, אֶרֶץ וְיַמִּים
כָּל צְבָא מָרוֹם גְּבוֹהִים וְרָמִים
תַּנִּין וְאָדָם וְחַיַּת רְאֵמִים
כִּי בְּיָהּ יהוה צוּר עוֹלָמִים.

הוּא אֲשֶׁר דִּבֶּר לְעַם סְגֻלָּתוֹ
שָׁמוֹר לְקַדְּשׁוֹ מִבּוֹאוֹ עַד צֵאתוֹ
שַׁבַּת קֹדֶשׁ יוֹם חֶמְדָּתוֹ
כִּי בוֹ שָׁבַת אֵל מִכָּל מְלַאכְתּוֹ.

בְּמִצְוַת שַׁבָּת אֵל יַחֲלִיצָךְ
קוּם קְרָא אֵלָיו, יָחִישׁ לְאַמְּצָךְ
נִשְׁמַת כָּל חַי וְגַם נַעֲרִיצָךְ
אֱכֹל בְּשִׂמְחָה כִּי כְבָר רָצָךְ.

בְּמִשְׁנֶה לֶחֶם וְקִדּוּשׁ רַבָּה
בְּרֹב מַטְעַמִּים וְרוּחַ נְדִיבָה
יִזְכּוּ לְרַב טוּב הַמִּתְעַנְּגִים בָּהּ
בְּבִיאַת גּוֹאֵל לְחַיֵּי הָעוֹלָם הַבָּא.

IYUN TEFILLA • עיון תפילה

כִּי בְּיָהּ ידוד צוּר עוֹלָמִים – *Were created by God, the Lord, who formed all worlds.* The Gemara (*Menaḥot* 29b) relates that, the name of God used here is comprised of two letters, *yod* and *heh* which represent God's creation respectively of the World to Come and this world. The letter *heh* represents

BIUR TEFILLA • ביאור תפילה

מְנוּחָה וְשִׂמְחָה – *Rest and joy.* The song speaks to the testimony Shabbat observance bears to creation in both the upper and lower worlds. In the merit of keeping the positive aspects of the day including praying, eating, making kiddush and the like, man will acquire the World to Come.

מַה־יְּדִידוּת How beloved[B] is your rest, Sabbath Queen, / We run to greet you: Come, royal bride, / Dressed in fine robes. We light the light with blessing. / All labors end [as is said:] "You shall do no work."
To savor the delights of fowl, quail and fish.

In advance all kinds of tasty food have been prepared, / Fattened chickens made ready while it was still day. / Varied dishes set out, and fragrant wines to drink, / And special delicacies all three times.
To savor the delights of fowl, quail and fish.

They shall inherit Jacob's heritage, a heritage unbounded, / Rich and poor will honor [the Sabbath] and be worthy of redemption, / If you keep the Sabbath day you will be My special treasure, / Six days shall you labor – and on the seventh let us rejoice.
To savor the delights of fowl, quail and fish.

Your secular concerns are forbidden; so too are calculations. / Reflections are permitted, and arranging matches for girls, / And teaching a child a book, and singing songs of praise, / And meditating on fine words at every place and gathering.
To savor the delights of fowl, quail and fish.

Your walk shall be unhurried; you shall call the Sabbath a delight. / Sleep too is praiseworthy, for it refreshes the spirit. / Therefore my soul yearns for you, to rest in you in love, / As if within a fence of roses: on it son and daughter rest.
To savor the delights of fowl, quail and fish.

A foretaste of the World to Come[B] is the day of Sabbath rest. / All who take delight in it will be worthy of great joy. / They will be delivered with relief from the birthpangs of the Messiah, / May our redemption spring forth, and sadness and sighing flee away.
To savor the delights of fowl, quail and fish.

Shabbat in particular is not simply passive, a state of inactivity, but rather something which each of us must actively create, as it were. On the verse (*Bereshit* 2:1) which says that God finished creation on the seventh day, Rashi cites the midrash which wonders how it is that God could finish creation on that day when in fact He was supposed to have finished creating on the sixth day. One answer offered is that He actually did create something on Shabbat, namely rest. What distinguishes Shabbat rest from pure relaxation is partially outlined in the rest of the song.

Refer to the appendix on *kavod* and *oneg* (on page 851) and see how many laws that one finds there can be found in this poem.

מֵעֵין עוֹלָם הַבָּא – *A foretaste of the World to Come.* The Gemara (*Berakhot* 57b) says that Shabbat is one-sixtieth of what the World to Come is like.

What do you think this might mean?

מַה־יְּדִידוּת מְנוּחָתֵךְ, אַתְּ שַׁבָּת הַמַּלְכָּה
בְּכֵן נָרוּץ לִקְרָאתֵךְ, בּוֹאִי כַלָּה נְסוּכָה
לְבוּשׁ בִּגְדֵי חֲמוּדוֹת, לְהַדְלִיק נֵר בִּבְרָכָה
וַתֵּכֶל כָּל הָעֲבוֹדוֹת, לֹא תַעֲשׂוּ מְלָאכָה.
לְהִתְעַנֵּג בְּתַעֲנוּגִים בַּרְבּוּרִים וּשְׂלָו וְדָגִים.

מֵעֶרֶב מַזְמִינִים כָּל מִינֵי מַטְעַמִּים
מִבְּעוֹד יוֹם מוּכָנִים תַּרְנְגוֹלִים מְפֻטָּמִים
וְלַעֲרֹךְ כַּמָּה מִינִים, שְׁתוֹת יֵינוֹת מְבֻשָּׂמִים
וְתַפְנוּקֵי מַעֲדַנִּים בְּכָל שָׁלֹשׁ פְּעָמִים.
לְהִתְעַנֵּג בְּתַעֲנוּגִים בַּרְבּוּרִים וּשְׂלָו וְדָגִים.

נַחֲלַת יַעֲקֹב יִירָשׁ, בְּלִי מְצָרִים נַחֲלָה
וִיכַבְּדוּהוּ עָשִׁיר וָרָשׁ, וְתִזְכּוּ לִגְאֻלָּה
יוֹם שַׁבָּת אִם תְּכַבֵּדוּ וִהְיִיתֶם לִי סְגֻלָּה
שֵׁשֶׁת יָמִים תַּעֲבֵדוּ וּבַשְּׁבִיעִי נָגִילָה.
לְהִתְעַנֵּג בְּתַעֲנוּגִים בַּרְבּוּרִים וּשְׂלָו וְדָגִים.

חֲפָצֶיךָ אֲסוּרִים וְגַם לַחְשֹׁב חֶשְׁבּוֹנוֹת
הִרְהוּרִים מֻתָּרִים וּלְשַׁדֵּךְ הַבָּנוֹת
וְתִינוֹק לְלַמְּדוֹ סֵפֶר, לַמְנַצֵּחַ בִּנְגִינוֹת
וְלַהֲגוֹת בְּאִמְרֵי שֶׁפֶר בְּכָל פִּנּוֹת וּמַחֲנוֹת.
לְהִתְעַנֵּג בְּתַעֲנוּגִים בַּרְבּוּרִים וּשְׂלָו וְדָגִים.

הִלּוּכָךְ יְהֵא בְנַחַת, עֹנֶג קְרָא לַשַּׁבָּת
וְהַשֵּׁנָה מְשֻׁבַּחַת כְּדָת נֶפֶשׁ מְשִׁיבַת
בְּכֵן נַפְשִׁי לְךָ עָרְגָה וְלָנוּחַ בְּחִבַּת
כַּשּׁוֹשַׁנִּים סוּגָה, בּוֹ יָנוּחוּ בֵּן וּבַת. לְהִתְעַנֵּג בְּתַעֲנוּגִים בַּרְבּוּרִים וּשְׂלָו וְדָגִים.

מֵעֵין עוֹלָם הַבָּא יוֹם שַׁבָּת מְנוּחָה
כָּל הַמִּתְעַנְּגִים בָּהּ יִזְכּוּ לְרֹב שִׂמְחָה
מֵחֶבְלֵי מָשִׁיחַ יֻצָּלוּ לִרְוָחָה
פְּדוּתֵנוּ תַצְמִיחַ, וְנָס יָגוֹן וַאֲנָחָה. לְהִתְעַנֵּג בְּתַעֲנוּגִים בַּרְבּוּרִים וּשְׂלָו וְדָגִים.

BIUR TEFILLA • ביאור תפילה

מַה־יְּדִידוּת – *How beloved.* The first stanza contains references to the source and spirit of the *Kabbalat Shabbat* service that was just recited in the synagogue. Rest on

יוֹם זֶה לְיִשְׂרָאֵל This day for Israel[B] is light and joy,
a Sabbath of serenity.
At the assembly at Sinai You decreed the laws,
Sabbath and the festivals – to keep them all my years;
Setting a table before me with courses of fine food – A Sabbath of serenity.
This day, for Israel, is light and joy, a Sabbath of serenity.

Heart's delight to a shattered people,[B]
To suffering spirits, an extra soul.
From troubled hearts may it banish sighs – A Sabbath of serenity.
This day, for Israel, is light and joy, a Sabbath of serenity.

You sanctified and blessed it above all other days.
In six days You finished the making of all worlds.
On it sad souls find quiet and safety – A Sabbath of serenity.
This day, for Israel, is light and joy, a Sabbath of serenity.

All work is forbidden by the revered One's commandment,
I will merit royal glory if I keep the Sabbath day,
Bringing the awesome One a sweetly scented gift – A Sabbath of serenity.
This day, for Israel, is light and joy, a Sabbath of serenity.

Renew our Sanctuary, remember the ruined city.
Bestow Your goodness, Savior, on one who is sad,
Yet still she spends the Sabbath in song and praise – A Sabbath of serenity.
This day, for Israel, is light and joy, a Sabbath of serenity.

---

stanzas might have been inserted later in tribute to him.

Shabbat is a day of light, happiness and rest. Elsewhere we have noted the midrash (*Bereshit Raba* 11) which claims that the added blessing that man receives on Shabbat is an increased glow. This is a theme that has already appeared in the first line of the song *Menuḥa VeSimḥa* which appears above. How might one explain this extra light? Is it the joy that comes from spending time with friends and family? Is it the glow that comes from being more well rested than any other day of the week? Is it the extra soul (*neshama yeteira*) which man receives on this day? Is it just the sheer happiness that comes from observing this day like no other?

חֶמְדַּת הַלְּבָבוֹת לְאֻמָּה שְׁבוּרָה–*Heart's delight to a shattered people.* The stanza contains a number of descriptions of the pains of a diaspora experience and personal angst. **Shabbat can provide a temporary reprieve for those feelings. How?**

יוֹם זֶה לְיִשְׂרָאֵל[ב] אוֹרָה וְשִׂמְחָה, שַׁבַּת מְנוּחָה.
צִוִּיתָ פִּקּוּדִים בְּמַעֲמַד סִינַי
שַׁבָּת וּמוֹעֲדִים לִשְׁמֹר בְּכָל שָׁנַי
לַעֲרֹךְ לְפָנַי מַשְׂאֵת וַאֲרוּחָה שַׁבַּת מְנוּחָה.
יוֹם זֶה לְיִשְׂרָאֵל אוֹרָה וְשִׂמְחָה, שַׁבַּת מְנוּחָה.

חֶמְדַּת הַלְּבָבוֹת לְאֻמָּה שְׁבוּרָה[ב]
לִנְפָשׁוֹת נִכְאָבוֹת נְשָׁמָה יְתֵרָה
לְנֶפֶשׁ מְצֵרָה יָסִיר אֲנָחָה שַׁבַּת מְנוּחָה.
יוֹם זֶה לְיִשְׂרָאֵל אוֹרָה וְשִׂמְחָה, שַׁבַּת מְנוּחָה.

קִדַּשְׁתָּ בֵּרַכְתָּ אוֹתוֹ מִכָּל יָמִים
בְּשֵׁשֶׁת כִּלִּיתָ מְלֶאכֶת עוֹלָמִים
בּוֹ מָצְאוּ עֲגוּמִים הַשְׁקֵט וּבִטְחָה שַׁבַּת מְנוּחָה.
יוֹם זֶה לְיִשְׂרָאֵל אוֹרָה וְשִׂמְחָה, שַׁבַּת מְנוּחָה.

לְאִסּוּר מְלָאכָה צִוִּיתָנוּ נוֹרָא
אֶזְכֶּה הוֹד מְלוּכָה אִם שַׁבָּת אֶשְׁמְרָה
אַקְרִיב שַׁי לַמּוֹרָא, מִנְחָה מֶרְקָחָה שַׁבַּת מְנוּחָה.
יוֹם זֶה לְיִשְׂרָאֵל אוֹרָה וְשִׂמְחָה, שַׁבַּת מְנוּחָה.

חַדֵּשׁ מִקְדָּשֵׁנוּ, זָכְרָה נֶחֱרֶבֶת
טוּבְךָ, מוֹשִׁיעֵנוּ, תְּנָה לַנֶּעֱצֶבֶת
בְּשַׁבָּת יוֹשֶׁבֶת בְּזֶמֶר וּשְׁבָחָה שַׁבַּת מְנוּחָה.
יוֹם זֶה לְיִשְׂרָאֵל אוֹרָה וְשִׂמְחָה, שַׁבַּת מְנוּחָה.

BIUR TEFILLA • ביאור תפילה

יוֹם זֶה לְיִשְׂרָאֵל – *This day for Israel.* This is yet another liturgical poem whose author is unknown. There is an acrostic in the first refrain and subsequent four stanzas that spells the name Yitzḥak, but there are different versions of the poem which include even more stanzas which would spell Yitzḥak Luria *ḥazak*, that is, the Ari; these

יָהּ רִבּוֹן Master of all worlds, our God, adored,
King of kings, over all the LORD:
Your wondrous deeds to applaud
We sing to You with one accord.
God of all worlds, our God, adored; King of kings, over all, the LORD.

Early and late my praise shall ring,
To You, holy Author of every thing:
Beasts of the field, birds that take wing.
Angels and mortals to You shall sing.
God of all worlds, our God, adored; King of kings, over all, the LORD.

Your great good deeds are vast in scale,
You humble the proud, You lift the frail.
A thousand years would not avail
Of Your works to tell the tale.
God of all worlds, our God, adored; King of kings, over all, the LORD.

Yours is the glory, the greatness too,
From the lion's jaw, Your flock rescue.
Bring Your exiles home to You:
The people You chose, deliver anew.
God of all worlds, our God, adored; King of kings, over all, the LORD.

Come back to Your Temple, Your sacred shrine,
That there in joy our souls may entwine.
In song our voices to combine,
When Jerusalem's beauty again will shine.
God of all worlds, our God, adored; King of kings, over all, the LORD.

---

who was born in Damascus, moved to Tzefat and later became the rabbi of Gaza. The poem is unusual in a few ways beginning with the fact that it is written in Aramaic rather than Hebrew. More importantly, it contains no explicit reference to Shabbat and there is no indication that it was written for that purpose. Yet it's extolling the greatness of Hashem, especially as Creator, and our unique relationship with Him has made it a standard addition to the Friday night tradition.

It is said that the poem was frequently sung during the Holocaust during particularly difficult moments.

What themes can you find that might explain this choice?

יָהּ רִבּוֹן עָלַם וְעָלְמַיָּא
אַנְתְּ הוּא מַלְכָּא מֶלֶךְ מַלְכַיָּא
עוֹבַד גְּבוּרְתָךְ וְתִמְהַיָּא
שְׁפַר קָדָמָךְ לְהַחֲוָיָא.
יָהּ רִבּוֹן עָלַם וְעָלְמַיָּא, אַנְתְּ הוּא מַלְכָּא מֶלֶךְ מַלְכַיָּא.

שְׁבָחִין אֲסַדֵּר צַפְרָא וְרַמְשָׁא
לָךְ אֱלָהָא קַדִּישָׁא דִּי בְרָא כָּל נַפְשָׁא
עִירִין קַדִּישִׁין וּבְנֵי אֱנָשָׁא
חֵיוַת בָּרָא וְעוֹפֵי שְׁמַיָּא.
יָהּ רִבּוֹן עָלַם וְעָלְמַיָּא, אַנְתְּ הוּא מַלְכָּא מֶלֶךְ מַלְכַיָּא.

רַבְרְבִין עוֹבְדָיךְ וְתַקִּיפִין
מָכֵךְ רָמַיָּא וְזָקֵף כְּפִיפִין
לוּ יְחֵי גְבַר שְׁנִין אַלְפִין
לָא יֵעֹל גְּבוּרְתָּךְ בְּחֻשְׁבְּנַיָּא.
יָהּ רִבּוֹן עָלַם וְעָלְמַיָּא, אַנְתְּ הוּא מַלְכָּא מֶלֶךְ מַלְכַיָּא.

אֱלָהָא דִּי לֵהּ יְקָר וּרְבוּתָא
פְּרֹק יָת עָנָךְ מִפֻּם אַרְיָוָתָא
וְאַפֵּק יָת עַמָּךְ מִגּוֹ גָלוּתָא
עַמָּא דִּי בְחַרְתְּ מִכָּל אֻמַּיָּא.
יָהּ רִבּוֹן עָלַם וְעָלְמַיָּא, אַנְתְּ הוּא מַלְכָּא מֶלֶךְ מַלְכַיָּא.

לְמַקְדְּשָׁךְ תּוּב וּלְקֹדֶשׁ קֻדְשִׁין
אֲתַר דִּי בֵהּ יֶחֱדוּן רוּחִין וְנַפְשִׁין
וִיזַמְּרוּן לָךְ שִׁירִין וְרַחֲשִׁין
בִּירוּשְׁלֵם קַרְתָּא דְשֻׁפְרַיָּא.
יָהּ רִבּוֹן עָלַם וְעָלְמַיָּא, אַנְתְּ הוּא מַלְכָּא מֶלֶךְ מַלְכַיָּא.

BIUR TEFILLA • ביאור תפילה

יָהּ רִבּוֹן – *Master of all.* The acrostic at the beginning of each stanza spells the name Israel, a reference to its author, Rabbi Yisrael Najara, one of the greatest poets,

צָמְאָה נַפְשִׁי My soul thirsts[B] for God, the living God
My heart and flesh will sing joyfully to the living God. *Ps. 84*
The One God created me, and said "As I live,
no one shall see Me and live."[I]

My soul thirsts for God, the living God
My heart and flesh will sing joyfully
to the living God.

He created all with wisdom, design and deliberation,
Deeply hidden though it is from the eyes of all that live.
His glory is high above all, every mouth makes known His splendor,
Blessed is He in whose hands is the life-force of all that lives.

My soul thirsts for God, the living God
My heart and flesh will sing joyfully
to the living God.

He set apart the quiet one's offspring,[B] to teach them decrees,
Which if one performs them, thereby he shall live.
Who can vindicate himself? We are like specks of dust,
Truly none can vindicate itself before You, nothing that lives.

My soul thirsts for God, the living God
My heart and flesh will sing joyfully
to the living God.

As the body needs water for its survival, so too does the soul need a connection to God. Both body and soul need their sustenance in order to thrive and feel healthy and alive. Indeed, note the motif word **חַי** *ḥai*, live or life, which appears twice in the first two lines and once in every line thereafter. The Jewish people lives, as does its faith in God.

הִבְדִּיל נִינֵי תָם – *He set apart the quiet one's offspring.* This is a reference to Yaakov who was known as a *tam* or quiet one (*Bereshit* 25:27).

IYUN TEFILLA • עיון תפילה

אֵל אֶחָד בְּרָאַנִי, וְאָמַר חַי אָנִי, כִּי לֹא יִרְאַנִי הָאָדָם וָחָי – *The One God created me, and said "As I live, no one shall see Me and live."* As sure as I am alive, says God, My word is true (Ibn Ezra on *Shemot* 33:20). And in this case, what is true is that He cannot be seen. The message is clear: God exists, even if we cannot always physically see Him. Even so, my soul knows that He is there. The heart has its reasons, said Pascal, of which reason has no knowledge.

תהלים פד

צָמְאָה נַפְשִׁי ב לֵאלֹהִים לְאֵל חָי:
לִבִּי וּבְשָׂרִי יְרַנְּנוּ אֶל אֵל־חָי:
אֵל אֶחָד בְּרָאֲנִי, וְאָמַר חַי אָנִי
כִּי לֹא יִרְאַנִי הָאָדָם וָחָי.ע

צָמְאָה נַפְשִׁי לֵאלֹהִים לְאֵל חָי
לִבִּי וּבְשָׂרִי יְרַנְּנוּ אֶל אֵל־חָי.

בָּרָא כֹל בְּחָכְמָה, בְּעֵצָה וּבִמְזִמָּה
מְאֹד נֶעְלָמָה מֵעֵינֵי כָּל חָי.
רָם עַל כֹּל כְּבוֹדוֹ, כָּל פֶּה יְחַוֶּה הוֹדוֹ
בָּרוּךְ אֲשֶׁר בְּיָדוֹ נֶפֶשׁ כָּל חָי.

צָמְאָה נַפְשִׁי לֵאלֹהִים לְאֵל חָי
לִבִּי וּבְשָׂרִי יְרַנְּנוּ אֶל אֵל־חָי.

הִבְדִּיל נִינֵי תָם,ב חֻקִּים לְהוֹרוֹתָם
אֲשֶׁר יַעֲשֶׂה אוֹתָם הָאָדָם וָחָי.
מִי זֶה יִצְטַדָּק, נִמְשַׁל לְאָבָק דָּק
אֱמֶת, כִּי לֹא יִצְדַּק לְפָנֶיךָ כָּל חָי.

צָמְאָה נַפְשִׁי לֵאלֹהִים לְאֵל חָי
לִבִּי וּבְשָׂרִי יְרַנְּנוּ אֶל אֵל־חָי.

BIUR TEFILLA • ביאור תפילה

צָמְאָה נַפְשִׁי – *My soul thirsts.* Aside from its opening line, the first letter of every stanza spells out the name of Rabbi Avraham ibn Ezra, the famous Spanish exegete and poet whose varied interests extended to mathematics and astronomy in the twelfth century.

The first line, based on *Tehillim* 42:3, sets the stage for a focal point of religious life in general and Shabbat in particular. We all long to be touched, we all long for connection. The poet expresses that search in terms of a thirst that yearns to be quenched.

In the heart, the inclination is like a viper's poison,
How then can we return, and be like flesh that lives?
Those who have gone astray, if they wished,
could turn from their way,
Before they go to their rest in the place destined
for all that lives.

My soul thirsts for God, the living God
My heart and flesh will sing joyfully
mto the living God.

For everything, I shall thank You, every mouth
shall declare Your oneness,
You who open Your hand and satisfy all that lives.
Recall the love of ancient times, and revive those
who slumber,
Bring near the days when the Messiah shall live.

My soul thirsts for God, the living God
My heart and flesh will sing joyfully
to the living God.

See who is the true mistress,[B] when the handmaid says,
"No, your son is dead while my son lives."
I will bow face down and spread my hands toward you,
When I open my mouth to say: "The soul of all that lives."

My soul thirsts for God, the living God
My heart and flesh will sing joyfully
to the living God.

---

is Sarah, the handmaid is Hagar, the mother of Yishmael, and the speech she gives is based upon that of the case of the two mothers who came before King Shlomo (*Melakhim* I 20:31).

בְּלֵב יֵצֶר חָשׁוּב כִּדְמוּת חֲמַת עַכְשׁוּב
וְאֵיכָכָה יָשׁוּב הַבָּשָׂר הֶחָי.
נְסוֹגִים אִם אָבוּ, וּמִדַּרְכָּם שָׁבוּ
טֶרֶם יִשְׁכָּבוּ בֵּית מוֹעֵד לְכָל חָי.

צָמְאָה נַפְשִׁי לֵאלֹהִים לְאֵל חָי
לִבִּי וּבְשָׂרִי יְרַנְּנוּ אֶל אֵל־חָי.

עַל כֹּל אֲהוֹדֶךָ, כָּל פֶּה תְּיַחֲדֶךָ
פּוֹתֵחַ אֶת יָדֶךָ וּמַשְׂבִּיעַ לְכָל חָי.
זְכֹר אַהֲבַת קְדוּמִים, וְהַחֲיֵה נִרְדָּמִים
וְקָרֵב הַיָּמִים אֲשֶׁר בֶּן יִשַׁי חָי.

צָמְאָה נַפְשִׁי לֵאלֹהִים לְאֵל חָי
לִבִּי וּבְשָׂרִי יְרַנְּנוּ אֶל אֵל־חָי.

רְאֵה לִגְבֶרֶת אֱמֶת,ב שִׁפְחָה נוֹאֶמֶת
לֹא כִי, בְּנֵךְ הַמֵּת וּבְנִי הֶחָי.
אֶקֹּד עַל אַפִּי, וְאֶפְרֹשׂ לְךָ כַּפִּי
עֵת אֶפְתַּח פִּי בְּנִשְׁמַת כָּל חָי.

צָמְאָה נַפְשִׁי לֵאלֹהִים לְאֵל חָי
לִבִּי וּבְשָׂרִי יְרַנְּנוּ אֶל אֵל־חָי.

BIUR TEFILLA • ביאור תפילה

רְאֵה לִגְבֶרֶת אֱמֶת – *See who is the true mistress*…The references in this stanza may be a polemic against the Islamic world where Ibn Ezra first lived. The true mistress

צוּר מִשֶּׁלּוֹ The Rock from whom we have eaten: Bless Him, my faithful friends;
we have sufficed, we have left over, just as the LORD said.

He feeds His world – our Shepherd, our Father,
we have eaten of His bread, His wine we have drunk.
So let us thank His name, let us praise Him with our mouths,
saying, singing: None is holy like the LORD.
The Rock from whom we have eaten: Bless Him, my faithful friends;
we have sufficed, we have left over, just as the LORD said.

With song and sound of thanks, we shall bless our God,
for the gift He gave our fathers: A lovely land.
With food and sustenance He has satisfied our souls.
His kindness overwhelms us: True is the LORD.
The Rock from whom we have eaten: Bless Him, my faithful friends;
we have sufficed, we have left over, just as the LORD said.

Have compassion in Your love for Your people, our Rock,
for Zion, Your home of glory, Temple of our splendor.
The son of David Your servant: may he come and redeem us,
breath of our life, anointed of the LORD.
The Rock from whom we have eaten: Bless Him, my faithful friends;
we have sufficed, we have left over, just as the LORD said.

May the Temple be rebuilt, Zion's city full again;
there we will sing a new song as we go up in joy,
to the Compassionate, the Holy One – may He be blessed and raised on high –
with a full cup of wine, sign of the blessing of the LORD.
The Rock from whom we have eaten: Bless Him, my faithful friends;
we have sufficed, we have left over, just as the LORD said.

Birkat HaMazon can be found on page 734.

---

the themes of first three blessings of *Birkat HaMazon*. (See if you can find the language in each that connects them. *Birkat HaMazon* can be found on page 739). The final stanza's reference to a cup of wine alludes to the custom of saying *Birkat HaMazon* over wine which is drunk at the conclusion of the blessing.

The opening is apparently based upon a midrash (*Bereshit Raba* 43:7) in which Avraham, the paradigm of *ḥesed* (kindness) to others is said to have offered food and drink to passersby. At the conclusion of the meal he instructed them to say a blessing of thanks and they inquired to whom it should be directed, whereupon he replied "Bless the God of the world, whose food (מִשֶּׁלּוֹ) we have eaten." In other words, the food we eat is not ours, no matter how hard we worked for it, prepared it, or shared it with others. Rather, everything comes from Hashem, "the Rock from whom we have eaten."

צוּר מִשֶּׁלּוֹ אָכַלְנוּ בָּרְכוּ אֱמוּנַי
שָׂבַעְנוּ וְהוֹתַרְנוּ כִּדְבַר יהוה.

הַזָּן אֶת עוֹלָמוֹ רוֹעֵנוּ אָבִינוּ
אָכַלְנוּ אֶת לַחְמוֹ וְיֵינוֹ שָׁתִינוּ
עַל כֵּן נוֹדֶה לִשְׁמוֹ וּנְהַלְּלוֹ בְּפִינוּ
אָמַרְנוּ וְעָנִינוּ אֵין קָדוֹשׁ כַּיהוה.
צוּר מִשֶּׁלּוֹ אָכַלְנוּ, בָּרְכוּ אֱמוּנַי, שָׂבַעְנוּ וְהוֹתַרְנוּ כִּדְבַר יהוה.

בְּשִׁיר וְקוֹל תּוֹדָה נְבָרֵךְ אֱלֹהֵינוּ
עַל אֶרֶץ חֶמְדָּה שֶׁהִנְחִיל לַאֲבוֹתֵינוּ
מָזוֹן וְצֵידָה הִשְׂבִּיעַ לְנַפְשֵׁנוּ
חַסְדּוֹ גָּבַר עָלֵינוּ וֶאֱמֶת יהוה.
צוּר מִשֶּׁלּוֹ אָכַלְנוּ, בָּרְכוּ אֱמוּנַי, שָׂבַעְנוּ וְהוֹתַרְנוּ כִּדְבַר יהוה.

רַחֵם בְּחַסְדֶּךָ עַל עַמְּךָ צוּרֵנוּ
עַל צִיּוֹן מִשְׁכַּן כְּבוֹדֶךָ זְבוּל בֵּית תִּפְאַרְתֵּנוּ
בֶּן דָּוִד עַבְדֶּךָ יָבוֹא וְיִגְאָלֵנוּ
רוּחַ אַפֵּינוּ מְשִׁיחַ יהוה.
צוּר מִשֶּׁלּוֹ אָכַלְנוּ, בָּרְכוּ אֱמוּנַי, שָׂבַעְנוּ וְהוֹתַרְנוּ כִּדְבַר יהוה.

יִבָּנֶה הַמִּקְדָּשׁ עִיר צִיּוֹן תְּמַלֵּא
וְשָׁם נָשִׁיר שִׁיר חָדָשׁ וּבִרְנָנָה נַעֲלֶה
הָרַחֲמָן הַנִּקְדָּשׁ יִתְבָּרַךְ וְיִתְעַלֶּה
עַל כּוֹס יַיִן מָלֵא כְּבִרְכַּת יהוה.
צוּר מִשֶּׁלּוֹ אָכַלְנוּ, בָּרְכוּ אֱמוּנַי, שָׂבַעְנוּ וְהוֹתַרְנוּ כִּדְבַר יהוה.

ברכת המזון *can be found on page 735.*

BIUR TEFILLA • ביאור תפילה

צוּר מִשֶּׁלּוֹ אָכַלְנוּ – *The Rock from whom we have eaten.* This song is traditionally the last one sung for the evening as it was apparently intended as a prelude to *Birkat HaMazon*, the blessing said at the conclusion of the meal. The first three stanzas reflect

Shaharit for Shabbat

The following order of prayers and blessings, which departs from that of most prayer books, is based on the consensus of recent halakhic authorities.

ON WAKING

On waking, our first thought should be that we are in the presence of God. Since we are forbidden to speak God's name until we have washed our hands, the following prayer is said, which, without mentioning God's name, acknowledges His presence and gives thanks for a new day and for the gift of life.

מוֹדֶה I thank You,[A] living and eternal King,
for giving me back my soul in mercy.
Great is Your faithfulness.[B]

---

necessarily gets out of bed every morning bursting with energy, although Jewish law recommends it, but it does enable one to meet the day knowing that one is not alone.

HILKHOT TEFILLA • הלכות תפילה

The custom is to say the preliminary blessings after waking in the morning but, if one did not, then they may be recited before communal services begin.

ANI TEFILLA • אני תפילה

מוֹדֶה אֲנִי – *I thank You.* Many people wake up in the morning and think only of the challenges or routines that lie ahead. But waking up thankful means that one's very first thought in the day consists of thinking about the miracle of being alive. Perhaps that is why the sentence isn't written *ani modeh* (I thank) but rather *modeh ani* (literally, thankful am I); the very first word from a Jew's lips in the morning is gratitude. **Think for a moment about the miracle of your own life. Be thankful.**

BIUR TEFILLA • ביאור תפילה

רַבָּה אֱמוּנָתֶךָ – *Great is Your faithfulness.* The phrase could just as easily mean "Your faith in us is great," that is to say, each day begins anew with Hashem believing we can do better and confident that we can make today different. No one should feel stuck in yesterday.

שחרית לשבת

The following order of prayers and blessings, which departs from that of most prayer books, is based on the consensus of recent halakhic authorities.

השכמת הבוקר

On waking, our first thought should be that we are in the presence of God. Since we are forbidden to speak God's name until we have washed our hands, the following prayer is said, which, without mentioning God's name, acknowledges His presence and gives thanks for a new day and for the gift of life.

מוֹדֶה/ *women* מוֹדָה/ אֲנִי[א] לְפָנֶיךָ מֶלֶךְ חַי וְקַיָּם
שֶׁהֶחֱזַרְתָּ בִּי נִשְׁמָתִי בְּחֶמְלָה
רַבָּה אֱמוּנָתֶךָ.[ב]

INTRODUCTION TO THE PRELIMINARY BLESSINGS AND KORBANOT

We tend to be a little self-absorbed in the morning and understandably so. We are tired from the night before or anxious or excited about the day ahead. It takes us a while to get our act together, to gather our wits, take care of our bodily needs, get dressed and greet the day. During the week, in the intense world that many of us live in, there is barely time to think as we check the paper or our electronic media before rushing out the door to begin our day. On Shabbat, there is more time to be present in the moment to appreciate that it is another new day, that one has one's health, that the sun is shining (somewhere, even if not in our part of the world), that there is much to be grateful for. Yet, we still need to be reminded. The siddur is designed to help do that.

The prayers which follow in this introductory section, then, are really quite personal; indeed, many of them were intended to be said before we even get to the synagogue, some even before we have gotten out of bed and put our feet on the floor. In Judaism, taking stock means first and foremost not only an awareness of oneself but God-awareness as well, the sense that there is a higher, transcendent Being and meaning to life. That awareness is ideally what provides perspective to one's day, it anchors you in a value system and direction that other people can spend years searching for. That doesn't mean that one

Wash hands and say the following blessings.
Some have the custom to say "Wisdom begins" below at this point.

בָּרוּךְ Blessed are You, LORD our God, King of the Universe,
who has made us holy through His commandments,
and has commanded us about washing hands.[A]

בָּרוּךְ Blessed are You, LORD our God, King of the Universe,
who formed[I] man in wisdom
and created in him many orifices and cavities.
It is revealed and known before the throne of Your glory
that were one of them to be ruptured or blocked,
it would be impossible to survive
and stand before You.
Blessed are You, LORD,
Healer of all flesh who does wondrous deeds.

Some say:

רֵאשִׁית חָכְמָה Wisdom begins in awe of the LORD; *Ps. 111*
all who fulfill [His commandments] gain good understanding;
His praise is ever-lasting.
The Torah Moses commanded us *Deut. 33*
is the heritage of the congregation of Jacob.
Listen, my son, to your father's instruction, *Prov. 1*
and do not forsake your mother's teaching.
May the Torah be my faith and Almighty God my help.
Blessed be the name of His glorious kingdom for ever and all time.

IYUN TEFILLA • עיון תפילה

אֲשֶׁר יָצַר – *Who formed.* If one wants to see the beauty of creation, the complexity of life, if one wants to be in awe, one need look no further than the miracle of one's own body. And rather than think only about the noblest things that the body can do, we focus, too, on the most base, on that which is generally not spoken of. For therein lies one of the most miraculous aspects of bodily function, the ability to distinguish between good and bad, the needed and the superfluous. Imagine what would happen if we could not relieve ourselves! Every time one uses the bathroom is an opportunity for thankfulness and to recognize the presence of the Divine.

Wash hands and say the following blessings.
Some have the custom to say רֵאשִׁית חָכְמָה *below at this point.*

בָּרוּךְ אַתָּה יהוה אֱלֹהֵינוּ מֶלֶךְ הָעוֹלָם
אֲשֶׁר קִדְּשָׁנוּ בְּמִצְוֹתָיו וְצִוָּנוּ עַל נְטִילַת יָדָיִם.[א]

בָּרוּךְ אַתָּה יהוה אֱלֹהֵינוּ מֶלֶךְ הָעוֹלָם
אֲשֶׁר יָצַר[ע] אֶת הָאָדָם בְּחָכְמָה
וּבָרָא בוֹ נְקָבִים נְקָבִים, חֲלוּלִים חֲלוּלִים.
גָּלוּי וְיָדוּעַ לִפְנֵי כִסֵּא כְבוֹדֶךָ
שֶׁאִם יִפָּתֵחַ אֶחָד מֵהֶם אוֹ יִסָּתֵם אֶחָד מֵהֶם
אִי אֶפְשָׁר לְהִתְקַיֵּם וְלַעֲמֹד לְפָנֶיךָ.
בָּרוּךְ אַתָּה יהוה, רוֹפֵא כָל בָּשָׂר וּמַפְלִיא לַעֲשׂוֹת.

Some say:

רֵאשִׁית חָכְמָה יִרְאַת יהוה, שֵׂכֶל טוֹב לְכָל־עֹשֵׂיהֶם, תְּהִלָּתוֹ עֹמֶדֶת לָעַד: תהלים קיא
תּוֹרָה צִוָּה־לָנוּ מֹשֶׁה, מוֹרָשָׁה קְהִלַּת יַעֲקֹב: דברים לג
שְׁמַע בְּנִי מוּסַר אָבִיךָ וְאַל־תִּטֹּשׁ תּוֹרַת אִמֶּךָ: משלי א
תּוֹרָה תְּהֵא אֱמוּנָתִי, וְאֵל שַׁדַּי בְּעֶזְרָתִי.
בָּרוּךְ שֵׁם כְּבוֹד מַלְכוּתוֹ לְעוֹלָם וָעֶד.

ANI TEFILLA • אני תפילה

עַל נְטִילַת יָדָיִם – *About washing hands.* It is the custom to wash one's hands ritually upon waking in the morning but this goes beyond the normal hygienic reasons.

An old Jew is known for his wisdom and clairvoyance despite the fact that he has been blind from birth. Some young men come to taunt him and, worse, threaten his life if he does not come up with the correct answer to this one question. "I have a bird in my hand," says their leader. "Is the bird alive or dead?" The old man is silent and again the young thug demands, "Is the bird alive or dead?!" Finally, the old man responds: "I do not know whether it is dead or alive. What I do know is that it is in your hands."

The story is told in many cultures, a testament to its enduring lesson. In Jewish life, we begin our day by ritually washing our hands, a reminder to ourselves that each day is a new one. Much of how we spend it is in our hands.

אֱלֹהַי My God,
the soul[1] You placed within me is pure.
You created it, You formed it, You breathed it into me,
and You guard it while it is within me.
One day You will take it from me,
and restore it to me in the time to come.
As long as the soul is within me,
I will thank You,
LORD my God and God of my ancestors,
Master of all works, LORD of all souls.
Blessed are You, LORD,
who restores souls to lifeless bodies.

TZITZIT

The following blessing is said before putting on tzitzit.
However, neither it nor the subsequent prayer is said by those who wear a tallit. The blessing over the latter, found on page 172, exempts the former.

בָּרוּךְ Blessed are You, LORD our God, King of the Universe,
who has made us holy through His commandments,
and has commanded us about the command of tasseled garments.

After putting on tzitzit, say:

יְהִי רָצוֹן May it be Your will, LORD my God and God of my ancestors,
that the commandment of the tasseled garment be considered before You
as if I had fulfilled it in all its specifics,
details and intentions,
as well as the 613 commandments
dependent on it, Amen, Selah.

---

contain. We are a mass of cells and muscles and nerve endings. But that will not describe the totality of who I am as a person, my identity and feelings and what it is that makes me be me. I am the force that animates me and defines me, and I acknowledge my uniqueness with this blessing at the very beginning of the day, thanking God that I have woken to live another day.

אֱלֹהַי
נְשָׁמָה[ע] שֶׁנָּתַתָּ בִּי טְהוֹרָה הִיא.
אַתָּה בְרָאתָהּ, אַתָּה יְצַרְתָּהּ, אַתָּה נְפַחְתָּהּ בִּי
וְאַתָּה מְשַׁמְּרָהּ בְּקִרְבִּי, וְאַתָּה עָתִיד לִטְּלָהּ מִמֶּנִּי
וּלְהַחֲזִירָהּ בִּי לֶעָתִיד לָבוֹא.
כָּל זְמַן שֶׁהַנְּשָׁמָה בְקִרְבִּי, מוֹדֶה/ *women* מוֹדָה/ אֲנִי לְפָנֶיךָ
יהוה אֱלֹהַי וֵאלֹהֵי אֲבוֹתַי
רִבּוֹן כָּל הַמַּעֲשִׂים, אֲדוֹן כָּל הַנְּשָׁמוֹת.
בָּרוּךְ אַתָּה יהוה, הַמַּחֲזִיר נְשָׁמוֹת לִפְגָרִים מֵתִים.

לבישת ציצית

The following blessing is said before putting on a טלית קטן*.*
However, neither it nor יְהִי רָצוֹן *is said by those who wear a* טלית*.*
The blessing over the latter, found on page 173, exempts the former.

בָּרוּךְ אַתָּה יהוה אֱלֹהֵינוּ מֶלֶךְ הָעוֹלָם
אֲשֶׁר קִדְּשָׁנוּ בְּמִצְוֹתָיו וְצִוָּנוּ עַל מִצְוַת צִיצִית.

After putting on the טלית קטן*, say:*

יְהִי רָצוֹן מִלְּפָנֶיךָ, יהוה אֱלֹהַי וֵאלֹהֵי אֲבוֹתַי
שֶׁתְּהֵא חֲשׁוּבָה מִצְוַת צִיצִית לְפָנֶיךָ
כְּאִלּוּ קִיַּמְתִּיהָ בְּכָל פְּרָטֶיהָ וְדִקְדּוּקֶיהָ וְכַוָּנוֹתֶיהָ
וְתַרְיַ״ג מִצְוֹת הַתְּלוּיוֹת בָּהּ, אָמֵן סֶלָה.

IYUN TEFILLA • עיון תפילה

אֱלֹהַי נְשָׁמָה – *My God, the soul.* Having just recited a blessing over the body, we now recognize that there is another side of us. To be sure, our bodies could be described in terms of the amount of oxygen, carbon, hydrogen and other elements they

BLESSINGS OVER THE TORAH[B]

In Judaism, study is greater even than prayer. So, before beginning to pray, we engage in a miniature act of study, preceded by the appropriate blessings. The blessings are followed by brief selections from Scripture, Mishna and Gemara, the three foundational texts of Judaism.

בָּרוּךְ Blessed are You, LORD our God, King of the Universe,
who has made us holy through His commandments,
and has commanded us to engage in study
of the words of Torah.
Please, LORD our God, make the words of Your Torah
sweet in our mouths and in the mouths of Your people,
the house of Israel,
so that we, our descendants (and their descendants)
and the descendants of Your people,
the house of Israel,
may all know Your name and study Your Torah for its own sake.
Blessed are You, LORD,
who teaches Torah to His people Israel.

בָּרוּךְ Blessed are You, LORD our God, King of the Universe,
who has chosen us from all the peoples
and given us His Torah.
Blessed are You, LORD,
Giver of the Torah.

---

because the very nature of Torah is that its commandments and values are a part of the very fabric of the life of a Jew. We never stop trying to live Torah or be Torah during the course of a day. Our lives are one continuous fulfillment of the blessing. I know that I exist yet I do not go running around declaring that I exist. A parent always has an inner awareness that they have a child even when not actually thinking about the child, just as a child always has that same inner awareness of a parent. That is the same as the Jew's relationship with Torah. Say it once in the morning, and try to fulfill it the rest of the day.

ברכות התורה[ב]

In Judaism, study is greater even than prayer. So, before beginning to pray, we engage in a miniature act of study, preceded by the appropriate blessings. The blessings are followed by brief selections from תנ״ך, משנה and גמרא, the three foundational texts of Judaism.

בָּרוּךְ אַתָּה יהוה אֱלֹהֵינוּ מֶלֶךְ הָעוֹלָם
אֲשֶׁר קִדְּשָׁנוּ בְּמִצְוֹתָיו
וְצִוָּנוּ לַעֲסֹק בְּדִבְרֵי תוֹרָה.
וְהַעֲרֶב נָא יהוה אֱלֹהֵינוּ אֶת דִּבְרֵי תוֹרָתְךָ
בְּפִינוּ וּבְפִי עַמְּךָ בֵּית יִשְׂרָאֵל
וְנִהְיֶה אֲנַחְנוּ וְצֶאֱצָאֵינוּ (וְצֶאֱצָאֵי צֶאֱצָאֵינוּ)
וְצֶאֱצָאֵי עַמְּךָ בֵּית יִשְׂרָאֵל
כֻּלָּנוּ יוֹדְעֵי שְׁמֶךָ וְלוֹמְדֵי תוֹרָתְךָ לִשְׁמָהּ.
בָּרוּךְ אַתָּה יהוה, הַמְלַמֵּד תּוֹרָה לְעַמּוֹ יִשְׂרָאֵל.

בָּרוּךְ אַתָּה יהוה אֱלֹהֵינוּ מֶלֶךְ הָעוֹלָם
אֲשֶׁר בָּחַר בָּנוּ מִכָּל הָעַמִּים
וְנָתַן לָנוּ אֶת תּוֹרָתוֹ.
בָּרוּךְ אַתָּה יהוה, נוֹתֵן הַתּוֹרָה.

BIUR TEFILLA • ביאור תפילה

ברכות התורה – *Blessings over the Torah.* These blessings are said over the learning of Torah at the beginning of the day. There is here a halakhic anomaly however. Every time one fulfills a mitzva, say before one eats, one is required to say a blessing; no matter how many times one does it during the course of the day, one must recite a blessing beforehand. And yet, for learning Torah reciting them once in the morning is enough. Why should this be so? Rabbi J. B. Soloveitchik once suggested that it is

יְבָרֶכְךָ May the LORD bless you[H] and protect you. *Num. 6*
May the LORD make His face shine on you
and be gracious to you.
May the LORD turn His face toward you
and grant you peace.

אֵלּוּ These are the things *Mishna Pe'ah 1:1*
for which there is no fixed measure:
the corner of the field,
first-fruits,
appearances before the LORD [on festivals, with offerings],
acts of kindness
and the study of Torah.

אֵלּוּ These are the things *Shabbat 127a*
whose fruits we eat in this world
but whose full reward awaits us
in the World to Come:
honoring parents;
acts of kindness;
arriving early at the house of study
morning and evening;
hospitality to strangers;
visiting the sick;
helping the needy bride;
attending to the dead;
devotion in prayer;
and bringing peace between people –
but the study of Torah is equal to them all.

---

after the recitation of the blessing. The next three paragraphs thus represent selections respectively from Torah, Mishna, and Gemara, thereby symbolically incorporating all of the Written Torah and the Oral Torah into our learning – for its own sake.

במדבר ו

יְבָרֶכְךָ יהוה וְיִשְׁמְרֶךָ:
יָאֵר יהוה פָּנָיו אֵלֶיךָ וִיחֻנֶּךָּ:
יִשָּׂא יהוה פָּנָיו אֵלֶיךָ וְיָשֵׂם לְךָ שָׁלוֹם:

משנה, פאה א:א

אֵלּוּ דְבָרִים שֶׁאֵין לָהֶם שִׁעוּר
הַפֵּאָה וְהַבִּכּוּרִים וְהָרֵאָיוֹן
וּגְמִילוּת חֲסָדִים וְתַלְמוּד תּוֹרָה.

שבת קכז.

אֵלּוּ דְבָרִים שֶׁאָדָם אוֹכֵל פֵּרוֹתֵיהֶם בָּעוֹלָם הַזֶּה
וְהַקֶּרֶן קַיֶּמֶת לוֹ לָעוֹלָם הַבָּא
וְאֵלּוּ הֵן
כִּבּוּד אָב וָאֵם
וּגְמִילוּת חֲסָדִים
וְהַשְׁכָּמַת בֵּית הַמִּדְרָשׁ שַׁחֲרִית וְעַרְבִית
וְהַכְנָסַת אוֹרְחִים
וּבִקּוּר חוֹלִים
וְהַכְנָסַת כַּלָּה
וּלְוָיַת הַמֵּת
וְעִיּוּן תְּפִלָּה
וַהֲבָאַת שָׁלוֹם בֵּין אָדָם לַחֲבֵרוֹ
וְתַלְמוּד תּוֹרָה כְּנֶגֶד כֻּלָּם.

HILKHOT TEFILLA • הלכות תפילה

יְבָרֶכְךָ – *May the Lord bless you*. We just recited blessings over Torah study. In order to ensure that the blessings not be in vain, the custom is to learn some Torah immediately

TALLIT

Say the following meditation before putting on the tallit. Meditations before the fulfillment of mitzvot are to ensure that we do so with the requisite intention (kavana). This particularly applies to mitzvot whose purpose is to induce in us certain states of mind, as is the case with tallit and tefillin, both of which are external symbols of inward commitment to the life of observance of the mitzvot.

בָּרְכִי נַפְשִׁי Bless the LORD, my soul. LORD, my God, You are very Ps. 104
great, clothed in majesty and splendor, wrapped in a robe of light, spreading out the heavens like a tent.

Some say:

For the sake of the unification of the Holy One, blessed be He, and His Divine Presence, in reverence and love, to unify the name *Yod-Heh* with *Vav-Heh* in perfect unity in the name of all Israel.

I am about to wrap myself in this tasseled garment (tallit). So may my soul, my 248 limbs and 365 sinews be wrapped in the light of the tassel (*hatzitzit*) which amounts to 613 [commandments]. And just as I cover myself with a tasseled garment in this world, so may I be worthy of rabbinical dress and a fine garment in the World to Come in the Garden of Eden. Through the commandment of tassels may my life's-breath, spirit, soul and prayer be delivered from external impediments, and
may the tallit spread its wings over them like an eagle stirring up its nest, hovering Deut. 32
over its young. May the commandment of the tasseled garment be considered before the Holy One, blessed be He, as if I had fulfilled it in all its specifics, details and intentions, as well as the 613 commandments dependent on it, Amen, Selah.

Before wrapping oneself in the tallit, say:

בָּרוּךְ Blessed are You, LORD our God, King of the Universe,
who has made us holy through His commandments,
and has commanded us to wrap ourselves in the tasseled garment.

According to the Shela (Rabbi Isaiah Horowitz), one should say these verses after wrapping oneself in the tallit:

מַה־יָּקָר How precious is Your loving-kindness, O God, Ps. 36
and the children of men find refuge under the shadow of Your wings.
They are filled with the rich plenty of Your House.
You give them drink from Your river of delights.
For with You is the fountain of life; in Your light, we see light.
Continue Your loving-kindness to those who know You,
and Your righteousness to the upright in heart.

עטיפת טלית

Say the following meditation before putting on the טלית. Meditations before the fulfillment of מצוות are to ensure that we do so with the requisite intention (כוונה). This particularly applies to מצוות whose purpose is to induce in us certain states of mind, as is the case with טלית and תפילין, both of which are external symbols of inward commitment to the life of observance of the מצוות.

תהלים קד בָּרְכִי נַפְשִׁי אֶת־יהוה, יהוה אֱלֹהַי גָּדַלְתָּ מְּאֹד, הוֹד וְהָדָר לָבָשְׁתָּ:
עֹטֶה־אוֹר כַּשַּׂלְמָה, נוֹטֶה שָׁמַיִם כַּיְרִיעָה:

Some say:

לְשֵׁם יִחוּד קֻדְשָׁא בְּרִיךְ הוּא וּשְׁכִינְתֵּהּ בִּדְחִילוּ וּרְחִימוּ, לְיַחֵד שֵׁם י״ה בו״ה בְּיִחוּדָא שְׁלִים בְּשֵׁם כָּל יִשְׂרָאֵל.

הֲרֵינִי מִתְעַטֵּף בְּצִיצִית. כֵּן תִּתְעַטֵּף נִשְׁמָתִי וּרְמַ״ח אֵבָרַי וּשְׁסָ״ה גִּידַי בְּאוֹר הַצִּיצִית הָעוֹלָה תַּרְיַ״ג. וּכְשֵׁם שֶׁאֲנִי מִתְכַּסֶּה בְּטַלִּית בָּעוֹלָם הַזֶּה, כָּךְ אֶזְכֶּה לַחֲלוּקָא דְרַבָּנָן וּלְטַלִּית נָאָה לָעוֹלָם הַבָּא בְּגַן עֵדֶן. וְעַל יְדֵי מִצְוַת צִיצִית תִּנָּצֵל נַפְשִׁי רוּחִי וְנִשְׁמָתִי וּתְפִלָּתִי מִן הַחִיצוֹנִים. וְהַטַּלִּית תִּפְרֹשׂ כְּנָפֶיהָ
דברים לב עֲלֵיהֶם וְתַצִּילֵם, כְּנֶשֶׁר יָעִיר קִנּוֹ, עַל גּוֹזָלָיו יְרַחֵף: וּתְהֵא חֲשׁוּבָה מִצְוַת צִיצִית לִפְנֵי הַקָּדוֹשׁ בָּרוּךְ הוּא, כְּאִלּוּ קִיַּמְתִּיהָ בְּכָל פְּרָטֶיהָ וְדִקְדּוּקֶיהָ וְכַוָּנוֹתֶיהָ וְתַרְיַ״ג מִצְוֹת הַתְּלוּיוֹת בָּהּ, אָמֵן סֶלָה.

Before wrapping oneself in the טלית, say:

בָּרוּךְ אַתָּה יהוה אֱלֹהֵינוּ מֶלֶךְ הָעוֹלָם
אֲשֶׁר קִדְּשָׁנוּ בְּמִצְוֹתָיו וְצִוָּנוּ לְהִתְעַטֵּף בַּצִּיצִית.

According to the Shela (Rabbi Isaiah Horowitz), one should say these verses after wrapping oneself in the טלית:

תהלים לו מַה־יָּקָר חַסְדְּךָ אֱלֹהִים, וּבְנֵי אָדָם בְּצֵל כְּנָפֶיךָ יֶחֱסָיוּן:
יִרְוְיֻן מִדֶּשֶׁן בֵּיתֶךָ, וְנַחַל עֲדָנֶיךָ תַשְׁקֵם:
כִּי־עִמְּךָ מְקוֹר חַיִּים, בְּאוֹרְךָ נִרְאֶה־אוֹר:
מְשֹׁךְ חַסְדְּךָ לְיֹדְעֶיךָ, וְצִדְקָתְךָ לְיִשְׁרֵי־לֵב:

PREPARATION FOR PRAYER

On entering the synagogue:

HOW GOODLY[B] *Num. 24*

are your tents, Jacob, your dwelling places, Israel.

As for me, *Ps. 5*
in Your great loving-kindness,
I will come into Your House.
I will bow down to Your holy Temple
in awe of You.

Lord, I love the habitation of Your House, *Ps. 26*
the place where Your glory dwells.

As for me,
I will bow in worship;
I will bend the knee
before the Lord my Maker.

As for me, *Ps. 69*
may my prayer come to You, Lord,
at a time of favor.
God, in Your great loving-kindness,
answer me with Your faithful salvation.

---

provides them with a blessing. Here he seems to focus on the tightly knit nature of community for which the Jewish people is known. The Rabbis suggested that it was also a comment on the spiritual institutions of the nation where tents and camps allude to the study halls and synagogues (מִשְׁכְּנֹתֶיךָ – *mishkenotekha* means dwelling places but can also be related to the word *mishkan* or Tabernacle where the *Shekhina* or Divine Presence rests). How odd that we should begin our prayers with an observation by a non-Jew. But the truth is that sometimes the outsider sees truths that we ourselves forget or do not see.

הכנה לתפילה

On entering the בית כנסת:

במדבר כד
מַה־טֹּבוּ
אֹהָלֶיךָ יַעֲקֹב, מִשְׁכְּנֹתֶיךָ יִשְׂרָאֵל:
תהלים ה
וַאֲנִי בְּרֹב חַסְדְּךָ אָבוֹא בֵיתֶךָ
אֶשְׁתַּחֲוֶה אֶל־הֵיכַל־קָדְשְׁךָ
בְּיִרְאָתֶךָ:
תהלים כו
יהוה אָהַבְתִּי מְעוֹן בֵּיתֶךָ
וּמְקוֹם מִשְׁכַּן כְּבוֹדֶךָ:

וַאֲנִי אֶשְׁתַּחֲוֶה
וְאֶכְרָעָה
אֶבְרְכָה לִפְנֵי יהוה עֹשִׂי.

תהלים סט
וַאֲנִי תְפִלָּתִי־לְךָ יהוה
עֵת רָצוֹן
אֱלֹהִים בְּרָב־חַסְדֶּךָ
עֲנֵנִי בֶּאֱמֶת יִשְׁעֶךָ:

BIUR TEFILLA • ביאור תפילה

מַה־טֹּבוּ – *How goodly.* This verse is taken from the chapter in *Bemidbar* wherein the non-Jewish prophet Bilaam sets out to curse the Jewish people but instead

The following poems, on this page and the next, both from the Middle Ages, are summary statements of Jewish faith, orienting us to the spiritual contours of the world that we actualize in the mind by the act of prayer.

LORD OF THE UNIVERSE,[A]
who reigned before the birth of any thing –

When by His will all things were made
then was His name proclaimed King.

And when all things shall cease to be
He alone will reign in awe.

He was, He is, and He shall be
glorious for evermore.

He is One, there is none else,
alone, unique, beyond compare;

Without beginning, without end,
His might, His rule are everywhere.

He is my God; my Redeemer lives.
He is the Rock on whom I rely –

My banner and my safe retreat,
my cup, my portion when I cry.

Into His hand my soul I place,
when I awake and when I sleep.

The LORD is with me, I shall not fear;
body and soul from harm will He keep.

---

theme is His exaltedness on the one hand, and His intimate contact with the world on the other, themes that we will return to over and over again for they speak to the heart of religious experience and belief: He is far but He is close; He is before time but He is this-worldly; He is beyond our grasp and comprehension, yet He is within reach and knowable; He is distant, yet He is my refuge. These are not contradictions but different aspects of an ongoing relationship. At times we feel one way, at others we feel differently. The bottom line is that we can feel both and both are normal.

For more commentary on *Adon Olam* see page 469 (in Musaf).

The following poems, on this page and the next, both from the Middle Ages, are summary statements of Jewish faith, orienting us to the spiritual contours of the world that we actualize in the mind by the act of prayer.

אֲדוֹן עוֹלָם[א]

אֲשֶׁר מָלַךְ בְּטֶרֶם כָּל־יְצִיר נִבְרָא.
לְעֵת נַעֲשָׂה בְחֶפְצוֹ כֹּל אֲזַי מֶלֶךְ שְׁמוֹ נִקְרָא.
וְאַחֲרֵי כִּכְלוֹת הַכֹּל לְבַדּוֹ יִמְלֹךְ נוֹרָא.
וְהוּא הָיָה וְהוּא הֹוֶה וְהוּא יִהְיֶה בְּתִפְאָרָה.
וְהוּא אֶחָד וְאֵין שֵׁנִי לְהַמְשִׁיל לוֹ לְהַחְבִּירָה.
בְּלִי רֵאשִׁית בְּלִי תַכְלִית וְלוֹ הָעֹז וְהַמִּשְׂרָה.
וְהוּא אֵלִי וְחַי גּוֹאֲלִי וְצוּר חֶבְלִי בְּעֵת צָרָה.
וְהוּא נִסִּי וּמָנוֹס לִי מְנָת כּוֹסִי בְּיוֹם אֶקְרָא.
בְּיָדוֹ אַפְקִיד רוּחִי בְּעֵת אִישַׁן וְאָעִירָה.
וְעִם רוּחִי גְּוִיָּתִי יהוה לִי וְלֹא אִירָא.

BIUR TEFILLA • ביאור תפילה

אֲדוֹן עוֹלָם – *Lord of the universe.*
The author of this famous hymn is unknown (it dates back to the eleventh century or perhaps even hundreds of years earlier) but it is firmly placed in the canon of prayer. It is recited by some individuals on their own before services begin, it is part of the liturgy recited at bedtime (*Keriat Shema al HaMita*), yet it is also commonly sung by the entire congregation at the conclusion of the service on Shabbat and Yom Tov. In some Moroccan communities, it is sung as the bride enters the wedding canopy. What is its appeal? The first half, actually the first six lines, speak about aspects of God, His essence, or who He is to the extent that we can know such a thing, while the remainder speaks about His relationship with man. In short, its

GREAT[B]

is the living God and praised.
He exists, and His existence is beyond time.

He is One, and there is no unity like His.
Unfathomable, His oneness is infinite.

He has neither bodily form nor substance;
His holiness is beyond compare.

He preceded all that was created.
He was first: there was no beginning to His beginning.

Behold He is Master of the Universe; and every creature
shows His greatness and majesty.

The rich flow of His prophecy He gave
to His treasured people in whom He gloried.

Never in Israel has there arisen another like Moses,
a prophet who beheld God's image.

God gave His people a Torah of truth
by the hand of His prophet, most faithful of His House.

God will not alter or change His law
for any other, for eternity.

He sees and knows our secret thoughts;
as soon as something is begun, He foresees its end.

He rewards people with loving-kindness according to their deeds;
He punishes the wicked according to his wickedness.

At the end of days He will send our Messiah
to redeem those who await His final salvation.

God will revive the dead in His great loving-kindness.
Blessed for evermore is His glorious name!

---

been spilled by philosophers about the meaning of each one of these statements but for the Jew at prayer they are simple declarations of faith. "We start our devotions as *faithful* Jews, believing in the existence of a Creator – one, spiritual and eternal; believing in Prophecy and the Torah of Moses; in the rule of justice in God's universe; in the Messiah, and in the immortality of the soul" (Rabbi Joseph Hertz).

יִגְדַּל ב

אֱלֹהִים חַי וְיִשְׁתַּבַּח, נִמְצָא וְאֵין עֵת אֶל מְצִיאוּתוֹ.
אֶחָד וְאֵין יָחִיד כְּיִחוּדוֹ, נֶעְלָם וְגַם אֵין סוֹף לְאַחְדוּתוֹ.
אֵין לוֹ דְּמוּת הַגּוּף וְאֵינוֹ גוּף, לֹא נַעֲרֹךְ אֵלָיו קְדֻשָּׁתוֹ.
קַדְמוֹן לְכָל דָּבָר אֲשֶׁר נִבְרָא, רִאשׁוֹן וְאֵין רֵאשִׁית לְרֵאשִׁיתוֹ.
הִנּוֹ אֲדוֹן עוֹלָם, וְכָל נוֹצָר יוֹרֶה גְדֻלָּתוֹ וּמַלְכוּתוֹ.
שֶׁפַע נְבוּאָתוֹ נְתָנוֹ אֶל־אַנְשֵׁי סְגֻלָּתוֹ וְתִפְאַרְתּוֹ.
לֹא קָם בְּיִשְׂרָאֵל כְּמֹשֶׁה עוֹד נָבִיא וּמַבִּיט אֶת תְּמוּנָתוֹ.
תּוֹרַת אֱמֶת נָתַן לְעַמּוֹ אֵל עַל יַד נְבִיאוֹ נֶאֱמַן בֵּיתוֹ.
לֹא יַחֲלִיף הָאֵל וְלֹא יָמִיר דָּתוֹ לְעוֹלָמִים לְזוּלָתוֹ.
צוֹפֶה וְיוֹדֵעַ סְתָרֵינוּ, מַבִּיט לְסוֹף דָּבָר בְּקַדְמָתוֹ.
גּוֹמֵל לְאִישׁ חֶסֶד כְּמִפְעָלוֹ, נוֹתֵן לְרָשָׁע רָע כְּרִשְׁעָתוֹ.
יִשְׁלַח לְקֵץ יָמִין מְשִׁיחֵנוּ לִפְדּוֹת מְחַכֵּי קֵץ יְשׁוּעָתוֹ.
מֵתִים יְחַיֶּה אֵל בְּרֹב חַסְדּוֹ, בָּרוּךְ עֲדֵי עַד שֵׁם תְּהִלָּתוֹ.

BIUR TEFILLA • ביאור תפילה

יִגְדַּל – *Great.* Judaism has no systematic system of dogma or a creedal formulation of belief. Maimonides, famed halakhist and philosopher of the twelfth century, composed a list of thirteen principles – although it is unlikely that he meant these to serve as a definitive list to the exclusion of others. Nevertheless, these thirteen have taken on a life of their own, due in no small part to their popularization by their recitation by some at the conclusion of services every morning and by their reformulation in this hymn known simply by its first word, *Yigdal,* which may have been written as early as the fourteenth century. It is recited by some individuals to themselves at the beginning of services but also often sung by the entire congregation at the conclusion of services on Friday night or Shabbat morning.

Each line consists of a poetic reconstruction of one of the thirteen principles laid out by Maimonides. Much ink has

MORNING BLESSINGS

The following blessings are said aloud by the Leader, but each individual should say them quietly as well. It is our custom to say them standing.

בָּרוּךְ Blessed are You, Lord our God, King of the Universe,
who gives the heart understanding
to distinguish day from night.

Blessed are You, Lord our God, King of the Universe,
who has not made me a heathen.

Blessed are You, Lord our God, King of the Universe,
who has not made me a slave.

Blessed are You, Lord our God, King of the Universe,
men: who has not made me a woman.
women: who has made me according to His will.

Blessed are You, Lord our God, King of the Universe,
who gives sight to the blind.[B]

Even so, the siddur provides us with a way to start our day. Why blessings over such small everyday acts? The answer lies in that very description – we take nothing for granted in life. Especially when you are caught up in routine, when one day seems to merge with another, the siddur awakens us to the everyday miracles in our lives. The siddur is the antidote for complacency and fatigue.

BIUR TEFILLA • ביאור תפילה

פּוֹקֵחַ עִוְרִים – *Who gives sight to the blind.* The phrase is no doubt taken from the account in *Bereshit* about the forbidden fruit, of which it is said that when Adam and Ḥava (Eve) ate from the tree, their eyes "were opened and they knew they were naked." Given that, as Rashi explains, even a blind person knows when he is naked, the opening of the eyes must refer not to sight but to insight. Are you blind?! Open your eyes! Can't you see?! These are all expressions which speak to the same failing.

What insight do you have that you are grateful for?

ברכות השחר

The following blessings are said aloud by the שליח ציבור*, but each individual should say them quietly as well. It is our custom to say them standing.*

בָּרוּךְ אַתָּה יהוה אֱלֹהֵינוּ מֶלֶךְ הָעוֹלָם
אֲשֶׁר נָתַן לַשֶּׂכְוִי בִינָה
לְהַבְחִין בֵּין יוֹם וּבֵין לָיְלָה.

בָּרוּךְ אַתָּה יהוה אֱלֹהֵינוּ מֶלֶךְ הָעוֹלָם
שֶׁלֹּא עָשַׂנִי גּוֹי.

בָּרוּךְ אַתָּה יהוה אֱלֹהֵינוּ מֶלֶךְ הָעוֹלָם
שֶׁלֹּא עָשַׂנִי עָבֶד.

בָּרוּךְ אַתָּה יהוה אֱלֹהֵינוּ מֶלֶךְ הָעוֹלָם
men שֶׁלֹּא עָשַׂנִי אִשָּׁה. / *women* שֶׁעָשַׂנִי כִּרְצוֹנוֹ.

בָּרוּךְ אַתָּה יהוה אֱלֹהֵינוּ מֶלֶךְ הָעוֹלָם
פּוֹקֵחַ עִוְרִים.[ב]

INTRODUCTION TO BIRKHOT HASHAHAR

The Talmud (*Berakhot* 60a) relates that each of these blessings was to be recited upon a different experience upon awakening in the morning. For example, when you hear the rooster crow or first wake up, you say the first blessing; when you open your eyes, you say, "Who gives sight to the blind"; when you put on clothes, you say, "Who clothes the naked"; "Who has provided me my every need," when you put on your shoes, and so on. Over time, however, people forgot which blessing was associated with each act, and so the blessings were made part of the synagogue service instead. In most communities, the *ḥazan* recites the blessing and the congregation recites "Amen." But in so doing, by divorcing the blessings from those first moments of awareness when we wake up in the morning, have we perhaps lost something?

Blessed are You, LORD our God, King of the Universe,
who clothes the naked.

Blessed are You, LORD our God, King of the Universe,
who sets captives free.

Blessed are You, LORD our God, King of the Universe,
who raises those bowed down.

Blessed are You, LORD our God, King of the Universe,
who spreads the earth above the waters.

Blessed are You, LORD our God, King of the Universe,
who has provided me with all I need.[1]

Blessed are You, LORD our God, King of the Universe,
who makes firm the steps of man.

Blessed are You, LORD our God, King of the Universe,
who girds Israel with strength.

Blessed are You, LORD our God, King of the Universe,
who crowns Israel with glory.

Blessed are You, LORD our God, King of the Universe,
who gives strength to the weary.

In the Talmud (*Shabbat* 129a), we are told: "Rav Yehuda said in Rav's name: One should always sell [even] the beams of his house and buy shoes for his feet." In the labor and death camp Majdanek, one of the central exhibits that conveys the enormity of the Holocaust is a barracks filled with nothing but thousands of pairs of shoes confiscated from the victims. Pick any image you want or construct your own. Be thankful not only for your shoes but for what they represent.

ANI TEFILLA

I was recently told the story of a deeply religious man who had suffered horrible losses which cast him into a state of sadness so profound that he could no longer bring himself to pray to God. Distraught that he had separated himself from a lifetime of devotion, he traveled to a see a rabbi in whom he could confide. "Start small," the rabbi said. "Just say one thing but say it every day." And so he did, until eventually he was able to find his faith in prayer again. The story ended there, until it suddenly occurred to me that I had not asked what the chosen prayer was that brought him back. The answer: "Blessed are You, LORD our God, King of the Universe, who gives strength to the weary." (Dr. David Pelcovitz)

בָּרוּךְ אַתָּה יהוה אֱלֹהֵינוּ מֶלֶךְ הָעוֹלָם
מַלְבִּישׁ עֲרֻמִּים.

בָּרוּךְ אַתָּה יהוה אֱלֹהֵינוּ מֶלֶךְ הָעוֹלָם
מַתִּיר אֲסוּרִים.

בָּרוּךְ אַתָּה יהוה אֱלֹהֵינוּ מֶלֶךְ הָעוֹלָם
זוֹקֵף כְּפוּפִים.

בָּרוּךְ אַתָּה יהוה אֱלֹהֵינוּ מֶלֶךְ הָעוֹלָם
רוֹקַע הָאָרֶץ עַל הַמָּיִם.

בָּרוּךְ אַתָּה יהוה אֱלֹהֵינוּ מֶלֶךְ הָעוֹלָם
שֶׁעָשָׂה לִי כָּל צָרְכִּי.[ע]

בָּרוּךְ אַתָּה יהוה אֱלֹהֵינוּ מֶלֶךְ הָעוֹלָם
הַמֵּכִין מִצְעֲדֵי גָבֶר.

בָּרוּךְ אַתָּה יהוה אֱלֹהֵינוּ מֶלֶךְ הָעוֹלָם
אוֹזֵר יִשְׂרָאֵל בִּגְבוּרָה.

בָּרוּךְ אַתָּה יהוה אֱלֹהֵינוּ מֶלֶךְ הָעוֹלָם
עוֹטֵר יִשְׂרָאֵל בְּתִפְאָרָה.

בָּרוּךְ אַתָּה יהוה אֱלֹהֵינוּ מֶלֶךְ הָעוֹלָם
הַנּוֹתֵן לַיָּעֵף כֹּחַ.

IYUN TEFILLA • עיון תפילה

שֶׁעָשָׂה לִי כָּל צָרְכִּי – *Who has provided me with all I need.* This particular blessing was originally said when one put on shoes in the morning. Do we ever think of the significance of our shoes? My grandmother, ז״ל used to get very upset when we walked around the house without a pair of shoes. To her, walking barefoot was a sign of mourning.

בָּרוּךְ Blessed are You, LORD our God, King of the Universe,
who removes sleep from my eyes
and slumber from my eyelids.
And may it be Your will,[B] LORD our God
and God of our ancestors,
to accustom us to Your Torah,
and make us attached to Your commandments.
Lead us not into error, transgression,
iniquity, temptation or disgrace.
Do not let the evil instinct dominate us.
Keep us far from a bad man and a bad companion.
Help us attach ourselves to the good instinct and to good deeds
and bend our instincts to be subservient to You.
Grant us, this day and every day,
grace, loving-kindness and compassion in Your eyes
and in the eyes of all who see us,
and bestow loving-kindness upon us.
Blessed are You, LORD,
who bestows loving-kindness on His people Israel.

יְהִי רָצוֹן May it be Your will, LORD my God and God of my ancestors, to save me today and every day, from the arrogant and from arrogance itself, from a bad man, a bad friend, a bad neighbor, a bad mishap, a destructive adversary, a harsh trial and a harsh opponent, whether or not he is a son of the covenant. *Berakhot 16b*

The message is clear: waking up, being aware, is itself a huge gift, if only we would recognize it as such every day (Tosafot *Berakhot* 46).

יְהִי רָצוֹן... – *May it be Your will...* This prayer was a personal one, originally written by Rabbi Yehuda the Nasi (the Prince) in the third century, redactor of the Mishna and leader of the Jewish community in Israel. In it we pray for the ability to take full advantage of the opportunities in the coming day, to improve our relationships with God, with other people, and with ourselves. So important is this challenge every day, so important is it to take stock before the day begins, that the *Tur* (46) rules one may add even further requests if one wishes, ones presumably that match the concerns you personally have for the coming day.

בָּרוּךְ אַתָּה יהוה אֱלֹהֵינוּ מֶלֶךְ הָעוֹלָם
הַמַּעֲבִיר שֵׁנָה מֵעֵינַי וּתְנוּמָה מֵעַפְעַפָּי.
וִיהִי רָצוֹן[ב] מִלְּפָנֶיךָ יהוה אֱלֹהֵינוּ וֵאלֹהֵי אֲבוֹתֵינוּ
שֶׁתַּרְגִּילֵנוּ בְּתוֹרָתֶךָ, וְדַבְּקֵנוּ בְּמִצְוֹתֶיךָ
וְאַל תְּבִיאֵנוּ לֹא לִידֵי חֵטְא, וְלֹא לִידֵי עֲבֵרָה וְעָוֹן
וְלֹא לִידֵי נִסָּיוֹן וְלֹא לִידֵי בִזָּיוֹן
וְאַל תַּשְׁלֶט בָּנוּ יֵצֶר הָרָע
וְהַרְחִיקֵנוּ מֵאָדָם רָע וּמֵחָבֵר רָע
וְדַבְּקֵנוּ בְּיֵצֶר הַטּוֹב וּבְמַעֲשִׂים טוֹבִים
וְכֹף אֶת יִצְרֵנוּ לְהִשְׁתַּעְבֶּד לָךְ
וּתְנֵנוּ הַיּוֹם וּבְכָל יוֹם לְחֵן וּלְחֶסֶד וּלְרַחֲמִים
בְּעֵינֶיךָ, וּבְעֵינֵי כָל רוֹאֵינוּ
וְתִגְמְלֵנוּ חֲסָדִים טוֹבִים.
בָּרוּךְ אַתָּה יהוה, גּוֹמֵל חֲסָדִים טוֹבִים לְעַמּוֹ יִשְׂרָאֵל.

ברכות טז: יְהִי רָצוֹן מִלְּפָנֶיךָ יהוה אֱלֹהַי וֵאלֹהֵי אֲבוֹתַי, שֶׁתַּצִּילֵנִי הַיּוֹם וּבְכָל יוֹם מֵעַזֵּי פָנִים וּמֵעַזּוּת פָּנִים, מֵאָדָם רָע, וּמֵחָבֵר רָע, וּמִשָּׁכֵן רָע, וּמִפֶּגַע רָע, וּמִשָּׂטָן הַמַּשְׁחִית, מִדִּין קָשֶׁה, וּמִבַּעַל דִּין קָשֶׁה בֵּין שֶׁהוּא בֶן בְּרִית וּבֵין שֶׁאֵינוֹ בֶן בְּרִית.

BIUR TEFILLA • ביאור תפילה

הַמַּעֲבִיר שֵׁנָה מֵעֵינַי... יְהִי רָצוֹן – *Who removes sleep... May it be Your will.* From a purely technical point of view, this section raises a question. In Jewish law, a long blessing is one that begins and ends with the same formula of "*Blessed are You...*" However, the stipulation is that the theme at the end of the blessing must be consistent with the theme at the beginning of the blessing. Yet here it begins with gratitude for removing sleep from my eyes but it ends with the acknowledgment that He bestows loving-kindness upon us.

THE BINDING OF ISAAC

On the basis of Jewish mystical tradition, some have the custom of saying daily the biblical passage recounting the Binding of Isaac, the supreme trial of faith in which Abraham demonstrated his love of God above all other loves. On Shabbat most omit the introductory and concluding prayers, "Our God and God of our ancestors" and "Master of the Universe." Others skip to "A person should" on page 190.

Our God and God of our ancestors, remember us with a favorable memory, and recall us with a remembrance of salvation and compassion from the highest of high heavens. Remember, LORD our God, on our behalf, the love of the ancients, Abraham, Isaac and Yisrael Your servants; the covenant, the loving-kindness, and the oath You swore to Abraham our father on Mount Moriah, and the Binding, when he bound Isaac his son on the altar, as is written in Your Torah:

It happened after these things that God tested Abraham. He said to him, "Abraham!" "Here I am," he replied. He said, "Take your son, your only son, Isaac, whom you love, and go to the land of Moriah and offer him there as a burnt-offering on one of the mountains which I shall say to you." Early the next morning Abraham rose and saddled his donkey and took his two lads with him, and Isaac his son, and he cut wood for the burnt-offering, and he set out for the place of which God had told him. On the third day Abraham looked up and saw the place from afar. Abraham said to his lads, "Stay here with the donkey while I and the boy go on ahead. We will worship and we will return to you." Abraham took the wood for the burnt-offering and placed it on Isaac his son, and he took in his hand the fire and the knife, and the two of them went together. Isaac said to Abraham his father, "Father?" and he said "Here I am, my son." And he said, "Here are the fire and the wood, but where is the sheep for the burnt-offering?" Abraham said, "God will see to the sheep for the burnt-offering, my son." And the two of them went together. They came to the place God had told him about, and Abraham built there an altar and arranged the *Gen. 22*

פרשת העקדה

On the basis of Jewish mystical tradition, some have the custom of saying daily the biblical passage recounting the Binding of Isaac, the supreme trial of faith in which Abraham demonstrated his love of God above all other loves. On שבת *most omit the introductory and concluding prayers,* אֱלֹהֵינוּ וֵאלֹהֵי אֲבוֹתֵינוּ *and* רִבּוֹנוֹ שֶׁל עוֹלָם. *Others skip to* לְעוֹלָם יְהֵא אָדָם *on page 191.*

אֱלֹהֵינוּ וֵאלֹהֵי אֲבוֹתֵינוּ, זָכְרֵנוּ בְּזִכָּרוֹן טוֹב לְפָנֶיךָ, וּפָקְדֵנוּ בִּפְקֻדַּת יְשׁוּעָה וְרַחֲמִים מִשְּׁמֵי שְׁמֵי קֶדֶם, וּזְכָר לָנוּ יהוה אֱלֹהֵינוּ, אַהֲבַת הַקַּדְמוֹנִים אַבְרָהָם יִצְחָק וְיִשְׂרָאֵל עֲבָדֶיךָ, אֶת הַבְּרִית וְאֶת הַחֶסֶד וְאֶת הַשְּׁבוּעָה שֶׁנִּשְׁבַּעְתָּ לְאַבְרָהָם אָבִינוּ בְּהַר הַמּוֹרִיָּה, וְאֶת הָעֲקֵדָה שֶׁעָקַד אֶת יִצְחָק בְּנוֹ עַל גַּבֵּי הַמִּזְבֵּחַ, כַּכָּתוּב בְּתוֹרָתֶךָ:

וַיְהִי אַחַר הַדְּבָרִים הָאֵלֶּה, וְהָאֱלֹהִים נִסָּה אֶת־אַבְרָהָם, וַיֹּאמֶר אֵלָיו אַבְרָהָם, וַיֹּאמֶר הִנֵּנִי: וַיֹּאמֶר קַח־נָא אֶת־בִּנְךָ אֶת־יְחִידְךָ אֲשֶׁר־אָהַבְתָּ, אֶת־יִצְחָק, וְלֶךְ־לְךָ אֶל־אֶרֶץ הַמֹּרִיָּה, וְהַעֲלֵהוּ שָׁם לְעֹלָה עַל אַחַד הֶהָרִים אֲשֶׁר אֹמַר אֵלֶיךָ: וַיַּשְׁכֵּם אַבְרָהָם בַּבֹּקֶר, וַיַּחֲבֹשׁ אֶת־חֲמֹרוֹ, וַיִּקַּח אֶת־שְׁנֵי נְעָרָיו אִתּוֹ וְאֵת יִצְחָק בְּנוֹ, וַיְבַקַּע עֲצֵי עֹלָה, וַיָּקָם וַיֵּלֶךְ אֶל־הַמָּקוֹם אֲשֶׁר־אָמַר־לוֹ הָאֱלֹהִים: בַּיּוֹם הַשְּׁלִישִׁי וַיִּשָּׂא אַבְרָהָם אֶת־עֵינָיו וַיַּרְא אֶת־הַמָּקוֹם מֵרָחֹק: וַיֹּאמֶר אַבְרָהָם אֶל־נְעָרָיו, שְׁבוּ־לָכֶם פֹּה עִם־הַחֲמוֹר, וַאֲנִי וְהַנַּעַר נֵלְכָה עַד־כֹּה, וְנִשְׁתַּחֲוֶה וְנָשׁוּבָה אֲלֵיכֶם: וַיִּקַּח אַבְרָהָם אֶת־עֲצֵי הָעֹלָה וַיָּשֶׂם עַל־יִצְחָק בְּנוֹ, וַיִּקַּח בְּיָדוֹ אֶת־הָאֵשׁ וְאֶת־הַמַּאֲכֶלֶת, וַיֵּלְכוּ שְׁנֵיהֶם יַחְדָּו: וַיֹּאמֶר יִצְחָק אֶל־אַבְרָהָם אָבִיו, וַיֹּאמֶר אָבִי, וַיֹּאמֶר הִנֶּנִּי בְנִי, וַיֹּאמֶר, הִנֵּה הָאֵשׁ וְהָעֵצִים, וְאַיֵּה הַשֶּׂה לְעֹלָה: וַיֹּאמֶר אַבְרָהָם, אֱלֹהִים יִרְאֶה־לּוֹ הַשֶּׂה לְעֹלָה, בְּנִי, וַיֵּלְכוּ שְׁנֵיהֶם יַחְדָּו: וַיָּבֹאוּ אֶל־הַמָּקוֹם אֲשֶׁר אָמַר־לוֹ בראשית כב

wood and bound Isaac his son and laid him on the altar on top of the wood. He reached out his hand and took the knife to slay his son. Then an angel of the LORD called out to him from heaven, "Abraham! Abraham!" He said, "Here I am." He said, "Do not reach out your hand against the boy; do not do anything to him, for now I know that you fear God, because you have not held back your son, your only son, from Me." Abraham looked up and there he saw a ram caught in a thicket by its horns, and Abraham went and took the ram and offered it as a burnt-offering instead of his son. Abraham called that place "The LORD will see," as is said to this day, "On the mountain of the LORD He will be seen." The angel of the LORD called to Abraham a second time from heaven, and said, "By Myself I swear, declares the LORD, that because you have done this and have not held back your son, your only son, I will greatly bless you and greatly multiply your descendants, as the stars of heaven and the sand of the seashore, and your descendants shall take possession of the gates of their enemies. Through your descendants, all the nations of the earth will be blessed, because you have heeded My voice." Then Abraham returned to his lads, and they rose and went together to Beersheba, and Abraham stayed in Beersheba.

Most omit this passage on Shabbat.

Master of the Universe, just as Abraham our father suppressed his compassion to do Your will wholeheartedly, so may Your compassion suppress Your anger from us and may Your compassion prevail over Your other attributes. Deal with us, LORD our God, with the attributes of loving-kindness and compassion, and in Your great goodness may Your anger be turned away from Your people, Your city, Your land and Your inheritance. Fulfill in us, LORD our God, the promise You made in Your Torah through the hand of Moses Your servant, as it is said: "I will remember My covenant with Jacob, and also My covenant with Isaac, and also My covenant with Abraham I will remember, and the land I will remember." *Lev. 26*

הָאֱלֹהִים, וַיִּבֶן שָׁם אַבְרָהָם אֶת־הַמִּזְבֵּחַ וַיַּעֲרֹךְ אֶת־הָעֵצִים,
וַיַּעֲקֹד אֶת־יִצְחָק בְּנוֹ, וַיָּשֶׂם אֹתוֹ עַל־הַמִּזְבֵּחַ מִמַּעַל לָעֵצִים:
וַיִּשְׁלַח אַבְרָהָם אֶת־יָדוֹ, וַיִּקַּח אֶת־הַמַּאֲכֶלֶת, לִשְׁחֹט אֶת־
בְּנוֹ: וַיִּקְרָא אֵלָיו מַלְאַךְ יהוה מִן־הַשָּׁמַיִם, וַיֹּאמֶר אַבְרָהָם
אַבְרָהָם, וַיֹּאמֶר הִנֵּנִי: וַיֹּאמֶר אַל־תִּשְׁלַח יָדְךָ אֶל־הַנַּעַר, וְאַל־
תַּעַשׂ לוֹ מְאוּמָה, כִּי עַתָּה יָדַעְתִּי כִּי־יְרֵא אֱלֹהִים אַתָּה, וְלֹא
חָשַׂכְתָּ אֶת־בִּנְךָ אֶת־יְחִידְךָ מִמֶּנִּי: וַיִּשָּׂא אַבְרָהָם אֶת־עֵינָיו,
וַיַּרְא וְהִנֵּה־אַיִל, אַחַר נֶאֱחַז בַּסְּבַךְ בְּקַרְנָיו, וַיֵּלֶךְ אַבְרָהָם
וַיִּקַּח אֶת־הָאַיִל, וַיַּעֲלֵהוּ לְעֹלָה תַּחַת בְּנוֹ: וַיִּקְרָא אַבְרָהָם
שֵׁם־הַמָּקוֹם הַהוּא יהוה יִרְאֶה, אֲשֶׁר יֵאָמֵר הַיּוֹם בְּהַר יהוה
יֵרָאֶה: וַיִּקְרָא מַלְאַךְ יהוה אֶל־אַבְרָהָם שֵׁנִית מִן־הַשָּׁמָיִם:
וַיֹּאמֶר, בִּי נִשְׁבַּעְתִּי נְאֻם־יהוה, כִּי יַעַן אֲשֶׁר עָשִׂיתָ אֶת־הַדָּבָר
הַזֶּה, וְלֹא חָשַׂכְתָּ אֶת־בִּנְךָ אֶת־יְחִידֶךָ: כִּי־בָרֵךְ אֲבָרֶכְךָ,
וְהַרְבָּה אַרְבֶּה אֶת־זַרְעֲךָ כְּכוֹכְבֵי הַשָּׁמַיִם, וְכַחוֹל אֲשֶׁר עַל־
שְׂפַת הַיָּם, וְיִרַשׁ זַרְעֲךָ אֵת שַׁעַר אֹיְבָיו: וְהִתְבָּרְכוּ בְזַרְעֲךָ
כֹּל גּוֹיֵי הָאָרֶץ, עֵקֶב אֲשֶׁר שָׁמַעְתָּ בְּקֹלִי: וַיָּשָׁב אַבְרָהָם
אֶל־נְעָרָיו, וַיָּקֻמוּ וַיֵּלְכוּ יַחְדָּו אֶל־בְּאֵר שָׁבַע, וַיֵּשֶׁב אַבְרָהָם
בִּבְאֵר שָׁבַע:

Most omit this passage on שבת.

רִבּוֹנוֹ שֶׁל עוֹלָם, כְּמוֹ שֶׁכָּבַשׁ אַבְרָהָם אָבִינוּ אֶת רַחֲמָיו לַעֲשׂוֹת רְצוֹנְךָ בְּלֵבָב
שָׁלֵם, כֵּן יִכְבְּשׁוּ רַחֲמֶיךָ אֶת כַּעַסְךָ מֵעָלֵינוּ וְיִגֹּלּוּ רַחֲמֶיךָ עַל מִדּוֹתֶיךָ. וְתִתְנַהֵג
עִמָּנוּ יהוה אֱלֹהֵינוּ בְּמִדַּת הַחֶסֶד וּבְמִדַּת הָרַחֲמִים, וּבְטוּבְךָ הַגָּדוֹל יָשׁוּב חֲרוֹן
אַפְּךָ מֵעַמְּךָ וּמֵעִירְךָ וּמֵאַרְצְךָ וּמִנַּחֲלָתֶךָ. וְקַיֶּם לָנוּ יהוה אֱלֹהֵינוּ אֶת הַדָּבָר
שֶׁהִבְטַחְתָּנוּ בְּתוֹרָתֶךָ עַל יְדֵי מֹשֶׁה עַבְדֶּךָ, כָּאָמוּר: וְזָכַרְתִּי אֶת־בְּרִיתִי יַעֲקוֹב ויקרא כו
וְאַף אֶת־בְּרִיתִי יִצְחָק, וְאַף אֶת־בְּרִיתִי אַבְרָהָם אֶזְכֹּר, וְהָאָרֶץ אֶזְכֹּר:

ACCEPTING THE SOVEREIGNTY OF HEAVEN[B]

לְעוֹלָם A person should always be God-fearing, privately and publicly, acknowledging the truth and speaking it in his heart. *Tanna DeVei Eliyahu, ch. 21*
He should rise early and say:

Master of all worlds,
not because of our righteousness *Dan. 9*
do we lay our pleas before You,
but because of Your great compassion.

What are we?
What are our lives?
What is our loving-kindness?
What is our righteousness?
What is our salvation?
What is our strength?
What is our might?
What shall we say before You,
LORD our God and God of our ancestors?
Are not all the mighty like nothing before You,
the men of renown as if they had never been,
the wise as if they know nothing,
and the understanding as if they lack intelligence?
For their many works are in vain,
and the days of their lives like a fleeting breath before You.
The pre-eminence of man over the animals is nothing, *Eccl. 3*
for all is but a fleeting breath.

---

could also explain the phrase toward the end, "those who sanctify Your name," which could be read as an allusion to those as martyrs who died *al Kiddush HaShem*, "for the sanctification of God's name."

But the truth is that even in our own day, living in completely open societies, there are many of us who are still afraid to go public with our Jewishness.

What aspects of your Jewishness could you permit to be seen more often where you work?

Among your friends? By your family? By yourself?

קבלת עול מלכות שמים[ב]

תנא דבי אליהו, פרק כא

לְעוֹלָם יְהֵא אָדָם יְרֵא שָׁמַיִם בְּסֵתֶר וּבְגָלוּי
וּמוֹדֶה עַל הָאֱמֶת, וְדוֹבֵר אֱמֶת בִּלְבָבוֹ
וְיַשְׁכֵּם וְיֹאמַר

רִבּוֹן כָּל הָעוֹלָמִים
דניאל ט לֹא עַל־צִדְקוֹתֵינוּ אֲנַחְנוּ מַפִּילִים תַּחֲנוּנֵינוּ לְפָנֶיךָ
כִּי עַל־רַחֲמֶיךָ הָרַבִּים:

מָה אָנוּ, מֶה חַיֵּינוּ, מֶה חַסְדֵּנוּ, מַה צִּדְקוֹתֵינוּ
מַה יְּשׁוּעָתֵנוּ, מַה כֹּחֵנוּ, מַה גְּבוּרָתֵנוּ
מַה נֹּאמַר לְפָנֶיךָ, יהוה אֱלֹהֵינוּ וֵאלֹהֵי אֲבוֹתֵינוּ
הֲלֹא כָּל הַגִּבּוֹרִים כְּאַיִן לְפָנֶיךָ
וְאַנְשֵׁי הַשֵּׁם כְּלֹא הָיוּ
וַחֲכָמִים כִּבְלִי מַדָּע, וּנְבוֹנִים כִּבְלִי הַשְׂכֵּל
כִּי רֹב מַעֲשֵׂיהֶם תֹּהוּ, וִימֵי חַיֵּיהֶם הֶבֶל לְפָנֶיךָ
קהלת ג וּמוֹתַר הָאָדָם מִן־הַבְּהֵמָה אָיִן
כִּי הַכֹּל הָבֶל:

BIUR TEFILLA • ביאור תפילה

קבלת עול מלכות שמים – *Accepting the sovereignty of heaven.* This section comes from a tenth-century midrash, *Tanna DeVei Eliyahu.* Its opening line raises questions, for why would it even be necessary to suggest that one should be God-fearing in private and in public – surely a God-fearing person is always so? Why distinguish? One answer suggests a historical source: In the times of the persecution under Persian rule in the fifth century, it was forbidden for Jews to observe Shabbat or read the Torah or recite the *Shema*. Jews therefore kept these things in private and recited the *Shema* at an earlier time so as not to be detected. This explains the opening line here as well as the inclusion of the first couple of lines of the *Shema* (*Shibbolei HaLeket*). It

אֲבָל Yet we are Your people, the children of Your covenant,
the children of Abraham, Your beloved,
to whom You made a promise on Mount Moriah;
the offspring of Isaac his only one who was bound on the altar;
the congregation of Jacob Your firstborn son
whom – because of the love with which You loved him
and the joy with which You rejoiced in him –
You called Yisrael and Yeshurun.

לְפִיכָךְ Therefore it is our duty
to thank You, and to praise, glorify, bless, sanctify
and give praise and thanks to Your name.
Happy are we, how good is our portion,
how lovely our fate, how beautiful our heritage.

▸ Happy are we who, early and late,
evening and morning, say twice each day –

Listen, Israel: the LORD is our God, the LORD is One. *Deut. 6*

Quietly: Blessed be the name of His glorious kingdom for ever and all time.

Some congregations say the entire first paragraph of the Shema (below) at this point. If there is a concern that the Shema will not be recited within the prescribed time, then all three paragraphs should be said.

Love the LORD your God with all your heart, with all your soul, and with all your might. These words which I command you today shall be on your heart. Teach them repeatedly to your children, speaking of them when you sit at home and when you travel on the way, when you lie down and when you rise. Bind them as a sign on your hand, and they shall be an emblem between your eyes. Write them on the doorposts of your house and gates.

אַתָּה הוּא It was You who existed
before the world was created,
it is You now that the world has been created.
It is You in this world
and You in the World to Come.

אֲבָל אֲנַחְנוּ עַמְּךָ בְּנֵי בְרִיתֶךָ
בְּנֵי אַבְרָהָם אֹהַבְךָ שֶׁנִּשְׁבַּעְתָּ לּוֹ בְּהַר הַמּוֹרִיָּה
זֶרַע יִצְחָק יְחִידוֹ שֶׁנֶּעֱקַד עַל גַּבֵּי הַמִּזְבֵּחַ
עֲדַת יַעֲקֹב בִּנְךָ בְּכוֹרֶךָ
שֶׁמֵּאַהֲבָתְךָ שֶׁאָהַבְתָּ אוֹתוֹ, וּמִשִּׂמְחָתְךָ שֶׁשָּׂמַחְתָּ בּוֹ
קָרָאתָ אֶת שְׁמוֹ יִשְׂרָאֵל וִישֻׁרוּן.

לְפִיכָךְ אֲנַחְנוּ חַיָּבִים לְהוֹדוֹת לְךָ וּלְשַׁבֵּחֲךָ וּלְפָאֶרְךָ
וּלְבָרֵךְ וּלְקַדֵּשׁ וְלָתֵת שֶׁבַח וְהוֹדָיָה לִשְׁמֶךָ.
אַשְׁרֵינוּ, מַה טּוֹב חֶלְקֵנוּ, וּמַה נָּעִים גּוֹרָלֵנוּ, וּמַה יָּפָה יְרֻשָּׁתֵנוּ.

אַשְׁרֵינוּ, שֶׁאֲנַחְנוּ מַשְׁכִּימִים וּמַעֲרִיבִים עֶרֶב וָבֹקֶר
וְאוֹמְרִים פַּעֲמַיִם בְּכָל יוֹם

דברים ו

שְׁמַע יִשְׂרָאֵל, יהוה אֱלֹהֵינוּ, יהוה אֶחָד:

Quietly בָּרוּךְ שֵׁם כְּבוֹד מַלְכוּתוֹ לְעוֹלָם וָעֶד.

Some congregations say the entire first paragraph of the שמע *(below) at this point. If there is a concern that the* שמע *will not be recited within the prescribed time, then all three paragraphs should be said.*

וְאָהַבְתָּ אֵת יהוה אֱלֹהֶיךָ, בְּכָל־לְבָבְךָ, וּבְכָל־נַפְשְׁךָ, וּבְכָל־מְאֹדֶךָ: וְהָיוּ הַדְּבָרִים הָאֵלֶּה, אֲשֶׁר אָנֹכִי מְצַוְּךָ הַיּוֹם, עַל־לְבָבֶךָ: וְשִׁנַּנְתָּם לְבָנֶיךָ, וְדִבַּרְתָּ בָּם, בְּשִׁבְתְּךָ בְּבֵיתֶךָ, וּבְלֶכְתְּךָ בַדֶּרֶךְ, וּבְשָׁכְבְּךָ וּבְקוּמֶךָ: וּקְשַׁרְתָּם לְאוֹת עַל־יָדֶךָ וְהָיוּ לְטֹטָפֹת בֵּין עֵינֶיךָ: וּכְתַבְתָּם עַל־מְזֻזוֹת בֵּיתֶךָ וּבִשְׁעָרֶיךָ:

אַתָּה הוּא עַד שֶׁלֹּא נִבְרָא הָעוֹלָם
אַתָּה הוּא מִשֶּׁנִּבְרָא הָעוֹלָם.
אַתָּה הוּא בָּעוֹלָם הַזֶּה
וְאַתָּה הוּא לָעוֹלָם הַבָּא.

Sanctify Your name through those who sanctify Your name,
and sanctify Your name
throughout Your world.
By Your salvation may our pride be exalted;
raise high our pride.
Blessed are You, Lord,
who sanctifies His name among the multitudes.

אַתָּה הוּא You are the Lord our God
in heaven and on earth,
and in the highest heaven of heavens.
Truly, You are the first
and You are the last,
and besides You there is no god.
Gather those who hope in You
from the four quarters of the earth.
May all mankind recognize and know
that You alone are God
over all the kingdoms on earth.

You made the heavens and the earth,
the sea and all they contain.
Who among all the works of Your hands,
above and below,
can tell You what to do?

Heavenly Father, deal kindly with us
for the sake of Your great name by which we are called,
and fulfill for us, Lord our God,
that which is written:

> "At that time I will bring you home, and at that time I will gather you, for I will give you renown and praise among all the peoples of the earth when I bring back your exiles before your eyes, says the Lord." *Zeph. 3*

קַדֵּשׁ אֶת שִׁמְךָ עַל מַקְדִּישֵׁי שְׁמֶךָ
וְקַדֵּשׁ אֶת שִׁמְךָ בְּעוֹלָמֶךָ
וּבִישׁוּעָתְךָ תָּרוּם וְתַגְבִּיהַּ קַרְנֵנוּ.
בָּרוּךְ אַתָּה יהוה, הַמְקַדֵּשׁ אֶת שִׁמְךָ בָּרַבִּים.

אַתָּה הוּא יהוה אֱלֹהֵינוּ
בַּשָּׁמַיִם וּבָאָרֶץ, וּבִשְׁמֵי הַשָּׁמַיִם הָעֶלְיוֹנִים.
אֱמֶת, אַתָּה הוּא רִאשׁוֹן
וְאַתָּה הוּא אַחֲרוֹן
וּמִבַּלְעָדֶיךָ אֵין אֱלֹהִים.
קַבֵּץ קֹוֶיךָ מֵאַרְבַּע כַּנְפוֹת הָאָרֶץ.
יַכִּירוּ וְיֵדְעוּ כָּל בָּאֵי עוֹלָם
כִּי אַתָּה הוּא הָאֱלֹהִים לְבַדְּךָ לְכֹל מַמְלְכוֹת הָאָרֶץ.

אַתָּה עָשִׂיתָ אֶת הַשָּׁמַיִם וְאֶת הָאָרֶץ
אֶת הַיָּם וְאֶת כָּל אֲשֶׁר בָּם
וּמִי בְּכָל מַעֲשֵׂי יָדֶיךָ בָּעֶלְיוֹנִים אוֹ בַתַּחְתּוֹנִים
שֶׁיֹּאמַר לְךָ מַה תַּעֲשֶׂה.

אָבִינוּ שֶׁבַּשָּׁמַיִם, עֲשֵׂה עִמָּנוּ חֶסֶד
בַּעֲבוּר שִׁמְךָ הַגָּדוֹל שֶׁנִּקְרָא עָלֵינוּ
וְקַיֶּם לָנוּ יהוה אֱלֹהֵינוּ
מַה שֶּׁכָּתוּב:
בָּעֵת הַהִיא אָבִיא אֶתְכֶם, וּבָעֵת קַבְּצִי אֶתְכֶם, צפניה ג
כִּי־אֶתֵּן אֶתְכֶם לְשֵׁם וְלִתְהִלָּה בְּכֹל עַמֵּי הָאָרֶץ,
בְּשׁוּבִי אֶת־שְׁבוּתֵיכֶם לְעֵינֵיכֶם, אָמַר יהוה:

OFFERINGS

The sages held that, in the absence of the Temple, studying the laws of sacrifices is the equivalent of offering them. Hence the following texts. There are different customs as to how many passages are to be said, and one should follow the custom of one's congregation.

The minimum requirement is to say the verses relating to The Daily Sacrifice on the next page.

THE BASIN[B]

The LORD spoke to Moses, saying: Make a bronze basin, with its bronze stand for washing, and place it between the Tent of Meeting and the altar, and put water in it. From it, Aaron and his sons are to wash their hands and feet. When they enter the Tent of Meeting, they shall wash with water so that they will not die; likewise when they approach the altar to minister, presenting a fire-offering to the LORD. They must wash their hands and feet so that they will not die. This shall be an everlasting ordinance for Aaron and his descendants throughout their generations. *Ex. 30*

---

of the entire corpus of Jewish law relating to the *korbanot* (sacrifices). The first major selection (*Tamid*) comes from the Torah, the second comes from Mishna (*Eizehu mekoman*), and the third (*R. Yishmael omer*) comes from Gemara (Tosafot, *Kiddushin* 30a). We thus bring to bear all aspects of Torah in both its written and oral forms. Over time, other passages were added, each for its own reason.

It is not clear whether the passages need to be learned such that one strives to understand all of their detail, thus making it a fulfillment of the mitzva of learning Torah (*Mishna Berura* 48:1), or whether simply reading it is enough – just as prayer with sincere intentions can compensate for a lack of comprehension of the prayers' meaning. (cf. *Magen Avraham* 50:2). Ideally, then, one should try to understand the words but, in the absence of that, reading these passages alone, allowing the recitation to bring one *karov* or in closer proximity to Hashem, may be all the offering necessary.

BIUR TEFILLA • בִּיאוּר תְּפִלָּה

פרשת הכיור – *The basin.* This passage is a description of the laver with which the *kohanim* (priests) washed their hands and feet before they went about their work. It thus became an introduction to the passages about the *korbanot* (sacrifices) since it preceded them. As they prepared themselves for the sacrifices, we prepare ourselves through its recitation. One's hands and feet are the primary appendages for accomplishing our goals as humans. With our hands we do, and with our legs we go. **How can you sanctify your hands and legs today?**

סדר הקרבנות

חז״ל held that, in the absence of the Temple, studying the laws of sacrifices is the equivalent of offering them. Hence the following texts. There are different customs as to how many passages are to be said, and one should follow the custom of one's congregation.

The minimum requirement is to say the verses relating to the קרבן תמיד on the next page.

פרשת הכיור[ב]

וַיְדַבֵּר יהוה אֶל־מֹשֶׁה לֵּאמֹר: וְעָשִׂיתָ כִּיּוֹר נְחֹשֶׁת וְכַנּוֹ נְחֹשֶׁת לְרָחְצָה, שמות ל
וְנָתַתָּ אֹתוֹ בֵּין־אֹהֶל מוֹעֵד וּבֵין הַמִּזְבֵּחַ, וְנָתַתָּ שָׁמָּה מָיִם: וְרָחֲצוּ אַהֲרֹן
וּבָנָיו מִמֶּנּוּ אֶת־יְדֵיהֶם וְאֶת־רַגְלֵיהֶם: בְּבֹאָם אֶל־אֹהֶל מוֹעֵד יִרְחֲצוּ־
מַיִם, וְלֹא יָמֻתוּ, אוֹ בְגִשְׁתָּם אֶל־הַמִּזְבֵּחַ לְשָׁרֵת, לְהַקְטִיר אִשֶּׁה לַיהוה:
וְרָחֲצוּ יְדֵיהֶם וְרַגְלֵיהֶם וְלֹא יָמֻתוּ, וְהָיְתָה לָהֶם חָק־עוֹלָם, לוֹ וּלְזַרְעוֹ
לְדֹרֹתָם:

AN INTRODUCTION TO KORBANOT (OFFERINGS)

Prayer is called "service of the heart," a parallel to the "service of the Temple" that took place for hundreds of years until the year 70 CE when the Second Temple was destroyed. In the aftermath of the destruction, prayer became more formalized and was seen as a substitute for the sacrifices which could no longer be offered as expressed by the prophet Hoshea (14:3): **וּנְשַׁלְּמָה פָרִים שְׂפָתֵינוּ** – "and let our lips substitute for bulls."

The word "sacrifice" in Hebrew is *korban* which comes from the same root as the word *karov*, meaning close in proximity. Sacrifices brought man closer to God, both individually and communally, in a way that no other worship could. Foreign as it may be for the modern sensibilities of some, one can nevertheless imagine the pageantry, the anticipation and the elation that came with visiting the place most identified with God's presence on earth. Our prayers are supposed to mimic that experience.

The Written and Oral Law (Torah and Talmud) provide enormous amounts of meticulous detail about these rituals and how they were carried out, some quite mystifying. This led many commentaries to try to additionally discern symbolic significance to many of these details, something that you are certainly free to try on your own. On the simplest level, however, the Gemara (*Ta'anit* 27b; *Megilla* 31b) recounts in the name of Hashem that "If they read about the sacrifices before Me, I will count it as if they offered them before Me, and I will forgive them for their sins." Before moving on to the core of the morning service, we therefore take a few moments to familiarize ourselves with some of these rituals, to learn them, to relive them and to offer them up with our words and our hearts.

The selections are but representative

TAKING OF THE ASHES[B]

The LORD spoke to Moses, saying: Instruct Aaron and his sons, saying, *Lev. 6*
This is the law of the burnt-offering. The burnt-offering shall remain on the altar hearth throughout the night until morning, and the altar fire shall be kept burning on it. The priest shall then put on his linen garments, and linen breeches next to his body, and shall remove the ashes of the burnt-offering that the fire has consumed on the altar and place them beside the altar. Then he shall take off these clothes and put on others, and carry the ashes outside the camp to a clean place. The fire on the altar must be kept burning; it must not go out. Each morning the priest shall burn wood on it, and prepare on it the burnt-offering and burn the fat of the peace-offerings. A perpetual fire must be kept burning on the altar; it must not go out.

May it be Your will, LORD our God and God of our ancestors, that You have compassion on us and pardon us all our sins, grant atonement for all our iniquities and forgive all our transgressions. May You rebuild the Temple swiftly in our days so that we may offer You the continual-offering that it may atone for us as You have prescribed for us in Your Torah through Moses Your servant, from the mouthpiece of Your glory, as it is said:

THE DAILY SACRIFICE[B]

וַיְדַבֵּר The LORD said to Moses, "Command the Israelites and *Num. 28*
tell them: 'Be careful to offer to Me at the appointed time My food-offering consumed by fire, as an aroma pleasing to Me.' Tell them: 'This is the fire-offering you shall offer to the LORD – two lambs a year old without blemish, as a regular burnt-offering each day. Prepare one lamb in the morning and the other toward

---

for taking care not to soil one's garments, but, at the same time, it is a reminder that, afterwards, one should maintain appropriate dress in Divine service. Hence the requirement that one be careful about how one dresses for prayer in general and, in the context of Shabbat, that one change into "Shabbat clothes" in honor of Shabbat, even if one does not attend synagogue services (Maharsha, *Shabbat* 114a).

פרשת קרבן התמיד – *The daily sacrifice.* Of all of the sacrifices mentioned in this section, the one describing the *Korban Tamid* is the one considered most obligatory (Rema 48:1). It is of special significance because the timing of the three prayer services in the day corresponds to three periods related to the sacrifice of the daily *Tamid* offering (*Berakhot* 26b). It was a communal offering, paid for by a communal tax for which everyone contributed a half-shekel. In the morning it was sacrificed amidst a festive air, accompanied by the songs of the Levites who chanted the song of that particular day, as we will do at the end of our morning service.

פרשת תרומת הדשן

וַיְדַבֵּר יהוה אֶל־מֹשֶׁה לֵּאמֹר: צַו אֶת־אַהֲרֹן וְאֶת־בָּנָיו לֵאמֹר, זֹאת תּוֹרַת ויקרא ו
הָעֹלָה, הִוא הָעֹלָה עַל מוֹקְדָה עַל־הַמִּזְבֵּחַ כָּל־הַלַּיְלָה עַד־הַבֹּקֶר, וְאֵשׁ
הַמִּזְבֵּחַ תּוּקַד בּוֹ: וְלָבַשׁ הַכֹּהֵן מִדּוֹ בַד, וּמִכְנְסֵי־בַד יִלְבַּשׁ עַל־בְּשָׂרוֹ, וְהֵרִים
אֶת־הַדֶּשֶׁן אֲשֶׁר תֹּאכַל הָאֵשׁ אֶת־הָעֹלָה, עַל־הַמִּזְבֵּחַ, וְשָׂמוֹ אֵצֶל הַמִּזְבֵּחַ:
וּפָשַׁט אֶת־בְּגָדָיו, וְלָבַשׁ בְּגָדִים אֲחֵרִים, וְהוֹצִיא אֶת־הַדֶּשֶׁן אֶל־מִחוּץ לַמַּחֲנֶה,
אֶל־מָקוֹם טָהוֹר: וְהָאֵשׁ עַל־הַמִּזְבֵּחַ תּוּקַד־בּוֹ, לֹא תִכְבֶּה, וּבִעֵר עָלֶיהָ הַכֹּהֵן
עֵצִים בַּבֹּקֶר בַּבֹּקֶר, וְעָרַךְ עָלֶיהָ הָעֹלָה, וְהִקְטִיר עָלֶיהָ חֶלְבֵי הַשְּׁלָמִים: אֵשׁ,
תָּמִיד תּוּקַד עַל־הַמִּזְבֵּחַ, לֹא תִכְבֶּה:

יְהִי רָצוֹן מִלְּפָנֶיךָ יהוה אֱלֹהֵינוּ וֵאלֹהֵי אֲבוֹתֵינוּ, שֶׁתְּרַחֵם עָלֵינוּ, וְתִמְחֹל לָנוּ עַל כָּל חַטֹּאתֵינוּ וּתְכַפֶּר לָנוּ עַל כָּל עֲוֹנוֹתֵינוּ וְתִסְלַח לָנוּ עַל כָּל פְּשָׁעֵינוּ, וְתִבְנֶה בֵּית הַמִּקְדָּשׁ בִּמְהֵרָה בְיָמֵינוּ, וְנַקְרִיב לְפָנֶיךָ קָרְבַּן הַתָּמִיד שֶׁיְּכַפֵּר בַּעֲדֵנוּ, כְּמוֹ שֶׁכָּתַבְתָּ עָלֵינוּ בְּתוֹרָתֶךָ עַל יְדֵי מֹשֶׁה עַבְדֶּךָ מִפִּי כְבוֹדֶךָ, כָּאָמוּר

פרשת קרבן התמיד

וַיְדַבֵּר יהוה אֶל־מֹשֶׁה לֵּאמֹר: צַו אֶת־בְּנֵי יִשְׂרָאֵל וְאָמַרְתָּ אֲלֵהֶם, במדבר כח
אֶת־קָרְבָּנִי לַחְמִי לְאִשַּׁי, רֵיחַ נִיחֹחִי, תִּשְׁמְרוּ לְהַקְרִיב לִי בְּמוֹעֲדוֹ:
וְאָמַרְתָּ לָהֶם, זֶה הָאִשֶּׁה אֲשֶׁר תַּקְרִיבוּ לַיהוה, כְּבָשִׂים בְּנֵי־
שָׁנָה תְמִימִם שְׁנַיִם לַיּוֹם, עֹלָה תָמִיד: אֶת־הַכֶּבֶשׂ אֶחָד תַּעֲשֶׂה
בַבֹּקֶר, וְאֵת הַכֶּבֶשׂ הַשֵּׁנִי תַּעֲשֶׂה בֵּין הָעַרְבָּיִם: וַעֲשִׂירִית הָאֵיפָה

BIUR TEFILLA • ביאור תפילה

פרשת תרומת הדשן – *Taking of the ashes.* The removal of the ashes from the altar was another necessary prerequisite to the beginning of the sacrificial order of the day and so it too came to be included in this section. As with all of the sacrificial order, some of the procedures mentioned are practical, such as the occasional removal of the ashes when too much of it accumulates. But others may be more symbolic. For example, the passage makes reference to the need to take a small amount of ash remaining from the previous day's sacrifices and place it on the floor of the courtyard near the ramp to the altar. Perhaps this is a reminder that one must try to first rid oneself of the old before beginning anew. Alternatively, perhaps this is a reminder that we will continue to serve God, just as we did yesterday (Rabbi S. Hirsch).

Similarly, the requirement that the *kohen* (priest) change his clothes before removing the ash is a practical reminder

evening, together with a meal-offering of a tenth of an ephah of fine flour mixed with a quarter of a hin of oil from pressed olives. This is the regular burnt-offering instituted at Mount Sinai as a pleasing aroma, a fire-offering made to the LORD. Its libation is to be a quarter of a hin [of wine] with each lamb, poured in the Sanctuary as a libation of strong drink to the LORD. Prepare the second lamb in the afternoon, along with the same meal-offering and libation as in the morning. This is a fire-offering, an aroma pleasing to the LORD.'"

וְשָׁחַט He shall slaughter it at the north side of the altar before the LORD, and Aaron's sons the priests shall sprinkle its blood against the altar on all sides. *Lev. 1*

May it be Your will, LORD our God and God of our ancestors,
that this recitation be considered accepted and favored before You
as if we had offered the daily sacrifice at its appointed time and place, according to its laws.

It is You, LORD our God, to whom our ancestors offered fragrant incense when the Temple stood, as You commanded them through Moses Your prophet, as is written in Your Torah:

THE INCENSE[B]

The LORD said to Moses: Take fragrant spices – balsam, onycha, galbanum and pure frankincense, all in equal amounts – and make a fragrant blend of incense, the work of a perfumer, well mixed, pure and holy. Grind it very finely and place it in front of the [Ark of] Testimony in the Tent of Meeting, where I will meet with you. It shall be most holy to you. *Ex. 30*

And it is said:

Aaron shall burn fragrant incense on the altar every morning when he cleans the lamps. He shall burn incense again when he lights the lamps toward evening so that there will be incense before the LORD at all times, throughout your generations.

---

of ethics (Love your neighbor) but rather in the day-to-day consistency of service.

Tamid means consistency, a reflection of the daily service in the *Beit HaMikdash* and the daily service of the heart that we perform today.

BIUR TEFILLA • ביאור תפילה

פרשת הקטורת – *The incense.* Incense was burned on the Golden Altar (the one inside the Sanctuary as opposed to the much larger one outside, used for offerings every day. The incense was made from a very precise formula that is described here in great detail and will be referred to again at the end of the Shabbat service.

This **BIUR TEFILLA** *continues on page 203.*

סֹלֶת לְמִנְחָה, בְּלוּלָה בְּשֶׁמֶן כָּתִית רְבִיעִת הַהִין: עֹלַת תָּמִיד,
הָעֲשֻׂיָה בְּהַר סִינַי, לְרֵיחַ נִיחֹחַ אִשֶּׁה לַיהוה: וְנִסְכּוֹ רְבִיעִת הַהִין
לַכֶּבֶשׂ הָאֶחָד, בַּקֹּדֶשׁ הַסֵּךְ נֶסֶךְ שֵׁכָר לַיהוה: וְאֵת הַכֶּבֶשׂ הַשֵּׁנִי
תַּעֲשֶׂה בֵּין הָעַרְבָּיִם, כְּמִנְחַת הַבֹּקֶר וּכְנִסְכּוֹ תַּעֲשֶׂה, אִשֵּׁה רֵיחַ
נִיחֹחַ לַיהוה:

וְשָׁחַט אֹתוֹ עַל יֶרֶךְ הַמִּזְבֵּחַ צָפֹנָה לִפְנֵי יהוה, וְזָרְקוּ בְּנֵי אַהֲרֹן ויקרא א
הַכֹּהֲנִים אֶת־דָּמוֹ עַל־הַמִּזְבֵּחַ, סָבִיב:

יְהִי רָצוֹן מִלְּפָנֶיךָ, יהוה אֱלֹהֵינוּ וֵאלֹהֵי אֲבוֹתֵינוּ
שֶׁתְּהֵא אֲמִירָה זוֹ חֲשׁוּבָה וּמְקֻבֶּלֶת וּמְרֻצָּה לְפָנֶיךָ
כְּאִלּוּ הִקְרַבְנוּ קָרְבַּן הַתָּמִיד בְּמוֹעֲדוֹ וּבִמְקוֹמוֹ וּכְהִלְכָתוֹ.

אַתָּה הוּא יהוה אֱלֹהֵינוּ שֶׁהִקְטִירוּ אֲבוֹתֵינוּ לְפָנֶיךָ אֶת קְטֹרֶת הַסַּמִּים בִּזְמַן שֶׁבֵּית
הַמִּקְדָּשׁ הָיָה קַיָּם, כַּאֲשֶׁר צִוִּיתָ אוֹתָם עַל יְדֵי מֹשֶׁה נְבִיאֶךָ, כַּכָּתוּב בְּתוֹרָתֶךָ:

פרשת הקטורת[ב]

וַיֹּאמֶר יהוה אֶל־מֹשֶׁה, קַח־לְךָ סַמִּים נָטָף וּשְׁחֵלֶת וְחֶלְבְּנָה, סַמִּים וּלְבֹנָה זַכָּה, שמות ל
בַּד בְּבַד יִהְיֶה: וְעָשִׂיתָ אֹתָהּ קְטֹרֶת, רֹקַח מַעֲשֵׂה רוֹקֵחַ, מְמֻלָּח, טָהוֹר קֹדֶשׁ:
וְשָׁחַקְתָּ מִמֶּנָּה הָדֵק, וְנָתַתָּה מִמֶּנָּה לִפְנֵי הָעֵדֻת בְּאֹהֶל מוֹעֵד אֲשֶׁר אִוָּעֵד לְךָ
שָׁמָּה, קֹדֶשׁ קָדָשִׁים תִּהְיֶה לָכֶם:

וְנֶאֱמַר
וְהִקְטִיר עָלָיו אַהֲרֹן קְטֹרֶת סַמִּים, בַּבֹּקֶר בַּבֹּקֶר בְּהֵיטִיבוֹ אֶת־הַנֵּרֹת יַקְטִירֶנָּה:
וּבְהַעֲלֹת אַהֲרֹן אֶת־הַנֵּרֹת בֵּין הָעַרְבַּיִם יַקְטִירֶנָּה, קְטֹרֶת תָּמִיד לִפְנֵי יהוה
לְדֹרֹתֵיכֶם:

ANI TEFILLA • אני תפילה

Ben Zoma said: "We find the most all-inclusive statement in 'Shema Yisrael… – Listen, O Israel, the Lord *is our God, the* Lord *is One.'" Ben Nanes said: "The most all-inclusive statement, is 'Love your neighbor as yourself.'" Shimon ben Pazi said: "The most all-inclusive statement, is "Prepare one lamb in the morning, and the other toward evening.'" Rabbi Ploni stood up and declared: "The law is in accordance with Ben Pazi."* (*Introduction to Ein Yaakov*)

Why is the third opinion, which takes its cues from our verses here which speak of the *Tamid* offering, considered the most authoritative? Perhaps it is that the single most important aspect of religious life is not in theology (*Shema Yisrael*) nor in the realm

The rabbis taught: How was the incense prepared? It weighed 368 manehs, 365 corresponding to the number of days in a solar year, a maneh for each day, half to be offered in the morning and half in the afternoon, and three additional manehs from which the High Priest took two handfuls on Yom Kippur. These were put back into the mortar on the day before Yom Kippur and ground again very thoroughly so as to be extremely fine. The incense contained eleven kinds of spices: balsam, onycha, galbanum and frankincense, each weighing seventy manehs; myrrh, cassia, spikenard and saffron, each weighing sixteen manehs; twelve manehs of costus, three of aromatic bark; nine of cinnamon; nine kabs of Carsina lye; three seahs and three kabs of Cyprus wine. If Cyprus wine was not available, old white wine might be used. A quarter of a kab of Sodom salt, and a minute amount of a smoke-raising herb. Rabbi Nathan the Babylonian says: also a minute amount of Jordan amber. If one added honey to the mixture, he rendered it unfit for sacred use. If he omitted any one of its ingredients, he is guilty of a capital offense. *Keritot 6a*

Rabban Simeon ben Gamliel says: "Balsam" refers to the sap that drips from the balsam tree. The Carsina lye was used for bleaching the onycha to improve it. The Cyprus wine was used to soak the onycha in it to make it pungent. Though urine is suitable for this purpose, it is not brought into the Temple out of respect.

It was taught, Rabbi Nathan says: While it was being ground, another would say, "Grind well, well grind," because the [rhythmic] sound is good for spices. If it was mixed in half-quantities, it is fit for use, but we have not heard whether this applies to a third or a quarter. Rabbi Judah said: The general rule is that if it was made in the correct proportions, it is fit for use even if made in half-quantity, but if he omitted any one of its ingredients, he is guilty of a capital offense.

It was taught, Bar Kappara says: Once every sixty or seventy years, the accumulated surpluses amounted to half the yearly quantity. Bar Kappara also taught: If a minute quantity of honey had been mixed into the incense, no one could have resisted the scent. Why did they not put honey into it? Because the Torah says, "For you are not to burn any leaven or honey in a fire-offering made to the Lord." *JT Yoma 4:5* *Lev. 2*

The following three verses are each said three times:

The Lord of hosts is with us; the God of Jacob is our stronghold, Selah. *Ps. 46*
Lord of hosts, happy is the one who trusts in You. *Ps. 84*
Lord, save! May the King answer us on the day we call. *Ps. 20*

---

utilitarian. Our sense of smell may be different from our other senses in that it cannot be as easily quantified. It is certainly something physical but its benefits may instead be primarily spiritual. "What is something that the soul benefits from but the body does not?" asks the Talmud (*Berakhot* 43b); to which it answers: "One must perforce say that it is the sense of smell" (Rabbi S. Aviner).

כריתות ו.
תָּנוּ רַבָּנָן: פִּטּוּם הַקְּטֹרֶת כֵּיצַד, שְׁלֹשׁ מֵאוֹת וְשִׁשִּׁים וּשְׁמוֹנָה מָנִים הָיוּ בָהּ. שְׁלֹשׁ מֵאוֹת וְשִׁשִּׁים וַחֲמִשָּׁה כְּמִנְיַן יְמוֹת הַחַמָּה, מָנֶה לְכָל יוֹם, פְּרַס בְּשַׁחֲרִית וּפְרַס בֵּין הָעַרְבַּיִם, וּשְׁלֹשָׁה מָנִים יְתֵרִים שֶׁמֵּהֶם מַכְנִיס כֹּהֵן גָּדוֹל מְלֹא חָפְנָיו בְּיוֹם הַכִּפּוּרִים, וּמַחֲזִירָן לְמַכְתֶּשֶׁת בְּעֶרֶב יוֹם הַכִּפּוּרִים וְשׁוֹחֲקָן יָפֶה יָפֶה, כְּדֵי שֶׁתְּהֵא דַקָּה מִן הַדַּקָּה. וְאַחַד עָשָׂר סַמָּנִים הָיוּ בָהּ, וְאֵלּוּ הֵן: הַצֳּרִי, וְהַצִּפֹּרֶן, וְהַחֶלְבְּנָה, וְהַלְּבוֹנָה מִשְׁקַל שִׁבְעִים שִׁבְעִים מָנֶה, מוֹר, וּקְצִיעָה, שִׁבֹּלֶת נֵרְדְּ, וְכַרְכֹּם מִשְׁקַל שִׁשָּׁה עָשָׂר שִׁשָּׁה עָשָׂר מָנֶה, הַקֹּשְׁטְ שְׁנֵים עָשָׂר, קִלּוּפָה שְׁלֹשָׁה, קִנָּמוֹן תִּשְׁעָה, בֹּרִית כַּרְשִׁינָה תִּשְׁעָה קַבִּין, יֵין קַפְרִיסִין סְאִין תְּלָת וְקַבִּין תְּלָתָא, וְאִם לֹא מָצָא יֵין קַפְרִיסִין, מֵבִיא חֲמַר חִוַּרְיָן עַתִּיק. מֶלַח סְדוֹמִית רֹבַע, מַעֲלֶה עָשָׁן כָּל שֶׁהוּא. רַבִּי נָתָן הַבַּבְלִי אוֹמֵר: אַף כִּפַּת הַיַּרְדֵּן כָּל שֶׁהוּא, וְאִם נָתַן בָּהּ דְּבַשׁ פְּסָלָהּ, וְאִם חִסַּר אֶחָד מִכָּל סַמָּנֶיהָ, חַיָּב מִיתָה.

רַבָּן שִׁמְעוֹן בֶּן גַּמְלִיאֵל אוֹמֵר: הַצֳּרִי אֵינוֹ אֶלָּא שְׂרָף הַנּוֹטֵף מֵעֲצֵי הַקְּטָף. בֹּרִית כַּרְשִׁינָה שֶׁשָּׁפִין בָּהּ אֶת הַצִּפֹּרֶן כְּדֵי שֶׁתְּהֵא נָאָה, יֵין קַפְרִיסִין שֶׁשּׁוֹרִין בּוֹ אֶת הַצִּפֹּרֶן כְּדֵי שֶׁתְּהֵא עַזָּה, וַהֲלֹא מֵי רַגְלַיִם יָפִין לָהּ, אֶלָּא שֶׁאֵין מַכְנִיסִין מֵי רַגְלַיִם בַּמִּקְדָּשׁ מִפְּנֵי הַכָּבוֹד.

תַּנְיָא, רַבִּי נָתָן אוֹמֵר: כְּשֶׁהוּא שׁוֹחֵק אוֹמֵר, הָדֵק הֵיטֵב הֵיטֵב הָדֵק, מִפְּנֵי שֶׁהַקּוֹל יָפֶה לַבְּשָׂמִים. פִּטְּמָהּ לַחֲצָאִין כְּשֵׁרָה, לִשְׁלִישׁ וְלִרְבִיעַ לֹא שָׁמַעְנוּ. אָמַר רַבִּי יְהוּדָה: זֶה הַכְּלָל, אִם כְּמִדָּתָהּ כְּשֵׁרָה לַחֲצָאִין, וְאִם חִסַּר אֶחָד מִכָּל סַמָּנֶיהָ חַיָּב מִיתָה.

ירושלמי יומא ד, הלכה ה
תַּנְיָא, בַּר קַפָּרָא אוֹמֵר: אַחַת לְשִׁשִּׁים אוֹ לְשִׁבְעִים שָׁנָה הָיְתָה בָאָה שֶׁל שִׁירַיִם לַחֲצָאִין. וְעוֹד תָּנֵי בַּר קַפָּרָא: אִלּוּ הָיָה נוֹתֵן בָּהּ קוֹרְטוֹב שֶׁל דְּבַשׁ אֵין אָדָם יָכוֹל
ויקרא ב
לַעֲמֹד מִפְּנֵי רֵיחָהּ, וְלָמָּה אֵין מְעָרְבִין בָּהּ דְּבַשׁ, מִפְּנֵי שֶׁהַתּוֹרָה אָמְרָה: כִּי כָל־שְׂאֹר וְכָל־דְּבַשׁ לֹא־תַקְטִירוּ מִמֶּנּוּ אִשֶּׁה לַיהוה:

The following three verses are each said three times:

תהלים מו
יהוה צְבָאוֹת עִמָּנוּ, מִשְׂגָּב לָנוּ אֱלֹהֵי יַעֲקֹב סֶלָה:

תהלים פד
יהוה צְבָאוֹת, אַשְׁרֵי אָדָם בֹּטֵחַ בָּךְ:

תהלים כ
יהוה הוֹשִׁיעָה, הַמֶּלֶךְ יַעֲנֵנוּ בְיוֹם־קָרְאֵנוּ:

The Torah does not explain the reason for this practice and so its symbolic meaning is left to the individual to discover, although its practice does not seem to have been

You are my hiding place; You will protect me from distress Ps. 32
and surround me with songs of salvation, Selah.
Then the offering of Judah and Jerusalem will be pleasing to the LORD Mal. 3
as in the days of old and as in former years.

THE ORDER OF THE PRIESTLY FUNCTIONS[B]

Abaye related the order of the daily priestly functions in the name of tradition and in accordance with Abba Shaul: The large pile [of wood] comes before the second pile for the incense; the second pile for the incense precedes the laying in order of the two logs of wood; the laying in order of the two logs of wood comes before the removing of ashes from the inner altar; the removing of ashes from the inner altar precedes the cleaning of the five lamps; the cleaning of the five lamps comes before the blood of the daily offering; the blood of the daily offering precedes the cleaning of the [other] two lamps; the cleaning of the two lamps comes before the incense-offering; the incense-offering precedes the burning of the limbs; the burning of the limbs comes before the meal-offering; the meal-offering precedes the pancakes; the pancakes come before the wine-libations; the wine-libations precede the additional offerings; the additional offerings come before the [frankincense] censers; the censers precede the daily afternoon offering; as it is said, "On it he shall arrange burnt-offerings, and on it he shall burn the fat of the peace-offerings" – "on it" [the daily offering] all the offerings were completed. Yoma 33a Lev. 6

Please, by the power of Your great right hand, set the captive nation free.
Accept Your people's prayer. Strengthen us, purify us, You who are revered.
Please, Mighty One, guard like the pupil of the eye those who seek Your unity.
Bless them, cleanse them, have compassion on them,
grant them Your righteousness always.
Mighty One, Holy One, in Your great goodness guide Your congregation.
Only One, Exalted One, turn to Your people, who proclaim Your holiness.
Accept our plea and heed our cry, You who know all secret thoughts.
Blessed be the name of His glorious kingdom for ever and all time.

Master of the Universe, You have commanded us to offer the daily sacrifice at its appointed time with the priests at their service, the Levites on their platform, and the Israelites at their post. Now, because of our sins, the Temple is destroyed and the daily sacrifice discontinued, and we have no priest at his service, no Levite on his platform, no Israelite at his post. But You said: "We will offer in place of bullocks [the prayer of] our lips." Therefore may it be Your will, LORD our God and God of our ancestors, that the prayer of our lips be considered, accepted and favored before You as if we had offered the daily sacrifice at its appointed time and place, according to its laws. Hos. 14

It, in turn, is followed by a passage of mystical significance that is described a little more in the commentary on the service for Friday night (page 57).

אַתָּה סֵתֶר לִי, מִצַּר תִּצְּרֵנִי, רָנֵּי פַלֵּט תְּסוֹבְבֵנִי סֶלָה: תהלים לב
וְעָרְבָה לַיהוה מִנְחַת יְהוּדָה וִירוּשָׁלָםִ, כִּימֵי עוֹלָם וּכְשָׁנִים קַדְמֹנִיּוֹת: מלאכי ג

סדר המערכה[ב]

אַבַּיֵּי הֲוָה מְסַדֵּר סֵדֶר הַמַּעֲרָכָה מִשְּׁמָא דִּגְמָרָא, וְאַלִּבָּא דְאַבָּא שָׁאוּל: יומא לג.
מַעֲרָכָה גְדוֹלָה קוֹדֶמֶת לְמַעֲרָכָה שְׁנִיָּה שֶׁל קְטֹרֶת, וּמַעֲרָכָה שְׁנִיָּה שֶׁל
קְטֹרֶת קוֹדֶמֶת לְסִדּוּר שְׁנֵי גִזְרֵי עֵצִים, וְסִדּוּר שְׁנֵי גִזְרֵי עֵצִים קוֹדֵם לְדִשּׁוּן
מִזְבֵּחַ הַפְּנִימִי, וְדִשּׁוּן מִזְבֵּחַ הַפְּנִימִי קוֹדֵם לַהֲטָבַת חָמֵשׁ נֵרוֹת, וַהֲטָבַת
חָמֵשׁ נֵרוֹת קוֹדֶמֶת לְדַם הַתָּמִיד, וְדַם הַתָּמִיד קוֹדֵם לַהֲטָבַת שְׁתֵּי נֵרוֹת,
וַהֲטָבַת שְׁתֵּי נֵרוֹת קוֹדֶמֶת לִקְטֹרֶת, וּקְטֹרֶת קוֹדֶמֶת לְאֵבָרִים, וְאֵבָרִים
לְמִנְחָה, וּמִנְחָה לַחֲבִתִּין, וַחֲבִתִּין לִנְסָכִין, וּנְסָכִין לְמוּסָפִין, וּמוּסָפִין
לְבָזִיכִין, וּבָזִיכִין קוֹדְמִין לְתָמִיד שֶׁל בֵּין הָעַרְבָּיִם. שֶׁנֶּאֱמַר: וְעָרַךְ עָלֶיהָ ויקרא ו
הָעֹלָה, וְהִקְטִיר עָלֶיהָ חֶלְבֵי הַשְּׁלָמִים: עָלֶיהָ הַשְׁלֵם כָּל הַקָּרְבָּנוֹת כֻּלָּם.

אָנָּא, בְּכֹחַ גְּדֻלַּת יְמִינְךָ, תַּתִּיר צְרוּרָה.
קַבֵּל רִנַּת עַמְּךָ, שַׂגְּבֵנוּ, טַהֲרֵנוּ, נוֹרָא.
נָא גִבּוֹר, דּוֹרְשֵׁי יִחוּדְךָ כְּבָבַת שָׁמְרֵם.
בָּרְכֵם, טַהֲרֵם, רַחֲמֵם, צִדְקָתְךָ תָּמִיד גָּמְלֵם.
חֲסִין קָדוֹשׁ, בְּרֹב טוּבְךָ נַהֵל עֲדָתֶךָ.
יָחִיד גֵּאֶה, לְעַמְּךָ פְּנֵה, זוֹכְרֵי קְדֻשָּׁתֶךָ.
שַׁוְעָתֵנוּ קַבֵּל וּשְׁמַע צַעֲקָתֵנוּ, יוֹדֵעַ תַּעֲלוּמוֹת.
בָּרוּךְ שֵׁם כְּבוֹד מַלְכוּתוֹ לְעוֹלָם וָעֶד.

רִבּוֹן הָעוֹלָמִים, אַתָּה צִוִּיתָנוּ לְהַקְרִיב קָרְבַּן הַתָּמִיד בְּמוֹעֲדוֹ וְלִהְיוֹת כֹּהֲנִים
בַּעֲבוֹדָתָם וּלְוִיִּם בְּדוּכָנָם וְיִשְׂרָאֵל בְּמַעֲמָדָם, וְעַתָּה בַּעֲוֹנוֹתֵינוּ חָרַב בֵּית
הַמִּקְדָּשׁ וּבָטַל הַתָּמִיד וְאֵין לָנוּ לֹא כֹהֵן בַּעֲבוֹדָתוֹ וְלֹא לֵוִי בְּדוּכָנוֹ וְלֹא יִשְׂרָאֵל
בְּמַעֲמָדוֹ, וְאַתָּה אָמַרְתָּ: וּנְשַׁלְּמָה פָרִים שְׂפָתֵינוּ: לָכֵן יְהִי רָצוֹן מִלְּפָנֶיךָ יהוה הושע יד
אֱלֹהֵינוּ וֵאלֹהֵי אֲבוֹתֵינוּ, שֶׁיְּהֵא שִׂיחַ שִׂפְתוֹתֵינוּ חָשׁוּב וּמְקֻבָּל וּמְרֻצֶּה לְפָנֶיךָ,
כְּאִלּוּ הִקְרַבְנוּ קָרְבַּן הַתָּמִיד בְּמוֹעֲדוֹ וּבִמְקוֹמוֹ וּכְהִלְכָתוֹ.

BIUR TEFILLA • ביאור תפילה

סדר המערכה – *The order of the priestly functions.* This is another additional passage that describes the overall order of the daily service as described by Abaye, a leading scholar in the Babylonian Talmud and community who lived in the fourth century CE.

וּבְיוֹם הַשַּׁבָּת On the Shabbat day, *Num. 28*
make an offering of two lambs a year old, without blemish,
together with two-tenths of an ephah of fine flour mixed with oil
as a meal-offering, and its appropriate libation.
This is the burnt-offering for every Shabbat,
in addition to the regular daily burnt-offering and its libation.

On Rosh Ḥodesh say:

וּבְרָאשֵׁי חָדְשֵׁיכֶם On your new moons, present as a burnt-offering to the LORD, two young bulls, one ram, and seven yearling lambs without blemish. There shall be a meal-offering of three-tenths of an ephah of fine flour mixed with oil for each bull, two-tenths of an ephah of fine flour mixed with oil for the ram, and one-tenth of an ephah of fine flour mixed with oil for each lamb. This is the burnt-offering – a fire-offering of pleasing aroma to the LORD. Their libations shall be: half a hin of wine for each bull, a third of a hin for the ram, and a quarter of a hin for each lamb. This is the monthly burnt-offering to be made at each new moon throughout the year. One male goat should be offered as a sin-offering to God, in addition to the regular daily burnt-offering and its libation. *Num. 28*

LAWS OF OFFERINGS, MISHNA ZEVAḤIM[B]

אֵיזֶהוּ מְקוֹמָן What is the location for sacrifices? The holiest offerings were slaughtered on the north side. The bull and he-goat of Yom Kippur were slaughtered on the north side. Their blood was received in a sacred vessel on the north side, and had to be sprinkled between the poles [of the Ark], toward the veil [screening the Holy of Holies], and on the golden altar. [The omission of] one of these sprinklings invalidated [the atonement ceremony]. The leftover blood was to be poured onto the western base of the outer altar. If this was not done, however, the omission did not invalidate [the ceremony]. *Zevaḥim Ch. 5*

The bulls and he-goats that were completely burnt were slaughtered on the north side, their blood was received in a sacred vessel on the north side, and had to be sprinkled toward the veil and on the golden altar. [The omission of] one of these sprinklings invalidated [the ceremony]. The leftover blood was to be poured onto the western base of the outer altar. If this was not done, however, the omission did not invalidate [the ceremony]. All these offerings were burnt where the altar ashes were deposited.

The communal and individual sin-offerings – these are the communal sin-offerings: the he-goats offered on Rosh Ḥodesh and Festivals were slaughtered on the north side, their blood was received in a sacred vessel on the north side, and required four

---

and, unlike the discussions in so many other chapters of the Mishna, this one contains no disputes among authorities. It thus represents the most "pure" form of oral tradition.

במדבר כח

וּבְיוֹם הַשַּׁבָּת
שְׁנֵי־כְבָשִׂים בְּנֵי־שָׁנָה תְּמִימִם
וּשְׁנֵי עֶשְׂרֹנִים סֹלֶת מִנְחָה בְּלוּלָה בַשֶּׁמֶן, וְנִסְכּוֹ:
עֹלַת שַׁבַּת בְּשַׁבַּתּוֹ, עַל־עֹלַת הַתָּמִיד וְנִסְכָּהּ:

On ראש חודש *say:*

במדבר כח

וּבְרָאשֵׁי חָדְשֵׁיכֶם תַּקְרִיבוּ עֹלָה לַיהוה, פָּרִים בְּנֵי־בָקָר שְׁנַיִם, וְאַיִל אֶחָד, כְּבָשִׂים בְּנֵי־שָׁנָה שִׁבְעָה, תְּמִימִם: וּשְׁלֹשָׁה עֶשְׂרֹנִים סֹלֶת מִנְחָה בְּלוּלָה בַשֶּׁמֶן לַפָּר הָאֶחָד, וּשְׁנֵי עֶשְׂרֹנִים סֹלֶת מִנְחָה בְּלוּלָה בַשֶּׁמֶן לָאַיִל הָאֶחָד: וְעִשָּׂרֹן עִשָּׂרוֹן סֹלֶת מִנְחָה בְּלוּלָה בַשֶּׁמֶן לַכֶּבֶשׂ הָאֶחָד, עֹלָה רֵיחַ נִיחֹחַ, אִשֶּׁה לַיהוה: וְנִסְכֵּיהֶם, חֲצִי הַהִין יִהְיֶה לַפָּר, וּשְׁלִישִׁת הַהִין לָאַיִל, וּרְבִיעִת הַהִין לַכֶּבֶשׂ, יָיִן, זֹאת עֹלַת חֹדֶשׁ בְּחָדְשׁוֹ לְחָדְשֵׁי הַשָּׁנָה: וּשְׂעִיר עִזִּים אֶחָד לְחַטָּאת לַיהוה, עַל־עֹלַת הַתָּמִיד יֵעָשֶׂה, וְנִסְכּוֹ:

דיני זבחים[ב]

זבחים פרק ה

אֵיזֶהוּ מְקוֹמָן שֶׁל זְבָחִים. קָדְשֵׁי קָדָשִׁים שְׁחִיטָתָן בַּצָּפוֹן. פַּר וְשָׂעִיר שֶׁל יוֹם הַכִּפּוּרִים, שְׁחִיטָתָן בַּצָּפוֹן, וְקִבּוּל דָּמָן בִּכְלֵי שָׁרֵת בַּצָּפוֹן, וְדָמָן טָעוּן הַזָּיָה עַל בֵּין הַבַּדִּים, וְעַל הַפָּרֹכֶת, וְעַל מִזְבַּח הַזָּהָב. מַתָּנָה אַחַת מֵהֶן מְעַכָּבֶת. שְׁיָרֵי הַדָּם הָיָה שׁוֹפֵךְ עַל יְסוֹד מַעֲרָבִי שֶׁל מִזְבֵּחַ הַחִיצוֹן, אִם לֹא נָתַן לֹא עִכֵּב.

פָּרִים הַנִּשְׂרָפִים וּשְׂעִירִים הַנִּשְׂרָפִים, שְׁחִיטָתָן בַּצָּפוֹן, וְקִבּוּל דָּמָן בִּכְלֵי שָׁרֵת בַּצָּפוֹן, וְדָמָן טָעוּן הַזָּיָה עַל הַפָּרֹכֶת וְעַל מִזְבַּח הַזָּהָב. מַתָּנָה אַחַת מֵהֶן מְעַכָּבֶת. שְׁיָרֵי הַדָּם הָיָה שׁוֹפֵךְ עַל יְסוֹד מַעֲרָבִי שֶׁל מִזְבֵּחַ הַחִיצוֹן, אִם לֹא נָתַן לֹא עִכֵּב. אֵלּוּ וָאֵלּוּ נִשְׂרָפִין בְּבֵית הַדֶּשֶׁן.

חַטֹּאת הַצִּבּוּר וְהַיָּחִיד. אֵלּוּ הֵן חַטֹּאת הַצִּבּוּר: שְׂעִירֵי רָאשֵׁי חֳדָשִׁים וְשֶׁל מוֹעֲדוֹת. שְׁחִיטָתָן בַּצָּפוֹן, וְקִבּוּל דָּמָן בִּכְלֵי שָׁרֵת בַּצָּפוֹן, וְדָמָן טָעוּן

BIUR TEFILLA • ביאור תפילה

דיני זבחים – *Laws of offerings, Mishna Zevaḥim.* These passages about various sacrifices come from the Mishna and were chosen perhaps because they lists all of the sacrifices

sprinklings, one on each of the four corners of the altar. How was this done? The priest ascended the ramp and turned [right] onto the surrounding ledge. He came to the southeast corner, then went to the northeast, then to the northwest, then to the southwest. The leftover blood he poured onto the southern base. [The meat of these offerings], prepared in any manner, was eaten within the [courtyard] curtains, by males of the priest-hood, on that day and the following night, until midnight.

The burnt-offering was among the holiest of sacrifices. It was slaughtered on the north side, its blood was received in a sacred vessel on the north side, and required two sprinklings [at opposite corners of the altar], making four in all. The offering had to be flayed, dismembered and wholly consumed by fire.

The communal peace-offerings and the guilt-offerings – these are the guilt-offerings: the guilt-offering for robbery; the guilt-offering for profane use of a sacred object; the guilt-offering [for violating] a betrothed maidservant; the guilt-offering of a Nazirite [who had become defiled by a corpse]; the guilt-offering of a leper [at his cleansing]; and the guilt-offering in case of doubt. All these were slaughtered on the north side, their blood was received in a sacred vessel on the north side, and required two sprinklings [at opposite corners of the altar], making four in all. [The meat of these offerings], prepared in any manner, was eaten within the [courtyard] curtains, by males of the priesthood, on that day and the following night, until midnight.

The thanksgiving-offering and the ram of a Nazirite were offerings of lesser holiness. They could be slaughtered anywhere in the Temple court, and their blood required two sprinklings [at opposite corners of the altar], making four in all. The meat of these offerings, prepared in any manner, was eaten anywhere within the city [Jerusalem], by anyone during that day and the following night until midnight. This also applied to the portion of these sacrifices [given to the priests], except that the priests' portion was only to be eaten by the priests, their wives, children and servants.

Peace-offerings were [also] of lesser holiness. They could be slaughtered anywhere in the Temple court, and their blood required two sprinklings [at opposite corners of the altar], making four in all. The meat of these offerings, prepared in any manner, was eaten anywhere within the city [Jerusalem], by anyone, for two days and one night. This also applied to the portion of these sacrifices [given to the priests], except that the priests' portion was only to be eaten by the priests, their wives, children and servants.

The firstborn and tithe of cattle and the Pesaḥ lamb were sacrifices of lesser holiness. They could be slaughtered anywhere in the Temple court, and their blood required only one sprinkling, which had to be done at the base of the altar. They differed in their consumption: the firstborn was eaten only by priests, while the tithe could be eaten by anyone. Both could be eaten anywhere within the city, prepared in any manner, during two days and one night. The Pesaḥ lamb had to be eaten that night until midnight. It could only be eaten by those who had been numbered for it, and eaten only roasted.

אַרְבַּע מַתָּנוֹת עַל אַרְבַּע קְרָנוֹת. כֵּיצַד, עָלָה בַכֶּבֶשׁ, וּפָנָה לַסּוֹבֵב, וּבָא לוֹ לְקֶרֶן דְּרוֹמִית מִזְרָחִית, מִזְרָחִית צְפוֹנִית, צְפוֹנִית מַעֲרָבִית, מַעֲרָבִית דְּרוֹמִית. שְׁיָרֵי הַדָּם הָיָה שׁוֹפֵךְ עַל יְסוֹד דְּרוֹמִי. וְנֶאֱכָלִין לִפְנִים מִן הַקְּלָעִים, לְזִכְרֵי כְהֻנָּה, בְּכָל מַאֲכָל, לְיוֹם וָלַיְלָה עַד חֲצוֹת.

הָעוֹלָה קֹדֶשׁ קָדָשִׁים. שְׁחִיטָתָהּ בַּצָּפוֹן, וְקִבּוּל דָּמָהּ בִּכְלִי שָׁרֵת בַּצָּפוֹן, וְדָמָהּ טָעוּן שְׁתֵּי מַתָּנוֹת שֶׁהֵן אַרְבַּע, וּטְעוּנָה הֶפְשֵׁט וְנִתּוּחַ, וְכָלִיל לָאִשִּׁים.

זִבְחֵי שַׁלְמֵי צִבּוּר וַאֲשָׁמוֹת. אֵלּוּ הֵן אֲשָׁמוֹת: אֲשַׁם גְּזֵלוֹת, אֲשַׁם מְעִילוֹת, אֲשַׁם שִׁפְחָה חֲרוּפָה, אֲשַׁם נָזִיר, אֲשַׁם מְצֹרָע, אָשָׁם תָּלוּי. שְׁחִיטָתָן בַּצָּפוֹן, וְקִבּוּל דָּמָן בִּכְלִי שָׁרֵת בַּצָּפוֹן, וְדָמָן טָעוּן שְׁתֵּי מַתָּנוֹת שֶׁהֵן אַרְבַּע. וְנֶאֱכָלִין לִפְנִים מִן הַקְּלָעִים, לְזִכְרֵי כְהֻנָּה, בְּכָל מַאֲכָל, לְיוֹם וָלַיְלָה עַד חֲצוֹת.

הַתּוֹדָה וְאֵיל נָזִיר קָדָשִׁים קַלִּים. שְׁחִיטָתָן בְּכָל מָקוֹם בָּעֲזָרָה, וְדָמָן טָעוּן שְׁתֵּי מַתָּנוֹת שֶׁהֵן אַרְבַּע, וְנֶאֱכָלִין בְּכָל הָעִיר, לְכָל אָדָם, בְּכָל מַאֲכָל, לְיוֹם וָלַיְלָה עַד חֲצוֹת. הַמּוּרָם מֵהֶם כַּיּוֹצֵא בָהֶם, אֶלָּא שֶׁהַמּוּרָם נֶאֱכָל לַכֹּהֲנִים, לִנְשֵׁיהֶם, וְלִבְנֵיהֶם וּלְעַבְדֵיהֶם.

שְׁלָמִים קָדָשִׁים קַלִּים. שְׁחִיטָתָן בְּכָל מָקוֹם בָּעֲזָרָה, וְדָמָן טָעוּן שְׁתֵּי מַתָּנוֹת שֶׁהֵן אַרְבַּע, וְנֶאֱכָלִין בְּכָל הָעִיר, לְכָל אָדָם, בְּכָל מַאֲכָל, לִשְׁנֵי יָמִים וְלַיְלָה אֶחָד. הַמּוּרָם מֵהֶם כַּיּוֹצֵא בָהֶם, אֶלָּא שֶׁהַמּוּרָם נֶאֱכָל לַכֹּהֲנִים, לִנְשֵׁיהֶם, וְלִבְנֵיהֶם וּלְעַבְדֵיהֶם.

הַבְּכוֹר וְהַמַּעֲשֵׂר וְהַפֶּסַח קָדָשִׁים קַלִּים. שְׁחִיטָתָן בְּכָל מָקוֹם בָּעֲזָרָה, וְדָמָן טָעוּן מַתָּנָה אֶחָת, וּבִלְבָד שֶׁיִּתֵּן כְּנֶגֶד הַיְסוֹד. שִׁנָּה בַאֲכִילָתָן, הַבְּכוֹר נֶאֱכָל לַכֹּהֲנִים וְהַמַּעֲשֵׂר לְכָל אָדָם, וְנֶאֱכָלִין בְּכָל הָעִיר, בְּכָל מַאֲכָל, לִשְׁנֵי יָמִים וְלַיְלָה אֶחָד. הַפֶּסַח אֵינוֹ נֶאֱכָל אֶלָּא בַלַּיְלָה, וְאֵינוֹ נֶאֱכָל אֶלָּא עַד חֲצוֹת, וְאֵינוֹ נֶאֱכָל אֶלָּא לִמְנוּיָו, וְאֵינוֹ נֶאֱכָל אֶלָּא צָלִי.

THE INTERPRETIVE PRINCIPLES OF RABBI YISHMAEL[B]

רַבִּי יִשְׁמָעֵאל Rabbi Yishmael says:

The Torah is expounded by thirteen principles:

1. An inference from a lenient law to a strict one, and vice versa.
2. An inference drawn from identical words in two passages.
3. A general principle derived from one text or two related texts.
4. A general law followed by specific examples
   [where the law applies exclusively to those examples].
5. A specific example followed by a general law
   [where the law applies to everything implied in the general statement].
6. A general law followed by specific examples and concluding with a general law: here you may infer only cases similar to the examples.
7. When a general statement requires clarification by a specific example, or a specific example requires clarification by a general statement
   [then rules 4 and 5 do not apply].
8. When a particular case, already included in the general statement, is expressly mentioned to teach something new, that special provision applies to all other cases included in the general statement.
9. When a particular case, though included in the general statement, is expressly mentioned with a provision similar to the general law, such a case is singled out to lessen the severity of the law, not to increase it.
10. When a particular case, though included in the general statement, is explicitly mentioned with a provision differing from the general law, it is singled out to lessen in some respects, and in others to increase, the severity of the law.
11. When a particular case, though included in the general statement, is explicitly mentioned with a new provision, the terms of the general statement no longer apply to it, unless Scripture indicates explicitly that they do apply.
12. A matter elucidated from its context, or from the following passage.
13. ▸ Also, when two passages [seem to] contradict each other,
   [they are to be elucidated by] a third passage that reconciles them.

May it be Your will, LORD our God and God of our ancestors, that the Temple be speedily rebuilt in our days, and grant us our share in Your Torah. And may we serve You there in reverence, as in the days of old and as in former years.

---

interpretation. This passage is a listing of thirteen of those principles, first laid down in a midrashic work that is dedicated to an understanding of the book of *Vayikra* (*Leviticus*) which is the major source for the laws of the sacrifices. Ideally, these principles are not simply to be recited but to be learned as well.

ברייתא דרבי ישמעאלב

רַבִּי יִשְׁמָעֵאל אוֹמֵר: בִּשְׁלֹשׁ עֶשְׂרֵה מִדּוֹת הַתּוֹרָה נִדְרֶשֶׁת

א מִקַּל וָחֹמֶר

ב וּמִגְּזֵרָה שָׁוָה

ג מִבִּנְיַן אָב מִכָּתוּב אֶחָד, וּמִבִּנְיַן אָב מִשְּׁנֵי כְתוּבִים

ד מִכְּלָל וּפְרָט

ה מִפְּרָט וּכְלָל

ו כְּלָל וּפְרָט וּכְלָל, אִי אַתָּה דָן אֶלָּא כְּעֵין הַפְּרָט

ז מִכְּלָל שֶׁהוּא צָרִיךְ לִפְרָט, וּמִפְּרָט שֶׁהוּא צָרִיךְ לִכְלָל

ח כָּל דָּבָר שֶׁהָיָה בִּכְלָל, וְיָצָא מִן הַכְּלָל לְלַמֵּד
לֹא לְלַמֵּד עַל עַצְמוֹ יָצָא, אֶלָּא לְלַמֵּד עַל הַכְּלָל כֻּלּוֹ יָצָא

ט כָּל דָּבָר שֶׁהָיָה בִּכְלָל, וְיָצָא לִטְעֹן טֹעַן אֶחָד שֶׁהוּא כְעִנְיָנוֹ
יָצָא לְהָקֵל וְלֹא לְהַחֲמִיר

י כָּל דָּבָר שֶׁהָיָה בִּכְלָל, וְיָצָא לִטְעֹן טֹעַן אַחֵר שֶׁלֹּא כְעִנְיָנוֹ
יָצָא לְהָקֵל וּלְהַחֲמִיר

יא כָּל דָּבָר שֶׁהָיָה בִּכְלָל, וְיָצָא לִדּוֹן בַּדָּבָר הֶחָדָשׁ
אִי אַתָּה יָכוֹל לְהַחֲזִירוֹ לִכְלָלוֹ
עַד שֶׁיַּחֲזִירֶנּוּ הַכָּתוּב לִכְלָלוֹ בְּפֵרוּשׁ

יב דָּבָר הַלָּמֵד מֵעִנְיָנוֹ, וְדָבָר הַלָּמֵד מִסּוֹפוֹ

◂ יג וְכֵן שְׁנֵי כְתוּבִים הַמַּכְחִישִׁים זֶה אֶת זֶה
עַד שֶׁיָּבוֹא הַכָּתוּב הַשְּׁלִישִׁי וְיַכְרִיעַ בֵּינֵיהֶם.

יְהִי רָצוֹן מִלְּפָנֶיךָ, יהוה אֱלֹהֵינוּ וֵאלֹהֵי אֲבוֹתֵינוּ, שֶׁיִּבָּנֶה בֵּית הַמִּקְדָּשׁ בִּמְהֵרָה בְיָמֵינוּ, וְתֵן חֶלְקֵנוּ בְּתוֹרָתֶךָ, וְשָׁם נַעֲבָדְךָ בְּיִרְאָה כִּימֵי עוֹלָם וּכְשָׁנִים קַדְמוֹנִיּוֹת.

BIUR TEFILLA • ביאור תפילה

ברייתא דרבי ישמעאל – *The interpretive principles of Rabbi Yishmael.* Like almost any written code, Jewish law is an intricate legal system that has accepted rules of

THE RABBIS' KADDISH

The following prayer, said by mourners, requires the presence of a minyan. In Ashkenazi practice it is customary to stand for this prayer because of the holiness associated with the sanctification of Hashem's name in the prayer in general and in the central response by the congregation in particular. (In Sephardic communities the custom is to sit, while others have the custom to remain standing if they are already doing so.)

A transliteration can be found on page 891.

Mourner: יִתְגַּדַּל Magnified and sanctified
may His great name be,
in the world He created by His will.
May He establish His kingdom
in your lifetime
and in your days,
and in the lifetime of all the house of Israel,
swiftly and soon –
and say: Amen.

All: May His great name[A] be blessed
for ever and all time.

Mourner: Blessed and praised,
glorified and exalted,
raised and honored,
uplifted and lauded
be the name of the Holy One,
blessed be He,
beyond any blessing,
song, praise and consolation
uttered in the world –
and say: Amen.

FOR AN INTRODUCTION TO KADDISH, see page 73.

קדיש דרבנן

The following prayer, said by mourners, requires the presence of a מנין*. In Ashkenazi practice it is customary to stand for this prayer because of the holiness associated with the sanctification of Hashem's name in the prayer in general and in the central response by the congregation in particular. (In Sephardic communities the custom is to sit, while others have the custom to remain standing if they are already doing so.)*

A transliteration can be found on page 891.

אבל: יִתְגַּדַּל וְיִתְקַדַּשׁ שְׁמֵהּ רַבָּא (קהל: אָמֵן)
בְּעָלְמָא דִּי בְרָא כִרְעוּתֵהּ
וְיַמְלִיךְ מַלְכוּתֵהּ
בְּחַיֵּיכוֹן וּבְיוֹמֵיכוֹן וּבְחַיֵּי דְכָל בֵּית יִשְׂרָאֵל
בַּעֲגָלָא וּבִזְמַן קָרִיב
וְאִמְרוּ אָמֵן. (קהל: אָמֵן)

קהל ואבל: יְהֵא שְׁמֵהּ רַבָּא[א] מְבָרַךְ לְעָלַם וּלְעָלְמֵי עָלְמַיָּא.

אבל: יִתְבָּרַךְ וְיִשְׁתַּבַּח וְיִתְפָּאַר וְיִתְרוֹמַם וְיִתְנַשֵּׂא
וְיִתְהַדָּר וְיִתְעַלֶּה וְיִתְהַלָּל
שְׁמֵהּ דְּקֻדְשָׁא בְּרִיךְ הוּא (קהל: בְּרִיךְ הוּא)
לְעֵלָּא מִן כָּל בִּרְכָתָא / בשבת שובה לְעֵלָּא לְעֵלָּא מִכָּל בִּרְכָתָא/
וְשִׁירָתָא, תֻּשְׁבְּחָתָא וְנֶחֱמָתָא
דַּאֲמִירָן בְּעָלְמָא
וְאִמְרוּ אָמֵן. (קהל: אָמֵן)

ANI TEFILLA • אני תפילה

יְהֵא שְׁמֵהּ רַבָּא – *May His great name.* *Whoever says "yeheh shemeh raba..." with all his strength, the Heavenly Court rips up any negative decree against him (*Shabbat *119b).*

To Israel,
to the teachers,
their disciples and their disciples' disciples,
and to all who engage in the study of Torah,
in this (*in Israel add:* holy) place or elsewhere,
may there come to them and you great peace,
grace, kindness and compassion,
long life, ample sustenance and deliverance,
from their Father in Heaven –
and say: Amen.

May there be great peace from heaven,
and (good) life for us and all Israel –
and say: Amen.

Bow and take three steps back as if taking leave of the Divine Presence.
Bow left: May He who makes peace in His high places,
Bow right: in His compassion make peace *Bow forward:* for us
and all Israel –
and say: Amen.

עַל יִשְׂרָאֵל וְעַל רַבָּנָן
וְעַל תַּלְמִידֵיהוֹן וְעַל כָּל תַּלְמִידֵי תַלְמִידֵיהוֹן
וְעַל כָּל מָאן דְּעָסְקִין בְּאוֹרַיְתָא
דִּי בְּאַתְרָא (בארץ ישראל: קַדִּישָׁא) הָדֵין, וְדִי בְּכָל אֲתַר וַאֲתַר
יְהֵא לְהוֹן וּלְכוֹן שְׁלָמָא רַבָּא
חִנָּא וְחִסְדָּא
וְרַחֲמֵי, וְחַיֵּי אֲרִיכֵי, וּמְזוֹנֵי רְוִיחֵי
וּפֻרְקָנָא מִן קֳדָם אֲבוּהוֹן דִּי בִשְׁמַיָּא
וְאִמְרוּ אָמֵן. (קהל: אָמֵן)

יְהֵא שְׁלָמָא רַבָּא מִן שְׁמַיָּא
וְחַיִּים (טוֹבִים) עָלֵינוּ וְעַל כָּל יִשְׂרָאֵל
וְאִמְרוּ אָמֵן. (קהל: אָמֵן)

Bow and take three steps back as if taking leave of the Divine Presence.

Bow left עֹשֶׂה שָׁלוֹם/ בשבת שובה: הַשָּׁלוֹם/ בִּמְרוֹמָיו
Bow right הוּא יַעֲשֶׂה בְרַחֲמָיו שָׁלוֹם *Bow forward* עָלֵינוּ
וְעַל כָּל יִשְׂרָאֵל, וְאִמְרוּ אָמֵן.

A PSALM BEFORE VERSES OF PRAISE

מִזְמוֹר שִׁיר A psalm of David. Ps. 30
A song for the dedication of the House.
I will exalt You, LORD, for You have lifted me up,
and not let my enemies rejoice over me.
LORD, my God, I cried to You for help and You healed me.
LORD, You lifted my soul from the grave;
You spared me from going down to the pit.
Sing to the LORD, you His devoted ones,
and give thanks to His holy name.
For His anger is for a moment, but His favor for a lifetime.
At night there may be weeping, but in the morning there is joy.
When I felt secure, I said, "I shall never be shaken."
LORD, when You favored me,
You made me stand firm as a mountain,
but when You hid Your face, I was terrified.
To You, LORD, I called; I pleaded with my LORD:
"What gain would there be if I died and went down to the grave?
Can dust thank You? Can it declare Your truth?
Hear, LORD, and be gracious to me; LORD, be my help."
You have turned my sorrow into dancing.
▸ You have removed my sackcloth and clothed me with joy,
so that my soul may sing to You and not be silent.
LORD my God, for ever will I thank You.

---

we already have from Him? Don't we need to acknowledge what He is capable of doing for us? Don't we need to first remind ourselves of the beauty of creation, the wonder of the cosmos, the miracle of life, the marvel of God's presence in our history? Only when we know before whom we are standing, when we can admit what His power is relative to our own, can we dare to ask. That's what these seemingly random verses of song, *Pesukei DeZimra*, are supposed to accomplish.

That is why the *Menorat HaMaor* once suggested that the word used here for "song" is related to another Hebrew word, a homonym – זֶמֶר (*zemer*) – meaning "to

This **INTRODUCTION** *continues on page 219.*

מזמור לפני פסוקי דזמרה

מִזְמוֹר שִׁיר־חֲנֻכַּת הַבַּיִת לְדָוִד: תהלים ל
אֲרוֹמִמְךָ יהוה כִּי דִלִּיתָנִי, וְלֹא־שִׂמַּחְתָּ אֹיְבַי לִי:
יהוה אֱלֹהָי, שִׁוַּעְתִּי אֵלֶיךָ וַתִּרְפָּאֵנִי:
יהוה, הֶעֱלִיתָ מִן־שְׁאוֹל נַפְשִׁי, חִיִּיתַנִי מִיָּרְדִי־בוֹר:
זַמְּרוּ לַיהוה חֲסִידָיו, וְהוֹדוּ לְזֵכֶר קָדְשׁוֹ:
כִּי רֶגַע בְּאַפּוֹ, חַיִּים בִּרְצוֹנוֹ, בָּעֶרֶב יָלִין בֶּכִי וְלַבֹּקֶר רִנָּה:
וַאֲנִי אָמַרְתִּי בְשַׁלְוִי, בַּל־אֶמּוֹט לְעוֹלָם:
יהוה, בִּרְצוֹנְךָ הֶעֱמַדְתָּה לְהַרְרִי עֹז
הִסְתַּרְתָּ פָנֶיךָ הָיִיתִי נִבְהָל:
אֵלֶיךָ יהוה אֶקְרָא, וְאֶל־אֲדֹנָי אֶתְחַנָּן:
מַה־בֶּצַע בְּדָמִי, בְּרִדְתִּי אֶל שָׁחַת, הֲיוֹדְךָ עָפָר, הֲיַגִּיד אֲמִתֶּךָ:
שְׁמַע־יהוה וְחָנֵּנִי, יהוה הֱיֵה־עֹזֵר לִי:
◂ הָפַכְתָּ מִסְפְּדִי לְמָחוֹל לִי, פִּתַּחְתָּ שַׂקִּי, וַתְּאַזְּרֵנִי שִׂמְחָה:
לְמַעַן יְזַמֶּרְךָ כָבוֹד וְלֹא יִדֹּם, יהוה אֱלֹהַי, לְעוֹלָם אוֹדֶךָּ:

AN INTRODUCTION TO THE INTRODUCTION – PESUKEI DEZIMRA

Praying isn't always easy – especially in the morning; especially when you have been up late the night before. The Rabbis understood that even in the best of times, prayer required psyching yourself, getting into the mood or the zone that is familiar to athletes before they play or performers before they go on stage. That's what *Pesukei DeZimra* is: the prelude to *tefilla*. It is a kind of prayer before one prays.

The Rabbis mandated, based upon a request that Moshe made to God, that before one asks anything of God, one should first praise Him. When I was younger, I cynically thought that this was like trying to bribe God, to butter Him up before I got what I wanted. Yet it gnawed at me: if God is so great, does He really need my praise?! It wasn't until later that I realized that in fact God doesn't need our praise; we do. If we're going to ask God for something, don't we need to first acknowledge the good that

MOURNER'S KADDISH

The following prayer, said by mourners, requires the presence of a minyan.
A transliteration can be found on page 892.

Mourner: יִתְגַּדַּל Magnified and sanctified may His great name be,
in the world He created by His will.
May He establish His kingdom
in your lifetime and in your days,
and in the lifetime of all the house of Israel,
swiftly and soon – and say: Amen.

All: May His great name be blessed for ever and all time.

Mourner: Blessed and praised, glorified and exalted,
raised and honored, uplifted and lauded
be the name of the Holy One, blessed be He,
beyond any blessing, song, praise and consolation
uttered in the world – and say: Amen.

May there be great peace from heaven,
and life for us and all Israel – and say: Amen.

Bow and take three steps back as if taking leave of the Divine Presence.
Bow left: May He who makes peace in His high places,
Bow right: make peace *Bow forward:* for us and all Israel –
and say: Amen.

---

is to cut away the thoughts and feelings that get in the way of our ability to grow spiritually. Reciting these verses is designed to prepare our souls for the encounter that we are hopefully to have with Hashem during the *Amida* a little later on. We first need to nurture our soul, to give it fresh air to breathe and the space to be able to come to the fore, before the demands of our day send it back into the recesses of our being. *Pesukei DeZimra* is an opportunity to get back in touch with the core of who we are and the One before whom we stand.

The goal here, then, is to get into the mood, to get focused. As such, it is all about quality not quantity. Go slow. Skip parts if necessary in order to maintain your own slower pace (see the guide on what to do when you are pressed for time, in the Halakha section in the back of this Siddur, law 23). Our sages tell us that we should utter each word as if it were a valuable coin being counted. Make the words count.

קדיש יתום

The following prayer, said by mourners, requires the presence of a מנין.
A transliteration can be found on page 892.

אבל: יִתְגַּדַּל וְיִתְקַדַּשׁ שְׁמֵהּ רַבָּא (קהל: אָמֵן)
בְּעָלְמָא דִּי בְרָא כִרְעוּתֵהּ
וְיַמְלִיךְ מַלְכוּתֵהּ
בְּחַיֵּיכוֹן וּבְיוֹמֵיכוֹן וּבְחַיֵּי דְכָל בֵּית יִשְׂרָאֵל
בַּעֲגָלָא וּבִזְמַן קָרִיב, וְאִמְרוּ אָמֵן. (קהל: אָמֵן)

קהל ואבל: יְהֵא שְׁמֵהּ רַבָּא מְבָרַךְ לְעָלַם וּלְעָלְמֵי עָלְמַיָּא.

אבל: יִתְבָּרַךְ וְיִשְׁתַּבַּח וְיִתְפָּאַר
וְיִתְרוֹמַם וְיִתְנַשֵּׂא וְיִתְהַדָּר וְיִתְעַלֶּה וְיִתְהַלָּל
שְׁמֵהּ דְּקֻדְשָׁא בְּרִיךְ הוּא (קהל: בְּרִיךְ הוּא)
לְעֵלָּא מִן כָּל בִּרְכָתָא / בשבת שובה: לְעֵלָּא לְעֵלָּא מִכָּל בִּרְכָתָא/
וְשִׁירָתָא, תֻּשְׁבְּחָתָא וְנֶחֱמָתָא
דַּאֲמִירָן בְּעָלְמָא, וְאִמְרוּ אָמֵן. (קהל: אָמֵן)

יְהֵא שְׁלָמָא רַבָּא מִן שְׁמַיָּא
וְחַיִּים, עָלֵינוּ וְעַל כָּל יִשְׂרָאֵל, וְאִמְרוּ אָמֵן. (קהל: אָמֵן)

Bow and take three steps back as if taking leave of the Divine Presence.

Bow left עֹשֶׂה שָׁלוֹם/ בשבת שובה: הַשָּׁלוֹם/ בִּמְרוֹמָיו
Bow right הוּא יַעֲשֶׂה שָׁלוֹם *Bow forward* עָלֵינוּ
וְעַל כָּל יִשְׂרָאֵל, וְאִמְרוּ אָמֵן.

---

prune." When one wants a plant to grow to be healthy and strong, one often needs to prune it, to cut back the limbs or foliage that prevent it from getting the full measure of air and light required for continued sustenance. So, too, in *Pesukei DeZimra* our goal

PESUKEI DEZIMRA

It is the general custom to stand for this blessing.
Some men also have a custom to hold onto the two front tzitziot of their tallit and kiss them upon conclusion of the prayer, at "songs of praise" (on the next page). From the beginning of this prayer to the end of the Amida, conversation is forbidden.

Some say:

I hereby prepare my mouth to thank, praise and laud my Creator, for the sake of the unification of the Holy One, blessed be He, and His Divine Presence, through that which is hidden and concealed, in the name of all Israel.

BLESSED IS HE WHO SPOKE[HB]

and the world came into being, blessed is He.
Blessed is He who creates the universe.
Blessed is He who speaks and acts.
Blessed is He who decrees and fulfills.
Blessed is He who shows compassion to the earth.
Blessed is He who shows compassion to all creatures.
Blessed is He who gives a good reward to those who fear Him.
Blessed is He who lives for ever and exists to eternity.
Blessed is He who redeems and saves.
Blessed is His name.

---

for other reasons. It could also be related to the tradition that the prayer was found on a note that fell from Heaven (Baḥ 53) and is thus considered so holy as to merit standing for its recitation. Similarly, the holding of the *tzitzit* may be tied to this association of holiness, for there are various Kabbalistic connections between the number of knots and/or strings with Kabbalistic understandings of the ways of Heaven and the names of God (e.g. Responsa *Zikhron Yehuda* 9). At the very least, one sees that the prayer itself is not "just" an introductory blessing, but the portal to a different awareness. Prepare yourself.

HILKHOT TEFILLA • הלכות תפילה

בָּרוּךְ שֶׁאָמַר – *Blessed is He who spoke.* The following is the opening blessing of *Pesukei DeZimra*. If you are running out of time, you should minimally say this prayer before moving on to *Ashrei* (Psalm 145).

If one understands the purpose of the

This **HILKHOT TEFILLA** *continues on page 223.*

פסוקי דזמרה

It is the general custom to stand for this blessing.
Some men also have a custom to hold onto the two front ציציות *of their* טלית *and kiss them upon conclusion of the prayer, at* בְּתִשְׁבָּחוֹת *(on the next page). From the beginning of this prayer to the end of the* עמידה*, conversation is forbidden.*

Some say:

הֲרֵינִי מְזַמֵּן אֶת פִּי לְהוֹדוֹת וּלְהַלֵּל וּלְשַׁבֵּחַ אֶת בּוֹרְאִי, לְשֵׁם יִחוּד קֻדְשָׁא בְּרִיךְ הוּא וּשְׁכִינְתֵּהּ עַל יְדֵי הַהוּא טָמִיר וְנֶעְלָם בְּשֵׁם כָּל יִשְׂרָאֵל.

בָּרוּךְ
שֶׁאָמַר הב
וְהָיָה הָעוֹלָם, בָּרוּךְ הוּא.
בָּרוּךְ עוֹשֶׂה בְרֵאשִׁית
בָּרוּךְ אוֹמֵר וְעוֹשֶׂה
בָּרוּךְ גּוֹזֵר וּמְקַיֵּם
בָּרוּךְ מְרַחֵם עַל הָאָרֶץ
בָּרוּךְ מְרַחֵם עַל הַבְּרִיּוֹת
בָּרוּךְ מְשַׁלֵּם שָׂכָר טוֹב לִירֵאָיו
בָּרוּךְ חַי לָעַד וְקַיָּם לָנֶצַח
בָּרוּךְ פּוֹדֶה וּמַצִּיל
בָּרוּךְ שְׁמוֹ

HILKHOT TEFILLA • הלכות תפילה

The rationale for standing for this prayer is not clear (*Mishna Berura* 51:1). It may be because as the opening blessing of this section of the siddur (*Pesukei DeZimra*) it parallels the closing blessing of *Yishtabaḥ* (page 291) where the custom is also to stand

Blessed are You, Lord our God, King of the Universe,
God, compassionate Father, extolled by the mouth of His people,
praised and glorified by the tongue of His devoted ones
and those who serve Him.
With the songs of Your servant David[B]
we will praise You, O Lord our God.
With praises and psalms
we will magnify and praise You, glorify You,
Speak Your name and proclaim Your kingship,
our King, our God, ▸ the only One, Giver of life to the worlds
the King whose great name is praised
and glorified to all eternity.
Blessed are You, Lord, the King extolled with songs of praise.

But it doesn't end there. The second line, בָּרוּךְ עוֹשֶׂה בְרֵאשִׁית, refers not to the world in general but specifically to the rest of creation. In fact, over and over again in the following verses in *Bereshit* (according to *Ḥazal* ten times in total), God spoke and the different parts of creation came into being. But what is especially noteworthy is the difference between the verb tense here and in the previous line. Do you see it? The verb here is in the present tense whereas the previous line is in the past tense. Perhaps that's because the initial creation of the world happened only once, but if you look around you, you can see the world being re-created every day: the dawn of a new day, the birth of a baby, the changing of the seasons – all point to ongoing creation. That's why בָּרוּךְ עוֹשֶׂה בְרֵאשִׁית is written in the present tense, because if I would just open my eyes (sleepy as they may be this time of morning) I would realize how amazing the world is.

BIUR TEFILLA • ביאור תפילה

וּבְשִׁירֵי דָוִד עַבְדֶּךָ – *With the songs of Your servant David.* This is a reference to King David and the songs referred to are the psalms that we know as the book of *Tehillim* which he authored. This opening blessing thus says that we will praise God specifically using David's *Tehillim* and it therefore alludes to the core of *Pesukei DeZimra*, namely, the last six chapters of the book of *Tehillim* which we will begin to say a little later on, starting with the prayer *Ashrei*.

ANI TEFILLA • אני תפילה

"The more you appreciate your life the more your life appreciates." (Rabbi David Aaron)

בָּרוּךְ אַתָּה יהוה אֱלֹהֵינוּ מֶלֶךְ הָעוֹלָם
הָאֵל הָאָב הָרַחֲמָן הַמְהֻלָּל בְּפִי עַמּוֹ
מְשֻׁבָּח וּמְפֹאָר בִּלְשׁוֹן חֲסִידָיו וַעֲבָדָיו
וּבְשִׁירֵי דָוִד עַבְדֶּךָ נְהַלֶּלְךָ יהוה אֱלֹהֵינוּ.
בִּשְׁבָחוֹת וּבִזְמִירוֹת, נְגַדֶּלְךָ וּנְשַׁבֵּחֲךָ וּנְפָאֶרְךָ
וְנַזְכִּיר שִׁמְךָ וְנַמְלִיכְךָ מַלְכֵּנוּ אֱלֹהֵינוּ. › יָחִיד חֵי הָעוֹלָמִים
מֶלֶךְ, מְשֻׁבָּח וּמְפֹאָר עֲדֵי עַד שְׁמוֹ הַגָּדוֹל
בָּרוּךְ אַתָּה יהוה, מֶלֶךְ מְהֻלָּל בַּתִּשְׁבָּחוֹת.

BIUR TEFILLA • ביאור תפילה

בָּרוּךְ שֶׁאָמַר – *Blessed is He who spoke.* The first section of the *tefilla*, which you can easily tell consists of a number of repetitions of the word בָּרוּךְ (ten of them if you don't include בָּרוּךְ הוּא, which is part of Hashem's name and not a blessing), followed by some descriptions of what Hashem can do and does.

In the very first one, for example, בָּרוּךְ שֶׁאָמַר וְהָיָה הָעוֹלָם בָּרוּךְ הוּא, we declare that Hashem created the world. Sounds like an appropriate way to start off *tefilla*, no? After all, if we are about to pray, it makes sense for us to remind ourselves to whom we are praying. But note that it's not just about the fact that He created the world, but the *way* in which He created it: simply by uttering His desire to do so. Recall the phrase at the beginning of *Bereshit*, "And God *said*, 'Let there be...' And there was..." Hashem simply willed the world into existence through speech.

different parts of *Pesukei DeZimra* as being a single unit of praise that is designed to prepare us psychologically and spiritually for the *Amida*, then one can appreciate the fact that Halakha deems it important that its recitation not be interrupted by unnecessary speech. Its identity as a single unit is indicated by the opening blessing we are about to recite and the similar concluding blessing at the end of *Yishtabaḥ*, thereby making *Pesukei DeZimra* one long blessing of praise. This is also the reason why during its recitation one may respond *Amen* on hearing someone else's blessing, since *Amen*, too, is considered a song of praise, something that cannot be said of extraneous conversation.

בָּרוּךְ שֶׁאָמַר – *Blessed is He who spoke.* The origin of this prayer is shrouded in mystery. One source (as mentioned above) claims that a note fell down from heaven upon which this prayer was written. In fact, it may date as far back as the *Tanna'im*, but the legend attests to the mystical content of the prayer as well. So holy was this prayer considered, so important was it deemed to be as an introduction to *Pesukei DeZimra*, that there are reports of some communities in medieval Germany that used to spend one full hour reciting it.

הודו Thank the LORD,[B] call on His name, make His acts known among the peoples. Sing to Him, make music to Him, tell of all His wonders. Glory in His holy name; let the hearts of those who seek the LORD rejoice. Search out the LORD and His strength; seek His presence at all times. Remember the wonders He has done, His miracles, and the judgments He pronounced. Descendants of Yisrael His servant, sons of Jacob His chosen ones: He is the LORD our God. His judgments are throughout the earth. Remember His covenant for ever, the word He commanded for a thousand generations. He made it with Abraham, vowed it to Isaac, and confirmed it to Jacob as a statute and to Israel as an everlasting covenant, saying, "To you I will give the land of Canaan as your allotted heritage." You were then small in number, few, strangers there, wandering from nation to nation, from one kingdom to another, but He let no man oppress them, and for their sake He rebuked kings: "Do not touch My anointed ones, and do My prophets no harm." Sing to the LORD, all the earth; proclaim His salvation daily. Declare His glory among the nations, His marvels among all the peoples. For great is the LORD and greatly to be praised; He is awesome beyond all heavenly powers. ▸ For all the gods of the peoples are mere idols; it was the LORD who made the heavens. *I Chr. 16*

Before Him are majesty and splendor; there is strength and beauty in His holy place. Render to the LORD, families of the peoples, render to the LORD honor and might. Render to the LORD the glory due to His name; bring an offering and come before Him; bow down to the LORD in the splendor of holiness. Tremble before Him,

---

Beit HaMikdash was built by King Solomon. At that point, different sacrifices and songs were instituted.

This historical information explains the difference between Ashkenazic and Sephardic practice regarding this prayer. Sephardim associate it with the sacrifices and therefore recite it before the prayer of *Barukh She'amar* which marks the beginning of *Pesukei DeZimra*. Ashkenazim, however, associate it with the *Tehillim* composed and recited by David since, once the *Beit HaMikdash* was built, this prayer was no longer said with the sacrifices and thus stands on its own as a song of David (*Beit Yosef* 50, Tur 51).

דברי הימים א׳ טז

הוֹדוּ לַיהוה קִרְאוּ בִשְׁמוֹ, הוֹדִיעוּ בָעַמִּים עֲלִילֹתָיו: שִׁירוּ לוֹ, זַמְּרוּ־לוֹ, שִׂיחוּ בְּכָל־נִפְלְאֹתָיו: הִתְהַלְלוּ בְּשֵׁם קָדְשׁוֹ, יִשְׂמַח לֵב מְבַקְשֵׁי יהוה: דִּרְשׁוּ יהוה וְעֻזּוֹ, בַּקְּשׁוּ פָנָיו תָּמִיד: זִכְרוּ נִפְלְאֹתָיו אֲשֶׁר עָשָׂה, מֹפְתָיו וּמִשְׁפְּטֵי־פִיהוּ: זֶרַע יִשְׂרָאֵל עַבְדּוֹ, בְּנֵי יַעֲקֹב בְּחִירָיו: הוּא יהוה אֱלֹהֵינוּ, בְּכָל־הָאָרֶץ מִשְׁפָּטָיו: זִכְרוּ לְעוֹלָם בְּרִיתוֹ, דָּבָר צִוָּה לְאֶלֶף דּוֹר: אֲשֶׁר כָּרַת אֶת־אַבְרָהָם, וּשְׁבוּעָתוֹ לְיִצְחָק: וַיַּעֲמִידֶהָ לְיַעֲקֹב לְחֹק, לְיִשְׂרָאֵל בְּרִית עוֹלָם: לֵאמֹר, לְךָ אֶתֵּן אֶרֶץ־כְּנָעַן, חֶבֶל נַחֲלַתְכֶם: בִּהְיוֹתְכֶם מְתֵי מִסְפָּר, כִּמְעַט וְגָרִים בָּהּ: וַיִּתְהַלְּכוּ מִגּוֹי אֶל־גּוֹי, וּמִמַּמְלָכָה אֶל־עַם אַחֵר: לֹא־הִנִּיחַ לְאִישׁ לְעָשְׁקָם, וַיּוֹכַח עֲלֵיהֶם מְלָכִים: אַל־תִּגְּעוּ בִּמְשִׁיחָי, וּבִנְבִיאַי אַל־תָּרֵעוּ: שִׁירוּ לַיהוה כָּל־הָאָרֶץ, בַּשְּׂרוּ מִיּוֹם־אֶל־יוֹם יְשׁוּעָתוֹ: סַפְּרוּ בַגּוֹיִם אֶת־כְּבוֹדוֹ, בְּכָל־הָעַמִּים נִפְלְאֹתָיו: כִּי גָדוֹל יהוה וּמְהֻלָּל מְאֹד, וְנוֹרָא הוּא עַל־כָּל־אֱלֹהִים: ‹ כִּי כָּל־אֱלֹהֵי הָעַמִּים אֱלִילִים, וַיהוה שָׁמַיִם עָשָׂה:

הוֹד וְהָדָר לְפָנָיו, עֹז וְחֶדְוָה בִּמְקֹמוֹ: הָבוּ לַיהוה מִשְׁפְּחוֹת עַמִּים, הָבוּ לַיהוה כָּבוֹד וָעֹז: הָבוּ לַיהוה כְּבוֹד שְׁמוֹ, שְׂאוּ מִנְחָה וּבֹאוּ לְפָנָיו, הִשְׁתַּחֲווּ לַיהוה בְּהַדְרַת־קֹדֶשׁ: חִילוּ מִלְּפָנָיו כָּל־הָאָרֶץ, אַף־תִּכּוֹן תֵּבֵל בַּל־תִּמּוֹט: יִשְׂמְחוּ הַשָּׁמַיִם וְתָגֵל הָאָרֶץ,

---

BIUR TEFILLA • ביאור תפילה

הוֹדוּ לַיהוה – *Thank the Lord.* The first set of verses was recited by David and actually come from *Divrei HaYamim* I 16:8–36. Once the Ark had been returned by the Pelishtim, David built a special enclosure in Yerushalayim to protect it there. A special *Tamid* sacrifice in its honor was instituted, once in the morning and once in the evening, each with its own song sung by a choir of *Levi'im*. And thus it was for 43 years until the

all the earth; the world stands firm, it will not be shaken. Let the heavens rejoice and the earth be glad; let them declare among the nations, "The Lord is King." Let the sea roar, and all that is in it; let the fields be jubilant, and all they contain. Then the trees of the forest will sing for joy before the Lord, for He is coming to judge the earth. Thank the Lord for He is good; His loving-kindness is for ever. Say: "Save us, God of our salvation; gather us and rescue us from the nations, to acknowledge Your holy name and glory in Your praise. Blessed is the Lord, God of Israel, from this world to eternity." And let all the people say "Amen" and "Praise the Lord."

▸ Exalt the Lord our God and bow before His footstool: He is *Ps. 99*
holy. Exalt the Lord our God and bow at His holy mountain; for holy is the Lord our God.

He is compassionate. He forgives iniquity and does not destroy. *Ps. 78*
Repeatedly He suppresses His anger, not rousing His full wrath.
You, Lord: do not withhold Your compassion from me. May Your *Ps. 40*
loving-kindness and truth always guard me. Remember, Lord, Your *Ps. 25*
acts of compassion and love, for they have existed for ever. Ascribe *Ps. 68*
power to God, whose majesty is over Israel and whose might is in the skies. You are awesome, God, in Your holy places. It is the God of Israel who gives might and strength to the people, may God
be blessed. God of retribution, Lord, God of retribution, appear. *Ps. 94*
Arise, Judge of the earth, to repay the arrogant their just deserts.
Salvation belongs to the Lord; may Your blessing rest upon Your *Ps. 3*
people, Selah! ▸ The Lord of hosts is with us, the God of Jacob is *Ps. 46*
our stronghold, Selah! Lord of hosts, happy is the one who trusts *Ps. 84*
in You. Lord, save! May the King answer us on the day we call. *Ps. 20*

Save Your people and bless Your heritage; tend them and carry *Ps. 28*
them for ever. Our soul longs for the Lord; He is our Help and *Ps. 33*
Shield. For in Him our hearts rejoice, for in His holy name we have trusted. May Your loving-kindness, Lord, be upon us, as we have
put our hope in You. Show us, Lord, Your loving-kindness and grant *Ps. 85*
us Your salvation. Arise, help us and redeem us for the sake of Your *Ps. 44*
love. I am the Lord your God who brought you up from the land of *Ps. 81*

וְיֹאמְרוּ בַגּוֹיִם יהוה מָלָךְ: יִרְעַם הַיָּם וּמְלוֹאוֹ, יַעֲלֹץ הַשָּׂדֶה
וְכָל־אֲשֶׁר־בּוֹ: אָז יְרַנְּנוּ עֲצֵי הַיָּעַר, מִלִּפְנֵי יהוה, כִּי־בָא לִשְׁפּוֹט
אֶת־הָאָרֶץ: הוֹדוּ לַיהוה כִּי טוֹב, כִּי לְעוֹלָם חַסְדּוֹ: וְאִמְרוּ,
הוֹשִׁיעֵנוּ אֱלֹהֵי יִשְׁעֵנוּ, וְקַבְּצֵנוּ וְהַצִּילֵנוּ מִן־הַגּוֹיִם, לְהֹדוֹת
לְשֵׁם קָדְשֶׁךָ, לְהִשְׁתַּבֵּחַ בִּתְהִלָּתֶךָ: בָּרוּךְ יהוה אֱלֹהֵי יִשְׂרָאֵל
מִן־הָעוֹלָם וְעַד־הָעֹלָם, וַיֹּאמְרוּ כָל־הָעָם אָמֵן, וְהַלֵּל לַיהוה:

◄ רוֹמְמוּ יהוה אֱלֹהֵינוּ וְהִשְׁתַּחֲווּ לַהֲדֹם רַגְלָיו, קָדוֹשׁ הוּא: תהלים צט
רוֹמְמוּ יהוה אֱלֹהֵינוּ וְהִשְׁתַּחֲווּ לְהַר קָדְשׁוֹ, כִּי־קָדוֹשׁ יהוה
אֱלֹהֵינוּ:

וְהוּא רַחוּם, יְכַפֵּר עָוֹן וְלֹא־יַשְׁחִית, וְהִרְבָּה לְהָשִׁיב אַפּוֹ, תהלים עח
וְלֹא־יָעִיר כָּל־חֲמָתוֹ: אַתָּה יהוה לֹא־תִכְלָא רַחֲמֶיךָ מִמֶּנִּי, חַסְדְּךָ תהלים מ
וַאֲמִתְּךָ תָּמִיד יִצְּרוּנִי: זְכֹר־רַחֲמֶיךָ יהוה וַחֲסָדֶיךָ, כִּי מֵעוֹלָם תהלים כה
הֵמָּה: תְּנוּ עֹז לֵאלֹהִים, עַל־יִשְׂרָאֵל גַּאֲוָתוֹ, וְעֻזּוֹ בַּשְּׁחָקִים: תהלים סח
נוֹרָא אֱלֹהִים מִמִּקְדָּשֶׁיךָ, אֵל יִשְׂרָאֵל הוּא נֹתֵן עֹז וְתַעֲצֻמוֹת
לָעָם, בָּרוּךְ אֱלֹהִים: אֵל־נְקָמוֹת יהוה, אֵל נְקָמוֹת הוֹפִיעַ: הִנָּשֵׂא תהלים צד
שֹׁפֵט הָאָרֶץ, הָשֵׁב גְּמוּל עַל־גֵּאִים: לַיהוה הַיְשׁוּעָה, עַל־עַמְּךָ תהלים ג
בִרְכָתֶךָ סֶּלָה: ◄ יהוה צְבָאוֹת עִמָּנוּ, מִשְׂגָּב לָנוּ אֱלֹהֵי יַעֲקֹב תהלים מו
סֶלָה: יהוה צְבָאוֹת, אַשְׁרֵי אָדָם בֹּטֵחַ בָּךְ: יהוה הוֹשִׁיעָה, תהלים פד תהלים כ
הַמֶּלֶךְ יַעֲנֵנוּ בְיוֹם־קָרְאֵנוּ:

הוֹשִׁיעָה אֶת־עַמֶּךָ, וּבָרֵךְ אֶת־נַחֲלָתֶךָ, וּרְעֵם וְנַשְּׂאֵם עַד־ תהלים כח
הָעוֹלָם: נַפְשֵׁנוּ חִכְּתָה לַיהוה, עֶזְרֵנוּ וּמָגִנֵּנוּ הוּא: כִּי־בוֹ יִשְׂמַח תהלים לג
לִבֵּנוּ, כִּי בְשֵׁם קָדְשׁוֹ בָטָחְנוּ: יְהִי־חַסְדְּךָ יהוה עָלֵינוּ, כַּאֲשֶׁר
יִחַלְנוּ לָךְ: הַרְאֵנוּ יהוה חַסְדֶּךָ, וְיֶשְׁעֲךָ תִּתֶּן־לָנוּ: קוּמָה עֶזְרָתָה תהלים פה תהלים מד
לָּנוּ, וּפְדֵנוּ לְמַעַן חַסְדֶּךָ: אָנֹכִי יהוה אֱלֹהֶיךָ הַמַּעַלְךָ מֵאֶרֶץ תהלים פא

Egypt: open your mouth wide and I will fill it. Happy is the people *Ps. 144* for whom this is so; happy is the people whose God the LORD. ▸ As *Ps. 13* for me, I trust in Your loving-kindness; my heart rejoices in Your salvation. I will sing to the LORD for He has been good to me.

לַמְנַצֵּחַ For the conductor of music. A psalm of David. The heavens *Ps. 19* declare the glory of God; the skies proclaim the work of His hands.[1] Day to day they pour forth speech; night to night they communicate

---

off all the station's external lights so we can see the outside?" He stuck us in front of the windows and said, "Stay here for an orbit," about 90 minutes. He gave us that pause because on a flight, you're so busy that unless somebody forces you to take a moment like that, you don't get one. I'm so grateful for that. (Astronaut Tracy Caldwell Dyson)

Look around you. What are you taking for granted?

BIUR TEFILLA • ביאור תפילה

לַמְנַצֵּחַ – *TEHILLIM 19.* This psalm essentially divides into two. The first half praises God and the wonders of creation; the second half praises the Torah and the desire to fulfill it. Described here, then, are "the sources from which one could come to recognize God and worship Him." From nature, one can discern the existence of God, from the Torah one can discern what one should do with that knowledge (Rabbi S. Hirsch). From nature one learns the what, from Torah one learns the why. From the history of mankind one learns over and over again that science is no guarantor of a moral or religious life, and from Torah one cannot learn everything there is to know about how the natural world operates. One needs both to live a balanced life.

IYUN TEFILLA • עיון תפילה

הַשָּׁמַיִם מְסַפְּרִים כְּבוֹד־אֵל, וּמַעֲשֵׂה יָדָיו מַגִּיד הָרָקִיעַ – *The heavens declare the glory of God; the skies proclaim the work of His hands.* One possible reading of this passage is that it is man who is the one who looks at the universe and tells the story. Alternatively, it is the sky, the sun and the moon and the way that they keep to their appointed courses, the working of nature within its boundaries that tells its story all by itself – it is the story told silently without any words. The glory of Hashem is visible, perceivable yet indescribable, like a work of art drawn upon man's heart, a feeling, a thought, that words cannot describe (Radak). The word "*lehagid,*" "to declare," is usually used to convey something which someone did not know before, to inform.

What aspect of nature have you never really looked at before?

Look at it now in your mind's eye. Hear its story.

The **IYUN TEFILLA** *continues on page 231.*

תהלים קמד מִצְרָיִם, הַרְחֶב־פִּיךָ וַאֲמַלְאֵהוּ: אַשְׁרֵי הָעָם שֶׁכָּכָה לּוֹ, אַשְׁרֵי
תהלים יג הָעָם שֶׁיהוה אֱלֹהָיו: › וַאֲנִי בְּחַסְדְּךָ בָטַחְתִּי, יָגֵל לִבִּי בִּישׁוּעָתֶךָ,
אָשִׁירָה לַיהוה, כִּי גָמַל עָלָי:

תהלים יט לַמְנַצֵּחַ מִזְמוֹר לְדָוִד: הַשָּׁמַיִם מְסַפְּרִים כְּבוֹד־אֵל, וּמַעֲשֵׂה
יָדָיו מַגִּיד הָרָקִיעַ: ע יוֹם לְיוֹם יַבִּיעַ אֹמֶר, וְלַיְלָה לְּלַיְלָה יְחַוֶּה־

AN INTRODUCTION TO THE ADDITIONAL TEHILLIM OF SHABBAT MORNING

On Shabbat and Yom Tov additional selections of psalms (*Tehillim*) are added to the morning service. There is more time to reflect, more mental space to allow for the messages we want to permeate and penetrate, fewer distractions to drag us away from considering life's priorities.

There are seven new psalms introduced here (in addition to Psalms 92 and 93 which we recited for the first time last evening), one apparently for each day of the week or perhaps, too, an echo of the seven blessings said beneath the marriage canopy at a wedding (Ya'avetz). Unlike the *Tehillim* that were recited last night during Ma'ariv, or like others which will follow in the next section, these particular chapters are not in sequential order as they appear in the book of *Tehillim*. They may instead have some thematic order which includes topics such as Shabbat and the giving of the Torah (which tradition says took place on Shabbat) (*Levush*) or, as another observed, there may be three themes: "the memorial to Creation, the memorial to the exodus from Egypt, and the anticipation of the "world-wide Sabbath to come" (Munk). How these may tie together and which may resonate most will vary with each of us–and sometimes will vary from one Shabbat to the next.

The important thing is that they be said slowly, qualitatively, in a pleasant voice and cadence (*Or Zarua*), else we will have said many words but with little chance to be impacted by them.

ANI TEFILLA • אני תפילה

The first time I glimpsed Earth from space, I stared long and hard... No adjective can convey the feeling of knowing I was one of a small fraction of humans to see it with my own eyes: the richness of the changing colors, the glow of the atmosphere, the opalescence of the sun glinting off the water. It was overwhelming. You have these emotions going through your body because you've worked a lifetime to be there.

It wasn't until the middle of my first flight – day five or six – when my commander brought the rookies onto the flight deck, and asked, "Can you ask Mission Control to turn

knowledge.[I] There is no speech, there are no words, their voice is not heard.[B] Yet their music carries throughout the earth, their words to the end of the world. In them He has set a tent for the sun. It emerges like a groom from his marriage chamber, rejoicing like a champion about to run a race. It rises at one end of the heaven and makes its circuit to the other: nothing is hidden from its heat. The LORD's Torah is perfect, refreshing the soul.[B] The LORD's testimony is faithful, making the simple wise. The LORD's precepts are just, gladdening the heart. The LORD's commandment is radiant, giving light to the eyes.[I] The fear of the LORD is pure, enduring for ever.[A] The LORD's judgments are true, altogether righteous.[I] More precious than gold, than much fine gold. They are sweeter than honey,[I] than honey from the comb. Your

---

its owner but too much of it can make one ill, whereas wisdom, the more it is imbibed, the longer it will stay with you and the more beneficial and satisfying it will be (Radak). **How can you add to your knowledge of Judaism today?**

BIUR TEFILLA • ביאור תפילה

אֵין־אֹמֶר וְאֵין דְּבָרִים, בְּלִי נִשְׁמָע קוֹלָם – *There is no speech, there are no words, their voice is not heard.* The messages that nature sends us cannot always be put into words. Sometimes it's alright to just feel something and know it to be true without being able to articulate it. Shabbat can be that kind of day.

תּוֹרַת יהוה תְּמִימָה, מְשִׁיבַת נָפֶשׁ – *The LORD's Torah is perfect, refreshing the soul.* Torah generally refers not only to the Five Books of Moses but to the entire corpus of Jewish law. The Midrash finds a hint to this in the fact that the next verses contain five words each (corresponding to the five books of the Torah); furthermore, a total of six different categories of law (corresponding to the six divisions of the Oral Law, *Sidrei Mishna*) are mentioned, and Hashem's name is attached to each. The written law and the oral law all in essence have the same source and all can be "refreshing" if only one opens one's eyes to them, investing one's soul as well as one's mind.

ANI TEFILLA • אני תפילה

יִרְאַת יהוה טְהוֹרָה, עוֹמֶדֶת לָעַד – *The fear of the LORD is pure, enduring for ever.*

Imagine a tall building in the middle of a crowded area. Someone announces that the building is tilting and it is about to fall, thereby creating a huge panic as people run away to avoid being crushed. One lone person arrives on the scene and quickly realizes that the fault lay not with the structure of the building but with the eyesight of the person who first raised the concern. "Get him to a doctor," said the observer, "for he is clearly about to lose his sight altogether." And so it is with those who would claim that the Torah's laws need to be changed because the structure of the system is faulty. Such people do not realize that the structure is what has kept and will keep the building standing forever. (Ḥafetz Ḥayyim)

How can you change your perspective today?

דָּֽעַת׃ [ע] אֵין־אֹמֶר וְאֵין דְּבָרִים, בְּלִי נִשְׁמָע קוֹלָם׃ [ב] בְּכָל־הָאָֽרֶץ
יָצָא קַוָּם, וּבִקְצֵה תֵבֵל מִלֵּיהֶם, לַשֶּֽׁמֶשׁ שָׂם־אֹֽהֶל בָּהֶם׃ וְהוּא
כְּחָתָן יֹצֵא מֵחֻפָּתוֹ, יָשִׂישׂ כְּגִבּוֹר לָרוּץ אֹֽרַח׃ מִקְצֵה הַשָּׁמַֽיִם
מוֹצָאוֹ, וּתְקוּפָתוֹ עַל־קְצוֹתָם, וְאֵין נִסְתָּר מֵחַמָּתוֹ׃ תּוֹרַת יהוה
תְּמִימָה, מְשִֽׁיבַת נָֽפֶשׁ, [ב] עֵדוּת יהוה נֶאֱמָנָה, מַחְכִּֽימַת פֶּֽתִי׃
פִּקּוּדֵי יהוה יְשָׁרִים, מְשַׂמְּחֵי־לֵב, מִצְוַת יהוה בָּרָה, מְאִירַת
עֵינָֽיִם׃ [ע] יִרְאַת יהוה טְהוֹרָה, עוֹמֶֽדֶת לָעַד, [א] מִשְׁפְּטֵי־יהוה אֱמֶת,
צָֽדְקוּ יַחְדָּו׃ [ע] הַנֶּחֱמָדִים מִזָּהָב וּמִפַּז רָב, וּמְתוּקִים מִדְּבַשׁ [ע] וְנֹֽפֶת
צוּפִים׃ גַּם־עַבְדְּךָ נִזְהָר בָּהֶם, בְּשָׁמְרָם עֵֽקֶב רָב׃ שְׁגִיאוֹת מִי־

IYUN TEFILLA • עיון תפילה

יוֹם לְיוֹם יַבִּֽיעַ אֹֽמֶר, וְלַֽיְלָה לְּלַֽיְלָה יְחַוֶּה־דָּֽעַת – *Day to day they pour forth speech; night to night they communicate knowledge.* From a purely technical view, watch the globe from outer space via time lapse and see how one day turns into the next seamlessly. Alternatively, each day informs the next; days and nights can have a life of their own, almost animate. They share their beauty with the next day. Life is cumulative. Even as every day is a new creation, a fresh beginning, what we do or say today will inform our tomorrow. Viewed in this way, our Shabbat can inform the rest of our week.

מִצְוַת יהוה בָּרָה, מְאִירַת עֵינָֽיִם – *The Lord's commandment is radiant, giving light to the eyes.* Here lies the connection between the two sources of knowledge of God. Both the sun and the Torah provide light, both enable us to see through the dark, both provide a new way of taking in the life around us, the one in the natural sphere, the other in the moral sphere. Yet there are also differences: looking for a long time at the sun can make one blind; looking more at the Torah can enable one to keep seeing more.

מִשְׁפְּטֵי־יהוה אֱמֶת, צָֽדְקוּ יַחְדָּו – *The Lord's judgments are true, altogether righteous.* The Torah's laws of morality go where secular laws dare not. The latter are often predicated on the notion of not interfering with other people's rights. Jewish law is predicated on the notion that one is responsible for other people's welfare. These are two very different views of the world and of social justice. What examples can you think of?

הַנֶּחֱמָדִים מִזָּהָב וּמִפַּז רָב, וּמְתוּקִים מִדְּבַשׁ – *More precious than gold, than much fine gold. They are sweeter than honey.* Material wealth can be stolen or lost whereas one's knowledge of Torah and one's heritage are forever in one's possession. One can give one's money away and be left with nothing, but knowledge can be shared without any loss and can even be enhanced. Money is sweet like honey to

servant, too, is careful of them, for in observing them there is great reward. Yet who can discern his errors? Cleanse me of hidden faults. Keep Your servant also from willful sins; let them not have dominion over me. Then shall I be blameless, and innocent of grave sin. ▸ May the words of my mouth and the meditation of my heart find favor before You, LORD, my Rock and my Redeemer.

לְדָוִד Of David. When he pretended to be insane before Abimelech, who drove him away, and he left. Ps. 34

I will bless the LORD at all times;[I]
His praise will be always on my lips.
My soul will glory in the LORD;
let the lowly hear this and rejoice.
Magnify the LORD with me;
let us exalt His name together.
I sought the LORD, and He answered me;
He saved me from all my fears.
Those who look to Him are radiant;
Their faces are never downcast.
This poor man called,[I] and the LORD heard;
He saved him from all his troubles.

IYUN TEFILLA • עיון תפילה

בְּכָל־עֵת – *At all times.* Everything and everyone was created at just the right point in history. Avraham could not have been born at the time of Adam or vice versa. Each of us is born at a particular time in human history to fulfill our unique role that no one before or after us could do (*Midrash Shoḥer Tov*). The challenge is for us is to discover what that role is. During the week it is sometimes hard to do so. Shabbat presents that opportunity.

What can you do this week to come closer to fulfilling or finding your unique role?

זֶה עָנִי קָרָא - *This poor man called.* The *Zohar* says the prayers of a poor person are more readily accepted than those of other people and that the prayers of others do not appear before God until those of the poor have been presented first. (*Me'am Lo'ez*) What is it about the prayer of the poor that takes precedence? David, King of Israel, calls himself a poor person here.

In what way was he so? Consider yourself poor. Now pray.

יָבִין, מִנִּסְתָּרוֹת נַקֵּנִי: גַּם מִזֵּדִים חֲשֹׂךְ עַבְדֶּךָ, אַל־יִמְשְׁלוּ־בִי אָז אֵיתָם, וְנִקֵּיתִי מִפֶּשַׁע רָב: • יִהְיוּ לְרָצוֹן אִמְרֵי־פִי וְהֶגְיוֹן לִבִּי לְפָנֶיךָ, יהוה, צוּרִי וְגֹאֲלִי:

תהלים לד

לְדָוִד, בְּשַׁנּוֹתוֹ אֶת־טַעְמוֹ לִפְנֵי אֲבִימֶלֶךְ, וַיְגָרְשֵׁהוּ וַיֵּלַךְ:
אֲבָרְכָה אֶת־יהוה בְּכָל־עֵת, תָּמִיד תְּהִלָּתוֹ בְּפִי:
בַּיהוה תִּתְהַלֵּל נַפְשִׁי, יִשְׁמְעוּ עֲנָוִים וְיִשְׂמָחוּ:
גַּדְּלוּ לַיהוה אִתִּי, וּנְרוֹמְמָה שְׁמוֹ יַחְדָּו:
דָּרַשְׁתִּי אֶת־יהוה וְעָנָנִי, וּמִכָּל־מְגוּרוֹתַי הִצִּילָנִי:
הִבִּיטוּ אֵלָיו וְנָהָרוּ, וּפְנֵיהֶם אַל־יֶחְפָּרוּ:
זֶה עָנִי קָרָא, וַיהוה שָׁמֵעַ, וּמִכָּל־צָרוֹתָיו הוֹשִׁיעוֹ:

ANI TEFILLA • אני תפילה

Science is about explanation. Religion is about meaning. Science analyzes, religion integrates. Science breaks things down to their component parts. Religion binds people together in relationships of trust. Science tells us what is. Religion tells us what ought to be. Science describes. Religion beckons, summons, calls. Science sees objects. Religion speaks to us as subjects. (Rabbi J. Sacks)

BIUR TEFILLA • ביאור תפילה

לְדָוִד – *TEHILLIM 34.* The Bible (Shmuel I 21) relates that as David fled for his life from King Shaul, and while he prayed for deliverance, he found himself in the midst of the Pelishtim (Philistines) who thought they recognized him and also sought him harm. David feigned madness and was promptly released whereupon, according to tradition, he composed this psalm. Above all else, then, it is a testimony to the efficacy of prayer, even as each of us is required to be as creative as possible in first helping ourselves.

The psalm is one of those that is an alphabetical **acrostic**. Some say that one letter is missing; others say it really is there. (Can you find it?) Regardless, there are 22 verses, the same number as the letters in the Hebrew alphabet.

The LORD's angel encamps around those who fear Him,
and He rescues them.
Taste and see that the LORD is good;[B]
happy is the man who takes refuge in Him.
Fear the LORD, you His holy ones,
for those who fear Him lack nothing.[I]
Young lions may grow weak and hungry,
but those who seek the LORD lack no good thing.
Come, my children,
listen to me;
I will teach you the fear of the LORD.
Who desires life,
loving each day to see good?
Then guard your tongue from evil
and your lips from speaking deceit.[I]

ANI TEFILLA • אני תפילה

Rabbi Eliyahu Meir Bloch, the head of the Telz yeshiva in Cleveland, once went to visit a potential donor who was very wealthy. "Explain something to me," said the man. "I really am lacking nothing. I have a house in New York and another in Florida and a summer home in California. I have my own small private jet, a yacht and numerous cars and yet there is one thing I am still missing – happiness. I'm just not happy. And yet, I see you, a person with limited means who travels around the country with your hand out for donations, and yet it seems to me from the look on your face that you are a happy man. Why the difference between us?" Rabbi Bloch answered: "You know that we are both Jews and both of us possess a pure soul that accompanies us all day. Yet we know that we also have a body and that body needs to be fed, needs to be given water in order to survive, else we would shrivel up and die. The same is true of the soul. It too needs to be nourished and fed and that is what I try to do by learning Torah and living a life of mitzvot. Your soul, too, craves attention. Yet you try to satisfy it with houses and cars and boats – material things."

That is why "lions," powerful people can still feel "hungry." The soul cannot be nourished with material things. But "those who seek Hashem" will not lack.

חֹנֶה מַלְאַךְ־יהוה סָבִיב לִירֵאָיו, וַיְחַלְּצֵם:
טַעֲמוּ וּרְאוּ כִּי־טוֹב יהוה,ב אַשְׁרֵי הַגֶּבֶר יֶחֱסֶה־בּוֹ:
יְראוּ אֶת־יהוה קְדֹשָׁיו, כִּי־אֵין מַחְסוֹר לִירֵאָיו:ע
כְּפִירִים רָשׁוּ וְרָעֵבוּ, וְדֹרְשֵׁי יהוה לֹא־יַחְסְרוּ כָל־טוֹב:
לְכוּ־בָנִים שִׁמְעוּ־לִי, יִרְאַת יהוה אֲלַמֶּדְכֶם:
מִי־הָאִישׁ הֶחָפֵץ חַיִּים, אֹהֵב יָמִים לִרְאוֹת טוֹב:
נְצֹר לְשׁוֹנְךָ מֵרָע, וּשְׂפָתֶיךָ מִדַּבֵּר מִרְמָה:ע

BIUR TEFILLA • ביאור תפילה

טַעֲמוּ וּרְאוּ כִּי־טוֹב יהוה – *Taste and see that the Lord is good.* The word "see" can refer to one's eyesight: Look around you and see the actual good aspects of your life that surround you. But it can also mean to understand as in "Can't you see what I mean?"

The word **טַעַם** in this context can mean to think or to consider. But it can also mean to taste in the sense of an experience that goes beyond the cognitive. We are encouraged to experience a relationship with God not just try to understand it; only by actually living a Jewish life, getting to know it as an insider will we come to see how good and pleasant and fulfilling it can be. One cannot describe a sunset to a person who has been blind since birth. So, too, one cannot explain the beauty of Shabbat until it has been repeatedly experienced.

IYUN TEFILLA • עיון תפילה

כִּי־אֵין מַחְסוֹר לִירֵאָיו – *For those who fear Him lack nothing.* Note that it does not say that those who fear God will have riches; rather, that they will not be wanting. Do not be envious looking at those who have more wealth than you, for as long as you feel that you have enough, you will be satisfied. (*Etz HaDa'at Tov*). A traditional blessing in our family is: "May you always have just enough."

"Who is wealthy?" asks the Mishna in Avot (4:1), "the person who is happy with what he has."

נְצֹר לְשׁוֹנְךָ מֵרָע, וּשְׂפָתֶיךָ מִדַּבֵּר מִרְמָה – *Then guard your tongue from evil and your lips from speaking deceit.* Herein lies a source for the expression *lashon hara*, or gossip, which is forbidden by Jewish law. The path to having one's prayers answered lies not only in the ritual sphere but in the interpersonal as well. To be religious means to strive for wholeness in all facets of one's life, not just in the synagogue, not just on Shabbat.

Turn from evil and do good;[B]
seek peace and pursue it.[B]
The eyes of the LORD are on the righteous
and His ears attentive to their cry;
The LORD's face is set against those who do evil,
to erase their memory from the earth.
The righteous cry out, and the LORD hears them;
delivering them from all their troubles.
The LORD is close to the brokenhearted,
and saves those who are crushed in spirit.
Many troubles may befall the righteous,
but the LORD delivers him from them all;
He protects all his bones,
so that none of them will be broken.
Evil will slay the wicked;
the enemies of the righteous will be condemned.
▸ The LORD redeems His servants;
none who take refuge in Him shall be condemned.

תְּפִלָּה לְמֹשֶׁה A prayer of Moses, the man of God. LORD, You have been our shelter[I] in every generation. Before the mountains were born, before You brought forth the earth and the world, from everlasting to everlasting You are God. You turn men back to dust, saying, "Return, you children of men."[IB] For a thousand years *Ps. 90*

IYUN TEFILLA • עיון תפילה

מָעוֹן אַתָּה – *You have been our shelter.* There are those religions that believe that God is distant and unreachable, a transcendent being who is impossible to approach, with whom one has no connection. There are others that believe that God is immanent, close to man, a part of this world, a part of nature. Judaism believes in neither of these. Rather, God is both distant and near. The world is not His place, yet He is also close to us, watches over us and protects us, His place is in the world (*Midrash Shoḥer Tov, Bereshit Raba* 68:9).

שׁוּבוּ בְנֵי־אָדָם – *Return, you children of men.* Sometimes a person cannot emerge from the doldrums on his own. One needs the kindness and care of others who remind us to return to our former selves (*Menaḥem Tzyion*). Shabbat is an opportunity to spend time with those people and to reach out to others.

The **BIUR TEFILLA** *on psalm 90 is on page 239.*

סוּר מֵרָע וַעֲשֵׂה־טוֹב, בַּקֵּשׁ שָׁלוֹם וְרׇדְפֵהוּ: ב
עֵינֵי יהוה אֶל־צַדִּיקִים, וְאׇזְנָיו אֶל־שַׁוְעָתָם:
פְּנֵי יהוה בְּעֹשֵׂי רָע, לְהַכְרִית מֵאֶרֶץ זִכְרָם:
צָעֲקוּ וַיהוה שָׁמֵעַ, וּמִכׇּל־צָרוֹתָם הִצִּילָם:
קָרוֹב יהוה לְנִשְׁבְּרֵי־לֵב, וְאֶת־דַּכְּאֵי־רוּחַ יוֹשִׁיעַ:
רַבּוֹת רָעוֹת צַדִּיק, וּמִכֻּלָּם יַצִּילֶנּוּ יהוה:
שֹׁמֵר כׇּל־עַצְמוֹתָיו, אַחַת מֵהֵנָּה לֹא נִשְׁבָּרָה:
תְּמוֹתֵת רָשָׁע רָעָה, וְשֹׂנְאֵי צַדִּיק יֶאְשָׁמוּ:
◂ פּוֹדֶה יהוה נֶפֶשׁ עֲבָדָיו, וְלֹא יֶאְשְׁמוּ כׇּל־הַחֹסִים בּוֹ:

תהלים צ
תְּפִלָּה לְמֹשֶׁה אִישׁ־הָאֱלֹהִים, אֲדֹנָי, מָעוֹן אַתָּה הָיִיתָ לָּנוּ בְּדֹר
וָדֹר: בְּטֶרֶם הָרִים יֻלָּדוּ, וַתְּחוֹלֵל אֶרֶץ וְתֵבֵל, וּמֵעוֹלָם עַד־עוֹלָם
אַתָּה אֵל: תָּשֵׁב אֱנוֹשׁ עַד־דַּכָּא, וַתֹּאמֶר שׁוּבוּ בְנֵי־אָדָם: עב

BIUR TEFILLA • ביאור תפילה

תְּפִלָּה לְמֹשֶׁה – *TEHILLIM 90.* This psalm can be divided into two parts: the fleeting nature of life on the one hand, and the prayer for happiness and satisfaction on the other. It is one of the more sobering of all the psalms in *Tehillim*, yet it can also be hopeful, somber yet joyful, depending upon which part one emphasizes. One tradition suggests that the psalm was written by Moshe specifically before his death and thus serves as both a reflection on life and a mandate for how to live it. Throughout, there is an emphasis on time consciousness, a particularly important theme for the island of time that is Shabbat.

סוּר מֵרָע וַעֲשֵׂה־טוֹב – *Turn from evil and do good.* "Turn from evil" refers to the negative commandments; "do good" refers to the positive commandments (Ibn Ezra). In Jewish society it is not enough to "do no harm." The very definition of morality is where one also proactively seeks to do good.

בַּקֵּשׁ שָׁלוֹם וְרׇדְפֵהוּ – *Seek peace and pursue it.* Peace is not simply an ideal to be dreamed about nor is it something that one should just wait for (Rashi); rather, it is something to be actively pursued whether in human relations, in the political sphere (Malbim), or in one's inner life (Seforno).

How can you pursue peace today?

in Your sight are like yesterday[IA] when it has passed, like a watch in the night. You sweep men away; they sleep.[A] In the morning they are like grass newly grown: in the morning it flourishes and is new, but by evening it withers and dries up.[I] For we are consumed by Your anger, terrified by Your fury. You have set our iniquities before You, our secret sins in the light of Your presence. All our days pass away in Your wrath, we spend our years like a sigh. The span of our life is seventy years, or if we are strong, eighty years; but the best of them is trouble and sorrow, for they quickly pass, and we fly away. Who can know the force of Your anger? Your wrath matches the fear due to You. Teach us rightly to number our days, that we may gain a heart of wisdom. Relent, O Lord! How much longer?[I] Be sorry for Your servants.[I]

Until now, one might have thought that life is without meaning given how short and fleeting it is. This could be the stance of the human being before a distant eternal God. But here the verse speaks of "Your servants," which represents another perspective; namely, that of the loyal servant who finds meaning in service. Life's brevity thus leads not to hopelessness but to purpose, not to futility but to meaning (*Da'at Mikra*).

ANI TEFILLA • אני תפילה

כִּי אֶלֶף שָׁנִים בְּעֵינֶיךָ, כְּיוֹם אֶתְמוֹל – *For a thousand years in Your sight are like yesterday.* *A man once pleaded with God to bestow a bit of His abundance upon him. He implored and begged his Creator for long life and wealth. After all, the poor soul figured, God had an abundance of everything; why then, wouldn't He spare something for a Jew in need. He entered a huge, empty synagogue and began to cry."Ribono Shel Olam (Master of the Universe), in the great extent of Your eternity what is a million years?" The man began to tremble. He imagined that he actually heard a response."To Me a million years is but a mere second!" boomed a voice inside his mind. The man continued, "And to the magnitude of Your great bounty, what, may I ask, is a billion dollars?" "A billion dollars is just a mere penny," came the resonating reply. "Then," begged the man, "can I not have just one of your pennies?" "Surely!" came the response. And then a pause. "But you must wait a mere second."*

זְרַמְתָּם, שֵׁנָה יִהְיוּ – *You sweep men away; they sleep.* How often do we feel like we have slept life away? One wakens with a start only to realize with remorse how much time and opportunity have been lost. We sleep about one-third of our lives on earth.

How often can our waking hours be called sleep of a different kind?

How many opportunities did you lose last week? How will this Shabbat and next week be different?

Are you living your eulogy or your resume?

The **ANI TEFILLA** *continues on page 241.*

כִּי אֶלֶף שָׁנִים בְּעֵינֶיךָ, כְּיוֹם אֶתְמוֹל[עא] כִּי יַעֲבֹר, וְאַשְׁמוּרָה בַלָּיְלָה:
זְרַמְתָּם, שֵׁנָה יִהְיוּ,[א] בַּבֹּקֶר כֶּחָצִיר יַחֲלֹף: בַּבֹּקֶר יָצִיץ וְחָלָף,
לָעֶרֶב יְמוֹלֵל וְיָבֵשׁ:[ע] כִּי־כָלִינוּ בְאַפֶּךָ, וּבַחֲמָתְךָ נִבְהָלְנוּ: שַׁתָּ
עֲוֹנֹתֵינוּ לְנֶגְדֶּךָ, עֲלֻמֵנוּ לִמְאוֹר פָּנֶיךָ: כִּי כָל־יָמֵינוּ פָּנוּ בְעֶבְרָתֶךָ,
כִּלִּינוּ שָׁנֵינוּ כְמוֹ־הֶגֶה: יְמֵי־שְׁנוֹתֵינוּ בָהֶם שִׁבְעִים שָׁנָה, וְאִם
בִּגְבוּרֹת שְׁמוֹנִים שָׁנָה, וְרָהְבָּם עָמָל וָאָוֶן, כִּי־גָז חִישׁ וַנָּעֻפָה:
מִי־יוֹדֵעַ עֹז אַפֶּךָ, וּכְיִרְאָתְךָ עֶבְרָתֶךָ, לִמְנוֹת יָמֵינוּ כֵּן הוֹדַע,
וְנָבִא לְבַב חָכְמָה:[א] שׁוּבָה יהוה עַד־מָתָי,[ע] וְהִנָּחֵם עַל־עֲבָדֶיךָ:[ע]

BIUR TEFILLA • ביאור תפילה

שׁוּבוּ בְנֵי־אָדָם – *Return, you children of men.* The juxtaposition of this verse with the one which precedes, led the Rabbis to suggest that repentance was created before the world itself was. The implication is that it is part of the very fabric of creation, it is a natural element. Change is always possible.

IYUN TEFILLA • עיון תפילה

כִּי אֶלֶף שָׁנִים בְּעֵינֶיךָ, כְּיוֹם אֶתְמוֹל – *For a thousand years in Your sight are like yesterday.* Hashem is eternal and time, when measured by man, is relative. There are those who often turn to this verse to suggest that when the Bible speaks of the world being created in six days, it speaks metaphorically, for a day in God's reckoning is very different than a period of 24 hours and could be a thousand years, millions of years or more.

בַּבֹּקֶר יָצִיץ וְחָלָף, לָעֶרֶב יְמוֹלֵל וְיָבֵשׁ – *In the morning it flourishes and is new, but by evening it withers and dries up.* The imagery here is the basis of part of the famous prayer *Untaneh Tokef*, said on the High Holy Days: "Man is founded in dust and ends in dust. He lays down his soul to bring home bread. He is like a broken shard, like grass dried up, like a faded flower, like a fleeting shadow, like a passing cloud, like a breath of wind, like whirling dust, like a dream that slips away." Unfortunately, we tend to think of these things only at times of judgment. Yet every day is an opportunity to begin anew.

How can you treat today as a fresh new beginning?

שׁוּבָה יהוה עַד־מָתָי – *Relent, O Lord! How much longer?* The Rabbis homiletically understand these two verses as a call to man to repent on the day before he dies. Since one does not know that day with any certainty, one must therefore repent every day; hence these two verses say "teach us to number our days," to be conscious of each day as if it were our last, "Return, (*shuvu*) for how long?" until the day of one's death (*Midrash Shoḥer Tov*).

וְהִנָּחֵם עַל־עֲבָדֶיךָ – *Be sorry for Your servants.*

Satisfy us in the morning with Your loving-kindness, that we may sing and rejoice all our days. Grant us joy for as many days as You have afflicted us, for as many years as we saw trouble. Let Your deeds be seen by Your servants, and Your glory by their children. ▸ May the pleasantness of the LORD our God be upon us. Establish for us the work of our hands, O establish the work of our hands.[1]

יֹשֵׁב בְּסֵתֶר He who lives in the shelter of the Most High dwells in the shadow of the Almighty. I say of the LORD, my Refuge and Stronghold, my God in whom I trust, that He will save you from the fowler's snare and the deadly pestilence.[B] With His pinions He will cover you, and beneath His wings you will find shelter; His faithfulness is an encircling shield. You need not fear terror by night,[B] nor the arrow that flies by day; not the pestilence that stalks in darkness,[B] *Ps. 91*

---

should accompany him with regard to the various dangers that lurk in his life... a person must be aware of the existential dangers that surround him; he should not live under the false illusion that the world is a tranquil, safe place. On the other hand, this awareness should not embitter him or cause him to live in constant fear. Admittedly, the world is full of all sorts of dangers, but it is not ownerless: God watches over His creatures and treats each according to its needs. A person who trusts in God and makes Him his abode and his refuge will enjoy His protection from all of the dangers in the world. As his trust in God and closeness to Him grow, so God's Divine patronage in his regard will assume deeper and broader significance." (Rabbi Elchanan Samet)

כִּי הוּא יַצִּילְךָ מִפַּח יָקוּשׁ, מִדֶּבֶר הַוּוֹת – *He will save you from the fowler's snare and the deadly pestilence.* The first speaks to the dangers that can come suddenly from one's fellow man, the traps laid by men; the other, comes from nature. Notice how many other such allusions there are in the verses that follow.

לֹא תִירָא, מִפַּחַד לָיְלָה – *You need not fear terror by night.* Fear (*yira*) and terror (*paḥad*) are two different things. The one has a rational basis; the other is irrational bordering on the phobic. To be sure, there are real threats that lurk in the dark of the night. Some come from without, many come from within. The person of faith is able to cope, put them at bay or push them away.

מִדֶּבֶר בָּאֹפֶל יַהֲלֹךְ – *The pestilence that stalks in darkness.* What might be the difference between the pestilence here and the one mentioned above in the third verse?

שַׂבְּעֵנוּ בַבֹּקֶר חַסְדֶּךָ, וּנְרַנְּנָה וְנִשְׂמְחָה בְּכָל־יָמֵינוּ: שַׂמְּחֵנוּ
כִּימוֹת עִנִּיתָנוּ, שְׁנוֹת רָאִינוּ רָעָה: יֵרָאֶה אֶל־עֲבָדֶיךָ פָעֳלֶךָ,
וַהֲדָרְךָ עַל־בְּנֵיהֶם: ‹ וִיהִי נֹעַם אֲדֹנָי אֱלֹהֵינוּ עָלֵינוּ, וּמַעֲשֵׂה
יָדֵינוּ כּוֹנְנָה עָלֵינוּ, וּמַעֲשֵׂה יָדֵינוּ כּוֹנְנֵהוּ:ע

תהלים צא
יֹשֵׁב בְּסֵתֶר עֶלְיוֹן, בְּצֵל שַׁדַּי יִתְלוֹנָן: אֹמַר לַיהוה מַחְסִי וּמְצוּדָתִי,
אֱלֹהַי אֶבְטַח־בּוֹ: כִּי הוּא יַצִּילְךָ מִפַּח יָקוּשׁ, מִדֶּבֶר הַוּוֹת:ב
בְּאֶבְרָתוֹ יָסֶךְ לָךְ, וְתַחַת־כְּנָפָיו תֶּחְסֶה, צִנָּה וְסֹחֵרָה אֲמִתּוֹ:
לֹא־תִירָא מִפַּחַד לָיְלָה,ב מֵחֵץ יָעוּף יוֹמָם: מִדֶּבֶר בָּאֹפֶל יַהֲלֹךְ,ב

IYUN TEFILLA • עיון תפילה

וַהֲדָרְךָ עַל־בְּנֵיהֶם... וּמַעֲשֵׂה יָדֵינוּ כּוֹנְנָה עָלֵינוּ – *Your glory by their children... establish for us the work of our hands.* The religious personality knows that life is neither hopeless nor pointless despite one's mortality. One's children, one's contributions to others, can stand for posterity and negate any despondency about the limits of one's life.

לִמְנוֹת יָמֵינוּ כֵּן הוֹדַע, וְנָבִא לְבַב חָכְמָה – *Teach us rightly to number our days, that we may gain a heart of wisdom. Life is short. The days of our lives should not be counted but weighed (*Menaḥem Tzyion*). Help me not to count my days but to make each day count.*

BIUR TEFILLA • ביאור תפילה

יֹשֵׁב בְּסֵתֶר – *TEHILLIM 91.* This psalm is considered by many to be an extension of the one which precedes and, indeed, if you look closely you can find some parallels in language. It too is divided into two parts, though in this case the division is equal – there are eight verses consisting of 56 words in each. The themes in each of the halves sound similar but in truth, one builds on the other. It has been suggested that there are represented here at least two different voices – a husband and wife, or a parent and child, or a teacher and student – and that it should therefore be read as if it was said responsively.

The psalm is known by the Rabbis as "The Song of Mishaps" (*Shir Shel Pega'im*) for it speaks dramatically about the various forces, human and natural, that can appear out of nowhere to upend a person's life.

Our psalm contains a didactic theme: it guides the person – especially if he is young – to the proper awareness that

nor the plague that ravages at noon. A thousand may fall at your side, ten thousand at your right hand, but it will not come near you. You will only look with your eyes and see the punishment of the wicked. Because you said "The LORD is my Refuge,"[B] taking the Most High as your shelter, no harm will befall you, no plague will come near your tent, for He will command His angels about you, to guard you in all your ways. They will lift you in their hands, lest your foot stumble on a stone. You will tread on lions and vipers, you will trample on young lions and snakes. [God says] "Because he loves Me, I will rescue him; I will protect him, because he acknowledges My name. When he calls on Me, I will answer him,[B] I will be with him in distress,[I] I will deliver him and bring him honor.[I]
▸ With long life I will satisfy him, and show him My salvation.
With long life I will satisfy him, and show him My salvation."

When a person is not always conscious of the presence of God in his life, when he is separated from God, then God is also separated from him and then he is exposed to any evil that might befall him (Maimonides, *Guide for the Perplexed* 3:51).

Look around you. Who could benefit from your imitating God today?

ANI TEFILLA • אני תפילה

Eli Wiesel, the Nobel Laureate and famed Holocaust writer, was asked: "Did you lose your God after the Holocaust?" He answered, "God was my friend as a boy. I was a young Hasid, and God accompanied me everywhere. And for a time, after the war, I did not wish to have a relationship with Him. But He never left me completely, and now He is back fully in my life. But the relationship has changed. I have a right to assert my place. It is now more a rapport, not of equals, of course, but of two parties with a real and painful dialogue."

Someone once asked the Ba'al Shem Tov: "Why is it that one who clings to God and knows He is close to him, sometimes experiences a sense of interruption and remoteness?" The Ba'al Shem explained: "When a father sets out to teach his little child to walk, he stands in front of him and holds his two hands on either side of the child to catch him just in case he falls, and the child goes toward his father between his father's outstretched hands. But the moment he is close to his father, his father moves away a little, and holds his hands further apart, and he does this over and over, so that the child may learn to walk."

Believe that He is there, waiting for you to move forward.

מִקֶּטֶב יָשׁוּד צׇהֳרָיִם: יִפֹּל מִצִּדְּךָ אֶלֶף, וּרְבָבָה מִימִינֶךָ, אֵלֶיךָ
לֹא יִגָּשׁ: רַק בְּעֵינֶיךָ תַבִּיט, וְשִׁלֻּמַת רְשָׁעִים תִּרְאֶה: כִּי־אַתָּה
יהוה מַחְסִי,ב עֶלְיוֹן שַׂמְתָּ מְעוֹנֶךָ: לֹא־תְאֻנֶּה אֵלֶיךָ רָעָה, וְנֶגַע
לֹא־יִקְרַב בְּאׇהֳלֶךָ: כִּי מַלְאָכָיו יְצַוֶּה־לָּךְ, לִשְׁמׇרְךָ בְּכׇל־דְּרָכֶיךָ:
עַל־כַּפַּיִם יִשָּׂאוּנְךָ, פֶּן־תִּגֹּף בָּאֶבֶן רַגְלֶךָ: עַל־שַׁחַל וָפֶתֶן תִּדְרֹךְ,
תִּרְמֹס כְּפִיר וְתַנִּין: כִּי בִי חָשַׁק וַאֲפַלְּטֵהוּ, אֲשַׂגְּבֵהוּ כִּי־יָדַע
שְׁמִי: יִקְרָאֵנִי וְאֶעֱנֵהוּ,ב עִמּוֹ אָנֹכִי בְצָרָה,ע אֲחַלְּצֵהוּ וַאֲכַבְּדֵהוּ:ע
◂ אֹרֶךְ יָמִים אַשְׂבִּיעֵהוּ, וְאַרְאֵהוּ בִּישׁוּעָתִי:
אֹרֶךְ יָמִים אַשְׂבִּיעֵהוּ, וְאַרְאֵהוּ בִּישׁוּעָתִי:

BIUR TEFILLA • ביאור תפילה

יִקְרָאֵנִי וְאֶעֱנֵהוּ – *When he calls on Me, I will answer him.* Prophecy and prayer are similar. But in prophecy, it is God who initiates the conversation; in prayer, it is man. Man must first call out to God if he ever expects an answer.

כִּי־אַתָּה יהוה מַחְסִי – *Because you said "The Lord is my Refuge" [or "Because You are Hashem my Refuge].* Here is where the second half of the psalm begins. How does it compare and contrast with the parallel verse found in the second line above?

IYUN TEFILLA • עיון תפילה

עִמּוֹ אָנֹכִי בְצָרָה, אֲחַלְּצֵהוּ וַאֲכַבְּדֵהוּ – *I will be with him in distress, I will deliver him and bring him honor.* Herein lies an opportunity for *imitatio Dei*, to imitate the ways of the Creator, by being prepared to participate in the sorrows of others and to declare "I am with him in times of trouble." I will "deliver him" to the extent that I am able by relieving his suffering, I will "bring him honor" by extending my hand in a respectful and honorable way so that he will not be embarrassed (*Menaḥem Tzyion*).

עִמּוֹ אָנֹכִי בְצָרָה – *I will be with him in distress.* Moshe asked God why of all the trees in the world, did He decide to reveal Himself to him for the first time from within a lowly thornbush rather than from a more regal tree. Hashem answered: "My people are suffering in slavery and I should reveal myself from a more exalted tree?" – "I will be with him in distress (*Yalkut Shimoni* 843) .When man suffers, God, as it were, suffers too.

הַלְלוּיָהּ Halleluya! Praise the name of the LORD. Praise Him, you servants of the LORD who stand in the LORD's House, in the courtyards of the House of our God. Praise the LORD, for the LORD is good;[B] sing praises to His name, for it is lovely. For the LORD has chosen Jacob as His own, Israel as his treasure. For I know that the LORD is great, that our LORD is above all heavenly powers. Whatever pleases the LORD, He does,[I] in heaven and on earth, in the seas and all the depths. He raises clouds from the ends of the earth;[I] He sends lightning with the rain; He brings out the wind from His storehouses. He struck down the firstborn of Egypt, of both man and animals.[B] He sent signs and wonders into your midst, Egypt – against Pharaoh and all his servants. He struck down[I] many nations and slew mighty kings: Siḥon, King of the Amorites,[B] Og, King of Bashan, and all the kingdoms of Canaan, giving their land as a heritage, a heritage for His people Israel. Your name, LORD, endures for ever; Your renown, LORD, for all generations. For the LORD will bring justice to His people, and have compassion on Ps. 135

לְסִיחוֹן מֶלֶךְ הָאֱמֹרִי – *Siḥon, king of the Amorites.* This could be a symbolic reference to the 31 kings whom Yehoshua conquered when entering the Promised Land.

IYUN TEFILLA • עיון תפילה

כֹּל אֲשֶׁר־חָפֵץ יהוה עָשָׂה – *Whatever pleases the LORD, He does.* God can do whatever He wishes. Alternatively, God does many things that we cannot understand, that are not revealed to us until some point in history or in our lives when their true purpose is discovered.

Can you recall any events in your life that you thought were bad but ultimately turned out for the best?

מַעֲלֶה נְשִׂאִים מִקְצֵה הָאָרֶץ – *He raises clouds from the ends of the earth.* This is an example of God's power. The endless cycle of evaporation and precipitation that keeps us alive is something that we can be oblivious to except when we notice its absence during times of drought. The siddur reminds us that God's power, and our sense of wonder, lies especially in the things that we take for granted.

שֶׁהִכָּה – *He struck down.* Sometimes man needs to be hit with a "smack" in order to wake up to the Divine will. There were numerous smaller, less consequential plagues before the final one, but Pharaoh and the Egyptians did not pay heed. How many of us really do?

תהלים קלה

הַלְלוּיָהּ, הַלְלוּ אֶת־שֵׁם יהוה, הַלְלוּ עַבְדֵי יהוה: שֶׁעֹמְדִים בְּבֵית
יהוה, בְּחַצְרוֹת בֵּית אֱלֹהֵינוּ: הַלְלוּיָהּ כִּי־טוֹב יהוה,ב זַמְּרוּ
לִשְׁמוֹ כִּי נָעִים: כִּי־יַעֲקֹב בָּחַר לוֹ יָהּ, יִשְׂרָאֵל לִסְגֻלָּתוֹ: כִּי אֲנִי
יָדַעְתִּי כִּי־גָדוֹל יהוה, וַאֲדֹנֵינוּ מִכָּל־אֱלֹהִים: כֹּל אֲשֶׁר־חָפֵץ יהוה
עָשָׂה,ע בַּשָּׁמַיִם וּבָאָרֶץ, בַּיַּמִּים וְכָל־תְּהֹמוֹת: מַעֲלֶה נְשִׂאִים
מִקְצֵה הָאָרֶץ,ע בְּרָקִים לַמָּטָר עָשָׂה, מוֹצֵא־רוּחַ מֵאוֹצְרוֹתָיו:
שֶׁהִכָּהע בְּכוֹרֵי מִצְרָיִם, מֵאָדָם עַד־בְּהֵמָה:ב שָׁלַח אוֹתֹת וּמֹפְתִים
בְּתוֹכֵכִי מִצְרָיִם, בְּפַרְעֹה וּבְכָל־עֲבָדָיו: שֶׁהִכָּה גּוֹיִם רַבִּים, וְהָרַג
מְלָכִים עֲצוּמִים: לְסִיחוֹן מֶלֶךְ הָאֱמֹרִי,ב וּלְעוֹג מֶלֶךְ הַבָּשָׁן, וּלְכֹל
מַמְלְכוֹת כְּנָעַן: וְנָתַן אַרְצָם נַחֲלָה, נַחֲלָה לְיִשְׂרָאֵל עַמּוֹ: יהוה
שִׁמְךָ לְעוֹלָם, יהוה זִכְרְךָ לְדֹר־וָדֹר: כִּי־יָדִין יהוה עַמּוֹ, וְעַל־

BIUR TEFILLA • ביאור תפילה

הַלְלוּיָהּ – *TEHILLIM 135.* This psalm and the next one form an almost independent unit thematically. Similarly, they appear together at the concluding part of the Passover Seder because of the relevant themes they contain. Here they serve the function of furthering the themes of God's continuing presence in the natural world and the world of man. In the present psalm, one might discern three distinct parts: a call to recognize His Presence; a call to acknowledge His Presence in history; a call to recognize that His is the only Presence. Each part consists of five, seven and nine verses respectively, perhaps reflecting the ever-expanding realization of the Divine in all aspects of our lives that can begin with small steps and grow exponentially.

כִּי־טוֹב יהוה – *For the Lord is good.* Praise Him because He is Good. Alternatively, praise Him because of the good that He does.

Which speaks to you most today?

שֶׁהִכָּה בְּכוֹרֵי מִצְרָיִם, מֵאָדָם עַד־בְּהֵמָה – *He struck down the firstborn of Egypt, of both man and animals.* This is a reference to the last of the ten plagues during the exodus, the one which convinced Pharaoh to free us. At the same time, none of the firstborn of the Israelites was killed, thus making it a miracle within a miracle (Ibn Ezra). Above all else, it could not be dismissed as a mere coincidence or act of nature.

What historical events can you think of which might be seen as natural but within which could also be sensed the miraculous?

What event in your personal life could you view in the same way?

His servants. The idols of the nations are silver and gold,[l] the work of human hands.[l] They have mouths, but cannot speak; eyes, but cannot see; ears, but cannot hear; there is no breath in their mouths. Those who make them will become like them: so will all who trust in them. ▸ House of Israel, bless the LORD. House of Aaron, bless the LORD. House of Levi, bless the LORD. You who fear the LORD,[B] bless the LORD. Blessed is the LORD from Zion, He who dwells in Jerusalem. Halleluya!

The custom is to stand for the following psalm.

הוֹדוּ Thank the LORD for He is good; His loving-kindness is for ever.[A] *Ps. 136*
Thank the God of gods, His loving-kindness is for ever.
Thank the LORD of lords, His loving-kindness is for ever.

---

the fact that it has 26 verses: there were 26 generations from Adam until the giving of the Torah at Sinai (*Pesaḥim* 118a); 26 is the *gematria* (numerical equivalent) of God's four-letter name (Abudarham); remove the four verses of introduction and there remain 22 verses, one for each letter of the *Alef-Beit.*

One of the reasons for the search for greater meaning is perhaps the sheer scope and grandeur of the prayer. It speaks of the greatness of Hashem as manifest by the many kindnesses that He has done for the world at large, and then the kindnesses that He has done specifically for the Jewish People, and then concluding once again with all of mankind. Look closely and one will find an almost chronological unfolding of God's involvement in nature and history from the time of creation to Israel's entry into the Promised Land. But the climax, as it were, comes at the very end in a most surprising way.

ANI TEFILLA • אני תפילה

הודו לַיהוה כִּי־טוֹב, כִּי לְעוֹלָם חַסְדּוֹ – *Thank the LORD, for He is good, His loving-kindness is for ever.* It is important for a person to give praise to God not for His sake, but as a reminder to oneself. For the more that one can admit to the good things that one has in one's life and acknowledge that they are a result of God's blessing, then the more one is likely to live one's life a particular way and thus the more open one becomes to receiving more of His kindness. (*Da'at Sofrim*)

What are two of the good things in your life that you can acknowledge today?

עֲבָדָיו יִתְנֶחָם: עֲצַבֵּי הַגּוֹיִם כֶּסֶף וְזָהָב,[ע] מַעֲשֵׂה יְדֵי אָדָם:[ע] פֶּה־
לָהֶם וְלֹא יְדַבֵּרוּ, עֵינַיִם לָהֶם וְלֹא יִרְאוּ: אָזְנַיִם לָהֶם וְלֹא יַאֲזִינוּ,
אַף אֵין־יֶשׁ־רוּחַ בְּפִיהֶם: כְּמוֹהֶם יִהְיוּ עֹשֵׂיהֶם, כֹּל אֲשֶׁר־בֹּטֵחַ
בָּהֶם: ◂ בֵּית יִשְׂרָאֵל בָּרְכוּ אֶת־יהוה, בֵּית אַהֲרֹן בָּרְכוּ אֶת־
יהוה: בֵּית הַלֵּוִי בָּרְכוּ אֶת־יהוה, יִרְאֵי יהוה[ב] בָּרְכוּ אֶת־יהוה:
בָּרוּךְ יהוה מִצִּיּוֹן, שֹׁכֵן יְרוּשָׁלָםִ, הַלְלוּיָהּ:

The custom is to stand for the following psalm.

הוֹדוּ לַיהוה כִּי־טוֹב כִּי לְעוֹלָם חַסְדּוֹ: א תהלים קלו
הוֹדוּ לֵאלֹהֵי הָאֱלֹהִים כִּי לְעוֹלָם חַסְדּוֹ:
הוֹדוּ לַאֲדֹנֵי הָאֲדֹנִים כִּי לְעוֹלָם חַסְדּוֹ:

BIUR TEFILLA • ביאור תפילה

בֵּית יִשְׂרָאֵל...בֵּית אַהֲרֹן...בית הלוי...יִרְאֵי יהוה – *House of Israel... House of Aaron... House of Levi... You who fear the Lord.* In these two verses there are four categories of people mentioned. In the first three, they are referred to as the House of... This is because, like a family, anyone born into it is automatically a member, an organic part of the whole, who accepts upon himself the mission and destiny of that house. So, the priests of the House of Aaron, the Levites and Israel, each a family within a family, accept upon themselves to fulfill the obligations thrust upon them by virtue of their birth as a family. But so too is the demand made of each individual who has "fear of God" in his heart, to actualize it as a Jew and as a human being. (Rabbi S. Hirsch)

IYUN TEFILLA • עיון תפילה

עֲצַבֵּי הַגּוֹיִם כֶּסֶף וְזָהָב – *The idols of the nations are silver and gold.* We tend to look at polytheistic cultures as primitive and naive. But if in ancient times, the idols were made of silver and gold, it sometimes seems that today's idols are often the silver and gold themselves.

מַעֲשֵׂה יְדֵי אָדָם – *The work of human hands.* In Judaism, there are no intermediaries. Everyone can have a direct personal connection with God.

BIUR TEFILLA • ביאור תפילה

תהלים קלו – *TEHILLIM 136.* This particular psalm is referred to as *Hallel Gadol*, (the Great Praise). Many try to find symbolic meanings, each with its own message, in

To the One who alone
works great wonders,[I] His loving-kindness is for ever.
Who made the heavens with wisdom,[B] His loving-kindness is for ever.
Who spread the earth upon the waters, His loving-kindness is for ever.
Who made the great lights, His loving-kindness is for ever.
The sun to rule by day, His loving-kindness is for ever.
The moon and the stars to rule by night; His loving-kindness is for ever.
Who struck Egypt
through their firstborn, His loving-kindness is for ever.
And brought out Israel from their midst, His loving-kindness is for ever.
With a strong hand
and outstretched arm, His loving-kindness is for ever.
Who split the Reed Sea into parts, His loving-kindness is for ever.
And made Israel pass through it, His loving-kindness is for ever.
Casting Pharaoh and his army
into the Reed Sea; His loving-kindness is for ever.
Who led His people
through the wilderness;[I] His loving-kindness is for ever.
Who struck down great kings, His loving-kindness is for ever.
And slew mighty kings, His loving-kindness is for ever.
Siḥon, King of the Amorites, His loving-kindness is for ever.

BIUR TEFILLA • ביאור תפילה

לְעֹשֵׂה הַשָּׁמַיִם בִּתְבוּנָה – *Who made the heavens with wisdom.* He creates the heavens with His own wisdom and insight. Alternatively, He made creation with its own wisdom so that it operates according to its own internal logical principles (*Tehillot Hashem*). Alternatively, if you contemplate the heavens, you will understand that there is a Creator (Rabbi Simcha Bunim). Think of a place where you once saw how awesome the sky was. **Which of these interpretations speaks most to that experience?**

ANI TEFILLA • אני תפילה

Forty-one days after the revelation at Mount Sinai, the Israelites were making a golden calf to worship (Exodus 32). Faith is about seeing the miraculous in the everyday, not about waiting every day for miracles (Rabbi Jonathan Sacks).

לְעֹשֵׂה נִפְלָאוֹת גְּדֹלוֹת לְבַדּוֹ[ע] כִּי לְעוֹלָם חַסְדּוֹ:
לְעֹשֵׂה הַשָּׁמַיִם בִּתְבוּנָה[ב] כִּי לְעוֹלָם חַסְדּוֹ:
לְרֹקַע הָאָרֶץ עַל־הַמָּיִם כִּי לְעוֹלָם חַסְדּוֹ:
לְעֹשֵׂה אוֹרִים גְּדֹלִים כִּי לְעוֹלָם חַסְדּוֹ:
אֶת־הַשֶּׁמֶשׁ לְמֶמְשֶׁלֶת בַּיּוֹם כִּי לְעוֹלָם חַסְדּוֹ:
אֶת־הַיָּרֵחַ וְכוֹכָבִים לְמֶמְשְׁלוֹת בַּלָּיְלָה כִּי לְעוֹלָם חַסְדּוֹ:
לְמַכֵּה מִצְרַיִם בִּבְכוֹרֵיהֶם כִּי לְעוֹלָם חַסְדּוֹ:
וַיּוֹצֵא יִשְׂרָאֵל מִתּוֹכָם כִּי לְעוֹלָם חַסְדּוֹ:
בְּיָד חֲזָקָה וּבִזְרוֹעַ נְטוּיָה כִּי לְעוֹלָם חַסְדּוֹ:
לְגֹזֵר יַם־סוּף לִגְזָרִים כִּי לְעוֹלָם חַסְדּוֹ:
וְהֶעֱבִיר יִשְׂרָאֵל בְּתוֹכוֹ כִּי לְעוֹלָם חַסְדּוֹ:
וְנִעֵר פַּרְעֹה וְחֵילוֹ בְיַם־סוּף כִּי לְעוֹלָם חַסְדּוֹ:
לְמוֹלִיךְ עַמּוֹ בַּמִּדְבָּר[ע] כִּי לְעוֹלָם חַסְדּוֹ:
לְמַכֵּה מְלָכִים גְּדֹלִים כִּי לְעוֹלָם חַסְדּוֹ:
וַיַּהֲרֹג מְלָכִים אַדִּירִים כִּי לְעוֹלָם חַסְדּוֹ:
לְסִיחוֹן מֶלֶךְ הָאֱמֹרִי כִּי לְעוֹלָם חַסְדּוֹ:

IYUN TEFILLA • עיון תפילה

לְעֹשֵׂה נִפְלָאוֹת גְּדֹלוֹת לְבַדּוֹ – *To the One who alone works great wonders.* God does wonders for us every day, even if we are not always conscious of them. Think of the threats that present themselves, the germs averted, the accidents avoided, the coming together of seemingly random forces of destruction or disaster or illness. These too are wonders which God does "by Himself," without people knowing. (*Meam Loez*)

Take a moment to acknowledge this absence as provided by His Presence.

לְמוֹלִיךְ עַמּוֹ בַּמִּדְבָּר – *Who led His people through the wilderness.* One might think that being forced to enter and live in the desert is anything but a *ḥesed* or act of kindness. Yet the desert is the place where God provided for us and where we learned to be a people. The Torah was given in the desert and not in a specific country to symbolize the fact that anyone could join and acquire the knowledge and commitment of a life enriched by the Torah even if it means that sometimes one needs to travel in a desert to get there.

And Og, King of Bashan, His loving-kindness is for ever.
And gave their land as a heritage, His loving-kindness is for ever.
A heritage for His servant Israel; His loving-kindness is for ever.
Who remembered us in our lowly state, His loving-kindness is for ever.
And rescued us from our tormentors, His loving-kindness is for ever.
▸ Who gives food to all flesh,[B] His loving-kindness is for ever.
Give thanks to the God of heaven. His loving-kindness is for ever.

רַנְּנוּ Sing joyfully to the LORD, you righteous, for praise from the upright is seemly. Give thanks to the LORD with the harp; make music to Him on the ten-stringed lute. Sing Him a new song,[B] play skillfully with shouts of joy. For the LORD's word is right, and all His deeds are done in faith.[A] He loves righteousness and justice; Ps. 33

---

this psalm that opens with three lines of praise and concludes with three expressions of faith and requests for His kindness, thus totaling twenty-two verses altogether – the same number of letters in the Hebrew *Alef-Beit*. The verses in between contain seven elements of praise, and there are seven synonyms for praise throughout. The first three lines of the psalm speak directly to the listener ("Sing...you righteous") whereas the last three lines switch change to first person plural ("our soul..."), which is expressed no fewer than seven times in the Hebrew. Perhaps the allusion to the *Alef-Beit* symbolically represents the complete set of praises that is possible, while the number seven is itself a symbolic representation of completion representing here the Shabbat. The leader invites us to sing His praises, the very call to praise becomes praise itself, and we are drawn in, and we are left feeling ourselves a little more complete and whole.

שִׁירוּ־לוֹ שִׁיר חָדָשׁ – *Sing Him a new song.* Say something completely different (Radak) for every miracle that He does for you (Meiri). Alternatively, sing the same song anew every day (Rabbi Saadia Gaon).

How might your song this week be different from the one you might have sung last week?

ANI TEFILLA • אני תפילה

וְכָל־מַעֲשֵׂהוּ בֶּאֱמוּנָה – *And all of his deeds are done in faith.*

A man once received a wound on his leg. His friend came to console him and said how bad he felt for him. Said the injured man: "I thank God that it was only my leg that was hurt and not my eyes." Some see in misfortunes only the bad while people of faith see Hashem's hand in keeping the glass half-full (*Me'am Loez*).

Make your challenges today into a glass half-full.

וּלְעוֹג מֶלֶךְ הַבָּשָׁן כִּי לְעוֹלָם חַסְדּוֹ:
וְנָתַן אַרְצָם לְנַחֲלָה כִּי לְעוֹלָם חַסְדּוֹ:
נַחֲלָה לְיִשְׂרָאֵל עַבְדּוֹ כִּי לְעוֹלָם חַסְדּוֹ:
שֶׁבְּשִׁפְלֵנוּ זָכַר לָנוּ כִּי לְעוֹלָם חַסְדּוֹ:
וַיִּפְרְקֵנוּ מִצָּרֵינוּ כִּי לְעוֹלָם חַסְדּוֹ:
◂ נֹתֵן לֶחֶם לְכָל־בָּשָׂר[ב] כִּי לְעוֹלָם חַסְדּוֹ:
הוֹדוּ לְאֵל הַשָּׁמָיִם כִּי לְעוֹלָם חַסְדּוֹ:

רַנְּנוּ צַדִּיקִים בַּיהוה, לַיְשָׁרִים נָאוָה תְהִלָּה: הוֹדוּ לַיהוה בְּכִנּוֹר, תהלים לג
בְּנֵבֶל עָשׂוֹר זַמְּרוּ־לוֹ: שִׁירוּ־לוֹ שִׁיר חָדָשׁ,[ב] הֵיטִיבוּ נַגֵּן בִּתְרוּעָה:
כִּי־יָשָׁר דְּבַר־יהוה, וְכָל־מַעֲשֵׂהוּ בֶּאֱמוּנָה:[א] אֹהֵב צְדָקָה וּמִשְׁפָּט,

BIUR TEFILLA • ביאור תפילה

נֹתֵן לֶחֶם לְכָל־בָּשָׂר – *Who gives food to all flesh.* Note the way in which this concluding line stands out. Whereas all of the preceding verses generally speak of the past, this one speaks of the ongoing present. Whereas the others speak of events natural and supernatural in history, this one speaks of the basic staple of daily life. For in the small crumb of bread lies the same revelation of God that was displayed to mankind in general and the Jewish people in particular over the course of time. This morsel contains within it the same *ḥesed*, the same care, the same concern and support from on High. It is up to us to acknowledge it as such.

From here derives the mandate for man to acquire his needs in the most honest way from the hand of God. One's food comes not alone from the social or personal circumstances of one's life, but from Hashem. That is the meaning of the Gemara *Pesaḥim* 118a: "Making a living is as difficult as it was for Hashem to split the Red Sea at the time of the exodus." (Rabbi S. R. Hirsch)

ANI TEFILLA • אני תפילה

Which is a greater miracle, a sheaf of wheat or a loaf of bread?

BIUR TEFILLA • ביאור תפילה

תהלים לג – *TEHILLIM 33.* As we have seen before, sometimes form and content, the medium and message, go hand in hand. That is to say, sometimes in the siddur the way something is said can parallel or complement what is being said. Consider

the earth is full of the LORD's loving-kindness. By the LORD's word the heavens were made, and all their starry host by the breath of His mouth. He gathers the sea waters as a heap, and places the deep in storehouses. Let all the earth fear the LORD, and all the world's inhabitants stand in awe of Him. For He spoke, and it was; He commanded, and it stood firm. The LORD foils the plans of nations; He thwarts the intentions of peoples. The LORD's plans stand for ever, His heart's intents for all generations. Happy is the nation whose God is the LORD, the people He has chosen as His own. From heaven the LORD looks down and sees all mankind; from His dwelling place He oversees all who live on earth. He forms the hearts of all, and discerns all their deeds. No king is saved by the size of his army; no warrior is delivered by great strength. A horse is a vain hope for deliverance; despite its great strength, it cannot save. The eye of the LORD is on those who fear Him, on those who place their hope in His unfailing love, to rescue their soul from death, and keep them alive in famine. Our soul waits for the LORD; He is our Help and Shield. ▸ In Him our hearts rejoice, for we trust in His holy name. Let Your unfailing love be upon us, LORD, as we have put our hope in You.

You in the bad times when our hearts are more broken than they are now and our sense of dependence greater than we might be feeling right now (*Ohel Yaakov*).

IYUN TEFILLA • עיון תפילה

בִּדְבַר יהוה שָׁמַיִם נַעֲשׂוּ – *By the LORD's word the heavens were made.* The reference is to the days of Creation where it says throughout, "And God said let there be..." All of creation took place by Divine command, by an utterance. Creations are the expressions of God's will. From which the Gemara concludes that speech is like action. When a person merely recites the text of *Kiddush* over wine which attests to Creation, then it is as if he becomes a partner of God in the creation of the world (*Shabbat* 119b). Our words have the power to create worlds... or destroy them. **How will I use my words today?**

חֶסֶד יהוה מָלְאָה הָאָֽרֶץ:[ב] בִּדְבַר יהוה שָׁמַיִם נַעֲשׂוּ,[ע] וּבְרוּחַ
פִּיו כָּל־צְבָאָם: כֹּנֵס כַּנֵּד מֵי הַיָּם, נֹתֵן בְּאוֹצָרוֹת תְּהוֹמוֹת:
יִירְאוּ מֵיהוה כָּל־הָאָֽרֶץ, מִמֶּנּוּ יָגֽוּרוּ כָּל־יֹשְׁבֵי תֵבֵל: כִּי הוּא
אָמַר וַיֶּֽהִי, הוּא־צִוָּה וַיַּעֲמֹד: יהוה הֵפִיר עֲצַת־גּוֹיִם, הֵנִיא
מַחְשְׁבוֹת עַמִּים: עֲצַת יהוה לְעוֹלָם תַּעֲמֹד, מַחְשְׁבוֹת לִבּוֹ
לְדֹר וָדֹר: אַשְׁרֵי הַגּוֹי אֲשֶׁר־יהוה אֱלֹהָיו, הָעָם בָּחַר לְנַחֲלָה לוֹ:
מִשָּׁמַיִם הִבִּיט יהוה, רָאָה אֶת־כָּל־בְּנֵי הָאָדָם: מִמְּכוֹן־שִׁבְתּוֹ
הִשְׁגִּיחַ, אֶל כָּל־יֹשְׁבֵי הָאָֽרֶץ: הַיֹּצֵר יַחַד לִבָּם, הַמֵּבִין אֶל־כָּל־
מַעֲשֵׂיהֶם: אֵין־הַמֶּלֶךְ נוֹשָׁע בְּרָב־חָֽיִל, גִּבּוֹר לֹא־יִנָּצֵל בְּרָב־כֹּֽחַ:
שֶׁקֶר הַסּוּס לִתְשׁוּעָה, וּבְרֹב חֵילוֹ לֹא יְמַלֵּט: הִנֵּה עֵין יהוה
אֶל־יְרֵאָיו, לַמְיַחֲלִים לְחַסְדּוֹ: לְהַצִּיל מִמָּֽוֶת נַפְשָׁם, וּלְחַיּוֹתָם
בָּרָעָב: נַפְשֵׁנוּ חִכְּתָה לַיהוה, עֶזְרֵנוּ וּמָגִנֵּנוּ הוּא: ‹ כִּי־בוֹ יִשְׂמַח
לִבֵּנוּ, כִּי בְשֵׁם קָדְשׁוֹ בָטָֽחְנוּ: יְהִי־חַסְדְּךָ יהוה עָלֵינוּ, כַּאֲשֶׁר
יִחַֽלְנוּ לָךְ:[ב]

BIUR TEFILLA • ביאור תפילה

יְהִי־חַסְדְּךָ יהוה עָלֵינוּ, כַּאֲשֶׁר יִחַלְנוּ לָךְ – *Let Your unfailing love be upon us, Lord, as we have put our hope in You.* Let Your kindness be upon us because we have been waiting for You.

Alternatively, let Your kindness be upon us to the extent that we have waited for You, i.e., to the same measure that we have put our faith in Him (Ba'al Shem Tov).

Alternatively, be with us [even in good times] to the same extent that we rely upon

אֹהֵב צְדָקָה וּמִשְׁפָּט, חֶסֶד יהוה מָלְאָה הָאָרֶץ – *He loves righteousness and justice; the earth is full of the Lord's loving-kindness.* Hashem loves justice but, says the Radak, He loves loving-kindness more.

What indication is there of this from the verse? What indication is there of this in the Bible?

What indication of this is there in your life?

מִזְמוֹר שִׁיר A psalm. A song for the Sabbath day. It is good to thank the LORD and sing psalms to Your name, Most High – to tell of Your loving-kindness in the morning and Your faithfulness at night,[1] to the music of the ten-stringed lyre and the melody of the harp. For You have made me rejoice by Your work, O LORD; I sing for joy at the deeds of Your hands. How great are Your deeds, LORD, and how very deep Your thoughts. A boor cannot know, nor can a fool understand, that though the wicked spring up like grass and all evildoers flourish, it is only that they may be destroyed for ever. But You, LORD, are eternally exalted. For behold Your enemies, LORD, behold Your enemies will perish; all evildoers will be scattered. You have raised my pride like that of a wild ox; I am anointed with fresh oil. My eyes shall look in triumph on my adversaries, my ears shall hear the downfall of the wicked who rise against me. ▸ The righteous will flourish like a palm tree and grow tall like a cedar in Lebanon.[B] Planted in the LORD's House, blossoming in our God's courtyards, they will still bear fruit in old age, and stay vigorous and fresh, proclaiming that the LORD is upright: He is my Rock, in whom there is no wrong. *Ps. 92*

יהוה מָלָךְ The LORD reigns. He is robed in majesty. The LORD is robed, girded with strength. The world is firmly established; it *Ps. 93*

---

different as well. In the evening, we tend to feel more vulnerable and are thus called upon to have faith (*emuna*) that everything will work out. In the morning, when things are bright, there is the most potential to be thankful for the *hesed* that fills one's life. This is especially so on Shabbat when one does not have to put such thoughts aside in order to rush to work. Shabbat morning is different than any other morning of the week.

Take a moment to feel it.

There is more time to reflect upon all of the good things in the world and in your life.

Take a moment to count them.

BIUR TEFILLA • ביאור תפילה

תהלים צג – *TEHILLIM 93*. This is the second time that this psalm is recited on Shabbat. For further commentary, see page 71.

This psalm marks the conclusion of the additional psalms that are added on Shabbat morning.

This **BIUR TEFILLA** *continues on page 254.*

תהלים צב מִזְמוֹר שִׁיר לְיוֹם הַשַּׁבָּת: טוֹב לְהֹדוֹת לַיהוה, וּלְזַמֵּר לְשִׁמְךָ
עֶלְיוֹן: לְהַגִּיד בַּבֹּקֶר חַסְדֶּךָ, וֶאֱמוּנָתְךָ בַּלֵּילוֹת: עֲלֵי־עָשׂוֹר
וַעֲלֵי־נָבֶל, עֲלֵי הִגָּיוֹן בְּכִנּוֹר: כִּי שִׂמַּחְתַּנִי יהוה בְּפָעֳלֶךָ, בְּמַעֲשֵׂי
יָדֶיךָ אֲרַנֵּן: מַה־גָּדְלוּ מַעֲשֶׂיךָ יהוה, מְאֹד עָמְקוּ מַחְשְׁבֹתֶיךָ:
אִישׁ־בַּעַר לֹא יֵדָע, וּכְסִיל לֹא־יָבִין אֶת־זֹאת: בִּפְרֹחַ רְשָׁעִים
כְּמוֹ עֵשֶׂב, וַיָּצִיצוּ כָּל־פֹּעֲלֵי אָוֶן, לְהִשָּׁמְדָם עֲדֵי־עַד: וְאַתָּה מָרוֹם
לְעֹלָם יהוה: כִּי הִנֵּה אֹיְבֶיךָ יהוה, כִּי־הִנֵּה אֹיְבֶיךָ יֹאבֵדוּ, יִתְפָּרְדוּ
כָּל־פֹּעֲלֵי אָוֶן: וַתָּרֶם כִּרְאֵים קַרְנִי, בַּלֹּתִי בְּשֶׁמֶן רַעֲנָן: וַתַּבֵּט עֵינִי
בְּשׁוּרָי, בַּקָּמִים עָלַי מְרֵעִים תִּשְׁמַעְנָה אָזְנָי: צַדִּיק כַּתָּמָר יִפְרָח,
כְּאֶרֶז בַּלְּבָנוֹן יִשְׂגֶּה: שְׁתוּלִים בְּבֵית יהוה, בְּחַצְרוֹת אֱלֹהֵינוּ
יַפְרִיחוּ: עוֹד יְנוּבוּן בְּשֵׂיבָה, דְּשֵׁנִים וְרַעֲנַנִּים יִהְיוּ: לְהַגִּיד כִּי־
יָשָׁר יהוה, צוּרִי, וְלֹא־עַוְלָתָה בּוֹ:

תהלים צג יהוה מָלָךְ, גֵּאוּת לָבֵשׁ, לָבֵשׁ יהוה עֹז הִתְאַזָּר, אַף־תִּכּוֹן תֵּבֵל
בַּל־תִּמּוֹט: נָכוֹן כִּסְאֲךָ מֵאָז, מֵעוֹלָם אָתָּה: נָשְׂאוּ נְהָרוֹת יהוה,

---

BIUR TEFILLA • ביאור תפילה

תהלים צב – *TEHILLIM 92*. This is the second time that this psalm is recited on Shabbat. For further commentary, see page 67.

צַדִּיק כַּתָּמָר יִפְרָח, כְּאֶרֶז בַּלְּבָנוֹן יִשְׂגֶּה – *The righteous will flourish like a palm tree and grow tall like a cedar in Lebanon*. Unlike the evil who are compared to grass, the *tzaddik* or righteous person is compared to two of the most exquisite trees in the Middle East – the palm and the cedar. The one is known for its leaves and fruit, the other for its stature, but as the next verse indicates, both must be firmly rooted to grow, just as must one's life in religious faith in order to flourish.

IYUN TEFILLA • עיון תפילה

לְהַגִּיד בַּבֹּקֶר חַסְדֶּךָ, וֶאֱמוּנָתְךָ בַּלֵּילוֹת – *To tell of Your loving-kindness in the morning and Your faithfulness at night*. Jewish prayer is both time-sensitive and sensitive to time. Different prayers are recited at different times of the day because our moods are different throughout the day and the ways that we relate to the world around us are

cannot be moved. Your throne stands firm as of old; You are eternal. Rivers lift up, LORD, rivers lift up their voice, rivers lift up their Crashing waves. ▸ Mightier than the noise of many waters, than the mighty waves of the sea is the LORD on high. Your testimonies are very sure; holiness adorns Your House, LORD, for evermore.

יְהִי כְבוֹד May the LORD's glory[IAB] be for ever; may the LORD rejoice Ps. 104
in His works. May the LORD's name be blessed, now and for ever. Ps. 113
From the rising of the sun to its setting, may the LORD's name be
praised. The LORD is high above all nations; His glory is above the
heavens. LORD, Your name is for ever. Your renown, LORD, is for all Ps. 135
generations. The LORD has established His throne in heaven; His Ps. 103
kingdom rules all. Let the heavens rejoice and the earth be glad. Let 1 Chr. 16
them say among the nations, "The LORD is King." The LORD is King,
the LORD was King, the LORD will be King for ever and all time.
The LORD is King for ever and all time; nations will perish from Ps. 10
His land. The LORD foils the plans of nations; He frustrates the Ps. 33
intentions of peoples. Many are the intentions in a person's mind, Prov. 19
but the LORD's plan prevails. The LORD's plan shall stand for ever, Ps. 33

IYUN TEFILLA • עיון תפילה

יְהִי כְבוֹד – *May the LORD's glory.* "May Hashem's glory be forever; may Hashem rejoice in His works." Hashem's "glory" parallels "His works" and is thus a reference to creation. The Gemara says that when an angel uttered this verse at the time of creation, all of the plants began to emerge (*Ḥullin* 60a). The phrase thus introduces the theme of God's presence in nature that will be at the center of *Pesukei DeZimra*.

ANI TEFILLA • אני תפילה

יְהִי כְבוֹד – *May the LORD's glory.* The Gemara (*Berakhot* 10a) notes that "there is no artist like God."

Where can you see Hashem's artistry this morning?

BIUR TEFILLA • ביאור תפילה

יְהִי כְבוֹד – *May the LORD's glory.*
Numbers: There is a tradition that in this prayer there are 21 references to Hashem's name, paralleling the 21 verses in the prayer of *Ashrei* which follows (*Tehilla* 145). Can you find the 21? (Hint: most are explicit; one is hidden in the initials of the first four words of one of the verses.)

נָשְׂאוּ נְהָרוֹת קוֹלָם, יִשְׂאוּ נְהָרוֹת דָּכְיָם: ◂ מִקֹּלוֹת מַיִם רַבִּים,
אַדִּירִים מִשְׁבְּרֵי־יָם, אַדִּיר בַּמָּרוֹם יהוה: עֵדֹתֶיךָ נֶאֶמְנוּ מְאֹד
לְבֵיתְךָ נַאֲוָה־קֹדֶשׁ, יהוה לְאֹרֶךְ יָמִים:

יְהִי כְבוֹד [עאב] יהוה לְעוֹלָם, יִשְׂמַח יהוה בְּמַעֲשָׂיו: יְהִי שֵׁם יהוה תהלים קד / תהלים קיג
מְבֹרָךְ, מֵעַתָּה וְעַד־עוֹלָם: מִמִּזְרַח־שֶׁמֶשׁ עַד־מְבוֹאוֹ, מְהֻלָּל
שֵׁם יהוה: רָם עַל־כָּל־גּוֹיִם יהוה, עַל הַשָּׁמַיִם כְּבוֹדוֹ: יהוה תהלים קלה
שִׁמְךָ לְעוֹלָם, יהוה זִכְרְךָ לְדֹר־וָדֹר: יהוה בַּשָּׁמַיִם הֵכִין כִּסְאוֹ, תהלים קג
וּמַלְכוּתוֹ בַּכֹּל מָשָׁלָה: יִשְׂמְחוּ הַשָּׁמַיִם וְתָגֵל הָאָרֶץ, וְיֹאמְרוּ דברי הימים א׳ טז
בַגּוֹיִם יהוה מָלָךְ: יהוה מֶלֶךְ, יהוה מָלָךְ, יהוה יִמְלֹךְ לְעוֹלָם וָעֶד.
יהוה מֶלֶךְ עוֹלָם וָעֶד, אָבְדוּ גוֹיִם מֵאַרְצוֹ: יהוה הֵפִיר עֲצַת־גּוֹיִם, תהלים י / תהלים לג
הֵנִיא מַחְשְׁבוֹת עַמִּים: רַבּוֹת מַחֲשָׁבוֹת בְּלֶב־אִישׁ, וַעֲצַת יהוה משלי יט
הִיא תָקוּם: עֲצַת יהוה לְעוֹלָם תַּעֲמֹד, מַחְשְׁבוֹת לִבּוֹ לְדֹר וָדֹר: תהלים לג

What follows is the same service that occurs during weekdays until one gets to the prayer known as *Nishmat* ("The soul") on page 283.

ANI TEFILLA • אני תפילה

Six days shall you be a workaholic; on the seventh day, shall you join the serene company of human beings.

Six days shall you take orders from your boss; on the seventh day, shall you be a master/mistress of your own life.

Six days shall you toil in the market; on the seventh day, shall you detach from money matters.

Six days shall you create, drive, create, invent, push, drive; on the seventh day shall you reflect.

Six days shall you be the perfect success; on the seventh day, shall you remember that not everything is in your power.

Six days shall you be a miserable failure; on the seventh day, shall you be on top of the world.

Six days shall you enjoy the blessings of work; on the seventh day shall you understand that being as important as doing. (Blu Greenberg)

His mind's intent for all generations. For He spoke and it was; He
commanded and it stood firm. For the LORD has chosen Zion; He Ps. 132
desired it for His dwelling. For the LORD has chosen Jacob, Israel Ps. 135
as His special treasure. For the LORD will not abandon His people; Ps. 94
nor will He forsake His heritage. ▸ He is compassionate. He forgives Ps. 78
iniquity and does not destroy. Repeatedly He suppresses His anger,
not rousing His full wrath. LORD, save! May the King answer us on Ps. 20
the day we call.

The line beginning with "You open Your hand" should be said with special concentration, representing as it does the key idea of this psalm, and of Pesukei DeZimra as a whole, that God is the creator and sustainer of all.

אַשְׁרֵי Happy are those who dwell in Your House;[AB] Ps. 84
they shall continue to praise You, Selah!
Happy are the people for whom this is so; Ps. 144
happy are the people whose God is the LORD.

A song of praise by David. Ps. 145
א I will elevate You, my God, the King,
and bless Your name for ever and all time.
ב Every day I will bless You,
and praise Your name for ever and all time.

Research shows that people who pray regularly are healthier, have greater coping skills and resilience than those who don't. In short, they can indeed be happier.

BIUR TEFILLA • ביאור תפילה

אשרי יושבי ביתך – *Happy are those who dwell in Your House.* This verse is from *Tehilla* 84:5 and the next one is from *Tehilla* 144:15. They were added as a prelude to *Tehilla* 145 but the combination is known as *Ashrei*. Rabbi Soloveitchik once suggested that they were added because, viewed in context, they are a declaration of a longing to be in God's presence, just as Jews felt it during the times of the *Beit HaMikdash*. The language is therefore similar to the very first verse of *Tehillim* which also begins with the word אַשְׁרֵי. But *Hazal* added a verse at the end of this prayer that is not part of the original psalm and thereby makes the last word הַלְלוּיָהּ. Stylistically it is thus similar to the end of the book of *Tehillim* (and all of the ones we are about to say) which also ends with הַלְלוּיָהּ. This psalm thus reflects the entire book of *Tehillim* both in substance (the acrostic representing the entire *Alef-Beit*) and in form.

כִּי הוּא אָמַר וַיֶּהִי, הוּא־צִוָּה וַיַּעֲמֹד: כִּי־בָחַר יהוה בְּצִיּוֹן, אִוָּהּ תהלים קלב
לְמוֹשָׁב לוֹ: כִּי־יַעֲקֹב בָּחַר לוֹ יָהּ, יִשְׂרָאֵל לִסְגֻלָּתוֹ: כִּי לֹא־יִטֹּשׁ תהלים קלה תהלים צד
יהוה עַמּוֹ, וְנַחֲלָתוֹ לֹא יַעֲזֹב: • וְהוּא רַחוּם, יְכַפֵּר עָוֹן וְלֹא־יַשְׁחִית, תהלים עח
וְהִרְבָּה לְהָשִׁיב אַפּוֹ, וְלֹא־יָעִיר כָּל־חֲמָתוֹ: יהוה הוֹשִׁיעָה, הַמֶּלֶךְ תהלים כ
יַעֲנֵנוּ בְיוֹם־קָרְאֵנוּ:

The line beginning with פּוֹתֵחַ אֶת יָדֶךָ *should be said with special concentration, representing as it does the key idea of this psalm, and of* פסוקי דזמרה *as a whole, that God is the creator and sustainer of all.*

אַשְׁרֵי יוֹשְׁבֵי בֵיתֶךָ,[אב] עוֹד יְהַלְלוּךָ סֶּלָה: תהלים פד
אַשְׁרֵי הָעָם שֶׁכָּכָה לּוֹ, אַשְׁרֵי הָעָם שֶׁיהוה אֱלֹהָיו: תהלים קמד
תְּהִלָּה לְדָוִד תהלים קמה
א אֲרוֹמִמְךָ אֱלוֹהַי הַמֶּלֶךְ, וַאֲבָרְכָה שִׁמְךָ לְעוֹלָם וָעֶד:
ב בְּכָל־יוֹם אֲבָרְכֶךָּ, וַאֲהַלְלָה שִׁמְךָ לְעוֹלָם וָעֶד:

INTRODUCTION TO THE LAST SIX PSALMS

What follows next is the "core" of *Pesukei DeZimra*, the oldest and most significant parts of this section of *tefilla*. Rabbi J.B. Soloveitchik suggested that it derives from the practice reported in the Gemara (*Berakhot* 30b), wherein the pious men of old would wait for an hour before praying *Shemoneh Esreh* in order to properly collect and direct their thoughts. They recited psalms of praise in keeping with the directive of Rav Simlai (*Berakhot* 32a) that one must first praise Hashem and only afterwards ask for one's needs.

This next section we are about to say comprises a discrete unit since, rather than being seemingly random verses, it consists of the last six psalms of the book of *Tehillim* (chapters 145–150), as if to say that with their recitation, it is as if we recited the entire book of praises. Even so, these psalms share a common theme; they are a kind of *Hallel* in which Hashem reveals Himself not through miracles but through the forces of nature that surround us daily. Nourishment of one's faith lies in the everyday, not in supernatural wonders. As Rabbi Soloveitchik once noted, is there truly any greater miracle than the sun rising in the morning?

ANI TEFILLA • אני תפילה

אַשְׁרֵי יוֹשְׁבֵי בֵיתֶךָ – *Happy are those who dwell in Your House.* Happy are those who take time out every morning to get back in touch with You and with themselves.

ג Great is the Lord and greatly to be praised;
His greatness is unfathomable.
ד One generation will praise Your works to the next,
and tell of Your mighty deeds.
ה On the glorious splendor of Your majesty I will meditate,
and on the acts of Your wonders.
ו They shall talk of the power of Your awesome deeds,
and I will tell of Your greatness.
ז They shall recite the record of Your great goodness,
and sing with joy of Your righteousness.
ח The Lord is generous and compassionate,
slow to anger and great in loving-kindness.
ט The Lord is good to all,
and His compassion extends to all His works.
י All Your works shall thank You, Lord,
and Your devoted ones shall bless You.
כ They shall talk of the glory of Your kingship,
and speak of Your might.
ל To make known to mankind His mighty deeds
and the glorious majesty of His kingship.
מ Your kingdom is an everlasting kingdom,
and Your reign is for all generations.

---

visit their sick and bury their dead and to support their poor. (Rambam)

Even when seemingly bad things happen, one must believe that ultimately there is some good that will result, for "God is good... to all His works." (*Me'am Loez*)

"God's mercy is in all of His creations." He has implanted His mercy in each of us so that we too can act toward others with compassion. (*Bereshit Raba* 33:3)

יוֹדוּךָ יהוה כָּל מַעֲשֶׂיךָ – *All Your works shall thank You.* The moon and stars, the sea creatures, the deserts, the mountains and valleys, the vegetation and trees and animals and insects and birds; a song to God emanates from all of them. (*Tehillot Hashem*)

ANI TEFILLA • אני תפילה

יוֹדוּךָ יהוה כָּל מַעֲשֶׂיךָ – *All Your works shall thank You.*

Imagine yourself in a place where you have heard nature sing.

ג גָּדוֹל יהוה וּמְהֻלָּל מְאֹד, וְלִגְדֻלָּתוֹ אֵין חֵקֶר:
ד דּוֹר לְדוֹר יְשַׁבַּח מַעֲשֶׂיךָ, וּגְבוּרֹתֶיךָ יַגִּידוּ:
ה הֲדַר כְּבוֹד הוֹדֶךָ, וְדִבְרֵי נִפְלְאֹתֶיךָ אָשִׂיחָה:
ו וֶעֱזוּז נוֹרְאֹתֶיךָ יֹאמֵרוּ, וּגְדוּלָּתְךָ אֲסַפְּרֶנָּה:
ז זֵכֶר רַב־טוּבְךָ יַבִּיעוּ, וְצִדְקָתְךָ יְרַנֵּנוּ:
ח חַנּוּן וְרַחוּם יהוה, אֶרֶךְ אַפַּיִם וּגְדָל־חָסֶד:
ט טוֹב־יהוה לַכֹּל, וְרַחֲמָיו עַל־כָּל־מַעֲשָׂיו:
י יוֹדוּךָ יהוה כָּל־מַעֲשֶׂיךָ, וַחֲסִידֶיךָ יְבָרְכוּכָה:
כ כְּבוֹד מַלְכוּתְךָ יֹאמֵרוּ, וּגְבוּרָתְךָ יְדַבֵּרוּ:
ל לְהוֹדִיעַ לִבְנֵי הָאָדָם גְּבוּרֹתָיו, וּכְבוֹד הֲדַר מַלְכוּתוֹ:
מ מַלְכוּתְךָ מַלְכוּת כָּל־עֹלָמִים, וּמֶמְשַׁלְתְּךָ בְּכָל־דּוֹר וָדֹר:

ANI TEFILLA • אני תפילה

דּוֹר לְדוֹר יְשַׁבַּח מַעֲשֶׂיךָ – *One generation will praise Your works to the next.* Every generation passes its firsthand experience along to the next generation. We are who we are thanks to the traditions passed along to us by our parents, grandparents and previous generations (Radak).

What has the previous generation contributed to your development and growth as a person and as a Jew?

דּוֹר לְדוֹר יְשַׁבַּח מַעֲשֶׂיךָ – *One generation will praise Your works to the next.* Every generation is capable of uncovering scientific knowledge that was unavailable to its predecessors, so that in each generation it is possible to gain an even better and more accurate understanding and appreciation of God's world (Malbim).

What inventions or discoveries have previous generations enabled you to benefit from?

IYUN TEFILLA • עיון תפילה

וְצִדְקָתְךָ יְרַנֵּנוּ – *And sing with joy of Your righteousness. Tzedaka* may be understood as righteousness or charity. I sing with joy to Hashem, because when I think about it, everything good that I have in my life is really just a result of His charity and *ḥesed*. (Malbim)

טוֹב־יהוה לַכֹּל – *The Lord is good to all.* "God is good to all, and His compassion extends to all His works." Therefore, so too should we be careful to preserve animal life unless it is to protect ourselves or for some other worthwhile purpose. (Radak)

"God is good to all, and His compassion extends to all His works." Therefore, so too should we act this way toward people who are not of our faith, to

ס The Lord supports all who fall,
and raises all who are bowed down.
ע All raise their eyes to You in hope,
and You give them their food in due season.
פ You open Your hand,
and satisfy every living thing with favor.
צ The Lord is righteous in all His ways,
and kind in all He does.
ק The Lord is close to all who call on Him,
to all who call on Him in truth.
ר He fulfills the will of those who fear Him;
He hears their cry and saves them.
ש The Lord guards all who love Him,
but all the wicked He will destroy.
ת ▸ My mouth shall speak the praise of the Lord,
and all creatures shall bless His holy name for ever and all time.
We will bless the Lord now and for ever. Halleluya! *Ps. 115*

---

any amount of kavana any time I prayed, even as I mumbled the rest of the words of the prayer.

As I grew older, I realized two things: the first was that prayer didn't really work that way. It is not a magic incantation that you recite and then, poof, you get what you want, even if you pray really, really hard. And so I thought that Mr. Deutsch had really just led me on. But secondly, I came to learn that this prayer appears not in a section related to requests, bakashot, but that it was in a section of the siddur that is related to shevaḥ, giving praise to Hashem. In other words, I wasn't necessarily supposed to be asking for anything at all at this point in the service but rather was supposed to be praising God for giving all people the food that they need. And so I thought of the corn fields and wheat fields that make this country so rich and so prosperous and praised God for that.

As I grew yet older and became more sensitive to the people around me, I realized that there were a lot of people who were starving in the world and it made me wonder whether in fact God really was satisfying all of the needs of every living thing. I continued to say the verse, but I had my nagging doubts.

It was only later that I came to believe that perhaps God provides all of the resources necessary for all of the world's needs, but it is man's fault that those resources are not shared fairly. And so, whenever I recited the verse, I asked myself what I was doing to ensure that people in need were being helped. After all, if I want God to provide for my needs, shouldn't I be doing my share to provide for others? Perhaps my role was to be an agent for God's generosity to those around me. And every time I praised God, I also challenged myself to be a better person.

And then, while I became more sensitive to the needs of others, I became more aware of how much I already have in my own life, how many of my needs are already satisfied, how much I take for granted and how I am so fortunate and in many ways so very, very rich.

And then I realized that maybe Mr. Deutsch was right after all.

ס סוֹמֵךְ יהוה לְכָל־הַנֹּפְלִים, וְזוֹקֵף לְכָל־הַכְּפוּפִים:
ע עֵינֵי־כֹל אֵלֶיךָ יְשַׂבֵּרוּ, וְאַתָּה נוֹתֵן־לָהֶם אֶת־אָכְלָם בְּעִתּוֹ:
פ פּוֹתֵחַ אֶת־יָדֶךָ, וּמַשְׂבִּיעַ לְכָל־חַי רָצוֹן:
צ צַדִּיק יהוה בְּכָל־דְּרָכָיו, וְחָסִיד בְּכָל־מַעֲשָׂיו:
ק קָרוֹב יהוה לְכָל־קֹרְאָיו, לְכֹל אֲשֶׁר יִקְרָאֻהוּ בֶאֱמֶת:
ר רְצוֹן־יְרֵאָיו יַעֲשֶׂה, וְאֶת־שַׁוְעָתָם יִשְׁמַע, וְיוֹשִׁיעֵם:
ש שׁוֹמֵר יהוה אֶת־כָּל־אֹהֲבָיו, וְאֵת כָּל־הָרְשָׁעִים יַשְׁמִיד:
ת ◂ תְּהִלַּת יהוה יְדַבֶּר פִּי, וִיבָרֵךְ כָּל־בָּשָׂר שֵׁם קָדְשׁוֹ לְעוֹלָם וָעֶד:
וַאֲנַחְנוּ נְבָרֵךְ יָהּ מֵעַתָּה וְעַד־עוֹלָם, הַלְלוּיָהּ: תהלים קטו

IYUN TEFILLA • עיון תפילה

וְחָסִיד בְּכָל־מַעֲשָׂיו – *And kind in all He does.* If a person is punished, one can look at it as a lack of kindness; alternatively, it is possible that he is getting less of a punishment than he really deserves. (*Me'am Loez*)

קָרוֹב יהוה לְכָל־קֹרְאָיו – *The Lord is close to all who call on Him.* To all those who call out to Him in sincerity." God is close to everyone who calls out to Him; but only those who are sincere walk away realizing that He is close. (Rabbi S.R. Hirsch)

סוֹמֵךְ יהוה לְכָל הַנֹּפְלִים – *The Lord supports all who fall.* Even people who sin – Hashem supports them so that they do not fall even further (Maharsha). Remember that self improvement is always possible.

צַדִּיק יהוה בְּכָל־דְּרָכָיו – *The Lord is righteous in all His ways.* And should one wonder why some people have some things while others do not, know that Hashem gives each according to his unique needs, just as a doctor does not give the same medicine to each person. (Ibn Ezra)

ANI TEFILLA • אני תפילה

פּוֹתֵחַ אֶת־יָדֶךָ – *You open Your hand.*
When I was in elementary school, my teacher Mr. Deutsch told us that if we just said the phrase from Ashrei, פּוֹתֵחַ אֶת־יָדֶךָ וּמַשְׂבִּיעַ לְכָל־חַי רָצוֹן*, "You open Your hand, and satisfy every living thing with favor," then we would grow up to be very rich. As a young child, I understood it almost as a magic formula: acknowledge God's ability to make you rich, tell Him so as if you really mean it, and you will get rich. No doubt, this interpretation is one of the things that kept me saying that phrase with*

HILKHOT TEFILLA • הלכות תפילה

פּוֹתֵחַ אֶת־יָדֶךָ – *You open Your hand.* So critical is this verse that the *Shulḥan Arukh* says (51:7) that if one did not recite it with proper *kavana*, then one must go back and repeat it again, apparently because it contains the essence of *Pesukei DeZimra*. Why do you think this is so?

הַלְלוּיָהּ Halleluya! Praise the LORD, my soul.| I will praise the LORD Ps. 146
all my life;|A I will sing to my God as long as I live. Put not your trust in princes,| or in mortal man who cannot save. His breath expires,| he returns to the earth; on that day his plans come to an end. Happy is he whose help is the God of Jacob,| whose hope is in the LORD his God who made heaven and earth, the sea and all they contain; He who keeps faith for ever. He secures justice for the oppressed.| He gives food to the hungry.| The LORD sets captives free. The LORD gives sight to the blind.| The LORD raises those bowed down. The LORD loves the righteous. The LORD protects the stranger. He gives courage to the orphan and widow. He thwarts the way of the wicked. ▸ The LORD shall reign for ever. He is your God, Zion, for all generations. Halleluya!

---

day his plans come to an end." Man is finite. God is eternal. Whose values and plans will last longer?

אַשְׁרֵי שֶׁאֵל יַעֲקֹב בְּעֶזְרוֹ – *Happy is he whose help is the God of Jacob.* He is called the God of Yaakov here because Yaakov (see *Bereshit* 34:10) represents the survival of the Jewish people long after the other nations of the world have disappeared (Seforno). God has continued to watch over us. History proves it.

עֹשֶׂה מִשְׁפָּט לַעֲשׁוּקִים – *He secures justice for the oppressed.* Someone who sets out to harm another, very often inadvertently ends up helping him. The brothers of Yosef thought they were oppressing him when, in fact, their plot against him played right into God's plan. (Rabbi Yosef Albo)

נֹתֵן לֶחֶם לָרְעֵבִים – *He gives food to the hungry.* There is hunger that comes from not eating, and there is the hunger of the soul that comes from being out of touch. God can satisfy both.

יהוה פֹּקֵחַ עִוְרִים – *The LORD gives sight to the blind.* There are those whose eyesight is 20/20, yet they can still be described as being blind. Belief in God can open one's eyes.

ANI TEFILLA • אני תפילה

When I went to the moon, I was as pragmatic a test pilot, engineer, and scientist as any of my colleagues... But there was another aspect to my experience during Apollo 14, and it contradicted the "pragmatic engineer" attitude. It began with the breathtaking experience of seeing planet Earth floating in the vastness of space...the presence of divinity

This **ANI TEFILLA** *continues on page 267.*

הַלְלוּיָהּ, הַלְלִי נַפְשִׁי אֶת־יהוה:ע אֲהַלְלָה יהוה בְּחַיָּי,עא אֲזַמְּרָה לֵאלֹהַי בְּעוֹדִי: אַל־תִּבְטְחוּ בִנְדִיבִים,ע בְּבֶן־אָדָם שֶׁאֵין לוֹ תְשׁוּעָה: תֵּצֵא רוּחוֹ,ע יָשֻׁב לְאַדְמָתוֹ, בַּיּוֹם הַהוּא אָבְדוּ עֶשְׁתֹּנֹתָיו: אַשְׁרֵי שֶׁאֵל יַעֲקֹב בְּעֶזְרוֹ,ע שִׂבְרוֹ עַל־יהוה אֱלֹהָיו: עֹשֶׂה שָׁמַיִם וָאָרֶץ, אֶת־הַיָּם וְאֶת־כָּל־אֲשֶׁר־בָּם, הַשֹּׁמֵר אֱמֶת לְעוֹלָם: עֹשֶׂה מִשְׁפָּט לַעֲשׁוּקִים,ע נֹתֵן לֶחֶם לָרְעֵבִים,ע יהוה מַתִּיר אֲסוּרִים: יהוה פֹּקֵחַ עִוְרִים,ע יהוה זֹקֵף כְּפוּפִים, יהוה אֹהֵב צַדִּיקִים: יהוה שֹׁמֵר אֶת־גֵּרִים, יָתוֹם וְאַלְמָנָה יְעוֹדֵד, וְדֶרֶךְ רְשָׁעִים יְעַוֵּת: ◂ יִמְלֹךְ יהוה לְעוֹלָם, אֱלֹהַיִךְ צִיּוֹן לְדֹר וָדֹר, הַלְלוּיָהּ: תהלים קמו

IYUN TEFILLA • עיון תפילה

הַלְלִי נַפְשִׁי אֶת־יהוה – *Praise the Lord, my soul.* Besides the human soul, there is no other creation that is able to recognize God's presence in the world. (Rabbi S.R. Hirsch)

אֲהַלְלָה יהוה בְּחַיָּי – *I will praise the Lord all my life.* "I will praise Hashem while I live; I will sing praises to my God while I have my being."

The verse can also be read: "I will praise Hashem for the fact that I am alive and I will sing praises for the fact that He also watches over me" (Malbim).

No matter what else is going on in my life, I have much to be thankful for.

ANI TEFILLA • אני תפילה

אֲהַלְלָה יהוה בְּחַיָּי – *I will praise the Lord all my life.*

Compare these interpretations:

I will praise Hashem as long as I am alive. (Meiri)

I will praise Hashem while I still have my health. (Roke'aḥ)

I will praise Hashem with the way I live my life.

Which of these speaks most to you today?

IYUN TEFILLA • עיון תפילה

אַל־תִּבְטְחוּ בִנְדִיבִים – *Put not your trust in princes.* King David, himself a monarch and a wealthy man, warns us that only God is worthy of our trust; people who are wealthier than us may seem to "have it all," but money and prestige can disappear quickly. Faith in God is the only way to maintain one's true self-worth.

תֵּצֵא רוּחוֹ – *His breath expires.* "His breath expires, he returns to the earth; on that

הַלְלוּיָהּ Halleluya! How good it is to sing songs to our God; how pleasant and fitting to praise Him. The LORD rebuilds Jerusalem. He gathers the scattered exiles of Israel. He heals the broken-hearted[I] and binds up their wounds. He counts the number of the stars,[AI] calling each by name. Great is our LORD and mighty in power; His understanding has no limit.[I] The LORD gives courage to the humble, but casts the wicked to the ground. Sing to the LORD in thanks; make music to our God on the harp.[I] He covers the sky with clouds. He provides the earth with rain and makes grass grow on the hills.[A] He gives food to the cattle and to the ravens when they cry. He does not take delight in the strength of horses nor pleasure in the fleetness of man.[I] The LORD takes pleasure in those who fear Him, who put their hope in His loving care. Praise the LORD, Jerusalem;[I] sing to your God, Zion, for He has strengthened the bars of your gates and blessed your children in your midst. He has brought peace to your borders, and satisfied you with the finest wheat. He sends His commandment to earth; *Ps. 147*

---

according to the actions of that person. (*Midrash Shoḥer Tov 148:1*)

Hashem knows the name of every one of His creations – including me.

לִתְבוּנָתוֹ אֵין מִסְפָּר – *His understanding has no limit.* The full capacity of one's understanding cannot be measured by standardized tests such as SATs or IQs. And what is true of man is all the more true of God. (Based on Rabbi S.R. Hirsch)

זַמְּרוּ לֵאלֹהֵינוּ בְכִנּוֹר – *Make music to our God on the harp.* Song and music are both instruments for praising Hashem. They both can express emotions of thanks when words might otherwise fail. Sing.

לֹא־בְשׁוֹקֵי הָאִישׁ יִרְצֶה – *Nor pleasure in the fleetness of man.* The true value of a person is not in his physical prowess, but in how much he fears God. Even if he has athletic talents, he needs to acknowledge that those come from Hashem.

שַׁבְּחִי יְרוּשָׁלַםִ אֶת־יהוה – *Praise the LORD, Jerusalem.* "Sing to your God, Zion, for He has strengthened the bars of your gates and blessed your children in your midst." Since 1948, the Jewish people have had sovereignty over Jerusalem.

תהלים קמז
הַלְלוּיָהּ, כִּי־טוֹב זַמְּרָה אֱלֹהֵינוּ, כִּי־נָעִים נָאוָה תְהִלָּה: בּוֹנֵה
יְרוּשָׁלַיִם יהוה, נִדְחֵי יִשְׂרָאֵל יְכַנֵּס: הָרוֹפֵא לִשְׁבוּרֵי לֵב,ע וּמְחַבֵּשׁ
לְעַצְּבוֹתָם: מוֹנֶה מִסְפָּר לַכּוֹכָבִים,א״ע לְכֻלָּם שֵׁמוֹת יִקְרָא: גָּדוֹל
אֲדוֹנֵינוּ וְרַב־כֹּחַ, לִתְבוּנָתוֹ אֵין מִסְפָּר: ע מְעוֹדֵד עֲנָוִים יהוה,
מַשְׁפִּיל רְשָׁעִים עֲדֵי־אָרֶץ: עֱנוּ לַיהוה בְּתוֹדָה, זַמְּרוּ לֵאלֹהֵינוּ
בְכִנּוֹר: ע הַמְכַסֶּה שָׁמַיִם בְּעָבִים, הַמֵּכִין לָאָרֶץ מָטָר, הַמַּצְמִיחַ
הָרִים חָצִיר: א נוֹתֵן לִבְהֵמָה לַחְמָהּ, לִבְנֵי עֹרֵב אֲשֶׁר יִקְרָאוּ: לֹא
בִגְבוּרַת הַסּוּס יֶחְפָּץ, לֹא־בְשׁוֹקֵי הָאִישׁ יִרְצֶה: ע רוֹצֶה יהוה
אֶת־יְרֵאָיו, אֶת־הַמְיַחֲלִים לְחַסְדּוֹ: שַׁבְּחִי יְרוּשָׁלַיִם אֶת־יהוה,ע
הַלְלִי אֱלֹהַיִךְ צִיּוֹן: כִּי־חִזַּק בְּרִיחֵי שְׁעָרָיִךְ, בֵּרַךְ בָּנַיִךְ בְּקִרְבֵּךְ:
הַשָּׂם־גְּבוּלֵךְ שָׁלוֹם, חֵלֶב חִטִּים יַשְׂבִּיעֵךְ: הַשֹּׁלֵחַ אִמְרָתוֹ אָרֶץ,

---

became almost palpable, and I knew that life in the universe was not just an accident based on random processes… It was knowledge gained through private subjective awareness, but it was – and still is – every bit as real as the objective data upon which, say, the navigational program or the communications system was based. (Captain Edgar D. Mitchell)

IYUN TEFILLA • עיון תפילה

הָרוֹפֵא לִשְׁבוּרֵי לֵב – *He heals the brokenhearted.* Sometimes when other people cannot understand you, Hashem is the only One who can.

מוֹנֶה מִסְפָּר לַכּוֹכָבִים – *He counts the number of the stars.* Hashem counts each one of His creations because He cares about them. (Rashi)

Every person has a star in the heavens which corresponds to him and shines

ANI TEFILLA • אני תפילה

מוֹנֶה מִסְפָּר לַכּוֹכָבִים – *He counts the number of the stars.*

Imagine yourself in a place where you have seen a star-filled sky. Close your eyes. Count them.

הַמַּצְמִיחַ הָרִים חָצִיר – *Makes grass grow on the hills.*

Have you ever seen lush foliage, green pastures, mountains covered with clouds and vegetation? Imagine yourself there now.

swiftly runs His word. He spreads snow like fleece,[A] sprinkles frost like ashes, scatters hail like crumbs. Who can stand His cold? He sends His word and melts them; He makes the wind blow and the waters flow. ▸ He has declared His words to Jacob, His statutes and laws to Israel. He has done this for no other nation; such laws they do not know. Halleluya!

הַלְלוּיָהּ Halleluya! Praise the LORD from the heavens,[BI] praise Him in the heights. Praise Him, all His angels; praise Him, all His hosts. Praise Him, sun and moon; praise Him, all shining stars. Praise Him, highest heavens and the waters above the heavens. Let them praise the name of the LORD, for He commanded and they were created. He established them for ever and all time, issuing a decree that will never change. Praise the Ps. 148

ANI TEFILLA • אני תפילה

Think about the complexity of creation as you know it from biology or any of the other physical sciences. Close your eyes and imagine being in a place where you were once overwhelmed by the beauty, symmetry and complexity of nature.

IYUN TEFILLA • עיון תפילה

הַלְלוּיָהּ, הַלְלוּ אֶת־יהוה מִן־הַשָּׁמַיִם – *Halleluya! Praise the LORD from the heavens.* This psalm describes the entire universe in dynamic terms. Borrowing heavily from the terminology and images used in *Bereshit*, the psalm in both content and structure reflects one who is overcome by the realization of the varied yet unified nature of the world around us. The first section begins "Praise Hashem from the heavens"; the second section begins "Praise Hashem from the earth"; the concluding section begins "His majesty is above [both] the earth and the heavens."

ANI TEFILLA • אני תפילה

At a meeting of Alcoholics Anonymous (AA), a man related that he had been sober for seven years.

"I walked out on my first contact with AA. They were talking about having a Higher Power, and I was an avowed atheist. When I could not get sober, I returned and said that I want to join the program, but I don't want any of the God talk, and they said 'Okay.' They told me I had to get a sponsor, which I did, and

This **ANI TEFILLA** *continues on page 271.*

עַד־מְהֵרָה יָרוּץ דְּבָרוֹ: הַנֹּתֵן שֶׁלֶג כַּצָּמֶר,[א] כְּפוֹר כָּאֵפֶר יְפַזֵּר:
מַשְׁלִיךְ קַרְחוֹ כְפִתִּים, לִפְנֵי קָרָתוֹ מִי יַעֲמֹד: יִשְׁלַח דְּבָרוֹ וְיַמְסֵם,
יַשֵּׁב רוּחוֹ יִזְּלוּ־מָיִם: · מַגִּיד דְּבָרָו לְיַעֲקֹב, חֻקָּיו וּמִשְׁפָּטָיו
לְיִשְׂרָאֵל: לֹא עָשָׂה כֵן לְכָל־גּוֹי, וּמִשְׁפָּטִים בַּל־יְדָעוּם, הַלְלוּיָהּ:

הַלְלוּיָהּ, הַלְלוּ אֶת־יהוה מִן־הַשָּׁמַיִם,[בע] הַלְלוּהוּ בַּמְּרוֹמִים: תהלים קמח
הַלְלוּהוּ כָל־מַלְאָכָיו, הַלְלוּהוּ כָּל־צְבָאָו: הַלְלוּהוּ שֶׁמֶשׁ וְיָרֵחַ,
הַלְלוּהוּ כָּל־כּוֹכְבֵי אוֹר: הַלְלוּהוּ שְׁמֵי הַשָּׁמָיִם, וְהַמַּיִם אֲשֶׁר מֵעַל
הַשָּׁמָיִם: יְהַלְלוּ אֶת־שֵׁם יהוה, כִּי הוּא צִוָּה וְנִבְרָאוּ: וַיַּעֲמִידֵם
לָעַד לְעוֹלָם, חָק־נָתַן וְלֹא יַעֲבוֹר: הַלְלוּ אֶת־יהוה מִן־הָאָרֶץ,

---

ANI TEFILLA • אני תפילה

הַנֹּתֵן שֶׁלֶג כַּצָּמֶר – *He spreads snow like fleece.* The next three verses speak of Hashem's control over precipitation and the weather, which can have both positive and negative effects on man. The religious personality sees God's hand in the cycle of nature; "when the snow melts...the waters flow," and the cycle of life continues.

Look outside. What is the weather like today? Don't take it for granted.

BIUR TEFILLA • ביאור תפילה

הַלְלוּיָהּ, הַלְלוּ אֶת־יהוה מִן־הַשָּׁמַיִם – *Halleluya! Praise the Lord from the heavens.* The diversity of creation is highlighted by the listing of creations. In the first section (verses 1–6) they are listed according to their stature, moving mostly from "higher" to "lower." In the second section, the reverse is true: the creations are listed from the bottom of the sea up to the sky and back down again but according to their stature not their place. Especially toward the end, one sees movement from the inanimate (mountains) to the animate (animals) to mankind. Indeed, even within each category there is an attempt to convey a sense of all of its members by the use of opposites (fire and hail etc.). The all-encompassing nature of the description in both sections is emphasized by the recurring use of the word **כָּל**. It is as if the reader is immersed in all of the parts of creation. Man, reflecting upon the world around him, is overwhelmed by its diversity and complexity. At the same time, however, man is called upon to recognize the thread which ties together all of these diverse elements: namely, the One who created them all.

Lord from the earth: sea monsters and all the deep seas; fire and hail, snow and mist, storm winds that obey His word; mountains and all hills, fruit trees and all cedars; wild animals and all cattle, creeping things and winged birds; kings of the earth and all nations, princes and all judges on earth; youths and maidens, old and young. ▸ Let them praise the name of the Lord, for His name alone is sublime; His majesty is above earth and heaven. He has raised the pride of His people, for the glory of all His devoted ones, the children of Israel, the people close to Him. Halleluya!

הַלְלוּיָהּ Halleluya! Sing to the Lord a new song,[1] His praise in the assembly of the devoted. Let Israel rejoice in its Maker; let the children of Zion exult in their King. Let them praise His name with dancing; sing praises to Him with timbrel and harp. For the Lord delights in His people; He adorns the humble with salvation. Let the devoted revel in glory; let them sing for joy on their beds. Let high praises of God be in their throats, and a two-edged sword in their hand: to impose retribution on the nations, punishment on the peoples, ▸ binding their kings with chains, their nobles with iron fetters, carrying out the judgment written against them. This is the glory of all His devoted ones. Halleluya! Ps. 149

ANI TEFILLA • אני תפילה

One night I dreamed I was walking on the beach with God. I saw many scenes from my life flash across the sky. In each scene I noticed footprints in the sand. Sometimes there were two sets of footprints and sometimes there was only one.

This bothered me because I noticed that during the low periods in my life, when I was suffering from anguish, sorrow or defeat, I could see only one set of footprints, so I said to God, "You promised me that if I followed You, You would walk with me always. But I have noticed that during the most trying periods of my life there has been only one set of footprints in the sand. Why, when I have needed You most, have You not been there for me?"

God replied, "The years when you have seen only one set of footprints, my child, is when I carried you." (Author unknown)

תַּנִּינִים וְכָל־תְּהֹמוֹת: אֵשׁ וּבָרָד שֶׁלֶג וְקִיטוֹר, רְוּחַ סְעָרָה עֹשָׂה דְבָרוֹ: הֶהָרִים וְכָל־גְּבָעוֹת, עֵץ פְּרִי וְכָל־אֲרָזִים: הַחַיָּה וְכָל־בְּהֵמָה, רֶמֶשׂ וְצִפּוֹר כָּנָף: מַלְכֵי־אֶרֶץ וְכָל־לְאֻמִּים, שָׂרִים וְכָל־שֹׁפְטֵי אָרֶץ: בַּחוּרִים וְגַם־בְּתוּלוֹת, זְקֵנִים עִם־נְעָרִים: ◂ יְהַלְלוּ אֶת־שֵׁם יהוה, כִּי־נִשְׂגָּב שְׁמוֹ לְבַדּוֹ, הוֹדוֹ עַל־אֶרֶץ וְשָׁמָיִם: וַיָּרֶם קֶרֶן לְעַמּוֹ, תְּהִלָּה לְכָל־חֲסִידָיו, לִבְנֵי יִשְׂרָאֵל עַם קְרֹבוֹ, הַלְלוּיָהּ:

תהלים קמט

הַלְלוּיָהּ, שִׁירוּ לַיהוה שִׁיר חָדָשׁ,ע תְּהִלָּתוֹ בִּקְהַל חֲסִידִים: יִשְׂמַח יִשְׂרָאֵל בְּעֹשָׂיו, בְּנֵי־צִיּוֹן יָגִילוּ בְמַלְכָּם: יְהַלְלוּ שְׁמוֹ בְמָחוֹל, בְּתֹף וְכִנּוֹר יְזַמְּרוּ־לוֹ: כִּי־רוֹצֶה יהוה בְּעַמּוֹ, יְפָאֵר עֲנָוִים בִּישׁוּעָה: יַעְלְזוּ חֲסִידִים בְּכָבוֹד, יְרַנְּנוּ עַל־מִשְׁכְּבוֹתָם: רוֹמְמוֹת אֵל בִּגְרוֹנָם, וְחֶרֶב פִּיפִיּוֹת בְּיָדָם: לַעֲשׂוֹת נְקָמָה בַּגּוֹיִם, תּוֹכֵחוֹת בַּלְאֻמִּים: ◂ לֶאְסֹר מַלְכֵיהֶם בְּזִקִּים, וְנִכְבְּדֵיהֶם בְּכַבְלֵי בַרְזֶל: לַעֲשׂוֹת בָּהֶם מִשְׁפָּט כָּתוּב, הָדָר הוּא לְכָל־חֲסִידָיו, הַלְלוּיָהּ:

IYUN TEFILLA • עיון תפילה

הַלְלוּיָהּ, שִׁירוּ לַיהוה שִׁיר חָדָשׁ – *Halleluya! Sing to the Lord a new song.* Each of us is called upon to create our own personal praise of Hashem's presence in our lives. Each day we should create our own new song. Alternatively, each day we are different than we were the day before and so our song is a new one, unlike the one we sang yesterday, not because the words are different but because we are.

What's your song today?

my sponsor told me I had to pray every day. I said: 'Hold it! I was assured that I would not be bothered about God.' My sponsor said, 'Look here, do you want to get sober or stay drunk? If you want to get sober, you're going to pray every day.'

"Well, I prayed every day, but I didn't pray to God because I didn't believe in God. But when I prayed, that reminded me that I was not God."

The first step in recovery from addiction and in the effort to achieve a relationship with God, is humility, the realization that we are not God. Only then can we have emuna. Until then, our prayers may only help us realize that we are not God. (Rabbi A.J. Twerski)

הַלְלוּיָהּ Halleluya! Praise God in His holy place;[1] Ps. 150
praise Him in the heavens of His power.
Praise Him for His mighty deeds;
praise Him for His surpassing greatness.[1]
Praise Him with blasts of the shofar;
praise Him with the harp and lyre.
Praise Him with timbrel and dance;
praise Him with strings and flute.
Praise Him with clashing cymbals;
praise Him with resounding cymbals.
▸ Let all that breathes praise the LORD. Halleluya![1]
Let all that breathes praise the LORD. Halleluya![B]

כֹּל הַנְּשָׁמָה תְּהַלֵּל יָהּ – *Let all that breathes praise the* LORD. Words, music and song are all but modes of expression for that which lies at our core – the human soul. It is like "an inner drive that breaks out like a flame inside a volcano, but cannot do so in the form of words or logical sentences" (Rabbi J.B. Soloveitchik). Alternatively, the word for soul is related to the word for breath (נְשִׁימָה) – wherever we are, we should look for God's presence in our lives and celebrate with every breath we take.

BIUR TEFILLA • ביאור תפילה

כֹּל הַנְּשָׁמָה תְּהַלֵּל יָהּ – *Let all that breathes praise the* LORD. The repetition of the final sentence is a traditional way of conveying the fact that this represents the conclusion of a section; here it marks the end of the last chapter of *Tehillim*, the core of *Pesukei DeZimra* (*Tur* 51, *Sefer Pardes*).

ANI TEFILLA • אני תפילה

We can only pray the way prayer is supposed to be when we recognize that in fact the soul is always praying.

Without stop, the soul soars and yearns for its Beloved. It is at the time of outward prayer [as we are doing now], that the perpetual prayer of the soul reveals itself in the realm of action.

This is prayer's pleasure and joy, its glory and beauty. It is like a rose, opening its elegant petals toward the dew, facing the rays of the sun as they shine over it with the sun's light. (Rabbi A.Y. Kook)

Your soul is always praying. Now is the time to hear its voice.

תהלים קנ

הַלְלוּיָהּ, הַלְלוּ־אֵל בְּקָדְשׁוֹ
הַלְלוּהוּ בִּרְקִיעַ עֻזּוֹ:
הַלְלוּהוּ בִגְבוּרֹתָיו
הַלְלוּהוּ כְּרֹב גֻּדְלוֹ:
הַלְלוּהוּ בְּתֵקַע שׁוֹפָר
הַלְלוּהוּ בְּנֵבֶל וְכִנּוֹר:
הַלְלוּהוּ בְּתֹף וּמָחוֹל
הַלְלוּהוּ בְּמִנִּים וְעֻגָב:
הַלְלוּהוּ בְצִלְצְלֵי־שָׁמַע
הַלְלוּהוּ בְּצִלְצְלֵי תְרוּעָה:
› כֹּל הַנְּשָׁמָה תְּהַלֵּל יָהּ, הַלְלוּיָהּ:
כֹּל הַנְּשָׁמָה תְּהַלֵּל יָהּ, הַלְלוּיָהּ:

IYUN TEFILLA • עיון תפילה

הַלְלוּ־אֵל בְּקָדְשׁוֹ – *Halleluya! Praise God in His holy place. praise Him in the heavens.* His holy place is the *Beit HaMikdash* and represents God's revelation to man in the moral sphere. The heavens represent His revelation to man in the world of nature (Rabbi S.R. Hirsch). The study of Torah represents man's education about what God wants in the moral sphere; the study of the sciences represents man's education about God's presence in the physical sphere.

Science can be a religious quest.

הַלְלוּהוּ כְּרֹב גֻּדְלוֹ – *Praise Him for His surpassing greatness.* Says the psalm. However, sometimes words are inadequate to express how beautiful, complex, and overwhelming the beauty of the world and its creations can be. Did you ever witness something so amazing that it was indescribable? And so, when words fail, sometimes only music and song can best express what our heart is feeling. What follows, then, is reference to a variety of ancient musical instruments whose sounds are sometimes better equipped to express the praise we feel.

בָּרוּךְ Blessed be the LORD for ever.[B] Amen and Amen. *Ps. 89*
Blessed from Zion be the LORD *Ps. 135*
who dwells in Jerusalem. Halleluya!
Blessed be the LORD, God of Israel, who alone does wonders. *Ps. 72*
▸ Blessed be His glorious name for ever,
and may all the earth be filled with His glory.
Amen and Amen.[B]

Stand until "The soul" on page 282.

וַיְבָרֶךְ David blessed the LORD in front of the entire assembly. David said, "Blessed are You, LORD, God of our father Yisrael, for ever and ever. Yours, LORD, are the greatness and the power, the glory, majesty and splendor, for everything in heaven and earth is Yours. Yours, LORD, is the kingdom; You are exalted as Head over all. Both riches and honor are in Your gift and You reign over all things. In Your hand are strength and might. It is in Your power to make great and give strength to all. Therefore, our God, we thank You and praise Your glorious name." *1 Chr. 29*

You alone are the LORD.[B] You *Neh. 9*

Some suggest that prevalent custom to stand comes from the fact that people would stand to give charity or any other mitzva, or in deference to those who would come around to collect charity at this point. Our custom to stand on Shabbat, when handling money is forbidden, may be a vestige of the weekday practice or, alternatively, a symbolic show of deference to King David and the House of David.

While many Sephardim sit down after the recitation of this paragraph, Ashkenazi custom is to continue standing since one will soon have to stand for *Kaddish* and *Barekhu* in any event.

BIUR TEFILLA • ביאור תפילה

אַתָּה־הוּא יהוה לְבַדֶּךָ – *You alone are the Lord.* What follows in the next prayers is a brief history of our relationship with Hashem from Creation until the splitting of the Sea at the time of the exodus. This represents a shift from focusing primarily on Hashem's presence in nature to Hashem's presence in history. The bridge between the two is Avraham who, according to one tradition, discovered Hashem in nature and then went on to find His place in human affairs.

בָּרוּךְ יהוה לְעוֹלָם, אָמֵן וְאָמֵן: תהלים פט
בָּרוּךְ יהוה מִצִּיּוֹן, שֹׁכֵן יְרוּשָׁלָםִ, הַלְלוּיָהּ: תהלים קלה
בָּרוּךְ יהוה אֱלֹהִים אֱלֹהֵי יִשְׂרָאֵל, עֹשֵׂה נִפְלָאוֹת לְבַדּוֹ: תהלים עב
• וּבָרוּךְ שֵׁם כְּבוֹדוֹ לְעוֹלָם, וְיִמָּלֵא כְבוֹדוֹ אֶת־כָּל־הָאָרֶץ
אָמֵן וְאָמֵן:

Stand until נִשְׁמַת *on page 283.*

דברי הימים א׳ כט
וַיְבָרֶךְ דָּוִיד אֶת־יהוה לְעֵינֵי כָּל־הַקָּהָל, וַיֹּאמֶר דָּוִיד, בָּרוּךְ
אַתָּה יהוה, אֱלֹהֵי יִשְׂרָאֵל אָבִינוּ, מֵעוֹלָם וְעַד־עוֹלָם: לְךָ יהוה
הַגְּדֻלָּה וְהַגְּבוּרָה וְהַתִּפְאֶרֶת וְהַנֵּצַח וְהַהוֹד, כִּי־כֹל בַּשָּׁמַיִם
וּבָאָרֶץ, לְךָ יהוה הַמַּמְלָכָה וְהַמִּתְנַשֵּׂא לְכֹל לְרֹאשׁ: וְהָעֹשֶׁר
וְהַכָּבוֹד מִלְּפָנֶיךָ, וְאַתָּה מוֹשֵׁל בַּכֹּל, וּבְיָדְךָ כֹּחַ וּגְבוּרָה, וּבְיָדְךָ
לְגַדֵּל וּלְחַזֵּק לַכֹּל: וְעַתָּה אֱלֹהֵינוּ מוֹדִים אֲנַחְנוּ לָךְ, וּמְהַלְלִים
לְשֵׁם תִּפְאַרְתֶּךָ: אַתָּה־הוּא יהוה לְבַדֶּךָ, אַתָּ עָשִׂיתָ נחמיה ט

BIUR TEFILLA • ביאור תפילה

בָּרוּךְ יהוה לְעוֹלָם – *Blessed be the* Lord *for ever.* The prayers which follow add other dimensions to the *Pesukei DeZimra*. As they are not directly a part of the core *Tehillim* we just concluded, the Maharam would recite the following series of verses, reminiscent of the language of a closing blessing, in order to separate the two sections. (Abudarham)

אָמֵן וְאָמֵן – *Amen and Amen.* The word *amen* can have two meanings:

(a) a declaration – I agree with everything that was just said;

(b) a prayer – I pray that everything that was just said will come true. (*Tzeluta DeAvraham*)

HILKHOT TEFILLA • הלכות תפילה

These verses of praise were recited by King David toward the end of his life when he had amassed the wealth necessary to build the *Beit HaMikdash* that would be constructed by his son. As a result, there is a custom during the week to set aside a token amount of money at this point to donate to charity (*Magen Avraham* 51) as a concrete way of saying that the money I have is really from God and is to be used for a life of holiness, which in this case means sharing with others.

made the heavens, even the highest heavens, and all their hosts, the earth and all that is on it, the seas and all they contain. You give life to them all, and the hosts of heaven worship You. ▸ You are the LORD God who chose Abram and brought him out of Ur of the Chaldees, changing his name to Abraham. You found his heart faithful toward You, ◂ and You made a covenant with him to give to his descendants the land of the Canaanites, Hittites, Amorites, Perizzites, Jebusites and Girgashites. You fulfilled Your promise for You are righteous. You saw the suffering of our ancestors in Egypt. You heard their cry at the Sea of Reeds. You sent signs and wonders against Pharaoh, all his servants and all the people of his land, because You knew how arrogantly the Egyptians treated them. You created for Yourself renown that remains to this day. ▸ You divided the sea before them, so that they passed through the sea on dry land, but You cast their pursuers into the depths, like a stone into mighty waters.

וַיּוֹשַׁע That day the LORD saved Israel from the hands of the Egyp- *Ex. 14*
tians, and Israel saw the Egyptians lying dead on the seashore. ▸ When Israel saw the great power[1] the LORD had displayed against the Egyptians, the people feared the LORD, and believed in the LORD and in His servant, Moses.

---

be your seed," so shall be the history of your people, your children. Your great destiny is just as enigmatic and mysterious and incomprehensible as the great story of the heavens. Why try to rationalize it? ... The story of your people is the story of the heavens; no one will ever be able to understand it. (Rabbi J.B. Soloveitchik)

IYUN TEFILLA • עיון תפילה

וַיַּרְא יִשְׂרָאֵל אֶת־הַיָּד הַגְּדֹלָה – *When Israel saw the great power.* But were there not times subsequently when *Benei Yisrael* did not believe in Hashem?! What happened to their faith? Rather, faith is not something that is binary, an either/or proposition. Instead, faith is akin to an analog signal that varies with different intensities and strengths at different points in one's life. (Rabbi. S. Aviner)

Indeed, it can be argued that a faith that relies upon supernatural miracles is inferior. The stronger faith is the one that sees the miracles in the everyday.

What miracles surround your life this morning?

אֶת־הַשָּׁמַיִם, שְׁמֵי הַשָּׁמַיִם וְכָל־צְבָאָם, הָאָרֶץ וְכָל־אֲשֶׁר עָלֶיהָ, הַיַּמִּים וְכָל־אֲשֶׁר בָּהֶם, וְאַתָּה מְחַיֶּה אֶת־כֻּלָּם, וּצְבָא הַשָּׁמַיִם לְךָ מִשְׁתַּחֲוִים: ◄ אַתָּה הוּא יהוה הָאֱלֹהִים אֲשֶׁר בָּחַרְתָּ בְּאַבְרָם, וְהוֹצֵאתוֹ מֵאוּר כַּשְׂדִּים, וְשַׂמְתָּ שְּׁמוֹ אַבְרָהָם: וּמָצָאתָ אֶת־לְבָבוֹ נֶאֱמָן לְפָנֶיךָ, ◄ וְכָרוֹת עִמּוֹ הַבְּרִית לָתֵת אֶת־אֶרֶץ הַכְּנַעֲנִי הַחִתִּי הָאֱמֹרִי וְהַפְּרִזִּי וְהַיְבוּסִי וְהַגִּרְגָּשִׁי, לָתֵת לְזַרְעוֹ, וַתָּקֶם אֶת־דְּבָרֶיךָ, כִּי צַדִּיק אָתָּה: וַתֵּרֶא אֶת־עֳנִי אֲבֹתֵינוּ בְּמִצְרָיִם, וְאֶת־זַעֲקָתָם שָׁמַעְתָּ עַל־יַם־סוּף: וַתִּתֵּן אֹתֹת וּמֹפְתִים בְּפַרְעֹה וּבְכָל־עֲבָדָיו וּבְכָל־עַם אַרְצוֹ, כִּי יָדַעְתָּ כִּי הֵזִידוּ עֲלֵיהֶם, וַתַּעַשׂ־לְךָ שֵׁם כְּהַיּוֹם הַזֶּה: ◄ וְהַיָּם בָּקַעְתָּ לִפְנֵיהֶם, וַיַּעַבְרוּ בְתוֹךְ־הַיָּם בַּיַּבָּשָׁה, וְאֶת־רֹדְפֵיהֶם הִשְׁלַכְתָּ בִמְצוֹלֹת כְּמוֹ־אֶבֶן, בְּמַיִם עַזִּים:

וַיּוֹשַׁע יהוה בַּיּוֹם הַהוּא אֶת־יִשְׂרָאֵל מִיַּד מִצְרָיִם, וַיַּרְא יִשְׂרָאֵל אֶת־מִצְרַיִם מֵת עַל־שְׂפַת הַיָּם: ◄ וַיַּרְא יִשְׂרָאֵל אֶת־הַיָּד הַגְּדֹלָה ע אֲשֶׁר עָשָׂה יהוה בְּמִצְרַיִם, וַיִּירְאוּ הָעָם אֶת־יהוה, וַיַּאֲמִינוּ בַּיהוה וּבְמֹשֶׁה עַבְדּוֹ: שמות יד

ANI TEFILLA • אני תפילה

When Avraham was a lad, when he was a shepherd and remained in the field at night, he couldn't sleep because he was restless. He could not understand the cosmos; the grandeur of the cosmic drama puzzled him. Chaldea [Ur Kasdim] was the land where astronomy was born. They were the first ones to describe the skies, draw maps of the heavens. Avraham counted the stars; he discovered God with the stars. When a sensitive and refined person lifts his eyes and watches the stars and the heavenly drama, he begins to think of the enormous distances and is confronted by the Ein Sof, by infinity, by endlessness itself. The sensitive soul will sense the complete worthlessness of man in comparison with infinity and will finally find God in the infinite spaces separating galaxies and stars...

God tells Avraham not merely to count the stars, but to try to comprehend them. Can you enumerate the stars, Avraham? Can you explain the cosmic drama, the flying nebulae on the outskirts of the universe? ... "So shall

אָז יָשִׁיר־מֹשֶׁה Then Moses and the Israelites sang this song[HA] *Ex. 15*
to the LORD, saying:
I will sing to the LORD, for He has triumphed gloriously;
horse and rider He has hurled into the sea.
The LORD is my strength and song; He has become my salvation.
This is my God, and I will beautify Him,
my father's God, and I will exalt Him.
The LORD is a Master of war; LORD is His name.
Pharaoh's chariots and army He cast into the sea;
the best of his officers drowned in the Sea of Reeds.
The deep waters covered them;
they went down to the depths like a stone.
Your right hand, LORD, is majestic in power.
Your right hand, LORD, shatters the enemy.
In the greatness of Your majesty, You overthrew those who rose against You.
You sent out Your fury; it consumed them like stubble.
By the blast of Your nostrils the waters piled up.
The surging waters stood straight like a wall;
the deeps congealed in the heart of the sea.
The enemy said, "I will pursue. I will overtake. I will divide the spoil.
My desire shall have its fill of them.
I will draw my sword. My hand will destroy them."
You blew with Your wind; the sea covered them.
They sank in the mighty waters like lead.
Who is like You, LORD, among the mighty?
Who is like You – majestic in holiness, awesome in glory, working wonders?
You stretched out Your right hand, the earth swallowed them.
In Your loving-kindness, You led the people You redeemed.
In Your strength, You guided them to Your holy abode.

---

crossing of the Reed Sea, they all lifted up the hems of their clothes to keep them from getting wet, for it actually seemed to them that they had gone down into the Sea which had split before them. Such is the power of imagination during tefilla.

אָז יָשִׁיר־מֹשֶׁה וּבְנֵי יִשְׂרָאֵל אֶת־הַשִּׁירָה הַזֹּאת לַיהוה, וַיֹּאמְרוּ שמות טו
לֵאמֹר, אָשִׁירָה לַיהוה כִּי־גָאֹה גָּאָה, סוּס
וְרֹכְבוֹ רָמָה בַיָּם: עָזִּי וְזִמְרָת יָהּ וַיְהִי־לִי
לִישׁוּעָה, זֶה אֵלִי וְאַנְוֵהוּ, אֱלֹהֵי
אָבִי וַאֲרֹמְמֶנְהוּ: יהוה אִישׁ מִלְחָמָה, יהוה
שְׁמוֹ: מַרְכְּבֹת פַּרְעֹה וְחֵילוֹ יָרָה בַיָּם, וּמִבְחַר
שָׁלִשָׁיו טֻבְּעוּ בְיַם־סוּף: תְּהֹמֹת יְכַסְיֻמוּ, יָרְדוּ בִמְצוֹלֹת כְּמוֹ־
אָבֶן: יְמִינְךָ יהוה נֶאְדָּרִי בַּכֹּחַ, יְמִינְךָ
יהוה תִּרְעַץ אוֹיֵב: וּבְרֹב גְּאוֹנְךָ תַּהֲרֹס
קָמֶיךָ, תְּשַׁלַּח חֲרֹנְךָ יֹאכְלֵמוֹ כַּקַּשׁ: וּבְרוּחַ
אַפֶּיךָ נֶעֶרְמוּ מַיִם, נִצְּבוּ כְמוֹ־נֵד
נֹזְלִים, קָפְאוּ תְהֹמֹת בְּלֶב־יָם: אָמַר
אוֹיֵב אֶרְדֹּף, אַשִּׂיג, אֲחַלֵּק שָׁלָל, תִּמְלָאֵמוֹ
נַפְשִׁי, אָרִיק חַרְבִּי תּוֹרִישֵׁמוֹ יָדִי: נָשַׁפְתָּ
בְרוּחֲךָ כִּסָּמוֹ יָם, צָלְלוּ כַּעוֹפֶרֶת בְּמַיִם
אַדִּירִים: מִי־כָמֹכָה בָּאֵלִם יהוה, מִי
כָּמֹכָה נֶאְדָּר בַּקֹּדֶשׁ, נוֹרָא תְהִלֹּת עֹשֵׂה
פֶלֶא: נָטִיתָ יְמִינְךָ תִּבְלָעֵמוֹ אָרֶץ: נָחִיתָ
בְחַסְדְּךָ עַם־זוּ גָּאָלְתָּ, נֵהַלְתָּ בְעָזְּךָ אֶל־נְוֵה

ANI TEFILLA • אני תפילה

אָז יָשִׁיר־מֹשֶׁה וּבְנֵי יִשְׂרָאֵל – *Then Moses and the Israelites sang. Once, Rabbi Shmelke of Nikolsburg said the Song at the Sea as Ḥazan with such power that when the congregation recited with him the verses about the*

HILKHOT TEFILLA • הלכות תפילה

אָז יָשִׁיר־מֹשֶׁה וּבְנֵי יִשְׂרָאֵל – *Then Moses and the Israelites sang.* One should say the Song at the Sea with great joy, and imagine that at that very moment he crossed through it and was liberated. And if one does so, then all of his sins will be forgiven (*Mishna Berura* 51:17). In other words, this is not just about reciting or retelling the event; it is about reliving it.

Nations heard and trembled;
terror gripped Philistia's inhabitants.
The chiefs of Edom were dismayed,
Moab's leaders were seized with trembling,
the people of Canaan melted away.
Fear and dread fell upon them.
By the power of Your arm, they were still as stone –
until Your people crossed, LORD,
until the people You acquired crossed over.
You will bring them and plant them on the mountain of Your heritage –
the place, LORD, You made for Your dwelling,
the Sanctuary, LORD, Your hands established.
The LORD will reign for ever and all time.

The LORD will reign for ever and all time.
The LORD's kingship is established for ever and to all eternity.

When Pharaoh's horses, chariots and riders went into the sea,
the LORD brought the waters of the sea back over them,
but the Israelites walked on dry land through the sea.

▸ For kingship is the LORD's and He rules over the nations. *Ps. 22*
Saviors shall go up to Mount Zion to judge Mount Esau, *Ob. 1*
and the LORD's shall be the kingdom.
Then the LORD shall be King over all the earth; *Zech. 14*
on that day the LORD shall be One and His name One,

(as it is written in Your Torah, saying:
Listen, Israel: the LORD is our God, the LORD is One.) *Deut. 6*

---

of God's plan. Hence he said, "I will bless Hashem at all times," during the good and what seems like the bad. In the midst of crisis, it is hard to see the positive, unless you believe that it too is ultimately for the good. So ingrained is this worldview in Jewish life that it has been given expression in numerous ways, both popular and legal. As early as the first century, there was a sage who was known by the name Nahum ish Gamzu presumably because he would forever say "*gam zu le'tova*" meaning, "this too is for the good," a phrase still used colloquially today. In a similar vein, there is actually a blessing on hearing bad news, not because one ignores its sadness but because one prays that ultimately it is for the good. Judaism by its nature is forever optimistic.

קָדְשֶׁךָ: שָׁמְעוּ עַמִּים יִרְגָּזוּן, חִיל
אָחַז יֹשְׁבֵי פְּלָשֶׁת: אָז נִבְהֲלוּ אַלּוּפֵי
אֱדוֹם, אֵילֵי מוֹאָב יֹאחֲזֵמוֹ רָעַד, נָמֹגוּ
כֹּל יֹשְׁבֵי כְנָעַן: תִּפֹּל עֲלֵיהֶם אֵימָתָה
וָפַחַד, בִּגְדֹל זְרוֹעֲךָ יִדְּמוּ כָּאָבֶן, עַד־
יַעֲבֹר עַמְּךָ יהוה, עַד־יַעֲבֹר עַם־זוּ
קָנִיתָ: תְּבִאֵמוֹ וְתִטָּעֵמוֹ בְּהַר נַחֲלָתְךָ, מָכוֹן
לְשִׁבְתְּךָ פָּעַלְתָּ יהוה, מִקְּדָשׁ אֲדֹנָי כּוֹנְנוּ
יָדֶיךָ: יהוה ׀ יִמְלֹךְ לְעֹלָם וָעֶד:

יהוה יִמְלֹךְ לְעֹלָם וָעֶד.
יהוה מַלְכוּתֵהּ קָאֵם לְעָלַם וּלְעָלְמֵי עָלְמַיָּא.

כִּי
בָא סוּס פַּרְעֹה בְּרִכְבּוֹ וּבְפָרָשָׁיו בַּיָּם, וַיָּשֶׁב יהוה עֲלֵהֶם אֶת־מֵי
הַיָּם, וּבְנֵי יִשְׂרָאֵל הָלְכוּ בַיַּבָּשָׁה בְּתוֹךְ הַיָּם:

◂ כִּי לַיהוה הַמְּלוּכָה וּמֹשֵׁל בַּגּוֹיִם: תהלים כב
וְעָלוּ מוֹשִׁעִים בְּהַר צִיּוֹן לִשְׁפֹּט אֶת־הַר עֵשָׂו עובדיה א
וְהָיְתָה לַיהוה הַמְּלוּכָה:
וְהָיָה יהוה לְמֶלֶךְ עַל־כָּל־הָאָרֶץ זכריה יד
בַּיּוֹם הַהוּא יִהְיֶה יהוה אֶחָד וּשְׁמוֹ אֶחָד:

(וּבְתוֹרָתְךָ כָּתוּב לֵאמֹר, שְׁמַע יִשְׂרָאֵל, יהוה אֱלֹהֵינוּ יהוה אֶחָד:) דברים ו

ANI TEFILLA • אני תפילה

Rabbi Levi Yitzḥak of Berditchev said that David thought that one should praise God when good things happen but he couldn't understand why one should do so when bad things happen. But when David saw that he was saved as a result of having to lower himself by acting as if he had lost his senses, he realized that this too was part

THE SOUL[B]

of all that lives shall bless Your name,[I] LORD our God,
and the spirit of all flesh shall always glorify
and exalt Your remembrance, our King.
From eternity to eternity You are God.
Without You, we have no King, Redeemer or Savior,
who liberates, rescues, sustains
and shows compassion in every time of trouble and distress.
We have no King but You, God of the first and last,
God of all creatures,[B] Master of all ages,
extolled by a multitude of praises,
who guides His world with loving-kindness
and His creatures with compassion.
The LORD neither slumbers nor sleeps.
He rouses the sleepers and wakens the slumberers.
He makes the dumb speak, sets the bound free,
supports the fallen, and raises those bowed down.

---

think more clearly. We feel more profoundly. Indeed, the word for soul (*neshama*) and breath (*neshima*) are closely related. "In the still silence of the turning world it is as if we hear all that lives sing a song of praise to God who brought the universe into being, sustains it, and guides the destinies of all things" (Rabbi J. Sacks).

Take a deep breath or two, recite the prayer and feel.

IYUN TEFILLA • עיון תפילה

נִשְׁמַת כָּל חַי תְּבָרֵךְ אֶת שִׁמְךָ – *The soul of all that lives will bless Your name.* The constant prayer of our soul is always striving to emerge from concealment to revelation, to spread through all the life-powers of our entire spirit and all the life-powers of our entire body (Rav Kook, *Olat Reiya*). As I read this prayer, I will try to allow my soul to peek out from its hiding place.

BIUR TEFILLA • ביאור תפילה

אֱלֹהֵי הָרִאשׁוֹנִים וְהָאַחֲרוֹנִים, אֱלוֹהַּ כָּל בְּרִיּוֹת אֲדוֹן כָּל תּוֹלָדוֹת – *Literally: God of the first and the last, God of all creations, Master of all nature.* Each phrase represents a different aspect of his dominion: He is the God of man, of animals, of the inanimate (Hida). On this day, our goal is to see ourselves as a part of and not apart from.

נִשְׁמַת[ב]

כָּל חַי תְּבָרֵךְ אֶת שִׁמְךָ,[ע] יהוה אֱלֹהֵינוּ
וְרוּחַ כָּל בָּשָׂר תְּפָאֵר וּתְרוֹמֵם זִכְרְךָ מַלְכֵּנוּ תָּמִיד.
מִן הָעוֹלָם וְעַד הָעוֹלָם אַתָּה אֵל
וּמִבַּלְעָדֶיךָ אֵין לָנוּ מֶלֶךְ גּוֹאֵל וּמוֹשִׁיעַ
פּוֹדֶה וּמַצִּיל וּמְפַרְנֵס וּמְרַחֵם
בְּכָל עֵת צָרָה וְצוּקָה אֵין לָנוּ מֶלֶךְ אֶלָּא אָתָּה.
אֱלֹהֵי הָרִאשׁוֹנִים וְהָאַחֲרוֹנִים, אֱלוֹהַּ כָּל בְּרִיּוֹת
אֲדוֹן כָּל תּוֹלָדוֹת,[ב] הַמְהֻלָּל בְּרֹב הַתִּשְׁבָּחוֹת
הַמְנַהֵג עוֹלָמוֹ בְּחֶסֶד וּבְרִיּוֹתָיו בְּרַחֲמִים.
וַיהוה לֹא יָנוּם וְלֹא יִישָׁן
הַמְעוֹרֵר יְשֵׁנִים וְהַמֵּקִיץ נִרְדָּמִים
וְהַמֵּשִׂיחַ אִלְּמִים וְהַמַּתִּיר אֲסוּרִים
וְהַסּוֹמֵךְ נוֹפְלִים וְהַזּוֹקֵף כְּפוּפִים.

BIUR TEFILLA • ביאור תפילה

נִשְׁמַת – *NISHMAT.*
As the *Psukei DeZimra* section nears its conclusion, as we get closer to the *Amida,* we move ever higher. We just spoke of the emergence of Israel from the splitting of the Sea and of a day when all will go up to Jerusalem, to Mount Zion. Now, on Shabbat and Yom Tov, we can speak as well about the ascendancy of our own soul. During the week, we immerse ourselves as we have these past minutes in God's presence in creation and in history but we do not necessarily have time to linger and pursue their impact upon us. Today, however, we can push ourselves a little further, reaching further inward even as we strive upward.

Hassidic tradition suggests that at this juncture we acquire a small piece of the *neshama yeteira* or "extra soul" that is a hallmark of Shabbat (Arizal, cited in *Petura deAba*). We breathe more deeply. We

To You alone we give thanks:
If our mouths were as full of song as the sea,
and our tongue with jubilation as its myriad waves,
if our lips were full of praise like the spacious heavens,
and our eyes shone like the sun and moon,
if our hands were outstretched like eagles of the sky,
and our feet as swift as hinds –
still we could not thank You enough,
LORD our God and God of our ancestors,
or bless Your name
for even one of the thousand thousands
and myriad myriads of favors
You did for our ancestors and for us.
You redeemed us from Egypt, LORD our God,
and freed us from the house of bondage.
In famine You nourished us;
in times of plenty You sustained us.
You delivered us from the sword, saved us from the plague,
and spared us from serious and lasting illness.
Until now Your mercies have helped us.
Your love has not forsaken us.
May You, LORD our God, never abandon us.[A]

ANI TEFILLA • אני תפילה

מֵחֶרֶב הִצַּלְתָּנוּ... וְאַל תִּטְּשֵׁנוּ... לָנֶצַח – *You delivered us from the sword... May You... never abandon us.* I must share with you what I experienced at a meeting of revering recovering alcoholics. It was a "gratitude meeting," at which one person after another expressed thankfulness for the second chance in life and for all of the wonderful things that happened since giving up drinking. The last person to speak said, "I am now sober for four years, and I wish I could tell you that they have been good. I lost my job when my company downsized. My wife divorced me and took custody of the children. I was unable to pay the mortgage, and the bank foreclosed on my house. Last week, the finance company repossessed my car. But I know that God did not bring me all this way only to walk out on me now." That is what we say in the *Nishmat* prayer... As individuals and as a nation, God did not allow us to survive much travail only to walk out on us now (Rabbi Abraham Twerski).

לְךָ לְבַדְּךָ אֲנַחְנוּ מוֹדִים.
אִלּוּ פִינוּ מָלֵא שִׁירָה כַּיָּם,ע וּלְשׁוֹנֵנוּ רִנָּה כַּהֲמוֹן גַּלָּיו
וְשִׂפְתוֹתֵינוּ שֶֽׁבַח כְּמֶרְחֲבֵי רָקִיעַ
וְעֵינֵינוּ מְאִירוֹת כַּשֶּֽׁמֶשׁ וְכַיָּרֵֽחַ
וְיָדֵינוּ פְרוּשׂוֹת כְּנִשְׁרֵי שָׁמָֽיִם, וְרַגְלֵינוּ קַלּוֹת כָּאַיָּלוֹת
אֵין אֲנַחְנוּ מַסְפִּיקִים לְהוֹדוֹת לְךָ
יהוה אֱלֹהֵינוּ וֵאלֹהֵי אֲבוֹתֵינוּ
וּלְבָרֵךְ אֶת שְׁמֶךָ
עַל אַחַת מֵאֶֽלֶף אֶֽלֶף אַלְפֵי אֲלָפִים
וְרִבֵּי רְבָבוֹת פְּעָמִים הַטּוֹבוֹת
שֶׁעָשִֽׂיתָ עִם אֲבוֹתֵינוּ וְעִמָּנוּ.
מִמִּצְרַיִם גְּאַלְתָּנוּ,ע יהוה אֱלֹהֵינוּ, וּמִבֵּית עֲבָדִים פְּדִיתָנוּ
בְּרָעָב זַנְתָּנוּ וּבְשָׂבָע כִּלְכַּלְתָּנוּ
מֵחֶֽרֶב הִצַּלְתָּנוּ וּמִדֶּֽבֶר מִלַּטְתָּנוּ
וּמֵחֳלָיִם רָעִים וְנֶאֱמָנִים דִּלִּיתָנוּ.
עַד הֵֽנָּה עֲזָרֽוּנוּ רַחֲמֶֽיךָ, וְלֹא עֲזָבֽוּנוּ חֲסָדֶֽיךָ
וְאַל תִּטְּשֵֽׁנוּ, יהוה אֱלֹהֵינוּ, לָנֶֽצַח.א

IYUN TEFILLA • עיון תפילה

אִלּוּ פִינוּ מָלֵא שִׁירָה כַּיָּם – *If our mouths were as full of song as the sea.* Of course, the sea is never really full. Neither should be our appreciation.

מִמִּצְרַיִם גְּאַלְתָּנוּ – *You redeemed us from Egypt.* The word for Egypt (*Mitzrayim*) is often associated with the word *meitzarim* which means straits, a bad or difficult situation. Just as Hashem saved us there, so too does the redemption from Egypt spill easily into other areas of human suffering where we acknowledge His relieving hand: famine, wars, plague, illness.

Perhaps, too, this is the source for a custom ascribed to Rabbi Yehuda HaḤasid (twelfth century) that before one travels on a journey, something that was filled with danger in those days, one should vow to recite this prayer (*Nishmat*) upon arrival at one's destination (*Ḥemdat Yamim*).

Therefore the limbs You formed within us,
the spirit and soul You breathed into our nostrils,
and the tongue You placed in our mouth –
they will thank and bless,[I]
praise and glorify, exalt and esteem,
hallow and do homage to Your name, O our King.
For every mouth shall give thanks to You,
every tongue vow allegiance to You,
every knee shall bend to You,[B]
every upright body shall bow to You,
all hearts shall fear You,
and our innermost being sing praises to Your name,
as is written:

"All my bones shall say:[I] LORD, who is like You? Ps. 35
You save the poor from one stronger than him,
the poor and needy from one who would rob him."

Who is like You?
Who is equal to You?
Who can be compared to You?
O great, mighty and awesome God, God Most High,
Maker of heaven and earth.

---

yet others who use their hands and their actions to praise You or bring attention to You. I alone could not do it all but, as a community, we can merge our strengths to form a powerful unified voice (Hatam Sofer). My praise merges with that of others and we become a sum of all our parts. We are a praying community to whom I contribute what I can and from whom I draw the strength I do not have.

כָּל עַצְמֹתַי תֹּאמַרְנָה – *All of my bones will say.* From here one may learn that one should sway one's body during prayer (*Sefer Hassidim*).

BIUR TEFILLA • ביאור תפילה

וְכָל קוֹמָה לְפָנֶיךָ תִשְׁתַּחֲוֶה – *Every upright body shall bow to You.* Rabbi Barukh of Mezbizh said that the meaning is not that every person standing will bow; rather, a person can bow down even if he is standing upright, as long as his heart his broken.

עַל כֵּן אֵבָרִים שֶׁפִּלַּגְתָּ בָּנוּ
וְרוּחַ וּנְשָׁמָה שֶׁנָּפַחְתָּ בְּאַפֵּנוּ
וְלָשׁוֹן אֲשֶׁר שַׂמְתָּ בְּפִינוּ
הֵן הֵם יוֹדוּ וִיבָרְכוּ[ע] וִישַׁבְּחוּ וִיפָאֲרוּ
וִירוֹמְמוּ וְיַעֲרִיצוּ וְיַקְדִּישׁוּ וְיַמְלִיכוּ אֶת שִׁמְךָ מַלְכֵּנוּ
כִּי כָל פֶּה לְךָ יוֹדֶה
וְכָל לָשׁוֹן לְךָ תִשָּׁבַע
וְכָל בֶּרֶךְ לְךָ תִכְרַע
וְכָל קוֹמָה לְפָנֶיךָ תִשְׁתַּחֲוֶה[ב]
וְכָל לְבָבוֹת יִירָאוּךָ
וְכָל קֶרֶב וּכְלָיוֹת יְזַמְּרוּ לִשְׁמֶךָ
כַּדָּבָר שֶׁכָּתוּב

כָּל עַצְמֹתַי תֹּאמַרְנָה[ע] יהוה מִי כָמוֹךָ תהלים לה
מַצִּיל עָנִי מֵחָזָק מִמֶּנּוּ, וְעָנִי וְאֶבְיוֹן מִגֹּזְלוֹ:

מִי יִדְמֶה לָּךְ
וּמִי יִשְׁוֶה לָּךְ
וּמִי יַעֲרָךְ לָךְ
הָאֵל הַגָּדוֹל, הַגִּבּוֹר וְהַנּוֹרָא
אֵל עֶלְיוֹן, קֹנֵה שָׁמַיִם וָאָרֶץ.

IYUN TEFILLA • עיון תפילה

עַל כֵּן אֵבָרִים שֶׁפִּלַּגְתָּ בָּנוּ וְרוּחַ וּנְשָׁמָה... וְלָשׁוֹן... הֵן הֵם יוֹדוּ וִיבָרְכוּ – *Therefore The limbs You formed within us, the spirit and soul…the tongue...they will thank and bless.* I cannot do it all alone. But there are people standing beside me right now who have great voices or use their voices for positive purpose, there are those who use their intellects and

▸ We will laud, praise and glorify You and bless Your holy name,
as it is said:

"Of David. Bless the LORD, O my soul, *Ps. 103*
and all that is within me bless His holy name."

הָאֵל God – in Your absolute power,
Great – in the glory of Your name,
Mighty – for ever,
Awesome[B] – in Your awe-inspiring deeds,
The King – who sits on a throne.
High and lofty

The Leader begins here:

HE INHABITS ETERNITY;
exalted and holy is His name.
And it is written:

Sing joyfully to the LORD, you righteous, *Ps. 33*
for praise from the upright is seemly.

▸ By the mouth of the upright You shall be praised.
By the words of the righteous You shall be blessed.
By the tongue of the devout You shall be extolled,
And in the midst of the holy You shall be sanctified.

HILKHOT TEFILLA • הלכות תפילה

There is often a change in the *ḥazan* (prayer leader) at this point as we make the transition from the *Psukei DeZimra* section of the service which we are completing, to the next section (called *Birkhot Shema*) which is of greater *halakhic* significance. However, there are different customs about where the new *ḥazan* takes over and different communities chose different lines as the starting point depending upon the theme of the day (e.g. *Kol Bo*, 37). Nowadays, most commonly, on Shabbat, he begins with the words "He inhabits eternity" (שׁוֹכֵן עַד), focusing on His role as Creator; on Yom Tov, he begins "God in Your absolute power" (הָאֵל בְּתַעֲצוּמוֹת עֻזֶּךָ) to emphasize His power

This **HILKHOT TEFILLA** *continues on page 291.*

◂ נְהַלֶּלְךָ וּנְשַׁבֵּחֲךָ וּנְפָאֶרְךָ וּנְבָרֵךְ אֶת שֵׁם קָדְשֶׁךָ
כָּאָמוּר

תהלים קג
לְדָוִד, בָּרְכִי נַפְשִׁי אֶת־יהוה
וְכָל־קְרָבַי אֶת־שֵׁם קָדְשׁוֹ:

הָאֵל בְּתַעֲצוּמוֹת עֻזֶּךָ
הַגָּדוֹל בִּכְבוֹד שְׁמֶךָ
הַגִּבּוֹר לָנֶצַח וְהַנּוֹרָא[ב] בְּנוֹרְאוֹתֶיךָ
הַמֶּלֶךְ הַיּוֹשֵׁב עַל כִּסֵּא
רָם וְנִשָּׂא

The שליח ציבור *begins here:*

שׁוֹכֵן עַד

מָרוֹם וְקָדוֹשׁ שְׁמוֹ
וְכָתוּב

תהלים לג
רַנְּנוּ צַדִּיקִים בַּיהוה, לַיְשָׁרִים נָאוָה תְהִלָּה:

◂ בְּפִי יְשָׁרִים תִּתְהַלָּל
וּבְדִבְרֵי צַדִּיקִים תִּתְבָּרַךְ
וּבִלְשׁוֹן חֲסִידִים תִּתְרוֹמָם
וּבְקֶרֶב קְדוֹשִׁים תִּתְקַדָּשׁ

BIUR TEFILLA • ביאור תפילה

הָאֵל בְּתַעֲצֻמוֹת עֻזֶּךָ... הַגָּדוֹל... הַגִּבּוֹר... וְהַנּוֹרָא – *God – in Your absolute power, Great... Mighty... Awesome.* Look a few lines above for these very same adjectives, though here they are explained. These lines are a kind of midrash on those which precede.

וּבְמַקְהֲלוֹת And in the assemblies
of tens of thousands of Your people, the house of Israel,
with joyous song shall Your name, our King,
be glorified in every generation.
‣ For this is the duty of all creatures before You,
LORD our God and God of our ancestors:
to thank, praise, laud, glorify, exalt,
honor, bless, raise high and acclaim –
even beyond all the words of song and praise
of David, son of Jesse, Your servant, Your anointed.

The custom is to stand from the beginning of "Yishtabaḥ" until after "Barekhu" on page 296.

יִשְׁתַּבַּח May Your name be praised[B] for ever, our King,
the great and holy God, King in heaven and on earth.
For to You, LORD our God and God of our ancestors,

Shema) has not yet begun, should any talking be permitted?

There are those authorities who say it is not (Rif on *Berakhot* 23a; Rosh 5, 5; *Kol Bo*, *siman* 4). Their reasoning is because if *Pesukei DeZimra* is really intended as the praise one should say before one prays, then isn't it contradictory to interrupt that process? After all, when traveling on a straight path it makes no sense to take a detour, especially one that will get in the way of reaching one's destination with the right frame of mind. Why work so hard getting into the mood, only to get sidetracked and have to start over? Nevertheless, one sees that interrupting at this point, between units, is probably different from interrupting in the middle of a unit itself, and so some communities have the practice to allow certain interruptions (such as the recitation of *Shir HaMa'alot*) that are still related to the act of prayer or some other community related need (See Rema and *Mishna Berura* 54:3).

HILKHOT TEFILLA • הלכות תפילה

The reason for standing probably has less to do with anything intrinsic to the blessing itself (though recall we stood for the opening blessing of *Barukh She'Amar* as well) than to its context. We want to make sure that there is no interruption from one section to another of the prayer service. Parenthetically, that is why the *ḥazan* or leader who

This **HILKHOT TEFILLA** *continues on page 293.*

וּבְמַקְהֲלוֹת רִבְבוֹת עַמְּךָ בֵּית יִשְׂרָאֵל
בְּרִנָּה יִתְפָּאַר שִׁמְךָ מַלְכֵּנוּ בְּכָל דּוֹר וָדוֹר
◂ שֶׁכֵּן חוֹבַת כָּל הַיְצוּרִים
לְפָנֶיךָ יהוה אֱלֹהֵינוּ וֵאלֹהֵי אֲבוֹתֵינוּ
לְהוֹדוֹת, לְהַלֵּל, לְשַׁבֵּחַ, לְפָאֵר, לְרוֹמֵם
לְהַדֵּר, לְבָרֵךְ, לְעַלֵּה וּלְקַלֵּס
עַל כָּל דִּבְרֵי שִׁירוֹת וְתִשְׁבְּחוֹת
דָּוִד בֶּן יִשַׁי, עַבְדְּךָ מְשִׁיחֶךָ.

The custom is to stand from the beginning of יִשְׁתַּבַּח *until after* בָּרְכוּ *on page 297.*

יִשְׁתַּבַּח[ב] שִׁמְךָ לָעַד, מַלְכֵּנוּ
הָאֵל הַמֶּלֶךְ הַגָּדוֹל וְהַקָּדוֹשׁ בַּשָּׁמַיִם וּבָאָרֶץ
כִּי לְךָ נָאֶה, יהוה אֱלֹהֵינוּ וֵאלֹהֵי אֲבוֹתֵינוּ

---

symbolized in the Exodus (*Levush*), and on Rosh HaShana and Yom Kippur, he begins with "The King" (הַמֶּלֶךְ) to emphasize Hashem's sovereignty.

BIUR TEFILLA • ביאור תפילה

יִשְׁתַּבַּח – *May Your name be praised.* As we have noted, *Pesukei DeZimra* is a single unit bounded by the blessing *Barukh She'amar* at the beginning and the blessing *Yishtabaḥ* at the end. As such, no interruptions are generally permitted. What about between *Yishtabaḥ* and *Barekhu*? If the first unit (*Pesukei DeZimra*) is complete, and the next unit (*Birkhot Keriat*

ANI TEFILLA • אני תפילה

When I was a child, a group of us were sitting on the ground enjoying one another's company. I was absentmindedly picking at the blades of grass around me when an adult began to yell at me that it was forbidden to tear plants on Shabbat. I recall thinking, "what's the big deal? The world will not come to a crashing end simply because I tore this blade of grass! What difference should it make to God that I do this?" It was only later that I realized that on Shabbat, our task is not to display our ability to control nature but, rather, to display our understanding that we are a part of nature. In this respect, on Shabbat, I am no different than a blade of grass.

it is right to offer song and praise,
hymn and psalm,
strength and dominion,
eternity, greatness and power,
song of praise and glory,
holiness and kingship,
▸ blessings and thanks, from now and for ever.
Blessed are You, LORD, God and King,
exalted in praises,
God of thanksgivings,
Master of wonders,
who delights in hymns of song,
King, God, Giver of life to the worlds.[B]

On Shabbat Shuva, many congregations open the Ark and say this psalm responsively, verse by verse.

שִׁיר הַמַּעֲלוֹת A song of ascents. From the depths I have called to You, LORD. LORD, hear my voice; let Your ears be attentive to my plea. If You, LORD, should keep account of sins, O LORD, who could stand? But with You there is forgiveness, that You may be held in awe. I wait for the LORD, my soul waits, and in His word I put my hope. My soul waits for the LORD more than watchmen wait for the morning, more than watchmen wait for the morning. Israel, put your hope in the LORD, for with the LORD there is loving-kindness, and great is His power to redeem. It is He who will redeem Israel from all their sins. *Ps. 130*

BIUR TEFILLA • ביאור תפילה

יִשְׁתַּבַּח...מֶלֶךְ, אֵל, חֵי הָעוֹלָמִים – *May Your name be praised... King, God, Giver of life to the worlds.* At the beginning of *Pesukei DeZimra* we said that we would praise Hashem and make His name great in our eyes via the recitation of *Tehillim*: "With praises...we will exalt" (בִּשְׁבָחוֹת...נְגַדֶּלְךָ) We conclude here by saying that, thanks to our focusing on the *Tehillim* that we just said, we are now more aware of how

This **BIUR TEFILLA** *continues on page 93.*

שִׁיר וּשְׁבָחָה, הַלֵּל וְזִמְרָה
עֹז וּמֶמְשָׁלָה, נֶצַח, גְּדֻלָּה וּגְבוּרָה
תְּהִלָּה וְתִפְאֶרֶת, קְדֻשָּׁה וּמַלְכוּת
בְּרָכוֹת וְהוֹדָאוֹת, מֵעַתָּה וְעַד עוֹלָם.
בָּרוּךְ אַתָּה יהוה
אֵל מֶלֶךְ גָּדוֹל בַּתִּשְׁבָּחוֹת
אֵל הַהוֹדָאוֹת
אֲדוֹן הַנִּפְלָאוֹת
הַבּוֹחֵר בְּשִׁירֵי זִמְרָה
מֶלֶךְ, אֵל, חֵי הָעוֹלָמִים.[ב]

On שבת שובה*, many congregations open the* ארון קודש *and say this psalm responsively, verse by verse.*

תהלים קל

שִׁיר הַמַּעֲלוֹת, מִמַּעֲמַקִּים קְרָאתִיךָ יהוה: אֲדֹנָי שִׁמְעָה בְקוֹלִי, תִּהְיֶינָה אָזְנֶיךָ קַשֻּׁבוֹת לְקוֹל תַּחֲנוּנָי: אִם־עֲוֹנוֹת תִּשְׁמָר־יָהּ, אֲדֹנָי מִי יַעֲמֹד: כִּי־עִמְּךָ הַסְּלִיחָה, לְמַעַן תִּוָּרֵא: קִוִּיתִי יהוה קִוְּתָה נַפְשִׁי, וְלִדְבָרוֹ הוֹחָלְתִּי: נַפְשִׁי לַאדֹנָי, מִשֹּׁמְרִים לַבֹּקֶר, שֹׁמְרִים לַבֹּקֶר: יַחֵל יִשְׂרָאֵל אֶל יהוה, כִּי־עִם־יהוה הַחֶסֶד, וְהַרְבֵּה עִמּוֹ פְדוּת: וְהוּא יִפְדֶּה אֶת־יִשְׂרָאֵל, מִכֹּל עֲוֹנוֹתָיו:

---

takes over for the next upcoming section of the service already does so for this prayer even though the *Psukei DeZimra* section is not yet complete. Since we do not want any interruption between *Yishtabaḥ* and the *Kaddish* and *Barekhu* which follow, for which we have to stand, everyone stands in anticipation of those prayers so that no movement is necessary (Rema 51:7, *Baḥ* 51).

As indicated previously (page 213), Ashkenazic practice is generally to stand for any prayer like *Kaddish* and *Barekhu* which are considered a *davar she-be-kedusha*, an opportunity to publicly sanctify Hashem's Name.

HALF KADDISH

Leader: יִתְגַּדַּל Magnified and sanctified
may His great name be,
in the world He created by His will.
May He establish His kingdom
in your lifetime and in your days,
and in the lifetime of all the house of Israel,
swiftly and soon –
and say: Amen.

All: May His great name[A] be blessed
for ever and all time.

Leader: Blessed and praised,
glorified and exalted,
raised and honored,
uplifted and lauded
be the name of the Holy One,
blessed be He,
beyond any blessing,
song, praise and consolation
uttered in the world –
and say: Amen.

ANI TEFILLA • אני תפילה

יְהֵא שְׁמֵהּ רַבָּא – *May His great name. Whoever says "yeheh shemeh raba..." with all his strength, the Heavenly Court rips up any negative decree against him.* (*Shabbat* 119b)

"With all his strength" – with his complete concentration (Rashi).

חצי קדיש

ש״ץ: יִתְגַּדַּל וְיִתְקַדַּשׁ שְׁמֵהּ רַבָּא (קהל: אָמֵן)
בְּעָלְמָא דִּי בְרָא כִרְעוּתֵהּ
וְיַמְלִיךְ מַלְכוּתֵהּ
בְּחַיֵּיכוֹן וּבְיוֹמֵיכוֹן
וּבְחַיֵּי דְכָל בֵּית יִשְׂרָאֵל
בַּעֲגָלָא וּבִזְמַן קָרִיב
וְאִמְרוּ אָמֵן. (קהל: אָמֵן)

קהל וש״ץ: יְהֵא שְׁמֵהּ רַבָּא[א] מְבָרַךְ לְעָלַם וּלְעָלְמֵי עָלְמַיָּא.

ש״ץ: יִתְבָּרַךְ וְיִשְׁתַּבַּח וְיִתְפָּאַר וְיִתְרוֹמַם וְיִתְנַשֵּׂא
וְיִתְהַדָּר וְיִתְעַלֶּה וְיִתְהַלָּל
שְׁמֵהּ דְּקֻדְשָׁא בְּרִיךְ הוּא (קהל: בְּרִיךְ הוּא)
לְעֵלָּא מִן כָּל בִּרְכָתָא
/ בשבת שובה: לְעֵלָּא לְעֵלָּא מִכָּל בִּרְכָתָא/
וְשִׁירָתָא, תֻּשְׁבְּחָתָא וְנֶחֱמָתָא
דַּאֲמִירָן בְּעָלְמָא
וְאִמְרוּ אָמֵן. (קהל: אָמֵן)

---

great You are: "exalted in praises" (מֶלֶךְ גָּדוֹל בַּתִּשְׁבָּחוֹת).

It is said that the 15 nouns here correspond to the 15 steps leading from one part of the *Beit HaMikdash* to another. On Shabbat, it may also be said to symbolize the 15 psalms that we just finished reciting (the nine added for Shabbat plus the six said every day). As we conclude this part of the service, we get one step closer to our personal encounter with Hashem in the *Amida*.

BLESSINGS OF THE SHEMA

The following blessing and response are said only in the presence of a minyan.

Leader: *Bow* **BLESS**
Stand straight the LORD, the blessed One.

Congregation: *Bow* Bless *Stand straight* the LORD, the blessed One, for ever and all time.

Leader: *Bow* Bless *Stand straight* the LORD, the blessed One, for ever and all time.

---

join him in the recitation of the *berakhot* of *Keriat Shema* which are about to follow. In effect, he says, "Please join me so that I am not saying this alone, but rather we can all say this together as a community. Join with me, and have the intention to sanctify God's name, to fulfill the commandment regarding the recitation of the *Shema.* Join me, so that I can help you, and you can help me. We're on the verge of entering the palace of the *Amida*; let's go together." Implied here as well is the thought that if for some reason you are having a particularly difficult time focusing today, then listen to me, answer *Amen* to the blessings of the *Shema* and to the *Shema* itself. We thus transform our prayer from being not only a private affair, but a communal one as well.

INTRODUCTION TO KERIAT SHEMA AND ITS BLESSINGS

The next section of the service has at its center the *Shema*, one of the most significant prayers in all of Jewish liturgy. Its recitation twice a day, in the morning and the evening, is considered a commandment, and like most commandments it is accompanied by blessings. In this particular case, however, the Rabbis mandated that there be two blessings before the *Shema* and one after it (*Berakhot* 11a). Each blessing, moreover, has its own theme, one which is inextricably tied to each of the different themes of the *Shema* itself.

This **INTRODUCTION** *continues on page 299.*

קריאת שמע וברכותיה

The following blessing and response are said only in the presence of a מנין.

ש״ץ: *Bow* בָּרְכוּ

אֶת *Stand straight* יהוה הַמְבֹרָךְ.

קהל: *Bow* בָּרוּךְ *Stand straight* יהוה הַמְבֹרָךְ לְעוֹלָם וָעֶד.

ש״ץ: *Bow* בָּרוּךְ *Stand straight* יהוה הַמְבֹרָךְ לְעוֹלָם וָעֶד.

INTRODUCTION TO BAREKHU

The custom of bowing at this point is based on Divrei HaYamim I 29:20, "David said to the whole assembly, 'Now bless the Lord your God.' All the assembly blessed the Lord God of their fathers and bowed their heads low to the Lord and the King."

Until this point, although we have been praying with a *minyan*, the truth is that our prayer has been relatively individualistic. The service until now has been a warm-up exercise, a way for us to begin to get into the right frame of mind for the prayers which are to come, especially the *Amida*.

At this point, then, we move one step closer to our encounter with Hashem by formally joining together with the rest of the *tzibbur* or congregation.

One benefit of joining with others is that I am sometimes able to get "into it" much better, when everyone around me is doing the same thing, than when I am alone. Have you ever been to a sporting event or a concert and looked around at the thousands of people surrounding you, all experiencing the same emotions as you at that moment? That can be such a powerful experience. We aspire to that same experience in communal prayer. If I'm not in the mood, or am having a difficult time focusing, the presence of other people helps me to get into the right frame of mind. I allow myself to be drawn in to their devotion or excitement or participation. And so the *Ḥazan* here issues an invitation to the entire congregation to

The custom is to sit from this point until the Amida, since the predominant emotion of this section of the prayers is love rather than awe. Conversation is forbidden until after the Amida.

בָּרוּךְ Blessed are You, LORD our God,
King of the Universe,
who forms light and creates darkness,[B] *Is. 45*
makes peace and creates all.[B]

All will thank You.
All will praise You.
All[B] will declare: Nothing is as holy as the LORD.
All will exalt You, Selah, You who form all –

BIUR TEFILLA • ביאור תפילה

יוֹצֵר אוֹר וּבוֹרֵא חֹשֶׁךְ – *Who forms light and creates darkness.* Continuing the theme of *Pesukei DeZimra,* the theme of this first blessing before the *Shema* is "Hashem as Creator." From the beginning, we acknowledge that He is the One solely responsible for the world as we know it in all of its perfect harmony. At the same time, the blessing slides a step further into the theme of a similar relationship that Hashem has with the heavenly world, where He is also acknowledged as Creator. There is thus a balance between the lower world and the upper, which means that the whole universe is in harmony. The blessing thereby serves as an important prelude to our recitation of the *Shema* where we are called upon to declare His Oneness.

וּבוֹרֵא אֶת הַכֹּל – *And creates all.* There are those who say that the phrasing of this blessing was chosen specifically to deny the claim of those believers in ancient religions who thought there was a god of light and a god of darkness, one who reigned when good things happened and one who reigned when bad things happened. Interestingly, the phrasing is taken from a verse in *Yeshayahu* but was actually changed here. The original says that God "makes peace and creates evil," whereas here the Rabbis changed the ending to say "makes peace and creates everything" (*Yeshayahu* 45:7). The lesson is clear as we approach the *Shema* – there is only one God.

הַכֹּל...וְהַכֹּל...וְהַכֹּל – *All...all...all.* The opening blessing of this section spoke of Hashem as the one who "fashions light" and "created all." During the weekday service, the next passage primarily emphasizes the first theme, light. But today, another section is inserted, this one emphasizing the word "all," as indicated by the unusual number of times it appears.

What do you think this is meant to convey and why might it be an appropriate theme for today?

The custom is to sit from this point until the עמידה*, since the predominant emotion of this section of the prayers is love rather than awe. Conversation is forbidden until after the* עמידה*.*

בָּרוּךְ אַתָּה יהוה אֱלֹהֵינוּ מֶלֶךְ הָעוֹלָם
יוֹצֵר אוֹר וּבוֹרֵא חֹשֶׁךְ ישעיה מה
עֹשֶׂה שָׁלוֹם וּבוֹרֵא אֶת הַכֹּל.

הַכֹּל יוֹדְוּךָ וְהַכֹּל יְשַׁבְּחְוּךָ
וְהַכֹּל יֹאמְרוּ אֵין קָדוֹשׁ כַּיהוה
הַכֹּל יְרוֹמְמְוּךָ סֶּלָה, יוֹצֵר הַכֹּל.

The structure might therefore be described as follows:

	NAME		CONTENT	THEME
Blessing 1	יוֹצֵר אוֹר	*Yotzer Or*	Creator of light	Creation
Blessing 2	אַהֲבָה רַבָּה	*Ahava Raba*	Love of Israel as manifest in the giving of the Torah	Revelation
Shema	שְׁמַע יִשְׂרָאֵל	Paragraph 1 Paragraph 2 Paragraph 3		Acceptance of Sovereignty of God Acceptance of the Commandments (revelation) Exodus from Egypt (redemption)
Blessing 3	גָּאַל יִשְׂרָאֵל	*Ga'al Yisrael*	The Exodus from Egypt	Redemption. The one overarching theme of the unit is that there is only one God (*Hashem eḥad*), whose Presence can be felt in all three of the particular domains mentioned in the blessings and in the *Shema*. Think about these themes as we move ever closer to our rendezvous with the One.

HILKHOT TEFILLA • הלכות תפילה

Because this entire section is viewed as one indivisible unit, no talking is permitted unless it is an emergency or for the sake of the prayer service itself. See Table of Permitted Responses page 848.

the God who daily opens the doors of the gates of the East
and cleaves the windows of the sky,
who brings out the sun from its place and the moon from its abode,
giving light to the whole world and its inhabitants
whom He created by the attribute of compassion.
In compassion He gives light to the earth and its inhabitants,
and in His goodness daily, continually, renews the work of creation.
He is the King who alone was exalted since time began,
praised, glorified and raised high from days of old.
Eternal God, in Your great compassion,
have compassion on us,
Lord of our strength, Rock of our refuge,
Shield of our salvation, Stronghold of our safety.

אֵין כְּעֶרְכְּךָ None can be compared to You,
there is none besides You;
None without You.
Who is like You?

▸ None can be compared to You,
Lord our God – in this world.
There is none besides You, our King –
in the life of the World to Come.
There is none but You, our Redeemer –
in the days of the Messiah.
There is none like You, our Savior –
at the resurrection of the dead.

מְחַדֵּשׁ בְּכָל יוֹם – *Daily... renews the work of creation.* Creation was not a one-time event. It happens anew every day; one need only open one's eyes to the miracle of it all. The sun comes up, the flowers reappear, babies are born. Creation is dynamic and ongoing; life is beautiful.

If at the beginning of the blessing there was a refutation of there being more than one God, here the siddur refutes the idea advanced by the Greek philosopher Aristotle that God created the world and walked away. Instead, Hashem's presence is always felt, if one only looks for it.

Where have you seen it thus far today? Where can you see it?

הָאֵל הַפּוֹתֵחַ בְּכָל יוֹם דַּלְתוֹת שַׁעֲרֵי מִזְרָח
וּבוֹקֵעַ חַלּוֹנֵי רָקִיעַ
מוֹצִיא חַמָּה מִמְּקוֹמָהּ וּלְבָנָה מִמְּכוֹן שִׁבְתָּהּ
וּמֵאִיר לָעוֹלָם כֻּלּוֹ וּלְיוֹשְׁבָיו שֶׁבָּרָא בְּמִדַּת הָרַחֲמִים.
הַמֵּאִיר לָאָרֶץ וְלַדָּרִים עָלֶיהָ בְּרַחֲמִים[ע]
וּבְטוּבוֹ מְחַדֵּשׁ בְּכָל יוֹם[ע] תָּמִיד מַעֲשֵׂה בְרֵאשִׁית.
הַמֶּלֶךְ הַמְרוֹמָם לְבַדּוֹ מֵאָז
הַמְשֻׁבָּח וְהַמְפֹאָר וְהַמִּתְנַשֵּׂא מִימוֹת עוֹלָם.
אֱלֹהֵי עוֹלָם, בְּרַחֲמֶיךָ הָרַבִּים רַחֵם עָלֵינוּ
אֲדוֹן עֻזֵּנוּ, צוּר מִשְׂגַּבֵּנוּ, מָגֵן יִשְׁעֵנוּ, מִשְׂגָּב בַּעֲדֵנוּ.

אֵין כְּעֶרְכֶּךָ
וְאֵין זוּלָתֶךָ
אֶפֶס בִּלְתֶּךָ
וּמִי דּוֹמֶה לָּךְ.

◂ אֵין כְּעֶרְכְּךָ, יהוה אֱלֹהֵינוּ, בָּעוֹלָם הַזֶּה
וְאֵין זוּלָתְךָ, מַלְכֵּנוּ, לְחַיֵּי הָעוֹלָם הַבָּא
אֶפֶס בִּלְתְּךָ, גּוֹאֲלֵנוּ, לִימוֹת הַמָּשִׁיחַ
וְאֵין דּוֹמֶה לְּךָ, מוֹשִׁיעֵנוּ, לִתְחִיַּת הַמֵּתִים.

IYUN TEFILLA • עיון תפילה

הַמֵּאִיר לָאָרֶץ וְלַדָּרִים עָלֶיהָ בְּרַחֲמִים – *In compassion He gives light to the earth and its inhabitants.* If the sun were closer to the Earth, we would be like Venus – the oceans would boil away. If it were further away, we would be like Mars – the oceans would be frozen. We would no longer be in what astronomers call a Goldilocks Zone, a place that is situated in just the right location relative to its star. The continued existence of the planet is dependent upon His *raḥamim* (mercy).

אֵל אָדוֹן God, Lord of all creation,[BI]
the Blessed, is blessed by every soul.
His greatness and goodness fill the world;
knowledge and wisdom surround Him.[I]

Exalted above the holy Ḥayyot,
adorned in glory on the Chariot;
Merit and right are before His throne,
kindness and compassion before His glory.

---

with the old question of why did God bring the world into being? The letters of the *Alef-Beit* symbolize the written word of the Torah, the demands of which bring purpose and meaning to our world (Rabbi I. Wohlgemuth).

ANI TEFILLA • אני תפילה

A young illiterate boy came to shul and wanted to pray but had never been taught how to read. And so he simply recited the Alef-Beit over and over again. He then said to God: "I don't know the prayers. All I know are the letters of the Alef-Beit. Please take the letters and turn them into the right words to reflect what I feel in my heart." The Ba'al Shem Tov said that the boy's prayer broke through the gates of heaven, and enabled everyone else's prayers to enter as well.

IYUN TEFILLA • עיון תפילה

גָּדְלוֹ וְטוּבוֹ מָלֵא עוֹלָם, דַּעַת וּתְבוּנָה סוֹבְבִים אוֹתוֹ – *His greatness and goodness fill the world; knowledge and wisdom surround Him.* Hashem cannot be seen but that does not mean that He cannot be perceived. When one views the intricacy of creation, the sheer complexity of all of life down to the most basic unit that science will allow, one cannot help but feel that it is filled with "knowledge and wisdom." They surround Him, even as they leave Him invisible (*Dover Shalom*).

ANI TEFILLA • אני תפילה

A philosopher once came to Rabbi Meir and told him, "I don't believe in God. I feel that the universe came into being by itself, of its own accord, without any outside help." Rabbi Meir did not reply. A few days later, he came to the philosopher, and showed him a beautiful piece of poetry, written in a find hand on smooth white parchment. The philosopher looked at the parchment and admired it. He asked, "Who is the great poet who wrote this lovely poem? Who was the talented scribe who copied it?" Rabbi Meir

This **ANI TEFILLA** *continues on page 305.*

אֵל אָדוֹן עַל כָּל הַמַּעֲשִׂים
בָּרוּךְ וּמְבֹרָךְ בְּפִי כָּל נְשָׁמָה
גָּדְלוֹ וְטוּבוֹ מָלֵא עוֹלָם
דַּעַת וּתְבוּנָה סוֹבְבִים אוֹתוֹ.

הַמִּתְגָּאֶה עַל חַיּוֹת הַקֹּדֶשׁ
וְנֶהְדָּר בְּכָבוֹד עַל הַמֶּרְכָּבָה
זְכוּת וּמִישׁוֹר לִפְנֵי כִסְאוֹ
חֶסֶד וְרַחֲמִים לִפְנֵי כְבוֹדוֹ.

IYUN TEFILLA • עיון תפילה

אֵל אָדוֹן עַל כָּל הַמַּעֲשִׂים – *God, Lord of all creation.* Whereas the weekday prayer has 22 words in alphabetical order to describe this (...אֵל בָּרוּךְ גְּדוֹל דֵּעָה), today we add 22 complete lines, each of which begins with a successive letter of the *Alef-Beit.*

Why are certain prayers constructed this way? There is no one correct answer. One possibility comes from the experience that some of us have had of being in a place that was of such overwhelming beauty, a place that filled us with such awe, that we could not adequately describe it. There is a word here for every letter of the alphabet, but these are just representatives for every word in the entire language that we could possibly use to describe the feelings that we have at this moment. It's not only about what the words mean but about how they help us feel.

Alternatively, the blessing grapples

BIUR TEFILLA • ביאור תפילה

אֵל אָדוֹן עַל כָּל הַמַּעֲשִׂים – *God, Lord of all creation.* Only on Shabbat and Yom Tov is this special hymn added. Its mystical overtones are reminiscent of the vision of the divine chariot recorded in *Yeḥezkel* 1 and are reflected as well in the insistence of some that not a letter of it be changed (*Yesod veShoresh haAvoda*). Yet it also stands on its own as a song of great mystery and splendor inviting all to recognize not only the world's beauty but its dynamism as well. The sun and moon and stars are filled with vitality, they are miracles that dance across the heavens lighting up the sky. So, too, should they have that effect upon us as their "happiness" becomes our own, for on this day in particular we are all creations.

When did you last notice the miracle of the sun? The mystery of the moon? Consider them now.

Good are the radiant stars our God created;
He formed them with knowledge,
understanding, and deliberation.[1]
He gave them strength and might
to rule throughout the world.

Full of splendor, radiating light,
beautiful is their splendor throughout the world.
Glad as they go forth, joyous as they return,
they fulfill with awe their Creator's will.

Glory and honor they give to His name,
jubilation and song at the mention of His majesty.
He called the sun into being and it shone with light.
He looked and fashioned the form of the moon.

All the hosts on high give Him praise;
the Seraphim, Ophanim and holy Hayyot
ascribe glory and greatness –

IYUN TEFILLA • עיון תפילה

יְצָרָם בְּדַעַת בְּבִינָה וּבְהַשְׂכֵּל – *He formed them with knowledge, understanding, and deliberation.* If you want to know God, look carefully at all of His creations. As the Rambam (*Yesodei HaTorah* 2:2) says: "What is the path [a person should take] to attain love and fear of Him? When a person contemplates His wondrous and great deeds and creations, and appreciates His infinite wisdom that surpasses all comparison, he will immediately love, praise, and glorify [Him], yearning with tremendous desire to know [God's] great name, as David stated: 'My soul thirsts for Hashem, for the living God' [Psalms 42:3]."

Seen in this light, the siddur may be understood to mean that astronomy, biology, anatomy, and the like can all be used as vehicles for getting to know God better.

When you read about these subjects, do you see them as aspects of human knowledge or as a way to come to a better knowledge of God?

טוֹבִים מְאוֹרוֹת שֶׁבָּרָא אֱלֹהֵינוּ
יְצָרָם בְּדַעַת בְּבִינָה וּבְהַשְׂכֵּל
כֹּחַ וּגְבוּרָה נָתַן בָּהֶם
לִהְיוֹת מוֹשְׁלִים בְּקֶרֶב תֵּבֵל.

מְלֵאִים זִיו וּמְפִיקִים נֹגַהּ
נָאֶה זִיוָם בְּכָל הָעוֹלָם
שְׂמֵחִים בְּצֵאתָם וְשָׂשִׂים בְּבוֹאָם
עוֹשִׂים בְּאֵימָה רְצוֹן קוֹנָם.

פְּאֵר וְכָבוֹד נוֹתְנִים לִשְׁמוֹ
צָהֳלָה וְרִנָּה לְזֵכֶר מַלְכוּתוֹ
קָרָא לַשֶּׁמֶשׁ וַיִּזְרַח אוֹר
רָאָה וְהִתְקִין צוּרַת הַלְּבָנָה.

שֶׁבַח נוֹתְנִים לוֹ כָּל צְבָא מָרוֹם
תִּפְאֶרֶת וּגְדֻלָּה, שְׂרָפִים וְאוֹפַנִּים וְחַיּוֹת הַקֹּדֶשׁ.

---

shook his head and answered, "You are completely wrong. There was no poet. There was no scribe. This is what really happened. The parchment was lying on my desk next to a bottle of ink. A cat accidentally knocked over the bottle, spilling ink all over the parchment. This poem was the result." The philosopher looked at Rabbi Meir in amazement. He said, "But that is impossible! Such a lovely poem! Such perfect script! Such things do not come into being by themselves. There must be an author! There must be a scribe!" Rabbi Meir smiled. He answered the philosopher, "You yourself have said it! How could the universe, which is much more beautiful than any poem, come into being by itself? There must be an Author. There must be a Creator." (Rabbi Aryeh Kaplan citing *Ḥovot Halevavot* 1:6)

לָאֵל To God who rested[I] from all works,
and on the seventh day ascended and sat on His throne of glory.
He robed the day of rest in glory[I]
and called the Sabbath day a delight.[B]
This is the praise of the seventh day,
that on it God rested from all His work.
The seventh day itself gives praise, saying,
"A psalm, a song for the Sabbath day. *Ps. 92*
It is good to give thanks to the LORD."
Therefore let all He has formed glorify and bless God.
Let them give praise, honor and grandeur to God,
the King, who formed all things
and in His holiness gave a heritage of rest
to His people Israel on the holy Sabbath day.
May Your name, O LORD our God, be sanctified,
and Your renown, O our King, be glorified
in the heavens above and on earth below.
May You be blessed, our Deliverer,
by the praises of Your handiwork,
and by the radiant lights You have made:
may they glorify You. Selah!

---

coming into our midst. In legal terms, this is referred to as part of *kavod Shabbat*, the honor that one is required to give the day in anticipation of its arrival.

When one speaks therefore of wanting to "dress to impress" on this day, who is it that one should be dressing for–oneself? Other people? Shabbat? Hashem?

BIUR TEFILLA • ביאור תפילה

עֹנֶג קָרָא לְיוֹם הַשַּׁבָּת – *And called the Sabbath day a delight. Oneg Shabbat* is not simply a poetic description of the day but a legal term which refers to the commandment to enjoy the day by eating and drinking in its honor. "If you refrain from work on Shabbat...," says the prophet Yeshayahu in the name of Hashem, "if you proclaim the Shabbat day a delight (*oneg*), then I will mount you atop the heights of the world, I will provide you your heritage" (*Yeshayahu* 58:13–14).

לָאֵל אֲשֶׁר שָׁבַת[ע] מִכָּל הַמַּעֲשִׂים
בַּיּוֹם הַשְּׁבִיעִי נִתְעַלָּה וְיָשַׁב עַל כִּסֵּא כְבוֹדוֹ.
תִּפְאֶרֶת עָטָה לְיוֹם הַמְּנוּחָה[ע]
עֹנֶג קָרָא לְיוֹם הַשַּׁבָּת.[ב]
זֶה שֶׁבַח שֶׁלְּיוֹם הַשְּׁבִיעִי
שֶׁבּוֹ שָׁבַת אֵל מִכָּל מְלַאכְתּוֹ
וְיוֹם הַשְּׁבִיעִי מְשַׁבֵּחַ וְאוֹמֵר
מִזְמוֹר שִׁיר לְיוֹם הַשַּׁבָּת, טוֹב לְהֹדוֹת לַיהוה: תהלים צב
לְפִיכָךְ יְפָאֲרוּ וִיבָרְכוּ לָאֵל כָּל יְצוּרָיו
שֶׁבַח יְקָר וּגְדֻלָּה יִתְּנוּ לָאֵל מֶלֶךְ יוֹצֵר כֹּל
הַמַּנְחִיל מְנוּחָה לְעַמּוֹ יִשְׂרָאֵל בִּקְדֻשָּׁתוֹ בְּיוֹם שַׁבַּת קֹדֶשׁ.
שִׁמְךָ יהוה אֱלֹהֵינוּ יִתְקַדַּשׁ, וְזִכְרְךָ מַלְכֵּנוּ יִתְפָּאַר
בַּשָּׁמַיִם מִמַּעַל וְעַל הָאָרֶץ מִתָּחַת.
תִּתְבָּרַךְ מוֹשִׁיעֵנוּ עַל שֶׁבַח מַעֲשֵׂה יָדֶיךָ
וְעַל מְאוֹרֵי אוֹר שֶׁעָשִׂיתָ, יְפָאֲרוּךָ סֶּלָה.

IYUN TEFILLA • עיון תפילה

לָאֵל אֲשֶׁר שָׁבַת – *To God who rested.* In the midst of this lively description of how the world came into being, the Shabbat of Creation takes center stage, just as she does today. Hashem rested, as it were, not because of fatigue (which is an absurdity) but to remind us that there is something larger than our own lives, something even grander than the cosmos we toil so hard to discover and conquer. The day itself thus testifies to its Creator, it sings to Him "a song sung by the Shabbat day," it pays homage to Him, as do we (see the commentary on *Tehillim* 92 in *Kabbalat Shabbat* on page 67).

תִּפְאֶרֶת עָטָה לְיוֹם הַמְּנוּחָה – *He robed the day of rest in glory.* Just as Hashem "dressed" the day, so, too, do we. Quite literally, our clothes for Shabbat should be different than those we wear during the week, just as we would dress up for any important guest who was

תִּתְבָּרַךְ May You be blessed,
our Rock, King and Redeemer,
Creator of holy beings.[1]
May Your name be praised for ever,
our King, Creator of the ministering angels,
all of whom stand in the universe's heights,
proclaiming together,
in awe, aloud,
the words of the living God, the eternal King.
They are all beloved,
all pure,
all mighty,
and all perform in awe and reverence the will of their Maker.
► All open their mouths in holiness and purity,
with song and psalm,
and bless, praise, glorify,
revere, sanctify, and declare the sovereignty[A] of – ◄
The name of the great, mighty
and awesome God and King,
holy is He.

---

which in many ways parallels our own. Alternatively, in Hebrew, the word "angel" and the word for "emissary" are the same, in which case we could say that aspects of nature are themselves the angels/emissaries of Hashem. Thus, the sun and moon and stars are "angels," that is, emissaries and servants of God, who obey His will and sing His praises, as it were, just by the way they function.

When was the last time you listened to their song? Listen to it now if you can.

ANI TEFILLA · אני תפילה

וּמְבָרְכִים וּמְשַׁבְּחִים וּמְפָאֲרִים וּמַעֲרִיצִים וּמַקְדִּישִׁים וּמַמְלִיכִים – *And bless, praise, glorify, revere, sanctify, and declare the sovereignty.* There are six verbs here listed in rapid succession. It has been suggested that these reflect the six wings that Yeshayahu saw on each one of the angels in his vision.

Close your eyes. What does it sound like?

תִּתְבָּרַךְ
צוּרֵנוּ מַלְכֵּנוּ וְגוֹאֲלֵנוּ
בּוֹרֵא קְדוֹשִׁים[ע]
יִשְׁתַּבַּח שִׁמְךָ לָעַד
מַלְכֵּנוּ, יוֹצֵר מְשָׁרְתִים
וַאֲשֶׁר מְשָׁרְתָיו כֻּלָּם עוֹמְדִים בְּרוּם עוֹלָם
וּמַשְׁמִיעִים בְּיִרְאָה יַחַד בְּקוֹל
דִּבְרֵי אֱלֹהִים חַיִּים וּמֶלֶךְ עוֹלָם.
כֻּלָּם אֲהוּבִים
כֻּלָּם בְּרוּרִים
כֻּלָּם גִּבּוֹרִים
וְכֻלָּם עוֹשִׂים בְּאֵימָה וּבְיִרְאָה רְצוֹן קוֹנָם
◂ וְכֻלָּם פּוֹתְחִים אֶת פִּיהֶם בִּקְדֻשָּׁה וּבְטָהֳרָה
בְּשִׁירָה וּבְזִמְרָה
וּמְבָרְכִים וּמְשַׁבְּחִים וּמְפָאֲרִים
וּמַעֲרִיצִים וּמַקְדִּישִׁים וּמַמְלִיכִים[א] ◂
אֶת שֵׁם הָאֵל הַמֶּלֶךְ הַגָּדוֹל, הַגִּבּוֹר וְהַנּוֹרָא
קָדוֹשׁ הוּא.

IYUN TEFILLA • עיון תפילה

בּוֹרֵא קְדוֹשִׁים – *Creator of holy beings.* What goes on in our world of ongoing creation takes place in the upper worlds as well. While focusing on the skies above us, the blessing now shifts from the physical world to the spiritual world, from the sun and the moon and the stars to the angels, the Seraphim and Ophanim. Our knowledge of these angels comes from the prophetic visions of Yeshayahu and Yeḥezkel, and therefore our understanding is limited. But the blessing assures us that there is such a world, one

All accept on themselves, one from another,
the yoke of the kingdom of heaven,[B]
granting permission to one another[I]
to sanctify the One who formed them, in serene spirit,
pure speech and sweet melody.
All, as one, proclaim His holiness, saying in awe:

All say aloud: Holy, holy, holy[H] is the LORD of hosts; *Is. 6*
the whole world is filled with His glory.[I]

▸ Then the Ophanim and the Holy Ḥayyot,
with a roar of noise,
raise themselves toward the Seraphim and,
facing them, give praise, saying:

All say aloud: Blessed is the LORD's glory from His place. *Ezek. 3*

HILKHOT TEFILLA • הלכות תפילה

קָדוֹשׁ, קָדוֹשׁ, קָדוֹשׁ – *Holy, holy, holy.* This section of the prayer is known in halakhic literature as the "sitting *Kedusha*" (קְדֻשָּׁה דִּישִׁיבָה) as opposed to the "standing *Kedusha*" (קְדֻשָּׁה דַּעֲמִידָה) which is found in *Shemoneh Esreh*. What distinguishes the two is that in this one we do not actually sanctify God's name, otherwise we would not be able to sit down when reciting it, nor would we be able to say it without a *minyan* as normally required in a **דָּבָר שֶׁבִּקְדֻשָּׁה** (a prayer of such sanctity that it requires a *minyan*); rather, we merely describe the way that the angels praise Him and sanctify His name. The description is one step removed from our own experience.

IYUN TEFILLA • עיון תפילה

קָדוֹשׁ, קָדוֹשׁ, קָדוֹשׁ... בָּרוּךְ כְּבוֹד – *Holy, holy, holy… Blessed is the LORD's glory.* The two primary lines of the *Kedusha* contain a contradiction of sorts. On the one hand, God is distant, unfathomable, beyond anything we can understand or relate to – **קָדוֹשׁ, קָדוֹשׁ, קָדוֹשׁ**. The distance between infinity and mortality is too huge for us to cross. On the other hand, it says that God is nearby – **בָּרוּךְ כְּבוֹד יהוה מִמְּקוֹמוֹ**. He is located in a particular place, able to be perceived and praised. His Presence thus fills the entire universe and yet He can be found in one place. He is *Kadosh* in a way that we cannot fathom; on the other hand, the whole world is filled with His glory. How can He be far and yet be here? Yet this is precisely the relationship we have with Him. Like a parent who is far away; we can feel very close despite the distance. And we can send messages and thereby maintain our relationship even though

This IYUN TEFILLA *continues on page 313.*

וְכֻלָּם מְקַבְּלִים עֲלֵיהֶם עֹל מַלְכוּת שָׁמַיִם זֶה מִזֶּה[ב]
וְנוֹתְנִים רְשׁוּת זֶה לָזֶה[ע] לְהַקְדִּישׁ לְיוֹצְרָם בְּנַחַת רוּחַ
בְּשָׂפָה בְרוּרָה וּבִנְעִימָה
קְדֻשָּׁה כֻּלָּם כְּאֶחָד, עוֹנִים וְאוֹמְרִים בְּיִרְאָה

All say aloud קָדוֹשׁ, קָדוֹשׁ, קָדוֹשׁ[ה] יהוה צְבָאוֹת
מְלֹא כָל־הָאָרֶץ כְּבוֹדוֹ:[ע] ישעיה ו

וְהָאוֹפַנִּים וְחַיּוֹת הַקֹּדֶשׁ
בְּרַעַשׁ גָּדוֹל מִתְנַשְּׂאִים לְעֻמַּת שְׂרָפִים
לְעֻמָּתָם מְשַׁבְּחִים וְאוֹמְרִים

All say aloud בָּרוּךְ כְּבוֹד־יהוה מִמְּקוֹמוֹ: יחזקאל ג

BIUR TEFILLA • ביאור תפילה

וְכֻלָּם מְקַבְּלִים עֲלֵיהֶם עֹל מַלְכוּת שָׁמַיִם זֶה מִזֶּה – *All accept on themselves, one from another, the yoke of the kingdom of heaven.* Just as there is a unity and balance in the physical world, so too is there unity in the spiritual world. Here the emissaries gather together, as it were, to take upon themselves the yoke of heaven, קַבָּלַת עֹל מַלְכוּת שָׁמַיִם, just as we are about to do in the first paragraph of the *Shema*. And they do so as a prelude to sanctifying God's name in the *Kedusha*, just as we will do in the *Shemoneh Esreh*. In our collective praise, the upper and lower worlds, the physical and the spiritual, will be united.

ANI TEFILLA • אני תפילה

From the angels one learns that spirituality can be found in acknowledging the holiness of the other person. For in the other person I recognize that all of us are created in the image of Hashem. As one anonymous person wrote:

"I searched for God but could not find Thee. I searched for myself but could not find me. I searched for the other and there I found all three."

IYUN TEFILLA • עיון תפילה

וְנוֹתְנִים רְשׁוּת זֶה לָזֶה – *Granting permission to one another.* "They give permission to one another." In the spiritual world there is no place for selfishness. At first, they defer to one another, "You go first." "No, it's really ok, you go first." But in the end, they join together as one, כְּאֶחָד, in keeping with the theme of the *Shema* that we are about to say. The Midrash says that herein lies a challenge to all of us – to get rid of our selfishness in all aspects of life, both physical and spiritual.

לָאֵל To the blessed God[B] they offer melodies.
To the King, living and eternal God,
they say psalms and proclaim praises.
For it is He alone
who does mighty deeds
and creates new things,
who is Master of battles
and sows righteousness,
who makes salvation grow
and creates cures,
who is is revered in praises,
the LORD of wonders,
who in His goodness,
continually renews the work of creation,
day after day,
as it is said:
"[Praise] Him who made the great lights,
for His love endures for ever." Ps. 136
▸ May You make a new light shine over Zion,[B]
and may we all soon be worthy of its light.
Blessed are You, LORD,
who forms the radiant lights.

אוֹר חָדָשׁ עַל צִיּוֹן תָּאִיר – *May You make a new light shine over Zion.* It is not clear what this "new light" is. In *Bereshit* it says that God created light before He created the luminaries. According to *Ḥazal*, this therefore refers not to the light that we know but to one that was subsequently hidden from man for some future time. Here we pray for its restoration. Others suggest that it is a metaphoric light, the light of redemption or the restoration of the entire Jewish people to the Land.

ANI TEFILLA • אני תפילה

It is told that Rabbi Menachem Mendel Morgenstern, known as the Kotzker Rebbe, once asked a group of scholars "Where does God live?" They laughed and replied, "Doesn't it say that the whole world is filled with His glory!" But the Kotzker Rebbe then responded to his own question:

"God lives wherever man decides to let Him in."

לְאֵל בָּרוּךְ[ב] נְעִימוֹת יִתֵּנוּ, לְמֶלֶךְ אֵל חַי וְקַיָּם
זְמִירוֹת יֹאמֵרוּ וְתִשְׁבָּחוֹת יַשְׁמִיעוּ
כִּי הוּא לְבַדּוֹ
פּוֹעֵל גְּבוּרוֹת, עוֹשֶׂה חֲדָשׁוֹת
בַּעַל מִלְחָמוֹת, זוֹרֵעַ צְדָקוֹת
מַצְמִיחַ יְשׁוּעוֹת, בּוֹרֵא רְפוּאוֹת
נוֹרָא תְהִלּוֹת, אֲדוֹן הַנִּפְלָאוֹת
הַמְחַדֵּשׁ בְּטוּבוֹ בְּכָל יוֹם תָּמִיד מַעֲשֵׂה בְרֵאשִׁית
כָּאָמוּר
לְעֹשֵׂה אוֹרִים גְּדֹלִים, כִּי לְעוֹלָם חַסְדּוֹ: תהלים קלו
◂ אוֹר חָדָשׁ עַל צִיּוֹן תָּאִיר[ב] וְנִזְכֶּה כֻלָּנוּ מְהֵרָה לְאוֹרוֹ.
בָּרוּךְ אַתָּה יהוה, יוֹצֵר הַמְּאוֹרוֹת.

---

sometimes the gap which separates seems huge.

Alternatively, there are times when belief is very difficult, when God cannot be seen. Yet at other times, belief is easy and natural, times when God feels close. Sometimes we feel one way, sometimes we feel the other. Both are natural.

BIUR TEFILLA • ביאור תפילה

לְאֵל בָּרוּךְ – *To the blessed God.* As the blessing draws to a close, we return to the original theme. The angels sing about the wonderful things that God continues to do for the entire universe, including us, through His involvement in the ongoing creation of the world.

Each of the expressions can be understood to reflect some aspect of His role in nature or in human affairs. For example:

פּוֹעֵל גְּבוּרוֹת, *Who does mighty deeds* – He is the force behind hurricanes and man's ability to conquer space.

עוֹשֶׂה חֲדָשׁוֹת, *Creates new things* – from the cotton gin to the microchip.

בַּעַל מִלְחָמוֹת, *Master of battles* – the force behind successful human military strategy; victory and defeat.

אֲדוֹן הַנִּפְלָאוֹת, *Lord of wonders* – from the Seven Wonders of the World to the birth of a baby.

Look around you right now. Where can His hand be seen?

אַהֲבָה You have loved us with great love,[B] Lord our God,
and with surpassing compassion
have You had compassion on us.[1]
Our Father, our King,
for the sake of our ancestors who trusted in You,
and to whom You taught the laws of life,
be gracious also to us and teach us.
Our Father, compassionate Father, ever compassionate,
have compassion on us.
Instill in our hearts the desire to understand and discern,
to listen, learn and teach, to observe, perform and fulfill[B]
all the teachings of Your Torah in love.
Enlighten our eyes in Your Torah[B]
and let our hearts cling to Your commandments.[B]
Unite our hearts to love and revere Your name,[B]
so that we may never be ashamed.

BIUR TEFILLA • ביאור תפילה

לְהָבִין – *understand* the difficult theoretical issues of Torah study.

וּלְהַשְׂכִּיל – *discern* in order to be able to carry out in practice what we learn in theory.

לִשְׁמֹעַ – *listen* to the Rabbis as the qualified interpreters of Torah tradition.

לִלְמֹד – we have to review what we *learn* until it becomes part of our Torah knowledge.

וּלְלַמֵּד – *teach/share our knowledge* with others.

לִשְׁמֹר – *observe/review* our knowledge lest we forget it.

וְלַעֲשׂוֹת – *perform/carry out* the commandments.

וּלְקַיֵּם – *fulfill* the commandments in a meaningful way. (Rabbi I. Wohlgemuth)

וְהָאֵר עֵינֵינוּ בְּתוֹרָתֶךָ – *Enlighten our eyes in Your Torah.* We declare our willingness to learn the Torah for which you chose us. The two blessings of *Keriat Shema* are thus connected: the first blessing spoke of the lights of creation which help our physical lives. Here we speak about the enlightenment of Torah, a key to our spiritual lives.

וְדַבֵּק לִבֵּנוּ בְּמִצְוֹתֶיךָ – *And let our hearts cling to Your commandments.* We want not only to learn Torah, but to actualize it in our lives through the mitzvot.

וְיַחֵד לְבָבֵנוּ לְאַהֲבָה וּלְיִרְאָה אֶת שְׁמֶךָ – *Unite our hearts to love and revere Your name.* And through Torah and mitzvot we wish to unify our hearts in both love and awe. Chosenness, Torah, mitzvot, love, awe, unity, the Land – these are all themes that we will further describe in the *Shema*.

אַהֲבָה רַבָּה[ב] אֲהַבְתָּנוּ, יהוה אֱלֹהֵינוּ
חֶמְלָה גְדוֹלָה וִיתֵרָה חָמַלְתָּ עָלֵינוּ.[ע]
אָבִינוּ מַלְכֵּנוּ, בַּעֲבוּר אֲבוֹתֵינוּ שֶׁבָּטְחוּ בְךָ
וַתְּלַמְּדֵם חֻקֵּי חַיִּים, כֵּן תְּחָנֵּנוּ וּתְלַמְּדֵנוּ.
אָבִינוּ, הָאָב הָרַחֲמָן, הַמְרַחֵם
רַחֵם עָלֵינוּ, וְתֵן בְּלִבֵּנוּ לְהָבִין וּלְהַשְׂכִּיל
לִשְׁמֹעַ, לִלְמֹד וּלְלַמֵּד, לִשְׁמֹר וְלַעֲשׂוֹת, וּלְקַיֵּם[ב]
אֶת כָּל דִּבְרֵי תַלְמוּד תּוֹרָתֶךָ בְּאַהֲבָה.
וְהָאֵר עֵינֵינוּ בְּתוֹרָתֶךָ,[ב] וְדַבֵּק לִבֵּנוּ בְּמִצְוֹתֶיךָ[ב]
וְיַחֵד לְבָבֵנוּ לְאַהֲבָה וּלְיִרְאָה אֶת שְׁמֶךָ[ב]
וְלֹא נֵבוֹשׁ לְעוֹלָם וָעֶד.

BIUR TEFILLA • ביאור תפילה

אַהֲבָה רַבָּה – *Great love.* The first blessing, *Yotzer Or*, focused on Hashem's role as Creator. Its theme was quite universalistic. This second blessing, however, is more particularistic, moving us one step closer to focusing on our special relationship with Hashem. That unique relationship is exemplified by the Torah, which was given to us as a gift. Just as a groom presents his bride with a ring under the *ḥuppa*, so, too, Hashem gave us the Torah at Sinai. This relationship also carries with it certain responsibilities, including the requirement to declare our belief in Him as the One God, which we will do shortly in the *Shema*.

אַהֲבָה רַבָּה – *Great love.* רַבָּה in this context could mean not only "great" but also "constantly increasing" (Rabbi S. Schwab). His love is manifest in the fact that He helped expand the understanding of Torah over time. Torah has been at the center of Jewish intellectual history and Jewish identity for millennia. In each generation, scholars and lay people alike have expanded and enhanced our appreciation of its depth, beauty, and relevance to contemporary life. And the older we get, the more mature is our ability to understand and to appreciate what a gift it is. Appreciate Torah as our families did in previous generations.

IYUN TEFILLA • עיון תפילה

חֶמְלָה גְדוֹלָה וִיתֵרָה חָמַלְתָּ עָלֵינוּ – *And with surpassing compassion have You had compassion on us.* The only person in the Torah who is described as having the kind of compassion meant by חֶמְלָה was the daughter of Pharaoh (*Shemot* 2:6), who had pity on the baby she found. Hashem, You have had that kind of compassion for us.

And because we have trusted in Your holy, great and revered name,
may we be glad and rejoice in Your salvation.

At this point, gather the four tzitziot of the tallit, holding them in the left hand.

Bring us back[H] in peace from the four quarters of the earth
and lead us upright to our land.
▸ For You are a God who performs acts of salvation,
and You chose us from all peoples and tongues,
bringing us close to Your great name for ever in truth,
that we may thank You
and proclaim Your oneness in love.
Blessed are You, LORD, who chooses His people Israel in love.[A]

ANI TEFILLA • אני תפילה

הַבּוֹחֵר בְּעַמּוֹ יִשְׂרָאֵל בְּאַהֲבָה – *Who chooses His people Israel in love.* In terms of responsibility to God and doing His will through mitzvot, the concept of Israel means, first of all, me. When one recites in prayer, "Who chooses His people Israel with love," one is not thinking of the Chief Rabbi, but of oneself. When one says, 'You alone will we worship with awe and reverence,' one is also not thinking of any official body at the head of the community, but, again, of oneself. In other words, when one says 'we' in this context, or 'we Jews,' or 'we, the People of Israel,' one means 'I' or, at least, primarily 'I.' As it was once expressed, 'A person should pray in the synagogue as though he were in a forest, with a tree here and a tree there, and feel that he alone is communicating with God in worship' (Rabbi Adin Steinsaltz).

INTRODUCTION TO KERIAT SHEMA

In the first blessing, *Yotzer Or,* we focused on God as Creator; in the second it was the God of Israel. In the first, God is distant; in the second He is close. In the first, our relationship is marked by awe and wonder, or יִרְאָה; in the second it is marked by love, אַהֲבָה. Having experienced both emotions, we are now ready to speak about the Unity of God. (Rabbi M. Angel)

Contrary to popular belief, the *Shema* is not a prayer, as is commonly understood, as much as it is a declaration. That's why it is not called תְּפִלַּת שְׁמַע but rather קְרִיאַת שְׁמַע, for it is similar to reading a proclamation. Think of it a little like a national anthem. We sing it as much for ourselves as for anyone else. Rabbi Yitzḥak Arama in *Akedat Yitzḥak* (58:1) explains that it is a description of the roots of faith upon which prayer and belief are built. If in much of the rest of prayer man talks to God, here God talks to man. "Listen Israel" to what He has to say.

The first paragraph is about קַבָּלַת עֹל מַלְכוּת שָׁמַיִם – accepting God as the ultimate ruler in one's life.

The second paragraph is about קַבָּלַת עֹל מִצְווֹת – accepting the responsibility of doing mitzvot.

The first paragraph focuses on love.

The second paragraph focuses on awe and the concept of reward and punishment.

This **INTRODUCTION** *continues on page 319.*

כִּי בְשֵׁם קָדְשְׁךָ הַגָּדוֹל וְהַנּוֹרָא בָּטָחְנוּ
נָגִילָה וְנִשְׂמְחָה בִּישׁוּעָתֶךָ.

At this point, gather the four ציציות *of the* טלית*, holding them in the left hand.*

וַהֲבִיאֵנוּ[ה] לְשָׁלוֹם מֵאַרְבַּע כַּנְפוֹת הָאָרֶץ
וְתוֹלִיכֵנוּ קוֹמְמִיּוּת לְאַרְצֵנוּ.
‹ כִּי אֵל פּוֹעֵל יְשׁוּעוֹת אָתָּה
וּבָנוּ בָחַרְתָּ מִכָּל עַם וְלָשׁוֹן
וְקֵרַבְתָּנוּ לְשִׁמְךָ הַגָּדוֹל סֶלָה, בֶּאֱמֶת
לְהוֹדוֹת לְךָ וּלְיַחֶדְךָ בְּאַהֲבָה.
בָּרוּךְ אַתָּה יהוה, הַבּוֹחֵר בְּעַמּוֹ יִשְׂרָאֵל בְּאַהֲבָה.[א]

IYUN TEFILLA • עיון תפילה

The Maggid of Mezeritch said that the *Shema* is not a command to love God, nor is it a way to manipulate yourself into thinking you do. Rather it is a call for mindfulness. Be mindful. Hashem is our God. If you get that, says the Maggid, then *ve'ahavta* will be an inevitable result.

HILKHOT TEFILLA • הלכות תפילה

וַהֲבִיאֵנוּ – *Bring us back.* Because *tzitzit* figure prominently in the third paragraph of *Shema* there arose a very old custom to gather the *tzitzit* of all four corners of the *tallit* at this point in the blessing of *Ahava Raba* (which mentions the ingathering from the four corners of the world) and to hold on to them until shortly after the completion of the *Shema.* Others gather only the two front ones (Vilna Gaon), citing the reason that double the 5 knots and 8 strings on each amounts to 26, the numerical equivalent of the Tetragrammaton name of God. Some hold only one of the *tzitzit* since the numerical equivalent of the word is 600 to which one adds the 5 knots and 8 strings to equal 613, the traditional count of all *mitzvot* in the Torah (Mahari Beruna) which one then holds near the heart (*al levavkhem – Hagahot Maimoni*). Still others avoid the custom altogether (Rav Natroni Gaon), suggesting that the *tztizit* need to be seen not necessarily touched.

There are numerous other customs that arose as well including the practice of kissing the *tzitzit* every time the word is mentioned in the third paragraph of *Shema.* All of these customs arose simply because at the very mention of the mitzva itself, in the words of the Rema, one wants to show how beloved it is.

The Shema must be said with intense concentration. In the first paragraph one should accept, with love, the sovereignty of God; in the second, the mitzvot as the will of God. The end of the third paragraph constitutes fulfillment of the mitzva to remember, morning and evening, the exodus from Egypt. See laws 24–32.

When not praying with a minyan, say:

God, faithful King!

The following verse should be said aloud, while covering the eyes with the right hand:

Listen, Israel:[A] the LORD is our God, the LORD is One. *Deut. 6*

Quietly: Blessed be the name of His glorious kingdom for ever and all time.[H]

Arukh 61:4). The reading of this verse is considered by most to be a commandment of Torah origin and is seen as a statement of accepting upon oneself the "the yoke of Heaven," i.e., to accept the God of Israel as one's own. It is actually more of a declaration and, as such, the custom is to say it aloud.

For additional laws and customs, see appendix on laws of daily prayer 24–32.

ANI TEFILLA • אני תפילה

שְׁמַע יִשְׂרָאֵל – *Listen, Israel.*

Rabbi Eliezer Silver, a leader of American Orthodox Jewry in the twentieth century, was president of the Va'ad Hatzala or the Rescue Committee for Jews who survived the Shoah. In that capacity he traveled in post-war Europe looking for Jewish children who had ended up in non-Jewish orphanages, most often sponsored by the Church. In one such case he came to an orphanage in Alsace Lorraine asking if there were Jewish children there. He was told that there were none or that they could not be identified as such; their origins were unknown and they themselves had forgotten where they were from. Rabbi Silver insisted that he nevertheless be permitted to see the children and he was finally allowed to do so for a few moments before their bedtime. He walked into a room filled with beds of children preparing to go to sleep. He called out "Shema Yisrael Hashem Elokeinu Hashem Eḥad" and immediately a young child cried out "Mommy!" Soon other voices joined in as children began to come forward crying out for their mothers. "These children are mine," he said to the priest. "I will take them now."

HILKHOT TEFILLA • הלכות תפילה

בָּרוּךְ שֵׁם כְּבוֹד מַלְכוּתוֹ לְעוֹלָם וָעֶד – *Blessed be the name of His glorious kingdom for ever and all time.* The custom is to recite this verse in a whisper except on Yom Kippur when it is said using the same tone as the first line. A purely technical reason may be that unlike all of the verses of the *Shema* which come from the Torah, this line does not (*Pesaḥim* 56a) and lest one think that it was part of the original text, it is recited quietly.

The שמע must be said with intense concentration. In the first paragraph one should accept, with love, the sovereignty of God; in the second, the מצוות as the will of God. The end of the third paragraph constitutes fulfillment of the מצווה to remember, morning and evening, the exodus from Egypt. See laws 24–32.

When not praying with a מנין, say:

אֵל מֶלֶךְ נֶאֱמָן

The following verse should be said aloud, while covering the eyes with the right hand:

דברים ו **שְׁמַע יִשְׂרָאֵל,**[א] **יהוה אֱלֹהֵינוּ, יהוה ׀ אֶחָד:**

Quietly בָּרוּךְ שֵׁם כְּבוֹד מַלְכוּתוֹ לְעוֹלָם וָעֶד.[ה]

The first paragraph is in the singular.

The second paragraph is in the plural.

The path to accepting God in one's life is through love not fear.

The path to accepting the mitzvot is through reward and punishment.

WHY THESE DIFFERENCES?

Love of God is a matter for the individual who strives to attain it through self-perfection, whilst the acceptance of the yoke of the mitzvot and their fulfillment is only conceivable in human society. Robinson Crusoe living on his desert island isolated from human society could indeed have implemented "you should love Hashem your God," but he could not have fulfilled "if you [plural] listen to my commandments" which, for the most part, relate to the life of man amidst society and his bonds with his family, friends, the state, and the human race. (Nechama Leibowitz)

The third paragraph contains the mitzva to recall the exodus from Egypt, another basic tenet of Jewish life, without which the Jewish people would have disappeared from the stage of history. It also contains a reference to *tzitzit*, as well as a reminder that our eyes and our hearts can sometimes mislead us.

In sum, it has been suggested that *Birkhot HaShaḥar* are about Hashem's providence over our individual lives, *Pesukei DeZimra* are about Hashem's mastery over the world, and *Keriat Shema* is about our relationship with the God of Israel. The first paragraph of the *Shema* focuses on Hashem as King – similar to the theme of the first blessing of *Birkhot Keriat Shema;* the second paragraph of the *Shema* speaks of Hashem's unique relationship with the Jewish people – similar to the theme of the second blessing of *Birkhot Keriat Shema*. The third paragraph speaks to Hashem's involvement in history, just like the third blessing of *Birkhot Keriat Shema*.

Step by step we move closer to our personal encounter with Hashem in the *Shemoneh Esreh* where all of these themes, and more, will come together. We are almost there.

HILKHOT TEFILLA • הלכות תפילה

The prevailing custom is to cover one's eyes when one recites the first line of the Shema, primarily to be able to enhance one's concentration (*Berakhot* 13b; *Shulḥan*

וְאָהַבְתָּ Love the Lord your God with all your heart, with all your soul, and with all your might. These words which I command you today shall be on your heart. Teach them repeatedly to your children, speaking of them when you sit at home and when you travel on the way, when you lie down and when you rise. Bind them as a sign on your hand, and they shall be an emblem between your eyes. Write them on the doorposts of your house and gates. *Deut. 6*

וְהָיָה If you indeed heed My commandments with which I charge you today, to love the Lord your God and worship Him with all your heart and with all your soul, I will give rain in your land in its season, the early and late rain; and you shall gather in your grain, wine and oil. I will give grass in your field for your cattle, and you shall eat and be satisfied. Be careful lest your heart be tempted and you go astray and worship other gods, bowing down to them. Then the Lord's anger will flare against you and He will close the heavens so that there will be no rain. The land will not yield its crops, and you will perish swiftly from the good land that the Lord is *Deut. 11*

---

yourself? When someone says "I love fish" it's not really the fish he loves, but himself! So too here, do you love Hashem or do you love yourself? (*Sneh Bo'er BeKotzk* p. 110)

It was Friday, a few hours before we boarded the helicopter. Emmanuel asked me, "What would you do if, God forbid, our helicopter were to be hit by a missile and we would have just minutes to live before we crashed?" I answered him: "I don't know. I imagine I would be very sad and scared; I'd close my eyes and wait for it be over as quickly as possible and with as little pain as possible." Emmanuel thought for a moment and said: "What I would do, and what I think you should do, would be to say Shema Yisrael." I looked at him and said, "OK, fine, you'll say Shema Yisrael, but what will that accomplish since in any event in another second the helicopter will crash and we will all die?!" He answered me with one sentence that follows me to this day and I believe will continue to follow me the rest of my life. "If a person has five seconds left to live and there is still significance to his life and aspirations for what comes after it then that means that his life has meaning. But, if on the other hand, a person has five seconds to live and he does not understand the significance of those five seconds, then apparently there is no meaning to his entire life, because we do not live in order to satisfy our drives, or to enjoy or live for the moment. Rather, life is one added step on the way to the next."

Lt. Colonel Emmanuel Yehuda Moreno was killed in battle the next day Shabbat, August 19, 2006.

דברים ו וְאָהַבְתָּ אֵת יהוה אֱלֹהֶיךָ, בְּכָל־לְבָבְךָ וּבְכָל־נַפְשְׁךָ וּבְכָל־
מְאֹדֶךָ: וְהָיוּ הַדְּבָרִים הָאֵלֶּה, אֲשֶׁר אָנֹכִי מְצַוְּךָ הַיּוֹם, עַל־
לְבָבֶךָ: וְשִׁנַּנְתָּם לְבָנֶיךָ וְדִבַּרְתָּ בָּם, בְּשִׁבְתְּךָ בְּבֵיתֶךָ וּבְלֶכְתְּךָ
בַדֶּרֶךְ, וּבְשָׁכְבְּךָ וּבְקוּמֶךָ: וּקְשַׁרְתָּם לְאוֹת עַל־יָדֶךָ וְהָיוּ לְטֹטָפֹת
בֵּין עֵינֶיךָ: וּכְתַבְתָּם עַל־מְזֻזוֹת בֵּיתֶךָ וּבִשְׁעָרֶיךָ:

דברים יא וְהָיָה אִם־שָׁמֹעַ תִּשְׁמְעוּ אֶל־מִצְוֹתַי אֲשֶׁר אָנֹכִי מְצַוֶּה אֶתְכֶם
הַיּוֹם, לְאַהֲבָה אֶת־יהוה אֱלֹהֵיכֶם וּלְעָבְדוֹ, בְּכָל־לְבַבְכֶם וּבְכָל־
נַפְשְׁכֶם: וְנָתַתִּי מְטַר־אַרְצְכֶם בְּעִתּוֹ, יוֹרֶה וּמַלְקוֹשׁ, וְאָסַפְתָּ
דְגָנֶךָ וְתִירֹשְׁךָ וְיִצְהָרֶךָ: וְנָתַתִּי עֵשֶׂב בְּשָׂדְךָ לִבְהֶמְתֶּךָ, וְאָכַלְתָּ
וְשָׂבָעְתָּ: הִשָּׁמְרוּ לָכֶם פֶּן־יִפְתֶּה לְבַבְכֶם, וְסַרְתֶּם וַעֲבַדְתֶּם
אֱלֹהִים אֲחֵרִים וְהִשְׁתַּחֲוִיתֶם לָהֶם: וְחָרָה אַף־יהוה בָּכֶם, וְעָצַר
אֶת־הַשָּׁמַיִם וְלֹא־יִהְיֶה מָטָר, וְהָאֲדָמָה לֹא תִתֵּן אֶת־יְבוּלָהּ,
וַאֲבַדְתֶּם מְהֵרָה מֵעַל הָאָרֶץ הַטֹּבָה אֲשֶׁר יהוה נֹתֵן לָכֶם:

IYUN TEFILLA • עיון תפילה

וְאָהַבְתָּ – *Love.* How does one come to love God? By studying His Torah and by studying nature, for through His creations, one comes to better understand and know the Creator.

מְאֹדֶךָ – *Your might.* The phrase literally means "very much." I would translate the phrase as, "You shall love Hashem your God with all of your *very-muchness.*" This would refer to the extra talents or abilities which *HaKadosh Barukh Hu* has given a person, **מְאֹד**, more than that which he has given to other people. Examples would be utilizing one's great intelligence or musical or artistic ability, or building skills, to demonstrate his love for *HaKadosh Barukh Hu.* (Rabbi S. Schwab)

Which part of your מְאֹד can you better use today to enhance your spirituality?

וּלְעָבְדוֹ, בְּכָל לְבַבְכֶם – *And worship Him with all your heart.* What is service of the heart? *Tefilla.* (*Ta'anit* 2a)

ANI TEFILLA • אני תפילה

וְאָהַבְתָּ אֵת יהוה אֱלֹהֶיךָ – *Love the Lord your God.*

The Kotzker rebbe once called over one of his followers whom he heard reciting the Shema. Tell me the truth, he said, when you said v'ahavta, is it really Hashem you love or

giving you. Therefore, set these, My words, on your heart and soul. Bind them as a sign on your hand, and they shall be an emblem between your eyes. Teach them to your children, speaking of them when you sit at home and when you travel on the way, when you lie down and when you rise. Write them on the doorposts of your house and gates, so that you and your children may live long in the land that the LORD swore to your ancestors to give them, for as long as the heavens are above the earth.

Hold the tzitziot in the right hand also (some transfer to the right hand), kissing them at °.

וַיֹּאמֶר The LORD spoke to Moses, saying: Speak to the Israelites *Num. 15*
and tell them to make °tassels on the corners of their garments for all generations. They shall attach to the °tassel at each corner a thread of blue. This shall be your °tassel, and you shall see it and remember all of the LORD's commandments and keep them, not straying after your heart and after your eyes,[A] following your own sinful desires. Thus you will be reminded to keep all My commandments, and be holy to your God. I am the LORD your God, who brought you out of the land of Egypt[I] to be your God. I am the LORD your God.

°True[B] –

The Leader repeats:

▸ The LORD your God is true[I] –

HILKHOT TEFILLA • הלכות תפילה

יהוה אֱלֹהֵיכֶם אֱמֶת – *The LORD your God is true.* There is a very old custom in which the leader or *ḥazan* connects the last two words of the *Shema* to the first word of the next paragraph so as to form a single phrase. The source, which is rather mystical, suggests that there are 248 words in the *Keriat Shema* which corresponds to the 248 organs that rabbinic tradition says are in the human body. Reciting each part of the *Shema* carefully will result in the healing of each part of the body. But the truth is that there are only 245 words in the three paragraphs of *Shema*, and so the leader adds the three words at the end in order to round out the number. In Ashkenazic practice, if one is praying alone, since we do not repeat words when it can be avoided, one instead adds the three words "God, faithful King" (*El Melekh ne'eman*) at the beginning of the *Shema* (see page 319 in order to arrive at the required number).

וְשַׂמְתֶּם אֶת־דְּבָרַי אֵלֶּה עַל־לְבַבְכֶם וְעַל־נַפְשְׁכֶם, וּקְשַׁרְתֶּם
אֹתָם לְאוֹת עַל־יֶדְכֶם, וְהָיוּ לְטוֹטָפֹת בֵּין עֵינֵיכֶם: וְלִמַּדְתֶּם
אֹתָם אֶת־בְּנֵיכֶם לְדַבֵּר בָּם, בְּשִׁבְתְּךָ בְּבֵיתֶךָ וּבְלֶכְתְּךָ בַדֶּרֶךְ,
וּבְשָׁכְבְּךָ וּבְקוּמֶךָ: וּכְתַבְתָּם עַל־מְזוּזוֹת בֵּיתֶךָ וּבִשְׁעָרֶיךָ: לְמַעַן
יִרְבּוּ יְמֵיכֶם וִימֵי בְנֵיכֶם עַל הָאֲדָמָה אֲשֶׁר נִשְׁבַּע יהוה לַאֲבֹתֵיכֶם
לָתֵת לָהֶם, כִּימֵי הַשָּׁמַיִם עַל־הָאָרֶץ:

Hold the ציציות *in the right hand also (some transfer to the right hand), kissing them at °.*

במדבר טו
וַיֹּאמֶר יהוה אֶל־מֹשֶׁה לֵּאמֹר: דַּבֵּר אֶל־בְּנֵי יִשְׂרָאֵל וְאָמַרְתָּ
אֲלֵהֶם, וְעָשׂוּ לָהֶם °צִיצִת עַל־כַּנְפֵי בִגְדֵיהֶם לְדֹרֹתָם, וְנָתְנוּ °עַל־
צִיצִת הַכָּנָף פְּתִיל תְּכֵלֶת: וְהָיָה לָכֶם °לְצִיצִת, וּרְאִיתֶם אֹתוֹ
וּזְכַרְתֶּם אֶת־כָּל־מִצְוֺת יהוה וַעֲשִׂיתֶם אֹתָם, וְלֹא תָתוּרוּ אַחֲרֵי
לְבַבְכֶם וְאַחֲרֵי עֵינֵיכֶם,[א] אֲשֶׁר־אַתֶּם זֹנִים אַחֲרֵיהֶם: לְמַעַן תִּזְכְּרוּ
וַעֲשִׂיתֶם אֶת־כָּל־מִצְוֺתָי, וִהְיִיתֶם קְדֹשִׁים לֵאלֹהֵיכֶם: אֲנִי יהוה
אֱלֹהֵיכֶם, אֲשֶׁר הוֹצֵאתִי אֶתְכֶם מֵאֶרֶץ מִצְרַיִם,[ע] לִהְיוֹת לָכֶם
לֵאלֹהִים, אֲנִי יהוה אֱלֹהֵיכֶם:

°אֱמֶת[ב]

The שליח ציבור *repeats:*

◂ יהוה אֱלֹהֵיכֶם אֱמֶת[ה]

ANI TEFILLA • אני תפילה

וְלֹא תָתוּרוּ אַחֲרֵי לְבַבְכֶם וְאַחֲרֵי עֵינֵיכֶם – *Not straying after your heart and after your eyes.* "You should not wander after your hearts and your eyes."

Do your eyes follow your heart or do you let your heart follow your eyes?

IYUN TEFILLA • עיון תפילה

אֲנִי יהוה אֱלֹהֵיכֶם, אֲשֶׁר הוֹצֵאתִי אֶתְכֶם מֵאֶרֶץ מִצְרָיִם – *I am the* Lord *your God, who brought you out of the land of Egypt.* In an age when might triumphed over right, the Torah records one of the great turning points in the human story, when the Creator of heaven and earth intervened in defense of the powerless. (Rabbi J. Sacks)

וְיַצִּיב And firm, established and enduring, right, faithful,
beloved, cherished, delightful, pleasant,
awesome, mighty, perfect, accepted, good and beautiful
is this faith[B] for us for ever.

True is the eternal God, our King, Rock of Jacob,
Shield of our salvation.
He exists and His name exists through all generations.
His throne is established,
His kingship and faithfulness endure for ever.

At °, kiss the tzitziot and release them.

His words live and persist, faithful and desirable
°for ever and all time.
▸ So they were for our ancestors, so they are for us,
and so they will be for our children
and all our generations and for all future generations
of the seed of Israel, Your servants.

שִׁיר הַמַּעֲלוֹת (song of *ascents*), which in turn are reminiscent of the 15 steps in the *Beit HaMikdash* leading from the outer courtyard to the inner courtyard, as well as the 15 מַעֲלוֹת טובות (rising levels of favors) which Hashem did for us during and after the exodus mentioned in *Dayeinu* in the Haggada (Abudarham). These allusions remind us that we are moving ever closer to the encounter with Hashem in the *Amida*.

Imagine yourself at the bottom of a long staircase or at the end of a long hallway leading up to the office of the King. You are about to have a private audience with Him. Imagine yourself 15 steps away.

Alternatively, it has been suggested that including the word אֱמֶת there are 16 adjectives corresponding to the 16 verses from *Shema* to the end of the second paragraph. We declare each one of those verses to be true (*Etz Yosef*).

BIUR TEFILLA • ביאור תפילה

הַדָּבָר הַזֶּה – *Is this faith.* There are numerous adjectives added here, all of which describe "הַדָּבָר הַזֶּה." What is "this thing?" Most likely it is a reference to the final theme we mentioned in the *Shema*, namely, we hereby reaffirm our belief in the fact that "I am Hashem your God who took you out of Egypt." It is thus a reference to our belief in the historical truth of the exodus (*Tosafot, Berakhot* 12a). Alternatively, there are those who say it is a reference to our belief in Hashem, that it was He who took us out (*Emek Berakha*).

וְיַצִּיב, וְנָכוֹן וְקַיָּם, וְיָשָׁר וְנֶאֱמָן
וְאָהוּב וְחָבִיב, וְנֶחְמָד וְנָעִים
וְנוֹרָא וְאַדִּיר, וּמְתֻקָּן וּמְקֻבָּל, וְטוֹב וְיָפֶה
הַדָּבָר הַזֶּה[ב] עָלֵינוּ לְעוֹלָם וָעֶד.

אֱמֶת אֱלֹהֵי עוֹלָם מַלְכֵּנוּ
צוּר יַעֲקֹב מָגֵן יִשְׁעֵנוּ
לְדוֹר וָדוֹר הוּא קַיָּם וּשְׁמוֹ קַיָּם
וְכִסְאוֹ נָכוֹן, וּמַלְכוּתוֹ וֶאֱמוּנָתוֹ לָעַד קַיֶּמֶת.

At °, kiss the ציציות *and release them.*

וּדְבָרָיו חָיִים וְקַיָּמִים, נֶאֱמָנִים וְנֶחֱמָדִים
°לָעַד וּלְעוֹלְמֵי עוֹלָמִים
◂ עַל אֲבוֹתֵינוּ וְעָלֵינוּ
עַל בָּנֵינוּ וְעַל דּוֹרוֹתֵינוּ
וְעַל כָּל דּוֹרוֹת זֶרַע יִשְׂרָאֵל עֲבָדֶיךָ.

BIUR TEFILLA • ביאור תפילה

We now begin the third and final *berakha* before the *Amida*, called *Birkat Geula*, referring to our being freed from Egypt. The last paragraph of the *Shema* served as an introduction to this theme in its declaration that God took us out of Egypt in order to be His people. The blessing here conveys the point that it wasn't just that He gave us our freedom at that one point in history, but, like a parent, He continued to watch over us and protect us. This relationship is highlighted by the subsequent threat at *Yam Suf* and the destruction of our enemies in spite of overwhelming odds, a phenomenon that has repeated itself numerous times throughout our history. Here we therefore emphasize not the God of Creation (*Yotzer or*), or the God of Sinai (*Ahava raba*), but the God of history who remains a powerful force in our personal and collective lives.

IYUN TEFILLA • עיון תפילה

There are 15 adjectives here connected with one another by the conjunction "and," thus indicating that they are intended to form a single unit. This 15 is reminiscent of the 15 chapters of *Tehillim* composed by King David which begin with the phrase

For the early and the later generations[1]
this faith has proved good and enduring for ever –

True and faithful, an irrevocable law.

True You are the LORD: our God and God of our ancestors,
▸ our King and King of our ancestors,
our Redeemer and Redeemer of our ancestors,
our Maker,
Rock of our salvation,
our Deliverer and Rescuer:
this has ever been Your name.
There is no God but You.

עֶזְרַת You have always been the help of our ancestors,
Shield and Savior of their children after them
in every generation.
Your dwelling is in the heights of the universe,
and Your judgments and righteousness
reach to the ends of the earth.
Happy is the one who obeys Your commandments
and takes to heart Your teaching and Your word.

True You are the Master of Your people
and a mighty King who pleads their cause.

True You are the first and You are the last.
Besides You, we have no king,
redeemer or savior.

---

knew them all to be true because they saw "Truth" when God revealed Himself to them. We approach faith based upon their experiences which they handed down to us. But we can also have our own absolute faith that the Torah is true, for it has proven itself as the foundation of the laws of civilization, from one generation to the next, and it will never disappear.

עַל הָרִאשׁוֹנִים וְעַל הָאַחֲרוֹנִים[ע]
דָּבָר טוֹב וְקַיָּם לְעוֹלָם וָעֶד
אֱמֶת וֶאֱמוּנָה, חֹק וְלֹא יַעֲבֹר.
אֱמֶת שָׁאַתָּה הוּא יהוה אֱלֹהֵינוּ וֵאלֹהֵי אֲבוֹתֵינוּ
› מַלְכֵּנוּ מֶלֶךְ אֲבוֹתֵינוּ
גּוֹאֲלֵנוּ גּוֹאֵל אֲבוֹתֵינוּ
יוֹצְרֵנוּ צוּר יְשׁוּעָתֵנוּ
פּוֹדֵנוּ וּמַצִּילֵנוּ מֵעוֹלָם שְׁמֶךָ
אֵין אֱלֹהִים זוּלָתֶךָ.

עֶזְרַת אֲבוֹתֵינוּ אַתָּה הוּא מֵעוֹלָם
מָגֵן וּמוֹשִׁיעַ לִבְנֵיהֶם אַחֲרֵיהֶם בְּכָל דּוֹר וָדוֹר.
בְּרוּם עוֹלָם מוֹשָׁבֶךָ
וּמִשְׁפָּטֶיךָ וְצִדְקָתְךָ עַד אַפְסֵי אָרֶץ.
אַשְׁרֵי אִישׁ שֶׁיִּשְׁמַע לְמִצְוֹתֶיךָ
וְתוֹרָתְךָ וּדְבָרְךָ יָשִׂים עַל לִבּוֹ.
אֱמֶת אַתָּה הוּא אָדוֹן לְעַמֶּךָ
וּמֶלֶךְ גִּבּוֹר לָרִיב רִיבָם.
אֱמֶת אַתָּה הוּא רִאשׁוֹן וְאַתָּה הוּא אַחֲרוֹן
וּמִבַּלְעָדֶיךָ אֵין לָנוּ מֶלֶךְ גּוֹאֵל וּמוֹשִׁיעַ.

IYUN TEFILLA • עיון תפילה

עַל הָרִאשׁוֹנִים וְעַל הָאַחֲרוֹנִים – *For the early and the later generations.* There are some mitzvot in the Torah that make sense to us, and others that do not. Our ancestors

From Egypt You redeemed us,[B] Lord our God,
and from the slave-house You delivered us.
All their firstborn You killed,
but Your firstborn You redeemed.
You split the Sea of Reeds
and drowned the arrogant.
You brought Your beloved ones across.
The water covered their foes; *Ps. 106*
not one of them was left.

For this, the beloved ones praised and exalted God,
the cherished ones sang psalms, songs and praises,
blessings and thanksgivings to the King,
the living and enduring God.
High and exalted, great and awesome,
He humbles the haughty and raises the lowly,
freeing captives and redeeming those in need,
helping the poor
and answering His people when they cry out to Him.

Stand in preparation for the Amida. Take three steps back before beginning the Amida.

Praises to God Most High,
the Blessed One who is blessed.
Moses and the children of Israel
recited to You a song with great joy,
and they all exclaimed:
"Who is like You, Lord, among the mighty? *Ex. 15*
Who is like You, majestic in holiness,
awesome in praises, doing wonders?"

---

servant." So powerful was that experience that they burst into song and praise of Hashem, just as we are about to do in the first three blessings of the *Amida*. We thus fulfill the Rabbis' insistence that we precede our prayer by recalling that we were freed from Egypt and saved as a people (סוֹמֵךְ גְּאֻלָּה לִתְפִלָּה).

מִמִּצְרַיִם גְּאַלְתָּנוּ, יהוה אֱלֹהֵינוּ
וּמִבֵּית עֲבָדִים פְּדִיתָנוּ
כָּל בְּכוֹרֵיהֶם הָרָגְתָּ, וּבְכוֹרְךָ גָּאָלְתָּ
וְיַם סוּף בָּקַעְתָּ, וְזֵדִים טִבַּעְתָּ
וִידִידִים הֶעֱבַרְתָּ
וַיְכַסּוּ־מַיִם צָרֵיהֶם, אֶחָד מֵהֶם לֹא נוֹתָר: תהלים קו

עַל זֹאת שִׁבְּחוּ אֲהוּבִים, וְרוֹמְמוּ אֵל
וְנָתְנוּ יְדִידִים זְמִירוֹת, שִׁירוֹת וְתִשְׁבָּחוֹת
בְּרָכוֹת וְהוֹדָאוֹת לַמֶּלֶךְ אֵל חַי וְקַיָּם
רָם וְנִשָּׂא, גָּדוֹל וְנוֹרָא
מַשְׁפִּיל גֵּאִים וּמַגְבִּיהַּ שְׁפָלִים
מוֹצִיא אֲסִירִים, וּפוֹדֶה עֲנָוִים וְעוֹזֵר דַּלִּים
וְעוֹנֶה לְעַמּוֹ בְּעֵת שַׁוְּעָם אֵלָיו.

Stand in preparation for the עמידה*. Take three steps back before beginning the* עמידה*.*

◄ תְּהִלּוֹת לְאֵל עֶלְיוֹן, בָּרוּךְ הוּא וּמְבֹרָךְ
מֹשֶׁה וּבְנֵי יִשְׂרָאֵל
לְךָ עָנוּ שִׁירָה בְּשִׂמְחָה רַבָּה
וְאָמְרוּ כֻלָּם
מִי־כָמֹכָה בָּאֵלִם, יהוה שמות טו
מִי כָּמֹכָה נֶאְדָּר בַּקֹּדֶשׁ, נוֹרָא תְהִלֹּת, עֹשֵׂה פֶלֶא:

BIUR TEFILLA • ביאור תפילה

מִמִּצְרַיִם גְּאַלְתָּנוּ – *From Egypt You redeemed us.* The Torah says that when Israel saw the splitting of the *Yam Suf (the Red Sea)*, they "believed in God and in Moshe His

With a new song, the redeemed people praised
Your name at the seashore.
Together they all gave thanks, proclaimed Your kingship,
and declared:
"The LORD shall reign for ever and ever." *Ex. 15*

Congregants should end the following blessing together with the Leader so as to be able to move directly from the words "redeemed Israel" to the Amida, without the interruption of saying Amen.

צוּר יִשְׂרָאֵל Rock of Israel! Arise to the help of Israel.
Deliver, as You promised, Judah and Israel.
Our Redeemer, the LORD of hosts is His name, *Is. 47*
the Holy One of Israel.
Blessed are You, LORD, who redeemed Israel.

INTRODUCTION TO THE AMIDA

For an overview of the Amida prayer in general, see page 100 (at *Kabbalat Shabbat*).

The first three blessings and the last three blessings of the *Amida* are identical for every version of the *Amida* that there is, both throughout this day and for every other prayer service.

The first blessing, called *Avot* (Patriarchs) is an acknowledgment of the historic relationship that Hashem has had with the Jewish people since the days of our forefathers who brought monotheism to the world.

The second blessing called *Gevurot* (Divine Might) is an acknowledgment of God's power, particularly over nature but also in the affairs of man, for how could we speak to God if we were not ready to first admit to our dependence and inferiority?

The third blessing, called *Kedusha* (Holiness) speaks to God's immanence and transcendence. He is totally beyond us and yet, a close and personal relationship is possible as well.

In sum, our posture is "like a servant who organizes his praise before his master" (*Berakhot* 34a). One speaks to God this way not to engage in small talk, nor to be falsely ingratiating, but rather for us to realize before Whom we stand and to admit as much before Him.

The last three blessings similarly appear in every version of the *Amida* that there is. These blessings are "like a servant who received his allotment from his master and takes his leave" (*Berakhot* 34a). One does not turn one's back on the King, nor does one end the conversation abruptly, rather one leaves with a sense of ongoing commitment going forward, a sense of gratitude for having been heard and a sense of peace, both physical and spiritual.

By bracketing the middle blessing this way, the siddur seeks to help us frame our encounter with the Divine in an appropriate and very Jewish manner. The themes and posture are laid out for us, but what we bring to them, how we internalize them, how we are ultimately impacted by them, is up to each and every one of us in our own way.

This **INTRODUCTION** *continues on page 333.*

שִׁירָה חֲדָשָׁה שִׁבְּחוּ גְאוּלִים
לְשִׁמְךָ עַל שְׂפַת הַיָּם
יַחַד כֻּלָּם הוֹדוּ וְהִמְלִיכוּ
וְאָמְרוּ
יהוה יִמְלֹךְ לְעֹלָם וָעֶד: שמות טו

The קהל *should end the following blessing together with the* שליח ציבור *so as to be able to move directly from the words* גָּאַל יִשְׂרָאֵל *to the* עמידה*, without the interruption of saying* אמן.

◄ צוּר יִשְׂרָאֵל, קוּמָה בְּעֶזְרַת יִשְׂרָאֵל
וּפְדֵה כִנְאֻמֶךָ יְהוּדָה וְיִשְׂרָאֵל.
גֹּאֲלֵנוּ יהוה צְבָאוֹת שְׁמוֹ, קְדוֹשׁ יִשְׂרָאֵל: ישעיה מז
בָּרוּךְ אַתָּה יהוה, גָּאַל יִשְׂרָאֵל.

ANI TEFILLA • אני תפילה

Rabbi Yose ben Elyakim testified in the name of the holy community of Jerusalem:

If one joins the blessing of Geula to the Tefilla [Shemoneh Esreh], he will not meet with any mishap for the whole of the day. (Berakhot 9b)

ANI TEFILLA • אני תפילה

At this point we transport ourselves in time, seeing ourselves as having been there at the moment of liberation. Imagine the joy, the gratitude, the sense of awe and wonder, the sense of intimacy with Hashem and with one another.

Close your eyes and imagine actually coming into contact with the Presence of the Divine. Now begin the *Amida*.

IYUN TEFILLA • עיון תפילה

We know these events took place because they have been passed along to us by our parents and their parents going back to the moment when it all happened. We are living only a short period of time after the Holocaust, though there are people who deny it ever took place. It is all the more understandable that there are those who would deny the exodus and the splitting of the Sea. Yet, says Rabbi Yehuda HaLevi, our tradition has been unbroken and our historical experience ever since has proven over and over again that God has been an ongoing presence in our history, even if He is sometimes hard to see.

ANI TEFILLA • אני תפילה

"Looking for God is like a drop in the ocean looking for water." (Rabbi David Aaron)

THE AMIDA

The following prayer, until "in former years" on page 362, is said silently, standing with feet together.

Take three steps forward.

O Lord, open my lips, so that my mouth may declare Your praise. *Ps. 51*

PATRIARCHS

▾ *Bend the knees:* Blessed *Bow:* are You, *Stand straight:* Lord[B]
our God and God of our fathers,
God of Abraham, God of Isaac and God of Jacob;[1]
the great, mighty and awesome God, God Most High,
who bestows acts of loving-kindness and creates all,
who remembers the loving-kindness of the fathers
and will bring a Redeemer to their children's children
for the sake of His name, in love.

These words are added on Shabbat Shuva: Remember us for life, O King who desires life, and write us in the book of life – for Your sake, O God of life.

King, Helper, Savior, Shield:
▾ *Bend the knees:* Blessed *Bow:* are You, *Stand straight:* Lord,
Shield of Abraham.[1]

---

submission. It is thus both an acknowledgment of before Whom one stands as well as an act of prayer itself (Rabbi H. Vidal). People often make the mistake of rushing through these movements out of rote. It pays to take your time.

IYUN TEFILLA • עיון תפילה

אַבְרָהָם... יִצְחָק... יַעֲקֹב – *Abraham…Isaac…Jacob.* If Moses was so great, why don't we refer to the "God of Moses" just as we refer to God of Abraham, Isaac and Jacob? There is an inherent difference between Abraham and Moses. Abraham searched for God, but God did not react immediately. It was only much later, according to the Midrash, after Abraham had come to believe in Him, that God appeared to him. Moses was just the opposite. Moses did not search for the Almighty. He was a shepherd for Jethro, and "he hid his face because he feared to look at God (*Shemot* 3:6)." God searched for Moses, and He found him. Abraham, Isaac, and Jacob are the only true forefathers; God's revelation to them came after a long time and many frustrated efforts (Rabbi Joseph B. Soloveitchik). In short, the search for God lies at the heart of our prayer, even if He does not react immediately.

This **IYUN TEFILLA** *continues on page 335.*

עמידה

The following prayer, until קַדְמֹנִיּוֹת *on page 363, is said silently, standing with feet together. Take three steps forward.*

אֲדֹנָי, שְׂפָתַי תִּפְתָּח, וּפִי יַגִּיד תְּהִלָּתֶךָ: תהלים נא

אבות

▾ *Bend the knees* בָּרוּךְ *Bow* אַתָּה *Stand straight* יהוה

אֱלֹהֵינוּ וֵאלֹהֵי אֲבוֹתֵינוּ

אֱלֹהֵי אַבְרָהָם, אֱלֹהֵי יִצְחָק, וֵאלֹהֵי יַעֲקֹב

הָאֵל הַגָּדוֹל הַגִּבּוֹר וְהַנּוֹרָא, אֵל עֶלְיוֹן

גּוֹמֵל חֲסָדִים טוֹבִים, וְקוֹנֵה הַכֹּל, וְזוֹכֵר חַסְדֵי אָבוֹת

וּמֵבִיא גוֹאֵל לִבְנֵי בְנֵיהֶם לְמַעַן שְׁמוֹ בְּאַהֲבָה.

בשבת שובה: זָכְרֵנוּ לְחַיִּים, מֶלֶךְ חָפֵץ בַּחַיִּים

וְכָתְבֵנוּ בְּסֵפֶר הַחַיִּים, לְמַעַנְךָ אֱלֹהִים חַיִּים.

מֶלֶךְ עוֹזֵר וּמוֹשִׁיעַ וּמָגֵן.

▾ *Bend the knees* בָּרוּךְ *Bow* אַתָּה *Stand straight* יהוה, מָגֵן אַבְרָהָם.

STRUCTURE OF THE AMIDA FOR ALL SHABBAT SERVICES

STANDARDIZED FIRST THREE BLESSINGS OF PRAISE

1. **אבות** – Patriarchs
2. **גבורות** – Divine Might
3. **קדושת שם** – Holiness

THE MIDDLE BLESSING – THE HOLINESS OF SHABBAT

4. **קדושת היום** – Holiness of the day

Consists of: (a) Statement about Shabbat appropriate to the theme of this particular Shabbat service (changes for *Ma'ariv, Shaharit, Musaf and Minha*). (b) Verses from the Torah that speak about Shabbat. (c) Another thematic statement about Shabbat. (d) The conclusion of the blessing which is the same for every Shabbat service.

STANDARDIZED LAST THREE BLESSINGS OF GRATITUDE

5. **עבודה** – Temple Service
6. **מודים** – Thanksgiving
7. **שלום** – Peace

PRIVATE MEDITATION

אלהי נצור – My God, guard my tongue…

BIUR TEFILLA • ביאור תפילה

בָּרוּךְ אַתָּה יהוה – *Blessed are You, Lord.* The physical act of bowing is both the last preparation for prayer as well as its introduction. The very act of bowing is an act of

DIVINE MIGHT

אַתָּה גִּבּוֹר You are eternally mighty,[A] LORD.
You give life to the dead[I] and have great power to save.

The phrase "He makes the wind blow and the rain fall" is added from Simhat Torah until Pesah. In Israel the phrase "He causes the dew to fall" is added from Pesah until Shemini Atzeret.

In fall & winter: He makes the wind blow and the rain fall.
In Israel, in spring & summer: He causes the dew to fall.

He sustains the living with loving-kindness,
and with great compassion revives the dead.
He supports the fallen, heals the sick, sets captives free,
and keeps His faith with those who sleep in the dust.
Who is like You, Master of might, and who can compare to You,
O King who brings death and gives life, and makes salvation grow?

Between Rosh HaShana & Yom Kippur: Who is like You, compassionate Father,
who remembers His creatures in compassion, for life?

Faithful are You to revive the dead.
Blessed are You, LORD, who revives the dead.[B]

When saying the Amida silently, continue with "You are holy" on page 340.

ANI TEFILLA • אני תפילה

אַתָּה גִּבּוֹר לְעוֹלָם – *You are eternally mighty.* Have you ever been in a place in nature where you felt the presence of God? Have you ever witnessed a natural phenomenon when you felt like there was a force or Presence beyond yourself? **Close your eyes. Imagine yourself there now.**

IYUN TEFILLA • עיון תפילה

מְחַיֵּה מֵתִים אַתָּה – *You give life to the dead.* The blessing speaks about Hashem both as one who "brings death," and "gives life." Life and death are both part of living. A seed seems to decompose when it is actually beginning to sprout. What looks like death is actually the beginning of life. What looks like something bad is actually something good. That is the way Hashem works. **What "bad" can you point to in your life or the life of someone else that really turned out to be "good" in the end?**

BIUR TEFILLA • ביאור תפילה

מְחַיֵּה הַמֵּתִים – *Who revives the dead.* The blessing mentions the cardinal Jewish belief in the revival of the dead no less than five times, for there can be no greater example of Hashem's power over the physical world than that. Even so, many have suggested

This **BIUR TEFILLA** *continues on page 337.*

גבורות

אַתָּה גִּבּוֹר לְעוֹלָם,[א] אֲדֹנָי, מְחַיֵּה מֵתִים אַתָּה,[ע] רַב לְהוֹשִׁיעַ

The phrase מַשִּׁיב הָרְוּחַ *is added from* שמחת תורה *until* פסח.
In ארץ ישראל *the phrase* מוֹרִיד הַטָּל *is added from* פסח *until* שמיני עצרת.

בחורף: מַשִּׁיב הָרְוּחַ וּמוֹרִיד הַגֶּשֶׁם / בארץ ישראל בקיץ: מוֹרִיד הַטָּל

מְכַלְכֵּל חַיִּים בְּחֶסֶד, מְחַיֵּה מֵתִים בְּרַחֲמִים רַבִּים
סוֹמֵךְ נוֹפְלִים, וְרוֹפֵא חוֹלִים, וּמַתִּיר אֲסוּרִים
וּמְקַיֵּם אֱמוּנָתוֹ לִישֵׁנֵי עָפָר.
מִי כָמְוֹךָ, בַּעַל גְּבוּרוֹת, וּמִי דְּוֹמֶה לָּךְ
מֶלֶךְ, מֵמִית וּמְחַיֶּה וּמַצְמִיחַ יְשׁוּעָה.

בשבת שובה: מִי כָמְוֹךָ אַב הָרַחֲמִים
זוֹכֵר יְצוּרָיו לְחַיִּים בְּרַחֲמִים.

וְנֶאֱמָן אַתָּה לְהַחֲיוֹת מֵתִים.
בָּרוּךְ אַתָּה יהוה, מְחַיֵּה הַמֵּתִים.[ב]

When saying the עמידה *silently, continue with* אַתָּה קָדוֹשׁ *on page 341.*

בָּרוּךְ אַתָּה יהוה, מָגֵן אַבְרָהָם – *Blessed are You, Lord, Shield of Abraham.* Each of the Patriarchs may be seen as representing a different approach to the relationship with God and the Land. Avraham, according to the Rabbis, discovered God on his own, without the benefit of a Jewish education or tradition, boldly charting the path toward faith as a rationalist or a romantic, depending on how one views him. He was born outside the Land, made *aliya*, left for a period and then returned. Yitzḥak lived the life of a holy person, named by God, ready for the ultimate sacrifice, he never left the Land of Israel. Yaakov was born in Israel, lived in the Diaspora, returned to Israel, and then died in the Diaspora. His was a life of trials and tribulations, in which God was ever present but not necessarily always heard. We mention each of the Patriarchs perhaps in part because each of them points toward a different path toward interacting with Hashem and with the Land. Paths that speaks to each of us differently, perhaps at different points in our lives, perhaps at different points in our day. The path to faith or the Land isn't always a straight one but, as indicated by the concluding blessing, we all aspire to be like Avraham.

KEDUSHA[B]

During the Leader's Repetition, the following is said standing with feet together, rising on the toes at the words indicated by ▲.

Cong. then Leader: נְקַדֵּשׁ We will sanctify Your name on earth,
as they sanctify it in the highest heavens,
as is written by Your prophet,
"And they [the angels] call to one another saying: *Is. 6*

---

on cymbals struck the instrument only three times the entire evening. The Rav wondered whether they both got paid the same amount since the amount of effort they expended was certainly not equal, and so he went and asked the cymbalist if it were so. The musician not only confirmed that they were paid the same but that their importance was equal. "Without those three clashes of the cymbals," he said, "the entire concert would fall apart, for the essential thing about an orchestra is that every single sound is balanced with another; if one sound is missing, then the entire combination fails."

The Rav said that it was at that moment that he understood the gemara's statement (Berakhot 8a) that whoever has a synagogue in his community and does not attend, is called a bad neighbor.

BIUR TEFILLA • ביאור תפילה

קדושה – *KEDUSHA* (also see the commentary on kedusha during Minḥa on page 513

We have been on a journey moving ever higher, ever closer to an encounter with the Divine, which ideally found its most personal expression in the *Amida*. Now, before we descend, we join together as a community of people who have raised ourselves above ourselves, striving for the summit as a collective. Putting this into words, we adopt the stance of angels, as it were, describing Hashem's awesome distance and His intimate closeness. It is called simply *Kedusha*, holiness, for that is what we describe and it is for that we strive. Apparently in the times of the Geonim, at least in Israel, the *Kedusha* was only said on Shabbat (*Tosafot, Sanhedrin* 37b). To explain this custom, the story is told that the angels had six wings (*Yeshayahu* 6) and each wing would sing a song to *Hashem* on one of the six days of the week. The angels turned to Him and said, "*Hashem*, we only have six wings, and what of the seventh day?" To which He responded, "Don't worry, I have one more wing that can sing before Me, as the verse says: 'From the edge (*kenaf*) of the earth we have heard songs'" (*Yeshayahu* 24:16). The implication is clear: on Shabbat we are that wing.

As in the *Amida* itself, there is a widespread custom to stand with one's feet together as they if they were a single entity, similar to the vision of *Yeḥezkel* (1:7), one of the most mystical in all of *Tanakh* in which he described the angels as: "their legs were as one straight leg." At this moment, we see ourselves as wholly spiritual creatures.

It is as if our feet are bound and our will is not our own (Rabbeinu Baḥye, *Bemidbar* 16:22). One should have in mind the commandment "and I will be sanctified among the children of Israel" (Ḥida 18:13 in the name of Arizal)

קדושה[ב]

During the חזרת הש״ץ, *the following is said standing with feet together, rising on the toes at the words indicated by* ▲.

קהל *then* ש״ץ: נְקַדֵּשׁ אֶת שִׁמְךָ בָּעוֹלָם
כְּשֵׁם שֶׁמַּקְדִּישִׁים אוֹתוֹ בִּשְׁמֵי מָרוֹם
כַּכָּתוּב עַל יַד נְבִיאֶךָ:
ישעיה ו וְקָרָא זֶה אֶל־זֶה וְאָמַר

alternative possibilities for the meaning of the phrase "gives life to the dead."

(1) He supports and cures those who were at death's door whom doctors said could not be cured. Hashem thus revives the dead in this way (Abudarham).

(2) By virtue of the fact that He provides good to those who are still alive, this provides life/satisfaction to those who are dead (*Tiferet Shlomo*).

(3) Hashem grants life to those who are downcast or enveloped by sadness, who may feel like they are dead.

(4) Hashem sends rain on a regular basis which revives life on earth.

(5) Hashem enables us to awake every morning when we are otherwise like dead people.

Which interpretation appeals to you the most today?

INTRODUCTION TO *ḤAZARAT HASHATZ* – The Reader's repetition of the *Amida*

The repetition of the *Amida* by the *ḥazan* was established for a very functional reason, namely, to enable those who could not read the prayer to nevertheless fulfill their obligation by listening to the *ḥazan* recite it and answering *amen* to each of its blessings. Such a response is considered tantamount to saying the blessing oneself. In halakhic discourse this is known as *shome'a k'oneh*, the listener is like one who recited it. It is a statement that everyone should be able to participate in communal prayer, regardless of their background or ability.

At the same time, Rabbi Soloveitchik maintained that the repetition had another function, namely, it was a prayer not with the community, but of the community. That is to say, it is another *Amida*, said not by a group of individuals, but by a collective, represented by the *ḥazan*. We pray not just as individuals for ourselves and for others but for the single entity called community. As such, there are some who have the custom to remain standing, feet together, for the entire repetition as if they were saying the *Amida* yet again. Too often some people think of this practice as being repetitious; think of it instead as a totally new prayer, a new opportunity to come together as something larger than oneself.

ANI TEFILLA • אני תפילה

The story is told that Rav Soloveitchik once went to hear the Boston Symphony Orchestra and observed that the harpist worked so hard throughout the performance but the person

Cong. then Leader: ▲Holy, ▲holy, ▲holy[BH] is the LORD of hosts
the whole world is filled with His glory."
Then with a sound of mighty noise,[B] majestic and strong,
they make their voice heard, raising themselves
toward the Seraphim, and facing them say: "Blessed…

Cong. then Leader: ▲"Blessed is the LORD's glory from His place." *Ezek. 3*
Reveal Yourself from Your place,[A] O our King, and reign over us,
for we are waiting for You.[I]
When will You reign in Zion? May it be soon in our days,
and may You dwell there for ever and all time.
May You be exalted and sanctified in the midst of Jerusalem,
Your city, from generation to generation for evermore.
May our eyes see Your kingdom,
as is said in the songs of Your splendor,
written by David your righteous anointed one:

Cong. then Leader: ▲"The LORD shall reign for ever. He is your God, Zion, *Ps. 146*
from generation to generation, Halleluya!"

Leader: From generation to generation we will declare Your greatness,
and we will proclaim Your holiness for evermore.
Your praise, our God, shall not leave our mouth forever,
for You, God, are a great and holy King. Blessed are You, LORD,
the holy God. / *On Shabbat Shuva:* the holy King./

The Leader continues with "Moses rejoiced" on the next page.

ANI TEFILLA • אני תפילה

מִמְּקוֹמְךָ מַלְכֵּנוּ תוֹפִיעַ – *Reveal Yourself from Your place.* I once heard a convert say that one of the biggest adjustments to Jewish prayer was the absence of some physical representation of God to pray to. When I was a child, I recall wondering what would happen if the ark suddenly opened and God revealed Himself there or somewhere else at the front of the synagogue. How would all of us act differently at that moment?

How would your prayer be different right now if Hashem were suddenly to appear before you?

IYUN TEFILLA • עיון תפילה

כִּי מְחַכִּים אֲנַחְנוּ לָךְ – *For we are waiting for You.* The king is about to arrive. The troops are rallied and preparations are made. The officers make sure that everything is in order and the troops are gathered on the parade grounds in full regalia standing at attention

This **IYUN TEFILLA** *continues on page 341.*

קהל then ש״ץ: ״קָדוֹשׁ, ״קָדוֹשׁ, ״קָדוֹשׁ, בה יהוה צְבָאוֹת, מְלֹא כָל־הָאָרֶץ כְּבוֹדוֹ:
אָז בְּקוֹל[ב] רַעַשׁ גָּדוֹל אַדִּיר וְחָזָק, מַשְׁמִיעִים קוֹל
מִתְנַשְּׂאִים לְעֻמַּת שְׂרָפִים, לְעֻמָּתָם בָּרוּךְ יֹאמֵרוּ

קהל then ש״ץ: ״בָּרוּךְ כְּבוֹד־יהוה מִמְּקוֹמוֹ: יחזקאל ג
מִמְּקוֹמְךָ מַלְכֵּנוּ תוֹפִיעַ[א] וְתִמְלֹךְ עָלֵינוּ, כִּי מְחַכִּים אֲנַחְנוּ לָךְ[ע]
מָתַי תִּמְלֹךְ בְּצִיּוֹן, בְּקָרוֹב בְּיָמֵינוּ לְעוֹלָם וָעֶד תִּשְׁכֹּן
תִּתְגַּדַּל וְתִתְקַדַּשׁ בְּתוֹךְ יְרוּשָׁלַיִם עִירְךָ, לְדוֹר וָדוֹר וּלְנֵצַח נְצָחִים.
וְעֵינֵינוּ תִרְאֶינָה מַלְכוּתֶךָ
כַּדָּבָר הָאָמוּר בְּשִׁירֵי עֻזֶּךָ, עַל יְדֵי דָוִד מְשִׁיחַ צִדְקֶךָ

קהל then ש״ץ: ״יִמְלֹךְ יהוה לְעוֹלָם, אֱלֹהַיִךְ צִיּוֹן לְדֹר וָדֹר, הַלְלוּיָהּ: תהלים קמו

ש״ץ: לְדוֹר וָדוֹר נַגִּיד גָּדְלֶךָ, וּלְנֵצַח נְצָחִים קְדֻשָּׁתְךָ נַקְדִּישׁ
וְשִׁבְחֲךָ אֱלֹהֵינוּ מִפִּינוּ לֹא יָמוּשׁ לְעוֹלָם וָעֶד
כִּי אֵל מֶלֶךְ גָּדוֹל וְקָדוֹשׁ אָתָּה.
בָּרוּךְ אַתָּה יהוה הָאֵל הַקָּדוֹשׁ./בשבת שובה: הַמֶּלֶךְ הַקָּדוֹשׁ./

The שליח ציבור *continues with* יִשְׂמַח מֹשֶׁה *on the next page.*

BIUR TEFILLA • ביאור תפילה

קָדוֹשׁ, קָדוֹשׁ, קָדוֹשׁ – *Holy, holy, holy.* When reciting these words, one might have in mind the Aramaic translation that Hashem is holy above, He is holy on earth, and He will be holy forever (see the prayer *Uva LeTziyon* on page 495). He defies our limitations of space and time.

קָדוֹשׁ, קָדוֹשׁ, קָדוֹשׁ – *Holy, holy, holy.* This is in effect an admission that Hashem is beyond us. We shouldn't get upset that He sometimes seems elusive and untouchable. Were He not, He would not be God.

אָז בְּקוֹל – *Then with a mighty noise.* This *Kedusha* is a little different from the one said during the week, and has echoes of the description of the praise by the angels in the first of the *birkhot Keriat Shema* (page 321).

HILKHOT TEFILLA • הלכות תפילה

קָדוֹשׁ, קָדוֹשׁ, קָדוֹשׁ – *Holy, holy, holy.* Some have the custom here to go up and down on one's tiptoes with the recitation of each one of these words, as if one is reaching higher and higher.

HOLINESS

אַתָּה קָדוֹשׁ You are holy[B] and Your name is holy,
and holy ones praise You daily, Selah!
Blessed are You, LORD,
the holy God. / *On Shabbat Shuva:* the holy King./
(*If forgotten, repeat the Amida.*)

HOLINESS OF THE DAY

יִשְׂמַח Moses rejoiced at the gift of his portion[1]
when You called him "faithful servant."
A crown of glory
You placed on his head
when he stood before You on Mount Sinai.
He brought down in his hands two tablets of stone
on which was engraved the observance of the Sabbath.
So it is written in Your Torah:

---

praised Hashem in history (the first blessing – *Avot*) and in nature (the second blessing – *Gevurot*), we here admit that those descriptions are limited and that, in the end, He is beyond our understanding.

This is the meaning of the declaration at the beginning of the blessing which states simply "You are *Kadosh*." There is simply no better way to describe how indescribable You really are.

IYUN TEFILLA • עיון תפילה

יִשְׂמַח מֹשֶׁה בְּמַתְּנַת חֶלְקוֹ – *Moses rejoiced at the gift of his portion.* This passage describes Moshe's happiness at being able to bring the word of God to the Jewish people. In particular, the Rabbis understood that the presence of Shabbat in the Ten Commandments was especially joyful. Some commentaries point to the Gemara which describes a conversation between Moshe and Hashem atop Mount Sinai: "Hashem said to Moshe: 'I have a wonderful gift from my treasure house and its name is Shabbat. I want to give it to Israel. Go and let them know" (*Shabbat* 10b). It must always be remembered that Shabbat is a gift, not alone an obligation, not alone a yoke, not alone a lifestyle, but a gift.

If you were to look at this day more as a gift, how might it change the way you observe it today?

At the same time, perhaps it is an echo of the tradition that the Torah was given on Shabbat (*Shabbat* 86a). One can then understand Moshe's great joy... and the need for us to follow. Knowing Torah brings one joy.

What about this day generally gives you joy?

How can you make this Shabbat into more of a day of joy?

קדושת השם

אַתָּה קָדוֹשׁ[ב] וְשִׁמְךָ קָדוֹשׁ
וּקְדוֹשִׁים בְּכָל יוֹם יְהַלְלוּךָ סֶּלָה.
בָּרוּךְ אַתָּה יהוה, הָאֵל הַקָּדוֹשׁ. / בשבת שובה: הַמֶּלֶךְ הַקָּדוֹשׁ./

(*If forgotten, repeat the* עמידה.)

קדושת היום

יִשְׂמַח מֹשֶׁה בְּמַתְּנַת חֶלְקוֹ[ע]
כִּי עֶבֶד נֶאֱמָן קָרָאתָ לּוֹ
כְּלִיל תִּפְאֶרֶת בְּרֹאשׁוֹ נָתַתָּ לּוֹ
בְּעָמְדוֹ לְפָנֶיךָ עַל הַר סִינַי
וּשְׁנֵי לוּחוֹת אֲבָנִים הוֹרִיד בְּיָדוֹ
וְכָתוּב בָּהֶם שְׁמִירַת שַׁבָּת
וְכֵן כָּתוּב בְּתוֹרָתֶךָ

---

example did this officer set, what did it say about his allegiance and commitment? So, too, with us. With a full heart we say "we are waiting for You" but as time goes on we tire, we sleep, forgetting that at any moment, the King could arrive (Ḥafetz Ḥayyim).

awaiting the arrival of their commander in chief. But the king is delayed and one officer, try as he might, begins to get drowsy and falls asleep on a chair in front of the troops. When the king finally appears, he is sympathetic but unforgiving, for what kind of

BIUR TEFILLA • ביאור תפילה

אַתָּה קָדוֹשׁ – *You are holy.* What does the word "holy" (*kadosh*) really mean? At its core, the word is derived from the Hebrew word for "separation." The Hebrew word for betrothal (*kiddushin*), for example, suggests that, once engaged, the woman is off limits or *separated* from any other man who may want to marry her. Similarly, *Kiddush,* the blessing we say on wine on Friday night, is designed to establish that we are acknowledging that Shabbat is a day *separate* from all others. Finally, there is the portion in the Torah (*Vayikra* 19ff) which is called *kedoshim tihiyu* (You should be holy) – the commandment that the Jewish people be *separate* from all other nations.

Based on this, the meaning of the present blessing becomes clear: we declare Hashem as being *Kadosh* – totally separate, not only from man but from all life as we know it. Here we acknowledge that He is indescribable, seemingly distant, and beyond anything we can imagine. After having

וְשָׁמְרוּ The children of Israel must keep the Sabbath,
observing the Sabbath in every generation
as an everlasting covenant.
It is a sign between Me and the children of Israel for ever,
for in six days God made the heavens and the earth,
but on the seventh day
He ceased work and refreshed Himself. Ex. 31

וּבַיּוֹם הַשְּׁבִיעִי שָׁבַת וַיִּנָּפַשׁ – *But on the seventh day He ceased work and refreshed Himself.* Did God really need to recharge His batteries, as it were? The Gemara (*Beitza* 16a) homiletically learns from here instead that on Shabbat one receives an "added soul" (*neshama yeteira*), often understood as an added measure of spirituality. Rashi explains that in practical terms it means that one has a greater capacity for relaxation and joy, and that even one's eating and drinking on this day have a different dimension.

According to Rabbi Tzaddok of Lublin, the extra soul that we receive on Shabbat is not the same one that returns every week but a totally new one every Shabbat. "Hence, Shabbat is not a comfortably familiar ritual, the spiritual equivalent of a pair of old shoes... Rather, it bespeaks spiritual adventurousness, a pioneering drive, a fascination with the unknown and untried, and readiness to embrace the new as a way to *avodat Hashem* (service of *Hashem*)" (Rabbi Norman Lamm).

How can you engage your *neshama yeteira* (extra soul) this Shabbat?

וַיִּנָּפַשׁ – *He... refreshed Himself.* Shabbat is about refreshing one's soul, creating it anew, reliving being born into a new world. This highlights one of the main differences between the Western notion of relaxing and the Shabbat version of rest; the one is about recreation, the other is about re-creation.

ANI TEFILLA • אני תפילה

The story is told of a fool from Chelm who was so forgetful that before he went to bed he made a list of where everything was so that he could find it all in the morning: my pants are on the chair, my shirt is hanging in the closet, my shoes are near the door, and I, I am lying in bed. When he got up the next morning he consulted the list and found everything – except he could not find himself lying in the bed. Rabbi Ḥanokh Henikh Alexander would tell this story to his followers and when asked why, he responded, "Because we are all like that fool. We are so involved in everyday life that we spend all of our time keeping tabs on our material things, but not enough time asking ourselves 'Where am I?'"

שמות לא

וְשָׁמְרוּ בְנֵי־יִשְׂרָאֵל אֶת־הַשַּׁבָּת
לַעֲשׂוֹת אֶת־הַשַּׁבָּת לְדֹרֹתָם בְּרִית עוֹלָם:
בֵּינִי וּבֵין בְּנֵי יִשְׂרָאֵל אוֹת הִוא לְעֹלָם
כִּי־שֵׁשֶׁת יָמִים עָשָׂה יהוה אֶת־הַשָּׁמַיִם וְאֶת־הָאָרֶץ
וּבַיּוֹם הַשְּׁבִיעִי שָׁבַת וַיִּנָּפַשׁ:

IYUN TEFILLA • עיון תפילה

וְשָׁמְרוּ בְנֵי־יִשְׂרָאֵל אֶת־הַשַּׁבָּת – *The children of Israel must keep the Shabbat.* The Ten Commandments are written twice in the Torah. In one, the commandment is given to "keep the Shabbat" (*Devarim* 5:12); in the other, it is to "remember the Shabbat" (*Shemot* 20:8). But the expression "keep the Shabbat" regarding the seventh day of the week appears seven times throughout the Torah. The expression "remember the Shabbat" appears only once (*Iyun Tefilla*). The siddur here seeks to remind us to observe the day, to keep it and not just to remember it with words. We are good at mouthing our commitments but we must also act upon them.

How will you do a better job of that today?

בֵּינִי וּבֵין בְּנֵי יִשְׂרָאֵל אוֹת הִיא לְעוֹלָם – *It is a sign between Me and the children of Israel for ever.* The Rabbis point to this verse from *Shemot* 31:17 to explain why tefillin are not worn on Shabbat and Yom Tov. For tefillin are also referred to as a "sign" (**אות** *Shemot* 13:9). Thus, donning tefillin is considered disrespectful to the "sign" of Shabbat (*Shulhan Arukh*, 31:1). Shabbat is a connecting link between the Jewish people and Hashem, a distinguishing sign that even the non-Jewish world has come to recognize as one of our most unique characteristics.

בֵּינִי וּבֵין בְּנֵי יִשְׂרָאֵל אוֹת הִיא לְעוֹלָם – *It is a sign between Me and the children of Israel for ever.* "Rabbi Yehoshua ben Levi said: All of the commandments that Hashem gave to Israel were given publicly, except for the Shabbat which was given in private (*Beitza* 16a)." But what does this mean?! Isn't the commandment of Shabbat one of the Ten Commandments that were given in public for all to see and hear? Rather, what the Rabbis meant to say was that the commandment may have been public but the inner essence of Shabbat–its meaning, its taste, its secret–that is what was given in private. That is why it says it is "between me and Israel" (*Rabbeinu Beḥaye*).

How would you define the essence of Shabbat to someone else?

How can you yet experience it yourself today?

וְלֹא You, O Lord our God, did not give it
to the other nations of the world,[1]
nor did You, our King, give it as a heritage
to those who worship idols.
In its rest the uncircumcised do not dwell,
for You gave it in love to Israel Your people,
to the descendants of Jacob whom You chose.
May the people who sanctify the seventh day
all find satisfaction and delight in Your goodness,[B]
for You favored the seventh day
and made it holy,
calling it the most cherished of days,[IA]
a remembrance of the act of creation.

IYUN TEFILLA • עיון תפילה

חֶמְדַּת יָמִים אוֹתוֹ קָרָאתָ – *Calling it the most cherished of days.* What a person does with this day can have an impact on the following week, for your actions generate a sense of blessing that is implanted within you.

Create the opportunities for blessing today that you can take with you into next week.

ANI TEFILLA • אני תפילה

חֶמְדַּת יָמִים אוֹתוֹ קָרָאתָ – *Calling it the most cherished of days.* My grandfather, ז״ל, used to say, "Shabbos! I love the Shabbos! I don't know how the non-Jews survive without it."

What can you do today that will impact the rest of your week?

ANI TEFILLA • אני תפילה

"Mr. Speaker, allow me just one further point. This House should know, it is not necessary to be an observant Jew to appreciate the full historic and sacred aura that enshrines the 'perfect gift' called Shabbat. Its prohibitions are not arbitrary. They provide insulation against corrosive everydayness, they build fences against invasions by the profane, and they enrich the soul by creating a space for sacred time. In a word, one need not be pious to accept the cherished principle of Shabbat. One merely needs to be a proud Jew" (Prime Minister Menachem Begin speaking to the Knesset).

וְלֹא נְתַתּוֹ, יהוה אֱלֹהֵינוּ, לְגוֹיֵי הָאֲרָצוֹת[ע]
וְלֹא הִנְחַלְתּוֹ, מַלְכֵּנוּ, לְעוֹבְדֵי פְסִילִים
וְגַם בִּמְנוּחָתוֹ לֹא יִשְׁכְּנוּ עֲרֵלִים
כִּי לְיִשְׂרָאֵל עַמְּךָ נְתַתּוֹ בְּאַהֲבָה
לְזֶרַע יַעֲקֹב אֲשֶׁר בָּם בָּחָרְתָּ.
עַם מְקַדְּשֵׁי שְׁבִיעִי
כֻּלָּם יִשְׂבְּעוּ וְיִתְעַנְּגוּ מִטּוּבֶךָ[ב]
וּבַשְּׁבִיעִי רָצִיתָ בּוֹ וְקִדַּשְׁתּוֹ
חֶמְדַּת יָמִים אוֹתוֹ קָרָאתָ[עא]
זֵכֶר לְמַעֲשֵׂה בְרֵאשִׁית.

IYUN TEFILLA • עיון תפילה

וְלֹא נְתַתּוֹ, יהוה אֱלֹהֵינוּ, לְגוֹיֵי הָאֲרָצוֹת – *You, O Lord our God, did not give it to the other nations of the world.* Were Shabbat only about rest from fatigue or the eroding impact of the work week, then it would be the property of all mankind, for everyone understands the need to take a break, to recharge one's batteries so that one can return to work refreshed. But Shabbat is not only about that kind of rest; it is about refreshing one's soul, about gaining perspective, about one's relationship with God, with one's family and with oneself. That understanding, that goal, was given to the Jewish people alone.

BIUR TEFILLA • ביאור תפילה

כֻּלָּם יִשְׂבְּעוּ וְיִתְעַנְּגוּ מִטּוּבֶךָ – *All find satisfaction and delight in Your goodness.* Shouldn't it be the reverse – first one experiences the delight or joy (*oneg*) of eating and then one eats and becomes satiated? That is true of physical pleasure: one eats delicious food but then comes to a point at which one cannot eat any more. But in spiritual matters, there is no limit to one's growth and satisfaction. Hence one can be satisfied but still be delighted by more Torah, more song, more Shabbat (*Barukh SheAmar*).

אֱלֹהֵינוּ Our God and God of our ancestors, find favor in our rest.
Make us holy through Your commandments[ǀ]
and grant us our share in Your Torah.[ǀ]
Satisfy us with Your goodness, grant us joy in Your salvation,
and purify our hearts to serve You in truth.
In love and favor, LORD our God,
grant us as our heritage Your holy Sabbath,
so that Israel who sanctify Your name may find rest on it.
Blessed are You, LORD, who sanctifies the Sabbath.[ǀ]

---

place in Your Torah. Through actions comes understanding.

וְתֵן חֶלְקֵנוּ בְּתוֹרָתֶךָ – *And grant us our share in Your Torah.* There is a mystical tradition which says that every Jewish soul yet to be born stood at Sinai at the time of the revelation. As such, each of us actually owns a share in the Torah for we were there when it was originally given. We need only reclaim our rightful place in its tradition. If so, then the prayer takes on new meaning: Help us to find ourselves. Help us to get in touch with what we already have.

בָּרוּךְ אַתָּה יהוה, מְקַדֵּשׁ הַשַּׁבָּת – *Blessed are You, LORD, who sanctifies the Sabbath.* Shabbat derives its sanctity directly from God. The day itself therefore maintains its holiness regardless of what people do on that day, even if they do not know it is there. But we know that it is there, waiting to be discovered.

ANI TEFILLA • אני תפילה

"The revelation at Sinai, which is our focus in the Sabbath morning service, is about destiny. It is not about what we are. It is about what we are destined to become and how following the commandments Moses received from God on Sinai can help us become that. By telling us how to live, the commandments give us our mission – if we choose to accept it – of bettering, even perfecting, the world God created… I was taught that the Children of Israel became a nation not when they were liberated from slavery, but when the Law was revealed to them on Sinai – because that gave them their reason for being, their national destiny. Those same values give each of us a personal destiny. But you can't be passive about your destiny. It isn't fulfilled unless you decide to work to make it happen.

The commandment to observe the Sabbath is… at the heart of our destiny. But the Sabbath doesn't automatically enter our lives. We have to decide to bring it in, to seize that part of our destiny. And that can be difficult."

This **ANI TEFILLA** *continues on page 349.*

אֱלֹהֵינוּ וֵאלֹהֵי אֲבוֹתֵינוּ, רְצֵה בִמְנוּחָתֵנוּ
קַדְּשֵׁנוּ בְּמִצְוֹתֶיךָ[ע] וְתֵן חֶלְקֵנוּ בְּתוֹרָתֶךָ[ע]
שַׂבְּעֵנוּ מִטּוּבֶךָ וְשַׂמְּחֵנוּ בִּישׁוּעָתֶךָ
וְטַהֵר לִבֵּנוּ לְעָבְדְּךָ בֶּאֱמֶת
וְהַנְחִילֵנוּ, יהוה אֱלֹהֵינוּ, בְּאַהֲבָה וּבְרָצוֹן שַׁבַּת קָדְשֶׁךָ
וְיָנוּחוּ בוֹ יִשְׂרָאֵל מְקַדְּשֵׁי שְׁמֶךָ.
בָּרוּךְ אַתָּה יהוה, מְקַדֵּשׁ הַשַּׁבָּת.[ע]

IYUN TEFILLA • עיון תפילה

For more commentary on this blessing, see *Ma'ariv* (pages 108) and *Musaf* (pages 427).

קַדְּשֵׁנוּ בְּמִצְוֹתֶיךָ – *Make us holy through Your commandments.*

In what ways do you wish your life would be more holy?

How could you make the commandments that you already do make your life or your being more holy than you feel it is?

קַדְּשֵׁנוּ בְּמִצְוֹתֶיךָ וְתֵן חֶלְקֵנוּ בְּתוֹרָתֶךָ – *Make us holy through Your commandments and grant us our share in Your Torah.* In most other instances, the order is reversed, we first ask for a part in the Torah and then ask for help in fulfilling commandments. To what may this be compared? When accepting the Torah at Sinai, the Jewish people responded "we will do and we will listen," as if to say, we will commit ourselves to a Jewish life even if there are parts of the system which we do not yet fully understand. It is our prayer that through immersing ourselves in the commandments, we will come to find our

ANI TEFILLA • אני תפילה

The story is told of the day when the first train from Minsk to Pinsk rolled into town for its maiden voyage and two men bought tickets to see what it would be like to ride this new invention. Reuven was so amazed by this huge machine that he spent all of his time walking around the train, measuring its wheels, examining the locomotive and the passenger cars. He became so engrossed that he did not notice the final boarding call and the train pulled out of the station leaving him behind on the platform. Shimon, on the other hand, got onto the train as soon as it pulled into the station, thinking that he would come to better understand how it worked while he was on the journey.

When it comes to Shabbat, to prayer, and to other commandments, it pays to get on the train first.

TEMPLE SERVICE[B]

רְצֵה Find favor,[B] LORD our God, in Your people Israel
and their prayer.[B]
Restore the service to Your most holy House,[B]
and accept in love and favor
the fire-offerings[B] of Israel
and their prayer.[B]
May the service of Your people Israel
always find favor with You.

The "service" could be a reference to the prayers which were offered then and which we offer now, the *avoda shebalev* – service of the heart.

Which interpretation speaks to you most today?

וְאִשֵּׁי – *The fire-offerings.* This could refer to the fire-offerings in the *Beit HaMikdash.* We ask that the Temple service be restored. Prayers there are different from our prayers here.

How do you think they might be so?

וְאִשֵּׁי could refer to the martyrs of Israel (from the word אִישׁ, man) who sacrificed their lives for Your name. Accept their sacrifice and their prayers (*Tosafot Menaḥot* 110a).

וְאִשֵּׁי could refer to the fire that was always lit on the altar. So, too, in the heart of every Jew there is a hidden flame that seeks to cleave to Hashem, that is never extinguished.

Which interpretation speaks to you today?

ואשי ישראל ותפלתם באהבה תקבל בְּרָצוֹן – *And accept in love and favor the fire-offerings of Israel and their prayer.* "Love" could describe the prayers – we ask that the prayers we offer out of love should be accepted.

"Love" could describe the acceptance – we ask that the prayers we offer should be accepted with love.

ANI TEFILLA • אני תפילה

Make a picture in your mind when you are praying that you are really standing in Israel and in the Holy Temple and that you are actually seeing everything with your own eyes... And when you imagine this is so, that you are standing in Israel, you will achieve great clarity in your prayer (Rabbi Elimelekh of Lizhensk).

עבודה ב

רְצֵה ב יהוה אֱלֹהֵינוּ בְּעַמְּךָ יִשְׂרָאֵל וּבִתְפִלָּתָם ב
וְהָשֵׁב אֶת הָעֲבוֹדָה לִדְבִיר בֵּיתֶךָ ב
וְאִשֵּׁי ב יִשְׂרָאֵל וּתְפִלָּתָם בְּאַהֲבָה תְקַבֵּל בְּרָצוֹן ב
וּתְהִי לְרָצוֹן תָּמִיד עֲבוֹדַת יִשְׂרָאֵל עַמֶּךָ.

My religious observance, including my Sabbath observance, has taught me that it's ok to be different... When you choose your own path – whether in faith, politics, or whatever you do – you will not only feel better, but people will respect you for your choice"

(Senator Joe Lieberman, Vice-Presidential candidate, 2000)

BIUR TEFILLA • ביאור תפילה

עבודה – *Temple Service.* This is the first of the final three blessings of the *Shemoneh Esreh*, the *birkhot hodaya*, blessings of thanks. What they all have in common, despite elements of additional requests, is the acknowledgment of and gratitude to Hashem for the personal and communal relationship we have with Him.

רְצֵה – *Find favor.* Here we ask that our prayers be found acceptable in terms of their content.

Here we ask that our prayers be found acceptable in terms of their sincerity.

בְּעַמְּךָ יִשְׂרָאֵל, וּבִתְפִלָּתָם – *In Your people Israel and their prayer.* We first ask Hashem to find favor in "Your people," and only afterwards in "their prayer." This is to teach us that if we make a sincere effort to make our own lives worthy, to become better people and better Jews, only then can we hope that our prayers will be found worthy. (Rabbi S.R. Hirsch)

How have your prayers until this point moved you to become a better person today?

How can you make yourself a better person and a better Jew today?

וְהָשֵׁב אֶת הָעֲבוֹדָה לִדְבִיר בֵּיתֶךָ – *Restore the service to Your most holy House.* The "service" could be a reference to general worship in the *Beit HaMikdash*.

The "service" could be a reference to the specific Service/*Avoda* of Yom Kippur performed by the *Kohen Gadol* in the Holy of Holies. (*Devir beitekha* refers to the place where the word (*dibbur*) of God is heard.)

On Rosh Ḥodesh and Ḥol HaMo'ed, say:

אֱלֹהֵינוּ Our God and God of our ancestors, may there rise, come,[l] reach, appear, be favored, heard, regarded and remembered before You, our recollection and remembrance, as well as the remembrance of our ancestors, and of the Messiah son of David Your servant, and of Jerusalem Your holy city, and of all Your people the house of Israel – for deliverance and well-being, grace, loving-kindness and compassion, life and peace, on this day of:

On Rosh Ḥodesh: Rosh Ḥodesh.
On Pesaḥ: the Festival of Matzot.
On Sukkot: the Festival of Sukkot.

On it remember us, LORD our God, for good; recollect us for blessing, and deliver us for life. In accord with Your promise of salvation and compassion, spare us and be gracious to us; have compassion on us and deliver us, for our eyes are turned to You because You, God, are a gracious and compassionate King.

וְתֶחֱזֶינָה And may our eyes witness[B] Your return
to Zion in compassion.
Blessed are You, LORD,
who restores His Presence to Zion.[l]

BIUR TEFILLA · ביאור תפילה

וְתֶחֱזֶינָה עֵינֵינוּ – *And may our eyes witness.* Another possible translation: "and may You enable us to see." The existence of the State of Israel can be seen as a sign that You are a presence in history and that the State is the beginning of Your return to Zion. May You enable our eyes to see Israel not only as a political entity, but as the miracle that it really is.

What aspect of the modern State of Israel is the most miraculous in your opinion?

IYUN TEFILLA · עיון תפילה

הַמַּחֲזִיר שְׁכִינָתוֹ לְצִיּוֹן – *Who restores His Presence to Zion.* I thank You Hashem because I know that You will return Your Presence to Jerusalem. I only pray that it be sooner rather than later.

While this *berakha* is found in the final section of the *Amida*, the section of "Thanks," it sounds like a request for the restoration of the Temple service there. However, if we approach this as a statement of faith rather than a request, that we have total faith that this will happen, and we merely desire it in a speedy fashion, then it certainly belongs here.

On ראש חודש *and* חול המועד*, say:*

אֱלֹהֵינוּ וֵאלֹהֵי אֲבוֹתֵינוּ, יַעֲלֶה וְיָבוֹא[ע] וְיַגִּיעַ, וְיֵרָאֶה וְיֵרָצֶה וְיִשָּׁמַע, וְיִפָּקֵד וְיִזָּכֵר זִכְרוֹנֵנוּ וּפִקְדוֹנֵנוּ וְזִכְרוֹן אֲבוֹתֵינוּ, וְזִכְרוֹן מָשִׁיחַ בֶּן דָּוִד עַבְדֶּךָ, וְזִכְרוֹן יְרוּשָׁלַיִם עִיר קָדְשֶׁךָ, וְזִכְרוֹן כָּל עַמְּךָ בֵּית יִשְׂרָאֵל, לְפָנֶיךָ, לִפְלֵיטָה לְטוֹבָה, לְחֵן וּלְחֶסֶד וּלְרַחֲמִים, לְחַיִּים וּלְשָׁלוֹם בְּיוֹם

בראש חודש: **רֹאשׁ הַחֹדֶשׁ** / בפסח: **חַג הַמַּצּוֹת** / בסוכות: **חַג הַסֻּכּוֹת**

הַזֶּה. זָכְרֵנוּ יהוה אֱלֹהֵינוּ בּוֹ לְטוֹבָה, וּפָקְדֵנוּ בוֹ לִבְרָכָה, וְהוֹשִׁיעֵנוּ בוֹ לְחַיִּים. וּבִדְבַר יְשׁוּעָה וְרַחֲמִים, חוּס וְחָנֵּנוּ וְרַחֵם עָלֵינוּ וְהוֹשִׁיעֵנוּ, כִּי אֵלֶיךָ עֵינֵינוּ, כִּי אֵל מֶלֶךְ חַנּוּן וְרַחוּם אָתָּה.

וְתֶחֱזֶינָה עֵינֵינוּ[ב] בְּשׁוּבְךָ לְצִיּוֹן בְּרַחֲמִים.
בָּרוּךְ אַתָּה יהוה, הַמַּחֲזִיר שְׁכִינָתוֹ לְצִיּוֹן.[ע]

IYUN TEFILLA • עיון תפילה

יַעֲלֶה וְיָבוֹא – *May there rise, come.* Why is there so much discussion here about remembering; after all, does Hashem really forget anything? Rather, just as there are distractions which cause us to be unable to recall things we really know, so too there are things about our actions which act as barriers to Hashem's "remembering" the good things that we do. For example, each person is born with his own unique potential which he must realize on his own. We ask that Hashem remember (וְיִפָּקֵד) the potential that we have and that he recall (וְיִזָּכֵר) the good deeds we have done to try to realize that potential. Rosh Ḥodesh and the holy days are times for introspection, for that, too, is a form of service of the heart.

ANI TEFILLA • אני תפילה

Rabbi Refael of Bershad once told that he complained to his teacher Rabbi Pinḥas of Koretz that in difficult times it's very hard to have perfect faith in the belief that God watches out for every person. It actually seems as if God is hiding his face from such an unhappy person. What could he do to restore his faith? Rabbi Pinḥas answered him: "It ceases to be a hiding if you know that it is hiding."

THANKSGIVING

▾*Bow:* We give thanks to You,
for You are *Stand straight*
the LORD our God
and God of our ancestors
for ever and all time.
You are the Rock of our lives,
Shield of our salvation
from generation to generation.
We will thank You and
declare Your praise for our lives,[A]
which are entrusted into Your hand;
for our souls,
which are placed in Your charge;
for Your miracles
which are with us every day;
and for Your wonders[I] and favors
at all times,
evening, morning and midday.
You are good –
for Your compassion never fails.
You are compassionate –
for Your loving-kindnesses never cease.
We have always placed our hope in You.

During the Leader's Repetition, the congregation says quietly:

▾*Bow:* We give thanks to You,
for You are *Stand straight*
the LORD our God
and God of our ancestors,
God of all flesh,
who formed us
and formed the universe.
Blessings and thanks
are due to Your great
and holy name
for giving us life
and sustaining us.
May You continue
to give us life and sustain us;
and may You gather our
exiles to Your holy courts,
to keep Your decrees,
do Your will and serve You
with a perfect heart,
for it is for us
to give You thanks.
Blessed be God
to whom thanksgiving is due.

---

moment when my life was imperiled on my way here today but I walked by, totally unaware.

וְעַל נִפְלְאוֹתֶיךָ – *And for Your wonders.* We thank You for the everyday wonders to which we may be oblivious. I will not take for granted the vibrant life which surrounds me.

וְטוֹבוֹתֶיךָ – *And favors.* We thank You even for the things which seem bad, because ultimately we know that You want good to emerge from them.

מוֹדִים אֲנַחְנוּ לָךְ – *We give thanks to You.* In short, one can thank God here for anything and everything: the people in our lives who care about us, our family, our relatives, our friends and acquaintances, the material comforts we have, the air we breathe. Sometimes we do not appreciate things enough until they are gone. Don't wait. Be thankful.

What is on your list today?

IYUN TEFILLA • עיון תפילה

מודים דרבנן – *The Rabbis' Modim.* The Gemara (*Sota* 40a) asks what the congregation is supposed to recite when the *Ḥazan* reaches this point. Yet why ask? After all, in

This IYUN TEFILLA *continues on page 355.*

הודאה

▾ Bow מוֹדִים אֲנַחְנוּ לָךְ
Stand straight שָׁאַתָּה הוּא
יהוה אֱלֹהֵינוּ וֵאלֹהֵי אֲבוֹתֵינוּ
לְעוֹלָם וָעֶד.
צוּר חַיֵּינוּ, מָגֵן יִשְׁעֵנוּ
אַתָּה הוּא לְדוֹר וָדוֹר.
נוֹדֶה לְּךָ וּנְסַפֵּר תְּהִלָּתֶךָ
עַל חַיֵּינוּ[א] הַמְּסוּרִים בְּיָדֶךָ
וְעַל נִשְׁמוֹתֵינוּ הַפְּקוּדוֹת לָךְ
וְעַל נִסֶּיךָ שֶׁבְּכָל יוֹם עִמָּנוּ
וְעַל נִפְלְאוֹתֶיךָ[ע] וְטוֹבוֹתֶיךָ
שֶׁבְּכָל עֵת, עֶרֶב וָבֹקֶר וְצָהֳרָיִם.
הַטּוֹב, כִּי לֹא כָלוּ רַחֲמֶיךָ
וְהַמְרַחֵם, כִּי לֹא תַמּוּ חֲסָדֶיךָ
מֵעוֹלָם קִוִּינוּ לָךְ.

During the חזרת הש״ץ, *the* קהל *says quietly:*

▾ *Bow* מוֹדִים אֲנַחְנוּ לָךְ
Stand straight שָׁאַתָּה הוּא
יהוה אֱלֹהֵינוּ וֵאלֹהֵי אֲבוֹתֵינוּ
אֱלֹהֵי כָל בָּשָׂר
יוֹצְרֵנוּ, יוֹצֵר בְּרֵאשִׁית.
בְּרָכוֹת וְהוֹדָאוֹת
לְשִׁמְךָ הַגָּדוֹל וְהַקָּדוֹשׁ
עַל שֶׁהֶחֱיִיתָנוּ וְקִיַּמְתָּנוּ.
כֵּן תְּחַיֵּנוּ וּתְקַיְּמֵנוּ
וְתֶאֱסֹף גָּלֻיּוֹתֵינוּ
לְחַצְרוֹת קָדְשֶׁךָ
לִשְׁמֹר חֻקֶּיךָ
וְלַעֲשׂוֹת רְצוֹנֶךָ וּלְעָבְדְּךָ
בְּלֵבָב שָׁלֵם
עַל שֶׁאֲנַחְנוּ מוֹדִים לָךְ.
בָּרוּךְ אֵל הַהוֹדָאוֹת.

BIUR TEFILLA • ביאור תפילה

מוֹדִים אֲנַחְנוּ לָךְ – *We give thanks to You.* The word can mean "thank" in which case the sense is that we thank You for all of the good that there is in our lives.

The word can mean "acknowledge" in which case the sense is that we acknowledge that You are our God and the God of our ancestors. We acknowledge that God exists based upon all of the good things we have in our lives.

Do you want to thank God today or to acknowledge His existence?

עַל חַיֵּינוּ – *For our lives.* We thank You for our physical lives. I will not take my physical health for granted. There are so many people who are worse off than I.

וְעַל נִשְׁמוֹתֵינוּ – *For our souls.* We thank You for our souls which animate our bodies.

I will not take my spiritual life for granted. I know that there is more to me as a person than my physical body.

וְעַל נִסֶּיךָ – *For Your miracles.* We thank You for the everyday miracles in our lives of which we are not aware, for example, a virus I did not catch, a

The Amida continues on the next page with "For all these." On Ḥanukka and on Purim say "We thank You" below.

On Ḥanukka:

עַל הַנִּסִּים [We thank You also] for the miracles,[1] the redemption, the mighty deeds, the salvations, and the victories in battle which You performed for our ancestors in those days, at this time.

בִּימֵי מַתִּתְיָהוּ In the days of Mattityahu, son of Yoḥanan, the High Priest, the Hasmonean, and his sons, the wicked Greek kingdom rose up against Your people Israel to make them forget Your Torah and to force them to transgress the statutes of Your will. It was then that You in Your great compassion stood by them in the time of their distress. You championed their cause, judged their claim, and avenged their wrong. You delivered the strong into the hands of the weak, the many into the hands of the few, the impure into the hands of the pure, the wicked into the hands of the righteous, and the arrogant into the hands of those who were engaged in the study of Your Torah. You made for Yourself great and holy renown in Your world, and for Your people Israel You performed a great salvation and redemption as of this very day. Your children then entered the holiest part of Your House, cleansed Your Temple, purified Your Sanctuary, kindled lights in Your holy courts, and designated these eight days of Ḥanukka for giving thanks and praise to Your great name.

Continue with "For all these things."

On Shushan Purim in Jerusalem:

עַל הַנִּסִּים [We thank You also] for the miracles, the redemption, the mighty deeds, the salvations, and the victories in battle which You performed for our ancestors in those days, at this time.

בִּימֵי מָרְדְּכַי In the days of Mordekhai and Esther, in Shushan the capital, the wicked Haman rose up against them and sought to destroy, slay and exterminate all the Jews, young and old, children and women, on one day, the thirteenth day of the twelfth month, which is the month of Adar, and to plunder their possessions. Then You in Your great compassion thwarted his counsel, frustrated his plans, and caused his scheme to recoil on his own head, so that they hanged him and his sons on the gallows. *Esther 3*

Continue with "For all these things."

---

was completely spiritual. In the times of Mordekhai and Esther, the enemy wanted "to kill and annihilate" us. The threat was completely physical. In every generation there have been those who have continued to seek to attack us spiritually or physically. Yet, as a people, we have miraculously survived so that we can stand here today proud and tall.

Be thankful.

The עמידה *continues on the next page with* וְעַל כֻּלָּם. *On* חנוכה *and on* פורים *say* עַל הַנִּסִּים *below.*

בחנוכה:

עַל הַנִּסִּים[ע] וְעַל הַפֻּרְקָן וְעַל הַגְּבוּרוֹת וְעַל הַתְּשׁוּעוֹת וְעַל הַמִּלְחָמוֹת שֶׁעָשִׂיתָ לַאֲבוֹתֵינוּ בַּיָּמִים הָהֵם בַּזְּמַן הַזֶּה.

בִּימֵי מַתִּתְיָהוּ בֶּן יוֹחָנָן כֹּהֵן גָּדוֹל חַשְׁמוֹנַאי וּבָנָיו, כְּשֶׁעָמְדָה מַלְכוּת יָוָן הָרְשָׁעָה עַל עַמְּךָ יִשְׂרָאֵל לְהַשְׁכִּיחָם תּוֹרָתֶךָ וּלְהַעֲבִירָם מֵחֻקֵּי רְצוֹנֶךָ, וְאַתָּה בְּרַחֲמֶיךָ הָרַבִּים עָמַדְתָּ לָהֶם בְּעֵת צָרָתָם, רַבְתָּ אֶת רִיבָם, דַּנְתָּ אֶת דִּינָם, נָקַמְתָּ אֶת נִקְמָתָם, מָסַרְתָּ גִבּוֹרִים בְּיַד חַלָּשִׁים, וְרַבִּים בְּיַד מְעַטִּים, וּטְמֵאִים בְּיַד טְהוֹרִים, וּרְשָׁעִים בְּיַד צַדִּיקִים, וְזֵדִים בְּיַד עוֹסְקֵי תוֹרָתֶךָ, וּלְךָ עָשִׂיתָ שֵׁם גָּדוֹל וְקָדוֹשׁ בְּעוֹלָמֶךָ, וּלְעַמְּךָ יִשְׂרָאֵל עָשִׂיתָ תְּשׁוּעָה גְדוֹלָה וּפֻרְקָן כְּהַיּוֹם הַזֶּה. וְאַחַר כֵּן בָּאוּ בָנֶיךָ לִדְבִיר בֵּיתֶךָ, וּפִנּוּ אֶת הֵיכָלֶךָ, וְטִהֲרוּ אֶת מִקְדָּשֶׁךָ, וְהִדְלִיקוּ נֵרוֹת בְּחַצְרוֹת קָדְשֶׁךָ, וְקָבְעוּ שְׁמוֹנַת יְמֵי חֲנֻכָּה אֵלּוּ, לְהוֹדוֹת וּלְהַלֵּל לְשִׁמְךָ הַגָּדוֹל.

Continue with וְעַל כֻּלָּם.

בשושן פורים בירושלים:

עַל הַנִּסִּים וְעַל הַפֻּרְקָן וְעַל הַגְּבוּרוֹת וְעַל הַתְּשׁוּעוֹת וְעַל הַמִּלְחָמוֹת שֶׁעָשִׂיתָ לַאֲבוֹתֵינוּ בַּיָּמִים הָהֵם בַּזְּמַן הַזֶּה.

בִּימֵי מָרְדְּכַי וְאֶסְתֵּר בְּשׁוּשַׁן הַבִּירָה, כְּשֶׁעָמַד עֲלֵיהֶם הָמָן הָרָשָׁע, בִּקֵּשׁ לְהַשְׁמִיד לַהֲרֹג וּלְאַבֵּד אֶת־כָּל־הַיְּהוּדִים מִנַּעַר וְעַד־זָקֵן טַף וְנָשִׁים בְּיוֹם אֶחָד, בִּשְׁלוֹשָׁה עָשָׂר לְחֹדֶשׁ שְׁנֵים־עָשָׂר, הוּא־חֹדֶשׁ אֲדָר, וּשְׁלָלָם לָבוֹז: וְאַתָּה בְּרַחֲמֶיךָ הָרַבִּים הֵפַרְתָּ אֶת עֲצָתוֹ, וְקִלְקַלְתָּ אֶת מַחֲשַׁבְתּוֹ, וַהֲשֵׁבוֹתָ לּוֹ גְמוּלוֹ בְּרֹאשׁוֹ, וְתָלוּ אוֹתוֹ וְאֶת בָּנָיו עַל הָעֵץ. אסתר ג

Continue with וְעַל כֻּלָּם.

IYUN TEFILLA • עיון תפילה

עַל הַנִּסִּים – *For the miracles.* In the times of Matityahu, the enemy wanted to force us to "forget" the Torah, to "abandon our laws" and customs; in effect, they wanted us to assimilate. The threat

no other blessing during the *Ḥazan*'s repetition of the *Amida* is there a different blessing that we ourselves say; the ḥazan is our emissary for all of those other blessings. Why might it be different here? One answer was offered by Abudarham: because when it comes to saying "thank you" one cannot appoint a messenger. Each of us must offer thanks in our own personal way.

וְעַל כֻּלָּם For all these things
may Your name be blessed and exalted,
our King, continually, for ever and all time.

These words are added on Shabbat Shuva: And write, for a good life,
all the children of Your covenant.

Let all that lives thank You, Selah!
and praise Your name in truth,
God, our Savior and Help, Selah!
▾*Bend the knees:* Blessed *Bow:* are You, *Stand straight:* LORD,
whose name is "the Good" and to whom thanks are due.

BIRKAT KOHANIM[B]

The following is said by the Leader during the Repetition of the Amida.
In Israel, if Kohanim bless the congregation, *turn to page 732.*

Our God and God of our fathers, bless us with the threefold blessing in the Torah, written by the hand of Moses Your servant and pronounced by Aaron and his sons the priests, Your holy people, as it is said:

May the LORD bless you and protect you. *Num. 6*
Cong: May it be Your will.
May the LORD make His face shine on you and be gracious to you.
Cong: May it be Your will.
May the LORD turn His face toward you, and grant you peace.
Cong: May it be Your will.

BIUR TEFILLA • ביאור תפילה

ברכת כהנים – *Birkat Kohanim, The Priestly Blessing.* In the times of the *Beit HaMikdash*, after the sacrifices were offered, the priests (*kohanim*) would fulfill the positive commandment of blessing the people (*Bemidbar* 6:22–26.; *Vayikra* 9:22). Ultimately, however, it is understood that the blessing comes from Hashem, whose love for Israel is manifest in the blessings that we receive in our daily lives all around us. Note that each phrase has two verbs with Hashem at the center, and the phrases have 3, 5 and 7 words respectively, symbolizing the incremental growth inherent in each blessing (*berakha*), like a spring of water (*bereikha*) which bubbles up and gives life.

וְעַל כֻּלָּם יִתְבָּרַךְ וְיִתְרוֹמַם שִׁמְךָ מַלְכֵּנוּ תָּמִיד לְעוֹלָם וָעֶד.

בשבת שובה: וּכְתֹב לְחַיִּים טוֹבִים כָּל בְּנֵי בְרִיתֶךָ.

וְכֹל הַחַיִּים יוֹדְוּךָ סֶּלָה, וִיהַלְלוּ אֶת שִׁמְךָ בֶּאֱמֶת
הָאֵל יְשׁוּעָתֵנוּ וְעֶזְרָתֵנוּ סֶלָה.

▼ *Bend the knees* בָּרוּךְ *Bow* אַתָּה *Stand straight* יהוה
הַטּוֹב שִׁמְךָ וּלְךָ נָאֶה לְהוֹדוֹת.

ברכת כהנים[ב]

The following is said by the שליח ציבור *during* חזרת הש״ץ.
In ארץ ישראל, *if* כהנים *say* ברכת כהנים, *turn to page* 733.

אֱלֹהֵינוּ וֵאלֹהֵי אֲבוֹתֵינוּ, בָּרְכֵנוּ בַבְּרָכָה הַמְשֻׁלֶּשֶׁת בַּתּוֹרָה, הַכְּתוּבָה עַל
יְדֵי מֹשֶׁה עַבְדֶּךָ, הָאֲמוּרָה מִפִּי אַהֲרֹן וּבָנָיו כֹּהֲנִים עַם קְדוֹשֶׁךָ, כָּאָמוּר

יְבָרֶכְךָ יהוה וְיִשְׁמְרֶךָ: קהל: כֵּן יְהִי רָצוֹן במדבר ו
יָאֵר יהוה פָּנָיו אֵלֶיךָ וִיחֻנֶּךָּ: קהל: כֵּן יְהִי רָצוֹן
יִשָּׂא יהוה פָּנָיו אֵלֶיךָ וְיָשֵׂם לְךָ שָׁלוֹם: קהל: כֵּן יְהִי רָצוֹן

ANI TEFILLA • אני תפילה

The story is told of two angels who were assigned the task of going around the world to collect people's prayers. Each one set out with a bag, determined to beat the other one out. At the end of the prescribed time, one angel returned with a bag that was bulging, he was bent over from the burden of his load. The other angel, however, clearly did not have the same success. His bag was half empty, or, at best, half full, and as he turned his bag over to empty it, it became clear that he had returned with a paltry sum of prayers. What accounted for the difference?

It turns out that they were collecting different prayers. The first angel was collecting only those prayers which contained requests, people's expressions of the things they wanted or thought they wanted or thought they needed. The other angel, however, the one with the emptier bag, only collected prayers of thanks.

The point of the story is clear. We simply do not thank as much as we could, as much as we should.

PEACE

שִׂים שָׁלוֹם Grant peace,[1] goodness and blessing,
grace, loving-kindness and compassion to us[B]
and all Israel Your people.
Bless us, our Father, all as one, with the light of Your face,
for by the light of Your face[B] You have given us, LORD our God,
the Torah of life and love of kindness,
righteousness, blessing, compassion, life and peace.
May it be good in Your eyes to bless Your people Israel
at every time, in every hour, with Your peace.

שִׂים שָׁלוֹם – *Grant peace.* Shalom comes about when everyone knows his or her place in the world, where there is no struggle because there is acceptance of others.

Can you think of someone whom you might have a hard time accepting?

What small change can you try to make today in your relationship?

שִׂים שָׁלוֹם – *Grant peace.* When one says this blessing, one should have in mind the mitzva of וְאָהַבְתָּ לְרֵעֲךָ כָּמוֹךָ – love your neighbor as yourself (*Ya'arot Devash).*

Whom can you have in mind for this mitzva today?

BIUR TEFILLA • ביאור תפילה

חֵן וָחֶסֶד וְרַחֲמִים - *Grace, loving-kindness and compassion.*

Ḥen, grace, is when the receiver finds favor in the eyes of the giver.

Ḥesed, loving-kindness, comes from the generosity of the giver, whether the recipient deserves it or not.

Raḥamim, mercy, is granted when it is not deserved.

Which ones are most relevant for you today?

בְּאוֹר פָּנֶיךָ – *With the light of Your face.* "Bless us with the light of Your face"

This could be a request to God to stop hiding from us. The Ba'al HaTanya wrote that we are asking Him to enlighten us with belief in Him so that we can live with the clear understanding that everything comes from Him, and that He should reveal Himself to us in our daily lives. Peace can come from that knowledge.

How can you try harder to see the presence of God somewhere in your life today?

ANI TEFILLA • אני תפילה

If you saw somebody pulling a boat to the shore and were mistaken about mechanics and motion, you might think that he was pulling the shore to the boat. That's what prayer is like. You think that you're pulling God to you, but in fact, if you pray well, you pull yourself to God (attributed to Yehuda Aryeh MiModena).

ברכת שלום

שִׂים שָׁלוֹם[ע] טוֹבָה וּבְרָכָה
חֵן וָחֶסֶד וְרַחֲמִים[ב]
עָלֵינוּ וְעַל כָּל יִשְׂרָאֵל עַמֶּךָ.
בָּרְכֵנוּ אָבִינוּ כֻּלָּנוּ כְּאֶחָד בְּאוֹר פָּנֶיךָ
כִּי בְאוֹר פָּנֶיךָ[ב] נָתַתָּ לָּנוּ, יהוה אֱלֹהֵינוּ
תּוֹרַת חַיִּים וְאַהֲבַת חֶסֶד
וּצְדָקָה וּבְרָכָה וְרַחֲמִים וְחַיִּים וְשָׁלוֹם.
וְטוֹב בְּעֵינֶיךָ לְבָרֵךְ אֶת עַמְּךָ יִשְׂרָאֵל
בְּכָל עֵת וּבְכָל שָׁעָה בִּשְׁלוֹמֶךָ.

IYUN TEFILLA • עיון תפילה

שִׂים שָׁלוֹם – *Grant peace.* One vision of peace is surely that all Jews live together harmoniously. Although no one person can unify the world, every person is still obligated to feel united and connected to the Jewish people. (*Rinat Ḥayyim*).

To whom in your world could you feel more connected than you do?

שִׂים שָׁלוֹם – *Grant peace. Shalom* is related to the word *shalem*, meaning "whole" or "complete." There cannot be peace unless people feel complete within themselves; until they are at peace with their physical selves, their ethical selves, their moral selves. We ask Hashem to help us become more complete people today so that we may be at peace with ourselves and with others.

What can you do today to make yourself into a more complete person physically? Ethically? Emotionally? Religiously?

שִׂים שָׁלוֹם – *Grant peace.* Where there is anger, there cannot be peace. In a place where there is holiness, anger cannot exist. Therefore we ask Hashem to help us not be angry so that peace and holiness can reign.

שִׂים שָׁלוֹם – *Grant peace.* With whom am I angry?

I resolve to let my anger go so that I can feel more complete, so that the other person can feel more complete, so that the world can be more complete.

There can be no inner peace and no peace with others in a place where there is jealousy.

I resolve not to be jealous of others today.

There can be no inner peace or peace with others where there is unhealthy competitiveness.

I resolve not to be competitive today in an unhealthy way.

These words are added on Shabbat Shuva: In the book of life, blessing, peace and prosperity,
may we and all Your people
the house of Israel be remembered and written
before You for a good life, and for peace.*

Blessed are You, LORD, who blesses His people Israel with peace.

**On Shabbat Shuva outside Israel, many end the blessing:*
Blessed are You, LORD, who makes peace.

The following verse concludes the Leader's Repetition of the Amida. Some also say it here as part of the silent Amida.

May the words of my mouth[H] and the meditation of my heart
find favor before You, LORD, my Rock and Redeemer. *Ps. 19*

אֱלֹהַי My God, *Berakhot 17a*
guard[BI] my tongue from evil
and my lips from deceitful speech.

The *Shulhan Arukh* (122:1) rules that one should not utter any interruption until one has said יִהְיוּ לְרָצוֹן, "May the words of my mouth…" The Rema disagrees, clearly believing that one's *Amida* already formally concluded after *Sim Shalom*. The *Mishna Berura* suggests that one should say the verse יִהְיוּ לְרָצוֹן "May the words of my mouth…" twice, once here and once in *Elokai Netzor* in order to remove oneself from doubt.

BIUR TEFILLA • ביאור תפילה

אֱלֹהַי נְצֹר – *My God, guard.* The major theme of this concluding prayer is the request that we be protected against the sin of *lashon hara* (gossip or slander). Think about what negative effects *lashon hara* has upon us, our relationships, and our daily lives. Think about it enough, suffer from it once, try not speaking it for any length of time, and you'll begin to understand why we need God's help.

IYUN TEFILLA • עיון תפילה

אֱלֹהַי נְצֹר – *My God, guard.* The Ḥafetz Ḥayyim once said:

To be sure, in this prayer we ask Hashem for His help. We ask Him to help us to not speak *lashon hara* (gossip or slander) and not speak lies. But do we do our part? Do we expend energy to "protect our tongue from speaking evil and our lips from uttering deceit?" Do we do our part?

And if we do not do our part, then how can we possibly ask Him for His help? For we have learned that there is a law (*Devarim* 22:4) that if you see someone's donkey fallen under too heavy a load, you must help the owner pick it up. And the verse says "you shall surely lift it *with him*." From here the Gemara (*Bava Metzia* 32b) says it must happen "with him," meaning with the owner of the

This **IYUN TEFILLA** *continues on page 363.*

בשבת שובה: בְּסֵפֶר חַיִּים, בְּרָכָה וְשָׁלוֹם, וּפַרְנָסָה טוֹבָה
נִזָּכֵר וְנִכָּתֵב לְפָנֶיךָ, אֲנַחְנוּ וְכָל עַמְּךָ בֵּית יִשְׂרָאֵל
לְחַיִּים טוֹבִים וּלְשָׁלוֹם.*

בָּרוּךְ אַתָּה יהוה, הַמְבָרֵךְ אֶת עַמּוֹ יִשְׂרָאֵל בַּשָּׁלוֹם.

**On* שבת שובה *in* חוץ לארץ, *many end the blessing:*

בָּרוּךְ אַתָּה יהוה, עוֹשֶׂה הַשָּׁלוֹם.

The following verse concludes the חזרת הש״ץ.
Some also say it here as part of the silent עמידה.

תהלים יט
יִהְיוּ לְרָצוֹן אִמְרֵי־פִי וְהֶגְיוֹן לִבִּי לְפָנֶיךָ, יהוה צוּרִי וְגֹאֲלִי:

ברכות יז.
אֱלֹהַי
נְצֹר לְשׁוֹנִי מֵרָע, וּשְׂפָתַי מִדַּבֵּר מִרְמָה

HILKHOT TEFILLA • הלכות תפילה

יִהְיוּ לְרָצוֹן אִמְרֵי־פִי... – *May the words of my mouth...* The Gemara (*Berakhot* 9b) says that one should conclude one's *Amida* with this verse from *Tehillim* 19 just as one began one's prayer with the words, "Hashem, open my lips so that my mouth may declare Your praise." Now at the conclusion, we therefore say this parallel request: "May the words of my mouth and the meditation of my heart find favor..." We thus begin and end the prayer with a very personal request (unlike all of the other blessings, these words are in the singular and not the plural) that our prayers be heard, both those uttered aloud and those expressed in the inner recesses of our soul.

The question is whether this verse is part and parcel of the *Amida* itself or, given that it is not really a blessing and given that it is in the singular and not the plural, whether it is part of a private supplication. The practical difference would be if, for example, you had not yet said the verse but had already concluded *Sim Shalom* and, in the meantime the rest of the congregation had reached *Kedusha;* would you respond or would you have to remain silent because you haven't really finished *Amida* yet?

At the same time, there developed a practice to add even more supplications after the *Tefilla* was over. One such supplication, *Elokai Netzor* which appears next, was authored by one of the last of the Amoraim, Mar the son of Ravina (fifth century CE), and it was ultimately incorporated into the fixed text. Note that towards the end he includes this concluding verse of "May the words of my mouth…" (**יִהְיוּ לְרָצוֹן...**). As such, where exactly does the *Amida* end - after *Sim Shalom*? after the recitation of the verse **יִהְיוּ לְרָצוֹן** the first time? after the recitation of *Elokai Netzor*?

To those who curse me, let my soul be silent;[AB]
may my soul be to all like the dust.
Open my heart to Your Torah
and let my soul pursue Your commandments.
As for all who plan evil against me,
swiftly thwart their counsel and frustrate their plans.
Act for the sake of Your name; act for the sake of Your right hand;
act for the sake of Your holiness; act for the sake of Your Torah.
That Your beloved ones may be delivered,[B] *Ps. 60*
save with Your right hand and answer me.
May the words of my mouth *Ps. 19*
and the meditation of my heart
find favor before You, LORD, my Rock and Redeemer.

Bow and take three steps back as if taking leave of the Divine Presence.

Bow left: May He who makes peace in His high places,
Bow right: make peace *Bow forward:* for us and all Israel –
and say: Amen.

יְהִי רָצוֹן May it be Your will, LORD our God and God of our ancestors,
that the Temple be rebuilt speedily in our days,
and grant us a share in Your Torah.
And there we will serve You with reverence,
as in the days of old and as in former years.
Then the offering of Judah and Jerusalem *Mal. 3*
will be pleasing to the LORD as in the days of old and as in former years.

On Rosh Ḥodesh and Ḥanukka, the service continues with Hallel on page 680.

BIUR TEFILLA • ביאור תפילה

וְלִמְקַלְלַי נַפְשִׁי תִדֹּם – *To those who curse me, let my soul be silent.* Perhaps this is a reference to being on the receiving end of *lashon hara* (gossip or slander); if I am ever put in that position where people speak about me or against me, I hope I have the strength not to answer them in kind; otherwise, I will be no different to them, and my prayer will now be meaningless.

לְמַעַן יֵחָלְצוּן יְדִידֶיךָ – *That Your beloved ones may be delivered.* The Meiri suggests that the word יֵחָלְצוּן comes not from the word "to free," but rather from the word "to rest" (just as we say on Shabbat רְצֵה וְהַחֲלִיצֵנוּ in ברכת המזון). If so, then in this prayer I am asking that Hashem allow me to achieve mental rest, a release from pressure, tension, and worry.

וְלִמְקַלְלַי נַפְשִׁי תִדֹּם,[אב] וְנַפְשִׁי כֶּעָפָר לַכֹּל תִּהְיֶה.
פְּתַח לִבִּי בְּתוֹרָתֶךָ, וּבְמִצְוֹתֶיךָ תִּרְדֹּף נַפְשִׁי.
וְכָל הַחוֹשְׁבִים עָלַי רָעָה, מְהֵרָה הָפֵר עֲצָתָם וְקַלְקֵל מַחֲשַׁבְתָּם.
עֲשֵׂה לְמַעַן שְׁמֶךָ, עֲשֵׂה לְמַעַן יְמִינֶךָ
עֲשֵׂה לְמַעַן קְדֻשָּׁתֶךָ, עֲשֵׂה לְמַעַן תּוֹרָתֶךָ.
לְמַעַן יֵחָלְצוּן יְדִידֶיךָ,[ב] הוֹשִׁיעָה יְמִינְךָ וַעֲנֵנִי: תהלים ס
יִהְיוּ לְרָצוֹן אִמְרֵי־פִי וְהֶגְיוֹן לִבִּי לְפָנֶיךָ, יהוה צוּרִי וְגֹאֲלִי: תהלים יט

Bow and take three steps back as if taking leave of the Divine Presence.

Bow left עֹשֶׂה שָׁלוֹם/ בשבת שובה: הַשָּׁלוֹם/ בִּמְרוֹמָיו
Bow right הוּא יַעֲשֶׂה שָׁלוֹם *Bow forward* עָלֵינוּ וְעַל כָּל יִשְׂרָאֵל
וְאִמְרוּ אָמֵן.

יְהִי רָצוֹן מִלְּפָנֶיךָ יהוה אֱלֹהֵינוּ וֵאלֹהֵי אֲבוֹתֵינוּ
שֶׁיִּבָּנֶה בֵּית הַמִּקְדָּשׁ בִּמְהֵרָה בְיָמֵינוּ, וְתֵן חֶלְקֵנוּ בְּתוֹרָתֶךָ
וְשָׁם נַעֲבָדְךָ בְּיִרְאָה כִּימֵי עוֹלָם וּכְשָׁנִים קַדְמֹנִיּוֹת.
וְעָרְבָה לַיהוה מִנְחַת יְהוּדָה וִירוּשָׁלָםִ כִּימֵי עוֹלָם וּכְשָׁנִים קַדְמֹנִיּוֹת: מלאכי ג

On ראש חודש *and* חנוכה*, the service continues with* הלל *on page 681.*

So, too, in our case, said the Ḥafetz Ḥayyim, if we ask Hashem to help unload us from this sin, then Hashem may say, "Help Me by doing your share, otherwise I am under no obligation to help you." (Introduction to *Ḥovat HaShemira*)

donkey; for the owner might sit by the wayside and say "Okay, since you are obligated to lift up your fellow man's donkey, you lift it up while I sit back and watch." Hence the Gemara says "you must lift it *with him*," meaning, the owner of the donkey must participate.

ANI TEFILLA • אני תפילה

וְלִמְקַלְלַי נַפְשִׁי תִדֹּם – *To those who curse me, let my soul be silent.* One sees from here that one of the goals of prayer is to imbue you with a sense of serenity, of being at peace with yourself. When people make you angry or insult you or get on your bad side, there is something to be said for not allowing that to ruin your day or create within you a feeling of anger or resentment or a desire for revenge. Let their taunts not bother me, says this *tefilla*. I am better than that. My self-esteem comes from within me not from what others think of me. It is their pettiness. There are more important things in life to get upset about. Seen in this light, when you walk away from *tefilla*, you walk away transformed.

FULL KADDISH

Leader: יִתְגַּדַּל Magnified and sanctified may His great name be,
in the world He created by His will.
May He establish His kingdom
in your lifetime and in your days,
and in the lifetime of all the house of Israel,
swiftly and soon –
and say: Amen.

All: May His great name[A] be blessed for ever and all time.

Leader: Blessed and praised, glorified and exalted,
raised and honored, uplifted and lauded
be the name of the Holy One, blessed be He,
beyond any blessing, song, praise and consolation
uttered in the world –
and say: Amen.

May the prayers and pleas of all Israel
be accepted by their Father in heaven –
and say: Amen.

May there be great peace from heaven,
and life for us and all Israel –
and say: Amen.

Bow, take three steps back, as if taking leave of the Divine Presence, then bow, first left, then right, then center, while saying:

May He who makes peace in His high places,
make peace for us and all Israel –
and say: Amen.

ANI TEFILLA • אני תפילה

יְהֵא שְׁמֵהּ רַבָּא – *May His great name.* *Whoever says "yeheh shemeh raba..." with all his strength, the Heavenly Court rips up any negative decree against him* (*Shabbat* 119b). "With all his strength" – with all of one's heart and soul (*Mishna Berura* 56:1).

קדיש שלם

ש״ץ: יִתְגַּדַּל וְיִתְקַדַּשׁ שְׁמֵהּ רַבָּא (קהל: אָמֵן)
בְּעָלְמָא דִּי בְרָא כִרְעוּתֵהּ
וְיַמְלִיךְ מַלְכוּתֵהּ
בְּחַיֵּיכוֹן וּבְיוֹמֵיכוֹן וּבְחַיֵּי דְכָל בֵּית יִשְׂרָאֵל
בַּעֲגָלָא וּבִזְמַן קָרִיב, וְאִמְרוּ אָמֵן. (קהל: אָמֵן)

קהל וש״ץ: יְהֵא שְׁמֵהּ רַבָּא[א] מְבָרַךְ לְעָלַם וּלְעָלְמֵי עָלְמַיָּא.

ש״ץ: יִתְבָּרַךְ וְיִשְׁתַּבַּח וְיִתְפָּאַר
וְיִתְרוֹמַם וְיִתְנַשֵּׂא וְיִתְהַדָּר וְיִתְעַלֶּה וְיִתְהַלָּל
שְׁמֵהּ דְּקֻדְשָׁא בְּרִיךְ הוּא (קהל: בְּרִיךְ הוּא)
לְעֵלָּא מִן כָּל בִּרְכָתָא
/בשבת שובה: לְעֵלָּא לְעֵלָּא מִכָּל בִּרְכָתָא/
וְשִׁירָתָא, תֻּשְׁבְּחָתָא וְנֶחֱמָתָא
דַּאֲמִירָן בְּעָלְמָא, וְאִמְרוּ אָמֵן. (קהל: אָמֵן)

תִּתְקַבַּל צְלוֹתְהוֹן וּבָעוּתְהוֹן דְּכָל יִשְׂרָאֵל
קֳדָם אֲבוּהוֹן דִּי בִשְׁמַיָּא, וְאִמְרוּ אָמֵן. (קהל: אָמֵן)

יְהֵא שְׁלָמָא רַבָּא מִן שְׁמַיָּא
וְחַיִּים, עָלֵינוּ וְעַל כָּל יִשְׂרָאֵל, וְאִמְרוּ אָמֵן. (קהל: אָמֵן)

Bow, take three steps back, as if taking leave of the Divine Presence, then bow, first left, then right, then center, while saying:

עֹשֶׂה שָׁלוֹם/ בשבת שובה: הַשָּׁלוֹם/ בִּמְרוֹמָיו
הוּא יַעֲשֶׂה שָׁלוֹם עָלֵינוּ
וְעַל כָּל יִשְׂרָאֵל, וְאִמְרוּ אָמֵן. (קהל: אָמֵן)

REMOVING THE TORAH FROM THE ARK

אֵין־כָּמְוֹךָ There is none like You among the heavenly powers, *Ps. 86*
Lord, and there are no works like Yours.
Your kingdom is an eternal kingdom, *Ps. 145*
and Your dominion is for all generations.

The Lord is King, the Lord was King,
the Lord shall be King for ever and all time.
The Lord will give strength to His people; *Ps. 29*
the Lord will bless His people with peace.

---

communicate with them. This revelation at Sinai was not to a single prophet but to an entire nation of millions, and each parent passed on what they saw and heard to their children who did the same with their children in a chain of tradition that brings us here today. If one ever wanted proof of the truth of Torah and revelation and God, said Rabbi Yehuda HaLevi in the early twelfth century, then this unbroken unending chain of tradition is it.

In addition to the set number of people who are called up on Shabbat and holy days, there is another *aliya* that is added at the end, called *maftir*, or conclusion. This person will also be given the honor of reading from the portion from the *Navi* or book of Prophets that is also read subsequently on this day. He is given an *aliya* for the Torah as well, in deference to the honor of the Torah, lest one think that a reading from the Prophets is equal in status to that of the Torah itself (*Megilla* 23a).

IYUN TEFILLA · עיון תפילה

קריאת התורה – *PUBLIC READING OF THE TORAH.* Education in Jewish life has always been democratic. It is not only for the elite but for every person, rich or poor. Amazingly, universal schooling has been a part of Jewish life for close to 2000 years. So it should come as no surprise that from the very outset Moshe instituted that the Torah be read publicly three times a week (*Bava Kama* 82a), not just to keep the content of Torah alive, for that would happen in schools and private study regardless, but, rather, to remind us as a community that Torah is our life, as water is to a thirsty person, as water is to fish. We cannot live without it. According to Rabbi Soloveitchik, that is why there is not necessarily a need to even understand this public Torah reading or to learn from it (perhaps that is why it is simply called *Keriat HaTorah*: the reading, and not the learning, of Torah). The mere act of reading or hearing it sanctifies the listener. In doing so, I attach myself to my people, my tradition, my God. I am a part of something bigger than myself, and I am uplifted.

הוצאת ספר תורה[ע]

אֵין־כָּמְוֹךָ בָאֱלֹהִים, אֲדֹנָי, וְאֵין כְּמַעֲשֶׂיךָ: תהלים פו
מַלְכוּתְךָ מַלְכוּת כָּל־עֹלָמִים, וּמֶמְשַׁלְתְּךָ בְּכָל־דּוֹר וָדֹר: תהלים קמה

יהוה מֶלֶךְ, יהוה מָלָךְ, יהוה יִמְלֹךְ לְעֹלָם וָעֶד.
יהוה עֹז לְעַמּוֹ יִתֵּן, יהוה יְבָרֵךְ אֶת־עַמּוֹ בַשָּׁלוֹם: תהלים כט

INTRODUCTION TO KERIAT HATORAH

The Gemara (*Berakhot* 8a-b) teaches that one should repeat the weekly portion for oneself three times, twice in the original and once in translation. Today, only the Yemenite community actually maintains this practice, known as *shnayim mikra v'eḥad targum*, in the morning service, replete with a translator. For most others, however, the practice became to find ongoing time during the week to do this review, often using the commentary of Rashi as a replacement for a literal translation (*Shulḥan Arukh* 285:2 and *Mishna Berura*). The entire practice ensures that one has an ongoing intimate relationship with the weekly reading. The Torah is not something that lives in a building, but in the fabric of one's being.

Tradition has it that Moshe himself decreed that there be a regular Torah reading on Shabbat and all holy days (*Soferim* 10:1). The Torah has 54 divisions, or portions, each one called a *parasha*, one for each Shabbat of the year during a leap year. In a non-leap year, some of the portions (*parshiyot*) are doubled up, so that the entire Torah is completed annually, a collective reaffirmation of our identity.

The portion that is read is itself divided into a different number of sections depending on the sanctity of the occasion, and each section is apportioned to a different person in the congregation. On Shabbat there are 7 people called up, on Yom Kippur there are 6, on a *yom tov* there are 5, on Rosh Ḥodesh and Ḥol HaMoed (intermediate days of a festival) there are 4 and during the week there are 3 (*Megilla* 4:1-2). Each division is called an *aliya*, or ascent, a reference to the physical ascent to the platform where the Torah is read, as well as an echo of the ascent to Mount Sinai where the Torah was given. A minimum of ten verses are read, according to one tradition as a symbolic representation of the Ten Commandments (*Megilla* 21b; *Yerushalmi Taanit* 4:3). A minimum of three people are called up, reminiscent perhaps of Moshe, Aharon and Miriam, under whose watch the Torah was given. Minimally, a *Kohen*, *Levi* and *Yisrael* are called up to the Torah, thus representing the collective of the entire nation. Indeed, the entire procedure is highly reminiscent of the giving of the Torah at Mount Sinai, when the entire Jewish people heard the voice of God

Father of compassion,
favor Zion with Your goodness; rebuild the walls of Jerusalem. *Ps. 51*
For we trust in You alone, King, God, high and exalted,
Master of worlds.

The Ark is opened and the congregation stands. All say:

וַיְהִי בִּנְסֹעַ Whenever the Ark set out,[B] Moses would say, *Num. 10*
"Arise, LORD, and may Your enemies be scattered.
May those who hate You flee before You."
For the Torah shall come forth from Zion, *Is. 2*
and the word of the LORD from Jerusalem.
Blessed is He who in His Holiness
gave the Torah to His people Israel.

Blessed is the name[B] of the Master of the Universe. Blessed is Your crown and Your place. May Your favor always be with Your people Israel. Show Your people the salvation of Your right hand in Your Temple. Grant us the gift of Your good light, and accept our prayers in mercy. May it be Your will to prolong our life in goodness. May I be counted among the righteous, so that You will have compassion on me and protect me and all that is mine and all that is Your people Israel's. You feed all; You sustain all; You rule over all; You rule over kings, for sovereignty is Yours. I am a servant of the Holy One, blessed be He, before whom and before whose glorious Torah I bow at all times. Not in man do I trust, nor on any angel do I rely, but on the God of heaven who is the God of truth, whose Torah is truth, whose prophets speak truth, and who abounds in acts of love and truth. ▸ In Him I trust, and to His holy and glorious name I offer praises. May it be Your will to open my heart to the Torah, and to fulfill the wishes of my heart and of the hearts of all Your people Israel for good, for life, and for peace. *Zohar, Vayak-hel*

בְּרִיךְ שְׁמֵהּ – *Blessed is the name.* Added to the service by kabbalists about four centuries ago or more, this prayer is really a quote from the *Zohar* which says that "when the congregation takes the Torah from the Ark to read from it, the Gates of Mercy are opened in heaven and love is awakened on high; therefore this prayer should be spoken." Thus this prayer makes use, as it were, of a favorable circumstance to pray for the fulfillment of our hearts' deepest desires. (Rabbi E. Munk)

אַב הָרַחֲמִים

הֵיטִיבָה בִרְצוֹנְךָ אֶת־צִיּוֹן תִּבְנֶה חוֹמוֹת יְרוּשָׁלָםִ: תהלים נא
כִּי בְךָ לְבַד בָּטָחְנוּ, מֶלֶךְ אֵל רָם וְנִשָּׂא, אֲדוֹן עוֹלָמִים.

The ארון קודש *is opened and the* קהל *stands. All say:*

וַיְהִי בִּנְסֹעַ הָאָרֹן וַיֹּאמֶר מֹשֶׁה במדבר י
קוּמָה יהוה וְיָפֻצוּ אֹיְבֶיךָ וְיָנֻסוּ מְשַׂנְאֶיךָ מִפָּנֶיךָ:
כִּי מִצִּיּוֹן תֵּצֵא תוֹרָה וּדְבַר־יהוה מִירוּשָׁלָםִ: ישעיה ב
בָּרוּךְ שֶׁנָּתַן תּוֹרָה לְעַמּוֹ יִשְׂרָאֵל בִּקְדֻשָּׁתוֹ.

בְּרִיךְ שְׁמֵהּ דְּמָרֵא עָלְמָא, בְּרִיךְ כִּתְרָךְ וְאַתְרָךְ. יְהֵא רְעוּתָךְ עִם עַמָּךְ יִשְׂרָאֵל לְעָלַם, וּפֻרְקַן יְמִינָךְ אַחֲזֵי לְעַמָּךְ בְּבֵית מַקְדְּשָׁךְ, וּלְאַמְטוֹיֵי לָנָא מִטּוּב נְהוֹרָךְ, וּלְקַבֵּל צְלוֹתָנָא בְּרַחֲמִין. יְהֵא רַעֲוָא קֳדָמָךְ דְּתוֹרִיךְ לַן חַיִּין בְּטִיבוּ, וְלֶהֱוֵי אֲנָא פְקִידָא בְּגוֹ צַדִּיקַיָּא, לְמִרְחַם עָלַי וּלְמִנְטַר יָתִי וְיָת כָּל דִּי לִי וְדִי לְעַמָּךְ יִשְׂרָאֵל. אַנְתְּ הוּא זָן לְכֹלָּא וּמְפַרְנֵס לְכֹלָּא, אַנְתְּ הוּא שַׁלִּיט עַל כֹּלָּא, אַנְתְּ הוּא דְּשַׁלִּיט עַל מַלְכַיָּא, וּמַלְכוּתָא דִּילָךְ הִיא. אֲנָא עַבְדָּא דְקֻדְשָׁא בְּרִיךְ הוּא, דְּסָגֵדְנָא קַמֵּהּ וּמִקַּמֵּי דִּיקַר אוֹרַיְתֵהּ בְּכָל עִדָּן וְעִדָּן. לָא עַל אֱנָשׁ רָחִיצְנָא וְלָא עַל בַּר אֱלָהִין סָמִיכְנָא, אֶלָּא בֶּאֱלָהָא דִשְׁמַיָּא, דְּהוּא אֱלָהָא קְשׁוֹט, וְאוֹרַיְתֵהּ קְשׁוֹט, וּנְבִיאוֹהִי קְשׁוֹט, וּמַסְגֵּא לְמֶעְבַּד טַבְוָן וּקְשׁוֹט. ◂ בֵּהּ אֲנָא רָחִיץ, וְלִשְׁמֵהּ קַדִּישָׁא יַקִּירָא אֲנָא אֵמַר תֻּשְׁבְּחָן. יְהֵא רַעֲוָא קֳדָמָךְ דְּתִפְתַּח לִבַּאי בְּאוֹרַיְתָא, וְתַשְׁלִים מִשְׁאֲלִין דְּלִבַּאי וְלִבָּא דְכָל עַמָּךְ יִשְׂרָאֵל לְטָב וּלְחַיִּין וְלִשְׁלָם. זוהר ויקהל

BIUR TEFILLA • ביאור תפילה

וַיְהִי בִּנְסֹעַ הָאָרֹן – *Whenever the ark set out.* These words (*Bemidbar* 10:35) were recited in the desert whenever the Ark of the Covenant was moved from its resting place. It declares that the Torah will always emerge victorious over its enemies (Rabbi S. R. Hirsch), whether the enemies from without or the forces of doubt from within. As we open the ark for the Torah, so too, do we need to open our minds and our hearts to what it has to tell us.

The Leader takes the Torah scroll in his right arm. Leader then congregation:

Listen, Israel: the LORD is our God, the LORD is One. *Deut. 6*

Leader then congregation:

One is our God; great is our Master; holy is His name.

The Leader turns to face the Ark, bows and says:

Magnify the LORD with me, and let us exalt His name together.[B] *Ps. 34*

The Ark is closed. The Leader carries the Torah scroll to the bima and the congregation says:

לְךָ Yours, LORD, are the greatness and the power, the glory and the majesty and splendor, for everything in heaven and earth is Yours. Yours, LORD, is the kingdom; You are exalted as Head over all. *1 Chr. 29*

רוֹמְמוּ Exalt the LORD our God and bow to His footstool; He is holy. Exalt the LORD our God, and bow at His holy mountain, for holy is the LORD our God. *Ps. 99*

Over all may the name of the Supreme King of kings, the Holy One blessed be He, be magnified and sanctified, praised and glorified, exalted and extolled, in the worlds that He has created – this world and the World to Come – in accordance with His will, and the will of those who fear Him, and the will of the whole house of Israel. He is the Rock of worlds, LORD of all creatures, God of all souls, who dwells in

---

HILKHOT TEFILLA • הלכות תפילה

There is a custom for one to physically approach the Torah as it passes by, if it is possible, and in order to show one's enthusiasm and love, to kiss it either directly or by using one's siddur or tzitzit.

In truth, there is something distorted in having the Torah come to us. Were it physically possible, each of us should go to it.

ANI TEFILLA • אני תפילה

Prayer is about man reaching out to communicate with God.

Learning Torah is about God reaching out to communicate with man.

"How does one read a chapter of the Bible?" my teacher Nechama Leibowitz, ז״ל, would frequently ask. She would then answer her own question: "Exactly like a young woman who receives a letter from her lover and pours over every period and apostrophe. Why did he write the word *shalom* the way he did, why did he add this word or that, and leave out another? That is the way to read *Tanakh*." Torah, in other words, is a love letter, from Hashem to us. Read it that way. See if it makes a difference.

The שליח ציבור *takes the* ספר תורה *in his right arm.* שליח ציבור *then* קהל:

שְׁמַע יִשְׂרָאֵל, יהוה אֱלֹהֵינוּ, יהוה אֶחָד: דברים ו

שליח ציבור *then* קהל:

אֶחָד אֱלֹהֵינוּ, גָּדוֹל אֲדוֹנֵינוּ, קָדוֹשׁ שְׁמוֹ.

The שליח ציבור *turns to face the* ארון קודש*, bows and says:*

גַּדְּלוּ לַיהוה אִתִּי וּנְרוֹמְמָה שְׁמוֹ יַחְדָּו: תהלים לד

The ארון קודש *is closed. The* שליח ציבור *carries the* ספר תורה *to the* בימה *and the* קהל *says:*

לְךָ יהוה הַגְּדֻלָּה וְהַגְּבוּרָה וְהַתִּפְאֶרֶת וְהַנֵּצַח וְהַהוֹד, כִּי־כֹל בַּשָּׁמַיִם וּבָאָרֶץ, לְךָ יהוה הַמַּמְלָכָה וְהַמִּתְנַשֵּׂא לְכֹל לְרֹאשׁ: דברי הימים א׳ כט

רוֹמְמוּ יהוה אֱלֹהֵינוּ וְהִשְׁתַּחֲווּ לַהֲדֹם רַגְלָיו, קָדוֹשׁ הוּא: רוֹמְמוּ יהוה אֱלֹהֵינוּ וְהִשְׁתַּחֲווּ לְהַר קָדְשׁוֹ, כִּי־קָדוֹשׁ יהוה אֱלֹהֵינוּ: תהלים צט

עַל הַכֹּל יִתְגַּדַּל וְיִתְקַדַּשׁ וְיִשְׁתַּבַּח וְיִתְפָּאַר וְיִתְרוֹמַם וְיִתְנַשֵּׂא שְׁמוֹ שֶׁל מֶלֶךְ מַלְכֵי הַמְּלָכִים הַקָּדוֹשׁ בָּרוּךְ הוּא בָּעוֹלָמוֹת שֶׁבָּרָא, הָעוֹלָם הַזֶּה וְהָעוֹלָם הַבָּא, כִּרְצוֹנוֹ וְכִרְצוֹן יְרֵאָיו וְכִרְצוֹן כָּל בֵּית יִשְׂרָאֵל. צוּר הָעוֹלָמִים, אֲדוֹן כָּל הַבְּרִיּוֹת, אֱלוֹהַּ כָּל הַנְּפָשׁוֹת, הַיּוֹשֵׁב בְּמֶרְחֲבֵי מָרוֹם, הַשּׁוֹכֵן בִּשְׁמֵי שְׁמֵי קֶדֶם, קְדֻשָּׁתוֹ עַל הַחַיּוֹת, וּקְדֻשָּׁתוֹ עַל כִּסֵּא הַכָּבוֹד. וּבְכֵן יִתְקַדַּשׁ שִׁמְךָ בָּנוּ יהוה

BIUR TEFILLA • ביאור תפילה

גַּדְּלוּ לַיהוה אִתִּי וּנְרוֹמְמָה שְׁמוֹ יַחְדָּו – *Magnify the Lord with me and let us exalt His name together.* There is a custom for the one holding the Torah to literally "magnify" and "exalt" the Torah by raising it up. The Abudarham suggests that this is to symbolize the raising up of the ark to Jerusalem by King David after it had been captured by the Philistines. The prooftext he cites from that story is "Whenever the bearers of the ark walked six paces" they would celebrate with another sacrifice (*Shemuel* II 6:13). Interestingly, the Hebrew phrase we recite here itself has six words. Each step the *ḥazan* takes, therefore, each word we recite, is intended as a celebration of a renewed relationship with a long lost friend. Imagine what it was like for David on that day. Let his excitement inspire you.

the spacious heights and inhabits the high heavens of old. His holiness is over the Ḥayyot and over the throne of glory. Therefore may Your name, LORD our God, be sanctified among us in the sight of all that lives. Let us sing before Him a new song, as it is written: "Sing to God, make music for His name, extol Him who rides the clouds – the LORD is His name – and exult before Him." And may we see Him eye to eye when He returns to His abode as it is written: "For they shall see eye to eye when the LORD returns to Zion." And it is said: "Then will the glory of the LORD be revealed, and all mankind together shall see that the mouth of the LORD has spoken."

Ps. 68
Is. 52
Is. 40

Father of mercy, have compassion on the people borne by Him. May He remember the covenant with the mighty (patriarchs), and deliver us from evil times. May He reproach the evil instinct in the people by Him, and graciously grant that we be an eternal remnant. May He fulfill in good measure our requests for salvation and compassion.

The Torah scroll is placed on the bima and the Gabbai calls a Kohen to the Torah.

וְיַעֲזֹר May He help, shield and save all who seek refuge in Him, and let us say: Amen. Let us all render greatness to our God and give honor to the Torah. *Let the Kohen come forward. Arise (*name* son of *father's name*), the Kohen.

**If no Kohen is present, a Levi or Yisrael is called up as follows:*
/As there is no Kohen, arise (*name* son of *father's name*) in place of a Kohen./

Blessed is He who, in His holiness, gave the Torah to His people Israel.

The congregation followed by the Gabbai:

You who cling to the LORD your God are all alive today. *Deut. 4*

---

3. Since you are about to "read" the Torah, it makes sense to see exactly what you are about to "read" before making the blessing. That's why there is a custom for the *ba'al keria* to show you the place where your *aliya* begins. There is another custom to make a motion to touch that spot with one's tallit or some other material and then kiss it in order to display one's love of Torah and one's excitement at this opportunity.
4. There is a custom to hold onto the wooden handles which are called the *Etzei Ḥayyim* or "Trees (lit. wood) of Life." (Recall the verse [*Mishlei* 3:18] עֵץ־חַיִּים הִיא לַמַּחֲזִיקִים בָּהּ... – "It is a tree of life to those who grasp it.") One reason may be purely practical – you need to open the Torah to find the place (*Megilla* 32a). Another suggestion is that it is as if one is actually *receiving* the Torah on Mount Sinai (*Orkhot Ḥayyim*). And yet another suggestion is that there is a need to hold onto any article over which one is reciting a blessing, similar to a *lulav* (*Beit Yosef*). The custom is to keep holding at least one of the handles until one is completely finished with one's *aliya*.
5. The Gemara (*Megilla* 32a) relates a dispute about how one should recite the blessings. Rabbi Meir was concerned that if you look into the *sefer Torah* when

This **HILKHOT TEFILLA** *continues on page 375.*

אֱלֹהֵינוּ לְעֵינֵי כָּל חָי, וְנֹאמַר לְפָנָיו שִׁיר חָדָשׁ, כַּכָּתוּב: שִׁירוּ לֵאלֹהִים זַמְּרוּ תהלים סח
שְׁמוֹ, סֹלּוּ לָרֹכֵב בָּעֲרָבוֹת, בְּיָהּ שְׁמוֹ, וְעִלְזוּ לְפָנָיו: וְנִרְאֵהוּ עַיִן בְּעַיִן בְּשׁוּבוֹ אֶל
נָוֵהוּ, כַּכָּתוּב: כִּי עַיִן בְּעַיִן יִרְאוּ בְּשׁוּב יהוה צִיּוֹן: וְנֶאֱמַר: וְנִגְלָה כְּבוֹד יהוה, ישעיה נב ישעיה מ
וְרָאוּ כָל־בָּשָׂר יַחְדָּו כִּי פִּי יהוה דִּבֵּר:

אַב הָרַחֲמִים הוּא יְרַחֵם עַם עֲמוּסִים, וְיִזְכֹּר בְּרִית אֵיתָנִים, וְיַצִּיל נַפְשׁוֹתֵינוּ מִן הַשָּׁעוֹת הָרָעוֹת, וְיִגְעַר בְּיֵצֶר הָרָע מִן הַנְּשׂוּאִים, וְיָחֹן אוֹתָנוּ לִפְלֵיטַת עוֹלָמִים, וִימַלֵּא מִשְׁאֲלוֹתֵינוּ בְּמִדָּה טוֹבָה יְשׁוּעָה וְרַחֲמִים.

The ספר תורה is placed on the שולחן and the גבאי calls a כהן to the תורה.

וְיַעֲזֹר וְיָגֵן וְיוֹשִׁיעַ לְכָל הַחוֹסִים בּוֹ, וְנֹאמַר אָמֵן. הַכֹּל הָבוּ גֹדֶל לֵאלֹהֵינוּ וּתְנוּ כָבוֹד לַתּוֹרָה. *כֹּהֵן קְרַב, יַעֲמֹד (פלוני בֶּן פלוני) הַכֹּהֵן.

**If no כהן is present, a לוי or ישראל is called up as follows:*

/אֵין כָּאן כֹּהֵן, יַעֲמֹד (פלוני בֶּן פלוני) בִּמְקוֹם כֹּהֵן./

בָּרוּךְ שֶׁנָּתַן תּוֹרָה לְעַמּוֹ יִשְׂרָאֵל בִּקְדֻשָּׁתוֹ.

The קהל followed by the גבאי:

וְאַתֶּם הַדְּבֵקִים בַּיהוה אֱלֹהֵיכֶם חַיִּים כֻּלְּכֶם הַיּוֹם: דברים ד

HILKHOT TEFILLA • הלכות תפילה

A GUIDE TO GETTING AN ALIYA

1. Getting an *aliya* is a big deal. It's important to recall that the *kavod* (honor) is not only yours but the Torah's. In fact Rabbi Yehuda (*Berakhot* 55a) suggested that, except in certain extenuating circumstances, one's life might be shortened, God forbid, if one turns down an *aliya*. After all, the Torah is described as כִּי הוּא חַיֶּיךָ וְאֹרֶךְ יָמֶיךָ (*Devarim* 30:20) – "Torah is your life and the length of your days." Why would you want to give it up?
2. In order to show your love of the Torah and what an honor it is to get an *aliya*, and in order that everyone else doesn't have to wait unnecessarily long until you get from your seat to the *bima*, the custom is to take the shortest route to the Torah. If you are equidistant from both sides of the *bima*, the custom is to go up on the right side and leave via the left side. This is just because there is a preference in Judaism for the right (*Yoma* 15b). Hence, some halakhic authorities prefer that you always go up the right side even if it is further away from you (*Ḥatam Sofer OḤ* 187). The prophet Yeḥezkel (46:9) noted that in the *Beit HaMikdash* the custom was to enter via one gate and leave via another. Consider this *aliya*, then, a kind of *going up* to the *Beit HaMikdash*.

The appropriate Torah portion is read.

The Reader shows the oleh the section to be read. The oleh touches the scroll at that place with the tzitzit of his tallit, which he then kisses. Holding the handles of the scroll, he says:

Oleh: Bless[B] the LORD, the blessed One.

Cong: Bless the LORD, the blessed One, for ever and all time.

Oleh: Bless the LORD, the blessed One, for ever and all time.
Blessed are You, LORD our God, King of the Universe,
who has chosen us from all peoples and has given us His Torah.
Blessed are You, LORD, Giver of the Torah.

After the reading, the oleh says:

Oleh: Blessed are You, LORD our God, King of the Universe,
who has given us the Torah of truth,
planting everlasting life in our midst.
Blessed are You, LORD, Giver of the Torah.

---

along in a whisper with the *ba'al keria* as if to fulfill his own obligation to read, and so as to reinforce that the blessing he said was on his own reading.

8. Upon completion of the final blessing, the custom is to remain at the *bima* standing beside the *gabbai* until the completion of the next *aliya*. This is considered a fulfillment of giving honor to the Torah by not abandoning it prematurely (*Levush*). While theoretically one could leave once the next person getting an *aliya* is standing in front of the Torah, the custom is to wait until the end of his *aliya* and to try to get back to one's seat before the next *aliya* so that one does not miss any of the reading (*Magen Avraham* 141:8).
9. When returning to one's seat, the custom is to take the longer route back, as if to symbolize your sadness at leaving the Torah (*Levush*) or lest it look like you are trying to make a hasty getaway (*Arukh HaShulhan*). If the routes are equidistant, then leave from the opposite side you came from.
10. Finally, it is customary for people to wish you a יְיִשַׁר כֹּחַ (*yishar ko'ah/kohakha*), "may your strength be increased" or "more power to you," to which the traditional reply is בָּרוּךְ תִּהְיֶה (*barukh tihiyeh*), "May you be blessed." In Sepharadi tradition, the greeting is חֲזַק וּבָרוּךְ (*hazak uba-rukh*) "may your strength be increased and may you be blessed," to which the traditional reply is חֲזַק וֶאֱמָץ (*hazak ve'ematz*) "Be strong and courageous."

BIUR TEFILLA • ביאור תפילה

בָּרְכוּ – *Bless.* Here the person getting the *aliya* invites us all to join in with him. Indeed, there was a time when there was only one blessing cited before the first *aliya*

This **BIUR TEFILLA** *continues on page 377.*

The appropriate תורה *portion is read.*

The קורא *shows the* עולה *the section to be read. The* עולה *touches the scroll at that place with the* ציצית *of his* טלית*, which he then kisses. Holding the handles of the scroll, he says:*

עולה: **בָּרְכוּ**6 **אֶת יהוה הַמְבֹרָךְ.**

קהל: בָּרוּךְ יהוה הַמְבֹרָךְ לְעוֹלָם וָעֶד.

עולה: **בָּרוּךְ יהוה הַמְבֹרָךְ לְעוֹלָם וָעֶד.**
בָּרוּךְ אַתָּה יהוה, אֱלֹהֵינוּ מֶלֶךְ הָעוֹלָם
אֲשֶׁר בָּחַר בָּנוּ מִכָּל הָעַמִּים וְנָתַן לָנוּ אֶת תּוֹרָתוֹ.
בָּרוּךְ אַתָּה יהוה, נוֹתֵן הַתּוֹרָה.

After the קריאת התורה*, the* עולה *says:*

עולה: **בָּרוּךְ אַתָּה יהוה אֱלֹהֵינוּ מֶלֶךְ הָעוֹלָם**
אֲשֶׁר נָתַן לָנוּ תּוֹרַת אֱמֶת וְחַיֵּי עוֹלָם נָטַע בְּתוֹכֵנוּ.
בָּרוּךְ אַתָּה יהוה, נוֹתֵן הַתּוֹרָה.

---

reciting the blessings, people might think that the blessings were actually printed inside the Torah and were part of the Torah itself. Those who follow his opinion therefore suggest that one turn one's head to the left (*Magen Avraham* 139:8) or the right (*Arukh HaShulḥan* 139:13), or close one's eyes (*Ḥayyei Adam*), or do anything but look down. Rabbi Yehuda, on the other hand, said that you don't really need to worry about that since most people know the blessings are separate from the Torah itself; therefore, just recite the blessing however you want.

6. Reciting *Barekhu* is in effect an invitation to the community to join with you in learning Torah together, with you as their representative. They, in turn, answer in order to convey their presence and their participation. It is therefore important to recite the words loudly enough so that everyone (or at least a *minyan*'s worth) can hear you.

7. Ideally, each person is supposed to read the Torah portion for his own *aliya*. But if that were always enforced, then some people who could not read it accurately might be embarrassed (Ran), or he might read it with so many errors that those present would not be fulfilling their obligation to hear the Torah reading (Rosh), or a person who could not read Hebrew would never get an *aliya*, nor could a blind person. As such, the custom evolved to have a *ba'al keria*, who would be in charge of the reading and act as a *shaliaḥ* or messenger for the person getting the *aliya*. Nevertheless, there is a custom that the person getting an *aliya* should do his best to read

One who has survived a situation of danger says:

Blessed are You, LORD our God, King of the Universe, who bestows good on the unworthy, who has bestowed on me much good.

The congregation responds:

Amen. May He who bestowed much good on you continue to bestow on you much good, Selah.

After a Bar Mitzva boy has finished the Torah blessing, his father says aloud:

Blessed is He who has released me from the responsibility for this child.

FOR AN OLEH

May He who blessed our fathers, Abraham, Isaac and Jacob, bless (*name*, son of *father's name*) who has been called up in honor of the All-Present, in honor of the Torah, and in honor of Shabbat. As a reward for this, may the Holy One, blessed be He, protect and deliver him from all trouble and distress, all infection and illness, and send blessing and success to all the work of his hands, together with all Israel, his brethren, and let us say: Amen.

FOR A SICK MAN

May He who blessed our fathers, Abraham, Isaac and Jacob, Moses and Aaron, David and Solomon, bless and heal one who is ill, (*sick person's name*, son of *mother's name*), on whose behalf (*name of the one making the offering*) is making a contribution to charity. As a reward for this, may the Holy One, blessed be He, be filled with compassion for him, to restore his health, cure him, strengthen and revive him, sending him a swift and full recovery from heaven to all his 248 organs and 365 sinews, amongst the other sick ones in Israel, a healing of the spirit and a healing of the body – though on Shabbat it is forbidden to cry out, may healing be quick to come – now, swiftly and soon, and let us say: Amen.

FOR A SICK WOMAN

May He who blessed our fathers, Abraham, Isaac and Jacob, Moses and Aaron, David and Solomon, bless and heal one who is ill, (*sick person's name*, daughter of *mother's name*), on whose behalf (*name of the one making the offering*) is making a contribution to charity. As a reward for this, may the Holy One, blessed be He, be filled with compassion for her, to restore her health, cure her,

---

that the Torah is now a part of us. Perhaps that is the goal of this reading; namely, that we should walk away feeling like it is part of us.

One who has survived a situation of danger says:

בָּרוּךְ אַתָּה יהוה אֱלֹהֵינוּ מֶלֶךְ הָעוֹלָם הַגּוֹמֵל לְחַיָּבִים טוֹבוֹת שֶׁגְּמָלַנִי כָּל טוֹב.

The קהל *responds:*

אָמֵן. מִי שֶׁגְּמָלְךָ כָּל טוֹב הוּא יִגְמָלְךָ כָּל טוֹב, סֶלָה.

After a בר מצווה *has finished the* תורה *blessing, his father says aloud:*

בָּרוּךְ שֶׁפְּטָרַנִי מֵעָנְשׁוֹ שֶׁלָּזֶה.

מי שברך לעולה לתורה

מִי שֶׁבֵּרַךְ אֲבוֹתֵינוּ אַבְרָהָם יִצְחָק וְיַעֲקֹב, הוּא יְבָרֵךְ אֶת (פלוני בֶּן פלוני), בַּעֲבוּר שֶׁעָלָה לִכְבוֹד הַמָּקוֹם וְלִכְבוֹד הַתּוֹרָה וְלִכְבוֹד הַשַּׁבָּת. בִּשְׂכַר זֶה הַקָּדוֹשׁ בָּרוּךְ הוּא יִשְׁמְרֵהוּ וְיַצִּילֵהוּ מִכָּל צָרָה וְצוּקָה וּמִכָּל נֶגַע וּמַחֲלָה, וְיִשְׁלַח בְּרָכָה וְהַצְלָחָה בְּכָל מַעֲשֵׂה יָדָיו עִם כָּל יִשְׂרָאֵל אֶחָיו, וְנֹאמַר אָמֵן.

מי שברך לחולֶה

מִי שֶׁבֵּרַךְ אֲבוֹתֵינוּ אַבְרָהָם יִצְחָק וְיַעֲקֹב, מֹשֶׁה וְאַהֲרֹן דָּוִד וּשְׁלֹמֹה הוּא יְבָרֵךְ וִירַפֵּא אֶת הַחוֹלֶה (פלוני בֶּן פלונית) בַּעֲבוּר שֶׁ(פלוני בֶּן פלוני) נוֹדֵר צְדָקָה בַּעֲבוּרוֹ. בִּשְׂכַר זֶה הַקָּדוֹשׁ בָּרוּךְ הוּא יִמָּלֵא רַחֲמִים עָלָיו לְהַחֲלִימוֹ וּלְרַפְּאתוֹ וּלְהַחֲזִיקוֹ וּלְהַחֲיוֹתוֹ וְיִשְׁלַח לוֹ מְהֵרָה רְפוּאָה שְׁלֵמָה מִן הַשָּׁמַיִם לִרְמַ״ח אֵבָרָיו וּשְׁסָ״ה גִּידָיו בְּתוֹךְ שְׁאָר חוֹלֵי יִשְׂרָאֵל, רְפוּאַת הַנֶּפֶשׁ וּרְפוּאַת הַגּוּף. שַׁבָּת הִיא מִלִּזְעֹק וּרְפוּאָה קְרוֹבָה לָבוֹא, הַשְׁתָּא בַּעֲגָלָא וּבִזְמַן קָרִיב, וְנֹאמַר אָמֵן.

מי שברך לחולָה

מִי שֶׁבֵּרַךְ אֲבוֹתֵינוּ אַבְרָהָם יִצְחָק וְיַעֲקֹב, מֹשֶׁה וְאַהֲרֹן דָּוִד וּשְׁלֹמֹה הוּא יְבָרֵךְ וִירַפֵּא אֶת הַחוֹלָה (פלונית בַּת פלונית) בַּעֲבוּר שֶׁ(פלוני בֶּן פלוני) נוֹדֵר צְדָקָה בַּעֲבוּרָהּ. בִּשְׂכַר זֶה הַקָּדוֹשׁ בָּרוּךְ הוּא יִמָּלֵא רַחֲמִים עָלֶיהָ לְהַחֲלִימָהּ

(*Megilla* 4a). Today, each individual recites two blessings. The first refers to "His [God's] Torah" while the second seems to suggest and a second blessing recited only at the end of all of the *aliyot* as if it were one long reading in which all were involved

strengthen and revive her, sending her a swift and full recovery from heaven to all her organs and sinews, amongst the other sick ones in Israel, a healing of the spirit and a healing of the body – though on Shabbat it is forbidden to cry out, may healing be quick to come – now, swiftly and soon, and let us say: Amen.

ON THE BIRTH OF A SON

May He who blessed our fathers, Abraham, Isaac and Jacob, Moses and Aaron, David and Solomon, Sarah, Rebecca, Rachel and Leah, bless the woman (*name*, daughter of *father's name*) who has given birth, and her son who has been born to her as an auspicious sign. Her husband, the child's father, is making a contribution to charity. As a reward for this, may father and mother merit to bring the child into the covenant of Abraham and to a life of Torah, to the marriage canopy and to good deeds, and let us say: Amen.

ON THE BIRTH OF A DAUGHTER

May He who blessed our fathers, Abraham, Isaac and Jacob, Moses and Aaron, David and Solomon, Sarah, Rebecca, Rachel and Leah, bless the woman (*name*, daughter of *father's name*) who has given birth, and her daughter who has been born to her as an auspicious sign; and may her name be called in Israel (*baby's name*, daughter of *father's name*). Her husband, the child's father, is making a contribution to charity. As a reward for this, may father and mother merit to raise her to a life of Torah, to the marriage canopy, and to good deeds, and let us say: Amen.

FOR A BAR MITZVA

May He who blessed our fathers, Abraham, Isaac and Jacob, bless (*name*, son of *father's name*) who has completed thirteen years and attained the age of the commandments, who has been called to the Torah to give praise and thanks to God, may His name be blessed, for all the good He has bestowed on him. May the Holy One, blessed be He, protect and sustain him and direct his heart to be perfect with God, to walk in His ways and keep the commandments all the days of his life, and let us say: Amen.

FOR A BAT MITZVA

May He who blessed our fathers, Abraham, Isaac and Jacob, Sarah, Rebecca, Rachel and Leah, bless (*name*, daughter of *father's name*) who has completed twelve years and attained the age of the commandments, and gives praise and thanks to God, may His name be blessed, for all the good He has bestowed on her. May the Holy One, blessed be He, protect and sustain her and direct her heart to be perfect with God, to walk in His ways and keep the commandments all the days of her life, and let us say: Amen.

וּלְרַפּאתָהּ וּלְהַחֲזִיקָהּ וּלְהַחֲיוֹתָהּ וְיִשְׁלַח לָהּ מְהֵרָה רְפוּאָה שְׁלֵמָה מִן הַשָּׁמַיִם לְכָל אֵבָרֶיהָ וּלְכָל גִּידֶיהָ בְּתוֹךְ שְׁאָר חוֹלֵי יִשְׂרָאֵל, רְפוּאַת הַנֶּפֶשׁ וּרְפוּאַת הַגּוּף. שַׁבָּת הִיא מִלִּזְעֹק וּרְפוּאָה קְרוֹבָה לָבוֹא, הַשְׁתָּא בַּעֲגָלָא וּבִזְמַן קָרִיב, וְנֹאמַר אָמֵן.

מי שברך ליולדת בן

מִי שֶׁבֵּרַךְ אֲבוֹתֵינוּ אַבְרָהָם יִצְחָק וְיַעֲקֹב, מֹשֶׁה וְאַהֲרֹן דָּוִד וּשְׁלֹמֹה, שָׂרָה רִבְקָה רָחֵל וְלֵאָה הוּא יְבָרֵךְ אֶת הָאִשָּׁה הַיּוֹלֶדֶת (פלונית בַּת פלוני) וְאֶת בְּנָהּ שֶׁנּוֹלַד לָהּ לְמַזָּל טוֹב בַּעֲבוּר שֶׁבַּעְלָהּ וְאָבִיו נוֹדֵר צְדָקָה בַּעֲדָם. בִּשְׂכַר זֶה יִזְכּוּ אָבִיו וְאִמּוֹ לְהַכְנִיסוֹ בִּבְרִיתוֹ שֶׁל אַבְרָהָם אָבִינוּ וּלְגַדְּלוֹ לְתוֹרָה וּלְחֻפָּה וּלְמַעֲשִׂים טוֹבִים, וְנֹאמַר אָמֵן.

מי שברך ליולדת בת

מִי שֶׁבֵּרַךְ אֲבוֹתֵינוּ אַבְרָהָם יִצְחָק וְיַעֲקֹב, מֹשֶׁה וְאַהֲרֹן דָּוִד וּשְׁלֹמֹה, שָׂרָה רִבְקָה רָחֵל וְלֵאָה הוּא יְבָרֵךְ אֶת הָאִשָּׁה הַיּוֹלֶדֶת (פלונית בַּת פלוני) וְאֶת בִּתָּהּ שֶׁנּוֹלְדָה לָהּ לְמַזָּל טוֹב וְיִקָּרֵא שְׁמָהּ בְּיִשְׂרָאֵל (פלונית בַּת פלוני), בַּעֲבוּר שֶׁבַּעְלָהּ וְאָבִיהָ נוֹדֵר צְדָקָה בַּעֲדָן. בִּשְׂכַר זֶה יִזְכּוּ אָבִיהָ וְאִמָּהּ לְגַדְּלָהּ לְתוֹרָה וּלְחֻפָּה וּלְמַעֲשִׂים טוֹבִים, וְנֹאמַר אָמֵן.

מי שברך לבר מצווה

מִי שֶׁבֵּרַךְ אֲבוֹתֵינוּ אַבְרָהָם יִצְחָק וְיַעֲקֹב הוּא יְבָרֵךְ אֶת (פלוני בֶּן פלוני) שֶׁמָּלְאוּ לוֹ שְׁלֹשׁ עֶשְׂרֵה שָׁנָה וְהִגִּיעַ לְמִצְוֹת, וְעָלָה לַתּוֹרָה, לָתֵת שֶׁבַח וְהוֹדָיָה לְהַשֵּׁם יִתְבָּרַךְ עַל כָּל הַטּוֹבָה שֶׁגָּמַל אִתּוֹ. יִשְׁמְרֵהוּ הַקָּדוֹשׁ בָּרוּךְ הוּא וִיחַיֵּהוּ, וִיכוֹנֵן אֶת לִבּוֹ לִהְיוֹת שָׁלֵם עִם יהוה וְלָלֶכֶת בִּדְרָכָיו וְלִשְׁמֹר מִצְוֹתָיו כָּל הַיָּמִים, וְנֹאמַר אָמֵן.

מי שברך לבת מצווה

מִי שֶׁבֵּרַךְ אֲבוֹתֵינוּ אַבְרָהָם יִצְחָק וְיַעֲקֹב, שָׂרָה רִבְקָה רָחֵל וְלֵאָה, הוּא יְבָרֵךְ אֶת (פלונית בַּת פלוני) שֶׁמָּלְאוּ לָהּ שְׁתֵּים עֶשְׂרֵה שָׁנָה וְהִגִּיעָה לְמִצְוֹת, וְנוֹתֶנֶת שֶׁבַח וְהוֹדָיָה לְהַשֵּׁם יִתְבָּרַךְ עַל כָּל הַטּוֹבָה שֶׁגָּמַל אִתָּהּ. יִשְׁמְרֶהָ הַקָּדוֹשׁ בָּרוּךְ הוּא וִיחַיֶּהָ, וִיכוֹנֵן אֶת לִבָּהּ לִהְיוֹת שָׁלֵם עִם יהוה וְלָלֶכֶת בִּדְרָכָיו וְלִשְׁמֹר מִצְוֹתָיו כָּל הַיָּמִים, וְנֹאמַר אָמֵן.

In some congregations, during the week before a yahrzeit, "God, full of mercy" for a relative is said.

For a male close relative:

אֵל מָלֵא רַחֲמִים God, full of mercy, who dwells on high, grant fitting rest on the wings of the Divine Presence, in the heights of the holy and the pure who shine like the radiance of heaven, to the soul of (*name* son of *father's name*) who has gone to his eternal home, and to this I pledge (without formal vow) to give charity in his memory, may his resting place be in the Garden of Eden. Therefore, Master of compassion, shelter him in the shadow of Your wings forever and bind his soul in the bond of everlasting life. The LORD is his heritage; may he rest in peace, and let us say: Amen.

For a female close relative:

אֵל מָלֵא רַחֲמִים God, full of mercy, who dwells on high, grant fitting rest on the wings of the Divine Presence, in the heights of the holy and the pure who shine like the radiance of heaven, to the soul of (*name* daughter of *father's name*) who has gone to her eternal home, and to this I pledge (without formal vow) to give charity in her memory, may her resting place be in the Garden of Eden. Therefore, Master of compassion, shelter her in the shadow of Your wings forever and bind her soul in the bond of everlasting life. The LORD is her heritage; may she rest in peace, and let us say: Amen.

HALF KADDISH

Before Maftir is read, the Reader says Half Kaddish:

Reader: יִתְגַּדַּל Magnified and sanctified may His great name be,
in the world He created by His will.
May He establish His kingdom in your lifetime and in your days,
and in the lifetime of all the house of Israel,
swiftly and soon – and say: Amen.

All: May His great name[A] be blessed for ever and all time.

Reader: Blessed and praised, glorified and exalted,
raised and honored, uplifted and lauded
be the name of the Holy One, blessed be He,
beyond any blessing, song, praise and consolation
uttered in the world – and say: Amen.

ANI TEFILLA • אני תפילה

יְהֵא שְׁמֵהּ רַבָּא – *May His great name. Whoever says "yeheh shemeh raba..." with all his strength, the Heavenly Court rips up any negative decree against him* (Shabbat 119b). "With all his strength" – in a loud voice (Tosafot).

In some congregations, during the week before a yahrzeit, אֵל מָלֵא רַחֲמִים *for a relative is said.*

For a male close relative:

אֵל מָלֵא רַחֲמִים, שׁוֹכֵן בַּמְּרוֹמִים, הַמְצֵא מְנוּחָה נְכוֹנָה עַל כַּנְפֵי הַשְּׁכִינָה, בְּמַעֲלוֹת קְדוֹשִׁים וּטְהוֹרִים, כְּזֹהַר הָרָקִיעַ מַזְהִירִים, לְנִשְׁמַת (פלוני בֶּן פלוני) שֶׁהָלַךְ לְעוֹלָמוֹ, בַּעֲבוּר שֶׁבְּלִי נֶדֶר אֶתֵּן צְדָקָה בְּעַד הַזְכָּרַת נִשְׁמָתוֹ, בְּגַן עֵדֶן תְּהֵא מְנוּחָתוֹ. לָכֵן, בַּעַל הָרַחֲמִים יַסְתִּירֵהוּ בְּסֵתֶר כְּנָפָיו לְעוֹלָמִים, וְיִצְרֹר בִּצְרוֹר הַחַיִּים אֶת נִשְׁמָתוֹ, יהוה הוּא נַחֲלָתוֹ, וְיָנְוּחַ בְּשָׁלוֹם עַל מִשְׁכָּבוֹ, וְנֹאמַר אָמֵן.

For a female close relative:

אֵל מָלֵא רַחֲמִים, שׁוֹכֵן בַּמְּרוֹמִים, הַמְצֵא מְנוּחָה נְכוֹנָה עַל כַּנְפֵי הַשְּׁכִינָה, בְּמַעֲלוֹת קְדוֹשִׁים וּטְהוֹרִים, כְּזֹהַר הָרָקִיעַ מַזְהִירִים, לְנִשְׁמַת (פלונית בַּת פלוני) שֶׁהָלְכָה לְעוֹלָמָהּ, בַּעֲבוּר שֶׁבְּלִי נֶדֶר אֶתֵּן צְדָקָה בְּעַד הַזְכָּרַת נִשְׁמָתָהּ, בְּגַן עֵדֶן תְּהֵא מְנוּחָתָהּ. לָכֵן, בַּעַל הָרַחֲמִים יַסְתִּירֶהָ בְּסֵתֶר כְּנָפָיו לְעוֹלָמִים, וְיִצְרֹר בִּצְרוֹר הַחַיִּים אֶת נִשְׁמָתָהּ, יהוה הוּא נַחֲלָתָהּ, וְתָנְוּחַ בְּשָׁלוֹם עַל מִשְׁכָּבָהּ, וְנֹאמַר אָמֵן.

חצי קדיש

Before מפטיר *is read, the* קורא *says* חצי קדיש:

קורא: יִתְגַּדַּל וְיִתְקַדַּשׁ שְׁמֵהּ רַבָּא (קהל: אָמֵן)
בְּעָלְמָא דִּי בְרָא כִרְעוּתֵהּ וְיַמְלִיךְ מַלְכוּתֵהּ
בְּחַיֵּיכוֹן וּבְיוֹמֵיכוֹן וּבְחַיֵּי דְכָל בֵּית יִשְׂרָאֵל
בַּעֲגָלָא וּבִזְמַן קָרִיב, וְאִמְרוּ אָמֵן. (קהל: אָמֵן)

קהל וקורא: יְהֵא שְׁמֵהּ רַבָּא[א] מְבָרַךְ לְעָלַם וּלְעָלְמֵי עָלְמַיָּא.

קורא: יִתְבָּרַךְ וְיִשְׁתַּבַּח וְיִתְפָּאַר וְיִתְרוֹמַם וְיִתְנַשֵּׂא
וְיִתְהַדָּר וְיִתְעַלֶּה וְיִתְהַלָּל
שְׁמֵהּ דְּקֻדְשָׁא בְּרִיךְ הוּא (קהל: בְּרִיךְ הוּא)
לְעֵלָּא מִן כָּל בִּרְכָתָא / בשבת שובה: לְעֵלָּא לְעֵלָּא מִכָּל בִּרְכָתָא/
וְשִׁירָתָא, תֻּשְׁבְּחָתָא וְנֶחֱמָתָא
דַּאֲמִירָן בְּעָלְמָא, וְאִמְרוּ אָמֵן. (קהל: אָמֵן)

HAGBAHA AND GELILA

The Torah scroll is lifted and the congregation says:

וְזֹאת הַתּוֹרָה This is the Torah Deut. 4
that Moses placed before the children of Israel,
at the LORD's commandment, by the hand of Moses. Num. 9

Some add: It is a tree of life to those who grasp it, Prov. 3
and those who uphold it are happy.
Its ways are ways of pleasantness, and all its paths are peace.
Long life is in its right hand; in its left, riches and honor.
It pleased the LORD for the sake of [Israel's] righteousness, Is. 42
to make the Torah great and glorious.

The Torah scroll is bound and covered.

BLESSINGS BEFORE AND AFTER READING THE HAFTARA

Before reading the Haftara, the person called up for Maftir says:

בָּרוּךְ Blessed are You, LORD our God, King of the Universe, who chose good prophets and was pleased with their words, spoken in truth. Blessed are You, LORD, who chose the Torah, His servant Moses, His people Israel, and the prophets of truth and righteousness.

---

before the *haftara*, then read a minimum of 21 verses from a selection of a book of the Prophets that is related in some way to the weekly Torah portion and then four blessings afterwards for a total of eight blessings.

Finally, there is an opinion which suggests that the public reading from the Prophets is the remnant of an old custom to take time out on Shabbat to do some learning after finishing *Shaḥarit*, something that is more difficult to do during the week when everyone needs to rush off to work (Rashi). Seen in this light, the reading is a way for us to extend our individual and communal commitment to learning beyond that which some may think of as the minimum. In particular, we focus on the books that are too often ignored in education (*Shakh* in *Yoreh De'ah* 245:5), the Prophets, whose prophecies and speeches were written down because they have a message not only for their own time but for future generations as well. The essence of our listening intently to this recitation, then, is our ability to discern and internalize those messages, as has been done for generations of Jews since these words were first uttered.

The Gemara (*Megilla* 14a) informs us that there were far more prophets who lived over the course of biblical times than the ones which we know of. However, the only prophecies that were actually written down were the ones that would be needed for

This **INTRODUCTION TO HAFTARA** *continues on page 385.*

הגבהה וגלילה

The ספר תורה *is lifted and the* קהל *says:*

וְזֹאת הַתּוֹרָה אֲשֶׁר־שָׂם מֹשֶׁה לִפְנֵי בְּנֵי יִשְׂרָאֵל: דברים ד

עַל־פִּי יהוה בְּיַד מֹשֶׁה: במדבר ט

Some add עֵץ־חַיִּים הִיא לַמַּחֲזִיקִים בָּהּ וְתֹמְכֶיהָ מְאֻשָּׁר: משלי ג

דְּרָכֶיהָ דַרְכֵי־נֹעַם וְכָל־נְתִיבוֹתֶיהָ שָׁלוֹם:

אֹרֶךְ יָמִים בִּימִינָהּ, בִּשְׂמֹאולָהּ עֹשֶׁר וְכָבוֹד:

יהוה חָפֵץ לְמַעַן צִדְקוֹ יַגְדִּיל תּוֹרָה וְיַאְדִּיר: ישעיה מב

The ספר תורה *is bound and covered.*

ברכות ההפטרה

Before reading the הפטרה*, the person called up for* מפטיר *says:*

בָּרוּךְ אַתָּה יהוה אֱלֹהֵינוּ מֶלֶךְ הָעוֹלָם אֲשֶׁר בָּחַר בִּנְבִיאִים טוֹבִים, וְרָצָה בְדִבְרֵיהֶם הַנֶּאֱמָרִים בֶּאֱמֶת. בָּרוּךְ אַתָּה יהוה, הַבּוֹחֵר בַּתּוֹרָה וּבְמֹשֶׁה עַבְדּוֹ וּבְיִשְׂרָאֵל עַמּוֹ וּבִנְבִיאֵי הָאֱמֶת וָצֶדֶק.

INTRODUCTION TO HAFTARA

In addition to the weekly Torah portion, there is also a tradition to read a relatively short selection, called the *Haftara,* from a book of the Prophets. The exact source for this custom is not definitively known. One opinion has it that it was instituted by Ezra the Scribe in the fifth century BCE once all of the books of the Bible were canonized.

A more widely accepted theory is that there was a time in Jewish history when the public reading of the Torah was banned by the government (perhaps during the time of the Ḥanukka story in the second century BCE or even later during the time of the Roman empire). In order to nevertheless keep echoes of the tradition alive, the community resorted to reading a selection of the Prophets that was related in some way (e.g., in theme or language) to what would have been the Torah portion for that week. They established that the selection be a minimum of 21 verses long (to correspond to the minimum of three verses of the Torah read by each of the seven people who would have gotten an *aliya*) and that there be seven introductory blessings (to correspond to the missing blessings made by the seven people who would have gotten an *aliya*) (*Mishna Berura* 284:2). When the decree was rescinded, the practice nevertheless continued such that today one person is called up at the end of the Torah reading to make one blessing before and another after that reading (= two blessings), then two blessings

After the Haftara, the person called up for Maftir says the following blessings:

בָּרוּךְ Blessed are You, LORD our God, King of the Universe, Rock of all worlds, righteous for all generations, the faithful God who says and does, speaks and fulfills, all of whose words are truth and righteousness. You are faithful, LORD our God, and faithful are Your words, not one of which returns unfulfilled, for You, God, are a faithful (and compassionate) King. Blessed are You, LORD, faithful in all His words.

רַחֵם Have compassion on Zion for it is the source of our life, and save the one grieved in spirit swiftly in our days. Blessed are You, LORD, who makes Zion rejoice in her children.

שַׂמְּחֵנוּ Grant us joy, LORD our God, through Elijah the prophet Your servant, and through the kingdom of the house of David Your anointed – may he soon come and make our hearts glad. May no stranger sit on his throne, and may others not continue to inherit his glory, for You promised him by Your holy name that his light would never be extinguished. Blessed are You, LORD, Shield of David.

עַל הַתּוֹרָה For the Torah, for divine worship, for the prophets, and for this Sabbath day which You, LORD our God, have given us for holiness and rest, honor and glory – for all these we thank and bless You, LORD our God, and may Your name be blessed by the mouth of all that lives, continually, for ever and all time. Blessed are You, LORD, who sanctifies the Sabbath.

The following three paragraphs are only said when praying with a minyan (some say the first paragraph without a minyan).

יְקוּם פֻּרְקָן May deliverance arise[B] from heaven, bringing grace, love and compassion, long life, ample sustenance and heavenly help, physical health and enlightenment of mind, living and thriving children who

---

BIUR TEFILLA • ביאור תפילה

יְקוּם פֻּרְקָן – *May deliverance arise*. As indicated by the fact that they are in Aramaic and not Hebrew, these two prayers come from Talmudic and Geonic times (first century and onwards) in Babylonia. They are prayers for leadership, religious as well as lay people, professional as well as voluntary, those who contribute their time as well as those who contribute their money. Without them our communities could not function. Perhaps

This **BIUR TEFILLA** *continues on page 387.*

After the הפטרה, *the person called up for* מפטיר *says the following blessings:*

בָּרוּךְ אַתָּה יהוה אֱלֹהֵינוּ מֶלֶךְ הָעוֹלָם, צוּר כָּל הָעוֹלָמִים, צַדִּיק בְּכָל הַדּוֹרוֹת, הָאֵל הַנֶּאֱמָן, הָאוֹמֵר וְעוֹשֶׂה, הַמְדַבֵּר וּמְקַיֵּם, שֶׁכָּל דְּבָרָיו אֱמֶת וָצֶדֶק. נֶאֱמָן אַתָּה הוּא יהוה אֱלֹהֵינוּ וְנֶאֱמָנִים דְּבָרֶיךָ, וְדָבָר אֶחָד מִדְּבָרֶיךָ אָחוֹר לֹא יָשׁוּב רֵיקָם, כִּי אֵל מֶלֶךְ נֶאֱמָן (וְרַחֲמָן) אָתָּה. בָּרוּךְ אַתָּה יהוה, הָאֵל הַנֶּאֱמָן בְּכָל דְּבָרָיו.

רַחֵם עַל צִיּוֹן כִּי הִיא בֵּית חַיֵּינוּ, וְלַעֲלוּבַת נֶפֶשׁ תּוֹשִׁיעַ בִּמְהֵרָה בְיָמֵינוּ. בָּרוּךְ אַתָּה יהוה, מְשַׂמֵּחַ צִיּוֹן בְּבָנֶיהָ.

שַׂמְּחֵנוּ יהוה אֱלֹהֵינוּ בְּאֵלִיָּהוּ הַנָּבִיא עַבְדֶּךָ, וּבְמַלְכוּת בֵּית דָּוִד מְשִׁיחֶךָ, בִּמְהֵרָה יָבוֹא וְיָגֵל לִבֵּנוּ. עַל כִּסְאוֹ לֹא יֵשֶׁב זָר, וְלֹא יִנְחֲלוּ עוֹד אֲחֵרִים אֶת כְּבוֹדוֹ, כִּי בְשֵׁם קָדְשְׁךָ נִשְׁבַּעְתָּ לּוֹ שֶׁלֹּא יִכְבֶּה נֵרוֹ לְעוֹלָם וָעֶד. בָּרוּךְ אַתָּה יהוה, מָגֵן דָּוִד.

עַל הַתּוֹרָה וְעַל הָעֲבוֹדָה וְעַל הַנְּבִיאִים וְעַל יוֹם הַשַּׁבָּת הַזֶּה, שֶׁנָּתַתָּ לָּנוּ יהוה אֱלֹהֵינוּ לִקְדֻשָּׁה וְלִמְנוּחָה, לְכָבוֹד וּלְתִפְאָרֶת. עַל הַכֹּל יהוה אֱלֹהֵינוּ אֲנַחְנוּ מוֹדִים לָךְ וּמְבָרְכִים אוֹתָךְ, יִתְבָּרַךְ שִׁמְךָ בְּפִי כָּל חַי תָּמִיד לְעוֹלָם וָעֶד. בָּרוּךְ אַתָּה יהוה, מְקַדֵּשׁ הַשַּׁבָּת.

The following three paragraphs are only said when praying with a מנין *(some say the first paragraph without a* מנין*).*

יְקוּם פֻּרְקָן[ב] מִן שְׁמַיָּא, חִנָּא וְחִסְדָּא וְרַחֲמֵי וְחַיֵּי אֲרִיכֵי וּמְזוֹנֵי רְוִיחֵי, וְסִיַּעְתָּא דִשְׁמַיָּא, וּבַרְיוּת גּוּפָא וּנְהוֹרָא מְעַלְיָא, זַרְעָא חַיָּא וְקַיָּמָא,

---

future generations, that is to say, the ones whose messages were timeless. The challenge in following the *Haftara* reading is therefore not only to figure out the connection between the Torah reading and the *Haftara* reading for that particular week, but to figure out the connection between the *Haftara* reading and one's own life.

What message in this week's *Haftara* can you take with you into next week?

will neither interrupt nor cease from the words of the Torah – to our masters and teachers of the holy communities in the land of Israel and Babylon; to the leaders of assemblies and the leaders of communities in exile; to the heads of academies and to the judges in the gates; to all their disciples and their disciples' disciples, and to all who occupy themselves in study of the Torah. May the King of the Universe bless them, prolonging their lives, increasing their days, and adding to their years. May they be redeemed and delivered from all distress and illness. May our Master in heaven be their help at all times and seasons; and let us say: Amen.

יְקוּם פֻּרְקָן May deliverance arise from heaven, bringing grace, love and compassion, long life, ample sustenance and heavenly help, physical health and enlightenment of mind, living and thriving children who will neither interrupt nor cease from the words of the Torah – to all this holy congregation, great and small, women and children. May the King of the Universe bless you, prolonging your lives, increasing your days, and adding to your years. May you be redeemed and delivered from all distress and illness. May our Master in heaven be your help at all times and seasons; and let us say: Amen.

מִי שֶׁבֵּרַךְ May He who blessed our fathers, Abraham, Isaac and Jacob, bless all this holy congregation, together with all other holy congregations: them, their wives, their sons and daughters, and all that is theirs. May He bless those who unite to form synagogues for prayer and those who come there to pray; those who provide lamps for light and wine for Kiddush and Havdala, food for visitors and charity for the poor, and all who faithfully occupy themselves with the needs of the community. May the Holy One, blessed be He, give them their reward; may He remove from them all illness, grant them complete healing, and forgive all their sins. May He send blessing and success to all the work of their hands, together with all Israel their brethren; and let us say: Amen.

---

paid to religious leadership, and the wisdom and hard work contributed by people who have been prepared to step up to the plate. These are the ones who enable us to support one another, to be welcomed into a new community, to educate our children, to acquire and operate cemeteries and charities, hospitals and free loan societies, social service agencies, and, of course, the very synagogue in which you may now be standing. What kind of contribution can you make to keep this communal infrastructure alive?

זְרְעָא דִּי לָא יִפְסֻק וְדִי לָא יִבְטֻל מִפִּתְגָּמֵי אוֹרַיְתָא, לְמָרָנָן וְרַבָּנָן חֲבוּרָתָא קַדִּישָׁתָא דִּי בְאַרְעָא דְיִשְׂרָאֵל וְדִי בְּבָבֶל, לְרֵישֵׁי כַלָּה, וּלְרֵישֵׁי גַלְוָתָא, וּלְרֵישֵׁי מְתִיבָתָא, וּלְדַיָּנֵי דְבָבָא, לְכָל תַּלְמִידֵיהוֹן, וּלְכָל תַּלְמִידֵי תַלְמִידֵיהוֹן, וּלְכָל מָאן דְּעָסְקִין בְּאוֹרַיְתָא. מַלְכָּא דְעָלְמָא יְבָרֵךְ יָתְהוֹן, יַפֵּשׁ חַיֵּיהוֹן וְיַסְגֵּא יוֹמֵיהוֹן, וְיִתֵּן אַרְכָא לִשְׁנֵיהוֹן, וְיִתְפָּרְקוּן וְיִשְׁתֵּיזְבוּן מִן כָּל עָקָא וּמִן כָּל מַרְעִין בִּישִׁין. מָרַן דִּי בִשְׁמַיָּא יְהֵא בְסַעְדְּהוֹן כָּל זְמַן וְעִדָּן, וְנֹאמַר אָמֵן.

יְקוּם פֻּרְקָן מִן שְׁמַיָּא, חִנָּא וְחִסְדָּא וְרַחֲמֵי וְחַיֵּי אֲרִיכֵי וּמְזוֹנֵי רְוִיחֵי, וְסִיַּעְתָּא דִשְׁמַיָּא, וּבַרְיוּת גּוּפָא וּנְהוֹרָא מְעַלְּיָא, זַרְעָא חַיָּא וְקַיָּמָא, זַרְעָא דִּי לָא יִפְסֻק וְדִי לָא יִבְטֻל מִפִּתְגָּמֵי אוֹרַיְתָא, לְכָל קְהָלָא קַדִּישָׁא הָדֵין, רַבְרְבַיָּא עִם זְעֵרַיָּא, טַפְלָא וּנְשַׁיָּא. מַלְכָּא דְעָלְמָא יְבָרֵךְ יָתְכוֹן, יַפֵּשׁ חַיֵּיכוֹן וְיַסְגֵּא יוֹמֵיכוֹן, וְיִתֵּן אַרְכָא לִשְׁנֵיכוֹן, וְתִתְפָּרְקוּן וְתִשְׁתֵּיזְבוּן מִן כָּל עָקָא וּמִן כָּל מַרְעִין בִּישִׁין. מָרַן דִּי בִשְׁמַיָּא יְהֵא בְסַעְדְּכוֹן כָּל זְמַן וְעִדָּן, וְנֹאמַר אָמֵן.

מִי שֶׁבֵּרַךְ אֲבוֹתֵינוּ אַבְרָהָם יִצְחָק וְיַעֲקֹב, הוּא יְבָרֵךְ אֶת כָּל הַקָּהָל הַקָּדוֹשׁ הַזֶּה עִם כָּל קְהִלּוֹת הַקֹּדֶשׁ, הֵם וּנְשֵׁיהֶם וּבְנֵיהֶם וּבְנוֹתֵיהֶם וְכָל אֲשֶׁר לָהֶם, וּמִי שֶׁמְּיַחֲדִים בָּתֵּי כְנֵסִיּוֹת לִתְפִלָּה, וּמִי שֶׁבָּאִים בְּתוֹכָם לְהִתְפַּלֵּל, וּמִי שֶׁנּוֹתְנִים נֵר לַמָּאוֹר וְיַיִן לְקִדּוּשׁ וּלְהַבְדָּלָה וּפַת לָאוֹרְחִים וּצְדָקָה לָעֲנִיִּים, וְכָל מִי שֶׁעוֹסְקִים בְּצָרְכֵי צִבּוּר בֶּאֱמוּנָה. הַקָּדוֹשׁ בָּרוּךְ הוּא יְשַׁלֵּם שְׂכָרָם, וְיָסִיר מֵהֶם כָּל מַחֲלָה, וְיִרְפָּא לְכָל גּוּפָם, וְיִסְלַח לְכָל עֲוֹנָם, וְיִשְׁלַח בְּרָכָה וְהַצְלָחָה בְּכָל מַעֲשֵׂה יְדֵיהֶם עִם כָּל יִשְׂרָאֵל אֲחֵיהֶם, וְנֹאמַר אָמֵן.

For surely among the keys to Jewish survival over the millennia have been the value placed on education, the deference

the very use of the foreign language of Aramaic is a testimony to the longevity and consistency of this tradition.

The Prayer for the Welfare of the Canadian Government is on the next page.

PRAYER FOR THE WELFARE OF THE AMERICAN GOVERNMENT

The Leader says the following:

הַנּוֹתֵן תְּשׁוּעָה May He who gives salvation to kings and dominion to princes, whose kingdom is an everlasting kingdom, who delivers His servant David from the evil sword, who makes a way in the sea and a path through the mighty waters, bless and protect, guard and help, exalt, magnify and uplift the President, Vice President and all officials of this land. May the Supreme King of kings in His mercy put into their hearts and the hearts of all their counselors and officials, to deal kindly with us and all Israel. In their days and in ours, may Judah be saved and Israel dwell in safety, and may the Redeemer come to Zion. May this be His will, and let us say: Amen.

PRAYER FOR THE SAFETY OF THE AMERICAN MILITARY

The Leader says the following:

אַדִּיר בַּמָּרוֹם God on high who dwells in might, the King to whom peace belongs, look down from Your holy habitation and bless the soldiers of the American military forces who risk their lives for the sake of peace on earth. Be their shelter and stronghold, and let them not falter. Give them the strength and courage to thwart the plans of the enemy and end the rule of evil. May their enemies be scattered and their foes flee before them, and may they rejoice in Your salvation. Bring them back safely to their homes, as is written: "The Lord will guard you from all harm, He will guard your life. The Lord will guard your going and coming, now and for evermore." And may there be fulfilled for us the verse: "Nation shall not lift up sword against nation, nor shall they learn war any more." Let all the inhabitants on earth know that sovereignty is Yours and Your name inspires awe over all You have created – and let us say: Amen.

Ps. 121

Is. 2

---

sea, and as the creeping things, that have no ruler over them?' Why is man compared to the fishes of the sea? Just as among fish of the sea, the greater swallow up the smaller ones, so with men; were it not for fear of the government, men would swallow each other alive. This is just what we learned: R. Ḥanina, the Deputy High Priest, said, Pray for the welfare of the government, for were it not for the fear thereof, men would

This **INTRODUCTION** *continues on page 391.*

The Prayer for the Welfare of the Canadian Government is on the next page.

תפילה לשלום המלכות

The שליח ציבור *says the following:*

הַנּוֹתֵן תְּשׁוּעָה לַמְּלָכִים וּמֶמְשָׁלָה לַנְּסִיכִים, מַלְכוּתוֹ מַלְכוּת כָּל עוֹלָמִים, הַפּוֹצֶה אֶת דָּוִד עַבְדּוֹ מֵחֶרֶב רָעָה, הַנּוֹתֵן בַּיָּם דֶּרֶךְ וּבְמַיִם עַזִּים נְתִיבָה, הוּא יְבָרֵךְ וְיִשְׁמֹר וְיִנְצֹר וְיַעֲזֹר וִירוֹמֵם וִיגַדֵּל וִינַשֵּׂא לְמַעְלָה אֶת הַנָּשִׂיא וְאֵת מִשְׁנֵהוּ וְאֵת כָּל שָׂרֵי הָאָרֶץ הַזֹּאת. מֶלֶךְ מַלְכֵי הַמְּלָכִים, בְּרַחֲמָיו יִתֵּן בְּלִבָּם וּבְלֵב כָּל יוֹעֲצֵיהֶם וְשָׂרֵיהֶם לַעֲשׂוֹת טוֹבָה עִמָּנוּ וְעִם כָּל יִשְׂרָאֵל. בִּימֵיהֶם וּבְיָמֵינוּ תִּוָּשַׁע יְהוּדָה, וְיִשְׂרָאֵל יִשְׁכֹּן לָבֶטַח, וּבָא לְצִיּוֹן גּוֹאֵל. וְכֵן יְהִי רָצוֹן, וְנֹאמַר אָמֵן.

תפילה לשלום חיילי צבא ארצות הברית

The שליח ציבור *says the following:*

אַדִּיר בַּמָּרוֹם שׁוֹכֵן בִּגְבוּרָה, מֶלֶךְ שֶׁהַשָּׁלוֹם שֶׁלּוֹ, הַשְׁקִיפָה מִמְּעוֹן
קָדְשֶׁךָ, וּבָרֵךְ אֶת חַיָּלֵי צְבָא אַרְצוֹת הַבְּרִית, הַמְחָרְפִים נַפְשָׁם
בְּלֶכְתָּם לָשִׂים שָׁלוֹם בָּאָרֶץ. הֱיֵה נָא לָהֶם מַחֲסֶה וּמָעוֹז, וְאַל תִּתֵּן
לַמּוֹט רַגְלָם, חַזֵּק יְדֵיהֶם וְאַמֵּץ רוּחָם לְהָפֵר עֲצַת אוֹיֵב וּלְהַעֲבִיר
מֶמְשֶׁלֶת זָדוֹן, יָפוּצוּ אוֹיְבֵיהֶם וְיָנוּסוּ מְשַׂנְאֵיהֶם מִפְּנֵיהֶם, וְיִשְׂמְחוּ
בִּישׁוּעָתֶךָ. הֲשִׁיבֵם בְּשָׁלוֹם אֶל בֵּיתָם, כַּכָּתוּב בְּדִבְרֵי קָדְשֶׁךָ: יהוה תהלים קכא
יִשְׁמָרְךָ מִכָּל־רָע, יִשְׁמֹר אֶת־נַפְשֶׁךָ: יהוה יִשְׁמָר־צֵאתְךָ וּבוֹאֶךָ,
מֵעַתָּה וְעַד־עוֹלָם: וְקַיֵּם בָּנוּ מִקְרָא שֶׁכָּתוּב: לֹא־יִשָּׂא גוֹי אֶל־גּוֹי ישעיה ב
חֶרֶב, וְלֹא־יִלְמְדוּ עוֹד מִלְחָמָה: וְיֵדְעוּ כָּל יוֹשְׁבֵי תֵבֵל כִּי לְךָ מְלוּכָה
יָאֲתָה, וְשִׁמְךָ נוֹרָא עַל כָּל מַה שֶּׁבָּרָאתָ. וְנֹאמַר אָמֵן.

INTRODUCTION TO THE PRAYER FOR THE GOVERNMENT

Already in biblical times the prophet Yirmiyahu (29:7) instructed "Seek the peace of the city to which I have carried you in exile. Pray to Hashem for it, because in its peace, you shall find peace." And the Gemara (*Avoda Zara* 3a-b) adds: "Rav Judah says in the name of Samuel: Why is it written, (*Ḥavakkuk* 1:14) 'And You make man as the fishes of the

PRAYER FOR THE WELFARE OF THE CANADIAN GOVERNMENT

The Leader says the following:

הַנּוֹתֵן תְּשׁוּעָה May He who gives salvation to kings and dominion to princes, whose kingdom is an everlasting kingdom, who delivers His servant David from the evil sword, who makes a way in the sea and a path through the mighty waters, bless and protect, guard and help, exalt, magnify and uplift the Prime Minister and all the elected and appointed officials of Canada. May the Supreme King of kings in His mercy put into their hearts and the hearts of all their counselors and officials, to deal kindly with us and all Israel. In their days and in ours, may Judah be saved and Israel dwell in safety, and may the Redeemer come to Zion. May this be His will, and let us say: Amen.

PRAYER FOR THE SAFETY OF THE CANADIAN MILITARY FORCES

The Leader says the following:

אַדִּיר בַּמָּרוֹם God on high who dwells in might, the King to whom peace belongs, look down from Your holy habitation and bless the soldiers of the Canadian Forces who risk their lives for the sake of peace on earth. Be their shelter and stronghold, and let them not falter. Give them the strength and courage to thwart the plans of the enemy and end the rule of evil. May their enemies be scattered and their foes flee before them, and may they rejoice in Your salvation. Bring them back safely to their homes, as is written: "The Lord will guard you from all harm, He will *Ps. 121*
guard your life. The Lord will guard your going and coming, now and for evermore." And may there be fulfilled for us the verse: "Nation shall *Is. 2*
not lift up sword against nation, nor shall they learn war any more." Let all the inhabitants on earth know that sovereignty is Yours and Your name inspires awe over all You have created – and let us say: Amen.

---

us to thrive as a Jewish community in unprecedented ways in our history, even as it has granted us the rights to see ourselves as proud citizens who can make our own contributions to its development for all of its people.

Think about the most oppressive and repressive regimes under which the Jewish people have lived over time. Then say this blessing with gratitude and hope.

תפילה לשלום המלכות

The שליח ציבור *says the following:*

הַנּוֹתֵן תְּשׁוּעָה לַמְּלָכִים וּמֶמְשָׁלָה לַנְּסִיכִים, מַלְכוּתוֹ מַלְכוּת כָּל עוֹלָמִים, הַפּוֹצֶה אֶת דָּוִד עַבְדּוֹ מֵחֶרֶב רָעָה, הַנּוֹתֵן בַּיָּם דֶּרֶךְ וּבְמַיִם עַזִּים נְתִיבָה, הוּא יְבָרֵךְ וְיִשְׁמֹר וְיִנְצֹר וְיַעֲזֹר וִירוֹמֵם וִיגַדֵּל וִינַשֵּׂא לְמַעְלָה אֶת רֹאשׁ הַמֶּמְשָׁלָה וְאֶת כָּל שָׂרֵי הָאָרֶץ הַזֹּאת. מֶלֶךְ מַלְכֵי הַמְּלָכִים, בְּרַחֲמָיו יִתֵּן בְּלִבָּם וּבְלֵב כָּל יוֹעֲצֵיהֶם וְשָׂרֵיהֶם לַעֲשׂוֹת טוֹבָה עִמָּנוּ וְעִם כָּל יִשְׂרָאֵל. בִּימֵיהֶם וּבְיָמֵינוּ תִּוָּשַׁע יְהוּדָה, וְיִשְׂרָאֵל יִשְׁכֹּן לָבֶטַח, וּבָא לְצִיּוֹן גּוֹאֵל. וְכֵן יְהִי רָצוֹן, וְנֹאמַר אָמֵן.

תפילה לשלום חיילי צבא קנדה

The שליח ציבור *says the following:*

אַדִּיר בַּמָּרוֹם שׁוֹכֵן בִּגְבוּרָה, מֶלֶךְ שֶׁהַשָּׁלוֹם שֶׁלּוֹ, הַשְׁקִיפָה מִמְּעוֹן קָדְשְׁךָ, וּבָרֵךְ אֶת חַיָּלֵי צְבָא קָנָדָה, הַמְחָרְפִים נַפְשָׁם בְּלֶכְתָּם לָשִׂים שָׁלוֹם בָּאָרֶץ. הֱיֵה נָא לָהֶם מַחֲסֶה וּמָעוֹז, וְאַל תִּתֵּן לַמּוֹט רַגְלָם, חַזֵּק יְדֵיהֶם וְאַמֵּץ רוּחָם לְהָפֵר עֲצַת אוֹיֵב וּלְהַעֲבִיר מֶמְשֶׁלֶת זָדוֹן, יָפוּצוּ אוֹיְבֵיהֶם וְיָנוּסוּ מְשַׂנְאֵיהֶם מִפְּנֵיהֶם, וְיִשְׂמְחוּ בִּישׁוּעָתֶךָ.
הֲשִׁיבֵם בְּשָׁלוֹם אֶל בֵּיתָם, כַּכָּתוּב בְּדִבְרֵי קָדְשֶׁךָ: יהוה יִשְׁמָרְךָ תהלים קכא
מִכָּל־רָע, יִשְׁמֹר אֶת־נַפְשֶׁךָ: יהוה יִשְׁמָר־צֵאתְךָ וּבוֹאֶךָ, מֵעַתָּה
וְעַד־עוֹלָם: וְקַיֵּם בָּנוּ מִקְרָא שֶׁכָּתוּב: לֹא־יִשָּׂא גוֹי אֶל־גּוֹי חֶרֶב, ישעיה ב
וְלֹא־יִלְמְדוּ עוֹד מִלְחָמָה: וְיֵדְעוּ כָּל יוֹשְׁבֵי תֵבֵל כִּי לְךָ מְלוּכָה יָאֲתָה, וְשִׁמְךָ נוֹרָא עַל כָּל מַה שֶּׁבָּרָאתָ. וְנֹאמַר אָמֵן.

At the same time, in our own times, many of us have been blessed to live in countries where the governments have provided not only for our physical safety, but have enabled

swallow each other alive." This is the most minimalist view of a prayer for the government, the protection it provides for physical welfare.

PRAYER FOR THE STATE OF ISRAEL[B]

The Leader says the following prayer:

אָבִינוּ שֶׁבַּשָּׁמַיִם Heavenly Father, Israel's Rock and Redeemer,[I] bless the State of Israel, the first flowering of our redemption.[I] Shield it under the wings of Your loving-kindness and spread over it the Tabernacle of Your peace.[I] Send Your light and truth to its leaders, ministers and counselors, and direct them with good counsel before You.

Strengthen the hands of the defenders of our Holy Land; grant them deliverance, our God, and crown them with the crown of victory. Grant peace in the land and everlasting joy to its inhabitants.

As for our brothers, the whole house of Israel, remember them in all the lands of our (*In Israel say:* their) dispersion, and swiftly lead us (*In Israel say:* them) upright to Zion Your city, and Jerusalem Your dwelling place, as is written in the Torah of Moses Your servant:

IYUN TEFILLA • עיון תפילה

צוּר יִשְׂרָאֵל וְגוֹאֲלוֹ – *Israel's Rock and Redeemer.* Note the names of Hashem that are used here. Why were these chosen?

When the Declaration of Independence was being drafted in 1948 there was much controversy over whether to include God's name in the text. Secular Zionists were offended at the notion that the achievements of Zionism should be attributed to God, and Religious Zionists were insistent that they should be. The compromise was to include the term "צוּר יִשְׂרָאֵל," a name of God that can also be interpreted in other ways. Now reflect on why the Chief Rabbis in 1948 chose these two names in their prayer for the state.

רֵאשִׁית צְמִיחַת גְּאֻלָּתֵנוּ – *The first flowering of our redemption.* The phrase which declares that Israel is "the first flowering of our redemption" is one that some have objected to, especially those who would claim that the State of Israel has no religious significance, and they therefore leave out the prayer altogether. Still others have objected to the wish that all Jews eventually settle there. We believe, however, that the modern State, for all of its faults, is the instrument through which Hashem will bring the Jewish people its redemption. For the first time in 2000 years we live in our own sovereign state; that fact alone is cause for thanks and for hope.

סֻכַּת שְׁלוֹמֶךָ – *The Tabernacle of Your peace.* **Why do you think it is called the "*sukka*" of peace? What does a *sukka* represent?**

תפילה לשלום מדינת ישראל[ב]

The שליח ציבור *says the following prayer:*

אָבִינוּ שֶׁבַּשָּׁמַיִם, צוּר יִשְׂרָאֵל וְגוֹאֲלוֹ,[ע] בָּרֵךְ אֶת מְדִינַת יִשְׂרָאֵל,
רֵאשִׁית צְמִיחַת גְּאֻלָּתֵנוּ.[ע] הָגֵן עָלֶיהָ בְּאֶבְרַת חַסְדֶּךָ וּפְרֹשׂ עָלֶיהָ
סֻכַּת שְׁלוֹמֶךָ,[ע] וּשְׁלַח אוֹרְךָ וַאֲמִתְּךָ לְרָאשֶׁיהָ, שָׂרֶיהָ וְיוֹעֲצֶיהָ,
וְתַקְּנֵם בְּעֵצָה טוֹבָה מִלְּפָנֶיךָ.

חַזֵּק אֶת יְדֵי מְגִנֵּי אֶרֶץ קָדְשֵׁנוּ, וְהַנְחִילֵם אֱלֹהֵינוּ יְשׁוּעָה וַעֲטֶרֶת
נִצָּחוֹן תְּעַטְּרֵם, וְנָתַתָּ שָׁלוֹם בָּאָרֶץ וְשִׂמְחַת עוֹלָם לְיוֹשְׁבֶיהָ.

וְאֶת אַחֵינוּ כָּל בֵּית יִשְׂרָאֵל, פְּקָד נָא בְּכָל אַרְצוֹת פְּזוּרֵינוּ,
וְתוֹלִיכֵנוּ /בארץ ישראל: פְּזוּרֵיהֶם, וְתוֹלִיכֵם/ מְהֵרָה קוֹמְמִיּוּת לְצִיּוֹן
עִירֶךָ וְלִירוּשָׁלַיִם מִשְׁכַּן שְׁמֶךָ, כַּכָּתוּב בְּתוֹרַת מֹשֶׁה עַבְדֶּךָ:
אִם־יִהְיֶה נִדַּחֲךָ בִּקְצֵה הַשָּׁמָיִם, מִשָּׁם יְקַבֶּצְךָ יהוה אֱלֹהֶיךָ דברים ל

BIUR TEFILLA • ביאור תפילה

תפילה לשלום מדינת ישראל – *PRAYER FOR THE STATE OF ISRAEL.* The Prayer for the State of Israel was written by Chief Rabbis Herzog and Uziel in 1948 (allegedly with some minor revisions made by Noble Laureate Shai Agnon). This prayer is a modern contribution to the ongoing millennial development of the siddur as a microcosm of Jewish history, wherein each generation adds its own concerns and aspirations.

ANI TEFILLA • אני תפילה

Once I sat on the steps by a gate at David's Tower, I placed my two heavy baskets at my side. A group of tourists was standing around their guide and I became their target marker. "You see that man with the baskets? Just right of his head there's an arch from the Roman period. Just right of his head." "But he's moving, he's moving!" I said to myself: redemption will come only if their guide tells them, "You see that arch from the Roman period? It's not important: but next to it, left and down a bit, there sits a man who's bought fruit and vegetables for his family." (Yehuda Amichai, *Tourists*)

'Even if you are scattered to the furthermost lands under the heavens, from there the LORD your God will gather you and take you back. The LORD your God will bring you to the land your ancestors possessed and you will possess it; and He will make you more prosperous and numerous than your ancestors. Then the LORD your God will open up your heart and the heart of your descendants, to love the LORD your God with all your heart and with all your soul, that you may live." *Deut. 30*

Unite our hearts to love and revere Your name and observe all the words of Your Torah, and swiftly send us Your righteous anointed one of the house of David, to redeem those who long for Your salvation.

Appear in Your glorious majesty over all the dwellers on earth, and let all who breathe declare: The LORD God of Israel is King and His kingship has dominion over all. Amen, Selah.

PRAYER FOR ISRAEL'S DEFENSE FORCES[A]

The Leader says the following prayer:

מִי שֶׁבֵּרַךְ May He who blessed our ancestors, Abraham, Isaac and Jacob, bless the members of Israel's Defense Forces and its security services who stand guard over our land and the cities of our

---

this, it simply strengthens our faith, Mr. Chief Justice, that the day will yet come when there will be a Sanhedrin of 71 elders and the Jews from all four corners of the world will come to this place, to hang on your every word. Thank you, thank you, thank you, for your letter. With blessings, appreciation, and profound respect, Nechama Leibowitz."

ANI TEFILLA • אני תפילה

מי שברך לחיילי צה"ל – *PRAYER FOR ISRAEL'S DEFENSE FORCES.*

Rabbi Aryeh Levin saw a young soldier on short furlough from the army. He knew him from the neighborhood in Jerusalem and so he crossed the street in order to extend his hand in greeting. "Shalom aleichem," he said, "please come to my home. I would very much like to drink tea with you and hear about your activities."

This **ANI TEFILLA** *continues on page 397.*

וּמִשָּׁם יִקָּחֶךָ: וֶהֱבִיאֲךָ יהוה אֱלֹהֶיךָ אֶל־הָאָרֶץ אֲשֶׁר־יָרְשׁוּ אֲבֹתֶיךָ וִירִשְׁתָּהּ, וְהֵיטִבְךָ וְהִרְבְּךָ מֵאֲבֹתֶיךָ: וּמָל יהוה אֱלֹהֶיךָ אֶת־לְבָבְךָ וְאֶת־לְבַב זַרְעֶךָ, לְאַהֲבָה אֶת־יהוה אֱלֹהֶיךָ בְּכָל־לְבָבְךָ וּבְכָל־נַפְשְׁךָ, לְמַעַן חַיֶּיךָ:

וְיַחֵד לְבָבֵנוּ לְאַהֲבָה וּלְיִרְאָה אֶת שְׁמֶךָ, וְלִשְׁמֹר אֶת כָּל דִּבְרֵי תוֹרָתֶךָ, וּשְׁלַח לָנוּ מְהֵרָה בֶּן דָּוִד מְשִׁיחַ צִדְקֶךָ, לִפְדּוֹת מְחַכֵּי קֵץ יְשׁוּעָתֶךָ.

וְהוֹפַע בַּהֲדַר גְּאוֹן עֻזֶּךָ עַל כָּל יוֹשְׁבֵי תֵבֵל אַרְצֶךָ וְיֹאמַר כֹּל אֲשֶׁר נְשָׁמָה בְאַפּוֹ, יהוה אֱלֹהֵי יִשְׂרָאֵל מֶלֶךְ וּמַלְכוּתוֹ בַּכֹּל מָשָׁלָה, אָמֵן סֶלָה.

מי שברך לחיילי צה״ל[א]

The שליח ציבור *says the following prayer:*

מִי שֶׁבֵּרַךְ אֲבוֹתֵינוּ אַבְרָהָם יִצְחָק וְיַעֲקֹב הוּא יְבָרֵךְ אֶת חַיָּלֵי צְבָא הַהֲגָנָה לְיִשְׂרָאֵל וְאַנְשֵׁי כֹּחוֹת הַבִּטָּחוֹן, הָעוֹמְדִים

ANI TEFILLA • אני תפילה

Israel Supreme Court justice Tzvi Tal once sent a letter to Nechama Leibowitz with a reference to rabbinic literature (*Tosafot* on *Ḥullin*) that supported something that Nechama had written in one of her books. She wrote back to him: "Had someone told me in my youth in the Diaspora at the beginning of this century (for I am 90 years old) that I would merit to see a Supreme Court in Jerusalem, and that a Chief Justice would send me a reference to the Talmud, my brother, of blessed memory, and I would have thought that this was some sort of legend like the Leviathan that we are told the righteous will eat in the World to Come, the kind of legends that father used to tell us in order to strengthen our Zionist education. Yet this is no legend…for I am holding the envelope in my hands and it clearly says "Israel Supreme Court" on it! Since we have merited

God from the Lebanese border to the Egyptian desert, from the Mediterranean sea to the approach of the Aravah, and wherever else they are, on land, in air and at sea. May the LORD make the enemies who rise against us be struck down before them. May the Holy One, blessed be He, protect and deliver them from all trouble and distress, affliction and illness, and send blessing and success to all the work of their hands. May He subdue our enemies under them and crown them with deliverance and victory. And may there be fulfilled in them the verse, "It is the LORD your God who goes with you to fight for you against your enemies, to deliver you." And let us say: Amen. *Deut. 20*

PRAYER FOR THOSE BEING HELD IN CAPTIVITY

If Israeli soldiers or civilians are being held in captivity, the Leader says the following:

מִי שֶׁבֵּרַךְ May He who blessed our ancestors, Abraham, Isaac and Jacob, Joseph, Moses and Aaron, David and Solomon, bless, protect and guard the members of Israel's Defense Forces missing in action or held captive, and other captives among our brethren, the whole house of Israel, who are in distress or captivity, as we, the members of this holy congregation, pray on their behalf. May the Holy One, blessed be He, have compassion on them and bring them out from darkness and the shadow of death; may He break their bonds, deliver them from their distress, and bring them swiftly back to their families' embrace. Give thanks to the LORD for His loving-kindness and for the wonders He does for the children of men; and may there be fulfilled in them the verse: "Those redeemed by the LORD will return; they will enter Zion with singing, and everlasting joy will crown their heads. Gladness and joy will overtake them, and sorrow and sighing will flee away." And let us say: Amen. *Ps. 107* *Is. 35*

---

not look up so high as to notice whether you are wearing a kippa. But I can see your heart – and your heart is big and kind and that's what counts. You are also a soldier placing your life at risk for all of us in Israel. Please drink tea with me; your kippa is probably bigger than mine."

עַל מִשְׁמַר אַרְצֵנוּ וְעָרֵי אֱלֹהֵינוּ, מִגְּבוּל הַלְּבָנוֹן וְעַד מִדְבַּר
מִצְרַיִם וּמִן הַיָּם הַגָּדוֹל עַד לְבוֹא הָעֲרָבָה וּבְכָל מָקוֹם שֶׁהֵם,
בַּיַּבָּשָׁה, בָּאֲוִיר וּבַיָּם. יִתֵּן יהוה אֶת אוֹיְבֵינוּ הַקָּמִים עָלֵינוּ
נִגָּפִים לִפְנֵיהֶם. הַקָּדוֹשׁ בָּרוּךְ הוּא יִשְׁמֹר וְיַצִּיל אֶת חַיָּלֵינוּ
מִכָּל צָרָה וְצוּקָה וּמִכָּל נֶגַע וּמַחֲלָה, וְיִשְׁלַח בְּרָכָה וְהַצְלָחָה
בְּכָל מַעֲשֵׂי יְדֵיהֶם. יַדְבֵּר שׂוֹנְאֵינוּ תַּחְתֵּיהֶם וִיעַטְּרֵם בְּכֶתֶר
יְשׁוּעָה וּבַעֲטֶרֶת נִצָּחוֹן. וִיקֻיַּם בָּהֶם הַכָּתוּב: כִּי יהוה אֱלֹהֵיכֶם דברים כ
הַהֹלֵךְ עִמָּכֶם לְהִלָּחֵם לָכֶם עִם־אֹיְבֵיכֶם לְהוֹשִׁיעַ אֶתְכֶם:
וְנֹאמַר אָמֵן.

מי שברך לשבויים

If Israeli soldiers or civilians are being held in captivity, the שליח ציבור *says the following:*

מִי שֶׁבֵּרַךְ אֲבוֹתֵינוּ אַבְרָהָם יִצְחָק וְיַעֲקֹב, יוֹסֵף מֹשֶׁה וְאַהֲרֹן,
דָּוִד וּשְׁלֹמֹה, הוּא יְבָרֵךְ וְיִשְׁמֹר וְיִנְצֹר אֶת נֶעְדְּרֵי צְבָא הַהֲגָנָה
לְיִשְׂרָאֵל וּשְׁבוּיָו, וְאֶת כָּל אַחֵינוּ הַנְּתוּנִים בְּצָרָה וּבְשִׁבְיָה,
בַּעֲבוּר שֶׁכָּל הַקָּהָל הַקָּדוֹשׁ הַזֶּה מִתְפַּלֵּל בַּעֲבוּרָם. הַקָּדוֹשׁ
בָּרוּךְ הוּא יִמָּלֵא רַחֲמִים עֲלֵיהֶם, וְיוֹצִיאֵם מֵחֹשֶׁךְ וְצַלְמָוֶת,
וּמוֹסְרוֹתֵיהֶם יְנַתֵּק, וּמִמְּצוּקוֹתֵיהֶם יוֹשִׁיעֵם, וִישִׁיבֵם מְהֵרָה
לְחֵיק מִשְׁפְּחוֹתֵיהֶם. יוֹדוּ לַיהוה חַסְדּוֹ וְנִפְלְאוֹתָיו לִבְנֵי אָדָם: תהלים קז
וִיקֻיַּם בָּהֶם מִקְרָא שֶׁכָּתוּב: וּפְדוּיֵי יהוה יְשֻׁבוּן, וּבָאוּ צִיּוֹן ישעיה לה
בְּרִנָּה, וְשִׂמְחַת עוֹלָם עַל־רֹאשָׁם, שָׂשׂוֹן וְשִׂמְחָה יַשִּׂיגוּ, וְנָסוּ
יָגוֹן וַאֲנָחָה: וְנֹאמַר אָמֵן.

The young soldier said, "I don't think it's right for me to come visit you. I don't wear a kippa anymore.

Rabbi Levin, in his black hat and black kaftan, took the young man's hand in his own. "Don't you see, he said. I'm a very short man. I see you but I can-

BLESSING THE NEW MONTH

On the Shabbat before Rosh Ḥodesh, the following is said by the congregation, and repeated by the Leader:

יְהִי רָצוֹן May it be Your will, *Berakhot 16b*
LORD our God and God of our fathers,
to renew for us this coming month
for good and blessing.
Grant us long life,
a life of peace,
a life of goodness,
a life of blessing,
a life of sustenance,
a life of physical health,
a life marked by reverence for heaven
and dread of sin,
a life without shame or disgrace,
a life of wealth and honor,
a life in which we have love for the Torah
and reverence for heaven,
a life in which our hearts' desires
are fulfilled for good.
Amen, Selah.

Rosh Ḥodesh can be one day or two days long.

Originally, in order to ensure uniformity, authority for the official declaration of the new month was given to the supreme court of the Land, the Sanhedrin in Jerusalem, which announced the beginning of the month after the testimony of witnesses who had seen the first sliver of the new moon, and then word was subsequently spread to the rest of Israel and beyond with a system of bonfire signals atop the mountains. Although authority was subsequently invested in a calendar system in the fourth century, we maintain the echoes of the earlier system by announcing the days of the new month communally in this prayer to alert people for on this day there are special prayers and observances. We therefore stand, as did the witnesses themselves.

ברכת החודש

On the שבת *before* ראש חודש*, the following is said by the* קהל*, and repeated by the* שליח ציבור*:*

ברכות טז:

יְהִי רָצוֹן מִלְּפָנֶיךָ, יהוה אֱלֹהֵינוּ וֵאלֹהֵי אֲבוֹתֵינוּ
שֶׁתְּחַדֵּשׁ עָלֵינוּ אֶת הַחֹדֶשׁ הַזֶּה לְטוֹבָה וְלִבְרָכָה.
וְתִתֶּן לָנוּ חַיִּים אֲרוּכִים
חַיִּים שֶׁל שָׁלוֹם
חַיִּים שֶׁל טוֹבָה
חַיִּים שֶׁל בְּרָכָה
חַיִּים שֶׁל פַּרְנָסָה
חַיִּים שֶׁל חִלּוּץ עֲצָמוֹת
חַיִּים שֶׁיֵּשׁ בָּהֶם יִרְאַת שָׁמַיִם וְיִרְאַת חֵטְא
חַיִּים שֶׁאֵין בָּהֶם בּוּשָׁה וּכְלִמָּה
חַיִּים שֶׁל עֹשֶׁר וְכָבוֹד
חַיִּים שֶׁתְּהֵא בָנוּ אַהֲבַת תּוֹרָה וְיִרְאַת שָׁמַיִם
חַיִּים שֶׁיִּמָּלְאוּ מִשְׁאֲלוֹת לִבֵּנוּ לְטוֹבָה
אָמֵן סֶלָה.

INTRODUCTION TO BIRKAT HAḤODESH

The following prayer is recited on the Shabbat before Rosh Ḥodesh, the new month in the Hebrew calendar. It is recited standing.

The Jewish calendar is primarily lunar (though not exclusively so). The word month is derived from the word moon, just as the Hebrew word for month, *ḥodesh,* is related to the word *ḥadash*, meaning "new," for the new month begins when a new moon appears. But the moon is not always so easily visible when it first appears thus leaving room for error of a day before being sure of its appearance. Thus,

The new moon is announced, then the Leader takes the Torah scroll in his right arm and says:

מִי שֶׁעָשָׂה May He who performed miracles for our ancestors
and redeemed them from slavery to freedom,
redeem us soon, and gather in our dispersed people
from the four quarters of the earth,
so that all Israel may be united in friendship,[1]
and let us say: Amen.

The Leader, then the congregation:

The new month of (*Hebrew month*) will occur on (*day of week*).
May it come to us and all Israel for good.

The congregation and Leader continue:

Outside Israel:

May the Holy One,
blessed be He,
renew this new month
for us and
for all His people,
the house of Israel,
for life and peace,
gladness and joy,
salvation and consolation;
and let us say: Amen.

In Israel:

May the Holy One, blessed be He,
renew this month
for us and for all His people
the house of Israel, wherever they are,
for good and blessing, gladness and joy,
for salvation and consolation,
livelihood and sustenance,
for life and peace,
good tidings and good news,
(*In winter:* for rain in its due season,)
for complete healing
and imminent redemption,
and let us say: Amen.

(כָּל יִשְׂרָאֵל לִירוּשָׁלַיִם עִיר הַקֹּדֶשׁ) (*Maḥzor Vitry*). This version has historical echoes of the days when the Sanhedrin in Jerusalem established the month, but it also is a powerful statement that what unites us as a people is the centrality of Jerusalem to our national life. Just look at the variety of Jews walking the streets of Yerushalayim.

חֲבֵרִים כָּל יִשְׂרָאֵל – *All Israel may be united in friendship.* These words symbolize the collectivity of Israel, whom the *Beit Din* (court) represents when it declares the new month. In a similar vein, the *ḥazan* holds the Torah scroll, emblematic of the collective Jewish People. The Torah scroll unifies all our people into this one collective and it is this unification which provides the *ḥazan* with the authority to declare the new month (Rabbi Joseph B. Soloveitchik).

The מולד *is announced, then the* שליח ציבור *takes the* ספר תורה *in his right arm and says:*

מִי שֶׁעָשָׂה נִסִּים לַאֲבוֹתֵינוּ
וְגָאַל אוֹתָם מֵעַבְדוּת לְחֵרוּת
הוּא יִגְאַל אוֹתָנוּ בְּקָרוֹב
וִיקַבֵּץ נִדָּחֵינוּ מֵאַרְבַּע כַּנְפוֹת הָאָרֶץ
חֲבֵרִים כָּל יִשְׂרָאֵל[ע]
וְנֹאמַר אָמֵן.

The שליח ציבור*, then the* קהל*:*

רֹאשׁ חֹדֶשׁ *month* יִהְיֶה בְּיוֹם *day* (*וּבְיוֹם *day*)
הַבָּא עָלֵינוּ וְעַל כָּל יִשְׂרָאֵל לְטוֹבָה.

**if the second day falls on Sunday, then substitute:* וּלְמָחֳרָתוֹ בְּיוֹם

The קהל *and* שליח ציבור *continue:*

In חוץ לארץ *say:*

יְחַדְּשֵׁהוּ
הַקָּדוֹשׁ בָּרוּךְ הוּא
עָלֵינוּ
וְעַל כָּל עַמּוֹ
בֵּית יִשְׂרָאֵל
לְחַיִּים וּלְשָׁלוֹם
לְשָׂשׂוֹן וּלְשִׂמְחָה
לִישׁוּעָה וּלְנֶחָמָה
וְנֹאמַר אָמֵן.

in ארץ ישראל *say:*

יְחַדְּשֵׁהוּ הַקָּדוֹשׁ בָּרוּךְ הוּא
עָלֵינוּ וְעַל כָּל עַמּוֹ בֵּית יִשְׂרָאֵל
בְּכָל מָקוֹם שֶׁהֵם
לְטוֹבָה וְלִבְרָכָה, לְשָׂשׂוֹן וּלְשִׂמְחָה
לִישׁוּעָה וּלְנֶחָמָה
לְפַרְנָסָה וּלְכַלְכָּלָה
לְחַיִּים וּלְשָׁלוֹם
לִשְׁמוּעוֹת טוֹבוֹת וְלִבְשׂוֹרוֹת טוֹבוֹת
(בחורף: וְלִגְשָׁמִים בְּעִתָּם)
וְלִרְפוּאָה שְׁלֵמָה, וְלִגְאֻלָּה קְרוֹבָה, וְנֹאמַר אָמֵן.

IYUN TEFILLA • עיון תפילה

חֲבֵרִים כָּל יִשְׂרָאֵל – *All Israel may be united in friendship.* An earlier manuscript of this text from the twelfth century reads "all Israel friends to Jerusalem the holy city" (**חֲבֵרִים**

The following is omitted on days when Taḥanun is not said. It is also omitted on a Shabbat before Rosh Ḥodesh (except for the Shabbat before Rosh Ḥodesh Iyar and Rosh Ḥodesh Sivan) and on Shabbat Shekalim, Zakhor, Para and HaḤodesh.

אַב הָרַחֲמִים Father of compassion, who dwells on high: may He remember in His compassion the pious, the upright and the blameless – holy communities who sacrificed their lives for the sanctification of God's name. Lovely and pleasant in their lives, in death they were not parted. They were swifter than eagles and stronger than lions to do the will of their Maker and the desire of their Creator. O our God, remember them for good with the other righteous of the world, and may He exact retribution for the shed blood of His servants, as it is written in the Torah of Moses, the man of God: "O nations, acclaim *Deut. 32*
His people, for He will avenge the blood of His servants, wreak vengeance on His foes, and make clean His people's land." And by Your servants, the prophets, it is written: "I shall cleanse their blood which *Joel 4*
I have not yet cleansed, says the LORD who dwells in Zion." And in the holy Writings it says: "Why should the nations say: Where is their *Ps. 79*
God? Before our eyes, may those nations know that You avenge the shed blood of Your servants." And it also says: "For the Avenger of *Ps. 9*
blood remembers them and does not forget the cry of the afflicted." And it further says: "He will execute judgment among the nations, *Ps. 110*
filled with the dead, crushing rulers far and wide. From the brook by the wayside he will drink, then he will hold his head high."

---

not a remnant or a residue escape, even an infant or a suckling in the cradle." They then came and struck those who had remained in their houses – comely young men and comely and lovely young women along with elders. All of them stretched forth their necks. Even manumitted serving men and serving women were killed along with them for the sanctification of the name which is awesome and sublime ... Who rules above and below, Who was and will be. Indeed the LORD of Hosts is His name." (Robert Chazan, *European Jewry and the First Crusade*).

Because of its more somber content, it is not recited on happier occasions, such as Festivals or Rosh Ḥodesh or their related days, which may also coincide with Shabbat. However, most have the custom to continue to recite the prayer during the time from Pesaḥ to Shavuot, regardless of any happier day, even on Rosh Ḥodesh itself, because that is the time of year historically when these horrific events took place.

The following is omitted on days when תחנון *is not said.*
It is also omitted on שבת מברכים *(except for the* שבת *before* ראש חודש אייר *and* ראש חודש סיון*) and on the "*ארבע פרשיות*,"* שקלים, זכור, פרה *and* החודש.

אַב הָרַחֲמִים שׁוֹכֵן מְרוֹמִים, בְּרַחֲמָיו הָעֲצוּמִים הוּא יִפְקֹד בְּרַחֲמִים
הַחֲסִידִים וְהַיְשָׁרִים וְהַתְּמִימִים, קְהִלּוֹת הַקֹּדֶשׁ שֶׁמָּסְרוּ נַפְשָׁם עַל
קְדֻשַּׁת הַשֵּׁם, הַנֶּאֱהָבִים וְהַנְּעִימִים בְּחַיֵּיהֶם, וּבְמוֹתָם לֹא נִפְרָדוּ,
מִנְּשָׁרִים קַלּוּ וּמֵאֲרָיוֹת גָּבֵרוּ לַעֲשׂוֹת רְצוֹן קוֹנָם וְחֵפֶץ צוּרָם. יִזְכְּרֵם
אֱלֹהֵינוּ לְטוֹבָה עִם שְׁאָר צַדִּיקֵי עוֹלָם, וְיִנְקֹם לְעֵינֵינוּ נִקְמַת דַּם
עֲבָדָיו הַשָּׁפוּךְ, כַּכָּתוּב בְּתוֹרַת מֹשֶׁה אִישׁ הָאֱלֹהִים: הַרְנִינוּ גוֹיִם דברים לב
עַמּוֹ, כִּי דַם־עֲבָדָיו יִקּוֹם, וְנָקָם יָשִׁיב לְצָרָיו, וְכִפֶּר אַדְמָתוֹ עַמּוֹ: וְעַל
יְדֵי עֲבָדֶיךָ הַנְּבִיאִים כָּתוּב לֵאמֹר: וְנִקֵּיתִי, דָּמָם לֹא־נִקֵּיתִי, וַיהוה יואל ד
שֹׁכֵן בְּצִיּוֹן: וּבְכִתְבֵי הַקֹּדֶשׁ נֶאֱמַר: לָמָּה יֹאמְרוּ הַגּוֹיִם אַיֵּה אֱלֹהֵיהֶם, תהלים עט
יִוָּדַע בַּגּוֹיִם לְעֵינֵינוּ נִקְמַת דַּם־עֲבָדֶיךָ הַשָּׁפוּךְ: וְאוֹמֵר: כִּי־דֹרֵשׁ דָּמִים תהלים ט
אוֹתָם זָכָר, לֹא־שָׁכַח צַעֲקַת עֲנָוִים: וְאוֹמֵר: יָדִין בַּגּוֹיִם מָלֵא גְוִיּוֹת, תהלים קי
מָחַץ רֹאשׁ עַל־אֶרֶץ רַבָּה: מִנַּחַל בַּדֶּרֶךְ יִשְׁתֶּה, עַל־כֵּן יָרִים רֹאשׁ:

INTRODUCTION TO AV HARAHAMIM

On a day like Shabbat, when we have the time to reflect upon things like who we are and how we got here, there developed a custom to recite a prayer on behalf of martyrs who perished for no other reason than that they were Jews. This prayer finds its roots in the massacres that took place in the Rhine Valley during the period of the First Crusades, when the Jewish communities there were decimated and blood literally ran through the streets.

Consider the words of one chronicler from the town of Worms where the Jewish community divided itself into two groups in order to avoid complete annihilation.

"It came to pass on the tenth of Iyyar, on Sunday, they plotted craftily against them. They took a trampled corpse of theirs, that had been buried thirty days previously and carried it through the city, saying: "Behold what the Jews have done to our comrade. They took a gentile and boiled him in water. They then poured the water into our wells in order to kill us." When the crusaders and burghers heard this, they cried out and gathered – all who bore and unsheathed [a sword], from great to small – saying: "Behold the time has come to avenge him who was crucified, whom their ancestors slew. Now let

אַשְׁרֵי Happy[1] are those who dwell in Your House; Ps. 84
they shall continue to praise You, Selah!
Happy are the people for whom this is so; Ps. 144
happy are the people whose God is the LORD.
A song of praise by David. Ps. 145

א I will elevate You, my God, the King, and bless Your name for ever and all time. ב Every day I will bless You, and praise Your name for ever and all time. ג Great is the Lord and greatly to be praised; His greatness is unfathomable. ד One generation will praise Your works to the next, and tell of Your mighty deeds. ה On the glorious splendor of Your majesty I will meditate, and on the acts of Your wonders. ו They shall talk of the power of Your awesome deeds, and I will tell of Your greatness. ז They shall recite the record of Your great goodness, and sing with joy of Your righteousness. ח The Lord is generous and compassionate, slow to anger and great in loving-kindness. ט The Lord is good to all, and His compassion extends to all His works. י All Your works shall thank You, Lord, and Your devoted ones shall bless You. כ They shall talk of the glory of Your kingship, and speak of Your might. ל To make known to mankind His mighty deeds and the glorious majesty of His kingship. מ Your kingdom is an everlasting kingdom, and Your reign is for all generations. ס The Lord supports all who fall, and raises all who are bowed down. ע All raise their eyes to You in hope, and You give them their food in due season. פ You open Your hand, and satisfy every living thing

---

Therefore let each letter of the alphabet represent all of the praises that begin with that letter, of which I will offer just one line as an example." In a certain sense, then, the alphabetic listing of words is designed to convey the impression that all words fall short. It's not only about the meaning of the words but the feeling of the *Alef-Beit*.

ANI TEFILLA • אני תפילה

On the Sabbath, a Jew comes to know himself, not as twenty, or thirty, or sixty years old, but as four thousand years old, the bearer of an eternal witness of which the Sabbath is the sign (Michael S. Kogan).

אַשְׁרֵי[ע] יוֹשְׁבֵי בֵיתֶךָ, עוֹד יְהַלְלוּךָ סֶּלָה: תהלים פד

אַשְׁרֵי הָעָם שֶׁכָּכָה לּוֹ, אַשְׁרֵי הָעָם שֶׁיהוה אֱלֹהָיו: תהלים קמד

תְּהִלָּה לְדָוִד תהלים קמה

א אֲרוֹמִמְךָ אֱלוֹהַי הַמֶּלֶךְ, וַאֲבָרְכָה שִׁמְךָ לְעוֹלָם וָעֶד:

ב בְּכָל־יוֹם אֲבָרְכֶךָּ, וַאֲהַלְלָה שִׁמְךָ לְעוֹלָם וָעֶד:

ג גָּדוֹל יהוה וּמְהֻלָּל מְאֹד, וְלִגְדֻלָּתוֹ אֵין חֵקֶר:

ד דּוֹר לְדוֹר יְשַׁבַּח מַעֲשֶׂיךָ, וּגְבוּרֹתֶיךָ יַגִּידוּ:

ה הֲדַר כְּבוֹד הוֹדֶךָ, וְדִבְרֵי נִפְלְאֹתֶיךָ אָשִׂיחָה:

ו וֶעֱזוּז נוֹרְאֹתֶיךָ יֹאמֵרוּ, וּגְדוּלָּתְךָ אֲסַפְּרֶנָּה:

ז זֵכֶר רַב־טוּבְךָ יַבִּיעוּ, וְצִדְקָתְךָ יְרַנֵּנוּ:

ח חַנּוּן וְרַחוּם יהוה, אֶרֶךְ אַפַּיִם וּגְדָל־חָסֶד:

ט טוֹב־יהוה לַכֹּל, וְרַחֲמָיו עַל־כָּל־מַעֲשָׂיו:

י יוֹדוּךָ יהוה כָּל־מַעֲשֶׂיךָ, וַחֲסִידֶיךָ יְבָרְכוּכָה:

כ כְּבוֹד מַלְכוּתְךָ יֹאמֵרוּ, וּגְבוּרָתְךָ יְדַבֵּרוּ:

ל לְהוֹדִיעַ לִבְנֵי הָאָדָם גְּבוּרֹתָיו, וּכְבוֹד הֲדַר מַלְכוּתוֹ:

מ מַלְכוּתְךָ מַלְכוּת כָּל־עֹלָמִים, וּמֶמְשַׁלְתְּךָ בְּכָל־דּוֹר וָדֹר:

ס סוֹמֵךְ יהוה לְכָל־הַנֹּפְלִים, וְזוֹקֵף לְכָל־הַכְּפוּפִים:

ע עֵינֵי־כֹל אֵלֶיךָ יְשַׂבֵּרוּ, וְאַתָּה נוֹתֵן־לָהֶם אֶת־אָכְלָם בְּעִתּוֹ:

פ פּוֹתֵחַ אֶת־יָדֶךָ, וּמַשְׂבִּיעַ לְכָל־חַי רָצוֹן:

IYUN TEFILLA • עיון תפילה

אַשְׁרֵי – *Happy*. The Gemara (*Berakhot* 4b) relates that anyone who says this chapter of Psalms three times a day is guaranteed a place in the World to Come (It was recited once in *Pesukei DeZimra*, a second time here, and the third will be during *Minḥa*.) One of the reasons was because it is written as an acrostic, wherein each line begins with another letter of the *Alef-Beit*. It is as if one is saying, "Any praise I give You is incomplete.

with favor. צ The Lord is righteous in all His ways, and kind in all He does. ק The Lord is close to all who call on Him, to all who call on Him in truth. ר He fulfills the will of those who fear Him; He hears their cry and saves them. ש The Lord guards all who love Him, but all the wicked He will destroy. ת ▸ My mouth shall speak the praise of the Lord, and all creatures shall bless His holy name for ever and all time.

We will bless the LORD now and for ever. Halleluya! *Ps. 115*

RETURNING THE TORAH TO THE ARK

The Ark is opened. All stand.
The Leader takes the Torah scroll and says:

יְהַלְלוּ Let them praise the name of the LORD, *Ps. 148*
for His name alone is sublime.

The congregation responds:

הוֹדוֹ His majesty[H] is above earth and heaven.[I]
He has raised the horn of His people,
for the glory of all His devoted ones,
the children of Israel, the people close to Him.
Halleluya!

---

want to confuse our adoration for the Torah itself with that of its Author. Our respect for it, is essentially our respect for Him. To be sure, the Torah is holy, but it derives its holiness from Hashem and it is He that we honor (Rokeach).

IYUN TEFILLA • עיון תפילה

הוֹדוֹ עַל־אֶרֶץ וְשָׁמָיִם – *His majesty is above earth and heaven.* Alternatively, "on the earth and heaven." Why does the earth come first? This could mean that, contrary to one's initial thought, Hashem is not only located in heaven, as it were, but is also here on earth, watching over it and us (Meiri 149:13). Alternatively, Hashem is primarily located, as it were, on earth, and through our actions the heavens are influenced (*Shir Hashirim Raba* 8).

צ צַדִּיק יהוה בְּכָל־דְּרָכָיו, וְחָסִיד בְּכָל־מַעֲשָׂיו:
ק קָרוֹב יהוה לְכָל־קֹרְאָיו, לְכֹל אֲשֶׁר יִקְרָאֻהוּ בֶאֱמֶת:
ר רְצוֹן־יְרֵאָיו יַעֲשֶׂה, וְאֶת־שַׁוְעָתָם יִשְׁמַע, וְיוֹשִׁיעֵם:
ש שׁוֹמֵר יהוה אֶת־כָּל־אֹהֲבָיו, וְאֵת כָּל־הָרְשָׁעִים יַשְׁמִיד:
◂ ת תְּהִלַּת יהוה יְדַבֶּר פִּי, וִיבָרֵךְ כָּל־בָּשָׂר שֵׁם קָדְשׁוֹ לְעוֹלָם וָעֶד:
וַאֲנַחְנוּ נְבָרֵךְ יָהּ מֵעַתָּה וְעַד־עוֹלָם, הַלְלוּיָהּ: תהלים קטו

הכנסת ספר תורה

The ארון קודש *is opened. All stand.*
The שליח ציבור *takes the* ספר תורה *and says:*

יְהַלְלוּ אֶת־שֵׁם יהוה, כִּי־נִשְׂגָּב שְׁמוֹ, לְבַדּוֹ תהלים קמח

The קהל *responds:*

הוֹדוֹ עַל־אֶרֶץ וְשָׁמָיִם:
וַיָּרֶם קֶרֶן לְעַמּוֹ
תְּהִלָּה לְכָל־חֲסִידָיו
לִבְנֵי יִשְׂרָאֵל עַם קְרֹבוֹ
הַלְלוּיָהּ:

HILKHOT TEFILLA • הלכות תפילה

יְהַלְלוּ... הוֹדוֹ – *Let them praise… His majesty.* Two strange details: The *ḥazan* here recites the first part of a verse and the congregation responds with the other part when the custom is generally not to divide verses this way (*Magen Avraham* 51:9). Moreover, the focus of this responsive interaction between the *ḥazan* and the congregation is all about Hashem, as opposed to about the Torah which we are returning to the ark. The reason for these anomalies may be the important principle that we never

While the Torah scroll is being returned to the Ark, say:

מִזְמוֹר לְדָוִד A psalm of David.[B] Render to the LORD, you angelic powers, *Ps. 29*
render to the LORD glory and might. Render to the LORD the glory due to His name. Bow to the LORD in the beauty of holi-ness. The LORD's voice echoes over the waters; the God of glory thunders; the LORD is over the mighty waters. The LORD's voice in power,[I] the LORD's voice in beauty, the LORD's voice breaks cedars, the LORD shatters the cedars of Lebanon. He makes Lebanon skip like a calf, Sirion like a young wild ox. The LORD's voice cleaves flames of fire. The LORD's voice makes the desert quake, the LORD shakes the desert of Kadesh. The LORD's voice makes hinds calve and strips the forests bare, and in His temple all say: "Glory!" The LORD sat enthroned at the Flood, the LORD sits enthroned as King for ever. The LORD will give strength to His people; the LORD will bless His people with peace.

As the Torah scroll is placed into the Ark, all say:

וּבְנֻחֹה יֹאמַר When the Ark came to rest, Moses would say: "Return, O *Num. 10*
LORD, to the myriad thousands of Israel." Advance, LORD, to Your resting *Ps. 132*
place, You and Your mighty Ark. Your priests are clothed in righteousness, and Your devoted ones sing in joy. For the sake of Your servant David,
do not reject Your anointed one. For I give you good instruction; do not *Prov. 4*
forsake My Torah. It is a tree of life to those who grasp it, and those who *Prov. 3*
uphold it are happy. Its ways are ways of pleasantness, and all its paths
are peace. ▸ Turn us back, O LORD, to You, and we will return. Renew *Lam. 5*
our days as of old.

The Ark is closed.

IYUN TEFILLA • עיון תפילה

קוֹל־יהוה בַּכֹּחַ – *The LORD's voice in power.* The first of the Ten Commandments is "I am the LORD your God." The word "your" is written in the singular, not in the plural as one would expect. From here the midrash learns that each individual heard this commandment in his or her own way. It is similar to the manna which fell from heaven, which had the unique property that its taste conformed to the wishes of each person, so too this commandment was understood and experienced differently by each person. That is why David said "Hashem's voice was heard with power/ability" rather than "with His power," for it is in the power of each person individually to hear the voice of God in his or her own way (*Yalkut Shimoni, Yitro* 286).

While the ספר תורה *is being returned to the* ארון קודש, *say:*

תהלים כט
מִזְמוֹר לְדָוִד, הָבוּ לַיהוה בְּנֵי אֵלִים, הָבוּ לַיהוה כָּבוֹד וָעֹז: הָבוּ לַיהוה כְּבוֹד שְׁמוֹ, הִשְׁתַּחֲווּ לַיהוה בְּהַדְרַת־קֹדֶשׁ: קוֹל יהוה עַל־הַמָּיִם, אֵל־הַכָּבוֹד הִרְעִים, יהוה עַל־מַיִם רַבִּים: קוֹל־יהוה בַּכֹּחַ, קוֹל יהוה בֶּהָדָר: קוֹל יהוה שֹׁבֵר אֲרָזִים, וַיְשַׁבֵּר יהוה אֶת־אַרְזֵי הַלְּבָנוֹן: וַיַּרְקִידֵם כְּמוֹ־עֵגֶל, לְבָנוֹן וְשִׂרְיוֹן כְּמוֹ בֶן־רְאֵמִים: קוֹל־יהוה חֹצֵב לַהֲבוֹת אֵשׁ: קוֹל יהוה יָחִיל מִדְבָּר, יָחִיל יהוה מִדְבַּר קָדֵשׁ: קוֹל יהוה יְחוֹלֵל אַיָּלוֹת וַיֶּחֱשֹׂף יְעָרוֹת, וּבְהֵיכָלוֹ, כֻּלּוֹ אֹמֵר כָּבוֹד: יהוה לַמַּבּוּל יָשָׁב, וַיֵּשֶׁב יהוה מֶלֶךְ לְעוֹלָם: יהוה עֹז לְעַמּוֹ יִתֵּן, יהוה יְבָרֵךְ אֶת־עַמּוֹ בַשָּׁלוֹם:

As the ספר תורה *is placed into the* ארון קודש, *all say:*

במדבר י
תהלים קלב
וּבְנֻחֹה יֹאמַר, שׁוּבָה יהוה רִבְבוֹת אַלְפֵי יִשְׂרָאֵל: קוּמָה יהוה לִמְנוּחָתֶךָ, אַתָּה וַאֲרוֹן עֻזֶּךָ: כֹּהֲנֶיךָ יִלְבְּשׁוּ־צֶדֶק, וַחֲסִידֶיךָ יְרַנֵּנוּ:

משלי ד
בַּעֲבוּר דָּוִד עַבְדֶּךָ אַל־תָּשֵׁב פְּנֵי מְשִׁיחֶךָ: כִּי לֶקַח טוֹב נָתַתִּי

משלי ג
לָכֶם, תּוֹרָתִי אַל־תַּעֲזֹבוּ: עֵץ־חַיִּים הִיא לַמַּחֲזִיקִים בָּהּ, וְתֹמְכֶיהָ

איכה ה
מְאֻשָּׁר: דְּרָכֶיהָ דַרְכֵי־נֹעַם וְכָל־נְתִיבוֹתֶיהָ שָׁלוֹם: ◂ הֲשִׁיבֵנוּ יהוה אֵלֶיךָ וְנָשׁוּבָה, חַדֵּשׁ יָמֵינוּ כְּקֶדֶם:

The ארון קודש *is closed.*

BIUR TEFILLA • ביאור תפילה

מִזְמוֹר לְדָוִד – *A psalm of David.* The psalm is traditionally associated with the giving of the Torah (*Zevaḥim* 116a), perhaps because of its repeated mention of the "voice" of Hashem which was heard at Sinai (HaManhig). The word is mentioned seven times, a number clearly related to Shabbat which objectifies the number of completion, the seventh day of the week and, as mentioned, the day on which according to one tradition the Torah was given. See commentary on this psalm in Kabbalat Shabbat page 55.

HALF KADDISH

Leader: יִתְגַּדַּל Magnified and sanctified
may His great name be,
in the world He created by His will.
May He establish His kingdom
in your lifetime and in your days,
and in the lifetime of all the house of Israel,
swiftly and soon –
and say: Amen.

All: May His great name be blessed
for ever and all time.

Leader: Blessed and praised, glorified and exalted,
raised and honored, uplifted and lauded
be the name of the Holy One,
blessed be He,
beyond any blessing, song,
praise and consolation
uttered in the world –
and say: Amen.

---

words of the prophet *Hoshea* (14:3), "Instead of bulls we will pay the offering of our lips" took on even greater importance. While animal sacrifices can sometimes feel at odds with contemporary sensibilities (and this from a culture whose overindulgence and waste of food can be an embarrassment to the rest of the world), the world and all of its resources were put on earth by God for man's positive use, as a way of enhancing the world through his own development. And it is God Himself who decreed that the very limited and prescribed use of sacrifices was a way for man and God to bridge the gap between them. The Hebrew word for sacrifice, *korban*, is related to the Hebrew word *karov*, meaning close or proximity. As sacrifices force us to confront the end of a life, finitude, they offer us the possibility of getting closer to the Infinite.

For a general introduction to the Amida, see "Introduction to the Amida" on page 100 in Ma'ariv. For an overview of the structure of the Amida and further commentary, see page 333 in Shaḥarit.

חצי קדיש

ש״ץ: יִתְגַּדַּל וְיִתְקַדַּשׁ שְׁמֵהּ רַבָּא (קהל: אָמֵן)
בְּעָלְמָא דִּי בְרָא כִרְעוּתֵהּ
וְיַמְלִיךְ מַלְכוּתֵהּ
בְּחַיֵּיכוֹן וּבְיוֹמֵיכוֹן וּבְחַיֵּי דְכָל בֵּית יִשְׂרָאֵל
בַּעֲגָלָא וּבִזְמַן קָרִיב
וְאִמְרוּ אָמֵן. (קהל: אָמֵן)

קהל וש״ץ: יְהֵא שְׁמֵהּ רַבָּא מְבָרַךְ לְעָלַם וּלְעָלְמֵי עָלְמַיָּא.

ש״ץ: יִתְבָּרַךְ וְיִשְׁתַּבַּח וְיִתְפָּאַר וְיִתְרוֹמַם וְיִתְנַשֵּׂא
וְיִתְהַדָּר וְיִתְעַלֶּה וְיִתְהַלָּל
שְׁמֵהּ דְּקֻדְשָׁא בְּרִיךְ הוּא (קהל: בְּרִיךְ הוּא)
לְעֵלָּא מִן כָּל בִּרְכָתָא
/בשבת שובה: לְעֵלָּא לְעֵלָּא מִכָּל בִּרְכָתָא/
וְשִׁירָתָא, תֻּשְׁבְּחָתָא וְנֶחֱמָתָא
דַּאֲמִירָן בְּעָלְמָא
וְאִמְרוּ אָמֵן. (קהל: אָמֵן)

INTRODUCTION TO MUSAF

The number of prayer services generally parallels the daily sacrifices that took place in the *Beit HaMikdash*, there being one for each of the three periods of the day, evening, morning and afternoon (*Berakhot* 26b). On Shabbat and Holy Days, there was another sacrificial service which took place in honor of the day. It was, if you will, an additional service, and hence the name of this prayer, called *Musaf* or addition. Whereas the other prayer services reflect different themes and moods of the day, this one takes as its primary motif the sacrifices themselves. When the *Beit HaMikdash* was destroyed, then the

Musaf for Shabbat

On Shabbat Ḥol HaMo'ed say the Musaf on page 696.

THE AMIDA

The following prayer, until "in former years" on page 440, is said silently, standing with feet together. If there is a minyan, the Amida is repeated aloud by the Leader.

Take three steps forward.

When I proclaim the LORD's name, give glory to our God. *Deut. 32*

O LORD, open my lips, so that my mouth may declare Your praise. *Ps. 51*

PATRIARCHS

▼ *Bend the knees:* Blessed *Bow:* are You, *Stand straight:* LORD
our God and God of our fathers,
God of Abraham, God of Isaac and God of Jacob;
the great, mighty and awesome God, God Most High,
who bestows acts of loving-kindness and creates all,
who remembers the loving-kindness of the fathers
and will bring a Redeemer to their children's children
for the sake of His name, in love.

These words are added on Shabbat Shuva: Remember us for life, O King who desires life,
and write us in the book of life – for Your sake,
O God of life.

King, Helper, Savior, Shield:
▼ *Bend the knees:* Blessed *Bow:* are You, *Stand straight:* LORD,
Shield of Abraham.

---

was characterized by the spiritual and physical journeys and travails he endured. We invoke the example of each of them, even as we also say beforehand "our God," for our encounter this morning needs to reflect our own personality and relationship with Him as well as those of our ancestors.

What is your relationship with Hashem today? Which of the Patriarchs does it most resemble?

מָגֵן אַבְרָהָם – *Shield of Abraham.* Why is Avraham singled out from all of the patriarchs we mentioned above? Perhaps because his attribute of loving-kindness is so important. It is through the attribute of kindness that we are able to make room for others and to get in touch with our own ability to be more selfless and to withstand the challenges that life throws our way. Research shows that people who give are happier.

How can you better internalize the values of Avraham?

מוסף לשבת

On שבת חול המועד *say the* מוסף *on page 697.*

עמידה

The following prayer, until קַדְמֹנִיּוֹת *on page 441, is said standing with feet together. If there is a* מנין*, the* עמידה *is repeated aloud by the* שליח ציבור*.*

Take three steps forward.

כִּי שֵׁם יהוה אֶקְרָא, הָבוּ גֹדֶל לֵאלֹהֵינוּ: דברים לב
אֲדֹנָי, שְׂפָתַי תִּפְתָּח, וּפִי יַגִּיד תְּהִלָּתֶךָ: תהלים נא

אבות

▾ *Bend the knees* בָּרוּךְ *Bow* אַתָּה *Stand straight* יהוה
אֱלֹהֵינוּ וֵאלֹהֵי אֲבוֹתֵינוּ
אֱלֹהֵי אַבְרָהָם, אֱלֹהֵי יִצְחָק, וֵאלֹהֵי יַעֲקֹב[ע]
הָאֵל הַגָּדוֹל הַגִּבּוֹר וְהַנּוֹרָא, אֵל עֶלְיוֹן
גּוֹמֵל חֲסָדִים טוֹבִים, וְקוֹנֵה הַכֹּל, וְזוֹכֵר חַסְדֵי אָבוֹת
וּמֵבִיא גוֹאֵל לִבְנֵי בְנֵיהֶם לְמַעַן שְׁמוֹ בְּאַהֲבָה.

בשבת שובה: זָכְרֵנוּ לְחַיִּים, מֶלֶךְ חָפֵץ בַּחַיִּים
וְכָתְבֵנוּ בְּסֵפֶר הַחַיִּים, לְמַעַנְךָ אֱלֹהִים חַיִּים.

מֶלֶךְ עוֹזֵר וּמוֹשִׁיעַ וּמָגֵן.
▾ *Bend the knees* בָּרוּךְ *Bow* אַתָּה *Stand straight* יהוה, מָגֵן אַבְרָהָם.[ע]

IYUN TEFILLA • עיון תפילה

אֱלֹהֵי אַבְרָהָם, אֱלֹהֵי יִצְחָק, וֵאלֹהֵי יַעֲקֹב – *God of Abraham, God of Isaac and God of Jacob.* Note that it says "God of…" three times instead of just saying once, "God of the Patriarchs." Many suggest that this is because, based on what we know from the biblical narratives about their lives, each of the patriarchs related to God in his own personal way, though the defining characteristics are left to the reader. Avraham, for example, could be said to have expressed his relationship in terms of loving-kindness for others and through a bold spiritual adventurousness; Yitzḥak's life was characterized by the self-sacrifice he displayed at the *Akeida* (Binding of Isaac) and Yaakov's life

DIVINE MIGHT

אַתָּה גִּבּוֹר You are eternally mighty, LORD.
You give life to the dead and have great power to save.

The phrase "He makes the wind blow and the rain fall" is added from Simḥat Torah until Pesaḥ. In Israel the phrase "He causes the dew to fall" is added from Pesaḥ until Shemini Atzeret.

In fall & winter: He makes the wind blow and the rain fall.
In Israel, in spring & summer: He causes the dew to fall.

He sustains the living with loving-kindness,
and with great compassion revives the dead.
He supports the fallen,[1] heals the sick, sets captives free,
and keeps His faith with those who sleep in the dust.
Who is like You, Master of might, and who can compare to You,
O King who brings death and gives life, and makes salvation grow?

Between Rosh HaShana & Yom Kippur: Who is like You, compassionate Father,
who remembers His creatures in compassion, for life?

Faithful are You to revive the dead.
Blessed are You, LORD, who revives the dead.

During the Repetition of the Amida, the Leader continues with Kedusha on the next page.

HOLINESS

אַתָּה קָדוֹשׁ You are holy[1] and Your name is holy,
and holy ones praise You daily, Selah!
Blessed are You, LORD,
the holy God. / *On Shabbat Shuva:* the holy King./
(If forgotten, repeat the Amida.)

When saying the Amida silently, continue with "You instituted the Sabbath" on Shabbat and "Long ago You formed" on Rosh Ḥodesh on page 420.

IYUN TEFILLA • עיון תפילה

אַתָּה קָדוֹשׁ – *You are holy.* Rabbi Shimon Schwab wrote that Hashem asks that we separate ourselves from our *yetzer hara* (inclination to act badly) because Hashem is holy (*kadosh*). That is, you can be *kadosh* (holy), because I have placed within you a spark of My own holiness (*kedusha*), namely, the image of God (*tzelem Elohim*) implanted within man, which is the ability of the human being to overpower and separate

*This **IYUN TEFILLA** continues on page 417.*

גבורות

אַתָּה גִּבּוֹר לְעוֹלָם, אֲדֹנָי
מְחַיֵּה מֵתִים אַתָּה, רַב לְהוֹשִׁיעַ

The phrase מַשִּׁיב הָרְוּחַ *is added from* שמחת תורה *until* פסח.
In ארץ ישראל *the phrase* מוֹרִיד הַטָּל *is added from* פסח *until* שמיני עצרת.

בחורף: **מַשִּׁיב הָרְוּחַ וּמוֹרִיד הַגֶּשֶׁם** / בארץ ישראל בקיץ: **מוֹרִיד הַטָּל**

מְכַלְכֵּל חַיִּים בְּחֶסֶד, מְחַיֵּה מֵתִים בְּרַחֲמִים רַבִּים
סוֹמֵךְ נוֹפְלִים,[ע] **וְרוֹפֵא חוֹלִים, וּמַתִּיר אֲסוּרִים**
וּמְקַיֵּם אֱמוּנָתוֹ לִישֵׁנֵי עָפָר.
מִי כָמְוֹךָ, בַּעַל גְּבוּרוֹת, וּמִי דּוֹמֶה לָּךְ
מֶלֶךְ, מֵמִית וּמְחַיֶּה וּמַצְמִיחַ יְשׁוּעָה.

בשבת שובה: **מִי כָמְוֹךָ אַב הָרַחֲמִים, זוֹכֵר יְצוּרָיו לְחַיִּים בְּרַחֲמִים.**

וְנֶאֱמָן אַתָּה לְהַחֲיוֹת מֵתִים.
בָּרוּךְ אַתָּה יהוה, מְחַיֵּה הַמֵּתִים.

During the חזרת הש״ץ*, the* שליח ציבור *continues with* קדושה *on the next page.*

קדושת השם

אַתָּה קָדוֹשׁ[ע] **וְשִׁמְךָ קָדוֹשׁ, וּקְדוֹשִׁים בְּכָל יוֹם יְהַלְלְוּךָ סֶּלָה.**
בָּרוּךְ אַתָּה יהוה, הָאֵל הַקָּדוֹשׁ. / בשבת שובה: **הַמֶּלֶךְ הַקָּדוֹשׁ.**/
(*If forgotten, repeat the* עמידה.)

When saying the עמידה *silently, continue with*
אַתָּה יָצַרְתָּ *on* ראש חודש *and* תִּכַּנְתָּ שַׁבָּת *on* שבת *on page 421.*

IYUN TEFILLA • עיון תפילה

סוֹמֵךְ נוֹפְלִים – *He supports the fallen.* Rabbi Avraham Weinberg, a leader of the Hasidim of Slonim, noted that the phrase "who raises those who fall" is written in the present tense and not in the past tense. From here one learns that no matter how many times you may have stumbled or fallen, Hashem is still there every day, in the present, to support you and make sure that you can get up again. Every day brings with it new hope for a fresh beginning.

KEDUSHA[B]

During the Leader's Repetition, the following is said standing with feet together, rising on the toes at the words indicated by ▲.

Cong. then Leader: נַעֲרִיצְךָ We will revere and sanctify You[I]
with the words uttered by the holy Seraphim
who sanctify Your name in the Sanctuary;
as is written by Your prophet:
"They call out to one another, saying: *Is. 6*

Cong. then Leader: ▲Holy, ▲holy, ▲holy is the LORD of hosts;
the whole world is filled with His glory."
His glory fills the universe.[I]
His ministering angels ask each other,
"Where is the place of His glory?"
Those facing them reply "Blessed –

ANI TEFILLA • אני תפילה

As much as we here mimic the angels who sanctify the name of God on high, we must never forget that our goal is to sanctify His name here on earth (Ḥafetz Ḥayyim).

IYUN TEFILLA • עיון תפילה

נַעֲרִיצְךָ וְנַקְדִּישְׁךָ – *We will revere and sanctify You.* To revere God is to have a sense of awe based upon the actions He does. To sanctify Him is based upon His holiness, on that which is hidden from us. The revealed and the hidden can both be sources of faith and inspiration (*Dover Shalom*). In the birth of a baby, for example, or the sprouting of a flower are revealed both the obvious birth and hidden mystery of life.

כְּבוֹדוֹ מָלֵא עוֹלָם... – *His glory fills the universe.* His glory fills the universe, and yet we ask one another where is His place of glory and then we respond His glory is to be found in His place. What to make of this confusing search? One answer is that in the end God cannot really be "found" for He is beyond the limits of our understanding. At the same time, one can find traces of His presence everywhere, if one is only willing to look. Counterintuitively, then, His presence at those moments points to His absence.

קדושה[ב]

During the חזרת הש״ץ, *the following is said standing with feet together, rising on the toes at the words indicated by* ▲.

then קהל then ש״ץ:
נַעֲרִיצְךָ וְנַקְדִּישְׁךָ[ע] כְּסוֹד שִׂיחַ שַׂרְפֵי קֹדֶשׁ
הַמַּקְדִּישִׁים שִׁמְךָ בַּקֹּדֶשׁ
כַּכָּתוּב עַל יַד נְבִיאֶךָ:
ישעיה ו וְקָרָא זֶה אֶל־זֶה וְאָמַר

then קהל then ש״ץ:
▲קָדוֹשׁ, ▲קָדוֹשׁ, ▲קָדוֹשׁ, יהוה צְבָאוֹת
מְלֹא כָל הָאָרֶץ כְּבוֹדוֹ:
כְּבוֹדוֹ מָלֵא עוֹלָם[ע]
מְשָׁרְתָיו שׁוֹאֲלִים זֶה לָזֶה
אַיֵּה מְקוֹם כְּבוֹדוֹ
לְעֻמָּתָם בָּרוּךְ יֹאמֵרוּ

BIUR TEFILLA • ביאור תפילה

קדושה – *KEDUSHA*. This *Kedusha* is referred to as *Kedusha Rabba* or in the language of the Zohar *Kedusha Ila'a* (the High *Kedusha*). While in the other versions (e.g. in *Birkhot Keriat Shema*) we mimic what the angels say and thereby we strive to be like the angels, as it were, here we sing the *kedusha* together with them. For the line of *Shema* is described as being Israel's own *kedusha* (Ḥullin 91b). The midrashic source for this particular version of the *Kedusha* describes the angels surrounding God's throne, responsively answering one another (*Pirkei deRabbi Eliezer* 4) and we now imagine that dialogue with them.

himself from his drives and negative inclinations (*yetzer hara*). Just as the Holy One, Blessed be He, (*HaKadosh Barukh Hu*) is holy and not bound by His nature, He has imbued the human being with a similar power of holiness: that of being able to transcend his own urges and inclinations, and separate himself from them.

What inclination can you try to overcome just once today?

The Ramban says that we can become holy by living a life of balance. How can you make your life a little more balanced today?

Cong. then Leader: ▲"Blessed is the LORD's glory from His place." *Ezek. 3*
From His place may He turn with compassion
and be gracious to the people who proclaim the unity
of His name, morning and evening, every day, continually,
twice each day reciting in love the Shema:

Cong. then Leader: "Listen, Israel, the LORD is our God, the LORD is One." *Deut.6*
He is our God, He is our Father, He is our King,
He is our Savior – and He, in His compassion,
will let us hear a second time in the presence of all that lives,
His promise to be "Your God." *Num. 15*
"I am the LORD your God."

Leader: And in Your holy Writings it is written:

Cong. then Leader: ▲"The LORD shall reign for ever. He is your God, Zion, *Ps. 146*
from generation to generation, Halleluya!"

Leader: From generation to generation
we will declare Your greatness,
and we will proclaim Your holiness for evermore.
Your praise, our God, shall not leave our mouth forever,
for You, God, are a great and holy King.
Blessed are You, LORD,
the holy God. / *On Shabbat Shuva:* the holy King./

The Leader continues on the next page with "You instituted the Sabbath" on Shabbat and "Long ago You formed" on Rosh Ḥodesh.

---

recited in the *Musaf* service and as a testament to what belief and commitment can bring to a community (Abudarham, *Levush* 421).

אֲנִי יהוה אֱלֹהֵיכֶם – *I am the* LORD *your God.* I will be with you in your times of distress (*Pirkei deRabbi Eliezer*).

ANI TEFILLA • אני תפילה

A student of Rav Aaron of Karlin complained that he had not reached the level of spirituality that he really wanted to. "What can I do?" the Rabbi asked. "I have tried but have thus far been unable to find the key that will help you unlock your heart." "The key?!" cried the student. "Who needs a key? Use an axe to open my heart if you have to!" "No need," the Rabbi replied. "Your heart has just opened."

קהל then ש״ץ: ׳בָּרוּךְ כְּבוֹד־יהוה מִמְּקוֹמוֹ: יחזקאל ג
מִמְּקוֹמוֹ הוּא יִפֶן בְּרַחֲמִים וְיָחֹן עַם הַמְיַחֲדִים שְׁמוֹ
עֶרֶב וָבֹקֶר בְּכָל יוֹם תָּמִיד
פַּעֲמַיִם בְּאַהֲבָה שְׁמַע אוֹמְרִים

קהל then ש״ץ: שְׁמַע יִשְׂרָאֵל, יהוה אֱלֹהֵינוּ, יהוה אֶחָד: דברים ו
הוּא אֱלֹהֵינוּ, הוּא אָבִינוּ, הוּא מַלְכֵּנוּ, הוּא מוֹשִׁיעֵנוּ
וְהוּא יַשְׁמִיעֵנוּ בְּרַחֲמָיו שֵׁנִית לְעֵינֵי כָּל חָי
לִהְיוֹת לָכֶם לֵאלֹהִים במדבר טו
אֲנִי יהוה אֱלֹהֵיכֶם:ב

ש״ץ: וּבְדִבְרֵי קָדְשְׁךָ כָּתוּב לֵאמֹר

קהל then ש״ץ: ׳יִמְלֹךְ יהוה לְעוֹלָם, אֱלֹהַיִךְ צִיּוֹן לְדֹר וָדֹר, הַלְלוּיָהּ: תהלים קמו

ש״ץ: לְדוֹר וָדוֹר נַגִּיד גָּדְלֶךָ
וּלְנֵצַח נְצָחִים קְדֻשָּׁתְךָ נַקְדִּישׁ
וְשִׁבְחֲךָ אֱלֹהֵינוּ מִפִּינוּ לֹא יָמוּשׁ לְעוֹלָם וָעֶד
כִּי אֵל מֶלֶךְ גָּדוֹל וְקָדוֹשׁ אָתָּה.
בָּרוּךְ אַתָּה יהוה, הָאֵל הַקָּדוֹשׁ./ בשבת שובה: הַמֶּלֶךְ הַקָּדוֹשׁ./

The שליח ציבור *continues on the next page with* תִּכַּנְתָּ שַׁבָּת *on* שבת *and* אַתָּה יָצַרְתָּ *on* ראש חודש.

BIUR TEFILLA • ביאור תפילה

שְׁמַע יִשְׂרָאֵל... אֲנִי יהוה אֱלֹהֵיכֶם – *Listen, Israel... I am the Lord your God.* It is interesting to note that this section begins and ends with the first words and the last words of *Kriat Shema*. There is a tradition from at least the Geonic period that the passage was written in a time of persecution when the recitation of *Kriat Shema* was forbidden and the community surreptitiously inserted a responsive reading of the first and last lines here in order not to give up their statement of belief. The edict was miraculously rescinded as a result but it was kept here as a reminder of the centrality of *Shema* even though it is not

On Shabbat Rosh Ḥodesh say "Long ago You formed" below the line.

HOLINESS OF THE DAY

תִּכַּנְתָּ שַׁבָּת You instituted the Sabbath, You favored its offerings.
You commanded its specific laws
along with the order of its libations.
Those who delight in it inherit eternal glory,

Continue on the top of the next page.

On Shabbat Rosh Ḥodesh:

אַתָּה יָצַרְתָּ Long ago You formed Your world,
completing Your work on the seventh day.
You loved us. You favored us, raising us above all languages.
You made us holy through Your commandments,
brought us near, O our King, to Your service,
and called us by Your great and holy name.

Continue below the line on the next page.

IYUN TEFILLA • עיון תפילה

מְעַנְּגֶיהָ – *Those who delight in it.* Rabbi Yehuda said in Rav's name: "He who delights in the Sabbath is granted his heart's desires, for it is said, 'Delight yourself also in Hashem; And He will give you the desires of your heart' (*Tehillim* 37:3). Now, I do not know what this 'delight' refers to; but when it is said, 'and you shall call the Sabbath a delight" (*Yeshayahu* 58:13), you must say that it refers to the delight of the Sabbath" (*Shabbat* 118b). **What one thing could you do today to make Shabbat more delightful?**

HILKHOT TEFILLA • הלכות תפילה

אַתָּה יָצַרְתָּ עוֹלָמְךָ –*You formed Your world.* Whenever Rosh Ḥodesh (the beginning of a new Hebrew month) occurs on Shabbat, the text of the *Musaf* prayer needs to be changed to accommodate the extra themes of that day. This text, then, replaces the middle blessing that is traditionally said every Shabbat, with each day, as it were, making its own contribution to the content.

IYUN TEFILLA • עיון תפילה

אַתָּה יָצַרְתָּ עוֹלָמְךָ מִקֶּדֶם – *Long ago You formed Your world.* The word *mi-kedem*, long ago, can also be translated more narrowly as in primordial time, literally before the world existed. A midrash (*Bereshit Rabba* 1:9) relates that already in the first century, a philosopher came to Rabban Gamliel to suggest that God had help in the creation of the world from the sources of nature such as the wind and water. This is the ancient version of the debate about the origins of matter and whether it predates God's existence. The prayer here states at the outset that God was the Creator, no matter what science ultimately tells us about how old the universe is or whence derives its most basic elements.

On שבת ראש חודש *say* אַתָּה יָצַרְתָּ *below the line.*

קדושת היום

תִּכַּנְתָּ שַׁבָּת,ב רָצִיתָ קָרְבְּנוֹתֶיהָ
צִוִּיתָ פֵּרוּשֶׁיהָ עִם סִדּוּרֵי נְסָכֶיהָ
מְעַנְּגֶיהָבע לְעוֹלָם כָּבוֹד יִנְחָלוּ

Continue on the top of the next page.

בשבת ראש חודש:

אַתָּה יָצַרְתָּ עוֹלָמְךָה מִקֶּדֶם,ע כִּלִּיתָ מְלַאכְתְּךָ בַּיּוֹם הַשְּׁבִיעִי
אָהַבְתָּ אוֹתָנוּ וְרָצִיתָ בָּנוּ, וְרוֹמַמְתָּנוּ מִכָּל הַלְּשׁוֹנוֹת
וְקִדַּשְׁתָּנוּ בְּמִצְוֹתֶיךָ, וְקֵרַבְתָּנוּ מַלְכֵּנוּ לַעֲבוֹדָתֶךָ
וְשִׁמְךָ הַגָּדוֹל וְהַקָּדוֹשׁ עָלֵינוּ קָרָאתָ.

Continue below the line on the next page.

BIUR TEFILLA • ביאור תפילה

תִּכַּנְתָּ שַׁבָּת... – *You instituted the Sabbath.* Each of the following words begins with a different letter of the Hebrew alphabet but while we have seen such acrostics in the siddur before, this is the only instance in which it is arranged in reverse alphabetical order. Some might suggest that it is a fancy literary device. Others suggest that it has mystical significance: this reverse acrostic is known as **תשר"ק** because these are the last four letters of the *Alef-beit* in reverse order but it also forms a word which means to whistle as in *Zekharia* 10:8 "I will whistle and gather them because I will have redeemed them," thus making this whole paragraph an allusion to the ultimate redemption (*Tur* 286). Another, more philosophical reason, suggests that the form is there to convey that the world was created by Hashem *ex nihilo,* out of absolutely nothing, i.e., contrary to the laws of nature which require that everything be created out of some pre-existing matter. In order to stress this reversal of the law of nature, the wording of the paragraph was reversed (Yaavetz). Regardless of the meaning you decide to bring to it, allow the form to influence your perception of the content.

מְעַנְּגֶיהָ – *Those who delight in it. "Oneg"* is the word used to describe the enjoyment of Shabbat including the festive meals which are considered an obligatory part of the day. The prayer thus seems to equate the joy of the sacrifices of the day with the joy of the meals that we are soon to enjoy when the service is shortly over.

מְעַנְּגֶיהָ – *Those who delight in it.* "Those who delight" refers to those who equate Shabbat not with a sense of loss or handicap but with actual gain and true delight (Rabbi S. R. Hirsch).

For you today, is Shabbat an intrusion or an infusion?

those who relish it merit life,[1]
and those who love its teachings have chosen greatness.[B]
Even before Sinai they were commanded about it.
Then You, LORD our God, commanded us to offer on it
the additional offering of the Sabbath in the proper way.

יְהִי רָצוֹן May it be Your will, LORD our God
and God of our ancestors,
to lead us back in joy to our land and to plant us within our borders.
There we will prepare for You our obligatory offerings:
the regular daily offerings in their order,
and the additional offerings according to their laws.

Continue on the top of the next page.

You also gave us in love, LORD our God,
Sabbaths for rest and New Moons for atonement.[1]
But because we and our ancestors sinned against You,
our city was laid waste, our Sanctuary made desolate,
our splendor exiled, and the glory gone from our House of life.
We can no longer fulfill our obligations in Your chosen House,
the great and holy Temple called by Your name,
because of the hand that was stretched out against Your Sanctuary.

May it be Your will, LORD our God and God of our ancestors,
to lead us back in joy to our land, and to plant us within our borders.
There we will prepare for You our obligatory offerings:
the regular daily offerings in their order,
and the additional offerings according to their laws.

Continue below the line on the next page.

IYUN TEFILLA · עיון תפילה

וְרָאשֵׁי חֳדָשִׁים לְכַפָּרָה – *New Moons for atonement.* The identification of the new moon (and the new month) has always held symbolic significance in Judaism. The moon derives its light not by its own merit but through the sun, the source of light. So, too, the Jewish people gets its light from God, not because it is inherently better than any other nation. The waxing and waning of the moon, from its shining bright in its fullness, to its immersion in complete darkness, are often understood in terms of the changing fortunes of the Jewish people and its inconsistent ability to accurately reflect the light of its Maker. The reappearance of the moon is thus a cause for celebration, a period of collective atonement, or at-one-ment with the One who created the world, the moon and the Shabbat.

Use this *Rosh Ḥodesh* to be at one.

טוֹעֲמֶיהָ חַיִּים זָכוּ,ע וְגַם הָאוֹהֲבִים דְּבָרֶיהָ גְּדֻלָּה בָּחָרוּ.ב
אָז מִסִּינַי נִצְטַוּוּ עָלֶיהָ
וַתְּצַוֵּנוּ יהוה אֱלֹהֵינוּ לְהַקְרִיב בָּהּ קָרְבַּן מוּסַף שַׁבָּת כָּרָאוּי.

יְהִי רָצוֹן מִלְּפָנֶיךָ, יהוה אֱלֹהֵינוּ וֵאלֹהֵי אֲבוֹתֵינוּ
שֶׁתַּעֲלֵנוּ בְשִׂמְחָה לְאַרְצֵנוּ וְתִטָּעֵנוּ בִּגְבוּלֵנוּ
וְשָׁם נַעֲשֶׂה לְפָנֶיךָ אֶת קָרְבְּנוֹת חוֹבוֹתֵינוּ
תְּמִידִים כְּסִדְרָם וּמוּסָפִים כְּהִלְכָתָם.

Continue on the top of the next page.

וַתִּתֶּן לָנוּ יהוה אֱלֹהֵינוּ בְּאַהֲבָה, שַׁבָּתוֹת לִמְנוּחָה וְרָאשֵׁי חֳדָשִׁים לְכַפָּרָה.ע
וּלְפִי שֶׁחָטָאנוּ לְפָנֶיךָ אֲנַחְנוּ וַאֲבוֹתֵינוּ
חָרְבָה עִירֵנוּ, וְשָׁמֵם בֵּית מִקְדָּשֵׁנוּ, וְגָלָה יְקָרֵנוּ, וְנִטַּל כָּבוֹד מִבֵּית חַיֵּינוּ
וְאֵין אֲנַחְנוּ יְכוֹלִים לַעֲשׂוֹת חוֹבוֹתֵינוּ בְּבֵית בְּחִירָתֶךָ
בַּבַּיִת הַגָּדוֹל וְהַקָּדוֹשׁ שֶׁנִּקְרָא שִׁמְךָ עָלָיו, מִפְּנֵי הַיָּד שֶׁנִּשְׁתַּלְּחָה בְּמִקְדָּשֶׁךָ.

יְהִי רָצוֹן מִלְּפָנֶיךָ, יהוה אֱלֹהֵינוּ וֵאלֹהֵי אֲבוֹתֵינוּ
שֶׁתַּעֲלֵנוּ בְשִׂמְחָה לְאַרְצֵנוּ וְתִטָּעֵנוּ בִּגְבוּלֵנוּ
וְשָׁם נַעֲשֶׂה לְפָנֶיךָ אֶת קָרְבְּנוֹת חוֹבוֹתֵינוּ
תְּמִידִים כְּסִדְרָם וּמוּסָפִים כְּהִלְכָתָם.

Continue below the line on the next page.

BIUR TEFILLA • ביאור תפילה

וְגַם הָאוֹהֲבִים דְּבָרֶיהָ גְּדֻלָּה בָּחָרוּ – *And those who love its teachings have chosen greatness.* The word *devareha* can also allude to speech, in which case the meaning would be those who love the speech of Shabbat, i.e., that which is permitted to be spoken about on Shabbat (Vilna Gaon). Our desire to protect the atmosphere of Shabbat is so great, our passion to protect its specialness is so intense, that we avoid speaking on Shabbat of "mundane" matters that occupy us during the week. Hence the avoidance of talk about business or other topics that may detract from the spiritual.

What things can you avoid talking about today?

IYUN TEFILLA • עיון תפילה

טוֹעֲמֶיהָ חַיִּים זָכוּ – *Those who relish it merit life.* The word for "relish" can also mean "taste." From here there developed a tradition that it was a "meritorious" act to taste the Shabbat food on Friday afternoon (*Maḥzor Vitry*). Alternatively, it is a reference to those who delight in Shabbat merit eternal life. Or, perhaps, it's both – tasting the food in advance gives one a taste of the world to come!

וְאֶת מוּסַף And the additional offering of this Sabbath day
we will prepare and offer before You in love,
in accord with Your will's commandment,
as You wrote for us in Your Torah through Your servant Moses,
by Your own word, as it is said:

"On the Sabbath day, *Num. 28*
make an offering of two lambs a year old, without blemish,
together with two-tenths[B] of an ephah of fine flour
mixed with oil as a meal-offering, and its appropriate libation.[I]
This is the burnt-offering for every Sabbath,[I]
in addition to the regular daily burnt-offering and its libation."

Continue on the top of the next page.

And the additional offerings of this Sabbath day, and of this New Moon day,
we will prepare and offer before You in love,
in accord with Your will's commandment,
as You wrote for us in Your Torah through Your servant Moses,
by Your own word, as it is said:

"On the Sabbath day, make an offering of two lambs a year old, without blemish, together with two-tenths[B] of an ephah of fine flour mixed with oil as a meal-offering, and its appropriate libation.[I] This is the burnt-offering for every Sabbath,[I] in addition to the regular daily burnt-offering and its libation." *Num. 28*

"And on your new moons, present as a burnt-offering to the Lord two young bulls, one ram, and seven yearling lambs without blemish." *Num. 28*

And their meal-offerings and wine-libations as ordained: three-tenths of an ephah for each bull, two-tenths of an ephah for the ram, one-tenth of an ephah for each lamb, wine for the libations, a male goat for atonement, and two regular daily offerings according to their law.

Continue below the line on the next page.

---

significance wherein each offering represents a different facet of our lives. The showbread, for example, which was baked and replaced for each Shabbat, could represent the food we eat, the flour and oil represent our material possessions and the wine libation symbolizes our happiness (Rabbi S.R. Hirsch). **Think about each one of these things (food, possessions, happiness) and the role that they play in your life. How could you elevate each one of them into something more?**

עֹלַת שַׁבַּת בְּשַׁבַּתּוֹ – *The burnt-offering for every Shabbat.* Unlike other days, even holy days, when a sin offering (*korban ḥatat*) was offered, Shabbat is not a day to be marred by a public display of our failings. It's a day to feel whole.
Focus on the positive in your life right now.

וְאֶת מוּסַף יוֹם הַשַּׁבָּת הַזֶּה
נַעֲשֶׂה וְנַקְרִיב לְפָנֶיךָ בְּאַהֲבָה כְּמִצְוַת רְצוֹנֶךָ
כְּמוֹ שֶׁכָּתַבְתָּ עָלֵינוּ בְּתוֹרָתֶךָ, עַל יְדֵי מֹשֶׁה עַבְדֶּךָ מִפִּי כְבוֹדֶךָ
כָּאָמוּר

במדבר כח וּבְיוֹם הַשַּׁבָּת שְׁנֵי־כְבָשִׂים בְּנֵי־שָׁנָה תְּמִימִם
וּשְׁנֵי עֶשְׂרֹנִים סֹלֶת מִנְחָה בְּלוּלָה בַשֶּׁמֶן וְנִסְכּוֹ:
עֹלַת שַׁבַּת בְּשַׁבַּתּוֹ, עַל־עֹלַת הַתָּמִיד וְנִסְכָּהּ:

Continue on the top of the next page.

וְאֶת מוּסְפֵי יוֹם הַשַּׁבָּת הַזֶּה וְיוֹם רֹאשׁ הַחֹדֶשׁ הַזֶּה
נַעֲשֶׂה וְנַקְרִיב לְפָנֶיךָ בְּאַהֲבָה כְּמִצְוַת רְצוֹנֶךָ
כְּמוֹ שֶׁכָּתַבְתָּ עָלֵינוּ בְּתוֹרָתֶךָ עַל יְדֵי מֹשֶׁה עַבְדֶּךָ מִפִּי כְבוֹדֶךָ, כָּאָמוּר

במדבר כח וּבְיוֹם הַשַּׁבָּת שְׁנֵי־כְבָשִׂים בְּנֵי־שָׁנָה תְּמִימִם, וּשְׁנֵי עֶשְׂרֹנִים סֹלֶת מִנְחָה בְּלוּלָה בַשֶּׁמֶן וְנִסְכּוֹ: עֹלַת שַׁבַּת בְּשַׁבַּתּוֹ, עַל־עֹלַת הַתָּמִיד וְנִסְכָּהּ:

במדבר כח וּבְרָאשֵׁי חָדְשֵׁיכֶם תַּקְרִיבוּ עֹלָה לַיהוה, פָּרִים בְּנֵי־בָקָר שְׁנַיִם, וְאַיִל אֶחָד, כְּבָשִׂים בְּנֵי־שָׁנָה שִׁבְעָה, תְּמִימִם:

וּמִנְחָתָם וְנִסְכֵּיהֶם כִּמְדֻבָּר, שְׁלֹשָׁה עֶשְׂרֹנִים לַפָּר, וּשְׁנֵי עֶשְׂרֹנִים לָאָיִל, וְעִשָּׂרוֹן לַכֶּבֶשׂ, וְיַיִן כְּנִסְכּוֹ, וְשָׂעִיר לְכַפֵּר, וּשְׁנֵי תְמִידִים כְּהִלְכָתָם.

Continue below the line on the next page.

BIUR TEFILLA • ביאור תפילה

שְׁנֵי־כְבָשִׂים... וּשְׁנֵי עֶשְׂרֹנִים – *two lambs... with two-tenths.* The number two is significant on this day, in particular because of the double portion of manna that fell in the desert on Friday during the time of the Exodus so that no work would have to be done on Shabbat. That is why we have two loaves of bread on the table at each meal. For Shabbat represents a "double measure" of blessing, and that is what the Musaf service portrays and celebrates (Rabbi E. Munk).

What blessings in your life can you focus more on today?

IYUN TEFILLA • עיון תפילה

סֹלֶת מִנְחָה בְּלוּלָה בַשֶּׁמֶן וְנִסְכּוֹ – *Ephah of fine flour mixed with oil as a meal offering, and its appropriate libation.* The sacrifices are deemed by some to have symbolic

יִשְׂמְחוּ Those who keep the Sabbath and call it a delight
shall rejoice in Your kingship.
The people who sanctify the seventh day shall all be satisfied
and take delight in Your goodness,
for You favored the seventh day and declared it holy.
You called it "most desirable of days"
in remembrance of Creation.

אֱלֹהֵינוּ Our God and God of our ancestors, find favor in our rest.
Make us holy through Your commandments
and grant us our share in Your Torah.

Continue on the top of the next page.

Those who keep the Sabbath and call it a delight shall rejoice in Your kingship.
The people who sanctify the seventh day shall all be satisfied
and take delight in Your goodness,
for You favored the seventh day and declared it holy.
You called it "most desirable of days"
in remembrance of Creation.

Our God and God of our ancestors, find favor in our rest,
and on this Sabbath day renew for us the coming month

Continue below the line on the next page.

רְצֵה בִמְנוּחָתֵנוּ – *Find favor in our rest.* We rest because we are tired. We rest because we need a break. Ultimately, however, on this day we rest because God commanded that we do so. Perhaps part of the prayer here is that to the extent that I may be resting for selfish reasons as well, I pray that it ultimately be seen as a fulfillment of His command.

Alternatively, perhaps there is a play on words here, and the Hebrew word for "our rest," *menuḥateinu*, is supposed to echo the word *minḥateinu*, our offerings. Accept our rest as a sacrifice that we offer up to You.

In what ways might your rest today be a sacrifice?

וְתֵן חֶלְקֵנוּ בְּתוֹרָתֶךָ – *And grant us our share in Your Torah.* The gemara (*Nidda* 30b) suggests that when a baby is in the womb it learns the entire Torah and just before birth an angel comes, touches it on the upper lip (hence the indentation) and the baby forgets all that it learned. One could ask, if the child was going to forget everything it learned, then why was it taught all of that to begin with?! One answer might be so that when we ultimately learn about Torah on our own, we find thoughts and ideas that resonate with us. That is the remnant of the Torah that we learned in the womb. Our soul seeks to reclaim our share.

יִשְׂמְחוּ בְמַלְכוּתְךָ ע שׁוֹמְרֵי שַׁבָּת וְקוֹרְאֵי עֹנֶג
עַם מְקַדְּשֵׁי שְׁבִיעִי, כֻּלָּם יִשְׂבְּעוּ וְיִתְעַנְּגוּ מִטּוּבֶךָ
וּבַשְּׁבִיעִי רָצִיתָ בּוֹ וְקִדַּשְׁתּוֹ
חֶמְדַּת יָמִים אוֹתוֹ קָרָאתָ, זֵכֶר לְמַעֲשֵׂה בְרֵאשִׁית.

אֱלֹהֵינוּ וֵאלֹהֵי אֲבוֹתֵינוּ, ע רְצֵה בִמְנוּחָתֵנוּ ע
קַדְּשֵׁנוּ בְּמִצְוֹתֶיךָ וְתֵן חֶלְקֵנוּ בְּתוֹרָתֶךָ ע

Continue on the top of the next page.

יִשְׂמְחוּ בְמַלְכוּתְךָ ע שׁוֹמְרֵי שַׁבָּת וְקוֹרְאֵי עֹנֶג
עַם מְקַדְּשֵׁי שְׁבִיעִי, כֻּלָּם יִשְׂבְּעוּ וְיִתְעַנְּגוּ מִטּוּבֶךָ
וּבַשְּׁבִיעִי רָצִיתָ בּוֹ וְקִדַּשְׁתּוֹ
חֶמְדַּת יָמִים אוֹתוֹ קָרָאתָ, זֵכֶר לְמַעֲשֵׂה בְרֵאשִׁית.

אֱלֹהֵינוּ וֵאלֹהֵי אֲבוֹתֵינוּ, ע רְצֵה בִמְנוּחָתֵנוּ ע
וְחַדֵּשׁ עָלֵינוּ בְּיוֹם הַשַּׁבָּת הַזֶּה אֶת הַחֹדֶשׁ הַזֶּה

Continue below the line on the next page.

IYUN TEFILLA • עיון תפילה

יִשְׂמְחוּ בְמַלְכוּתְךָ – *Shall rejoice in your kingship.* People usually associate holy days as being happy, hence the greeting *Ḥag Same'aḥ.* But happiness is a hallmark of Shabbat as well (*Sifri, Bemidbar* 10:10). There is little room for sadness on Shabbat.

Recall that in *Shaḥarit* it spoke about Moshe being happy when we received the gift of Shabbat. As we move further into the day, we hopefully can now speak about our own joy.

אֱלֹהֵינוּ וֵאלֹהֵי אֲבוֹתֵינוּ – *Our God and God of our ancestors.* Whereas during the week, the *Amida* is filled with as many as 19 different requests many of them quite personal, on Shabbat we tend to forgo these kinds of requests in favor of those that are primarily more communal and national. Here, however, in this paragraph that is repeated in every *Amida* we recite on Shabbat, the focus may in fact be more personal. The difference is that they are entirely of a spiritual nature, in keeping with the focus of the day and the expanded capacity of our souls.

What spiritual requests for yourself can you associate with each of these phrases?

Satisfy us with Your goodness,
grant us joy in Your salvation,
and purify our hearts to serve You in truth.[A]
In love and favor, LORD our God,
grant us as our heritage Your holy Sabbath,[I]
so that Israel who sanctify Your name
may find rest on it.
Blessed are You, LORD,
who sanctifies the Sabbath.

Continue with "Find favor" on the next page.

---

for good and blessing, joy and gladness,
deliverance and consolation, sustenance and support,
life and peace, pardon of sin and forgiveness of iniquity
(*From Marḥeshvan to Adar II in a Jewish leap year:* and atonement of transgression).
For You have chosen Your people Israel from all nations;
You have made known to them Your holy Sabbath,
and instituted for them rules for the New Moon.
Blessed are You, LORD,
who sanctifies the Sabbath, Israel and the New Moons.[B]

Continue with "Find favor" on the next page.

ANI TEFILLA • אני תפילה

The rabbi was deathly ill and the inhabitants of the town declared a communal fast and day of prayer for his speedy recovery. A villager came along and made his way to the local bar where he wanted an alcoholic drink. He was told that none was available because of the fast. And so he made his way to the synagogue and prayed: "Master of Universe, please cure the Holy Rabbi so that I may have my drink."

When the rabbi began to recover he said: "The prayer of the villager was more effective than any of yours for he expressed his greatest longing with the greatest intent for my speedy recovery."

How badly do you want what you are praying for?

BIUR TEFILLA • ביאור תפילה

מְקַדֵּשׁ הַשַּׁבָּת וְיִשְׂרָאֵל וְרָאשֵׁי חֳדָשִׁים – *Who sanctifies the Shabbat, Israel and the New Moons.* The Rabbis inform us that the order here is instructive. Hashem Himself sanctified the Shabbat day as evidenced in the verses from *Bereshit* found in Kiddush "And He blessed the seventh day and sanctified it." The Shabbat is a holy day regardless of whether we observe it or not. But the very first commandment in the Torah appears at the time of the Exodus, when we were told to sanctify each new month. In Talmudic times this meant that men came to the central court (Sanhedrin)

This **BIUR TEFILLA** *continues on page 431.*

שַׂבְּעֵנוּ מִטּוּבֶךָ, וְשַׂמְּחֵנוּ בִּישׁוּעָתֶךָ
וְטַהֵר לִבֵּנוּ לְעָבְדְּךָ בֶּאֱמֶת[א]
וְהַנְחִילֵנוּ יהוה אֱלֹהֵינוּ בְּאַהֲבָה וּבְרָצוֹן שַׁבַּת קָדְשֶׁךָ[ע]
וְיָנוּחוּ בוֹ יִשְׂרָאֵל מְקַדְּשֵׁי שְׁמֶךָ.
בָּרוּךְ אַתָּה יהוה, מְקַדֵּשׁ הַשַּׁבָּת.

Continue with רְצֵה *on the next page.*

לְטוֹבָה וְלִבְרָכָה, לְשָׂשׂוֹן וּלְשִׂמְחָה
לִישׁוּעָה וּלְנֶחָמָה, לְפַרְנָסָה וּלְכַלְכָּלָה
לְחַיִּים וּלְשָׁלוֹם, לִמְחִילַת חֵטְא וְלִסְלִיחַת עָוֹן
(*From* מרחשון *to* אדר שני *in a Jewish leap year* **וּלְכַפָּרַת פָּשַׁע**)
כִּי בְעַמְּךָ יִשְׂרָאֵל בָּחַרְתָּ מִכָּל הָאֻמּוֹת
וְשַׁבַּת קָדְשְׁךָ לָהֶם הוֹדַעְתָּ, וְחֻקֵּי רָאשֵׁי חֳדָשִׁים לָהֶם קָבָעְתָּ.
בָּרוּךְ אַתָּה יהוה, מְקַדֵּשׁ הַשַּׁבָּת וְיִשְׂרָאֵל וְרָאשֵׁי חֳדָשִׁים.[ב]

Continue with רְצֵה *on the next page.*

ANI TEFILLA • אני תפילה

וְטַהֵר לִבֵּנוּ לְעָבְדְּךָ בֶּאֱמֶת – *And purify our hearts to serve You in truth.*

Which aspects of your life do you do by rote? Which ones do you pray you could do with more feeling and more intention "in truth?"

וְטַהֵר לִבֵּנוּ לְעָבְדְּךָ בֶּאֱמֶת – *And purify our hearts to serve You in truth.*

Rav Aharon of Karlin said to someone: You and I both say the same blessing over an apple before we eat it. But do you see that apple tree outside the window? When I see it, I am so overwhelmed by what a miracle from God it is that I just want to erupt in saying the blessing "bori pri ha-etz" (the blessing said before one eats a fruit), yet I cannot because I cannot partake of its fruit from a distance. So you see, I eat in order to say the blessing, but you say the blessing in order to eat.

IYUN TEFILLA • עיון תפילה

וְהַנְחִילֵנוּ... שַׁבַּת קָדְשֶׁךָ – *Grant us as our heritage Your holy Shabbat.* The word is sometimes translated as "inheritance" rather than "heritage."

What, if any, might be the difference? What might be the difference to you with regard to Shabbat?

TEMPLE SERVICE

רְצֵה Find favor, LORD our God,
in Your people Israel and their prayer.
Restore the service to Your most holy House,
and accept in love and favor
the fire-offerings of Israel and their prayer.
May the service of Your people Israel
always find favor with You.
And may our eyes witness
Your return to Zion in compassion.
Blessed are You, LORD,
who restores His Presence to Zion.

רְצֵה – *Find favor.* We are near spent. We have invested ourselves to the extent possible today in the words that we have uttered. Some days are better than others. Today was a little better or a little worse. Nevertheless, it is the best that we could do for now and we hope that Hashem will accept them. Like the sacrifices that are designed to bring one closer, so too we hope that our prayers have brought us closer to Him ...and He to us.

ANI TEFILLA · אני תפילה

Where Joseph-who-honors-the-Sabbaths lived there was a certain gentile who owned much property. Fortunetellers told him, 'Joseph-who-honors-the-Sabbaths will consume all your property. So he went, sold all his property, and bought a precious stone with the proceeds, which he hid in his turban. As he was crossing a bridge the wind blew it off and cast it into the water, [and] a fish swallowed it. Subsequently the fish was hauled up and brought to market on the eve of Shabbat towards sunset. "Who will buy now that it is so late?" cried the fisherman. "Go and take them to Joseph-who-honors-the-Sabbaths," they were told, "as he is accustomed to buy." So they took it to him. He bought it, opened it, found the jewel therein, and sold it for thirteen roomfuls of gold denarii. A certain old man met him [and] said, "He who lends to the Sabbath, the Sabbath repays him." (*Shabbat* 119a)

עבודה

רְצֵה יהוה אֱלֹהֵינוּ בְּעַמְּךָ יִשְׂרָאֵל וּבִתְפִלָּתָם
וְהָשֵׁב אֶת הָעֲבוֹדָה לִדְבִיר בֵּיתֶךָ
וְאִשֵּׁי יִשְׂרָאֵל וּתְפִלָּתָם בְּאַהֲבָה תְקַבֵּל בְּרָצוֹן
וּתְהִי לְרָצוֹן תָּמִיד עֲבוֹדַת יִשְׂרָאֵל עַמֶּךָ.
וְתֶחֱזֶינָה עֵינֵינוּ בְּשׁוּבְךָ לְצִיּוֹן בְּרַחֲמִים.
בָּרוּךְ אַתָּה יהוה, הַמַּחֲזִיר שְׁכִינָתוֹ לְצִיּוֹן.

to testify that they saw the first sliver of the moon and only then was the new month declared, independent of the calculation of a calendrical system which already was known in any event. The slaves of Egypt who had no time consciousness, where every day was the same monotonous routine as the day before, were given the gift of being time-aware and having a hand in the establishment of how the days are counted. On this day, then, when Shabbat meets Rosh Ḥodesh, God and we join together to sanctify our respective views of time, one of the most precious commodities we own.

ANI TEFILLA • אני תפילה

On the day following his bar mitzva, Rabbi Binyamin Kaminetsky was summoned to the office of his father, the great Rabbi Yaakov Kaminetsky. "When I came in, I raised my inquiring eyes towards him, but he said nothing. He simply stepped on a bench and took down a small, carefully wrapped package from the bookcase.

"My father took the package in his hand and said to me, 'Today, now that you're an adult, I want to give you the most precious piece of merchandise in the world. But first, I want you to promise me that you will protect it like your own life!'

"My father untied the strings that bound the package, removed the wrapping, and handed me a watch as a gift! In seeing the look on my face, he said: 'My son, know that Rabbi Israel Salanter used to say that time is life. If we lose time, we lose life!'"

How can you master time today? How can you sanctify it?

For further commentary on these final three blessings, see *Ma'ariv* (pages 111–118), *Shaharit* (pages 349–362) and *Minha* (pages 519–526).

THANKSGIVING

▾*Bow:* We give thanks to You,
for You are *Stand straight*
the LORD our God
and God of our ancestors
for ever and all time.
You are the Rock of our lives,
Shield of our salvation
from generation to generation.
We will thank You and
declare Your praise for our lives,[A]
which are entrusted into Your hand;
for our souls,
which are placed in Your charge;
for Your miracles
which are with us every day;
and for Your wonders[I] and favors
at all times,
evening, morning and midday.
You are good –
for Your compassion never fails.
You are compassionate –
for Your loving-kindnesses never cease.
We have always placed our hope
in You.

During the Leader's Repetition, the congregation says quietly:

▾*Bow:* We give thanks to You,
for You are *Stand straight*
the LORD our God
and God of our ancestors,
God of all flesh,
who formed us
and formed the universe.
Blessings and thanks
are due to Your great
and holy name
for giving us life
and sustaining us.
May You continue
to give us life
and sustain us;
and may You gather our
exiles to Your holy courts,
to keep Your decrees,
do Your will
and serve You
with a perfect heart,
for it is for us
to give You thanks.
Blessed be God
to whom thanksgiving
is due.

---

and praise. Hence it is written, 'Your anger is turned away, and You comfort me'. This is indeed in line with what R. Elazar stated: What is implied by the Scriptural text (*Tehillim* 72:18), 'Who does wondrous things alone…?' Even the person for whom a miracle is performed is unaware of the miracle (*Nidda* 31a). **What are some of the miracles that could have happened to you today of which you might be unaware?**

ANI TEFILLA • אני תפילה

"In my speeches and workshops, I sometimes ask my audiences to shut their eyes and think about someone who, at some point in their lives, has rekindled their inner light. It is always a profound experience for everyone as they remember the joy they received from being appreciated by someone when they needed it most.

This **ANI TEFILLA** *continues on page 435.*

הודאה

▾ Bow מוֹדִים אֲנַחְנוּ לָךְ
Stand straight שָׁאַתָּה הוּא
יהוה אֱלֹהֵינוּ וֵאלֹהֵי אֲבוֹתֵינוּ
לְעוֹלָם וָעֶד.
צוּר חַיֵּינוּ, מָגֵן יִשְׁעֵנוּ
אַתָּה הוּא לְדוֹר וָדוֹר.
נוֹדֶה לְּךָ וּנְסַפֵּר תְּהִלָּתֶךָ
עַל חַיֵּינוּ[א] הַמְּסוּרִים בְּיָדֶךָ
וְעַל נִשְׁמוֹתֵינוּ הַפְּקוּדוֹת לָךְ
וְעַל נִסֶּיךָ שֶׁבְּכָל יוֹם עִמָּנוּ
וְעַל נִפְלְאוֹתֶיךָ[ע] וְטוֹבוֹתֶיךָ
שֶׁבְּכָל עֵת, עֶרֶב וָבֹקֶר וְצָהֳרָיִם.
הַטּוֹב, כִּי לֹא כָלוּ רַחֲמֶיךָ
וְהַמְרַחֵם, כִּי לֹא תַמּוּ חֲסָדֶיךָ
מֵעוֹלָם קִוִּינוּ לָךְ.

During the חזרת הש״ץ, *the* קהל *says quietly:*

▾ Bow מוֹדִים אֲנַחְנוּ לָךְ
Stand straight שָׁאַתָּה הוּא
יהוה אֱלֹהֵינוּ וֵאלֹהֵי אֲבוֹתֵינוּ
אֱלֹהֵי כָל בָּשָׂר
יוֹצְרֵנוּ, יוֹצֵר בְּרֵאשִׁית.
בְּרָכוֹת וְהוֹדָאוֹת
לְשִׁמְךָ הַגָּדוֹל וְהַקָּדוֹשׁ
עַל שֶׁהֶחֱיִיתָנוּ וְקִיַּמְתָּנוּ.
כֵּן תְּחַיֵּנוּ וּתְקַיְּמֵנוּ
וְתֶאֱסֹף גָּלֻיּוֹתֵינוּ
לְחַצְרוֹת קָדְשֶׁךָ
לִשְׁמֹר חֻקֶּיךָ
וְלַעֲשׂוֹת רְצוֹנֶךָ וּלְעָבְדְּךָ
בְּלֵבָב שָׁלֵם
עַל שֶׁאֲנַחְנוּ מוֹדִים לָךְ.
בָּרוּךְ אֵל הַהוֹדָאוֹת.

ANI TEFILLA • אני תפילה

עַל חַיֵּינוּ – *For our lives.*

When was the last time you were truly thankful for just being alive? How might acknowledgment of this change the way you view today's challenges?

IYUN TEFILLA • עיון תפילה

וְעַל נִפְלְאוֹתֶיךָ – *And for Your wonders.* R. Joseph gave the following exposition: What is the purport of the Scriptural text, (*Yeshayahu* 12:1) 'I will give thanks unto You, O Lord; for though You were angry with me, Your anger is turned away, and You comfort me.' The text alludes to two men who set out on a trading expedition when a thorn got into [the foot of] one of them who began to blaspheme and to revile. After a time, however, when he heard that his friend's ship had sunk into the sea he began to laud

The Amida continues on the next page with "For all these." On Ḥanukka say "We thank You" below; on Purim say "We thank You" on the next page.

On Ḥanukka:

עַל הַנִּסִּים [We thank You also] for the miracles,[1] the redemption, the mighty deeds, the salvations, and the victories in battle which You performed for our ancestors in those days, at this time.

בִּימֵי מַתִּתְיָהוּ In the days of Mattityahu, son of Yoḥanan, the High Priest, the Hasmonean, and his sons, the wicked Greek kingdom rose up against Your people Israel to make them forget Your Torah and to force them to transgress the statutes of Your will. It was then that You in Your great compassion stood by them in the time of their distress. You championed their cause, judged their claim, and avenged their wrong. You delivered the strong into the hands of the weak, the many into the hands of the few, the impure into the hands of the pure, the wicked into the hands of the righteous, and the arrogant into the hands of those who were engaged in the study of Your Torah. You made for Yourself great and holy renown in Your world, and for Your people Israel You performed a great salvation and redemption as of this very day. Your children then entered the holiest part of Your House, cleansed Your Temple, purified Your Sanctuary, kindled lights in Your holy courts, and designated these eight days of Ḥanukka for giving thanks and praise to Your great name.

Continue with "For all these things" on the next page.

IYUN TEFILLA • עיון תפילה

עַל הַנִּסִּים – *For the miracles.* Ḥanuka is about the little jar of oil that miraculously lasted for eight days when the *Bet HaMikdash* (Temple) was retaken by the Hasmoneans in their revolt against the Syrian-Greeks. And yet, curiously, in this particular prayer there is little or no mention of that miracle. Rather, it emphasizes the military victory which preceded it. As Jews, our view of the world is not limited to the "religious." Geopolitical events can also have the hand of God even as man is the actor exercising his own will. In 1967, when Israel won an unprecedented victory over her attackers, there were those who said that one day people would reinterpret the six days it took to win the war as a symbol of a speedy victory and the extent to which her military forces were outnumbered would not be taken literally but as a euphemism for a difficult foe. And yet, for those who lived through it, for those who witnessed it, it was nothing short of a miracle. So, too, in those days of Ḥanuka, when the strong were delivered to the weak, and the many to the few.

The עמידה *continues on the next page with* וְעַל כֻּלָּם. *On* חנוכה *say* עַל הַנִּסִּים *below; on* פורים *say* עַל הַנִּסִּים *on the next page.*

בחנוכה:

עַל הַנִּסִּים וְעַל הַפֻּרְקָן וְעַל הַגְּבוּרוֹת וְעַל הַתְּשׁוּעוֹת וְעַל הַמִּלְחָמוֹת שֶׁעָשִׂיתָ לַאֲבוֹתֵינוּ בַּיָּמִים הָהֵם בַּזְּמַן הַזֶּה.

בִּימֵי מַתִּתְיָהוּ בֶּן יוֹחָנָן כֹּהֵן גָּדוֹל חַשְׁמוֹנַאי וּבָנָיו, כְּשֶׁעָמְדָה מַלְכוּת יָוָן הָרְשָׁעָה עַל עַמְּךָ יִשְׂרָאֵל לְהַשְׁכִּיחָם תּוֹרָתֶךָ וּלְהַעֲבִירָם מֵחֻקֵּי רְצוֹנֶךָ, וְאַתָּה בְּרַחֲמֶיךָ הָרַבִּים עָמַדְתָּ לָהֶם בְּעֵת צָרָתָם, רַבְתָּ אֶת רִיבָם, דַּנְתָּ אֶת דִּינָם, נָקַמְתָּ אֶת נִקְמָתָם, מָסַרְתָּ גִבּוֹרִים בְּיַד חַלָּשִׁים, וְרַבִּים בְּיַד מְעַטִּים, וּטְמֵאִים בְּיַד טְהוֹרִים, וּרְשָׁעִים בְּיַד צַדִּיקִים, וְזֵדִים בְּיַד עוֹסְקֵי תוֹרָתֶךָ, וּלְךָ עָשִׂיתָ שֵׁם גָּדוֹל וְקָדוֹשׁ בְּעוֹלָמֶךָ, וּלְעַמְּךָ יִשְׂרָאֵל עָשִׂיתָ תְּשׁוּעָה גְדוֹלָה וּפֻרְקָן כְּהַיּוֹם הַזֶּה. וְאַחַר כֵּן בָּאוּ בָנֶיךָ לִדְבִיר בֵּיתֶךָ, וּפִנּוּ אֶת הֵיכָלֶךָ, וְטִהֲרוּ אֶת מִקְדָּשֶׁךָ, וְהִדְלִיקוּ נֵרוֹת בְּחַצְרוֹת קָדְשֶׁךָ, וְקָבְעוּ שְׁמוֹנַת יְמֵי חֲנֻכָּה אֵלּוּ, לְהוֹדוֹת וּלְהַלֵּל לְשִׁמְךָ הַגָּדוֹל.

Continue with וְעַל כֻּלָּם *on the next page.*

After one session, a gentleman thanked me for creating a new awareness. He had immediately thought of his eighth grade literature teacher who had really made an impact on his life. He planned to track her down and thank her.

A few months later he called me to say that he had written his teacher. She had gotten his letter and the following week she sent him her response…

'Dear John,

You will never know how much your letter meant to me. I am 83 years old and I am living alone in one room. My friends are all gone, and my family's gone.

I taught for 50 years and yours is the first "thank you" letter I have ever gotten from a student. Sometimes I wonder what I did with my life. I will read and reread your letter until the day I die.'

He was very emotional on the phone. He said, "She is always the one we talk about at every reunion. She was everyone's favorite teacher. We loved her… But no one ever told her…" (Barbara Glantz)

We do not thank enough, not the people around us who do good things for us, nor God who is forever giving us things, especially the smaller things that we take for granted. But we never tell Him. The Jew takes this opportunity every day. Take it now. Think of something that you have otherwise taken for granted in your life and say Modim, "we thank You."

On Shushan Purim in Jerusalem:

עַל הַנִּסִּים [We thank You also] for the miracles, the redemption, the mighty deeds, the salvations, and the victories in battle which You performed for our ancestors in those days at this time.

בִּימֵי מָרְדְּכַי In the days of Mordekhai and Esther, in Shushan the capital, the wicked Haman rose up against them and sought to destroy, slay and exterminate all the Jews, young and old, children and women, on one day, the thirteenth day of the twelfth month, which is the month of Adar, and to plunder their possessions. Then You in Your great compassion thwarted his counsel, frustrated his plans, and caused his scheme to recoil on his own head, so that they hanged him and his sons on the gallows. *Esther 3*

Continue with "For all these things."

וְעַל כֻּלָּם For all these things
may Your name be blessed and exalted,
our King, continually, for ever and all time.

These words are added on Shabbat Shuva: And write, for a good life,
all the children of Your covenant.

Let all that lives thank You, Selah!
and praise Your name in truth,
God, our Savior and Help, Selah!
▾*Bend the knees:* Blessed *Bow:* are You, *Stand straight:* LORD,
whose name is "the Good" and to whom thanks are due.

The following is said by the Leader during the Repetition of the Amida.
In Israel, if Kohanim bless the congregation, turn to page 732.

Our God and God of our fathers, bless us with the threefold blessing in the Torah, written by the hand of Moses Your servant and pronounced by Aaron and his sons the priests, Your holy people, as it is said:

May the LORD bless you and protect you. *Num. 6*
Cong: May it be Your will.
May the LORD make His face shine on you and be gracious to you.
Cong: May it be Your will.
May the LORD turn His face toward you, and grant you peace.
Cong: May it be Your will.

בשושן פורים בירושלים:

עַל הַנִּסִּים וְעַל הַפֻּרְקָן וְעַל הַגְּבוּרוֹת וְעַל הַתְּשׁוּעוֹת וְעַל הַמִּלְחָמוֹת שֶׁעָשִׂיתָ לַאֲבוֹתֵינוּ בַּיָּמִים הָהֵם בַּזְּמַן הַזֶּה.

בִּימֵי מָרְדְּכַי וְאֶסְתֵּר בְּשׁוּשַׁן הַבִּירָה, כְּשֶׁעָמַד עֲלֵיהֶם הָמָן הָרָשָׁע,
בִּקֵּשׁ לְהַשְׁמִיד לַהֲרֹג וּלְאַבֵּד אֶת־כָּל־הַיְּהוּדִים מִנַּעַר וְעַד־זָקֵן טַף אסתר ג
וְנָשִׁים בְּיוֹם אֶחָד, בִּשְׁלוֹשָׁה עָשָׂר לְחֹדֶשׁ שְׁנֵים־עָשָׂר, הוּא־חֹדֶשׁ
אֲדָר, וּשְׁלָלָם לָבוֹז: וְאַתָּה בְּרַחֲמֶיךָ הָרַבִּים הֵפַרְתָּ אֶת עֲצָתוֹ, וְקִלְקַלְתָּ
אֶת מַחֲשַׁבְתּוֹ, וַהֲשֵׁבוֹתָ לּוֹ גְּמוּלוֹ בְּרֹאשׁוֹ, וְתָלוּ אוֹתוֹ וְאֶת בָּנָיו
עַל הָעֵץ.

Continue with וְעַל כֻּלָּם.

וְעַל כֻּלָּם יִתְבָּרַךְ וְיִתְרוֹמַם שִׁמְךָ מַלְכֵּנוּ תָּמִיד לְעוֹלָם וָעֶד.

בשבת שובה: וּכְתֹב לְחַיִּים טוֹבִים כָּל בְּנֵי בְרִיתֶךָ.

וְכֹל הַחַיִּים יוֹדְוּךָ סֶּלָה
וִיהַלְלוּ אֶת שִׁמְךָ בֶּאֱמֶת
הָאֵל יְשׁוּעָתֵנוּ וְעֶזְרָתֵנוּ סֶלָה.

▼ *Bend the knees* בָּרוּךְ *Bow* אַתָּה *Stand straight* יהוה
הַטּוֹב שִׁמְךָ וּלְךָ נָאֶה לְהוֹדוֹת.

The following is said by the שליח ציבור *during* חזרת הש״ץ.
In ארץ ישראל *if* כהנים *say* ברכת כהנים *turn to page 733.*

אֱלֹהֵינוּ וֵאלֹהֵי אֲבוֹתֵינוּ, בָּרְכֵנוּ בַּבְּרָכָה הַמְשֻׁלֶּשֶׁת בַּתּוֹרָה הַכְּתוּבָה עַל יְדֵי מֹשֶׁה עַבְדֶּךָ, הָאֲמוּרָה מִפִּי אַהֲרֹן וּבָנָיו כֹּהֲנִים עַם קְדוֹשֶׁיךָ, כָּאָמוּר

יְבָרֶכְךָ יהוה וְיִשְׁמְרֶךָ: קהל: כֵּן יְהִי רָצוֹן במדבר ו
יָאֵר יהוה פָּנָיו אֵלֶיךָ וִיחֻנֶּךָּ: קהל: כֵּן יְהִי רָצוֹן
יִשָּׂא יהוה פָּנָיו אֵלֶיךָ וְיָשֵׂם לְךָ שָׁלוֹם: קהל: כֵּן יְהִי רָצוֹן

PEACE

שִׂים שָׁלוֹם Grant peace, goodness[1] and blessing, grace,
loving-kindness and compassion to us
and all Israel Your people.
Bless us, our Father, all as one,
with the light of Your face,
for by the light of Your face You have given us,
LORD our God, the Torah of life and love of kindness,
righteousness, blessing, compassion, life and peace.
May it be good in Your eyes
to bless Your people Israel
at every time, in every hour, with Your peace.

These words are added on Shabbat Shuva: In the book of life, blessing, peace and prosperity,
may we and all Your people the house of Israel
be remembered and written before You
for a good life, and for peace.*

Blessed are You, LORD, who blesses His people Israel with peace.

**On Shabbat Shuva outside Israel, many end the blessing:*
Blessed are You, LORD, who makes peace.

The following verse concludes the Leader's Repetition of the Amida. Some also say it here as part of the silent Amida.

May the words of my mouth and the meditation of my heart
find favor before You, LORD, my Rock and Redeemer. *Ps. 19*

---

that mean? One interpretation suggests that it means that it conformed to its purpose, that is, it was ready to fulfill its role in Creation. When we ask for goodness, then, we ask that we too be able to live up to the task for which we were created. True peace comes from being our true selves, the self that Hashem created and wanted us to be (Rabbi David Aaron).

How can you be your true self today?

ברכת שלום

שִׂים שָׁלוֹם טוֹבָה^ע וּבְרָכָה
חֵן וָחֶסֶד וְרַחֲמִים עָלֵינוּ וְעַל כָּל יִשְׂרָאֵל עַמֶּךָ.
בָּרְכֵנוּ אָבִינוּ כֻּלָּנוּ כְּאֶחָד בְּאוֹר פָּנֶיךָ
כִּי בְאוֹר פָּנֶיךָ נָתַתָּ לָּנוּ, יהוה אֱלֹהֵינוּ
תּוֹרַת חַיִּים וְאַהֲבַת חֶסֶד
וּצְדָקָה וּבְרָכָה וְרַחֲמִים וְחַיִּים וְשָׁלוֹם.
וְטוֹב בְּעֵינֶיךָ לְבָרֵךְ אֶת עַמְּךָ יִשְׂרָאֵל
בְּכָל עֵת וּבְכָל שָׁעָה בִּשְׁלוֹמֶךָ.

בשבת שובה: בְּסֵפֶר חַיִּים, בְּרָכָה וְשָׁלוֹם, וּפַרְנָסָה טוֹבָה
נִזָּכֵר וְנִכָּתֵב לְפָנֶיךָ
אֲנַחְנוּ וְכָל עַמְּךָ בֵּית יִשְׂרָאֵל
לְחַיִּים טוֹבִים וּלְשָׁלוֹם.*

בָּרוּךְ אַתָּה יהוה, הַמְבָרֵךְ אֶת עַמּוֹ יִשְׂרָאֵל בַּשָּׁלוֹם.

On שבת שובה in חוץ לארץ, many end the blessing:

בָּרוּךְ אַתָּה יהוה, עוֹשֶׂה הַשָּׁלוֹם.

The following verse concludes the חזרת הש״ץ.
Some also say it here as part of the silent עמידה.

יִהְיוּ לְרָצוֹן אִמְרֵי־פִי וְהֶגְיוֹן לִבִּי לְפָנֶיךָ, יהוה צוּרִי וְגֹאֲלִי: תהלים יט

IYUN TEFILLA • עיון תפילה

טוֹבָה – *Goodness.* The word *tov* appears in the account of Creation wherein Hashem says that He saw each of the things that He created and said "it was good." What does

אֱלֹהַי My God,[B]
guard my tongue from evil and my lips from deceitful speech. *Berakhot 17a*
To those who curse me, let my soul be silent;
may my soul be to all like the dust.
Open my heart to Your Torah
and let my soul pursue Your commandments.
As for all who plan evil against me,
swiftly thwart their counsel and frustrate their plans.
Act for the sake of Your name; act for the sake of Your right hand;
act for the sake of Your holiness; act for the sake of Your Torah.
That Your beloved ones may be delivered, *Ps. 60*
save with Your right hand and answer me.
May the words of my mouth and the meditation of my heart *Ps. 19*
find favor[I] before You, LORD, my Rock and Redeemer.

Bow and take three steps back as if taking leave of the Divine Presence.
Bow left: May He who makes peace in His high places,
Bow right: make peace *Bow forward:* for us and all Israel –
and say: Amen.

יְהִי רָצוֹן May it be Your will, LORD our God and God of our ancestors,
that the Temple be rebuilt speedily in our days, and grant us a share in Your Torah.
And there we will serve You with reverence,
as in the days of old and as in former years.
Then the offering of Judah and Jerusalem *Mal. 3*
will be pleasing to the LORD as in the days of old and as in former years.

---

us to use that intelligence to its fullest, to ask and answer questions, to describe abstract thoughts, to speak to God. One might say, therefore, that a person who uses speech for petty purposes, for speaking about others for no purpose, is abusing the power that was given to him and, indeed, may even be said to deny his own uniqueness as a human being as opposed to an animal. We thus conclude the *Amida* with a reminder to use our power of speech not to denigrate others but to raise ourselves up, as friends, as servants of Hashem, as members of the human race who aspire to peaceful coexistence. **What will you do when you hear people talking about other people later today?**

ANI TEFILLA • אני תפילה

People with great minds talk about ideas. People with average minds talk about events. And people with small minds, talk about other people (Attributed to Eleanor Roosevelt).

אֱלֹהַי ברכות יז.

נְצֹר לְשׁוֹנִי מֵרָע וּשְׂפָתַי מִדַּבֵּר מִרְמָה
וְלִמְקַלְלַי נַפְשִׁי תִדֹּם, וְנַפְשִׁי כֶּעָפָר לַכֹּל תִּהְיֶה.
פְּתַח לִבִּי בְּתוֹרָתֶךָ, וּבְמִצְוֹתֶיךָ תִּרְדֹּף נַפְשִׁי.
וְכָל הַחוֹשְׁבִים עָלַי רָעָה
מְהֵרָה הָפֵר עֲצָתָם וְקַלְקֵל מַחֲשַׁבְתָּם.
עֲשֵׂה לְמַעַן שְׁמֶךָ, עֲשֵׂה לְמַעַן יְמִינֶךָ
עֲשֵׂה לְמַעַן קְדֻשָּׁתֶךָ, עֲשֵׂה לְמַעַן תּוֹרָתֶךָ.
לְמַעַן יֵחָלְצוּן יְדִידֶיךָ, הוֹשִׁיעָה יְמִינְךָ וַעֲנֵנִי: תהלים ס
יִהְיוּ לְרָצוֹן אִמְרֵי־פִי וְהֶגְיוֹן לִבִּי לְפָנֶיךָ, יהוה צוּרִי וְגֹאֲלִי: תהלים יט

Bow and take three steps back as if taking leave of the Divine Presence.

Bow left **עֹשֶׂה שָׁלוֹם**/ בשבת שובה: הַשָּׁלוֹם/ **בִּמְרוֹמָיו**
Bow right **הוּא יַעֲשֶׂה שָׁלוֹם** *Bow forward* **עָלֵינוּ וְעַל כָּל יִשְׂרָאֵל**
וְאִמְרוּ אָמֵן.

יְהִי רָצוֹן מִלְּפָנֶיךָ יהוה אֱלֹהֵינוּ וֵאלֹהֵי אֲבוֹתֵינוּ
שֶׁיִּבָּנֶה בֵּית הַמִּקְדָּשׁ בִּמְהֵרָה בְיָמֵינוּ, וְתֵן חֶלְקֵנוּ בְּתוֹרָתֶךָ
וְשָׁם נַעֲבָדְךָ בְּיִרְאָה כִּימֵי עוֹלָם וּכְשָׁנִים קַדְמֹנִיּוֹת.
וְעָרְבָה לַיהוה מִנְחַת יְהוּדָה וִירוּשָׁלָםִ כִּימֵי עוֹלָם וּכְשָׁנִים קַדְמֹנִיּוֹת: מלאכי ג

IYUN TEFILLA • עיון תפילה

יִהְיוּ לְרָצוֹן אִמְרֵי־פִי וְהֶגְיוֹן לִבִּי – *May the words of my mouth and the meditation of my heart find favor.* We began the *Amida* by asking that Hashem open our lips and here we ask that those words, both spoken and unspoken, be found worthy. Words are the tools that we use to achieve our highest ideals, to define and live up to our humanity. Man was made in the image of God which is often understood to be related to our intelligence, that which differentiates us from the animals. Communication is the tool that enables

BIUR TEFILLA • ביאור תפילה

אֱלֹהַי – *My God.* If we began the *Amida* by referring to God as "our God and the God of my fathers…" here we refer to Him as "my God." Hopefully by this point in the services, there is a little more comfort, a little more intimacy, a little more of a personal relationship that we can take with us when we leave.

FULL KADDISH

Leader: יִתְגַּדַּל Magnified and sanctified
may His great name be,
in the world He created by His will.
May He establish His kingdom
in your lifetime and in your days,
and in the lifetime of all the house of Israel,
swiftly and soon –
and say: Amen.

All: May His great name[A] be blessed for ever and all time.

Leader: Blessed and praised, glorified and exalted,
raised and honored,
uplifted and lauded be the name of the Holy One,
blessed be He, beyond any blessing,
song, praise and consolation uttered in the world –
and say: Amen.

May the prayers and pleas of all Israel
be accepted by their Father in heaven –
and say: Amen.

May there be great peace from heaven,
and life for us and all Israel –
and say: Amen.

Bow, take three steps back, as if taking leave of the Divine Presence, then bow, first left, then right, then center, while saying:

May He who makes peace in His high places,
make peace for us and all Israel –
and say: Amen.

ANI TEFILLA • אני תפילה

יְהֵא שְׁמֵהּ רַבָּא – *May His great name. Whoever says "yeheh shemeh raba..." with all his strength, the Heavenly Court rips up any negative decree against him* (*Shabbat* 119b). "With all his strength" – one should enunciate the words clearly (Maharal).

קדיש שלם

ש״ץ: יִתְגַּדַּל וְיִתְקַדַּשׁ שְׁמֵהּ רַבָּא (קהל: אָמֵן)
בְּעָלְמָא דִּי בְרָא כִרְעוּתֵהּ
וְיַמְלִיךְ מַלְכוּתֵהּ
בְּחַיֵּיכוֹן וּבְיוֹמֵיכוֹן וּבְחַיֵּי דְכָל בֵּית יִשְׂרָאֵל
בַּעֲגָלָא וּבִזְמַן קָרִיב
וְאִמְרוּ אָמֵן. (קהל: אָמֵן)

קהל וש״ץ: יְהֵא שְׁמֵהּ רַבָּא[א] מְבָרַךְ לְעָלַם וּלְעָלְמֵי עָלְמַיָּא.

ש״ץ: יִתְבָּרַךְ וְיִשְׁתַּבַּח וְיִתְפָּאַר
וְיִתְרוֹמַם וְיִתְנַשֵּׂא וְיִתְהַדָּר וְיִתְעַלֶּה וְיִתְהַלָּל
שְׁמֵהּ דְּקֻדְשָׁא בְּרִיךְ הוּא (קהל: בְּרִיךְ הוּא)
לְעֵלָּא מִן כָּל בִּרְכָתָא / בשבת שובה: לְעֵלָּא לְעֵלָּא מִכָּל בִּרְכָתָא/
וְשִׁירָתָא, תֻּשְׁבְּחָתָא וְנֶחֱמָתָא
דַּאֲמִירָן בְּעָלְמָא
וְאִמְרוּ אָמֵן. (קהל: אָמֵן)

תִּתְקַבַּל צְלוֹתְהוֹן וּבָעוּתְהוֹן דְּכָל יִשְׂרָאֵל
קֳדָם אֲבוּהוֹן דִּי בִשְׁמַיָּא
וְאִמְרוּ אָמֵן. (קהל: אָמֵן)

יְהֵא שְׁלָמָא רַבָּא מִן שְׁמַיָּא
וְחַיִּים, עָלֵינוּ וְעַל כָּל יִשְׂרָאֵל
וְאִמְרוּ אָמֵן. (קהל: אָמֵן)

Bow, take three steps back, as if taking leave of the Divine Presence, then bow, first left, then right, then center, while saying:

עֹשֶׂה שָׁלוֹם/ בשבת שובה: הַשָּׁלוֹם/ בִּמְרוֹמָיו
הוּא יַעֲשֶׂה שָׁלוֹם עָלֵינוּ וְעַל כָּל יִשְׂרָאֵל
וְאִמְרוּ אָמֵן. (קהל: אָמֵן)

אֵין כֵּאלֹהֵינוּ There is none like our God,[B] none like our LORD,
none like our King, none like our Savior.
Who is like our God? Who is like our LORD?
Who is like our King? Who is like our Savior?
We will thank our God, we will thank our LORD,
we will thank our King, we will thank our Savior.
Blessed is our God, blessed is our LORD,
blessed is our King, blessed is our Savior.
You are our God, You are our LORD,
You are our King, You are our Savior.
You are He to whom our ancestors offered the fragrant incense.

פִּטּוּם הַקְּטֹרֶת The incense mixture[B] consisted of balsam, onycha, galbanum[B] and frankincense, each weighing seventy manehs; myrrh, cassia, spikenard and saffron, each *Keritot 6a*

---

stanzas. The first three are an acrostic: the first letter of each Hebrew line spells out the Hebrew word amen (א־מ־ן). The first word in the next stanza is "Blessed" (*barukh*) and the first word in the next stanza is "You" (*ata*). We thus have the repetition of *amen, barukh ata* (Amen, Blessed are You), a kind of affirmation of the entire prayer service until now.

Alternatively, it has been suggested that each one of the names of Hashem that appears here is revealed in the same chronological order in the Torah – *Elohim* (*Bereshit* 1:1), *Adon* (*Bereshit* 15:2), *Melekh* (*Shemot* 15:18), *Moshia* (*Devarim* 33:29). Perhaps, then, the intention is to remind us of an unfolding revelation of our own that we have had this morning, ending in our ability to address Hashem most directly in the second person, *Blessed are You* (*Dover Shalom*).

פִּטּוּם הַקְּטֹרֶת – *The incense mixture.* This passage is actually a portion of the Talmud (*Keritut* 6a; *Yerushalmi Yoma* 4:5) which describes the composition of the incense that burned in the *Beit HaMikdash* every morning and evening on the smaller altar which was located in the sanctuary (*Shemot* 30:7-9). It is hoped that our recitation of the ingredients will act as a substitute for the real thing, just as we found at the very beginning of the service (see page 203).

The purpose of the incense is not known. Among the various rationales offered: as the sacrifice atoned for the body, the intangible scent of the incense atoned for the intangible soul (*Kli Yakar*); the pleasing aroma of the incense was to draw us into having a pleasing association with the awe one has for the Temple and its service, for the connection between one's sense of smell and one's memory is obvious (*Sefer HaḤinukh*); the incense was offered just before the Menora candles were lit, reminding us that our moral actions (= incense) must be more pleasing to God than our intellectual attainments (= lights of the Menora). "In the Jewish conception of life, genius is no license for nonobservation of the laws of morality, but on the contrary, the highest degree of morality is made the test for the highest degree of true intelligence…" (Rabbi S. R. Hirsch);

This **BIUR TEFILLA** *continues on page 447.*

אֵין כֵּאלֹהֵינוּ, אֵין כַּאדוֹנֵינוּ, אֵין כְּמַלְכֵּנוּ, אֵין כְּמוֹשִׁיעֵנוּ.
מִי כֵאלֹהֵינוּ, מִי כַאדוֹנֵינוּ, מִי כְמַלְכֵּנוּ, מִי כְמוֹשִׁיעֵנוּ.
נוֹדֶה לֵאלֹהֵינוּ, נוֹדֶה לַאדוֹנֵינוּ, נוֹדֶה לְמַלְכֵּנוּ, נוֹדֶה לְמוֹשִׁיעֵנוּ.
בָּרוּךְ אֱלֹהֵינוּ, בָּרוּךְ אֲדוֹנֵינוּ, בָּרוּךְ מַלְכֵּנוּ, בָּרוּךְ מוֹשִׁיעֵנוּ.
אַתָּה הוּא אֱלֹהֵינוּ, אַתָּה הוּא אֲדוֹנֵינוּ,
אַתָּה הוּא מַלְכֵּנוּ, אַתָּה הוּא מוֹשִׁיעֵנוּ.
אַתָּה הוּא שֶׁהִקְטִירוּ אֲבוֹתֵינוּ לְפָנֶיךָ אֶת קְטֹרֶת הַסַּמִּים.

פִּטּוּם הַקְּטֹרֶת. הַצֳּרִי, וְהַצִּפֹּרֶן, וְהַחֶלְבְּנָה, וְהַלְּבוֹנָה מִשְׁקַל שִׁבְעִים שִׁבְעִים מָנֶה, מֹר, וּקְצִיעָה, שִׁבֹּלֶת נֵרְדְּ, וְכַרְכֹּם מִשְׁקַל שִׁשָּׁה עָשָׂר שִׁשָּׁה עָשָׂר מָנֶה, כריתות ו.

INTRODUCTION TO THE CONCLUSION OF THE SERVICE

The service draws to a close with some of the same themes with which it began, messages for us to take with us as we embrace the rest of the Shabbat day. Hopefully by now we feel a little closer to the Divine Presence, and we try to hold on to that feeling through our recollection of the symbolism of the sacrifices, the value of peace, and the commitment to live our lives today in a more prayerful way.

BIUR TEFILLA • ביאור תפילה

אֵין כֵּאלֹהֵינוּ – *There is none like our God.* This prayer dates back to the days of the Geonim, and acts as a kind of introduction to the concluding parts of the service. Interestingly, it was supposed to be recited at the conclusion of the morning service every day, but since the words were supposed to be read very carefully rather than recited quickly by rote, just as the eleven incense ingredients themselves were supposed to be measured out very precisely (lest one omit one on punishment of death), there was a concern that in the rush to get to work, people would not give it the attention it deserved. In Ashkenazi communities outside of Israel, it is thus reserved for Shabbat and Yom Tov only (Rema 132:2). In Sephardic tradition, the daily recitation has been maintained.

Spend a moment enjoying a "Shabbat pace of life" and not needing to rush anywhere. Think about what this passage could mean to you.

On Shabbat and Yom Tov, when people have more time, there is a greater likelihood that they will have the necessary focus. Unfortunately, human nature is such that one often gets restless as the end of a journey nears, and the same can be true for the journey that we have been on this morning. The Ashkenazi custom should thus serve as a reminder that there is still much to be gained in these final moments. We need to hang in there.

The prayer, which is usually sung by everyone together, consists of a series of five

weighing sixteen manehs; twelve manehs of costus, three of aromatic bark; nine of cinnamon; nine kabs of Carsina lye; three seahs and three kabs of Cyprus wine. If Cyprus wine was not available, old white wine might be used. A quarter of a kab of Sodom salt, and a minute amount of a smoke-raising herb. Rabbi Nathan says: Also a minute amount of Jordan amber. If one added honey to the mixture, he rendered it unfit for sacred use. If he omitted any one of its ingredients, he is guilty of a capital offense.

Rabban Shimon ben Gamliel says: "Balsam" refers to the sap that drips from the balsam tree. The Carsina lye was used for bleaching the onycha to improve it. The Cyprus wine was used to soak the onycha in it to make it pungent. Though urine is suitable for this purpose, it is not brought into the Temple out of respect.

These were the psalms which the Levites used to recite[B] in the Temple: *Mishna, Tamid 7*

On the first day of the week they used to say: "The earth is the LORD's and all it contains, the world and all who live in it." *Ps. 24*

On the second day they used to say: "Great is the LORD and greatly to be praised in the city of God, on His holy mountain." *Ps. 48*

On the third day they used to say: "God stands in the divine assembly. Among the judges He delivers judgment." *Ps. 82*

On the fourth day they used to say: "God of retribution, LORD, God of retribution, appear." *Ps. 94*

On the fifth day they used to say: "Sing for joy to God, our strength. Shout aloud to the God of Jacob." *Ps. 81*

On the sixth day they used to say: "The LORD reigns: He is robed in majesty; the LORD is robed, girded with strength; the world is firmly established; it cannot be moved." *Ps. 93*

On the Sabbath they used to say: "A psalm, a song for the Sabbath day" – [meaning] a psalm and song for the time to come, for the day which will be entirely Sabbath and rest for life everlasting. *Ps. 92*

---

a different song for each day of the week. So too do we, except that on this day, when there is a little more time, we recite the source for this custom as it is described in the Mishna (*Tamid* 7:4) which highlights the day and the first line of the chapter of Psalms that comprised the song of that day. In the weekday *ANI TEFILLA Siddur*, pages 259–267, each one is explained individually. For now, the overall message is perhaps "that each day has its own character, its own tasks, its own tonality in the symphony of time" (Rabbi J. Sacks). Alternatively, it could serve as an opportunity to reflect quickly upon each day of the week that has just passed, and what we made of it. Or, it could be seen as in introduction to the song of Shabbat that we will recite momentarily; an opportunity to revel in the way that this day is so wonderfully different from the rest of the week.

How was this past week different to the one before it?

How will this Shabbat help bring the rest of your week into focus?

How will this Shabbat help next week be different?

הַקֹּשְׁטְ שְׁנֵים עָשָׂר, קִלּוּפָה שְׁלֹשָׁה, וְקִנָּמוֹן תִּשְׁעָה, בֹּרִית כַּרְשִׁינָה תִּשְׁעָה קַבִּין, יֵין קַפְרִיסִין סְאִין תְּלָת וְקַבִּין תְּלָתָא, וְאִם אֵין לוֹ יֵין קַפְרִיסִין, מֵבִיא חֲמַר חִוַּרְיָן עַתִּיק. מֶלַח סְדוֹמִית רֹבַע, מַעֲלֶה עָשָׁן כָּל שֶׁהוּא. רַבִּי נָתָן הַבַּבְלִי אוֹמֵר: אַף כִּפַּת הַיַּרְדֵּן כָּל שֶׁהוּא, וְאִם נָתַן בָּהּ דְּבַשׁ פְּסָלָהּ, וְאִם חִסַּר אֶחָד מִכָּל סַמָּנֶיהָ, חַיָּב מִיתָה.

רַבָּן שִׁמְעוֹן בֶּן גַּמְלִיאֵל אוֹמֵר: הַצֳּרִי אֵינוֹ אֶלָּא שְׂרָף הַנּוֹטֵף מֵעֲצֵי הַקְּטָף. בֹּרִית כַּרְשִׁינָה שֶׁשָּׁפִין בָּהּ אֶת הַצִּפֹּרֶן כְּדֵי שֶׁתְּהֵא נָאָה, יֵין קַפְרִיסִין שֶׁשּׁוֹרִין בּוֹ אֶת הַצִּפֹּרֶן כְּדֵי שֶׁתְּהֵא עַזָּה, וַהֲלֹא מֵי רַגְלַיִם יָפִין לָהּ, אֶלָּא שֶׁאֵין מַכְנִיסִין מֵי רַגְלַיִם בַּמִּקְדָּשׁ מִפְּנֵי הַכָּבוֹד.

משנה תמיד ז — הַשִּׁיר שֶׁהַלְוִיִּם הָיוּ אוֹמְרִים בְּבֵית הַמִּקְדָּשׁ:

תהלים כד — בַּיּוֹם הָרִאשׁוֹן הָיוּ אוֹמְרִים, לַיהוה הָאָרֶץ וּמְלוֹאָהּ, תֵּבֵל וְיֹשְׁבֵי בָהּ:

תהלים מח — בַּשֵּׁנִי הָיוּ אוֹמְרִים, גָּדוֹל יהוה וּמְהֻלָּל מְאֹד, בְּעִיר אֱלֹהֵינוּ הַר־קָדְשׁוֹ:

תהלים פב — בַּשְּׁלִישִׁי הָיוּ אוֹמְרִים, אֱלֹהִים נִצָּב בַּעֲדַת־אֵל, בְּקֶרֶב אֱלֹהִים יִשְׁפֹּט:

תהלים צד — בָּרְבִיעִי הָיוּ אוֹמְרִים, אֵל־נְקָמוֹת יהוה, אֵל נְקָמוֹת הוֹפִיעַ:

תהלים פא — בַּחֲמִישִׁי הָיוּ אוֹמְרִים, הַרְנִינוּ לֵאלֹהִים עוּזֵּנוּ, הָרִיעוּ לֵאלֹהֵי יַעֲקֹב:

תהלים צג — בַּשִּׁשִּׁי הָיוּ אוֹמְרִים, יהוה מָלָךְ גֵּאוּת לָבֵשׁ
לָבֵשׁ יהוה עֹז הִתְאַזָּר, אַף־תִּכּוֹן תֵּבֵל בַּל־תִּמּוֹט:

תהלים צב — בַּשַּׁבָּת הָיוּ אוֹמְרִים, מִזְמוֹר שִׁיר לְיוֹם הַשַּׁבָּת:
מִזְמוֹר שִׁיר לֶעָתִיד לָבוֹא, לְיוֹם שֶׁכֻּלּוֹ שַׁבָּת וּמְנוּחָה לְחַיֵּי הָעוֹלָמִים.

From the recitation of this passage, then, one can minimally take away the cleansing feeling of atonement, the pleasing smell of spirituality, or the call to moral action. It all depends on you.

וְהַחֶלְבְּנָה – *Galbanum.* This particular spice was known for its horrible smell. It was nevertheless included in the *ketoret*, for rather than causing the mixture to smell worse, it was transformed into something that made the *ketoret* itself smell even more pleasant. The galbanum is symbolic of the sinners among Israel and the *Ketoret* thus teaches us that when all the forces of Israel gather together for a common goal, then the inner sweetness of each of us emerges, such that each of us has a part to play the improvement of the Jewish people and the world (Rabbi A. Y. Kook).

BIUR TEFILLA • ביאור תפילה

הַשִּׁיר שֶׁהַלְוִיִּם הָיוּ אוֹמְרִים – *These were the psalms that the Levites used to recite.* The morning service in the *Beit HaMikdash* was marked by the singing of a song by the Levites,

It was taught in the Academy of Elijah: Whoever studies [Torah] laws every day is assured that he will be destined for the World to Come, as it is said, *Megilla 28b*
"The ways of the world are His" – read not, "ways" [*halikhot*] but "laws" [*halakhot*]. *Hab. 3*

Rabbi Elazar said in the name of Rabbi Ḥanina: The disciples of the sages increase *Berakhot 64a*
peace in the world, as it is said, "And all your children shall be taught of the LORD, *Is. 54*
and great shall be the peace of your children [*banayikh*]." Read not *banayikh*,
"your children," but *bonayikh*, "your builders." Those who love Your Torah have *Ps. 119*
great peace; there is no stumbling block for them. May there be peace within your *Ps. 122*
ramparts, prosperity in your palaces. For the sake of my brothers and friends, I
shall say, "Peace be within you." For the sake of the House of the LORD our God,
I will seek your good. ▸ May the LORD grant strength to His people; may the *Ps. 29*
LORD bless His people with peace.

THE RABBIS' KADDISH

The following prayer, said by mourners, requires the presence of a minyan.
A transliteration can be found on page 891.

Mourner: יִתְגַּדַּל Magnified and sanctified
may His great name be,
in the world He created by His will.
May He establish His kingdom in your lifetime
and in your days,
and in the lifetime of all the house of Israel,
swiftly and soon – and say: Amen.

All: May His great name[A] be blessed for ever and all time.

---

disagreements of interpretation and arguments ensue; where will there be peace? There are many who mistakenly think that world peace will be brought about through uniformity of opinions, and therefore when they see scholars exploring wisdom and knowledge of Torah, and different opinions emerging, they believe this causes dispute which is the opposite of peace. The truth is otherwise, that true peace can only emerge through the proliferation of peace, and the proliferation of peace entails seeing all the different aspects and opinions. (Rabbi A. Y. Kook)

ANI TEFILLA • אני תפילה

יְהֵא שְׁמֵהּ רַבָּא – *May His great name. Whoever says "yeheh shemeh raba..." with all his strength, the Heavenly Court rips up any negative decree against him* (*Shabbat* 119b). "With all his strength" – with all of your physical strength (Ritva).

תָּנָא דְבֵי אֵלִיָּהוּ:ע כָּל הַשּׁוֹנֶה הֲלָכוֹת בְּכָל יוֹם מגילה כח:
מֻבְטָח לוֹ שֶׁהוּא בֶּן עוֹלָם הַבָּא, שֶׁנֶּאֱמַר
הֲלִיכוֹת עוֹלָם לוֹ: אַל תִּקְרֵי הֲלִיכוֹת אֶלָּא הֲלָכוֹת. חבקוק ג

אָמַר רַבִּי אֶלְעָזָר, אָמַר רַבִּי חֲנִינָא: תַּלְמִידֵי חֲכָמִים מַרְבִּים שָׁלוֹם בָּעוֹלָם, ברכות סד.
שֶׁנֶּאֱמַר, וְכָל־בָּנַיִךְ לִמּוּדֵי יהוה, וְרַב שְׁלוֹם בָּנָיִךְ: אַל תִּקְרֵי בָּנָיִךְ, אֶלָּא ישעיה נד
בּוֹנָיִךְ. שָׁלוֹם רָב לְאֹהֲבֵי תוֹרָתֶךָ, וְאֵין־לָמוֹ מִכְשׁוֹל: יְהִי־שָׁלוֹם בְּחֵילֵךְ, תהלים קיט תהלים קכב
שַׁלְוָה בְּאַרְמְנוֹתָיִךְ: לְמַעַן אַחַי וְרֵעָי אֲדַבְּרָה־נָּא שָׁלוֹם בָּךְ: לְמַעַן בֵּית־יהוה
אֱלֹהֵינוּ אֲבַקְשָׁה טוֹב לָךְ: ‹ יהוה עֹז לְעַמּוֹ יִתֵּן, יהוה יְבָרֵךְ אֶת־עַמּוֹ בַשָּׁלוֹם: תהלים כט

קדיש דרבנן

The following prayer, said by mourners, requires the presence of a מנין*.*
A transliteration can be found on page 891.

אבל: יִתְגַּדַּל וְיִתְקַדַּשׁ שְׁמֵהּ רַבָּא (קהל: אָמֵן)
בְּעָלְמָא דִּי בְרָא כִרְעוּתֵהּ
וְיַמְלִיךְ מַלְכוּתֵהּ
בְּחַיֵּיכוֹן וּבְיוֹמֵיכוֹן וּבְחַיֵּי דְכָל בֵּית יִשְׂרָאֵל
בַּעֲגָלָא וּבִזְמַן קָרִיב, וְאִמְרוּ אָמֵן. (קהל: אָמֵן)

קהל ואבל: יְהֵא שְׁמֵהּ רַבָּאא מְבָרַךְ לְעָלַם וּלְעָלְמֵי עָלְמַיָּא.

IYUN TEFILLA • עיון תפילה

תָּנָא דְבֵי אֵלִיָּהוּ – *In the Academy of Elijah.* In deference to the opinion which says that *Kaddish DeRabbanan* should be recited after rabbinic homiletic (as opposed to purely legal) interpretations from the Oral Law (Rambam; *Magen Avraham* 54) this section of learning concludes with two such teachings. The first praises those who incorporate daily Torah into their lives. The second speaks of the way in which doing so can bring peace to the world. The word *shalom* (peace) is mentioned no fewer than six times, an allusion perhaps to the blessing of peace which we desire for the six days of the week (*Kol Bo*). Such teachings please the heart, and so the Kaddish recited afterwards is said out of happiness (*Birkei Yosef* 55:1; *Mishna Berura* 55:9).

What is the connection between Torah study and peace? After all, would not

Mourner: Blessed and praised,
glorified and exalted,
raised and honored,
uplifted and lauded
be the name of the Holy One,
blessed be He,
beyond any blessing, song, praise
and consolation uttered in the world –
and say: Amen.

To Israel, to the teachers,
their disciples and their disciples' disciples,
and to all who engage
in the study of Torah,
in this (*in Israel add:* holy) place or elsewhere,
may there come to them and you great peace,
grace, kindness and compassion,
long life, ample sustenance and deliverance,
from their Father in Heaven –
and say: Amen.

May there be great peace from heaven,
and (good) life for us and all Israel –
and say: Amen.

Bow and take three steps back as if taking leave of the Divine Presence.

Bow left: May He who makes peace
in His high places,
Bow right: in His compassion make peace *Bow forward:* for us and all Israel –
and say: Amen.

אבל: יִתְבָּרַךְ וְיִשְׁתַּבַּח וְיִתְפָּאַר וְיִתְרוֹמַם וְיִתְנַשֵּׂא
וְיִתְהַדָּר וְיִתְעַלֶּה וְיִתְהַלָּל
שְׁמֵהּ דְּקֻדְשָׁא בְּרִיךְ הוּא (קהל: בְּרִיךְ הוּא)
לְעֵלָּא מִן כָּל בִּרְכָתָא
/בשבת שובה: לְעֵלָּא לְעֵלָּא מִכָּל בִּרְכָתָא/
וְשִׁירָתָא, תֻּשְׁבְּחָתָא וְנֶחֱמָתָא
דַּאֲמִירָן בְּעָלְמָא
וְאִמְרוּ אָמֵן. (קהל: אָמֵן)

עַל יִשְׂרָאֵל וְעַל רַבָּנָן
וְעַל תַּלְמִידֵיהוֹן וְעַל כָּל תַּלְמִידֵי תַלְמִידֵיהוֹן
וְעַל כָּל מָאן דְּעָסְקִין בְּאוֹרַיְתָא
דִּי בְּאַתְרָא (בארץ ישראל: קַדִּישָׁא) הָדֵין, וְדִי בְּכָל אֲתַר וַאֲתַר
יְהֵא לְהוֹן וּלְכוֹן שְׁלָמָא רַבָּא
חִנָּא וְחִסְדָּא, וְרַחֲמֵי, וְחַיֵּי אֲרִיכֵי, וּמְזוֹנֵי רְוִיחֵי
וּפֻרְקָנָא מִן קֳדָם אֲבוּהוֹן דִּי בִשְׁמַיָּא
וְאִמְרוּ אָמֵן. (קהל: אָמֵן)

יְהֵא שְׁלָמָא רַבָּא מִן שְׁמַיָּא
וְחַיִּים (טוֹבִים) עָלֵינוּ וְעַל כָּל יִשְׂרָאֵל
וְאִמְרוּ אָמֵן. (קהל: אָמֵן)

Bow and take three steps back as if taking leave of the Divine Presence.

Bow left עֹשֶׂה שָׁלוֹם/ בשבת שובה: הַשָּׁלוֹם/ בִּמְרוֹמָיו
Bow right הוּא יַעֲשֶׂה בְרַחֲמָיו שָׁלוֹם *Bow forward* עָלֵינוּ
וְעַל כָּל יִשְׂרָאֵל
וְאִמְרוּ אָמֵן.

Stand while saying Aleinu.

עָלֵינוּ It is our duty to praise the Master of all,
and ascribe greatness to the Author of creation,
who has not made us like the nations of the lands
nor placed us like the families of the earth;
who has not made our portion like theirs,
nor our destiny like all their multitudes.
(For they worship vanity and emptiness,
and pray to a god who cannot save.)
▾ *Bow:* But we bow in worship and thank the Supreme King of kings,
the Holy One, blessed be He,
who extends the heavens and establishes the earth,
whose throne of glory is in the heavens above,
and whose power's Presence is in the highest of heights.
He is our God; there is no other.
Truly He is our King, there is none else,
as it is written in His Torah:
"You shall know and take to heart this day that the LORD is God, *Deut. 4*
in heaven above and on earth below. There is no other."

Therefore, we place our hope in You, LORD our God,
that we may soon see the glory of Your power,
when You will remove abominations from the earth,
and idols will be utterly destroyed,
when the world will be perfected
under the sovereignty of the Almighty,
when all humanity will call on Your name,
to turn all the earth's wicked toward You.
All the world's inhabitants will realize and know
that to You every knee must bow and every tongue swear loyalty.
Before You, LORD our God, they will kneel and bow down
and give honor to Your glorious name.
They will all accept the yoke of Your kingdom,
and You will reign over them soon and for ever.
For the kingdom is Yours,
and to all eternity You will reign in glory,
as it is written in Your Torah: "The LORD will reign for ever and ever." *Ex. 15*

Stand while saying עָלֵינוּ.

עָלֵינוּ לְשַׁבֵּחַ לַאֲדוֹן הַכֹּל, לָתֵת גְּדֻלָּה לְיוֹצֵר בְּרֵאשִׁית
שֶׁלֹּא עָשָׂנוּ כְּגוֹיֵי הָאֲרָצוֹת, וְלֹא שָׂמָנוּ כְּמִשְׁפְּחוֹת הָאֲדָמָה
שֶׁלֹּא שָׂם חֶלְקֵנוּ כָּהֶם וְגוֹרָלֵנוּ כְּכָל הֲמוֹנָם.
(שֶׁהֵם מִשְׁתַּחֲוִים לְהֶבֶל וָרִיק וּמִתְפַּלְלִים אֶל אֵל לֹא יוֹשִׁיעַ.)
▾ *Bow* וַאֲנַחְנוּ כּוֹרְעִים וּמִשְׁתַּחֲוִים וּמוֹדִים
לִפְנֵי מֶלֶךְ מַלְכֵי הַמְּלָכִים, הַקָּדוֹשׁ בָּרוּךְ הוּא
שֶׁהוּא נוֹטֶה שָׁמַיִם וְיוֹסֵד אָרֶץ
וּמוֹשַׁב יְקָרוֹ בַּשָּׁמַיִם מִמַּעַל
וּשְׁכִינַת עֻזּוֹ בְּגָבְהֵי מְרוֹמִים.
הוּא אֱלֹהֵינוּ, אֵין עוֹד.
אֱמֶת מַלְכֵּנוּ, אֶפֶס זוּלָתוֹ
כַּכָּתוּב בְּתוֹרָתוֹ, וְיָדַעְתָּ הַיּוֹם וַהֲשֵׁבֹתָ אֶל־לְבָבֶךָ דברים ד
כִּי יהוה הוּא הָאֱלֹהִים בַּשָּׁמַיִם מִמַּעַל וְעַל־הָאָרֶץ מִתָּחַת
אֵין עוֹד:

עַל כֵּן נְקַוֶּה לְּךָ יהוה אֱלֹהֵינוּ, לִרְאוֹת מְהֵרָה בְּתִפְאֶרֶת עֻזֶּךָ
לְהַעֲבִיר גִּלּוּלִים מִן הָאָרֶץ, וְהָאֱלִילִים כָּרוֹת יִכָּרֵתוּן
לְתַקֵּן עוֹלָם בְּמַלְכוּת שַׁדַּי.
וְכָל בְּנֵי בָשָׂר יִקְרְאוּ בִשְׁמֶךָ לְהַפְנוֹת אֵלֶיךָ כָּל רִשְׁעֵי אָרֶץ.
יַכִּירוּ וְיֵדְעוּ כָּל יוֹשְׁבֵי תֵבֵל
כִּי לְךָ תִּכְרַע כָּל בֶּרֶךְ, תִּשָּׁבַע כָּל לָשׁוֹן.
לְפָנֶיךָ יהוה אֱלֹהֵינוּ יִכְרְעוּ וְיִפֹּלוּ, וְלִכְבוֹד שִׁמְךָ יְקָר יִתֵּנוּ
וִיקַבְּלוּ כֻלָּם אֶת עֹל מַלְכוּתֶךָ
וְתִמְלֹךְ עֲלֵיהֶם מְהֵרָה לְעוֹלָם וָעֶד.
כִּי הַמַּלְכוּת שֶׁלְּךָ הִיא וּלְעוֹלְמֵי עַד תִּמְלֹךְ בְּכָבוֹד
כַּכָּתוּב בְּתוֹרָתֶךָ, יהוה יִמְלֹךְ לְעֹלָם וָעֶד: שמות טו

And it is said: "Then the LORD shall be King over all the earth; *Zech. 14*
on that day the LORD shall be One and His name One."

Some add:

Have no fear of sudden terror or of the ruin when it overtakes the wicked. *Prov. 3*
Devise your strategy, but it will be thwarted; *Is. 8*
propose your plan, but it will not stand, for God is with us.
When you grow old, I will still be the same.
When your hair turns gray, I will still carry you. *Is. 46*
I made you, I will bear you, I will carry you, and I will rescue you.

MOURNER'S KADDISH

The following prayer, said by mourners, requires the presence of a minyan.
A transliteration can be found on page 892.

Mourner: יִתְגַּדַּל Magnified and sanctified
may His great name be,
in the world He created by His will.
May He establish His kingdom
in your lifetime and in your days,
and in the lifetime of all the house of Israel,
swiftly and soon –
and say: Amen.

All: May His great name be blessed
for ever and all time.

Mourner: Blessed and praised, glorified and exalted,
raised and honored, uplifted and lauded
be the name of the Holy One,
blessed be He,

---

unfettered, if man is suspicious, envious, petty, and obscene it is only due to the fact that man is still a heathen, his life pagan, and his cult idolatrous. He has not yet understood and intellectually digested the doctrine of (*Devarim* 6:4) "the Lord our God, the Lord is one" (Rabbi Joseph B. Soloveitchik).

וְנֶאֱמַר, וְהָיָה יהוה לְמֶלֶךְ עַל־כָּל־הָאָרֶץ בַּיּוֹם הַהוּא יִהְיֶה יהוה אֶחָד וּשְׁמוֹ אֶחָד: זכריה יד

Some add:

אַל־תִּירָא מִפַּחַד פִּתְאֹם וּמִשֹּׁאַת רְשָׁעִים כִּי תָבֹא: משלי ג

עֻצוּ עֵצָה וְתֻפָר, דַּבְּרוּ דָבָר וְלֹא יָקוּם, כִּי עִמָּנוּ אֵל: ישעיה ח

וְעַד־זִקְנָה אֲנִי הוּא, וְעַד־שֵׂיבָה אֲנִי אֶסְבֹּל אֲנִי עָשִׂיתִי וַאֲנִי אֶשָּׂא וַאֲנִי אֶסְבֹּל וַאֲמַלֵּט: ישעיה מו

קדיש יתום

The following prayer, said by mourners, requires the presence of a מנין.
A transliteration can be found on page 892.

אבל: יִתְגַּדַּל וְיִתְקַדַּשׁ שְׁמֵהּ רַבָּא (קהל: אָמֵן)
בְּעָלְמָא דִּי בְרָא כִרְעוּתֵהּ
וְיַמְלִיךְ מַלְכוּתֵהּ
בְּחַיֵּיכוֹן וּבְיוֹמֵיכוֹן וּבְחַיֵּי דְכָל בֵּית יִשְׂרָאֵל
בַּעֲגָלָא וּבִזְמַן קָרִיב
וְאִמְרוּ אָמֵן. (קהל: אָמֵן)

קהל ואבל: יְהֵא שְׁמֵהּ רַבָּא מְבָרַךְ לְעָלַם וּלְעָלְמֵי עָלְמַיָּא.

אבל: יִתְבָּרַךְ וְיִשְׁתַּבַּח וְיִתְפָּאַר
וְיִתְרוֹמַם וְיִתְנַשֵּׂא וְיִתְהַדָּר וְיִתְעַלֶּה וְיִתְהַלָּל
שְׁמֵהּ דְּקֻדְשָׁא בְּרִיךְ הוּא (קהל: בְּרִיךְ הוּא)

IYUN TEFILLA • עיון תפילה

בַּיּוֹם הַהוּא יִהְיֶה יהוה אֶחָד וּשְׁמוֹ אֶחָד – *On that day the Lord will be One and His name One.* The conclusion one must derive from this prayer is that heathendom still rules our civilized world. If we are dissatisfied with the many imperfections of our social and moral order, if we encounter injustice, brutality, and cruel, ruthless stupidity, if falsehood, wickedness, violence, and evil forces are still rampant and

beyond any blessing, song, praise and consolation
uttered in the world – and say: Amen.

May there be great peace from heaven,
and life for us and all Israel – and say: Amen.

Bow and take three steps back as if taking leave of the Divine Presence.

Bow left: May He who makes peace in His high places,
Bow right: make peace *Bow forward:* for us and all Israel –
and say: Amen.

Many congregations say the Daily Psalm after the Song of Glory, page 462. (In Israel on Shabbat Rosh Ḥodesh, some say Barekhi Nafshi, page 536, as the Daily Psalm.)

Today is the holy Sabbath,
on which the Levites used to say this psalm in the Temple:

מִזְמוֹר A psalm. A song for the Sabbath day.[A] It is good to thank the LORD *Ps. 92* and sing psalms to Your name, Most High – to tell of Your loving-kindness in the morning and Your faithfulness at night, to the music of the ten-stringed lyre and the melody of the harp. For You have made me rejoice by Your work, O LORD; I sing for joy at the deeds of Your hands. How great are Your deeds, LORD, and how very deep Your thoughts. A boor cannot know, nor can a fool understand, that though the wicked spring up like grass and all evildoers flourish, it is only that they may be destroyed for ever. But You, LORD, are eternally exalted. For behold Your enemies, LORD, behold Your enemies will perish; all evildoers will be scattered. You have raised my pride like that of a wild ox; I am anointed with fresh oil. My eyes shall look in triumph on my adversaries; my ears shall hear the downfall of the wicked who rise against me. The righteous will flourish like a palm

---

Shabbat, and it is the third time we will be reciting it since Friday evening. (See pages 67 in Ma'ariv and 255 in Pesukei deZimra for more commentary). The Malbim informs us that one of the messages of Shabbat is the fact that Hashem is not the watchmaker who created something and then walked away. Rather, he watches out for the world and its inhabitants, and takes care of them every day, albeit operating within the confines of nature when He does so. Shabbat is a day to become more in tune with that Divine Providence (*hashgaḥa pratit*), which is the very theme of this psalm.

Where can you see Hashem's role in your life?

Where do you wish you could see Hashem's role in your life?

לְעֵלָּא מִן כָּל בִּרְכָתָא / בשבת שובה: לְעֵלָּא לְעֵלָּא מִכָּל בִּרְכָתָא/
וְשִׁירָתָא, תֻּשְׁבְּחָתָא וְנֶחֱמָתָא
דַּאֲמִירָן בְּעָלְמָא, וְאִמְרוּ אָמֵן. (קהל: אָמֵן)

יְהֵא שְׁלָמָא רַבָּא מִן שְׁמַיָּא
וְחַיִּים, עָלֵינוּ וְעַל כָּל יִשְׂרָאֵל, וְאִמְרוּ אָמֵן. (קהל: אָמֵן)

Bow and take three steps back as if taking leave of the Divine Presence.

Bow left עֹשֶׂה שָׁלוֹם/ בשבת שובה: הַשָּׁלוֹם/ בִּמְרוֹמָיו
Bow right הוּא יַעֲשֶׂה שָׁלוֹם *Bow forward* עָלֵינוּ
וְעַל כָּל יִשְׂרָאֵל, וְאִמְרוּ אָמֵן.

Many congregations say the שיר של יום *after the* שיר הכבוד, *page 463.*
(*In* ארץ ישראל *on* שבת ראש חודש, *some say* בָּרְכִי נַפְשִׁי, *page 537, as the* שיר של יום.)

הַיּוֹם יוֹם שַׁבַּת קֹדֶשׁ,[א] שֶׁבּוֹ הָיוּ הַלְוִיִּם אוֹמְרִים בְּבֵית הַמִּקְדָּשׁ:

מִזְמוֹר שִׁיר לְיוֹם הַשַּׁבָּת: טוֹב לְהֹדוֹת לַיהוה, וּלְזַמֵּר לְשִׁמְךָ עֶלְיוֹן: תהלים צב
לְהַגִּיד בַּבֹּקֶר חַסְדֶּךָ, וֶאֱמוּנָתְךָ בַּלֵּילוֹת: עֲלֵי־עָשׂוֹר וַעֲלֵי־נָבֶל, עֲלֵי
הִגָּיוֹן בְּכִנּוֹר: כִּי שִׂמַּחְתַּנִי יהוה בְּפָעֳלֶךָ, בְּמַעֲשֵׂי יָדֶיךָ אֲרַנֵּן: מַה־גָּדְלוּ
מַעֲשֶׂיךָ יהוה, מְאֹד עָמְקוּ מַחְשְׁבֹתֶיךָ: אִישׁ־בַּעַר לֹא יֵדָע, וּכְסִיל
לֹא־יָבִין אֶת־זֹאת: בִּפְרֹחַ רְשָׁעִים כְּמוֹ־עֵשֶׂב, וַיָּצִיצוּ כָּל־פֹּעֲלֵי אָוֶן,
לְהִשָּׁמְדָם עֲדֵי־עַד: וְאַתָּה מָרוֹם לְעֹלָם יהוה: כִּי הִנֵּה אֹיְבֶיךָ יהוה,
כִּי־הִנֵּה אֹיְבֶיךָ יֹאבֵדוּ, יִתְפָּרְדוּ כָּל־פֹּעֲלֵי אָוֶן: וַתָּרֶם כִּרְאֵים קַרְנִי,
בַּלֹּתִי בְּשֶׁמֶן רַעֲנָן: וַתַּבֵּט עֵינִי בְּשׁוּרָי, בַּקָּמִים עָלַי מְרֵעִים תִּשְׁמַעְנָה

ANI TEFILLA • אני תפילה

הַיּוֹם יוֹם שַׁבַּת קֹדֶשׁ – *Today is the holy Shabbat.* As mentioned above, in the times of the Beit HaMikdash, a different song was sung on each day of the week to mark that day. The following passage is the psalm for

It is told that one of the Hasidic greats once said that anyone who is not prepared to greet a dog or a tree with the greeting "*Shabbat Shalom*" does not understand what Shabbat is truly all about.

tree and grow tall like a cedar in Lebanon. Planted in the LORD's House,[A] blossoming in our God's courtyards, ▸ they will still bear fruit in old age, and stay vigorous and fresh, proclaiming that the LORD is upright: He is my Rock, in whom there is no wrong.

Mourner's Kaddish on the next page

On Rosh Ḥodesh, say Barekhi Nafshi on page 536 followed by Mourner's Kaddish. On Ḥanukka, many congregations add Psalm 30 on page 216 followed by Mourner's Kaddish.

From the second day of Rosh Ḥodesh Elul through Shemini Atzeret (in Israel through Hoshana Raba), the following psalm is said:

לְדָוִד A psalm of David. The LORD is my light and my salvation – whom then shall I fear? The LORD is the stronghold of my life – of whom shall I be afraid? When evil men close in on me to devour my flesh, it is they, my enemies and foes, who stumble and fall. Should an army besiege me, my heart would not fear. Should war break out against me, still I would be confident. One thing I ask of the LORD, only this do I seek: to live in the House of the LORD all the days of my life, to gaze on the beauty of the LORD and worship in His Temple. For He will keep me safe in His pavilion on the day of trouble. He will hide me under the cover of His tent. He will set me high upon a rock. Now my head is high above my enemies who surround me. I will sacrifice in His tent with shouts of joy. I will sing and chant praises to the LORD. LORD, hear my voice when I call. Be gracious to me and answer me. On Your behalf my heart says, "Seek My face." Your face, LORD, will I seek. Do not hide Your face from me. Do not turn Your servant away in anger. You have been my help. Do not reject or forsake me, God, my Savior. Were my father and my mother to forsake me, the LORD would take me in. Teach me Your way, LORD, and lead me on a level path, because of my oppressors. Do not abandon me to the will of my foes, for false witnesses have risen against me, breathing violence. ▸ Were it not for my faith that I shall see the LORD's goodness in the land of the living. Hope in the LORD. Be strong and of good courage, and hope in the LORD! *Ps. 27*

Mourner's Kaddish on the next page

---

becomes ritually pure again. From here there is a lesson to the person who uproots himself from the roots of his Judaism and attaches himself to things which are impure; namely, that he can always return, he can always replant himself anew in the vineyard that is the Jewish community and he can have a new start in the courtyard of Hashem, leading ultimately to giving fruit to happiness and produce that will gladden his or her own heart as well those of others (*Menaḥem Tziyon*).

אֲדֹנָי: צַדִּיק כַּתָּמָר יִפְרָח, כְּאֶרֶז בַּלְּבָנוֹן יִשְׂגֶּה: שְׁתוּלִים בְּבֵית יהוה,[א]
בְּחַצְרוֹת אֱלֹהֵינוּ יַפְרִיחוּ: › עוֹד יְנוּבוּן בְּשֵׂיבָה, דְּשֵׁנִים וְרַעֲנַנִּים יִהְיוּ:
לְהַגִּיד כִּי־יָשָׁר יהוה, צוּרִי, וְלֹא־עַוְלָֽתָה בּוֹ: קדיש יתום *on the next page*

On ראש חודש, *say* בָּרְכִי נַפְשִׁי *on page 537 followed by* קדיש יתום.
On חנוכה, *many congregations add* מִזְמוֹר שִׁיר־חֲנֻכַּת הַבַּיִת *on page 217 followed by* קדיש יתום.

From the second day of ראש חודש אלול *through* שמיני עצרת
(*in* ארץ ישראל *through* הושענא רבה), *the following psalm is said:*

לְדָוִד, יהוה אוֹרִי וְיִשְׁעִי, מִמִּי אִירָא, יהוה מָעוֹז־חַיַּי, מִמִּי אֶפְחָד: תהלים כז
בִּקְרֹב עָלַי מְרֵעִים לֶאֱכֹל אֶת־בְּשָׂרִי, צָרַי וְאֹיְבַי לִי, הֵמָּה כָשְׁלוּ וְנָפָלוּ:
אִם־תַּחֲנֶה עָלַי מַחֲנֶה, לֹא־יִירָא לִבִּי, אִם־תָּקוּם עָלַי מִלְחָמָה, בְּזֹאת
אֲנִי בוֹטֵחַ: אַחַת שָׁאַלְתִּי מֵאֵת־יהוה, אוֹתָהּ אֲבַקֵּשׁ, שִׁבְתִּי בְּבֵית־
יהוה כָּל־יְמֵי חַיַּי, לַחֲזוֹת בְּנֹעַם־יהוה, וּלְבַקֵּר בְּהֵיכָלוֹ: כִּי יִצְפְּנֵנִי
בְּסֻכֹּה בְּיוֹם רָעָה, יַסְתִּרֵנִי בְּסֵתֶר אָהֳלוֹ, בְּצוּר יְרוֹמְמֵנִי: וְעַתָּה יָרוּם
רֹאשִׁי עַל אֹיְבַי סְבִיבוֹתַי, וְאֶזְבְּחָה בְאָהֳלוֹ זִבְחֵי תְרוּעָה, אָשִׁירָה
וַאֲזַמְּרָה לַיהוה: שְׁמַע־יהוה קוֹלִי אֶקְרָא, וְחָנֵּנִי וַעֲנֵנִי: לְךָ אָמַר לִבִּי
בַּקְּשׁוּ פָנָי, אֶת־פָּנֶיךָ יהוה אֲבַקֵּשׁ: אַל־תַּסְתֵּר פָּנֶיךָ מִמֶּנִּי, אַל תַּט־
בְּאַף עַבְדֶּךָ, עֶזְרָתִי הָיִיתָ, אַל־תִּטְּשֵׁנִי וְאַל־תַּעַזְבֵנִי, אֱלֹהֵי יִשְׁעִי:
כִּי־אָבִי וְאִמִּי עֲזָבוּנִי, וַיהוה יַאַסְפֵנִי: הוֹרֵנִי יהוה דַּרְכֶּךָ, וּנְחֵנִי בְּאֹרַח
מִישׁוֹר, לְמַעַן שׁוֹרְרָי: אַל־תִּתְּנֵנִי בְּנֶפֶשׁ צָרָי, כִּי קָמוּ־בִי עֵדֵי־שֶׁקֶר,
וִיפֵחַ חָמָס: › לוּלֵא הֶאֱמַנְתִּי לִרְאוֹת בְּטוּב־יהוה בְּאֶרֶץ חַיִּים: קַוֵּה
אֶל־יהוה, חֲזַק וְיַאֲמֵץ לִבֶּךָ, וְקַוֵּה אֶל־יהוה: קדיש יתום *on the next page*

ANI TEFILLA • אני תפילה

שְׁתוּלִים בְּבֵית יהוה – *Planted in the Lord's House*…In the days of the Temple, gifts of food were tithed to the priests (*terumah*) and were thereby considered holy, such that they were actually capable of becoming ritually impure. The Mishna (*Terumah* 9:7) relates that if a tithed seedling which has become impure is replanted then it

MOURNER'S KADDISH

The following prayer, said by mourners, requires the presence of a minyan.
A transliteration can be found on page 892.

Mourner: יִתְגַּדַּל Magnified and sanctified
may His great name be,
in the world He created by His will.
May He establish His kingdom
in your lifetime and in your days,
and in the lifetime of all the house of Israel,
swiftly and soon – and say: Amen.

All: May His great name be blessed
for ever and all time.

Mourner: Blessed and praised,
glorified and exalted,
raised and honored,
uplifted and lauded
be the name of the Holy One,
blessed be He,
beyond any blessing,
song, praise and consolation
uttered in the world –
and say: Amen.

May there be great peace from heaven,
and life for us and all Israel –
and say: Amen.

Bow and take three steps back as if taking leave of the Divine Presence.

Bow left: May He who makes peace in His high places,
Bow right: make peace *Bow forward:* for us
and all Israel –
and say: Amen.

קדיש יתום

The following prayer, said by mourners, requires the presence of a מנין*.*
A transliteration can be found on page 892.

אבל: יִתְגַּדַּל וְיִתְקַדַּשׁ שְׁמֵהּ רַבָּא (קהל: אָמֵן)
בְּעָלְמָא דִּי בְרָא כִרְעוּתֵהּ
וְיַמְלִיךְ מַלְכוּתֵהּ
בְּחַיֵּיכוֹן וּבְיוֹמֵיכוֹן וּבְחַיֵּי דְכָל בֵּית יִשְׂרָאֵל
בַּעֲגָלָא וּבִזְמַן קָרִיב, וְאִמְרוּ אָמֵן. (קהל: אָמֵן)

קהל ואבל: יְהֵא שְׁמֵהּ רַבָּא מְבָרַךְ לְעָלַם וּלְעָלְמֵי עָלְמַיָּא.

אבל: יִתְבָּרַךְ וְיִשְׁתַּבַּח וְיִתְפָּאַר
וְיִתְרוֹמַם וְיִתְנַשֵּׂא וְיִתְהַדָּר וְיִתְעַלֶּה וְיִתְהַלָּל
שְׁמֵהּ דְּקֻדְשָׁא בְּרִיךְ הוּא (קהל: בְּרִיךְ הוּא)
לְעֵלָּא מִן כָּל בִּרְכָתָא / בשבת שובה: לְעֵלָּא לְעֵלָּא מִכָּל בִּרְכָתָא/
וְשִׁירָתָא, תֻּשְׁבְּחָתָא וְנֶחֱמָתָא
דַּאֲמִירָן בְּעָלְמָא
וְאִמְרוּ אָמֵן. (קהל: אָמֵן)

יְהֵא שְׁלָמָא רַבָּא מִן שְׁמַיָּא
וְחַיִּים, עָלֵינוּ וְעַל כָּל יִשְׂרָאֵל
וְאִמְרוּ אָמֵן. (קהל: אָמֵן)

Bow and take three steps back as if taking leave of the Divine Presence.

Bow left עֹשֶׂה שָׁלוֹם/ בשבת שובה: הַשָּׁלוֹם/ בִּמְרוֹמָיו
Bow right הוּא יַעֲשֶׂה שָׁלוֹם *Bow forward* עָלֵינוּ
וְעַל כָּל יִשְׂרָאֵל, וְאִמְרוּ אָמֵן.

SONG OF GLORY

The Ark is opened and all stand.

Leader: I will sing sweet psalms and I will weave songs,[B]
to You for whom my soul longs.

Cong: My soul yearns for the shelter of Your hand,
that all Your mystic secrets I might understand.[B]

Leader: Whenever I speak of Your glory above,
my heart is yearning for Your love.

Cong: So Your glories I will proclaim,
and in songs of love give honor to Your name.

---

to do, and to place a crown upon His head. Beneath the surface, then, may lie mystical allusions that only the initiated can perceive. Here too is a source of its perceived holiness.

As we have seen in other places, there is a swing back and forth between addressing Hashem in the second person ("To You for Whom my soul longs") and then in the third person ("He wore") and then back to the second person again. It is as if after all of our prayers this morning, we feel we have a slightly more intimate relationship with Him than we did when we arrived, yet when we realize the chasm that separates us, we recoil and address Him as King, only to long for that personal connection again before we depart.

The theme in all of its lyrical, mystical beauty is the indescribability of God, His relationship with His people, and ours with Him. As described in the first line and the last "For You my soul will always long."

BIUR TEFILLA • ביאור תפילה

אַנְעִים זְמִירוֹת וְשִׁירִים אֶאֱרֹג – *I will sing sweet psalms and I will weave songs.* Just as the weaver ties strands of thread together, so too will I weave these melodies into one big tapestry of praise to You.

נַפְשִׁי חִמְּדָה... לָדַעַת כָּל רָז סוֹדֶךָ – *My soul yearns... that all your mystic secrets I might understand.* I want to be close to You, to understand You, even as I know that You are impossible to understand, and no matter how many secrets or insights I uncover, there will always be more.

שיר הכבוד

The ארון קודש *is opened and all stand.*

ש״ץ: אַנְעִים זְמִירוֹת וְשִׁירִים אֶאֱרֹג, כִּי אֵלֶיךָ נַפְשִׁי תַעֲרֹג.

קהל: נַפְשִׁי חִמְּדָה בְּצֵל יָדֶךָ, לָדַעַת כָּל רָז סוֹדֶךָ.

ש״ץ: מִדֵּי דַבְּרִי בִּכְבוֹדֶךָ, הוֹמֶה לִבִּי אֶל דּוֹדֶיךָ.

קהל: עַל כֵּן אֲדַבֵּר בְּךָ נִכְבָּדוֹת, וְשִׁמְךָ אֲכַבֵּד בְּשִׁירֵי יְדִידוֹת.

INRODUCTION TO ANIM ZEMIROT אנעים זמרות

Perhaps one can learn something about the inclusion of this prayer in the siddur from those who objected to its recitation. This prayer was considered so holy and uplifting that it was deemed by some inappropriate to be said every day, lest we come to take its content for granted. Rather, said one halakhic authority, we should use as our model the fact that the Kohen Gadol (The High Priest) used to enter the Holy of Holies only once a year on Yom Kippur. So, too, should we recite this particular prayer only on that one day.

Many congregations therefore now limit its recitation to Shabbat and Yom Tov. Because of its content, some recite it at the beginning of the service, while others do so just before the reading of the Torah, while still others leave it for the end of the service, ironically a time when its sanctity can sometimes be overlooked because of its proximity to the close. It is often led by a child below the age of Bar Mitzva, perhaps because it gives him an opportunity to practice his skills in leading the congregation on a prayer that is not really part of the core service. Alternatively, perhaps it is because the innocent faith of a younger child is the stance that we must all take for this most awe inspiring poem.

Attributed Rabbi Yehuda HaḤasid over 800 years ago, the prayer has four lines at the beginning and three lines at the end (in addition to a couple of verses recited afterwards), but at its center is an alphabetical acrostic. The first half of each stanza rhymes with the second half, a scheme that was maintained in the English translation. Variations of the word *rosh* (head) figure prominently (its first letter *reish* is also the only one that receives two lines in the acrostic) as does the word *kavod* (glory), from which the poem derives its name (*Shir HaKavod* / Song of Glory). It is as if the poet is trying to aspire to see the full glory of God, something that even the prophet Moshe was unable

Leader: I will tell of Your glory though I have not seen You,
imagine and describe You, though I have not known You.

Cong: By the hand of Your prophets, through Your servants' mystery,
You gave a glimpse[B] of Your wondrous majesty.

Leader: Recounting Your grandeur and Your glory,
of Your great deeds they told the story.

Cong: They depicted You, though not as You are,
but as You do: Your acts, Your power.

Leader: They represented You in many visions;
through them all You are One without divisions.

Cong: They saw You, now old, then young,
Your head with gray, with black hair hung.

Leader: Aged on the day of judgment, yet on the day of war,
a young warrior with mighty hands they saw.

Cong: Triumph like a helmet He wore on his head;
His right hand and holy arm to victory have led.

Leader: His curls are filled with dew drops of light,
His locks with fragments of the night.

Cong: He will glory in me, for He delights in me;
My diadem of beauty He shall be.

Leader: His head is like pure beaten gold;
Engraved on His brow, His sacred name behold.

Cong: For grace and glory, beauty and renown,
His people have adorned Him with a crown.

Leader: Like a youth's, His hair in locks unfurls;
Its black tresses flowing in curls.

Cong: Jerusalem, His splendor, is the dwelling place of right;
may He prize it as His highest delight.

ANI TEFILLA • אני תפילה

The Maggid of Mezeritch used to say that one can learn three things from a child: always be happy, never be idle, and when you want something, ask for it vigorously.

ש״ץ: אֲסַפְּרָה כְבוֹדְךָ וְלֹא רְאִיתִיךָ, אֲדַמְּךָ אֲכַנְּךָ וְלֹא יְדַעְתִּיךָ.
קהל: בְּיַד נְבִיאֶיךָ בְּסוֹד עֲבָדֶיךָ, דִּמִּיתָ הֲדַר כְּבוֹד הוֹדֶךָ.

ש״ץ: גְּדֻלָּתְךָ וּגְבוּרָתֶךָ, כִּנּוּ לְתֹקֶף פְּעֻלָּתֶךָ.
קהל: דִּמּוּ אוֹתְךָ וְלֹא כְּפִי יֶשְׁךָ, וַיְשַׁוּוּךָ לְפִי מַעֲשֶׂיךָ.

ש״ץ: הִמְשִׁילוּךָ בְּרֹב חֶזְיוֹנוֹת, הִנְּךָ אֶחָד בְּכָל דִּמְיוֹנוֹת.
קהל: וַיֶּחֱזוּ בְךָ זִקְנָה וּבַחֲרוּת, וּשְׂעַר רֹאשְׁךָ בְּשֵׂיבָה וְשַׁחֲרוּת.

ש״ץ: זִקְנָה בְּיוֹם דִּין וּבַחֲרוּת בְּיוֹם קְרָב, כְּאִישׁ מִלְחָמוֹת יָדָיו לוֹ רָב.
קהל: חָבַשׁ כּוֹבַע יְשׁוּעָה בְּרֹאשׁוֹ, הוֹשִׁיעָה לּוֹ יְמִינוֹ וּזְרוֹעַ קָדְשׁוֹ.

ש״ץ: טַלְלֵי אוֹרוֹת רֹאשׁוֹ נִמְלָא, קְוֻצּוֹתָיו רְסִיסֵי לָיְלָה.
קהל: יִתְפָּאֵר בִּי כִּי חָפֵץ בִּי, וְהוּא יִהְיֶה לִּי לַעֲטֶרֶת צְבִי.

ש״ץ: כֶּתֶם טָהוֹר פָּז דְּמוּת רֹאשׁוֹ, וְחַק עַל מֵצַח כְּבוֹד שֵׁם קָדְשׁוֹ.
קהל: לְחֵן וּלְכָבוֹד צְבִי תִפְאָרָה, אֻמָּתוֹ לוֹ עִטְּרָה עֲטָרָה.

ש״ץ: מַחְלְפוֹת רֹאשׁוֹ כְּבִימֵי בְחוּרוֹת, קְוֻצּוֹתָיו תַּלְתַּלִּים שְׁחוֹרוֹת.
קהל: נְוֵה הַצֶּדֶק צְבִי תִפְאַרְתּוֹ, יַעֲלֶה נָּא עַל רֹאשׁ שִׂמְחָתוֹ.

BIUR TEFILLA • ביאור תפילה

דִּמּוּ אוֹתְךָ וְלֹא כְּפִי יֶשְׁךָ, וַיְשַׁוּוּךָ לְפִי מַעֲשֶׂיךָ – *They depicted You, though not as You are, but as You do: Your acts, Your power.* The Bible describes Your deeds. We can discern some of Your characteristics only through Your actions since we can never really perceive You. Deeds that we understand as kind, just, punishing, loving, all give us insight into the contours of who You really are. You can be described as a lion (*Amos* 3:8) or as a panther (*Hoshea* 13:7), yet these are but human perceptions and terms for that which we cannot ever really see (Yaavetz).

בְּיַד נְבִיאֶיךָ... דִּמִּיתָ – *By the hand of Your prophets…You gave a glimpse.* All we know of God is what the Bible tells us. The prophets can describe their visions which are but metaphors or vague shapes seen through the thickness of a veil, but even the greatest prophet of all, Moshe, was told "No man can see Me and live" (*Shemot* 33:20).

Leader: Like a crown in His hand may His treasured people be,
a turban of beauty and of majesty.

Cong: He bore them, carried them, with a crown He adorned them.
They were precious in His sight, and He honored them.

Leader: His glory is on me; my glory is on Him.
He is near to me when I call to Him.[B]

Cong: He is bright and rosy; red will be His dress,
when He comes from Edom, treading the winepress.

Leader: He showed the tefillin-knot to Moses, humble, wise,
when the LORD's likeness was before his eyes.

Cong: He delights in His people; the humble He does raise –
He glories in them; He sits enthroned upon their praise.

Leader: Your first word, Your call to every age, is true:
O seek the people who seek You.

Cong: My many songs please take and hear
and may my hymn of joy to You come near.

Leader: May my praise be a crown for Your head,
and like incense before You, the prayers I have said.

Cong: May a poor man's song be precious in Your eyes,
like a song sung over sacrifice.

Leader: To the One who sustains all, may my blessing take flight:
Creator, Life-Giver, God of right and might.

Cong: And when I offer blessing, to me Your head incline:
accepting it as spice, fragrant and fine.

Leader: May my prayer be to You sweet song.
For You my soul will always long.

The Ark is closed.

Yours, LORD, are the greatness and the power, the glory, the majesty *1 Chr. 29*
and splendor, for everything in heaven and earth is Yours. Yours, LORD,
is the kingdom; You are exalted as Head over all. ▸ Who can tell of the *Ps. 106*
mighty acts of the LORD and make all His praise be heard?

Mourner's Kaddish (page 460)

ש״ץ: סְגֻלָּתוֹ תְּהִי בְיָדוֹ עֲטֶרֶת, וּצְנִיף מְלוּכָה צְבִי תִפְאֶרֶת.
קהל: עֲמוּסִים נְשָׂאָם, עֲטֶרֶת עִנְּדָם, מֵאֲשֶׁר יָקְרוּ בְעֵינָיו כִּבְּדָם.

ש״ץ: פְּאֵרוֹ עָלַי וּפְאֵרִי עָלָיו, וְקָרוֹב אֵלַי בְּקָרְאִי אֵלָיו.ב
קהל: צַח וְאָדֹם לִלְבוּשׁוֹ אָדֹם, פּוּרָה בְדָרְכוֹ בְּבוֹאוֹ מֵאֱדוֹם.

ש״ץ: קֶשֶׁר תְּפִלִּין הֶרְאָה לֶעָנָו, תְּמוּנַת יהוה לְנֶגֶד עֵינָיו.
קהל: רוֹצֶה בְעַמּוֹ עֲנָוִים יְפָאֵר, יוֹשֵׁב תְּהִלּוֹת בָּם לְהִתְפָּאֵר.

ש״ץ: רֹאשׁ דְּבָרְךָ אֱמֶת קוֹרֵא מֵרֹאשׁ דּוֹר וָדוֹר, עַם דּוֹרֶשְׁךָ דְּרֹשׁ.
קהל: שִׁית הֲמוֹן שִׁירַי נָא עָלֶיךָ, וְרִנָּתִי תִּקְרַב אֵלֶיךָ.

ש״ץ: תְּהִלָּתִי תְּהִי לְרֹאשְׁךָ עֲטֶרֶת, וּתְפִלָּתִי תִּכּוֹן קְטֹרֶת.
קהל: תִּיקַר שִׁירַת רָשׁ בְּעֵינֶיךָ, כַּשִּׁיר יוּשַׁר עַל קָרְבָּנֶיךָ.

ש״ץ: בִּרְכָתִי תַעֲלֶה לְרֹאשׁ מַשְׁבִּיר, מְחוֹלֵל וּמוֹלִיד, צַדִּיק כַּבִּיר.
קהל: וּבְבִרְכָתִי תְנַעֲנַע לִי רֹאשׁ, וְאוֹתָהּ קַח לְךָ כִּבְשָׂמִים רֹאשׁ.

ש״ץ: יֶעֱרַב נָא שִׂיחִי עָלֶיךָ, כִּי נַפְשִׁי תַעֲרֹג אֵלֶיךָ.

The ארון קודש *is closed.*

לְךָ יהוה הַגְּדֻלָּה וְהַגְּבוּרָה וְהַתִּפְאֶרֶת וְהַנֵּצַח וְהַהוֹד, כִּי־כֹל בַּשָּׁמַיִם וּבָאָרֶץ, לְךָ יהוה הַמַּמְלָכָה וְהַמִּתְנַשֵּׂא לְכֹל לְרֹאשׁ: • מִי יְמַלֵּל גְּבוּרוֹת יהוה, יַשְׁמִיעַ כָּל־תְּהִלָּתוֹ: (דברי הימים א׳ כט; תהלים קו)

קדיש יתום (*page 461*)

BIUR TEFILLA • ביאור תפילה

פְּאֵרוֹ עָלַי וּפְאֵרִי עָלָיו, וְקָרוֹב אֵלַי בְּקָרְאִי אֵלָיו – *His glory is on me; my glory is on Him. He is near to me when I call Him.* The word *pe'er*, glory or adornment, is also an allusion to tefillin (*Berakhot* 11a). The bond between the Jewish people and Hashem is so close that not only do we wear tefillin with His name in them, but He also wears tefillin that bear our name (*Berakhot* 6a). Today, however, the tefillin that adorn our heads are the prayers that we offer up; the praises that we hope, in the end, will be "like a crown for Your head" (תְּהִלָּתִי תְּהִי לְרֹאשְׁךָ עֲטֶרֶת).

LORD OF THE UNIVERSE,[BI]
who reigned before the birth of any thing –

When by His will all things were made
then was His name proclaimed King.

And when all things shall cease to be
He alone will reign in awe.

He was, He is, and He shall be[I]
glorious for evermore.

---

yet He is within reach and knowable. He is distant, yet He is my refuge. These are not contradictions but different aspects of an ongoing relationship. At times we feel one way, other times we feel differently. The bottom line is that we can feel both, and both are normal.

בְּטֶרֶם כָּל־יְצִיר נִבְרָא – *Who reigned before the birth of any thing.* This is a cardinal statement of faith. Hashem existed before the world did, before the raw material of matter. As such, the world was not created from something but from nothing, what is referred to as *creation ex nihilo* (*yesh me-ayin*). Our minds cannot fathom "nothing." That perhaps is just one of the many reasons that we cannot be God; but that does not mean that such a thing is impossible.

וְאַחֲרֵי כִּכְלוֹת הַכֹּל לְבַדּוֹ יִמְלֹךְ נוֹרָא. וְהוּא הָיָה וְהוּא הֹוֶה וְהוּא יִהְיֶה – And when all things shall cease to be, He alone will reign in awe. *He was, He is, He shall be.* Past, present and future are concepts in time that exist only for us, based upon our human perceptions. In Hashem's view there are no such things. He sees everything.

How might that view change the way my life is seen?

ANI TEFILLA • אני תפילה

My father used to tell the story of a very simple man, just barely literate, who came to a bookstore asking to buy a siddur. The proprietor, realizing that the man had limited knowledge, offered him the simplest siddur, but the man asked for something more elaborate. He continued asking for a more sophisticated siddur until finally the storekeeper offered him the Otzar HaTefillot, a massive volume with numerous pages of commentary. The customer was delighted but the storekeeper could not contain himself and finally asked, "Are you really going to be able to understand this book?" "Not at all," the customer answered. "But I have young children at home and whenever they want to pretend to pray they handle the siddur so roughly that they tear the first pages apart. Since the Adon Olam prayer is always at the

This **ANI TEFILLA** *continues on page 471.*

אֲדוֹן עוֹלָם בע

אֲשֶׁר מָלַךְ בְּטֶרֶם כָּל־יְצִיר נִבְרָא.

לְעֵת נַעֲשָׂה בְחֶפְצוֹ כֹּל אֲזַי מֶלֶךְ שְׁמוֹ נִקְרָא.

וְאַחֲרֵי כִּכְלוֹת הַכֹּל לְבַדּוֹ יִמְלֹךְ נוֹרָא.

וְהוּא הָיָה וְהוּא הֹוֶה וְהוּא יִהְיֶה ע בְּתִפְאָרָה.

BIUR TEFILLA • ביאור תפילה

אֲדוֹן עוֹלָם – *Lord of the universe.* The word *olam* in Hebrew can have multiple meanings or nuances. The phrase may therefore be translated as "Lord of the Universe" or "Lord of the Earth," denoting one of these places. The word could also conjure up an association with the word "forever," and would thus be translated as "Lord who reigns forever," thus denoting that He is beyond time. Or it could remind one of the word for "hidden" suggesting that Hashem is mysterious and unknowable.

Which of these appeals to you most today?

In any event, learning Hebrew can provide one with added dimensions of understanding and intent.

IYUN TEFILLA • עיון תפילה

אֲדוֹן עוֹלָם – *Lord of the universe.* The author of this famous hymn is unknown (it dates back to the eleventh century or perhaps even hundreds of years earlier), but it has found a firm place in the canon of prayer. It is recited by some individuals on their own before services begin, it is part of the liturgy recited at bedtime (*keriat Shema al ha-mita*) yet it is also commonly sung by the entire congregation at the conclusion of the service on Shabbat and Yom Tov. In some Moroccan communities, it is sung as the bride enters the wedding canopy.

What is its appeal? The first half, actually the first six lines, speak about aspects of God, His essence or who He is to the extent that we can know such a thing, while the other four lines speak about His relationship with man. In short, its theme is His exaltedness on the one hand, and His intimate contact with the world on the other, themes that we will return to over and over again, for they speak to the heart of religious experience and belief: He is far but He is close. He is before time but He is this-worldly. He is beyond our grasp and comprehension,

He is One, there is none else,
alone, unique, beyond compare;

Without beginning, without end,
His might, His rule are everywhere.

He is my God;[1] my Redeemer lives.
He is the Rock on whom I rely[A] –

My banner and my safe retreat,[B]
my cup, my portion when I cry.

Into His hand my soul I place,
when I awake and when I sleep.

The Lord is with me, I shall not fear;
body and soul from harm will He keep.[1]

Alternatively, He is my miracle, meaning, perhaps, that the daily miracles that surround me come from Him.

What miracles can you identify around you thus far today?

IYUN TEFILLA • עיון תפילה

בְּיָדוֹ אַפְקִיד רוּחִי בְּעֵת אִישַׁן וְאָעִירָה. וְעִם רוּחִי גְּוִיָּתִי יהוה לִי וְלֹא אִירָא – *Into His hand my soul I place, when I awake and when I sleep. The Lord is with me, I shall not fear; body and soul from harm will He keep.* R. Alexander said: A person loans an article to someone and it gets returned used and tattered, but *HaKadosh Barukh Hu*, the Holy One Blessed be He, is different. For at night we give Him our souls and He returns them to us in the morning refreshed and like new. We go to bed at night spent and exhausted but we awake ready to begin the day as if we are born anew. And if we have the faith to believe that this will happen every morning, then we must have the faith that it will happen after we die as well (*Shoḥer Tov* 25:2).

It was said in the name of Rav Shrira Gaon and Rav Hai his son that whoever had the proper intention during the recitation of this prayer was assured that his prayers would be answered (*Mateh Moshe*). "The beauty of its form, the easy rhythm of its verse, and the tender passion of its contents have an invigorating effect upon spirit and soul. It strengthens in man that attitude of optimism toward life… (Rabbi E. Munk).

וְהוּא אֶחָד וְאֵין שֵׁנִי לְהַמְשִׁיל לוֹ לְהַחְבִּירָה.
בְּלִי רֵאשִׁית בְּלִי תַכְלִית וְלוֹ הָעֹז וְהַמִּשְׂרָה.
וְהוּא אֵלִי[יא] וְחַי גּוֹאֲלִי וְצוּר חֶבְלִי בְּעֵת צָרָה.[א]
וְהוּא נִסִּי וּמָנוֹס לִי[יב] מְנָת כּוֹסִי בְּיוֹם אֶקְרָא.
בְּיָדוֹ אַפְקִיד רוּחִי בְּעֵת אִישַׁן וְאָעִירָה.
וְעִם רוּחִי גְּוִיָּתִי יהוה לִי וְלֹא אִירָא.[ע]

Father said, "The many customs and practices that were added to the Torah are there to assure that we keep the Adon Olam [i.e., the Master of the Universe] intact." (Rabbi Abraham Twerski)

beginning, it always gets ripped out but with the Otzar HaTefillot siddur, there are so many pages of commentary at the beginning, the kids will have a long way to go before they ever get to Adon Olam."

ANI TEFILLA • אני תפילה

וְצוּר חֶבְלִי בְּעֵת צָרָה – *He is the Rock on whom I rely.* When I'm in pain, when I'm anxious or hurting, He is a rock. Think of a rock and its properties.

Why is Hashem compared to one?

What support can it provide you with in a time of need?

IYUN TEFILLA • עיון תפילה

וְהוּא אֵלִי – *He is my God.* He knows me personally and He is interested in me, to watch over me. This is what Rav Kook said: "It is as if there was no one else in the world but me." They once asked an educator, "Which child is your favorite?" and he answered, "The one I am with in the moment." Hashem does not play favorites. Each of us who is present with Him is His favorite (Rabbi S. Aviner). Be present.

BIUR TEFILLA • ביאור תפילה

וְהוּא נִסִּי וּמָנוֹס לִי – *My banner and my safe retreat.* A banner was originally a flag on a pole used as the standard of a monarch, an army, or knight. It could be used as an identifying mark, or as a way that others could see the leader, or that outsiders could see one from afar.

How can Hashem be a banner in your life?

Kiddush and Zemirot for Shabbat Day

SHABBAT MORNING KIDDUSH

Some say:

אִם־תָּשִׁיב If you keep your feet from breaking the Sabbath, *Is. 58*
and from pursuing your affairs on My holy day,
if you call the Sabbath a delight, and the LORD's holy day honorable,
and if you honor it by not going your own way
or attending to your own affairs, or speaking idle words,
then you will find joy in the LORD,
and I will cause you to ride on the heights of the earth
and to feast on the inheritance of your father Jacob,
for the mouth of the LORD has spoken.

Most begin Kiddush here.

וְשָׁמְרוּ The children of Israel must keep the Sabbath, *Ex. 31*
observing the Sabbath in every generation
as an everlasting covenant.
It is a sign between Me and the children of Israel for ever,
for in six days the LORD made the heavens and the earth,
but on the seventh day He ceased work
and refreshed Himself.

HILKHOT TEFILLA • הלכות תפילה

Unlike the Kiddush of Friday night, this one has no prescribed text or theme. In theory, one need only recite the blessing over wine in order to fulfill one's obligation. Ironically, it is known in the literature as *Kiddusha Raba* ("The Great Kiddush") despite or perhaps because of its brevity. In practice, however, different customs have developed to introduce the blessing with added passages from Tanakh which highlight one theme or another about the special nature of Shabbat. It is known popularly simply as Kiddush. Some just say the blessing over wine; others add a line or lines of other passages but it is always followed by food in keeping with the principle outlined on Friday evening that kiddush is recited together with one's meal. As to how to conduct oneself at a communal kiddush after services, one should consult with one's rabbi.

קידוש וזמירות ליום שבת

קידושא רבה

Some say:

אִם־תָּשִׁיב מִשַּׁבָּת רַגְלֶךָ עֲשׂוֹת חֲפָצֶךָ בְּיוֹם קָדְשִׁי ישעיה נח
וְקָרָאתָ לַשַּׁבָּת עֹנֶג לִקְדוֹשׁ יהוה מְכֻבָּד
וְכִבַּדְתּוֹ מֵעֲשׂוֹת דְּרָכֶיךָ מִמְּצוֹא חֶפְצְךָ וְדַבֵּר דָּבָר:
אָז תִּתְעַנַּג עַל־יהוה
וְהִרְכַּבְתִּיךָ עַל־בָּמֳתֵי אָרֶץ
וְהַאֲכַלְתִּיךָ נַחֲלַת יַעֲקֹב אָבִיךָ
כִּי פִּי יהוה דִּבֵּר:

Most begin קידוש *here.*

וְשָׁמְרוּ בְנֵי־יִשְׂרָאֵל אֶת־הַשַּׁבָּת שמות לא
לַעֲשׂוֹת אֶת־הַשַּׁבָּת לְדֹרֹתָם בְּרִית עוֹלָם:
בֵּינִי וּבֵין בְּנֵי יִשְׂרָאֵל אוֹת הִוא לְעֹלָם
כִּי־שֵׁשֶׁת יָמִים עָשָׂה יהוה אֶת־הַשָּׁמַיִם וְאֶת־הָאָרֶץ
וּבַיּוֹם הַשְּׁבִיעִי שָׁבַת וַיִּנָּפַשׁ:

INTRODUCTION TO KIDDUSH FOR SHABBAT MORNING

When the Torah commands that one should "Remember the Shabbat *day* to keep it holy," the Rabbis learned that one should recite Kiddush during the day just as one did when the Shabbat arrived in the previous evening (*Pesaḥim* 106a). We are thus reminded once again of the sanctity of the day, appropriately just at the moment when we might fall prey to the assumption that the sumptuous food we are about to eat is solely for our own benefit and pleasure. Kiddush reminds us that we can raise the act of eating from an animalistic drive to a humanizing and holy gesture.

זָכוֹר Remember the Sabbath day[H] to keep it holy. *Ex. 20*
Six days you shall labor and do all your work,
but the seventh day is a Sabbath of the Lord your God;
on it you shall not do any work –
you, your son or daughter,
your male or female slave, or your cattle,
or the stranger within your gates.
For in six days the Lord made heaven and earth
and sea and all that is in them,
and rested on the seventh day;
therefore the Lord blessed the Sabbath day
and declared it holy.

When saying Kiddush for others, add:
Please pay attention, my masters.

בָּרוּךְ Blessed are You, Lord our God,
King of the Universe,
who creates the fruit of the vine.[H]

ANI TEFILLA • אני תפילה

Let me share with you a conversation I had with the director of a large retirement home in Miami. The residents' children all lived far away – New York, Washington, Chicago. There were three categories of children. Some sent a check every month to their parents. Sometimes the son or daughter would include a short note; sometimes, not even that. In any event, the parent knew that the child remembered him every month. Others sent the monthly check straight to the retirement home office. It didn't go direct to the parent but at least they remembered the parents every month. The third type, explained the director, comprised those who made use of a standing bank order, such that the money was sent each month by a teller at the bank without the child having any idea as to whether his parent was even still alive. Everything was conducted automatically. (Rabbi Yehuda Amital)

What kind of relationship do you have with God?

זָכוֹר אֶת־יוֹם הַשַּׁבָּת^ה לְקַדְּשׁוֹ: שמות כ

שֵׁשֶׁת יָמִים תַּעֲבֹד, וְעָשִׂיתָ כָּל־מְלַאכְתֶּךָ:

וְיוֹם הַשְּׁבִיעִי שַׁבָּת לַיהוה אֱלֹהֶיךָ

לֹא־תַעֲשֶׂה כָל־מְלָאכָה

אַתָּה וּבִנְךָ וּבִתֶּךָ

עַבְדְּךָ וַאֲמָתְךָ וּבְהֶמְתֶּךָ

וְגֵרְךָ אֲשֶׁר בִּשְׁעָרֶיךָ:

כִּי שֵׁשֶׁת־יָמִים עָשָׂה יהוה אֶת־הַשָּׁמַיִם וְאֶת־הָאָרֶץ

אֶת־הַיָּם וְאֶת־כָּל־אֲשֶׁר־בָּם

וַיָּנַח בַּיּוֹם הַשְּׁבִיעִי

עַל־כֵּן בֵּרַךְ יהוה אֶת־יוֹם הַשַּׁבָּת וַיְקַדְּשֵׁהוּ:

When saying קידוש *for others, add:*

סַבְרִי מָרָנָן

בָּרוּךְ אַתָּה יהוה אֱלֹהֵינוּ מֶלֶךְ הָעוֹלָם

בּוֹרֵא פְּרִי הַגָּפֶן.[ה]

HILKHOT TEFILLA • הלכות תפילה

בּוֹרֵא פְּרִי הַגָּפֶן – *Who creates the fruit of the vine.* The blessings over foods are generally broken down into categories. There is one blessing for all fruits, another for all vegetables. Why does wine get its own specific blessing? The answer, says the Gemara (*Berakhot* 35a), is related to the verse in *Tehillim* 104, "And wine cheers the heart of man." Wine has the special property of lightening one's mood, opening one's heart and soul to the messages of Shabbat.

BIUR TEFILLA • ביאור תפילה

זָכוֹר אֶת־יוֹם הַשַּׁבָּת – *Remember the Shabbat day.* This passage is from *Shemot* 20:7. It is the seventh verse in the chapter, it begins with the seventh letter of the alphabet and it goes on to recall seven people who must rest on the seventh day (*Tur*).

ZEMIROT FOR SHABBAT DAY

בָּרוּךְ Blessed be the LORD who, day by day, carries our burden with salvation and redemption. We will rejoice in His name all day long, and raise our head high in His salvation. For He is a stronghold for the poor and a refuge for the needy.

The LORD's tribes are Israel's testimony: He was distressed in their distress, in their suffering and slavery. Through a pavement of sapphire He showed them the strength of His love, He revealed Himself, lifting them from the depths of the pit. For with the LORD is loving- *Ps. 130* kindness; He abounds in redemption.

How precious is His loving-kindness; He shelters them under His shade. For their sake He went with them into exile in Babylon. When they went down in ships, He was counted among them. He ensured that they were treated mercifully by those who took them captive. For the LORD will not forsake His people, for the sake of His great name.

In Eilam He placed His throne, to rescue His beloved, to remove from them the stronghold of His rebels. He redeemed His servants from passing under the sword. He raised the pride of His people, for the glory of all His devoted ones. For though He afflicts, He also shows *Lam. 3* compassion and loving-kindness.

When the he-goat [Greece] extended its power, and the vision of the four ascended to the heights, And in their hearts they intended to destroy those He loved, through His priests He laid low those who rose against Him: The LORD's kindness has not ended nor His *Lam. 3* compassion ceased.

I was handed over to Edom [Rome] by my quarrelsome friends, who daily sated their appetite with my treasures. His help was with me, supporting my foundations, He will not forsake me all the days of my age. For the LORD does not reject forever. *Lam. 3*

When He comes from Edom with garments stained crimson, there will be slaughter in Botzra, and an execution of traitors, their blood will turn His garments red, in His great strength He will bring the leaders low. With His mighty blast like a day of the east wind. *Is. 27*

When the oppressor from Edom sees how it will be, He will think Botzra to be a refuge like Betzer, giving protection to angels and men, willful and accidental sinners alike. Love the *Ps. 31* LORD, all His devoted ones: all His faithful ones He will guard.

The Rock in His kindness will command His communities to gather, coming together from the four winds, He will settle them upon the high mountains, He will return with us, gathering the dispersed, for it does not say, "He will bring back" but "He will return" and gather.

Blessed is our God who has bestowed good upon us. In His compassion and abundant kindness, He has done great things for us. Like these and those, may He do yet more for us, to magnify His great, mighty and awesome name, by which we are called.

Blessed is our God who created us for His glory, To praise and laud Him and tell of His majesty, His loving-kindness is greater to us than to any other nation. Therefore with all our heart and soul and might, let us proclaim His kingship and His unity.

---

in stanza two through the first letters of stanza nine. The lack of cohesion with the first and last two stanzas both in form and content lead some to believe that these are later interpolations.

The overall theme speaks to the various

This **BIUR TEFILLA** *continues on page 479.*

זמירות ליום שבת

בָּרוּךְ אֲדֹנָי יוֹם יוֹם, יַעֲמָס לָֽנוּ יֶֽשַׁע וּפִדְיוֹם, וּבִשְׁמוֹ נָגִיל כָּל הַיּוֹם, וּבִישׁוּעָתוֹ נָרִים
רֹאשׁ עֶלְיוֹן. כִּי הוּא מָעוֹז לַדָּל וּמַחְסֶה לָאֶבְיוֹן.

שִׁבְטֵי יָהּ לְיִשְׂרָאֵל עֵדוּת, בְּצָרָתָם לוֹ צָר בְּסִבְלוּת וּבְעַבְדוּת, בִּלְבְנַת הַסַּפִּיר הֶרְאָם
עֹז יְדִידוּת, וְנִגְלָה לְהַעֲלוֹתָם מֵעֹמֶק בּוֹר וָדוּת. כִּי־עִם־יהוה הַחֶסֶד, וְהַרְבֵּה עִמּוֹ פְדוּת: תהלים קל

מַה יָּקָר חַסְדּוֹ בְּצִלּוֹ לְגוֹנְנֵמוֹ, בְּגָלוּת בָּבֶלָה שֻׁלַּח לְמַעֲנֵמוֹ, לְהוֹרִיד בָּרִיחִים נִמְנָה
בֵינֵימוֹ, וַיִּתְּנֵם לְרַחֲמִים לִפְנֵי שׁוֹבֵימוֹ. כִּי לֹא יִטֹּשׁ יהוה אֶת עַמּוֹ, בַּעֲבוּר הַגָּדוֹל שְׁמוֹ.

עֵילָם שָׁת כִּסְאוֹ לְהַצִּיל יְדִידָיו, לְהַאֲבִיד מִשָּׁם מָעֻזְנֵי מוֹרְדָיו, מֵעֲבֹר בַּשֶּֽׁלַח פָּדָה
אֶת עֲבָדָיו, קֶרֶן לְעַמּוֹ יָרִים, תְּהִלָּה לְכָל חֲסִידָיו. כִּי אִם־הוֹגָה, וְרִחַם כְּרֹב חֲסָדָו: איכה ג

וּצְפִיר הָעִזִּים הִגְדִּיל עֲצוּמָיו, וְגַם חָזוּת אַרְבַּע עָלוּ לִמְרוֹמָיו, וּבְלִבָּם דִּמּוּ לְהַשְׁחִית אֶת
רְחוּמָיו, עַל יְדֵי כֹהֲנָיו מִגֵּר מִתְקוֹמְמָיו. חַסְדֵי יהוה כִּי לֹא־תָֽמְנוּ, כִּי לֹא כָלוּ רַחֲמָיו: איכה ג

נִסְגַּֽרְתִּי לֶאֱדוֹם בְּיַד רֵעַי מְדָנַי, שֶׁבְּכָל יוֹם מְמַלְּאִים כְּרֵסָם מֵעֲדָנַי, עֶזְרָתוֹ עִמִּי לִסְמֹךְ
אֶת אֲדָנַי, וְלֹא נְטַשְׁתַּֽנִי כָּל יְמֵי עִדָּנַי. כִּי לֹא יִזְנַח לְעוֹלָם אֲדֹנָי: איכה ג

בְּבוֹאוֹ מֵאֱדוֹם חֲמוּץ בְּגָדִים, זֶֽבַח לוֹ בְּבָצְרָה וְטֶֽבַח לוֹ בְּבוֹגְדִים, וְיֵז נִצְחָם מַלְבּוּשָׁיו
לְהַאְדִּים, בְּכֹחוֹ הַגָּדוֹל יִבְצֹר רֽוּחַ נְגִידִים. הָגָה בְּרוּחוֹ הַקָּשָׁה בְּיוֹם קָדִים: ישעיה כז

רְאוֹתוֹ כִּי כֵן אֲדוֹמִי הָעוֹצֵר, יַחְשָׁב לוֹ בָּצְרָה תִּקְלֹט כְּבֶֽצֶר, וּמַלְאָךְ כְּאָדָם בְּתוֹכָהּ
יִנָּצֵר, וּמֵזִיד כַּשּׁוֹגֵג בְּמִקְלָט יֵעָצֵר. אֶֽהֱבוּ אֶת־יהוה כָּל־חֲסִידָיו, אֱמוּנִים נֹצֵר: תהלים לא

יְצַוֶּה צוּר חַסְדּוֹ קְהִלּוֹתָיו לְקַבֵּץ, מֵאַרְבַּע רוּחוֹת עָדָיו לְהִקָּבֵץ, וּבְהַר מְרוֹם הָרִים
אוֹתָֽנוּ לְהַרְבֵּץ, וְאִתָּֽנוּ יָשׁוּב נִדָּחִים קוֹבֵץ. יָשִׁיב לֹא נֶאֱמַר, כִּי אִם וְשָׁב וְקִבֵּץ.

בָּרוּךְ הוּא אֱלֹהֵינוּ אֲשֶׁר טוֹב גְּמָלָֽנוּ, כְּרַחֲמָיו וּכְרֹב חֲסָדָיו הִגְדִּיל לָֽנוּ, אֵֽלֶּה וְכָאֵֽלֶּה
יוֹסֵף עִמָּֽנוּ, לְהַגְדִּיל שְׁמוֹ הַגָּדוֹל הַגִּבּוֹר וְהַנּוֹרָא, שֶׁנִּקְרָא עָלֵֽינוּ.

בָּרוּךְ הוּא אֱלֹהֵֽינוּ שֶׁבְּרָאָֽנוּ לִכְבוֹדוֹ, לְהַלְּלוֹ וּלְשַׁבְּחוֹ וּלְסַפֵּר הוֹדוֹ, מִכָּל אֹם גָּבַר
עָלֵֽינוּ חַסְדּוֹ, לָכֵן בְּכָל לֵב וּבְכָל נֶֽפֶשׁ וּבְכָל מְאוֹדוֹ, נַמְלִיכוֹ וּנְיַחֲדוֹ.

BIUR TEFILLA • ביאור תפילה

בָּרוּךְ אֲדֹנָי יוֹם יוֹם – *Blessed be the Lord who, day by day.* This poem was written by Shimon HaGadol ben Yitzḥak of Magence in the tenth century, one of the earliest poets of Ashkenazic Jewry. His name can be found hidden in acrostic form beginning

May He to whom peace belongs, send us blessing and peace. From left and right, may Israel have peace. May the Compassionate One bless His people with peace, and may they merit to see children and children's children, occupied with Torah and the commandments, bringing Israel peace. Wondrous Counselor, mighty God, everlasting Father, Prince of peace. *Is. 9*

בָּרוּךְ אֵל עֶלְיוֹן Blessed is God Most High[B] who has given us rest, / To relieve our souls from distress and pain. / May He seek the good of Zion, the outcast city. / How long must she grieve, her spirits downcast?

All who keep the Sabbath, man and woman alike, find favor like an offering made to God.

He who rides the heavens, King of worlds, / Gently told His people to rest, / With tasty food and delicacies of all kinds, / With elegant dress, as at a family feast.

All who keep the Sabbath, man and woman alike, find favor like an offering made to God.

Happy are all who await a double reward / From the One who sees all, though He dwells in dense dark. / He will grant him a heritage in hill and valley, / A heritage and resting place like [Jacob] on whom the sun shone.

All who keep the Sabbath, man and woman alike, find favor like an offering made to God.

Whoever keeps the Sabbath fully, not profaning it, / Shows that he is worthy; holy is his lot. / Happy is he who fulfills the day's duty; / It is like a gift presented to God who fashioned him.

All who keep the Sabbath, man and woman alike, find favor like an offering made to God.

The Rock, my God, called it "Beloved of days." / Happy are the faithful if it is kept intact. / He will set on their head a close-fitting crown. / On them the Rock of Eternity will make His spirit rest.

All who keep the Sabbath, man and woman alike, find favor like an offering made to God.

He who remembers the Sabbath day to keep it holy / Will gain high honor like a diadem on his head. / Therefore let each give to his soul / Delight and joy with which to be exalted.

All who keep the Sabbath, man and woman alike, find favor like an offering made to God.

Let her be holy to you – Sabbath the queen – / Placing a blessing in your home. / In all your dwellings, do no work, / Nor your sons and daughters, your servant or maid.

All who keep the Sabbath, man and woman alike, find favor like an offering made to God.

---

exiled, the Divine Presence went with them…and when the day comes when they will be redeemed and return to the Land, the Divine Presence will return with them."

BIUR TEFILLA • ביאור תפילה

בָּרוּךְ אֵל עֶלְיוֹן – *Blessed is God Most High.* This poem was written by Rabbi Barukh ben Rabbi Shmuel of Mainz (Magence).The acrostic spells only his first name with the word chazak as in בָּרוּךְ חֲזַק."

שֶׁהַשָּׁלוֹם שֶׁלּוֹ יָשִׂים עָלֵינוּ בְּרָכָה וְשָׁלוֹם, מִשְּׂמֹאל וּמִיָּמִין עַל יִשְׂרָאֵל שָׁלוֹם, הָרַחֲמָן
הוּא יְבָרֵךְ אֶת עַמּוֹ בַשָּׁלוֹם, וְיִזְכּוּ לִרְאוֹת בָּנִים וּבְנֵי בָנִים, עוֹסְקִים, בַּתּוֹרָה וּבְמִצְוֹת,
עַל יִשְׂרָאֵל שָׁלוֹם. פֶּלֶא יוֹעֵץ אֵל גִּבּוֹר אֲבִי־עַד שַׂר־שָׁלוֹם: ישעיה ט

בָּרוּךְ אֵל עֶלְיוֹן,ב אֲשֶׁר נָתַן מְנוּחָה, לְנַפְשֵׁנוּ פִדְיוֹן מִשֵּׁאת וַאֲנָחָה
וְהוּא יִדְרֹשׁ לְצִיּוֹן, עִיר הַנִּדָּחָה, עַד אָנָה תּוּגְיוֹן נֶפֶשׁ נֶאֱנָחָה.
הַשּׁוֹמֵר שַׁבָּת הַבֵּן עִם הַבַּת, לָאֵל יֵרָצוּ כְּמִנְחָה עַל מַחֲבַת.

רוֹכֵב בָּעֲרָבוֹת, מֶלֶךְ עוֹלָמִים, אֶת עַמּוֹ לִשְׁבֹּת אִזֵּן בַּנְּעִימִים
בְּמַאֲכָלוֹת עֲרֵבוֹת בְּמִינֵי מַטְעַמִּים, בְּמַלְבּוּשֵׁי כָבוֹד זֶבַח מִשְׁפָּחָה.
הַשּׁוֹמֵר שַׁבָּת הַבֵּן עִם הַבַּת, לָאֵל יֵרָצוּ כְּמִנְחָה עַל מַחֲבַת.

וְאַשְׁרֵי כָּל חוֹכֶה לְתַשְׁלוּמֵי כֵפֶל, מֵאֵת כֹּל סוֹכֶה, שׁוֹכֵן בָּעֲרָפֶל
נַחֲלָה לוֹ יִזְכֶּה בָּהָר וּבַשָּׁפֶל, נַחֲלָה וּמְנוּחָה כַּשֶּׁמֶשׁ לוֹ זָרְחָה.
הַשּׁוֹמֵר שַׁבָּת הַבֵּן עִם הַבַּת, לָאֵל יֵרָצוּ כְּמִנְחָה עַל מַחֲבַת.

כָּל שׁוֹמֵר שַׁבָּת כַּדָּת מֵחַלְּלוֹ, הֵן הֶכְשַׁר חִבַּת קֹדֶשׁ גּוֹרָלוֹ
וְאִם יֵצֵא חוֹבַת הַיּוֹם, אַשְׁרֵי לוֹ, אֶל אֵל אָדוֹן מְחוֹלְלוֹ מִנְחָה הִיא שְׁלוּחָה.
הַשּׁוֹמֵר שַׁבָּת הַבֵּן עִם הַבַּת, לָאֵל יֵרָצוּ כְּמִנְחָה עַל מַחֲבַת.

חֶמְדַּת הַיָּמִים קְרָאוֹ אֵלִי צוּר, וְאַשְׁרֵי לִתְמִימִים אִם יִהְיֶה נָצוּר
כֶּתֶר הִלּוּמִים עַל רֹאשָׁם יָצוּר, צוּר הָעוֹלָמִים, רוּחוֹ בָּם נָחָה.
הַשּׁוֹמֵר שַׁבָּת הַבֵּן עִם הַבַּת, לָאֵל יֵרָצוּ כְּמִנְחָה עַל מַחֲבַת.

זָכוֹר אֶת יוֹם הַשַּׁבָּת לְקַדְּשׁוֹ, קַרְנוֹ כִּי גָבְהָה נֵזֶר עַל רֹאשׁוֹ
עַל כֵּן יִתֵּן הָאָדָם לְנַפְשׁוֹ, עֹנֶג וְגַם שִׂמְחָה בָּהֶם לְמָשְׁחָה.
הַשּׁוֹמֵר שַׁבָּת הַבֵּן עִם הַבַּת, לָאֵל יֵרָצוּ כְּמִנְחָה עַל מַחֲבַת.

קֹדֶשׁ הִיא לָכֶם שַׁבָּת הַמַּלְכָּה, אֶל תּוֹךְ בָּתֵּיכֶם לְהָנִיחַ בְּרָכָה
בְּכָל מוֹשְׁבוֹתֵיכֶם לֹא תַעֲשׂוּ מְלָאכָה, בְּנֵיכֶם וּבְנוֹתֵיכֶם עֶבֶד וְגַם שִׁפְחָה.
הַשּׁוֹמֵר שַׁבָּת הַבֵּן עִם הַבַּת, לָאֵל יֵרָצוּ כְּמִנְחָה עַל מַחֲבַת.

---

with us. As the Gemara relates (*Megilla* 29a) "R. Shimon bar Yoḥai said: 'See how beloved Israel is to the Holy One Blessed be He, for in every place where Israel was exiles that the Jewish people have endured over time. The key to our survival of those and any future exile lies in the knowledge that Hashem has always been

יוֹם זֶה מְכֻבָּד This day is honored[B] above all others,
For on it He who formed worlds found rest.

For six days, do your work
But the seventh day is God's:
On the Sabbath you shall do no work,
For in six days He made all.

This day is honored above all others,
for on it He who formed worlds found rest.

Foremost among sacred days[B]
Is this day of rest, this holy Sabbath.
So let each say Kiddush over wine,
And break bread over two complete loaves.[B]

This day is honored above all others,
for on it He who formed worlds found rest.

Eat choice food, drink sweet wine,
For God will give to those who cleave to Him
Clothes to wear, due portions of bread,
Meat and fish, and all tasty foods.

This day is honored above all others,
for on it He who formed worlds found rest.

רִאשׁוֹן הוּא לְמִקְרָאֵי קֹדֶשׁ... – *Foremost among sacred days…* This is a reference to the verses in *Vayikra* 23:2-3 in which the commandments given to observe each of the holidays is preceded with the command to rest on Shabbat. It is thus the first and foremost among the sacred days and so is also called "*Shabbat Shabbaton*" – the Sabbath of Sabbaths.

עַל שְׁתֵּי לֶחֶם יִבְצְעוּ תְמִימִים – *And break bread over two complete loaves.* The requirement is that the two loaves of bread over which one says the blessing of *HaMotzi* at the beginning of the meal must be whole rather than pre-sliced or cut (*Shulḥan Arukh* 274:1).

Alternatively, it has been suggested that the word "complete" refers not to the bread but to the person who breaks the bread and says kiddush, the person who is thereby whole.

Where else in the poem can you find the similar Hebrew word *tamim* (whole, complete, perfect)? What might be the connection?

יוֹם זֶה מְכֻבָּד ב מִכָּל יָמִים, כִּי בוֹ שָׁבַת צוּר עוֹלָמִים.

שֵׁשֶׁת יָמִים תַּעֲשֶׂה מְלַאכְתֶּךָ
וְיוֹם הַשְּׁבִיעִי לֵאלֹהֶיךָ
שַׁבָּת לֹא תַעֲשֶׂה בוֹ מְלָאכָה
כִּי כֹל עָשָׂה שֵׁשֶׁת יָמִים.

יוֹם זֶה מְכֻבָּד מִכָּל יָמִים, כִּי בוֹ שָׁבַת צוּר עוֹלָמִים.

רִאשׁוֹן הוּא לְמִקְרָאֵי קֹדֶשׁ ב
יוֹם שַׁבָּתוֹן יוֹם שַׁבַּת קֹדֶשׁ
עַל כֵּן כָּל אִישׁ בְּיֵינוֹ יְקַדֵּשׁ
עַל שְׁתֵּי לֶחֶם יִבְצְעוּ תְמִימִים. ב

יוֹם זֶה מְכֻבָּד מִכָּל יָמִים, כִּי בוֹ שָׁבַת צוּר עוֹלָמִים.

אֱכֹל מַשְׁמַנִּים, שְׁתֵה מַמְתַּקִּים
כִּי אֵל יִתֵּן לְכֹל בּוֹ דְבֵקִים
בֶּגֶד לִלְבֹּשׁ, לֶחֶם חֻקִּים
בָּשָׂר וְדָגִים וְכָל מַטְעַמִּים.

יוֹם זֶה מְכֻבָּד מִכָּל יָמִים, כִּי בוֹ שָׁבַת צוּר עוֹלָמִים.

BIUR TEFILLA • ביאור תפילה

יוֹם זֶה מְכֻבָּד – *This day is honored.* The composer is an anonymous person named Yisrael whose name appears in an acrostic in all of the stanzas but the last one which curiously also does not fit entirely with the themes of the previous ones.

The poem focuses on aspects of Shabbat which we are already familiar with from the songs of Friday evening: Hashem's rest on Shabbat, the mandate for us to observe not only the prohibitions against work but to sanctify the day with kiddush and *HaMotzi* (the blessing over bread) and by eating and drinking, and saying *Birkat HaMazon*. The day is thus "honored above all others" not alone by the actions of God, but through the meaning that we human beings bring to it.

On it you shall lack nothing – so eat,
Be satisfied and bless
The LORD your God, whom you love,
For He has blessed you from all peoples.

This day is honored above all others,
for on it He who formed worlds found rest.

The heavens declare His glory
And the earth is full of His loving-kindness.
See all these things His hand has made
For He is the Rock, His work is perfect.

This day is honored above all others,
for on it He who formed worlds found rest.

שַׁבָּת הַיּוֹם Today is the Sabbath of the LORD.
Celebrate greatly with my songs,
Multiply my delicacies,
Keep it like the LORD's command. Today is the Sabbath of the LORD.

Do not travel beyond boundaries,
Do not labor on this day:
Eat, drink, make merry.
This is the day the LORD has made. Today is the Sabbath of the LORD.

If you keep it God will guard you like the pupil of His eye,
You, your son and daughter too.
If you call the Sabbath a delight
Then you will find delight before the LORD.
Today is the Sabbath of the LORD.

Eat rich foods and delicacies, Tasty dishes of many kinds,
Soft-shelled nuts and pomegranates:
Eat, be satisfied and bless the LORD. Today is the Sabbath of the LORD.

Make ready on the table delicious bread,
And make, this day, three meals.
Bless and thank His glorious name.
Take care, observe and do, my sons. Today is the Sabbath of the LORD.

לֹא תֶחְסַר כֹּל בּוֹ, וְאָכַלְתָּ
וְשָׂבָעְתָּ וּבֵרַכְתָּ
אֶת יהוה אֱלֹהֶיךָ אֲשֶׁר אָהַבְתָּ
כִּי בֵרַכְךָ מִכָּל הָעַמִּים.
יוֹם זֶה מְכֻבָּד מִכָּל יָמִים, כִּי בוֹ שָׁבַת צוּר עוֹלָמִים.

הַשָּׁמַיִם מְסַפְּרִים כְּבוֹדוֹ
וְגַם הָאָרֶץ מָלְאָה חַסְדּוֹ
רְאוּ כָּל אֵלֶּה עָשְׂתָה יָדוֹ
כִּי הוּא הַצּוּר פָּעֳלוֹ תָמִים.
יוֹם זֶה מְכֻבָּד מִכָּל יָמִים, כִּי בוֹ שָׁבַת צוּר עוֹלָמִים.

שַׁבָּת הַיּוֹם לַיהוה, מְאֹד צַהֲלוּ בְּרִנּוּנַי
וְגַם הַרְבּוּ מַעֲדַנַּי, אוֹתוֹ לִשְׁמֹר כְּמִצְוַת יהוה.
שַׁבָּת הַיּוֹם לַיהוה.

מֵעֲבֹר דֶּרֶךְ וּגְבוּלִים, מֵעֲשׂוֹת הַיּוֹם פְּעָלִים
לֶאֱכֹל וְלִשְׁתּוֹת בְּהִלּוּלִים, זֶה הַיּוֹם עָשָׂה יהוה.
שַׁבָּת הַיּוֹם לַיהוה.

וְאִם תִּשְׁמְרֶנּוּ, יָהּ יִנְצָרְךָ כְּבָבַת, אַתָּה וּבִנְךָ וְגַם הַבַּת
וְקָרָאתָ עֹנֶג לַשַּׁבָּת, אָז תִּתְעַנַּג עַל יהוה.
שַׁבָּת הַיּוֹם לַיהוה.

אֱכֹל מַשְׁמַנִּים וּמַעֲדַנִּים, וּמַטְעַמִּים הַרְבֵּה מִינִים
אֱגוֹזֵי פֶרֶךְ וְרִמּוֹנִים, וְאָכַלְתָּ וְשָׂבָעְתָּ וּבֵרַכְתָּ אֶת יהוה.
שַׁבָּת הַיּוֹם לַיהוה.

לַעֲרֹךְ בְּשֻׁלְחָן לֶחֶם חֲמוּדוֹת, לַעֲשׂוֹת הַיּוֹם שָׁלֹשׁ סְעוּדוֹת
אֶת הַשֵּׁם הַנִּכְבָּד לְבָרֵךְ וּלְהוֹדוֹת, שִׁקְדוּ וְשִׁמְרוּ וַעֲשׂוּ בָנַי.
שַׁבָּת הַיּוֹם לַיהוה.

יוֹם שַׁבָּתוֹן The day of rest[B] should not be forgotten,
Its memory is like sweet fragrance,
On it the dove found rest, And in it the exhausted rest.

This day is honored by the people of faith.
Parents and children guard it with care.
It was engraved on two tablets of stone,
By the greatness of His power and His unfailing strength.
On it the dove found rest, And in it the exhausted rest.

All came together in a covenant:
"We will do and we will obey," they said as one.
Then they responded, saying, "The Lord is One" –
Blessed is He who gives the weary strength.
On it the dove found rest, And in it the exhausted rest.

He spoke in His holiness on the Mount of Myrrh [Sinai]:
"Remember and observe the seventh day."
And learn together all His commands:
Gird your loins and muster strength.
On it the dove found rest, And in it the exhausted rest.

The people who have wandered like a straying flock –
May He remember the covenant and the oath,
So that no harm should happen to them,
As You swore at the end of Noah's flood.
On it the dove found rest, And in it the exhausted rest.

Who exactly is the dove?

The Gemara (*Shabbat* 49a) points to the verse in *Tehillim* 68:14 "the wings of a dove are coated in silver" and concludes that just as the wings of a dove protect her, so too the mitzvot or commandments protect Israel. In that case, the dove might be the Jewish people who find protective rest in Shabbat.

Alternatively, the *Tikkunei Zohar* 6 22b says that while in exile the Divine Presence did not rest except on Shabbat and holy days, and so the dove is really God's Presence.

Alternatively, it is both man and God, as it were, who share their rest and the peace that comes with it.

יוֹם שַׁבָּתוֹן[ב] אֵין לִשְׁכֹּחַ, זִכְרוֹ כְּרֵיחַ הַנִּיחֹחַ
יוֹנָה מָצְאָה בוֹ מָנוֹחַ וְשָׁם יָנוּחוּ יְגִיעֵי כֹחַ.

הַיּוֹם נִכְבָּד לִבְנֵי אֱמוּנִים
זְהִירִים לְשָׁמְרוֹ אָבוֹת וּבָנִים
חָקוּק בִּשְׁנֵי לוּחוֹת אֲבָנִים
מֵרֹב אוֹנִים וְאַמִּיץ כֹּחַ. יוֹנָה מָצְאָה בוֹ מָנוֹחַ וְשָׁם יָנוּחוּ יְגִיעֵי כֹחַ.

וּבָאוּ כֻלָּם בִּבְרִית יַחַד
נַעֲשֶׂה וְנִשְׁמַע אָמְרוּ כְּאֶחָד
וּפָתְחוּ וְעָנוּ יהוה אֶחָד
בָּרוּךְ נֹתֵן לַיָּעֵף כֹּחַ. יוֹנָה מָצְאָה בוֹ מָנוֹחַ וְשָׁם יָנוּחוּ יְגִיעֵי כֹחַ.

דִּבֶּר בְּקָדְשׁוֹ בְּהַר הַמֹּר
יוֹם הַשְּׁבִיעִי זָכוֹר וְשָׁמוֹר
וְכָל פִּקּוּדָיו יַחַד לִגְמֹר
חַזֵּק מָתְנַיִם וְאַמֵּץ כֹּחַ. יוֹנָה מָצְאָה בוֹ מָנוֹחַ וְשָׁם יָנוּחוּ יְגִיעֵי כֹחַ.

הָעָם אֲשֶׁר נָע, כַּצֹּאן תָּעָה
יִזְכֹּר לְפָקְדוֹ בְּרִית וּשְׁבוּעָה
לְבַל יַעֲבָר בָּם מִקְרֵה רָעָה
כַּאֲשֶׁר נִשְׁבַּעְתָּ עַל מֵי נֹחַ. יוֹנָה מָצְאָה בוֹ מָנוֹחַ וְשָׁם יָנוּחוּ יְגִיעֵי כֹחַ.

BIUR TEFILLA • ביאור תפילה

יוֹם שַׁבָּתוֹן – *The day of rest*. The author was Rabbi Yehuda HaLevi (d. 1141), one of the foremost poets and philosophers in Jewish history.

The refrain speaks of a dove who found rest on Shabbat, just as can those who are exhausted. The image is most commonly connected to the story of Noaḥ who sent out a dove "on the seventh day" (*Bereshit* 8:12). The dove did not return and thus one can assume that it found a place on land to rest after the travails of the Flood.

שִׁמְרוּ שַׁבְּתוֹתַי Observe My Sabbaths,[B] so that you are nourished and sated,
From the radiance of My blessings,
when you come to rest. Borrow on My account, My children,
Delight in My pleasures: Today is the Sabbath of the Lord.

Borrow on My account, My children,
Delight in My pleasures: Today is the Sabbath of the Lord.

Proclaim freedom from toil, then I will grant My blessing,
joining one to the next,
bringing gladness on My day of joy. Wear clothes of fine linen and wool.
And learn from My elders: Today is the Sabbath of the Lord.

Borrow on My account, My children,
Delight in My pleasures: Today is the Sabbath of the Lord.

Quickly bring the portion, obey Esther's command.[I]
Make a reckoning with the Creator,
He will repay you for the food, and more. Trust in Me, My faithful ones,
And drink wine from My plentiful supply. Today is the Sabbath of the Lord.

Borrow on My account, My children,
Delight in My pleasures: Today is the Sabbath of the Lord.

Today is a day of redemption, if you observe the Sabbath;
Then you will be My special treasure.
Stay [for the night of exile], then pass on. Then you will live before Me.
And be filled from My hidden store. Today is the Sabbath of the Lord.

Borrow on My account, My children,
Delight in My pleasures: Today is the Sabbath of the Lord.

Make my city strong, God, the God most high.
Bring back my Temple,
With joy and words of song. There may my singers chant,
My Levites and my priests.
Then you will delight in the Lord. Today is the Sabbath of the Lord.

Borrow on My account, My children,
Delight in My pleasures: Today is the Sabbath of the Lord.

(*Etz Yosef*) (although the wording of the phrase here is a play on Esther 5:5). The reference to haste is found in the Gemara (*Shabbat* 117b) which encourages one to get up early to prepare for Shabbat as a way of honoring the day, as opposed to leaving everything for the last minute. Alternatively, it could be a reference to *Shabbat* 119a which encourages one not to put off eating the Shabbat meal, but to do so as soon as one can, as a way of honoring the day.

שִׁמְרוּ שַׁבְּתוֹתַי,ב לְמַעַן תִּינְקוּ וּשְׂבַעְתֶּם, מִזִּיו בִּרְכוֹתַי
אֶל הַמְּנוּחָה כִּי בָאתֶם, וּלְווּ עָלַי בָּנַי, וְעִדְנוּ מַעֲדָנַי שַׁבָּת הַיּוֹם לַיהוה.
וּלְווּ עָלַי בָּנַי, וְעִדְנוּ מַעֲדָנַי, שַׁבָּת הַיּוֹם לַיהוה.

לְעָמֵל קִרְאוּ דְרוֹר, וְנָתַתִּי אֶת בִּרְכָתִי, אִשָּׁה אֶל אֲחוֹתָהּ לִצְרוֹר
לְגַלּוֹת עַל יוֹם שִׂמְחָתִי, בִּגְדֵי שֵׁשׁ עִם שָׁנִי, וְהִתְבּוֹנְנוּ מִזְּקֵנַי
שַׁבָּת הַיּוֹם לַיהוה.
וּלְווּ עָלַי בָּנַי, וְעִדְנוּ מַעֲדָנַי, שַׁבָּת הַיּוֹם לַיהוה.

מַהֲרוּ אֶת הַמָּנֶה, לַעֲשׂוֹת אֶת דְּבַר אֶסְתֵּר,ע וְחִשְׁבוּ עִם הַקּוֹנֶה
לְשַׁלֵּם אָכוֹל וְהוֹתֵר, בִּטְחוּ בִי אֱמוּנַי, וּשְׁתוּ יֵין מִשְׁמַנַּי שַׁבָּת הַיּוֹם לַיהוה.
וּלְווּ עָלַי בָּנַי, וְעִדְנוּ מַעֲדָנַי, שַׁבָּת הַיּוֹם לַיהוה.

הִנֵּה יוֹם גְּאֻלָּה, יוֹם שַׁבָּת אִם תִּשְׁמֹרוּ, וִהְיִיתֶם לִי סְגֻלָּה
לִינוּ וְאַחַר תַּעֲבֹרוּ, וְאָז תִּחְיוּ לְפָנַי, וּתְמַלְּאוּ צְפוּנַי שַׁבָּת הַיּוֹם לַיהוה.
וּלְווּ עָלַי בָּנַי, וְעִדְנוּ מַעֲדָנַי, שַׁבָּת הַיּוֹם לַיהוה.

חַזֵּק קִרְיָתִי, אֵל אֱלֹהִים עֶלְיוֹן, וְהָשֵׁב אֶת נְוָתִי
בְּשִׂמְחָה וּבְהִגָּיוֹן, יְשׁוֹרְרוּ שָׁם רְנָנַי, לְוִיַּי וְכֹהֲנַי, אָז תִּתְעַנַּג עַל יהוה
שַׁבָּת הַיּוֹם לַיהוה.
וּלְווּ עָלַי בָּנַי, וְעִדְנוּ מַעֲדָנַי, שַׁבָּת הַיּוֹם לַיהוה.

BIUR TEFILLA • ביאור תפילה

שִׁמְרוּ שַׁבְּתוֹתַי – *Observe My Sabbaths.* Here Hashem calls on the Jewish people to keep the Shabbat, and promises that whatever expenditures they must incur He will repay them in kind. The theme comes from the Gemara (*Beitza* 15b) in which Hashem is quoted as saying "spend what you need to in order to sanctify the day" and then adds "believe in Me." Shabbat has always been a focal point of Jewish life, both in terms of the rhythms of our workweek, and the way that we spend our resources, putting our money as it were, where our values are. In return, as in so many of the other songs which are sung this day, there is the promise of redemption.

IYUN TEFILLA • עיון תפילה

מַהֲרוּ אֶת הַמָּנֶה, לַעֲשׂוֹת אֶת דְּבַר אֶסְתֵּר – *Quickly bring the portion, obey Esther's command.* The Shabbat is sometimes referred to in kabbalistic literature as Esther

כִּי אֶשְׁמְרָה If I keep the Sabbath, God will keep me,[I]
It is an eternal sign between God and me.
It is an eternal sign between God and me.

It is forbidden to engage in business or to travel,[H]
Even to speak about the things we need, or about matters of trade or state.
Instead I will study God's Torah and it will make me wise.[I]
It is an eternal sign between God and me.

On it I always find refreshment for my soul.
See: My Holy One gave the first generation,
A sign, by giving them a double portion on the sixth day.
So may my food be doubled every sixth day!
It is an eternal sign between God and me.

Engraved in God's law is His priests' decree,
To prepare the Show-Bread in His presence.
So, His sages ruled, on it fasting is forbidden, except on sins' Atonement Day.
It is an eternal sign between God and me.

It is a day of honor, a day of delight, with bread and fine wine, meat and fish. On it those who mourn are turned around,
For it is a joyous day and it will bring me joy.
It is an eternal sign between God and me.

Those who desecrate it by working will, in the end, be cut off.
Therefore I cleanse my heart with it as if with soap.[I]
Evening and morning I will pray to God,
Additional and afternoon prayer also, and He will answer me.
It is an eternal sign between God and me.

IYUN TEFILLA • עיון תפילה

אֶהְגֶּה בְּתוֹרַת אֵל וּתְחַכְּמֵנִי – *I will study God's Torah and it will make me wise.* Ibn Ezra, the author of this poem (his first name is formed by an acrostic), writes in his commentary on the Torah (*Shemot* 20:8) that on Shabbat one receives greater wisdom than one might have during the week (*Yalkut Lekaḥ Tov*). Surely being well rested and not having to be in so many other places can help focus one's concentration. No matter what your experience during the week, therefore, the Torah one learns on Shabbat feels different.

עַל כֵּן אֲכַבֵּס בּוֹ לִבִּי כְּבוֹרִית – *Therefore I cleanse my heart with it as if with soap.* Shabbat itself is like a bar of soap that has the potential to cleanse one's soul (Rabbi Meir of Permishlan).

כִּי אֶשְׁמְרָה שַׁבָּת אֵל יִשְׁמְרֵנִי. אוֹת הִיא לְעוֹלְמֵי עַד בֵּינוֹ וּבֵינִי.
אוֹת הִיא לְעוֹלְמֵי עַד בֵּינוֹ וּבֵינִי.

אָסוּר מְצֹא חֵפֶץ, עֲשׂוֹת דְּרָכִים, גַּם מִלְּדַבֵּר בּוֹ דִּבְרֵי צְרָכִים
דִּבְרֵי סְחוֹרָה אַף דִּבְרֵי מְלָכִים, אֶהְגֶּה בְּתוֹרַת אֵל וּתְחַכְּמֵנִי.
אוֹת הִיא לְעוֹלְמֵי עַד בֵּינוֹ וּבֵינִי.

בּוֹ אֶמְצָא תָמִיד נֹפֶשׁ לְנַפְשִׁי, הִנֵּה לְדוֹר רִאשׁוֹן נָתַן קְדוֹשִׁי
מוֹפֵת, בְּתֵת לֶחֶם מִשְׁנֶה בַּשִּׁשִּׁי, כָּכָה בְּכָל שִׁשִּׁי יַכְפִּיל מְזוֹנִי.
אוֹת הִיא לְעוֹלְמֵי עַד בֵּינוֹ וּבֵינִי.

רָשַׁם בְּדַת הָאֵל חֹק אֶל סְגָנָיו, בּוֹ לַעֲרֹךְ לֶחֶם פָּנִים בְּפָנָיו
עַל כֵּן לְהִתְעַנּוֹת בּוֹ עַל פִּי נְבוֹנָיו, אָסוּר, לְבַד מִיּוֹם כִּפּוּר עֲוֹנִי.
אוֹת הִיא לְעוֹלְמֵי עַד בֵּינוֹ וּבֵינִי.

הוּא יוֹם מְכֻבָּד, הוּא יוֹם תַּעֲנוּגִים, לֶחֶם וְיַיִן טוֹב, בָּשָׂר וְדָגִים
הַמִּתְאַבְּלִים בּוֹ אָחוֹר נְסוֹגִים, כִּי יוֹם שְׂמָחוֹת הוּא וּתְשַׂמְּחֵנִי.
אוֹת הִיא לְעוֹלְמֵי עַד בֵּינוֹ וּבֵינִי.

מֵחֵל מְלָאכָה בּוֹ סוֹפוֹ לְהַכְרִית, עַל כֵּן אֲכַבֵּס בּוֹ לִבִּי כְּבוֹרִית
וְאֶתְפַּלְלָה אֶל אֵל עַרְבִית וְשַׁחֲרִית, מוּסָף וְגַם מִנְחָה הוּא יַעֲנֵנִי.
אוֹת הִיא לְעוֹלְמֵי עַד בֵּינוֹ וּבֵינִי.

HILKHOT TEFILLA • הלכות תפילה

אָסוּר מְצֹא חֵפֶץ, עֲשׂוֹת דְּרָכִים – *It is forbidden to engage in business or to travel.* One is not permitted to travel beyond certain limits of one's town but neither is one permitted to travel somewhere within the permitted limits if it is to tend to one's possessions or the like (*Eiruvin 38b and Rashi* there).

IYUN TEFILLA • עיון תפילה

כִּי אֶשְׁמְרָה שַׁבָּת אֵל יִשְׁמְרֵנִי – *If I keep the Sabbath, God will keep me.* "Rabbi Yoḥanan said: 'whoever keeps the Shabbat according to its laws, even if he is an idolater, will be forgiven'" (*Shabbat* 118b).

דְּרוֹר יִקְרָא God proclaims freedom[B] to boy and girl,
And guards you like the pupil of His eye.
Your name is pleasant, never will it cease.
Rest and be at ease on the Sabbath day.

Seek my Temple and my hall,
And show me a sign of salvation.
Plant a shoot in my vineyard.[B]
Hear the cry of my people.

Tread the winepress in Botzra,
And in Babylon which overpowered.
Crush my foes in anger and wrath,
Hear my voice on the day I cry.

God, let there be on the desert mountain,
Myrtle, acacia, cypress and box tree.[B]
To one who warns and one who is warned,[B]
Let peace flow like river waters.

Crush those who rise against me, zealous God,
Melting their heart with grief.
Then we will open and fill our mouths,
And tongues with songs of joy to You.

Know what is wisdom for your soul,
And it will be a crown for your head.
Keep your Holy One's command,
Observe your holy Sabbath day.

Birkat HaMazon can be found on page 734.

---

is whole again. Similarly, there is expressed the hope of freedom from our enemies who would prevent us from fulfilling our national aspirations.

נְטַע שׂוֹרֵק בְּתוֹךְ כַּרְמִי – *Plant a shoot in my vineyard.* This is generally a reference to the Messiah.

הֲדַס שִׁטָּה בְּרוֹשׁ תִּדְהָר – *Myrtle, acacia, cypress and box tree.* May these trees provide shade for those who leave the desert of exile on their way to Israel.

וְלַמַּזְהִיר וְלַנִּזְהָר – *To one who warns and one who is warned.* One who warns others about the need to keep the Shabbat, and the one who heeds the warning himself.

דְּרוֹר יִקְרָא‎ב לְבֵן עִם בַּת, וְיִנְצָרְכֶם כְּמוֹ בָבַת
נְעִים שִׁמְכֶם וְלֹא יֻשְׁבַּת, שְׁבוּ נְוּחוּ בְּיוֹם שַׁבָּת

דְּרֹשׁ נָוִי וְאוּלַמִּי, וְאוֹת יֶשַׁע עֲשֵׂה עִמִּי
נְטַע שׂוֹרֵק בְּתוֹךְ כַּרְמִי,‎ב שְׁעֵה שַׁוְעַת בְּנֵי עַמִּי.

דְּרֹךְ פּוּרָה בְּתוֹךְ בָּצְרָה, וְגַם בָּבֶל אֲשֶׁר גָּבְרָה
נְתֹץ צָרַי בְּאַף עֶבְרָה, שְׁמַע קוֹלִי בְּיוֹם אֶקְרָא.

אֱלֹהִים תֵּן בְּמִדְבָּר הַר, הֲדַס שִׁטָּה בְּרוֹשׁ תִּדְהָר‎ב
וְלַמַּזְהִיר וְלַנִּזְהָר,‎ב שְׁלוֹמִים תֵּן כְּמֵי נָהָר.

הֲדֹךְ קָמַי, אֵל קַנָּא, בְּמוֹג לֵבָב וּבִמְגִנָּה
וְנַרְחִיב פֶּה וּנְמַלְּאֶנָּה, לְשׁוֹנֵנוּ לְךָ רִנָּה.

דְּעֶה חָכְמָה לְנַפְשֶׁךָ, וְהִיא כֶתֶר לְרֹאשֶׁךָ
נְצֹר מִצְוַת קְדוֹשֶׁךָ, שְׁמֹר שַׁבַּת קָדְשֶׁךָ.

ברכת המזון *can be found on page 735.*

BIUR TEFILLA • ביאור תפילה

דְּרוֹר יִקְרָא – *God proclaims freedom.* This could be one of the earliest liturgical poems written exclusively about Shabbat. The composer was Dunash ibn Librat, one of the pioneers of Jewish grammar and poetry, a student of Rav Saadia Gaon in the tenth century. The poem speaks to the spiritual freedom and redemption given to us by Hashem with the Shabbat. As a bride and bridegroom take care of one another, so too do the Jews preserve Shabbat, and Shabbat, in turn, protects us from our enemies, as Hashem protects us like the pupil of His eye.

The word "freedom" with which the poem opens goes on to have multiple meanings. It is taken from the law of the jubilee year when "freedom is declared throughout the Land" (*Vayikra* 25:10) when all slaves go free, when property returns to its owners and debts are canceled. Perhaps the allusion in the poem is to a world that

Minḥa for Shabbat

אַשְׁרֵי Happy[1] are those who dwell in Your House; Ps. 84
they shall continue to praise You, Selah!
Happy are the people for whom this is so; Ps. 144
happy are the people whose God is the LORD.

A song of praise by David. Ps. 145

א I will elevate You, my God, the King, and bless Your name for ever and all time. ב Every day I will bless You, and praise Your name for ever and all time. ג Great is the Lord and greatly to be praised; His greatness is unfathomable. ד One generation will praise Your works to the next, and tell of Your mighty deeds. ה On the glorious splendor of Your majesty I will meditate, and on the acts of Your wonders. ו They shall talk of the power of Your awesome deeds, and I will tell of Your greatness. ז They shall recite the record of Your great goodness, and sing with joy of Your righteousness. ח The Lord is generous and compassionate, slow to anger and great in loving-kindness. ט The Lord is good to all, and His compassion extends to all His works. י All Your works shall thank You, Lord, and Your devoted ones shall bless You. כ They shall talk of the glory of Your kingship, and speak of Your might. ל To make known to mankind His mighty deeds and the glorious majesty of His kingship. מ Your kingdom is an everlasting kingdom, and Your reign is for all generations. ס The Lord supports all who fall, and raises all who are bowed down. ע All raise their

---

out of a sense of frivolity, or sadness, or while carrying on trivial conversation, but rather with a sense of joy. Rashi explains that reminding us of the joy in our lives is exactly the purpose of *Ashrei* – "Hashem protects those who love Him," "Hashem will fulfill the desires of those who are in awe of Him." We are reminded that we are not alone, that we have much to be thankful for. Once we acknowledge that, we are ready to say the *Amida*. **What do you have to be thankful for this afternoon? Let *Ashrei* point the way.**

מנחה לשבת

תהלים פד — אַשְׁרֵי[ע] יוֹשְׁבֵי בֵיתֶךָ, עוֹד יְהַלְלְוּךָ סֶּלָה:
תהלים קמד — אַשְׁרֵי הָעָם שֶׁכָּכָה לּוֹ, אַשְׁרֵי הָעָם שֶׁיהוה אֱלֹהָיו:
תהלים קמה — תְּהִלָּה לְדָוִד

א אֲרוֹמִמְךָ אֱלוֹהַי הַמֶּלֶךְ, וַאֲבָרְכָה שִׁמְךָ לְעוֹלָם וָעֶד:
ב בְּכָל־יוֹם אֲבָרְכֶךָּ, וַאֲהַלְלָה שִׁמְךָ לְעוֹלָם וָעֶד:
ג גָּדוֹל יהוה וּמְהֻלָּל מְאֹד, וְלִגְדֻלָּתוֹ אֵין חֵקֶר:
ד דּוֹר לְדוֹר יְשַׁבַּח מַעֲשֶׂיךָ, וּגְבוּרֹתֶיךָ יַגִּידוּ:
ה הֲדַר כְּבוֹד הוֹדֶךָ, וְדִבְרֵי נִפְלְאֹתֶיךָ אָשִׂיחָה:
ו וֶעֱזוּז נוֹרְאֹתֶיךָ יֹאמֵרוּ, וּגְדוּלָּתְךָ אֲסַפְּרֶנָּה:
ז זֵכֶר רַב־טוּבְךָ יַבִּיעוּ, וְצִדְקָתְךָ יְרַנֵּנוּ:
ח חַנּוּן וְרַחוּם יהוה, אֶרֶךְ אַפַּיִם וּגְדָל־חָסֶד:
ט טוֹב־יהוה לַכֹּל, וְרַחֲמָיו עַל־כָּל־מַעֲשָׂיו:
י יוֹדוּךָ יהוה כָּל־מַעֲשֶׂיךָ, וַחֲסִידֶיךָ יְבָרְכוּכָה:
כ כְּבוֹד מַלְכוּתְךָ יֹאמֵרוּ, וּגְבוּרָתְךָ יְדַבֵּרוּ:
ל לְהוֹדִיעַ לִבְנֵי הָאָדָם גְּבוּרֹתָיו, וּכְבוֹד הֲדַר מַלְכוּתוֹ:
מ מַלְכוּתְךָ מַלְכוּת כָּל־עֹלָמִים, וּמֶמְשַׁלְתְּךָ בְּכָל־דּוֹר וָדֹר:
ס סוֹמֵךְ יהוה לְכָל־הַנֹּפְלִים, וְזוֹקֵף לְכָל־הַכְּפוּפִים:
ע עֵינֵי־כֹל אֵלֶיךָ יְשַׂבֵּרוּ, וְאַתָּה נוֹתֵן־לָהֶם אֶת־אָכְלָם בְּעִתּוֹ:

IYUN TEFILLA • עיון תפילה

אַשְׁרֵי – *Happy.* In some ways, *Ashrei* here serves the same function as all of *Pesukei DeZimra* did in *Shaḥarit*. It is a prelude to *Tefilla* (the *Shemoneh Esreh*), a way for us to get into the right mindset before our afternoon rendezvous with *HaKadosh Barukh Hu.*

What is that mindset? The Gemara (*Berakhot* 31a) explains that one should not pray

eyes to You in hope, and You give them their food in due season.
פ You open Your hand, and satisfy every living thing with favor.
צ The Lord is righteous in all His ways, and kind in all He does.
ק The Lord is close to all who call on Him, to all who call on Him
in truth. ר He fulfills the will of those who fear Him; He hears their
cry and saves them. ש The Lord guards all who love Him, but all
the wicked He will destroy. ת ▸ My mouth shall speak the praise
of the Lord, and all creatures shall bless His holy name for ever
and all time. We will bless the LORD now and for ever. Halleluya! Ps. 115

וּבָא לְצִיּוֹן גּוֹאֵל "A redeemer will come to Zion,[B] Is. 59
to those of Jacob who repent of their sins," declares the LORD.
"As for Me, this is My covenant with them,"[I] says the LORD.
"My spirit, that is on you,
and My words I have placed in your mouth
will not depart from your mouth,
or from the mouth of your children,
or from the mouth of their descendants from
this time on and for ever," says the LORD.

---

service was already long enough, especially for those who for health reasons could not put off getting to lunch (*Kol Bo*).

Regardless of the historical reasons, the overall emphasis seems to be on putting one's faith in God and in His Torah, an appropriate theme for the public reading of the Torah that we are about to perform, and for the *Amida* that we are about to recite.

IYUN TEFILLA • עיון תפילה

וַאֲנִי זֹאת בְּרִיתִי אוֹתָם – *As for Me, this is My covenant with them.* The words can literally be read "this is My covenant to them," as if to say that it is a one-sided affair rather than a two way street. The Ḥafetz Ḥayyim once remarked that this is because in some ways the covenant of living the life of a Jew was forced upon us, and cannot be erased no matter how we might try. This explains why in every generation there are Jews who come back to the fold, who assume a life of greater observance than their parents, for the covenant is something from which one cannot escape.

פ פּוֹתֵחַ אֶת־יָדֶךָ, וּמַשְׂבִּיעַ לְכָל־חַי רָצוֹן:
צ צַדִּיק יהוה בְּכָל־דְּרָכָיו, וְחָסִיד בְּכָל־מַעֲשָׂיו:
ק קָרוֹב יהוה לְכָל־קֹרְאָיו, לְכֹל אֲשֶׁר יִקְרָאֻהוּ בֶאֱמֶת:
ר רְצוֹן־יְרֵאָיו יַעֲשֶׂה, וְאֶת־שַׁוְעָתָם יִשְׁמַע, וְיוֹשִׁיעֵם:
ש שׁוֹמֵר יהוה אֶת־כָּל־אֹהֲבָיו, וְאֵת כָּל־הָרְשָׁעִים יַשְׁמִיד:
◂ ת תְּהִלַּת יהוה יְדַבֶּר פִּי, וִיבָרֵךְ כָּל־בָּשָׂר שֵׁם קָדְשׁוֹ לְעוֹלָם וָעֶד:
תהלים קטו
וַאֲנַחְנוּ נְבָרֵךְ יָהּ מֵעַתָּה וְעַד־עוֹלָם, הַלְלוּיָהּ:

ישעיה נט
וּבָא לְצִיּוֹן גּוֹאֵל,ב וּלְשָׁבֵי פֶשַׁע בְּיַעֲקֹב, נְאֻם יהוה:
וַאֲנִי זֹאת בְּרִיתִי אוֹתָם,ע אָמַר יהוה
רוּחִי אֲשֶׁר עָלֶיךָ וּדְבָרַי אֲשֶׁר־שַׂמְתִּי בְּפִיךָ
לֹא־יָמוּשׁוּ מִפִּיךָ וּמִפִּי זַרְעֲךָ וּמִפִּי זֶרַע זַרְעֲךָ
אָמַר יהוה, מֵעַתָּה וְעַד־עוֹלָם:

BIUR TEFILLA • ביאור תפילה

וּבָא לְצִיּוֹן גּוֹאֵל – *A redeemer will come to Zion.* Those who come to morning services every day during the week will recognize this prayer as one of the last that is said then. It contains a number of themes and elements: a version of the *Kedusha* that we have seen before in the morning's blessing before the *Shema* and in the repetition of the *Amida* although here it includes an Aramaic translation, verses about redemption, faithfulness, and trust in God, and a blessing thanking God for the Torah and the ability to fulfill the commandments.

While its appearance here in Shabbat afternoon *Minḥa* dates back at least to the times of the Geonim over a thousand years ago, the reason for its institution is not so clear. One theory suggests that Shabbat afternoon was a time when classes would be given and they would be concluded with verses about redemption and holiness of the kind contained in this prayer (Abudarham). Another theory suggests that it was in fact supposed to be said in the morning, just as on any other day, but it was pushed off until the afternoon because the morning

You are the Holy One, enthroned on the praises of Israel. *Ps. 22*
And [the angels] call to one another, saying, ◂ "Holy, holy, holy is the LORD of hosts; the whole world is filled with His glory."
And they receive permission from one another, saying: *Targum Yonatan Is. 6*
'Holy in the highest heavens, home of His Presence; holy on earth, the work of His strength; holy for ever and all time is the LORD of hosts; the whole earth is full of His radiant glory."

Then a wind lifted me up and I heard behind me the sound of a great noise, saying, ◂ "Blessed is the LORD's glory from His place." *Ezek. 3*
Then a wind lifted me up and I heard behind me the sound of a great tempest of those who uttered praise, saying, "Blessed is the LORD's glory from the place of the home of His Presence." *Targum Yonatan Ezek. 3*

The LORD shall reign for ever and all time. *Ex. 15*
The LORD's kingdom is established for ever and all time. *Targum Onkelos Ex. 15*

יהוה LORD, God of Abraham, Isaac and Yisrael, our ancestors, may You keep this for ever so that it forms the thoughts in Your people's heart, and directs their heart toward You. He is compassionate. He forgives iniquity and does not destroy. Repeatedly He suppresses His anger, not rousing His full wrath. For You, my LORD, are good and forgiving, abundantly kind to all who call on You. Your righteousness is eternally righteous, and Your Torah is truth. Grant truth to Jacob, loving-kindness to Abraham, as You promised our ancestors in ancient times. Blessed is my LORD for day after day He burdens us [with His blessings]; is our salvation, Selah! The LORD of hosts is with us; the God of Jacob is our refuge, Selah! LORD of hosts, happy is the one who trusts in You. LORD, save. May the King answer us on the day we call.

1 Chr. 29; Ps. 78; Ps. 86; Ps. 119; Micah 7; Ps. 68; Ps. 46; Ps. 84; Ps. 20

בָּרוּךְ Blessed is He, our God, who created us for His glory, separating us from those who go astray; who gave us the Torah of truth, planting within us eternal life. May He open our heart to His Torah, imbuing our heart with the love and awe of Him, that we may do His will and serve Him with a perfect heart, so that we neither toil in vain nor give birth to confusion.

תהלים כב / ישעיה ו
וְאַתָּה קָדוֹשׁ יוֹשֵׁב תְּהִלּוֹת יִשְׂרָאֵל: וְקָרָא זֶה אֶל־זֶה וְאָמַר ◂
קָדוֹשׁ, קָדוֹשׁ, קָדוֹשׁ, יהוה צְבָאוֹת, מְלֹא כָל־הָאָרֶץ כְּבוֹדוֹ:

תרגום יונתן ישעיה ו
וּמְקַבְּלִין דֵּין מִן דֵּין וְאָמְרִין, קַדִּישׁ בִּשְׁמֵי מְרוֹמָא עִלָּאָה בֵּית שְׁכִינְתֵהּ
קַדִּישׁ עַל אַרְעָא עוֹבַד גְּבוּרְתֵהּ, קַדִּישׁ לְעָלַם וּלְעָלְמֵי עָלְמַיָּא
יהוה צְבָאוֹת, מַלְיָא כָל אַרְעָא זִיו יְקָרֵהּ.

יחזקאל ג
וַתִּשָּׂאֵנִי רוּחַ, וָאֶשְׁמַע אַחֲרַי קוֹל רַעַשׁ גָּדוֹל ◂
בָּרוּךְ כְּבוֹד־יהוה מִמְּקוֹמוֹ:

תרגום יונתן יחזקאל ג
וּנְטָלַתְנִי רוּחָא, וּשְׁמָעִית בַּתְרַי קָל זִיעַ סַגִּיא, דִּמְשַׁבְּחִין וְאָמְרִין
בְּרִיךְ יְקָרָא דַיהוה מֵאֲתַר בֵּית שְׁכִינְתֵהּ.

שמות טו
יהוה יִמְלֹךְ לְעֹלָם וָעֶד:

תרגום אונקלוס שמות טו
יהוה מַלְכוּתֵהּ קָאֵם לְעָלַם וּלְעָלְמֵי עָלְמַיָּא.

דברי הימים א, כט
יהוה אֱלֹהֵי אַבְרָהָם יִצְחָק וְיִשְׂרָאֵל אֲבֹתֵינוּ, שָׁמְרָה־זֹּאת לְעוֹלָם
תהלים עח
לְיֵצֶר מַחְשְׁבוֹת לְבַב עַמֶּךָ, וְהָכֵן לְבָבָם אֵלֶיךָ: וְהוּא רַחוּם יְכַפֵּר
תהלים פו
עָוֹן וְלֹא־יַשְׁחִית, וְהִרְבָּה לְהָשִׁיב אַפּוֹ, וְלֹא־יָעִיר כָּל־חֲמָתוֹ: כִּי־
תהלים קיט
אַתָּה אֲדֹנָי טוֹב וְסַלָּח, וְרַב־חֶסֶד לְכָל־קֹרְאֶיךָ: צִדְקָתְךָ צֶדֶק
מיכה ז
לְעוֹלָם וְתוֹרָתְךָ אֱמֶת: תִּתֵּן אֱמֶת לְיַעֲקֹב, חֶסֶד לְאַבְרָהָם, אֲשֶׁר־
תהלים סח
נִשְׁבַּעְתָּ לַאֲבֹתֵינוּ מִימֵי קֶדֶם: בָּרוּךְ אֲדֹנָי יוֹם יוֹם יַעֲמָס־לָנוּ, הָאֵל
תהלים מו
יְשׁוּעָתֵנוּ סֶלָה: יהוה צְבָאוֹת עִמָּנוּ, מִשְׂגָּב לָנוּ אֱלֹהֵי יַעֲקֹב סֶלָה:
תהלים כ / תהלים פד
יהוה צְבָאוֹת, אַשְׁרֵי אָדָם בֹּטֵחַ בָּךְ: יהוה הוֹשִׁיעָה, הַמֶּלֶךְ יַעֲנֵנוּ
בְיוֹם־קָרְאֵנוּ:

בָּרוּךְ הוּא אֱלֹהֵינוּ שֶׁבְּרָאָנוּ לִכְבוֹדוֹ, וְהִבְדִּילָנוּ מִן הַתּוֹעִים, וְנָתַן לָנוּ תּוֹרַת אֱמֶת, וְחַיֵּי עוֹלָם נָטַע בְּתוֹכֵנוּ. הוּא יִפְתַּח לִבֵּנוּ בְּתוֹרָתוֹ, וְיָשֵׂם בְּלִבֵּנוּ אַהֲבָתוֹ וְיִרְאָתוֹ וְלַעֲשׂוֹת רְצוֹנוֹ וּלְעָבְדוֹ בְּלֵבָב שָׁלֵם, לְמַעַן לֹא נִיגַע לָרִיק וְלֹא נֵלֵד לַבֶּהָלָה.

יְהִי רָצוֹן May it be Your will, O Lord our God and God of our ancestors, that we keep Your laws in this world, and thus be worthy to live, see and inherit goodness and blessing in the Messianic Age and in
the life of the World to Come. So that my soul may sing to You and *Ps. 30*
not be silent. Lord, my God, for ever I will thank You. Blessed is *Jer. 17*
the man who trusts in the Lord, whose trust is in the Lord alone.
Trust in the Lord for evermore, for God, the Lord, is an everlasting *Is. 26*
Rock. ▸ Those who know Your name trust in You, for You, Lord, do *Ps. 9*
not forsake those who seek You. The Lord desired, for the sake of *Is. 42*
Israel's merit, to make the Torah great and glorious.

HALF KADDISH

Leader: יִתְגַּדַּל Magnified and sanctified
may His great name be,
in the world He created by His will.
May He establish His kingdom
in your lifetime and in your days,
and in the lifetime of all the house of Israel,
swiftly and soon –
and say: Amen.

All: May His great name be blessed
for ever and all time.

Leader: Blessed and praised,
glorified and exalted,
raised and honored,
uplifted and lauded
be the name of the Holy One,
blessed be He,
beyond any blessing,
song, praise and consolation
uttered in the world –
and say: Amen.

יְהִי רָצוֹן מִלְּפָנֶיךָ יהוה אֱלֹהֵינוּ וֵאלֹהֵי אֲבוֹתֵינוּ, שֶׁנִּשְׁמֹר חֻקֶּיךָ
בָּעוֹלָם הַזֶּה, וְנִזְכֶּה וְנִחְיֶה וְנִרְאֶה וְנִירַשׁ טוֹבָה וּבְרָכָה, לִשְׁנֵי
יְמוֹת הַמָּשִׁיחַ וּלְחַיֵּי הָעוֹלָם הַבָּא. לְמַעַן יְזַמֶּרְךָ כָבוֹד וְלֹא יִדֹּם, תהלים ל
יהוה אֱלֹהַי, לְעוֹלָם אוֹדֶךָּ: בָּרוּךְ הַגֶּבֶר אֲשֶׁר יִבְטַח בַּיהוה, וְהָיָה ירמיה יז
יהוה מִבְטַחוֹ: בִּטְחוּ בַיהוה עֲדֵי־עַד, כִּי בְּיָהּ יהוה צוּר עוֹלָמִים: ישעיה כו
› וְיִבְטְחוּ בְךָ יוֹדְעֵי שְׁמֶךָ, כִּי לֹא־עָזַבְתָּ דֹרְשֶׁיךָ, יהוה: יהוה חָפֵץ תהלים ט ישעיה מב
לְמַעַן צִדְקוֹ, יַגְדִּיל תּוֹרָה וְיַאְדִּיר:

חצי קדיש

ש״ץ: יִתְגַּדַּל וְיִתְקַדַּשׁ שְׁמֵהּ רַבָּא (קהל: אָמֵן)
בְּעָלְמָא דִּי בְרָא כִרְעוּתֵהּ
וְיַמְלִיךְ מַלְכוּתֵהּ
בְּחַיֵּיכוֹן וּבְיוֹמֵיכוֹן וּבְחַיֵּי דְכָל בֵּית יִשְׂרָאֵל
בַּעֲגָלָא וּבִזְמַן קָרִיב
וְאִמְרוּ אָמֵן. (קהל: אָמֵן)

קהל וש״ץ: יְהֵא שְׁמֵהּ רַבָּא מְבָרַךְ לְעָלַם וּלְעָלְמֵי עָלְמַיָּא.

ש״ץ: יִתְבָּרַךְ וְיִשְׁתַּבַּח וְיִתְפָּאַר וְיִתְרוֹמַם וְיִתְנַשֵּׂא
וְיִתְהַדָּר וְיִתְעַלֶּה וְיִתְהַלָּל
שְׁמֵהּ דְּקֻדְשָׁא בְּרִיךְ הוּא (קהל: בְּרִיךְ הוּא)
לְעֵלָּא מִן כָּל בִּרְכָתָא
/ בשבת שובה: לְעֵלָּא לְעֵלָּא מִכָּל בִּרְכָתָא/
וְשִׁירָתָא, תֻּשְׁבְּחָתָא וְנֶחֱמָתָא
דַּאֲמִירָן בְּעָלְמָא
וְאִמְרוּ אָמֵן. (קהל: אָמֵן)

REMOVING THE TORAH FROM THE ARK

וַאֲנִי As for me, may my prayer come to You,[1] LORD, at a time of favor. O God, in Your great love, answer me with Your faithful salvation. *Ps. 69*

The Ark is opened and the congregation stands. All say:

וַיְהִי בִּנְסֹעַ Whenever the Ark set out, Moses would say, *Num. 10*
"Arise, LORD, and may Your enemies be scattered.[B]
May those who hate You flee before You."
For the Torah shall come forth from Zion, *Is. 2*
and the word of the LORD from Jerusalem.
Blessed is He who in His Holiness
gave the Torah to His people Israel.

Blessed is the name of the Master of the Universe. Blessed is Your crown and Your place. May Your favor always be with Your people Israel. Show Your people the salvation of Your right hand in Your Temple. Grant us the gift of Your good light, and accept our prayers in mercy. May it be Your will to prolong our life in goodness. May I be counted among the righteous, so that You will have compassion on me and protect me and all that is mine and all that is Your people Israel's. You feed all; *Zohar, Vayak-hel*

---

at *Minha*, and on Mondays and Thursdays at *Shaharit* – so that we would not go for more than three days without being infused with the lifeblood of our existence that is Torah. And yet, we just finished reading the entire week's portion at the services this morning! Why do we need to read again? Perhaps the gesture is a symbolic one; that our commitment to Torah is never complete or finished. No sooner do we end one portion then we begin the next. On the holiday of Simhat Torah we complete the last portion in the book of *Devarim* and immediately begin all over again with *Bereshit*. In the Oral Law, the Talmud, every individual tractate begins with page number 2; there is no first page. For Torah learning is as continuous and essential to life as breathing.

For further commentary see pages 367–374.

BIUR TEFILLA • ביאור תפילה

וְיָפֻצוּ אֹיְבֶיךָ וְיָנֻסוּ מְשַׂנְאֶיךָ – *May Your enemies be scattered. May those who hate you flee before You.* What is the difference between enemies and those who hate you? Rashi explains that the latter are the people who hate the Jews, for whoever hates the Jews hates God. In contemporary terms this may mean that when looking for sources of anti-Semitism, one need not resort to theories about the Jews being strangers, about our successes, about our character traits and the like. Rather, the source of animosity against us is our religion.

What evidence can you find for this?

הוצאת ספר תורה

וַאֲנִי תְפִלָּתִי־לְךָ יהוה, עֵת רָצוֹן, אֱלֹהִים בְּרָב־חַסְדֶּךָ תהלים סט
עֲנֵנִי בֶּאֱמֶת יִשְׁעֶךָ:

The ארון קודש *is opened and the* קהל *stands. All say:*

וַיְהִי בִּנְסֹעַ הָאָרֹן וַיֹּאמֶר מֹשֶׁה במדבר י
קוּמָה יהוה וְיָפֻצוּ אֹיְבֶיךָ וְיָנֻסוּ מְשַׂנְאֶיךָ מִפָּנֶיךָ:
כִּי מִצִּיּוֹן תֵּצֵא תוֹרָה וּדְבַר־יהוה מִירוּשָׁלָםִ: ישעיה ב
בָּרוּךְ שֶׁנָּתַן תּוֹרָה לְעַמּוֹ יִשְׂרָאֵל בִּקְדֻשָּׁתוֹ.

בְּרִיךְ שְׁמֵהּ דְּמָרֵא עָלְמָא, בְּרִיךְ כִּתְרָךְ וְאַתְרָךְ. יְהֵא רְעוּתָךְ עִם עַמָּךְ יִשְׂרָאֵל לְעָלַם, וּפֻרְקַן יְמִינָךְ אַחֲזֵי לְעַמָּךְ בְּבֵית מַקְדְּשָׁךְ, וּלְאַמְטוּיֵי לַנָא מִטּוּב נְהוֹרָךְ, וּלְקַבֵּל צְלוֹתַנָא בְּרַחֲמִין. יְהֵא רַעֲוָא קֳדָמָךְ דְּתוֹרִיךְ לַן חַיִּין בְּטִיבוּ, וְלֶהֱוֵי אֲנָא פְקִידָא בְּגוֹ צַדִּיקַיָּא, לְמִרְחַם עָלַי וּלְמִנְטַר יָתִי וְיַת כָּל דִּי לִי וְדִי לְעַמָּךְ יִשְׂרָאֵל. זוהר ויקהל

IYUN TEFILLA • עיון תפילה

וַאֲנִי תְפִלָּתִי־לְךָ – *As for me, may my prayer come to You.* In its original context (*Tehillim* 69:14) this verse is immediately preceded by one which says "I am the taunt of drunkards." The Midrash homiletically suggests that the connection is that in other cultures there may be a custom to drink and revel to excess on a day of celebration, but in Judaism pleasure is tempered by reminding ourselves that it is for the sake of Heaven, and that our physical enjoyment should be an outgrowth of our spirituality (Abudarham). On a day that we have spent in no small measure feasting and relaxing, if we have spent too much of today focused on our own physicality and not enough on our need for spirituality, then this statement provides us with an opportunity to begin to restore the balance.

Yet another rationale is that the verse's reference to "a time of favor" is an apt description of *Minḥa* which was described as such by Eliyahu the prophet atop Mount Carmel (*Melakhim I* 18:36), and is taken here to be particularly associated with the notion of the ultimate redemption, a theme that we will soon focus on in our *Amida* (*Shibbolei HaLeket, Berakhot* 6b).

INTRODUCTION TO KERIAT HATORAH

Tradition has it that the prophet Ezra established the public reading of the first ten verses of the following shabbat's portion of the Torah on a regular basis – on Shabbat

You sustain all; You rule over all; You rule over kings, for sovereignty is Yours. I am a servant of the Holy One, blessed be He, before whom and before whose glorious Torah I bow at all times. Not in man do I trust, nor on any angel do I rely, but on the God of heaven who is the God of truth, whose Torah is truth, whose prophets speak truth, and who abounds in acts of love and truth. ▸ In Him I trust, and to His holy and glorious name I offer praises. May it be Your will to open my heart to the Torah, and to fulfill the wishes of my heart and of the hearts of all Your people Israel for good, for life, and for peace.

The Leader takes the Torah scroll in his right arm, bows toward the Ark and says:

Magnify the LORD with me,
and let us exalt His name together. *Ps. 34*

The Ark is closed. The Leader carries the Torah scroll to the bima and the congregation says:

לְךָ Yours, LORD, are the greatness and the power, the glory and the majesty and splendor, for everything in heaven and earth is Yours. Yours, LORD, is the kingdom; You are exalted as Head over all. *1 Chr. 29*

רוֹמְמוּ Exalt the LORD our God and bow to His footstool; He is holy. Exalt the LORD our God, and bow at His holy mountain, for holy is the LORD our God. *Ps. 99*

אַב הָרַחֲמִים May the Father of compassion have compassion on the people borne by Him. May He remember the covenant with the mighty [patriarchs], and deliver us from evil times. May He reproach the evil instinct in the people carried by Him, and graciously grant that we be an everlasting remnant. May He fulfill in good measure our requests for salvation and compassion.

The Torah scroll is placed on the bima and the Gabbai calls a Kohen to the Torah.

וְתִגָּלֶה May His kingship over us be soon revealed and made manifest. May He be gracious to our surviving remnant, the remnant of His people the house of Israel in grace, loving-kindness, compassion and favor, and let us say: Amen. Let us all render greatness to our God and give honor to the Torah. *Let the Kohen come forward. Arise (*name* son of *father's name*), the Kohen.

**If no Kohen is present, a Levi or Yisrael is called up as follows:*

/As there is no Kohen, arise (*name* son of *father's name*) in place of a Kohen./

Blessed is He who, in His holiness, gave the Torah to His people Israel.

The congregation followed by the Gabbai:

You who cling to the LORD your God are all alive today. *Deut. 4*

אַנְתְּ הוּא זָן לְכְלָּא וּמְפַרְנֵס לְכְלָּא, אַנְתְּ הוּא שַׁלִּיט עַל כְּלָּא, אַנְתְּ הוּא דְּשַׁלִּיט עַל מַלְכַיָּא, וּמַלְכוּתָא דִּילָךְ הִיא. אֲנָא עַבְדָּא דְקֻדְשָׁא בְּרִיךְ הוּא, דְּסָגֵדְנָא קַמֵּהּ וּמִקַּמֵּי דִּיקַר אוֹרַיְתֵהּ בְּכָל עִדָּן וְעִדָּן. לָא עַל אֱנָשׁ רָחִיצְנָא וְלָא עַל בַּר אֱלָהִין סָמִיכְנָא, אֶלָּא בֶּאֱלָהָא דִשְׁמַיָּא, דְּהוּא אֱלָהָא קְשׁוֹט, וְאוֹרַיְתֵהּ קְשׁוֹט, וּנְבִיאוֹהִי קְשׁוֹט, וּמַסְגֵּא לְמֶעְבַּד טַבְוָן וּקְשׁוֹט. ‹ בֵּהּ אֲנָא רָחִיץ, וְלִשְׁמֵהּ קַדִּישָׁא יַקִּירָא אֲנָא אֵמַר תֻּשְׁבְּחָן. יְהֵא רַעֲוָא קֳדָמָךְ דְּתִפְתַּח לִבַּאי בְּאוֹרַיְתָא, וְתַשְׁלִים מִשְׁאֲלִין דְּלִבַּאי וְלִבָּא דְכָל עַמָּךְ יִשְׂרָאֵל לְטָב וּלְחַיִּין וְלִשְׁלָם.

The שליח ציבור *takes the* ספר תורה *in his right arm, bows toward the* ארון קודש *and says:*

תהלים לד גַּדְּלוּ לַיהוה אִתִּי וּנְרוֹמְמָה שְׁמוֹ יַחְדָּו:

The ארון קודש *is closed. The* שליח ציבור *carries the* ספר תורה *to the* בימה *and the* קהל *says:*

דברי הימים א׳ כט לְךָ יהוה הַגְּדֻלָּה וְהַגְּבוּרָה וְהַתִּפְאֶרֶת וְהַנֵּצַח וְהַהוֹד, כִּי־כֹל בַּשָּׁמַיִם וּבָאָרֶץ: לְךָ יהוה הַמַּמְלָכָה וְהַמִּתְנַשֵּׂא לְכֹל לְרֹאשׁ:

תהלים צט רוֹמְמוּ יהוה אֱלֹהֵינוּ וְהִשְׁתַּחֲווּ לַהֲדֹם רַגְלָיו, קָדוֹשׁ הוּא: רוֹמְמוּ יהוה אֱלֹהֵינוּ וְהִשְׁתַּחֲווּ לְהַר קָדְשׁוֹ, כִּי־קָדוֹשׁ יהוה אֱלֹהֵינוּ:

אַב הָרַחֲמִים הוּא יְרַחֵם עַם עֲמוּסִים, וְיִזְכֹּר בְּרִית אֵיתָנִים, וְיַצִּיל נַפְשׁוֹתֵינוּ מִן הַשָּׁעוֹת הָרָעוֹת, וְיִגְעַר בְּיֵצֶר הָרָע מִן הַנְּשׂוּאִים, וְיָחֹן אוֹתָנוּ לִפְלֵיטַת עוֹלָמִים, וִימַלֵּא מִשְׁאֲלוֹתֵינוּ בְּמִדָּה טוֹבָה יְשׁוּעָה וְרַחֲמִים.

The ספר תורה *is placed on the* שולחן *and the* גבאי *calls a* כהן *to the* תורה.

וְתִגָּלֶה וְתֵרָאֶה מַלְכוּתוֹ עָלֵינוּ בִּזְמַן קָרוֹב, וְיָחֹן פְּלֵיטָתֵנוּ וּפְלֵיטַת עַמּוֹ בֵּית יִשְׂרָאֵל לְחֵן וּלְחֶסֶד וּלְרַחֲמִים וּלְרָצוֹן וְנֹאמַר אָמֵן. הַכֹּל הָבוּ גֹדֶל לֵאלֹהֵינוּ וּתְנוּ כָבוֹד לַתּוֹרָה. *כֹּהֵן קְרַב, יַעֲמֹד (פלוני בֶּן פלוני) הַכֹּהֵן.

**If no* כהן *is present, a* לוי *or* ישראל *is called up as follows:*

/אֵין כָּאן כֹּהֵן, יַעֲמֹד (פלוני בֶּן פלוני) בִּמְקוֹם כֹּהֵן./

בָּרוּךְ שֶׁנָּתַן תּוֹרָה לְעַמּוֹ יִשְׂרָאֵל בִּקְדֻשָּׁתוֹ.

The קהל *followed by the* גבאי*:*

דברים ד וְאַתֶּם הַדְּבֵקִים בַּיהוה אֱלֹהֵיכֶם חַיִּים כֻּלְּכֶם הַיּוֹם:

*The appropriate Torah portion is read (**pages 778–826**).*

The Reader shows the oleh the section to be read. The oleh touches the scroll at that place with the tzitzit of his tallit or the fabric belt of the Torah scroll, which he then kisses. Holding the handles of the scroll, he says:

Oleh: Bless the LORD, the blessed One.

Cong: Bless the LORD, the blessed One,
for ever and all time.

Oleh: Bless the LORD, the blessed One,
for ever and all time.
Blessed are You, LORD our God, King of the Universe,
who has chosen us from all peoples
and has given us His Torah.
Blessed are You, LORD, Giver of the Torah.

After the reading, the oleh says:

Oleh: Blessed are You, LORD our God, King of the Universe,
who has given us the Torah of truth,
planting everlasting life in our midst.
Blessed are You, LORD, Giver of the Torah.

The Torah scroll is lifted and the congregation says:

וְזֹאת הַתּוֹרָה This is the Torah that *Deut. 4*
Moses placed before the children of Israel,
at the LORD's commandment, by the hand of Moses. *Num. 9*

Some add: It is a tree of life to those who grasp it, and those who uphold it are happy. *Prov. 3*
Its ways are ways of pleasantness, and all its paths are peace.
Long life is in its right hand; in its left, riches and honor.
It pleased the LORD for the sake of [Israel's] righteousness, *Is. 42*
to make the Torah great and glorious.

The Torah scroll is bound and covered.

IYUN TEFILLA • עיון תפילה

נוֹתֵן הַתּוֹרָה – *Giver of the Torah.* Both blessings emphasize Hashem as the Giver of the Torah. Surely that is significant only if you are prepared to be a recipient. Prepare to receive the Torah again.

The appropriate תורה *portion is read (pages 778–826).*

The קורא *shows the* עולה *the section to be read.*
The עולה *touches the scroll at that place with the* ציצית
of his טלית *or the gartel of the* ספר תורה*, which he then kisses.*
Holding the handles of the scroll, he says:

עולה: **בָּרְכוּ אֶת יהוה הַמְבֹרָךְ.**

קהל: **בָּרוּךְ יהוה הַמְבֹרָךְ לְעוֹלָם וָעֶד.**

עולה: **בָּרוּךְ יהוה הַמְבֹרָךְ לְעוֹלָם וָעֶד.**

בָּרוּךְ אַתָּה יהוה, אֱלֹהֵינוּ מֶלֶךְ הָעוֹלָם
אֲשֶׁר בָּחַר בָּנוּ מִכָּל הָעַמִּים
וְנָתַן לָנוּ אֶת תּוֹרָתוֹ.
בָּרוּךְ אַתָּה יהוה, נוֹתֵן הַתּוֹרָה.

After the קריאת התורה*, the* עולה *says:*

עולה: **בָּרוּךְ אַתָּה יהוה אֱלֹהֵינוּ מֶלֶךְ הָעוֹלָם**
אֲשֶׁר נָתַן לָנוּ תּוֹרַת אֱמֶת
וְחַיֵּי עוֹלָם נָטַע בְּתוֹכֵנוּ.
בָּרוּךְ אַתָּה יהוה, נוֹתֵן הַתּוֹרָה.

The ספר תורה *is lifted and the* קהל *says:*

וְזֹאת הַתּוֹרָה אֲשֶׁר־שָׂם מֹשֶׁה לִפְנֵי בְּנֵי יִשְׂרָאֵל: דברים ד
עַל־פִּי יהוה בְּיַד מֹשֶׁה: במדבר ט

Some add עֵץ־חַיִּים הִיא לַמַּחֲזִיקִים בָּהּ וְתֹמְכֶיהָ מְאֻשָּׁר: משלי ג
דְּרָכֶיהָ דַרְכֵי־נֹעַם וְכָל־נְתִיבוֹתֶיהָ שָׁלוֹם:
אֹרֶךְ יָמִים בִּימִינָהּ, בִּשְׂמֹאולָהּ עֹשֶׁר וְכָבוֹד:
יהוה חָפֵץ לְמַעַן צִדְקוֹ יַגְדִּיל תּוֹרָה וְיַאְדִּיר: ישעיה מב

The ספר תורה *is bound and covered.*

The Ark is opened. The Leader takes the Torah scroll and says:

יְהַלְלוּ Let them praise the name of the Lord, *Ps. 148*
for His name alone is sublime.

The congregation responds:

הוֹדוֹ His majesty is above earth and heaven.
He has raised the horn of His people,
for the glory of all His devoted ones,
the children of Israel, the people close to Him. Halleluya!

As the Torah scroll is returned to the Ark say:

לְדָוִד מִזְמוֹר A psalm of David. The earth is the Lord's and all it contains, *Ps. 24* the world and all who live in it. For He founded it on the seas and established it on the streams. Who may climb the mountain of the Lord? Who may stand in His holy place? He who has clean hands and a pure heart, who has not taken My name in vain, or sworn deceitfully. He shall receive blessing from the Lord, and just reward from God, his salvation. This is a generation of those who seek Him, the descendants of Jacob who seek Your presence, Selah! Lift up your heads, O gates; be uplifted, eternal doors, so that the King of glory may enter. Who is the King of glory? It is the Lord, strong and mighty, the Lord mighty in battle. Lift up your heads, O gates; lift them up, eternal doors, so that the King of glory may enter. Who is He, the King of glory? The Lord of hosts, He is the King of glory, Selah!

As the Torah scroll is placed into the Ark, say:

וּבְנֻחֹה יֹאמַר When the Ark came to rest, Moses would say: "Return, *Num. 10* O Lord, to the myriad thousands of Israel." Advance, Lord, to Your *Ps. 132* resting place, You and Your mighty Ark. Your priests are clothed in righteousness, and Your devoted ones sing in joy. For the sake of Your servant David, do not reject Your anointed one. For I give you good *Prov. 4* instruction; do not forsake My Torah. It is a tree of life to those who *Prov. 3* grasp it, and those who uphold it are happy. Its ways are ways of pleasantness, and all its paths are peace. ▸ Turn us back, O Lord, to You, and *Lam. 5* we will return. Renew our days as of old.

The Ark is closed.

The ארון קודש *is opened. The* שליח ציבור *takes the* ספר תורה *and says:*

תהלים קמח
יְהַלְלוּ אֶת־שֵׁם יהוה, כִּי־נִשְׂגָּב שְׁמוֹ, לְבַדּוֹ

The קהל *responds:*

הוֹדוֹ עַל־אֶרֶץ וְשָׁמָיִם:
וַיָּרֶם קֶרֶן לְעַמּוֹ, תְּהִלָּה לְכָל־חֲסִידָיו
לִבְנֵי יִשְׂרָאֵל עַם קְרֹבוֹ, הַלְלוּיָהּ:

As the ספר תורה *is returned to the* ארון קודש*, say:*

תהלים כד
לְדָוִד מִזְמוֹר, לַיהוה הָאָרֶץ וּמְלוֹאָהּ, תֵּבֵל וְיֹשְׁבֵי בָהּ: כִּי־הוּא עַל־
יַמִּים יְסָדָהּ, וְעַל־נְהָרוֹת יְכוֹנְנֶהָ: מִי־יַעֲלֶה בְהַר־יהוה, וּמִי־יָקוּם
בִּמְקוֹם קָדְשׁוֹ: נְקִי כַפַּיִם וּבַר־לֵבָב, אֲשֶׁר לֹא־נָשָׂא לַשָּׁוְא נַפְשִׁי
וְלֹא נִשְׁבַּע לְמִרְמָה: יִשָּׂא בְרָכָה מֵאֵת יהוה, וּצְדָקָה מֵאֱלֹהֵי יִשְׁעוֹ:
זֶה דּוֹר דֹּרְשָׁו, מְבַקְשֵׁי פָנֶיךָ, יַעֲקֹב, סֶלָה: שְׂאוּ שְׁעָרִים רָאשֵׁיכֶם,
וְהִנָּשְׂאוּ פִּתְחֵי עוֹלָם, וְיָבוֹא מֶלֶךְ הַכָּבוֹד: מִי זֶה מֶלֶךְ הַכָּבוֹד,
יהוה עִזּוּז וְגִבּוֹר, יהוה גִּבּוֹר מִלְחָמָה: שְׂאוּ שְׁעָרִים רָאשֵׁיכֶם,
וּשְׂאוּ פִּתְחֵי עוֹלָם, וְיָבֹא מֶלֶךְ הַכָּבוֹד: מִי הוּא זֶה מֶלֶךְ הַכָּבוֹד,
יהוה צְבָאוֹת הוּא מֶלֶךְ הַכָּבוֹד, סֶלָה:

As the ספר תורה *is placed into the* ארון קודש*, say:*

במדבר י
וּבְנֻחֹה יֹאמַר, שׁוּבָה יהוה רִבְבוֹת אַלְפֵי יִשְׂרָאֵל: קוּמָה יהוה
תהלים קלב
לִמְנוּחָתֶךָ, אַתָּה וַאֲרוֹן עֻזֶּךָ: כֹּהֲנֶיךָ יִלְבְּשׁוּ־צֶדֶק, וַחֲסִידֶיךָ יְרַנֵּנוּ:
משלי ד
בַּעֲבוּר דָּוִד עַבְדֶּךָ אַל־תָּשֵׁב פְּנֵי מְשִׁיחֶךָ: כִּי לֶקַח טוֹב נָתַתִּי
משלי ג
לָכֶם, תּוֹרָתִי אַל־תַּעֲזֹבוּ: עֵץ־חַיִּים הִיא לַמַּחֲזִיקִים בָּהּ, וְתֹמְכֶיהָ
איכה ה
מְאֻשָּׁר: דְּרָכֶיהָ דַרְכֵי־נֹעַם וְכָל־נְתִיבֹתֶיהָ שָׁלוֹם: ◂ הֲשִׁיבֵנוּ יהוה
אֵלֶיךָ וְנָשׁוּבָה, חַדֵּשׁ יָמֵינוּ כְּקֶדֶם:

The ארון קודש *is closed.*

HALF KADDISH

Leader: יִתְגַּדַּל Magnified and sanctified may His great name be,
in the world He created by His will.
May He establish His kingdom
in your lifetime and in your days,
and in the lifetime of all the house of Israel,
swiftly and soon – and say: Amen.

All: May His great name[A] be blessed for ever and all time.

Leader: Blessed and praised, glorified and exalted,
raised and honored, uplifted and lauded
be the name of the Holy One, blessed be He,
beyond any blessing, song, praise and consolation
uttered in the world – and say: Amen.

THE AMIDA

The following prayer, until "in former years" on page 528, is said silently, standing with feet together. If there is a minyan, the Amida is repeated aloud by the Leader. Take three steps forward.

When I proclaim the LORD's name, give glory to our God. *Deut. 32*
O LORD, open my lips, so that my mouth may declare Your praise. *Ps. 51*

PATRIARCHS

▾*Bend the knees:* Blessed *Bow:* are You, *Stand straight:* LORD
our God and God of our fathers,[I]
God of Abraham, God of Isaac and God of Jacob;
the great, mighty and awesome God, God Most High,
who bestows acts of loving-kindness and creates all,

IYUN TEFILLA • עיון תפילה

For an overview of the Amida prayer in general, see page 100 . For a discussion of the first and last blessings including more commentary see page 333.

אֱלֹהֵינוּ וֵאלֹהֵי אֲבוֹתֵינוּ – *Our God and God of our fathers.* Did you ever have difficulty relating to the existence of God? Some people find strength in recalling that Hashem has had a historical relationship with the Jewish people going all the way back to the Avot, that is, with our Forefathers, and with our fathers.

What event or phenomenon in Jewish history gives you reason to believe?

חצי קדיש

ש״ץ: יִתְגַּדַּל וְיִתְקַדַּשׁ שְׁמֵהּ רַבָּא (קהל: אָמֵן)
בְּעָלְמָא דִּי בְרָא כִרְעוּתֵהּ וְיַמְלִיךְ מַלְכוּתֵהּ
בְּחַיֵּיכוֹן וּבְיוֹמֵיכוֹן, וּבְחַיֵּי דְכָל בֵּית יִשְׂרָאֵל
בַּעֲגָלָא וּבִזְמַן קָרִיב, וְאִמְרוּ אָמֵן. (קהל: אָמֵן)

קהל וש״ץ: יְהֵא שְׁמֵהּ רַבָּא[א] מְבָרַךְ לְעָלַם וּלְעָלְמֵי עָלְמַיָּא.

ש״ץ: יִתְבָּרַךְ וְיִשְׁתַּבַּח וְיִתְפָּאַר וְיִתְרוֹמַם וְיִתְנַשֵּׂא
וְיִתְהַדָּר וְיִתְעַלֶּה וְיִתְהַלָּל שְׁמֵהּ דְּקֻדְשָׁא בְּרִיךְ הוּא (קהל: בְּרִיךְ הוּא)
לְעֵלָּא מִן כָּל בִּרְכָתָא / בשבת שובה: לְעֵלָּא לְעֵלָּא מִכָּל בִּרְכָתָא/
וְשִׁירָתָא, תֻּשְׁבְּחָתָא וְנֶחֱמָתָא
דַּאֲמִירָן בְּעָלְמָא, וְאִמְרוּ אָמֵן. (קהל: אָמֵן)

עמידה

The following prayer, until קַדְמֹנִיּוֹת *on page 529, is said silently, standing with feet together. If there is a* מנין, *the* עמידה *is repeated aloud by the* שליח ציבור.

Take three steps forward.

דברים לב כִּי שֵׁם יהוה אֶקְרָא, הָבוּ גֹדֶל לֵאלֹהֵינוּ:
תהלים נא אֲדֹנָי, שְׂפָתַי תִּפְתָּח, וּפִי יַגִּיד תְּהִלָּתֶךָ:

אבות

Bend the knees בָּרוּךְ *Bow* אַתָּה *Stand straight* יהוה
אֱלֹהֵינוּ וֵאלֹהֵי אֲבוֹתֵינוּ[ע]
אֱלֹהֵי אַבְרָהָם, אֱלֹהֵי יִצְחָק, וֵאלֹהֵי יַעֲקֹב
הָאֵל הַגָּדוֹל הַגִּבּוֹר וְהַנּוֹרָא, אֵל עֶלְיוֹן
גּוֹמֵל חֲסָדִים טוֹבִים, וְקוֹנֵה הַכֹּל

ANI TEFILLA • אני תפילה

יְהֵא שְׁמֵהּ רַבָּא – *May His great name. Whoever says "yeheh shemeh raba..." with all his strength, the Heavenly Court rips up any negative decree against him (Shabbat* 119b). "With all his strength" – with all of His strength, for through the power of one's *tefilla*, one strengthens the hand of Hashem to destroy the decree (Maharsha).

who remembers the loving-kindness of the fathers
and will bring a Redeemer to their children's children
for the sake of His name, in love.

These words are added on Shabbat Shuva: Remember us for life, O King who desires life, and write us in the book of life – for Your sake, O God of life.

King, Helper, Savior, Shield:
▾ *Bend the knees:* Blessed *Bow:* are You, *Stand straight:* LORD,
Shield of Abraham.[1]

DIVINE MIGHT

אַתָּה גִּבּוֹר You are eternally mighty, LORD.
You give life to the dead and have great power to save.

The phrase "He makes the wind blow and the rain fall" is added from Simḥat Torah until Pesaḥ. In Israel, the phrase "He causes the dew to fall" is added from Pesaḥ until Shemini Atzeret.

In fall & winter: He makes the wind blow and the rain fall.
In Israel, in spring & summer: He causes the dew to fall.

He sustains the living with loving-kindness,
and with great compassion revives the dead.
He supports the fallen, heals the sick, sets captives free,
and keeps His faith with those who sleep in the dust.
Who is like You, Master of might,
and who can compare to You,
O King who brings death and gives life, and makes salvation grow?

These words are added on Shabbat Shuva: Who is like You, compassionate Father, who remembers His creatures in compassion, for life?

Faithful are You to revive the dead.
Blessed are You, LORD, who revives the dead.

When saying the Amida silently, continue with "You are holy" on page 514.

---

not only found God but enabled others to do so as well. Therefore, how could one dare recite this blessing without committing oneself to act like Avraham: to reach out to one's fellow man, to have pity on those in need, to have empathy for others even as one is struggling with one's own life challenges, and to accept with faith that Hashem has one's best interests in mind (*Ye'arot Devash*).

וְזוֹכֵר חַסְדֵי אָבוֹת
וּמֵבִיא גוֹאֵל לִבְנֵי בְנֵיהֶם לְמַעַן שְׁמוֹ בְּאַהֲבָה.

בשבת שובה: זָכְרֵנוּ לְחַיִּים, מֶלֶךְ חָפֵץ בַּחַיִּים
וְכָתְבֵנוּ בְּסֵפֶר הַחַיִּים, לְמַעַנְךָ אֱלֹהִים חַיִּים.

מֶלֶךְ עוֹזֵר וּמוֹשִׁיעַ וּמָגֵן.

Bend the knees בָּרוּךְ *Bow* אַתָּה *Stand straight* יהוה, מָגֵן אַבְרָהָם.ע

גבורות

אַתָּה גִּבּוֹר לְעוֹלָם, אֲדֹנָי
מְחַיֵּה מֵתִים אַתָּה, רַב לְהוֹשִׁיעַ

The phrase מַשִּׁיב הָרְוּחַ *is added from* שמחת תורה *until* פסח.
In ארץ ישראל, *the phrase* מוֹרִיד הַטָּל *is added from* פסח *until* שמיני עצרת.

בחורף: מַשִּׁיב הָרְוּחַ וּמוֹרִיד הַגֶּשֶׁם / בארץ ישראל בקיץ: מוֹרִיד הַטָּל

מְכַלְכֵּל חַיִּים בְּחֶסֶד, מְחַיֵּה מֵתִים בְּרַחֲמִים רַבִּים
סוֹמֵךְ נוֹפְלִים, וְרוֹפֵא חוֹלִים, וּמַתִּיר אֲסוּרִים
וּמְקַיֵּם אֱמוּנָתוֹ לִישֵׁנֵי עָפָר.
מִי כָמְוֹךָ, בַּעַל גְּבוּרוֹת, וּמִי דּוֹמֶה לָּךְ
מֶלֶךְ, מֵמִית וּמְחַיֶּה וּמַצְמִיחַ יְשׁוּעָה.

בשבת שובה: מִי כָמְוֹךָ אַב הָרַחֲמִים, זוֹכֵר יְצוּרָיו לְחַיִּים בְּרַחֲמִים.

וְנֶאֱמָן אַתָּה לְהַחֲיוֹת מֵתִים.
בָּרוּךְ אַתָּה יהוה, מְחַיֵּה הַמֵּתִים.

When saying the עמידה *silently, continue with* אַתָּה קָדוֹשׁ *on page 515.*

IYUN TEFILLA • עיון תפילה

מָגֵן אַבְרָהָם – *Shield of Abraham.* Abraham was known for being a person of enormous loving-kindness. And he was the knight of faith, the founder of monotheism who

KEDUSHA[B]

During the Leader's Repetition, the following is said standing with feet together, rising on the toes at the words indicated by ▲.

Cong. then Leader: נְקַדֵּשׁ We will sanctify Your name on earth,
as they sanctify it in the highest heavens,
as is written by Your prophet,
"And they [the angels] call to one another saying: *Is. 6*

Cong. then Leader: ▲Holy, ▲holy, ▲holy is the LORD of hosts
the whole world is filled with His glory."
Those facing them say "Blessed – "

Cong. then Leader: ▲"Blessed is the LORD's glory from His place." *Ezek. 3*
And in Your holy Writings it is written thus:

Cong. then Leader: ▲"The LORD shall reign for ever. *Ps. 146*
He is your God, Zion,
from generation to generation, Halleluya!"

Leader: From generation to generation
we will declare Your greatness,
and we will proclaim Your holiness for evermore.
Your praise, our God, shall not leave our mouth forever,
for You, God, are a great and holy King.
Blessed are You, LORD,
the holy God. / *On Shabbat Shuva:* the holy King./

The Leader continues with "You are One" on the next page.

---

from the Land together with Her people. He thus speaks of a time in the present when God's glory, as it were, is blessed "in its place," where it may be in the Diaspora. These two visions, past and present, are then reconciled by a third vision, not of the angels but of man, that one day in the future, to use the words of King David, "Hashem will reign forever" in Zion. (Rabbi I. Wohlgemuth) In this short prayer, therefore, we have a merging of past and present, and a millennia old vision of the future that we recited daily.

קדושה[ב]

During the חזרת הש״ץ, *the following is said standing with feet together, rising on the toes at the words indicated by* ˄.

קהל *then* ש״ץ: נְקַדֵּשׁ אֶת שִׁמְךָ בָּעוֹלָם
כְּשֵׁם שֶׁמַּקְדִּישִׁים אוֹתוֹ בִּשְׁמֵי מָרוֹם
כַּכָּתוּב עַל יַד נְבִיאֶךָ: וְקָרָא זֶה אֶל־זֶה וְאָמַר ישעיה ו

קהל *then* ש״ץ: ˄קָדוֹשׁ, ˄קָדוֹשׁ, ˄קָדוֹשׁ, יהוה צְבָאוֹת
מְלֹא כָל־הָאָרֶץ כְּבוֹדוֹ:
לְעֻמָּתָם בָּרוּךְ יֹאמֵרוּ

קהל *then* ש״ץ: ˄בָּרוּךְ כְּבוֹד־יהוה מִמְּקוֹמוֹ: יחזקאל ג
וּבְדִבְרֵי קָדְשְׁךָ כָּתוּב לֵאמֹר

קהל *then* ש״ץ: ˄יִמְלֹךְ יהוה לְעוֹלָם, אֱלֹהַיִךְ צִיּוֹן לְדֹר וָדֹר, הַלְלוּיָהּ: תהלים קמו

ש״ץ: לְדוֹר וָדוֹר נַגִּיד גָּדְלֶךָ
וּלְנֵצַח נְצָחִים קְדֻשָּׁתְךָ נַקְדִּישׁ
וְשִׁבְחֲךָ אֱלֹהֵינוּ מִפִּינוּ לֹא יָמוּשׁ לְעוֹלָם וָעֶד
כִּי אֵל מֶלֶךְ גָּדוֹל וְקָדוֹשׁ אָתָּה.
בָּרוּךְ אַתָּה יהוה
הָאֵל הַקָּדוֹשׁ. / בשבת שובה: הַמֶּלֶךְ הַקָּדוֹשׁ./

The שליח ציבור *continues with* אַתָּה אֶחָד *on the next page.*

BIUR TEFILLA • ביאור תפילה

קדושה – *KEDUSHA.*
The line quoted from Yeshayahu's vision (*kadosh, kadosh, kadosh…*) perhaps reflects a time when the kingdom of Judah was strong and independent, and the Hand of God was spread over the Land. As Yeshayahu says in the rest of the verse, "the land is filled with His glory." In the time of Yeḥezkel, however, the Temple was destroyed and the Divine Presence was exiled, as it were,

HOLINESS

אַתָּה קָדוֹשׁ You are holy[1] and Your name is holy,
and holy ones praise You daily, Selah!
Blessed are You, LORD,
the holy God. / *On Shabbat Shuva:* the holy King./
(*If forgotten, repeat the Amida.*)

HOLINESS OF THE DAY

אַתָּה You are One, Your name is One;
and who is like Your people Israel,
a nation unique[1] on earth?[1]

---

tionship we have with Shabbat, even as we sense that the day is drawing to a close. It has taken us almost an entire day to get to this point. It pays to stop for a moment to reflect on what we have (and have not yet) accomplished in this relationship thus far.

IYUN TEFILLA • עיון תפילה

אַתָּה אֶחָד...גּוֹי אֶחָד – *You are One… a nation unique.* A midrash relates that the three parties – Israel, Shabbat and Hashem – testify about one another: Israel and Hashem testify that Shabbat is a day of rest. Israel and Shabbat testify about Hashem that He is One. Hashem and Shabbat testify to the uniqueness of Israel in the world (Tosafot, *Ḥagiga* 3a).

Think about each of these. How is each unique? How could that potentially impact your life?

גּוֹי אֶחָד בָּאָרֶץ – *A nation unique on earth.*

In what ways do you think the Jewish people is unique?

The Gemara (*Yevamot* 79) suggests that we are unique in that we are "merciful, bashful and benevolent…

Only he who cultivates these three characteristics is fit to join this nation."

What evidence of this can you point to?

How can you become a greater part of the nation in this way?

In what other ways do you think we might be unique?

ANI TEFILLA • אני תפילה

"Shabbat enshrines a social-ethical principle without peer. Shabbat is one of the loftiest values in all of humanity. It originated with us, the Jews. It is all ours. No other civilization in history knew a day of rest. Ancient Egypt had a great culture whose treasures are on view to this day, yet the Egypt of antiquity did not know a day of rest. The Greeks of old excelled in philosophy and the arts, yet they did not know a day of rest. Rome established mighty empires and instituted a system of law which is relevant to this day, yet they did not know a day of rest. Neither did the civilizations of Assyria, Babylon, Persia, India, China – not one of them knew a day of rest." (Prime Minister Menachem Begin).

קדושת השם

אַתָּה קָדוֹשׁ ע וְשִׁמְךָ קָדוֹשׁ
וּקְדוֹשִׁים בְּכָל יוֹם יְהַלְלוּךָ סֶּלָה.
בָּרוּךְ אַתָּה יהוה, הָאֵל הַקָּדוֹשׁ. / בשבת שובה: **הַמֶּלֶךְ הַקָּדוֹשׁ.**/
(If forgotten, repeat the עמידה*.)*

קדושת היום

אַתָּה אֶחָד וְשִׁמְךָ אֶחָד
וּמִי כְּעַמְּךָ יִשְׂרָאֵל גּוֹי אֶחָד ע בָּאָרֶץ.ע

IYUN TEFILLA • עיון תפילה

אַתָּה קָדוֹשׁ – *You are holy.* This is admission that Hashem is beyond us. We shouldn't get upset that He sometimes seems elusive and untouchable. Were He not, He would not be God.

INTRODUCTION TO THE MIDDLE BLESSING, *KEDUSHAT HA-YOM*

We have previously noted that the middle blessing of the *Amida* is unique for each version recited on Shabbat, and different commentaries have discerned different themes that are developed which reflect the different moods of the day

We began on Friday evening by focusing on the Shabbat of the Creation (*Ma'ariv*), then the Shabbat of revelation (*Shaharit*) and the Shabbat of the Temple (*Musaf*). Here we focus on the Shabbat of the ideal future, the day when all of humanity will recognize its value and its Source. This may also explain why, unlike the other versions, in *Minḥa* there are no biblical verses brought as support, for Judaism is otherwise very focused on the here and now of daily life and not on some idealized view of the future. As we have absorbed all of the pleasures and messages of Shabbat during the majority of this past day, however, we allow ourselves to imagine what such an ideal world might look like.

Recall, too, the suggestion that the different versions of the *Amida* might represent different stages in the wedding between ourselves and Shabbat: the betrothal (*Ma'ariv*); the happiness (*Shaḥarit*); the festive meal (*Musaf*); and finally, now, at *Minḥa*, the joining of bride and groom. (The Hebrew term for this uniting is *yiḥud*, a word which is similar to the word *eḥad*, meaning "one," the word we use here to describe Hashem's unity.) Alternatively, whereas in *Ma'ariv* we talked about Hashem sanctifying the day, and in *Shaḥarit* we spoke about our own sanctification of the day, here we speak about our coming together (Rabbi Yaakov M. Ḥarlap). In certain ways, then, this prayer represents the most intimate rela-

Splendor of greatness and a crown of salvation
is the day of rest[I] and holiness You have given Your people.
Abraham will rejoice,
Isaac will sing for joy,
Jacob and his children will find rest in it[B] –
a rest of love and generosity,
a rest of truth and faith,
a rest of peace and tranquility, calm and trust;
a complete rest in which You find favor.
May Your children recognize and know
that their rest comes from You,
and that by their rest they sanctify Your name.

אֱלֹהֵינוּ Our God and God of our ancestors,
find favor in our rest.
Make us holy through Your commandments
and grant us our share in Your Torah.[I]
Satisfy us with Your goodness,
grant us joy in Your salvation,
and purify our hearts to serve You in truth.

ANI TEFILLA • אני תפילה

Meditation, though it begins as something one does at a particular stated time, is also often interpreted as the key to a total way of life. Shabbat, on the other hand, is one day out of seven. It never becomes a complete way of life. It represents the Israelites' recognition that although human beings can catch a glimpse of the pure realm of unity and innocence, they also live in the fractured world of division, greed, and sorrow. Shabbat is Israel's ingenious attempt to live both in history and beyond it, both in time and eternity (Harvey Cox, a preeminent non-Jewish theologian, author and teacher at Harvard Divinity School).

IYUN TEFILLA • עיון תפילה

וְתֵן חֶלְקֵנוּ בְּתוֹרָתֶךָ – *And grant us our share in Your Torah.*
What share would you like to have? To what kind of Torah knowledge do you aspire? What next step could you take to get there?

תִּפְאֶרֶת גְּדֻלָּה וַעֲטֶרֶת יְשׁוּעָה
יוֹם מְנוּחָה[ע] וּקְדֻשָּׁה לְעַמְּךָ נָתָתָּ.
אַבְרָהָם יָגֵל, יִצְחָק יְרַנֵּן, יַעֲקֹב וּבָנָיו יָנוּחוּ בוֹ[ב]
מְנוּחַת אַהֲבָה וּנְדָבָה
מְנוּחַת אֱמֶת וֶאֱמוּנָה
מְנוּחַת שָׁלוֹם וְשַׁלְוָה וְהַשְׁקֵט וָבֶטַח
מְנוּחָה שְׁלֵמָה שֶׁאַתָּה רוֹצֶה בָּהּ.
יַכִּירוּ בָנֶיךָ וְיֵדְעוּ, כִּי מֵאִתְּךָ הִיא מְנוּחָתָם
וְעַל מְנוּחָתָם יַקְדִּישׁוּ אֶת שְׁמֶךָ.

אֱלֹהֵינוּ וֵאלֹהֵי אֲבוֹתֵינוּ, רְצֵה בִמְנוּחָתֵנוּ
קַדְּשֵׁנוּ בְּמִצְוֹתֶיךָ וְתֵן חֶלְקֵנוּ בְּתוֹרָתֶךָ[ע]
שַׂבְּעֵנוּ מִטּוּבֶךָ וְשַׂמְּחֵנוּ בִּישׁוּעָתֶךָ
וְטַהֵר לִבֵּנוּ לְעָבְדְּךָ בֶּאֱמֶת.

BIUR TEFILLA • ביאור תפילה

מְנוּחָה – *Rest.*

How many times is the word *menuḥa*/ rest mentioned in this one paragraph?

אַבְרָהָם יָגֵל, יִצְחָק יְרַנֵּן, יַעֲקֹב וּבָנָיו יָנוּחוּ בוֹ – *Abraham will rejoice, Isaac will sing for joy, Jacob and his children will find rest in it.* Why are the *Avot* (Patriarchs) mentioned here? Perhaps because, given the theme here, they were the first to recognize and foster monotheism (*Kol Bo*). Alternatively, note that it is only Yaakov who is mentioned as having sons, us among them, who ultimately embraced the Shabbat. Why does the text not mention the sons of Avraham and Yitzḥak as well (*Beit Yosef*)?

מְנוּחַת אַהֲבָה וּנְדָבָה – *A rest of love and generosity.*

מְנוּחַת אֱמֶת וֶאֱמוּנָה – *A rest of truth and faith.*

מְנוּחַת שָׁלוֹם וְשַׁלְוָה וְהַשְׁקֵט וָבֶטַח – *A rest of peace and tranquility, calm and trust.*

מְנוּחָה שְׁלֵמָה שֶׁאַתָּה רוֹצֶה בָּהּ – *A complete rest in which You find favor.*

How would you define each of these kinds of "rest?"

How have you experienced any of these today?

In love and favor, Lord our God,
grant us as our heritage Your holy Sabbaths,
so that Israel who sanctify Your name may find rest on them.
Blessed are You, Lord, who sanctifies the Sabbath.

TEMPLE SERVICE

רְצֵה Find favor, Lord our God, in Your people Israel and their prayer.
Restore the service to Your most holy House,[B]
and accept in love and favor
the fire-offerings of Israel and their prayer.
May the service of Your people Israel always find favor with You.

On Rosh Ḥodesh and Ḥol HaMo'ed, say:

אֱלֹהֵינוּ Our God and God of our ancestors, may there rise, come,[B] reach, appear, be favored, heard, regarded and remembered before You, our recollection and remembrance, as well as the remembrance of our ancestors, and of the Messiah son of David Your servant, and of Jerusalem Your holy city, and of all Your people the house of Israel – for deliverance and well-being, grace, loving-kindness and compassion, life and peace, on this day of:

On Rosh Ḥodesh: Rosh Ḥodesh.
On Pesaḥ: the Festival of Matzot.
On Sukkot: the Festival of Sukkot.

On it remember us, Lord our God, for good; recollect us for blessing, and deliver us for life. In accord with Your promise of salvation and compassion, spare us and be gracious to us; have compassion on us and deliver us, for our eyes are turned to You because You, God, are a gracious and compassionate King.

IYUN TEFILLA · עיון תפילה

וְיָבוֹא וְיַגִּיעַ, וְיֵרָאֶה וְיֵרָצֶה וְיִשָּׁמַע, וְיִפָּקֵד וְיִזָּכֵר – *Come, reach, appear, be favored, heard, regarded, and remembered before You.* There are seven expressions here related to Hashem's remembering of us. The Vilna Gaon suggested that these correspond to the Kabbalistic concept of seven spheres which separate us from the spiritual realm (*Ḥagiga* 12b). Remembering, like prayer itself, is a process that does not happen in one fell swoop. It takes time and practice, effort and determination, and not a little courage. With time, however, one can get past each of the veils to ultimately see things that one did not see before.

In return, perhaps, the prayer suggests that we be rewarded in seven ways. Can you find them?

וְהַנְחִילֵנוּ יהוה אֱלֹהֵינוּ בְּאַהֲבָה וּבְרָצוֹן שַׁבְּתוֹת קָדְשֶׁךָ
וְיָנוּחוּ בָם יִשְׂרָאֵל מְקַדְּשֵׁי שְׁמֶךָ.
בָּרוּךְ אַתָּה יהוה, מְקַדֵּשׁ הַשַּׁבָּת.

עבודה
רְצֵה יהוה אֱלֹהֵינוּ בְּעַמְּךָ יִשְׂרָאֵל וּבִתְפִלָּתָם
וְהָשֵׁב אֶת הָעֲבוֹדָה לִדְבִיר בֵּיתֶךָ[ב]
וְאִשֵּׁי יִשְׂרָאֵל וּתְפִלָּתָם בְּאַהֲבָה תְקַבֵּל בְּרָצוֹן
וּתְהִי לְרָצוֹן תָּמִיד עֲבוֹדַת יִשְׂרָאֵל עַמֶּךָ.

On ראש חודש *and* חול המועד*, say:*

אֱלֹהֵינוּ וֵאלֹהֵי אֲבוֹתֵינוּ, יַעֲלֶה וְיָבוֹא וְיַגִּיעַ, וְיֵרָאֶה וְיֵרָצֶה וְיִשָּׁמַע, וְיִפָּקֵד וְיִזָּכֵר[ע] זִכְרוֹנֵנוּ וּפִקְדוֹנֵנוּ וְזִכְרוֹן אֲבוֹתֵינוּ, וְזִכְרוֹן מָשִׁיחַ בֶּן דָּוִד עַבְדֶּךָ, וְזִכְרוֹן יְרוּשָׁלַיִם עִיר קָדְשֶׁךָ, וְזִכְרוֹן כָּל עַמְּךָ בֵּית יִשְׂרָאֵל, לְפָנֶיךָ, לִפְלֵיטָה לְטוֹבָה, לְחֵן וּלְחֶסֶד וּלְרַחֲמִים, לְחַיִּים וּלְשָׁלוֹם בְּיוֹם
בראש חודש: רֹאשׁ הַחֹדֶשׁ / בפסח: חַג הַמַּצּוֹת / בסוכות: חַג הַסֻּכּוֹת
הַזֶּה. זָכְרֵנוּ יהוה אֱלֹהֵינוּ בּוֹ לְטוֹבָה, וּפָקְדֵנוּ בוֹ לִבְרָכָה, וְהוֹשִׁיעֵנוּ בוֹ לְחַיִּים. וּבִדְבַר יְשׁוּעָה וְרַחֲמִים, חוּס וְחָנֵּנוּ וְרַחֵם עָלֵינוּ וְהוֹשִׁיעֵנוּ, כִּי אֵלֶיךָ עֵינֵינוּ, כִּי אֵל מֶלֶךְ חַנּוּן וְרַחוּם אָתָּה.

BIUR TEFILLA • ביאור תפילה

For more commentary on these final blessings, see *Ma'ariv* (pages 111–118), *Shaharit* (pages 349–362), and *Musaf* (pages 431–440).

לִדְבִיר בֵּיתֶךָ – *Your most holy House.* The *Devir*, or House, is a reference to the Holy of Holies (*Kodesh HaKedoshim*), the innermost sanctuary of the Temple. What took place here? It was not the sacrifices which took place in the outer courtyard. It was not the offering of incense or the lighting of the Menora, which took place within the sanctuary itself. Rather, it was the location of the Holy Ark within which was found the Torah. Our expressed desire for its return in this context, therefore, is not to be able to do the rituals per se, but rather to return to the Source, to stand as close to His Presence as one could on this earth.

See yourself there now.

וְתֶחֱזֶינָה And may our eyes witness[I] Your return
to Zion in compassion.
Blessed are You, Lord, who restores His Presence to Zion.

THANKSGIVING

▾ *Bow:* We give thanks to You,
for You are *Stand straight*
the Lord our God
and God of our ancestors
for ever and all time.
You are the Rock of our lives,
Shield of our salvation
from generation to generation.
We will thank You and
declare Your praise for our lives,[A]
which are entrusted into Your hand;
for our souls,
which are placed in Your charge;
for Your miracles
which are with us every day;
and for Your wonders[I] and favors
at all times,
evening, morning and midday.
You are good –
for Your compassion never fails.
You are compassionate –
for Your loving-kindnesses never cease.
We have always placed our hope in You.

During the Leader's Repetition, the congregation says quietly:
▾ *Bow:* We give thanks to You,
for You are *Stand straight*
the Lord our God
and God of our ancestors,
God of all flesh,
who formed us
and formed the universe.
Blessings and thanks
are due to Your great
and holy name
for giving us life
and sustaining us.
May You continue
to give us life and sustain us;
and may You gather our
exiles to Your holy courts,
to keep Your decrees,
do Your will and serve You
with a perfect heart,
for it is for us
to give You thanks.
Blessed be God
to whom thanksgiving
is due.

IYUN TEFILLA • עיון תפילה

שֶׁבְּכָל עֵת – *Are with us… at all times.* Relationships are all about giving. A relationship that is one sided doesn't work. Both sides need to give to the other. It's like parents who in many ways are more connected to their children than the other way around, because they give more. It's only when the children grow up that they realize how much their parents had given them all of those years.

Think of Hashem as a parent. What has He given you? It is time to give thanks in return.

וְתֶחֱזֶינָה עֵינֵינוּ[ע] בְּשׁוּבְךָ לְצִיּוֹן בְּרַחֲמִים.
בָּרוּךְ אַתָּה יהוה, הַמַּחֲזִיר שְׁכִינָתוֹ לְצִיּוֹן.

הודאה

▾ Bow מוֹדִים אֲנַחְנוּ לָךְ
Stand straight שָׁאַתָּה הוּא
יהוה אֱלֹהֵינוּ וֵאלֹהֵי אֲבוֹתֵינוּ
לְעוֹלָם וָעֶד.
צוּר חַיֵּינוּ, מָגֵן יִשְׁעֵנוּ
אַתָּה הוּא לְדוֹר וָדוֹר.
נוֹדֶה לְּךָ וּנְסַפֵּר תְּהִלָּתֶךָ
עַל חַיֵּינוּ[א] הַמְּסוּרִים בְּיָדֶךָ
וְעַל נִשְׁמוֹתֵינוּ הַפְּקוּדוֹת לָךְ
וְעַל נִסֶּיךָ שֶׁבְּכָל יוֹם עִמָּנוּ
וְעַל נִפְלְאוֹתֶיךָ[ע] וְטוֹבוֹתֶיךָ
שֶׁבְּכָל עֵת, עֶרֶב וָבֹקֶר וְצָהֳרָיִם.
הַטּוֹב, כִּי לֹא כָלוּ רַחֲמֶיךָ וְהַמְרַחֵם,
כִּי לֹא תַמּוּ חֲסָדֶיךָ, מֵעוֹלָם קִוִּינוּ לָךְ.

During the חזרת הש״ץ, *the* קהל *says quietly:*

▾ Bow מוֹדִים אֲנַחְנוּ לָךְ
Stand straight שָׁאַתָּה הוּא
יהוה אֱלֹהֵינוּ וֵאלֹהֵי אֲבוֹתֵינוּ
אֱלֹהֵי כָל בָּשָׂר
יוֹצְרֵנוּ, יוֹצֵר בְּרֵאשִׁית.
בְּרָכוֹת וְהוֹדָאוֹת
לְשִׁמְךָ הַגָּדוֹל וְהַקָּדוֹשׁ
עַל שֶׁהֶחֱיִיתָנוּ וְקִיַּמְתָּנוּ.
כֵּן תְּחַיֵּנוּ וּתְקַיְּמֵנוּ
וְתֶאֱסֹף גָּלֻיּוֹתֵינוּ
לְחַצְרוֹת קָדְשֶׁךָ
לִשְׁמֹר חֻקֶּיךָ וְלַעֲשׂוֹת רְצוֹנֶךָ
וּלְעָבְדְּךָ בְּלֵבָב שָׁלֵם
עַל שֶׁאֲנַחְנוּ מוֹדִים לָךְ.
בָּרוּךְ אֵל הַהוֹדָאוֹת.

IYUN TEFILLA • עיון תפילה

וְתֶחֱזֶינָה עֵינֵינוּ – *May our eyes witness.* Every Jew is obligated to see him or herself as an Israeli. Even if he was born elsewhere – by historical error – he nonetheless belongs to the Land of Israel. A Jew should always say: "I come from *Eretz Yisrael*!" Rabbi Moshe from Coucy, the author of the *halakhic* work called the *Semag* and one of the Ba`alei Tosafot, would sign his name: "Moshe from the Exile of Jerusalem who is in France." It is true that I am in France, but I am from Jerusalem. When a Jew is asked: "Where are you from," he must therefore respond: I come from *Eretz Yisrael* (Rabbi Meir Yeḥiel of Ostrowiec).

ANI TEFILLA • אני תפילה

מוֹדִים – *We give thanks.*
Name five things that you have to be thankful for today.

The Amida continues on the next page with "For all these." On Ḥanukka and on Purim say "We thank You" below.

On Ḥanukka:

עַל הַנִּסִּים [We thank You also] for the miracles, the redemption, the mighty deeds, the salvations, and the victories in battle which You performed for our ancestors in those days, at this time.

בִּימֵי מַתִּתְיָהוּ In the days of Mattityahu, son of Yoḥanan, the High Priest,[1] the Hasmonean, and his sons, the wicked Greek kingdom rose up against Your people Israel to make them forget Your Torah[1] and to force them to transgress the statutes of Your will. It was then that You in Your great compassion stood by them in the time of their distress. You championed their cause, judged their claim, and avenged their wrong. You delivered the strong into the hands of the weak, the many into the hands of the few, the impure into the hands of the pure, the wicked into the hands of the righteous, and the arrogant into the hands of those who were engaged in the study of Your Torah. You made for Yourself great and holy renown in Your world, and for Your people Israel You performed a great salvation and redemption as of this very day. Your children then entered the holiest part of Your House, cleansed Your Temple, purified Your Sanctuary, kindled lights in Your holy courts, and designated these eight days of Ḥanukka for giving thanks and praise to Your great name.

Continue with "For all these things" on the next page.

On Shushan Purim in Jerusalem:

עַל הַנִּסִּים [We thank You also] for the miracles, the redemption, the mighty deeds, the salvations, and the victories in battle which You performed for our ancestors in those days, at this time.

בִּימֵי מָרְדְּכַי In the days of Mordekhai and Esther, in Shushan the capital, the wicked Haman rose up against them and sought to destroy, slay and exterminate all the Jews, young and old, children and women, on one day, the thirteenth day of the twelfth month, which is the month of Adar, and to plunder their possessions. Then You in Your great compassion thwarted his counsel, frustrated his plans, and caused his scheme to recoil on his own head, so that they hanged him and his sons on the gallows. *Esther 3*

Continue with "For all these things."

בִּימֵי מַתִּתְיָהוּ בֶּן יוֹחָנָן כֹּהֵן גָּדוֹל – *In the days of Matityahu, son of Yoḥanan, the High Priest.* Note that the day is not marked by the date or by the period of history in which it occurred but, rather, by the personalities who made it happen. Individuals can leave their mark on the world if only they would step up to the plate.

ANI TEFILLA • אני תפילה

David is driving in Jerusalem. He's late for a meeting, he's looking for a parking place, and can't find one. In desperation, he turns towards heaven and says: "Lord, if you find me a parking place, I promise that I'll eat only kosher, respect Shabbat

This **ANI TEFILLA** *continues on page 525.*

The עמידה *continues on the next page with* וְעַל כֻּלָּם. *On* חנוכה *and on* פורים *say* עַל הַנִּסִּים *below.*

בחנוכה:

עַל הַנִּסִּים וְעַל הַפֻּרְקָן וְעַל הַגְּבוּרוֹת וְעַל הַתְּשׁוּעוֹת וְעַל הַמִּלְחָמוֹת שֶׁעָשִׂיתָ לַאֲבוֹתֵינוּ בַּיָּמִים הָהֵם בִּזְּמַן הַזֶּה.

בִּימֵי מַתִּתְיָהוּ בֶּן יוֹחָנָן כֹּהֵן[ע] גָּדוֹל חַשְׁמוֹנַאי וּבָנָיו, כְּשֶׁעָמְדָה מַלְכוּת יָוָן הָרְשָׁעָה עַל עַמְּךָ יִשְׂרָאֵל לְהַשְׁכִּיחָם תּוֹרָתֶךָ[ע] וּלְהַעֲבִירָם מֵחֻקֵּי רְצוֹנֶךָ, וְאַתָּה בְּרַחֲמֶיךָ הָרַבִּים עָמַדְתָּ לָהֶם בְּעֵת צָרָתָם, רַבְתָּ אֶת רִיבָם, דַּנְתָּ אֶת דִּינָם, נָקַמְתָּ אֶת נִקְמָתָם, מָסַרְתָּ גִּבּוֹרִים בְּיַד חַלָּשִׁים, וְרַבִּים בְּיַד מְעַטִּים, וּטְמֵאִים בְּיַד טְהוֹרִים, וּרְשָׁעִים בְּיַד צַדִּיקִים, וְזֵדִים בְּיַד עוֹסְקֵי תוֹרָתֶךָ, וּלְךָ עָשִׂיתָ שֵׁם גָּדוֹל וְקָדוֹשׁ בְּעוֹלָמֶךָ, וּלְעַמְּךָ יִשְׂרָאֵל עָשִׂיתָ תְּשׁוּעָה גְדוֹלָה וּפֻרְקָן כְּהַיּוֹם הַזֶּה. וְאַחַר כֵּן בָּאוּ בָנֶיךָ לִדְבִיר בֵּיתֶךָ, וּפִנּוּ אֶת הֵיכָלֶךָ, וְטִהֲרוּ אֶת מִקְדָּשֶׁךָ, וְהִדְלִיקוּ נֵרוֹת בְּחַצְרוֹת קָדְשֶׁךָ, וְקָבְעוּ שְׁמוֹנַת יְמֵי חֲנֻכָּה אֵלּוּ, לְהוֹדוֹת וּלְהַלֵּל לְשִׁמְךָ הַגָּדוֹל.

Continue with וְעַל כֻּלָּם *on the next page.*

בשושן פורים בירושלים:

עַל הַנִּסִּים וְעַל הַפֻּרְקָן וְעַל הַגְּבוּרוֹת וְעַל הַתְּשׁוּעוֹת וְעַל הַמִּלְחָמוֹת שֶׁעָשִׂיתָ לַאֲבוֹתֵינוּ בַּיָּמִים הָהֵם בִּזְּמַן הַזֶּה.

בִּימֵי מָרְדְּכַי וְאֶסְתֵּר בְּשׁוּשַׁן הַבִּירָה, כְּשֶׁעָמַד עֲלֵיהֶם הָמָן הָרָשָׁע,
אסתר ג בִּקֵּשׁ לְהַשְׁמִיד לַהֲרֹג וּלְאַבֵּד אֶת־כָּל־הַיְּהוּדִים מִנַּעַר וְעַד־זָקֵן טַף
וְנָשִׁים בְּיוֹם אֶחָד, בִּשְׁלוֹשָׁה עָשָׂר לְחֹדֶשׁ שְׁנֵים־עָשָׂר, הוּא־חֹדֶשׁ אֲדָר,
וּשְׁלָלָם לָבוֹז: וְאַתָּה בְּרַחֲמֶיךָ הָרַבִּים הֵפַרְתָּ אֶת עֲצָתוֹ, וְקִלְקַלְתָּ אֶת
מַחֲשַׁבְתּוֹ, וַהֲשֵׁבוֹתָ לּוֹ גְּמוּלוֹ בְּרֹאשׁוֹ, וְתָלוּ אוֹתוֹ וְאֶת בָּנָיו עַל הָעֵץ.

Continue with וְעַל כֻּלָּם.

IYUN TEFILLA • עיון תפילה

לְהַשְׁכִּיחָם תּוֹרָתֶךָ – *To make them forget Your Torah.* Note that they did not seek to simply ban Torah learning but to resocialize or reeducate an entire generation so that Judaism would come to an end. That is a goal that other leaders and dictators sought to do in our history from Antiochus to the modern era when in some countries Jewish schools were banned, synagogues burned or closed, and Torah scrolls destroyed. And yet, we are still here because Jewish commitment to Torah persevered.

What can I do to make sure that the Torah is not forgotten?

וְעַל כֻּלָּם For all these things may Your name be blessed and exalted, our King, continually, for ever and all time.

These words are added on Shabbat Shuva: And write, for a good life, all the children of Your covenant.

Let all that lives thank You,[B] Selah!
and praise Your name in truth,
God, our Savior and Help, Selah!
▾ *Bend the knees:* Blessed *Bow:* are You, *Stand straight:* LORD,
whose name is "the Good" and to whom thanks are due.

PEACE

שָׁלוֹם רָב Grant
great peace
to Your people Israel
for ever,
for You are
the sovereign LORD
of all peace;[I]
and may it be good
in Your eyes
to bless Your people Israel
at every time,
at every hour,
with Your peace.

In Israel:
שִׂים שָׁלוֹם Grant peace,
goodness and blessing,
grace, loving-kindness and compassion
to us and all Israel Your people.
Bless us, our Father, all as one,
with the light of Your face,
for by the light of Your face
You have given us, LORD our God,
the Torah of life and love of kindness,
righteousness, blessing, compassion,
life and peace.
May it be good in Your eyes
to bless Your people Israel
at every time, in every hour,
with Your peace.

IYUN TEFILLA • עיון תפילה

כִּי אַתָּה הוּא מֶלֶךְ... לְכָל הַשָּׁלוֹם – *For You are the Sovereign…of all peace.* Peace comes about through shared values and ideals, through a common vision of the world that enables us to put our individual differences aside. The more that we can all come to accept God as the source of those values, the greater the chance for peace. Jealousy, unhealthy competition, egocentrism are the enemies of God, and of peace.

How will I carry those values into my week?

וְעַל כֻּלָּם יִתְבָּרַךְ וְיִתְרוֹמַם שִׁמְךָ מַלְכֵּנוּ תָּמִיד לְעוֹלָם וָעֶד.

בשבת שובה: וּכְתֹב לְחַיִּים טוֹבִים כָּל בְּנֵי בְרִיתֶךָ.

וְכֹל הַחַיִּים יוֹדְוּךָ[ב] סֶּלָה
וִיהַלְלוּ אֶת שִׁמְךָ בֶּאֱמֶת
הָאֵל יְשׁוּעָתֵנוּ וְעֶזְרָתֵנוּ סֶלָה.

Bend the knees בָּרוּךְ *Bow* אַתָּה *Stand straight* יהוה
הַטּוֹב שִׁמְךָ וּלְךָ נָאֶה לְהוֹדוֹת.

ברכת שלום

שָׁלוֹם רָב עַל יִשְׂרָאֵל עַמְּךָ
תָּשִׂים לְעוֹלָם
כִּי אַתָּה הוּא
מֶלֶךְ אָדוֹן לְכָל הַשָּׁלוֹם.[ע]
וְטוֹב בְּעֵינֶיךָ
לְבָרֵךְ אֶת עַמְּךָ יִשְׂרָאֵל
בְּכָל עֵת וּבְכָל שָׁעָה
בִּשְׁלוֹמֶךָ.

In ארץ ישראל:
שִׂים שָׁלוֹם טוֹבָה וּבְרָכָה
חֵן וָחֶסֶד וְרַחֲמִים
עָלֵינוּ וְעַל כָּל יִשְׂרָאֵל עַמֶּךָ.
בָּרְכֵנוּ אָבִינוּ כֻּלָּנוּ כְּאֶחָד בְּאוֹר פָּנֶיךָ
כִּי בְאוֹר פָּנֶיךָ נָתַתָּ לָּנוּ יהוה אֱלֹהֵינוּ
תּוֹרַת חַיִּים וְאַהֲבַת חֶסֶד
וּצְדָקָה וּבְרָכָה וְרַחֲמִים וְחַיִּים וְשָׁלוֹם.
וְטוֹב בְּעֵינֶיךָ לְבָרֵךְ אֶת עַמְּךָ יִשְׂרָאֵל
בְּכָל עֵת וּבְכָל שָׁעָה בִּשְׁלוֹמֶךָ.

---

and all the holidays." Miraculously, a place opens up just in front of him. He turns his face up to heaven and says, "Never mind, I just found one!"

BIUR TEFILLA • ביאור תפילה

וְכֹל הַחַיִּים יוֹדְוּךָ – *Let all that lives thank You.* This could be understood as "all living things" will thank You. Alternatively, it could mean "all of [my] life" will thank You, which would suggest that the way I live my life will be an acknowledgment of all of the good that You have given me.

What can you do to begin living that way?

These words are added on Shabbat Shuva: In the book of life, blessing, peace and prosperity,
may we and all Your people the house of Israel
be remembered and written before You
for a good life, and for peace.*

Blessed are You, LORD, who blesses His people Israel with peace.[1]

**On Shabbat Shuva outside Israel, many end the blessing:*
Blessed are You, LORD, who makes peace.

The following verse concludes the Leader's Repetition of the Amida.
Some also say it here as part of the silent Amida.
May the words of my mouth and the meditation of my heart *Ps. 19*
find favor before You, LORD, my Rock and Redeemer.

אֱלֹהַי My God, *Berakhot 17a*
guard my tongue from evil
and my lips from deceitful speech.
To those who curse me, let my soul be silent;
may my soul be to all like the dust.[B]
Open my heart to Your Torah
and let my soul pursue Your commandments.
As for all who plan evil against me,
swiftly thwart their counsel and frustrate their plans.
Act for the sake of Your name; act for the sake of Your right hand;
act for the sake of Your holiness; act for the sake of Your Torah.

Another possibility: Let me be selfless to the point of humility. This would be in keeping with our being descendants of Avraham who said (*Bereshit* 18:27) "I am mere dust and ashes." Just because one is selfless and humble does not mean that one is devoid of ego or promise. Recall that Avraham was to become the father of a nation, the one who despite or because of his humility God promised (*Bereshit* 13:16): "I will make your offspring like the dust of the earth."

Alternatively: Let me be humble and maintain perspective on what is important in life. After all, King Solomon said "everything comes from dust and returns to dust" (*Kohelet* 3:20). We come from dust and return to dust. Remembering that life is short and that you are made from dust can help give perspective to the little things that make you crazy during the day.

Another possibility: "Let me not become arrogant if I am praised." It was reported that Rav Shimon Schwab, the former rabbinic leader of the German community known as "Breuer's" in New York City, was honored at a dinner. As he entered the hall, he was heard to be quietly whispering in Hebrew "And may my soul be as dust to all."

בשבת שובה: בְּסֵפֶר חַיִּים, בְּרָכָה וְשָׁלוֹם, וּפַרְנָסָה טוֹבָה נִזָּכֵר וְנִכָּתֵב לְפָנֶיךָ, אֲנַחְנוּ וְכָל עַמְּךָ בֵּית יִשְׂרָאֵל לְחַיִּים טוֹבִים וּלְשָׁלוֹם.*

בָּרוּךְ אַתָּה יהוה, הַמְבָרֵךְ אֶת עַמּוֹ יִשְׂרָאֵל בַּשָּׁלוֹם.[ע]

**On* שבת שובה *in* חוץ לארץ *many end the blessing:*

בָּרוּךְ אַתָּה יהוה, עוֹשֶׂה הַשָּׁלוֹם.

The following verse concludes the חזרת הש״ץ.
Some also say it here as part of the silent עמידה.

תהלים יט
יִהְיוּ לְרָצוֹן אִמְרֵי־פִי וְהֶגְיוֹן לִבִּי לְפָנֶיךָ, יהוה צוּרִי וְגֹאֲלִי:

ברכות יז.
אֱלֹהַי
נְצֹר לְשׁוֹנִי מֵרָע וּשְׂפָתַי מִדַּבֵּר מִרְמָה
וְלִמְקַלְלַי נַפְשִׁי תִדֹּם, וְנַפְשִׁי כֶּעָפָר לַכֹּל תִּהְיֶה.[ב]
פְּתַח לִבִּי בְּתוֹרָתֶךָ, וּבְמִצְוֹתֶיךָ תִּרְדֹּף נַפְשִׁי.
וְכָל הַחוֹשְׁבִים עָלַי רָעָה, מְהֵרָה הָפֵר עֲצָתָם וְקַלְקֵל מַחֲשַׁבְתָּם.
עֲשֵׂה לְמַעַן שְׁמֶךָ, עֲשֵׂה לְמַעַן יְמִינֶךָ
עֲשֵׂה לְמַעַן קְדֻשָּׁתֶךָ, עֲשֵׂה לְמַעַן תּוֹרָתֶךָ.

IYUN TEFILLA • עיון תפילה

הַמְבָרֵךְ אֶת עַמּוֹ יִשְׂרָאֵל בַּשָּׁלוֹם – *Who blesses His people Israel with peace.* The midrash reports that "R. Shimon ben Ḥalafta said: 'Great is peace, for there is no vessel which contains blessings like peace, as it says (*Tehillim* 29:11) 'Hashem will bless His people with peace'" (*Bemidbar Rabba* 11:7). The midrash is actually understanding the phrase to say "in peace" rather than "with peace." All of the blessings that we ask for are contained within peace. Without peace there is nothing.

What can you do to make more peace this week?

BIUR TEFILLA • ביאור תפילה

וְנַפְשִׁי כֶּעָפָר לַכֹּל תִּהְיֶה – *May my soul be to all like the dust.* One possibility: May I be so insignificant that people not notice me to talk about me.

That Your beloved ones may be delivered, Ps. 60
save with Your right hand and answer me.
May the words of my mouth and the meditation of my heart Ps. 19
find favor before You, LORD, my Rock and Redeemer.

Bow and take three steps back as if taking leave of the Divine Presence.
Bow left: May He who makes peace in His high places,
Bow right: make peace *Bow forward:* for us and all Israel – and say: Amen.

יְהִי רָצוֹן May it be Your will, LORD our God and God of our ancestors, that the Temple be rebuilt speedily in our days, and grant us a share in Your Torah. And there we will serve You with reverence, as in the days of old and as in former years. Then the offering of Judah and Jerusalem will be pleasing to the LORD as in the days Mal. 3
of old and as in former years.

The following is omitted on days when Taḥanun is not said.

צִדְקָתְךָ Your righteousness is an everlasting righteousness,[B] Ps. 119
and Your Torah is truth.
Your righteousness, O God, reaches to the highest heights, Ps. 71
for You have done great things.
O God, who is like You?
Your righteousness is like the mighty mountains;[I] Ps. 36
Your judgments like the great depths.
O LORD, You save both man and beast.

---

coming week. These three statements may therefore be three principles that we need to recall going forward: (1) Hashem taught us to live a life of justice and righteousness. (2) Any deviation from this path would be deserving of our forfeiting our lives, were it not for Hashem's loving-kindness. (3) Despite that, there will be times when the "judgments" of Hashem, the decrees that determine trouble and sorrow, will also be unleashed by Him, for these are what affirm our free will and enable us to meet our potential (Rabbi S. R. Hirsch).

IYUN TEFILLA • עיון תפילה

צִדְקָתְךָ כְּהַרְרֵי־אֵל – *Your righteousness is like the mighty mountains.* Why the comparison to the mountains? Sometimes mountains are covered in darkness and haze and cannot be seen clearly. So, too, Hashem's righteousness is sometimes hard to see, and only becomes visible with the passing of time (*Menaḥem Tziyon*). As the week approaches, we pray that our vision will not be tested.

HILKHOT TEFILLA • הלכות תפילה

If today is a day when *Taḥanun* would not be said were it a regular weekday, then the following is not said either.

לְמַעַן יֵחָלְצוּן יְדִידֶיךָ, הוֹשִׁיעָה יְמִינְךָ וַעֲנֵנִי: תהלים ס
יִהְיוּ לְרָצוֹן אִמְרֵי־פִי וְהֶגְיוֹן לִבִּי לְפָנֶיךָ, יהוה צוּרִי וְגֹאֲלִי: תהלים יט

Bow and take three steps back as if taking leave of the Divine Presence.

Bow left עֹשֶׂה שָׁלוֹם/ בשבת שובה: הַשָּׁלוֹם/ בִּמְרוֹמָיו
Bow right הוּא יַעֲשֶׂה שָׁלוֹם *Bow forward* עָלֵינוּ וְעַל כָּל יִשְׂרָאֵל
וְאִמְרוּ אָמֵן.

יְהִי רָצוֹן מִלְּפָנֶיךָ יהוה אֱלֹהֵינוּ וֵאלֹהֵי אֲבוֹתֵינוּ, שֶׁיִּבָּנֶה בֵּית הַמִּקְדָּשׁ
בִּמְהֵרָה בְיָמֵינוּ, וְתֵן חֶלְקֵנוּ בְּתוֹרָתֶךָ, וְשָׁם נַעֲבָדְךָ בְּיִרְאָה כִּימֵי עוֹלָם
וּכְשָׁנִים קַדְמֹנִיּוֹת. וְעָרְבָה לַיהוה מִנְחַת יְהוּדָה וִירוּשָׁלָםִ כִּימֵי עוֹלָם מלאכי ג
וּכְשָׁנִים קַדְמֹנִיּוֹת:

The following is omitted on days when תחנון *is not said.*

צִדְקָתְךָ צֶדֶק לְעוֹלָם וְתוֹרָתְךָ אֱמֶת: תהלים קיט
וְצִדְקָתְךָ אֱלֹהִים עַד־מָרוֹם, אֲשֶׁר־עָשִׂיתָ גְדֹלוֹת תהלים עא
אֱלֹהִים, מִי כָמוֹךָ:
צִדְקָתְךָ כְּהַרְרֵי־אֵל, מִשְׁפָּטֶיךָ תְּהוֹם רַבָּה תהלים לו
אָדָם וּבְהֵמָה תוֹשִׁיעַ יהוה:

BIUR TEFILLA • ביאור תפילה

צִדְקָתְךָ צֶדֶק לְעוֹלָם - *Your* righteousness *is an everlasting righteousness.* There are a number of theories about the origin and significance of reciting these three individual verses from *Tehillim*, all of which begin with the same word, for while a single authoritative rationale has been lost to us, the custom goes back over a thousand years, and in Jewish life custom can be a more powerful a force than any rationale. There are those who suggest that the verses are a reference to Yosef, Moshe, and David, each of whom died on Shabbat afternoon, and, "like the words said at a funeral, they are an acceptance of loss as God's just decree" (Rabbi J. Sacks). Yet another suggests some messianic overtones (Abudarham) while still others suggest that it is reminiscent of the supplications that we make to Hashem after the *Amida* on a weekday (*Levush*). Alternatively, perhaps, as *Minḥa* comes to an end, and there is a palpable sense that the Shabbat is ebbing away, our thoughts turn toward the challenges and struggles that lay ahead of us in the

FULL KADDISH

Leader: יִתְגַּדַּל Magnified and sanctified may His great name be,
in the world He created by His will.
May He establish His kingdom
in your lifetime and in your days,
and in the lifetime of all the house of Israel,
swiftly and soon – and say: Amen.

All: May His great name[B] be blessed for ever and all time.

Leader: Blessed and praised, glorified and exalted,
raised and honored, uplifted and lauded be
the name of the Holy One,
blessed be He, beyond any blessing,
song, praise and consolation
uttered in the world – and say: Amen.

May the prayers and pleas of all Israel
be accepted by their Father in heaven – and say: Amen.

May there be great peace from heaven,
and life for us and all Israel – and say: Amen.

Bow, take three steps back, as if taking leave of the Divine Presence, then bow, first left, then right, then center, while saying:

May He who makes peace in His high places,
make peace for us and all Israel – and say: Amen.

BIUR TEFILLA · ביאור תפילה

יְהֵא שְׁמֵהּ רַבָּא – *May His great name. Maḥzor Vitry* suggests that the prayer is that His name will one day in the future be complete, i.e., when His enemies are destroyed and the world comes to accept that He is the One God.

The *Tur* (56) says that the prayer is that His name is great now at this moment in time, by virtue of the fact that we are all sanctifying it together.

Of course, one can choose to have only one of these in mind, but there is no reason that they cannot both be true at the same time.

קדיש שלם

ש״ץ: יִתְגַּדַּל וְיִתְקַדַּשׁ שְׁמֵהּ רַבָּא (קהל: אָמֵן)
בְּעָלְמָא דִּי בְרָא כִרְעוּתֵהּ
וְיַמְלִיךְ מַלְכוּתֵהּ
בְּחַיֵּיכוֹן וּבְיוֹמֵיכוֹן וּבְחַיֵּי דְכָל בֵּית יִשְׂרָאֵל
בַּעֲגָלָא וּבִזְמַן קָרִיב, וְאִמְרוּ אָמֵן. (קהל: אָמֵן)

קהל וש״ץ: יְהֵא שְׁמֵהּ רַבָּא מְבָרַךְ לְעָלַם וּלְעָלְמֵי עָלְמַיָּא.

ש״ץ: יִתְבָּרַךְ וְיִשְׁתַּבַּח וְיִתְפָּאַר
וְיִתְרוֹמַם וְיִתְנַשֵּׂא וְיִתְהַדָּר וְיִתְעַלֶּה וְיִתְהַלָּל
שְׁמֵהּ דְּקֻדְשָׁא בְּרִיךְ הוּא (קהל: בְּרִיךְ הוּא)
לְעֵלָּא מִן כָּל בִּרְכָתָא
/ בשבת שובה: לְעֵלָּא לְעֵלָּא מִכָּל בִּרְכָתָא/
וְשִׁירָתָא, תֻּשְׁבְּחָתָא וְנֶחֱמָתָא
דַּאֲמִירָן בְּעָלְמָא, וְאִמְרוּ אָמֵן. (קהל: אָמֵן)

תִּתְקַבַּל צְלוֹתְהוֹן וּבָעוּתְהוֹן דְּכָל יִשְׂרָאֵל
קֳדָם אֲבוּהוֹן דִּי בִשְׁמַיָּא, וְאִמְרוּ אָמֵן. (קהל: אָמֵן)

יְהֵא שְׁלָמָא רַבָּא מִן שְׁמַיָּא
וְחַיִּים, עָלֵינוּ וְעַל כָּל יִשְׂרָאֵל, וְאִמְרוּ אָמֵן. (קהל: אָמֵן)

Bow, take three steps back, as if taking leave of the Divine Presence, then bow, first left, then right, then center, while saying:

עֹשֶׂה שָׁלוֹם/ בשבת שובה: הַשָּׁלוֹם/ בִּמְרוֹמָיו
הוּא יַעֲשֶׂה שָׁלוֹם עָלֵינוּ
וְעַל כָּל יִשְׂרָאֵל, וְאִמְרוּ אָמֵן. (קהל: אָמֵן)

Between Sukkot and Pesaḥ, some recite Barekhi Nafshi, page 536, at this point.
Between Pesaḥ and Rosh HaShana some recite Ethics of the Fathers, page 544, at this point.

Stand while saying Aleinu.

עָלֵינוּ It is our duty to praise the Master of all,
and ascribe greatness to the Author of creation,
who has not made us like the nations of the lands
nor placed us like the families of the earth;
who has not made our portion like theirs,
nor our destiny like all their multitudes.
(For they worship vanity and emptiness,
and pray to a god who cannot save.)
▾ *Bow:* But we bow in worship
and thank the Supreme King of kings, the Holy One, blessed be He,
who extends the heavens and establishes the earth,
whose throne of glory is in the heavens above,
and whose power's Presence is in the highest of heights.
He is our God; there is no other.
Truly He is our King, there is none else,
as it is written in His Torah: "You shall know and take to heart this day *Deut. 4*
that the Lord is God, in heaven above and on earth below.
There is no other."

Therefore, we place our hope in You, Lord our God,
that we may soon see the glory of Your power,
when You will remove abominations from the earth,
and idols will be utterly destroyed,
when the world will be perfected under the sovereignty of the Almighty,
when all humanity will call on Your name,
to turn all the earth's wicked toward You.
All the world's inhabitants will realize and know
that to You every knee must bow and every tongue swear loyalty.
Before You, Lord our God, they will kneel and bow down
and give honor to Your glorious name.
They will all accept the yoke of Your kingdom,
and You will reign over them soon and for ever.
For the kingdom is Yours, and to all eternity You will reign in glory,
as it is written in Your Torah: "The Lord will reign for ever and ever." *Ex. 15*

Between סוכות *and* פסח*, some recite* ברכי נפשי*,* *page 537, at this point.*
Between פסח *and* ראש השנה *some recite* פרקי אבות*,* *page 545, at this point.*

Stand while saying עָלֵינוּ*.*

עָלֵינוּ לְשַׁבֵּחַ לַאֲדוֹן הַכֹּל, לָתֵת גְּדֻלָּה לְיוֹצֵר בְּרֵאשִׁית
שֶׁלֹּא עָשָׂנוּ כְּגוֹיֵי הָאֲרָצוֹת, וְלֹא שָׂמָנוּ כְּמִשְׁפְּחוֹת הָאֲדָמָה
שֶׁלֹּא שָׂם חֶלְקֵנוּ כָּהֶם וְגוֹרָלֵנוּ כְּכָל הֲמוֹנָם.
(שֶׁהֵם מִשְׁתַּחֲוִים לְהֶבֶל וָרִיק וּמִתְפַּלְלִים אֶל אֵל לֹא יוֹשִׁיעַ.)
▾ *Bow* וַאֲנַחְנוּ כּוֹרְעִים וּמִשְׁתַּחֲוִים וּמוֹדִים
לִפְנֵי מֶלֶךְ מַלְכֵי הַמְּלָכִים, הַקָּדוֹשׁ בָּרוּךְ הוּא
שֶׁהוּא נוֹטֶה שָׁמַיִם וְיוֹסֵד אָרֶץ, וּמוֹשַׁב יְקָרוֹ בַּשָּׁמַיִם מִמַּעַל
וּשְׁכִינַת עֻזּוֹ בְּגָבְהֵי מְרוֹמִים.
הוּא אֱלֹהֵינוּ, אֵין עוֹד.
אֱמֶת מַלְכֵּנוּ, אֶפֶס זוּלָתוֹ
כַּכָּתוּב בְּתוֹרָתוֹ, וְיָדַעְתָּ הַיּוֹם וַהֲשֵׁבֹתָ אֶל־לְבָבֶךָ דברים ד
כִּי יהוה הוּא הָאֱלֹהִים בַּשָּׁמַיִם מִמַּעַל וְעַל־הָאָרֶץ מִתָּחַת
אֵין עוֹד:

עַל כֵּן נְקַוֶּה לְּךָ יהוה אֱלֹהֵינוּ, לִרְאוֹת מְהֵרָה בְּתִפְאֶרֶת עֻזֶּךָ
לְהַעֲבִיר גִּלּוּלִים מִן הָאָרֶץ, וְהָאֱלִילִים כָּרוֹת יִכָּרֵתוּן
לְתַקֵּן עוֹלָם בְּמַלְכוּת שַׁדַּי.
וְכָל בְּנֵי בָשָׂר יִקְרְאוּ בִשְׁמֶךָ לְהַפְנוֹת אֵלֶיךָ כָּל רִשְׁעֵי אָרֶץ.
יַכִּירוּ וְיֵדְעוּ כָּל יוֹשְׁבֵי תֵבֵל
כִּי לְךָ תִּכְרַע כָּל בֶּרֶךְ, תִּשָּׁבַע כָּל לָשׁוֹן.
לְפָנֶיךָ יהוה אֱלֹהֵינוּ יִכְרְעוּ וְיִפֹּלוּ, וְלִכְבוֹד שִׁמְךָ יְקָר יִתֵּנוּ
וִיקַבְּלוּ כֻלָּם אֶת עֹל מַלְכוּתֶךָ
וְתִמְלֹךְ עֲלֵיהֶם מְהֵרָה לְעוֹלָם וָעֶד.
כִּי הַמַּלְכוּת שֶׁלְּךָ הִיא וּלְעוֹלְמֵי עַד תִּמְלֹךְ בְּכָבוֹד
כַּכָּתוּב בְּתוֹרָתֶךָ, יהוה יִמְלֹךְ לְעֹלָם וָעֶד: שמות טו

And it is said: "Then the LORD shall be King over all the earth; *Zech. 14*
on that day the LORD shall be One and His name One."

Some add:

Have no fear of sudden terror or of the ruin when it overtakes the wicked. *Prov. 3*
Devise your strategy, but it will be thwarted; propose your plan, *Is. 8*
but it will not stand, for God is with us.
When you grow old, I will still be the same. *Is. 46*
When your hair turns gray, I will still carry you.
I made you, I will bear you, I will carry you, and I will rescue you.

MOURNER'S KADDISH

The following prayer, said by mourners, requires the presence of a minyan. A transliteration can be found on page 892.

Mourner: יִתְגַּדַּל Magnified and sanctified may His great name be,
in the world He created by His will.
May He establish His kingdom in your lifetime
and in your days,
and in the lifetime of all the house of Israel,
swiftly and soon – and say: Amen.

All: May His great name be blessed for ever and all time.

Mourner: Blessed and praised, glorified and exalted,
raised and honored, uplifted and lauded
be the name of the Holy One,
blessed be He,
beyond any blessing, song, praise and consolation
uttered in the world –
and say: Amen.

May there be great peace from heaven,
and life for us and all Israel –
and say: Amen.

Bow and take three steps back as if taking leave of the Divine Presence.
Bow left: May He who makes peace in His high places,
Bow right: make peace *Bow forward:* for us and all Israel –
and say: Amen.

וְנֶאֱמַר, וְהָיָה יהוה לְמֶלֶךְ עַל־כָּל־הָאָרֶץ זכריה יד
בַּיּוֹם הַהוּא יִהְיֶה יהוה אֶחָד וּשְׁמוֹ אֶחָד:

Some add:

אַל־תִּירָא מִפַּחַד פִּתְאֹם וּמִשֹּׁאַת רְשָׁעִים כִּי תָבֹא: משלי ג
עֻצוּ עֵצָה וְתֻפָר, דַּבְּרוּ דָבָר וְלֹא יָקוּם, כִּי עִמָּנוּ אֵל: ישעיה ח
וְעַד־זִקְנָה אֲנִי הוּא, וְעַד־שֵׂיבָה אֲנִי אֶסְבֹּל אֲנִי עָשִׂיתִי וַאֲנִי אֶשָּׂא וַאֲנִי אֶסְבֹּל וַאֲמַלֵּט: ישעיה מו

קדיש יתום

The following prayer, said by mourners, requires the presence of a מנין.
A transliteration can be found on page 892.

אבל: יִתְגַּדַּל וְיִתְקַדַּשׁ שְׁמֵהּ רַבָּא (קהל: אָמֵן)
בְּעָלְמָא דִּי בְרָא כִרְעוּתֵהּ
וְיַמְלִיךְ מַלְכוּתֵהּ
בְּחַיֵּיכוֹן וּבְיוֹמֵיכוֹן וּבְחַיֵּי דְכָל בֵּית יִשְׂרָאֵל
בַּעֲגָלָא וּבִזְמַן קָרִיב, וְאִמְרוּ אָמֵן. (קהל: אָמֵן)

קהל ואבל: יְהֵא שְׁמֵהּ רַבָּא מְבָרַךְ לְעָלַם וּלְעָלְמֵי עָלְמַיָּא.

אבל: יִתְבָּרַךְ וְיִשְׁתַּבַּח וְיִתְפָּאַר
וְיִתְרוֹמַם וְיִתְנַשֵּׂא וְיִתְהַדָּר וְיִתְעַלֶּה וְיִתְהַלָּל
שְׁמֵהּ דְּקֻדְשָׁא בְּרִיךְ הוּא (קהל: בְּרִיךְ הוּא)
לְעֵלָּא מִן כָּל בִּרְכָתָא / בשבת שובה: לְעֵלָּא לְעֵלָּא מִכָּל בִּרְכָתָא/
וְשִׁירָתָא, תֻּשְׁבְּחָתָא וְנֶחֱמָתָא
דַּאֲמִירָן בְּעָלְמָא, וְאִמְרוּ אָמֵן. (קהל: אָמֵן)

יְהֵא שְׁלָמָא רַבָּא מִן שְׁמַיָּא
וְחַיִּים, עָלֵינוּ וְעַל כָּל יִשְׂרָאֵל, וְאִמְרוּ אָמֵן. (קהל: אָמֵן)

Bow and take three steps back as if taking leave of the Divine Presence.

Bow left עֹשֶׂה שָׁלוֹם/ בשבת שובה: הַשָּׁלוֹם/ בִּמְרוֹמָיו
Bow right הוּא יַעֲשֶׂה שָׁלוֹם *Bow forward* עָלֵינוּ
וְעַל כָּל יִשְׂרָאֵל, וְאִמְרוּ אָמֵן.

BAREKHI NAFSHI

The following psalms are said from the Shabbat after Simḥat Torah until (but not including) the Shabbat before Pesaḥ.

בָּרְכִי נַפְשִׁי Bless the LORD, my soul.[H] LORD, my God, You are very great, clothed in majesty and splendor, wrapped in a robe of light. You have spread out the heavens like a tent. He has laid the beams of His lofts in the waters. He makes the clouds His chariot, riding on the wings of the wind. He makes the winds His messengers, flames of fire His ministers. He has fixed the earth on its foundations so that it will never be shaken. You covered it with the deep like a cloak; the waters stood above the mountains. At Your rebuke they fled; at the sound of Your thunder they rushed away, flowing over the hills, pouring down into the valleys to the place You appointed for them. You fixed a boundary they were not to pass, so that they would never cover the earth again. He makes springs flow in the valleys; they make their way between the hills, giving drink to all the beasts of the field; the wild donkeys quench their thirst. The birds of the sky dwell beside them, singing among the foliage. He waters the mountains from His lofts: the earth is sated with the fruit of Your work. He makes grass grow for the cattle, and plants for the use of man, that he may produce bread from the earth, wine to cheer the heart of man, oil to make the face shine, and bread to sustain man's heart. The trees of the LORD drink their fill, the cedars of Lebanon which He planted. There, birds build their nests; the stork makes its home in the cypresses. High hills are for the wild goats; crags are shelter for the badgers. He made the moon to mark the seasons, and makes the sun know when to set. You bring darkness and it is night; then all the beasts of the forests stir. The young lions roar for prey, seeking their food from God. When the sun rises, they slink away and seek rest in their lairs. Man goes out to his work and his labor until evening. How numerous are Your works, LORD; You made them all in wisdom; the earth is full of Your creations. There is the vast, immeasurable sea with its countless swarming creatures, living things great and small. There ships sail. There is Leviathan You formed to sport there. All of them look to You in hope, to give them their food when it is due. What You give them, they gather up. When You open Your hand, they are sated with good. When You hide Your face, they are dismayed. When You take away their breath, they die and return to dust. When *Ps. 104*

---

the Songs of Ascent, the first two words of each of the chapters. There are fifteen of them in total, a number that carries symbolic and associative importance to creation in general and prayer in particular (*Sukka* 53a; Rabbeinu Baḥye on *Shemot* 25:7).

ברכי נפשי

The following psalms are said from שבת בראשית *until (but not including)* שבת הגדול.

בָּרְכִי נַפְשִׁי[ה] אֶת־יהוה, יהוה אֱלֹהַי גָּדַלְתָּ מְּאֹד, הוֹד וְהָדָר לָבָשְׁתָּ: עֹטֶה־ תהלים קד
אוֹר כַּשַּׂלְמָה, נוֹטֶה שָׁמַיִם כַּיְרִיעָה: הַמְקָרֶה בַמַּיִם עֲלִיּוֹתָיו, הַשָּׂם־עָבִים
רְכוּבוֹ, הַמְהַלֵּךְ עַל־כַּנְפֵי־רוּחַ: עֹשֶׂה מַלְאָכָיו רוּחוֹת, מְשָׁרְתָיו אֵשׁ לֹהֵט:
יָסַד־אֶרֶץ עַל־מְכוֹנֶיהָ, בַּל־תִּמּוֹט עוֹלָם וָעֶד: תְּהוֹם כַּלְּבוּשׁ כִּסִּיתוֹ, עַל־
הָרִים יַעַמְדוּ־מָיִם: מִן־גַּעֲרָתְךָ יְנוּסוּן, מִן־קוֹל רַעַמְךָ יֵחָפֵזוּן: יַעֲלוּ הָרִים,
יֵרְדוּ בְקָעוֹת, אֶל־מְקוֹם זֶה יָסַדְתָּ לָהֶם: גְּבוּל־שַׂמְתָּ בַּל־יַעֲבֹרוּן, בַּל־
יְשׁוּבוּן לְכַסּוֹת הָאָרֶץ: הַמְשַׁלֵּחַ מַעְיָנִים בַּנְּחָלִים, בֵּין הָרִים יְהַלֵּכוּן: יַשְׁקוּ
כָּל־חַיְתוֹ שָׂדָי, יִשְׁבְּרוּ פְרָאִים צְמָאָם: עֲלֵיהֶם עוֹף־הַשָּׁמַיִם יִשְׁכּוֹן, מִבֵּין
עֳפָאיִם יִתְּנוּ־קוֹל: מַשְׁקֶה הָרִים מֵעֲלִיּוֹתָיו, מִפְּרִי מַעֲשֶׂיךָ תִּשְׂבַּע הָאָרֶץ:
מַצְמִיחַ חָצִיר לַבְּהֵמָה, וְעֵשֶׂב לַעֲבֹדַת הָאָדָם, לְהוֹצִיא לֶחֶם מִן־הָאָרֶץ:
וְיַיִן יְשַׂמַּח לְבַב־אֱנוֹשׁ, לְהַצְהִיל פָּנִים מִשָּׁמֶן, וְלֶחֶם לְבַב־אֱנוֹשׁ יִסְעָד:
יִשְׂבְּעוּ עֲצֵי יהוה, אַרְזֵי לְבָנוֹן אֲשֶׁר נָטָע: אֲשֶׁר־שָׁם צִפֳּרִים יְקַנֵּנוּ, חֲסִידָה
בְּרוֹשִׁים בֵּיתָהּ: הָרִים הַגְּבֹהִים לַיְּעֵלִים, סְלָעִים מַחְסֶה לַשְׁפַנִּים: עָשָׂה יָרֵחַ
לְמוֹעֲדִים, שֶׁמֶשׁ יָדַע מְבוֹאוֹ: תָּשֶׁת־חֹשֶׁךְ וִיהִי לָיְלָה, בּוֹ־תִרְמֹשׂ כָּל־חַיְתוֹ־
יָעַר: הַכְּפִירִים שֹׁאֲגִים לַטָּרֶף, וּלְבַקֵּשׁ מֵאֵל אָכְלָם: תִּזְרַח הַשֶּׁמֶשׁ יֵאָסֵפוּן,
וְאֶל־מְעוֹנֹתָם יִרְבָּצוּן: יֵצֵא אָדָם לְפָעֳלוֹ, וְלַעֲבֹדָתוֹ עֲדֵי־עָרֶב: מָה־רַבּוּ
מַעֲשֶׂיךָ יהוה, כֻּלָּם בְּחָכְמָה עָשִׂיתָ, מָלְאָה הָאָרֶץ קִנְיָנֶךָ: זֶה הַיָּם גָּדוֹל
וּרְחַב יָדָיִם, שָׁם־רֶמֶשׂ וְאֵין מִסְפָּר, חַיּוֹת קְטַנּוֹת עִם־גְּדֹלוֹת: שָׁם אֳנִיּוֹת
יְהַלֵּכוּן, לִוְיָתָן זֶה־יָצַרְתָּ לְשַׂחֶק־בּוֹ: כֻּלָּם אֵלֶיךָ יְשַׂבֵּרוּן, לָתֵת אָכְלָם בְּעִתּוֹ:
תִּתֵּן לָהֶם יִלְקֹטוּן, תִּפְתַּח יָדְךָ יִשְׂבְּעוּן טוֹב: תַּסְתִּיר פָּנֶיךָ יִבָּהֵלוּן, תֹּסֵף

HILKHOT TEFILLA • הלכות תפילה

בָּרְכִי נַפְשִׁי – *Bless the Lord, my soul.* There is a custom to recite these chapters from *Tehillim* from *Shabbat Bereshit* (the Shabbat on which the first chapter of the book of *Bereshit* is read) until the Shabbat before Pesaḥ. It is appropriate perhaps that *Tehillim* 104, which extols the wonders of creation, should be recited every Shabbat during the winter months, for what better time to remind ourselves of the beauty and the miracles that lie dormant all around us. Chapters 120-134 are collectively known as

You send back Your breath, they are created, giving new life to the earth. May the glory of the Lord be for ever; may the Lord rejoice in His works. When He looks at the earth, it trembles. When He touches the mountains, they pour forth smoke. I will sing to the Lord as long as I live; I will sing psalms to my God all my life. May my meditation be pleasing to Him; I shall rejoice in the Lord. May sinners vanish from the earth, and the wicked be no more. Bless the Lord, my soul. Halleluya!

A song of ascents. I called to the Lord in my distress and He answered me. *Ps. 120*
"Lord, save my soul from lying lips, from a deceitful tongue." What will a deceitful tongue profit you? What will you gain? Only a warrior's sharp arrows, and hot coals of broom-wood. Woe to me that I dwell in Meshekh, that I live among the tents of Kedar. I have lived too long among those who hate peace. I am for peace, but whenever I speak of it, they are for war.

A song of ascents. I lift my eyes up to the hills; from where will my help come? *Ps. 121*
My help comes from the Lord, Maker of heaven and earth. He will not let your foot stumble; He who guards you does not slumber. See: the Guardian of Israel neither slumbers nor sleeps. The Lord is your Guardian; the Lord is your Shade at your right hand. The sun will not strike you by day, nor the moon by night. The Lord will guard you from all harm; He will guard your life. The Lord will guard your going and coming, now and for evermore.

A song of ascents. Of David. I rejoiced when they said to me, "Let us go to *Ps. 122*
the House of the Lord." Our feet stood within your gates, Jerusalem: Jerusalem built as a city joined together. There the tribes went up, the tribes of the Lord – as a testimony to Israel – to give thanks to the name of the Lord. For there the thrones of justice are set, the thrones of the house of David. Pray for the peace of Jerusalem: "May those who love you prosper. May there be peace within your ramparts, tranquility in your citadels." For the sake of my brothers and my friends, I shall say, "Peace be within you." For the sake of the House of the Lord our God, I shall seek your good.

A song of ascents. To You, enthroned in heaven, I lift my eyes. As the eyes *Ps. 123*
of slaves turn to their master's hand, or the eyes of a slave-girl to the hand of her mistress, so our eyes are turned to the Lord our God, awaiting His favor. Show us favor, Lord, show us favor, for we have suffered more than enough contempt. Too long have we suffered the scorn of the complacent, the contempt of arrogant men.

A song of ascents. Of David. Had the Lord not been on our side – let Israel *Ps. 124*
say it – had the Lord not been on our side when men rose up against us, they would have swallowed us alive when their anger raged against us. The waters

רוּחָם יִגְוָעוּן, וְאֶל־עֲפָרָם יְשׁוּבוּן: תְּשַׁלַּח רוּחֲךָ יִבָּרֵאוּן, וּתְחַדֵּשׁ פְּנֵי אֲדָמָה:
יְהִי כְבוֹד יהוה לְעוֹלָם, יִשְׂמַח יהוה בְּמַעֲשָׂיו: הַמַּבִּיט לָאָרֶץ וַתִּרְעָד, יִגַּע
בֶּהָרִים וְיֶעֱשָׁנוּ: אָשִׁירָה לַיהוה בְּחַיָּי, אֲזַמְּרָה לֵאלֹהַי בְּעוֹדִי: יֶעֱרַב עָלָיו
שִׂיחִי, אָנֹכִי אֶשְׂמַח בַּיהוה: יִתַּמּוּ חַטָּאִים מִן־הָאָרֶץ, וּרְשָׁעִים עוֹד אֵינָם,
בָּרְכִי נַפְשִׁי אֶת־יהוה, הַלְלוּיָהּ:

שִׁיר הַמַּעֲלוֹת, אֶל־יהוה בַּצָּרָתָה לִּי, קָרָאתִי וַיַּעֲנֵנִי: יהוה הַצִּילָה נַפְשִׁי תהלים קכ
מִשְּׂפַת־שֶׁקֶר, מִלָּשׁוֹן רְמִיָּה: מַה־יִּתֵּן לְךָ וּמַה־יֹּסִיף לָךְ, לָשׁוֹן רְמִיָּה: חִצֵּי
גִבּוֹר שְׁנוּנִים, עִם גַּחֲלֵי רְתָמִים: אוֹיָה־לִי כִּי־גַרְתִּי מֶשֶׁךְ, שָׁכַנְתִּי עִם־אָהֳלֵי
קֵדָר: רַבַּת שָׁכְנָה־לָּהּ נַפְשִׁי, עִם שׂוֹנֵא שָׁלוֹם: אֲנִי־שָׁלוֹם וְכִי אֲדַבֵּר, הֵמָּה
לַמִּלְחָמָה:

שִׁיר לַמַּעֲלוֹת, אֶשָּׂא עֵינַי אֶל־הֶהָרִים, מֵאַיִן יָבֹא עֶזְרִי: עֶזְרִי מֵעִם יהוה, תהלים קכא
עֹשֵׂה שָׁמַיִם וָאָרֶץ: אַל־יִתֵּן לַמּוֹט רַגְלֶךָ, אַל־יָנוּם שֹׁמְרֶךָ: הִנֵּה לֹא־יָנוּם וְלֹא
יִישָׁן, שׁוֹמֵר יִשְׂרָאֵל: יהוה שֹׁמְרֶךָ, יהוה צִלְּךָ עַל־יַד יְמִינֶךָ: יוֹמָם הַשֶּׁמֶשׁ
לֹא־יַכֶּכָּה, וְיָרֵחַ בַּלָּיְלָה: יהוה יִשְׁמָרְךָ מִכָּל־רָע, יִשְׁמֹר אֶת־נַפְשֶׁךָ: יהוה
יִשְׁמָר־צֵאתְךָ וּבוֹאֶךָ, מֵעַתָּה וְעַד־עוֹלָם:

שִׁיר הַמַּעֲלוֹת לְדָוִד, שָׂמַחְתִּי בְּאֹמְרִים לִי בֵּית יהוה נֵלֵךְ: עֹמְדוֹת הָיוּ תהלים קכב
רַגְלֵינוּ, בִּשְׁעָרַיִךְ יְרוּשָׁלָםִ: יְרוּשָׁלַםִ הַבְּנוּיָה, כְּעִיר שֶׁחֻבְּרָה־לָּהּ יַחְדָּו: שֶׁשָּׁם
עָלוּ שְׁבָטִים שִׁבְטֵי־יָהּ, עֵדוּת לְיִשְׂרָאֵל, לְהֹדוֹת לְשֵׁם יהוה: כִּי שָׁמָּה יָשְׁבוּ
כִסְאוֹת לְמִשְׁפָּט, כִּסְאוֹת לְבֵית דָּוִד: שַׁאֲלוּ שְׁלוֹם יְרוּשָׁלָםִ, יִשְׁלָיוּ אֹהֲבָיִךְ:
יְהִי־שָׁלוֹם בְּחֵילֵךְ, שַׁלְוָה בְּאַרְמְנוֹתָיִךְ: לְמַעַן אַחַי וְרֵעָי, אֲדַבְּרָה־נָּא שָׁלוֹם
בָּךְ: לְמַעַן בֵּית־יהוה אֱלֹהֵינוּ, אֲבַקְשָׁה טוֹב לָךְ:

שִׁיר הַמַּעֲלוֹת, אֵלֶיךָ נָשָׂאתִי אֶת־עֵינַי, הַיֹּשְׁבִי בַּשָּׁמָיִם: הִנֵּה כְעֵינֵי עֲבָדִים תהלים קכג
אֶל־יַד אֲדוֹנֵיהֶם, כְּעֵינֵי שִׁפְחָה אֶל־יַד גְּבִרְתָּהּ, כֵּן עֵינֵינוּ אֶל־יהוה אֱלֹהֵינוּ,
עַד שֶׁיְּחָנֵּנוּ: חָנֵּנוּ יהוה חָנֵּנוּ, כִּי־רַב שָׂבַעְנוּ בוּז: רַבַּת שָׂבְעָה־לָּהּ נַפְשֵׁנוּ,
הַלַּעַג הַשַּׁאֲנַנִּים, הַבּוּז לִגְאֵי יוֹנִים:

שִׁיר הַמַּעֲלוֹת לְדָוִד, לוּלֵי יהוה שֶׁהָיָה לָנוּ, יֹאמַר־נָא יִשְׂרָאֵל: לוּלֵי יהוה תהלים קכד
שֶׁהָיָה לָנוּ, בְּקוּם עָלֵינוּ אָדָם: אֲזַי חַיִּים בְּלָעוּנוּ, בַּחֲרוֹת אַפָּם בָּנוּ: אֲזַי הַמַּיִם

would have engulfed us; the torrent would have swept over us; over us would have swept the raging waters. Blessed be the LORD who did not leave us as a prey for their teeth. We escaped like a bird from the fowler's trap; the trap broke and we escaped. Our help is in the name of the LORD, Maker of heaven and earth.

A song of ascents. Those who trust in the LORD are like Mount Zion that cannot *Ps. 125*
be moved, that stands firm for ever. As hills surround Jerusalem so the LORD surrounds His people, now and forever. The scepter of the wicked shall not rest on the land allotted to the righteous, so that the righteous shall not set their hand to wrongdoing. Do good, LORD, to those who are good, to those who are upright in heart. As for those who turn aside to crooked ways, may the LORD make them go the way of evildoers. Peace be on Israel!

A song of ascents. When the LORD brought back the exiles of Zion we were like *Ps. 126*
people who dream. Then were our mouths filled with laughter, and our tongues with songs of joy. Then was it said among the nations, "The LORD has done great things for them." The LORD did do great things for us and we rejoiced. Bring back our exiles, LORD, like streams in a dry land. May those who sowed in tears, reap in joy. May one who goes out weeping, carrying a bag of seed, come back with songs of joy, carrying his sheaves.

A song of ascents. Of Solomon. Unless the LORD builds the house, its builders *Ps. 127*
labor in vain. Unless the LORD guards the city, in vain does the guard keep watch. In vain do you rise early and go late to rest, toiling for the bread you eat. He provides for His loved ones while they sleep. Children are a heritage from the LORD; the fruit of the womb, His reward. Like arrows in the hand of a warrior are the sons of one's youth. Happy is the man who fills his quiver with them; they shall not be put to shame when they contend with the enemy at the gate.

A song of ascents. Happy are all who fear the LORD, who walk in His ways. *Ps. 128*
When you eat the fruit of your labor, happy and fortunate are you. Your wife shall be like a fruitful vine within your house; your sons like olive saplings around your table. So shall the man who fears the LORD be blessed. May the LORD bless you from Zion; may you see the good of Jerusalem all the days of your life; and may you live to see your children's children. Peace be on Israel!

A song of ascents. Often since I was young I have been attacked – let Israel now *Ps. 129*
say – often since I was young I have been attacked, but never have my attackers prevailed. Ploughmen ploughed across my back, making long furrows. But the LORD is just; He has cut the bonds of the wicked. Let all who hate Zion be driven back in shame. Let them be like the grass on roofs that fades before it can be pulled up. It will never fill a reaper's hand nor yield an armful for the gatherer of sheaves. No passersby will say to them: "The LORD's blessing be upon you. We bless you in the name of the LORD."

שְׁטָפוּנוּ, נַחְלָה עָבַר עַל־נַפְשֵׁנוּ: אֲזַי עָבַר עַל־נַפְשֵׁנוּ, הַמַּיִם הַזֵּידוֹנִים: בָּרוּךְ יהוה, שֶׁלֹּא נְתָנָנוּ טֶרֶף לְשִׁנֵּיהֶם: נַפְשֵׁנוּ כְּצִפּוֹר נִמְלְטָה מִפַּח יוֹקְשִׁים, הַפַּח נִשְׁבָּר וַאֲנַחְנוּ נִמְלָטְנוּ: עֶזְרֵנוּ בְּשֵׁם יהוה, עֹשֵׂה שָׁמַיִם וָאָרֶץ:

תהלים קכה
שִׁיר הַמַּעֲלוֹת, הַבֹּטְחִים בַּיהוה, כְּהַר־צִיּוֹן לֹא־יִמּוֹט, לְעוֹלָם יֵשֵׁב: יְרוּשָׁלַםִ, הָרִים סָבִיב לָהּ, וַיהוה סָבִיב לְעַמּוֹ, מֵעַתָּה וְעַד־עוֹלָם: כִּי לֹא יָנוּחַ שֵׁבֶט הָרֶשַׁע עַל גּוֹרַל הַצַּדִּיקִים, לְמַעַן לֹא־יִשְׁלְחוּ הַצַּדִּיקִים בְּעַוְלָתָה יְדֵיהֶם: הֵיטִיבָה יהוה לַטּוֹבִים, וְלִישָׁרִים בְּלִבּוֹתָם: וְהַמַּטִּים עֲקַלְקַלּוֹתָם יוֹלִיכֵם יהוה אֶת־פֹּעֲלֵי הָאָוֶן, שָׁלוֹם עַל־יִשְׂרָאֵל:

תהלים קכו
שִׁיר הַמַּעֲלוֹת, בְּשׁוּב יהוה אֶת־שִׁיבַת צִיּוֹן, הָיִינוּ כְּחֹלְמִים: אָז יִמָּלֵא שְׂחוֹק פִּינוּ וּלְשׁוֹנֵנוּ רִנָּה, אָז יֹאמְרוּ בַגּוֹיִם הִגְדִּיל יהוה לַעֲשׂוֹת עִם־אֵלֶּה: הִגְדִּיל יהוה לַעֲשׂוֹת עִמָּנוּ, הָיִינוּ שְׂמֵחִים: שׁוּבָה יהוה אֶת־שְׁבִיתֵנוּ, כַּאֲפִיקִים בַּנֶּגֶב: הַזֹּרְעִים בְּדִמְעָה בְּרִנָּה יִקְצֹרוּ: הָלוֹךְ יֵלֵךְ וּבָכֹה נֹשֵׂא מֶשֶׁךְ־הַזָּרַע, בֹּא־יָבֹא בְרִנָּה נֹשֵׂא אֲלֻמֹּתָיו:

תהלים קכז
שִׁיר הַמַּעֲלוֹת לִשְׁלֹמֹה, אִם־יהוה לֹא־יִבְנֶה בַיִת, שָׁוְא עָמְלוּ בוֹנָיו בּוֹ, אִם־יהוה לֹא־יִשְׁמָר־עִיר, שָׁוְא שָׁקַד שׁוֹמֵר: שָׁוְא לָכֶם מַשְׁכִּימֵי קוּם מְאַחֲרֵי־שֶׁבֶת, אֹכְלֵי לֶחֶם הָעֲצָבִים, כֵּן יִתֵּן לִידִידוֹ שֵׁנָא: הִנֵּה נַחֲלַת יהוה בָּנִים, שָׂכָר פְּרִי הַבָּטֶן: כְּחִצִּים בְּיַד־גִּבּוֹר כֵּן בְּנֵי הַנְּעוּרִים: אַשְׁרֵי הַגֶּבֶר אֲשֶׁר מִלֵּא אֶת־אַשְׁפָּתוֹ מֵהֶם, לֹא־יֵבֹשׁוּ כִּי־יְדַבְּרוּ אֶת־אוֹיְבִים בַּשָּׁעַר:

תהלים קכח
שִׁיר הַמַּעֲלוֹת, אַשְׁרֵי כָּל־יְרֵא יהוה, הַהֹלֵךְ בִּדְרָכָיו: יְגִיעַ כַּפֶּיךָ כִּי תֹאכֵל, אַשְׁרֶיךָ וְטוֹב לָךְ: אֶשְׁתְּךָ כְּגֶפֶן פֹּרִיָּה בְּיַרְכְּתֵי בֵיתֶךָ, בָּנֶיךָ כִּשְׁתִלֵי זֵיתִים, סָבִיב לְשֻׁלְחָנֶךָ: הִנֵּה כִי־כֵן יְבֹרַךְ גָּבֶר יְרֵא יהוה: יְבָרֶכְךָ יהוה מִצִּיּוֹן, וּרְאֵה בְּטוּב יְרוּשָׁלָםִ, כֹּל יְמֵי חַיֶּיךָ: וּרְאֵה־בָנִים לְבָנֶיךָ, שָׁלוֹם עַל־יִשְׂרָאֵל:

תהלים קכט
שִׁיר הַמַּעֲלוֹת, רַבַּת צְרָרוּנִי מִנְּעוּרַי, יֹאמַר־נָא יִשְׂרָאֵל: רַבַּת צְרָרוּנִי מִנְּעוּרָי, גַּם לֹא־יָכְלוּ לִי: עַל־גַּבִּי חָרְשׁוּ חֹרְשִׁים, הֶאֱרִיכוּ לְמַעֲנִיתָם: יהוה צַדִּיק, קִצֵּץ עֲבוֹת רְשָׁעִים: יֵבֹשׁוּ וְיִסֹּגוּ אָחוֹר כֹּל שֹׂנְאֵי צִיּוֹן: יִהְיוּ כַּחֲצִיר גַּגּוֹת שֶׁקַּדְמַת שָׁלַף יָבֵשׁ: שֶׁלֹּא מִלֵּא כַפּוֹ קוֹצֵר, וְחִצְנוֹ מְעַמֵּר: וְלֹא אָמְרוּ הָעֹבְרִים, בִּרְכַּת־יהוה אֲלֵיכֶם, בֵּרַכְנוּ אֶתְכֶם בְּשֵׁם יהוה:

A song of ascents. From the depths I have called to You, O Lord. Lord, hear my voice; let Your ears be attentive to my plea. If You, Lord, should keep account of sins, O Lord, who could stand? But with You there is forgiveness, that You may be held in awe. I wait for the Lord, my soul waits, and in His word I put my hope. My soul waits for the Lord more than watchmen wait for the morning, more than watchmen wait for the morning. Israel, put your hope in the Lord, for with the Lord there is loving-kindness, and great is His power to redeem. It is He who will redeem Israel from all their sins. *Ps. 130*

A song of ascents. By David. Lord, my heart is not proud, nor are my eyes haughty. I do not busy myself with great affairs or with things beyond me. But I have made my soul still and quiet, like a weaned child with its mother; like a weaned child is my soul within me. Israel, put your hope in the Lord, now and for evermore. *Ps. 131*

A song of ascents. Lord, remember David and all the hardship he endured. He swore an oath to the Lord and made a vow to the Mighty One of Jacob: "I will not enter my house, nor go to bed; I will not give sleep to my eyes or slumber to my eyelids, until I find a place for the Lord, a dwelling for the Mighty One of Jacob." We heard of it in Efrat, we found it in the fields of Yaar. Let us enter His dwelling, worship at His footstool. Advance, Lord, to Your resting place, You and Your mighty Ark. Your priests are robed in righteousness; Your devoted ones sing for joy. For the sake of Your servant David, do not reject Your anointed one. The Lord swore to David a firm oath that He will not revoke: "One of your own descendants I will set upon your throne. If your sons keep My covenant and My decrees that I teach them, then their sons shall sit upon your throne for all time." For the Lord has chosen Zion; He desired it for His home. This is My resting place for all time; here I will dwell, for that is My desire. I will amply bless its store of food; its poor I will satisfy with bread. I will clothe its priests with salvation; its loyal ones shall sing for joy. There I will make David's dynasty flourish; I will prepare a lamp for My anointed one. I will clothe his enemies with shame, but on him will be a shining crown. *Ps. 132*

A song of ascents. By David. How good and pleasant it is when brothers dwell together. It is like fragrant oil on the head, running down onto the beard, Aaron's beard, that runs down over the collar of his robes. It is like the dew of Hermon that falls on the mountains of Zion. There the Lord bestows His blessing, life for evermore. *Ps. 133*

A song of ascents. Come, bless the Lord, all you servants of the Lord, who nightly stand in the House of the Lord. Lift up your hands toward the Sanctuary and bless the Lord. May the Lord, Maker of heaven and earth, bless you from Zion! *Ps. 134*

תהלים קל שִׁיר הַמַּעֲלוֹת, מִמַּעֲמַקִּים קְרָאתִיךָ יהוה: אֲדֹנָי שִׁמְעָה בְקוֹלִי, תִּהְיֶינָה אָזְנֶיךָ קַשֻּׁבוֹת לְקוֹל תַּחֲנוּנָי: אִם־עֲוֹנוֹת תִּשְׁמָר־יָהּ, אֲדֹנָי מִי יַעֲמֹד: כִּי־עִמְּךָ הַסְּלִיחָה, לְמַעַן תִּוָּרֵא: קִוִּיתִי יהוה קִוְּתָה נַפְשִׁי, וְלִדְבָרוֹ הוֹחָלְתִּי: נַפְשִׁי לַאדֹנָי, מִשֹּׁמְרִים לַבֹּקֶר, שֹׁמְרִים לַבֹּקֶר: יַחֵל יִשְׂרָאֵל אֶל־יהוה, כִּי־עִם־יהוה הַחֶסֶד, וְהַרְבֵּה עִמּוֹ פְדוּת: וְהוּא יִפְדֶּה אֶת־יִשְׂרָאֵל, מִכֹּל עֲוֹנוֹתָיו:

תהלים קלא שִׁיר הַמַּעֲלוֹת לְדָוִד, יהוה לֹא־גָבַהּ לִבִּי, וְלֹא־רָמוּ עֵינַי, וְלֹא־הִלַּכְתִּי בִּגְדֹלוֹת וּבְנִפְלָאוֹת מִמֶּנִּי: אִם־לֹא שִׁוִּיתִי וְדוֹמַמְתִּי נַפְשִׁי, כְּגָמֻל עֲלֵי אִמּוֹ, כַּגָּמֻל עָלַי נַפְשִׁי: יַחֵל יִשְׂרָאֵל אֶל־יהוה, מֵעַתָּה וְעַד־עוֹלָם:

תהלים קלב שִׁיר הַמַּעֲלוֹת, זְכוֹר־יהוה לְדָוִד אֵת כָּל־עֻנּוֹתוֹ: אֲשֶׁר נִשְׁבַּע לַיהוה, נָדַר לַאֲבִיר יַעֲקֹב: אִם־אָבֹא בְּאֹהֶל בֵּיתִי, אִם־אֶעֱלֶה עַל־עֶרֶשׂ יְצוּעָי: אִם־אֶתֵּן שְׁנָת לְעֵינָי, לְעַפְעַפַּי תְּנוּמָה: עַד־אֶמְצָא מָקוֹם לַיהוה, מִשְׁכָּנוֹת לַאֲבִיר יַעֲקֹב: הִנֵּה־שְׁמַעֲנוּהָ בְאֶפְרָתָה, מְצָאנוּהָ בִּשְׂדֵי־יָעַר: נָבוֹאָה לְמִשְׁכְּנוֹתָיו, נִשְׁתַּחֲוֶה לַהֲדֹם רַגְלָיו: קוּמָה יהוה לִמְנוּחָתֶךָ, אַתָּה וַאֲרוֹן עֻזֶּךָ: כֹּהֲנֶיךָ יִלְבְּשׁוּ־צֶדֶק, וַחֲסִידֶיךָ יְרַנֵּנוּ: בַּעֲבוּר דָּוִד עַבְדֶּךָ, אַל־תָּשֵׁב פְּנֵי מְשִׁיחֶךָ: נִשְׁבַּע־יהוה לְדָוִד, אֱמֶת לֹא־יָשׁוּב מִמֶּנָּה, מִפְּרִי בִטְנְךָ אָשִׁית לְכִסֵּא־לָךְ: אִם־יִשְׁמְרוּ בָנֶיךָ בְּרִיתִי, וְעֵדֹתִי זוֹ אֲלַמְּדֵם, גַּם־בְּנֵיהֶם עֲדֵי־עַד, יֵשְׁבוּ לְכִסֵּא־לָךְ: כִּי־בָחַר יהוה בְּצִיּוֹן, אִוָּהּ לְמוֹשָׁב לוֹ: זֹאת־מְנוּחָתִי עֲדֵי־עַד, פֹּה אֵשֵׁב כִּי אִוִּתִיהָ: צֵידָהּ בָּרֵךְ אֲבָרֵךְ, אֶבְיוֹנֶיהָ אַשְׂבִּיעַ לָחֶם: וְכֹהֲנֶיהָ אַלְבִּישׁ יֶשַׁע, וַחֲסִידֶיהָ רַנֵּן יְרַנֵּנוּ: שָׁם אַצְמִיחַ קֶרֶן לְדָוִד, עָרַכְתִּי נֵר לִמְשִׁיחִי: אוֹיְבָיו אַלְבִּישׁ בֹּשֶׁת, וְעָלָיו יָצִיץ נִזְרוֹ:

תהלים קלג שִׁיר הַמַּעֲלוֹת לְדָוִד, הִנֵּה מַה־טּוֹב וּמַה־נָּעִים, שֶׁבֶת אַחִים גַּם־יָחַד: כַּשֶּׁמֶן הַטּוֹב עַל־הָרֹאשׁ, יֹרֵד עַל־הַזָּקָן, זְקַן־אַהֲרֹן שֶׁיֹּרֵד עַל־פִּי מִדּוֹתָיו: כְּטַל־חֶרְמוֹן שֶׁיֹּרֵד עַל־הַרְרֵי צִיּוֹן, כִּי שָׁם צִוָּה יהוה אֶת־הַבְּרָכָה, חַיִּים עַד־הָעוֹלָם:

תהלים קלד שִׁיר הַמַּעֲלוֹת, הִנֵּה בָּרְכוּ אֶת־יהוה כָּל־עַבְדֵי יהוה, הָעֹמְדִים בְּבֵית־יהוה בַּלֵּילוֹת: שְׂאוּ־יְדֵכֶם קֹדֶשׁ, וּבָרְכוּ אֶת־יהוה: יְבָרֶכְךָ יהוה מִצִּיּוֹן, עֹשֵׂה שָׁמַיִם וָאָרֶץ:

ETHICS OF THE FATHERS

One of the following chapters is read each Shabbat after Pesaḥ until the Shabbat before Rosh HaShana. On the last three Shabbatot before Rosh HaShana, two chapters are read.

All Israel have a share in the World to Come,[B] as it is said: *Sanhedrin 90a*
"Your people are all righteous; they shall inherit the land for ever; *Is. 60*
they are a shoot of My own planting,
a work of My own hands, that I may be glorified."

CHAPTER I

1. Moses received the Torah at Sinai and handed it on to Yehoshua; Yehoshua to the elders; the elders to the prophets; and the prophets handed it on to the men of the Great Assembly. They (the men of the Great Assembly) said three things: Be careful in judgment; raise up many disciples; and make a fence for the Torah.

Why during this time of year in particular? Again, there is no one reason to be found. Some suggest that this is a period of "spring fever" when one needs reminders about being true to our values of ethics and propriety (*Midrash Shmuel*). Similarly, this period is generally considered a time of semi-mourning in Jewish life, the so-called Omer, which commemorates the death of 12,000 pairs of Rabbi Akiva's students, an event which should move us to further humility and self-improvement.

During this time of year, the days are longer and there is more time to do some learning that one may not be able to do during the week (*HaManhig*). This would explain why the custom to learn this material extends from Pesaḥ all the way to Rosh HaShana.

BIUR TEFILLA • ביאור תפילה

כָּל יִשְׂרָאֵל יֵשׁ לָהֶם חֵלֶק לָעוֹלָם הַבָּא – *All Israel have a share in the World to Come.* The recitation of this brief mishna from the tractate *Sanhedrin* was instituted, according to the twelfth-century Provencal scholar Rabbi Avraham ibn Yarḥi "so as to not question the status of those who are returnees to observant Judaism as well as those who are uneducated. If not for the words in that paragraph, those individuals who may not be as involved in Torah study nor in the appropriate performance of *mitzvot* might lose hope that they will merit entrance into the Next World" (*HaManhig*). The passage thus assures that all Jews have a place, regardless of how much they understand or how many commandments they have or haven't performed in the past. Change is always possible and welcome, even if it is only in small increments.

פרקי אבות

One of the following chapters is read each שבת *after* פסח *until the* שבת *before* ראש השנה*. On the last three* שבתות *before* ראש השנה*, two chapters are read.*

כָּל יִשְׂרָאֵל יֵשׁ לָהֶם חֵלֶק לָעוֹלָם הַבָּא.[ב] שֶׁנֶּאֱמַר: סנהדרין צ.
וְעַמֵּךְ כֻּלָּם צַדִּיקִים, לְעוֹלָם יִירְשׁוּ אָרֶץ ישעיה ס
נֵצֶר מַטָּעַי, מַעֲשֵׂה יָדַי לְהִתְפָּאֵר:

פרק ראשון

א מֹשֶׁה קִבֵּל תּוֹרָה מִסִּינַי וּמְסָרָהּ לִיהוֹשֻׁעַ, וִיהוֹשֻׁעַ לִזְקֵנִים, וּזְקֵנִים לִנְבִיאִים, וּנְבִיאִים מְסָרוּהָ לְאַנְשֵׁי כְנֶסֶת הַגְּדוֹלָה. הֵם אָמְרוּ שְׁלֹשָׁה דְבָרִים: הֱווּ מְתוּנִים בַּדִּין, וְהַעֲמִידוּ תַלְמִידִים הַרְבֵּה, וַעֲשׂוּ סְיָג לַתּוֹרָה.

INTRODUCTION TO PIRKEI AVOT

פרקי אבות – *PIRKEI AVOT* (*Chapters [Ethics] of the Fathers*) is an unusual tractate of the Mishna which deals almost entirely with ethical teachings of the Rabbis. Its style is short and concise, making it sometimes difficult to understand without commentary. While the values and virtues of Judaism can be found defined and debated throughout all of Mishna and Talmud, this is the only place where such teachings are gathered in one place to the near exclusion of other kinds of legal material. Hence the rabbinic view which said that, of all of the Oral Law, if one wants to be a pious person one should learn *Avot* (*Bava Kamma* 30a).

There are a number of rationales offered for why this section was traditionally learned on Shabbat afternoon and how often and therefore there were and remain numerous different customs related to its recitation. To cite but a few:

Shabbat afternoon was the time when Moshe died (though there is another tradition which says it was Friday evening) and there is a custom that one does not learn Talmud when a great sage dies but only Mishna as is our custom to this day in a house of mourning. In deference to the very first Mishna in this tractate which mentions Moshe's role in tradition, we restrict our learning to these chapters (*Otzar HaGeonim*). Alternatively, simply the fact that Moshe spent a total of four summer months atop Mount Sinai receiving the Torah, as indicated in the first line, would be enough to merit this selection of learning (Rabbi E. Munk).

A common custom was to do this learning only on Shabbat afternoon between Pesaḥ and Shavuot. This would explain why there is a chapter that was added to the original five chapters of the tractate, for there are six *Shabbatot* between the two holidays.

Shimon the Just was one of the last survivors of the Great Assembly. He used to say: On three things the world stands: on the Torah, on divine worship, and on acts of loving-kindness.

3. Antigonos of Sokho received [the Torah tradition] from Shimon the Just. He used to say: Do not be like servants who serve their master on condition of receiving a reward, but be like servants who serve their master not on condition of receiving a reward; and let the fear of Heaven be upon you.

4. Yose ben Yo'ezer of Zereda and Yose ben Yoḥanan of Jerusalem received [the tradition] from them. Yose ben Yo'ezer of Zereda used to say: Let your house be a meeting place for sages; sit in the dust at their feet, and with thirst, drink in their words.

5. Yose ben Yoḥanan of Jerusalem used to say: Let your house be open wide; let the poor join the members of your household; and do not gossip inordinately with women. This was said about one's own wife; all the more so does it apply to another man's wife. Hence the sages say: a man who talks too much with a woman brings trouble on himself, neglects the study of Torah, and in the end will inherit Gehinnom.

6. Yehoshua ben Peraḥya and Nittai the Arbelite received [the tradition] from them. Yehoshua ben Peraḥya used to say: Get yourself a teacher, acquire a companion, and give everyone the benefit of the doubt.

7. Nittai the Arbelite used to say: Keep far from a bad neighbor, do not associate with a bad person, and do not despair of divine retribution.

8. Yehuda ben Tabbai and Shimon ben Shataḥ received [the tradition] from them. Yehuda ben Tabbai used to say: [When sitting as a judge] do not act as an advocate; when the parties to a lawsuit appear before you, regard them both as guilty; but when they leave you, having accepted the verdict, regard them both as innocent.

9. Shimon ben Shataḥ used to say: Examine the witnesses thoroughly, and be careful in your words, lest through them they learn how to lie.

10. Shemaya and Avtalyon received [the tradition] from them. Shemaya used to say: Love work, hate public office, and do not become too intimate with the ruling power.

11. Avtalyon used to say: sages, be careful in what you say, lest you incur the penalty of exile and find yourself banished to a place of evil waters, where your disciples who follow you may drink from them and die, with the result that the name of Heaven will be profaned.

12. Hillel and Shammai received [the tradition] from them. Hillel said: Be among the disciples of Aaron, loving peace and pursuing peace, loving people and drawing them close to the Torah.

ב שִׁמְעוֹן הַצַּדִּיק הָיָה מִשְּׁיָרֵי כְּנֶסֶת הַגְּדוֹלָה. הוּא הָיָה אוֹמֵר: עַל שְׁלֹשָׁה דְּבָרִים הָעוֹלָם עוֹמֵד, עַל הַתּוֹרָה, וְעַל הָעֲבוֹדָה, וְעַל גְּמִילוּת חֲסָדִים.

ג אַנְטִיגְנוֹס אִישׁ סוֹכוֹ קִבֵּל מִשִּׁמְעוֹן הַצַּדִּיק. הוּא הָיָה אוֹמֵר: אַל תִּהְיוּ כַּעֲבָדִים הַמְשַׁמְּשִׁים אֶת הָרַב עַל מְנָת לְקַבֵּל פְּרָס, אֶלָּא הֱווּ כַּעֲבָדִים הַמְשַׁמְּשִׁים אֶת הָרַב שֶׁלֹּא עַל מְנָת לְקַבֵּל פְּרָס, וִיהִי מוֹרָא שָׁמַיִם עֲלֵיכֶם.

ד יוֹסֵי בֶּן יוֹעֶזֶר אִישׁ צְרֵדָה וְיוֹסֵי בֶּן יוֹחָנָן אִישׁ יְרוּשָׁלַיִם קִבְּלוּ מֵהֶם. יוֹסֵי בֶּן יוֹעֶזֶר אִישׁ צְרֵדָה אוֹמֵר: יְהִי בֵיתְךָ בֵּית וַעַד לַחֲכָמִים, וֶהֱוֵי מִתְאַבֵּק בַּעֲפַר רַגְלֵיהֶם, וֶהֱוֵי שׁוֹתֶה בַצָּמָא אֶת דִּבְרֵיהֶם.

ה יוֹסֵי בֶּן יוֹחָנָן אִישׁ יְרוּשָׁלַיִם אוֹמֵר: יְהִי בֵיתְךָ פָּתוּחַ לִרְוָחָה, וְיִהְיוּ עֲנִיִּים בְּנֵי בֵיתֶךָ, וְאַל תַּרְבֶּה שִׂיחָה עִם הָאִשָּׁה. בְּאִשְׁתּוֹ אָמְרוּ, קַל וָחֹמֶר בְּאֵשֶׁת חֲבֵרוֹ. מִכָּאן אָמְרוּ חֲכָמִים: כָּל הַמַּרְבֶּה שִׂיחָה עִם הָאִשָּׁה, גּוֹרֵם רָעָה לְעַצְמוֹ, וּבוֹטֵל מִדִּבְרֵי תוֹרָה, וְסוֹפוֹ יוֹרֵשׁ גֵּיהִנָּם.

ו יְהוֹשֻׁעַ בֶּן פְּרַחְיָה וְנִתַּאי הָאַרְבֵּלִי קִבְּלוּ מֵהֶם. יְהוֹשֻׁעַ בֶּן פְּרַחְיָה אוֹמֵר: עֲשֵׂה לְךָ רַב, וּקְנֵה לְךָ חָבֵר, וֶהֱוֵי דָן אֶת כָּל הָאָדָם לְכַף זְכוּת.

ז נִתַּאי הָאַרְבֵּלִי אוֹמֵר: הַרְחֵק מִשָּׁכֵן רָע, וְאַל תִּתְחַבֵּר לָרָשָׁע, וְאַל תִּתְיָאֵשׁ מִן הַפֻּרְעָנוּת.

ח יְהוּדָה בֶּן טַבַּאי וְשִׁמְעוֹן בֶּן שָׁטָח קִבְּלוּ מֵהֶם. יְהוּדָה בֶּן טַבַּאי אוֹמֵר: אַל תַּעַשׂ עַצְמְךָ כְּעוֹרְכֵי הַדַּיָּנִין, וּכְשֶׁיִּהְיוּ בַּעֲלֵי הַדִּין עוֹמְדִים לְפָנֶיךָ יִהְיוּ בְעֵינֶיךָ כִּרְשָׁעִים, וּכְשֶׁנִּפְטָרִים מִלְּפָנֶיךָ יִהְיוּ בְעֵינֶיךָ כְּזַכָּאִין, כְּשֶׁקִּבְּלוּ עֲלֵיהֶם אֶת הַדִּין.

ט שִׁמְעוֹן בֶּן שָׁטָח אוֹמֵר: הֱוֵי מַרְבֶּה לַחְקֹר אֶת הָעֵדִים, וֶהֱוֵי זָהִיר בִּדְבָרֶיךָ, שֶׁמָּא מִתּוֹכָם יִלְמְדוּ לְשַׁקֵּר.

י שְׁמַעְיָה וְאַבְטַלְיוֹן קִבְּלוּ מֵהֶם. שְׁמַעְיָה אוֹמֵר: אֱהֹב אֶת הַמְּלָאכָה, וּשְׂנָא אֶת הָרַבָּנוּת, וְאַל תִּתְוַדַּע לָרָשׁוּת.

יא אַבְטַלְיוֹן אוֹמֵר: חֲכָמִים הִזָּהֲרוּ בְּדִבְרֵיכֶם, שֶׁמָּא תָחוּבוּ חוֹבַת גָּלוּת, וְתִגְלוּ לִמְקוֹם מַיִם הָרָעִים, וְיִשְׁתּוּ הַתַּלְמִידִים הַבָּאִים אַחֲרֵיכֶם וְיָמוּתוּ, וְנִמְצָא שֵׁם שָׁמַיִם מִתְחַלֵּל.

יב הִלֵּל וְשַׁמַּאי קִבְּלוּ מֵהֶם. הִלֵּל אוֹמֵר: הֱוֵי מִתַּלְמִידָיו שֶׁל אַהֲרֹן, אוֹהֵב שָׁלוֹם וְרוֹדֵף שָׁלוֹם, אוֹהֵב אֶת הַבְּרִיּוֹת וּמְקָרְבָן לַתּוֹרָה.

13. He used to say: A name made great is a name destroyed. He who does not increase [his knowledge] loses it. He who does not study deserves to die, and he who makes worldly use of the crown [of Torah] passes away.

14. He used to say: If I am not for myself, who will be for me? And if I am only for myself, what am I? And if not now, when?

15. Shammai used to say: Make your Torah study a fixed habit. Say little and do much; and greet everyone cheerfully.

16. Rabban Gamliel used to say: Get yourself a teacher, avoid doubt, and do not make a habit of giving tithes by guessing.

17. Shimon, his son, used to say: All my life I grew up among sages and I found that nothing is better for a person than silence. Not learning but doing is the main thing; and one who talks too much causes sin.

18. Rabban Shimon ben Gamliel used to say: On three things does the world stand – on truth, justice and peace, as it is said, "Administer truth and the judgment of peace in your gates." *Zech. 8*

Rabbi Ḥananya ben Akashya said:[B] The Holy One, blessed be He, wanted to confer merit on Israel. That is why He gave them a copious Torah and many commandments, as it is said, "It pleased the Lord, for the sake of [Israel's] righteousness, to make the Torah great and glorious." *Makkot 23b* *Is. 42*

If there is a minyan, mourners say the Rabbis' Kaddish (page 448).

* * *

All Israel have a share in the World to Come, as it is said: *Sanhedrin 90a*
"Your people are all righteous; they shall inherit the land for ever; *Is. 60*
they are a shoot of My own planting,
a work of My own hands, that I may be glorified."

CHAPTER 2

1. Rabbi [Judah the Prince] said: What is the right path a person should choose for himself? Whatever is honorable to one who chooses it and honorable in the eyes of others. Be as meticulous in the observance of a minor mitzva as a major one, for you do not know the reward for each mitzva. Against the loss

---

content, this mishna may be understood to mean that, as Maimonides says, "It is a fundamental principle of Jewish faith that if a person fulfills even one of the 613 *mitzvot* fully and properly, without ulterior motive but simply for its own sake and out of love, he merits a share in the World to Come. Therefore Rabbi Ḥananya teaches that there are so many *mitzvot* that it is impossible that a person should not have fulfilled at least one in the course of a lifetime, and thereby merit eternal life."

יג הוּא הָיָה אוֹמֵר: נְגַד שְׁמָא אֲבַד שְׁמֵהּ, וּדְלָא מוֹסִיף יָסוּף, וּדְלָא יָלֵף קְטָלָא חַיָּב, וּדְאִשְׁתַּמַּשׁ בְּתָגָא חֳלָף.

יד הוּא הָיָה אוֹמֵר: אִם אֵין אֲנִי לִי מִי לִי, וּכְשֶׁאֲנִי לְעַצְמִי מָה אֲנִי, וְאִם לֹא עַכְשָׁו אֵימָתָי.

טו שַׁמַּאי אוֹמֵר: עֲשֵׂה תוֹרָתְךָ קֶבַע, אֱמֹר מְעַט וַעֲשֵׂה הַרְבֵּה, וֶהֱוֵי מְקַבֵּל אֶת כָּל הָאָדָם בְּסֵבֶר פָּנִים יָפוֹת.

טז רַבָּן גַּמְלִיאֵל אוֹמֵר: עֲשֵׂה לְךָ רַב, וְהִסְתַּלֵּק מִן הַסָּפֵק, וְאַל תַּרְבֶּה לְעַשֵּׂר אֻמָּדוֹת.

יז שִׁמְעוֹן בְּנוֹ אוֹמֵר: כָּל יָמַי גָּדַלְתִּי בֵּין הַחֲכָמִים, וְלֹא מָצָאתִי לַגּוּף טוֹב מִשְּׁתִיקָה, וְלֹא הַמִּדְרָשׁ עִקָּר אֶלָּא הַמַּעֲשֶׂה, וְכָל הַמַּרְבֶּה דְבָרִים מֵבִיא חֵטְא.

יח רַבָּן שִׁמְעוֹן בֶּן גַּמְלִיאֵל אוֹמֵר: עַל שְׁלֹשָׁה דְבָרִים הָעוֹלָם קַיָּם, עַל הַדִּין, וְעַל הָאֱמֶת, וְעַל הַשָּׁלוֹם. שֶׁנֶּאֱמַר: אֱמֶת וּמִשְׁפַּט שָׁלוֹם שִׁפְטוּ בְּשַׁעֲרֵיכֶם: זכריה ח

רַבִּי חֲנַנְיָא בֶּן עֲקַשְׁיָא אוֹמֵר:[ב] רָצָה הַקָּדוֹשׁ בָּרוּךְ הוּא לְזַכּוֹת אֶת יִשְׂרָאֵל, לְפִיכָךְ הִרְבָּה לָהֶם תּוֹרָה וּמִצְוֹת. שֶׁנֶּאֱמַר: יהוה חָפֵץ לְמַעַן צִדְקוֹ, יַגְדִּיל תּוֹרָה וְיַאְדִּיר: מכות כג: / ישעיה מב

If there is a מנין*, mourners say* קדיש דרבנן *(page 449).*

* * *

כָּל יִשְׂרָאֵל יֵשׁ לָהֶם חֵלֶק לָעוֹלָם הַבָּא. שֶׁנֶּאֱמַר: סנהדרין צ.
וְעַמֵּךְ כֻּלָּם צַדִּיקִים, לְעוֹלָם יִירְשׁוּ אָרֶץ ישעיה ס
נֵצֶר מַטָּעַי, מַעֲשֵׂה יָדַי לְהִתְפָּאֵר:

פרק שני

א רַבִּי אוֹמֵר: אֵיזוֹ הִיא דֶרֶךְ יְשָׁרָה שֶׁיָּבֹר לוֹ הָאָדָם, כָּל שֶׁהִיא תִּפְאֶרֶת לְעֹשֶׂיהָ וְתִפְאֶרֶת לוֹ מִן הָאָדָם. וֶהֱוֵי זָהִיר בְּמִצְוָה קַלָּה כְּבַחֲמוּרָה, שֶׁאֵין

BIUR TEFILLA • ביאור תפילה

רַבִּי חֲנַנְיָא בֶּן עֲקַשְׁיָא אוֹמֵר – *Rabbi Ḥananya ben Akashya said.* This passage is not part of the tractate of *Avot* but is appended at the conclusion of every learning session. From a purely technical point of view, it is because this teaching qualifies as *aggada*, a non-legal teaching, and there is a rule that *Kaddish DeRabbanan* is only recited after the recitation of *aggadic* material and not *halakhic*. But from the point of view of its

that fulfilling a mitzva may entail, reckon its reward, and against the benefit a transgression may bring, reckon the loss it involves. Reflect on three things and you will not fall into transgression: know what is above you – a seeing eye, a hearing ear, and a book in which all your deeds are written.

2. Rabban Gamliel, son of Rabbi Judah the Prince, said: It is good to combine Torah study with a worldly occupation, for the effort involved in both makes one forget sin. Torah study without an occupation will in the end fail and lead to sin. And all who work for the community should do so for the sake of Heaven, for their ancestral merit will support them and their righteousness endures for ever. And as for you [God will say], I count you worthy of great reward as though you yourselves had accomplished it all.

3. Be wary in your dealings with the ruling power, for they only befriend a man when it serves their needs. When it is to their advantage, they appear as friends, but they do not stand by a person in his hour of need.

4. He used to say: Do His will as if it were yours, so that He may do your will as if it were His. Set aside your will for the sake of His, that He may set aside the will of others before yours.

5. Hillel said: Do not separate yourself from the community. Do not be sure of yourself until the day you die. Do not judge your fellow until you have stood in his place. Do not say anything that cannot be understood [at once] in the hope that it will eventually be understood. And do not say, I will study when I have the time, for you may never have the time.

6. He used to say: An uncouth person cannot be sin-fearing, nor can an ignoramus be pious. A shy person cannot learn, nor can an impatient one teach. A person over-occupied in business does not always become wise. In a place where there are no worthy people, strive to be worthy.

7. Seeing a skull floating on the water, he said: "Because you drowned others, they drowned you, and those who drowned you will themselves eventually be drowned."

8. He used to say: The more flesh, the more worms. The more possessions, the more worries. The more wives, the more witchcraft. The more maidservants, the more lewdness. The more menservants, the more robbery. The more Torah, the more life. The more study, the more wisdom. The more counsel, the more understanding. The more charity, the more peace. Whoever acquires a good name acquires something for himself. Whoever acquires for himself words of Torah acquires for himself life in the World to Come.

9. Rabban Yoḥanan ben Zakkai received [the tradition] from Hillel and Shammai. He used to say: If you have learnt much Torah, take no special credit for yourself, for it was for this that you were created.

אַתָּה יוֹדֵעַ מַתַּן שְׂכָרָן שֶׁל מִצְוֹת. וֶהֱוֵי מְחַשֵּׁב הֶפְסֵד מִצְוָה כְּנֶגֶד שְׂכָרָהּ, וּשְׂכַר עֲבֵרָה כְּנֶגֶד הֶפְסֵדָהּ. הִסְתַּכֵּל בִּשְׁלֹשָׁה דְבָרִים, וְאֵין אַתָּה בָא לִידֵי עֲבֵרָה. דַּע מַה לְּמַעְלָה מִמְּךָ, עַיִן רוֹאָה, וְאֹזֶן שׁוֹמַעַת, וְכָל מַעֲשֶׂיךָ בַּסֵּפֶר נִכְתָּבִים.

ב רַבָּן גַּמְלִיאֵל בְּנוֹ שֶׁל רַבִּי יְהוּדָה הַנָּשִׂיא אוֹמֵר: יָפֶה תַּלְמוּד תּוֹרָה עִם דֶּרֶךְ אֶרֶץ, שֶׁיְּגִיעַת שְׁנֵיהֶם מְשַׁכַּחַת עָוֹן. וְכָל תּוֹרָה שֶׁאֵין עִמָּהּ מְלָאכָה, סוֹפָהּ בְּטֵלָה וְגוֹרֶרֶת עָוֹן. וְכָל הָעוֹסְקִים עִם הַצִּבּוּר, יִהְיוּ עוֹסְקִים עִמָּהֶם לְשֵׁם שָׁמַיִם, שֶׁזְּכוּת אֲבוֹתָם מְסַיַּעְתָּם, וְצִדְקָתָם עוֹמֶדֶת לָעַד. וְאַתֶּם, מַעֲלֶה אֲנִי עֲלֵיכֶם שָׂכָר הַרְבֵּה כְּאִלּוּ עֲשִׂיתֶם.

ג הֱווּ זְהִירִין בָּרָשׁוּת, שֶׁאֵין מְקָרְבִין לוֹ לָאָדָם אֶלָּא לְצֹרֶךְ עַצְמָן. נִרְאִין כְּאוֹהֲבִין בִּשְׁעַת הֲנָאָתָן, וְאֵין עוֹמְדִין לוֹ לָאָדָם בִּשְׁעַת דָּחְקוֹ.

ד הוּא הָיָה אוֹמֵר: עֲשֵׂה רְצוֹנוֹ כִּרְצוֹנְךָ, כְּדֵי שֶׁיַּעֲשֶׂה רְצוֹנְךָ כִּרְצוֹנוֹ. בַּטֵּל רְצוֹנְךָ מִפְּנֵי רְצוֹנוֹ, כְּדֵי שֶׁיְּבַטֵּל רְצוֹן אֲחֵרִים מִפְּנֵי רְצוֹנֶךָ.

ה הִלֵּל אוֹמֵר: אַל תִּפְרֹשׁ מִן הַצִּבּוּר, וְאַל תַּאֲמִין בְּעַצְמְךָ עַד יוֹם מוֹתְךָ, וְאַל תָּדִין אֶת חֲבֵרְךָ עַד שֶׁתַּגִּיעַ לִמְקוֹמוֹ. וְאַל תֹּאמַר דָּבָר שֶׁאִי אֶפְשָׁר לִשְׁמֹעַ, שֶׁסּוֹפוֹ לְהִשָּׁמַע. וְאַל תֹּאמַר לִכְשֶׁאֶפָּנֶה אֶשְׁנֶה, שֶׁמָּא לֹא תִפָּנֶה.

ו הוּא הָיָה אוֹמֵר: אֵין בּוּר יְרֵא חֵטְא, וְלֹא עַם הָאָרֶץ חָסִיד, וְלֹא הַבַּיְשָׁן לָמֵד, וְלֹא הַקַּפְּדָן מְלַמֵּד, וְלֹא כָל הַמַּרְבֶּה בִסְחוֹרָה מַחְכִּים. וּבִמְקוֹם שֶׁאֵין אֲנָשִׁים, הִשְׁתַּדֵּל לִהְיוֹת אִישׁ.

ז אַף הוּא רָאָה גֻּלְגֹּלֶת אַחַת שֶׁצָּפָה עַל פְּנֵי הַמָּיִם. אָמַר לָהּ: עַל דַּאֲטֵפְתְּ אַטְיפוּךְ, וְסוֹף מְטִיפַיִךְ יְטוּפוּן.

ח הוּא הָיָה אוֹמֵר: מַרְבֶּה בָשָׂר, מַרְבֶּה רִמָּה. מַרְבֶּה נְכָסִים, מַרְבֶּה דְאָגָה. מַרְבֶּה נָשִׁים, מַרְבֶּה כְשָׁפִים. מַרְבֶּה שְׁפָחוֹת, מַרְבֶּה זִמָּה. מַרְבֶּה עֲבָדִים, מַרְבֶּה גָזֵל. מַרְבֶּה תוֹרָה, מַרְבֶּה חַיִּים. מַרְבֶּה יְשִׁיבָה, מַרְבֶּה חָכְמָה. מַרְבֶּה עֵצָה, מַרְבֶּה תְבוּנָה. מַרְבֶּה צְדָקָה, מַרְבֶּה שָׁלוֹם. קָנָה שֵׁם טוֹב, קָנָה לְעַצְמוֹ. קָנָה לוֹ דִבְרֵי תוֹרָה, קָנָה לוֹ חַיֵּי הָעוֹלָם הַבָּא.

ט רַבָּן יוֹחָנָן בֶּן זַכַּאי קִבֵּל מֵהִלֵּל וּמִשַּׁמַּאי. הוּא הָיָה אוֹמֵר: אִם לָמַדְתָּ תּוֹרָה הַרְבֵּה, אַל תַּחֲזִיק טוֹבָה לְעַצְמְךָ, כִּי לְכָךְ נוֹצָרְתָּ.

10. Rabban Yoḥanan ben Zakkai had five [pre-eminent] disciples, namely: Rabbi Eliezer ben Hyrcanus, Rabbi Yehoshua ben Ḥananya, Rabbi Yose the Priest, Rabbi Shimon ben Netanel and Rabbi Elazar ben Arakh.

11. He used to recount their praise: Eliezer ben Hyrcanus: a plastered well that never loses a drop. Yehoshua ben Ḥananya: happy the one who gave him birth. Yose the Priest: a pious man. Shimon ben Netanel: a man who fears sin. Elazar ben Arakh: an ever-flowing spring.

12. He used to say: If all the sages of Israel were in one scale of a balance and Eliezer ben Hyrcanus in the other, he would outweigh them all. However, Abba Saul said in his name: If all the sages of Israel, including Eliezer ben Hyrcanus, were in one scale of a balance, and Elazar ben Arakh in the other, he would outweigh them all.

13. He said to them: Go and see which is the right way to which one should cling. Rabbi Eliezer said: a good eye [generosity of spirit]. Rabbi Yehoshua said: a good companion. Rabbi Yose said: a good neighbor. Rabbi Shimon said: one who considers the consequences. Rabbi Elazar said: a good heart. Then he said to them: I prefer the answer of Elazar ben Arakh, for his view includes all of yours.

14. He said to them: Go and see which is the wrong way one should avoid. Rabbi Eliezer said: an evil eye [envy]. Rabbi Yehoshua said: an evil companion. Rabbi Yose said: an evil neighbor. Rabbi Shimon said: one who borrows and does not repay, for borrowing from a person is like borrowing from God, as it is said, "The wicked borrows and does not repay, but the Righteous *Ps. 37* One is gracious and repays." Rabbi Elazar said: an evil heart. Then he said to them: I prefer the answer of Elazar ben Arakh, for his view includes all of yours.

15. Each of the disciples said three things. Rabbi Eliezer said: Let the honor of your fellow be as precious to you as your own. Do not be easily provoked to anger. Repent one day before you die. [He also said:] Warm yourself by the fire of the sages, but be careful of their glowing coals lest you be burnt; for their bite is the bite of a fox, their sting is the sting of a scorpion, their hiss is the hiss of a serpent, and all their words are like fiery coals.

16. Rabbi Yehoshua said: The evil eye [envy], the evil impulse, and hatred of humankind drive a person out of the world.

17. Rabbi Yose said: Let the property of your fellow be as precious to you as your own. Prepare yourself to study Torah, for it does not come to you as an inheritance. And let all your deeds be for the sake of Heaven.

י חֲמִשָּׁה תַלְמִידִים הָיוּ לְרַבָּן יוֹחָנָן בֶּן זַכַּאי. וְאֵלּוּ הֵן: רַבִּי אֱלִיעֶזֶר בֶּן הוּרְקְנוֹס, רַבִּי יְהוֹשֻׁעַ בֶּן חֲנַנְיָה, רַבִּי יוֹסֵי הַכֹּהֵן, רַבִּי שִׁמְעוֹן בֶּן נְתַנְאֵל, רַבִּי אֶלְעָזָר בֶּן עֲרָךְ.

יא הוּא הָיָה מוֹנֶה שִׁבְחָם: אֱלִיעֶזֶר בֶּן הוּרְקְנוֹס, בּוֹר סוּד שֶׁאֵינוֹ מְאַבֵּד טִפָּה. יְהוֹשֻׁעַ בֶּן חֲנַנְיָה, אַשְׁרֵי יוֹלַדְתּוֹ. יוֹסֵי הַכֹּהֵן, חָסִיד. שִׁמְעוֹן בֶּן נְתַנְאֵל, יְרֵא חֵטְא. אֶלְעָזָר בֶּן עֲרָךְ, כְּמַעְיָן הַמִּתְגַּבֵּר.

יב הוּא הָיָה אוֹמֵר: אִם יִהְיוּ כָּל חַכְמֵי יִשְׂרָאֵל בְּכַף מֹאזְנַיִם, וֶאֱלִיעֶזֶר בֶּן הוּרְקְנוֹס בְּכַף שְׁנִיָּה, מַכְרִיעַ אֶת כֻּלָּם. אַבָּא שָׁאוּל אוֹמֵר מִשְּׁמוֹ: אִם יִהְיוּ כָּל חַכְמֵי יִשְׂרָאֵל בְּכַף מֹאזְנַיִם, וֶאֱלִיעֶזֶר בֶּן הוּרְקְנוֹס אַף עִמָּהֶם, וְאֶלְעָזָר בֶּן עֲרָךְ בְּכַף שְׁנִיָּה, מַכְרִיעַ אֶת כֻּלָּם.

יג אָמַר לָהֶם: צְאוּ וּרְאוּ אֵיזוֹ הִיא דֶּרֶךְ טוֹבָה, שֶׁיִּדְבַּק בָּהּ הָאָדָם. רַבִּי אֱלִיעֶזֶר אוֹמֵר: עַיִן טוֹבָה. רַבִּי יְהוֹשֻׁעַ אוֹמֵר: חָבֵר טוֹב. רַבִּי יוֹסֵי אוֹמֵר: שָׁכֵן טוֹב. רַבִּי שִׁמְעוֹן אוֹמֵר: הָרוֹאֶה אֶת הַנּוֹלָד. רַבִּי אֶלְעָזָר אוֹמֵר: לֵב טוֹב. אָמַר לָהֶם, רוֹאֶה אֲנִי אֶת דִּבְרֵי אֶלְעָזָר בֶּן עֲרָךְ מִדִּבְרֵיכֶם, שֶׁבִּכְלַל דְּבָרָיו דִּבְרֵיכֶם.

יד אָמַר לָהֶם: צְאוּ וּרְאוּ, אֵיזוֹ הִיא דֶּרֶךְ רָעָה, שֶׁיִּתְרַחֵק מִמֶּנָּה הָאָדָם. רַבִּי אֱלִיעֶזֶר אוֹמֵר: עַיִן רָעָה. רַבִּי יְהוֹשֻׁעַ אוֹמֵר: חָבֵר רָע. רַבִּי יוֹסֵי אוֹמֵר: שָׁכֵן רָע. רַבִּי שִׁמְעוֹן אוֹמֵר: הַלֹּוֶה וְאֵינוֹ מְשַׁלֵּם, אֶחָד הַלֹּוֶה מִן הָאָדָם כְּלֹוֶה מִן הַמָּקוֹם, שֶׁנֶּאֱמַר: לֹוֶה רָשָׁע וְלֹא יְשַׁלֵּם, וְצַדִּיק חוֹנֵן וְנוֹתֵן: (תהלים לז) רַבִּי אֶלְעָזָר אוֹמֵר: לֵב רָע. אָמַר לָהֶם: רוֹאֶה אֲנִי אֶת דִּבְרֵי אֶלְעָזָר בֶּן עֲרָךְ מִדִּבְרֵיכֶם, שֶׁבִּכְלַל דְּבָרָיו דִּבְרֵיכֶם.

טו הֵם אָמְרוּ שְׁלֹשָׁה דְבָרִים. רַבִּי אֱלִיעֶזֶר אוֹמֵר: יְהִי כְבוֹד חֲבֵרְךָ חָבִיב עָלֶיךָ כְּשֶׁלָּךְ, וְאַל תְּהִי נוֹחַ לִכְעֹס. וְשׁוּב יוֹם אֶחָד לִפְנֵי מִיתָתְךָ. וֶהֱוֵי מִתְחַמֵּם כְּנֶגֶד אוּרָן שֶׁל חֲכָמִים, וֶהֱוֵי זָהִיר בְּגַחַלְתָּן שֶׁלֹּא תִכָּוֶה, שֶׁנְּשִׁיכָתָן נְשִׁיכַת שׁוּעָל, וַעֲקִיצָתָן עֲקִיצַת עַקְרָב, וּלְחִישָׁתָן לְחִישַׁת שָׂרָף, וְכָל דִּבְרֵיהֶם כְּגַחֲלֵי אֵשׁ.

טז רַבִּי יְהוֹשֻׁעַ אוֹמֵר: עַיִן הָרָע וְיֵצֶר הָרָע וְשִׂנְאַת הַבְּרִיּוֹת, מוֹצִיאִין אֶת הָאָדָם מִן הָעוֹלָם.

יז רַבִּי יוֹסֵי אוֹמֵר: יְהִי מָמוֹן חֲבֵרְךָ חָבִיב עָלֶיךָ כְּשֶׁלָּךְ. וְהַתְקֵן עַצְמְךָ לִלְמֹד תּוֹרָה, שֶׁאֵינָהּ יְרֻשָּׁה לָךְ. וְכָל מַעֲשֶׂיךָ יִהְיוּ לְשֵׁם שָׁמָיִם.

18. Rabbi Shimon said: Be meticulous in reciting the Shema and the [Amida] prayer. When you pray, do not do so as a fixed routine, but as a plea for mercy and grace before God, as it is said, "For He is gracious and compassionate, slow to anger, abounding in kindness, and renouncing punishment." Do not be evil in your own eyes. *Joel 2*

19. Rabbi Elazar said: Be diligent in the study of Torah. Know how to answer a heretic. Know for whom you labor and who is your Employer who will pay you the reward of your work.

20. Rabbi Tarfon said: The day is short, the task is great, the laborers are lazy, the reward is much, and the Master insistent.

21. He used to say: It is not for you to complete the task, but neither are you free to stand aside from it. If you have studied much Torah, you will be given great reward, for your Employer will faithfully reward your work. Know, though, that the reward of the righteous is granted in the time to come.

Rabbi Ḥananya ben Akashya said: The Holy One, blessed be He, wanted to confer merit on Israel. That is why He gave them a copious Torah and many commandments, as it is said, "It pleased the LORD, for the sake of [Israel's] righteousness, to make the Torah great and glorious." *Makkot 23b* *Is. 42*

If there is a minyan, mourners say the Rabbis' Kaddish (*page 448*).

* * *

All Israel have a share in the World to Come, as it is said, *Sanhedrin 90a*
"Your people are all righteous; they shall inherit the land for ever; *Is. 60*
they are a shoot of My own planting,
a work of My own hands, that I may be glorified."

CHAPTER 3

1. Akavya ben Mahalalel said: Reflect on three things and you will avoid transgression: Know where you came from, where you are going, and before whom you will have to give an account and reckoning. "Where you came from" – from a putrid drop. "Where you are going" – to a place of dust, worms and maggots. "And before whom you will have to give an account and reckoning" – before the Supreme King of kings, the Holy One, blessed be He.

2. Rabbi Ḥanina, the deputy High Priest, said: Pray for the welfare of the government, for were it not for fear of it, people would swallow one another alive.

3. Rabbi Ḥanina ben Teradyon said: When two people sit together and no words of Torah pass between them, they are regarded as a company of scoffers, as it is said, "He does not sit in the company of scoffers." But when two people sit together and words of Torah do pass between them, the Divine Presence rests with them, as it is said, "Then those who feared the LORD talked together, *Ps. 1* *Mal. 3*

יח רַבִּי שִׁמְעוֹן אוֹמֵר: הֱוֵי זָהִיר בִּקְרִיאַת שְׁמַע וּבִתְפִלָּה. וּכְשֶׁאַתָּה מִתְפַּלֵּל
אַל תַּעַשׂ תְּפִלָּתְךָ קֶבַע, אֶלָּא רַחֲמִים וְתַחֲנוּנִים לִפְנֵי הַמָּקוֹם, שֶׁנֶּאֱמַר: כִּי יואל ב
חַנּוּן וְרַחוּם הוּא, אֶרֶךְ אַפַּיִם וְרַב־חֶסֶד וְנִחָם עַל־הָרָעָה: וְאַל תְּהִי רָשָׁע
בִּפְנֵי עַצְמֶךָ.

יט רַבִּי אֶלְעָזָר אוֹמֵר: הֱוֵי שָׁקוּד לִלְמֹד תּוֹרָה. וְדַע מַה שֶׁתָּשִׁיב לְאֶפִּיקוֹרוֹס.
וְדַע לִפְנֵי מִי אַתָּה עָמֵל, וּמִי הוּא בַּעַל מְלַאכְתְּךָ, שֶׁיְּשַׁלֶּם לְךָ שְׂכַר פְּעֻלָּתֶךָ.

כ רַבִּי טַרְפוֹן אוֹמֵר: הַיּוֹם קָצֵר, וְהַמְּלָאכָה מְרֻבָּה, וְהַפּוֹעֲלִים עֲצֵלִים, וְהַשָּׂכָר
הַרְבֵּה, וּבַעַל הַבַּיִת דּוֹחֵק.

כא הוּא הָיָה אוֹמֵר: לֹא עָלֶיךָ הַמְּלָאכָה לִגְמֹר, וְלֹא אַתָּה בֶן חוֹרִין לִבָּטֵל מִמֶּנָּה.
אִם לָמַדְתָּ תּוֹרָה הַרְבֵּה, נוֹתְנִין לְךָ שָׂכָר הַרְבֵּה. וְנֶאֱמָן הוּא בַּעַל מְלַאכְתְּךָ,
שֶׁיְּשַׁלֶּם לְךָ שְׂכַר פְּעֻלָּתֶךָ. וְדַע, שֶׁמַּתַּן שְׂכָרָן שֶׁל צַדִּיקִים לֶעָתִיד לָבוֹא.

מכות כג: רַבִּי חֲנַנְיָא בֶּן עֲקַשְׁיָא אוֹמֵר: רָצָה הַקָּדוֹשׁ בָּרוּךְ הוּא לְזַכּוֹת אֶת יִשְׂרָאֵל, לְפִיכָךְ
ישעיה מב הִרְבָּה לָהֶם תּוֹרָה וּמִצְוֹת. שֶׁנֶּאֱמַר: יהוה חָפֵץ לְמַעַן צִדְקוֹ, יַגְדִּיל תּוֹרָה וְיַאְדִּיר:

If there is a מנין*, mourners say* קדיש דרבנן *(page 449).*

* * *

סנהדרין צ. כָּל יִשְׂרָאֵל יֵשׁ לָהֶם חֵלֶק לָעוֹלָם הַבָּא. שֶׁנֶּאֱמַר:
ישעיה ס וְעַמֵּךְ כֻּלָּם צַדִּיקִים, לְעוֹלָם יִירְשׁוּ אָרֶץ
נֵצֶר מַטָּעַי, מַעֲשֵׂה יָדַי לְהִתְפָּאֵר:

פרק שלישי

א עֲקַבְיָא בֶּן מַהֲלַלְאֵל אוֹמֵר: הִסְתַּכֵּל בִּשְׁלֹשָׁה דְבָרִים, וְאֵין אַתָּה בָא לִידֵי
עֲבֵרָה. דַּע מֵאַיִן בָּאתָ, וּלְאָן אַתָּה הוֹלֵךְ, וְלִפְנֵי מִי אַתָּה עָתִיד לִתֵּן דִּין
וְחֶשְׁבּוֹן. מֵאַיִן בָּאתָ, מִטִּפָּה סְרוּחָה. וּלְאָן אַתָּה הוֹלֵךְ, לִמְקוֹם עָפָר, רִמָּה
וְתוֹלֵעָה. וְלִפְנֵי מִי אַתָּה עָתִיד לִתֵּן דִּין וְחֶשְׁבּוֹן, לִפְנֵי מֶלֶךְ מַלְכֵי הַמְּלָכִים,
הַקָּדוֹשׁ בָּרוּךְ הוּא.

ב רַבִּי חֲנִינָא סְגַן הַכֹּהֲנִים אוֹמֵר: הֱוֵי מִתְפַּלֵּל בִּשְׁלוֹמָהּ שֶׁל מַלְכוּת, שֶׁאִלְמָלֵא
מוֹרָאָהּ, אִישׁ אֶת רֵעֵהוּ חַיִּים בְּלָעוֹ.

ג רַבִּי חֲנִינָא בֶּן תְּרַדְיוֹן אוֹמֵר: שְׁנַיִם שֶׁיּוֹשְׁבִין, וְאֵין בֵּינֵיהֶם דִּבְרֵי תוֹרָה, הֲרֵי
תהלים א זֶה מוֹשַׁב לֵצִים, שֶׁנֶּאֱמַר: וּבְמוֹשַׁב לֵצִים לֹא יָשָׁב: אֲבָל שְׁנַיִם שֶׁיּוֹשְׁבִין,

and the LORD listened and heard, and a scroll of remembrance was written before Him concerning those who feared the LORD and cherished His name." This verse tells me about two people; from where can I learn that even one person who sits alone and studies Torah, the Holy One, blessed be He, grants him a reward? From the verse, "Though he sits alone and meditates quietly, He will grant him a reward." *Lam. 3*

4. Rabbi Shimon said: Three who eat at one table, and do not speak words of Torah, are as if they had eaten of sacrifices of dead idols, as it is said, "For all the tables are full of vomit and filth, when God is absent." However, three who eat at one table and speak words of Torah, it is as if they had eaten at God's table, as it is said, "And He spoke to me: This is the table before the LORD." *Is. 28* *Ezek. 41*

5. Rabbi Ḥanina ben Ḥakhinai said: One who stays awake at night, travels alone, or turns his mind to idle thoughts, endangers his soul.

6. Rabbi Neḥunya ben HaKanna said: One who takes on himself the yoke of Torah will be spared the yoke of government and the yoke of worldly responsibilities, but one who throws off the yoke of the Torah will bear the yoke of government and the yoke of worldly responsibilities.

7. Rabbi Ḥalafta ben Dosa of Kfar Ḥananya said: When ten people sit together and study Torah, the Divine Presence rests among them, as it is said, "God stands in the divine assembly." How do we know that the same applies to five? From the verse, "He has founded His group on the earth." And how do we know that it applies even to three? From the verse, "He judges among the judges." How do we know that the same applies even to two? From the verse, "Then those who feared the LORD talked together, and the LORD listened and heard." And how do we know that it applies even to one? From the verse, "In every place where I cause My name to be mentioned, I will come to you and bless you." *Ps. 82* *Amos 9* *Ps. 82* *Mal. 3* *Ex. 20*

8. Rabbi Elazar of Bartota said: Give Him what is His, for you and yours are His. This was also said by David: "For all things come from You, and we have given You only what is Yours." *1 Chr. 29*

9. Rabbi Jacob said: One who is reviewing his Torah study while walking on the way, and interrupts his study to say, "What a beautiful tree" or "What a beautiful field," is regarded by Scripture as if he had endangered his soul.

10. Rabbi Dostai of Rabbi Yannai said in the name of Rabbi Meir: One who forgets even one thing of his Torah learning, Scripture regards him as if he had endangered his soul, for it is said, "Only take heed and guard your soul very carefully so that you do not forget the things that your eyes saw." One might think that this applies even to one who finds his studies too hard to remember. Therefore the verse adds, "Lest they be removed from your heart all the days of your life." Thus, one does not endanger his soul unless he deliberately removes teachings from his heart. *Deut. 4* *Ibid.*

וְיֵשׁ בֵּינֵיהֶם דִּבְרֵי תוֹרָה, שְׁכִינָה שְׁרוּיָה בֵינֵיהֶם, שֶׁנֶּאֱמַר: אָז נִדְבְּרוּ יִרְאֵי מלאכי ג
יהוה אִישׁ אֶל־רֵעֵהוּ, וַיַּקְשֵׁב יהוה וַיִּשְׁמָע, וַיִּכָּתֵב סֵפֶר זִכָּרוֹן לְפָנָיו לְיִרְאֵי
יהוה וּלְחֹשְׁבֵי שְׁמוֹ: אֵין לִי אֶלָּא שְׁנַיִם, מִנַּיִן אֲפִלּוּ אֶחָד שֶׁיּוֹשֵׁב וְעוֹסֵק
בַּתּוֹרָה שֶׁהַקָּדוֹשׁ בָּרוּךְ הוּא קוֹבֵעַ לוֹ שָׂכָר, שֶׁנֶּאֱמַר: יֵשֵׁב בָּדָד וְיִדֹּם כִּי נָטַל איכה ג
עָלָיו:

ד רַבִּי שִׁמְעוֹן אוֹמֵר: שְׁלֹשָׁה שֶׁאָכְלוּ עַל שֻׁלְחָן אֶחָד וְלֹא אָמְרוּ עָלָיו דִּבְרֵי
תוֹרָה, כְּאִלּוּ אָכְלוּ מִזִּבְחֵי מֵתִים, שֶׁנֶּאֱמַר: כִּי כָּל־שֻׁלְחָנוֹת מָלְאוּ קִיא ישעיה כח
צֹאָה בְּלִי מָקוֹם: אֲבָל שְׁלֹשָׁה שֶׁאָכְלוּ עַל שֻׁלְחָן אֶחָד, וְאָמְרוּ עָלָיו דִּבְרֵי
תוֹרָה, כְּאִלּוּ אָכְלוּ מִשֻּׁלְחָנוֹ שֶׁל מָקוֹם, שֶׁנֶּאֱמַר: וַיְדַבֵּר אֵלַי, זֶה הַשֻּׁלְחָן יחזקאל מא
אֲשֶׁר לִפְנֵי יהוה:

ה רַבִּי חֲנִינָא בֶּן חֲכִינַאי אוֹמֵר: הַנֵּעוֹר בַּלַּיְלָה, וְהַמְהַלֵּךְ בַּדֶּרֶךְ יְחִידִי, וְהַמְפַנֶּה לִבּוֹ לְבַטָּלָה, הֲרֵי זֶה מִתְחַיֵּב בְּנַפְשׁוֹ.

ו רַבִּי נְחוּנְיָא בֶּן הַקָּנָה אוֹמֵר: כָּל הַמְקַבֵּל עָלָיו עֹל תּוֹרָה, מַעֲבִירִין מִמֶּנּוּ עֹל מַלְכוּת וְעֹל דֶּרֶךְ אֶרֶץ. וְכָל הַפּוֹרֵק מִמֶּנּוּ עֹל תּוֹרָה, נוֹתְנִין עָלָיו עֹל מַלְכוּת וְעֹל דֶּרֶךְ אֶרֶץ.

ז רַבִּי חֲלַפְתָּא בֶּן דּוֹסָא אִישׁ כְּפַר חֲנַנְיָה אוֹמֵר: עֲשָׂרָה שֶׁיּוֹשְׁבִין וְעוֹסְקִין
בַּתּוֹרָה שְׁכִינָה שְׁרוּיָה בֵינֵיהֶם, שֶׁנֶּאֱמַר: אֱלֹהִים נִצָּב בַּעֲדַת־אֵל: וּמִנַּיִן אֲפִלּוּ תהלים פב
חֲמִשָּׁה, שֶׁנֶּאֱמַר: וַאֲגֻדָּתוֹ עַל־אֶרֶץ יְסָדָהּ: וּמִנַּיִן אֲפִלּוּ שְׁלֹשָׁה, שֶׁנֶּאֱמַר: עמוס ט
בְּקֶרֶב אֱלֹהִים יִשְׁפֹּט: וּמִנַּיִן אֲפִלּוּ שְׁנַיִם, שֶׁנֶּאֱמַר: אָז נִדְבְּרוּ יִרְאֵי יהוה אִישׁ תהלים פב מלאכי ג
אֶל־רֵעֵהוּ, וַיַּקְשֵׁב יהוה וַיִּשְׁמָע: וּמִנַּיִן אֲפִלּוּ אֶחָד, שֶׁנֶּאֱמַר: בְּכָל־הַמָּקוֹם שמות כ
אֲשֶׁר אַזְכִּיר אֶת־שְׁמִי, אָבוֹא אֵלֶיךָ וּבֵרַכְתִּיךָ:

ח רַבִּי אֶלְעָזָר אִישׁ בַּרְתּוֹתָא אוֹמֵר: תֶּן לוֹ מִשֶּׁלּוֹ, שֶׁאַתָּה וְשֶׁלְּךָ שֶׁלּוֹ. וְכֵן בְּדָוִד
הוּא אוֹמֵר: כִּי־מִמְּךָ הַכֹּל, וּמִיָּדְךָ נָתַנּוּ לָךְ: דברי הימים א׳ כט

ט רַבִּי יַעֲקֹב אוֹמֵר: הַמְהַלֵּךְ בַּדֶּרֶךְ וְשׁוֹנֶה, וּמַפְסִיק מִמִּשְׁנָתוֹ וְאוֹמֵר, מַה נָּאֶה אִילָן זֶה, מַה נָּאֶה נִיר זֶה, מַעֲלֶה עָלָיו הַכָּתוּב כְּאִלּוּ מִתְחַיֵּב בְּנַפְשׁוֹ.

י רַבִּי דוֹסְתַּאי בְּרַבִּי יַנַּאי מִשּׁוּם רַבִּי מֵאִיר אוֹמֵר: כָּל הַשּׁוֹכֵחַ דָּבָר אֶחָד
מִמִּשְׁנָתוֹ, מַעֲלֶה עָלָיו הַכָּתוּב כְּאִלּוּ מִתְחַיֵּב בְּנַפְשׁוֹ, שֶׁנֶּאֱמַר: רַק הִשָּׁמֶר דברים ד
לְךָ וּשְׁמֹר נַפְשְׁךָ מְאֹד, פֶּן־תִּשְׁכַּח אֶת־הַדְּבָרִים אֲשֶׁר־רָאוּ עֵינֶיךָ: יָכוֹל אֲפִלּוּ
תָּקְפָה עָלָיו מִשְׁנָתוֹ, תַּלְמוּד לוֹמַר: וּפֶן יָסוּרוּ מִלְּבָבְךָ כֹּל יְמֵי חַיֶּיךָ: הָא אֵינוֹ שם
מִתְחַיֵּב בְּנַפְשׁוֹ, עַד שֶׁיֵּשֵׁב וִיסִירֵם מִלִּבּוֹ.

11. Rabbi Ḥanina ben Dosa said: For one who puts fear of sin before wisdom, wisdom endures. For one who puts wisdom before fear of sin, wisdom does not endure.

12. He also used to say: For one whose good deeds exceed his wisdom, wisdom endures. For one whose wisdom exceeds his good deeds, wisdom does not endure.

13. He also used to say: In one in whom people delight, God delights. In one in whom people do not delight, God does not delight.

14. Rabbi Dosa ben Harkinas said: Sleeping late in the morning, drinking wine at midday, chattering with children and sitting in gatherings of the ignorant – these drive a person from the world.

15. Rabbi Elazar of Modin said: One who desecrates sacred things, despises the festivals, shames his fellow in public, nullifies the covenant of our father Abraham, or attributes meanings to the Torah contrary to normative law, even though he has to his credit Torah and good deeds, has no share in the World to Come.

16. Rabbi Yishmael said: Be yielding to a superior, pleasing to the young, and receive everyone cheerfully.

17. Rabbi Akiva said: Mocking and frivolity lead to immorality. The oral tradition (*Mesora*) is a fence protecting the Torah; tithes are a fence protecting wealth; vows are a fence protecting abstinence. The fence protecting wisdom is silence.

18. He used to say: Beloved is man, for he was created in the image of God. As a gesture of special love, it was made known to him that he was created in the
image of God, as it is said, "For in the image of God He made man." Beloved *Gen. 9*
are Israel for they are called God's children. As a gesture of special love, it was
made known to them that they are called God's children, as it is said, "You are *Deut. 14*
the children of the Lord your God." Beloved are Israel, for they were given a precious vessel [the Torah]. As a gesture of special love, it was made known to them that they were given the precious vessel through which the world was cre-
ated, as it is said, "I have given you good instruction; do not forsake My Torah." *Prov. 4*

19. All is foreseen, yet freedom of choice is given. The world is judged with goodness, but all depends on the majority of one's deeds.

20. He used to say: All is given on collateral, and a net is spread over all the living. The shop is open, the shopkeeper extends credit, the ledger is open, and the hand records. Whoever wishes to borrow may come and borrow. The collectors regularly make their daily rounds and collect payment from a person, whether he realizes it or not. They have [a record] on which they can rely; the judgment is just; and all is prepared for the banquet.

יא רַבִּי חֲנִינָא בֶּן דּוֹסָא אוֹמֵר: כָּל שֶׁיִּרְאַת חֶטְאוֹ קוֹדֶמֶת לְחָכְמָתוֹ, חָכְמָתוֹ מִתְקַיֶּמֶת. וְכָל שֶׁחָכְמָתוֹ קוֹדֶמֶת לְיִרְאַת חֶטְאוֹ, אֵין חָכְמָתוֹ מִתְקַיֶּמֶת.

יב הוּא הָיָה אוֹמֵר: כָּל שֶׁמַּעֲשָׂיו מְרֻבִּין מֵחָכְמָתוֹ, חָכְמָתוֹ מִתְקַיֶּמֶת. וְכָל שֶׁחָכְמָתוֹ מְרֻבָּה מִמַּעֲשָׂיו, אֵין חָכְמָתוֹ מִתְקַיֶּמֶת.

יג הוּא הָיָה אוֹמֵר: כָּל שֶׁרְוּחַ הַבְּרִיּוֹת נוֹחָה הֵימֶנּוּ, רְוּחַ הַמָּקוֹם נוֹחָה הֵימֶנּוּ. וְכָל שֶׁאֵין רְוּחַ הַבְּרִיּוֹת נוֹחָה הֵימֶנּוּ, אֵין רְוּחַ הַמָּקוֹם נוֹחָה הֵימֶנּוּ.

יד רַבִּי דוֹסָא בֶּן הַרְכִּינָס אוֹמֵר: שֵׁנָה שֶׁל שַׁחֲרִית, וְיַיִן שֶׁל צָהֳרַיִם, וְשִׂיחַת הַיְלָדִים, וִישִׁיבַת בָּתֵּי כְנֵסִיּוֹת שֶׁל עַמֵּי הָאָרֶץ, מוֹצִיאִין אֶת הָאָדָם מִן הָעוֹלָם.

טו רַבִּי אֶלְעָזָר הַמּוֹדָעִי אוֹמֵר: הַמְחַלֵּל אֶת הַקֳּדָשִׁים, וְהַמְבַזֶּה אֶת הַמּוֹעֲדוֹת, וְהַמַּלְבִּין פְּנֵי חֲבֵרוֹ בָּרַבִּים, וְהַמֵּפֵר בְּרִיתוֹ שֶׁל אַבְרָהָם אָבִינוּ, וְהַמְגַלֶּה פָנִים בַּתּוֹרָה שֶׁלֹּא כַהֲלָכָה, אַף עַל פִּי שֶׁיֵּשׁ בְּיָדוֹ תּוֹרָה וּמַעֲשִׂים טוֹבִים, אֵין לוֹ חֵלֶק לָעוֹלָם הַבָּא.

טז רַבִּי יִשְׁמָעֵאל אוֹמֵר: הֱוֵי קַל לְרֹאשׁ וְנְוֹחַ לְתִשְׁחֹרֶת, וֶהֱוֵי מְקַבֵּל אֶת כָּל הָאָדָם בְּשִׂמְחָה.

יז רַבִּי עֲקִיבָא אוֹמֵר: שְׂחוֹק וְקַלּוּת רֹאשׁ מַרְגִּילִין אֶת הָאָדָם לְעֶרְוָה. מַסֹּרֶת סְיָג לַתּוֹרָה, מַעְשְׂרוֹת סְיָג לָעֹשֶׁר, נְדָרִים סְיָג לַפְּרִישׁוּת, סְיָג לַחָכְמָה שְׁתִיקָה.

יח הוּא הָיָה אוֹמֵר, חָבִיב אָדָם שֶׁנִּבְרָא בְצֶלֶם, חִבָּה יְתֵרָה נוֹדַעַת לוֹ שֶׁנִּבְרָא
בְּצֶלֶם, שֶׁנֶּאֱמַר: כִּי בְּצֶלֶם אֱלֹהִים עָשָׂה אֶת־הָאָדָם: חֲבִיבִין יִשְׂרָאֵל שֶׁנִּקְרְאוּ בראשית ט
בָנִים לַמָּקוֹם, חִבָּה יְתֵרָה נוֹדַעַת לָהֶם שֶׁנִּקְרְאוּ בָנִים לַמָּקוֹם, שֶׁנֶּאֱמַר: בָּנִים דברים יד
אַתֶּם לַיהוה אֱלֹהֵיכֶם: חֲבִיבִין יִשְׂרָאֵל שֶׁנִּתַּן לָהֶם כְּלִי חֶמְדָּה, חִבָּה יְתֵרָה
נוֹדַעַת לָהֶם שֶׁנִּתַּן לָהֶם כְּלִי חֶמְדָּה שֶׁבּוֹ נִבְרָא הָעוֹלָם, שֶׁנֶּאֱמַר: כִּי לֶקַח משלי ד
טוֹב נָתַתִּי לָכֶם, תּוֹרָתִי אַל־תַּעֲזֹבוּ:

יט הַכֹּל צָפוּי, וְהָרְשׁוּת נְתוּנָה, וּבְטוֹב הָעוֹלָם נִדּוֹן, וְהַכֹּל לְפִי רֹב הַמַּעֲשֶׂה.

כ הוּא הָיָה אוֹמֵר: הַכֹּל נָתוּן בְּעֵרָבוֹן, וּמְצוּדָה פְרוּסָה עַל כָּל הַחַיִּים. הֶחָנוּת פְּתוּחָה, וְהַחֶנְוָנִי מַקִּיף, וְהַפִּנְקָס פָּתְוּחַ, וְהַיָּד כּוֹתֶבֶת, וְכָל הָרוֹצֶה לִלְווֹת יָבֹא וְיִלְוֶה. וְהַגַּבָּאִין מַחֲזִירִין תָּדִיר בְּכָל יוֹם, וְנִפְרָעִין מִן הָאָדָם מִדַּעְתּוֹ וְשֶׁלֹּא מִדַּעְתּוֹ, וְיֵשׁ לָהֶם עַל מַה שֶּׁיִּסְמֹכוּ. וְהַדִּין, דִּין אֱמֶת. וְהַכֹּל מְתֻקָּן לִסְעוּדָה.

21. Rabbi Elazar ben Azariah said: If there is no Torah, there is no respect; if there is no respect, there is no Torah. If there is no wisdom, there is no reverence; if there is no reverence, there is no wisdom. If there is no knowledge, there is no understanding; if there is no understanding, there is no knowledge. If there is no flour [sustenance], there is no Torah; if there is no Torah, there is no flour.

22. He used to say: To what may one whose wisdom exceeds his deeds be compared? To a tree with many branches but few roots. When a wind comes, it uproots and overturns it, as it is said, "He shall be like a juniper tree in the desert, *Jer. 17*
which does not sense the coming of good: it is set in the scorched places of the wilderness in a barren, uninhabited land." To what may one whose deeds exceed his wisdom be compared? To a tree with few branches but many roots. Even if all the winds of the world come and blow against it, they cannot dislodge it from its place, as it is said, "He shall be like a tree planted by waters, sending *Jer. 17*
forth its roots by a stream: it does not sense the coming of heat; its leaves are ever fresh; it has no care in a year of drought; it does not cease to bear fruit."

23. Rabbi Elazar ben Ḥisma said: The laws of bird offerings and the calculation of menstrual periods are essential laws; astronomy and mathematics are adjuncts to wisdom.

Rabbi Ḥananya ben Akashya said: The Holy One, blessed be He, wanted to confer *Makkot 23b*
merit on Israel. That is why He gave them a copious Torah and many commandments, as it is said, "It pleased the Lord, for the sake of [Israel's] righteousness, *Is. 42*
to make the Torah great and glorious."

If there is a minyan, mourners say the Rabbis' Kaddish (page 448).

* * *

All Israel have a share in the World to Come, as it is said: *Sanhedrin 90a*
"Your people are all righteous; they shall inherit the land for ever; *Is. 60*
they are a shoot of My own planting,
a work of My own hands, that I may be glorified."

CHAPTER 4

1. Ben Zoma said: Who is wise? One who learns from everyone, as it is said, "From all my teachers I have learned, for Your testimonies are my meditation." Who *Ps. 119*
is strong? One who masters his evil impulse, as it is said, "He who is slow to *Prov. 16*
anger is better than the mighty, and he who rules over his spirit is better than he who conquers a city." Who is rich? One who rejoices in what he has, as it is said, "When you eat from the labor of your hands, you will be happy and all *Ps. 128*
will be well with you." "You will be happy" – in this world, "and all will be well with you"– in the World to Come. Who is honored? One who honors others, as it is said, "Those who honor Me, I will honor; but those who scorn Me will *I Sam. 2*
be despised."

כא רַבִּי אֶלְעָזָר בֶּן עֲזַרְיָה אוֹמֵר: אִם אֵין תּוֹרָה אֵין דֶּרֶךְ אֶרֶץ, אִם אֵין דֶּרֶךְ אֶרֶץ אֵין תּוֹרָה. אִם אֵין חָכְמָה אֵין יִרְאָה, אִם אֵין יִרְאָה אֵין חָכְמָה. אִם אֵין דַּעַת אֵין בִּינָה, אִם אֵין בִּינָה אֵין דַּעַת. אִם אֵין קֶמַח אֵין תּוֹרָה, אִם אֵין תּוֹרָה אֵין קֶמַח.

כב הוּא הָיָה אוֹמֵר: כָּל שֶׁחָכְמָתוֹ מְרֻבָּה מִמַּעֲשָׂיו, לְמָה הוּא דוֹמֶה, לְאִילָן
שֶׁעֲנָפָיו מְרֻבִּין וְשָׁרָשָׁיו מֻעָטִין, וְהָרוּחַ בָּאָה וְעוֹקַרְתּוֹ וְהוֹפַכְתּוֹ עַל פָּנָיו.
שֶׁנֶּאֱמַר, וְהָיָה כְּעַרְעָר בָּעֲרָבָה, וְלֹא יִרְאֶה כִּי־יָבוֹא טוֹב, וְשָׁכַן חֲרֵרִים ירמיה יז
בַּמִּדְבָּר, אֶרֶץ מְלֵחָה וְלֹא תֵשֵׁב: אֲבָל כָּל שֶׁמַּעֲשָׂיו מְרֻבִּין מֵחָכְמָתוֹ, לְמָה
הוּא דוֹמֶה, לְאִילָן שֶׁעֲנָפָיו מֻעָטִין וְשָׁרָשָׁיו מְרֻבִּין, שֶׁאֲפִלּוּ כָּל הָרוּחוֹת
שֶׁבָּעוֹלָם בָּאוֹת וְנוֹשְׁבוֹת בּוֹ, אֵין מְזִיזִין אוֹתוֹ מִמְּקוֹמוֹ. שֶׁנֶּאֱמַר: וְהָיָה כְּעֵץ ירמיה יז
שָׁתוּל עַל־מַיִם, וְעַל־יוּבַל יְשַׁלַּח שָׁרָשָׁיו, וְלֹא יִרְאֶ כִּי־יָבֹא חֹם, וְהָיָה עָלֵהוּ
רַעֲנָן, וּבִשְׁנַת בַּצֹּרֶת לֹא יִדְאָג, וְלֹא יָמִישׁ מֵעֲשׂוֹת פֶּרִי:

כג רַבִּי אֶלְעָזָר בֶּן חִסְמָא אוֹמֵר: קִנִּין וּפִתְחֵי נִדָּה הֵן הֵן גּוּפֵי הֲלָכוֹת, תְּקוּפוֹת וְגִימַטְרִיָּאוֹת פַּרְפְּרָאוֹת לַחָכְמָה.

רַבִּי חֲנַנְיָא בֶּן עֲקַשְׁיָא אוֹמֵר: רָצָה הַקָּדוֹשׁ בָּרוּךְ הוּא לְזַכּוֹת אֶת יִשְׂרָאֵל, לְפִיכָךְ מכות כג:
הִרְבָּה לָהֶם תּוֹרָה וּמִצְוֹת. שֶׁנֶּאֱמַר: יהוה חָפֵץ לְמַעַן צִדְקוֹ, יַגְדִּיל תּוֹרָה וְיַאְדִּיר: ישעיה מב

If there is a מנין*, mourners say* קדיש דרבנן (*page 449*).

* * *

כָּל יִשְׂרָאֵל יֵשׁ לָהֶם חֵלֶק לָעוֹלָם הַבָּא. שֶׁנֶּאֱמַר: סנהדרין צ.
וְעַמֵּךְ כֻּלָּם צַדִּיקִים, לְעוֹלָם יִירְשׁוּ אָרֶץ ישעיה ס
נֵצֶר מַטָּעַי, מַעֲשֵׂה יָדַי לְהִתְפָּאֵר:

פרק רביעי

א בֶּן זוֹמָא אוֹמֵר: אֵיזֶהוּ חָכָם, הַלּוֹמֵד מִכָּל אָדָם, שֶׁנֶּאֱמַר: מִכָּל־מְלַמְּדַי תהלים קיט
הִשְׂכַּלְתִּי, כִּי עֵדְוֹתֶיךָ שִׂיחָה לִי: אֵיזֶהוּ גִבּוֹר, הַכּוֹבֵשׁ אֶת יִצְרוֹ, שֶׁנֶּאֱמַר: טוֹב משלי טז
אֶרֶךְ אַפַּיִם מִגִּבּוֹר וּמֹשֵׁל בְּרוּחוֹ מִלֹּכֵד עִיר: אֵיזֶהוּ עָשִׁיר, הַשָּׂמֵחַ בְּחֶלְקוֹ,
שֶׁנֶּאֱמַר: יְגִיעַ כַּפֶּיךָ כִּי תֹאכֵל אַשְׁרֶיךָ וְטוֹב לָךְ: אַשְׁרֶיךָ בָּעוֹלָם הַזֶּה וְטוֹב תהלים קכח
לָךְ לָעוֹלָם הַבָּא. אֵיזֶהוּ מְכֻבָּד, הַמְכַבֵּד אֶת הַבְּרִיּוֹת, שֶׁנֶּאֱמַר: כִּי־מְכַבְּדַי שמואל א׳ ב
אֲכַבֵּד, וּבֹזַי יֵקָלּוּ:

Ben Azzai said: Run to do even a minor mitzva, and flee from sin, for one mitzva leads to another, and one sin leads to another – for the reward of a mitzva is another mitzva, and the recompense of a sin is another sin.

3. He used to say: Despise no one and disdain nothing, for there is no one who does not have his hour and there is nothing that does not have its place.
4. Rabbi Levitas of Yavne said: Have extreme humility of spirit, for the end of mortal man is the worm [the grave].
5. Rabbi Yoḥanan ben Beroka said: Whoever profanes God's name in secret will be punished in public. Profaning the name is the same whether done inadvertently or deliberately.
6. Rabbi Yishmael his son said: One who learns in order to teach will be given the opportunity to learn and teach. One who learns in order to do will be given the opportunity to learn, teach, keep and do.
7. Rabbi Zadok said: Do not separate yourself from the community. [When sitting as a judge] do not act as a lawyer. Do not use [the Torah] as a crown for self-glorification, or as a spade with which to dig. Likewise Hillel used to say: One who makes worldly use of the crown [of the Torah] shall fade away. From this you learn that one who seeks personal benefit from the words of Torah risks destroying his life.
8. Rabbi Yose said: One who honors the Torah will be honored by mankind. One who disgraces the Torah will be disgraced by mankind.
9. Rabbi Yishmael his son said: One who avoids serving as a judge spares himself enmity, robbery and false swearing. One who is over-confident in giving decisions is foolish, wicked and arrogant.
10. He used to say: Do not act as a judge alone, for none may judge alone except the One. Do not say "Accept my view"; for they are permitted, not you.
11. Rabbi Yonatan said: Whoever keeps the Torah when poor will eventually keep it in wealth. Whoever neglects the Torah when wealthy will eventually neglect it in poverty.
12. Rabbi Meir said: Limit your business activities and occupy yourself with Torah. Have humility before everyone. If you neglect the Torah, you will have many excuses to neglect it, but if you labor in the Torah, He has great reward to give you.
13. Rabbi Eliezer ben Jacob said: One who performs a single mitzva acquires for himself an advocate. One who commits a single transgression acquires for himself an accuser. Repentance and good deeds are a shield against punishment.
14. Rabbi Yoḥanan the sandal maker said: Every gathering that meets for the sake of heaven will have an enduring effect. One that is not for the sake of heaven will not have an enduring effect.

ב בֶּן עַזַּאי אוֹמֵר: הֱוֵי רָץ לְמִצְוָה קַלָּה וּבוֹרֵחַ מִן הָעֲבֵרָה. שֶׁמִּצְוָה גוֹרֶרֶת מִצְוָה, וַעֲבֵרָה גוֹרֶרֶת עֲבֵרָה. שֶׁשְּׂכַר מִצְוָה מִצְוָה, וּשְׂכַר עֲבֵרָה עֲבֵרָה.

ג הוּא הָיָה אוֹמֵר: אַל תְּהִי בָז לְכָל אָדָם, וְאַל תְּהִי מַפְלִיג לְכָל דָּבָר. שֶׁאֵין לְךָ אָדָם שֶׁאֵין לוֹ שָׁעָה, וְאֵין לְךָ דָבָר שֶׁאֵין לוֹ מָקוֹם.

ד רַבִּי לְוִיטַס אִישׁ יַבְנֶה אוֹמֵר: מְאֹד מְאֹד הֱוֵי שְׁפַל רוּחַ, שֶׁתִּקְוַת אֱנוֹשׁ רִמָּה.

ה רַבִּי יוֹחָנָן בֶּן בְּרוֹקָא אוֹמֵר: כָּל הַמְחַלֵּל שֵׁם שָׁמַיִם בַּסֵּתֶר, נִפְרָעִין מִמֶּנּוּ בַּגָּלוּי. אֶחָד שׁוֹגֵג וְאֶחָד מֵזִיד בְּחִלּוּל הַשֵּׁם.

ו רַבִּי יִשְׁמָעֵאל בְּנוֹ אוֹמֵר: הַלּוֹמֵד עַל מְנָת לְלַמֵּד, מַסְפִּיקִין בְּיָדוֹ לִלְמֹד וּלְלַמֵּד. וְהַלּוֹמֵד עַל מְנָת לַעֲשׂוֹת, מַסְפִּיקִין בְּיָדוֹ לִלְמֹד וּלְלַמֵּד, לִשְׁמֹר וְלַעֲשׂוֹת.

ז רַבִּי צָדוֹק אוֹמֵר: אַל תִּפְרשׁ מִן הַצִּבּוּר, וְאַל תַּעַשׂ עַצְמְךָ כְּעוֹרְכֵי הַדַּיָּנִין, וְאַל תַּעֲשֶׂהָ עֲטָרָה לְהִתְגַּדֶּל בָּהּ, וְלֹא קַרְדֹּם לַחְפֹּר בָּהּ. וְכָךְ הָיָה הִלֵּל אוֹמֵר: וּדְאִשְׁתַּמֵּשׁ בְּתָגָא חֲלָף. הָא לָמַדְתָּ, כָּל הַנֶּהֱנֶה מִדִּבְרֵי תוֹרָה, נוֹטֵל חַיָּיו מִן הָעוֹלָם.

ח רַבִּי יוֹסֵי אוֹמֵר: כָּל הַמְכַבֵּד אֶת הַתּוֹרָה, גּוּפוֹ מְכֻבָּד עַל הַבְּרִיּוֹת. וְכָל הַמְחַלֵּל אֶת הַתּוֹרָה, גּוּפוֹ מְחֻלָּל עַל הַבְּרִיּוֹת.

ט רַבִּי יִשְׁמָעֵאל בְּנוֹ אוֹמֵר: הַחוֹשֵׂךְ עַצְמוֹ מִן הַדִּין, פּוֹרֵק מִמֶּנּוּ אֵיבָה וְגָזֵל וּשְׁבוּעַת שָׁוְא. וְהַגַּס לִבּוֹ בְּהוֹרָאָה, שׁוֹטֶה, רָשָׁע וְגַס רוּחַ.

י הוּא הָיָה אוֹמֵר: אַל תְּהִי דָן יְחִידִי, שֶׁאֵין דָּן יְחִידִי אֶלָּא אֶחָד. וְאַל תֹּאמַר קַבְּלוּ דַעְתִּי, שֶׁהֵן רַשָּׁאִין וְלֹא אָתָּה.

יא רַבִּי יוֹנָתָן אוֹמֵר: כָּל הַמְקַיֵּם אֶת הַתּוֹרָה מֵעֹנִי, סוֹפוֹ לְקַיְּמָהּ מֵעֹשֶׁר. וְכָל הַמְבַטֵּל אֶת הַתּוֹרָה מֵעֹשֶׁר, סוֹפוֹ לְבַטְּלָהּ מֵעֹנִי.

יב רַבִּי מֵאִיר אוֹמֵר: הֱוֵי מְמַעֵט בְּעֵסֶק וַעֲסֹק בַּתּוֹרָה, וֶהֱוֵי שְׁפַל רוּחַ בִּפְנֵי כָל אָדָם. וְאִם בָּטַלְתָּ מִן הַתּוֹרָה, יֶשׁ לְךָ בְּטֵלִים הַרְבֵּה כְּנֶגְדְּךָ. וְאִם עָמַלְתָּ בַּתּוֹרָה, יֶשׁ לוֹ שָׂכָר הַרְבֵּה לִתֶּן לָךְ.

יג רַבִּי אֱלִיעֶזֶר בֶּן יַעֲקֹב אוֹמֵר: הָעוֹשֶׂה מִצְוָה אַחַת, קוֹנֶה לּוֹ פְּרַקְלִיט אֶחָד. וְהָעוֹבֵר עֲבֵרָה אַחַת, קוֹנֶה לּוֹ קַטֵּגוֹר אֶחָד. תְּשׁוּבָה וּמַעֲשִׂים טוֹבִים, כִּתְרִיס בִּפְנֵי הַפֻּרְעָנוּת.

יד רַבִּי יוֹחָנָן הַסַּנְדְּלָר אוֹמֵר: כָּל כְּנֵסִיָּה שֶׁהִיא לְשֵׁם שָׁמַיִם, סוֹפָהּ לְהִתְקַיֵּם. וְשֶׁאֵינָהּ לְשֵׁם שָׁמַיִם, אֵין סוֹפָהּ לְהִתְקַיֵּם.

15. Rabbi Elazar ben Shammua said: Let your student's honor be as precious to you as your own; let your colleague's honor be like the reverence due to your teacher; and let the reverence you have for your teacher be like the reverence due to Heaven.
16. Rabbi Judah said: Be careful when you study, for an inadvertent error in study is tantamount to an intentional sin.
17. Rabbi Shimon said: There are three crowns: the crown of Torah, the crown of priesthood, and the crown of kingship – but the crown of a good name surpasses them all.
18. Rabbi Nehorai said: Exile yourself to a place of Torah, and do not assume that it will come after you, for your fellow students will ensure that it will remain with you. "Do not rely on your own understanding." *Prov. 3*
19. Rabbi Yannai said: It is not in our power to explain either the peace of the wicked or the suffering of the righteous.
20. Rabbi Matya ben Ḥarash said: Be first in greeting everyone. Be a tail to lions rather than a head to foxes.
21. Rabbi Jacob said: This world is like an antechamber before the World to Come. Prepare yourself in the antechamber so that you may enter the banqueting hall.
22. He used to say: Better one hour of repentance and good deeds in this world than all the life in the World to Come. Better one hour of bliss in the World to Come than the whole life of this world.
23. Rabbi Shimon ben Elazar said: Do not try to placate your fellow in his hour of anger. Do not try to comfort him while his dead lies before him. Do not question him about his vow at the time he is making it. Do not try to see him in his hour of disgrace.
24. Samuel the Younger used to quote: "If your enemy falls, do not rejoice; if he *Prov. 24* stumbles, let not your heart be glad; lest the Lord see it and be displeased, and divert His wrath from him to you."
25. Elisha ben Abuya said: When you learn as a child, what is it like? Like ink written on clean paper. When you learn in old age, what is it like? Like ink written on blotted paper.
26. Rabbi Yose bar Judah of Kfar Bavli said: When you learn from the young, what is it like? Like eating unripe grapes or drinking wine straight from the vat. When you learn from the old, what is it like? Like eating ripe grapes and drinking old wine.
27. Rabbi Meir said: Do not look at the container but at what it contains, for a new flask may contain old wine, and an old flask may not contain anything, even new wine.
28. Rabbi Elazar HaKappar said: Envy, lust, and the seeking of honor, drive a person out of the world.

טו רַבִּי אֶלְעָזָר בֶּן שַׁמּוּעַ אוֹמֵר: יְהִי כְבוֹד תַּלְמִידְךָ חָבִיב עָלֶיךָ כְּשֶׁלָּךְ, וּכְבוֹד חֲבֵרְךָ כְּמוֹרָא רַבָּךְ, וּמוֹרָא רַבָּךְ כְּמוֹרָא שָׁמָיִם.

טז רַבִּי יְהוּדָה אוֹמֵר: הֱוֵי זָהִיר בְּתַלְמוּד, שֶׁשִּׁגְגַת תַּלְמוּד עוֹלָה זָדוֹן.

יז רַבִּי שִׁמְעוֹן אוֹמֵר: שְׁלֹשָׁה כְתָרִים הֵן, כֶּתֶר תּוֹרָה וְכֶתֶר כְּהֻנָּה וְכֶתֶר מַלְכוּת, וְכֶתֶר שֵׁם טוֹב עוֹלֶה עַל גַּבֵּיהֶן.

יח רַבִּי נְהוֹרָאִי אוֹמֵר: הֱוֵי גוֹלֶה לִמְקוֹם תּוֹרָה. וְאַל תֹּאמַר שֶׁהִיא תָבוֹא אַחֲרֶיךָ, שֶׁחֲבֵרֶיךָ יְקַיְּמוּהָ בְיָדֶךָ. וְאֶל־בִּינָתְךָ אַל־תִּשָּׁעֵן: משלי ג

יט רַבִּי יַנַּאי אוֹמֵר: אֵין בְּיָדֵינוּ לֹא מִשַּׁלְוַת הָרְשָׁעִים וְאַף לֹא מִיִּסּוּרֵי הַצַּדִּיקִים.

כ רַבִּי מַתְיָא בֶּן חָרָשׁ אוֹמֵר: הֱוֵי מַקְדִּים בִּשְׁלוֹם כָּל אָדָם, וֶהֱוֵי זָנָב לָאֲרָיוֹת, וְאַל תְּהִי רֹאשׁ לַשּׁוּעָלִים.

כא רַבִּי יַעֲקֹב אוֹמֵר: הָעוֹלָם הַזֶּה דּוֹמֶה לִפְרוֹזְדוֹר בִּפְנֵי הָעוֹלָם הַבָּא. הַתְקֵן עַצְמְךָ בִּפְרוֹזְדוֹר, כְּדֵי שֶׁתִּכָּנֵס לַטְּרַקְלִין.

כב הוּא הָיָה אוֹמֵר: יָפָה שָׁעָה אַחַת בִּתְשׁוּבָה וּמַעֲשִׂים טוֹבִים בָּעוֹלָם הַזֶּה, מִכֹּל חַיֵּי הָעוֹלָם הַבָּא. וְיָפָה שָׁעָה אַחַת שֶׁל קוֹרַת רוּחַ בָּעוֹלָם הַבָּא, מִכֹּל חַיֵּי הָעוֹלָם הַזֶּה.

כג רַבִּי שִׁמְעוֹן בֶּן אֶלְעָזָר אוֹמֵר: אַל תְּרַצֶּה אֶת חֲבֵרְךָ בִּשְׁעַת כַּעְסוֹ, וְאַל תְּנַחֲמֵהוּ בְּשָׁעָה שֶׁמֵּתוֹ מֻטָּל לְפָנָיו, וְאַל תִּשְׁאַל לוֹ בִּשְׁעַת נִדְרוֹ, וְאַל תִּשְׁתַּדֵּל לִרְאוֹתוֹ בִּשְׁעַת קַלְקָלָתוֹ.

כד שְׁמוּאֵל הַקָּטָן אוֹמֵר: בִּנְפֹל אוֹיִבְךָ אַל־תִּשְׂמָח, וּבִכָּשְׁלוֹ אַל־יָגֵל לִבֶּךָ: פֶּן־ משלי כד
יִרְאֶה יהוה וְרַע בְּעֵינָיו, וְהֵשִׁיב מֵעָלָיו אַפּוֹ:

כה אֱלִישָׁע בֶּן אֲבוּיָה אוֹמֵר: הַלּוֹמֵד יֶלֶד, לְמָה הוּא דוֹמֶה, לִדְיוֹ כְתוּבָה עַל נְיָר חָדָשׁ. וְהַלּוֹמֵד זָקֵן, לְמָה הוּא דוֹמֶה, לִדְיוֹ כְתוּבָה עַל נְיָר מָחוּק.

כו רַבִּי יוֹסֵי בַּר יְהוּדָה אִישׁ כְּפַר הַבַּבְלִי אוֹמֵר: הַלּוֹמֵד מִן הַקְּטַנִּים, לְמָה הוּא דוֹמֶה, לְאוֹכֵל עֲנָבִים קֵהוֹת וְשׁוֹתֶה יַיִן מִגִּתּוֹ. וְהַלּוֹמֵד מִן הַזְּקֵנִים, לְמָה הוּא דוֹמֶה, לְאוֹכֵל עֲנָבִים בְּשׁוּלוֹת וְשׁוֹתֶה יַיִן יָשָׁן.

כז רַבִּי מֵאִיר אוֹמֵר: אַל תִּסְתַּכֵּל בַּקַּנְקַן, אֶלָּא בְּמַה שֶּׁיֵּשׁ בּוֹ. יֵשׁ קַנְקַן חָדָשׁ מָלֵא יָשָׁן, וְיָשָׁן שֶׁאֲפִלּוּ חָדָשׁ אֵין בּוֹ.

כח רַבִּי אֶלְעָזָר הַקַּפָּר אוֹמֵר: הַקִּנְאָה וְהַתַּאֲוָה וְהַכָּבוֹד, מוֹצִיאִין אֶת הָאָדָם מִן הָעוֹלָם.

29. He used to say: Those who are born will one day die, those who die will live again, and the living will be judged. It is for us to know, make known, and confirm that He is God, He is the Maker; He is the Creator; He is the Discerner; He is the Judge; He is the Witness; He is the Plaintiff; and He will deliver the judgment. Blessed is He before whom there is no unrighteousness, no forgetfulness, no favoritism and no taking of bribes; and know that all is according to a strict reckoning. Do not let your evil impulse persuade you that the grave is, for you, a place of refuge: for without your consent you were formed, without your consent you were born, without your consent you live, without your consent you will die, and without your consent you will in the future have to give an account and reckoning before the Supreme King of kings, the Holy One, blessed be He.

Rabbi Ḥananya ben Akashya said: The Holy One, blessed be He, wanted to confer merit on Israel. That is why He gave them a copious Torah and many commandments, as it is said, "It pleased the Lord, for the sake of [Israel's] righteousness, to make the Torah great and glorious." *Makkot 23b* *Is. 42*

If there is a minyan, mourners say the Rabbis' Kaddish (page 448).

* * *

All Israel have a share in the World to Come, as it is said, *Sanhedrin 90a*
"Your people are all righteous; they shall inherit the land for ever; *Is. 60*
they are a shoot of My own planting,
a work of My own hands, that I may be glorified."

CHAPTER 5

1. By ten acts of speech the world was created. What does this teach us? Could not the world have been created by a single act of speech? It is to exact punishment from the wicked who destroy a world created by ten acts of speech, and richly to reward the righteous who sustain the world created by ten acts of speech.
2. There were ten generations from Adam to Noah, to make known how patient God is, for all those generations increasingly provoked Him until He brought on them the waters of the Flood.
3. There were ten generations from Noah to Abraham, to make known how patient God is, for all those generations increasingly provoked Him until Abraham our father came and received the reward which could have been theirs.
4. Abraham our father was tested with ten trials and he withstood all of them, to make known how deep was our father Abraham's love of God.
5. Ten miracles were performed for our ancestors in Egypt, and ten at the Sea. The Holy One, blessed be He, brought ten plagues against the Egyptians in Egypt, and ten at the Sea.

כט הוּא הָיָה אוֹמֵר: הַיִּלּוֹדִים לָמוּת, וְהַמֵּתִים לְחְיוֹת, וְהַחַיִּים לִדּוֹן, לֵידַע וּלְהוֹדִיעַ וּלְהִוָּדַע, שֶׁהוּא אֵל, הוּא הַיּוֹצֵר, הוּא הַבּוֹרֵא, הוּא הַמֵּבִין, הוּא הַדַּיָּן, הוּא הָעֵד, הוּא בַּעַל דִּין, הוּא עָתִיד לָדוּן. בָּרוּךְ הוּא, שֶׁאֵין לְפָנָיו לֹא עַוְלָה וְלֹא שִׁכְחָה, וְלֹא מַשּׂוֹא פָנִים וְלֹא מִקַּח שֹׁחַד, שֶׁהַכֹּל שֶׁלּוֹ. וְדַע, שֶׁהַכֹּל לְפִי הַחֶשְׁבּוֹן. וְאַל יַבְטִיחֲךָ יִצְרְךָ שֶׁהַשְּׁאוֹל בֵּית מָנוֹס לָךְ, שֶׁעַל כָּרְחֲךָ אַתָּה נוֹצָר, וְעַל כָּרְחֲךָ אַתָּה נוֹלָד, וְעַל כָּרְחֲךָ אַתָּה חַי, וְעַל כָּרְחֲךָ אַתָּה מֵת, וְעַל כָּרְחֲךָ אַתָּה עָתִיד לִתֵּן דִּין וְחֶשְׁבּוֹן לִפְנֵי מֶלֶךְ מַלְכֵי הַמְּלָכִים הַקָּדוֹשׁ בָּרוּךְ הוּא.

רַבִּי חֲנַנְיָא בֶּן עֲקַשְׁיָא אוֹמֵר: רָצָה הַקָּדוֹשׁ בָּרוּךְ הוּא לְזַכּוֹת אֶת יִשְׂרָאֵל, לְפִיכָךְ מכות כג:
הִרְבָּה לָהֶם תּוֹרָה וּמִצְוֹת. שֶׁנֶּאֱמַר: יהוה חָפֵץ לְמַעַן צִדְקוֹ, יַגְדִּיל תּוֹרָה וְיַאְדִּיר: ישעיה מב

If there is a מנין, *mourners say* קדיש דרבנן *(page 449).*

* * *

כָּל יִשְׂרָאֵל יֵשׁ לָהֶם חֵלֶק לָעוֹלָם הַבָּא. שֶׁנֶּאֱמַר: סנהדרין צ.
וְעַמֵּךְ כֻּלָּם צַדִּיקִים, לְעוֹלָם יִירְשׁוּ אָרֶץ ישעיה ס
נֵצֶר מַטָּעַי, מַעֲשֵׂה יָדַי לְהִתְפָּאֵר:

פרק חמישי

א בַּעֲשָׂרָה מַאֲמָרוֹת נִבְרָא הָעוֹלָם. וּמַה תַּלְמוּד לוֹמַר, וַהֲלֹא בְּמַאֲמָר אֶחָד יָכוֹל לְהִבָּרְאוֹת, אֶלָּא לְהִפָּרַע מִן הָרְשָׁעִים, שֶׁמְּאַבְּדִין אֶת הָעוֹלָם שֶׁנִּבְרָא בַּעֲשָׂרָה מַאֲמָרוֹת, וְלִתֵּן שָׂכָר טוֹב לַצַּדִּיקִים, שֶׁמְּקַיְּמִין אֶת הָעוֹלָם שֶׁנִּבְרָא בַּעֲשָׂרָה מַאֲמָרוֹת.

ב עֲשָׂרָה דוֹרוֹת מֵאָדָם וְעַד נֹחַ, לְהוֹדִיעַ כַּמָּה אֶרֶךְ אַפַּיִם לְפָנָיו, שֶׁכָּל הַדּוֹרוֹת הָיוּ מַכְעִיסִין וּבָאִין, עַד שֶׁהֵבִיא עֲלֵיהֶם אֶת מֵי הַמַּבּוּל.

ג עֲשָׂרָה דוֹרוֹת מִנֹּחַ וְעַד אַבְרָהָם, לְהוֹדִיעַ כַּמָּה אֶרֶךְ אַפַּיִם לְפָנָיו, שֶׁכָּל הַדּוֹרוֹת הָיוּ מַכְעִיסִין וּבָאִין, עַד שֶׁבָּא אַבְרָהָם אָבִינוּ וְקִבֵּל שְׂכַר כֻּלָּם.

ד עֲשָׂרָה נִסְיוֹנוֹת נִתְנַסָּה אַבְרָהָם אָבִינוּ וְעָמַד בְּכֻלָּם, לְהוֹדִיעַ כַּמָּה חִבָּתוֹ שֶׁל אַבְרָהָם אָבִינוּ.

ה עֲשָׂרָה נִסִּים נַעֲשׂוּ לַאֲבוֹתֵינוּ בְּמִצְרַיִם, וַעֲשָׂרָה עַל הַיָּם. עֶשֶׂר מַכּוֹת הֵבִיא הַקָּדוֹשׁ בָּרוּךְ הוּא עַל הַמִּצְרִיִּים בְּמִצְרַיִם, וְעֶשֶׂר עַל הַיָּם.

With ten trials our ancestors tried the patience of the Holy One, blessed be He, in the wilderness, as it is written, "They have tested Me these ten times, and did not listen to My voice." *Num. 14*

7. Ten miracles were performed for our ancestors in the Temple: (1) No woman miscarried from the aroma of the sacrificial meat; (2) the sacrificial meat never became putrid; (3) no fly was seen in the slaughterhouse; (4) the High Priest never suffered ritual pollution on Yom Kippur; (5) rain never extinguished the fire of the wood-pile on the altar; (6) the wind never blew away the column of smoke that rose from the altar; (7) no defect was ever found in the Omer, the Two Loaves, or the Showbread; (8) the people stood crowded together, yet there was ample space when they prostrated themselves; (9) no serpent or scorpion ever harmed anyone in Jerusalem; and (10) no one ever said to his fellow, "There is no room for me to stay overnight in Jerusalem."
8. Ten things were created on the eve of the Sabbath at twilight. They were: (1) the mouth of the earth; (2) the mouth of the well; (3) the mouth of [Balaam's] ass; (4) the rainbow; (5) the manna; (6) the staff; (7) the Shamir; (8) the writing [on the Tablets]; (9) the inscription; and (10) the Tablets. Some say: also the demons, Moses' burial place, and the ram of our father Abraham. And some say: also tongs made with tongs.
9. Seven traits characterize an uncultured person, and seven a sage. A sage: (1) does not speak before one who is wiser than he; (2) does not interrupt the words of his fellow; (3) does not answer impetuously; (4) asks relevant questions and gives appropriate answers; (5) deals with first things first, and last things last; (6) about something he has not heard he says, "I have not heard"; and (7) he acknowledges the truth. The opposites of these characterize an uncultured person.
10. Seven types of punishment come into the world for seven kinds of transgression: (1) If some tithe and others do not, a famine caused by drought occurs, so that some go hungry while others have sufficient. (2) If all decide not to tithe, a famine comes through tumult [of war] as well as drought. (3) If they also decide not to set apart ḥalla, a fatal famine ensues.
11. (4) Pestilence comes to the world for crimes that, according to the Torah, carry the death penalty, but are not the preserve of a human tribunal, and also for violation of the laws relating to produce of the seventh year. (5) The sword comes to the world for delay of justice, the perversion of justice, and for those who give a legal decision in violation of normative Torah law.
12. (6) Wild beasts come to the world because of perjury and the desecration of God's name. (7) Exile comes to the world for idolatry, sexual immorality and bloodshed, and for violating the sabbatical year of the land.

ו עֲשָׂרָה נִסְיוֹנוֹת נִסּוּ אֲבוֹתֵינוּ אֶת הַקָּדוֹשׁ בָּרוּךְ הוּא בַּמִּדְבָּר, שֶׁנֶּאֱמַר:
וַיְנַסּוּ אֹתִי זֶה עֶשֶׂר פְּעָמִים, וְלֹא שָׁמְעוּ בְּקוֹלִי: במדבר יד

ז עֲשָׂרָה נִסִּים נַעֲשׂוּ לַאֲבוֹתֵינוּ בְּבֵית הַמִּקְדָּשׁ. לֹא הִפִּילָה אִשָּׁה מֵרֵיחַ בְּשַׂר הַקֹּדֶשׁ, וְלֹא הִסְרִיחַ בְּשַׂר הַקֹּדֶשׁ מֵעוֹלָם, וְלֹא נִרְאָה זְבוּב בְּבֵית הַמִּטְבְּחַיִם, וְלֹא אֵרַע קֶרִי לְכֹהֵן גָּדוֹל בְּיוֹם הַכִּפּוּרִים, וְלֹא כִבּוּ הַגְּשָׁמִים אֵשׁ שֶׁל עֲצֵי הַמַּעֲרָכָה, וְלֹא נִצְּחָה הָרוּחַ אֶת עַמּוּד הֶעָשָׁן, וְלֹא נִמְצָא פְסוּל בָּעֹמֶר וּבִשְׁתֵּי הַלֶּחֶם וּבְלֶחֶם הַפָּנִים, עוֹמְדִים צְפוּפִים וּמִשְׁתַּחֲוִים רְוָחִים, וְלֹא הִזִּיק נָחָשׁ וְעַקְרָב בִּירוּשָׁלַיִם מֵעוֹלָם, וְלֹא אָמַר אָדָם לַחֲבֵרוֹ: צַר לִי הַמָּקוֹם שֶׁאָלִין בִּירוּשָׁלָיִם.

ח עֲשָׂרָה דְבָרִים נִבְרְאוּ בְּעֶרֶב שַׁבָּת בֵּין הַשְּׁמָשׁוֹת. וְאֵלּוּ הֵן, פִּי הָאָרֶץ, פִּי הַבְּאֵר, פִּי הָאָתוֹן, הַקֶּשֶׁת, וְהַמָּן, וְהַמַּטֶּה, וְהַשָּׁמִיר, הַכְּתָב, וְהַמִּכְתָּב, וְהַלּוּחוֹת. וְיֵשׁ אוֹמְרִים, אַף הַמַּזִּיקִין, וּקְבוּרָתוֹ שֶׁל מֹשֶׁה, וְאֵילוֹ שֶׁל אַבְרָהָם אָבִינוּ. וְיֵשׁ אוֹמְרִים, אַף צְבָת בִּצְבָת עֲשׂוּיָה.

ט שִׁבְעָה דְבָרִים בְּגֹלֶם, וְשִׁבְעָה בְּחָכָם. חָכָם אֵינוֹ מְדַבֵּר לִפְנֵי מִי שֶׁגָּדוֹל מִמֶּנּוּ בְּחָכְמָה, וְאֵינוֹ נִכְנָס לְתוֹךְ דִּבְרֵי חֲבֵרוֹ, וְאֵינוֹ נִבְהָל לְהָשִׁיב, שׁוֹאֵל כָּעִנְיָן וּמֵשִׁיב כַּהֲלָכָה, וְאוֹמֵר עַל רִאשׁוֹן רִאשׁוֹן וְעַל אַחֲרוֹן אַחֲרוֹן, וְעַל מַה שֶּׁלֹּא שָׁמַע אוֹמֵר לֹא שָׁמַעְתִּי, וּמוֹדֶה עַל הָאֱמֶת. וְחִלּוּפֵיהֶן בְּגֹלֶם.

י שִׁבְעָה מִינֵי פֻרְעָנִיּוֹת בָּאִין לָעוֹלָם עַל שִׁבְעָה גוּפֵי עֲבֵרָה. מִקְצָתָן מְעַשְּׂרִין וּמִקְצָתָן אֵינָן מְעַשְּׂרִין, רָעָב שֶׁל בַּצֹּרֶת בָּא, מִקְצָתָן רְעֵבִים וּמִקְצָתָן שְׂבֵעִים. גָּמְרוּ שֶׁלֹּא לְעַשֵּׂר, רָעָב שֶׁל מְהוּמָה וְשֶׁל בַּצֹּרֶת בָּא. וְשֶׁלֹּא לִטּוֹל אֶת הַחַלָּה, רָעָב שֶׁל כְּלָיָה בָּא.

יא דֶּבֶר בָּא לָעוֹלָם עַל מִיתוֹת הָאֲמוּרוֹת בַּתּוֹרָה שֶׁלֹּא נִמְסְרוּ לְבֵית דִּין, וְעַל פֵּרוֹת שְׁבִיעִית. חֶרֶב בָּאָה לָעוֹלָם עַל עִנּוּי הַדִּין, וְעַל עִוּוּת הַדִּין, וְעַל הַמּוֹרִים בַּתּוֹרָה שֶׁלֹּא כַהֲלָכָה.

יב חַיָּה רָעָה בָּאָה לָעוֹלָם עַל שְׁבוּעַת שָׁוְא וְעַל חִלּוּל הַשֵּׁם. גָּלוּת בָּאָה לָעוֹלָם עַל עֲבוֹדָה זָרָה, וְעַל גִּלּוּי עֲרָיוֹת, וְעַל שְׁפִיכוּת דָּמִים, וְעַל שְׁמִטַּת הָאָרֶץ.

13. At four periods [of the seven-year sabbatical cycle] pestilence increases: in the fourth year, the seventh year, the year following the sabbatical year, and annually at the conclusion of the Festival of Sukkot. In the fourth year, [pestilence increases] because of neglect of the tithe for the poor in the third year; in the seventh year, because of neglect of the tithe for the poor in the sixth year; in the year following the sabbatical year, because of the violation of the laws of the seventh-year produce; and at the conclusion of the Festival of Sukkot, for robbing the poor of their gifts.
14. There are four types of human character: (1) One who says, "What is mine is mine, and what is yours is yours," is an average person, though some say this is a Sodom type. (2) One who says, "What is mine is yours and what is yours is mine," is an ignoramus. (3) One who says, "What is mine is yours and what is yours is yours," is pious. (4) One who says, "What is yours is mine and what is mine is mine," is wicked.
15. There are four types of temperament: (1) One who is easily angered and easily pacified – his loss is cancelled by his gain. (2) One who is hard to anger and hard to pacify – his gain is cancelled by his loss. (3) One who is hard to anger and easily pacified is pious. (4) One who is easily angered and hard to pacify is wicked.
16. There are four types of student: (1) One who learns quickly and forgets quickly – his gain is cancelled by his loss. (2) One who learns slowly and forgets slowly – his loss is cancelled by his gain. (3) One who learns quickly and forgets slowly – his is a happy lot. (4) One who learns slowly and forgets quickly – his is a sad lot.
17. There are four types of donor to charity: (1) One who wishes to give but does not want others to give, begrudges others. (2) One who wants others to give, but does not himself give, begrudges himself. (3) One who gives and wants others to give is pious. (4) One who does not himself give and does not want others to give is wicked.
18. There are four types among those who attend the House of Study: (1) One who goes but does not practice [what he learns] receives a reward for going. (2) One who practices but does not go receives a reward for practicing. (3) One who goes and also practices is pious. (4) One who neither goes nor practices is wicked.
19. There are four types among those who sit before the sages: the sponge, the funnel, the strainer and the sieve. The sponge absorbs everything. The funnel takes in at one end and lets out at the other. The strainer lets out the wine and retains the sediment. The sieve allows the flour dust to pass through and retains the fine flour.
20. If love depends on a specific cause, when the cause ends, so does the love. If love does not depend on a specific cause, then it never ends. What is an example of love depending on a specific cause? The love of Amnon for Tamar. What is an example of love not dependent on a specific cause? The love of David and Jonathan.

יג בְּאַרְבָּעָה פְרָקִים הַדֶּבֶר מִתְרַבֶּה, בָּרְבִיעִית, וּבַשְּׁבִיעִית, וּבְמוֹצָאֵי שְׁבִיעִית, וּבְמוֹצָאֵי הֶחָג שֶׁבְּכָל שָׁנָה וְשָׁנָה. בָּרְבִיעִית, מִפְּנֵי מַעְשַׂר עָנִי שֶׁבַּשְּׁלִישִׁית. בַּשְּׁבִיעִית, מִפְּנֵי מַעְשַׂר עָנִי שֶׁבַּשִּׁשִּׁית. בְּמוֹצָאֵי שְׁבִיעִית, מִפְּנֵי פֵּרוֹת שְׁבִיעִית. בְּמוֹצָאֵי הֶחָג שֶׁבְּכָל שָׁנָה וְשָׁנָה, מִפְּנֵי גֶזֶל מַתְּנוֹת עֲנִיִּים.

יד אַרְבַּע מִדּוֹת בָּאָדָם. הָאוֹמֵר שֶׁלִּי שֶׁלִּי וְשֶׁלְּךָ שֶׁלָּךְ, זוֹ מִדָּה בֵינוֹנִית, וְיֵשׁ אוֹמְרִים, זוֹ מִדַּת סְדוֹם. שֶׁלִּי שֶׁלָּךְ וְשֶׁלְּךָ שֶׁלִּי, עַם הָאָרֶץ. שֶׁלִּי שֶׁלָּךְ וְשֶׁלָּךְ שֶׁלָּךְ, חָסִיד. שֶׁלָּךְ שֶׁלִּי וְשֶׁלִּי שֶׁלִּי, רָשָׁע.

טו אַרְבַּע מִדּוֹת בַּדֵּעוֹת. נוֹחַ לִכְעוֹס וְנוֹחַ לִרְצוֹת, יָצָא הֶפְסֵדוֹ בִּשְׂכָרוֹ. קָשֶׁה לִכְעוֹס וְקָשֶׁה לִרְצוֹת, יָצָא שְׂכָרוֹ בְּהֶפְסֵדוֹ. קָשֶׁה לִכְעוֹס וְנוֹחַ לִרְצוֹת, חָסִיד. נוֹחַ לִכְעוֹס וְקָשֶׁה לִרְצוֹת, רָשָׁע.

טז אַרְבַּע מִדּוֹת בַּתַּלְמִידִים. מָהִיר לִשְׁמוֹעַ וּמָהִיר לְאַבֵּד, יָצָא שְׂכָרוֹ בְּהֶפְסֵדוֹ. קָשֶׁה לִשְׁמוֹעַ וְקָשֶׁה לְאַבֵּד, יָצָא הֶפְסֵדוֹ בִּשְׂכָרוֹ. מָהִיר לִשְׁמוֹעַ וְקָשֶׁה לְאַבֵּד, זֶה חֵלֶק טוֹב. קָשֶׁה לִשְׁמוֹעַ וּמָהִיר לְאַבֵּד, זֶה חֵלֶק רָע.

יז אַרְבַּע מִדּוֹת בְּנוֹתְנֵי צְדָקָה. הָרוֹצֶה שֶׁיִּתֵּן וְלֹא יִתְּנוּ אֲחֵרִים, עֵינוֹ רָעָה בְּשֶׁל אֲחֵרִים. יִתְּנוּ אֲחֵרִים וְהוּא לֹא יִתֵּן, עֵינוֹ רָעָה בְּשֶׁלּוֹ. יִתֵּן וְיִתְּנוּ אֲחֵרִים, חָסִיד. לֹא יִתֵּן וְלֹא יִתְּנוּ אֲחֵרִים, רָשָׁע.

יח אַרְבַּע מִדּוֹת בְּהוֹלְכֵי בֵית הַמִּדְרָשׁ. הוֹלֵךְ וְאֵינוֹ עוֹשֶׂה, שְׂכַר הֲלִיכָה בְּיָדוֹ. עוֹשֶׂה וְאֵינוֹ הוֹלֵךְ, שְׂכַר מַעֲשֶׂה בְּיָדוֹ. הוֹלֵךְ וְעוֹשֶׂה, חָסִיד. לֹא הוֹלֵךְ וְלֹא עוֹשֶׂה, רָשָׁע.

יט אַרְבַּע מִדּוֹת בְּיוֹשְׁבִים לִפְנֵי חֲכָמִים, סְפוֹג, וּמַשְׁפֵּךְ, מְשַׁמֶּרֶת, וְנָפָה. סְפוֹג, שֶׁהוּא סוֹפֵג אֶת הַכֹּל. וּמַשְׁפֵּךְ, שֶׁמַּכְנִיס בְּזוֹ וּמוֹצִיא בְזוֹ. מְשַׁמֶּרֶת, שֶׁמּוֹצִיאָה אֶת הַיַּיִן וְקוֹלֶטֶת אֶת הַשְּׁמָרִים. וְנָפָה, שֶׁמּוֹצִיאָה אֶת הַקֶּמַח וְקוֹלֶטֶת אֶת הַסֹּלֶת.

כ כָּל אַהֲבָה שֶׁהִיא תְלוּיָה בְדָבָר, בָּטֵל דָּבָר, בְּטֵלָה אַהֲבָה. וְשֶׁאֵינָהּ תְּלוּיָה בְדָבָר, אֵינָהּ בְּטֵלָה לְעוֹלָם. אֵיזוֹ הִיא אַהֲבָה שֶׁהִיא תְלוּיָה בְדָבָר, זוֹ אַהֲבַת אַמְנוֹן וְתָמָר. וְשֶׁאֵינָהּ תְּלוּיָה בְדָבָר, זוֹ אַהֲבַת דָּוִד וִיהוֹנָתָן.

21. Any dispute for the sake of Heaven will have enduring value, but any dispute not for the sake of Heaven will not have enduring value. What is an example of a dispute for the sake of heaven? The dispute between Hillel and Shammai. What is an example of one not for the sake of heaven? The dispute of Koraḥ and all his company.

22. One who brings merit to the many will not be the cause of sin. One who causes the many to sin will be denied the means to repent. Moses attained merit and brought merit to the many; therefore the merit of the many was attributed to him, as it is said, "He carried out the LORD's righteousness and His ordinances with Israel." Jeroboam, son of Nebat, sinned and caused the many to sin; therefore the sin of the many was attributed to him, as it is said, "For the sins of Jeroboam that he committed and that he caused Israel to commit." *Deut. 33* *1 Kings 15*

23. Whoever possesses these three traits is one of the disciples of our father Abraham; whoever possesses the three opposite traits is one of the disciples of the wicked Balaam. A generous eye, a modest demeanor and a humble soul are the traits of the disciples of our father Abraham. An evil eye, an arrogant demeanor and an insatiable soul are attributes of the disciples of the wicked Balaam. What is the difference between our father Abraham's disciples and those of the wicked Balaam? Our father Abraham's disciples enjoy this world and inherit the World to Come, as it is said, "That I may cause those who love me to inherit substance and so that I may fill their treasures." The wicked Balaam's disciples inherit Gehinnom and go down to the pit of destruction, as it is said, "But You, God, will bring them down to the pit of destruction; bloodthirsty and deceitful men shall not live out half their days; but I trust in You." *Prov. 8* *Ps. 55*

24. Judah ben Tema said: Be strong as a leopard, light as an eagle, swift as a gazelle, and brave as a lion, to do the will of your Father in heaven. He used to say: The shameless go to Gehinnom; those who have a sense of shame are destined for the Garden of Eden. May it be Your will, O LORD our God and God of our ancestors that the Temple be speedily rebuilt in our days; and grant us our portion in Your Torah.

25. He used to say: Five years old is the age to begin studying Scripture; ten for Mishna; thirteen for the obligation of the commandments; fifteen for the study of Talmud; eighteen for marriage; twenty for seeking a livelihood; thirty for full strength; forty for understanding; fifty for giving counsel; sixty for old age; seventy for ripe old age; eighty for exceptional strength; and ninety for a bent back; at a hundred, one is as if he were dead and had left and gone from the world.

כא כָּל מַחֲלֹקֶת שֶׁהִיא לְשֵׁם שָׁמַיִם, סוֹפָהּ לְהִתְקַיֵּם. וְשֶׁאֵינָהּ לְשֵׁם שָׁמַיִם,
אֵין סוֹפָהּ לְהִתְקַיֵּם. אֵיזוֹ הִיא מַחֲלֹקֶת שֶׁהִיא לְשֵׁם שָׁמַיִם, זוֹ מַחֲלֹקֶת
הִלֵּל וְשַׁמַּאי. וְשֶׁאֵינָהּ לְשֵׁם שָׁמַיִם, זוֹ מַחֲלֹקֶת קֹרַח וְכָל עֲדָתוֹ.

כב כָּל הַמְזַכֶּה אֶת הָרַבִּים, אֵין חֵטְא בָּא עַל יָדוֹ. וְכָל הַמַּחֲטִיא אֶת הָרַבִּים,
אֵין מַסְפִּיקִין בְּיָדוֹ לַעֲשׂוֹת תְּשׁוּבָה. מֹשֶׁה זָכָה וְזִכָּה אֶת הָרַבִּים, זְכוּת
הָרַבִּים תָּלוּי בּוֹ, שֶׁנֶּאֱמַר: צִדְקַת יהוה עָשָׂה וּמִשְׁפָּטָיו עִם־יִשְׂרָאֵל: יָרָבְעָם דברים לג
בֶּן נְבָט, חָטָא וְהֶחֱטִיא אֶת הָרַבִּים, חֵטְא הָרַבִּים תָּלוּי בּוֹ, שֶׁנֶּאֱמַר: עַל־ מלכים א׳ טו
חַטֹּאות יָרָבְעָם אֲשֶׁר חָטָא וַאֲשֶׁר הֶחֱטִיא אֶת־יִשְׂרָאֵל:

כג כָּל מִי שֶׁיֵּשׁ בּוֹ שְׁלֹשָׁה דְבָרִים הַלָּלוּ, הוּא מִתַּלְמִידָיו שֶׁל אַבְרָהָם אָבִינוּ,
וּשְׁלֹשָׁה דְבָרִים אֲחֵרִים, הוּא מִתַּלְמִידָיו שֶׁל בִּלְעָם הָרָשָׁע. עַיִן טוֹבָה,
וְרוּחַ נְמוּכָה, וְנֶפֶשׁ שְׁפָלָה, תַּלְמִידָיו שֶׁל אַבְרָהָם אָבִינוּ. עַיִן רָעָה, וְרוּחַ
גְּבוֹהָה וְנֶפֶשׁ רְחָבָה, תַּלְמִידָיו שֶׁל בִּלְעָם הָרָשָׁע. מַה בֵּין תַּלְמִידָיו שֶׁל
אַבְרָהָם אָבִינוּ לְתַלְמִידָיו שֶׁל בִּלְעָם הָרָשָׁע. תַּלְמִידָיו שֶׁל אַבְרָהָם אָבִינוּ
אוֹכְלִין בָּעוֹלָם הַזֶּה וְנוֹחֲלִין הָעוֹלָם הַבָּא, שֶׁנֶּאֱמַר: לְהַנְחִיל אֹהֲבַי יֵשׁ משלי ח
וְאֹצְרֹתֵיהֶם אֲמַלֵּא: אֲבָל תַּלְמִידָיו שֶׁל בִּלְעָם הָרָשָׁע יוֹרְשִׁין גֵּיהִנֹּם וְיוֹרְדִין
לִבְאֵר שַׁחַת, שֶׁנֶּאֱמַר: וְאַתָּה אֱלֹהִים תּוֹרִדֵם לִבְאֵר שַׁחַת, אַנְשֵׁי דָמִים תהלים נה
וּמִרְמָה לֹא־יֶחֱצוּ יְמֵיהֶם, וַאֲנִי אֶבְטַח־בָּךְ:

כד יְהוּדָה בֶּן תֵּימָא אוֹמֵר: הֱוֵי עַז כַּנָּמֵר וְקַל כַּנֶּשֶׁר, רָץ כַּצְּבִי וְגִבּוֹר כָּאֲרִי,
לַעֲשׂוֹת רְצוֹן אָבִיךָ שֶׁבַּשָּׁמָיִם. הוּא הָיָה אוֹמֵר: עַז פָּנִים לְגֵיהִנֹּם, וּבֹשֶׁת
פָּנִים לְגַן עֵדֶן. יְהִי רָצוֹן מִלְּפָנֶיךָ, יהוה אֱלֹהֵינוּ וֵאלֹהֵי אֲבוֹתֵינוּ, שֶׁיִּבָּנֶה
בֵּית הַמִּקְדָּשׁ בִּמְהֵרָה בְיָמֵינוּ, וְתֵן חֶלְקֵנוּ בְּתוֹרָתֶךָ.

כה הוּא הָיָה אוֹמֵר: בֶּן חָמֵשׁ שָׁנִים לַמִּקְרָא, בֶּן עֶשֶׂר שָׁנִים לַמִּשְׁנָה, בֶּן שְׁלֹשׁ
עֶשְׂרֵה לַמִּצְוֹת, בֶּן חֲמֵשׁ עֶשְׂרֵה לַגְּמָרָא, בֶּן שְׁמוֹנֶה עֶשְׂרֵה לַחֻפָּה, בֶּן
עֶשְׂרִים לִרְדֹּף, בֶּן שְׁלֹשִׁים לַכֹּחַ, בֶּן אַרְבָּעִים לַבִּינָה, בֶּן חֲמִשִּׁים לָעֵצָה,
בֶּן שִׁשִּׁים לַזִּקְנָה, בֶּן שִׁבְעִים לַשֵּׂיבָה, בֶּן שְׁמוֹנִים לַגְּבוּרָה, בֶּן תִּשְׁעִים
לָשׁוּחַ, בֶּן מֵאָה כְּאִלּוּ מֵת וְעָבַר וּבָטֵל מִן הָעוֹלָם.

26. Ben Bag-Bag said: Turn it [the Torah] over and over, for everything is in it. Reflect on it, grow old and gray in it and do not stir from it, for there is no better portion for you than this. Ben Heh-Heh said: According to the effort is the reward.

Rabbi Ḥananya ben Akashya said: The Holy One, blessed be He, wanted to confer merit on Israel. That is why He gave them a copious Torah and many commandments, as it is said, "It pleased the LORD, for the sake of [Israel's] righteousness, to make the Torah great and glorious." *Makkot 23b* *Is. 42*

If there is a minyan, mourners say the Rabbis' Kaddish (page 448).

* * *

Sanhedrin 90a

All Israel have a share in the World to Come, as it is said,
"Your people are all righteous; they shall inherit the land for ever; *Is. 60*
they are a shoot of My own planting,
a work of My own hands, that I may be glorified."

CHAPTER 6

The sages taught the following in the style of the Mishna – blessed be He who chose them and their teaching.

1. Rabbi Meir said: Whoever engages in Torah study for its own sake merits many things; moreover, the whole world is worthwhile for his sake alone. He is called friend, beloved, a lover of God and a lover of mankind. He brings joy to God; he brings joy to mankind. [The Torah] clothes him with humility and reverence. It prepares him to be righteous, pious, upright and faithful. It keeps him far from sin and near to virtue. People benefit from his advice and wisdom, understanding and courage, as it is said, "Mine are counsel and wisdom; I am understanding, courage is mine." It gives him sovereignty, dominion and discerning judgment. To him the secrets of the Torah are revealed. He becomes like a never-failing fountain, like a river that never runs dry. He becomes modest and patient; he forgives insults. It makes him great, exalting him above all things. *Prov. 8*

2. Rabbi Yehoshua ben Levi said: Every day a heavenly voice resounds from Mount Horeb, proclaiming and saying: "Woe to mankind for their contempt of the Torah!" For whoever does not occupy himself with the Torah is called reprehensible, as it is said, "Like a gold ring in the snout of a pig is a beautiful woman bereft of sense." It also says, "The tablets were the work of God, and the writing was the writing of God, engraved (*ḥarut*) on the tablets." Read not *ḥarut* ("engraved") but *ḥerut* ("freedom"), for the only person who is truly free is one who occupies himself with Torah study; and whoever occupies himself with Torah study will be exalted, as it is said, "And from Mattana to Naḥaliel, and from Naḥaliel to Bamot." *Prov. 11* *Ex. 32* *Num. 21*

כו בֶּן בַּג בַּג אוֹמֵר: הֲפָךְ בָּהּ וַהֲפָךְ בָּהּ דְּכֹלָּא בָהּ, וּבַהּ תֶּחֱזֵי, וְסִיב וּבְלֵה בַהּ, וּמִנַּהּ לָא תְזוּעַ, שֶׁאֵין לְךָ מִדָּה טוֹבָה הֵימֶנָּה. בֶּן הֵא הֵא אוֹמֵר: לְפוּם צַעֲרָא אַגְרָא.

רַבִּי חֲנַנְיָא בֶּן עֲקַשְׁיָא אוֹמֵר: רָצָה הַקָּדוֹשׁ בָּרוּךְ הוּא לְזַכּוֹת אֶת יִשְׂרָאֵל, לְפִיכָךְ הִרְבָּה לָהֶם תּוֹרָה וּמִצְוֹת. שֶׁנֶּאֱמַר: יהוה חָפֵץ לְמַעַן צִדְקוֹ, יַגְדִּיל תּוֹרָה וְיַאְדִּיר: מכות כג. ישעיה מב

If there is a מנין*, mourners say* קדיש דרבנן *(page 449).*

* * *

כָּל יִשְׂרָאֵל יֵשׁ לָהֶם חֵלֶק לָעוֹלָם הַבָּא. שֶׁנֶּאֱמַר: סנהדרין צ.
וְעַמֵּךְ כֻּלָּם צַדִּיקִים, לְעוֹלָם יִירְשׁוּ אָרֶץ ישעיה ס
נֵצֶר מַטָּעַי, מַעֲשֵׂה יָדַי לְהִתְפָּאֵר:

פרק ששי

שָׁנוּ חֲכָמִים בִּלְשׁוֹן הַמִּשְׁנָה, בָּרוּךְ שֶׁבָּחַר בָּהֶם וּבְמִשְׁנָתָם.

א רַבִּי מֵאִיר אוֹמֵר: כָּל הָעוֹסֵק בַּתּוֹרָה לִשְׁמָהּ, זוֹכֶה לִדְבָרִים הַרְבֵּה. וְלֹא עוֹד, אֶלָּא שֶׁכָּל הָעוֹלָם כֻּלּוֹ כְּדַאי הוּא לוֹ. נִקְרָא רֵעַ, אָהוּב, אוֹהֵב אֶת הַמָּקוֹם, אוֹהֵב אֶת הַבְּרִיּוֹת, מְשַׂמֵּחַ אֶת הַמָּקוֹם, מְשַׂמֵּחַ אֶת הַבְּרִיּוֹת, וּמַלְבַּשְׁתּוֹ עֲנָוָה וְיִרְאָה, וּמַכְשַׁרְתּוֹ לִהְיוֹת צַדִּיק, חָסִיד, יָשָׁר, וְנֶאֱמָן, וּמְרַחַקְתּוֹ מִן הַחֵטְא, וּמְקָרַבְתּוֹ לִידֵי זְכוּת, וְנֶהֱנִין מִמֶּנּוּ עֵצָה וְתוּשִׁיָּה, בִּינָה וּגְבוּרָה, שֶׁנֶּאֱמַר: לִי־עֵצָה וְתוּשִׁיָּה, אֲנִי בִינָה, לִי גְבוּרָה: וְנוֹתֶנֶת לוֹ מַלְכוּת וּמֶמְשָׁלָה, וְחִקּוּר דִּין, וּמְגַלִּין לוֹ רָזֵי תוֹרָה, וְנַעֲשֶׂה כְּמַעְיָן הַמִּתְגַּבֵּר וּכְנָהָר שֶׁאֵינוֹ פוֹסֵק, וְהֹוֶה צָנוּעַ, וְאֶרֶךְ רוּחַ, וּמוֹחֵל עַל עֶלְבּוֹנוֹ, וּמְגַדַּלְתּוֹ וּמְרוֹמַמְתּוֹ עַל כָּל הַמַּעֲשִׂים. משלי ח

ב אָמַר רַבִּי יְהוֹשֻׁעַ בֶּן לֵוִי: בְּכָל יוֹם וָיוֹם, בַּת קוֹל יוֹצֵאת מֵהַר חוֹרֵב וּמַכְרֶזֶת וְאוֹמֶרֶת, אוֹי לָהֶם לַבְּרִיּוֹת מֵעֶלְבּוֹנָהּ שֶׁל תּוֹרָה, שֶׁכָּל מִי שֶׁאֵינוֹ עוֹסֵק בַּתּוֹרָה נִקְרָא נָזוּף, שֶׁנֶּאֱמַר: נֶזֶם זָהָב בְּאַף חֲזִיר, אִשָּׁה יָפָה וְסָרַת טָעַם: משלי יא
וְאוֹמֵר: וְהַלֻּחֹת מַעֲשֵׂה אֱלֹהִים הֵמָּה, וְהַמִּכְתָּב מִכְתַּב אֱלֹהִים הוּא, חָרוּת עַל־הַלֻּחֹת: אַל תִּקְרָא חָרוּת אֶלָּא חֵרוּת, שֶׁאֵין לְךָ בֶּן חוֹרִין אֶלָּא מִי שֶׁעוֹסֵק בְּתַלְמוּד תּוֹרָה. וְכָל מִי שֶׁעוֹסֵק בְּתַלְמוּד תּוֹרָה, הֲרֵי זֶה מִתְעַלֶּה, שֶׁנֶּאֱמַר: שמות לב
וּמִמַּתָּנָה נַחֲלִיאֵל, וּמִנַּחֲלִיאֵל בָּמוֹת: במדבר כא

Whoever learns from someone else a single chapter, a single law, a single verse, a single word, even a single letter, must treat him with honor, for so we find in the case of David, King of Israel, who learned only two things from Aḥitophel, yet he called him his teacher, his guide, and his close friend, for so it says, "But it is you, my equal, my guide, my close friend." The following *Ps. 55* inference can be derived: If David, King of Israel, who learned only two things from Aḥitophel, called him his teacher, guide and close friend, how much more must one who learns from someone else a chapter, a law, a verse, a word or even a single letter, treat him with honor! And honor is due only to Torah, as it is written, "The wise shall inherit honor," and "The wholehearted *Prov. 3* *Prov. 28* shall attain good," and "good" signifies Torah, as it is said, "I have given you *Prov. 4* good instruction; do not forsake My Torah."

4. This is the way of Torah: Eat bread with salt, drink water by measure, sleep on the ground, live a life of hardship, but toil in the Torah! If you do so, "You will be happy and it will be well with you": "You will be happy" in this world, "and it shall be well with you" in the World to Come.

5. Do not seek greatness for yourself, and do not long for honor. Let your deeds exceed your learning. Do not crave the table of kings, for your table is greater than theirs, your crown is greater than their crown, and your Employer can be relied upon to pay you your labor's reward.

6. The Torah is greater than priesthood and kingship, for kingship is acquired with thirty attainments, and priesthood is endowed with twenty-four [gifts], but the Torah is acquired by forty-eight virtues. They are: study, attentive listening, well-ordered speech, intuitive understanding, awe, reverence, humility, joy, purity, serving the wise, association with colleagues, debate with students, serenity, knowledge of Scripture and Mishna; minimizing time spent on business, worldly matters, pleasure, sleep, small talk or laughter; patience, a kindly heart, faith in the sages, and acceptance of suffering; knowing one's place, being happy with one's lot, restraining one's words, and claiming no credit for oneself; being loved, loving God, loving mankind and loving righteousness, justice and admonishment; shunning honors, avoiding arrogance in one's learning or delight in giving decisions; sharing someone else's burden, giving him the benefit of the doubt, guiding him to truth and peace; concentrating on one's study, asking and answering questions, listening and adding to one's knowledge; learning in order to teach, learning in order to do, making one's teacher wiser, being precise in one's studies, and reporting a saying in the name of the one who said it. For you have learned: Whoever reports a saying in the name of the one who said it brings deliverance to the world, as it is said, "And Esther told the king in *Esther 2* the name of Mordekhai."

ג הַלּוֹמֵד מֵחֲבֵרוֹ פֶּרֶק אֶחָד, אוֹ הֲלָכָה אַחַת, אוֹ פָּסוּק אֶחָד, אוֹ דִבּוּר אֶחָד, אוֹ אֲפִלּוּ אוֹת אַחַת, צָרִיךְ לִנְהָג בּוֹ כָּבוֹד. שֶׁכֵּן מָצִינוּ בְּדָוִד מֶלֶךְ יִשְׂרָאֵל, שֶׁלֹּא לָמַד מֵאֲחִיתֹפֶל אֶלָּא שְׁנֵי דְבָרִים בִּלְבָד, קְרָאוֹ רַבּוֹ אַלּוּפוֹ וּמְיֻדָּעוֹ, שֶׁנֶּאֱמַר: וְאַתָּה אֱנוֹשׁ כְּעֶרְכִּי, אַלּוּפִי וּמְיֻדָּעִי: וַהֲלֹא דְבָרִים קַל וָחֹמֶר. וּמָה דָּוִד מֶלֶךְ יִשְׂרָאֵל, שֶׁלֹּא לָמַד מֵאֲחִיתֹפֶל אֶלָּא שְׁנֵי דְבָרִים בִּלְבָד, קְרָאוֹ רַבּוֹ אַלּוּפוֹ וּמְיֻדָּעוֹ, הַלּוֹמֵד מֵחֲבֵרוֹ פֶּרֶק אֶחָד, אוֹ הֲלָכָה אַחַת, אוֹ פָּסוּק אֶחָד, אוֹ דִבּוּר אֶחָד, אוֹ אֲפִלּוּ אוֹת אַחַת, עַל אַחַת כַּמָּה וְכַמָּה שֶׁצָּרִיךְ לִנְהָג בּוֹ כָּבוֹד. וְאֵין כָּבוֹד אֶלָּא תוֹרָה, שֶׁנֶּאֱמַר: כָּבוֹד חֲכָמִים יִנְחָלוּ: וּתְמִימִים יִנְחֲלוּ־טוֹב: וְאֵין טוֹב אֶלָּא תוֹרָה, שֶׁנֶּאֱמַר: כִּי לֶקַח טוֹב נָתַתִּי לָכֶם, תּוֹרָתִי אַל־תַּעֲזֹבוּ:

(תהלים נה; משלי ג; משלי כח; משלי ד)

ד כָּךְ הִיא דַּרְכָּהּ שֶׁל תּוֹרָה. פַּת בַּמֶּלַח תֹּאכַל, וּמַיִם בַּמְּשׂוּרָה תִּשְׁתֶּה, וְעַל הָאָרֶץ תִּישַׁן, וְחַיֵּי צַעַר תִּחְיֶה, וּבַתּוֹרָה אַתָּה עָמֵל. אִם אַתָּה עוֹשֶׂה כֵּן, אַשְׁרֶיךָ וְטוֹב לָךְ, אַשְׁרֶיךָ בָּעוֹלָם הַזֶּה, וְטוֹב לָךְ לָעוֹלָם הַבָּא.

ה אַל תְּבַקֵּשׁ גְּדֻלָּה לְעַצְמְךָ, וְאַל תַּחְמֹד כָּבוֹד. יוֹתֵר מִלִּמּוּדְךָ עֲשֵׂה. וְאַל תִּתְאַוֶּה לְשֻׁלְחָנָם שֶׁל מְלָכִים, שֶׁשֻּׁלְחָנְךָ גָּדוֹל מִשֻּׁלְחָנָם, וְכִתְרְךָ גָּדוֹל מִכִּתְרָם. וְנֶאֱמָן הוּא בַּעַל מְלַאכְתְּךָ, שֶׁיְּשַׁלֶּם לְךָ שְׂכַר פְּעֻלָּתֶךָ.

ו גְּדוֹלָה תוֹרָה יוֹתֵר מִן הַכְּהֻנָּה וּמִן הַמַּלְכוּת. שֶׁהַמַּלְכוּת נִקְנֵית בִּשְׁלֹשִׁים מַעֲלוֹת, וְהַכְּהֻנָּה בְּעֶשְׂרִים וְאַרְבַּע, וְהַתּוֹרָה נִקְנֵית בְּאַרְבָּעִים וּשְׁמוֹנָה דְבָרִים. וְאֵלּוּ הֵן, בְּתַלְמוּד, בִּשְׁמִיעַת הָאֹזֶן, בַּעֲרִיכַת שְׂפָתַיִם, בְּבִינַת הַלֵּב, בְּאֵימָה, בְּיִרְאָה, בַּעֲנָוָה, בְּשִׂמְחָה, בְּטָהֳרָה, בְּשִׁמּוּשׁ חֲכָמִים, בְּדִקְדּוּק חֲבֵרִים, בְּפִלְפּוּל הַתַּלְמִידִים, בְּיִשּׁוּב, בְּמִקְרָא, בְּמִשְׁנָה, בְּמִעוּט סְחוֹרָה, בְּמִעוּט דֶּרֶךְ אֶרֶץ, בְּמִעוּט תַּעֲנוּג, בְּמִעוּט שֵׁנָה, בְּמִעוּט שִׂיחָה, בְּמִעוּט שְׂחוֹק, בְּאֶרֶךְ אַפַּיִם, בְּלֵב טוֹב, בֶּאֱמוּנַת חֲכָמִים, בְּקַבָּלַת הַיִּסּוּרִין, הַמַּכִּיר אֶת מְקוֹמוֹ, וְהַשָּׂמֵחַ בְּחֶלְקוֹ, וְהָעוֹשֶׂה סְיָג לִדְבָרָיו, וְאֵינוֹ מַחֲזִיק טוֹבָה לְעַצְמוֹ, אָהוּב, אוֹהֵב אֶת הַמָּקוֹם, אוֹהֵב אֶת הַבְּרִיּוֹת, אוֹהֵב אֶת הַצְּדָקוֹת, אוֹהֵב אֶת הַמֵּישָׁרִים, אוֹהֵב אֶת הַתּוֹכָחוֹת, וּמִתְרַחֵק מִן הַכָּבוֹד, וְלֹא מֵגִיס לִבּוֹ בְּתַלְמוּדוֹ, וְאֵינוֹ שָׂמֵחַ בְּהוֹרָאָה, נוֹשֵׂא בְעֹל עִם חֲבֵרוֹ, וּמַכְרִיעוֹ לְכַף זְכוּת, וּמַעֲמִידוֹ עַל הָאֱמֶת, וּמַעֲמִידוֹ עַל הַשָּׁלוֹם, וּמִתְיַשֵּׁב לִבּוֹ בְּתַלְמוּדוֹ, שׁוֹאֵל וּמֵשִׁיב, שׁוֹמֵעַ וּמוֹסִיף, הַלּוֹמֵד עַל מְנָת לְלַמֵּד, וְהַלּוֹמֵד עַל מְנָת לַעֲשׂוֹת, הַמַּחְכִּים אֶת רַבּוֹ, וְהַמְכַוֵּן אֶת שְׁמוּעָתוֹ, וְהָאוֹמֵר דָּבָר בְּשֵׁם אוֹמְרוֹ. הָא לָמַדְתָּ, כָּל הָאוֹמֵר דָּבָר בְּשֵׁם אוֹמְרוֹ, מֵבִיא גְאֻלָּה לָעוֹלָם, שֶׁנֶּאֱמַר: וַתֹּאמֶר אֶסְתֵּר לַמֶּלֶךְ בְּשֵׁם מָרְדֳּכָי: אסתר ב

7. Great is Torah for it gives life to its practitioners in both this world and the World to Come, as it is said, "For they are life to those that find them, and healing to all their flesh"; and it says, "It shall be healing for your body and marrow for your bones"; and it says, "It is a tree of life to those who grasp it, and those who support it shall be happy"; and it says, "They shall be a garland of grace on your head, and pendants for your neck"; and it says, "It will adorn your head with a garland of grace, and bestow on you a crown of glory"; and it says, "Through me shall your days increase, and years of life shall be added to you"; and it says, "At its right hand is length of days; in its left, riches and honor"; and it says, "For length of days and years of life and peace shall they add to you." *Prov. 4* *Prov. 3* *Prov. 1* *Prov. 4* *Prov. 9* *Prov. 3* *Prov. 3*

8. Rabbi Shimon ben Menasya said in the name of Rabbi Shimon ben Yoḥai: Beauty, strength, wealth, honor, wisdom, old age, gray hair, and children are fitting for the righteous and for the world, as it is said: "Gray hair is a crown of glory; it is attained by the way of righteousness"; and it says, "The crown of the wise is their wealth"; and it says, "Grandchildren are the crown of their elders; the glory of children is their parents"; and it says, "The glory of the young is their strength; the majesty of the old is their gray hair"; and it says, "Then the moon shall be ashamed and the sun shall be abashed, for the LORD of hosts will reign on Mount Zion and in Jerusalem, and glory shall be before His elders." Rabbi Shimon ben Menasya said: These seven qualities which the sages attributed to the righteous were all present in Rabbi [Judah the Prince] and his sons. *Prov. 16* *Prov. 14* *Prov. 17* *Prov. 20* *Is. 24*

9. Rabbi Yose ben Kisma said: Once I was walking along the road when a man met and greeted me, and I returned his greeting. He said to me, "Rabbi, where do you come from?" I replied, "I come from a great city of sages and scribes." He said to me, "Rabbi, if you are willing to live with us in our place I will give you a million gold dinars, as well as precious stones and pearls." I replied, "Were you to give me all the silver and gold and precious stones and pearls in the world, I would not live anywhere except in a place of Torah, for so it is written in the book of Psalms by David, King of Israel, 'I prefer the Torah of your mouth to thousands of gold and silver pieces.' Furthermore, when a person departs from this world, neither silver nor gold nor precious stones nor pearls accompany him, but only Torah and good deeds, as it is said, 'When you walk, it will lead you; when you lie down, it will watch over you; and when you awake, it will talk with you.' 'When you walk, it will lead you' – in this world; 'when you lie down, it will watch over you' – in the grave; 'and when you awake, it will speak for you' – in the World to Come. And it says, 'Mine is the silver, and Mine is the gold, says the LORD of hosts.'" *Ps. 119* *Prov. 6* *Hag. 2*

ז גדולה תורה, שהיא נותנת חיים לעושיה בעולם הזה ובעולם הבא,
שנאמר: כי־חיים הם למצאיהם, ולכל־בשרו מרפא: ואומר: רפאות תהי משלי ד משלי ג
לשרך, ושקוי לעצמותיך: ואומר: עץ־חיים היא למחזיקים בה, ותמכיה
מאשר: ואומר: כי לוית חן הם לראשך, וענקים לגרגרתיך: ואומר: תתן משלי א משלי ד
לראשך לוית־חן, עטרת תפארת תמגנך: ואומר: כי־בי ירבו ימיך, ויוסיפו משלי ט
לך שנות חיים: ואומר: ארך ימים בימינה, בשמאולה עשר וכבוד: משלי ג
ואומר: כי ארך ימים ושנות חיים ושלום יוסיפו לך: משלי ג

ח רבי שמעון בן מנסיא משום רבי שמעון בן יוחאי אומר: הנוי, והכח,
והעשר, והכבוד, והחכמה, והזקנה, והשיבה, והבנים, נאה לצדיקים
ונאה לעולם, שנאמר: עטרת תפארת שיבה, בדרך צדקה תמצא: ואומר: משלי טז
עטרת חכמים עשרם: ואומר: עטרת זקנים בני בנים, ותפארת בנים משלי יז משלי יד
אבותם: ואומר: תפארת בחורים כחם, והדר זקנים שיבה: ואומר: וחפרה משלי כ ישעיה כד
הלבנה ובושה החמה, כי־מלך יהוה צבאות בהר ציון ובירושלים, ונגד
זקניו כבוד: רבי שמעון בן מנסיא אומר: אלו שבע מדות שמנו חכמים
לצדיקים, כלם נתקימו ברבי ובבניו.

ט אמר רבי יוסי בן קסמא: פעם אחת הייתי מהלך בדרך, ופגע בי אדם
אחד, ונתן לי שלום והחזרתי לו שלום. אמר לי, רבי, מאיזה מקום אתה.
אמרתי לו, מעיר גדולה של חכמים ושל סופרים אני. אמר לי, רבי, רצונך
שתדור עמנו במקומנו, ואני אתן לך אלף אלפים דינרי זהב ואבנים
טובות ומרגליות. אמרתי לו, אם אתה נותן לי כל כסף וזהב ואבנים
טובות ומרגליות שבעולם, איני דר אלא במקום תורה, וכן כתוב בספר
תהלים על ידי דוד מלך ישראל: טוב־לי תורת־פיך מאלפי זהב וכסף: תהלים קיט
ולא עוד, אלא שבשעת פטירתו של אדם, אין מלוין לו לאדם לא כסף
ולא זהב ולא אבנים טובות ומרגליות, אלא תורה ומעשים טובים בלבד,
שנאמר: בהתהלכך תנחה אתך, בשכבך תשמר עליך, והקיצות היא משלי ו
תשיחך: בהתהלכך תנחה אתך, בעולם הזה. בשכבך תשמר עליך,
בקבר. והקיצות היא תשיחך, לעולם הבא. ואומר: לי הכסף ולי הזהב, חגי ב
נאם יהוה צבאות:

10. Five possessions did the Holy One, blessed be He, declare as His own in His world, and they are: the Torah, heaven and earth, Abraham, Israel and the Temple. How do we know this about the Torah? Because it is written, "The LORD created me at the beginning of His way, as the first of His works in days of old." How do we know it about heaven and earth? Because it is written, "So says the LORD: the heaven is My throne, and the earth is My footstool; what house can you build for Me, and where is the place for My rest?"; and it also says, "How numerous are Your works, LORD; You made them all in wisdom; the earth is full of Your creations." How do we know it about Abraham? Because it is written, "And He blessed him and said, Blessed be Abram of God the Most High, owner of heaven and earth." How do we know it about Israel? Because it is written, "Until Your people pass over, O LORD, until this people You acquired pass over"; and it also says, "As for the holy ones who are on earth and for the mighty, all My delight is in them." How do we know it about the Temple? Because it is written, "Your dwelling place which You, LORD, have made; the Temple, O LORD, which Your hands established"; and it also says, "He brought them to His holy realm, the mountain His right hand had acquired."

Prov. 8 *Is. 66* *Ps. 104* *Gen. 14* *Ex. 15* *Ps. 16* *Ex. 15* *Ps. 78*

11. All that the Holy One, blessed be He, created in His world, He created solely for His glory, as it is said, "All that is called by My name, it is for My glory that I created it, formed it and made it"; and it also says, "The LORD shall reign for ever and ever."

Is. 43 *Ex. 15*

Rabbi Ḥananya ben Akashya said: The Holy One, blessed be He, wanted to confer merit on Israel. That is why He gave them a copious Torah and many commandments, as it is said, "It pleased the LORD, for the sake of [Israel's] righteousness, to make the Torah great and glorious."

Makkot 23b *Is. 42*

If there is a minyan, mourners say the Rabbis' Kaddish *(page 448).*

י חֲמִשָּׁה קִנְיָנִים קָנָה הַקָּדוֹשׁ בָּרוּךְ הוּא בְּעוֹלָמוֹ. וְאֵלּוּ הֵן, תּוֹרָה קִנְיָן אֶחָד,
שָׁמַיִם וָאָרֶץ קִנְיָן אֶחָד, אַבְרָהָם קִנְיָן אֶחָד, יִשְׂרָאֵל קִנְיָן אֶחָד, בֵּית הַמִּקְדָּשׁ
קִנְיָן אֶחָד. תּוֹרָה מִנַּיִן, דִּכְתִיב: יהוה קָנָנִי רֵאשִׁית דַּרְכּוֹ, קֶדֶם מִפְעָלָיו מֵאָז: משלי ח
שָׁמַיִם וָאָרֶץ מִנַּיִן, דִּכְתִיב: כֹּה אָמַר יהוה הַשָּׁמַיִם כִּסְאִי וְהָאָרֶץ הֲדֹם רַגְלָי, ישעיה סו
אֵי־זֶה בַיִת אֲשֶׁר תִּבְנוּ־לִי, וְאֵי־זֶה מָקוֹם מְנוּחָתִי: וְאוֹמֵר: מָה־רַבּוּ מַעֲשֶׂיךָ תהלים קד
יהוה, כֻּלָּם בְּחָכְמָה עָשִׂיתָ, מָלְאָה הָאָרֶץ קִנְיָנֶךָ: אַבְרָהָם מִנַּיִן, דִּכְתִיב:
וַיְבָרְכֵהוּ וַיֹּאמַר, בָּרוּךְ אַבְרָם לְאֵל עֶלְיוֹן, קֹנֵה שָׁמַיִם וָאָרֶץ: יִשְׂרָאֵל מִנַּיִן, בראשית יד
דִּכְתִיב: עַד־יַעֲבֹר עַמְּךָ יהוה, עַד־יַעֲבֹר עַם־זוּ קָנִיתָ: וְאוֹמֵר: לִקְדוֹשִׁים שמות טו תהלים טז
אֲשֶׁר־בָּאָרֶץ הֵמָּה, וְאַדִּירֵי כָּל־חֶפְצִי־בָם: בֵּית הַמִּקְדָּשׁ מִנַּיִן, דִּכְתִיב: מָכוֹן שמות טו
לְשִׁבְתְּךָ פָּעַלְתָּ יהוה, מִקְּדָשׁ אֲדֹנָי כּוֹנְנוּ יָדֶיךָ: וְאוֹמֵר: וַיְבִיאֵם אֶל־גְּבוּל תהלים עח
קָדְשׁוֹ, הַר־זֶה קָנְתָה יְמִינוֹ:

יא כָּל מַה שֶּׁבָּרָא הַקָּדוֹשׁ בָּרוּךְ הוּא בְּעוֹלָמוֹ, לֹא בְרָאוֹ אֶלָּא לִכְבוֹדוֹ,
שֶׁנֶּאֱמַר: כֹּל הַנִּקְרָא בִשְׁמִי וְלִכְבוֹדִי בְּרָאתִיו, יְצַרְתִּיו אַף־עֲשִׂיתִיו: וְאוֹמֵר: ישעיה מג
יהוה יִמְלֹךְ לְעֹלָם וָעֶד: שמות טו

רַבִּי חֲנַנְיָא בֶּן עֲקַשְׁיָא אוֹמֵר: רָצָה הַקָּדוֹשׁ בָּרוּךְ הוּא לְזַכּוֹת אֶת יִשְׂרָאֵל, לְפִיכָךְ מכות כג:
הִרְבָּה לָהֶם תּוֹרָה וּמִצְוֹת. שֶׁנֶּאֱמַר: יהוה חָפֵץ לְמַעַן צִדְקוֹ, יַגְדִּיל תּוֹרָה וְיַאְדִּיר: ישעיה מב

If there is a מנין*, mourners say* קדיש דרבנן *(page 449)**.*

Seuda Shelishit for Shabbat

מִזְמוֹר לְדָוִד A psalm of David. The LORD is my Shepherd, I shall not want. He makes me lie down in green pastures. He leads me beside the still waters. He refreshes my soul. He guides me in the paths of righteousness for His name's sake. Though I walk through the valley of the shadow of death, I will fear no evil, for You are with me; Your rod and Your staff, they comfort me. You set a table before me in the presence of my enemies; You anoint my head with oil; my cup is filled to overflowing. May goodness and kindness follow me all the days of my life, and may I live in the House of the LORD for evermore. *Ps. 23*

יְדִיד Beloved of the soul,[A] Father of compassion,
draw Your servant close to Your will.
Like a deer will Your servant run and fall prostrate before Your beauty.
To him Your love is sweeter than honey from the comb, than any taste.

הָדוּר Glorious, beautiful, radiance of the world,
my soul is sick with love for You.
Please, God, heal her now by showing her Your tender radiance.
Then she will recover her strength and be healed,
Be Your servant for eternity.

וָתִיק Ancient of Days, let Your mercy be aroused;
please have pity on Your beloved child.
How long have I yearned to see the glory of Your strength.
Please, my God, my heart's desire – hasten; do not hide Yourself.

הִגָּלֶה Reveal Yourself, beloved, and spread over me
the tabernacle of Your peace.
Let the earth shine with Your glory,
let us be overjoyed and rejoice in You.
Hurry, beloved, for the appointed time has come,
and be gracious to me as in the times of old.

---

he was declared the victor, the young man came to him to ask how it was possible that after having practiced for so long, rehearsed each word and sentence, he had nevertheless lost the competition. "It's true," said the little old man. "You knew every word and every sentence of 'The Lord is my Shepherd.' But you see, the difference is that I know the Shepherd."

Sing as if you know the Shepherd.

יְדִיד נֶפֶשׁ – *Beloved of the soul.* For commentary see page 35.

סעודה שלישית של שבת

מִזְמוֹר לְדָוִד, יהוה רֹעִי לֹא אֶחְסָר: בִּנְאוֹת דֶּשֶׁא יַרְבִּיצֵנִי, עַל־מֵי מְנוּחוֹת תהלים כג
יְנַהֲלֵנִי: נַפְשִׁי יְשׁוֹבֵב, יַנְחֵנִי בְמַעְגְּלֵי־צֶדֶק לְמַעַן שְׁמוֹ: גַּם כִּי־אֵלֵךְ
בְּגֵיא צַלְמָוֶת לֹא־אִירָא רָע, כִּי־אַתָּה עִמָּדִי, שִׁבְטְךָ וּמִשְׁעַנְתֶּךָ הֵמָּה
יְנַחֲמֻנִי: תַּעֲרֹךְ לְפָנַי שֻׁלְחָן נֶגֶד צֹרְרָי, דִּשַּׁנְתָּ בַשֶּׁמֶן רֹאשִׁי, כּוֹסִי רְוָיָה:
אַךְ טוֹב וָחֶסֶד יִרְדְּפוּנִי כָּל־יְמֵי חַיָּי, וְשַׁבְתִּי בְּבֵית־יהוה לְאֹרֶךְ יָמִים:

יְדִיד נֶפֶשׁ,[א] אָב הָרַחֲמָן, מְשֹׁךְ עַבְדְּךָ אֶל רְצוֹנֶךָ
יָרוּץ עַבְדְּךָ כְּמוֹ אַיָּל, יִשְׁתַּחֲוֶה מוּל הֲדָרֶךָ
כִּי יֶעֱרַב לוֹ יְדִידוּתֶךָ, מִנֹּפֶת צוּף וְכָל טָעַם.

הָדוּר, נָאֶה, זִיו הָעוֹלָם, נַפְשִׁי חוֹלַת אַהֲבָתֶךָ
אָנָּא, אֵל נָא, רְפָא נָא לָהּ, בְּהַרְאוֹת לָהּ נֹעַם זִיוֶךָ
אָז תִּתְחַזֵּק וְתִתְרַפֵּא, וְהָיְתָה לָךְ שִׁפְחַת עוֹלָם.

וָתִיק, יֶהֱמוּ רַחֲמֶיךָ, וְחוּס נָא עַל בֵּן אוֹהֲבָךְ
כִּי זֶה כַּמָּה נִכְסֹף נִכְסַף לִרְאוֹת בְּתִפְאֶרֶת עֻזָּךְ
אָנָּא, אֵלִי, מַחְמַד לִבִּי, חוּשָׁה נָּא, וְאַל תִּתְעַלָּם.

הִגָּלֵה נָא וּפְרֹשׂ, חָבִיב, עָלַי אֶת סֻכַּת שְׁלוֹמֶךָ
תָּאִיר אֶרֶץ מִכְּבוֹדֶךָ, נָגִילָה וְנִשְׂמְחָה בָּךְ.
מַהֵר, אָהוּב, כִּי בָא מוֹעֵד, וְחָנֵּנִי כִּימֵי עוֹלָם.

ANI TEFILLA • אני תפילה

The story is told about a poetry reading contest in Britain wherein contestants were required to provide a dramatic reading of the 23rd Psalm – "The Lord is my Shepherd, I shall not lack anything." One young British contestant, a well-rehearsed orator, gave a brilliant performance filled with all of the right enunciation and intonation. He was better than any of his predecessors and it was clear to all that he would be declared the victor. Until a little old Jewish man with a European accent got up and though there were initial giggles and murmurs, his rendition of the psalm touched their hearts and some were actually moved to tears. When

אֵל מִסְתַּתֵּר God hides Himself[B] in the beauty of concealment, His wisdom opaque to all human thought; / Cause of causes, adorned with the highest crown, they [the angels] give You, LORD, a crown.

In the beginning was Your primordial Torah, inscribed with Your hermetic wisdom. Where can it be found? It is hidden. Wisdom begins in awe of the LORD.

Wider than a river, like never-ending streams, deep waters, that only an understanding man can draw, / its outcomes are the fifty gates of understanding. The faithful are guarded by the LORD.

Great God, all eyes are turned toward You. Your great kindness is higher than the heavens. / God of Abraham, remember Your servant, I will tell of the LORD's kindness, sing praises to the LORD.

Sublime, majestic in strength and might, who brings forth unparalleled light, "Awe of Isaac," make our judgment light. Forever, LORD, is Your might.

Who is like You, God, doing great deeds, Mighty One of Jacob, awesome in praise, Splendor of Israel, who listens to prayers, LORD who listens to those in need.

God, may the merit of the fathers be our shield. Eternal One of Israel, redeem us from distress. / Draw us, raise us, from the pit of exile, that we may loudly sing in service at the House of the LORD.

From right and left the prophets were inspired, finding within them Eternity and Glory, / known by the names of Yakhin and Boaz, and all your children shall be learned of the LORD.

Foundation, the Righteous, is hidden in Seven, the sign of the covenant to the world. Source of blessing, Righteous, Foundation of the world, righteous are You, LORD.

Restore, please, David and Solomon's kingdom, with the crown with which his mother crowned it. / The congregation of Israel is sweetly called a bride, a crown of splendor in the hand of the LORD.

Mighty One, unite the ten Sefirot as one. Those who divide them from the LORD will see no light. / Together they shine like sapphire. Bring my song close to You, the LORD.

Birkat HaMazon can be found on page 734.

Moshe Cordevero, a central figure in the development of the Kabbala in Tzefat in the sixteenth century. Each of the first ten stanzas is based on one of the mystical *sefirot*, the divine emanations or attributes through which Hashem is revealed.

אֵל מִסְתַּתֵּר בְּשַׁפְרִיר חֶבְיוֹן, הַשֵּׂכֶל הַנֶּעְלָם מִכָּל רַעְיוֹן
עִלַּת הָעִלּוֹת מֻכְתָּר בְּכֶתֶר עֶלְיוֹן, כֶּתֶר יִתְּנוּ לְךָ יהוה.

בְּרֵאשִׁית תּוֹרָתְךָ הַקְּדוּמָה, רְשׁוּמָה חָכְמָתְךָ הַסְּתוּמָה
מֵאַיִן תִּמָּצֵא וְהִיא נֶעְלָמָה, רֵאשִׁית חָכְמָה יִרְאַת יהוה.

רְחוֹבוֹת הַנָּהָר נַחֲלֵי אֱמוּנָה, מַיִם עֲמֻקִּים יִדְלֵם אִישׁ תְּבוּנָה
תּוֹצְאוֹתֶיהָ חֲמִשִּׁים שַׁעֲרֵי בִינָה, אֱמוּנִים נוֹצֵר יהוה.

הָאֵל הַגָּדוֹל עֵינֵי כֹל נֶגְדֶּךָ, רַב חֶסֶד גָּדוֹל עַל הַשָּׁמַיִם חַסְדֶּךָ
אֱלֹהֵי אַבְרָהָם זְכֹר לְעַבְדֶּךָ, חַסְדֵי יהוה אַזְכִּיר תְּהִלּוֹת יהוה.

מָרוֹם נֶאְדָּר בְּכֹחַ וּגְבוּרָה, מוֹצִיא אוֹרָה מֵאֵין תְּמוּרָה
פַּחַד יִצְחָק מִשְׁפָּטֵנוּ הָאִירָה, אַתָּה גִּבּוֹר לְעוֹלָם יהוה.

מִי אֵל כָּמוֹךָ עוֹשֶׂה גְדוֹלוֹת, אֲבִיר יַעֲקֹב נוֹרָא תְהִלּוֹת
תִּפְאֶרֶת יִשְׂרָאֵל שׁוֹמֵעַ תְּפִלּוֹת, כִּי שׁוֹמֵעַ אֶל אֶבְיוֹנִים יהוה.

יָהּ, זְכוּת אָבוֹת יָגֵן עָלֵינוּ, נֵצַח יִשְׂרָאֵל, מִצָּרוֹתֵינוּ גְּאָלֵנוּ
וּמִבּוֹר גָּלוּת דְּלֵנוּ וְהַעֲלֵנוּ, לְנַצֵּחַ עַל מְלֶאכֶת בֵּית יהוה.

מִיָּמִין וּמִשְּׂמֹאל יְנִיקַת הַנְּבִיאִים, נֶצַח וָהוֹד מֵהֶם נִמְצָאִים
יָכִין וּבֹעַז בְּשֵׁם נִקְרָאִים, וְכָל בָּנַיִךְ לִמּוּדֵי יהוה.

יְסוֹד צַדִּיק בְּשִׁבְעָה נֶעְלָם, אוֹת בְּרִית הוּא לְעוֹלָם
מַעְיַן הַבְּרָכָה צַדִּיק יְסוֹד עוֹלָם, צַדִּיק אַתָּה יהוה.

נָא הָקֵם מַלְכוּת דָּוִד וּשְׁלֹמֹה, בָּעֲטָרָה שֶׁעִטְּרָה לּוֹ אִמּוֹ
כְּנֶסֶת יִשְׂרָאֵל כַּלָּה קְרוּאָה בִּנְעִימָה, עֲטֶרֶת תִּפְאֶרֶת בְּיַד יהוה.

חָזָק מְיַחֵד כְּאֶחָד עֶשֶׂר סְפִירוֹת, וּמַפְרִיד אַלּוּף לֹא יִרְאֶה מְאוֹרוֹת
סַפִּיר גִּזְרָתָם יַחַד מְאִירוֹת, תִּקְרַב רִנָּתִי לְפָנֶיךָ יהוה.

ברכת המזון *can be found on page 735.*

BIUR TEFILLA • ביאור תפילה

אֵל מִסְתַּתֵּר – *God hides Himself.* The poem was written by Avraham Maimin, as indicated by the first letter of each stanza which spells his name. He was a student of Rabbi

Ma'ariv for Motza'ei Shabbat

In many congregations, the following two psalms are sung before Ma'ariv at the end of Shabbat.

לְדָוִד Of David. Blessed is the Lord, my Rock, who trains my hands for war, my fingers for battle. He is my Benefactor, my Fortress, my Stronghold and my Refuge, my Shield in whom I trust, He who subdues nations under me. Lord, what is man that You care for him, what are mortals that You think of them? Man is no more than a breath, his days like a fleeting shadow. Lord, part Your heavens and come down; touch the mountains so that they pour forth smoke. Flash forth lightning and scatter them; shoot Your arrows and panic them. Reach out Your hand from on high; deliver me and rescue me from the mighty waters, from the hands of strangers, whose every word is worthless, whose right hands are raised in falsehood. To You, God, I will sing a new song; to You I will play music on a ten-stringed harp. He who gives salvation to kings, who saved His servant David from the cruel sword: may He deliver me and rescue me from the hands of strangers, whose every word is worthless, whose right hands are raised in falsehood. Then our sons will be like saplings, well nurtured in their youth. Our daughters will be like pillars carved for a palace. Our barns will be filled with every kind of provision. Our sheep will increase by thousands, even tens of thousands in our fields. Our oxen will draw heavy loads. There will be no breach in the walls, no going into captivity, no cries of distress in our streets. Happy are the people for whom this is so; happy are the people whose God is the Lord. *Ps. 144*

לַמְנַצֵּחַ For the conductor of music. With stringed instruments. A psalm, a song. May God be gracious to us and bless us. May He make His face shine on us, Selah. Then will Your way be known on earth, Your salvation among all the nations. Let the peoples praise You, God; let all peoples praise You. Let nations rejoice and sing for joy, for You judge the peoples with equity, and guide the nations of the earth, Selah. Let the peoples praise You, God; let all peoples praise You. The earth has yielded its harvest. May God, our God, bless us. God will bless us, and all the ends of the earth will fear Him. *Ps. 67*

מעריב למוצאי שבת

In many congregations, the following two psalms are sung before מעריב *on* מוצאי שבת.

תהלים קמד לְדָוִד, בָּרוּךְ יהוה צוּרִי, הַמְלַמֵּד יָדַי לַקְרָב, אֶצְבְּעוֹתַי לַמִּלְחָמָה:
חַסְדִּי וּמְצוּדָתִי מִשְׂגַּבִּי וּמְפַלְטִי לִי, מָגִנִּי וּבוֹ חָסִיתִי, הָרוֹדֵד עַמִּי
תַחְתָּי: יהוה מָה־אָדָם וַתֵּדָעֵהוּ, בֶּן־אֱנוֹשׁ וַתְּחַשְּׁבֵהוּ: אָדָם לַהֶבֶל
דָּמָה, יָמָיו כְּצֵל עוֹבֵר: יהוה הַט־שָׁמֶיךָ וְתֵרֵד, גַּע בֶּהָרִים וְיֶעֱשָׁנוּ:
בְּרוֹק בָּרָק וּתְפִיצֵם, שְׁלַח חִצֶּיךָ וּתְהֻמֵּם: שְׁלַח יָדֶיךָ מִמָּרוֹם,
פְּצֵנִי וְהַצִּילֵנִי מִמַּיִם רַבִּים, מִיַּד בְּנֵי נֵכָר: אֲשֶׁר פִּיהֶם דִּבֶּר־שָׁוְא,
וִימִינָם יְמִין שָׁקֶר: אֱלֹהִים שִׁיר חָדָשׁ אָשִׁירָה לָּךְ, בְּנֵבֶל עָשׂוֹר
אֲזַמְּרָה־לָּךְ: הַנּוֹתֵן תְּשׁוּעָה לַמְּלָכִים, הַפּוֹצֶה אֶת־דָּוִד עַבְדּוֹ מֵחֶרֶב
רָעָה: פְּצֵנִי וְהַצִּילֵנִי מִיַּד בְּנֵי נֵכָר, אֲשֶׁר פִּיהֶם דִּבֶּר־שָׁוְא, וִימִינָם
יְמִין שָׁקֶר: אֲשֶׁר בָּנֵינוּ כִּנְטִעִים, מְגֻדָּלִים בִּנְעוּרֵיהֶם, בְּנוֹתֵינוּ
כְזָוִיֹּת, מְחֻטָּבוֹת תַּבְנִית הֵיכָל: מְזָוֵינוּ מְלֵאִים, מְפִיקִים מִזַּן אֶל־
זַן, צֹאונֵנוּ מַאֲלִיפוֹת מְרֻבָּבוֹת בְּחוּצוֹתֵינוּ: אַלּוּפֵינוּ מְסֻבָּלִים, אֵין
פֶּרֶץ וְאֵין יוֹצֵאת, וְאֵין צְוָחָה בִּרְחֹבֹתֵינוּ: אַשְׁרֵי הָעָם שֶׁכָּכָה לּוֹ,
אַשְׁרֵי הָעָם שֶׁיהוה אֱלֹהָיו:

תהלים סז לַמְנַצֵּחַ בִּנְגִינֹת, מִזְמוֹר שִׁיר: אֱלֹהִים יְחָנֵּנוּ וִיבָרְכֵנוּ, יָאֵר פָּנָיו אִתָּנוּ
סֶלָה: לָדַעַת בָּאָרֶץ דַּרְכֶּךָ, בְּכָל־גּוֹיִם יְשׁוּעָתֶךָ: יוֹדוּךָ עַמִּים אֱלֹהִים,
יוֹדוּךָ עַמִּים כֻּלָּם: יִשְׂמְחוּ וִירַנְּנוּ לְאֻמִּים, כִּי־תִשְׁפֹּט עַמִּים מִישֹׁר,
וּלְאֻמִּים בָּאָרֶץ תַּנְחֵם סֶלָה: יוֹדוּךָ עַמִּים אֱלֹהִים, יוֹדוּךָ עַמִּים כֻּלָּם:
אֶרֶץ נָתְנָה יְבוּלָהּ, יְבָרְכֵנוּ אֱלֹהִים אֱלֹהֵינוּ: יְבָרְכֵנוּ אֱלֹהִים, וְיִירְאוּ
אוֹתוֹ כָּל־אַפְסֵי־אָרֶץ:

וְהוּא רַחוּם He is compassionate. Ps. 78
He forgives iniquity and does not destroy.
Repeatedly He suppresses His anger,
not rousing His full wrath. Ps. 20
LORD, save!
May the King, answer us on the day we call.

BLESSINGS OF THE SHEMA

Leader: *Bow* **BLESS**
Stand straight the LORD, the blessed One.

Congregation: *Bow* Bless *Stand straight* the LORD, the blessed One,
for ever and all time.

Leader: *Bow* Bless *Stand straight* the LORD, the blessed One,
for ever and all time.

בָּרוּךְ Blessed are You, LORD our God, King of the Universe,
who by His word brings on evenings,
by His wisdom opens the gates of heaven,
with understanding makes time change and the seasons rotate,
and by His will
orders the stars in their constellations in the sky.
He creates day and night,
rolling away the light before the darkness,
and darkness before the light.
▸ He makes the day pass and brings on night,
distinguishing day from night:
the LORD of hosts is His name.
May the living and forever enduring God rule over us for all time.
Blessed are You, LORD, who brings on evenings.

וְהוּא רַחוּם, יְכַפֵּר עָוֹן וְלֹא־יַשְׁחִית תהלים עח
וְהִרְבָּה לְהָשִׁיב אַפּוֹ, וְלֹא־יָעִיר כָּל־חֲמָתוֹ:
יהוה הוֹשִׁיעָה, הַמֶּלֶךְ יַעֲנֵנוּ בְיוֹם־קָרְאֵנוּ: תהלים כ

קריאת שמע וברכותיה

ש״ץ: *Bow* בָּרְכוּ

אֶת *Stand straight* יהוה הַמְבֹרָךְ.

קהל: *Bow* בָּרוּךְ *Stand straight* יהוה הַמְבֹרָךְ לְעוֹלָם וָעֶד.

ש״ץ: *Bow* בָּרוּךְ *Stand straight* יהוה הַמְבֹרָךְ לְעוֹלָם וָעֶד.

בָּרוּךְ אַתָּה יהוה אֱלֹהֵינוּ מֶלֶךְ הָעוֹלָם
אֲשֶׁר בִּדְבָרוֹ מַעֲרִיב עֲרָבִים
בְּחָכְמָה פּוֹתֵחַ שְׁעָרִים
וּבִתְבוּנָה מְשַׁנֶּה עִתִּים וּמַחֲלִיף אֶת הַזְּמַנִּים
וּמְסַדֵּר אֶת הַכּוֹכָבִים בְּמִשְׁמְרוֹתֵיהֶם בָּרָקִיעַ כִּרְצוֹנוֹ.
בּוֹרֵא יוֹם וָלָיְלָה, גּוֹלֵל אוֹר מִפְּנֵי חֹשֶׁךְ וְחֹשֶׁךְ מִפְּנֵי אוֹר
◂ וּמַעֲבִיר יוֹם וּמֵבִיא לָיְלָה
וּמַבְדִּיל בֵּין יוֹם וּבֵין לָיְלָה
יהוה צְבָאוֹת שְׁמוֹ.
אֵל חַי וְקַיָּם תָּמִיד, יִמְלֹךְ עָלֵינוּ לְעוֹלָם וָעֶד.
בָּרוּךְ אַתָּה יהוה, הַמַּעֲרִיב עֲרָבִים.

אַהֲבַת עוֹלָם With everlasting love
have You loved Your people, the house of Israel.
You have taught us Torah and commandments,
decrees and laws of justice.
Therefore, LORD our God, when we lie down and when we rise up
we will speak of Your decrees,
rejoicing in the words of Your Torah
and Your commandments for ever.
▸ For they are our life and the length of our days;
on them will we meditate day and night.
May You never take away Your love from us.
Blessed are You, LORD, who loves His people Israel.

The Shema must be said with intense concentration.

When not with a minyan, say:
God, faithful King!

The following verse should be said aloud, while covering the eyes with the right hand:

Listen, Israel: the LORD is our God, the LORD is One. Deut. 6

Quietly: Blessed be the name of His glorious kingdom for ever and all time.

וְאָהַבְתָּ Love the LORD your God with all your heart, with all your soul, and with all your might. These words which I command you today shall be on your heart. Teach them repeatedly to your children, speaking of them when you sit at home and when you travel on the way, when you lie down and when you rise. Bind them as a sign on your hand, and they shall be an emblem between your eyes. Write them on the doorposts of your house and gates. Deut. 6

וְהָיָה If you indeed heed My commandments with which I charge you today, to love the LORD your God and worship Him with all your heart and with all your soul, I will give rain in your land in its season, the early and late rain; and you shall gather in your Deut. 11

אַהֲבַת עוֹלָם בֵּית יִשְׂרָאֵל עַמְּךָ אָהָבְתָּ
תּוֹרָה וּמִצְוֹת, חֻקִּים וּמִשְׁפָּטִים, אוֹתָנוּ לִמַּדְתָּ
עַל כֵּן יהוה אֱלֹהֵינוּ בְּשָׁכְבֵנוּ וּבְקוּמֵנוּ נָשִׂיחַ בְּחֻקֶּיךָ
וְנִשְׂמַח בְּדִבְרֵי תוֹרָתֶךָ וּבְמִצְוֹתֶיךָ לְעוֹלָם וָעֶד
◄ כִּי הֵם חַיֵּינוּ וְאֹרֶךְ יָמֵינוּ
וּבָהֶם נֶהְגֶּה יוֹמָם וָלָיְלָה.
וְאַהֲבָתְךָ אַל תָּסִיר מִמֶּנּוּ לְעוֹלָמִים.
בָּרוּךְ אַתָּה יהוה, אוֹהֵב עַמּוֹ יִשְׂרָאֵל.

The שמע *must be said with intense concentration.*

When not with a מנין*, say:*

אֵל מֶלֶךְ נֶאֱמָן

The following verse should be said aloud, while covering the eyes with the right hand:

שְׁמַע יִשְׂרָאֵל, יהוה אֱלֹהֵינוּ, יהוה ׀ אֶחָד׃ דברים ו

Quietly בָּרוּךְ שֵׁם כְּבוֹד מַלְכוּתוֹ לְעוֹלָם וָעֶד.

וְאָהַבְתָּ אֵת יהוה אֱלֹהֶיךָ, בְּכָל־לְבָבְךָ וּבְכָל־נַפְשְׁךָ וּבְכָל־ דברים ו
מְאֹדֶךָ׃ וְהָיוּ הַדְּבָרִים הָאֵלֶּה, אֲשֶׁר אָנֹכִי מְצַוְּךָ הַיּוֹם, עַל־לְבָבֶךָ׃
וְשִׁנַּנְתָּם לְבָנֶיךָ וְדִבַּרְתָּ בָּם, בְּשִׁבְתְּךָ בְּבֵיתֶךָ וּבְלֶכְתְּךָ בַדֶּרֶךְ,
וּבְשָׁכְבְּךָ וּבְקוּמֶךָ׃ וּקְשַׁרְתָּם לְאוֹת עַל־יָדֶךָ וְהָיוּ לְטֹטָפֹת בֵּין
עֵינֶיךָ׃ וּכְתַבְתָּם עַל־מְזֻזוֹת בֵּיתֶךָ וּבִשְׁעָרֶיךָ׃

וְהָיָה אִם־שָׁמֹעַ תִּשְׁמְעוּ אֶל־מִצְוֹתַי אֲשֶׁר אָנֹכִי מְצַוֶּה אֶתְכֶם דברים יא
הַיּוֹם, לְאַהֲבָה אֶת־יהוה אֱלֹהֵיכֶם וּלְעָבְדוֹ, בְּכָל־לְבַבְכֶם וּבְכָל־
נַפְשְׁכֶם׃ וְנָתַתִּי מְטַר־אַרְצְכֶם בְּעִתּוֹ, יוֹרֶה וּמַלְקוֹשׁ, וְאָסַפְתָּ

grain, wine and oil. I will give grass in your field for your cattle, and you shall eat and be satisfied. Be careful lest your heart be tempted and you go astray and worship other gods, bowing down to them. Then the LORD's anger will flare against you and He will close the heavens so that there will be no rain. The land will not yield its crops, and you will perish swiftly from the good land that the LORD is giving you. Therefore, set these, My words, on your heart and soul. Bind them as a sign on your hand, and they shall be an emblem between your eyes. Teach them to your children, speaking of them when you sit at home and when you travel on the way, when you lie down and when you rise. Write them on the doorposts of your house and gates, so that you and your children may live long in the land that the LORD swore to your ancestors to give them, for as long as the heavens are above the earth.

וַיֹּאמֶר The LORD spoke to Moses, saying: Speak to the Israelites *Num. 15*
and tell them to make tassels on the corners of their garments for all generations. They shall attach to the tassel at each corner a thread of blue. This shall be your tassel, and you shall see it and remember all of the LORD's commandments and keep them, not straying after your heart and after your eyes, following your own sinful desires. Thus you will be reminded to keep all My commandments, and be holy to your God. I am the LORD your God, who brought you out of the land of Egypt to be your God. I am the LORD your God.

True –

The Leader repeats:

▸ The LORD your God is true –

דְגָנֶךָ וְתִירֹשְׁךָ וְיִצְהָרֶךָ: וְנָתַתִּי עֵשֶׂב בְּשָׂדְךָ לִבְהֶמְתֶּךָ, וְאָכַלְתָּ
וְשָׂבָעְתָּ: הִשָּׁמְרוּ לָכֶם פֶּן־יִפְתֶּה לְבַבְכֶם, וְסַרְתֶּם וַעֲבַדְתֶּם
אֱלֹהִים אֲחֵרִים וְהִשְׁתַּחֲוִיתֶם לָהֶם: וְחָרָה אַף־יהוה בָּכֶם, וְעָצַר
אֶת־הַשָּׁמַיִם וְלֹא־יִהְיֶה מָטָר, וְהָאֲדָמָה לֹא תִתֵּן אֶת־יְבוּלָהּ,
וַאֲבַדְתֶּם מְהֵרָה מֵעַל הָאָרֶץ הַטֹּבָה אֲשֶׁר יהוה נֹתֵן לָכֶם:
וְשַׂמְתֶּם אֶת־דְּבָרַי אֵלֶּה עַל־לְבַבְכֶם וְעַל־נַפְשְׁכֶם, וּקְשַׁרְתֶּם
אֹתָם לְאוֹת עַל־יֶדְכֶם, וְהָיוּ לְטוֹטָפֹת בֵּין עֵינֵיכֶם: וְלִמַּדְתֶּם
אֹתָם אֶת־בְּנֵיכֶם לְדַבֵּר בָּם, בְּשִׁבְתְּךָ בְּבֵיתֶךָ וּבְלֶכְתְּךָ בַדֶּרֶךְ,
וּבְשָׁכְבְּךָ וּבְקוּמֶךָ: וּכְתַבְתָּם עַל־מְזוּזוֹת בֵּיתֶךָ וּבִשְׁעָרֶיךָ: לְמַעַן
יִרְבּוּ יְמֵיכֶם וִימֵי בְנֵיכֶם עַל הָאֲדָמָה אֲשֶׁר נִשְׁבַּע יהוה לַאֲבֹתֵיכֶם
לָתֵת לָהֶם, כִּימֵי הַשָּׁמַיִם עַל־הָאָרֶץ:

במדבר טו וַיֹּאמֶר יהוה אֶל־מֹשֶׁה לֵּאמֹר: דַּבֵּר אֶל־בְּנֵי יִשְׂרָאֵל וְאָמַרְתָּ
אֲלֵהֶם, וְעָשׂוּ לָהֶם צִיצִת עַל־כַּנְפֵי בִגְדֵיהֶם לְדֹרֹתָם, וְנָתְנוּ
עַל־צִיצִת הַכָּנָף פְּתִיל תְּכֵלֶת: וְהָיָה לָכֶם לְצִיצִת, וּרְאִיתֶם אֹתוֹ
וּזְכַרְתֶּם אֶת־כָּל־מִצְוֹת יהוה וַעֲשִׂיתֶם אֹתָם, וְלֹא תָתֻרוּ אַחֲרֵי
לְבַבְכֶם וְאַחֲרֵי עֵינֵיכֶם, אֲשֶׁר־אַתֶּם זֹנִים אַחֲרֵיהֶם: לְמַעַן תִּזְכְּרוּ
וַעֲשִׂיתֶם אֶת־כָּל־מִצְוֹתָי, וִהְיִיתֶם קְדֹשִׁים לֵאלֹהֵיכֶם: אֲנִי יהוה
אֱלֹהֵיכֶם, אֲשֶׁר הוֹצֵאתִי אֶתְכֶם מֵאֶרֶץ מִצְרַיִם, לִהְיוֹת לָכֶם
לֵאלֹהִים, אֲנִי יהוה אֱלֹהֵיכֶם:

אֱמֶת

The שליח ציבור *repeats:*

◂ יהוה אֱלֹהֵיכֶם אֱמֶת

וֶאֱמוּנָה – and faithful is all this,
and firmly established for us
that He is the LORD our God,
and there is none besides Him,
and that we, Israel, are His people.
He is our King, who redeems us from the hand of kings
and delivers us from the grasp of all tyrants.
He is our God,
who on our behalf repays our foes
and brings just retribution on our mortal enemies;
who performs great deeds beyond understanding
and wonders beyond number;
who kept us alive, not letting our foot slip; *Ps. 66*
who led us on the high places of our enemies,
raising our pride above all our foes;
who did miracles for us
and brought vengeance against Pharaoh;
who performed signs and wonders
in the land of Ham's children;
who smote in His wrath all the firstborn of Egypt,
and brought out His people Israel from their midst
into everlasting freedom;
who led His children through the divided Reed Sea,
plunging their pursuers and enemies into the depths.
When His children saw His might,
they gave praise and thanks to His name,
▸ and willingly accepted His Sovereignty.
Moses and the children of Israel
then sang a song to You with great joy,
and they all exclaimed:

מִי־כָמְכָה "Who is like You, LORD, among the mighty? *Ex. 15*
Who is like You, majestic in holiness,
awesome in praises, doing wonders?"

וֶאֱמוּנָה כָּל זֹאת וְקַיָּם עָלֵינוּ
כִּי הוּא יהוה אֱלֹהֵינוּ וְאֵין זוּלָתוֹ
וַאֲנַחְנוּ יִשְׂרָאֵל עַמּוֹ.
הַפּוֹדֵנוּ מִיַּד מְלָכִים, מַלְכֵּנוּ
הַגּוֹאֲלֵנוּ מִכַּף כָּל הֶעָרִיצִים.
הָאֵל הַנִּפְרָע לָנוּ מִצָּרֵינוּ
וְהַמְשַׁלֵּם גְּמוּל לְכָל אוֹיְבֵי נַפְשֵׁנוּ.
הָעוֹשֶׂה גְדוֹלוֹת עַד אֵין חֵקֶר, וְנִפְלָאוֹת עַד אֵין מִסְפָּר
הַשָּׂם נַפְשֵׁנוּ בַּחַיִּים, וְלֹא־נָתַן לַמּוֹט רַגְלֵנוּ: (תהלים סו)
הַמַּדְרִיכֵנוּ עַל בָּמוֹת אוֹיְבֵינוּ
וַיָּרֶם קַרְנֵנוּ עַל כָּל שׂוֹנְאֵינוּ.
הָעוֹשֶׂה לָּנוּ נִסִּים וּנְקָמָה בְּפַרְעֹה
אוֹתוֹת וּמוֹפְתִים בְּאַדְמַת בְּנֵי חָם.
הַמַּכֶּה בְעֶבְרָתוֹ כָּל בְּכוֹרֵי מִצְרָיִם
וַיּוֹצֵא אֶת עַמּוֹ יִשְׂרָאֵל מִתּוֹכָם לְחֵרוּת עוֹלָם.
הַמַּעֲבִיר בָּנָיו בֵּין גִּזְרֵי יַם סוּף
אֶת רוֹדְפֵיהֶם וְאֶת שׂוֹנְאֵיהֶם בִּתְהוֹמוֹת טִבַּע
וְרָאוּ בָנָיו גְּבוּרָתוֹ, שִׁבְּחוּ וְהוֹדוּ לִשְׁמוֹ
◄ וּמַלְכוּתוֹ בְּרָצוֹן קִבְּלוּ עֲלֵיהֶם.
מֹשֶׁה וּבְנֵי יִשְׂרָאֵל, לְךָ עָנוּ שִׁירָה בְּשִׂמְחָה רַבָּה
וְאָמְרוּ כֻלָּם
מִי־כָמֹכָה בָּאֵלִם יהוה (שמות טו)
מִי כָּמֹכָה נֶאְדָּר בַּקֹּדֶשׁ
נוֹרָא תְהִלֹּת עֹשֵׂה פֶלֶא:

▸ Your children beheld Your majesty
as You parted the sea before Moses.
"This is my God!" they responded, and then said:
"The LORD shall reign for ever and ever." *Ex. 15*

▸ And it is said,
"For the LORD has redeemed Jacob and rescued him *Jer. 31*
from a power stronger than his own."
Blessed are You, LORD, who redeemed Israel.

הַשְׁכִּיבֵנוּ Help us lie down, O LORD our God, in peace,
and rise up, O our King, to life.
Spread over us Your canopy of peace.
Direct us with Your good counsel,
and save us for the sake of Your name.
Shield us and remove from us every enemy,
plague, sword, famine and sorrow.
Remove the adversary from before and behind us.
Shelter us in the shadow of Your wings,
for You, God, are our Guardian and Deliverer;
You, God, are a gracious and compassionate King.
▸ Guard our going out and our coming in,
for life and peace, from now and for ever.
Blessed are You, LORD, who guards His people Israel for ever.

In Israel the service continues with Half Kaddish on page 600.

בָּרוּךְ Blessed be the LORD for ever. Amen and Amen. *Ps. 89*
Blessed from Zion be the LORD *Ps. 135*
who dwells in Jerusalem. Halleluya!
Blessed be the LORD, God of Israel, *Ps. 72*
who alone does wondrous things.
Blessed be His glorious name for ever,
and may the whole earth be filled with His glory. Amen and Amen.

› מַלְכוּתְךָ רָאוּ בָנֶיךָ, בּוֹקֵעַ יָם לִפְנֵי מֹשֶׁה
זֶה אֵלִי עָנוּ, וְאָמְרוּ
יהוה יִמְלֹךְ לְעֹלָם וָעֶד: שמות טו
› וְנֶאֱמַר
כִּי־פָדָה יהוה אֶת־יַעֲקֹב, וּגְאָלוֹ מִיַּד חָזָק מִמֶּנּוּ: ירמיהו לא
בָּרוּךְ אַתָּה יהוה, גָּאַל יִשְׂרָאֵל.

הַשְׁכִּיבֵנוּ יהוה אֱלֹהֵינוּ לְשָׁלוֹם
וְהַעֲמִידֵנוּ מַלְכֵּנוּ לְחַיִּים
וּפְרֹשׂ עָלֵינוּ סֻכַּת שְׁלוֹמֶךָ
וְתַקְּנֵנוּ בְּעֵצָה טוֹבָה מִלְּפָנֶיךָ
וְהוֹשִׁיעֵנוּ לְמַעַן שְׁמֶךָ.
וְהָגֵן בַּעֲדֵנוּ, וְהָסֵר מֵעָלֵינוּ אוֹיֵב, דֶּבֶר וְחֶרֶב וְרָעָב וְיָגוֹן
וְהָסֵר שָׂטָן מִלְּפָנֵינוּ וּמֵאַחֲרֵינוּ, וּבְצֵל כְּנָפֶיךָ תַּסְתִּירֵנוּ
כִּי אֵל שׁוֹמְרֵנוּ וּמַצִּילֵנוּ אָתָּה
כִּי אֵל מֶלֶךְ חַנּוּן וְרַחוּם אָתָּה.
› וּשְׁמֹר צֵאתֵנוּ וּבוֹאֵנוּ לְחַיִּים וּלְשָׁלוֹם מֵעַתָּה וְעַד עוֹלָם.
בָּרוּךְ אַתָּה יהוה, שׁוֹמֵר עַמּוֹ יִשְׂרָאֵל לָעַד.

In ארץ ישראל *the service continues with* חצי קדיש *on page 601.*

בָּרוּךְ יהוה לְעוֹלָם, אָמֵן וְאָמֵן: תהלים פט
בָּרוּךְ יהוה מִצִּיּוֹן, שֹׁכֵן יְרוּשָׁלָֽם, הַלְלוּיָהּ: תהלים קלה
בָּרוּךְ יהוה אֱלֹהִים אֱלֹהֵי יִשְׂרָאֵל, עֹשֵׂה נִפְלָאוֹת לְבַדּוֹ: תהלים עב
וּבָרוּךְ שֵׁם כְּבוֹדוֹ לְעוֹלָם
וְיִמָּלֵא כְבוֹדוֹ אֶת־כָּל־הָאָרֶץ, אָמֵן וְאָמֵן:

May the glory of the LORD endure for ever; *Ps. 104*
may the LORD rejoice in His works.
May the name of the LORD be blessed now and for all time. *Ps. 113*
For the sake of His great name *I Sam. 12*
the LORD will not abandon His people,
for the LORD vowed to make you a people of His own.
When all the people saw [God's wonders] they fell on their faces *I Kings 18*
and said: "The LORD, He is God; the LORD, He is God."
Then the LORD shall be King over all the earth; *Zech. 14*
on that day the LORD shall be One and His name One.
May Your love, LORD, be upon us, *Ps. 33*
as we have put our hope in You.
Save us, LORD our God, gather us *Ps. 106*
and deliver us from the nations,
to thank Your holy name, and glory in Your praise.
All the nations You made shall come and bow before You, LORD, *Ps. 86*
and pay honor to Your name,
for You are great and You perform wonders:
You alone are God.
We, Your people, the flock of Your pasture, will praise You for ever. *Ps. 79*
For all generations we will relate Your praise.

בָּרוּךְ Blessed is the LORD by day, blessed is the LORD by night.
Blessed is the LORD when we lie down;
blessed is the LORD when we rise.
For in Your hand are the souls of the living and the dead,
[as it is written:] "In His hand is every living soul, *Job 12*
and the breath of all mankind."
Into Your hand I entrust my spirit: *Ps. 31*
You redeemed me, LORD, God of truth.
Our God in heaven, bring unity to Your name,
establish Your kingdom constantly
and reign over us for ever and all time.

יְהִי כְבוֹד יהוה לְעוֹלָם, יִשְׂמַח יהוה בְּמַעֲשָׂיו: תהלים קד
יְהִי שֵׁם יהוה מְבֹרָךְ מֵעַתָּה וְעַד־עוֹלָם: תהלים קיג
כִּי לֹא־יִטֹּשׁ יהוה אֶת־עַמּוֹ בַּעֲבוּר שְׁמוֹ הַגָּדוֹל שמואל א, יב
כִּי הוֹאִיל יהוה לַעֲשׂוֹת אֶתְכֶם לוֹ לְעָם:
וַיַּרְא כָּל־הָעָם וַיִּפְּלוּ עַל־פְּנֵיהֶם מלכים א, יח
וַיֹּאמְרוּ, יהוה הוּא הָאֱלֹהִים, יהוה הוּא הָאֱלֹהִים:
וְהָיָה יהוה לְמֶלֶךְ עַל־כָּל־הָאָרֶץ זכריה יד
בַּיּוֹם הַהוּא יִהְיֶה יהוה אֶחָד וּשְׁמוֹ אֶחָד:
יְהִי־חַסְדְּךָ יהוה עָלֵינוּ, כַּאֲשֶׁר יִחַלְנוּ לָךְ: תהלים לג
הוֹשִׁיעֵנוּ יהוה אֱלֹהֵינוּ, וְקַבְּצֵנוּ מִן־הַגּוֹיִם תהלים קו
לְהוֹדוֹת לְשֵׁם קָדְשֶׁךָ, לְהִשְׁתַּבֵּחַ בִּתְהִלָּתֶךָ:
כָּל־גּוֹיִם אֲשֶׁר עָשִׂיתָ, יָבוֹאוּ וְיִשְׁתַּחֲווּ לְפָנֶיךָ, אֲדֹנָי תהלים פו
וִיכַבְּדוּ לִשְׁמֶךָ:
כִּי־גָדוֹל אַתָּה וְעֹשֵׂה נִפְלָאוֹת, אַתָּה אֱלֹהִים לְבַדֶּךָ:
וַאֲנַחְנוּ עַמְּךָ וְצֹאן מַרְעִיתֶךָ, נוֹדֶה לְּךָ לְעוֹלָם תהלים עט
לְדוֹר וָדֹר נְסַפֵּר תְּהִלָּתֶךָ:

בָּרוּךְ יהוה בַּיּוֹם, בָּרוּךְ יהוה בַּלָּיְלָה
בָּרוּךְ יהוה בְּשָׁכְבֵנוּ, בָּרוּךְ יהוה בְּקוּמֵנוּ.
כִּי בְיָדְךָ נַפְשׁוֹת הַחַיִּים וְהַמֵּתִים.
אֲשֶׁר בְּיָדוֹ נֶפֶשׁ כָּל־חָי, וְרוּחַ כָּל־בְּשַׂר־אִישׁ: איוב יב
בְּיָדְךָ אַפְקִיד רוּחִי, פָּדִיתָה אוֹתִי יהוה אֵל אֱמֶת: תהלים לא
אֱלֹהֵינוּ שֶׁבַּשָּׁמַיִם, יַחֵד שִׁמְךָ וְקַיֵּם מַלְכוּתְךָ תָּמִיד
וּמְלֹךְ עָלֵינוּ לְעוֹלָם וָעֶד.

יִרְאוּ May our eyes see, our hearts rejoice,
and our souls be glad in Your true salvation,
when Zion is told, "Your God reigns."
The LORD is King, the LORD was King,
the LORD will be King for ever and all time.
▸ For sovereignty is Yours, and to all eternity You will reign in glory,
for we have no king but You.
Blessed are You, LORD,
the King who in His constant glory will reign over us
and all His creation for ever and all time.

HALF KADDISH

Leader: יִתְגַּדַּל Magnified and sanctified
may His great name be,
in the world He created by His will.
May He establish His kingdom
in your lifetime and in your days,
and in the lifetime of all the house of Israel,
swiftly and soon –
and say: Amen.

All: May His great name be blessed
for ever and all time.

Leader: Blessed and praised,
glorified and exalted,
raised and honored,
uplifted and lauded
be the name of the Holy One,
blessed be He,
beyond any blessing,
song, praise and consolation
uttered in the world –
and say: Amen.

יִרְאוּ עֵינֵינוּ וְיִשְׂמַח לִבֵּנוּ וְתָגֵל נַפְשֵׁנוּ בִּישׁוּעָתְךָ בֶּאֱמֶת
בֶּאֱמֹר לְצִיּוֹן מָלַךְ אֱלֹהָיִךְ.
יהוה מֶלֶךְ, יהוה מָלָךְ, יהוה יִמְלֹךְ לְעֹלָם וָעֶד.
כִּי הַמַּלְכוּת שֶׁלְּךָ הִיא, וּלְעוֹלְמֵי עַד תִּמְלֹךְ בְּכָבוֹד
כִּי אֵין לָנוּ מֶלֶךְ אֶלָּא אָתָּה.
בָּרוּךְ אַתָּה יהוה
הַמֶּלֶךְ בִּכְבוֹדוֹ תָּמִיד, יִמְלֹךְ עָלֵינוּ לְעוֹלָם וָעֶד וְעַל כָּל מַעֲשָׂיו.

חצי קדיש

ש״ץ: יִתְגַּדַּל וְיִתְקַדַּשׁ שְׁמֵהּ רַבָּא (קהל: אָמֵן)
בְּעָלְמָא דִּי בְרָא כִרְעוּתֵהּ
וְיַמְלִיךְ מַלְכוּתֵהּ
בְּחַיֵּיכוֹן וּבְיוֹמֵיכוֹן וּבְחַיֵּי דְכָל בֵּית יִשְׂרָאֵל
בַּעֲגָלָא וּבִזְמַן קָרִיב
וְאִמְרוּ אָמֵן. (קהל: אָמֵן)

קהל וש״ץ: יְהֵא שְׁמֵהּ רַבָּא מְבָרַךְ לְעָלַם וּלְעָלְמֵי עָלְמַיָּא.

ש״ץ: יִתְבָּרַךְ וְיִשְׁתַּבַּח וְיִתְפָּאַר וְיִתְרוֹמַם וְיִתְנַשֵּׂא
וְיִתְהַדָּר וְיִתְעַלֶּה וְיִתְהַלָּל
שְׁמֵהּ דְּקֻדְשָׁא בְּרִיךְ הוּא (קהל: בְּרִיךְ הוּא)
לְעֵלָּא מִן כָּל בִּרְכָתָא
/בעשרת ימי תשובה: לְעֵלָּא לְעֵלָּא מִכָּל בִּרְכָתָא/
וְשִׁירָתָא, תֻּשְׁבְּחָתָא וְנֶחֱמָתָא
דַּאֲמִירָן בְּעָלְמָא
וְאִמְרוּ אָמֵן. (קהל: אָמֵן)

THE AMIDA

The following prayer, until "in former years" on page 620, is said silently, standing with feet together.
Take three steps forward.

O Lord, open my lips, so that my mouth may declare Your praise. *Ps. 51*

PATRIARCHS

▾*Bend the knees:* Blessed *Bow:* are You, *Stand straight:* Lord
our God and God of our fathers,
God of Abraham, God of Isaac and God of Jacob;
the great, mighty and awesome God, God Most High,
who bestows acts of loving-kindness and creates all,
who remembers the loving-kindness of the fathers
and will bring a Redeemer to their children's children
for the sake of His name, in love.

These words are added between Rosh HaShana & Yom Kippur: Remember us for life, O King who desires life,
and write us in the book of life –
for Your sake, O God of life.

King, Helper, Savior, Shield:
▾*Bend the knees:* Blessed *Bow:* are You, *Stand straight:* Lord,
Shield of Abraham.

DIVINE MIGHT

אַתָּה גִּבּוֹר You are eternally mighty, Lord.
You give life to the dead
and have great power to save.

The phrase "He makes the wind blow and the rain fall" is added from Simḥat Torah until Pesaḥ. In Israel the phrase "He causes the dew to fall" is added from Pesaḥ until Shemini Atzeret.

In fall & winter: He makes the wind blow and the rain fall.
In Israel, in spring & summer: He causes the dew to fall.

He sustains the living with loving-kindness,
and with great compassion revives the dead.
He supports the fallen, heals the sick, sets captives free,
and keeps His faith with those who sleep in the dust.

עמידה

The following prayer, until קַדְמֹנִיּוֹת *on page 621, is said silently, standing with feet together. Take three steps forward.*

אֲדֹנָי, שְׂפָתַי תִּפְתָּח, וּפִי יַגִּיד תְּהִלָּתֶךָ: תהלים נא

אבות

▾ *Bend the knees* בָּרוּךְ *Bow* אַתָּה *Stand straight* יהוה
אֱלֹהֵינוּ וֵאלֹהֵי אֲבוֹתֵינוּ
אֱלֹהֵי אַבְרָהָם, אֱלֹהֵי יִצְחָק, וֵאלֹהֵי יַעֲקֹב
הָאֵל הַגָּדוֹל הַגִּבּוֹר וְהַנּוֹרָא, אֵל עֶלְיוֹן
גּוֹמֵל חֲסָדִים טוֹבִים, וְקוֹנֵה הַכֹּל
וְזוֹכֵר חַסְדֵי אָבוֹת
וּמֵבִיא גוֹאֵל לִבְנֵי בְנֵיהֶם לְמַעַן שְׁמוֹ בְּאַהֲבָה.

בעשרת ימי תשובה: זָכְרֵנוּ לְחַיִּים, מֶלֶךְ חָפֵץ בַּחַיִּים
וְכָתְבֵנוּ בְּסֵפֶר הַחַיִּים, לְמַעַנְךָ אֱלֹהִים חַיִּים.

מֶלֶךְ עוֹזֵר וּמוֹשִׁיעַ וּמָגֵן.
▾ *Bend the knees* בָּרוּךְ *Bow* אַתָּה *Stand straight* יהוה, מָגֵן אַבְרָהָם.

גבורות

אַתָּה גִּבּוֹר לְעוֹלָם, אֲדֹנָי
מְחַיֵּה מֵתִים אַתָּה, רַב לְהוֹשִׁיעַ

The phrase מַשִּׁיב הָרְוּחַ *is added from* שמחת תורה *until* פסח. *In* ארץ ישראל *the phrase* מוֹרִיד הַטָּל *is added from* פסח *until* שמיני עצרת.

בחורף: מַשִּׁיב הָרְוּחַ וּמוֹרִיד הַגֶּשֶׁם / בארץ ישראל בקיץ: מוֹרִיד הַטָּל

מְכַלְכֵּל חַיִּים בְּחֶסֶד
מְחַיֵּה מֵתִים בְּרַחֲמִים רַבִּים
סוֹמֵךְ נוֹפְלִים, וְרוֹפֵא חוֹלִים, וּמַתִּיר אֲסוּרִים
וּמְקַיֵּם אֱמוּנָתוֹ לִישֵׁנֵי עָפָר.

Who is like You, Master of might,
and who can compare to You,
O King who brings death and gives life,
and makes salvation grow?

These words are added between Rosh HaShana & Yom Kippur: Who is like You, compassionate Father,
who remembers His creatures
in compassion, for life?

Faithful are You to revive the dead.
Blessed are You, LORD,
who revives the dead.

HOLINESS

אַתָּה קָדוֹשׁ You are holy and Your name is holy,
and holy ones praise You daily, Selah!
Blessed are You, LORD,
the holy God. / *Between Rosh HaShana & Yom Kippur:* the holy King./
(*If forgotten, repeat the Amida.*)

KNOWLEDGE

אַתָּה חוֹנֵן You grace humanity with knowledge
and teach mortals understanding.
You have graced us[B] with the knowledge of Your Torah,
and taught us to perform the statutes of Your will.

---

and human, the Jewish people and the rest of humanity, the holy and the mundane. And so as we begin our week, we acknowledge these differences, we ourselves imitate God by using our intellect to differentiate, to distinguish, to separate out the lessons and challenges in the physical, moral and historical worlds in which we ourselves are also creators. In the coming week we have the ability to distinguish between the holy and the mundane, the light and the dark, the Jewish and the non-Jewish, by virtue of the way that we live our lives, by the decisions we make every day. If we do that, if we carry with us any of the lessons that we learned about ourselves, or others, or God over the course of the past 25 hours, then we will have surely fulfilled Hashem's wish that we distinguish between Shabbat and the other six days of the week.

מִי כָמְוֹךָ, בַּעַל גְּבוּרוֹת, וּמִי דְּוֹמֶה לָּךְ
מֶלֶךְ, מֵמִית וּמְחַיֶּה וּמַצְמִיחַ יְשׁוּעָה.

בעשרת ימי תשובה: מִי כָמְוֹךָ אַב הָרַחֲמִים
זוֹכֵר יְצוּרָיו לְחַיִּים בְּרַחֲמִים.

וְנֶאֱמָן אַתָּה לְהַחֲיוֹת מֵתִים.
בָּרוּךְ אַתָּה יהוה, מְחַיֵּה הַמֵּתִים.

קדושת השם

אַתָּה קָדוֹשׁ וְשִׁמְךָ קָדוֹשׁ
וּקְדוֹשִׁים בְּכָל יוֹם יְהַלְלְוּךָ סֶּלָה.
בָּרוּךְ אַתָּה יהוה, הָאֵל הַקָּדוֹשׁ./ בעשרת ימי תשובה: הַמֶּלֶךְ הַקָּדוֹשׁ./
(*If forgotten, repeat the* עמידה.)

דעת

אַתָּה חוֹנֵן לְאָדָם דַּעַת, וּמְלַמֵּד לֶאֱנוֹשׁ בִּינָה.
אַתָּה חוֹנַנְתָּנוּ[ב] לְמַדַּע תּוֹרָתֶךָ
וַתְּלַמְּדֵנוּ לַעֲשׂוֹת חֻקֵּי רְצוֹנֶךָ

BIUR TEFILLA • ביאור תפילה

אַתָּה חוֹנַנְתָּנוּ – *You have graced us.* We acknowledge the arrival of the new workweek with a formal statement for important transitions need to be articulated and not just allowed to happen.

This blessing is also known as a *havdala* (separation or differentiation), distinguishing between the experience we have just had and the week we are about to enter into. It is incorporated into the very first request of the new week which, appropriately, is a blessing whose theme is human intelligence, the core of our ability to think and distinguish one thing from another (*Berakhot* 33a).

Many of the themes highlighted during the past twenty-five hours reverberate here. Hashem created the world through acts of separation and differentiation: nothingness and matter, light and dark, heaven and earth, inanimate and animate, animal

You have distinguished, LORD our God,
between sacred and profane,
light and darkness, Israel and the nations,
and between the seventh day and the six days of work. Our Father, our King, may the days approaching us bring peace;
may we be free from all sin, cleansed from all iniquity,
holding fast to our reverence of You.
And Grace us with the knowledge, understanding
and discernment that come from You.
Blessed are You, LORD, who graciously grants knowledge.

REPENTANCE

הֲשִׁיבֵנוּ Bring us back, our Father, to Your Torah.
Draw us near, our King, to Your service.
Lead us back to You in perfect repentance.
Blessed are You, LORD, who desires repentance.

FORGIVENESS

Strike the left side of the chest at °.

סְלַח לָנוּ Forgive us, our Father, for we have °sinned.
Pardon us, our King, for we have °transgressed;
for You pardon and forgive.
Blessed are You, LORD, the gracious One who repeatedly forgives.

REDEMPTION

רְאֵה Look on our affliction, plead our cause,
and redeem us soon for Your name's sake,
for You are a powerful Redeemer.
Blessed are You, LORD, the Redeemer of Israel.

---

said nothing. "Well, then," he said, "it seems that you wasted your Shabbat" and he walked away. I recall being hurt by the remark for, after all, I certainly attended whatever learning sessions there were and I had had many interactions with other students and with some teachers. Surely, they left some impact upon me?! It is now decades later, and the sting of the remark has long since passed, but I don't recall any of the sessions I went to or any of the people I met, but that question still rears its head at the end of almost every Shabbat.

וַתַּבְדֵּל יהוה אֱלֹהֵינוּ בֵּין קֹדֶשׁ לְחֹל
בֵּין אוֹר לְחֹשֶׁךְ, בֵּין יִשְׂרָאֵל לָעַמִּים
בֵּין יוֹם הַשְּׁבִיעִי לְשֵׁשֶׁת יְמֵי הַמַּעֲשֶׂה.
אָבִינוּ מַלְכֵּנוּ, הָחֵל עָלֵינוּ הַיָּמִים הַבָּאִים לִקְרָאתֵנוּ לְשָׁלוֹם
חֲשׂוּכִים מִכָּל חֵטְא וּמְנֻקִּים מִכָּל עָוֹן וּמְדֻבָּקִים בְּיִרְאָתֶךָ.
וְחָנֵּנוּ מֵאִתְּךָ דֵּעָה בִּינָה וְהַשְׂכֵּל.
בָּרוּךְ אַתָּה יהוה, חוֹנֵן הַדָּעַת.

תשובה

הֲשִׁיבֵנוּ אָבִינוּ לְתוֹרָתֶךָ, וְקָרְבֵנוּ מַלְכֵּנוּ לַעֲבוֹדָתֶךָ
וְהַחֲזִירֵנוּ בִּתְשׁוּבָה שְׁלֵמָה לְפָנֶיךָ.
בָּרוּךְ אַתָּה יהוה, הָרוֹצֶה בִּתְשׁוּבָה.

סליחה

Strike the left side of the chest at °.

סְלַח לָנוּ אָבִינוּ כִּי °חָטָאנוּ
מְחַל לָנוּ מַלְכֵּנוּ כִּי °פָשָׁעְנוּ
כִּי מוֹחֵל וְסוֹלֵחַ אָתָּה.
בָּרוּךְ אַתָּה יהוה, חַנּוּן הַמַּרְבֶּה לִסְלֹחַ.

גאולה

רְאֵה בְעָנְיֵנוּ, וְרִיבָה רִיבֵנוּ, וּגְאָלֵנוּ מְהֵרָה לְמַעַן שְׁמֶךָ
כִּי גוֹאֵל חָזָק אָתָּה.
בָּרוּךְ אַתָּה יהוה, גּוֹאֵל יִשְׂרָאֵל.

ANI TEFILLA • אני תפילה

I recall once when I was younger, at the end of a shabbaton, a Shabbat-long gathering for students my age, that someone came over to me and wished me a good week and asked me what I had learned over the course of the Shabbat. I was a little caught off guard and

HEALING

רְפָאֵנוּ Heal us, LORD, and we shall be healed.
Save us and we shall be saved, for You are our praise.
Bring complete recovery for all our ailments,

The following prayer for a sick person may be said here:
May it be Your will, O LORD my God and God of my ancestors, that You speedily send a complete recovery from heaven, a healing of both soul and body, to the patient (*name*), son/daughter of (*mother's name*) among the other afflicted of Israel.

for You, God, King, are a faithful and compassionate Healer.
Blessed are You, LORD,
Healer of the sick of His people Israel.

PROSPERITY

The phrase "Grant dew and rain as a blessing" is said from December 4th (in the year before a civil leap year, December 5th) until Pesaḥ. In Israel, it is said from the 7th of Marḥeshvan. The phrase "Grant blessing" is said from Ḥol HaMo'ed Pesaḥ until December 3rd (in the year before a civil leap year, December 4th). In Israel it is said through the 6th of Marḥeshvan.

בָּרֵךְ Bless this year for us, LORD our God,
and all its types of produce for good.

In winter: Grant dew and rain as a blessing
In other seasons: Grant blessing

on the face of the earth, and from its goodness satisfy us,
blessing our year as the best of years.
Blessed are You, LORD, who blesses the years.

INGATHERING OF EXILES

תְּקַע Sound the great shofar for our freedom,
raise high the banner to gather our exiles,
and gather us together
from the four quarters of the earth.
Blessed are You, LORD,
who gathers the dispersed of His people Israel.

רפואה

רְפָאֵנוּ יהוה וְנֵרָפֵא
הוֹשִׁיעֵנוּ וְנִוָּשֵׁעָה, כִּי תְהִלָּתֵנוּ אָתָּה
וְהַעֲלֵה רְפוּאָה שְׁלֵמָה לְכָל מַכּוֹתֵינוּ

The following prayer for a sick person may be said here:

יְהִי רָצוֹן מִלְּפָנֶיךָ יהוה אֱלֹהַי וֵאלֹהֵי אֲבוֹתַי, שֶׁתִּשְׁלַח מְהֵרָה רְפוּאָה שְׁלֵמָה
מִן הַשָּׁמַיִם רְפוּאַת הַנֶּפֶשׁ וּרְפוּאַת הַגּוּף לַחוֹלֶה/לַחוֹלָה *name of patient*
בֶּן/בַּת *mother's name* בְּתוֹךְ שְׁאָר חוֹלֵי יִשְׂרָאֵל.

כִּי אֵל מֶלֶךְ רוֹפֵא נֶאֱמָן וְרַחֲמָן אָתָּה.
בָּרוּךְ אַתָּה יהוה, רוֹפֵא חוֹלֵי עַמּוֹ יִשְׂרָאֵל.

ברכת השנים

The phrase וְתֵן טַל וּמָטָר לִבְרָכָה *is said from December 4th (in the year before a civil leap year, December 5th) until* פסח*. In* ארץ ישראל*, it is said from* ז׳ מרחשון*. The phrase* וְתֵן בְּרָכָה *is said from* חול המועד פסח *until December 3rd (in the year before a civil leap year, December 4th). In* ארץ ישראל *it is said through* ו׳ מרחשון*.*

בָּרֵךְ עָלֵינוּ יהוה אֱלֹהֵינוּ אֶת הַשָּׁנָה הַזֹּאת
וְאֶת כָּל מִינֵי תְבוּאָתָהּ, לְטוֹבָה
בחורף: וְתֵן טַל וּמָטָר לִבְרָכָה / בקיץ: וְתֵן בְּרָכָה
עַל פְּנֵי הָאֲדָמָה, וְשַׂבְּעֵנוּ מִטּוּבָהּ
וּבָרֵךְ שְׁנָתֵנוּ כַּשָּׁנִים הַטּוֹבוֹת.
בָּרוּךְ אַתָּה יהוה, מְבָרֵךְ הַשָּׁנִים.

קבוץ גלויות

תְּקַע בְּשׁוֹפָר גָּדוֹל לְחֵרוּתֵנוּ, וְשָׂא נֵס לְקַבֵּץ גָּלֻיּוֹתֵינוּ
וְקַבְּצֵנוּ יַחַד מֵאַרְבַּע כַּנְפוֹת הָאָרֶץ.
בָּרוּךְ אַתָּה יהוה, מְקַבֵּץ נִדְחֵי עַמּוֹ יִשְׂרָאֵל.

JUSTICE

הָשִׁיבָה Restore our judges as at first,
and our counselors as at the beginning,
and remove from us sorrow and sighing.
May You alone, LORD, reign over us
with loving-kindness and compassion,
and vindicate us in justice.
Blessed are You, LORD,
the King who loves righteousness and justice.
/ *Between Rosh HaShana & Yom Kippur, end the blessing:* the King of justice./

AGAINST INFORMERS

וְלַמַּלְשִׁינִים For the slanderers let there be no hope,
and may all wickedness perish in an instant.
May all Your people's enemies swiftly be cut down.
May You swiftly uproot, crush, cast down
and humble the arrogant swiftly in our days.
Blessed are You, LORD,
who destroys enemies and humbles the arrogant.

THE RIGHTEOUS

עַל הַצַּדִּיקִים To the righteous, the pious,
the elders of Your people the house of Israel,
the remnant of their scholars,
the righteous converts, and to us,
may Your compassion be aroused, LORD our God.
Grant a good reward to all who sincerely trust in Your name.
Set our lot with them,
so that we may never be ashamed,
for in You we trust.
Blessed are You, LORD,
who is the support and trust of the righteous.

השבת המשפט

הָשִׁיבָה שׁוֹפְטֵינוּ כְּבָרִאשׁוֹנָה וְיוֹעֲצֵינוּ כְּבַתְּחִלָּה
וְהָסֵר מִמֶּנּוּ יָגוֹן וַאֲנָחָה
וּמְלֹךְ עָלֵינוּ אַתָּה יהוה לְבַדְּךָ בְּחֶסֶד וּבְרַחֲמִים
וְצַדְּקֵנוּ בַּמִּשְׁפָּט.
בָּרוּךְ אַתָּה יהוה
מֶלֶךְ אוֹהֵב צְדָקָה וּמִשְׁפָּט. / בעשרת ימי תשובה: הַמֶּלֶךְ הַמִּשְׁפָּט./

ברכת המינים

וְלַמַּלְשִׁינִים אַל תְּהִי תִקְוָה
וְכָל הָרִשְׁעָה כְּרֶגַע תֹּאבֵד
וְכָל אוֹיְבֵי עַמְּךָ מְהֵרָה יִכָּרֵתוּ
וְהַזֵּדִים מְהֵרָה תְעַקֵּר וּתְשַׁבֵּר וּתְמַגֵּר וְתַכְנִיעַ בִּמְהֵרָה בְיָמֵינוּ.
בָּרוּךְ אַתָּה יהוה, שׁוֹבֵר אוֹיְבִים וּמַכְנִיעַ זֵדִים.

על הצדיקים

עַל הַצַּדִּיקִים וְעַל הַחֲסִידִים
וְעַל זִקְנֵי עַמְּךָ בֵּית יִשְׂרָאֵל
וְעַל פְּלֵיטַת סוֹפְרֵיהֶם
וְעַל גֵּרֵי הַצֶּדֶק, וְעָלֵינוּ
יֶהֱמוּ רַחֲמֶיךָ יהוה אֱלֹהֵינוּ
וְתֵן שָׂכָר טוֹב לְכָל הַבּוֹטְחִים בְּשִׁמְךָ בֶּאֱמֶת
וְשִׂים חֶלְקֵנוּ עִמָּהֶם
וּלְעוֹלָם לֹא נֵבוֹשׁ כִּי בְךָ בָטָחְנוּ.
בָּרוּךְ אַתָּה יהוה, מִשְׁעָן וּמִבְטָח לַצַּדִּיקִים.

REBUILDING JERUSALEM

וְלִירוּשָׁלַיִם To Jerusalem, Your city, may You return in compassion,
and may You dwell in it as You promised.
May You rebuild it rapidly in our days as an everlasting structure,
and install within it soon the throne of David.
Blessed are You, Lord,
who builds Jerusalem.

KINGDOM OF DAVID

אֶת צֶמַח May the offshoot of Your servant David soon flower,
and may his pride be raised high by Your salvation,
for we wait for Your salvation all day.
Blessed are You, Lord,
who makes the glory of salvation flourish.

RESPONSE TO PRAYER

שְׁמַע קוֹלֵנוּ Listen to our voice, Lord our God.
Spare us and have compassion on us,
and in compassion and favor accept our prayer,
for You, God, listen to prayers and pleas.
Do not turn us away, O our King,
empty-handed from Your presence,*
for You listen with compassion
to the prayer of Your people Israel.
Blessed are You, Lord, who listens to prayer.

At this point, in times of drought in Israel, say "And answer us" on page 732.

TEMPLE SERVICE

רְצֵה Find favor, Lord our God,
in Your people Israel and their prayer.
Restore the service to Your most holy House,
and accept in love and favor
the fire-offerings of Israel and their prayer.
May the service of Your people Israel always find favor with You.

בניין ירושלים

וְלִירוּשָׁלַיִם עִירְךָ בְּרַחֲמִים תָּשׁוּב
וְתִשְׁכֹּן בְּתוֹכָהּ כַּאֲשֶׁר דִּבַּרְתָּ
וּבְנֵה אוֹתָהּ בְּקָרוֹב בְּיָמֵינוּ בִּנְיַן עוֹלָם
וְכִסֵּא דָוִד מְהֵרָה לְתוֹכָהּ תָּכִין.
בָּרוּךְ אַתָּה יהוה, בּוֹנֵה יְרוּשָׁלָיִם.

משיח בן דוד

אֶת צֶמַח דָּוִד עַבְדְּךָ מְהֵרָה תַצְמִיחַ, וְקַרְנוֹ תָּרוּם בִּישׁוּעָתֶךָ
כִּי לִישׁוּעָתְךָ קִוִּינוּ כָּל הַיּוֹם.
בָּרוּךְ אַתָּה יהוה, מַצְמִיחַ קֶרֶן יְשׁוּעָה.

שומע תפילה

שְׁמַע קוֹלֵנוּ יהוה אֱלֹהֵינוּ
חוּס וְרַחֵם עָלֵינוּ
וְקַבֵּל בְּרַחֲמִים וּבְרָצוֹן אֶת תְּפִלָּתֵנוּ
כִּי אֵל שׁוֹמֵעַ תְּפִלּוֹת וְתַחֲנוּנִים אָתָּה
וּמִלְּפָנֶיךָ מַלְכֵּנוּ רֵיקָם אַל תְּשִׁיבֵנוּ*
כִּי אַתָּה שׁוֹמֵעַ תְּפִלַּת עַמְּךָ יִשְׂרָאֵל בְּרַחֲמִים.
בָּרוּךְ אַתָּה יהוה, שׁוֹמֵעַ תְּפִלָּה.

At this point, in times of drought in ארץ ישראל, say וַעֲנֵנוּ on page 733.

עבודה

רְצֵה יהוה אֱלֹהֵינוּ בְּעַמְּךָ יִשְׂרָאֵל וּבִתְפִלָּתָם
וְהָשֵׁב אֶת הָעֲבוֹדָה לִדְבִיר בֵּיתֶךָ
וְאִשֵּׁי יִשְׂרָאֵל וּתְפִלָּתָם בְּאַהֲבָה תְקַבֵּל בְּרָצוֹן
וּתְהִי לְרָצוֹן תָּמִיד עֲבוֹדַת יִשְׂרָאֵל עַמֶּךָ.

On Rosh Ḥodesh and Ḥol HaMo'ed, say:

אֱלֹהֵינוּ Our God and God of our ancestors, may there rise, come, reach, appear, be favored, heard, regarded and remembered before You, our recollection and remembrance, as well as the remembrance of our ancestors, and of the Messiah son of David Your servant, and of Jerusalem Your holy city, and of all Your people the house of Israel – for deliverance and well-being, grace, loving-kindness and compassion, life and peace, on this day of:

On Rosh Ḥodesh: Rosh Ḥodesh.
On Pesaḥ: the Festival of Matzot.
On Sukkot: the Festival of Sukkot.

On it remember us, LORD our God, for good; recollect us for blessing, and deliver us for life. In accord with Your promise of salvation and compassion, spare us and be gracious to us; have compassion on us and deliver us, for our eyes are turned to You because You, God, are a gracious and compassionate King.

וְתֶחֱזֶינָה And may our eyes witness Your return
to Zion in compassion.
Blessed are You, LORD, who restores His Presence to Zion.

THANKSGIVING

▾*Bow:* We give thanks[1] to You,
for You are *Stand straight*
the LORD our God and God of our ancestors
for ever and all time.
You are the Rock of our lives,
Shield of our salvation from generation to generation.
We will thank You and declare Your praise for our lives,
which are entrusted into Your hand;
for our souls, which are placed in Your charge;
for Your miracles which are with us every day;
and for Your wonders and favors at all times,
evening, morning and midday.
You are good – for Your compassion never fails.
You are compassionate – for Your loving-kindnesses never cease.
We have always placed our hope in You.

On ראש חודש *and* חול המועד*, say:*

אֱלֹהֵינוּ וֵאלֹהֵי אֲבוֹתֵינוּ, יַעֲלֶה וְיָבוֹא וְיַגִּיעַ, וְיֵרָאֶה וְיֵרָצֶה וְיִשָּׁמַע, וְיִפָּקֵד וְיִזָּכֵר זִכְרוֹנֵנוּ וּפִקְדוֹנֵנוּ וְזִכְרוֹן אֲבוֹתֵינוּ, וְזִכְרוֹן מָשִׁיחַ בֶּן דָּוִד עַבְדֶּךָ, וְזִכְרוֹן יְרוּשָׁלַיִם עִיר קָדְשֶׁךָ, וְזִכְרוֹן כָּל עַמְּךָ בֵּית יִשְׂרָאֵל, לְפָנֶיךָ, לִפְלֵיטָה לְטוֹבָה, לְחֵן וּלְחֶסֶד וּלְרַחֲמִים, לְחַיִּים וּלְשָׁלוֹם בְּיוֹם

בראש חודש: **רֹאשׁ הַחֹדֶשׁ** / בפסח: **חַג הַמַּצּוֹת** / בסוכות: **חַג הַסֻּכּוֹת**

הַזֶּה. זָכְרֵנוּ יהוה אֱלֹהֵינוּ בּוֹ לְטוֹבָה, וּפָקְדֵנוּ בוֹ לִבְרָכָה, וְהוֹשִׁיעֵנוּ בוֹ לְחַיִּים. וּבִדְבַר יְשׁוּעָה וְרַחֲמִים, חוּס וְחָנֵּנוּ וְרַחֵם עָלֵינוּ וְהוֹשִׁיעֵנוּ, כִּי אֵלֶיךָ עֵינֵינוּ, כִּי אֵל מֶלֶךְ חַנּוּן וְרַחוּם אָתָּה.

וְתֶחֱזֶינָה עֵינֵינוּ בְּשׁוּבְךָ לְצִיּוֹן בְּרַחֲמִים.
בָּרוּךְ אַתָּה יהוה, הַמַּחֲזִיר שְׁכִינָתוֹ לְצִיּוֹן.

הודאה

▾ *Bow* מוֹדִים ע אֲנַחְנוּ לָךְ
שָׁאַתָּה הוּא *Stand straight*
יהוה אֱלֹהֵינוּ וֵאלֹהֵי אֲבוֹתֵינוּ לְעוֹלָם וָעֶד.
צוּר חַיֵּינוּ, מָגֵן יִשְׁעֵנוּ אַתָּה הוּא לְדוֹר וָדוֹר.
נוֹדֶה לְּךָ וּנְסַפֵּר תְּהִלָּתֶךָ
עַל חַיֵּינוּ הַמְּסוּרִים בְּיָדֶךָ
וְעַל נִשְׁמוֹתֵינוּ הַפְּקוּדוֹת לָךְ
וְעַל נִסֶּיךָ שֶׁבְּכָל יוֹם עִמָּנוּ
וְעַל נִפְלְאוֹתֶיךָ וְטוֹבוֹתֶיךָ
שֶׁבְּכָל עֵת, עֶרֶב וָבֹקֶר וְצָהֳרָיִם.
הַטּוֹב, כִּי לֹא כָלוּ רַחֲמֶיךָ, וְהַמְרַחֵם, כִּי לֹא תַמּוּ חֲסָדֶיךָ
מֵעוֹלָם קִוִּינוּ לָךְ.

On Ḥanukka:

עַל הַנִּסִּים [We thank You also] for the miracles, the redemption, the mighty deeds, the salvations, and the victories in battle which You performed for our ancestors in those days, at this time.

בִּימֵי מַתִּתְיָהוּ In the days of Mattityahu, son of Yoḥanan, the High Priest, the Hasmonean, and his sons, the wicked Greek kingdom rose up against Your people Israel to make them forget Your Torah and to force them to transgress the statutes of Your will. It was then that You in Your great compassion stood by them in the time of their distress. You championed their cause, judged their claim, and avenged their wrong. You delivered the strong into the hands of the weak, the many into the hands of the few, the impure into the hands of the pure, the wicked into the hands of the righteous, and the arrogant into the hands of those who were engaged in the study of Your Torah. You made for Yourself great and holy renown in Your world, and for Your people Israel You performed a great salvation and redemption as of this very day. Your children then entered the holiest part of Your House, cleansed Your Temple, purified Your Sanctuary, kindled lights in Your holy courts, and designated these eight days of Ḥanukka for giving thanks and praise to Your great name.

Continue with "For all these things."

On Purim:

עַל הַנִּסִּים [We thank You also] for the miracles, the redemption, the mighty deeds, the salvations, and the victories in battle which You performed for our ancestors in those days at this time.

בִּימֵי מָרְדְּכַי In the days of Mordekhai and Esther, in Shushan the capital, the wicked Haman rose up against them and sought to destroy, slay and exterminate *Esther 3*
all the Jews, young and old, children and women, on one day, the thirteenth day of the twelfth month, which is the month of Adar, and to plunder their possessions. Then You in Your great compassion thwarted his counsel, frustrated his plans, and caused his scheme to recoil on his own head, so that they hanged him and his sons on the gallows.

Continue with "For all these things."

וְעַל כֻּלָּם For all these things may Your name be blessed and exalted, our King, continually, for ever and all time.

These words are added between Rosh HaShana & Yom Kippur:	And write, for a good life, all the children of Your covenant.

Let all that lives thank You, Selah! and praise Your name in truth, God, our Savior and Help, Selah!

▾*Bend the knees:* Blessed *Bow:* are You, *Stand straight:* LORD, whose name is "the Good" and to whom thanks are due.

בחנוכה:

עַל הַנִּסִּים וְעַל הַפֻּרְקָן וְעַל הַגְּבוּרוֹת וְעַל הַתְּשׁוּעוֹת וְעַל הַמִּלְחָמוֹת שֶׁעָשִׂיתָ לַאֲבוֹתֵינוּ בַּיָּמִים הָהֵם בַּזְּמַן הַזֶּה.

בִּימֵי מַתִּתְיָהוּ בֶּן יוֹחָנָן כֹּהֵן גָּדוֹל חַשְׁמוֹנַאי וּבָנָיו, כְּשֶׁעָמְדָה מַלְכוּת יָוָן הָרְשָׁעָה עַל עַמְּךָ יִשְׂרָאֵל לְהַשְׁכִּיחָם תּוֹרָתֶךָ וּלְהַעֲבִירָם מֵחֻקֵּי רְצוֹנֶךָ, וְאַתָּה בְּרַחֲמֶיךָ הָרַבִּים עָמַדְתָּ לָהֶם בְּעֵת צָרָתָם, רַבְתָּ אֶת רִיבָם, דַּנְתָּ אֶת דִּינָם, נָקַמְתָּ אֶת נִקְמָתָם, מָסַרְתָּ גִבּוֹרִים בְּיַד חַלָּשִׁים, וְרַבִּים בְּיַד מְעַטִּים, וּטְמֵאִים בְּיַד טְהוֹרִים, וּרְשָׁעִים בְּיַד צַדִּיקִים, וְזֵדִים בְּיַד עוֹסְקֵי תוֹרָתֶךָ, וּלְךָ עָשִׂיתָ שֵׁם גָּדוֹל וְקָדוֹשׁ בְּעוֹלָמֶךָ, וּלְעַמְּךָ יִשְׂרָאֵל עָשִׂיתָ תְּשׁוּעָה גְדוֹלָה וּפֻרְקָן כְּהַיּוֹם הַזֶּה. וְאַחַר כֵּן בָּאוּ בָנֶיךָ לִדְבִיר בֵּיתֶךָ, וּפִנּוּ אֶת הֵיכָלֶךָ, וְטִהֲרוּ אֶת מִקְדָּשֶׁךָ, וְהִדְלִיקוּ נֵרוֹת בְּחַצְרוֹת קָדְשֶׁךָ, וְקָבְעוּ שְׁמוֹנַת יְמֵי חֲנֻכָּה אֵלּוּ, לְהוֹדוֹת וּלְהַלֵּל לְשִׁמְךָ הַגָּדוֹל.

Continue with וְעַל כֻּלָּם.

בפורים:

עַל הַנִּסִּים וְעַל הַפֻּרְקָן וְעַל הַגְּבוּרוֹת וְעַל הַתְּשׁוּעוֹת וְעַל הַמִּלְחָמוֹת שֶׁעָשִׂיתָ לַאֲבוֹתֵינוּ בַּיָּמִים הָהֵם בַּזְּמַן הַזֶּה.

בִּימֵי מָרְדְּכַי וְאֶסְתֵּר בְּשׁוּשַׁן הַבִּירָה, כְּשֶׁעָמַד עֲלֵיהֶם הָמָן הָרָשָׁע, בִּקֵּשׁ
לְהַשְׁמִיד לַהֲרֹג וּלְאַבֵּד אֶת־כָּל־הַיְּהוּדִים מִנַּעַר וְעַד־זָקֵן טַף וְנָשִׁים בְּיוֹם אסתר ג
אֶחָד, בִּשְׁלוֹשָׁה עָשָׂר לְחֹדֶשׁ שְׁנֵים־עָשָׂר, הוּא־חֹדֶשׁ אֲדָר, וּשְׁלָלָם לָבוֹז: וְאַתָּה בְּרַחֲמֶיךָ הָרַבִּים הֵפַרְתָּ אֶת עֲצָתוֹ, וְקִלְקַלְתָּ אֶת מַחֲשַׁבְתּוֹ, וַהֲשֵׁבוֹתָ לּוֹ גְּמוּלוֹ בְּרֹאשׁוֹ, וְתָלוּ אוֹתוֹ וְאֶת בָּנָיו עַל הָעֵץ.

Continue with וְעַל כֻּלָּם.

וְעַל כֻּלָּם יִתְבָּרַךְ וְיִתְרוֹמַם שִׁמְךָ מַלְכֵּנוּ תָּמִיד לְעוֹלָם וָעֶד.

בעשרת ימי תשובה: וּכְתֹב לְחַיִּים טוֹבִים כָּל בְּנֵי בְרִיתֶךָ.

וְכֹל הַחַיִּים יוֹדְוּךָ סֶּלָה, וִיהַלְלוּ אֶת שִׁמְךָ בֶּאֱמֶת הָאֵל יְשׁוּעָתֵנוּ וְעֶזְרָתֵנוּ סֶלָה.

▾ *Bend the knees* בָּרוּךְ *Bow* אַתָּה *Stand straight* יהוה הַטּוֹב שִׁמְךָ וּלְךָ נָאֶה לְהוֹדוֹת.

PEACE

שָׁלוֹם רָב Grant great peace to Your people Israel for ever,
for You are the sovereign LORD of all peace;
and may it be good in Your eyes
to bless Your people Israel
at every time, at every hour, with Your peace.

These words are added between Rosh HaShana & Yom Kippur:	In the book of life, blessing, peace and prosperity, may we and all Your people the house of Israel be remembered and written before You for a good life, and for peace.*

Blessed are You, LORD, who blesses His people Israel with peace.

**Between Rosh HaShana and Yom Kippur outside Israel, many end the blessing:*
Blessed are You, LORD, who makes peace.

Some say the following verse:
May the words of my mouth and the meditation of my heart *Ps. 19*
find favor before You, LORD, my Rock and Redeemer.

אֱלֹהַי My God, *Berakhot 17a*
guard my tongue from evil
and my lips from deceitful speech.
To those who curse me,
let my soul be silent;
may my soul be to all like the dust.
Open my heart to Your Torah
and let my soul pursue Your commandments.
As for all who plan evil against me,
swiftly thwart their counsel and frustrate their plans.
Act for the sake of Your name;
act for the sake of Your right hand;
act for the sake of Your holiness;
act for the sake of Your Torah.

ברכת שלום

שָׁלוֹם רָב עַל יִשְׂרָאֵל עַמְּךָ תָּשִׂים לְעוֹלָם
כִּי אַתָּה הוּא מֶלֶךְ אָדוֹן לְכָל הַשָּׁלוֹם.
וְטוֹב בְּעֵינֶיךָ לְבָרֵךְ אֶת עַמְּךָ יִשְׂרָאֵל
בְּכָל עֵת וּבְכָל שָׁעָה בִּשְׁלוֹמֶךָ.

בעשרת ימי תשובה: **בְּסֵפֶר חַיִּים, בְּרָכָה וְשָׁלוֹם, וּפַרְנָסָה טוֹבָה**
נִזָּכֵר וְנִכָּתֵב לְפָנֶיךָ, אֲנַחְנוּ וְכָל עַמְּךָ בֵּית יִשְׂרָאֵל
לְחַיִּים טוֹבִים וּלְשָׁלוֹם.*

בָּרוּךְ אַתָּה יהוה, הַמְבָרֵךְ אֶת עַמּוֹ יִשְׂרָאֵל בַּשָּׁלוֹם.

**During the* עשרת ימי תשובה *in* חוץ לארץ*, many end the blessing:*

בָּרוּךְ אַתָּה יהוה, עוֹשֵׂה הַשָּׁלוֹם.

Some say the following verse:

יִהְיוּ לְרָצוֹן אִמְרֵי־פִי וְהֶגְיוֹן לִבִּי לְפָנֶיךָ, יהוה צוּרִי וְגֹאֲלִי: תהלים יט

ברכות יז.

אֱלֹהַי
נְצֹר לְשׁוֹנִי מֵרָע וּשְׂפָתַי מִדַּבֵּר מִרְמָה
וְלִמְקַלְלַי נַפְשִׁי תִדֹּם, וְנַפְשִׁי כֶּעָפָר לַכֹּל תִּהְיֶה.
פְּתַח לִבִּי בְּתוֹרָתֶךָ, וּבְמִצְוֹתֶיךָ תִּרְדֹּף נַפְשִׁי.
וְכָל הַחוֹשְׁבִים עָלַי רָעָה
מְהֵרָה הָפֵר עֲצָתָם וְקַלְקֵל מַחֲשַׁבְתָּם.
עֲשֵׂה לְמַעַן שְׁמֶךָ
עֲשֵׂה לְמַעַן יְמִינֶךָ
עֲשֵׂה לְמַעַן קְדֻשָּׁתֶךָ
עֲשֵׂה לְמַעַן תּוֹרָתֶךָ.

That Your beloved ones may be delivered, *Ps. 60*
save with Your right hand and answer me.
May the words of my mouth *Ps. 19*
and the meditation of my heart find favor before You,
LORD, my Rock and Redeemer.

Bow and take three steps back as if taking leave of the Divine Presence.

Bow left: May He who makes peace in His high places,
Bow right: make peace *Bow forward:* for us and all Israel – and say: Amen.

יְהִי רָצוֹן May it be Your will, LORD our God and God of our ancestors,
that the Temple be rebuilt speedily in our days, and grant us a share in Your Torah.
And there we will serve You with reverence,
as in the days of old and as in former years.
Then the offering of Judah and Jerusalem *Mal. 3*
will be pleasing to the LORD as in the days of old and as in former years.

If Yom Tov falls in the following week,
the service continues with Full Kaddish on page 628.

HALF KADDISH

Leader: יִתְגַּדַּל Magnified and sanctified may His great name be,
in the world He created by His will.
May He establish His kingdom
in your lifetime and in your days,
and in the lifetime of all the house of Israel,
swiftly and soon –
and say: Amen.

All: May His great name be blessed for ever and all time.

Leader: Blessed and praised, glorified and exalted,
raised and honored,
uplifted and lauded be
the name of the Holy One,
blessed be He, beyond any blessing,
song, praise and consolation
uttered in the world –
and say: Amen.

לְמַעַן יֵחָלְצוּן יְדִידֶיךָ, הוֹשִׁיעָה יְמִינְךָ וַעֲנֵנִי: תהלים ס
יִהְיוּ לְרָצוֹן אִמְרֵי־פִי וְהֶגְיוֹן לִבִּי לְפָנֶיךָ, יהוה צוּרִי וְגֹאֲלִי: תהלים יט

Bow and take three steps back as if taking leave of the Divine Presence.

Bow left עֹשֶׂה שָׁלוֹם/ בשבת שובה: הַשָּׁלוֹם/ בִּמְרוֹמָיו
Bow right הוּא יַעֲשֶׂה שָׁלוֹם *Bow forward* עָלֵינוּ וְעַל כָּל יִשְׂרָאֵל
וְאִמְרוּ אָמֵן.

יְהִי רָצוֹן מִלְּפָנֶיךָ יהוה אֱלֹהֵינוּ וֵאלֹהֵי אֲבוֹתֵינוּ
שֶׁיִּבָּנֶה בֵּית הַמִּקְדָּשׁ בִּמְהֵרָה בְיָמֵינוּ, וְתֵן חֶלְקֵנוּ בְּתוֹרָתֶךָ
וְשָׁם נַעֲבָדְךָ בְּיִרְאָה כִּימֵי עוֹלָם וּכְשָׁנִים קַדְמֹנִיּוֹת.
וְעָרְבָה לַיהוה מִנְחַת יְהוּדָה וִירוּשָׁלָםִ כִּימֵי עוֹלָם וּכְשָׁנִים קַדְמֹנִיּוֹת: מלאכי ג

If יום טוב *falls in the following week, the service continues with* קדיש שלם *on page 629.*

חצי קדיש

ש״ץ: יִתְגַּדַּל וְיִתְקַדַּשׁ שְׁמֵהּ רַבָּא (קהל: אָמֵן)
בְּעָלְמָא דִּי בְרָא כִרְעוּתֵהּ
וְיַמְלִיךְ מַלְכוּתֵהּ
בְּחַיֵּיכוֹן וּבְיוֹמֵיכוֹן וּבְחַיֵּי דְכָל בֵּית יִשְׂרָאֵל
בַּעֲגָלָא וּבִזְמַן קָרִיב, וְאִמְרוּ אָמֵן. (קהל: אָמֵן)

קהל וש״ץ: יְהֵא שְׁמֵהּ רַבָּא מְבָרַךְ לְעָלַם וּלְעָלְמֵי עָלְמַיָּא.

ש״ץ: יִתְבָּרַךְ וְיִשְׁתַּבַּח וְיִתְפָּאַר וְיִתְרוֹמַם וְיִתְנַשֵּׂא
וְיִתְהַדָּר וְיִתְעַלֶּה וְיִתְהַלָּל
שְׁמֵהּ דְּקֻדְשָׁא בְּרִיךְ הוּא (קהל: בְּרִיךְ הוּא)
לְעֵלָּא מִן כָּל בִּרְכָתָא /בעשרת ימי תשובה: לְעֵלָּא לְעֵלָּא מִכָּל בִּרְכָתָא/
וְשִׁירָתָא, תֻּשְׁבְּחָתָא וְנֶחֱמָתָא
דַּאֲמִירָן בְּעָלְמָא, וְאִמְרוּ אָמֵן. (קהל: אָמֵן)

These paragraphs are not recited when Yom Tov is scheduled to take place during the coming week. In part, this is because it is not a full work week but, as well, it is hoped that the upcoming festival will serve as protection enough.

וִיהִי נֹעַם May the pleasantness[B] of the LORD our God be upon us. Establish for us the work of our hands, O establish the work of our hands. *Ps. 90*

יֹשֵׁב He who lives in the shelter of the Most High[I] dwells in the shadow of the Almighty. I say of the LORD, my Refuge and Stronghold, my God in whom I trust, that He will save you from the fowler's snare and the deadly pestilence. With His pinions He will cover you, and beneath His wings you will find shelter; His faithfulness is an encircling shield. You need not fear terror by night, nor the arrow that flies by day; not the pestilence that stalks in darkness, nor the plague that ravages at noon. A thousand may fall at your side, ten thousand at your right hand, but it will not come near you. You will only look with your eyes and see the punishment of the wicked. Because you said, "The LORD is my Refuge," taking the Most High as your shelter, no harm will befall you, no plague come near your tent, for He will command His angels about you, to guard you in all your ways. They will lift you in their hands, lest your foot stumble on a stone. You will tread on lions and vipers; you will trample on young lions and snakes. [God says:] "Because he loves Me, I will rescue him; I will protect him, because he acknowledges My name. When he calls on Me, I will answer him; I will be with him in distress, I will deliver him and bring him honor. *Ps. 91*
▸ With long life I will satisfy him and show him My salvation.
With long life I will satisfy him and show him My salvation.

---

as the warmth and peace of Shabbat begin to ebb away, there can be a rising feeling of anxiety and concern about the week ahead, the challenges, the trials, the work that has yet to be completed. We can feel more vulnerable than we did during the past 25 hours and that is an invitation to recall that we still need Hashem to watch over us.

ANI TEFILLA • אני תפילה

A group of women in a Bible study were puzzled by the quote in Malakhi 3:3, "He shall sit as a refiner and purifier of silver...." So one woman offered to find a silversmith

This **ANI TEFILLA** *continues on page 625.*

These paragraphs are not recited when יום טוב *is scheduled to take place during the coming week. In part, this is because it is not a full work week but, as well, it is hoped that the upcoming festival will serve as protection enough.*

תהלים צ וִיהִי נֹעַם אֲדֹנָי אֱלֹהֵינוּ עָלֵינוּ וּמַעֲשֵׂה יָדֵינוּ כּוֹנְנָה עָלֵינוּ וּמַעֲשֵׂה יָדֵינוּ כּוֹנְנֵהוּ:

תהלים צא יֹשֵׁב בְּסֵתֶר עֶלְיוֹן, בְּצֵל שַׁדַּי יִתְלוֹנָן: אֹמַר לַיהוה מַחְסִי וּמְצוּדָתִי, אֱלֹהַי אֶבְטַח־בּוֹ: כִּי הוּא יַצִּילְךָ מִפַּח יָקוּשׁ, מִדֶּבֶר הַוּוֹת: בְּאֶבְרָתוֹ יָסֶךְ לָךְ, וְתַחַת־כְּנָפָיו תֶּחְסֶה, צִנָּה וְסֹחֵרָה אֲמִתּוֹ: לֹא־תִירָא מִפַּחַד לָיְלָה, מֵחֵץ יָעוּף יוֹמָם: מִדֶּבֶר בָּאֹפֶל יַהֲלֹךְ, מִקֶּטֶב יָשׁוּד צָהֳרָיִם: יִפֹּל מִצִּדְּךָ אֶלֶף, וּרְבָבָה מִימִינֶךָ, אֵלֶיךָ לֹא יִגָּשׁ: רַק בְּעֵינֶיךָ תַבִּיט, וְשִׁלֻּמַת רְשָׁעִים תִּרְאֶה: כִּי־אַתָּה יהוה מַחְסִי, עֶלְיוֹן שַׂמְתָּ מְעוֹנֶךָ: לֹא־תְאֻנֶּה אֵלֶיךָ רָעָה, וְנֶגַע לֹא־יִקְרַב בְּאָהֳלֶךָ: כִּי מַלְאָכָיו יְצַוֶּה־לָּךְ, לִשְׁמָרְךָ בְּכָל־דְּרָכֶיךָ: עַל־כַּפַּיִם יִשָּׂאוּנְךָ, פֶּן־תִּגֹּף בָּאֶבֶן רַגְלֶךָ: עַל־שַׁחַל וָפֶתֶן תִּדְרֹךְ, תִּרְמֹס כְּפִיר וְתַנִּין: כִּי בִי חָשַׁק וַאֲפַלְּטֵהוּ, אֲשַׂגְּבֵהוּ כִּי־יָדַע שְׁמִי: יִקְרָאֵנִי וְאֶעֱנֵהוּ, עִמּוֹ אָנֹכִי בְצָרָה, אֲחַלְּצֵהוּ וַאֲכַבְּדֵהוּ:
◂ אֹרֶךְ יָמִים אַשְׂבִּיעֵהוּ, וְאַרְאֵהוּ בִּישׁוּעָתִי:
אֹרֶךְ יָמִים אַשְׂבִּיעֵהוּ, וְאַרְאֵהוּ בִּישׁוּעָתִי:

BIUR TEFILLA • ביאור תפילה

וִיהִי נֹעַם – *May the pleasantness.* This particular line is said to have been the verse which Moshe used to bless Israel after they had completed the building of the Tabernacle (*Mishkan*) in the desert (*Torat Kohanim Shemini,* and Rashi *Shemot* 39:43). In any event, the implication is perhaps that Hashem lend our work week the pleasantness and satisfaction that comes from successfully completing one's work. **What are your goals for this coming work week?**

IYUN TEFILLA • עיון תפילה

יֹשֵׁב בְּסֵתֶר עֶלְיוֹן – *He who lives in the shelter of the Most High.*

See the commentary on this psalm in *Pesukei DeZimra* page 241.).

It is recited here as a prayer for Hashem's protection during the coming week. Almost inevitably,

You are the Holy One,[B] enthroned on the praises of Israel. *Ps. 22*
And [the angels] call to one another, saying,
"Holy, holy, holy is the LORD of hosts; *Is. 6*
the whole world is filled with His glory."

And they receive permission from one another, saying: *Targum Yonatan Is. 6*
"Holy in the highest heavens, home of His Presence;
holy on earth, the work of His strength;
holy for ever and all time is the LORD of hosts;
the whole earth is full of His radiant glory."

▸ Then a wind lifted me up *Ezek. 3*
and I heard behind me the sound of a great noise, saying,
"Blessed is the LORD's glory from His place."

Then a wind lifted me up and I heard behind me *Targum Yonatan Ezek. 3*
the sound of a great tempest of those who uttered praise, saying,
"Blessed is the LORD's glory from the place
of the home of His Presence."

The LORD shall reign for ever and all time. *Ex. 15*

The LORD's kingdom is established for ever and all time. *Targum Onkelos Ex. 15*

BIUR TEFILLA · ביאור תפילה

וְאַתָּה קָדוֹשׁ – *You are the Holy One.* If in the previous prayer we asked for physical protection during the week ahead, here the emphasis is much more spiritual. Its focus is on holiness and on Torah, the things that should be the animating forces of our physical lives during the week. These, too, have been a focal point this past Shabbat. How will I carry them into my week even in some small new way?

The prayer appeared as well in the *Minḥa* service on Shabbat afternoon and in the weekday siddur at the conclusion of the service. See our commentaries there for the history and function of this prayer. Suffice it to say here that the other versions contain lines which speak to the concepts of redemption (וּבָא לְצִיּוֹן) and the covenant (וַאֲנִי זֹאת בְּרִיתִי) which do not fit into the theme here of spirituality that we wish to carry into our week (Munk cf. Tur 295).

תהלים כב
וְאַתָּה קָדוֹשׁ יוֹשֵׁב תְּהִלּוֹת יִשְׂרָאֵל:
וְקָרָא זֶה אֶל־זֶה וְאָמַר

ישעיה ו
קָדוֹשׁ, קָדוֹשׁ, קָדוֹשׁ, יהוה צְבָאוֹת, מְלֹא כָל־הָאָרֶץ כְּבוֹדוֹ:

תרגום יונתן ישעיה ו
וּמְקַבְּלִין דֵּין מִן דֵּין וְאָמְרִין
קַדִּישׁ בִּשְׁמֵי מְרוֹמָא עִלָּאָה בֵּית שְׁכִינְתֵהּ
קַדִּישׁ עַל אַרְעָא עוֹבַד גְּבוּרְתֵהּ
קַדִּישׁ לְעָלַם וּלְעָלְמֵי עָלְמַיָּא
יהוה צְבָאוֹת, מַלְיָא כָל אַרְעָא זִיו יְקָרֵהּ.

יחזקאל ג
וַתִּשָּׂאֵנִי רוּחַ, וָאֶשְׁמַע אַחֲרַי קוֹל רַעַשׁ גָּדוֹל
בָּרוּךְ כְּבוֹד־יהוה מִמְּקוֹמוֹ:

תרגום יונתן יחזקאל ג
וּנְטָלַתְנִי רוּחָא, וּשְׁמָעִית בַּתְרַי קָל זִיעַ סַגִּיא
דִּמְשַׁבְּחִין וְאָמְרִין
בְּרִיךְ יְקָרָא דַיהוה מֵאֲתַר בֵּית שְׁכִינְתֵהּ.

שמות טו
יהוה יִמְלֹךְ לְעֹלָם וָעֶד:

תרגום אונקלוס שמות טו
יהוה מַלְכוּתֵהּ קָאֵם לְעָלַם וּלְעָלְמֵי עָלְמַיָּא.

---

and seek clarification. She found a silversmith who would let her observe the process of refining silver and on the appointed day, she watched him holding a piece of silver over the fire and letting it heat up. He explained that refining meant holding the silver over the hottest part of the flame so as to burn away all the impurities. The woman grasped the significance of God holding us over the fire at times to burn away our impurities. But again the question the group began with, why the "He shall sit as a refiner and purifier of silver"? So she questioned the silversmith if it was necessary that he sit in front of the fire the whole time the refining was taking place "Oh, yes", he responded, "not only do I need to sit before the process but I must keep my eye on the silver the entire time – for if left in the fire a moment too long, the silver is destroyed. The woman now understood God watching as our refining took place – not wanting us to be destroyed in the process "But how do you know the exact moment of purification," she asked. Smiling, he responded, "Oh, that's easy, when I see my image in it."

יהוה LORD, God of Abraham, Isaac and Yisrael, our ancestors, may *1 Chr. 29* You keep this for ever so that it forms the thoughts in Your people's heart, and directs their heart toward You. He is compassionate. He *Ps. 78* forgives iniquity and does not destroy. Repeatedly He suppresses His anger, not rousing His full wrath. For You, my LORD, are good *Ps. 86* and forgiving, abundantly kind to all who call on You. Your righ- *Ps. 119* teousness is eternally righteous, and Your Torah is truth. Grant *Micah 7* truth to Jacob, loving-kindness to Abraham, as You promised our ancestors in ancient times. Blessed is my LORD for day after day He *Ps. 68* burdens us [with His blessings]; God is our salvation, Selah! The *Ps. 46* LORD of hosts is with us; the God of Jacob is our refuge, Selah! LORD of hosts, happy is the one who trusts in You. LORD, save! *Ps. 84* *Ps. 20* May the King answer us on the day we call.

בָּרוּךְ Blessed is He, our God, who created us for His glory, separating us from those who go astray; who gave us the Torah of truth, planting within us eternal life. May He open our heart to His Torah, imbuing our heart with the love and awe of Him, that we may do His will and serve Him with a perfect heart, so that we neither toil in vain nor give birth to confusion.

יְהִי רָצוֹן May it be Your will, O LORD our God and God of our ancestors, that we keep Your laws in this world, and thus be worthy to live, see and inherit goodness and blessing in the Messianic Age and in the life of the World to Come. So that my soul may sing to You and *Ps. 30* not be silent. LORD, my God, for ever I will thank You. Blessed is *Jer. 17* the man who trusts in the LORD, whose trust is in the LORD alone. Trust in the LORD for evermore, for God, the LORD, is an everlast- *Is. 26* ing Rock. ▸ Those who know Your name trust in You, for You, LORD, *Ps. 9* do not forsake those who seek You. The LORD desired, for the sake *Is. 42* of Israel's merit, to make the Torah great and glorious.

יהוה אֱלֹהֵי אַבְרָהָם יִצְחָק וְיִשְׂרָאֵל אֲבֹתֵינוּ, שָׁמְרָה־זֹּאת (דברי הימים א׳ כט)
לְעוֹלָם לְיֵצֶר מַחְשְׁבוֹת לְבַב עַמֶּךָ, וְהָכֵן לְבָבָם אֵלֶיךָ: וְהוּא (תהלים עח)
רַחוּם יְכַפֵּר עָוֺן וְלֹא־יַשְׁחִית, וְהִרְבָּה לְהָשִׁיב אַפּוֹ, וְלֹא־יָעִיר
כָּל־חֲמָתוֹ: כִּי־אַתָּה אֲדֹנָי טוֹב וְסַלָּח, וְרַב־חֶסֶד לְכָל־קֹרְאֶיךָ: (תהלים פו)
צִדְקָתְךָ צֶדֶק לְעוֹלָם וְתוֹרָתְךָ אֱמֶת: תִּתֵּן אֱמֶת לְיַעֲקֹב, חֶסֶד (תהלים קיט, מיכה ז)
לְאַבְרָהָם, אֲשֶׁר־נִשְׁבַּעְתָּ לַאֲבֹתֵינוּ מִימֵי קֶדֶם: בָּרוּךְ אֲדֹנָי (תהלים סח)
יוֹם יוֹם יַעֲמָס־לָנוּ, הָאֵל יְשׁוּעָתֵנוּ סֶלָה: יהוה צְבָאוֹת עִמָּנוּ, (תהלים מו)
מִשְׂגָּב לָנוּ אֱלֹהֵי יַעֲקֹב סֶלָה: יהוה צְבָאוֹת, אַשְׁרֵי אָדָם בֹּטֵחַ (תהלים פד)
בָּךְ: יהוה הוֹשִׁיעָה, הַמֶּלֶךְ יַעֲנֵנוּ בְיוֹם־קָרְאֵנוּ: (תהלים כ)

בָּרוּךְ הוּא אֱלֹהֵינוּ שֶׁבְּרָאָנוּ לִכְבוֹדוֹ, וְהִבְדִּילָנוּ מִן הַתּוֹעִים, וְנָתַן לָנוּ תּוֹרַת אֱמֶת, וְחַיֵּי עוֹלָם נָטַע בְּתוֹכֵנוּ. הוּא יִפְתַּח לִבֵּנוּ בְּתוֹרָתוֹ, וְיָשֵׂם בְּלִבֵּנוּ אַהֲבָתוֹ וְיִרְאָתוֹ וְלַעֲשׂוֹת רְצוֹנוֹ וּלְעָבְדוֹ בְּלֵבָב שָׁלֵם, לְמַעַן לֹא נִיגַע לָרִיק וְלֹא נֵלֵד לַבֶּהָלָה.

יְהִי רָצוֹן מִלְּפָנֶיךָ יהוה אֱלֹהֵינוּ וֵאלֹהֵי אֲבוֹתֵינוּ, שֶׁנִּשְׁמֹר חֻקֶּיךָ
בָּעוֹלָם הַזֶּה, וְנִזְכֶּה וְנִחְיֶה וְנִרְאֶה וְנִירַשׁ טוֹבָה וּבְרָכָה, לִשְׁנֵי
יְמוֹת הַמָּשִׁיחַ וּלְחַיֵּי הָעוֹלָם הַבָּא. לְמַעַן יְזַמֶּרְךָ כָבוֹד וְלֹא יִדֹּם, (תהלים ל)
יהוה אֱלֹהַי, לְעוֹלָם אוֹדֶךָּ: בָּרוּךְ הַגֶּבֶר אֲשֶׁר יִבְטַח בַּיהוה, (ירמיה יז)
וְהָיָה יהוה מִבְטַחוֹ: בִּטְחוּ בַיהוה עֲדֵי־עַד, כִּי בְּיָהּ יהוה צוּר (ישעיה כו)
עוֹלָמִים: ◂ וְיִבְטְחוּ בְךָ יוֹדְעֵי שְׁמֶךָ, כִּי לֹא־עָזַבְתָּ דֹרְשֶׁיךָ, יהוה: (תהלים ט)
יהוה חָפֵץ לְמַעַן צִדְקוֹ, יַגְדִּיל תּוֹרָה וְיַאְדִּיר: (ישעיה מב)

FULL KADDISH

Leader: יִתְגַּדַּל Magnified and sanctified may His great name be,
in the world He created by His will.
May He establish His kingdom in your lifetime
and in your days,
and in the lifetime of all the house of Israel,
swiftly and soon –
and say: Amen.

All: May His great name be blessed for ever and all time.

Leader: Blessed and praised,
glorified and exalted,
raised and honored,
uplifted and lauded be
the name of the Holy One,
blessed be He,
beyond any blessing,
song, praise and consolation uttered in the world –
and say: Amen.

On Purim and Tisha B'Av, omit the next verse and continue with "May there be great peace."

May the prayers and pleas of all Israel
be accepted by their Father in heaven –
and say: Amen.

May there be great peace from heaven,
and life for us and all Israel –
and say: Amen.

Bow, take three steps back, as if taking leave of the Divine Presence, then bow, first left, then right, then center, while saying:

May He who makes peace in His high places,
make peace for us and all Israel –
and say: Amen.

קדיש שלם

ש״ץ: יִתְגַּדַּל וְיִתְקַדַּשׁ שְׁמֵהּ רַבָּא (קהל: אָמֵן)
בְּעָלְמָא דִּי בְרָא כִרְעוּתֵהּ
וְיַמְלִיךְ מַלְכוּתֵהּ
בְּחַיֵּיכוֹן וּבְיוֹמֵיכוֹן וּבְחַיֵּי דְכָל בֵּית יִשְׂרָאֵל
בַּעֲגָלָא וּבִזְמַן קָרִיב, וְאִמְרוּ אָמֵן. (קהל: אָמֵן)

קהל וש״ץ: יְהֵא שְׁמֵהּ רַבָּא מְבָרַךְ לְעָלַם וּלְעָלְמֵי עָלְמַיָּא.

ש״ץ: יִתְבָּרַךְ וְיִשְׁתַּבַּח וְיִתְפָּאַר
וְיִתְרוֹמַם וְיִתְנַשֵּׂא וְיִתְהַדָּר וְיִתְעַלֶּה וְיִתְהַלָּל
שְׁמֵהּ דְּקֻדְשָׁא בְּרִיךְ הוּא (קהל: בְּרִיךְ הוּא)
לְעֵלָּא מִן כָּל בִּרְכָתָא
/בעשרת ימי תשובה: לְעֵלָּא לְעֵלָּא מִכָּל בִּרְכָתָא/
וְשִׁירָתָא, תֻּשְׁבְּחָתָא וְנֶחֱמָתָא
דַּאֲמִירָן בְּעָלְמָא, וְאִמְרוּ אָמֵן. (קהל: אָמֵן)

On פורים *and* תשעה באב*, omit the next verse and continue with* יְהֵא שְׁלָמָא.

תִּתְקַבַּל צְלוֹתְהוֹן וּבָעוּתְהוֹן דְּכָל יִשְׂרָאֵל
קֳדָם אֲבוּהוֹן דִּי בִשְׁמַיָּא, וְאִמְרוּ אָמֵן. (קהל: אָמֵן)

יְהֵא שְׁלָמָא רַבָּא מִן שְׁמַיָּא
וְחַיִּים, עָלֵינוּ וְעַל כָּל יִשְׂרָאֵל, וְאִמְרוּ אָמֵן. (קהל: אָמֵן)

Bow, take three steps back, as if taking leave of the Divine Presence, then bow, first left, then right, then center, while saying:

עֹשֶׂה שָׁלוֹם/ בעשרת ימי תשובה: הַשָּׁלוֹם/ בִּמְרוֹמָיו
הוּא יַעֲשֶׂה שָׁלוֹם עָלֵינוּ
וְעַל כָּל יִשְׂרָאֵל, וְאִמְרוּ אָמֵן. (קהל: אָמֵן)

Between Pesaḥ and Shavuot the Omer is counted at this point on page 660.

On Ḥanukka, the candles are lit at this point, page 724.

On Tisha B'Av, the following prayers are omitted and the service continues with Aleinu on page 638.

BIBLICAL VERSES OF BLESSING

וְיִתֶּן־לְךָ May God give you[B] dew from heaven and the richness of the earth, and corn and wine in plenty. May peoples serve you and nations bow down to you. Be lord over your brothers, and may your mother's sons bow down to you. A curse on those who curse you, but a blessing on those who bless you. *Gen. 27*

וְאֵל שַׁדַּי May God Almighty bless you; may He make you fruitful and numerous until you become an assembly of peoples. May He give you and your descendants the blessing of Abraham, that you may possess the land where you are now staying, the land God gave to Abraham. This comes from the God of your father – may He help you – and from the Almighty – may He bless you with blessings of the heaven above and the blessings of the deep that lies below, the blessings of breast and womb. The blessings of your father surpass the blessings of my fathers to the bounds of the endless hills. May they rest on the head of Joseph, on the brow of the prince among his brothers. He will love you and bless you and increase your numbers. He will bless the fruit of your womb and the fruit of your land: your corn, your wine and oil, the calves of your herds and the lambs of your flocks, in the land He swore to your fathers to give you. You will be blessed more than any other people. None of your men or women will be childless, nor any of your livestock without young. The Lord will keep you free from any disease. He will not inflict on you the terrible diseases you knew in Egypt, but He will inflict them on those who hate you. *Gen. 28* *Gen. 49* *Deut. 7*

הַמַּלְאָךְ May the angel who rescued me from all harm, bless these boys. May they be called by my name and the names of my fathers Abraham and Isaac, and may they increase greatly on the earth. The Lord your God has increased your numbers so that today you are as many as the stars in the sky. May the Lord, God of your fathers, increase you a thousand times, and bless you as He promised you. *Gen. 48* *Deut. 1*

---

and the land. The subsequent paragraphs contain other blessings for redemption, forgiveness, the absence of shame, the presence of joy, peace and consolation, all worthwhile dreams for the coming week. There is no way to know what the coming days will bring. We can only hope and pray.

What are your hopes and prayers for the coming week?

Between פסח *and* שבועות *the* עומר *is counted at this point on page 661.*

On חנוכה*, the candles are lit at this point, page 725.*

On תשעה באב*, the following prayers are omitted and the service continues with* עָלֵינוּ *on page 639.*

Between פסח *and* שבועות *the* עומר *is counted at this point on page 661.* *On* חנוכה*, the candles are lit at this point, page 725.* *On* תשעה באב*, the following prayers are omitted and the service continues with* עָלֵינוּ *on page 639.*

פסוקי ברכה

וְיִתֶּן־לְךָ הָאֱלֹהִים מִטַּל הַשָּׁמַיִם וּמִשְׁמַנֵּי הָאָרֶץ, וְרֹב דָּגָן וְתִירֹשׁ: יַעַבְדוּךָ עַמִּים וְיִשְׁתַּחֲוֻ לְךָ לְאֻמִּים, הֱוֵה גְבִיר לְאַחֶיךָ וְיִשְׁתַּחֲווּ לְךָ בְּנֵי אִמֶּךָ, אֹרְרֶיךָ אָרוּר וּמְבָרְכֶיךָ בָּרוּךְ: בראשית כז

וְאֵל שַׁדַּי יְבָרֵךְ אֹתְךָ וְיַפְרְךָ וְיַרְבֶּךָ, וְהָיִיתָ לִקְהַל עַמִּים: וְיִתֶּן־לְךָ אֶת־ בראשית כח
בִּרְכַּת אַבְרָהָם, לְךָ וּלְזַרְעֲךָ אִתָּךְ, לְרִשְׁתְּךָ אֶת־אֶרֶץ מְגֻרֶיךָ אֲשֶׁר־נָתַן
אֱלֹהִים לְאַבְרָהָם: מֵאֵל אָבִיךָ וְיַעְזְרֶךָּ וְאֵת שַׁדַּי וִיבָרְכֶךָּ, בִּרְכֹת שָׁמַיִם בראשית מט
מֵעָל בִּרְכֹת תְּהוֹם רֹבֶצֶת תָּחַת, בִּרְכֹת שָׁדַיִם וָרָחַם: בִּרְכֹת אָבִיךָ גָּבְרוּ
עַל־בִּרְכֹת הוֹרַי עַד־תַּאֲוַת גִּבְעֹת עוֹלָם, תִּהְיֶיןָ לְרֹאשׁ יוֹסֵף וּלְקָדְקֹד
נְזִיר אֶחָיו: וַאֲהֵבְךָ וּבֵרַכְךָ וְהִרְבֶּךָ, וּבֵרַךְ פְּרִי־בִטְנְךָ וּפְרִי־אַדְמָתֶךָ, דְּגָנְךָ דברים ז
וְתִירֹשְׁךָ וְיִצְהָרֶךָ, שְׁגַר־אֲלָפֶיךָ וְעַשְׁתְּרֹת צֹאנֶךָ, עַל הָאֲדָמָה אֲשֶׁר־נִשְׁבַּע
לַאֲבֹתֶיךָ לָתֶת לָךְ: בָּרוּךְ תִּהְיֶה מִכָּל־הָעַמִּים, לֹא־יִהְיֶה בְךָ עָקָר וַעֲקָרָה
וּבִבְהֶמְתֶּךָ: וְהֵסִיר יהוה מִמְּךָ כָּל־חֹלִי, וְכָל־מַדְוֵי מִצְרַיִם הָרָעִים אֲשֶׁר
יָדַעְתָּ, לֹא יְשִׂימָם בָּךְ, וּנְתָנָם בְּכָל־שֹׂנְאֶיךָ:

הַמַּלְאָךְ הַגֹּאֵל אֹתִי מִכָּל־רָע יְבָרֵךְ אֶת־הַנְּעָרִים, וְיִקָּרֵא בָהֶם שְׁמִי וְשֵׁם בראשית מח
אֲבֹתַי אַבְרָהָם וְיִצְחָק, וְיִדְגּוּ לָרֹב בְּקֶרֶב הָאָרֶץ: יהוה אֱלֹהֵיכֶם הִרְבָּה דברים א
אֶתְכֶם, וְהִנְּכֶם הַיּוֹם כְּכוֹכְבֵי הַשָּׁמַיִם לָרֹב: יהוה אֱלֹהֵי אֲבוֹתֵיכֶם יֹסֵף
עֲלֵיכֶם כָּכֶם אֶלֶף פְּעָמִים, וִיבָרֵךְ אֶתְכֶם כַּאֲשֶׁר דִּבֶּר לָכֶם:

BIUR TEFILLA • ביאור תפילה

וַיִּתֶּן־לְךָ – *May God give you.* What follows are a series of extra prayers that are added in some congregations. They are blessings for prosperity for the coming week and are drawn from the source, that is to say, from blessings which appear in chronological order in the Torah. It begins with a blessing given by Yitzḥak to Yaakov (*Bereshit* 27), a blessing by Yaakov to Yosef and his brothers (*Bereshit* 49) and a blessing by Moshe to Israel (*Devarim* 7) all referring to the blessings of children

בָּרוּךְ You will be blessed in the city, and blessed in the field. You will be blessed when you come in, and blessed when you go out. Your basket and your kneading trough will be blessed. The fruit of your womb will be blessed, and the crops of your land, and the young of your livestock, the calves of your herds and the lambs of your flocks. The LORD will send a blessing on your barns, and on everything you put your hand to. The LORD your God will bless you in the land He is giving you. The LORD will open for you the heavens, the storehouse of His bounty, to send rain on your land in season, and to bless all the work of your hands. You will lend to many nations but will borrow from none. For the LORD your God will bless you as He has promised: you will lend to many nations but will borrow from none. You will rule over many nations, but none will rule over you. Happy are you, Israel! Who is like you, a people saved by the LORD? He is your Shield and Helper and your glorious Sword. Your enemies will cower before you, and you will tread on their high places. *Deut. 28* *Deut. 15* *Deut. 33*

מָחִיתִי I have wiped away your transgressions like a cloud, your sins like the morning mist. Return to Me for I have redeemed you. Sing for joy, O heavens, for the LORD has done this; shout aloud, you depths of the earth; burst into song, you mountains, you forests and all your trees, for the LORD has redeemed Jacob, and will glory in Israel. Our Redeemer, the LORD of hosts is His name, the Holy One of Israel. *Is. 44* *Is. 47*

יִשְׂרָאֵל Israel is saved by the LORD with everlasting salvation. You will never be ashamed or disgraced to time everlasting. You will eat your fill and praise the name of the LORD your God, who has worked wonders for you. Never again shall My people be shamed. Then you will know that I am in the midst of Israel, that I am the LORD your God, and there is no other. Never again will My people be shamed. You will go out in joy and be led out in peace. The mountains and hills will burst into song before you, and all the trees of the field will clap their hands. Behold, God is my salvation, I will trust and not be afraid. The LORD, the LORD, is my strength and my song. He has become my salvation. With joy you will draw water from the springs of salvation. On that day you will say, "Thank the LORD, proclaim His name, make His deeds known among the nations." Declare that His name is exalted. Sing to the LORD, for He has done glorious things; let this be known throughout the world. Shout aloud and sing for joy, you who dwell in Zion, for great in your midst is the Holy One of Israel. On that day they will say, "See, this is our God; we set our hope in Him and He saved us. This is the LORD in whom we hoped; let us rejoice and be glad in His salvation." *Is. 45* *Joel 2* *Is. 55* *Is. 12* *Is. 25*

בֵּית Come, house of Jacob: let us walk in the light of the LORD. He will be the sure foundation of your times; a rich store of salvation, wisdom and knowledge – the fear of the LORD is a person's treasure. In everything he did, David was successful, for the LORD was with him. *Is. 2* *Is. 32* *I Sam. 18*

דברים כח בָּרוּךְ אַתָּה בָּעִיר, וּבָרוּךְ אַתָּה בַּשָּׂדֶה: בָּרוּךְ אַתָּה בְּבֹאֶךָ, וּבָרוּךְ אַתָּה
בְּצֵאתֶךָ: בָּרוּךְ טַנְאֲךָ וּמִשְׁאַרְתֶּךָ: בָּרוּךְ פְּרִי־בִטְנְךָ וּפְרִי אַדְמָתְךָ וּפְרִי
בְהֶמְתֶּךָ, שְׁגַר אֲלָפֶיךָ וְעַשְׁתְּרוֹת צֹאנֶךָ: יְצַו יהוה אִתְּךָ אֶת־הַבְּרָכָה
בַּאֲסָמֶיךָ וּבְכֹל מִשְׁלַח יָדֶךָ, וּבֵרַכְךָ בָּאָרֶץ אֲשֶׁר־יהוה אֱלֹהֶיךָ נֹתֵן לָךְ:
יִפְתַּח יהוה לְךָ אֶת־אוֹצָרוֹ הַטּוֹב אֶת־הַשָּׁמַיִם, לָתֵת מְטַר־אַרְצְךָ בְּעִתּוֹ,
דברים טו וּלְבָרֵךְ אֵת כָּל־מַעֲשֵׂה יָדֶךָ, וְהִלְוִיתָ גּוֹיִם רַבִּים וְאַתָּה לֹא תִלְוֶה: כִּי־יהוה
אֱלֹהֶיךָ בֵּרַכְךָ כַּאֲשֶׁר דִּבֶּר־לָךְ, וְהַעֲבַטְתָּ גּוֹיִם רַבִּים וְאַתָּה לֹא תַעֲבֹט,
דברים לג וּמָשַׁלְתָּ בְּגוֹיִם רַבִּים וּבְךָ לֹא יִמְשֹׁלוּ: אַשְׁרֶיךָ יִשְׂרָאֵל, מִי כָמוֹךָ, עַם
נוֹשַׁע בַּיהוה, מָגֵן עֶזְרֶךָ וַאֲשֶׁר־חֶרֶב גַּאֲוָתֶךָ, וְיִכָּחֲשׁוּ אֹיְבֶיךָ לָךְ, וְאַתָּה
עַל־בָּמוֹתֵימוֹ תִדְרֹךְ:

ישעיה מד מָחִיתִי כָעָב פְּשָׁעֶיךָ וְכֶעָנָן חַטֹּאותֶיךָ, שׁוּבָה אֵלַי כִּי גְאַלְתִּיךָ: רָנּוּ שָׁמַיִם
כִּי־עָשָׂה יהוה, הָרִיעוּ תַּחְתִּיּוֹת אָרֶץ, פִּצְחוּ הָרִים רִנָּה, יַעַר וְכָל־עֵץ בּוֹ,
ישעיה מז כִּי־גָאַל יהוה יַעֲקֹב וּבְיִשְׂרָאֵל יִתְפָּאָר: גֹּאֲלֵנוּ, יהוה צְבָאוֹת שְׁמוֹ, קְדוֹשׁ
יִשְׂרָאֵל:

ישעיה מה יִשְׂרָאֵל נוֹשַׁע בַּיהוה תְּשׁוּעַת עוֹלָמִים, לֹא־תֵבֹשׁוּ וְלֹא־תִכָּלְמוּ עַד־עוֹלְמֵי
יואל ב עַד: וַאֲכַלְתֶּם אָכוֹל וְשָׂבוֹעַ, וְהִלַּלְתֶּם אֶת־שֵׁם יהוה אֱלֹהֵיכֶם אֲשֶׁר־עָשָׂה
עִמָּכֶם לְהַפְלִיא, וְלֹא־יֵבֹשׁוּ עַמִּי לְעוֹלָם: וִידַעְתֶּם כִּי בְקֶרֶב יִשְׂרָאֵל אָנִי,
ישעיה נה וַאֲנִי יהוה אֱלֹהֵיכֶם וְאֵין עוֹד, וְלֹא־יֵבֹשׁוּ עַמִּי לְעוֹלָם: כִּי־בְשִׂמְחָה תֵצֵאוּ
וּבְשָׁלוֹם תּוּבָלוּן, הֶהָרִים וְהַגְּבָעוֹת יִפְצְחוּ לִפְנֵיכֶם רִנָּה, וְכָל־עֲצֵי הַשָּׂדֶה
ישעיה יב יִמְחֲאוּ־כָף: הִנֵּה אֵל יְשׁוּעָתִי אֶבְטַח, וְלֹא אֶפְחָד, כִּי־עָזִּי וְזִמְרָת יָהּ יהוה,
וַיְהִי־לִי לִישׁוּעָה: וּשְׁאַבְתֶּם־מַיִם בְּשָׂשׂוֹן, מִמַּעַיְנֵי הַיְשׁוּעָה: וַאֲמַרְתֶּם
בַּיּוֹם הַהוּא, הוֹדוּ לַיהוה קִרְאוּ בִשְׁמוֹ, הוֹדִיעוּ בָעַמִּים עֲלִילֹתָיו, הַזְכִּירוּ
כִּי נִשְׂגָּב שְׁמוֹ: זַמְּרוּ יהוה כִּי גֵאוּת עָשָׂה, מוּדַעַת זֹאת בְּכָל־הָאָרֶץ: צַהֲלִי
ישעיה כה וָרֹנִּי יוֹשֶׁבֶת צִיּוֹן, כִּי־גָדוֹל בְּקִרְבֵּךְ קְדוֹשׁ יִשְׂרָאֵל: וְאָמַר בַּיּוֹם הַהוּא,
הִנֵּה אֱלֹהֵינוּ זֶה קִוִּינוּ לוֹ וְיוֹשִׁיעֵנוּ, זֶה יהוה קִוִּינוּ לוֹ, נָגִילָה וְנִשְׂמְחָה
בִּישׁוּעָתוֹ:

ישעיה ב ישעיה לג בֵּית יַעֲקֹב לְכוּ וְנֵלְכָה בְּאוֹר יהוה: וְהָיָה אֱמוּנַת עִתֶּיךָ, חֹסֶן יְשׁוּעֹת חָכְמַת
שמואל א׳ יח וָדָעַת, יִרְאַת יהוה הִיא אוֹצָרוֹ: וַיְהִי דָוִד לְכָל־דְּרָכָו מַשְׂכִּיל, וַיהוה עִמּוֹ:

פְּדָה He redeemed my soul in peace from the battle waged against me, for the sake *Ps. 55*
of the many who were with me. The people said to Saul, "Shall Jonathan die – he *1 Sam. 14*
who has brought about this great deliverance in Israel? Heaven forbid! As surely as the LORD lives, not a hair of his head shall fall to the ground, for he did this
today with God's help." So the people rescued Jonathan and he did not die. Those *Is. 35*
redeemed by the LORD shall return; they will enter Zion singing; everlasting joy will crown their heads. Gladness and joy will overtake them, and sorrow and sighing will flee away.

הָפַכְתָּ You have turned my sorrow into dancing. You have removed my sackcloth *Ps. 30*
and clothed me with joy. The LORD your God refused to listen to Balaam; instead *Deut. 23*
the LORD your God turned the curse into a blessing, for the LORD your God
loves you. Then maidens will dance and be glad; so too will young men and old *Jer. 31*
together; I will turn their mourning into gladness; I will give them comfort and joy instead of sorrow.

בּוֹרֵא I create the speech of lips: Peace, peace to those far and near, says the LORD, *Is. 57*
and I will heal them. Then the spirit came upon Amasai, chief of the captains, *1 Chr. 12*
and he said: "We are yours, David! We are with you, son of Jesse! Peace, peace to you, and peace to those who help you; for your God will help you." Then David
received them and made them leaders of his troop. And you shall say: "To life! *1 Sam. 25*
Peace be to you, peace to your household, and peace to all that is yours!" The *Ps. 29*
LORD will give strength to His people; the LORD will bless His people with peace.

אָמַר Rabbi Yoḥanan said: Wherever you find the greatness of the Holy One, *Megilla 31a*
blessed be He, there you find His humility. This is written in the Torah, repeated in the Prophets, and stated a third time in the Writings. It is written in the
Torah: "For the LORD your God is God of gods and LORD of lords, the great, *Deut. 10*
mighty and awe-inspiring God, who shows no favoritism and accepts no bribe." Immediately afterwards it is written, "He upholds the cause of the orphan and widow, and loves the stranger, giving him food and clothing." It is repeated in the

---

be omens for good and for blessing instead (*Tur* 220).

אָמַר רַבִּי יוֹחָנָן – *Rabbi Yoḥanan said.* Herein are extolled the virtues of humility taking Hashem Himself as our role model for, as this passage from the Gemara explains (*Megilla* 31a), this attribute of God is extolled across the entire Bible as evidenced in passages from the Torah, the Prophets and the Writings. Perhaps the reason for this message here is that as we are about to enter into the week, we need to recall that the people who are the weakest in society are deserving of special protection by Hashem, something that we need to emulate or else run the risk of being held accountable. In Hashem's greatness lies His humility. In our humility and sensitivity to the weaker people around us, we may find our greatness.

פָּדָה בְשָׁלוֹם נַפְשִׁי מִקְּרָב־לִי, כִּי־בְרַבִּים הָיוּ עִמָּדִי: וַיֹּאמֶר הָעָם אֶל־ תהלים נה שמואל א׳ יד
שָׁאוּל, הֲיוֹנָתָן יָמוּת אֲשֶׁר עָשָׂה הַיְשׁוּעָה הַגְּדוֹלָה הַזֹּאת בְּיִשְׂרָאֵל,
חָלִילָה, חַי־יהוה אִם־יִפֹּל מִשַּׂעֲרַת רֹאשׁוֹ אַרְצָה, כִּי־עִם־אֱלֹהִים עָשָׂה
הַיּוֹם הַזֶּה, וַיִּפְדּוּ הָעָם אֶת־יוֹנָתָן וְלֹא־מֵת: וּפְדוּיֵי יהוה יְשֻׁבוּן וּבָאוּ צִיּוֹן ישעיה לה
בְּרִנָּה, וְשִׂמְחַת עוֹלָם עַל־רֹאשָׁם, שָׂשׂוֹן וְשִׂמְחָה יַשִּׂיגוּ, וְנָסוּ יָגוֹן וַאֲנָחָה:

הָפַכְתָּ מִסְפְּדִי לְמָחוֹל לִי, פִּתַּחְתָּ שַׂקִּי, וַתְּאַזְּרֵנִי שִׂמְחָה: וְלֹא־אָבָה יהוה תהלים ל דברים כג
אֱלֹהֶיךָ לִשְׁמֹעַ אֶל־בִּלְעָם, וַיַּהֲפֹךְ יהוה אֱלֹהֶיךָ לְּךָ אֶת־הַקְּלָלָה לִבְרָכָה,
כִּי אֲהֵבְךָ יהוה אֱלֹהֶיךָ: אָז תִּשְׂמַח בְּתוּלָה בְּמָחוֹל, וּבַחֻרִים וּזְקֵנִים יַחְדָּו, ירמיה לא
וְהָפַכְתִּי אֶבְלָם לְשָׂשׂוֹן, וְנִחַמְתִּים, וְשִׂמַּחְתִּים מִיגוֹנָם:

בּוֹרֵא נִיב[ע] שְׂפָתָיִם, שָׁלוֹם שָׁלוֹם לָרָחוֹק וְלַקָּרוֹב אָמַר יהוה, וּרְפָאתִיו: ישעיה נז
וְרוּחַ לָבְשָׁה אֶת־עֲמָשַׂי רֹאשׁ הַשָּׁלִישִׁים, לְךָ דָוִיד וְעִמְּךָ בֶן־יִשַׁי, שָׁלוֹם דברי הימים א׳ יב
שָׁלוֹם לְךָ וְשָׁלוֹם לְעֹזְרֶךָ, כִּי עֲזָרְךָ אֱלֹהֶיךָ, וַיְקַבְּלֵם דָּוִיד וַיִּתְּנֵם בְּרָאשֵׁי
הַגְּדוּד: וַאֲמַרְתֶּם כֹּה לֶחָי, וְאַתָּה שָׁלוֹם וּבֵיתְךָ שָׁלוֹם וְכֹל אֲשֶׁר־לְךָ שָׁלוֹם: שמואל א׳ כה
יהוה עֹז לְעַמּוֹ יִתֵּן, יהוה יְבָרֵךְ אֶת־עַמּוֹ בַשָּׁלוֹם: תהלים כט

אָמַר רַבִּי יוֹחָנָן:[ע] בְּכָל מָקוֹם שֶׁאַתָּה מוֹצֵא גְּדֻלָּתוֹ שֶׁל הַקָּדוֹשׁ בָּרוּךְ מגילה לא.
הוּא, שָׁם אַתָּה מוֹצֵא עַנְוְתָנוּתוֹ. דָּבָר זֶה כָּתוּב בַּתּוֹרָה, וְשָׁנוּי בַּנְּבִיאִים,
וּמְשֻׁלָּשׁ בַּכְּתוּבִים. כָּתוּב בַּתּוֹרָה: כִּי יהוה אֱלֹהֵיכֶם הוּא אֱלֹהֵי הָאֱלֹהִים דברים י
וַאֲדֹנֵי הָאֲדֹנִים, הָאֵל הַגָּדֹל הַגִּבֹּר וְהַנּוֹרָא, אֲשֶׁר לֹא־יִשָּׂא פָנִים וְלֹא יִקַּח
שֹׁחַד: וּכְתִיב בָּתְרֵהּ: עֹשֶׂה מִשְׁפַּט יָתוֹם וְאַלְמָנָה, וְאֹהֵב גֵּר לָתֶת לוֹ לֶחֶם

IYUN TEFILLA • עיון תפילה

פָּדָה... הָפַכְתָּ... בּוֹרֵא נִיב – *He redeemed... You have turned... I create the speech.* The Gemara (*Berakhot* 55b) instructs that when one has a bad dream, one should recite three sets of three verses, each set containing at least one reference to the words redemption, reversal and peace respectively. The siddur uses these themes in each of the following paragraphs, perhaps expressing the hope that just as we pray when we wake with a start that a bad dream ultimately turns out to be a good omen (or a purging of the fears of our inner consciousness) so, too, we hope that whatever ominous things may lie ahead of us in the coming hours and days, they should

Prophets, as it says: "So says the High and Exalted One, who lives for ever and *Is. 57*
whose name is Holy: I live in a high and holy place, but also with the contrite
and lowly in spirit, to revive the spirit of the lowly, and to revive the heart of the
contrite." It is stated a third time in the Writings: "Sing to God, make music for *Ps. 68*
His name, extol Him who rides the clouds – the LORD is His name – and exult
before Him." Immediately afterwards it is written: "Father of the orphans and
Justice of widows, is God in His holy habitation."

יְהִי May the LORD our God be with us, as He was with our ancestors. May He *1 Kings 8*
never abandon us or forsake us. You who cleave to the LORD your God are all alive *Deut. 4*
this day. For the LORD will comfort Zion, He will comfort all her ruins; He will *Is. 51*
make her wilderness like Eden, and her desert like a garden of the LORD. Joy and
gladness will be found there, thanksgiving and the sound of singing. It pleased the *Is. 42*
LORD for the sake of [Israel's] righteousness to make the Torah great and glorious.

שִׁיר הַמַּעֲלוֹת A song of ascents. Happy are all who fear the LORD, who walk in His *Ps. 128*
ways. When you eat the fruit of your labor, happy and fortunate are you. Your wife shall be like a fruitful vine within your house; your sons like olive saplings around your table. So shall the man who fears the LORD be blessed. May the LORD bless you from Zion; may you see the good of Jerusalem all the days of your life; and may you live to see your children's children. Peace be on Israel!

HAVDALA IN THE SYNAGOGUE

Some say the full Havdala on page 654.

The Leader takes the cup of wine in his right hand, and says:

Please pay attention, my masters.

Blessed are You, LORD our God, King of the Universe,
who creates the fruit of the vine.

Holding the spice box, the Leader says:

Blessed are You, LORD our God, King of the Universe,
who creates the various spices.

The Leader smells the spices and puts the spice box down.
He lifts his hands toward the flame of the Havdala candle, and says:

Blessed are You, LORD our God, King of the Universe,
who creates the lights of fire.

He lifts the cup of wine in his right hand, and says:

Blessed are You, LORD our God, King of the Universe, who distinguishes between sacred and secular, between light and darkness, between Israel and the nations, between the seventh day and the six days of work. Blessed are You, LORD, who distinguishes between sacred and secular.

וְשִׁמְלָה: שָׁנוּי בַּנְּבִיאִים, דִּכְתִיב: כִּי כֹה אָמַר רָם וְנִשָּׂא שֹׁכֵן עַד וְקָדוֹשׁ ישעיה נז
שְׁמוֹ, מָרוֹם וְקָדוֹשׁ אֶשְׁכּוֹן, וְאֶת־דַּכָּא וּשְׁפַל־רוּחַ, לְהַחֲיוֹת רוּחַ שְׁפָלִים
וּלְהַחֲיוֹת לֵב נִדְכָּאִים: מְשֻׁלָּשׁ בַּכְּתוּבִים, דִּכְתִיב: שִׁירוּ לֵאלֹהִים, זַמְּרוּ תהלים סח
שְׁמוֹ, סֹלּוּ לָרֹכֵב בָּעֲרָבוֹת בְּיָהּ שְׁמוֹ, וְעִלְזוּ לְפָנָיו: וּכְתִיב בָּתְרֵהּ: אֲבִי
יְתוֹמִים וְדַיַּן אַלְמָנוֹת, אֱלֹהִים בִּמְעוֹן קָדְשׁוֹ:

יְהִי יהוה אֱלֹהֵינוּ עִמָּנוּ כַּאֲשֶׁר הָיָה עִם־אֲבֹתֵינוּ, אַל־יַעַזְבֵנוּ וְאַל־יִטְּשֵׁנוּ: מלכים א׳ ח
וְאַתֶּם הַדְּבֵקִים בַּיהוה אֱלֹהֵיכֶם, חַיִּים כֻּלְּכֶם הַיּוֹם: כִּי־נִחַם יהוה צִיּוֹן, נִחַם דברים ד ישעיה נא
כָּל־חָרְבֹתֶיהָ, וַיָּשֶׂם מִדְבָּרָהּ כְּעֵדֶן וְעַרְבָתָהּ כְּגַן־יהוה, שָׂשׂוֹן וְשִׂמְחָה יִמָּצֵא
בָהּ, תּוֹדָה וְקוֹל זִמְרָה: יהוה חָפֵץ לְמַעַן צִדְקוֹ, יַגְדִּיל תּוֹרָה וְיַאְדִּיר: ישעיה מב

שִׁיר הַמַּעֲלוֹת, אַשְׁרֵי כָּל־יְרֵא יהוה, הַהֹלֵךְ בִּדְרָכָיו: יְגִיעַ כַּפֶּיךָ כִּי תֹאכֵל, תהלים קכח
אַשְׁרֶיךָ וְטוֹב לָךְ: אֶשְׁתְּךָ כְּגֶפֶן פֹּרִיָּה בְּיַרְכְּתֵי בֵיתֶךָ, בָּנֶיךָ כִּשְׁתִלֵי זֵיתִים,
סָבִיב לְשֻׁלְחָנֶךָ: הִנֵּה כִי־כֵן יְבֹרַךְ גָּבֶר יְרֵא יהוה: יְבָרֶכְךָ יהוה מִצִּיּוֹן, וּרְאֵה
בְּטוּב יְרוּשָׁלָםִ, כֹּל יְמֵי חַיֶּיךָ: וּרְאֵה־בָנִים לְבָנֶיךָ, שָׁלוֹם עַל־יִשְׂרָאֵל:

הבדלה בבית הכנסת

Some say the full הבדלה *on page 655.*

The שליח ציבור *takes the cup of wine in his right hand, and says:*

סַבְרִי מָרָנָן

בָּרוּךְ אַתָּה יהוה אֱלֹהֵינוּ מֶלֶךְ הָעוֹלָם, בּוֹרֵא פְּרִי הַגָּפֶן.

Holding the spice box, the שליח ציבור *says:*

בָּרוּךְ אַתָּה יהוה אֱלֹהֵינוּ מֶלֶךְ הָעוֹלָם, בּוֹרֵא מִינֵי בְשָׂמִים.

The שליח ציבור *smells the spices and puts the spice box down.*
He lifts his hands toward the flame of the הבדלה *candle, and says:*

בָּרוּךְ אַתָּה יהוה אֱלֹהֵינוּ מֶלֶךְ הָעוֹלָם, בּוֹרֵא מְאוֹרֵי הָאֵשׁ.

He lifts the cup of wine in his right hand, and says:

בָּרוּךְ אַתָּה יהוה אֱלֹהֵינוּ מֶלֶךְ הָעוֹלָם, הַמַּבְדִּיל בֵּין קֹדֶשׁ לְחֹל, בֵּין אוֹר לְחֹשֶׁךְ, בֵּין יִשְׂרָאֵל לָעַמִּים, בֵּין יוֹם הַשְּׁבִיעִי לְשֵׁשֶׁת יְמֵי הַמַּעֲשֶׂה.
בָּרוּךְ אַתָּה יהוה, הַמַּבְדִּיל בֵּין קֹדֶשׁ לְחֹל.

The commentary on *Havdala* can be found on page 655.

Stand while saying Aleinu.

עָלֵינוּ It is our duty to praise the Master of all,
and ascribe greatness to the Author of creation,
who has not made us like the nations of the lands
nor placed us like the families of the earth;
who has not made our portion like theirs,
nor our destiny like all their multitudes.
(For they worship vanity and emptiness,
and pray to a god who cannot save.)
▾ *Bow:* But we bow in worship and thank the Supreme King of kings,
the Holy One, blessed be He,
who extends the heavens and establishes the earth,
whose throne of glory is in the heavens above,
and whose power's Presence is in the highest of heights.
He is our God; there is no other.
Truly He is our King, there is none else, as it is written in His Torah:
"You shall know and take to heart this day that the LORD is God, *Deut. 4*
in heaven above and on earth below. There is no other."

Therefore, we place our hope in You, LORD our God,
that we may soon see the glory of Your power,
when You will remove abominations from the earth,
and idols will be utterly destroyed,
when the world will be perfected under the sovereignty of the Almighty,
when all humanity will call on Your name,
to turn all the earth's wicked toward You.
All the world's inhabitants will realize and know
that to You every knee must bow and every tongue swear loyalty.
Before You, LORD our God, they will kneel and bow down
and give honor to Your glorious name.
They will all accept the yoke of Your kingdom,
and You will reign over them soon and for ever.
For the kingdom is Yours, and to all eternity You will reign in glory,
as it is written in Your Torah: "The LORD will reign for ever and ever." *Ex. 15*
▸ And it is said: "Then the LORD shall be King over all the earth; *Zech. 14*
on that day the LORD shall be One and His name One."

Stand while saying עָלֵינוּ.

עָלֵינוּ לְשַׁבֵּחַ לַאֲדוֹן הַכֹּל, לָתֵת גְּדֻלָּה לְיוֹצֵר בְּרֵאשִׁית
שֶׁלֹּא עָשָׂנוּ כְּגוֹיֵי הָאֲרָצוֹת, וְלֹא שָׂמָנוּ כְּמִשְׁפְּחוֹת הָאֲדָמָה
שֶׁלֹּא שָׂם חֶלְקֵנוּ כָּהֶם וְגוֹרָלֵנוּ כְּכָל הֲמוֹנָם.
(שֶׁהֵם מִשְׁתַּחֲוִים לְהֶבֶל וָרִיק וּמִתְפַּלְלִים אֶל אֵל לֹא יוֹשִׁיעַ.)
▾ *Bow* וַאֲנַחְנוּ כּוֹרְעִים וּמִשְׁתַּחֲוִים וּמוֹדִים
לִפְנֵי מֶלֶךְ מַלְכֵי הַמְּלָכִים, הַקָּדוֹשׁ בָּרוּךְ הוּא
שֶׁהוּא נוֹטֶה שָׁמַיִם וְיוֹסֵד אָרֶץ
וּמוֹשַׁב יְקָרוֹ בַּשָּׁמַיִם מִמַּעַל
וּשְׁכִינַת עֻזּוֹ בְּגָבְהֵי מְרוֹמִים.
הוּא אֱלֹהֵינוּ, אֵין עוֹד.
אֱמֶת מַלְכֵּנוּ, אֶפֶס זוּלָתוֹ, כַּכָּתוּב בְּתוֹרָתוֹ
וְיָדַעְתָּ הַיּוֹם וַהֲשֵׁבֹתָ אֶל־לְבָבֶךָ דברים ד
כִּי יהוה הוּא הָאֱלֹהִים בַּשָּׁמַיִם מִמַּעַל וְעַל־הָאָרֶץ מִתָּחַת, אֵין עוֹד:

עַל כֵּן נְקַוֶּה לְּךָ יהוה אֱלֹהֵינוּ, לִרְאוֹת מְהֵרָה בְּתִפְאֶרֶת עֻזֶּךָ
לְהַעֲבִיר גִּלּוּלִים מִן הָאָרֶץ, וְהָאֱלִילִים כָּרוֹת יִכָּרֵתוּן
לְתַקֵּן עוֹלָם בְּמַלְכוּת שַׁדַּי.
וְכָל בְּנֵי בָשָׂר יִקְרְאוּ בִשְׁמֶךָ לְהַפְנוֹת אֵלֶיךָ כָּל רִשְׁעֵי אָרֶץ.
יַכִּירוּ וְיֵדְעוּ כָּל יוֹשְׁבֵי תֵבֵל, כִּי לְךָ תִּכְרַע כָּל בֶּרֶךְ, תִּשָּׁבַע כָּל לָשׁוֹן.
לְפָנֶיךָ יהוה אֱלֹהֵינוּ יִכְרְעוּ וְיִפֹּלוּ, וְלִכְבוֹד שִׁמְךָ יְקָר יִתֵּנוּ
וִיקַבְּלוּ כֻלָּם אֶת עֹל מַלְכוּתֶךָ וְתִמְלֹךְ עֲלֵיהֶם מְהֵרָה לְעוֹלָם וָעֶד.
כִּי הַמַּלְכוּת שֶׁלְּךָ הִיא וּלְעוֹלְמֵי עַד תִּמְלֹךְ בְּכָבוֹד
כַּכָּתוּב בְּתוֹרָתֶךָ, יהוה יִמְלֹךְ לְעֹלָם וָעֶד: שמות טו
◂ וְנֶאֱמַר, וְהָיָה יהוה לְמֶלֶךְ עַל־כָּל־הָאָרֶץ זכריה יד
בַּיּוֹם הַהוּא יִהְיֶה יהוה אֶחָד וּשְׁמוֹ אֶחָד:

Some add:

Have no fear of sudden terror or of the ruin when it overtakes the wicked. *Prov. 3*
Devise your strategy, but it will be thwarted; propose your plan, *Is. 8*
but it will not stand, for God is with us.
When you grow old, I will still be the same. *Is. 46*
When your hair turns gray, I will still carry you.
I made you, I will bear you, I will carry you, and I will rescue you.

MOURNER'S KADDISH

The following prayer, said by mourners, requires the presence of a minyan. A transliteration can be found on page 892.

Mourner: יִתְגַּדַּל Magnified and sanctified may His great name be,
in the world He created by His will.
May He establish His kingdom
in your lifetime and in your days,
and in the lifetime of all the house of Israel,
swiftly and soon –
and say: Amen.

All: May His great name be blessed for ever and all time.

Mourner: Blessed and praised,
glorified and exalted,
raised and honored,
uplifted and lauded
be the name of the Holy One,
blessed be He, beyond any blessing,
song, praise and consolation
uttered in the world –
and say: Amen.

May there be great peace from heaven,
and life for us and all Israel –
and say: Amen.

Bow and take three steps back as if taking leave of the Divine Presence.
Bow left: May He who makes peace in His high places,
Bow right: make peace *Bow forward:* for us and all Israel –
and say: Amen.

Some add:

אַל־תִּירָא מִפַּחַד פִּתְאֹם וּמִשֹּׁאַת רְשָׁעִים כִּי תָבֹא: משלי ג

עֻצוּ עֵצָה וְתֻפָר, דַּבְּרוּ דָבָר וְלֹא יָקוּם, כִּי עִמָּנוּ אֵל: ישעיה ח

וְעַד־זִקְנָה אֲנִי הוּא, וְעַד־שֵׂיבָה אֲנִי אֶסְבֹּל אֲנִי עָשִׂיתִי וַאֲנִי אֶשָּׂא וַאֲנִי אֶסְבֹּל וַאֲמַלֵּט: ישעיה מו

קדיש יתום

The following prayer, said by mourners, requires the presence of a מנין*.*
A transliteration can be found on page 892.

אבל: יִתְגַּדַּל וְיִתְקַדַּשׁ שְׁמֵהּ רַבָּא (קהל: אָמֵן)
בְּעָלְמָא דִּי בְרָא כִרְעוּתֵהּ
וְיַמְלִיךְ מַלְכוּתֵהּ
בְּחַיֵּיכוֹן וּבְיוֹמֵיכוֹן וּבְחַיֵּי דְכָל בֵּית יִשְׂרָאֵל
בַּעֲגָלָא וּבִזְמַן קָרִיב, וְאִמְרוּ אָמֵן. (קהל: אָמֵן)

קהל ואבל: יְהֵא שְׁמֵהּ רַבָּא מְבָרַךְ לְעָלַם וּלְעָלְמֵי עָלְמַיָּא.

אבל: יִתְבָּרַךְ וְיִשְׁתַּבַּח וְיִתְפָּאַר
וְיִתְרוֹמַם וְיִתְנַשֵּׂא וְיִתְהַדָּר וְיִתְעַלֶּה וְיִתְהַלָּל
שְׁמֵהּ דְּקֻדְשָׁא בְּרִיךְ הוּא (קהל: בְּרִיךְ הוּא)
לְעֵלָּא מִן כָּל בִּרְכָתָא / בעשרת ימי תשובה: לְעֵלָּא לְעֵלָּא מִכָּל בִּרְכָתָא/
וְשִׁירָתָא, תֻּשְׁבְּחָתָא וְנֶחֱמָתָא
דַּאֲמִירָן בְּעָלְמָא, וְאִמְרוּ אָמֵן. (קהל: אָמֵן)

יְהֵא שְׁלָמָא רַבָּא מִן שְׁמַיָּא
וְחַיִּים, עָלֵינוּ וְעַל כָּל יִשְׂרָאֵל, וְאִמְרוּ אָמֵן. (קהל: אָמֵן)

Bow and take three steps back as if taking leave of the Divine Presence.

Bow left עֹשֶׂה שָׁלוֹם/ בעשרת ימי תשובה: הַשָּׁלוֹם/ בִּמְרוֹמָיו
Bow right הוּא יַעֲשֶׂה שָׁלוֹם *Bow forward* עָלֵינוּ
וְעַל כָּל יִשְׂרָאֵל, וְאִמְרוּ אָמֵן.

From the second day of Rosh Ḥodesh Elul through Shemini Atzeret (in Israel through Hoshana Raba), the following psalm is said:

לְדָוִד By David. The LORD is my light and my salvation – whom then shall I fear? The LORD is the stronghold of my life – of whom shall I be afraid? When evil men close in on me to devour my flesh, it is they, my enemies and foes, who stumble and fall. Should an army besiege me, my heart would not fear. Should war break out against me, still I would be confident. One thing I ask of the LORD, only this do I seek: to live in the House of the LORD all the days of my life, to gaze on the beauty of the LORD and worship in His Temple. For He will keep me safe in His pavilion on the day of trouble. He will hide me under the cover of His tent. He will set me high upon a rock. Now my head is high above my enemies who surround me. I will sacrifice in His tent with shouts of joy. I will sing and chant praises to the LORD. LORD, hear my voice when I call. Be gracious to me and answer me. On Your behalf my heart says, "Seek My face." Your face, LORD, will I seek. Do not hide Your face from me. Do not turn Your servant away in anger. You have been my help. Do not reject or forsake me, God, my Savior. Were my father and my mother to forsake me, the LORD would take me in. Teach me Your way, LORD, and lead me on a level path, because of my oppressors. Do not abandon me to the will of my foes, for false witnesses have risen against me, breathing violence. ▸ Were it not for my faith that I shall see the LORD's goodness in the land of the living. Hope in the LORD. Be strong and of good courage, and hope in the LORD! Ps. 27

Mourner's Kaddish (on previous page)

---

but my family did not change. Then I realized: first, I must change myself. (Rabbi Israel Salanter)

How will you change yourself this week? This year?

From the second day of ראש חודש אלול *through* שמיני עצרת (*in* ארץ ישראל *through* הושענא רבה), *the following psalm is said:*

תהלים כז

לְדָוִד, יהוה אוֹרִי וְיִשְׁעִי, מִמִּי אִירָא, יהוה מָעוֹז־חַיַּי, מִמִּי אֶפְחָד: בִּקְרֹב עָלַי מְרֵעִים לֶאֱכֹל אֶת־בְּשָׂרִי, צָרַי וְאֹיְבַי לִי, הֵמָּה כָשְׁלוּ וְנָפָלוּ: אִם־תַּחֲנֶה עָלַי מַחֲנֶה, לֹא־יִירָא לִבִּי, אִם־תָּקוּם עָלַי מִלְחָמָה, בְּזֹאת אֲנִי בוֹטֵחַ: אַחַת שָׁאַלְתִּי מֵאֵת־יהוה, אוֹתָהּ אֲבַקֵּשׁ, שִׁבְתִּי בְּבֵית־יהוה כָּל־יְמֵי חַיַּי, לַחֲזוֹת בְּנֹעַם־יהוה, וּלְבַקֵּר בְּהֵיכָלוֹ: כִּי יִצְפְּנֵנִי בְּסֻכֹּה בְּיוֹם רָעָה, יַסְתִּרֵנִי בְּסֵתֶר אָהֳלוֹ, בְּצוּר יְרוֹמְמֵנִי: וְעַתָּה יָרוּם רֹאשִׁי עַל אֹיְבַי סְבִיבוֹתַי, וְאֶזְבְּחָה בְאָהֳלוֹ זִבְחֵי תְרוּעָה, אָשִׁירָה וַאֲזַמְּרָה לַיהוה: שְׁמַע־יהוה קוֹלִי אֶקְרָא, וְחָנֵּנִי וַעֲנֵנִי: לְךָ אָמַר לִבִּי בַּקְּשׁוּ פָנָי, אֶת־פָּנֶיךָ יהוה אֲבַקֵּשׁ: אַל־תַּסְתֵּר פָּנֶיךָ מִמֶּנִּי, אַל תַּט־בְּאַף עַבְדֶּךָ, עֶזְרָתִי הָיִיתָ, אַל־תִּטְּשֵׁנִי וְאַל־תַּעַזְבֵנִי, אֱלֹהֵי יִשְׁעִי: כִּי־אָבִי וְאִמִּי עֲזָבוּנִי, וַיהוה יַאַסְפֵנִי: הוֹרֵנִי יהוה דַּרְכֶּךָ, וּנְחֵנִי בְּאֹרַח מִישׁוֹר, לְמַעַן שׁוֹרְרָי: אַל־תִּתְּנֵנִי בְּנֶפֶשׁ צָרָי, כִּי קָמוּ־בִי עֵדֵי־שֶׁקֶר, וִיפֵחַ חָמָס: ▸ לוּלֵא הֶאֱמַנְתִּי לִרְאוֹת בְּטוּב־יהוה בְּאֶרֶץ חַיִּים: קַוֵּה אֶל־יהוה, חֲזַק וְיַאֲמֵץ לִבֶּךָ, וְקַוֵּה אֶל־יהוה:

קדיש יתום (*on previous page*)

ANI TEFILLA • אני תפילה

At first, I wanted to change the world. I tried, but the world did not change. Then I tried to change my town, but the town did not change. Then I tried to change my family,

BLESSING OF THE NEW MOON

Kiddush Levana, the Blessing of the New Moon, is said between the third day and the middle day of each month. If possible, it should be said at the end of Shabbat, under the open sky, and in the presence of a minyan.

הַלְלוּיָהּ Halleluya! Praise the LORD from the heavens, praise Him in the heights. Praise Him, all His angels; praise Him, all His hosts. Praise Him, sun and moon; praise Him, all shining stars. Praise Him, highest heavens and the waters above the heavens. Let them praise the name of the LORD, for He commanded and they were created. He established them for ever and all time, issuing a decree that will never change. *Ps. 148*

כִּי־אֶרְאֶה When I see Your heavens, the work of Your fingers, the moon and the stars which You have set in place: What is man that You are mindful of him, the son of man that You care for him? *Ps. 8*

Look at the moon, then say:

בָּרוּךְ Blessed are You, LORD our God, King of the Universe who by His word created the heavens, and by His breath all their host. He set for them laws and times, so that they should not deviate from their appointed task. They are joyous and glad to perform the will of their Owner, the Worker of truth whose work is truth. To the moon He said that it should renew itself as a crown of beauty for those He carried from the womb [Israel], for they are destined to be renewed like it, and to praise their Creator for the sake of His glorious majesty. Blessed are You, LORD, who renews the months.

The following five verses are each said three times:

Blessed is He who formed you; blessed is He who made you;
blessed is He who owns you; blessed is He who created you.

The following verse is said rising on the toes.

Just as I leap toward you but cannot touch you,
so may none of my enemies be able to touch me to do me harm.

May fear and dread fall upon them; *Ex. 15*
by the power of Your arm may they be still as stone.
May they be still as stone through the power of Your arm,
when dread and fear fall upon them.

קידוש לבנה

קידוש לבנה, the Blessing of the New Moon, is said between the third day and the middle day of each month. If possible, it should be said at the end of שבת, under the open sky, and in the presence of a מנין.

תהלים קמח
הַלְלוּיָהּ, הַלְלוּ אֶת־יהוה מִן־הַשָּׁמַיִם, הַלְלוּהוּ בַּמְּרוֹמִים: הַלְלוּהוּ כָל־מַלְאָכָיו, הַלְלוּהוּ כָּל־צְבָאָו: הַלְלוּהוּ שֶׁמֶשׁ וְיָרֵחַ, הַלְלוּהוּ כָּל־כּוֹכְבֵי אוֹר: הַלְלוּהוּ שְׁמֵי הַשָּׁמָיִם, וְהַמַּיִם אֲשֶׁר מֵעַל הַשָּׁמָיִם: יְהַלְלוּ אֶת־שֵׁם יהוה, כִּי הוּא צִוָּה וְנִבְרָאוּ: וַיַּעֲמִידֵם לָעַד לְעוֹלָם, חָק־נָתַן וְלֹא יַעֲבוֹר:

תהלים ח
כִּי־אֶרְאֶה שָׁמֶיךָ מַעֲשֵׂה אֶצְבְּעֹתֶיךָ, יָרֵחַ וְכוֹכָבִים אֲשֶׁר כּוֹנָנְתָּה: מָה־אֱנוֹשׁ כִּי־תִזְכְּרֶנּוּ, וּבֶן־אָדָם כִּי תִפְקְדֶנּוּ:

Look at the moon, then say:

בָּרוּךְ אַתָּה יהוה אֱלֹהֵינוּ מֶלֶךְ הָעוֹלָם, אֲשֶׁר בְּמַאֲמָרוֹ בָּרָא שְׁחָקִים, וּבְרוּחַ פִּיו כָּל צְבָאָם, חֹק וּזְמַן נָתַן לָהֶם שֶׁלֹּא יְשַׁנּוּ אֶת תַּפְקִידָם. שָׂשִׂים וּשְׂמֵחִים לַעֲשׂוֹת רְצוֹן קוֹנָם, פּוֹעֵל אֱמֶת שֶׁפְּעֻלָּתוֹ אֱמֶת. וְלַלְּבָנָה אָמַר שֶׁתִּתְחַדֵּשׁ, עֲטֶרֶת תִּפְאֶרֶת לַעֲמוּסֵי בָטֶן, שֶׁהֵם עֲתִידִים לְהִתְחַדֵּשׁ כְּמוֹתָהּ וּלְפָאֵר לְיוֹצְרָם עַל שֵׁם כְּבוֹד מַלְכוּתוֹ. בָּרוּךְ אַתָּה יהוה, מְחַדֵּשׁ חֳדָשִׁים.

The following five verses are each said three times:

בָּרוּךְ יוֹצְרֵךְ, בָּרוּךְ עוֹשֵׂךְ, בָּרוּךְ קוֹנֵךְ, בָּרוּךְ בּוֹרְאֵךְ.

The following verse is said rising on the toes.

כְּשֵׁם שֶׁאֲנִי רוֹקֵד כְּנֶגְדֵּךְ וְאֵינִי יָכוֹל לִנְגֹּעַ בָּךְ
כָּךְ לֹא יוּכְלוּ כָּל אוֹיְבַי לִנְגֹּעַ בִּי לְרָעָה.

שמות טו
תִּפֹּל עֲלֵיהֶם אֵימָתָה וָפַחַד, בִּגְדֹל זְרוֹעֲךָ יִדְּמוּ כָּאָבֶן:
כָּאָבֶן יִדְּמוּ זְרוֹעֲךָ בִּגְדֹל, וָפַחַד אֵימָתָה עֲלֵיהֶם תִּפֹּל.

David, King of Israel, lives and endures.

Turn to three people and say to each:

Peace upon you.

They respond:

Upon you, peace.

Say three times:

May it be a good sign and a good omen for us and all Israel. Amen.

קוֹל Hark! My beloved! Here he comes, leaping over the mountains, bounding over the hills. My beloved is like a gazelle, like a young deer. There he stands outside our wall, peering in through the windows, gazing through the lattice. *Song. 2*

שִׁיר לַמַּעֲלוֹת A song of ascents. I lift my eyes up to the hills; from where will my help come? My help comes from the LORD, Maker of heaven and earth. He will not let your foot stumble; He who guards you does not slumber. See: the Guardian of Israel neither slumbers nor sleeps. The LORD is your Guardian; the LORD is your Shade at your right hand. The sun will not strike you by day, nor the moon by night. The LORD will guard you from all harm; He will guard your life. The LORD will guard your going and coming, now and for evermore. *Ps. 121*

הַלְלוּיָהּ Halleluya! Praise God in His holy place; praise Him in the heavens of His power. Praise Him for His mighty deeds; praise Him for His surpassing greatness. Praise Him with blasts of the ram's horn; praise Him with the harp and lyre. Praise Him with timbrel and dance; praise Him with strings and flute. Praise Him with clashing cymbals; praise Him with resounding cymbals. Let all that breathes praise the LORD. Halleluya! *Ps. 150*

תָּנָא In the academy of Rabbi Yishmael it was taught: Were the people of Israel privileged to greet the presence of their heavenly Father only once a month, it would have been sufficient for them. Abaye said: Therefore it [the blessing of the moon] should be said standing. Who is this coming up from the desert, leaning on her beloved? *Sanhedrin 42a* *Song. 8*

דָּוִד מֶלֶךְ יִשְׂרָאֵל חַי וְקַיָּם.

Turn to three people and say to each:

שָׁלוֹם עֲלֵיכֶם.

They respond:

עֲלֵיכֶם שָׁלוֹם.

Say three times:

סִימָן טוֹב וּמַזָּל טוֹב יְהֵא לָנוּ וּלְכָל יִשְׂרָאֵל, אָמֵן.

קוֹל דּוֹדִי הִנֵּה־זֶה בָּא, מְדַלֵּג עַל־הֶהָרִים, מְקַפֵּץ עַל־הַגְּבָעוֹת: דּוֹמֶה דוֹדִי לִצְבִי אוֹ לְעֹפֶר הָאַיָּלִים, הִנֵּה־זֶה עוֹמֵד אַחַר כָּתְלֵנוּ, מַשְׁגִּיחַ מִן־הַחַלֹּנוֹת, מֵצִיץ מִן־הַחֲרַכִּים: שיר השירים ב

שִׁיר לַמַּעֲלוֹת, אֶשָּׂא עֵינַי אֶל־הֶהָרִים, מֵאַיִן יָבֹא עֶזְרִי: עֶזְרִי מֵעִם יהוה, עֹשֵׂה שָׁמַיִם וָאָרֶץ: אַל־יִתֵּן לַמּוֹט רַגְלֶךָ, אַל־יָנוּם שֹׁמְרֶךָ: הִנֵּה לֹא־יָנוּם וְלֹא יִישָׁן, שׁוֹמֵר יִשְׂרָאֵל: יהוה שֹׁמְרֶךָ, יהוה צִלְּךָ עַל־יַד יְמִינֶךָ: יוֹמָם הַשֶּׁמֶשׁ לֹא־יַכֶּכָּה, וְיָרֵחַ בַּלָּיְלָה: יהוה יִשְׁמָרְךָ מִכָּל־רָע, יִשְׁמֹר אֶת־נַפְשֶׁךָ: יהוה יִשְׁמָר־צֵאתְךָ וּבוֹאֶךָ, מֵעַתָּה וְעַד־עוֹלָם: תהלים קכא

הַלְלוּיָהּ, הַלְלוּ־אֵל בְּקָדְשׁוֹ, הַלְלוּהוּ בִּרְקִיעַ עֻזּוֹ: הַלְלוּהוּ בִגְבוּרֹתָיו, הַלְלוּהוּ כְּרֹב גֻּדְלוֹ: הַלְלוּהוּ בְּתֵקַע שׁוֹפָר, הַלְלוּהוּ בְּנֵבֶל וְכִנּוֹר: הַלְלוּהוּ בְתֹף וּמָחוֹל, הַלְלוּהוּ בְּמִנִּים וְעֻגָב: הַלְלוּהוּ בְצִלְצְלֵי־שָׁמַע, הַלְלוּהוּ בְּצִלְצְלֵי תְרוּעָה: כֹּל הַנְּשָׁמָה תְּהַלֵּל יָהּ, הַלְלוּיָהּ: תהלים קנ

תָּנָא דְבֵי רַבִּי יִשְׁמָעֵאל: אִלְמָלֵי לֹא זָכוּ יִשְׂרָאֵל אֶלָּא לְהַקְבִּיל פְּנֵי אֲבִיהֶם שֶׁבַּשָּׁמַיִם פַּעַם אַחַת בַּחֹדֶשׁ, דַּיָּם. אָמַר אַבַּיֵּי: הִלְכָּךְ צָרִיךְ לְמֵימְרָא מְעֻמָּד. מִי זֹאת עֹלָה מִן־הַמִּדְבָּר, מִתְרַפֶּקֶת עַל־דּוֹדָהּ: סנהדרין מב. שיר השירים ח

וִיהִי May it be Your will, LORD my God and God of my ancestors, to make good the deficiency of the moon, so that it is no longer in its diminished state. May the light of the moon be like the light of the sun and like the light of the seven days of creation as it was before it was diminished, as it says, "The two great luminaries." And may there *Gen. 1* be fulfilled for us the verse: "They shall seek the LORD their God, and *Hos. 3* David their king." Amen.

לַמְנַצֵּחַ For the conductor of music. With stringed instruments, a psalm. *Ps. 67* A song. May God be gracious to us and bless us. May He make His face shine on us, Selah. Then will Your way be known on earth, Your salvation among all the nations. Let the peoples praise You, God; let all peoples praise You. Let nations rejoice and sing for joy, for You judge the peoples with equity, and guide the nations of the earth, Selah. Let the peoples praise You, God; let all peoples praise You. The earth has yielded its harvest. May God, our God, bless us. God will bless us, and all the ends of the earth will fear Him.

Stand while saying Aleinu.

עָלֵינוּ It is our duty to praise the Master of all,
and ascribe greatness to the Author of creation,
who has not made us like the nations of the lands
nor placed us like the families of the earth;
who has not made our portion like theirs,
nor our destiny like all their multitudes.
(For they worship vanity and emptiness,
and pray to a god who cannot save.)
▾ *Bow:* But we bow in worship
and thank the Supreme King of kings, the Holy One, blessed be He,
who extends the heavens and establishes the earth,
whose throne of glory is in the heavens above,
and whose power's Presence is in the highest of heights.
He is our God; there is no other.
Truly He is our King, there is none else,
as it is written in His Torah: "You shall know and take to heart this day *Deut. 4*
that the LORD is God, in heaven above and on earth below.
There is no other."

וִיהִי רָצוֹן מִלְּפָנֶיךָ יהוה אֱלֹהַי וֵאלֹהֵי אֲבוֹתַי, לְמַלֹּאת פְּגִימַת הַלְּבָנָה וְלֹא יִהְיֶה בָּהּ שׁוּם מִעוּט. וִיהִי אוֹר הַלְּבָנָה כְּאוֹר הַחַמָּה וּכְאוֹר
בראשית א שִׁבְעַת יְמֵי בְרֵאשִׁית, כְּמוֹ שֶׁהָיְתָה קֹדֶם מִעוּטָהּ, שֶׁנֶּאֱמַר: אֶת־שְׁנֵי
הושע ג הַמְּאֹרֹת הַגְּדֹלִים: וְיִתְקַיֵּם בָּנוּ מִקְרָא שֶׁכָּתוּב: וּבִקְשׁוּ אֶת־יהוה אֱלֹהֵיהֶם וְאֵת דָּוִיד מַלְכָּם: אָמֵן.

תהלים סז לַמְנַצֵּחַ בִּנְגִינֹת, מִזְמוֹר שִׁיר: אֱלֹהִים יְחָנֵּנוּ וִיבָרְכֵנוּ, יָאֵר פָּנָיו אִתָּנוּ סֶלָה: לָדַעַת בָּאָרֶץ דַּרְכֶּךָ, בְּכָל־גּוֹיִם יְשׁוּעָתֶךָ: יוֹדוּךָ עַמִּים אֱלֹהִים, יוֹדוּךָ עַמִּים כֻּלָּם: יִשְׂמְחוּ וִירַנְּנוּ לְאֻמִּים, כִּי־תִשְׁפֹּט עַמִּים מִישֹׁר, וּלְאֻמִּים בָּאָרֶץ תַּנְחֵם סֶלָה: יוֹדוּךָ עַמִּים אֱלֹהִים, יוֹדוּךָ עַמִּים כֻּלָּם: אֶרֶץ נָתְנָה יְבוּלָהּ, יְבָרְכֵנוּ אֱלֹהִים אֱלֹהֵינוּ: יְבָרְכֵנוּ אֱלֹהִים, וְיִירְאוּ אוֹתוֹ כָּל־אַפְסֵי־אָרֶץ:

Stand while saying עָלֵינוּ.

עָלֵינוּ לְשַׁבֵּחַ לַאֲדוֹן הַכֹּל, לָתֵת גְּדֻלָּה לְיוֹצֵר בְּרֵאשִׁית
שֶׁלֹּא עָשָׂנוּ כְּגוֹיֵי הָאֲרָצוֹת, וְלֹא שָׂמָנוּ כְּמִשְׁפְּחוֹת הָאֲדָמָה
שֶׁלֹּא שָׂם חֶלְקֵנוּ כָּהֶם וְגוֹרָלֵנוּ כְּכָל הֲמוֹנָם.
(שֶׁהֵם מִשְׁתַּחֲוִים לְהֶבֶל וָרִיק וּמִתְפַּלְלִים אֶל אֵל לֹא יוֹשִׁיעַ.)
▾ *Bow* וַאֲנַחְנוּ כּוֹרְעִים וּמִשְׁתַּחֲוִים וּמוֹדִים
לִפְנֵי מֶלֶךְ מַלְכֵי הַמְּלָכִים, הַקָּדוֹשׁ בָּרוּךְ הוּא
שֶׁהוּא נוֹטֶה שָׁמַיִם וְיוֹסֵד אָרֶץ
וּמוֹשַׁב יְקָרוֹ בַּשָּׁמַיִם מִמַּעַל
וּשְׁכִינַת עֻזּוֹ בְּגָבְהֵי מְרוֹמִים.
הוּא אֱלֹהֵינוּ, אֵין עוֹד.
אֱמֶת מַלְכֵּנוּ, אֶפֶס זוּלָתוֹ, כַּכָּתוּב בְּתוֹרָתוֹ
דברים ד וְיָדַעְתָּ הַיּוֹם וַהֲשֵׁבֹתָ אֶל־לְבָבֶךָ
כִּי יהוה הוּא הָאֱלֹהִים בַּשָּׁמַיִם מִמַּעַל וְעַל־הָאָרֶץ מִתָּחַת, אֵין עוֹד:

Therefore, we place our hope in You, LORD our God,
that we may soon see the glory of Your power,
when You will remove abominations from the earth,
and idols will be utterly destroyed,
when the world will be perfected
under the sovereignty of the Almighty,
when all humanity will call on Your name,
to turn all the earth's wicked toward You.
All the world's inhabitants will realize and know
that to You every knee must bow and every tongue swear loyalty.
Before You, LORD our God, they will kneel and bow down
and give honor to Your glorious name.
They will all accept the yoke of Your kingdom,
and You will reign over them soon and for ever.
For the kingdom is Yours, and to all eternity You will reign in glory,
as it is written in Your Torah: "The LORD will reign for ever and ever." *Ex. 15*
▸ And it is said: "Then the LORD shall be King over all the earth; *Zech. 14*
on that day the LORD shall be One and His name One."

Some add:

Have no fear of sudden terror or of the ruin when it overtakes the wicked. *Prov. 3*
Devise your strategy, but it will be thwarted; propose your plan, *Is. 8*
but it will not stand, for God is with us.
When you grow old, I will still be the same. *Is. 46*
When your hair turns gray, I will still carry you.
I made you, I will bear you, I will carry you, and I will rescue you.

MOURNER'S KADDISH

The following prayer, said by mourners, requires the presence of a minyan.
A transliteration can be found on page 892.

Mourner: יִתְגַּדַּל Magnified and sanctified may His great name be,
in the world He created by His will.
May He establish His kingdom
in your lifetime and in your days,
and in the lifetime of all the house of Israel,
swiftly and soon – and say: Amen.

All: May His great name be blessed for ever and all time.

עַל כֵּן נְקַוֶּה לְּךָ יהוה אֱלֹהֵינוּ, לִרְאוֹת מְהֵרָה בְּתִפְאֶרֶת עֻזֶּךָ
לְהַעֲבִיר גִּלּוּלִים מִן הָאָרֶץ, וְהָאֱלִילִים כָּרוֹת יִכָּרֵתוּן
לְתַקֵּן עוֹלָם בְּמַלְכוּת שַׁדַּי.
וְכָל בְּנֵי בָשָׂר יִקְרְאוּ בִשְׁמֶךָ לְהַפְנוֹת אֵלֶיךָ כָּל רִשְׁעֵי אָרֶץ.
יַכִּירוּ וְיֵדְעוּ כָּל יוֹשְׁבֵי תֵבֵל
כִּי לְךָ תִּכְרַע כָּל בֶּרֶךְ, תִּשָּׁבַע כָּל לָשׁוֹן.
לְפָנֶיךָ יהוה אֱלֹהֵינוּ יִכְרְעוּ וְיִפֹּלוּ, וְלִכְבוֹד שִׁמְךָ יְקָר יִתֵּנוּ
וִיקַבְּלוּ כֻלָּם אֶת עֹל מַלְכוּתֶךָ
וְתִמְלֹךְ עֲלֵיהֶם מְהֵרָה לְעוֹלָם וָעֶד.
כִּי הַמַּלְכוּת שֶׁלְּךָ הִיא וּלְעוֹלְמֵי עַד תִּמְלֹךְ בְּכָבוֹד
כַּכָּתוּב בְּתוֹרָתֶךָ, יהוה יִמְלֹךְ לְעֹלָם וָעֶד: שמות טו
◂ וְנֶאֱמַר, וְהָיָה יהוה לְמֶלֶךְ עַל־כָּל־הָאָרֶץ זכריה יד
בַּיּוֹם הַהוּא יִהְיֶה יהוה אֶחָד וּשְׁמוֹ אֶחָד:

Some add:

אַל־תִּירָא מִפַּחַד פִּתְאֹם וּמִשֹּׁאַת רְשָׁעִים כִּי תָבֹא: משלי ג
עֻצוּ עֵצָה וְתֻפָר, דַּבְּרוּ דָבָר וְלֹא יָקוּם, כִּי עִמָּנוּ אֵל: ישעיה ח
וְעַד־זִקְנָה אֲנִי הוּא, וְעַד־שֵׂיבָה אֲנִי אֶסְבֹּל, אֲנִי עָשִׂיתִי וַאֲנִי אֶשָּׂא וַאֲנִי אֶסְבֹּל וַאֲמַלֵּט: ישעיה מו

קדיש יתום

The following prayer, said by mourners, requires the presence of a מנין.
A transliteration can be found on page 892.

אבל: יִתְגַּדַּל וְיִתְקַדַּשׁ שְׁמֵהּ רַבָּא (קהל: אָמֵן)
בְּעָלְמָא דִּי בְרָא כִרְעוּתֵהּ
וְיַמְלִיךְ מַלְכוּתֵהּ
בְּחַיֵּיכוֹן וּבְיוֹמֵיכוֹן וּבְחַיֵּי דְכָל בֵּית יִשְׂרָאֵל
בַּעֲגָלָא וּבִזְמַן קָרִיב, וְאִמְרוּ אָמֵן. (קהל: אָמֵן)

קהל ואבל: יְהֵא שְׁמֵהּ רַבָּא מְבָרַךְ לְעָלַם וּלְעָלְמֵי עָלְמַיָּא.

Mourner: Blessed and praised,
glorified and exalted,
raised and honored,
uplifted and lauded
be the name of the Holy One,
blessed be He,
beyond any blessing,
song, praise and consolation
uttered in the world –
and say: Amen.
May there be great peace from heaven,
and life for us and all Israel –
and say: Amen.

Bow and take three steps back as if taking leave of the Divine Presence.
Bow left: May He who makes peace in His high places,
Bow right: make peace *Bow forward:* for us and all Israel –
and say: Amen.

All sing:

טוֹבִים Good are the radiant stars our God created;
He formed them with knowledge,
understanding and deliberation.
He gave them strength and might
to rule throughout the world.

Full of splendor, radiating light,
beautiful is their splendor throughout the world.
Glad as they go forth, joyous as they return,
they fulfill with awe their Creator's will.

Glory and honor they give to His name,
jubilation and song at the mention of His majesty.
He called the sun into being and it shone with light.
He looked and fashioned the form of the moon.

אבל: יִתְבָּרַךְ וְיִשְׁתַּבַּח וְיִתְפָּאַר
וְיִתְרוֹמַם וְיִתְנַשֵּׂא וְיִתְהַדָּר וְיִתְעַלֶּה וְיִתְהַלָּל
שְׁמֵהּ דְּקֻדְשָׁא בְּרִיךְ הוּא (קהל: בְּרִיךְ הוּא)
לְעֵלָּא מִן כָּל בִּרְכָתָא
/ בעשרת ימי תשובה: לְעֵלָּא לְעֵלָּא מִכָּל בִּרְכָתָא/
וְשִׁירָתָא, תֻּשְׁבְּחָתָא וְנֶחֱמָתָא
דַּאֲמִירָן בְּעָלְמָא
וְאִמְרוּ אָמֵן. (קהל: אָמֵן)

יְהֵא שְׁלָמָא רַבָּא מִן שְׁמַיָּא
וְחַיִּים, עָלֵינוּ וְעַל כָּל יִשְׂרָאֵל
וְאִמְרוּ אָמֵן. (קהל: אָמֵן)

Bow and take three steps back as if taking leave of the Divine Presence.

Bow left עֹשֶׂה שָׁלוֹם/ בעשרת ימי תשובה: הַשָּׁלוֹם/ בִּמְרוֹמָיו
Bow right הוּא יַעֲשֶׂה שָׁלוֹם *Bow forward* עָלֵינוּ
וְעַל כָּל יִשְׂרָאֵל, וְאִמְרוּ אָמֵן.

All sing:

טוֹבִים מְאוֹרוֹת שֶׁבָּרָא אֱלֹהֵינוּ, יְצָרָם בְּדַעַת בְּבִינָה וּבְהַשְׂכֵּל
כֹּחַ וּגְבוּרָה נָתַן בָּהֶם, לִהְיוֹת מוֹשְׁלִים בְּקֶרֶב תֵּבֵל.

מְלֵאִים זִיו וּמְפִיקִים נֹגַהּ, נָאֶה זִיוָם בְּכָל הָעוֹלָם
שְׂמֵחִים בְּצֵאתָם וְשָׂשִׂים בְּבוֹאָם, עוֹשִׂים בְּאֵימָה רְצוֹן קוֹנָם.

פְּאֵר וְכָבוֹד נוֹתְנִים לִשְׁמוֹ, צָהֳלָה וְרִנָּה לְזֵכֶר מַלְכוּתוֹ
קָרָא לַשֶּׁמֶשׁ וַיִּזְרַח אוֹר, רָאָה וְהִתְקִין צוּרַת הַלְּבָנָה.

HAVDALA AT HOME

Taking a cup of wine in the right hand, say:

הִנֵּה Behold, God is my salvation. I will trust and not be afraid. *Is. 12*
The LORD, the LORD, is my strength and my song.
He has become my salvation.
With joy you will draw water from the springs of salvation.
Salvation is the LORD's; on Your people is Your blessing, Selah. *Ps. 3*
The LORD of hosts is with us, the God of Jacob is our stronghold, Selah. *Ps. 46*
LORD of hosts: happy is the one who trusts in You. *Ps. 84*
LORD, save! May the King answer us on the day we call. *Ps. 20*
For the Jews there was light and gladness, joy and honor – *Esther 8*
so may it be for us.
I will lift the cup of salvation and call on the name of the LORD. *Ps. 116*

---

fire was granted as a gift by God for man to join Him in becoming a creator, to continue the act of creation and help perfect the world. Beginning the week by lighting a match is also a way of highlighting the difference between Shabbat whose beginning is marked by the lighting of candles and the cessation of any further "work," and the end of Shabbat which is marked by our relighting a candle to show that "work" is now permitted. Alternatively, it is as if light was created anew (Rashba cited *Be'er Heiteiv* 299:14) and the process of creation begins once again. To see the light cast from the candle is to banish darkness and feel joy at the ability to control one's environment (*Pirkei DeRabbi Eliezer* 20).

And finally, there is a blessing which highlights the differences between light and darkness, the holy and the profane, Israel and the nations. Hopefully these are among the lessons that we have been reminded of over Shabbat, the ones that will help us approach the coming week with the right perspective as creators, as holy beings, and as people with a mission to be a holy light unto the nations.

The order of the blessings seems to go in order of the senses or faculties moving from the lower to the upper portions of our head, i.e., for wine we use our sense of taste, for spices our sense of smell, for light our sense of sight, and for the final blessing we use our intelligence to distinguish between the holy and the mundane (Rabbi Y. Jacobson).

HILKHOT TEFILLA • הלכות תפילה

Havdala is usually said while standing (Rema) although some do sit (*Shulḥan Arukh* 296:6). Although there is a custom to recite it in the synagogue, just we did

This **HILKHOT TEFILLA** *continues on page 657.*

סדר הבדלה בבית

Taking a cup of wine in the right hand, say:

הִנֵּה אֵל יְשׁוּעָתִי אֶבְטַח, וְלֹא אֶפְחָד ישעיה יב
כִּי־עָזִּי וְזִמְרָת יָהּ יהוה, וַיְהִי־לִי לִישׁוּעָה:
וּשְׁאַבְתֶּם־מַיִם בְּשָׂשׂוֹן, מִמַּעַיְנֵי הַיְשׁוּעָה:
לַיהוה הַיְשׁוּעָה, עַל־עַמְּךָ בִרְכָתֶךָ סֶּלָה: תהלים ג
יהוה צְבָאוֹת עִמָּנוּ, מִשְׂגָּב לָנוּ אֱלֹהֵי יַעֲקֹב סֶלָה: תהלים מו
יהוה צְבָאוֹת, אַשְׁרֵי אָדָם בֹּטֵחַ בָּךְ: תהלים פד
יהוה הוֹשִׁיעָה, הַמֶּלֶךְ יַעֲנֵנוּ בְיוֹם־קָרְאֵנוּ: תהלים כ
לַיְּהוּדִים הָיְתָה אוֹרָה וְשִׂמְחָה וְשָׂשֹׂן וִיקָר: כֵּן תִּהְיֶה לָּנוּ. אסתר ח
כּוֹס־יְשׁוּעוֹת אֶשָּׂא, וּבְשֵׁם יהוה אֶקְרָא: תהלים קטז

INTRODUCTION TO HAVDALA

Just as we ushered in the Shabbat with candles and wine, so too do we escort her out. This is an extension of the commandment to "remember the Shabbat and sanctify it" for remembering is as much an obligation as we cross over the threshold from the holy to the mundane as it was when we crossed from the mundane to the holy twenty-five hours ago. (Rambam, *Sefer HaMitzvot* 155). The very name of the ceremony, *Havdala*, derives from the Hebrew word "to separate" or "distinguish."

The Kiddush is preceded by the recitation of some verses that focus on the theme of salvation (mentioned seven times) and the name of Hashem (eight times), as if to say that rescue during the coming week will come from Hashem alone, and only to those who put their faith in Him.

Another blessing is said over fragrant spices, designed to provide consolation and rejuvenation, a kind of counterbalance to the loss of our *neshama yeteira*, the extra soul which helped to animate and spiritualize us over the course of Shabbat (Abudarham). This is to make the departure of Shabbat less abrupt and disconcerting.

Another blessing is then said over a candle with multiple wicks. It is the symbolic representation of our return to the creative process of the week. The Gemara (*Pesaḥim* 54a) relates that after the very first Shabbat, Adam decided to replicate the actions of God and brought two stones, rubbed them together, and created fire. Unlike Prometheus of Greek mythology who defied the gods by stealing fire and giving it to humanity, in the Jewish conception,

When making Havdala for others, add:
Please pay attention, my masters.

Blessed are You, LORD our God, King of the Universe,
who creates the fruit of the vine.

Hold the spice box and say:

Blessed are You, LORD our God, King of the Universe,
who creates the various spices.

Smell the spices and put the spice box down.
Lift the hands toward the flame of the Havdala candle and say:

Blessed are You, LORD our God, King of the Universe,
who creates the lights of fire.

Holding the cup of wine again in the right hand, say:

בָּרוּךְ Blessed are You, LORD our God, King of the Universe,
who distinguishes between sacred and secular,
between light and darkness,
between Israel and the nations,
between the seventh day and the six days of work.
Blessed are You, LORD,
who distinguishes between sacred and secular.

---

one's love for the mitzva or as a symbolic prayer for a week filled with insight and wisdom.

Regarding the blessing over the candle, since one does not recite a blessing of this kind without deriving some resulting benefit, the custom is to hold up one's hands to be able to see them in the light of the candle and thereby use the light that is cast from the flame. Some specifically look at the reflection from their fingernails to see the contrast between shadows and light. Some also look at their fingers in the bent position as if to say that they have been tied down from using fire or "work" during Shabbat, and then stretch them open in the light of the flame in order to show that they are now free again to be used as they wish (Maharam of Rothenburg).

When making הבדלה *for others, add:*

סַבְרִי מָרָנָן

בָּרוּךְ אַתָּה יהוה אֱלֹהֵינוּ מֶלֶךְ הָעוֹלָם
בּוֹרֵא פְּרִי הַגָּפֶן.

Hold the spice box and say:

בָּרוּךְ אַתָּה יהוה אֱלֹהֵינוּ מֶלֶךְ הָעוֹלָם
בּוֹרֵא מִינֵי בְשָׂמִים.

Smell the spices and put the spice box down.
Lift the hands toward the flame of the הבדלה *candle and say:*

בָּרוּךְ אַתָּה יהוה אֱלֹהֵינוּ מֶלֶךְ הָעוֹלָם
בּוֹרֵא מְאוֹרֵי הָאֵשׁ.

Holding the cup of wine again in the right hand, say:

בָּרוּךְ אַתָּה יהוה אֱלֹהֵינוּ מֶלֶךְ הָעוֹלָם
הַמַּבְדִּיל בֵּין קֹדֶשׁ לְחֹל
בֵּין אוֹר לְחֹשֶׁךְ
בֵּין יִשְׂרָאֵל לָעַמִּים
בֵּין יוֹם הַשְּׁבִיעִי לְשֵׁשֶׁת יְמֵי הַמַּעֲשֶׂה.
בָּרוּךְ אַתָּה יהוה, הַמַּבְדִּיל בֵּין קֹדֶשׁ לְחֹל.

---

kiddush on Friday night, the primary obligation is to recite it at home.

The tradition is that the glass is filled to the very brim (some fill it to overflowing) as a sign of impending wealth during the coming week in keeping with the rabbinic adage (*Eiruvin* 65a) that any house that has wine flowing like water is filled with blessing (Rema 296:1).

Similarly some have the custom to dip ones finger in the wine and dab the top of one's eyes or forehead as a sign of

הַמַּבְדִּיל He who distinguishes between sacred and secular,
may He forgive our sins.
May He multiply our offspring and wealth like the sand,
and like the stars at night.

The day has passed like a palm tree's shadow;
I call on God to fulfill what the watchman said: *Is. 21*
"Morning comes, though now it is night."

Your righteousness is as high as Mount Tabor.
May You pass high over my sins.
[Let them be] like yesterday when it has passed, *Ps. 90*
like a watch in the night.

The time of offerings has passed.
Would that I might rest.
I am weary with my sighing, *Ps. 6*
every night I drench [with tears].

Hear my voice; let it not be cast aside.
Open for me the lofty gate.
My head is filled with the dew of dawn, *Song. 5*
my hair with raindrops of the night.

Heed my prayer, revered and awesome God.
When I cry, grant me deliverance at twilight, *Prov. 7*
as the day fades, or in the darkness of the night.

I call to You, Lord: Save me.
Make known to me the path of life.
Rescue me from misery before day turns to night.

Cleanse the defilement of my deeds,
lest those who torment me say,
"Where is the God who made me, *Job 35*
who gives cause for songs in the night?"

We are in Your hands like clay:
please forgive our sins, light and grave.
Day to day they pour forth speech, *Ps. 19*
and night to night [they communicate knowledge].

הַמַּבְדִּיל בֵּין קֹדֶשׁ לְחוֹל, חַטֹּאתֵינוּ הוּא יִמְחֹל
זַרְעֵנוּ וְכַסְפֵּנוּ יַרְבֶּה כַחוֹל וְכַכּוֹכָבִים בַּלָּיְלָה.

יוֹם פָּנָה כְּצֵל תֹּמֶר, אֶקְרָא לָאֵל עָלַי גּוֹמֵר
אָמַר שֹׁמֵר, אָתָא בֹקֶר וְגַם־לָיְלָה: ישעיה כא

צִדְקָתְךָ כְּהַר תָּבוֹר, עַל חֲטָאַי עָבוֹר תַּעֲבֹר
כְּיוֹם אֶתְמוֹל כִּי יַעֲבֹר, וְאַשְׁמוּרָה בַלָּיְלָה: תהלים צ

חָלְפָה עוֹנַת מִנְחָתִי, מִי יִתֵּן מְנוּחָתִי
יָגַעְתִּי בְאַנְחָתִי, אַשְׂחֶה בְכָל־לַיְלָה: תהלים ו

קוֹלִי בַּל יֻנְטַל, פְּתַח לִי שַׁעַר הַמְנֻטָּל
שֶׁרֹּאשִׁי נִמְלָא טָל, קְוֻצּוֹתַי רְסִיסֵי לָיְלָה: שיר השירים ה

הֵעָתֵר נוֹרָא וְאָיֹם, אֲשַׁוֵּעַ, תְּנָה פִדְיוֹם
בְּנֶשֶׁף־בְּעֶרֶב יוֹם, בְּאִישׁוֹן לָיְלָה: משלי ז

קְרָאתִיךָ יָהּ, הוֹשִׁיעֵנִי, אֹרַח חַיִּים תּוֹדִיעֵנִי
מִדַּלָּה תְבַצְּעֵנִי, מִיּוֹם עַד לָיְלָה.

טַהֵר טִנּוּף מַעֲשַׂי, פֶּן יֹאמְרוּ מַכְעִיסַי
אַיֵּה אֱלוֹהַּ עֹשָׂי, נֹתֵן זְמִרוֹת בַּלָּיְלָה: איוב לה

נַחְנוּ בְיָדְךָ כַּחֹמֶר, סְלַח נָא עַל קַל וָחֹמֶר
יוֹם לְיוֹם יַבִּיעַ אֹמֶר, וְלַיְלָה לְּלָיְלָה: תהלים יט

COUNTING OF THE OMER[BA]

The Omer is counted each night from the second night of Pesaḥ until the night before Shavuot.
Some say the following meditation before the blessing:

For the sake of the unification of the Holy One, blessed be He,
and His Divine Presence, in reverence and love,
to unify the name *Yod-Heh* with *Vav-Heh*
in perfect unity in the name of all Israel.

הִנְנִי I am prepared and ready to fulfill the positive commandment of Counting the Omer, as is written in the Torah, "You shall count seven complete weeks from the day following the [Pesaḥ] rest day, when you brought the Omer as a wave-offering. To the day after the seventh week you shall count fifty days. Then you shall present a meal-offering of new grain to the LORD." May the pleasantness of the LORD our God be upon us. Establish for us the work of our hands, O establish the work of our hands.

Lev. 23

Ps. 90

בָּרוּךְ Blessed are You, LORD our God,
King of the Universe,
who has made us holy through His commandments,
and has commanded us about counting the Omer.

---

before a vacation, before seeing a friend or a loved one. People often count down the days and weeks before a life milestone such as a bar mitzva or a wedding. Counting is a way to mark time, to express our hopes and our longing. *Sefirat HaOmer,* the daily counting of the days and weeks from Pesaḥ to Shavuot, is that kind of counting. For without Shavuot, Pesaḥ would be meaningless. The giving of the Torah was the reason for our liberation, the essence of who we are as a people, our definition of ourselves. The giving of the Torah changed the course of history, and not just for the Jews. Shavuot is thus our spiritual birthday, the true source of our freedom, a rendezvous with an old friend, the marriage of the Jewish people with God. We count the days and weeks to express our excitement or to remind ourselves to get excited.

The *Ḥagim* are not just holidays whose task is to commemorate the past and provide opportunity for recreation; rather, they are holy days whose task is to reenact and to re-create. Especially because Shavuot has fewer symbols and rituals associated with it than say, Pesaḥ or Sukkot, it may need even more preparation. For as we know, most special events are made special because we prepare for them. The more we prepare, the more we anticipate, the more meaningful is the event when it finally arrives. How can I better prepare for the coming of the giving of the Torah? What can I do to make this coming Shavuot more meaningful? The counting of the Omer can be a beginning.

סדר ספירת העומר[בא]

The עומר *is counted each night from the second night of* פסח *until the night before* שבועות*.*
Some say the following meditation before the blessing:

לְשֵׁם יִחוּד קֻדְשָׁא בְּרִיךְ הוּא וּשְׁכִינְתֵּהּ בִּדְחִילוּ וּרְחִימוּ
לְיַחֵד שֵׁם י״ה בו״ה בְּיִחוּדָא שְׁלִים בְּשֵׁם כָּל יִשְׂרָאֵל.

הִנְנִי מוּכָן וּמְזֻמָּן לְקַיֵּם מִצְוַת עֲשֵׂה שֶׁל סְפִירַת הָעֹמֶר. כְּמוֹ שֶׁכָּתוּב בַּתּוֹרָה,
ויקרא כג וּסְפַרְתֶּם לָכֶם מִמָּחֳרַת הַשַּׁבָּת, מִיּוֹם הֲבִיאֲכֶם אֶת־עֹמֶר הַתְּנוּפָה, שֶׁבַע
שַׁבָּתוֹת תְּמִימֹת תִּהְיֶינָה: עַד מִמָּחֳרַת הַשַּׁבָּת הַשְּׁבִיעִת תִּסְפְּרוּ חֲמִשִּׁים
תהלים צ יוֹם, וְהִקְרַבְתֶּם מִנְחָה חֲדָשָׁה לַיהוה: וִיהִי נֹעַם אֲדֹנָי אֱלֹהֵינוּ עָלֵינוּ, וּמַעֲשֵׂה
יָדֵינוּ כּוֹנְנָה עָלֵינוּ, וּמַעֲשֵׂה יָדֵינוּ כּוֹנְנֵהוּ:

בָּרוּךְ אַתָּה יהוה אֱלֹהֵינוּ מֶלֶךְ הָעוֹלָם
אֲשֶׁר קִדְּשָׁנוּ בְּמִצְוֹתָיו וְצִוָּנוּ עַל סְפִירַת הָעֹמֶר.

BIUR TEFILLA • ביאור תפילה

ספירת העומר – *COUNTING OF THE OMER.* In the days of the *Beit HaMikdash*, on the first day after Pesaḥ, an offering was brought consisting of an *omer* (a unit of measurement, approximately 2–4 liters) of barley. Before this offering, any grains from new crops (*ḥadash*) were not permitted to be eaten. The Torah says that the next 49 days – seven weeks – of the "waving of the *omer*" were to be counted until the arrival of Shavuot, when another offering was brought to mark the beginning of the grain harvest. This is what became known as the period of the counting (*sefira*) of the *omer*. When the *Beit HaMikdash* was destroyed, the Rabbis mandated that we continue the practice of counting.

As for the requirement not to eat from crops that were planted before Pesaḥ until the day after Pesaḥ (*ḥadash*), it is generally accepted that this rule is independent of the existence of the *Beit HaMikdash;* it continues to be observed both in Israel and in the Diaspora, where people carefully calculate the dates of the growing and harvesting of the grains grown in their country and used in different products to make sure that they only eat from older crops (*yashan*). Others maintain that this is an act of piety that is untenable for most people and rely upon a more lenient *halakhic* view.

ANI TEFILLA • אני תפילה

ספירת העומר – *COUNTING OF THE OMER.* Do you recall the last time you counted the days before an important event in your life? Perhaps it was the days before a birthday,

16 Nisan

1. Today is the first day
of the Omer.

17 Nisan

2. Today is the second day
of the Omer.

18 Nisan

3. Today is the third day
of the Omer.

19 Nisan

4. Today is the fourth day
of the Omer.

20 Nisan

5. Today is the fifth day
of the Omer.

21 Nisan

6. Today is the sixth day
of the Omer.

22 Nisan

7. Today is the seventh day,
making one week
of the Omer.

23 Nisan

8. Today is the eighth day,
making one week and one day
of the Omer.

24 Nisan

9. Today is the ninth day,
making one week and two days
of the Omer.

25 Nisan

10. Today is the tenth day,
making one week and three
days of the Omer.

26 Nisan

11. Today is the eleventh day,
making one week
and four days
of the Omer.

27 Nisan

12. Today is the twelfth day,
making one week
and five days
of the Omer.

28 Nisan

13. Today is the thirteenth day,
making one week
and six days
of the Omer.

29 Nisan

14. Today is the fourteenth day,
making two weeks
of the Omer.

30 Nisan, 1st day Rosh Ḥodesh

15. Today is the fifteenth day,
making two weeks
and one day
of the Omer.

1 Iyar, 2nd day Rosh Ḥodesh

16. Today is the sixteenth day,
making two weeks
and two days
of the Omer.

2 Iyar

17. Today is the seventeenth day,
making two weeks
and three days
of the Omer.

טז בניסן

1. הַיּוֹם יוֹם אֶחָד בָּעֹמֶר.

חסד שבחסד

יז בניסן

2. הַיּוֹם שְׁנֵי יָמִים בָּעֹמֶר.

גבורה שבחסד

יח בניסן

3. הַיּוֹם שְׁלֹשָׁה יָמִים בָּעֹמֶר.

תפארת שבחסד

יט בניסן

4. הַיּוֹם אַרְבָּעָה יָמִים בָּעֹמֶר.

נצח שבחסד

כ בניסן

5. הַיּוֹם חֲמִשָּׁה יָמִים בָּעֹמֶר.

הוד שבחסד

כא בניסן

6. הַיּוֹם שִׁשָּׁה יָמִים בָּעֹמֶר.

יסוד שבחסד

כב בניסן

7. הַיּוֹם שִׁבְעָה יָמִים
שֶׁהֵם שָׁבוּעַ אֶחָד בָּעֹמֶר.

מלכות שבחסד

כג בניסן

8. הַיּוֹם שְׁמוֹנָה יָמִים
שֶׁהֵם שָׁבוּעַ אֶחָד וְיוֹם אֶחָד
בָּעֹמֶר.

חסד שבגבורה

כד בניסן

9. הַיּוֹם תִּשְׁעָה יָמִים
שֶׁהֵם שָׁבוּעַ אֶחָד וּשְׁנֵי יָמִים
בָּעֹמֶר.

גבורה שבגבורה

כה בניסן

10. הַיּוֹם עֲשָׂרָה יָמִים
שֶׁהֵם שָׁבוּעַ אֶחָד וּשְׁלֹשָׁה
יָמִים בָּעֹמֶר.

תפארת שבגבורה

כו בניסן

11. הַיּוֹם אַחַד עָשָׂר יוֹם
שֶׁהֵם שָׁבוּעַ אֶחָד וְאַרְבָּעָה
יָמִים בָּעֹמֶר.

נצח שבגבורה

כז בניסן

12. הַיּוֹם שְׁנֵים עָשָׂר יוֹם
שֶׁהֵם שָׁבוּעַ אֶחָד וַחֲמִשָּׁה
יָמִים בָּעֹמֶר.

הוד שבגבורה

כח בניסן

13. הַיּוֹם שְׁלֹשָׁה עָשָׂר יוֹם
שֶׁהֵם שָׁבוּעַ אֶחָד וְשִׁשָּׁה יָמִים
בָּעֹמֶר.

יסוד שבגבורה

כט בניסן

14. הַיּוֹם אַרְבָּעָה עָשָׂר יוֹם
שֶׁהֵם שְׁנֵי שָׁבוּעוֹת
בָּעֹמֶר.

מלכות שבגבורה

ל בניסן, א׳ דראש חודש

15. הַיּוֹם חֲמִשָּׁה עָשָׂר יוֹם
שֶׁהֵם שְׁנֵי שָׁבוּעוֹת וְיוֹם אֶחָד
בָּעֹמֶר.

חסד שבתפארת

א באייר, ב׳ דראש חודש

16. הַיּוֹם שִׁשָּׁה עָשָׂר יוֹם
שֶׁהֵם שְׁנֵי שָׁבוּעוֹת וּשְׁנֵי יָמִים
בָּעֹמֶר.

גבורה שבתפארת

ב באייר

17. הַיּוֹם שִׁבְעָה עָשָׂר יוֹם
שֶׁהֵם שְׁנֵי שָׁבוּעוֹת וּשְׁלֹשָׁה
יָמִים בָּעֹמֶר.

תפארת שבתפארת

3 Iyar

18. Today is the eighteenth day,
making two weeks
and four days
of the Omer.

4 Iyar

19. Today is the nineteenth day,
making two weeks
and five days
of the Omer.

5 Iyar, Yom HaAtzma'ut

20. Today is the twentieth day,
making two weeks
and six days
of the Omer.

6 Iyar

21. Today is the twenty-first day,
making three weeks
of the Omer.

7 Iyar

22. Today is the twenty-second day,
making three weeks
and one day
of the Omer.

8 Iyar

23. Today is the twenty-third day,
making three weeks
and two days
of the Omer.

9 Iyar

24. Today is the twenty-fourth day,
making three weeks
and three days
of the Omer.

10 Iyar

25. Today is the twenty-fifth day,
making three weeks
and four days
of the Omer.

11 Iyar

26. Today is the twenty-sixth day,
making three weeks
and five days
of the Omer.

12 Iyar

27. Today is the twenty-seventh
day, making three weeks
and six days
of the Omer.

13 Iyar

28. Today is the twenty-eighth day,
making four weeks
of the Omer.

14 Iyar, Pesaḥ Sheni

29. Today is the twenty-ninth day,
making four weeks
and one day
of the Omer.

15 Iyar

30. Today is the thirtieth day,
making four weeks
and two days
of the Omer.

16 Iyar

31. Today is the thirty-first day,
making four weeks
and three days
of the Omer.

ג באייר

18. הַיּוֹם שְׁמוֹנָה עָשָׂר יוֹם
שֶׁהֵם שְׁנֵי שָׁבוּעוֹת וְאַרְבָּעָה
יָמִים בָּעֹמֶר. נצח שבתפארת

ד באייר

19. הַיּוֹם תִּשְׁעָה עָשָׂר יוֹם
שֶׁהֵם שְׁנֵי שָׁבוּעוֹת וַחֲמִשָּׁה
יָמִים בָּעֹמֶר. הוד שבתפארת

ה באייר, יום העצמאות

20. הַיּוֹם עֶשְׂרִים יוֹם
שֶׁהֵם שְׁנֵי שָׁבוּעוֹת וְשִׁשָּׁה
יָמִים בָּעֹמֶר. יסוד שבתפארת

ו באייר

21. הַיּוֹם אֶחָד וְעֶשְׂרִים יוֹם
שֶׁהֵם שְׁלֹשָׁה שָׁבוּעוֹת בָּעֹמֶר.
מלכות שבתפארת

ז באייר

22. הַיּוֹם שְׁנַיִם וְעֶשְׂרִים יוֹם
שֶׁהֵם שְׁלֹשָׁה שָׁבוּעוֹת
וְיוֹם אֶחָד בָּעֹמֶר. חסד שבנצח

ח באייר

23. הַיּוֹם שְׁלֹשָׁה וְעֶשְׂרִים יוֹם
שֶׁהֵם שְׁלֹשָׁה שָׁבוּעוֹת
וּשְׁנֵי יָמִים בָּעֹמֶר. גבורה שבנצח

ט באייר

24. הַיּוֹם אַרְבָּעָה וְעֶשְׂרִים יוֹם
שֶׁהֵם שְׁלֹשָׁה שָׁבוּעוֹת
וּשְׁלֹשָׁה יָמִים בָּעֹמֶר.
תפארת שבנצח

י באייר

25. הַיּוֹם חֲמִשָּׁה וְעֶשְׂרִים יוֹם
שֶׁהֵם שְׁלֹשָׁה שָׁבוּעוֹת
וְאַרְבָּעָה יָמִים בָּעֹמֶר. נצח שבנצח

יא באייר

26. הַיּוֹם שִׁשָּׁה וְעֶשְׂרִים יוֹם
שֶׁהֵם שְׁלֹשָׁה שָׁבוּעוֹת
וַחֲמִשָּׁה יָמִים בָּעֹמֶר. הוד שבנצח

יב באייר

27. הַיּוֹם שִׁבְעָה וְעֶשְׂרִים יוֹם
שֶׁהֵם שְׁלֹשָׁה שָׁבוּעוֹת
וְשִׁשָּׁה יָמִים בָּעֹמֶר. יסוד שבנצח

יג באייר

28. הַיּוֹם שְׁמוֹנָה וְעֶשְׂרִים יוֹם
שֶׁהֵם אַרְבָּעָה שָׁבוּעוֹת
בָּעֹמֶר. מלכות שבנצח

יד באייר, פסח שני

29. הַיּוֹם תִּשְׁעָה וְעֶשְׂרִים יוֹם
שֶׁהֵם אַרְבָּעָה שָׁבוּעוֹת
וְיוֹם אֶחָד בָּעֹמֶר. חסד שבהוד

טו באייר

30. הַיּוֹם שְׁלֹשִׁים יוֹם
שֶׁהֵם אַרְבָּעָה שָׁבוּעוֹת
וּשְׁנֵי יָמִים בָּעֹמֶר. גבורה שבהוד

טז באייר

31. הַיּוֹם אֶחָד וּשְׁלֹשִׁים יוֹם
שֶׁהֵם אַרְבָּעָה שָׁבוּעוֹת
וּשְׁלֹשָׁה יָמִים בָּעֹמֶר.
תפארת שבהוד

17 Iyar

32. Today is the thirty-second day,
making four weeks
and four days
of the Omer.

18 Iyar, Lag BaOmer

33. Today is the thirty-third day,
making four weeks
and five days
of the Omer.

19 Iyar

34. Today is the thirty-fourth day,
making four weeks
and six days
of the Omer.

20 Iyar

35. Today is the thirty-fifth day,
making five weeks
of the Omer.

21 Iyar

36. Today is the thirty-sixth day,
making five weeks
and one day
of the Omer.

22 Iyar

37. Today is the thirty-seventh day,
making five weeks
and two days
of the Omer.

23 Iyar

38. Today is the thirty-eighth day,
making five weeks
and three days
of the Omer.

24 Iyar

39. Today is the thirty-ninth day,
making five weeks
and four days
of the Omer.

25 Iyar

40. Today is the fortieth day,
making five weeks
and five days
of the Omer.

26 Iyar

41. Today is the forty-first day,
making five weeks
and six days
of the Omer.

27 Iyar

42. Today is the forty-second day,
making six weeks
of the Omer.

28 Iyar, Yom Yerushalayim

43. Today is the forty-third day,
making six weeks
and one day
of the Omer.

29 Iyar

44. Today is the forty-fourth day,
making six weeks
and two days
of the Omer.

1 Sivan, Rosh Ḥodesh

45. Today is the forty-fifth day,
making six weeks
and three days
of the Omer.

יז באייר

32. הַיּוֹם שְׁנַיִם וּשְׁלֹשִׁים יוֹם
שֶׁהֵם אַרְבָּעָה שָׁבוּעוֹת
וְאַרְבָּעָה יָמִים בָּעֹֽמֶר. נצח שבהוד

יח באייר, לג בעומר

33. הַיּוֹם שְׁלֹשָׁה וּשְׁלֹשִׁים יוֹם
שֶׁהֵם אַרְבָּעָה שָׁבוּעוֹת
וַחֲמִשָּׁה יָמִים בָּעֹֽמֶר. הוד שבהוד

יט באייר

34. הַיּוֹם אַרְבָּעָה וּשְׁלֹשִׁים יוֹם
שֶׁהֵם אַרְבָּעָה שָׁבוּעוֹת
וְשִׁשָּׁה יָמִים בָּעֹֽמֶר. יסוד שבהוד

כ באייר

35. הַיּוֹם חֲמִשָּׁה וּשְׁלֹשִׁים יוֹם
שֶׁהֵם חֲמִשָּׁה שָׁבוּעוֹת
בָּעֹֽמֶר. מלכות שבהוד

כא באייר

36. הַיּוֹם שִׁשָּׁה וּשְׁלֹשִׁים יוֹם
שֶׁהֵם חֲמִשָּׁה שָׁבוּעוֹת
וְיוֹם אֶחָד בָּעֹֽמֶר. חסד שביסוד

כב באייר

37. הַיּוֹם שִׁבְעָה וּשְׁלֹשִׁים יוֹם
שֶׁהֵם חֲמִשָּׁה שָׁבוּעוֹת
וּשְׁנֵי יָמִים בָּעֹֽמֶר. גבורה שביסוד

כג באייר

38. הַיּוֹם שְׁמוֹנָה וּשְׁלֹשִׁים יוֹם
שֶׁהֵם חֲמִשָּׁה שָׁבוּעוֹת
וּשְׁלֹשָׁה יָמִים בָּעֹֽמֶר.
תפארת שביסוד

כד באייר

39. הַיּוֹם תִּשְׁעָה וּשְׁלֹשִׁים יוֹם
שֶׁהֵם חֲמִשָּׁה שָׁבוּעוֹת
וְאַרְבָּעָה יָמִים בָּעֹֽמֶר. נצח שביסוד

כה באייר

40. הַיּוֹם אַרְבָּעִים יוֹם
שֶׁהֵם חֲמִשָּׁה שָׁבוּעוֹת
וַחֲמִשָּׁה יָמִים בָּעֹֽמֶר. הוד שביסוד

כו באייר

41. הַיּוֹם אֶחָד וְאַרְבָּעִים יוֹם
שֶׁהֵם חֲמִשָּׁה שָׁבוּעוֹת
וְשִׁשָּׁה יָמִים בָּעֹֽמֶר. יסוד שביסוד

כז באייר

42. הַיּוֹם שְׁנַיִם וְאַרְבָּעִים יוֹם
שֶׁהֵם שִׁשָּׁה שָׁבוּעוֹת
בָּעֹֽמֶר. מלכות שביסוד

כח באייר, יום ירושלים

43. הַיּוֹם שְׁלֹשָׁה וְאַרְבָּעִים יוֹם
שֶׁהֵם שִׁשָּׁה שָׁבוּעוֹת
וְיוֹם אֶחָד בָּעֹֽמֶר. חסד שבמלכות

כט באייר

44. הַיּוֹם אַרְבָּעָה וְאַרְבָּעִים יוֹם
שֶׁהֵם שִׁשָּׁה שָׁבוּעוֹת
וּשְׁנֵי יָמִים בָּעֹֽמֶר. גבורה שבמלכות

א בסיון, ראש חודש

45. הַיּוֹם חֲמִשָּׁה וְאַרְבָּעִים יוֹם
שֶׁהֵם שִׁשָּׁה שָׁבוּעוֹת וּשְׁלֹשָׁה
יָמִים בָּעֹֽמֶר. תפארת שבמלכות

2 Sivan

46. Today is the forty-sixth day, making six weeks and four days of the Omer.

3 Sivan

47. Today is the forty-seventh day, making six weeks and five days of the Omer.

4 Sivan

48. Today is the forty-eighth day, making six weeks and six days of the Omer.

5 Sivan, Erev Shavuot

49. Today is the forty-ninth day, making seven weeks of the Omer.

הָרַחֲמָן May the Compassionate One restore the Temple service to its place speedily in our days. Amen, Selah.

Some add:

לַמְנַצֵּחַ For the conductor of music. With stringed instruments. A psalm, a song. May God be gracious to us and bless us. May He make His face shine on us, Selah. Then will Your way be known on earth, Your salvation among all the nations. Let the peoples praise You, God; let all peoples praise You. Let nations rejoice and sing for joy, for You judge the peoples with equity, and guide the nations of the earth, Selah. Let the peoples praise You, God; let all peoples praise You. The earth has yielded its harvest. May God, our God, bless us. God will bless us, and all the ends of the earth will fear Him. *Ps. 67*

אָנָּא Please, by the power of Your great right hand, set the captive nation free. Accept Your people's prayer. Strengthen us, purify us, You who are revered. Please, mighty One, guard like the pupil of the eye those who seek Your unity. Bless them, cleanse them, have compassion on them, grant them Your righteousness always. Mighty One, Holy One, in Your great goodness guide Your congregation. Only One, exalted One, turn to Your people, who proclaim Your holiness. Accept our plea and heed our cry, You who know all secret thoughts. Blessed be the name of His glorious kingdom for ever and all time.

רִבּוֹנוֹ שֶׁל עוֹלָם Master of the Universe, You commanded us through Your servant Moses to count the Omer, to cleanse our carapaces and impurities, as You have written in Your Torah: "You shall count seven complete weeks from the day following the [Pesaḥ] rest day, when you brought the Omer as a wave-offering. To the day after the seventh week, you shall count fifty days." *Lev. 23* This is so that the souls of Your people Israel may be purified from their uncleanliness. May it also be Your will, Lord our God and God of our ancestors, that in the merit of the Omer count that I have counted today, there may be rectified any defect on my part in the counting of (*insert the appropriate sefira for each day*). May I be cleansed and sanctified with Your holiness on high, and through this may there flow a rich stream through all worlds, to rectify our lives, spirits and souls from any dross and defect, purifying and sanctifying us with Your sublime holiness. Amen, Selah.

On Friday night the service continues with Aleinu on page 128.

On Motza'ei Shabbat the service continues with "May God give you dew" on page 630.

ב בסיון

46. הַיּוֹם שִׁשָּׁה וְאַרְבָּעִים יוֹם שֶׁהֵם שִׁשָּׁה שָׁבוּעוֹת וְאַרְבָּעָה יָמִים בָּעֹמֶר. נצח שבמלכות

ג בסיון

47. הַיּוֹם שִׁבְעָה וְאַרְבָּעִים יוֹם שֶׁהֵם שִׁשָּׁה שָׁבוּעוֹת וַחֲמִשָּׁה יָמִים בָּעֹמֶר. הוד שבמלכות

ד בסיון

48. הַיּוֹם שְׁמוֹנָה וְאַרְבָּעִים יוֹם שֶׁהֵם שִׁשָּׁה שָׁבוּעוֹת וְשִׁשָּׁה יָמִים בָּעֹמֶר. יסוד שבמלכות

ה בסיון, ערב שבועות

49. הַיּוֹם תִּשְׁעָה וְאַרְבָּעִים יוֹם שֶׁהֵם שִׁבְעָה שָׁבוּעוֹת בָּעֹמֶר. מלכות שבמלכות

הָרַחֲמָן הוּא יַחֲזִיר לָנוּ עֲבוֹדַת בֵּית הַמִּקְדָּשׁ לִמְקוֹמָהּ בִּמְהֵרָה בְיָמֵינוּ, אָמֵן סֶלָה.

Some add:

תהלים סז
לַמְנַצֵּחַ בִּנְגִינֹת, מִזְמוֹר שִׁיר: אֱלֹהִים יְחָנֵּנוּ וִיבָרְכֵנוּ, יָאֵר פָּנָיו אִתָּנוּ סֶלָה: לָדַעַת בָּאָרֶץ דַּרְכֶּךָ, בְּכָל־גּוֹיִם יְשׁוּעָתֶךָ: יוֹדוּךָ עַמִּים אֱלֹהִים, יוֹדוּךָ עַמִּים כֻּלָּם: יִשְׂמְחוּ וִירַנְּנוּ לְאֻמִּים, כִּי־תִשְׁפֹּט עַמִּים מִישֹׁר, וּלְאֻמִּים בָּאָרֶץ תַּנְחֵם סֶלָה: יוֹדוּךָ עַמִּים אֱלֹהִים, יוֹדוּךָ עַמִּים כֻּלָּם: אֶרֶץ נָתְנָה יְבוּלָהּ, יְבָרְכֵנוּ אֱלֹהִים אֱלֹהֵינוּ: יְבָרְכֵנוּ אֱלֹהִים, וְיִירְאוּ אוֹתוֹ כָּל־אַפְסֵי־אָרֶץ:

אָנָּא, בְּכֹחַ גְּדֻלַּת יְמִינְךָ, תַּתִּיר צְרוּרָה. קַבֵּל רִנַּת עַמְּךָ, שַׂגְּבֵנוּ, טַהֲרֵנוּ, נוֹרָא. נָא גִבּוֹר, דּוֹרְשֵׁי יִחוּדְךָ כְּבָבַת שָׁמְרֵם. בָּרְכֵם, טַהֲרֵם, רַחֲמֵם, צִדְקָתְךָ תָּמִיד גָּמְלֵם. חֲסִין קָדוֹשׁ, בְּרֹב טוּבְךָ נַהֵל עֲדָתֶךָ. יָחִיד גֵּאֶה, לְעַמְּךָ פְּנֵה, זוֹכְרֵי קְדֻשָּׁתֶךָ. שַׁוְעָתֵנוּ קַבֵּל וּשְׁמַע צַעֲקָתֵנוּ, יוֹדֵעַ תַּעֲלוּמוֹת. בָּרוּךְ שֵׁם כְּבוֹד מַלְכוּתוֹ לְעוֹלָם וָעֶד.

רִבּוֹנוֹ שֶׁל עוֹלָם, אַתָּה צִוִּיתָנוּ עַל יְדֵי מֹשֶׁה עַבְדְּךָ לִסְפֹּר סְפִירַת הָעֹמֶר, כְּדֵי לְטַהֲרֵנוּ מִקְּלִפּוֹתֵינוּ וּמִטֻּמְאוֹתֵינוּ. כְּמוֹ שֶׁכָּתַבְתָּ בְּתוֹרָתֶךָ: וּסְפַרְתֶּם לָכֶם מִמָּחֳרַת הַשַּׁבָּת, מִיּוֹם הֲבִיאֲכֶם אֶת־עֹמֶר הַתְּנוּפָה, שֶׁבַע שַׁבָּתוֹת תְּמִימֹת תִּהְיֶינָה: עַד מִמָּחֳרַת הַשַּׁבָּת הַשְּׁבִיעִת תִּסְפְּרוּ חֲמִשִּׁים יוֹם: כְּדֵי שֶׁיִּטָּהֲרוּ נַפְשׁוֹת עַמְּךָ יִשְׂרָאֵל מִזֻּהֲמָתָם. וּבְכֵן יְהִי רָצוֹן מִלְּפָנֶיךָ יהוה אֱלֹהֵינוּ וֵאלֹהֵי אֲבוֹתֵינוּ, שֶׁבִּזְכוּת סְפִירַת הָעֹמֶר שֶׁסָּפַרְתִּי הַיּוֹם, יְתֻקַּן מַה שֶּׁפָּגַמְתִּי בִּסְפִירָה (*insert appropriate* ספירה *for each day*) וְאֶטָּהֵר וְאֶתְקַדֵּשׁ בִּקְדֻשָּׁה שֶׁל מַעְלָה, וְעַל יְדֵי זֶה יֻשְׁפַּע שֶׁפַע רַב בְּכָל הָעוֹלָמוֹת, לְתַקֵּן אֶת נַפְשׁוֹתֵינוּ וְרוּחוֹתֵינוּ וְנִשְׁמוֹתֵינוּ מִכָּל סִיג וּפְגָם, וּלְטַהֲרֵנוּ וּלְקַדְּשֵׁנוּ בִּקְדֻשָּׁתְךָ הָעֶלְיוֹנָה, אָמֵן סֶלָה. ויקרא כג

On Friday night the service continues with עָלֵינוּ *on page 129.*
On מוצאי שבת *the service continues with* וְיִתֶּן־לְךָ *on page 631.*

SHEMA BEFORE SLEEP AT NIGHT[B]

הֲרֵינִי I hereby forgive anyone who has angered or provoked me or sinned against me, physically or financially or by failing to give me due respect, or in any other matter relating to me, involuntarily or willingly, inadvertently or deliberately, whether in word or deed: let no one incur punishment because of me.

בָּרוּךְ Blessed are You, Lord our God, King of the Universe,
who makes the bonds of sleep fall on my eyes,[IHB]
and slumber on my eyelids.
May it be Your will, Lord my God and God of my fathers,
that You make me lie down in peace
and arise in peace.
Let not my imagination, bad dreams or troubling thoughts disturb me.[B]

HILKHOT TEFILLA • הלכות תפילה

הַמַּפִּיל חֶבְלֵי שֵׁנָה עַל עֵינַי – *Who makes the bonds of sleep fall on my eyes.* There are two traditions regarding the sequence of the recitation of the *Shema* and the blessing. Which should be recited first? Which should be one's final prayer before drifting into sleep? Interestingly, the *Mishna Berura* suggests that it is up to each individual to decide according to one's own level of fatigue – if you don't think you can stay awake long enough to say the blessing, say it first; otherwise, leave it for the end. Each of us leaves our consciousness of the previous day and the presence of God in our lives in our own way. Also interesting is that unlike almost all other prayers, this one is in the singular, perhaps because it takes place at a most intimate and personal moment in our day.

BIUR TEFILLA • ביאור תפילה

הַמַּפִּיל חֶבְלֵי שֵׁנָה עַל עֵינַי – *Who makes the bonds of sleep fall on my eyes.* We say a blessing on it because sleep is something that man needs. The Midrash (*Bereshit Raba* 9:6) teaches that "*vehineh tov meod*" (and God saw that it was *very* good) is a reference to sleep. With it, man is able to get up in the morning and pursue Torah (Abudarham). Is this a statement of fact or of thanks?

וְאַל יְבַהֲלוּנִי רַעְיוֹנַי וַחֲלוֹמוֹת רָעִים וְהַרְהוֹרִים רָעִים – *Let not my imagination, bad dreams or troubling thoughts disturb me.* One's imagination, bad thoughts and bad dreams can shake one to the core at night, causing one to wake up startled, confused and ill at ease, and subsequently leaving one as tired, if not more so, than when one went to sleep. We pray that our sleep is restful and refreshing.

קריאת שמע על המיטה[ב]

הֲרֵינִי מוֹחֵל לְכָל מִי שֶׁהִכְעִיס וְהִקְנִיט אוֹתִי אוֹ שֶׁחָטָא כְּנֶגְדִּי, בֵּין בְּגוּפִי בֵּין בְּמָמוֹנִי בֵּין בִּכְבוֹדִי בֵּין בְּכָל אֲשֶׁר לִי, בֵּין בְּאֹנֶס בֵּין בְּרָצוֹן, בֵּין בְּשׁוֹגֵג בֵּין בְּמֵזִיד, בֵּין בְּדִבּוּר בֵּין בְּמַעֲשֶׂה, וְלֹא יֵעָנֵשׁ שׁוּם אָדָם בְּסִבָּתִי.

בָּרוּךְ אַתָּה יהוה אֱלֹהֵינוּ מֶלֶךְ הָעוֹלָם
הַמַּפִּיל חֶבְלֵי שֵׁנָה עַל עֵינַי[ע"ה ב] וּתְנוּמָה עַל עַפְעַפָּי.
וִיהִי רָצוֹן מִלְּפָנֶיךָ, יהוה אֱלֹהַי וֵאלֹהֵי אֲבוֹתַי
שֶׁתַּשְׁכִּיבֵנִי לְשָׁלוֹם וְתַעֲמִידֵנִי לְשָׁלוֹם
וְאַל יְבַהֲלוּנִי רַעְיוֹנַי וַחֲלוֹמוֹת רָעִים וְהִרְהוּרִים רָעִים[ב]

BIUR TEFILLA • ביאור תפילה

קריאת שמע על המיטה – *Shema before sleep at night.* The Gemara (*Berakhot* 4b) says that, separate from what one said in *Ma'ariv*, one should recite the [first paragraph of the] *Shema* again because of its reference to the timing of its recitation, namely, בְּשָׁכְבְּךָ, when you lie down. As a result there is a special recitation of the *Shema* which is said just before one nods off to sleep. In addition, the Gemara elsewhere (*Berakhot* 60b) mentions a blessing that should be said upon going to sleep. At its core, then, "the bedtime *Shema*" consists of a blessing and the recitation of the *Shema*; all of the other paragraphs represent additional prayers that are an expansion of one's request for protection during the night.

IYUN TEFILLA • עיון תפילה

הַמַּפִּיל חֶבְלֵי שֵׁנָה עַל עֵינַי – *Who makes the bonds of sleep fall on my eyes.* Here it sounds like sleep is something cast upon you, against your will. Some of us would like to stay up all night if we could, but the blessing assures us that sleep is a *ḥesed* provided by Hashem for the benefit of our bodies, and our souls. Alternatively, young children have a fear of the dark, as their imaginations run wild about the dangers. As adults, we often have our own fears and trepidations about the day prior, about the night and day ahead. Sleep is cast upon us to teach us that the dark is to be embraced before the dawn of a new day.

Compare the text above with the text of the blessing that we say in the morning:

> בָּרוּךְ אַתָּה יהוה אֱלֹהֵינוּ מֶלֶךְ הָעוֹלָם, הַמַּעֲבִיר שֵׁנָה מֵעֵינַי וּתְנוּמָה מֵעַפְעַפָּי.
>
> Blessed are You, Hashem our God, King of the Universe, who removes sleep from my eyes and slumber from my eyelids.

May my bed be flawless before You.
Enlighten my eyes lest I sleep the sleep of death,[B]
for it is You who illuminates the pupil of the eye.
Blessed are You, LORD, who gives light to the whole world in His glory.[B]

When saying all three paragraphs of Shema, say:
God, faithful King!

The following verse should be said aloud, while covering the eyes with the right hand:

Listen, Israel: the LORD is our God, the LORD is One.

Deut. 6

Quietly: Blessed be the name of His glorious kingdom for ever and all time.

וְאָהַבְתָּ Love the LORD your God with all your heart, with all your soul, and with all your might. These words which I command you today shall be on your heart. Teach them repeatedly to your children, speaking of them when you sit at home and when you travel on the way, when you lie down and when you rise. Bind them as a sign on your hand, and they shall be an emblem between your eyes. Write them on the doorposts of your house and gates. *Deut. 6*

וִיהִי May the pleasantness of the LORD our God be upon us. Establish for us the work of our hands, O establish the work of our hands. *Ps. 90*

יֹשֵׁב He who lives in the shelter of the Most High dwells in the shadow of the Almighty. I say of God, my Refuge and Stronghold, my LORD in whom I trust, that He will save you from the fowler's snare and the deadly pestilence. With His pinions He will cover you, and beneath His wings you will find shelter; His faithfulness is an encircling shield. You need not fear terror by night, nor *Ps. 91*

I will thank Hashem for the restoration of my soul and my reemergence from a state of slumber to a rejuvenated state of being alive.

הַמֵּאִיר לָעוֹלָם כֻּלּוֹ בִּכְבוֹדוֹ – *Who gives light to the whole world in His glory.* The blessing ends on a note of optimism. Dark as it may seem at night, we will awaken in the morning to acknowledge a new day, illuminated both literally and figuratively by the light which Hashem provides. Such a thought brings comfort, peace and rest.

וּתְהֵא מִטָּתִי שְׁלֵמָה לְפָנֶיךָ
וְהָאֵר עֵינַי פֶּן אִישַׁן הַמָּוֶת, כִּי אַתָּה הַמֵּאִיר לְאִישׁוֹן בַּת עָיִן.
בָּרוּךְ אַתָּה יהוה, הַמֵּאִיר לָעוֹלָם כֻּלּוֹ בִּכְבוֹדוֹ.

When saying all three paragraphs of שמע*, say:*

אֵל מֶלֶךְ נֶאֱמָן

The following verse should be said aloud, while covering the eyes with the right hand:

דברים ו
שְׁמַע יִשְׂרָאֵל, יהוה אֱלֹהֵינוּ, יהוה | אֶחָד:

Quietly בָּרוּךְ שֵׁם כְּבוֹד מַלְכוּתוֹ לְעוֹלָם וָעֶד.

דברים ו
וְאָהַבְתָּ אֵת יהוה אֱלֹהֶיךָ, בְּכָל־לְבָבְךָ וּבְכָל־נַפְשְׁךָ וּבְכָל־מְאֹדֶךָ: וְהָיוּ הַדְּבָרִים הָאֵלֶּה, אֲשֶׁר אָנֹכִי מְצַוְּךָ הַיּוֹם, עַל־לְבָבֶךָ: וְשִׁנַּנְתָּם לְבָנֶיךָ וְדִבַּרְתָּ בָּם, בְּשִׁבְתְּךָ בְּבֵיתֶךָ וּבְלֶכְתְּךָ בַדֶּרֶךְ, וּבְשָׁכְבְּךָ וּבְקוּמֶךָ: וּקְשַׁרְתָּם לְאוֹת עַל־יָדֶךָ וְהָיוּ לְטֹטָפֹת בֵּין עֵינֶיךָ: וּכְתַבְתָּם עַל־מְזֻזוֹת בֵּיתֶךָ וּבִשְׁעָרֶיךָ:

תהלים צ
וִיהִי נֹעַם אֲדֹנָי אֱלֹהֵינוּ עָלֵינוּ וּמַעֲשֵׂה יָדֵינוּ כּוֹנְנָה עָלֵינוּ וּמַעֲשֵׂה יָדֵינוּ כּוֹנְנֵהוּ:

תהלים צא
יֹשֵׁב בְּסֵתֶר עֶלְיוֹן, בְּצֵל שַׁדַּי יִתְלוֹנָן: אֹמַר לַיהוה מַחְסִי וּמְצוּדָתִי, אֱלֹהַי אֶבְטַח־בּוֹ: כִּי הוּא יַצִּילְךָ מִפַּח יָקוּשׁ, מִדֶּבֶר הַוּוֹת: בְּאֶבְרָתוֹ יָסֶךְ לָךְ, וְתַחַת־כְּנָפָיו תֶּחְסֶה, צִנָּה וְסֹחֵרָה אֲמִתּוֹ: לֹא־תִירָא מִפַּחַד

BIUR TEFILLA • ביאור תפילה

וְהָאֵר עֵינַי פֶּן אִישַׁן הַמָּוֶת – *Enlighten my eyes lest I sleep the sleep of death.* Only at the end does one admit to the biggest fear of them all – lest I not awake in the morning. The apprehension of death is not always present, but the possibility is. Here it receives its due mention, a prelude to the celebratory statement in the morning of *Modeh Ani,* wherein

the arrow that flies by day; not the pestilence that stalks in darkness, nor the plague that ravages at noon. A thousand may fall at your side, ten thousand at your right hand, but it will not come near you. You will only look with your eyes and see the punishment of the wicked. Because you said, "The LORD is my Refuge," taking the Most High as your shelter, no harm will befall you, no plague come near your tent, for He will command His angels about you, to guard you in all your ways. They will lift you in their hands, lest your foot stumble on a stone. You will tread on lions and vipers; you will trample on young lions and snakes. [God says:] "Because he loves Me, I will rescue him; I will protect him, because he acknowledges My name. When he calls on Me, I will answer him; I will be with him in distress, I will deliver him and bring him honor. With long life I will satisfy him and show him My salvation.
With long life I will satisfy him and show him My salvation.

יהוה LORD, how numerous are my enemies, how many rise against me. *Ps. 3*
Many say of me: "There is no help for him in God," Selah. But You, LORD, are a shield around me. You are my glory; You raise my head high. I cry aloud to the LORD, and He answers me from His holy mountain, Selah. I lie down to sleep and I wake again, for the LORD supports me. I will not fear the myriad forces ranged against me on all sides. Arise, LORD, save me, O my God; strike all my enemies across the cheek; break the teeth of the wicked. From the LORD comes deliverance; may Your blessing rest upon Your people, Selah.

הַשְׁכִּיבֵנוּ Help us lie down, O LORD our God, in peace, and rise up, O our King, to life. Spread over us Your canopy of peace. Direct us with Your good counsel, and save us for the sake of Your name. Shield us and remove from us every enemy, plague, sword, famine and sorrow. Remove the adversary from before and behind us. Shelter us in the shadow of Your wings, for You, God, are our Guardian and Deliverer; You, God, are a gracious and compassionate King. Guard our going out and our coming in, for life and peace, from now and for ever.

בָּרוּךְ Blessed is the LORD by day, blessed is the LORD by night. Blessed is
the LORD when we lie down; blessed is the LORD when we rise. For in Your
hand are the souls of the living and the dead, [as it is written:] "In His hand *Job 12*
is every living soul, and the breath of all mankind." Into Your hand I entrust *Ps. 31*
my spirit: You redeemed me, LORD, God of truth. Our God in heaven, bring unity to Your name, establish Your kingdom constantly and reign over us for ever and all time.

לַיְלָה, מֵחֵץ יָעוּף יוֹמָם: מִדֶּבֶר בָּאֹפֶל יַהֲלֹךְ, מִקֶּטֶב יָשׁוּד צָהֳרָיִם:
יִפֹּל מִצִּדְּךָ אֶלֶף, וּרְבָבָה מִימִינֶךָ, אֵלֶיךָ לֹא יִגָּשׁ: רַק בְּעֵינֶיךָ תַבִּיט,
וְשִׁלֻּמַת רְשָׁעִים תִּרְאֶה: כִּי־אַתָּה יהוה מַחְסִי, עֶלְיוֹן שַׂמְתָּ מְעוֹנֶךָ:
לֹא־תְאֻנֶּה אֵלֶיךָ רָעָה, וְנֶגַע לֹא־יִקְרַב בְּאָהֳלֶךָ: כִּי מַלְאָכָיו יְצַוֶּה־לָּךְ,
לִשְׁמָרְךָ בְּכָל־דְּרָכֶיךָ: עַל־כַּפַּיִם יִשָּׂאוּנְךָ, פֶּן־תִּגֹּף בָּאֶבֶן רַגְלֶךָ: עַל־
שַׁחַל וָפֶתֶן תִּדְרֹךְ, תִּרְמֹס כְּפִיר וְתַנִּין: כִּי בִי חָשַׁק וַאֲפַלְּטֵהוּ, אֲשַׂגְּבֵהוּ
כִּי־יָדַע שְׁמִי: יִקְרָאֵנִי וְאֶעֱנֵהוּ, עִמּוֹ־אָנֹכִי בְצָרָה, אֲחַלְּצֵהוּ וַאֲכַבְּדֵהוּ:
אֹרֶךְ יָמִים אַשְׂבִּיעֵהוּ, וְאַרְאֵהוּ בִּישׁוּעָתִי:
אֹרֶךְ יָמִים אַשְׂבִּיעֵהוּ, וְאַרְאֵהוּ בִּישׁוּעָתִי:

יהוה מָה־רַבּוּ צָרָי, רַבִּים קָמִים עָלָי: רַבִּים אֹמְרִים לְנַפְשִׁי, אֵין יְשׁוּעָתָה תהלים ג
לּוֹ בֵאלֹהִים, סֶלָה: וְאַתָּה יהוה מָגֵן בַּעֲדִי, כְּבוֹדִי וּמֵרִים רֹאשִׁי: קוֹלִי
אֶל־יהוה אֶקְרָא, וַיַּעֲנֵנִי מֵהַר קָדְשׁוֹ, סֶלָה: אֲנִי שָׁכַבְתִּי וָאִישָׁנָה,
הֱקִיצוֹתִי כִּי יהוה יִסְמְכֵנִי: לֹא־אִירָא מֵרִבְבוֹת עָם, אֲשֶׁר סָבִיב שָׁתוּ
עָלָי: קוּמָה יהוה, הוֹשִׁיעֵנִי אֱלֹהַי, כִּי־הִכִּיתָ אֶת־כָּל־אֹיְבַי לֶחִי, שִׁנֵּי
רְשָׁעִים שִׁבַּרְתָּ: לַיהוה הַיְשׁוּעָה, עַל־עַמְּךָ בִרְכָתֶךָ סֶּלָה:

הַשְׁכִּיבֵנוּ, יהוה אֱלֹהֵינוּ, לְשָׁלוֹם. וְהַעֲמִידֵנוּ, מַלְכֵּנוּ, לְחַיִּים. וּפְרֹשׂ עָלֵינוּ
סֻכַּת שְׁלוֹמֶךָ, וְתַקְּנֵנוּ בְּעֵצָה טוֹבָה מִלְּפָנֶיךָ, וְהוֹשִׁיעֵנוּ לְמַעַן שְׁמֶךָ. וְהָגֵן
בַּעֲדֵנוּ, וְהָסֵר מֵעָלֵינוּ אוֹיֵב, דֶּבֶר וְחֶרֶב וְרָעָב וְיָגוֹן. וְהָסֵר שָׂטָן מִלְּפָנֵינוּ
וּמֵאַחֲרֵינוּ, וּבְצֵל כְּנָפֶיךָ תַּסְתִּירֵנוּ, כִּי אֵל שׁוֹמְרֵנוּ וּמַצִּילֵנוּ אָתָּה, כִּי אֵל
מֶלֶךְ חַנּוּן וְרַחוּם אָתָּה. וּשְׁמֹר צֵאתֵנוּ וּבוֹאֵנוּ לְחַיִּים וּלְשָׁלוֹם מֵעַתָּה
וְעַד עוֹלָם.

בָּרוּךְ יהוה בַּיּוֹם, בָּרוּךְ יהוה בַּלָּיְלָה, בָּרוּךְ יהוה בְּשָׁכְבֵנוּ, בָּרוּךְ
יהוה בְּקוּמֵנוּ. כִּי בְיָדְךָ נַפְשׁוֹת הַחַיִּים וְהַמֵּתִים. אֲשֶׁר בְּיָדוֹ נֶפֶשׁ כָּל־ איוב יב
חָי, וְרוּחַ כָּל־בְּשַׂר־אִישׁ: בְּיָדְךָ אַפְקִיד רוּחִי, פָּדִיתָה אוֹתִי יהוה אֵל תהלים לא
אֱמֶת: אֱלֹהֵינוּ שֶׁבַּשָּׁמַיִם, יַחֵד שִׁמְךָ וְקַיֵּם מַלְכוּתְךָ תָּמִיד, וּמְלֹךְ עָלֵינוּ
לְעוֹלָם וָעֶד.

יִרְאוּ May our eyes see, our hearts rejoice, and our souls be glad in Your true salvation, when Zion is told, "Your God reigns." The LORD is King, the LORD was King, and the LORD will be King for ever and all time. For sovereignty is Yours, and to all eternity You will reign in glory, for we have no king but You.

הַמַּלְאָךְ May the angel who rescued me from all harm, bless these boys. May they be called by my name and the names of my fathers Abraham and Isaac, and may they increase greatly on the earth. *Gen. 48*

וַיֹּאמֶר He said, "If you listen carefully to the voice of the LORD your God and do what is right in His eyes, if you pay attention to His commandments and keep all His statutes, I will not bring on you any of the diseases I brought on the Egyptians, for I am the LORD who heals you." The LORD said to the accuser, "The LORD shall rebuke you, accuser. The LORD who has chosen Jerusalem shall rebuke you! Is not this man a burning stick snatched from the fire?" Look! It is Solomon's bed, escorted by sixty warriors, the noblest of Israel, all of them wearing the sword, experienced in battle, each with his sword at his side, prepared for the terror of the nights. *Ex. 15* *Zech. 3* *Song. 3*

Say three times:

יְבָרֶכְךָ May the LORD bless you and protect you. *Num. 6*
May the LORD make His face shine on you and be gracious to you.
May the LORD turn His face toward you and grant you peace.

Say three times:

הִנֵּה See – the Guardian of Israel *Ps. 121*
neither slumbers nor sleeps.

Say three times:

לִישׁוּעָתְךָ For Your salvation I hope, LORD. *Gen. 49*
I hope, LORD, for Your salvation.
LORD, for Your salvation I hope.

Say three times:

בְּשֵׁם In the name of the LORD, God of Israel:
may Michael be at my right hand,
Gabriel, at my left;
in front of me, Uriel,
behind me, Raphael;
and above my head the Presence of God.

יִרְאוּ עֵינֵינוּ וְיִשְׂמַח לִבֵּנוּ, וְתָגֵל נַפְשֵׁנוּ בִּישׁוּעָתְךָ בֶּאֱמֶת, בֶּאֱמֹר לְצִיּוֹן
מָלַךְ אֱלֹהָיִךְ. יהוה מֶלֶךְ, יהוה מָלָךְ, יהוה יִמְלֹךְ לְעוֹלָם וָעֶד. כִּי הַמַּלְכוּת
שֶׁלְּךָ הִיא, וּלְעוֹלְמֵי עַד תִּמְלֹךְ בְּכָבוֹד, כִּי אֵין לָנוּ מֶלֶךְ אֶלָּא אָתָּה.

בראשית מח הַמַּלְאָךְ הַגֹּאֵל אֹתִי מִכָּל־רָע יְבָרֵךְ אֶת־הַנְּעָרִים, וְיִקָּרֵא בָהֶם שְׁמִי וְשֵׁם
אֲבֹתַי אַבְרָהָם וְיִצְחָק, וְיִדְגּוּ לָרֹב בְּקֶרֶב הָאָרֶץ:

שמות טו וַיֹּאמֶר אִם־שָׁמוֹעַ תִּשְׁמַע לְקוֹל יהוה אֱלֹהֶיךָ, וְהַיָּשָׁר בְּעֵינָיו תַּעֲשֶׂה,
וְהַאֲזַנְתָּ לְמִצְוֹתָיו וְשָׁמַרְתָּ כָּל־חֻקָּיו, כָּל־הַמַּחֲלָה אֲשֶׁר־שַׂמְתִּי בְמִצְרַיִם
זכריה ג לֹא־אָשִׂים עָלֶיךָ, כִּי אֲנִי יהוה רֹפְאֶךָ: וַיֹּאמֶר יהוה אֶל־הַשָּׂטָן, יִגְעַר יהוה
בְּךָ הַשָּׂטָן, וְיִגְעַר יהוה בְּךָ הַבֹּחֵר בִּירוּשָׁלָםִ, הֲלוֹא זֶה אוּד מֻצָּל מֵאֵשׁ:
שיר השירים ג הִנֵּה מִטָּתוֹ שֶׁלִּשְׁלֹמֹה, שִׁשִּׁים גִּבֹּרִים סָבִיב לָהּ, מִגִּבֹּרֵי יִשְׂרָאֵל: כֻּלָּם
אֲחֻזֵי חֶרֶב, מְלֻמְּדֵי מִלְחָמָה, אִישׁ חַרְבּוֹ עַל־יְרֵכוֹ מִפַּחַד בַּלֵּילוֹת:

Say three times:

במדבר ו
יְבָרֶכְךָ יהוה וְיִשְׁמְרֶךָ:
יָאֵר יהוה פָּנָיו אֵלֶיךָ וִיחֻנֶּךָּ:
יִשָּׂא יהוה פָּנָיו אֵלֶיךָ וְיָשֵׂם לְךָ שָׁלוֹם:

Say three times:

תהלים קכא הִנֵּה לֹא־יָנוּם וְלֹא יִישָׁן שׁוֹמֵר יִשְׂרָאֵל:

Say three times:

בראשית מט
לִישׁוּעָתְךָ קִוִּיתִי יהוה:
קִוִּיתִי יהוה לִישׁוּעָתְךָ
יהוה לִישׁוּעָתְךָ קִוִּיתִי

Say three times:

בְּשֵׁם יהוה אֱלֹהֵי יִשְׂרָאֵל
מִימִינִי מִיכָאֵל, וּמִשְּׂמֹאלִי גַּבְרִיאֵל
וּמִלְּפָנַי אוּרִיאֵל, וּמֵאֲחוֹרַי רְפָאֵל
וְעַל רֹאשִׁי שְׁכִינַת אֵל.

שִׁיר הַמַּעֲלוֹת A song of ascents. *Ps. 128*
Happy are all who fear the LORD, who walk in His ways.
When you eat the fruit of your labor, happy and fortunate are you.
Your wife shall be like a fruitful vine within your house;
your sons like olive saplings around your table.
So shall the man who fears the LORD be blessed.
May the LORD bless you from Zion;
may you see the good of Jerusalem all the days of your life;
and may you live to see your children's children. Peace be on Israel!

Say three times:

רִגְזוּ Tremble, and do not sin. *Ps. 4*
Search your heart as you lie on your bed, and be silent. Selah.

אֲדוֹן עוֹלָם LORD of the Universe,
who reigned before the birth of any thing;
when by His will all things were made,
then was His name proclaimed King.
And when all things shall cease to be,
He alone will reign in awe.
He was, He is, and He shall be glorious for evermore.
He is One, there is none else, alone, unique, beyond compare;
Without beginning, without end, His might, His rule are everywhere.
He is my God; my Redeemer lives.
He is the Rock on whom I rely –
my banner and my safe retreat, my cup, my portion when I cry.
Into His hand my soul I place, when I awake and when I sleep.
The LORD is with me, I shall not fear;
body and soul from harm will He keep.

שִׁיר הַמַּעֲלוֹת, אַשְׁרֵי כָּל־יְרֵא יהוה, הַהֹלֵךְ בִּדְרָכָיו: תהלים קכח
יְגִיעַ כַּפֶּיךָ כִּי תֹאכֵל, אַשְׁרֶיךָ וְטוֹב לָךְ:
אֶשְׁתְּךָ כְּגֶפֶן פֹּרִיָּה בְּיַרְכְּתֵי בֵיתֶךָ
בָּנֶיךָ כִּשְׁתִלֵי זֵיתִים, סָבִיב לְשֻׁלְחָנֶךָ:
הִנֵּה כִי־כֵן יְבֹרַךְ גָּבֶר יְרֵא יהוה:
יְבָרֶכְךָ יהוה מִצִּיּוֹן, וּרְאֵה בְּטוּב יְרוּשָׁלָםִ, כֹּל יְמֵי חַיֶּיךָ:
וּרְאֵה־בָנִים לְבָנֶיךָ, שָׁלוֹם עַל־יִשְׂרָאֵל:

Say three times:

רִגְזוּ וְאַל־תֶּחֱטָאוּ תהלים ד
אִמְרוּ בִלְבַבְכֶם עַל־מִשְׁכַּבְכֶם, וְדֹמּוּ סֶלָה:

אֲדוֹן עוֹלָם אֲשֶׁר מָלַךְ בְּטֶרֶם כָּל־יְצִיר נִבְרָא.
לְעֵת נַעֲשָׂה בְחֶפְצוֹ כֹּל אֲזַי מֶלֶךְ שְׁמוֹ נִקְרָא.
וְאַחֲרֵי כִּכְלוֹת הַכֹּל לְבַדּוֹ יִמְלֹךְ נוֹרָא.
וְהוּא הָיָה וְהוּא הֹוֶה וְהוּא יִהְיֶה בְּתִפְאָרָה.
וְהוּא אֶחָד וְאֵין שֵׁנִי לְהַמְשִׁיל לוֹ לְהַחְבִּירָה.
בְּלִי רֵאשִׁית בְּלִי תַכְלִית וְלוֹ הָעֹז וְהַמִּשְׂרָה.
וְהוּא אֵלִי וְחַי גּוֹאֲלִי וְצוּר חֶבְלִי בְּעֵת צָרָה.
וְהוּא נִסִּי וּמָנוֹס לִי מְנָת כּוֹסִי בְּיוֹם אֶקְרָא.
בְּיָדוֹ אַפְקִיד רוּחִי בְּעֵת אִישַׁן וְאָעִירָה.
וְעִם רוּחִי גְּוִיָּתִי יהוה לִי וְלֹא אִירָא.

Hallel

On Ḥanukka and Ḥol HaMo'ed Pesaḥ, Full Hallel is said.
On Rosh Ḥodesh and Ḥol HaMo'ed Sukkot, Half Hallel is said.

בָּרוּךְ Blessed are You, LORD our God, King of the Universe, who has made us holy through His commandments and has commanded us to recite the Hallel.

הַלְלוּיָהּ Halleluya! Servants of the LORD,[A] give praise; praise the name *Ps. 113*
of the LORD. Blessed be the name of the LORD now and for evermore. From the rising of the sun to its setting, may the LORD's name be praised. High is the LORD above all nations; His glory is above the

new month as a new start, filled with hope for emerging from the limitations that may hold us back, and with the promise that Hashem is ever-present to help us out. **What are your hopes for the coming month?**

HILKHOT TEFILLA • הלכות תפילה

Each holiday has its own historical derivation and halakhic status, and this helps determine how much of Hallel is required. The core consists of six successive chapters of *Tehillim* (113–118) with a blessing at the beginning and at the end. Sometimes, the first parts of some of those chapters are omitted, resulting in two versions referred to as "Full Hallel" and "Half/Skipped Hallel." Full Hallel is generally recited for events of great national import, such as Pesaḥ, Shavuot, Sukkot and Ḥanukka, and, by the decree of the Chief Rabbinate of Israel, on Yom HaAtzma'ut and Yom Yerushalayim as well. The shortened version is recited on Rosh Ḥodesh which, while not a holiday in the classic sense, was nevertheless commemorated with the celebration of seeing the new moon.

ANI TEFILLA • אני תפילה

הַלְלוּיָהּ הַלְלוּ עַבְדֵי יהוה – *Halleluya! Servants of the LORD, give praise.* The first three verses speak of Hashem's presence in time – for eternity and in a single day.

The middle three verses speak of Hashem's presence in space – in the universe, and on earth.

The last three verses speak of Hashem's presence in the lives of man – helping the poor and the childless.

Where can you feel Hashem's presence most today?

סדר הלל

On חנוכה *and* חול המועד סוכות, הלל שלם *is said.*
On ראש חודש *and* חול המועד פסח, הלל בדילוג *is said.*

בָּרוּךְ אַתָּה יהוה אֱלֹהֵינוּ מֶלֶךְ הָעוֹלָם
אֲשֶׁר קִדְּשָׁנוּ בְּמִצְוֹתָיו וְצִוָּנוּ לִקְרֹא אֶת הַהַלֵּל.

הַלְלוּיָהּ, הַלְלוּ עַבְדֵי יהוה,[א] הַלְלוּ אֶת־שֵׁם יהוה: יְהִי שֵׁם יהוה תהלים קיג
מְבֹרָךְ, מֵעַתָּה וְעַד־עוֹלָם: מִמִּזְרַח־שֶׁמֶשׁ עַד־מְבוֹאוֹ, מְהֻלָּל שֵׁם
יהוה: רָם עַל־כָּל־גּוֹיִם יהוה, עַל הַשָּׁמַיִם כְּבוֹדוֹ: מִי כַּיהוה אֱלֹהֵינוּ,

---

AN INTRODUCTION TO HALLEL

The Talmud (*Pesaḥim* 117a) brings a number of opinions regarding the ancient roots of Hallel. There are those who suggest that it was recited by Moshe and *Benei Yisrael* at the splitting of the Sea, by Yehoshua and *Benei Yisrael* when faced by the kings of Canaan, and by Mordekhai and Esther when they were facing Haman, to name but three occasions. In short, say the sages, it was to be said whenever the Jewish people were redeemed from some potential calamity. In Rabbinic literature it is called *Hallel Mitzri*, or the Egyptian Hallel, based upon the reference in the second paragraph to the exodus from Egypt. The prayer marks our deliverance, often by seemingly supernatural means, throughout our history. "That is why we say it on Yom HaAtzma'ut and Yom Yerushalayim, two of the most most transformative events of modern Jewish history, in the faith that it is not human beings alone who shape the destiny of our people, but God working in and through His children" (Rabbi J. Sacks). In Hallel, we praise God's presence in world events, past and present.

Rosh Ḥodesh is not that exact same kind of holy day. Rather, Rosh Ḥodesh marks the beginning of a new month. Recall that the very first commandment that the Israelites were given in Egypt was to sanctify the new moon (*Shemot* 12:1), in effect to enable the measurement and marking of time, and establish the calendar. Each new month is thus not only a natural astrological event, but a psychological and theological one as well. On a national level, the fate of the Jewish people has been compared to the waxing and waning of the moon, from periods of darkness to periods when it fills the world with its reflected light. On a personal level, Rosh Ḥodesh represents a new beginning, one that is filled with optimism about the opportunities for growth and personal enlightenment. As such, we celebrate every

heavens. Who is like the LORD our God, who sits enthroned so high, yet turns so low to see the heavens and the earth? ▸ He raises the poor from the dust and the needy from the refuse heap, giving them a place alongside princes, the princes of His people. He makes the woman in a childless house a happy mother of children. Halleluya!

בְּצֵאת When Israel came out[1] of Egypt, the house of Jacob from a people of foreign tongue, Judah became His sanctuary, Israel His dominion. The sea saw and fled; the Jordan turned back. The mountains skipped like rams, the hills like lambs. ▸ Why was it, sea, that you fled? Jordan, why did you turn back? Why, mountains, did you skip like rams, and you, hills, like lambs? It was at the presence of the LORD, Creator of the earth, at the presence of the God of Jacob, who turned the rock into a pool of water, flint into a flowing spring. *Ps. 114*

Omit on Rosh Ḥodesh (except on Ḥanukka) and on Shabbat Ḥol HaMo'ed Pesaḥ:

לֹא לָנוּ Not to us, LORD, not to us, but to Your name give glory, for Your love, for Your faithfulness. Why should the nations say, "Where now is their God?" Our God is in heaven; whatever He wills He does. Their idols are silver and gold, made by human hands.[1] They have mouths but cannot speak; eyes but cannot see. They have ears but cannot hear; noses but cannot smell. They have hands but cannot feel; feet but cannot walk. No sound comes from their throat. Those who make them become like them; so will all who trust in them. ▸ Israel, trust in the LORD – He is their Help and their Shield. House of *Ps. 115*

---

are silver and gold, made by human hands. We cannot always see God. He sometimes seems absent or hidden from our lives. This psalm addresses this frustration by speaking of the folly of idolatry and of placing one's faith in other gods or non-Jewish beliefs. They are called idols, *atzabim* (from the word *itzev*, to make), because they are fashioned by man, but also because they bring sadness (from the word *atzuv*) and disappointment to their believers. Physical idols and images of gods are easily seen, but their abilities are not manifest. Hashem, however, cannot be physically seen but His actions can be seen everywhere (Rabbi S.R. Hirsch). The search for God is universal and it is a natural inclination to want to see some physical manifestation of Him. Judaism's response is that He cannot be seen but His impact is everywhere. Look around you.

הַמַּגְבִּיהִי לָשָׁבֶת: הַמַּשְׁפִּילִי לִרְאוֹת, בַּשָּׁמַיִם וּבָאָרֶץ: ‹ מְקִימִי מֵעָפָר דָּל, מֵאַשְׁפֹּת יָרִים אֶבְיוֹן: לְהוֹשִׁיבִי עִם־נְדִיבִים, עִם נְדִיבֵי עַמּוֹ: מוֹשִׁיבִי עֲקֶרֶת הַבַּיִת, אֵם־הַבָּנִים שְׂמֵחָה, הַלְלוּיָהּ:

תהלים קיד
בְּצֵאת יִשְׂרָאֵל ע מִמִּצְרָיִם, בֵּית יַעֲקֹב מֵעַם לֹעֵז: הָיְתָה יְהוּדָה לְקָדְשׁוֹ, יִשְׂרָאֵל מַמְשְׁלוֹתָיו: הַיָּם רָאָה וַיָּנֹס, הַיַּרְדֵּן יִסֹּב לְאָחוֹר: הֶהָרִים רָקְדוּ כְאֵילִים, גְּבָעוֹת כִּבְנֵי־צֹאן: ‹ מַה־לְּךָ הַיָּם כִּי תָנוּס, הַיַּרְדֵּן תִּסֹּב לְאָחוֹר: הֶהָרִים תִּרְקְדוּ כְאֵילִים, גְּבָעוֹת כִּבְנֵי־צֹאן: מִלִּפְנֵי אָדוֹן חוּלִי אָרֶץ, מִלִּפְנֵי אֱלוֹהַּ יַעֲקֹב: הַהֹפְכִי הַצּוּר אֲגַם־מָיִם, חַלָּמִישׁ לְמַעְיְנוֹ־מָיִם:

Omit on ראש חודש *(except on* חנוכה*) and on* שבת חול המועד פסח*:*

תהלים קטו
לֹא לָנוּ יהוה לֹא לָנוּ, כִּי־לְשִׁמְךָ תֵּן כָּבוֹד, עַל־חַסְדְּךָ עַל־אֲמִתֶּךָ: לָמָּה יֹאמְרוּ הַגּוֹיִם אַיֵּה־נָא אֱלֹהֵיהֶם: וֵאלֹהֵינוּ בַשָּׁמָיִם, כֹּל אֲשֶׁר־חָפֵץ עָשָׂה: עֲצַבֵּיהֶם כֶּסֶף וְזָהָב, מַעֲשֵׂה יְדֵי אָדָם: ע פֶּה־לָהֶם וְלֹא יְדַבֵּרוּ, עֵינַיִם לָהֶם וְלֹא יִרְאוּ: אָזְנַיִם לָהֶם וְלֹא יִשְׁמָעוּ, אַף לָהֶם וְלֹא יְרִיחוּן: יְדֵיהֶם וְלֹא יְמִישׁוּן, רַגְלֵיהֶם וְלֹא יְהַלֵּכוּ, לֹא־יֶהְגּוּ בִּגְרוֹנָם: כְּמוֹהֶם יִהְיוּ עֹשֵׂיהֶם, כֹּל אֲשֶׁר־בֹּטֵחַ בָּהֶם: ‹ יִשְׂרָאֵל בְּטַח בַּיהוה, עֶזְרָם וּמָגִנָּם

IYUN TEFILLA • עיון תפילה

בְּצֵאת יִשְׂרָאֵל – *When Israel came out.* Hashem is Master both of nature and of human history. No sooner is Israel freed from Egypt, than the entire natural world responds. The "sea saw and fled" by splitting for the Israelites; similarly "the Jordan [River] turned back" when they crossed over into the Promised Land. The natural world is thus a partner in the historical process. The inanimate world of seas and rivers, mountains and hills, comes alive when seen as part of the continuum of history, at least forty years of which is compressed here into one unified vision.

Have you ever felt in sync with nature? Imagine the whole world that way.

עֲצַבֵּיהֶם כֶּסֶף וְזָהָב, מַעֲשֵׂה יְדֵי אָדָם – *Their idols*

Aaron, trust in the LORD – He is their Help and their Shield. You who fear the LORD, trust in the LORD[B] – He is their Help and their Shield.

יהוה זְכָרָנוּ The LORD remembers us and will bless us. He will bless the house of Israel. He will bless the house of Aaron. He will bless those who fear the LORD, small and great alike. May the LORD give you increase: you and your children. May you be blessed by the LORD, Maker of heaven and earth. ▸ The heavens are the LORD's, but the earth He has given over to mankind.[B] It is not the dead who praise the LORD,[A] nor those who go down to the silent grave. But we will bless the LORD, now and for ever. Halleluya!

Omit on Rosh Ḥodesh (except on Ḥanukka) and on Shabbat Ḥol HaMo'ed Pesaḥ:

אָהַבְתִּי I love[A] the LORD, for He hears my voice, my pleas. He turns His ear to me whenever I call. The bonds of death encompassed me, the anguish of the grave came upon me, I was overcome by trouble and sorrow. Then I called on the name of the LORD: "LORD, I pray, save my life." Gracious is the LORD, and righteous; our God is full of compassion. The LORD protects the simple hearted. When I was brought low, He saved me.[B] My soul, be at peace once more,[A] for the *Ps. 116*

Look around you now. What can you see that is life affirming?

אָהַבְתִּי – *I love.* I stand before Hashem knowing that life has its challenges, troubles and sorrows, both physical and spiritual. Nevertheless, I know that Hashem listens whenever I speak to Him about them. I do not always get the response that I want, but sometimes just knowing that Someone is listening is relief enough.

Hashem is listening right now. What do you want to say to Him?

BIUR TEFILLA • ביאור תפילה

דַּלּוֹתִי וְלִי יְהוֹשִׁיעַ – *When I was brought low (daloti), He saved me.* The congregation of Israel spoke before the Holy One, blessed be He, Sovereign of the Universe! Though I am poor (*dala*) in mitzvot, and do not always do what I am supposed to do, nevertheless, I am Yours, my commitment is there, I try my best, and it is fitting that I should be saved (based on *Pesaḥim* 118b).

ANI TEFILLA • אני תפילה

שׁוּבִי נַפְשִׁי לִמְנוּחָיְכִי – *My soul, be at peace once more.* One can communicate with one's soul. Prayer can be a form of mindfulness and meditation that enables one to get in touch with one's inner being. Focusing on the realization that Hashem has been good to me can provide my soul with inner peace that I often lose track of in the hustle and bustle of my day. Here is such a moment. Focus: My soul, be at peace once again.

הוּא: בֵּית אַהֲרֹן בִּטְחוּ בַיהוה, עֶזְרָם וּמָגִנָּם הוּא: יִרְאֵי יהוה בִּטְחוּ
בַיהוה,ב עֶזְרָם וּמָגִנָּם הוּא:

יהוה זְכָרָנוּ יְבָרֵךְ, יְבָרֵךְ אֶת־בֵּית יִשְׂרָאֵל, יְבָרֵךְ אֶת־בֵּית אַהֲרֹן:
יְבָרֵךְ יִרְאֵי יהוה, הַקְּטַנִּים עִם־הַגְּדֹלִים: יֹסֵף יהוה עֲלֵיכֶם, עֲלֵיכֶם
וְעַל־בְּנֵיכֶם: בְּרוּכִים אַתֶּם לַיהוה, עֹשֵׂה שָׁמַיִם וָאָרֶץ: › הַשָּׁמַיִם
שָׁמַיִם לַיהוה, וְהָאָרֶץ נָתַן לִבְנֵי־אָדָם:ב לֹא הַמֵּתִים יְהַלְלוּ־יָהּ,א
וְלֹא כָּל־יֹרְדֵי דוּמָה: וַאֲנַחְנוּ נְבָרֵךְ יָהּ, מֵעַתָּה וְעַד־עוֹלָם, הַלְלוּיָהּ:

Omit on ראש חודש (*except on* חנוכה) *and on* שבת חול המועד פסח:

אָהַבְתִּי,א כִּי־יִשְׁמַע יהוה, אֶת־קוֹלִי תַּחֲנוּנָי: כִּי־הִטָּה אָזְנוֹ לִי, וּבְיָמַי תהלים קטז
אֶקְרָא: אֲפָפוּנִי חֶבְלֵי־מָוֶת, וּמְצָרֵי שְׁאוֹל מְצָאוּנִי, צָרָה וְיָגוֹן אֶמְצָא:
וּבְשֵׁם־יהוה אֶקְרָא, אָנָּה יהוה מַלְּטָה נַפְשִׁי: חַנּוּן יהוה וְצַדִּיק, וֵאלֹהֵינוּ
מְרַחֵם: שֹׁמֵר פְּתָאיִם יהוה, דַּלּוֹתִי וְלִי יְהוֹשִׁיעַ:ב שׁוּבִי נַפְשִׁי לִמְנוּחָיְכִי,א

BIUR TEFILLA • ביאור תפילה

וְהָאָרֶץ נָתַן לִבְנֵי־אָדָם – *But the earth He has given over to mankind.* "He gave the earth to man," not as a present but as a trust to be guarded and protected. Hashem gave the planet to mankind, not to be used and abused, but to be developed and nurtured. The Torah gives us the earth as a resource for our use (*Bereshit* 1:28), but also with the responsibility to protect and conserve it (ibid. 2:15). Our challenge is to find the appropriate balance between these two (Rabbi J.B. Soloveitchik).

יִרְאֵי יהוה בִּטְחוּ בַיהוה – *You who fear the Lord, trust in the Lord.* The verse says that Hashem will bless "those who fear" Him. But it already said He will bless the house of Israel and the house of Aharon – who else is left? A number of possibilities: it is a reference to converts (Rashi); the Torah scholars (Radak); the religious people of other faiths (Ibn Ezra); the righteous people of other faiths (Metzuda).

ANI TEFILLA • אני תפילה

לֹא הַמֵּתִים יְהַלְלוּ־יָהּ – *It is not the dead who praise the Lord.* True, life can be filled with tragedy, and the existence of death, natural as it may be, is still a reason for sadness. Yet knowing that such things exist should also be a reminder that every day presents a new opportunity to praise and thank Hashem for life, and for the things that we have. Even if one has a day when one might feel "down" and want to be in "silence," we are reminded that life in its totality is indeed beautiful and worth singing about.

Lord has been good to you. For You have rescued me from death, my eyes from weeping, my feet from stumbling. ▸ I shall walk in the presence of the Lord in the land of the living. I had faith, even when I said, "I am greatly afflicted," even when I said rashly, "All men are liars."

מָה־אָשִׁיב How can I repay the Lord[A] for all His goodness to me? I will lift the cup of salvation and call on the name of the Lord. I will fulfill my vows to the Lord in the presence of all His people. Grievous in the Lord's sight is the death of His devoted ones. Truly, Lord, I am Your servant;[IA] I am Your servant, the son of Your maidservant. You set me free from my chains. ▸ To You I shall bring a thanksgiving-offering and call on the Lord by name. I will fulfill my vows to the Lord in the presence of all His people, in the courts of the House of the Lord, in your midst, Jerusalem. Halleluya!

הַלְלוּ Praise the Lord,[I] all nations; acclaim Him, all you peoples; Ps. 117
for His loving-kindness to us is strong,
and the Lord's faithfulness is everlasting.
Halleluya!

---

na" ("Hashem, please, save us" [see page 693]) *The Rebbe responded, "No, you misunderstood. I wasn't referring to that phrase but to the one which says "Ana Hashem ki ani avdekha"* (*Truly,* Lord, *I am Your servant*). *First one must commit oneself to the King's service; only then can one presume to call on Him for help.*

IYUN TEFILLA • עיון תפילה

הַלְלוּ אֶת־יהוה – *Praise the* Lord.

This is the shortest of all of the psalms, a mere two verses. The psalmist speaks of the universal significance of Israel's history. It is not Israel alone, but all the nations, who will see in the story of this people, something beyond mere history. "The Jew is the emblem of eternity. He whom neither slaughter nor torture of thousands of years could destroy, he whom neither fire nor sword nor inquisition was able to wipe off the face of the earth, he who was the first to produce the oracles of God, who has been for so long the guardian of prophecy and transmitted it to the rest of the world – such a nation cannot be destroyed. The Jew is everlasting as eternity itself" (Tolstoy). (Rabbi J. Sacks)

Sometimes non-Jews see the miracle of our survival more clearly than we ourselves do (*Pesaḥim* 118b and Rashi).

כִּי־יהוה גָּמַל עָלָיְכִי: כִּי חִלַּצְתָּ נַפְשִׁי מִמָּוֶת, אֶת־עֵינִי מִן־דִּמְעָה, אֶת־
רַגְלִי מִדֶּחִי: ‹ אֶתְהַלֵּךְ לִפְנֵי יהוה, בְּאַרְצוֹת הַחַיִּים: הֶאֱמַנְתִּי כִּי אֲדַבֵּר,
אֲנִי עָנִיתִי מְאֹד: אֲנִי אָמַרְתִּי בְחָפְזִי, כָּל־הָאָדָם כֹּזֵב:

מָה־אָשִׁיב לַיהוה,[א] כָּל־תַּגְמוּלוֹהִי עָלָי: כּוֹס־יְשׁוּעוֹת אֶשָּׂא, וּבְשֵׁם
יהוה אֶקְרָא: נְדָרַי לַיהוה אֲשַׁלֵּם, נֶגְדָה־נָּא לְכָל־עַמּוֹ: יָקָר בְּעֵינֵי
יהוה, הַמָּוְתָה לַחֲסִידָיו: אָנָּה יהוה כִּי־אֲנִי עַבְדֶּךָ,[עא] אֲנִי־עַבְדְּךָ
בֶּן־אֲמָתֶךָ, פִּתַּחְתָּ לְמוֹסֵרָי: ‹ לְךָ־אֶזְבַּח זֶבַח תּוֹדָה, וּבְשֵׁם יהוה
אֶקְרָא: נְדָרַי לַיהוה אֲשַׁלֵּם, נֶגְדָה־נָּא לְכָל־עַמּוֹ: בְּחַצְרוֹת בֵּית
יהוה, בְּתוֹכֵכִי יְרוּשָׁלָםִ, הַלְלוּיָהּ:

תהלים קיז

הַלְלוּ אֶת־יהוה[ע] כָּל־גּוֹיִם, שַׁבְּחוּהוּ כָּל־הָאֻמִּים:
כִּי גָבַר עָלֵינוּ חַסְדּוֹ, וֶאֱמֶת־יהוה לְעוֹלָם, הַלְלוּיָהּ:

ANI TEFILLA • אני תפילה

מָה־אָשִׁיב לַיהוה – *How can I repay the Lord.* How can I possibly thank Hashem for everything I have? The answer: I can't. For no matter how difficult daily circumstances may be, I still have my life, which Judaism maintains is a supreme gift. The good always, always, outweighs the bad.

IYUN TEFILLA • עיון תפילה

אָנָּה יהוה כִּי־אֲנִי עַבְדֶּךָ – *Truly, Lord, I am Your servant.* I have come to serve You from two directions. First, I am Your servant; I try to do my best on my own, finding my own faith and my own way. Second, I am a product of my mother, whose traditions and teachings shaped me in becoming a Jew. I am thus a servant in my own right and the child of a servant (Radak). Both of those free me from (physical, social, intellectual or spiritual) chains that would otherwise tie me down. For that I am thankful.

ANI TEFILLA • אני תפילה

אָנָּה יְהוָה כִּי־אֲנִי עַבְדֶּךָ – *Truly, Lord, I am Your servant.*
A Hasid came to his Rebbe and asked for direction about how he might get help from Hashem. The Rebbe advised him to say the phrase that begins with the words "Ana Hashem" with all of his strength and devotion. The Hasid returned one day and complained that he had followed the Rebbe's advice but to no avail. The Rebbe asked him, "Which Ana Hashem did you recite?" The Hasid answered, "Ana Hashem hoshia

The following verses are chanted by the Leader. At the end of each verse, the congregation responds, "Thank the Lord for He is good; His loving-kindness is for ever."

הודו Thank the Lord for He is good;[B] His loving-kindness is for ever. *Ps. 118*
Let Israel say His loving-kindness is for ever.
Let the house of Aaron say His loving-kindness is for ever.
Let those who fear the Lord say His loving-kindness is for ever.

מִן־הַמֵּצַר In my distress I called on the Lord.[A] The Lord answered me and set me free. The Lord is with me; I will not be afraid. What can man do to me? The Lord is with me. He is my Helper. I will see the downfall of my enemies. It is better to take refuge in the Lord than to trust in man. It is better to take refuge in the Lord than to trust in princes. The nations all surrounded me, but in the Lord's name I drove them off. They surrounded me on every side, but in the Lord's name I drove them off. They surrounded me like bees,[A] they attacked me as fire attacks brushwood, but in the Lord's name I drove them off. They thrust so hard against me, I nearly fell, but the Lord came to my help. The Lord is my strength and my song; He has become

ANI TEFILLA • אני תפילה

מִן־הַמֵּצַר קָרָאתִי יָּהּ – *In my distress I called on the Lord.*

There were times when I thought my world was crashing around me, when I could not understand why this was happening to me, to my family, to people that I cared about. At those moments, I took strength from the belief that there must be a bigger plan, that Hashem had something in mind that I just couldn't see right now. That belief doesn't always take away the pain of the moment, but it gives one enough perspective to take it in stride and to move on with a sense of optimism. Though I sometimes find myself confined in narrow "straits" (metzar), my knowing that Hashem is there enables me to realize that there is a bigger, more "expansive" (merḥav) picture.

סַבּוּנִי כִדְבֹרִים – *They surrounded me like bees.* Sometimes those who attack us appear as a forest fire that burns the brush all around us; we see them coming but cannot get out of the way. Sometimes they appear as bees, attractive in color, full of life, bearing sweet honey for us, but if we let our guard down they sting us and quickly move off. Either way, my faith provides me with perspective that makes me strong and resilient.

The following verses are chanted by the שליח ציבור*.*
At the end of each verse, the קהל *responds:* הוֹדוּ לַיהוה כִּי־טוֹב, כִּי לְעוֹלָם חַסְדּוֹ.

תהלים קיח

הוֹדוּ לַיהוה כִּי־טוֹב[ב] כִּי לְעוֹלָם חַסְדּוֹ:
יֹאמַר־נָא יִשְׂרָאֵל כִּי לְעוֹלָם חַסְדּוֹ:
יֹאמְרוּ־נָא בֵית־אַהֲרֹן כִּי לְעוֹלָם חַסְדּוֹ:
יֹאמְרוּ־נָא יִרְאֵי יהוה כִּי לְעוֹלָם חַסְדּוֹ:

מִן־הַמֵּצַר קָרָאתִי יָּהּ,[א] עָנָנִי בַמֶּרְחָב יָהּ: יהוה לִי לֹא אִירָא, מַה־יַּעֲשֶׂה לִי אָדָם: יהוה לִי בְּעֹזְרָי, וַאֲנִי אֶרְאֶה בְשֹׂנְאָי: טוֹב לַחֲסוֹת בַּיהוה, מִבְּטֹחַ בָּאָדָם: טוֹב לַחֲסוֹת בַּיהוה, מִבְּטֹחַ בִּנְדִיבִים: כָּל־גּוֹיִם סְבָבוּנִי, בְּשֵׁם יהוה כִּי אֲמִילַם: סַבּוּנִי גַם־סְבָבוּנִי, בְּשֵׁם יהוה כִּי אֲמִילַם: סַבּוּנִי כִדְבֹרִים,[א] דֹּעֲכוּ כְּאֵשׁ קוֹצִים, בְּשֵׁם יהוה כִּי אֲמִילַם: דָּחֹה דְחִיתַנִי לִנְפֹּל, וַיהוה עֲזָרָנִי:

BIUR TEFILLA • ביאור תפילה

הוֹדוּ לַיהוה כִּי־טוֹב – *Thank the* Lord *for He is good.* The word *hodu* (thank) is related to the name Yehuda, whose mother, Leah, named him thus because she "thanked God" for his birth (*Bereshit* 29:35). The name "Jew" or "*Yehudi*" also comes from the name Yehuda (Judah). The implication is clear: to be a Jew means to be thankful.

הוֹדוּ לַיהוה כִּי־טוֹב – *Thank the* Lord *for He is good.* The last three of the groups mentioned here are the ones (referred to in Psalm 115 above) who were called upon to have faith that Hashem would protect and help them. It has been suggested that here there are four groups, the first being all of mankind, and that there is a closeness-to-God hierarchy of sorts from one group to the next (Rashbam). The greater the constant sense that everything comes from God, the more one knows that everything is a gift, the more one knows how fortunate one really is, the more thankful one can be.

How fortunate do you feel today? Give thanks.

הוֹדוּ לַיהוה כִּי־טוֹב – *Thank the* Lord *for He is good.* There are two possibilities for what "good" describes. One could be: "Thank God because He is good." Alternatively, "Thank God because all is good" (Ibn Ezra). The two are separate but certainly related. Have one or both in mind.

my salvation. Sounds of song and salvation resound in the tents of the righteous: "The LORD's right hand has done mighty deeds. The LORD's right hand is lifted high. The LORD's right hand has done mighty deeds." I will not die but live, and tell what the LORD has done. The LORD has chastened me severely, but He has not given me over to death. ▸ Open for me the gates of righteousness that I may enter them and thank the LORD. This is the gateway to the LORD; through it, the righteous shall enter.

אוֹדְךָ I will thank You, for You answered me,[B]
and became my salvation.
I will thank You, for You answered me,
and became my salvation.

The stone the builders rejected[I]
has become the main cornerstone.
The stone the builders rejected
has become the main cornerstone.

This is the LORD's doing; it is wondrous in our eyes.
This is the LORD's doing; it is wondrous in our eyes.

This is the day the LORD has made;
let us rejoice and be glad in it.
This is the day the LORD has made;
let us rejoice and be glad in it.

IYUN TEFILLA • עיון תפילה

אֶבֶן מָאֲסוּ הַבּוֹנִים – *The stone the builders rejected.* There are those who say that the "foundation stone rejected by the builders" is a reference to King David himself who, before he was anointed, was essentially misunderstood by his family, not unlike the way that Yosef was misunderstood by his brothers. David wasn't even considered to be a candidate for leadership. Nevertheless, he went on to become the cornerstone of Jewish sovereignty. One day a shepherd, the next a king of Israel (*Da'at Soferim*). We ignore the strengths of those around us just as we ourselves are sometimes ignored. But Hashem is aware of the potential in each of us, and for that I give thanks.

עָזִּי וְזִמְרָת יָהּ, וַיְהִי־לִי לִישׁוּעָה: קוֹל רִנָּה וִישׁוּעָה בְּאָהֳלֵי צַדִּיקִים, יְמִין יהוה עֹשָׂה חָיִל: יְמִין יהוה רוֹמֵמָה, יְמִין יהוה עֹשָׂה חָיִל: לֹא־אָמוּת כִּי־אֶחְיֶה, וַאֲסַפֵּר מַעֲשֵׂי יָהּ: יַסֹּר יִסְּרַנִּי יָּהּ, וְלַמָּוֶת לֹא נְתָנָנִי: › פִּתְחוּ־לִי שַׁעֲרֵי־צֶדֶק, אָבֹא־בָם אוֹדֶה יָהּ: זֶה־הַשַּׁעַר לַיהוה, צַדִּיקִים יָבֹאוּ בוֹ:

אוֹדְךָ כִּי עֲנִיתָנִי,[ב] וַתְּהִי־לִי לִישׁוּעָה:
אוֹדְךָ כִּי עֲנִיתָנִי, וַתְּהִי־לִי לִישׁוּעָה:

אֶבֶן מָאֲסוּ הַבּוֹנִים,[ע] הָיְתָה לְרֹאשׁ פִּנָּה:
אֶבֶן מָאֲסוּ הַבּוֹנִים, הָיְתָה לְרֹאשׁ פִּנָּה:

מֵאֵת יהוה הָיְתָה זֹּאת, הִיא נִפְלָאת בְּעֵינֵינוּ:
מֵאֵת יהוה הָיְתָה זֹּאת, הִיא נִפְלָאת בְּעֵינֵינוּ:

זֶה־הַיּוֹם עָשָׂה יהוה, נָגִילָה וְנִשְׂמְחָה בוֹ:
זֶה־הַיּוֹם עָשָׂה יהוה, נָגִילָה וְנִשְׂמְחָה בוֹ:

BIUR TEFILLA • ביאור תפילה

אוֹדְךָ כִּי עֲנִיתָנִי – *I will thank You, for You answered me.* Although the following nine verses are part of the same preceding Psalm 118, they are treated differently in that each one of them is repeated. This is because, when looking at the structure of the entire psalm, one notices that all of the verses are coupled, in that the theme or language of one is repeated, in one form or another, in the following verse. That is not the case, however, in these nine verses, each of which stands alone according to many commentators. And so it was decided that, in keeping with the rhythm, tone and theme of the psalm as a whole, each of these verses should be repeated in order to maintain the pattern (Rashi, *Sukka* 38a). The Gemara (*Pesaḥim* 119a) relates that there is also a conversational quality about these verses that lends itself to responsive reading or singing, as may have been done in the *Beit HaMikdash*.

Leader followed by congregation:

אָנָּא LORD, please, save us.[B]
LORD, please, save us.
LORD, please, grant us success.
LORD, please, grant us success.

בָּרוּךְ Blessed is one who comes in the name of the LORD;[I]
we bless you from the House of the LORD.
Blessed is one who comes in the name of the LORD;
we bless you from the House of the LORD.

The LORD is God; He has given us light.
Bind the festival offering with thick cords
[and bring it] to the horns of the altar.
The LORD is God; He has given us light. Bind the festival offering with thick cords [and bring it] to the horns of the altar.

You are my God and I will thank You;
You are my God, I will exalt You.
You are my God and I will thank You;
You are my God, I will exalt You.

Thank the LORD for He is good;
His loving-kindness is for ever.[A]
Thank the LORD for He is good;
His loving-kindness is for ever.

IYUN TEFILLA • עיון תפילה

בָּרוּךְ הַבָּא בְּשֵׁם יהוה – *Blessed is one who comes in the name of the LORD.* The blessing is given to those who show up. One cannot expect blessings if one does not first do one's part (*Me'am Loez*).

ANI TEFILLA • אני תפילה

הוֹדוּ לַיהוה כִּי־טוֹב, כִּי לְעוֹלָם חַסְדּוֹ – *Thank the LORD for He is good; His loving-kindness is for ever.* The chapter ends with the exact same phrase with which it began but, hopefully, we can now say it with added meaning.

שליח ציבור followed by קהל:

אָנָּא יהוה הוֹשִׁיעָה נָּא: [ב]

אָנָּא יהוה הוֹשִׁיעָה נָּא:

אָנָּא יהוה הַצְלִיחָה נָּא:

אָנָּא יהוה הַצְלִיחָה נָּא:

בָּרוּךְ הַבָּא בְּשֵׁם יהוה, [ע] **בֵּרַכְנוּכֶם מִבֵּית יהוה:**

בָּרוּךְ הַבָּא בְּשֵׁם יהוה, בֵּרַכְנוּכֶם מִבֵּית יהוה:

אֵל יהוה וַיָּאֶר לָנוּ, אִסְרוּ־חַג בַּעֲבֹתִים עַד־קַרְנוֹת הַמִּזְבֵּחַ:

אֵל יהוה וַיָּאֶר לָנוּ, אִסְרוּ־חַג בַּעֲבֹתִים עַד־קַרְנוֹת הַמִּזְבֵּחַ:

אֵלִי אַתָּה וְאוֹדֶךָּ, אֱלֹהַי אֲרוֹמְמֶךָּ:

אֵלִי אַתָּה וְאוֹדֶךָּ, אֱלֹהַי אֲרוֹמְמֶךָּ:

הוֹדוּ לַיהוה כִּי־טוֹב, [א] **כִּי לְעוֹלָם חַסְדּוֹ:**

הוֹדוּ לַיהוה כִּי־טוֹב, כִּי לְעוֹלָם חַסְדּוֹ:

BIUR TEFILLA • ביאור תפילה

אָנָּא יהוה הוֹשִׁיעָה נָּא – *Lord, please, save us.* *Yeshua*, being saved, refers to being freed from things which constrict us (Malbim) or, alternatively, it could be a reference to the personal happiness associated with being alive (Rabbi S.R. Hirsch).

Which speaks to you more today?

Hatzlaha, on the other hand, refers to success in our endeavors. Help from above, however, only comes about if we put in the effort to begin with.

יְהַלְלוּךָ All Your works will praise You, LORD our God,
and Your devoted ones –
the righteous who do Your will,
together with all Your people the house of Israel –
will joyously thank, bless, praise, glorify,
exalt, revere, sanctify, and proclaim
the sovereignty of Your name, our King.
▸ For it is good to thank You
and fitting to sing psalms to Your name,
for from eternity to eternity You are God.
Blessed are You, LORD,
King who is extolled with praises.

The service continues with Full Kaddish on page 364.

people were transported in the worst possible, inhumane way by railcar. They thought they were going to a work camp. We all know they were going to a death camp.

"After hours and hours in this inhumane corral with no light, no bathroom, cold, they arrived at the camps. The doors were swung wide open, and they were blinded by the light. Men were separated from women, mothers from daughters, fathers from sons. They went off to the bunkers to sleep.

Am I going to push the blanket to the other people, or am I going to pull it to stay warm?

"As they went into the area to sleep, only one person was given a blanket for every six. The person who received the blanket, when he went to bed, had to decide, 'Am I going to push the blanket to the five other people who did not get one, or am I going to pull it toward myself to stay warm?'"

"Larry, imagine you've come back from the store with a brand new radio. You plug it in and all you hear is static. No music. No news. No baseball games. Do you call the radio stations and complain?"

"Of course not."

"Exactly. The signal isn't being received properly. You have to adjust the dial so it can pick up the radio waves. Same thing with God. He is there. He is on the air. You have to tune yourself to receive his signal, his bounty, and his blessing. But if your life is full of static – distractions, false ego..." (Rabbi Irwin Katsof)

יְהַלְלְוּךָ יהוה אֱלֹהֵינוּ כָּל מַעֲשֶׂיךָ
וַחֲסִידֶיךָ צַדִּיקִים עוֹשֵׂי רְצוֹנֶךָ
וְכָל עַמְּךָ בֵּית יִשְׂרָאֵל
בְּרִנָּה יוֹדוּ וִיבָרְכוּ וִישַׁבְּחוּ
וִיפָאֲרוּ וִירוֹמְמוּ וְיַעֲרִיצוּ וְיַקְדִּישׁוּ
וְיַמְלִיכוּ אֶת שִׁמְךָ מַלְכֵּנוּ
◂ כִּי לְךָ טוֹב לְהוֹדוֹת וּלְשִׁמְךָ נָאֶה לְזַמֵּר
כִּי מֵעוֹלָם וְעַד עוֹלָם אַתָּה אֵל.
בָּרוּךְ אַתָּה יהוה, מֶלֶךְ מְהֻלָּל בַּתִּשְׁבָּחוֹת.

The service continues with קדיש שלם *on page 365.*

ANI TEFILLA • אני תפילה

When I was in Israel, I went to Mea Shearim, the ultra-Orthodox area within Jerusalem. Along with a group of businessmen I was with, I had the opportunity to have an audience with Rabbi Noson Tzvi Finkel, the head of a yeshiva there [Mir Yeshiva]. I had never heard of him and didn't know anything about him. We went into his study and waited 10 to 15 minutes for him. Finally, the doors opened.

Rabbi Finkel was severely afflicted with Parkinson's disease. Our inclination was to look away.

...He sat down at the head of the table, and...he asked, "Who can tell me what the lesson of the Holocaust is?" He called on one guy, who didn't know what to do - it was like being called on in the fifth grade without the answer. And the guy says something benign like, "We will never, ever forget?" And the rabbi completely dismisses him. I felt terrible for the guy until I realized the rabbi was getting ready to call on someone else. All of us were sort of under the table, looking away – you know, please, not me. He did not call me. I was sweating. He called on another guy, who had such a fantastic answer: "We will never, ever again be a victim or bystander."

The rabbi said, "You guys just don't get it. Okay, gentlemen, let me tell you the essence of the human spirit.

"As you know, during the Holocaust, the

Musaf for Shabbat Ḥol HaMo'ed

The following Amida is said on Shabbat Ḥol HaMo'ed Pesaḥ and on Shabbat Ḥol HaMo'ed Sukkot.

The following prayer, until "in former years" on page 716, is said silently, standing with feet together. If there is a minyan, the Amida is repeated aloud by the Leader. Take three steps forward.

When I proclaim the LORD's name, give glory to our God. *Deut. 32*
O LORD, open my lips, so that my mouth may declare Your praise. *Ps. 51*

PATRIARCHS

▾ *Bend the knees:* Blessed *Bow:* are You, *Stand straight:* LORD
our God and God of our fathers,
God of Abraham, God of Isaac and God of Jacob;
the great, mighty and awesome God, God Most High,
who bestows acts of loving-kindness and creates all,
who remembers the loving-kindness of the fathers
and will bring a Redeemer to their children's children
for the sake of His name, in love.
King, Helper, Savior, Shield:
▾ *Bend the knees:* Blessed *Bow:* are You, *Stand straight:* LORD,
Shield of Abraham.[1]

DIVINE MIGHT

אַתָּה גִּבּוֹר You are eternally mighty, LORD.
You give life to the dead and have great power to save.
In Israel: He causes the dew to fall.

---

the major festivals. The theme is thus one that echoes the loss of the *Beit HaMikdash*, and conjures up a time when the nation would make its way to *Yerushalayim* to celebrate together. If you have ever been to the Kotel on such a festival or even on a Friday night, you can begin to get a feel for what it must have been like.

Within this central theme, however, accommodations are made for mention of variations between one festival and the next. So, for example, because the kind and number of sacrifices varied for each of these occasions, then the blessing makes mention of these, listing the sacrifices that were unique to that particular occasion. On a day when festivals and the Shabbat overlap, then the Shabbat offerings are also mentioned.

מוסף לשבת חול המועד

The following עמידה *is said on* שבת חול המועד פסח *and on* שבת חול המועד סוכות.

The following prayer, until קַדְמֹנִיּוֹת *on page 717, is said silently, standing with feet together. If there is a* מנין*, the* עמידה *is repeated aloud by the* שליח ציבור.

Take three steps forward.

דברים לב כִּי שֵׁם יהוה אֶקְרָא, הָבוּ גֹדֶל לֵאלֹהֵינוּ:
תהלים נא אֲדֹנָי, שְׂפָתַי תִּפְתָּח, וּפִי יַגִּיד תְּהִלָּתֶךָ:

אבות

▼ *Bend the knees* בָּרוּךְ *Bow* אַתָּה *Stand straight* יהוה
אֱלֹהֵינוּ וֵאלֹהֵי אֲבוֹתֵינוּ,
אֱלֹהֵי אַבְרָהָם, אֱלֹהֵי יִצְחָק, וֵאלֹהֵי יַעֲקֹב
הָאֵל הַגָּדוֹל הַגִּבּוֹר וְהַנּוֹרָא, אֵל עֶלְיוֹן
גּוֹמֵל חֲסָדִים טוֹבִים, וְקוֹנֵה הַכֹּל, וְזוֹכֵר חַסְדֵי אָבוֹת
וּמֵבִיא גוֹאֵל לִבְנֵי בְנֵיהֶם לְמַעַן שְׁמוֹ בְּאַהֲבָה.
מֶלֶךְ עוֹזֵר וּמוֹשִׁיעַ וּמָגֵן.
▼ *Bend the knees* בָּרוּךְ *Bow* אַתָּה *Stand straight* יהוה, מָגֵן אַבְרָהָם.

גבורות

אַתָּה גִּבּוֹר לְעוֹלָם, אֲדֹנָי, מְחַיֵּה מֵתִים אַתָּה, רַב לְהוֹשִׁיעַ
בארץ ישראל: מוֹרִיד הַטָּל

INTRODUCTION TO MUSAF AMIDA SHALOSH REGALIM

The structure of the *Musaf Amida* is similar to that of Shabbat, i.e., the first three and last three blessings are the same as they are for every *Amida*; only the middle blessing, the one which declares and describes the sanctity of the day (*Kedushat HaYom*) is different. In terms of content, however, on Shabbat, the theme of the middle blessing is one that is appropriate to the themes of Shabbat. On a festival day, or on one of its intermediate days (*Ḥol HaMo'ed*), a different theme is emphasized and so there is need for a special version of the middle *Amida* blessing.

The *Musaf* service, it will be recalled, parallels the additional offerings that were made in the *Beit HaMikdash* on Shabbat and

He sustains the living with loving-kindness,
and with great compassion revives the dead.
He supports the fallen, heals the sick, sets captives free,
and keeps His faith with those who sleep in the dust.
Who is like You, Master of might,
and who can compare to You,
O King who brings death and gives life, and makes salvation grow?
Faithful are You to revive the dead.
Blessed are You, LORD, who revives the dead.

When saying the Amida silently, continue with "You are holy" on the next page.

KEDUSHA *During the Leader's Repetition, the following is said standing with feet together, rising on the toes at the words indicated by ▴.*

Cong. then Leader: נַעֲרִיצְךָ We will revere and sanctify You with the words uttered by the holy Seraphim who sanctify Your name in the Sanctuary; as is written by Your prophet: "They call out to one another, saying: *Is. 6*

Cong. then Leader: ▴Holy, ▴holy, ▴holy is the LORD of hosts; the whole world is filled with His glory."
His glory fills the universe. His ministering angels ask each other, "Where is the place of His glory?" Those facing them reply "Blessed –

Cong. then Leader: ▴"Blessed is the LORD's glory from His place." *Ezek. 3*
From His place may He turn with compassion and be gracious to the people who proclaim the unity of His name, morning and evening, every day, continually, twice each day reciting in love the Shema:

Cong. then Leader: "Listen, Israel: the LORD is our God, the LORD is One." *Deut. 6*
He is our God, He is our Father, He is our King, He is our Savior – and He, in His compassion, will let us hear a second time in the presence of all that lives, His promise "to be Your God. *Num. 15*
I am the LORD your God."

Leader: And in Your holy Writings it is written:

Cong. then Leader: ▴"The LORD shall reign for ever. He is your God, Zion, from generation to generation, Halleluya!" *Ps. 146*

Leader: From generation to generation we will declare Your greatness, and we will proclaim Your holiness for evermore. Your praise, our God, shall not leave our mouth forever, for You, God, are a great and holy King. Blessed are You, LORD, the holy God.

The Leader continues with "You have chosen us" on the next page.

מְכַלְכֵּל חַיִּים בְּחֶסֶד, מְחַיֵּה מֵתִים בְּרַחֲמִים רַבִּים
סוֹמֵךְ נוֹפְלִים, וְרוֹפֵא חוֹלִים, וּמַתִּיר אֲסוּרִים
וּמְקַיֵּם אֱמוּנָתוֹ לִישֵׁנֵי עָפָר.
מִי כָמְוֹךָ, בַּעַל גְּבוּרוֹת, וּמִי דּוֹמֶה לָּךְ
מֶלֶךְ, מֵמִית וּמְחַיֶּה וּמַצְמִיחַ יְשׁוּעָה.
וְנֶאֱמָן אַתָּה לְהַחֲיוֹת מֵתִים.
בָּרוּךְ אַתָּה יהוה, מְחַיֵּה הַמֵּתִים.

When saying the עמידה silently, continue with אַתָּה קָדוֹשׁ on the next page.

קדושה

*During the חזרת הש״ץ, the following is said standing with feet together, rising on the toes at the words indicated by *.*

then קהל ש״ץ: נַעֲרִיצְךָ וְנַקְדִּישְׁךָ כְּסוֹד שִׂיחַ שַׂרְפֵי קֹדֶשׁ, הַמַּקְדִּישִׁים שִׁמְךָ בַּקֹּדֶשׁ,
ישעיה ו כַּכָּתוּב עַל יַד נְבִיאֶךָ: וְקָרָא זֶה אֶל־זֶה וְאָמַר

then קהל ש״ץ: *קָדוֹשׁ, *קָדוֹשׁ, *קָדוֹשׁ, יהוה צְבָאוֹת, מְלֹא כָל הָאָרֶץ כְּבוֹדוֹ:
כְּבוֹדוֹ מָלֵא עוֹלָם, מְשָׁרְתָיו שׁוֹאֲלִים זֶה לָזֶה, אַיֵּה מְקוֹם כְּבוֹדוֹ,
לְעֻמָּתָם בָּרוּךְ יֹאמֵרוּ

יחזקאל ג then קהל ש״ץ: *בָּרוּךְ כְּבוֹד־יהוה מִמְּקוֹמוֹ:
מִמְּקוֹמוֹ הוּא יִפֶן בְּרַחֲמִים, וְיָחֹן עַם הַמְיַחֲדִים שְׁמוֹ, עֶרֶב וָבְקֶר בְּכָל
יוֹם תָּמִיד, פַּעֲמַיִם בְּאַהֲבָה שְׁמַע אוֹמְרִים

דברים ו then קהל ש״ץ: שְׁמַע יִשְׂרָאֵל, יהוה אֱלֹהֵינוּ, יהוה אֶחָד:
הוּא אֱלֹהֵינוּ, הוּא אָבִינוּ, הוּא מַלְכֵּנוּ, הוּא מוֹשִׁיעֵנוּ, וְהוּא יַשְׁמִיעֵנוּ
במדבר טו בְּרַחֲמָיו שֵׁנִית לְעֵינֵי כָּל חָי, לִהְיוֹת לָכֶם לֵאלֹהִים, אֲנִי יהוה אֱלֹהֵיכֶם:

ש״ץ: וּבְדִבְרֵי קָדְשְׁךָ כָּתוּב לֵאמֹר

תהלים קמו then קהל ש״ץ: *יִמְלֹךְ יהוה לְעוֹלָם, אֱלֹהַיִךְ צִיּוֹן לְדֹר וָדֹר, הַלְלוּיָהּ:

ש״ץ: לְדוֹר וָדוֹר נַגִּיד גָּדְלֶךָ, וּלְנֵצַח נְצָחִים קְדֻשָּׁתְךָ נַקְדִּישׁ, וְשִׁבְחֲךָ אֱלֹהֵינוּ
מִפִּינוּ לֹא יָמוּשׁ לְעוֹלָם וָעֶד, כִּי אֵל מֶלֶךְ גָּדוֹל וְקָדוֹשׁ אָתָּה. בָּרוּךְ
אַתָּה יהוה, הָאֵל הַקָּדוֹשׁ.

The שליח ציבור continues with אַתָּה בְחַרְתָּנוּ on the next page.

When saying the Amida silently, continue here with "You are holy":

HOLINESS

אַתָּה קָדוֹשׁ You are holy and Your name is holy,
and holy ones praise You daily, Selah!
Blessed are You, LORD, the holy God.

HOLINESS OF THE DAY

אַתָּה בְחַרְתָּנוּ You have chosen us[1] from among all peoples.
You have loved and favored us.
You have raised us above all tongues.
You have made us holy through Your commandments.
You have brought us near, our King, to Your service,
and have called us by Your great and holy name.

וַתִּתֶּן לָנוּ And You, LORD our God, have given us in love
Sabbaths for rest and festivals for rejoicing,
holy days and seasons for joy,
this Sabbath day and this day of:

On Pesaḥ: the festival of Matzot, the time of our freedom
On Sukkot: the festival of Sukkot, our time of rejoicing

with love, a holy assembly[B]
in memory of the exodus from Egypt.

BIUR TEFILLA • ביאור תפילה

מִקְרָא קֹדֶשׁ – *A holy assembly.* The holy days/festivals are each referred to in the Torah as a "holy assembly" although the understanding of the Hebrew word *mikra*, most commonly understood to derive from the word "to call out," is not uniform. Rabbi Yissachar Jacobson gathered a number of possibilities, each with its own implications:

• *Sanctify* it with food, with drink and clean clothes (*Mekhilta Bo* 12:16).

• A day *called* for the purpose of commemorating (Rashbam).

• A day when we are *called to gather* together to Jerusalem to *sanctify* it (Ramban). As is written in *Neḥemia* 8:10, "Then he said unto them: 'Go your way, eat rich foods, and drink sweet beverages, and send portions to him for whom nothing is prepared; for this day is holy unto our Lord; do not be sad; for the joy of Hashem is your strength.'

This BIUR TEFILLA *continues on page 703.*

When saying the עמידה *silently, continue here with* אַתָּה קָדוֹשׁ:

קדושת השם

אַתָּה קָדוֹשׁ וְשִׁמְךָ קָדוֹשׁ, וּקְדוֹשִׁים בְּכָל יוֹם יְהַלְלוּךָ סֶּלָה.
בָּרוּךְ אַתָּה יהוה, הָאֵל הַקָּדוֹשׁ.

קדושת היום

אַתָּה בְחַרְתָּנוּ[ע] מִכָּל הָעַמִּים
אָהַבְתָּ אוֹתָנוּ וְרָצִיתָ בָּנוּ
וְרוֹמַמְתָּנוּ מִכָּל הַלְּשׁוֹנוֹת
וְקִדַּשְׁתָּנוּ בְּמִצְוֹתֶיךָ
וְקֵרַבְתָּנוּ מַלְכֵּנוּ לַעֲבוֹדָתֶךָ
וְשִׁמְךָ הַגָּדוֹל וְהַקָּדוֹשׁ עָלֵינוּ קָרָאתָ.

וַתִּתֶּן לָנוּ יהוה אֱלֹהֵינוּ בְּאַהֲבָה
שַׁבָּתוֹת לִמְנוּחָה וּמוֹעֲדִים לְשִׂמְחָה, חַגִּים וּזְמַנִּים לְשָׂשׂוֹן
אֶת יוֹם הַשַּׁבָּת הַזֶּה וְאֶת יוֹם
פסח: חַג הַמַּצּוֹת הַזֶּה, זְמַן חֵרוּתֵנוּ
בסוכות: חַג הַסֻּכּוֹת הַזֶּה, זְמַן שִׂמְחָתֵנוּ
בְּאַהֲבָה מִקְרָא קֹדֶשׁ,[ב] זֵכֶר לִיצִיאַת מִצְרָיִם.

IYUN TEFILLA • עיון תפילה

אַתָּה בְחַרְתָּנוּ – *You have chosen us.* A careful review of the verses in the Torah that attest to our being chosen make it clear that we were not chosen because we had some sort of innate attribute that made us "better" than any other people. Rather, we are chosen simply fulfill a purpose, to live up to the responsibility of living our lives in a particular way. For our part, we find that responsibility ennobling, a badge of honor that we wear with pride.

What aspects of being Jewish make you proud?

וּמִפְּנֵי חֲטָאֵינוּ But because of our sins
we were exiled from our land
and driven far from our country.
We cannot go up to appear and bow before You,
and to perform our duties in Your chosen House,
the great and holy Temple that was called by Your name,
because of the hand that was stretched out
against Your Sanctuary.
May it be Your will, LORD our God and God of our ancestors,
merciful King,
that You in Your abounding compassion may once more
have mercy on us and on Your Sanctuary,
rebuilding it swiftly and adding to its glory.
Our Father, our King,
reveal the glory of Your kingdom to us swiftly.
Appear and be exalted over us in the sight of all that lives.
Bring back our scattered ones from among the nations,
and gather our dispersed people from the ends of the earth.[B]

---

to help trigger within us a sense of holiness that is spiritual and not material. This is the ultimate meaning of *mikra* – the soul of man *calls* out to his internal powers as if to say: "Let's all go together on the path of *holiness*, let us all be ready for holy service, let us all ascend to the levels of holiness (Rabbi Tzvi Mecklenberg). *Mikra kodesh* is a call to holiness.

Which explanation appeals to you the most today?

Which one will you use to help make a difference to the way you celebrate *Yom Tov* today?

BIUR TEFILLA • ביאור תפילה

וְקָרֵב פְּזוּרֵינוּ מִבֵּין הַגּוֹיִם, וּנְפוּצוֹתֵינוּ כַּנֵּס מִיַּרְכְּתֵי אָרֶץ – *Bring back our scattered ones from among the nations, and gather our dispersed people from the ends of the earth.* What is the difference between these two phrases? One suggestion is that there are two kinds of exile. The first is one in which Jews try to lose themselves among non-Jewish society; the second is the traditional understanding of the Jewish people scattered among the nations. One phrase thus prays that all Jews find their way back to their Jewish roots. The other, is a prayer for the ingathering of the Jewish people as a whole (Rabbi Shlomo Goldhar).

וּמִפְּנֵי חֲטָאֵינוּ גָּלִינוּ מֵאַרְצֵנוּ, וְנִתְרַחַקְנוּ מֵעַל אַדְמָתֵנוּ
וְאֵין אֲנַחְנוּ יְכוֹלִים לַעֲלוֹת וְלֵרָאוֹת וּלְהִשְׁתַּחֲווֹת לְפָנֶיךָ
וְלַעֲשׂוֹת חוֹבוֹתֵינוּ בְּבֵית בְּחִירָתֶךָ
בַּבַּיִת הַגָּדוֹל וְהַקָּדוֹשׁ שֶׁנִּקְרָא שִׁמְךָ עָלָיו
מִפְּנֵי הַיָּד שֶׁנִּשְׁתַּלְּחָה בְּמִקְדָּשֶׁךָ.
יְהִי רָצוֹן מִלְּפָנֶיךָ יהוה אֱלֹהֵינוּ וֵאלֹהֵי אֲבוֹתֵינוּ, מֶלֶךְ רַחֲמָן
שֶׁתָּשׁוּב וּתְרַחֵם עָלֵינוּ וְעַל מִקְדָּשְׁךָ בְּרַחֲמֶיךָ הָרַבִּים
וְתִבְנֵהוּ מְהֵרָה וּתְגַדֵּל כְּבוֹדוֹ.
אָבִינוּ מַלְכֵּנוּ, גַּלֵּה כְּבוֹד מַלְכוּתְךָ עָלֵינוּ מְהֵרָה
וְהוֹפַע וְהִנָּשֵׂא עָלֵינוּ לְעֵינֵי כָּל חָי
וְקָרֵב פְּזוּרֵינוּ מִבֵּין הַגּוֹיִם, וּנְפוּצוֹתֵינוּ כַּנֵּס מִיַּרְכְּתֵי אָרֶץ.[ב]

• These times are *appointed times* that I desire, but if you do not call them *holy appointed times* but rather they are appointed secular times, i.e., that you indulge in your own pleasure, they will not be called "my appointed times" but rather in the words of *Yeshayahu* 1:14 "My soul detests your new moons and your appointed seasons; they are a burden to Me; I am weary of bearing them" (Seforno).

• Days which were called, i.e., *established* legally by the court (Abravanel). The establishment of the new month or a festival was done not by a calendar but by the courts. These are legal days, which man is required to establish as holy.

• Each time has its own established name. Do not refer to them as you would any other day, in astronomical (morning, night), seasonal or agricultural terms, but call each according to its name (Biur). In other words, today is not Tuesday or Wednesday, for example, but rather *call* it a *holy* day with a name of its own.

• The word *mikra* comes from a similar word meaning "to prepare" (*Bemidbar* 35:11) suggesting in this context that one must prepare oneself for the holiness of the festivals. That is to say, one must engrave upon his soul the messages of these days and consider the foundations upon which they were created. For the truth is that they are not about eating, drinking and clean clothes, for these are but the symbolic reminders for the individual to prepare himself for the spiritual messages of the day. It is well known that emotions follow actions, and so these practices of eating etc. are there only

Lead us to Zion, Your city, in jubilation,
and to Jerusalem, home of Your Temple, with everlasting joy.
There we will prepare for You our obligatory offerings:
the regular daily offerings in their order
and the additional offerings according to their law.
And the additional offerings of this Sabbath day
and of this day of:

On Pesaḥ: the festival of Matzot.
On Sukkot: the festival of Sukkot.

we will prepare and offer before You in love,
in accord with Your will's commandment,
as You wrote for us in Your Torah
through Your servant Moses, by Your own word, as it is said:

וּבְיוֹם הַשַּׁבָּת On the Sabbath day,[H] *Num. 28*
make an offering of two lambs a year old, without blemish,
together with two-tenths of an ephah of fine flour mixed with oil
as a meal-offering, and its appropriate libation.
This is the burnt-offering for every Sabbath,
in addition to the regular daily burnt-offering and its libation.

On Ḥol HaMo'ed Pesaḥ say:

וְהִקְרַבְתֶּם And you shall bring an offering consumed by fire, a burnt-offering to the LORD: two young bullocks, one ram, and seven yearling male lambs; they shall be to you unblemished. And their meal-offerings and wine-libations as ordained: three-tenths of an ephah for each bull, two-tenths of an ephah for the ram, one-tenth of an ephah for each lamb, wine for the libations, a male goat for atonement, and two regular daily offerings according to their law. *Num. 28*

Continue with "Those who keep the Sabbath" on page 708.

---

savor the moment, to familiarize ourselves with a ritual that has become foreign to us, to acknowledge the realization that there is something dynamic and fundamental that is missing from our national life, not least of which is a concrete ritual that had the potential to bring us closer to Him and to ourselves.

וַהֲבִיאֵנוּ לְצִיּוֹן עִירְךָ בְּרִנָּה
וְלִירוּשָׁלַיִם בֵּית מִקְדָּשְׁךָ בְּשִׂמְחַת עוֹלָם
וְשָׁם נַעֲשֶׂה לְפָנֶיךָ אֶת קָרְבְּנוֹת חוֹבוֹתֵינוּ
תְּמִידִים כְּסִדְרָם וּמוּסָפִים כְּהִלְכָתָם
וְאֶת מוּסְפֵי יוֹם הַשַּׁבָּת הַזֶּה וְיוֹם

פסח: חַג הַמַּצּוֹת הַזֶּה

בסוכות: חַג הַסֻּכּוֹת הַזֶּה

נַעֲשֶׂה וְנַקְרִיב לְפָנֶיךָ בְּאַהֲבָה כְּמִצְוַת רְצוֹנֶךָ
כְּמוֹ שֶׁכָּתַבְתָּ עָלֵינוּ בְּתוֹרָתֶךָ
עַל יְדֵי מֹשֶׁה עַבְדֶּךָ מִפִּי כְבוֹדֶךָ, כָּאָמוּר

וּבְיוֹם הַשַּׁבָּת, שְׁנֵי־כְבָשִׂים בְּנֵי־שָׁנָה תְּמִימִם במדבר כח
וּשְׁנֵי עֶשְׂרֹנִים סֹלֶת מִנְחָה בְּלוּלָה בַשֶּׁמֶן וְנִסְכּוֹ:
עֹלַת שַׁבַּת בְּשַׁבַּתּוֹ, עַל־עֹלַת הַתָּמִיד וְנִסְכָּהּ:

On חול המועד פסח *say:*

וְהִקְרַבְתֶּם אִשֶּׁה עֹלָה לַיהוה, פָּרִים בְּנֵי־בָקָר שְׁנַיִם וְאַיִל אֶחָד, במדבר כח
וְשִׁבְעָה כְבָשִׂים בְּנֵי שָׁנָה, תְּמִימִם יִהְיוּ לָכֶם: וּמִנְחָתָם וְנִסְכֵּיהֶם
כִּמְדֻבָּר, שְׁלֹשָׁה עֶשְׂרֹנִים לַפָּר וּשְׁנֵי עֶשְׂרֹנִים לָאָיִל, וְעִשָּׂרוֹן לַכֶּבֶשׂ,
וְיַיִן כְּנִסְכּוֹ, וְשָׂעִיר לְכַפֵּר, וּשְׁנֵי תְמִידִים כְּהִלְכָתָם.

Continue with יִשְׂמְחוּ בְמַלְכוּתְךָ *on page 709.*

HILKHOT TEFILLA • הלכות תפילה

וּבְיוֹם הַשַּׁבָּת – *On the Shabbat day*. There is a dispute between Rashi and Tosafot as to whether the details of each of the sacrifices needs to be mentioned or whether it would be sufficient to say "There we will bring our obligatory and daily offerings in their order and our *Musaf* offerings according to their precepts." Our custom is to recite the more detailed description (*Shulḥan Arukh* 488:3) which enables us to

When Shabbat falls on the first day of Ḥol HaMo'ed Sukkot, say the following two paragraphs (in Israel say only the first):

וּבַיּוֹם הַשֵּׁנִי On the second day you shall offer twelve young bullocks, two rams, fourteen yearling male lambs without blemish. And their meal-offerings and wine-libations as ordained: three-tenths of an ephah for each bull, two-tenths of an ephah for each ram, one-tenth of an ephah for each lamb, wine for the libations, a male goat for atonement, and two regular daily offerings according to their law. *Num. 29*

וּבַיּוֹם הַשְּׁלִישִׁי On the third day you shall offer eleven bullocks, two rams, fourteen yearling male lambs without blemish. And their meal-offerings and wine-libations as ordained: three-tenths of an ephah for each bull, two-tenths of an ephah for the ram, one-tenth of an ephah for each lamb, wine for the libations, a male goat for atonement, and two regular daily offerings according to their law. *Num. 29*

Continue with "Those who keep the Sabbath" on the next page.

When Shabbat falls on the third day of Ḥol HaMo'ed Sukkot, say the following two paragraphs (in Israel say only the first):

וּבַיּוֹם הָרְבִיעִי On the fourth day you shall offer ten bullocks, two rams, fourteen yearling male lambs without blemish. And their meal-offerings and wine-libations as ordained: three-tenths of an ephah for each bull, two-tenths of an ephah for each ram, one-tenth of an ephah for each lamb, wine for the libations, a male goat for atonement, and two regular daily offerings according to their law. *Num. 29*

וּבַיּוֹם הַחֲמִישִׁי On the fifth day you shall offer nine bullocks, two rams, fourteen yearling male lambs without blemish. And their meal-offerings and wine-libations as ordained: three-tenths of an ephah for each bull, two-tenths of an ephah for each ram, one-tenth of an ephah for each lamb, wine for the libations, a male goat for atonement, and two regular daily offerings according to their law. *Num. 29*

Continue with "Those who keep the Sabbath" on the next page.

When Shabbat falls on the fourth day of Ḥol HaMo'ed Sukkot, say the following two paragraphs (in Israel say only the first):

וּבַיּוֹם הַחֲמִישִׁי On the fifth day you shall offer nine bullocks, two rams, fourteen yearling male lambs without blemish. And their meal-offerings and wine-libations as ordained: three-tenths of an ephah for each bull, two-tenths of an ephah for each ram, one-tenth of an ephah for each lamb, wine for the libations, a male goat for atonement, and two regular daily offerings according to their law. *Num. 29*

Continue with "On the sixth day" at the top of the next page.
In Israel continue with "Those who keep" on the next page.

When שבת falls on the first day of חול המועד סוכות,
say the following two paragraphs (in ארץ ישראל say only the first):

וּבַיּוֹם הַשֵּׁנִי, פָּרִים בְּנֵי־בָקָר שְׁנֵים עָשָׂר, אֵילִם שְׁנָיִם, כְּבָשִׂים בְּנֵי־שָׁנָה אַרְבָּעָה עָשָׂר, תְּמִימִם: וּמִנְחָתָם וְנִסְכֵּיהֶם כִּמְדֻבָּר, שְׁלֹשָׁה עֶשְׂרֹנִים לַפָּר, וּשְׁנֵי עֶשְׂרֹנִים לָאָיִל, וְעִשָּׂרוֹן לַכֶּבֶשׂ, וְיַיִן כְּנִסְכּוֹ, וְשָׂעִיר לְכַפֵּר, וּשְׁנֵי תְמִידִים כְּהִלְכָתָם. במדבר כט

וּבַיּוֹם הַשְּׁלִישִׁי, פָּרִים עַשְׁתֵּי־עָשָׂר, אֵילִם שְׁנָיִם, כְּבָשִׂים בְּנֵי־שָׁנָה אַרְבָּעָה עָשָׂר, תְּמִימִם: וּמִנְחָתָם וְנִסְכֵּיהֶם כִּמְדֻבָּר, שְׁלֹשָׁה עֶשְׂרֹנִים לַפָּר, וּשְׁנֵי עֶשְׂרֹנִים לָאָיִל, וְעִשָּׂרוֹן לַכֶּבֶשׂ, וְיַיִן כְּנִסְכּוֹ, וְשָׂעִיר לְכַפֵּר, וּשְׁנֵי תְמִידִים כְּהִלְכָתָם. במדבר כט

Continue with יִשְׂמְחוּ בְמַלְכוּתְךָ on the next page.

When שבת falls on the third day of חול המועד סוכות,
say the following two paragraphs (in ארץ ישראל say only the first):

וּבַיּוֹם הָרְבִיעִי, פָּרִים עֲשָׂרָה, אֵילִם שְׁנָיִם, כְּבָשִׂים בְּנֵי־שָׁנָה אַרְבָּעָה עָשָׂר, תְּמִימִם: וּמִנְחָתָם וְנִסְכֵּיהֶם כִּמְדֻבָּר, שְׁלֹשָׁה עֶשְׂרֹנִים לַפָּר, וּשְׁנֵי עֶשְׂרֹנִים לָאָיִל, וְעִשָּׂרוֹן לַכֶּבֶשׂ, וְיַיִן כְּנִסְכּוֹ, וְשָׂעִיר לְכַפֵּר, וּשְׁנֵי תְמִידִים כְּהִלְכָתָם. במדבר כט

וּבַיּוֹם הַחֲמִישִׁי, פָּרִים תִּשְׁעָה, אֵילִם שְׁנָיִם, כְּבָשִׂים בְּנֵי־שָׁנָה אַרְבָּעָה עָשָׂר, תְּמִימִם: וּמִנְחָתָם וְנִסְכֵּיהֶם כִּמְדֻבָּר, שְׁלֹשָׁה עֶשְׂרֹנִים לַפָּר, וּשְׁנֵי עֶשְׂרֹנִים לָאָיִל, וְעִשָּׂרוֹן לַכֶּבֶשׂ, וְיַיִן כְּנִסְכּוֹ, וְשָׂעִיר לְכַפֵּר, וּשְׁנֵי תְמִידִים כְּהִלְכָתָם. במדבר כט

Continue with יִשְׂמְחוּ בְמַלְכוּתְךָ on the next page.

When שבת falls on the fourth day of חול המועד סוכות, say the
following two paragraphs (in ארץ ישראל say only the first):

וּבַיּוֹם הַחֲמִישִׁי, פָּרִים תִּשְׁעָה, אֵילִם שְׁנָיִם, כְּבָשִׂים בְּנֵי־שָׁנָה אַרְבָּעָה עָשָׂר, תְּמִימִם: וּמִנְחָתָם וְנִסְכֵּיהֶם כִּמְדֻבָּר, שְׁלֹשָׁה עֶשְׂרֹנִים לַפָּר, וּשְׁנֵי עֶשְׂרֹנִים לָאָיִל, וְעִשָּׂרוֹן לַכֶּבֶשׂ, וְיַיִן כְּנִסְכּוֹ, וְשָׂעִיר לְכַפֵּר, וּשְׁנֵי תְמִידִים כְּהִלְכָתָם. במדבר כט

Continue with וּבַיּוֹם הַשִּׁשִּׁי at the top of the next page.
In Israel continue with יִשְׂמְחוּ בְמַלְכוּתְךָ on the next page.

וּבַיּוֹם הַשִּׁשִּׁי On the sixth day you shall offer eight bullocks, two rams, fourteen yearling male lambs without blemish. And their meal-offerings and wine-libations as ordained: three-tenths of an ephah for each bull, two-tenths of an ephah for each ram, one-tenth of an ephah for each lamb, wine for the libations, a male goat for atonement, and two regular daily offerings according to their law. *Num. 29*

Continue below.

יִשְׂמְחוּ Those who keep the Sabbath and call it a delight
shall rejoice in Your kingship.
The people who sanctify the seventh day
shall all be satisfied and take delight in Your goodness,
for You favored the seventh day and declared it holy.
You called it "most desirable of days" in remembrance of Creation.

אֱלֹהֵינוּ Our God and God of our ancestors,
merciful King, have compassion upon us.
You who are good and do good, respond to our call.
Return to us in Your abounding mercy
for the sake of our fathers who did Your will.
Rebuild Your Temple as at the beginning,
and establish Your Sanctuary on its site.
Let us witness its rebuilding and gladden us by its restoration.
Bring the priests back to their service,
the Levites to their song and music,
and the Israelites to their homes.

וְשָׁם נַעֲלֶה There we will go up and appear and bow before You
on the three pilgrimage festivals, as is written in Your Torah:

"Three times in the year *Deut. 16*
all your males shall appear before the Lord your God
at the place He will choose:
on Pesaḥ, Shavuot and Sukkot.
They shall not appear before the Lord empty-handed.
Each shall bring such a gift as he can,
in proportion to the blessing
that the Lord your God grants you."

וּבַיּוֹם הַשִּׁשִּׁי, פָּרִים שְׁמֹנָה, אֵילִם שְׁנָיִם, כְּבָשִׂים בְּנֵי־שָׁנָה אַרְבָּעָה עָשָׂר, תְּמִימִם: וּמִנְחָתָם וְנִסְכֵּיהֶם כִּמְדֻבָּר, שְׁלֹשָׁה עֶשְׂרֹנִים לַפָּר, וּשְׁנֵי עֶשְׂרֹנִים לָאָיִל, וְעִשָּׂרוֹן לַכֶּבֶשׂ, וְיַיִן כְּנִסְכּוֹ, וְשָׂעִיר לְכַפֵּר, וּשְׁנֵי תְמִידִים כְּהִלְכָתָם. במדבר כט

Continue below.

יִשְׂמְחוּ בְמַלְכוּתְךָ שׁוֹמְרֵי שַׁבָּת וְקוֹרְאֵי עֹנֶג.
עַם מְקַדְּשֵׁי שְׁבִיעִי כֻּלָּם יִשְׂבְּעוּ וְיִתְעַנְּגוּ מִטּוּבֶךָ
וּבַשְּׁבִיעִי רָצִיתָ בּוֹ וְקִדַּשְׁתּוֹ
חֶמְדַּת יָמִים אוֹתוֹ קָרָאתָ, זֵכֶר לְמַעֲשֵׂה בְרֵאשִׁית.

אֱלֹהֵינוּ וֵאלֹהֵי אֲבוֹתֵינוּ
מֶלֶךְ רַחֲמָן רַחֵם עָלֵינוּ, טוֹב וּמֵטִיב הִדָּרֶשׁ לָנוּ
שׁוּבָה אֵלֵינוּ בַּהֲמוֹן רַחֲמֶיךָ, בִּגְלַל אָבוֹת שֶׁעָשׂוּ רְצוֹנֶךָ.
בְּנֵה בֵיתְךָ כְּבַתְּחִלָּה, וְכוֹנֵן מִקְדָּשְׁךָ עַל מְכוֹנוֹ
וְהַרְאֵנוּ בְּבִנְיָנוֹ, וְשַׂמְּחֵנוּ בְּתִקּוּנוֹ
וְהָשֵׁב כֹּהֲנִים לַעֲבוֹדָתָם, וּלְוִיִּם לְשִׁירָם וּלְזִמְרָם
וְהָשֵׁב יִשְׂרָאֵל לִנְוֵיהֶם.

וְשָׁם נַעֲלֶה וְנֵרָאֶה וְנִשְׁתַּחֲוֶה לְפָנֶיךָ בְּשָׁלֹשׁ פַּעֲמֵי רְגָלֵינוּ
כַּכָּתוּב בְּתוֹרָתֶךָ

שָׁלוֹשׁ פְּעָמִים בַּשָּׁנָה יֵרָאֶה כָל־זְכוּרְךָ אֶת־פְּנֵי יהוה אֱלֹהֶיךָ דברים טז
בַּמָּקוֹם אֲשֶׁר יִבְחָר
בְּחַג הַמַּצּוֹת, וּבְחַג הַשָּׁבֻעוֹת, וּבְחַג הַסֻּכּוֹת
וְלֹא יֵרָאֶה אֶת־פְּנֵי יהוה רֵיקָם:
אִישׁ כְּמַתְּנַת יָדוֹ
כְּבִרְכַּת יהוה אֱלֹהֶיךָ אֲשֶׁר נָתַן־לָךְ:

וְהַשִּׂיאֵנוּ Bestow on us, LORD our God,
the blessing of Your festivals
for life and peace, joy and gladness,
as You desired and promised to bless us.
Our God and God of our ancestors, be pleased with our rest.
Make us holy through Your commandments
and grant us a share in Your Torah;
satisfy us with Your goodness,
gladden us with Your salvation,
and purify our hearts to serve You in truth.
And grant us a heritage, LORD our God, with love and favor,
with joy and gladness Your holy Sabbath and festivals.
May Israel, who sanctify Your name, rejoice in You.
Blessed are You, LORD,
who sanctifies the Sabbath and Israel, and the festive seasons.[B]

TEMPLE SERVICE

רְצֵה Find favor, LORD our God,
in Your people Israel and their prayer.
Restore the service to Your most holy House,
and accept in love and favor
the fire-offerings of Israel and their prayer.
May the service of Your people Israel always find favor with You.
And may our eyes witness Your return to Zion in compassion.
Blessed are You, LORD,
who restores His Presence to Zion.

---

of the authority given to the Sanhedrin to declare a new month, and by extension when the holidays would occur, based on the testimony of witnesses, the sanctification of time for the festivals was granted to the Jewish people. God, as it were, gave up that right to man. We are thus partners in the sanctification of time.

How will you make your day more holy even after having recited this blessing?

וְהַשִּׂיאֵנוּ יהוה אֱלֹהֵינוּ אֶת בִּרְכַּת מוֹעֲדֶיךָ
לְחַיִּים וּלְשָׁלוֹם, לְשִׂמְחָה וּלְשָׂשׂוֹן
כַּאֲשֶׁר רָצִיתָ וְאָמַרְתָּ לְבָרְכֵנוּ.
אֱלֹהֵינוּ וֵאלֹהֵי אֲבוֹתֵינוּ, רְצֵה בִמְנוּחָתֵנוּ
קַדְּשֵׁנוּ בְּמִצְוֹתֶיךָ, וְתֵן חֶלְקֵנוּ בְּתוֹרָתֶךָ
שַׂבְּעֵנוּ מִטּוּבֶךָ, וְשַׂמְּחֵנוּ בִּישׁוּעָתֶךָ
וְטַהֵר לִבֵּנוּ לְעָבְדְּךָ בֶּאֱמֶת
וְהַנְחִילֵנוּ יהוה אֱלֹהֵינוּ בְּאַהֲבָה וּבְרָצוֹן
בְּשִׂמְחָה וּבְשָׂשׂוֹן שַׁבָּת וּמוֹעֲדֵי קָדְשֶׁךָ
וְיִשְׂמְחוּ בְךָ יִשְׂרָאֵל מְקַדְּשֵׁי שְׁמֶךָ.
בָּרוּךְ אַתָּה יהוה, מְקַדֵּשׁ הַשַּׁבָּת וְיִשְׂרָאֵל וְהַזְּמַנִּים.[ב]

עבודה

רְצֵה יהוה אֱלֹהֵינוּ בְּעַמְּךָ יִשְׂרָאֵל וּבִתְפִלָּתָם
וְהָשֵׁב אֶת הָעֲבוֹדָה לִדְבִיר בֵּיתֶךָ
וְאִשֵּׁי יִשְׂרָאֵל וּתְפִלָּתָם בְּאַהֲבָה תְקַבֵּל בְּרָצוֹן
וּתְהִי לְרָצוֹן תָּמִיד עֲבוֹדַת יִשְׂרָאֵל עַמֶּךָ.
וְתֶחֱזֶינָה עֵינֵינוּ בְּשׁוּבְךָ לְצִיּוֹן בְּרַחֲמִים.
בָּרוּךְ אַתָּה יהוה, הַמַּחֲזִיר שְׁכִינָתוֹ לְצִיּוֹן.

BIUR TEFILLA • ביאור תפילה

מְקַדֵּשׁ הַשַּׁבָּת וְיִשְׂרָאֵל וְהַזְּמַנִּים – *Who sanctifies the Shabbat and Israel, and the festive seasons.* The order here is instructive for should not the people Israel be at the beginning, or at the end; why in the middle? The answer is that the Shabbat is sanctified entirely by Hashem. He is the one who declared the Shabbat day to be holy. By virtue

THANKSGIVING

▾*Bow:* We give thanks to You,
for You are *Stand straight*
the LORD our God
and God of our ancestors
for ever and all time.
You are the Rock of our lives,
Shield of our salvation
from generation to generation.
We will thank You and
declare Your praise for our lives,[A]
which are entrusted into Your hand;
for our souls,
which are placed in Your charge;
for Your miracles
which are with us every day;
and for Your wonders[l] and favors
at all times,
evening, morning and midday.
You are good –
for Your compassion never fails.
You are compassionate –
for Your loving-kindnesses never cease.
We have always placed our hope in You.

During the Leader's Repetition, the congregation says quietly:
▾*Bow:* We give thanks to You,
for You are *Stand straight*
the LORD our God
and God of our ancestors,
God of all flesh,
who formed us
and formed the universe.
Blessings and thanks
are due to Your great
and holy name
for giving us life
and sustaining us.
May You continue
to give us life and sustain us;
and may You gather our
exiles to Your holy courts,
to keep Your decrees,
do Your will and serve You
with a perfect heart,
for it is for us
to give You thanks.
Blessed be God
to whom thanksgiving
is due.

וְעַל כֻּלָּם For all these things may Your name be blessed and
exalted, our King, continually, for ever and all time.
Let all that lives thank You, Selah!
and praise Your name in truth,
God, our Savior and Help, Selah!
▾*Bend the knees:* Blessed *Bow:* are You, *Stand straight:* LORD,
whose name is "the Good" and to whom thanks are due.

הודאה

▾ *Bow* מוֹדִים אֲנַחְנוּ לָךְ
Stand straight שָׁאַתָּה הוּא
יהוה אֱלֹהֵינוּ וֵאלֹהֵי אֲבוֹתֵינוּ
לְעוֹלָם וָעֶד.
צוּר חַיֵּינוּ, מָגֵן יִשְׁעֵנוּ
אַתָּה הוּא לְדוֹר וָדוֹר.
נוֹדֶה לְּךָ וּנְסַפֵּר תְּהִלָּתֶךָ
עַל חַיֵּינוּ[א] הַמְּסוּרִים בְּיָדֶךָ
וְעַל נִשְׁמוֹתֵינוּ הַפְּקוּדוֹת לָךְ
וְעַל נִסֶּיךָ שֶׁבְּכָל יוֹם עִמָּנוּ
וְעַל נִפְלְאוֹתֶיךָ[ע] וְטוֹבוֹתֶיךָ
שֶׁבְּכָל עֵת, עֶרֶב וָבֹקֶר וְצָהֳרָיִם.
הַטּוֹב, כִּי לֹא כָלוּ רַחֲמֶיךָ
וְהַמְרַחֵם, כִּי לֹא תַמּוּ חֲסָדֶיךָ
מֵעוֹלָם קִוִּינוּ לָךְ.

During the חזרת הש״ץ, *the* קהל *says quietly:*

▾ *Bow* מוֹדִים אֲנַחְנוּ לָךְ
Stand straight שָׁאַתָּה הוּא
יהוה אֱלֹהֵינוּ וֵאלֹהֵי אֲבוֹתֵינוּ
אֱלֹהֵי כָל בָּשָׂר
יוֹצְרֵנוּ, יוֹצֵר בְּרֵאשִׁית.
בְּרָכוֹת וְהוֹדָאוֹת
לְשִׁמְךָ הַגָּדוֹל וְהַקָּדוֹשׁ
עַל שֶׁהֶחֱיִיתָנוּ וְקִיַּמְתָּנוּ.
כֵּן תְּחַיֵּנוּ וּתְקַיְּמֵנוּ
וְתֶאֱסֹף גָּלֻיּוֹתֵינוּ
לְחַצְרוֹת קָדְשֶׁךָ
לִשְׁמֹר חֻקֶּיךָ
וְלַעֲשׂוֹת רְצוֹנֶךָ
וּלְעָבְדְּךָ בְּלֵבָב שָׁלֵם
עַל שֶׁאֲנַחְנוּ מוֹדִים לָךְ.
בָּרוּךְ אֵל הַהוֹדָאוֹת.

וְעַל כֻּלָּם יִתְבָּרַךְ וְיִתְרוֹמַם שִׁמְךָ מַלְכֵּנוּ תָּמִיד לְעוֹלָם וָעֶד.
וְכֹל הַחַיִּים יוֹדוּךָ סֶּלָה
וִיהַלְלוּ אֶת שִׁמְךָ בֶּאֱמֶת
הָאֵל יְשׁוּעָתֵנוּ וְעֶזְרָתֵנוּ סֶלָה.
▾ *Bend the knees* בָּרוּךְ *Bow* אַתָּה *Stand straight* יהוה
הַטּוֹב שִׁמְךָ וּלְךָ נָאֶה לְהוֹדוֹת.

The following is said by the Leader during the Repetition of the Amida. In Israel, the regular Priestly Blessing on page 732 is said. If Kohanim do not ascend, the following is said. See laws 44–52.

Our God and God of our fathers, bless us with the threefold blessing in the Torah, written by the hand of Moses Your servant and pronounced by Aaron and his sons the priests, Your holy people, as it is said:

May the LORD bless you and protect you. (*Cong:* May it be Your will.) *Num. 6*
May the LORD make His face shine on you and be gracious to you.
(*Cong:* May it be Your will.)
May the LORD turn His face toward you, and grant you peace.
(*Cong:* May it be Your will.)

PEACE

שִׂים שָׁלוֹם Grant peace, goodness[1] and blessing, grace,
loving-kindness and compassion to us
and all Israel Your people.
Bless us, our Father, all as one,
with the light of Your face,
for by the light of Your face You have given us,
LORD our God, the Torah of life and love of kindness,
righteousness, blessing, compassion, life and peace.
May it be good in Your eyes to bless Your people Israel
at every time, in every hour, with Your peace.
Blessed are You, LORD, who blesses His people Israel with peace.

The following verse concludes the Leader's Repetition of the Amida. Some also say it here as part of the silent Amida. See law 42.

May the words of my mouth and the meditation of my heart *Ps. 19*
find favor before You, LORD, my Rock and Redeemer.

אֱלֹהַי My God, *Berakhot 17a*
guard my tongue from evil and my lips from deceitful speech.
To those who curse me, let my soul be silent;
may my soul be to all like the dust.[B]
Open my heart to Your Torah
and let my soul pursue Your commandments.
As for all who plan evil against me,
swiftly thwart their counsel and frustrate their plans.

The following is said by the שליח ציבור *during* חזרת הש״ץ.
In ארץ ישראל*, the regular* ברכת כהנים *on page 733 is said.*
If כהנים *do not ascend, the following is said. See laws 44–52.*

אֱלֹהֵינוּ וֵאלֹהֵי אֲבוֹתֵינוּ, בָּרְכֵנוּ בַּבְּרָכָה הַמְשֻׁלֶּשֶׁת בַּתּוֹרָה, הַכְּתוּבָה עַל יְדֵי מֹשֶׁה עַבְדֶּךָ, הָאֲמוּרָה מִפִּי אַהֲרֹן וּבָנָיו כֹּהֲנִים עַם קְדוֹשֶׁיךָ, כָּאָמוּר

יְבָרֶכְךָ יהוה וְיִשְׁמְרֶךָ: קהל: כֵּן יְהִי רָצוֹן במדבר ו

יָאֵר יהוה פָּנָיו אֵלֶיךָ וִיחֻנֶּךָּ: קהל: כֵּן יְהִי רָצוֹן

יִשָּׂא יהוה פָּנָיו אֵלֶיךָ וְיָשֵׂם לְךָ שָׁלוֹם: קהל: כֵּן יְהִי רָצוֹן

ברכת שלום

שִׂים שָׁלוֹם טוֹבָה וּבְרָכָה
חֵן וָחֶסֶד וְרַחֲמִים עָלֵינוּ וְעַל כָּל יִשְׂרָאֵל עַמֶּךָ.
בָּרְכֵנוּ אָבִינוּ כֻּלָּנוּ כְּאֶחָד בְּאוֹר פָּנֶיךָ
כִּי בְאוֹר פָּנֶיךָ נָתַתָּ לָּנוּ, יהוה אֱלֹהֵינוּ
תּוֹרַת חַיִּים וְאַהֲבַת חֶסֶד
וּצְדָקָה וּבְרָכָה וְרַחֲמִים וְחַיִּים וְשָׁלוֹם.
וְטוֹב בְּעֵינֶיךָ לְבָרֵךְ אֶת עַמְּךָ יִשְׂרָאֵל
בְּכָל עֵת וּבְכָל שָׁעָה בִּשְׁלוֹמֶךָ.
בָּרוּךְ אַתָּה יהוה, הַמְבָרֵךְ אֶת עַמּוֹ יִשְׂרָאֵל בַּשָּׁלוֹם.

The following verse concludes the חזרת הש״ץ.
Some also say it here as part of the silent עמידה*. See law 42.*

יִהְיוּ לְרָצוֹן אִמְרֵי־פִי וְהֶגְיוֹן לִבִּי לְפָנֶיךָ, יהוה צוּרִי וְגֹאֲלִי: תהלים יט

אֱלֹהַי ברכות יז.
נְצֹר לְשׁוֹנִי מֵרָע וּשְׂפָתַי מִדַּבֵּר מִרְמָה
וְלִמְקַלְלַי נַפְשִׁי תִדֹּם, וְנַפְשִׁי כֶּעָפָר לַכֹּל תִּהְיֶה.
פְּתַח לִבִּי בְּתוֹרָתֶךָ, וּבְמִצְוֹתֶיךָ תִּרְדֹּף נַפְשִׁי.
וְכָל הַחוֹשְׁבִים עָלַי רָעָה, מְהֵרָה הָפֵר עֲצָתָם וְקַלְקֵל מַחֲשַׁבְתָּם.

Act for the sake of Your name;
act for the sake of Your right hand;
act for the sake of Your holiness;
act for the sake of Your Torah.
That Your beloved ones may be delivered, *Ps. 60*
save with Your right hand and answer me.
May the words of my mouth and the meditation of my heart *Ps. 19*
find favor before You, LORD, my Rock and Redeemer.

Bow and take three steps back as if taking leave of the Divine Presence.
Bow left: May He who makes peace in His high places,
Bow right: make peace *Bow forward:* for us
and all Israel –
and say: Amen.

יְהִי רָצוֹן May it be Your will, LORD our God and God of our ancestors,
that the Temple be rebuilt speedily in our days,
and grant us a share in Your Torah.
And there we will serve You with reverence,
as in the days of old and as in former years.
Then the offering of Judah and Jerusalem will be pleasing to the LORD *Mal. 3*
as in the days of old and as in former years.

On Shabbat Ḥol HaMo'ed Sukkot, Hoshanot (on the next page) are said at this point.

On Shabbat Ḥol HaMo'ed Pesaḥ, Full Kaddish (page 442) is said and the service continues with "There is none like our God" on page 444.

עֲשֵׂה לְמַעַן שְׁמֶךָ
עֲשֵׂה לְמַעַן יְמִינֶךָ
עֲשֵׂה לְמַעַן קְדֻשָּׁתֶךָ
עֲשֵׂה לְמַעַן תּוֹרָתֶךָ.

תהלים ס
לְמַעַן יֵחָלְצוּן יְדִידֶיךָ, הוֹשִׁיעָה יְמִינְךָ וַעֲנֵנִי:

תהלים יט
יִהְיוּ לְרָצוֹן אִמְרֵי־פִי וְהֶגְיוֹן לִבִּי לְפָנֶיךָ, יהוה צוּרִי וְגֹאֲלִי:

Bow and take three steps back as if taking leave of the Divine Presence.

Bow left עֹשֶׂה שָׁלוֹם בִּמְרוֹמָיו

Bow right הוּא יַעֲשֶׂה שָׁלוֹם *Bow forward* עָלֵינוּ וְעַל כָּל יִשְׂרָאֵל

וְאִמְרוּ אָמֵן.

יְהִי רָצוֹן מִלְּפָנֶיךָ יהוה אֱלֹהֵינוּ וֵאלֹהֵי אֲבוֹתֵינוּ
שֶׁיִּבָּנֶה בֵּית הַמִּקְדָּשׁ בִּמְהֵרָה בְיָמֵינוּ
וְתֵן חֶלְקֵנוּ בְּתוֹרָתֶךָ
וְשָׁם נַעֲבָדְךָ בְּיִרְאָה כִּימֵי עוֹלָם וּכְשָׁנִים קַדְמֹנִיּוֹת.

מלאכי ג
וְעָרְבָה לַיהוה מִנְחַת יְהוּדָה וִירוּשָׁלָםִ כִּימֵי עוֹלָם וּכְשָׁנִים קַדְמֹנִיּוֹת:

On שבת חול המועד סוכות*,* הושענות *(on the next page) are said at this point.*

On שבת חול המועד פסח*,* קדיש שלם *(page 443) is said*
and the service continues with אֵין כֵּאלֹהֵינוּ *on page 445.*

Hoshanot for Shabbat

The Ark is opened but no Torah scrolls are taken out.
The congregation does not walk around the bima.

Leader then congregation:

Save us, please For Your sake, our God Save us, please.

Leader then congregation:

Save us, please For Your sake, our Creator Save us, please.

Leader then congregation:

Save us, please For Your sake, our Redeemer Save us, please.

Leader then congregation:

Save us, please For Your sake, You who seek us Save us, please.

Save us ,please–

אֹם נְצוּרָה A people guarded like the pupil of Your eye / who understand the Law that refreshes the spirit / who learn through all the laws of Shabbat / who unfold the rules of carrying on Shabbat / who fix two thousand cubits as our boundary for Shabbat / and keep our feet from breaking Shabbat / who remember early and keep hold of Shabbat / and speed to hasten in Shabbat / who for six days work hard for Shabbat / who sit patiently on before ending Shabbat / who call her an honor, delight, our Shabbat / who change their clothes, and dress for Shabbat / who prepare themselves feast and drink for Shabbat / laying a spread of sweet things on Shabbat / holding three festive meals for Shabbat / who break bread over two loaves on Shabbat / distinguishing four domains on Shabbat / who light the candles for the command, for

---

single individual stands in the center of the *bima* holding a Torah and the congregation, each one holding the four species, is led in responsive reading by the *ḥazan,* while making one complete circuit around the Torah.

There is a different poem for each day of the week, reflecting a theme unique to that day, although the refrain of *Hoshana* is repeated in each. On Shabbat, however, the four species are not taken in hand and so, in turn, the *Hoshana* ceremony is curtailed. The general custom is for the Ark to be opened, without a *sefer Torah* being removed, and a liturgical poem is recited but while everyone stands in place.

The poem is in the form of an alphabetical acrostic. Each stich makes reference to another mitzva or aspect of our observance of Shabbat. How many of them can you identify?

הושענות לשבת

The ארון קודש *is opened but no* ספרי תורה *are taken out. The* קהל *does not walk around the* בימה.

קהל *then* שליח ציבור:

הוֹשַׁע נָא לְמַעַנְךָ אֱלֹהֵינוּ הוֹשַׁע נָא.

קהל *then* שליח ציבור:

הוֹשַׁע נָא לְמַעַנְךָ בּוֹרְאֵנוּ הוֹשַׁע נָא.

קהל *then* שליח ציבור:

הוֹשַׁע נָא לְמַעַנְךָ גּוֹאֲלֵנוּ הוֹשַׁע נָא.

קהל *then* שליח ציבור:

הוֹשַׁע נָא לְמַעַנְךָ דּוֹרְשֵׁנוּ הוֹשַׁע נָא.

הוֹשַׁע נָא

אֹם נְצוּרָה כְּבָבַת. בּוֹנֶנֶת בְּדָת נֶפֶשׁ מְשִׁיבַת. גּוֹמֶרֶת הִלְכוֹת שַׁבָּת.
דּוֹרֶשֶׁת מַשְׂאַת שַׁבָּת. הַקּוֹבַעַת אַלְפַּיִם תְּחוּם שַׁבָּת. וּמְשִׁיבַת רֶגֶל
מִשַּׁבָּת. זָכוֹר וְשָׁמוֹר מְקַיֶּמֶת בַּשַּׁבָּת. חָשָׁה לְמַהֵר בִּיאַת שַׁבָּת. טוֹרַחַת
כֹּל מִשִּׁשָּׁה לַשַּׁבָּת. יוֹשֶׁבֶת וּמַמְתֶּנֶת עַד כְּלוֹת שַׁבָּת. כָּבוֹד וָעֹנֶג קוֹרְאָה
לַשַּׁבָּת. לְבוּשׁ וּכְסוּת מְחַלֶּפֶת בַּשַּׁבָּת. מַאֲכָל וּמִשְׁתֶּה מְכִינָה לַשַּׁבָּת.
נֹעַם מְגָדִים מַנְעֶמֶת לַשַּׁבָּת. סְעוּדוֹת שָׁלֹשׁ מְקַיֶּמֶת בַּשַּׁבָּת. עַל שְׁתֵּי
כִּכָּרוֹת בּוֹצַעַת בַּשַּׁבָּת. פּוֹרֶטֶת אַרְבַּע רְשֻׁיּוֹת שַׁבָּת. צִוּוּי הַדְלָקַת

INTRODUCTION TO HOSHANOT FOR SHABBAT ḤOL HAMOED

During the times of the *Beit HaMikdash,* on each of the days of Sukkot, long willow branches would be cut from just below the city and returned to the Courtyard where they would be leaned against the altar with their branches hanging over it. With their four species in hand, people would then do one circuit around the altar, reciting a prayer whose constant refrain was "*hoshana*" meaning "Please save" or "Save now" (*Sukka* 4:5).The ceremony thus took on the name *Hoshana* (or the plural *Hoshanot*). Despite the subsequent loss of the *Beit HaMikdash*, the ceremony continued, a symbolic representation of our longing for its complete restoration. In place of the altar, a

Shabbat / who sanctify the day on Shabbat / who speak seven blessings [in the Amida] of Shabbat / who read seven portions of Torah on Shabbat / bring us into what is ours, the day that will be entirely Shabbat. / Save us, please.

I and HE: save us, please.

כְּהוֹשַׁעְתָּ As You saved Adam, formed in Your hands, and protected him,
making the holy Shabbat his ransom, clemency – so, save us, please.

As You saved the people who remained distinct while longing for freedom –
their thoughts already marking out the seventh day for rest –
so, save us, please.

As You saved the people You led as a flock is guided,
and gave a Law at Mara, by the still waters – so, save us, please.

As You saved those who received Your gift in the Wilderness of Sin, the camp,
who were taught and collected two-fold bread on a Friday –
so, save us, please.

As You saved those who clung to You, who learned of their own mind to prepare for Shabbat,
and [Moses] their shepherd blessed their strength and concurred –
so, save us, please.

As You saved those who ate [manna] stored up on [their day of] delight,
and it looked no different and its scent had not spoiled –
so, save us, please.

As You saved those who learned every law of a journey on Shabbat,
who rested, stopped, and kept the boundaries of domain and encampment – so, save us, please.

As You saved those who could hear the fourth commandment at Sinai:
both "Remember" and "Keep" to make the seventh day holy –
so, save us, please.

As You saved those commanded to march seven times round Jericho,
besieging her to strike until she fell on Shabbat – so, save us, please.

As You saved Kohelet [Solomon] and his people in the eternal House,
when they came to please You for seven days and seven –
so, save us, please.

As You saved those who returned, rising up from exile, redeemed,
as they read Your Torah on this Festival, each day – so, save us, please.

נֵר מַדְלֶקֶת בַּשַּׁבָּת. קָדוֹשׁ הַיּוֹם מְקַדֶּשֶׁת בַּשַּׁבָּת. רֶנֶן שֶׁבַע מְפַלֶּלֶת בַּשַּׁבָּת. שִׁבְעָה בַּדָּת קוֹרְאָה בַּשַּׁבָּת. תַּנְחִילֶנָּה לְיוֹם שֶׁכֻּלּוֹ שַׁבָּת. הוֹשַׁע נָא.

אֲנִי וָהוּ הוֹשִׁיעָה נָּא.

כְּהוֹשַׁעְתָּ אָדָם יְצִיר כַּפֶּיךָ לְגוֹנְנָה.
בְּשַׁבַּת קֹדֶשׁ הִמְצֵאתוֹ כֹּפֶר וַחֲנִינָה. כֵּן הוֹשַׁע נָא.

כְּהוֹשַׁעְתָּ גּוֹי מְצֻיָּן מְקַוִּים חֹפֶשׁ.
דֵּעָה כִּוְּנוּ לָבֹר שְׁבִיעִי לְנֹפֶשׁ. כֵּן הוֹשַׁע נָא.

כְּהוֹשַׁעְתָּ הָעָם נִהַגְתָּ כַּצֹּאן לְהַנְחוֹת.
וְחֹק שַׂמְתָּ בְּמָרָה עַל מֵי מְנוּחוֹת. כֵּן הוֹשַׁע נָא.

כְּהוֹשַׁעְתָּ זְבוּדֶיךָ בְּמִדְבַּר סִין בַּמַּחֲנֶה.
חָכְמוּ וְלָקְטוּ בַּשִּׁשִּׁי לֶחֶם מִשְׁנֶה. כֵּן הוֹשַׁע נָא.

כְּהוֹשַׁעְתָּ טְפוּלֶיךָ הוֹרוּ הֲכָנָה בְּמַדָּעָם.
יָשַׁר כֹּחָם, וְהוֹדָה לָמוֹ רוֹעָם. כֵּן הוֹשַׁע נָא.

כְּהוֹשַׁעְתָּ כִּלְכַּלְתָּם בְּעֹנֶג מָן הַמְּשֻׁמָּר.
לֹא הָפַךְ עֵינוֹ וְרֵיחוֹ לֹא נָמָר. כֵּן הוֹשַׁע נָא.

כְּהוֹשַׁעְתָּ מִשְׁפְּטֵי מַשְּׂאוֹת שַׁבָּת גָּמָרוּ.
נָחוּ וְשָׁבְתוּ, רְשׁוּיוֹת וּתְחוּמִים שָׁמָרוּ. כֵּן הוֹשַׁע נָא.

כְּהוֹשַׁעְתָּ סִינַי הָשְׁמְעוּ בְּדִבּוּר רְבִיעִי.
עִנְיַן זָכוֹר וְשָׁמוֹר לְקַדֵּשׁ שְׁבִיעִי. כֵּן הוֹשַׁע נָא.

כְּהוֹשַׁעְתָּ פְּקֻדוּ יְרִיחוֹ שֶׁבַע לְהַקֵּף.
צָרוּ עַד רִדְתָּהּ בַּשַּׁבָּת לְתַקֵּף. כֵּן הוֹשַׁע נָא.

כְּהוֹשַׁעְתָּ קֹהֶלֶת וְעַמּוֹ בְּבֵית עוֹלָמִים.
רִצּוּךָ בְּחָגְגָם שִׁבְעָה וְשִׁבְעָה יָמִים. כֵּן הוֹשַׁע נָא.

כְּהוֹשַׁעְתָּ שָׁבִים עוֹלֵי גוֹלָה לְפִדְיוֹם.
תּוֹרָתְךָ בְּקָרְאָם בֶּחָג יוֹם יוֹם. כֵּן הוֹשַׁע נָא.

As You saved those who rejoiced for You in the second House, renewed,
in the Sanctuary where they took up the lulav all seven days –
so, save us, please.

As You saved those whose willow beating overrode Shabbat,
who placed branches from Motza at the base of the Altar –
so, save us, please.

As You saved those who rejoiced with supple, long, high willows,
as they parted from the place calling "Praise to you, Altar!" –
so, save us, please.

As You saved those who gave thanks and who prayed and were true to their words,
all of them repeating "We are the LORD's and to Him our eyes are turned" –
so, save us, please.

As You saved those circling [the Altar,] the wine-vat You carved out, with luscious willows,
as they sang out, "I and He: save us, please" – so, save us, please.

As You saved the eager legion [of priests], hastening to serve on the day of rest,
bringing a double Shabbat offering, burnt-offering and meal-offering –
so, save us, please.

As You saved Your Levites, making them many on their platform,
singing "A psalm. A song for the Sabbath day" – so, save us, please.

As You saved those You comforted, always delighting in Your commands,
and desired and delivered them, bringing them safe to respite and peace –
so, save us, please.

As You saved the returning exiles of the tribes of Jacob,
so come back and return the exiles of the tents of Jacob –
and save us, please.

As You saved those who kept Your commandments and waited for salvation,
God of all salvation – save us, please.

I and HE: save us, please.

הוֹשִׁיעָה Save Your people; bless Your legacy; tend them and carry them for- *Ps. 28*
ever. Let these words with which I have pleaded with the LORD be close to *1 Kings 8*
the LORD our God day and night, that they may do justice for His servant, and justice for His people Israel, day after day; so that all the peoples of the earth will know that the LORD is God. There is no other.

The Ark is closed and the Leader continues the service with Full Kaddish on *page 442.*

כְּהוֹשַׁעְתָּ מְשַׁמְּחֶיךָ בְּבִנְיַן שֵׁנִי הַמְחֻדָּשׁ.
נוֹטְלִין לוּלָב כָּל שִׁבְעָה בַּמִּקְדָּשׁ. כֵּן הוֹשַׁע נָא.

כְּהוֹשַׁעְתָּ חִבּוּט עֲרָבָה שַׁבָּת מַדְחִים.
מְרֻבִּיּוֹת מוֹצָא לִיסוֹד מִזְבֵּחַ מַנִּיחִים. כֵּן הוֹשַׁע נָא.

כְּהוֹשַׁעְתָּ בְּרֻכּוֹת וַאֲרֻכּוֹת וּגְבוֹהוֹת מְעַלְּסִים.
בִּפְטִירָתָן יֹפִי לְךָ מִזְבֵּחַ מְקַלְּסִים. כֵּן הוֹשַׁע נָא.

כְּהוֹשַׁעְתָּ מוֹדִים וּמְיַחֲלִים וְלֹא מְשַׁנִּים.
כֻּלָּנוּ אָנוּ לְיָהּ וְעֵינֵינוּ לְיָהּ שׁוֹנִים. כֵּן הוֹשַׁע נָא.

כְּהוֹשַׁעְתָּ יֶקֶב מַחְצָבֶיךָ סוֹבְבִים בְּרַעֲנָנָה.
רוֹנְנִים אֲנִי וָהוֹ הוֹשִׁיעָה נָּא. כֵּן הוֹשַׁע נָא.

כְּהוֹשַׁעְתָּ חֵיל זְרִיזִים מְשָׁרְתִים בִּמְנוּחָה.
קָרְבַּן שַׁבָּת כָּפוּל, עוֹלָה וּמִנְחָה. כֵּן הוֹשַׁע נָא.

כְּהוֹשַׁעְתָּ לְוִיֶּיךָ עַל דּוּכָנָם לְהַרְבַּת.
אוֹמְרִים מִזְמוֹר שִׁיר לְיוֹם הַשַּׁבָּת. כֵּן הוֹשַׁע נָא.

כְּהוֹשַׁעְתָּ נְחוּמֶיךָ בְּמִצְוֹתֶיךָ תָּמִיד יִשְׁתַּעַשְׁעוּן.
וּרְצֵם וְהַחֲלִיצֵם בְּשׁוּבָה וָנַחַת יִוָּשֵׁעוּן. כֵּן הוֹשַׁע נָא.

כְּהוֹשַׁעְתָּ שְׁבוּת שִׁבְטֵי יַעֲקֹב.
תָּשׁוּב וְתָשִׁיב שְׁבוּת אָהֳלֵי יַעֲקֹב. וְהוֹשִׁיעָה נָּא.

כְּהוֹשַׁעְתָּ שׁוֹמְרֵי מִצְוֹת וְחוֹכֵי יְשׁוּעוֹת.
אֵל לְמוֹשָׁעוֹת. וְהוֹשִׁיעָה נָּא.

אֲנִי וָהוֹ הוֹשִׁיעָה נָּא.

תהלים כח
מלכים א׳ ח

הוֹשִׁיעָה אֶת־עַמֶּךָ, וּבָרֵךְ אֶת־נַחֲלָתֶךָ, וּרְעֵם וְנַשְּׂאֵם עַד־הָעוֹלָם: וְיִהְיוּ דְבָרַי אֵלֶּה, אֲשֶׁר הִתְחַנַּנְתִּי לִפְנֵי יהוה, קְרֹבִים אֶל־יהוה אֱלֹהֵינוּ יוֹמָם וָלָיְלָה, לַעֲשׂוֹת מִשְׁפַּט עַבְדּוֹ וּמִשְׁפַּט עַמּוֹ יִשְׂרָאֵל, דְּבַר־יוֹם בְּיוֹמוֹ: לְמַעַן דַּעַת כָּל־עַמֵּי הָאָרֶץ כִּי יהוה הוּא הָאֱלֹהִים, אֵין עוֹד:

The ארון קודש *is closed and the* שליח ציבור *continues the service with* קדיש שלם *on page 443.*

SERVICE FOR ḤANUKKA

On each of the eight nights of Ḥanukka, the lights of the menora (ḥanukkia) are lit: one on the first night, two on the second, and so on. On the first night, the rightmost branch of the menora is used; on each subsequent night, an additional light is added to the left. Each night, the new light is lit first, then the others, moving rightwards. If possible, the menora should be displayed near a window so that it is visible from the street. The lights are lit using a separate flame known as the shamash. The lighting should be carried out as soon as possible after nightfall. On Friday night, it must be done before the beginning of Shabbat. Before lighting the Ḥanukka lights, say:

בָּרוּךְ Blessed are You, Lord our God, King of the Universe,
who has made us holy through His commandments,
and has commanded us to light the Ḥanukka lights.

בָּרוּךְ Blessed are You, Lord our God, King of the Universe,
who performed miracles for our ancestors in those days,
at this time.

On the first night, add:

בָּרוּךְ Blessed are You, Lord our God, King of the Universe,
who has given us life, sustained us,
and brought us to this time.

After lighting the first light, say:

הַנֵּרוֹת הַלָּלוּ We light these lights *Soferim ch. 20*
because of the miracles and wonders,
deliverances and victories
You performed for our ancestors
in those days, at this time,
through Your holy priests.

Throughout the eight days of Ḥanukka
these lights are holy
and we are not permitted
to make any other use of them,
except to look at them,

that we may give thanks and praise to Your great name
for Your miracles, Your wonders and Your deliverances.

סדר הדלקת נרות חנוכה

On each of the eight nights of חנוכה*, the lights of the* חנוכיה *are lit: one on the first night, two on the second, and so on. On the first night, the rightmost branch of the* חנוכיה *is used; on each subsequent night, an additional light is added to the left. Each night, the new light is lit first, then the others, moving rightwards. If possible, the* חנוכיה *should be displayed near a window so that it is visible from the street.*

The lights are lit using a separate flame known as the שמש*. The lighting should be carried out as soon as possible after nightfall. On Friday night, it must be done before the beginning of* שבת*. Before lighting the* חנוכה *lights, say:*

בָּרוּךְ אַתָּה יהוה אֱלֹהֵינוּ מֶלֶךְ הָעוֹלָם
אֲשֶׁר קִדְּשָׁנוּ בְּמִצְוֹתָיו וְצִוָּנוּ לְהַדְלִיק נֵר שֶׁל חֲנֻכָּה.

בָּרוּךְ אַתָּה יהוה אֱלֹהֵינוּ מֶלֶךְ הָעוֹלָם
שֶׁעָשָׂה נִסִּים לַאֲבוֹתֵינוּ בַּיָּמִים הָהֵם בַּזְּמַן הַזֶּה.

On the first night, add:

בָּרוּךְ אַתָּה יהוה אֱלֹהֵינוּ מֶלֶךְ הָעוֹלָם
שֶׁהֶחֱיָנוּ וְקִיְּמָנוּ וְהִגִּיעָנוּ לַזְּמַן הַזֶּה.

After lighting the first light, say:

מסכת סופרים פרק כ

הַנֵּרוֹת הַלָּלוּ אָנוּ מַדְלִיקִים
עַל הַנִּסִּים וְעַל הַנִּפְלָאוֹת וְעַל הַתְּשׁוּעוֹת וְעַל הַמִּלְחָמוֹת
שֶׁעָשִׂיתָ לַאֲבוֹתֵינוּ בַּיָּמִים הָהֵם בַּזְּמַן הַזֶּה
עַל יְדֵי כֹּהֲנֶיךָ הַקְּדוֹשִׁים.

וְכָל שְׁמוֹנַת יְמֵי חֲנֻכָּה
הַנֵּרוֹת הַלָּלוּ קֹדֶשׁ הֵם
וְאֵין לָנוּ רְשׁוּת לְהִשְׁתַּמֵּשׁ בָּהֶם
אֶלָּא לִרְאוֹתָם בִּלְבָד

כְּדֵי לְהוֹדוֹת וּלְהַלֵּל לְשִׁמְךָ הַגָּדוֹל
עַל נִסֶּיךָ וְעַל נִפְלְאוֹתֶיךָ וְעַל יְשׁוּעָתֶךָ.

After the lights are lit:

מָעוֹז צוּר Refuge, Rock of my salvation:
to You it is a delight to give praise.
Restore my House of prayer, so that there I may offer You thanksgiving.
When You silence the loud-mouthed foe,
Then will I complete, with song and psalm, the altar's dedication.

רָעוֹת Troubles sated my soul; my strength was spent with sorrow.
They embittered my life with hardship,
when I was enslaved under Egyptian rule.
But God with His great power brought out His treasured people,
While Pharaoh's host and followers sank like a stone into the deep.

דְּבִיר He brought me to His holy abode, but even there I found no rest.
The oppressor came and exiled me,
because I had served strange gods.
I had drunk poisoned wine. I almost perished.
Then Babylon fell, Zerubbabel came: within seventy years I was saved.

כְּרֹת The Agagite, son of Hammedatha,
sought to cut down the tall fir tree,
But it became a trap to him, and his arrogance was brought to an end.
You raised the head of the Benjaminite,
and the enemy's name You blotted out.
His many sons and his household You hanged on the gallows.

יְוָנִים Then the Greeks gathered against me,
in the days of the Hasmoneans.
They broke down the walls of my towers, and defiled all the oils.
But from the last remaining flask
a miracle was wrought for Your beloved.
Therefore the sages ordained these eight days for song and praise.

חֲשֹׂף Bare Your holy arm, and hasten the time of salvation.
Take retribution against the evil nation
on behalf of Your servants,
For the hour [of deliverance] has been too long delayed;
there seems no end to the evil days.
Thrust the enemy into the darkness of death,
and establish for us the seven Shepherds.

After the lights are lit:

מָעוֹז צוּר יְשׁוּעָתִי   לְךָ נָאֶה לְשַׁבֵּחַ
תִּכּוֹן בֵּית תְּפִלָּתִי   וְשָׁם תּוֹדָה נְזַבֵּחַ
לְעֵת תָּכִין מַטְבֵּחַ   מִצָּר הַמְנַבֵּחַ
אָז אֶגְמֹר   בְּשִׁיר מִזְמוֹר   חֲנֻכַּת הַמִּזְבֵּחַ.

רָעוֹת שָׂבְעָה נַפְשִׁי   בְּיָגוֹן כֹּחִי כָּלָה
חַיַּי מֵרְרוּ בְקֹשִׁי   בְּשִׁעְבּוּד מַלְכוּת עֶגְלָה
וּבְיָדוֹ הַגְּדוֹלָה   הוֹצִיא אֶת הַסְּגֻלָּה
חֵיל פַּרְעֹה   וְכָל זַרְעוֹ   יָרְדוּ כְּאֶבֶן מְצוּלָה.

דְּבִיר קָדְשׁוֹ הֱבִיאַנִי   וְגַם שָׁם לֹא שָׁקַטְתִּי
וּבָא נוֹגֵשׂ וְהִגְלַנִי   כִּי זָרִים עָבַדְתִּי
וְיֵין רַעַל מָסַכְתִּי   כִּמְעַט שֶׁעָבַרְתִּי
קֵץ בָּבֶל   זְרֻבָּבֶל   לְקֵץ שִׁבְעִים נוֹשַׁעְתִּי.

כְּרֹת קוֹמַת בְּרוֹשׁ בִּקֵּשׁ   אֲגָגִי בֶּן הַמְּדָתָא
וְנִהְיְתָה לוֹ לְפַח וּלְמוֹקֵשׁ   וְגַאֲוָתוֹ נִשְׁבָּתָה
רֹאשׁ יְמִינִי נִשֵּׂאתָ   וְאוֹיֵב שְׁמוֹ מָחִיתָ
רֹב בָּנָיו   וְקִנְיָנָיו   עַל הָעֵץ תָּלִיתָ.

יְוָנִים נִקְבְּצוּ עָלַי   אֲזַי בִּימֵי חַשְׁמַנִּים
וּפָרְצוּ חוֹמוֹת מִגְדָּלַי   וְטִמְּאוּ כָּל הַשְּׁמָנִים
וּמִנּוֹתַר קַנְקַנִּים   נַעֲשָׂה נֵס לַשּׁוֹשַׁנִּים
בְּנֵי בִינָה   יְמֵי שְׁמוֹנָה   קָבְעוּ שִׁיר וּרְנָנִים.

חֲשֹׂף זְרוֹעַ קָדְשֶׁךָ   וְקָרֵב קֵץ הַיְשׁוּעָה
נְקֹם נִקְמַת עֲבָדֶיךָ   מֵאֻמָּה הָרְשָׁעָה
כִּי אָרְכָה לָנוּ הַשָּׁעָה   וְאֵין קֵץ לִימֵי הָרָעָה
דְּחֵה אַדְמוֹן   בְּצֵל צַלְמוֹן   הָקֵם לָנוּ רוֹעִים שִׁבְעָה.

SERVICE FOR PURIM

Before the reading of the Megilla, the congregation stands and the Reader says the following three blessings:

בָּרוּךְ Blessed are You, LORD our God, King of the Universe,
who has made us holy through His commandments,
and has commanded us about reading the Megilla.

בָּרוּךְ Blessed are You, LORD our God, King of the Universe,
who performed miracles for our ancestors
in those days at this time.

בָּרוּךְ Blessed are You, LORD our God, King of the Universe,
who has given us life, sustained us, and brought us to this time.

The Megilla is read. When the reading is completed, the scroll is rolled up and, if a minyan is present, the Reader continues:

בָּרוּךְ Blessed are You, LORD our God, King of the Universe,
who pleads our cause, judges our claim, avenges our wrong,
brings retribution to our enemies, and punishes our foes.
Blessed are You, LORD, who on behalf of His people Israel,
exacts punishment from all their foes, the God who brings salvation.

The following is said after the reading of the Megilla:

אֲשֶׁר הֵנִיא [God] frustrated the plan of the nations,
Thwarted the intentions of the crafty.
An evil man rose up against us,
An arrogant branch of Amalek's tree,
Haughty, rich, he dug his own pit.
His hubris became his own snare.
He was trapped in the trap he set for others.
Seeking to destroy, he was destroyed.
Haman shared his ancestors' hate,
And stirred against children the hostility of brothers.
He did not remember Saul's act of mercy,
his pity for Agag, through which a new enemy was born.
The wicked planned to cut off the righteous,
but the impure were defeated by the pure.

סדר קריאת המגילה בפורים

Before the reading of the מגילה*, the* קהל *stands and the* קורא *says the following three blessings:*

בָּרוּךְ אַתָּה יהוה אֱלֹהֵינוּ מֶלֶךְ הָעוֹלָם
אֲשֶׁר קִדְּשָׁנוּ בְּמִצְוֹתָיו וְצִוָּנוּ עַל מִקְרָא מְגִלָּה.

בָּרוּךְ אַתָּה יהוה אֱלֹהֵינוּ מֶלֶךְ הָעוֹלָם
שֶׁעָשָׂה נִסִּים לַאֲבוֹתֵינוּ בַּיָּמִים הָהֵם בַּזְּמַן הַזֶּה.

בָּרוּךְ אַתָּה יהוה אֱלֹהֵינוּ מֶלֶךְ הָעוֹלָם
שֶׁהֶחֱיָנוּ וְקִיְּמָנוּ וְהִגִּיעָנוּ לַזְּמַן הַזֶּה.

The מגילה *is read. When the reading is completed, the scroll is rolled up and, if a* מנין *is present, the* קורא *continues:*

בָּרוּךְ אַתָּה יהוה אֱלֹהֵינוּ מֶלֶךְ הָעוֹלָם
הָרָב אֶת רִיבֵנוּ, וְהַדָּן אֶת דִּינֵנוּ, וְהַנּוֹקֵם אֶת נִקְמָתֵנוּ
וְהַמְשַׁלֵּם גְּמוּל לְכָל אוֹיְבֵי נַפְשֵׁנוּ, וְהַנִּפְרָע לָנוּ מִצָּרֵינוּ.
בָּרוּךְ אַתָּה יהוה
הַנִּפְרָע לְעַמּוֹ יִשְׂרָאֵל מִכָּל צָרֵיהֶם, הָאֵל הַמּוֹשִׁיעַ.

The following is said after the reading of the מגילה*:*

אֲשֶׁר הֵנִיא עֲצַת גּוֹיִם, וַיָּפֶר מַחְשְׁבוֹת עֲרוּמִים.
בְּקוּם עָלֵינוּ אָדָם רָשָׁע, נֵצֶר זָדוֹן מִזֶּרַע עֲמָלֵק.
גָּאָה בְעָשְׁרוֹ וְכָרָה לּוֹ בּוֹר, וּגְדֻלָּתוֹ יָקְשָׁה לּוֹ לָכֶד.
דִּמָּה בְנַפְשׁוֹ לִלְכֹּד וְנִלְכַּד, בִּקֵּשׁ לְהַשְׁמִיד וְנִשְׁמַד מְהֵרָה.
הָמָן הוֹדִיעַ אֵיבַת אֲבוֹתָיו, וְעוֹרֵר שִׂנְאַת אַחִים לַבָּנִים.
וְלֹא זָכַר רַחֲמֵי שָׁאוּל, כִּי בְחֶמְלָתוֹ עַל אֲגָג נוֹלַד אוֹיֵב.
זָמַם רָשָׁע לְהַכְרִית צַדִּיק, וְנִלְכַּד טָמֵא בִּידֵי טָהוֹר.

[Mordekhai's] goodness overcame the father's [Saul's] error,
    but the evil [Haman] piled sin upon sin.
He hid in his heart his cunning schemes,
    intent on his evildoing.
He stretched out his hand against God's holy ones;
    he spent his wealth to destroy every memory of them.
When Mordekhai saw the wrath go forth,
    and Haman's decrees issued in Shushan,
he put on sackcloth, wrapped himself in mourning,
    decreed a fast and sat on ashes.
"Who will arise to atone for error,
    and find forgiveness for our ancestors' sins?"
A flower blossomed from the palm tree;
    Hadassa arose to wake those who slept.
Her servants hastened Haman to come,
    to serve him wine with the venom of serpents.
He had risen by his wealth, but fell by his evil.
    He made the very gallows by which he was hanged.
All the inhabitants of the world were amazed
    When Haman's ploy (*pur*) became our joy (*Purim*).
The righteous was saved from evil hands,
    the perpetrator suffered the fate of his intended victim.
They undertook to celebrate Purim,
    and to rejoice on it year after year.
You heeded the prayer of Mordekhai and Esther;
    and Haman and his sons were hanged on the gallows.

All say:

שׁוֹשַׁנַּת יַעֲקֹב The lily of Jacob rejoiced and was glad,
When, together, they saw Mordekhai robed in royal blue.
You have been their eternal salvation, their hope in every generation;
To make known that all who hope in You will not be put to shame,
All who trust in You will never be humiliated.
Cursed be Haman who sought to destroy me. Blessed be Mordekhai the Yehudi.
Cursed be Zeresh, wife of him who terrified me.
Blessed be Esther [whose actions saved] me.
Cursed be all the wicked; blessed be all Israel.
And may Ḥarbona, too, be remembered for good.

Continues with "May the pleasantness" on page 622.

חֶסֶד גָּבַר עַל שִׁגְגַת אָב, וְרָשָׁע הוֹסִיף חֵטְא עַל חֲטָאָיו.
טָמַן בְּלִבּוֹ מַחְשְׁבוֹת עֲרוּמָיו, וַיִּתְמַכֵּר לַעֲשׂוֹת רָעָה.
יָדוֹ שָׁלַח בִּקְדוֹשֵׁי אֵל, כַּסְפּוֹ נָתַן לְהַכְרִית זִכְרָם.
כִּרְאוֹת מָרְדְּכַי כִּי יָצָא קֶצֶף, וְדָתֵי הָמָן נִתְּנוּ בְשׁוּשָׁן.
לָבַשׁ שַׂק וְקָשַׁר מִסְפֵּד וְגָזַר צוֹם וַיֵּשֶׁב עַל הָאֵפֶר.
מִי זֶה יַעֲמֹד לְכַפֵּר שְׁגָגָה, וְלִמְחֹל חַטַּאת עֲוֹן אֲבוֹתֵינוּ.
נֵץ פָּרַח מִלּוּלָב, הֵן הֲדַסָּה עָמְדָה לְעוֹרֵר יְשֵׁנִים.
סָרִיסֶיהָ הִבְהִילוּ לְהָמָן, לְהַשְׁקוֹתוֹ יֵין חֲמַת תַּנִּינִים.
עָמַד בְּעָשְׁרוֹ וְנָפַל בְּרִשְׁעוֹ, עָשָׂה לוֹ עֵץ וְנִתְלָה עָלָיו.
פִּיהֶם פָּתְחוּ כָּל יוֹשְׁבֵי תֵבֵל, כִּי פוּר הָמָן נֶהְפַּךְ לְפוּרֵנוּ.
צַדִּיק נֶחֱלַץ מִיַּד רָשָׁע, אוֹיֵב נִתַּן תַּחַת נַפְשׁוֹ.
קִיְּמוּ עֲלֵיהֶם לַעֲשׂוֹת פּוּרִים וְלִשְׂמֹחַ בְּכָל שָׁנָה וְשָׁנָה.
רָאִיתָ אֶת תְּפִלַּת מָרְדְּכַי וְאֶסְתֵּר, הָמָן וּבָנָיו עַל הָעֵץ תָּלִיתָ.

All say:

שׁוֹשַׁנַּת יַעֲקֹב צָהֲלָה וְשָׂמֵחָה
בִּרְאוֹתָם יַחַד תְּכֵלֶת מָרְדְּכָי.
תְּשׁוּעָתָם הָיִיתָ לָנֶצַח, וְתִקְוָתָם בְּכָל דּוֹר וָדוֹר.
לְהוֹדִיעַ שֶׁכָּל קוֶֹיךָ לֹא יֵבֹשׁוּ
וְלֹא יִכָּלְמוּ לָנֶצַח כָּל הַחוֹסִים בָּךְ.
אָרוּר הָמָן אֲשֶׁר בִּקֵּשׁ לְאַבְּדִי
בָּרוּךְ מָרְדְּכַי הַיְּהוּדִי.
אֲרוּרָה זֶרֶשׁ אֵשֶׁת מַפְחִידִי
בְּרוּכָה אֶסְתֵּר בַּעֲדִי.
אֲרוּרִים כָּל הָרְשָׁעִים, בְּרוּכִים כָּל יִשְׂרָאֵל
וְגַם חַרְבוֹנָה זָכוּר לַטּוֹב.

Continues with וִיהִי נֹעַם *on page 623.*

BIRKAT KOHANIM IN ISRAEL

In Israel, the following is said by the Leader during the Repetition of the Amida when Kohanim bless the congregation. If there is more than one Kohen, a member of the congregation calls:

Kohanim!

The Kohanim respond:

Blessed are You, Lord our God, King of the Universe, who has made us holy with the holiness of Aaron, and has commanded us to bless His people Israel with love.

The Leader calls word by word, followed by the Kohanim:

יְבָרֶכְךָ May the Lord bless you and protect you. (*Cong:* Amen.) *Num. 6*
May the Lord make His face shine on you
and be gracious to you. (*Cong:* Amen.)
May the Lord turn His face toward you,
and grant you peace. (*Cong:* Amen.)

The Leader continues with "Grant peace" at Shaharit on page 358, at Musaf of Shabbat on page 438 and at Musaf of Shabbat Hol HaMo'ed on page 714.

The congregation says:

אַדִּיר Majestic One on high who dwells in power: You are peace and Your name is peace. May it be Your will to bestow on us and on Your people the house of Israel, life and blessing as a safeguard for peace.

The Kohanim say:

רִבּוֹנוֹ Master of the Universe: we have done what You have decreed for us. So too may You deal with us as You have promised us. Look down from Your holy dwelling place, from heaven, and bless Your people Israel and the land You have given us as You promised on oath to our ancestors, a land flowing with milk and honey. *Deut. 26*

PRAYER IN TIMES OF DROUGHT

In times of drought in Israel, the following is added in the Response to Prayer blessing of the Amida:

וַעֲנֵנוּ And answer us through the attribute of compassion, Creator of the universe who chooses His people Israel to make known His greatness and majestic glory. You who listen to prayer, grant dew and rain on the face of the earth, satisfying the whole universe from Your goodness. Fill our hands from Your blessings and Your hand's rich gift. Guard and deliver this year from all evil, all kinds of destruction and punishment, and give it hope and a peaceful end. Spare us and have compassion on us and on all our produce and fruit, blessing us with bounteous rain. May we merit life, plenty and peace as in the good years. Remove from us plague, sword and famine, wild animals, captivity and plunder, the evil instinct and serious and dangerous illnesses and events. Decree for us goodly decrees, and may Your compassion prevail over Your other attributes, that You may act toward Your children through the attribute of compassion, and in compassion and favor accept our prayer.

Continue with "For You listen" at Minha for Erev Shabbat on page 16, and at Ma'ariv for Motza'ei Shabbat on page 612.

ברכת כהנים בארץ ישראל

In ארץ ישראל*, the following is said by the* שליח ציבור *during the* חזרת הש״ץ *when* כהנים *say* ברכת כהנים*. If there is more than one* כהן*, a member of the* קהל *calls:*

כֹּהֲנִים

The כהנים *respond:*

בָּרוּךְ אַתָּה יהוה אֱלֹהֵינוּ מֶלֶךְ הָעוֹלָם, אֲשֶׁר קִדְּשָׁנוּ בִּקְדֻשָּׁתוֹ שֶׁל אַהֲרֹן וְצִוָּנוּ לְבָרֵךְ אֶת עַמּוֹ יִשְׂרָאֵל בְּאַהֲבָה.

The שליח ציבור *calls word by word, followed by the* כהנים*:*

יְבָרֶכְךָ יהוה וְיִשְׁמְרֶךָ: קהל: אָמֵן במדבר ו
יָאֵר יהוה פָּנָיו אֵלֶיךָ וִיחֻנֶּךָּ: קהל: אָמֵן
יִשָּׂא יהוה פָּנָיו אֵלֶיךָ וְיָשֵׂם לְךָ שָׁלוֹם: קהל: אָמֵן

The שליח ציבור *continues with* שִׂים שָׁלוֹם *at* שחרית *on page 359, at* מוסף לשבת *on page 439 and at* מוסף לשבת חול המועד *on page 715.*

The קהל *says:*

אַדִּיר בַּמָּרוֹם שׁוֹכֵן בִּגְבוּרָה, אַתָּה שָׁלוֹם וְשִׁמְךָ שָׁלוֹם. יְהִי רָצוֹן שֶׁתָּשִׂים עָלֵינוּ וְעַל כָּל עַמְּךָ בֵּית יִשְׂרָאֵל חַיִּים וּבְרָכָה לְמִשְׁמֶרֶת שָׁלוֹם.

The כהנים *say:*

רִבּוֹנוֹ שֶׁל עוֹלָם, עָשִׂינוּ מַה שֶּׁגָּזַרְתָּ עָלֵינוּ, אַף אַתָּה עֲשֵׂה עִמָּנוּ כְּמוֹ שֶׁהִבְטַחְתָּנוּ. הַשְׁקִיפָה מִמְּעוֹן קָדְשְׁךָ מִן־הַשָּׁמַיִם, וּבָרֵךְ אֶת־עַמְּךָ אֶת־יִשְׂרָאֵל, וְאֵת הָאֲדָמָה אֲשֶׁר נָתַתָּה לָנוּ, כַּאֲשֶׁר נִשְׁבַּעְתָּ לַאֲבֹתֵינוּ, אֶרֶץ זָבַת חָלָב וּדְבָשׁ: דברים כו

תפילה לשעת עצירת גשמים

In times of drought in ארץ ישראל*, the following is added in the* שומע תפילה *blessing of the* עמידה*:*

וַעֲנֵנוּ בּוֹרֵא עוֹלָם בְּמִדַּת הָרַחֲמִים, בּוֹחֵר בְּעַמּוֹ יִשְׂרָאֵל לְהוֹדִיעַ גָּדְלוֹ וְהַדְרַת כְּבוֹדוֹ. שׁוֹמֵעַ תְּפִלָּה, תֵּן טַל וּמָטָר עַל פְּנֵי הָאֲדָמָה, וְתַשְׂבִּיעַ אֶת הָעוֹלָם כֻּלּוֹ מִטּוּבֶךָ, וּמַלֵּא יָדֵינוּ מִבִּרְכוֹתֶיךָ וּמֵעֹשֶׁר מַתְּנַת יָדֶךָ. שְׁמֹר וְהַצֵּל שָׁנָה זוֹ מִכָּל דָּבָר רָע, וּמִכָּל מִינֵי מַשְׁחִית וּמִכָּל מִינֵי פֻרְעָנִיּוֹת, וַעֲשֵׂה לָהּ תִּקְוָה וְאַחֲרִית שָׁלוֹם. חוּס וְרַחֵם עָלֵינוּ וְעַל כָּל תְּבוּאָתֵנוּ וּפֵרוֹתֵינוּ, וּבָרְכֵנוּ בְּגִשְׁמֵי בְרָכָה, וְנִזְכֶּה לְחַיִּים וָשֹׂבַע וְשָׁלוֹם כַּשָּׁנִים הַטּוֹבוֹת. וְהָסֵר מִמֶּנּוּ דֶּבֶר וְחֶרֶב וְרָעָב, וְחַיָּה רָעָה וּשְׁבִי וּבִזָּה, וְיֵצֶר הָרָע וָחֳלָיִים רָעִים וְקָשִׁים וּמְאֹרָעוֹת רָעִים וְקָשִׁים. וּגְזֹר עָלֵינוּ גְּזֵרוֹת טוֹבוֹת מִלְּפָנֶיךָ, וְיִגָּלוּ רַחֲמֶיךָ עַל מִדּוֹתֶיךָ, וְתִתְנַהֵג עִם בָּנֶיךָ בְּמִדַּת הָרַחֲמִים, וְקַבֵּל בְּרַחֲמִים וּבְרָצוֹן אֶת תְּפִלָּתֵנוּ.

Continue with כִּי אַתָּה שׁוֹמֵעַ *at* מנחה לערב שבת *on page 17, and at* מעריב למוצאי שבת *on page 613.*

THE MEAL AND ITS BLESSINGS

On washing hands before eating bread:

Blessed are You, Lord our God, King of the Universe,
who has made us holy through His commandments,
and has commanded us about washing hands.

Before eating bread:

Blessed are You, Lord our God, King of the Universe,
who brings forth bread from the earth.

BIRKAT HAMAZON / GRACE AFTER MEALS

שִׁיר הַמַּעֲלוֹת A song of ascents. When the Lord brought back the exiles of Zion we were like people who dream. Then were our mouths filled with laughter, and our tongues with songs of joy. Then was it said among the nations, "The Lord has done great things for them." The Lord did do great things for us and we rejoiced. Bring back our exiles, Lord, like streams in a dry land. May those who sowed in tears, reap in joy. May one who goes out weeping, carrying a bag of seed, come back with songs of joy, carrying his sheaves. *Ps. 126*

Some say:

תְּהִלַּת My mouth shall speak the praise of God, and all creatures *Ps. 145*
shall bless His holy name for ever and all time. We will bless God *Ps. 115*
now and for ever. Halleluya! Thank the Lord for He is good; His *Ps. 136*
loving-kindness is for ever. Who can tell of the Lord's mighty acts *Ps. 106*
and make all His praise be heard?

---

when we are in need; we tend to forget to be thankful when the need has passed. *Berakhot* are a reminder not to forget.

In this particular mitzva there is also a special opportunity, when we sit together in a group, to have a *zimmun* – a calling together of everyone who has eaten in the same place. Rabbi Hirsch suggests one possible rationale: When we recognize Hashem as the Provider, Preserver, Sustainer of us all, whose goodness enables us all to live and remain alive, we acknowledge that

This **INTRODUCTION** *continues on page 737.*

סדר סעודה וברכותיה

On washing hands before eating bread:

בָּרוּךְ אַתָּה יהוה אֱלֹהֵינוּ מֶלֶךְ הָעוֹלָם
אֲשֶׁר קִדְּשָׁנוּ בְּמִצְוֹתָיו וְצִוָּנוּ עַל נְטִילַת יָדַיִם.

Before eating bread:

בָּרוּךְ אַתָּה יהוה אֱלֹהֵינוּ מֶלֶךְ הָעוֹלָם
הַמּוֹצִיא לֶחֶם מִן הָאָרֶץ.

ברכת המזון

שִׁיר הַמַּעֲלוֹת, בְּשׁוּב יהוה אֶת־שִׁיבַת צִיּוֹן, הָיִינוּ כְּחֹלְמִים: אָז תהלים קכו
יִמָּלֵא שְׂחוֹק פִּינוּ וּלְשׁוֹנֵנוּ רִנָּה, אָז יֹאמְרוּ בַגּוֹיִם הִגְדִּיל יהוה
לַעֲשׂוֹת עִם־אֵלֶּה: הִגְדִּיל יהוה לַעֲשׂוֹת עִמָּנוּ, הָיִינוּ שְׂמֵחִים:
שׁוּבָה יהוה אֶת־שְׁבִיתֵנוּ, כַּאֲפִיקִים בַּנֶּגֶב: הַזֹּרְעִים בְּדִמְעָה
בְּרִנָּה יִקְצֹרוּ: הָלוֹךְ יֵלֵךְ וּבָכֹה נֹשֵׂא מֶשֶׁךְ־הַזָּרַע, בֹּא־יָבֹא
בְרִנָּה נֹשֵׂא אֲלֻמֹּתָיו:

Some say:

תְּהִלַּת יהוה יְדַבֶּר פִּי, וִיבָרֵךְ כָּל־בָּשָׂר שֵׁם קָדְשׁוֹ לְעוֹלָם וָעֶד: תהלים קמה
וַאֲנַחְנוּ נְבָרֵךְ יָהּ מֵעַתָּה וְעַד־עוֹלָם, הַלְלוּיָהּ: הוֹדוּ לַיהוה תהלים קטו תהלים קלו
כִּי־טוֹב, כִּי לְעוֹלָם חַסְדּוֹ: מִי יְמַלֵּל גְּבוּרוֹת יהוה, יַשְׁמִיעַ כָּל־ תהלים קו
תְּהִלָּתוֹ:

INTRODUCTION TO BIRKAT HAMAZON

The Torah mandated that we say a blessing after our meal, apparently because it is precisely when our stomachs are full that we have a tendency to forget where the meal ultimately came from (*Devarim* 8:12–18). We tend to be very thankful at those moments

ZIMMUN / INVITATION

For the zimmun said during the week of Sheva Berakhot, see page 774.
At a Brit, see page 764.

When three or more men say Birkat HaMazon together, the following zimmun is said. When three or more women say Birkat HaMazon, substitute "Friends" for "Gentlemen." The leader should ask permission from those with precedence to lead the Birkat HaMazon.

Leader Gentlemen, let us say grace.

Others May the name of the LORD be blessed Ps. 113
from now and for ever.

Leader May the name of the LORD be blessed
from now and for ever.
With your permission,
(my father and teacher /
my mother and teacher /
the Kohanim present /
our teacher the Rabbi /
the master of this house /
the mistress of this house)
my masters and teachers,
let us bless (*in a minyan:* our God,) the One
from whose food we have eaten.

Others Blessed be (*in a minyan:* our God,) the One
from whose food we have eaten,
and by whose goodness we live.

**People present who have not taken part in the meal say:*
*Blessed be (*in a minyan:* our God,) the One
whose name is continually blessed for ever and all time.

Leader Blessed be (*in a minyan:* our God,) the One
from whose food we have eaten,
and by whose goodness we live.

Blessed be He, and blessed be His name.

סדר הזימון

For the זימון *said during the week of* שבע ברכות*, see page 775.*
At a ברית*, see page 765.*

When three or more men say ברכת המזון *together, the following* זימון *is said.*
When three or more women say ברכת המזון*, substitute* חֲבֵרוֹתַי *for* רַבּוֹתַי*.*
The leader should ask permission from those with precedence to lead the ברכת המזון*.*

Leader רַבּוֹתַי, נְבָרֵךְ.

Others יְהִי שֵׁם יהוה מְבֹרָךְ מֵעַתָּה וְעַד־עוֹלָם: תהלים קיג

Leader יְהִי שֵׁם יהוה מְבֹרָךְ מֵעַתָּה וְעַד־עוֹלָם:
בִּרְשׁוּת (אָבִי מוֹרִי / אִמִּי מוֹרָתִי / כֹּהֲנִים / מוֹרֵנוּ הָרַב /
בַּעַל הַבַּיִת הַזֶּה / בַּעֲלַת הַבַּיִת הַזֶּה)
מָרָנָן וְרַבָּנָן וְרַבּוֹתַי
נְבָרֵךְ (במנין: אֱלֹהֵינוּ) שֶׁאָכַלְנוּ מִשֶּׁלּוֹ.

Others בָּרוּךְ (במנין: אֱלֹהֵינוּ) שֶׁאָכַלְנוּ מִשֶּׁלּוֹ וּבְטוּבוֹ חָיִינוּ.

**People present who have not taken part in the meal say:*
*בָּרוּךְ (במנין: אֱלֹהֵינוּ) וּמְבֹרָךְ שְׁמוֹ תָּמִיד לְעוֹלָם וָעֶד.

Leader בָּרוּךְ (במנין: אֱלֹהֵינוּ) שֶׁאָכַלְנוּ מִשֶּׁלּוֹ וּבְטוּבוֹ חָיִינוּ.
בָּרוּךְ הוּא וּבָרוּךְ שְׁמוֹ.

He is near to all of us, and so there is no reason to be envious of another's wealth. *Birkat HaMazon* is thus the great equalizer, reminding us that Hashem gives to each of us what is good and beneficial for us at any particular time. It makes us thankful, gives us perspective, and draws us closer to one another.

BLESSING OF NOURISHMENT

בָּרוּךְ Blessed are You, LORD our God, King of the Universe,
who in His goodness feeds the whole world
with grace, kindness and compassion.[B]
He gives food to all living things,
for His kindness is for ever.
Because of His continual great goodness,
we have never lacked food,
nor may we ever lack it,[A]
for the sake of His great name.
For He is God who feeds and sustains all,
does good to all,
and prepares food for all creatures He has created.
Blessed are You, LORD,
who feeds all.[A]

BLESSING OF LAND

נוֹדֶה We thank You,[A] LORD our God,
for having granted as a heritage to our ancestors
a desirable, good and spacious land;
for bringing us out, LORD our God, from the land of Egypt,
freeing us from the house of slavery;

ANI TEFILLA • אני תפילה

לֹא חָסַר לָנוּ וְאַל יֶחְסַר לָנוּ מָזוֹן לְעוֹלָם וָעֶד – *We have never lacked food, nor may we ever lack it.* The premise of the blessing is that Hashem provides sufficient food for the entire world. As such, the fact that some people do not have enough to eat is not a failure of God, but the failure of man.

הַזָּן אֶת הַכֹּל – *Who feeds all.* There is a motif word that is repeated six times in this paragraph. What is the word and what might be the significance?

נוֹדֶה לְּךָ – *We thank You.* There is one word that appears in this blessing no less than ten times! What is the word and what is its significance?

ברכת הזן

בָּרוּךְ אַתָּה יהוה אֱלֹהֵינוּ מֶלֶךְ הָעוֹלָם
הַזָּן אֶת הָעוֹלָם כֻּלּוֹ בְּטוּבוֹ
בְּחֵן בְּחֶסֶד וּבְרַחֲמִים[ב]
הוּא נוֹתֵן לֶחֶם לְכָל בָּשָׂר
כִּי לְעוֹלָם חַסְדּוֹ.
וּבְטוּבוֹ הַגָּדוֹל, תָּמִיד לֹא חָסַר לָנוּ
וְאַל יֶחְסַר לָנוּ מָזוֹן לְעוֹלָם וָעֶד[א]
בַּעֲבוּר שְׁמוֹ הַגָּדוֹל.
כִּי הוּא אֵל זָן וּמְפַרְנֵס לַכֹּל וּמֵטִיב לַכֹּל
וּמֵכִין מָזוֹן לְכָל בְּרִיּוֹתָיו אֲשֶׁר בָּרָא.
בָּרוּךְ אַתָּה יהוה, הַזָּן אֶת הַכֹּל.[א]

ברכת הארץ

נוֹדֶה לְּךָ,[א] יהוה אֱלֹהֵינוּ
עַל שֶׁהִנְחַלְתָּ לַאֲבוֹתֵינוּ אֶרֶץ חֶמְדָּה טוֹבָה וּרְחָבָה
וְעַל שֶׁהוֹצֵאתָנוּ יהוה אֱלֹהֵינוּ מֵאֶרֶץ מִצְרַיִם
וּפְדִיתָנוּ מִבֵּית עֲבָדִים

BIUR TEFILLA • ביאור תפילה

בְּחֵן בְּחֶסֶד וּבְרַחֲמִים – *With grace, kindness and compassion.*

What might each of these three terms represent? Where does each manifest itself in your life?

The terms might refer to the different kinds of support that one needs from Hashem at different points in one's life (Rabbi Yosef Albo).

Alternatively, they might refer to different kinds of help depending on the merits of the receiver (Rabbi Hirsch).

Alternatively, they might refer to different people's economic status (*Arukh HaShulḥan*).

for Your covenant which You sealed in our flesh;
for Your Torah which You taught us;
for Your laws which You made known to us;
for the life, grace and kindness You have bestowed on us;
and for the food by which You continually feed and sustain us,
every day, every season, every hour.

On Ḥanukka:

עַל הַנִּסִּים [We thank You also] for the miracles, the redemption, the mighty deeds, the salvations, and the victories in battle which You performed for our ancestors in those days, at this time.

בִּימֵי מַתִּתְיָהוּ In the days of Mattityahu, son of Yoḥanan, the High Priest, the Hasmonean, and his sons, the wicked Greek kingdom rose up against Your people Israel to make them forget Your Torah and to force them to transgress the statutes of Your will. It was then that You in Your great compassion stood by them in the time of their distress. You championed their cause, judged their claim, and avenged their wrong. You delivered the strong into the hands of the weak, the many into the hands of the few, the impure into the hands of the pure, the wicked into the hands of the righteous, and the arrogant into the hands of those who were engaged in the study of Your Torah. You made for Yourself great and holy renown in Your world, and for Your people Israel You performed a great salvation and redemption as of this very day. Your children then entered the holiest part of Your House, cleansed Your Temple, purified Your Sanctuary, kindled lights in Your holy courts, and designated these eight days of Ḥanukka for giving thanks and praise to Your great name.

Continue with "For all this."

On Shushan Purim in Jerusalem:

עַל הַנִּסִּים [We thank You also] for the miracles, the redemption, the mighty deeds, the salvations, and the victories in battle which You performed for our ancestors in those days, at this time.

בִּימֵי מָרְדְּכַי In the days of Mordekhai and Esther, in Shushan the capital,
the wicked Haman rose up against them and sought to destroy, slay and *Esther 3*
exterminate all the Jews, young and old, children and women, on one day, the thirteenth day of the twelfth month, which is the month of Adar, and to plunder their possessions. Then You in Your great compassion thwarted his counsel, frustrated his plans, and caused his scheme to recoil on his own head, so that they hanged him and his sons on the gallows.

Continue with "For all this."

וְעַל בְּרִיתְךָ שֶׁחָתַמְתָּ בִּבְשָׂרֵנוּ
וְעַל תּוֹרָתְךָ שֶׁלִּמַּדְתָּנוּ
וְעַל חֻקֶּיךָ שֶׁהוֹדַעְתָּנוּ
וְעַל חַיִּים חֵן וָחֶסֶד שֶׁחוֹנַנְתָּנוּ
וְעַל אֲכִילַת מָזוֹן שָׁאַתָּה זָן וּמְפַרְנֵס אוֹתָנוּ תָּמִיד
בְּכָל יוֹם וּבְכָל עֵת וּבְכָל שָׁעָה.

בחנוכה:

עַל הַנִּסִּים וְעַל הַפֻּרְקָן וְעַל הַגְּבוּרוֹת וְעַל הַתְּשׁוּעוֹת וְעַל הַמִּלְחָמוֹת שֶׁעָשִׂיתָ לַאֲבוֹתֵינוּ בַּיָּמִים הָהֵם בַּזְּמַן הַזֶּה.

בִּימֵי מַתִּתְיָהוּ בֶּן יוֹחָנָן כֹּהֵן גָּדוֹל חַשְׁמוֹנַאי וּבָנָיו, כְּשֶׁעָמְדָה מַלְכוּת יָוָן הָרְשָׁעָה עַל עַמְּךָ יִשְׂרָאֵל לְהַשְׁכִּיחָם תּוֹרָתֶךָ וּלְהַעֲבִירָם מֵחֻקֵּי רְצוֹנֶךָ, וְאַתָּה בְּרַחֲמֶיךָ הָרַבִּים עָמַדְתָּ לָהֶם בְּעֵת צָרָתָם, רַבְתָּ אֶת רִיבָם, דַּנְתָּ אֶת דִּינָם, נָקַמְתָּ אֶת נִקְמָתָם, מָסַרְתָּ גִּבּוֹרִים בְּיַד חַלָּשִׁים, וְרַבִּים בְּיַד מְעַטִּים, וּטְמֵאִים בְּיַד טְהוֹרִים, וּרְשָׁעִים בְּיַד צַדִּיקִים, וְזֵדִים בְּיַד עוֹסְקֵי תוֹרָתֶךָ, וּלְךָ עָשִׂיתָ שֵׁם גָּדוֹל וְקָדוֹשׁ בְּעוֹלָמֶךָ, וּלְעַמְּךָ יִשְׂרָאֵל עָשִׂיתָ תְּשׁוּעָה גְדוֹלָה וּפֻרְקָן כְּהַיּוֹם הַזֶּה. וְאַחַר כֵּן בָּאוּ בָנֶיךָ לִדְבִיר בֵּיתֶךָ, וּפִנּוּ אֶת הֵיכָלֶךָ, וְטִהֲרוּ אֶת מִקְדָּשֶׁךָ, וְהִדְלִיקוּ נֵרוֹת בְּחַצְרוֹת קָדְשֶׁךָ, וְקָבְעוּ שְׁמוֹנַת יְמֵי חֲנֻכָּה אֵלּוּ, לְהוֹדוֹת וּלְהַלֵּל לְשִׁמְךָ הַגָּדוֹל.

Continue with וְעַל הַכֹּל.

בשושן פורים בירושלים:

עַל הַנִּסִּים וְעַל הַפֻּרְקָן וְעַל הַגְּבוּרוֹת וְעַל הַתְּשׁוּעוֹת וְעַל הַמִּלְחָמוֹת שֶׁעָשִׂיתָ לַאֲבוֹתֵינוּ בַּיָּמִים הָהֵם בַּזְּמַן הַזֶּה.

בִּימֵי מָרְדְּכַי וְאֶסְתֵּר בְּשׁוּשַׁן הַבִּירָה, כְּשֶׁעָמַד עֲלֵיהֶם הָמָן הָרָשָׁע, בִּקֵּשׁ
אסתר ג לְהַשְׁמִיד לַהֲרֹג וּלְאַבֵּד אֶת־כָּל־הַיְּהוּדִים מִנַּעַר וְעַד־זָקֵן טַף וְנָשִׁים בְּיוֹם אֶחָד, בִּשְׁלוֹשָׁה עָשָׂר לְחֹדֶשׁ שְׁנֵים־עָשָׂר, הוּא־חֹדֶשׁ אֲדָר, וּשְׁלָלָם לָבוֹז: וְאַתָּה בְּרַחֲמֶיךָ הָרַבִּים הֵפַרְתָּ אֶת עֲצָתוֹ, וְקִלְקַלְתָּ אֶת מַחֲשַׁבְתּוֹ, וַהֲשֵׁבוֹתָ לּוֹ גְּמוּלוֹ בְּרֹאשׁוֹ, וְתָלוּ אוֹתוֹ וְאֶת בָּנָיו עַל הָעֵץ.

Continue with וְעַל הַכֹּל.

וְעַל הַכֹּל For all this, LORD our God,
we thank and bless You.
May Your name be blessed continually
by the mouth of all that lives, for ever and all time –
for so it is written:
"You will eat and be satisfied, *Deut. 8*
then you shall bless the LORD your God
for the good land He has given you."
Blessed are You, LORD, for the land and for the food.[1]

BLESSING FOR JERUSALEM

רַחֶם נָא Have compassion, please, LORD our God,
on Israel Your people, on Jerusalem Your city,
on Zion the dwelling place of Your glory,
on the royal house of David Your anointed,
and on the great and holy House that bears Your name.
Our God, our Father,
tend us, feed us, sustain us and support us,
relieve us and send us relief,
LORD our God, swiftly from all our troubles.
Please, LORD our God, do not make us dependent
on the gifts or loans of other people,
but only on Your full, open, holy and generous hand
so that we may suffer neither shame nor humiliation
for ever and all time.

BIUR TEFILLA • ביאור תפילה

רַחֶם נָא, יהוה אֱלֹהֵינוּ, עַל יִשְׂרָאֵל עַמֶּךָ – *Have compassion, please, LORD our God, on Israel Your people.* Commentators have tried to explain the connection between the requests for the restoration of the *Beit HaMikdash* and the request that our food and material needs be provided. One suggestion cites the Gemara (*Ḥagiga* 27a) which says that the Altar in the *Beit HaMikdash* atoned for the sins of mankind but, in its absence, the table where a person eats has the same impact. How might this connection be understood? Rashi suggests that it is because one has guests at one's table. How does this explain the Gemara's statement?

Can you suggest another connection between the themes of the *Beit HaMikdash* and the request for food?

וְעַל הַכֹּל, יהוה אֱלֹהֵינוּ
אֲנַחְנוּ מוֹדִים לָךְ וּמְבָרְכִים אוֹתָךְ
יִתְבָּרַךְ שִׁמְךָ בְּפִי כָּל חַי תָּמִיד לְעוֹלָם וָעֶד
כַּכָּתוּב: וְאָכַלְתָּ וְשָׂבָעְתָּ, וּבֵרַכְתָּ אֶת־יהוה אֱלֹהֶיךָ דברים ח
עַל־הָאָרֶץ הַטֹּבָה אֲשֶׁר נָתַן־לָךְ:
בָּרוּךְ אַתָּה יהוה, עַל הָאָרֶץ וְעַל הַמָּזוֹן.[ע]

ברכת ירושלים

רַחֵם נָא, יהוה אֱלֹהֵינוּ
עַל יִשְׂרָאֵל עַמֶּךָ, וְעַל יְרוּשָׁלַיִם עִירֶךָ
וְעַל צִיּוֹן מִשְׁכַּן כְּבוֹדֶךָ, וְעַל מַלְכוּת בֵּית דָּוִד מְשִׁיחֶךָ
וְעַל הַבַּיִת הַגָּדוֹל וְהַקָּדוֹשׁ שֶׁנִּקְרָא שִׁמְךָ עָלָיו.
אֱלֹהֵינוּ, אָבִינוּ
רְעֵנוּ, זוּנֵנוּ, פַּרְנְסֵנוּ וְכַלְכְּלֵנוּ
וְהַרְוִיחֵנוּ, וְהַרְוַח לָנוּ יהוה אֱלֹהֵינוּ מְהֵרָה מִכָּל צָרוֹתֵינוּ.
וְנָא אַל תַּצְרִיכֵנוּ, יהוה אֱלֹהֵינוּ
לֹא לִידֵי מַתְּנַת בָּשָׂר וָדָם, וְלֹא לִידֵי הַלְוָאָתָם
כִּי אִם לְיָדְךָ הַמְּלֵאָה, הַפְּתוּחָה, הַקְּדוֹשָׁה וְהָרְחָבָה
שֶׁלֹּא נֵבוֹשׁ וְלֹא נִכָּלֵם לְעוֹלָם וָעֶד.

IYUN TEFILLA • עיון תפילה

עַל הָאָרֶץ וְעַל הַמָּזוֹן – *For the land and for the food.* The blessing enumerates a number of things for which we should be grateful: the Land, the Exodus, the covenant represented by Brit Mila, the Torah, the laws, the life, favor and *ḥesed* that Hashem bestowed upon us, our never-ending supply of food, and for everything. Yet the blessing's signature relates only to the Land and food.

(a) The Gemara (*Berakhot* 49a) says that the ending or signature of a blessing may not have two different themes in it. Yet here there are two mentioned. How might they be seen as the same?

(b) What might be the connection between those two things and all of the others? For which should we be grateful?

What reason can you suggest for the order of the eight things that are listed for which we should be grateful?

רְצֵה Favor and strengthen us, LORD our God,
through Your commandments,
especially through the commandment of the seventh day,
this great and holy Sabbath.
For it is, for You, a great and holy day.
On it we cease work and rest in love
in accord with Your will's commandment.
May it be Your will, LORD our God,
to grant us rest without distress,
grief, or lament on our day of rest.
May You show us the consolation of Zion Your city,
and the rebuilding of Jerusalem Your holy city,
for You are the Master of salvation and consolation.

On Rosh Ḥodesh and Ḥol HaMo'ed, say:

אֱלֹהֵינוּ Our God and God of our ancestors,
may there rise, come, reach, appear, be favored, heard, regarded
and remembered before You, our recollection and remembrance,
as well as the remembrance of our ancestors,
and of the Messiah son of David Your servant,
and of Jerusalem Your holy city,
and of all Your people the house of Israel –
for deliverance and well-being,
grace, loving-kindness and compassion,
life and peace, on this day of:

On Rosh Ḥodesh: Rosh Ḥodesh.
On Pesaḥ: the Festival of Matzot.
On Sukkot: the Festival of Sukkot.

On it remember us, LORD our God, for good;
recollect us for blessing, and deliver us for life.
In accord with Your promise of salvation and compassion,
spare us and be gracious to us;
have compassion on us and deliver us,
for our eyes are turned to You because You are God,
gracious and compassionate.

רְצֵה וְהַחֲלִיצֵנוּ, יהוה אֱלֹהֵינוּ, בְּמִצְוֹתֶיךָ
וּבְמִצְוַת יוֹם הַשְּׁבִיעִי הַשַּׁבָּת הַגָּדוֹל וְהַקָּדוֹשׁ הַזֶּה
כִּי יוֹם זֶה גָּדוֹל וְקָדוֹשׁ הוּא לְפָנֶיךָ
לִשְׁבָּת בּוֹ, וְלָנוּחַ בּוֹ בְּאַהֲבָה כְּמִצְוַת רְצוֹנֶךָ
וּבִרְצוֹנְךָ הָנִיחַ לָנוּ, יהוה אֱלֹהֵינוּ
שֶׁלֹּא תְהֵא צָרָה וְיָגוֹן וַאֲנָחָה בְּיוֹם מְנוּחָתֵנוּ
וְהַרְאֵנוּ, יהוה אֱלֹהֵינוּ, בְּנֶחָמַת צִיּוֹן עִירֶךָ
וּבְבִנְיַן יְרוּשָׁלַיִם עִיר קָדְשֶׁךָ
כִּי אַתָּה הוּא בַּעַל הַיְשׁוּעוֹת וּבַעַל הַנֶּחָמוֹת.

On ראש חודש *and* חול המועד*, say:*

אֱלֹהֵינוּ וֵאלֹהֵי אֲבוֹתֵינוּ
יַעֲלֶה וְיָבוֹא וְיַגִּיעַ, וְיֵרָאֶה וְיֵרָצֶה וְיִשָּׁמַע
וְיִפָּקֵד וְיִזָּכֵר זִכְרוֹנֵנוּ וּפִקְדוֹנֵנוּ
וְזִכְרוֹן אֲבוֹתֵינוּ
וְזִכְרוֹן מָשִׁיחַ בֶּן דָּוִד עַבְדֶּךָ
וְזִכְרוֹן יְרוּשָׁלַיִם עִיר קָדְשֶׁךָ
וְזִכְרוֹן כָּל עַמְּךָ בֵּית יִשְׂרָאֵל
לְפָנֶיךָ, לִפְלֵיטָה לְטוֹבָה, לְחֵן וּלְחֶסֶד וּלְרַחֲמִים
לְחַיִּים וּלְשָׁלוֹם בְּיוֹם

בראש חודש: רֹאשׁ הַחֹדֶשׁ הַזֶּה.
בפסח: חַג הַמַּצּוֹת הַזֶּה.
בסוכות: חַג הַסֻּכּוֹת הַזֶּה.

זָכְרֵנוּ יהוה אֱלֹהֵינוּ בּוֹ לְטוֹבָה
וּפָקְדֵנוּ בוֹ לִבְרָכָה, וְהוֹשִׁיעֵנוּ בוֹ לְחַיִּים.
וּבִדְבַר יְשׁוּעָה וְרַחֲמִים
חוּס וְחָנֵּנוּ וְרַחֵם עָלֵינוּ, וְהוֹשִׁיעֵנוּ
כִּי אֵלֶיךָ עֵינֵינוּ, כִּי אֵל חַנּוּן וְרַחוּם אָתָּה.

וּבְנֵה And may Jerusalem the holy city be rebuilt soon, in our time.
Blessed are You, LORD, who in His compassion
will rebuild Jerusalem. Amen.

BLESSING OF GOD'S GOODNESS

בָּרוּךְ Blessed are You, LORD our God, King of the Universe –
God our Father, our King, our Sovereign,
our Creator, our Redeemer, our Maker,
our Holy One, the Holy One of Jacob.
He is our Shepherd, Israel's Shepherd,
the good King who does good to all.
Every day He has done, is doing, and will do good to us.
He has acted, is acting, and will always act kindly toward us for ever,
granting us grace, kindness and compassion, relief and rescue,
prosperity, blessing, redemption and comfort,
sustenance and support,
compassion, life, peace and all good things,
and of all good things may He never let us lack.

ADDITIONAL REQUESTS

הָרַחֲמָן May the Compassionate One reign over us
for ever and all time.

May the Compassionate One be blessed
in heaven and on earth.

---

the entire blessing consists of one theme, which is the criteria for having only one blessing formula at the beginning (Rashi on *Berakhot* 49a).

ANI TEFILLA · אני תפילה

הָרַחֲמָן – *The Compassionate One.* This series of eight short requests are a later addition but they make room for one to add one's own related personal requests. The rationale is that since one's table is like an altar where atonement is granted, then the table is a particularly good place to have one's prayers heard, assuming one conducted oneself appropriately at the meal (*Piskei Teshuvot* 189:2).

What prayer would you like to add today?

וּבְנֵה יְרוּשָׁלַיִם עִיר הַקֹּדֶשׁ בִּמְהֵרָה בְיָמֵינוּ.
בָּרוּךְ אַתָּה יהוה, בּוֹנֵה בְרַחֲמָיו יְרוּשָׁלָיִם, אָמֵן.

ברכת הטוב והמטיב

בָּרוּךְ אַתָּה יהוה אֱלֹהֵינוּ מֶלֶךְ הָעוֹלָם
הָאֵל אָבִינוּ, מַלְכֵּנוּ, אַדִּירֵנוּ
בּוֹרְאֵנוּ, גּוֹאֲלֵנוּ, יוֹצְרֵנוּ, קְדוֹשֵׁנוּ, קְדוֹשׁ יַעֲקֹב
רוֹעֵנוּ, רוֹעֵה יִשְׂרָאֵל, הַמֶּלֶךְ הַטּוֹב וְהַמֵּיטִיב לַכֹּל, שֶׁבְּכָל יוֹם וָיוֹם
הוּא הֵיטִיב, הוּא מֵיטִיב, הוּא יֵיטִיב לָנוּ
הוּא גְמָלָנוּ, הוּא גוֹמְלֵנוּ, הוּא יִגְמְלֵנוּ לָעַד
לְחֵן וּלְחֶסֶד וּלְרַחֲמִים, וּלְרֶוַח, הַצָּלָה וְהַצְלָחָה
בְּרָכָה וִישׁוּעָה, נֶחָמָה, פַּרְנָסָה וְכַלְכָּלָה
וְרַחֲמִים וְחַיִּים וְשָׁלוֹם וְכָל טוֹב, וּמִכָּל טוּב לְעוֹלָם אַל יְחַסְּרֵנוּ.

בקשות נוספות

הָרַחֲמָן הוּא יִמְלֹךְ עָלֵינוּ לְעוֹלָם וָעֶד.
הָרַחֲמָן הוּא יִתְבָּרַךְ בַּשָּׁמַיִם וּבָאָרֶץ.

BIUR TEFILLA • ביאור תפילה

אָמֵן – *Amen.* Answering "Amen" to one's own blessing is rare. In this case it serves as a marker to separate the end of the three blessings which are from the Torah and the beginning of the fourth blessing which is *deRabbanan,* instituted by the Rabbis.

הוּא הֵיטִיב, הוּא מֵיטִיב, הוּא יֵיטִיב לָנוּ – *He has done, is doing, and will do good to us.* The first blessing is in the present tense, thanking Hashem for the food which He gives us; the second is in the past, thanking Hashem for the gifts of the Land; while the third blessing about the rebuilding of Yerushalayim is in the future tense (Rabbi Munk). Here, we refer to Hashem's goodness toward us in all three tenses.

וּמִכָּל טוּב לְעוֹלָם אַל יְחַסְּרֵנוּ – *And of all good things may He never let us lack.* This is the end of the fourth blessing which is why it is appropriate to answer Amen when it is recited in a group. Despite its length, it does not end in the formula of *Barukh ata* because

May the Compassionate One
be praised from generation to generation,
be glorified by us to all eternity,
and honored among us for ever and all time.

May the Compassionate One
grant us an honorable livelihood.

May the Compassionate One
break the yoke from our neck
and lead us upright to our land.

May the Compassionate One
send us many blessings to this house
and this table at which we have eaten.

May the Compassionate One
send us Elijah the prophet –
may he be remembered for good –
to bring us good tidings of salvation and consolation.

May the Compassionate One
bless the State of Israel, first flowering of our redemption.

May the Compassionate One
bless the members of Israel's Defense Forces,
who stand guard over our land.

A guest says:

יְהִי רָצוֹן May it be Your will that the master of this house
shall not suffer shame in this world,
nor humiliation in the World to Come.
May all he owns prosper greatly,
and may his and our possessions be successful and close to hand.
Let not the Accuser hold sway over his deeds or ours,
and may no thought of sin, iniquity or transgression
enter him or us
from now and for evermore.

הָרַחֲמָן הוּא יִשְׁתַּבַּח לְדוֹר דּוֹרִים
וְיִתְפָּאַר בָּֽנוּ לָעַד וּלְנֵֽצַח נְצָחִים
וְיִתְהַדַּר בָּֽנוּ לָעַד וּלְעוֹלְמֵי עוֹלָמִים.

הָרַחֲמָן הוּא יְפַרְנְסֵֽנוּ בְּכָבוֹד.

הָרַחֲמָן הוּא יִשְׁבֹּר עֻלֵּֽנוּ מֵעַל צַוָּארֵֽנוּ
וְהוּא יוֹלִיכֵֽנוּ קוֹמְמִיּוּת לְאַרְצֵֽנוּ.

הָרַחֲמָן הוּא יִשְׁלַח לָֽנוּ בְּרָכָה מְרֻבָּה בַּבַּֽיִת הַזֶּה
וְעַל שֻׁלְחָן זֶה שֶׁאָכַֽלְנוּ עָלָיו.

הָרַחֲמָן הוּא יִשְׁלַח לָֽנוּ אֶת אֵלִיָּֽהוּ הַנָּבִיא זָכוּר לַטּוֹב
וִיבַשֶּׂר לָֽנוּ בְּשׂוֹרוֹת טוֹבוֹת יְשׁוּעוֹת וְנֶחָמוֹת.

הָרַחֲמָן הוּא יְבָרֵךְ אֶת מְדִינַת יִשְׂרָאֵל
רֵאשִׁית צְמִיחַת גְּאֻלָּתֵֽנוּ.

הָרַחֲמָן הוּא יְבָרֵךְ אֶת חַיָּלֵי צְבָא הַהֲגָנָה לְיִשְׂרָאֵל
הָעוֹמְדִים עַל מִשְׁמַר אַרְצֵֽנוּ.

A guest says:

יְהִי רָצוֹן שֶׁלֹּא יֵבוֹשׁ בַּֽעַל הַבַּֽיִת בָּעוֹלָם הַזֶּה
וְלֹא יִכָּלֵם לָעוֹלָם הַבָּא
וְיִצְלַח מְאֹד בְּכָל נְכָסָיו
וְיִהְיוּ נְכָסָיו וּנְכָסֵֽינוּ מֻצְלָחִים וּקְרוֹבִים לָעִיר
וְאַל יִשְׁלוֹט שָׂטָן לֹא בְּמַעֲשֵׂה יָדָיו וְלֹא בְּמַעֲשֵׂה יָדֵֽינוּ.
וְאַל יִזְדַּקֵּק לֹא לְפָנָיו וְלֹא לְפָנֵֽינוּ שׁוּם דְּבַר הִרְהוּר חֵטְא
עֲבֵירָה וְעָוֹן, מֵעַתָּה וְעַד עוֹלָם.

הָרַחֲמָן May the Compassionate One bless –

When eating at one's own table, say (include the words in parentheses that apply):
me, (my wife/husband, / my father, my teacher / my mother, my teacher/ my children,) and all that is mine,

A guest at someone else's table says (include the words in parentheses that apply):
the master of this house, him (and his wife, the mistress of this house / and his children,) and all that is his,

Children at their parents' table say (include the words in parentheses that apply):
my father, my teacher, (master of this house,) and my mother, my teacher, (mistress of this house,) them, their household, their children, and all that is theirs.

For all other guests, add:
and all the diners here,

אוֹתָנוּ – together with us and all that is ours.
Just as our forefathers
Abraham, Isaac and Jacob were blessed in all, from all, with all,[1]
so may He bless all of us together
with a complete blessing, and let us say: Amen.

בַּמָּרוֹם On high, may grace be invoked for them and for us,
as a safeguard of peace.
May we receive a blessing from the LORD
and a just reward from the God of our salvation,
and may we find grace and good favor
in the eyes of God and man.

At a circumcision feast add here "May the Compassionate One bless the father" on page 766.

I [Yitzḥak] have eaten from *everything*" (27:33); "for Hashem has been kind to me [Yaakov] and I have *everything* [I need]" (33:11). From here the Gemara (*Bava Batra* 17a) concludes that the *yetzer hara*, the evil inclination, had no power over the *Avot*.

What do you think the Gemara means by this? What is a lesson you can take away from here whenever you say this?

הָרַחֲמָן הוּא יְבָרֵךְ

When eating at one's own table, say (include the words in parentheses that apply):

אוֹתִי (וְאֶת אִשְׁתִּי / וְאֶת בַּעְלִי / וְאֶת אָבִי מוֹרִי /
וְאֶת אִמִּי מוֹרָתִי / וְאֶת זַרְעִי) וְאֶת כָּל אֲשֶׁר לִי.

A guest at someone else's table says (include the words in parentheses that apply):

אֶת בַּעַל הַבַּיִת הַזֶּה, אוֹתוֹ (וְאֶת אִשְׁתּוֹ בַּעֲלַת הַבַּיִת הַזֶּה /
וְאֶת זַרְעוֹ) וְאֶת כָּל אֲשֶׁר לוֹ.

Children at their parents' table say (include the words in parentheses that apply):

אֶת אָבִי מוֹרִי (בַּעַל הַבַּיִת הַזֶּה), וְאֶת אִמִּי מוֹרָתִי (בַּעֲלַת הַבַּיִת
הַזֶּה), אוֹתָם וְאֶת בֵּיתָם וְאֶת זַרְעָם וְאֶת כָּל אֲשֶׁר לָהֶם

For all other guests, add:

וְאֶת כָּל הַמְּסֻבִּין כָּאן

אוֹתָנוּ וְאֶת כָּל אֲשֶׁר לָנוּ
כְּמוֹ שֶׁנִּתְבָּרְכוּ אֲבוֹתֵינוּ
אַבְרָהָם יִצְחָק וְיַעֲקֹב, בַּכֹּל, מִכֹּל, כֹּל[ע]
כֵּן יְבָרֵךְ אוֹתָנוּ כֻּלָּנוּ יַחַד בִּבְרָכָה שְׁלֵמָה, וְנֹאמַר אָמֵן.

בַּמָּרוֹם יְלַמְּדוּ עֲלֵיהֶם וְעָלֵינוּ זְכוּת
שֶׁתְּהֵא לְמִשְׁמֶרֶת שָׁלוֹם
וְנִשָּׂא בְרָכָה מֵאֵת יהוה וּצְדָקָה מֵאֱלֹהֵי יִשְׁעֵנוּ
וְנִמְצָא חֵן וְשֵׂכֶל טוֹב בְּעֵינֵי אֱלֹהִים וְאָדָם.

At a meal after a ברית *add here* הָרַחֲמָן הוּא יְבָרֵךְ אֲבִי הַיֶּלֶד *on page 767.*

IYUN TEFILLA • עיון תפילה

בַּכֹּל, מִכֹּל, כֹּל – *In all, from all, with all.* Each of these words is a reference to one of the *Avot*: "And Hashem blessed Avraham with *everything*" (*Bereshit* 24:1); "and

May the Compassionate One let us inherit
the time, that will be entirely Shabbat and rest for life everlasting.

On Rosh Ḥodesh: May the Compassionate One renew this month for us, for good and blessing.

On Sukkot: May the Compassionate One restore for us, the fallen Tabernacle of David.

הָרַחֲמָן May the Compassionate One make us worthy
of the Messianic Age and life in the World to Come.
He is a tower of salvation to His king, *II Sam. 22*
showing kindness to His anointed,
to David and his descendants for ever.
He who makes peace in His high places,
may He make peace for us and all Israel, and let us say: Amen.

יְראוּ Fear the Lord, you His holy ones; those who fear Him lack nothing. *Ps. 34*
Young lions may grow weak and hungry,
but those who seek the Lord lack no good thing.
Thank the Lord for He is good; His loving-kindness is for ever. *Ps. 118*
You open Your hand, and satisfy every living thing with favor. *Ps. 145*
Blessed is the person who trusts in the Lord, *Jer. 17*
whose trust is in the Lord alone.
Once I was young, and now I am old, yet I have never watched *Ps. 37*
a righteous man forsaken or his children begging for bread.
The Lord will give His people strength. *Ps. 29*
The Lord will bless His people with peace.

If Birkat HaMazon was made on a cup of wine, then the blessing over wine is made and the majority of the cup is drunk, after which Al HaMiḥya, on the next page, is said. If Seuda Shelishit continues after sunset, then the blessing is not said, and the cup of wine is saved for Havdala.

At Sheva Berakhot, turn to page 776.

---

effort or exertion? But as for the righteous, they have no need to exert themselves when they pray; then, their minds are always pure and clear. But during the time of eating, that is when they have to use their energy to exert themselves.

BIUR TEFILLA • ביאור תפילה

נַעַר הָיִיתִי גַּם־זָקַנְתִּי, וְלֹא־רָאִיתִי צַדִּיק נֶעֱזָב – *Once I was young, and now I am old, yet I have never watched a righteous man forsaken.* The word **רָאִיתִי**, "I saw," can be understood

The **BIUR TEFILLA** *continues on page 755.*

הָרַחֲמָן הוּא יַנְחִילֵנוּ יוֹם שֶׁכֻּלּוֹ שַׁבָּת וּמְנוּחָה לְחַיֵּי הָעוֹלָמִים.

בראש חודש: הָרַחֲמָן הוּא יְחַדֵּשׁ עָלֵינוּ אֶת הַחֹדֶשׁ הַזֶּה לְטוֹבָה וְלִבְרָכָה.

בסוכות: הָרַחֲמָן הוּא יָקִים לָנוּ אֶת סֻכַּת דָּוִד הַנּוֹפֶלֶת.

הָרַחֲמָן הוּא יְזַכֵּנוּ לִימוֹת הַמָּשִׁיחַ וּלְחַיֵּי הָעוֹלָם הַבָּא
מִגְדּוֹל יְשׁוּעוֹת מַלְכּוֹ — שמואל ב׳ כב
וְעֹשֶׂה־חֶסֶד לִמְשִׁיחוֹ, לְדָוִד וּלְזַרְעוֹ עַד־עוֹלָם:
עֹשֶׂה שָׁלוֹם בִּמְרוֹמָיו
הוּא יַעֲשֶׂה שָׁלוֹם עָלֵינוּ וְעַל כָּל יִשְׂרָאֵל, וְאִמְרוּ אָמֵן.

יְראוּ אֶת־יהוה קְדֹשָׁיו, כִּי־אֵין מַחְסוֹר לִירֵאָיו: — תהלים לד
כְּפִירִים רָשׁוּ וְרָעֵבוּ, וְדֹרְשֵׁי יהוה לֹא־יַחְסְרוּ כָל־טוֹב:
הוֹדוּ לַיהוה כִּי־טוֹב, כִּי לְעוֹלָם חַסְדּוֹ: — תהלים קיח
פּוֹתֵחַ אֶת־יָדֶךָ, וּמַשְׂבִּיעַ לְכָל־חַי רָצוֹן: — תהלים קמה
בָּרוּךְ הַגֶּבֶר אֲשֶׁר יִבְטַח בַּיהוה, וְהָיָה יהוה מִבְטַחוֹ: — ירמיה יז
נַעַר הָיִיתִי גַּם־זָקַנְתִּי, וְלֹא־רָאִיתִי צַדִּיק נֶעֱזָב וְזַרְעוֹ מְבַקֶּשׁ־לָחֶם: — תהלים לז
יהוה עֹז לְעַמּוֹ יִתֵּן, יהוה יְבָרֵךְ אֶת־עַמּוֹ בַשָּׁלוֹם: — תהלים כט

If ברכת המזון *was made on a cup of wine, then* בּוֹרֵא פְּרִי הַגָּפֶן *is said and the majority of the cup is drunk, after which* ברכה מעין שלוש*, on the next page, is said. If* סעודה שלישית *continues after* שקיעה*, then the* ברכה *is not said, and the cup of wine is saved for* הבדלה*.*

At שבע ברכות*, turn to page 777.*

ANI TEFILLA • אני תפילה

יְראוּ אֶת־יהוה קְדֹשָׁיו, כִּי־אֵין מַחְסוֹר לִירֵאָיו – *Fear the* Lord*, you His holy ones; those who fear Him lack nothing.* The blessing claims that those who fear or believe in Hashem are not lacking anything, yet we know that there are God-fearing people who are poor or who have needs. How might this seeming contradiction be reconciled?

יהוה עֹז לְעַמּוֹ יִתֵּן – *The* Lord *will give His people strength.* Rav Elimelekh of Lizhensk said: Most people exert all of their energy in the time of prayer, to direct their heart and to ward off foreign thoughts. But when they eat they make no effort or exertion, since they eat only for their own pleasure – so where is there a place for

BLESSING AFTER FOOD – AL HAMIḤYA

Grace after eating from the "seven species" of produce with which Israel is blessed: food made from the five grains (but not bread); wine or grape juice; grapes, figs, pomegranates, olives, or dates.

בָּרוּךְ Blessed are You, Lord our God, King of the Universe,

After grain products (but not bread or matza):	*After wine or grape juice:*	*After grapes, figs, olives, pomegranates or dates:*
for the nourishment and sustenance,	for the vine and the fruit of the vine,	for the tree and the fruit of the tree,

After grain products (but not bread or matza), and wine or grape juice:
for the nourishment and sustenance
and for the vine and the fruit of the vine,

and for the produce of the field; for the desirable, good and spacious land that You willingly gave as heritage to our ancestors, that they might eat of its fruit and be satisfied with its goodness. Have compassion, please, Lord our God, on Israel Your people, on Jerusalem, Your city, on Zion the home of Your glory, on Your altar and Your Temple. May You rebuild Jerusalem, the holy city swiftly in our time, and may You bring us back there, rejoicing in its rebuilding, eating from its fruit, satisfied by its goodness, and blessing You for it in holiness and purity. Be pleased to refresh us on this Sabbath Day.

On Rosh Ḥodesh: Remember us for good on this day of the New Moon.
On Pesaḥ: Grant us joy on this Festival of Matzot.
On Sukkot: Grant us joy on this Festival of Sukkot.

For You, God, are good and do good to all and we thank You for the land

---

was forsaken," that is, it is a call to us to not be passive when others are in need, just as Hashem has not stood by and let me go hungry.

ברכה מעין שלוש

Grace after eating from the "seven species" of produce with which Israel is blessed: food made from the five grains (but not bread); wine or grape juice; grapes, figs, pomegranates, olives, or dates.

בָּרוּךְ אַתָּה יהוה אֱלֹהֵינוּ מֶלֶךְ הָעוֹלָם, עַל

After grain products (but not bread or מצה):
הַמִּחְיָה וְעַל הַכַּלְכָּלָה

After wine or grape juice:
הַגֶּפֶן וְעַל פְּרִי הַגֶּפֶן

After grapes, figs, olives, pomegranates or dates:
הָעֵץ וְעַל פְּרִי הָעֵץ

After grain products (but not bread or מצה), and wine or grape juice:
הַמִּחְיָה וְעַל הַכַּלְכָּלָה וְעַל הַגֶּפֶן וְעַל פְּרִי הַגֶּפֶן

וְעַל תְּנוּבַת הַשָּׂדֶה וְעַל אֶרֶץ חֶמְדָּה טוֹבָה וּרְחָבָה, שֶׁרָצִיתָ וְהִנְחַלְתָּ לַאֲבוֹתֵינוּ לֶאֱכֹל מִפִּרְיָהּ וְלִשְׂבֹּעַ מִטּוּבָהּ. רַחֵם נָא יהוה אֱלֹהֵינוּ עַל יִשְׂרָאֵל עַמֶּךָ וְעַל יְרוּשָׁלַיִם עִירֶךָ וְעַל צִיּוֹן מִשְׁכַּן כְּבוֹדֶךָ וְעַל מִזְבְּחֶךָ וְעַל הֵיכָלֶךָ. וּבְנֵה יְרוּשָׁלַיִם עִיר הַקֹּדֶשׁ בִּמְהֵרָה בְיָמֵינוּ, וְהַעֲלֵנוּ לְתוֹכָהּ וְשַׂמְּחֵנוּ בְּבִנְיָנָהּ וְנֹאכַל מִפִּרְיָהּ וְנִשְׂבַּע מִטּוּבָהּ, וּנְבָרֶכְךָ עָלֶיהָ בִּקְדֻשָּׁה וּבְטָהֳרָה. וּרְצֵה וְהַחֲלִיצֵנוּ בְּיוֹם הַשַּׁבָּת הַזֶּה

בראש חודש: וְזָכְרֵנוּ לְטוֹבָה בְּיוֹם רֹאשׁ הַחֹדֶשׁ הַזֶּה

בפסח: וְשַׂמְּחֵנוּ בְּיוֹם חַג הַמַּצּוֹת הַזֶּה

בסוכות: וְשַׂמְּחֵנוּ בְּיוֹם חַג הַסֻּכּוֹת הַזֶּה

כִּי אַתָּה יהוה טוֹב וּמֵטִיב לַכֹּל, וְנוֹדֶה לְּךָ עַל הָאָרֶץ

---

the destruction of my people." If so, then the translation here would be "I have never stood by silently while a righteous man instead as "I watched in silence" drawing from a similar usage in Esther 8:6 – "For how could I stand by silently and watch

After grain products (but not bread or matza):	*After wine or grape juice:*	*After grapes, figs, olives, pomegranates or dates:*
and for the nourishment. Blessed are You, Lord, for the land and for the nourishment.	and for the fruit of the vine. Blessed are You, Lord, for the land and for the fruit of the vine.	and for the fruit. Blessed are You, Lord, for the land and for the fruit.

After grain products (but not bread or matza), and wine or grape juice:

and for the nourishment and for the fruit of the vine.
Blessed are You, Lord, for the land
and for the nourishment
and the fruit of the vine.

BLESSING AFTER FOOD – BOREH NEFASHOT

After food or drink that does not require Birkat HaMazon or Al HaMiḥya – such as meat, fish, dairy products, vegetables, beverages, or fruit other than grapes, figs, pomegranates, olives or dates – say:

בָּרוּךְ Blessed are You, Lord our God, King of the Universe,
who creates the many forms of life and their needs.
For all You have created
to sustain the life of all that lives,
blessed be He, Giver of life to the worlds.

---

of foods from which we derive pleasure, even if they are not staples. Alternatively, we thank Hashem even if we do not have those staples.

The second opinion, however, sees this as one long blessing whose theme is Hashem's provision of our needs. As such, a comma after וְחֶסְרוֹנָן is unnecessary.

In any event, one sees that for all the focus on the spiritual, Judaism acknowledges the importance of the physical. The need to eat is a basic drive, no different from any other animal on the planet. But rather than succumbing to our bestial instincts, Judaism constantly raises the act of eating to a spiritual activity.

Have you ever seen people eating in a way that is more animalistic than human? How might the recitation of this blessing help you maintain your humanity?

After grain products (but not bread or מצה):

וְעַל הַמִּחְיָה.
בָּרוּךְ אַתָּה יהוה עַל
הָאָרֶץ וְעַל הַמִּחְיָה.

After wine or grape juice:

וְעַל פְּרִי הַגָּפֶן.*
בָּרוּךְ אַתָּה יהוה עַל
הָאָרֶץ וְעַל פְּרִי הַגָּפֶן.*

After grapes, figs, olives, pomegranates or dates:

וְעַל הַפֵּרוֹת.**
בָּרוּךְ אַתָּה יהוה עַל
הָאָרֶץ וְעַל הַפֵּרוֹת.**

After grain products (but not bread or מצה), and wine or grape juice:

וְעַל הַמִּחְיָה וְעַל פְּרִי הַגָּפֶן.*
בָּרוּךְ אַתָּה יהוה, עַל הָאָרֶץ וְעַל הַמִּחְיָה וְעַל פְּרִי הַגָּפֶן.*

**If the wine is from ארץ ישראל, then substitute גַּפְנָהּ for הַגָּפֶן.*
***If the fruit is from ארץ ישראל, then substitute פֵּרוֹתֶיהָ for הַפֵּרוֹת.*

בורא נפשות

After food or drink that does not require מעין שלוש or ברכת המזון – such as meat, fish, dairy products, vegetables, beverages, or fruit other than grapes, figs, pomegranates, olives or dates – say:

בָּרוּךְ אַתָּה יהוה אֱלֹהֵינוּ מֶלֶךְ הָעוֹלָם
בּוֹרֵא נְפָשׁוֹת רַבּוֹת וְחֶסְרוֹנָן
עַל כָּל מַה שֶּׁבָּרָאתָ
לְהַחֲיוֹת בָּהֶם נֶפֶשׁ כָּל חָי.
בָּרוּךְ חֵי הָעוֹלָמִים.

BOREH NEFASHOT

There is a dispute among the Rishonim as to whether the text of the blessing is interpreted as having two themes or just one. According to the first opinion, there should be a comma after the word וְחֶסְרוֹנָן (needs). We thank Hashem for the fact that He created us (**בּוֹרֵא נְפָשׁוֹת**) and we acknowledge our deficiencies, that is, our need for bread and water, the staples that we need in order to survive. The second part of the blessing, referring to "all You have created," is therefore a reference to all other kinds

BRIT MILA

When the baby is brought in, all stand and say:

Blessed is he who comes.

The mohel (in some congregations, all) say (in Israel omit):

וַיְדַבֵּר The LORD spoke to Moses, saying: *Num. 25*
Pinehas the son of Elazar, the son of Aaron the priest,
turned back My rage from the children of Israel,
when he was zealous for Me among them,
and I did not annihilate the children of Israel in My own zeal.
And so tell him, that I now give him My covenant for peace.

The following verses, through "LORD, please, grant us success," are only said in Israel.

Mohel: Happy are those You choose and bring near to dwell in Your courts. *Ps. 65*

All: May we be sated with the goodness of Your House,
Your holy Temple.

The father takes the baby in his hands and says quietly:

אִם אֶשְׁכָּחֵךְ If I forget you, O Jerusalem, *Ps. 137*
may my right hand forget its skill.
May my tongue cling to the roof of my mouth,
if I do not remember you,
if I do not set Jerusalem above my highest joy.

The father says aloud, followed by the congregation:

Listen, Israel: the LORD is our God, the LORD is One. *Deut. 6*

The Mohel, followed by the congregation,
recites each of the following three phrases:

The LORD is King, the LORD was King,
the LORD shall be King for ever and all time.
LORD, please, save us. *Ps. 118*
LORD, please, grant us success.

The baby is placed on Eliyahu's seat, and the Mohel says:

This is the throne of Elijah the prophet,
may he be remembered for good.

סדר ברית מילה

When the baby is brought in, all stand and say:

בָּרוּךְ הַבָּא.

The מוהל *(in some congregations, all) say (in* ארץ ישראל *omit):*

וַיְדַבֵּר יהוה אֶל־מֹשֶׁה לֵּאמֹר: במדבר כה
פִּינְחָס בֶּן־אֶלְעָזָר בֶּן־אַהֲרֹן הַכֹּהֵן הֵשִׁיב אֶת־חֲמָתִי
מֵעַל בְּנֵי־יִשְׂרָאֵל, בְּקַנְאוֹ אֶת־קִנְאָתִי בְּתוֹכָם
וְלֹא־כִלִּיתִי אֶת־בְּנֵי־יִשְׂרָאֵל בְּקִנְאָתִי:
לָכֵן אֱמֹר, הִנְנִי נֹתֵן לוֹ אֶת־בְּרִיתִי שָׁלוֹם:

The following verses, through אָנָּא יהוה הַצְלִיחָה נָא *are only said in Israel.*

המוהל: אַשְׁרֵי תִּבְחַר וּתְקָרֵב, יִשְׁכֹּן חֲצֵרֶיךָ תהלים סה
הקהל: נִשְׂבְּעָה בְּטוּב בֵּיתֶךָ, קְדֹשׁ הֵיכָלֶךָ:

The father takes the baby in his hands and says quietly:

אִם־אֶשְׁכָּחֵךְ יְרוּשָׁלָֽםִ, תִּשְׁכַּח יְמִינִי: תהלים קלז
תִּדְבַּק לְשׁוֹנִי לְחִכִּי אִם־לֹא אֶזְכְּרֵכִי
אִם־לֹא אַעֲלֶה אֶת־יְרוּשָׁלַ͏ִם עַל רֹאשׁ שִׂמְחָתִי:

The father says aloud, followed by the קהל*:*

שְׁמַע יִשְׂרָאֵל, יהוה אֱלֹהֵינוּ, יהוה אֶחָד: דברים ו

The מוהל*, followed by the* קהל*, repeats each of the following three phrases:*

יהוה מֶלֶךְ, יהוה מָלָךְ, יהוה יִמְלֹךְ לְעוֹלָם וָעֶד.
אָנָּא יהוה הוֹשִׁיעָה נָּא תהלים קיח
אָנָּא יהוה הַצְלִיחָה נָא:

The baby is placed on the כסא של אליהו*, and the* מוהל *says:*

זֶה הַכִּסֵּא שֶׁל אֵלִיָּהוּ הַנָּבִיא זָכוּר לַטּוֹב.

The Mohel continues:

לִישׁוּעָתְךָ For Your salvation I wait, O LORD. *Gen. 49*
I await Your deliverance, LORD, *Ps. 119*
and I observe Your commandments.
Elijah, angel of the covenant, behold:
yours is before you.
Stand at my right hand and be close to me.
I await Your deliverance, LORD. *Ps. 119*
I rejoice in Your word like one who finds much spoil.
Those who love Your Torah have great peace,
and there is no stumbling block before them.
Happy are those You choose and bring near *Ps. 65*
to dwell in Your courts.

All respond:

May we be sated with the goodness
of Your House, Your holy Temple.

The baby is placed on the knees of the Sandak, and the Mohel says:

בָּרוּךְ Blessed are You, LORD our God, King of the Universe,
who has made us holy through His commandments,
and has commanded us concerning circumcision.

Immediately after the circumcision, the father says:

בָּרוּךְ Blessed are You, LORD our God, King of the Universe,
who has made us holy through His commandments,
and has commanded us to bring him [our son]
into the covenant of Abraham, our father.

In Israel the father adds (some outside Israel add it as well):

בָּרוּךְ Blessed are You, LORD our God, King of the Universe,
who has given us life, sustained us, and brought us to this time.

All respond:

אָמֵן Amen. Just as he has entered into the covenant,
so may he enter into Torah, marriage and good deeds.

The מוהל *continues:*

לִישׁוּעָתְךָ קִוִּיתִי יהוה: בראשית מט

שִׂבַּרְתִּי לִישׁוּעָתְךָ יהוה, וּמִצְוֹתֶיךָ עָשִׂיתִי: תהלים קיט

אֵלִיָּהוּ מַלְאַךְ הַבְּרִית, הִנֵּה שֶׁלְּךָ לְפָנֶיךָ, עֲמֹד עַל יְמִינִי וְסָמְכֵנִי.

שִׂבַּרְתִּי לִישׁוּעָתְךָ יהוה: תהלים קיט

שָׂשׂ אָנֹכִי עַל־אִמְרָתֶךָ, כְּמוֹצֵא שָׁלָל רָב:

שָׁלוֹם רָב לְאֹהֲבֵי תוֹרָתֶךָ, וְאֵין־לָמוֹ מִכְשׁוֹל:

אַשְׁרֵי תִּבְחַר וּתְקָרֵב, יִשְׁכֹּן חֲצֵרֶיךָ תהלים סה

All respond:

נִשְׂבְּעָה בְּטוּב בֵּיתֶךָ, קְדֹשׁ הֵיכָלֶךָ:

The baby is placed on the knees of the סנדק*, and the* מוהל *says:*

בָּרוּךְ אַתָּה יהוה אֱלֹהֵינוּ מֶלֶךְ הָעוֹלָם
אֲשֶׁר קִדְּשָׁנוּ בְּמִצְוֹתָיו וְצִוָּנוּ עַל הַמִּילָה.

Immediately after the circumcision, the father says:

בָּרוּךְ אַתָּה יהוה אֱלֹהֵינוּ מֶלֶךְ הָעוֹלָם
אֲשֶׁר קִדְּשָׁנוּ בְּמִצְוֹתָיו וְצִוָּנוּ
לְהַכְנִיסוֹ בִּבְרִיתוֹ שֶׁל אַבְרָהָם אָבִינוּ.

In ארץ ישראל *the father adds (some in* חוץ לארץ *add it as well):*

בָּרוּךְ אַתָּה יהוה אֱלֹהֵינוּ מֶלֶךְ הָעוֹלָם
שֶׁהֶחֱיָנוּ וְקִיְּמָנוּ וְהִגִּיעָנוּ לַזְּמַן הַזֶּה.

All respond:

אָמֵן. כְּשֵׁם שֶׁנִּכְנַס לַבְּרִית
כֵּן יִכָּנֵס לְתוֹרָה וּלְחֻפָּה וּלְמַעֲשִׂים טוֹבִים.

After the circumcision has been completed, the Mohel (or another honoree) takes a cup of wine and says:

בָּרוּךְ Blessed are You, LORD our God, King of the Universe, who creates the fruit of the vine.

בָּרוּךְ Blessed are You, LORD our God, King of the Universe, who made the beloved one [Isaac] holy from the womb, marked the decree of circumcision in his flesh, and gave his descendants the seal and sign of the holy covenant. As a reward for this, the Living God, our Portion, our Rock, did order deliverance from destruction for the beloved of our flesh, for the sake of His covenant that He set in our flesh. Blessed are You, LORD, who establishes the covenant.

אֱלֹהֵינוּ Our God and God of our fathers, preserve this child to his father and mother, and let his name be called in Israel (*baby's name* son of *father's name*). May the father rejoice in the issue of his body, and the
mother be glad with the fruit of her womb, as is written, "May your *Prov. 23*
father and mother rejoice, and she who bore you be glad." And it is said,
"Then I passed by you and saw you downtrodden in your blood, and I *Ezek. 16*
said to you: In your blood, live; and I said to you: In your blood, live."

וְנֶאֱמַר And it is said, "He remembered His covenant for ever; the *Ps. 105*
word He ordained for a thousand generations; the covenant He made with Abraham and gave on oath to Isaac, confirming it as a statute for Jacob, an everlasting covenant for Israel." And it is said, "And Abraham
circumcised his son Isaac at the age of eight days, as God had com- *Gen. 21*
manded him." Thank the LORD for He is good; His loving-kindness *Ps. 118*
is for ever.

All respond:

Thank the LORD for He is good; His loving-kindness is for ever.

The Mohel (or honoree) continues:

May this child (*baby's name* son of *father's name*) become great. Just as he has entered into the covenant, so may he enter into Torah, marriage and good deeds.

The Sandak also drinks some of the wine; some drops are given to the baby. The cup is then sent to the mother, who also drinks from it.

All say Aleinu on page 452, and Mourner's Kaddish on page 454.

After the circumcision has been completed, the מוהל *(or another honoree) takes a cup of wine and says:*

בָּרוּךְ אַתָּה יהוה אֱלֹהֵינוּ מֶלֶךְ הָעוֹלָם, בּוֹרֵא פְּרִי הַגָּפֶן.

בָּרוּךְ אַתָּה יהוה אֱלֹהֵינוּ מֶלֶךְ הָעוֹלָם, אֲשֶׁר קִדֵּשׁ יְדִיד מִבֶּטֶן, וְחֹק בִּשְׁאֵרוֹ שָׂם, וְצֶאֱצָאָיו חָתַם בְּאוֹת בְּרִית קֹדֶשׁ. עַל כֵּן בִּשְׂכַר זֹאת, אֵל חַי חֶלְקֵנוּ צוּרֵנוּ צַוֵּה לְהַצִּיל יְדִידוּת שְׁאֵרֵנוּ מִשַּׁחַת, לְמַעַן בְּרִיתוֹ אֲשֶׁר שָׂם בִּבְשָׂרֵנוּ. בָּרוּךְ אַתָּה יהוה, כּוֹרֵת הַבְּרִית.

אֱלֹהֵינוּ וֵאלֹהֵי אֲבוֹתֵינוּ, קַיֵּם אֶת הַיֶּלֶד הַזֶּה לְאָבִיו וּלְאִמּוֹ, וְיִקָּרֵא שְׁמוֹ בְּיִשְׂרָאֵל (פלוני בֶּן פלוני). יִשְׂמַח הָאָב בְּיוֹצֵא חֲלָצָיו וְתָגֵל אִמּוֹ בִּפְרִי בִטְנָהּ, כַּכָּתוּב: יִשְׂמַח־אָבִיךָ וְאִמֶּךָ, וְתָגֵל יוֹלַדְתֶּךָ: משלי כג
וְנֶאֱמַר: וָאֶעֱבֹר עָלַיִךְ וָאֶרְאֵךְ מִתְבּוֹסֶסֶת בְּדָמָיִךְ, וָאֹמַר לָךְ בְּדָמַיִךְ חֲיִי, וָאֹמַר לָךְ בְּדָמַיִךְ חֲיִי: יחזקאל טז

וְנֶאֱמַר: זָכַר לְעוֹלָם בְּרִיתוֹ, דָּבָר צִוָּה לְאֶלֶף דּוֹר: אֲשֶׁר כָּרַת אֶת־אַבְרָהָם, וּשְׁבוּעָתוֹ לְיִשְׂחָק: וַיַּעֲמִידֶהָ לְיַעֲקֹב לְחֹק, לְיִשְׂרָאֵל בְּרִית עוֹלָם: תהלים קה
וְנֶאֱמַר: וַיָּמָל אַבְרָהָם אֶת־יִצְחָק בְּנוֹ בֶּן־שְׁמֹנַת יָמִים, כַּאֲשֶׁר צִוָּה אֹתוֹ אֱלֹהִים: בראשית כא
הוֹדוּ לַיהוה כִּי־טוֹב, כִּי לְעוֹלָם חַסְדּוֹ: תהלים קיח

All respond:

הוֹדוּ לַיהוה כִּי־טוֹב, כִּי לְעוֹלָם חַסְדּוֹ:

The מוהל *(or honoree) continues:*

(פלוני בֶּן פלוני) זֶה הַקָּטָן גָּדוֹל יִהְיֶה, כְּשֵׁם שֶׁנִּכְנַס לַבְּרִית, כֵּן יִכָּנֵס לְתוֹרָה וּלְחֻפָּה וּלְמַעֲשִׂים טוֹבִים.

The סנדק *also drinks some of the wine; some drops are given to the baby. The cup is then sent to the mother, who also drinks from it.*

All say עָלֵינוּ *on page 453, and* קדיש יתום *on page 455.*

BIRKAT HAMAZON AT A BRIT MILA

Leader Gentlemen, let us say grace.

Others May the name of the LORD be blessed
from now and for ever. *Ps. 113*

Leader May the name of the LORD be blessed
from now and for ever.

Leader then others We give thanks to Your name among the faithful.
Blessed are you to the LORD.

Leader With permission of the Almighty, awesome and revered,
a refuge in times of trouble,
Almighty, girded with strength –
majestic on high, the LORD.

Others We give thanks to Your name among the faithful.
Blessed are you to the LORD.

Leader With permission of the holy Torah,
pure and clear,
given to us as a heritage
by Moses the servant of the LORD.

Others We give thanks to Your name among the faithful.
Blessed are you to the LORD.

Leader With permission of the priests, the Levites,
I call upon the God of the Hebrews,
declaring His glory to the furthest isles,
and offering blessings to the LORD.

Others We give thanks to Your name among the faithful.
Blessed are you to the LORD.

ברכת המזון לברית מילה

Leader רַבּוֹתַי, נְבָרֵךְ.

Others יְהִי שֵׁם יהוה מְבֹרָךְ מֵעַתָּה וְעַד־עוֹלָם: תהלים קיג

Leader יְהִי שֵׁם יהוה מְבֹרָךְ מֵעַתָּה וְעַד־עוֹלָם:

Leader then others נוֹדֶה לְשִׁמְךָ בְּתוֹךְ אֱמוּנַי, בְּרוּכִים אַתֶּם לַיהוה.

Leader בִּרְשׁוּת אֵל אָיֹם וְנוֹרָא
מִשְׂגָּב לְעִתּוֹת בַּצָּרָה
אֵל נֶאְזָר בִּגְבוּרָה
אַדִּיר בַּמָּרוֹם יהוה.

Others נוֹדֶה לְשִׁמְךָ בְּתוֹךְ אֱמוּנַי, בְּרוּכִים אַתֶּם לַיהוה.

Leader בִּרְשׁוּת הַתּוֹרָה הַקְּדוֹשָׁה
טְהוֹרָה הִיא וְגַם פְּרוּשָׁה
צִוָּה לָנוּ מוֹרָשָׁה
מֹשֶׁה עֶבֶד יהוה.

Others נוֹדֶה לְשִׁמְךָ בְּתוֹךְ אֱמוּנַי, בְּרוּכִים אַתֶּם לַיהוה.

Leader בִּרְשׁוּת הַכֹּהֲנִים וְהַלְוִיִּם
אֶקְרָא לֵאלֹהֵי הָעִבְרִיִּים
אֲהוֹדֶנּוּ בְּכָל אִיִּים
אֲבָרְכָה אֶת יהוה.

Others נוֹדֶה לְשִׁמְךָ בְּתוֹךְ אֱמוּנַי, בְּרוּכִים אַתֶּם לַיהוה.

Leader With the permission of the rabbis, teachers and friends,
I open my lips with song,
saying from my innermost being:
"Blessed is he that comes in the name of the LORD."

Others We give thanks to Your name among the faithful.
Blessed are you to the LORD.

Leader With your permission, my masters and teachers,
let us bless (*in a minyan:* our God,) the One
from whose food we have eaten.

Others Blessed be (*in a minyan:* our God,) the One
from whose food we have eaten,
and by whose goodness we live.

Leader Blessed be (*in a minyan:* our God,) the One
from whose food we have eaten,
and by whose goodness we live.
Blessed be He, and blessed be His name.

Continue with Birkat HaMazon on page 738
until "in the eyes of God and man" on page 750. Then continue:

Someone other than the father says:

הָרַחֲמָן May the Compassionate One
bless the father and mother of this child.
May they be worthy to raise him,
educate him, and train him in wisdom.
From this eighth day onward
may his blood be accepted,
and may the LORD his God be with him always.

Someone other than the Sandak says:

הָרַחֲמָן May the Compassionate One bless him [the Sandak]
who assisted in the covenant of circumcision
and rejoiced to do this pious deed.
May God doubly reward him for his deed,
exalting him ever higher.

Leader בִּרְשׁוּת מָרָנָן וְרַבָּנָן וְרַבּוֹתַי

אֶפְתְּחָה בְּשִׁיר פִּי וּשְׂפָתַי

וְתֹאמַרְנָה עַצְמוֹתַי

בָּרוּךְ הַבָּא בְּשֵׁם יהוה.

Others נוֹדֶה לְשִׁמְךָ בְּתוֹךְ אֱמוּנַי, בְּרוּכִים אַתֶּם לַיהוה.

Leader בִּרְשׁוּת מָרָנָן וְרַבָּנָן וְרַבּוֹתַי

נְבָרֵךְ (במנין: אֱלֹהֵינוּ) שֶׁאָכַלְנוּ מִשֶּׁלּוֹ.

Others בָּרוּךְ (במנין: אֱלֹהֵינוּ) שֶׁאָכַלְנוּ מִשֶּׁלּוֹ וּבְטוּבוֹ חָיִינוּ.

Leader בָּרוּךְ (במנין: אֱלֹהֵינוּ) שֶׁאָכַלְנוּ מִשֶּׁלּוֹ וּבְטוּבוֹ חָיִינוּ.

בָּרוּךְ הוּא וּבָרוּךְ שְׁמוֹ.

Continue with ברכת המזון *on page 739 until* בְּעֵינֵי אֱלֹהִים וְאָדָם *on page 751. Then continue:*

Someone other than the father says:

הָרַחֲמָן הוּא יְבָרֵךְ אֲבִי הַיֶּלֶד וְאִמּוֹ

וְיִזְכּוּ לְגַדְּלוֹ וּלְחַנְּכוֹ וּלְחַכְּמוֹ

מִיּוֹם הַשְּׁמִינִי וָהָלְאָה יֵרָצֶה דָמוֹ

וִיהִי יהוה אֱלֹהָיו עִמּוֹ.

Someone other than the סנדק *says:*

הָרַחֲמָן הוּא יְבָרֵךְ בַּעַל בְּרִית הַמִּילָה

אֲשֶׁר שָׂשׂ לַעֲשׂוֹת צֶדֶק בְּגִילָה

וִישַׁלֵּם פָּעֳלוֹ וּמַשְׂכֻּרְתּוֹ כְּפוּלָה

וְיִתְּנֵהוּ לְמַעְלָה לְמָעְלָה.

הָרַחֲמָן May the Compassionate One
bless the tender child, circumcised on his eighth day.
May his heart and hands be firm with God,
and may he be worthy to witness the Divine Presence
three times a year.

Someone other than the Mohel says:

הָרַחֲמָן May the Compassionate One
bless him who performed the circumcision,
and fulfilled every part of the precept.
The service of the faint-hearted
would not be acceptable
if he failed to perform the three essentials
of the precept.

הָרַחֲמָן May the Compassionate One
send us His anointed, blameless in life,
through the merit of this child
groomed by the blood of circumcision,
to proclaim good news and consolations
to the unique people scattered
and dispersed among the nations.

הָרַחֲמָן May the Compassionate One
send us the righteous priest, who was taken into hiding,
until a throne, bright as the sun, radiant as a diamond,
is prepared for him;
the prophet who covered his face with his mantle
and wrapped himself in it [when God declared]:
My covenant is with him for life and peace.

Continue with "May the Compassionate One let us inherit" on page 752.

הָרַחֲמָן הוּא יְבָרֵךְ רַךְ הַנִּמּוֹל לִשְׁמוֹנָה
וְיִהְיוּ יָדָיו וְלִבּוֹ לָאֵל אֱמוּנָה
וְיִזְכֶּה לִרְאוֹת פְּנֵי הַשְּׁכִינָה
שָׁלֹשׁ פְּעָמִים בַּשָּׁנָה.

Someone other than the מוהל *says:*

הָרַחֲמָן הוּא יְבָרֵךְ הַמָּל בְּשַׂר הָעָרְלָה
וּפָרַע וּמָצַץ דְּמֵי הַמִּילָה
אִישׁ הַיָּרֵא וְרַךְ הַלֵּבָב עֲבוֹדָתוֹ פְּסוּלָה
אִם שְׁלָשׁ אֵלֶּה לֹא יַעֲשֶׂה לָהּ.

הָרַחֲמָן הוּא יִשְׁלַח לָנוּ מְשִׁיחוֹ הוֹלֵךְ תָּמִים
בִּזְכוּת חֲתַן לַמּוּלוֹת דָּמִים
לְבַשֵּׂר בְּשׂוֹרוֹת טוֹבוֹת וְנִחוּמִים
לְעַם אֶחָד מְפֻזָּר וּמְפֹרָד בֵּין הָעַמִּים.

הָרַחֲמָן הוּא יִשְׁלַח לָנוּ כֹּהֵן צֶדֶק אֲשֶׁר לֻקַּח לְעֵילוֹם
עַד הוּכַן כִּסְאוֹ כַּשֶּׁמֶשׁ וְיַהֲלֹם
וַיָּלֶט פָּנָיו בְּאַדַּרְתּוֹ וַיִּגְלֹם
בְּרִיתִי הָיְתָה אִתּוֹ הַחַיִּים וְהַשָּׁלוֹם.

Continue with הָרַחֲמָן הוּא יַנְחִילֵנוּ *on page 753.*

THANKSGIVING PRAYER AFTER CHILDBIRTH

On entering the synagogue, say:

וַאֲנִי As for me, by Your great love, *Ps. 5*
I will come into Your House.
I will bow down toward Your holy Temple in awe of You.

אָהַבְתִּי I love the Lord, for He hears my voice, my pleas. *Ps. 116*
He turns His ear to me whenever I call.
The bonds of death encompassed me,
the anguish of the grave came upon me,
I was overcome by trouble and sorrow.
Then I called on the name of the Lord:
"Lord, I pray, save my life."
Gracious is the Lord, and righteous;
our God is full of compassion.
The Lord protects the simple hearted.
When I was brought low, He saved me.
My soul, be at peace once more,
for the Lord has been good to you.
For You have rescued me from death,
my eyes from weeping, my feet from stumbling.
I shall walk in the presence of the Lord
in the land of the living.
I had faith, even when I said,
"I am greatly afflicted,"
even when I said rashly,
"All men are liars."

מָה־אָשִׁיב How can I repay the Lord for all His goodness to me? *Ps. 116*
To You I shall bring a thanksgiving-offering
and call on the Lord by name.
I will fulfill my vows to the Lord in the presence of all His people,
in the courts of the House of the Lord,
in your midst, Jerusalem. Halleluya!

סדר תפילה ליולדת

On entering the בית כנסת*, say:*

וַאֲנִי בְּרֹב חַסְדְּךָ אָבוֹא בֵיתֶךָ תהלים ה
אֶשְׁתַּחֲוֶה אֶל־הֵיכַל־קָדְשְׁךָ בְּיִרְאָתֶךָ:

אָהַבְתִּי, כִּי־יִשְׁמַע יהוה, אֶת־קוֹלִי תַּחֲנוּנָי: תהלים קטז
כִּי־הִטָּה אָזְנוֹ לִי, וּבְיָמַי אֶקְרָא:
אֲפָפוּנִי חֶבְלֵי־מָוֶת
וּמְצָרֵי שְׁאוֹל מְצָאוּנִי
צָרָה וְיָגוֹן אֶמְצָא:
וּבְשֵׁם־יהוה אֶקְרָא, אָנָּה יהוה מַלְּטָה נַפְשִׁי:
חַנּוּן יהוה וְצַדִּיק, וֵאלֹהֵינוּ מְרַחֵם:
שֹׁמֵר פְּתָאיִם יהוה, דַּלּוֹתִי וְלִי יְהוֹשִׁיעַ:
שׁוּבִי נַפְשִׁי לִמְנוּחָיְכִי, כִּי־יהוה גָּמַל עָלָיְכִי:
כִּי חִלַּצְתָּ נַפְשִׁי מִמָּוֶת
אֶת־עֵינִי מִן־דִּמְעָה
אֶת־רַגְלִי מִדֶּחִי:
אֶתְהַלֵּךְ לִפְנֵי יהוה, בְּאַרְצוֹת הַחַיִּים:
הֶאֱמַנְתִּי כִּי אֲדַבֵּר, אֲנִי עָנִיתִי מְאֹד:
אֲנִי אָמַרְתִּי בְחָפְזִי, כָּל־הָאָדָם כֹּזֵב:

מָה־אָשִׁיב לַיהוה, כָּל־תַּגְמוּלוֹהִי עָלָי: תהלים קטז
לְךָ־אֶזְבַּח זֶבַח תּוֹדָה, וּבְשֵׁם יהוה אֶקְרָא:
נְדָרַי לַיהוה אֲשַׁלֵּם, נֶגְדָה־נָּא לְכָל־עַמּוֹ:
בְּחַצְרוֹת בֵּית יהוה, בְּתוֹכֵכִי יְרוּשָׁלָםִ, הַלְלוּיָהּ:

The mother says:

בָּרוּךְ Blessed are You, Lord our God, King of the Universe,
who bestows good things on the unworthy,
who has bestowed on me much good.

All respond:

אָמֵן Amen. May He who bestowed much good on you,
continue to bestow on you much good. Selah.

אָנָּא O great, mighty and revered God. By Your great love I now come into Your House, to offer You a thanksgiving-offering for all the good You have bestowed on me. Travail beset me, pains seized me. In my distress I cried to You, and from Your habitation You heard my voice and helped me. You healed all my sickness, and crowned me with kindness and compassion. Until now Your mercy has helped me. I pray to You, God, never forsake me. Bestow Your blessing upon Your handmaid. Strengthen and support me together with my husband, that we may raise

For a boy:

הַיֶּלֶד the boy that has been born to us, to revere You and serve You in truth, and to walk in the path of righteousness. Protect our tender child in all his ways. Favor him with knowledge, understanding and discernment, and let his portion be in Your Torah, so that he may sanctify Your great name, and become a comfort to us as we grow old. As for me, may my prayer come to You, Lord, at a time of favor. *Ps. 69*
O God, in Your great love, answer me with Your faithful salvation.

For a girl:

הַיַּלְדָּה the girl that has been born to us, to revere You and serve You in truth, and to walk in the path of righteousness. Protect our tender child in all her ways. Favor her with knowledge, understanding and discernment, and let her portion be in Your Torah, so that she may sanctify Your great name, and become a comfort to us as we grow old. As for me, may my prayer come to You, Lord, at a time of favor. *Ps. 69*
O God, in Your great love, answer me with Your faithful salvation.

If the baby is brought to the synagogue, the Rabbi says the following blessings over him/her:

יְבָרֶכְךָ May the Lord bless you and protect you. *Num. 6*
May the Lord make His face shine on you and be gracious to you.
May the Lord turn His face toward you and grant you peace.

The mother says:

בָּרוּךְ אַתָּה יהוה אֱלֹהֵינוּ מֶלֶךְ הָעוֹלָם
הַגּוֹמֵל לְחַיָּבִים טוֹבוֹת, שֶׁגְּמָלַנִי כָּל טוֹב.

All respond:

אָמֵן. מִי שֶׁגְּמָלֵךְ כָּל טוֹב, הוּא יִגְמָלֵךְ כָּל טוֹב, סֶלָה.

אָנָּא הָאֵל הַגָּדוֹל הַגִּבּוֹר וְהַנּוֹרָא, בְּרֹב חַסְדְּךָ אָבוֹא בֵיתֶךָ, לִזְבֹּחַ לְךָ זֶבַח תּוֹדָה עַל כָּל הַטּוֹבוֹת אֲשֶׁר גָּמַלְתָּ עָלָי. אֲפָפוּנִי חֲבָלִים וְצִירִים אֲחָזוּנִי, בַּצַּר לִי קָרָאתִי אֵלֶיךָ, וְשָׁמַעְתָּ מֵהֵיכָלְךָ קוֹלִי וְהָיִיתָ בְּעֶזְרִי, וְרִפֵּאתָ לְכָל תַּחֲלוּאַי, עִטַּרְתַּנִי חֶסֶד וְרַחֲמִים, עַד הֵנָּה עֲזָרוּנִי רַחֲמֶיךָ, אָנָּא אַל תִּטְּשֵׁנִי לָנֶצַח. הוֹאֵל אֱלוֹהַּ, וּבָרֵךְ אֶת אֲמָתֶךָ, חַזְּקֵנִי וְאַמְּצֵנִי, אוֹתִי וְאֶת בַּעְלִי, וּנְגַדֵּל אֶת

For a boy:

הַיֶּלֶד אֲשֶׁר יֻלַּד לָנוּ, לְיִרְאָתֶךָ וּלְעָבְדְךָ בֶּאֱמֶת, וְלָלֶכֶת אֹרַח מֵישָׁרִים. שְׁמֹר אֶת הַיֶּלֶד הָרַךְ בְּכָל דְּרָכָיו, חָנֵּהוּ דֵּעָה בִּינָה וְהַשְׂכֵּל, וְתֵן חֶלְקוֹ בְּתוֹרָתֶךָ, וִיקַדֵּשׁ אֶת שִׁמְךָ הַגָּדוֹל, וְהָיָה לָנוּ לְמֵשִׁיב נֶפֶשׁ בִּימֵי שֵׂיבָתֵנוּ. וַאֲנִי תְפִלָּתִי־לְךָ יהוה עֵת רָצוֹן, תהלים סט
אֱלֹהִים בְּרָב־חַסְדֶּךָ, עֲנֵנִי בֶּאֱמֶת יִשְׁעֶךָ:

For a girl:

הַיַּלְדָּה אֲשֶׁר יֻלְּדָה לָנוּ, לְיִרְאָתֶךָ וּלְעָבְדְךָ בֶּאֱמֶת, וְלָלֶכֶת אֹרַח מֵישָׁרִים. שְׁמֹר אֶת הַיַּלְדָּה הָרַכָּה בְּכָל דְּרָכֶיהָ, חָנֶּהָ דֵּעָה בִּינָה וְהַשְׂכֵּל, וְתֵן חֶלְקָהּ בְּתוֹרָתֶךָ, וּתְקַדֵּשׁ אֶת שִׁמְךָ הַגָּדוֹל, וְהָיְתָה לָנוּ לְמְשִׁיבַת נֶפֶשׁ בִּימֵי שֵׂיבָתֵנוּ. וַאֲנִי תְפִלָּתִי־לְךָ יהוה עֵת רָצוֹן, תהלים סט
אֱלֹהִים בְּרָב־חַסְדֶּךָ, עֲנֵנִי בֶּאֱמֶת יִשְׁעֶךָ:

If the baby is brought to the בית כנסת*, the Rabbi says the following blessings over him/her:*

יְבָרֶכְךָ יהוה וְיִשְׁמְרֶךָ: יָאֵר יהוה פָּנָיו אֵלֶיךָ וִיחֻנֶּךָּ: במדבר ו
יִשָּׂא יהוה פָּנָיו אֵלֶיךָ, וְיָשֵׂם לְךָ שָׁלוֹם:

ZIMMUN FOR SHEVA BERAKHOT FEAST

The leader takes a cup of wine in his hand and says:

Leader Gentlemen, let us say grace.

Others May the name of the Lord be blessed from now and for ever. *Ps. 113*

Leader May the name of the Lord be blessed from now and for ever.

Banish grief and anger.
Let even the mute celebrate in song.
Guide us in the paths of righteousness.
Hear the blessing of the children of Aaron.

Add the appropriate words in parentheses:

With your permission,
(my father and teacher / my mother and teacher /
the Kohanim present / our teacher the Rabbi /
the master of this house / the mistress of this house)
my masters and teachers,
let us bless our God, in whose dwelling place is joy,
from whose food we have eaten.

Others Blessed be our God in whose dwelling place is joy,
from whose food we have eaten,
and by whose goodness we live.

Leader Blessed be our God in whose dwelling place is joy,
from whose food we have eaten,
and by whose goodness we live.

Blessed be He, and blessed be His name.

Continue with Birkat HaMazon on page 738, at the end of which say the Sheva Berakhot on the next page over a cup of wine.

זימון לסעודת שבע ברכות

The leader takes a cup of wine in his hand and says:

Leader רַבּוֹתַי, נְבָרֵךְ.

Others יְהִי שֵׁם יהוה מְבֹרָךְ מֵעַתָּה וְעַד־עוֹלָם: תהלים קיג

Leader יְהִי שֵׁם יהוה מְבֹרָךְ מֵעַתָּה וְעַד־עוֹלָם:

דְּוַי הָסֵר וְגַם חָרוֹן
וְאָז אִלֵּם בְּשִׁיר יָרֹן.
נְחֵנוּ בְּמַעְגְּלֵי צֶדֶק
שְׁעֵה בִּרְכַּת בְּנֵי אַהֲרֹן.

Add the appropriate words in parentheses:

בִּרְשׁוּת (אָבִי מוֹרִי / אִמִּי מוֹרָתִי / כֹּהֲנִים / מוֹרֵנוּ הָרַב /
בַּעַל הַבַּיִת הַזֶּה / בַּעֲלַת הַבַּיִת הַזֶּה)
מָרָנָן וְרַבָּנָן וְרַבּוֹתַי
נְבָרֵךְ אֱלֹהֵינוּ שֶׁהַשִּׂמְחָה בִּמְעוֹנוֹ וְשֶׁאָכַלְנוּ מִשֶּׁלּוֹ.

Others בָּרוּךְ אֱלֹהֵינוּ שֶׁהַשִּׂמְחָה בִּמְעוֹנוֹ
שֶׁאָכַלְנוּ מִשֶּׁלּוֹ וּבְטוּבוֹ חָיִינוּ.

Leader בָּרוּךְ אֱלֹהֵינוּ שֶׁהַשִּׂמְחָה בִּמְעוֹנוֹ
שֶׁאָכַלְנוּ מִשֶּׁלּוֹ וּבְטוּבוֹ חָיִינוּ.

בָּרוּךְ הוּא וּבָרוּךְ שְׁמוֹ.

Continue with ברכת המזון *on page 739, at the end of which say the* שבע ברכות *on the next page over a cup of wine.*

THE SEVEN BLESSINGS OF MARRIAGE

בָּרוּךְ Blessed are You, LORD our God, King of the Universe,
who has created all for His glory.

בָּרוּךְ Blessed are You, LORD our God, King of the Universe,
Creator of mankind.

בָּרוּךְ Blessed are You, LORD our God, King of the Universe,
who made humanity in His image, the image of His likeness,
and out of His very self formed a building for eternity.
Blessed are You, LORD,
Creator of mankind.

שׂוֹשׂ Bring great happiness and joy to one who was barren [Zion],
as her children return to her in joy.
Blessed are You, LORD,
who gladdens Zion through her children.

שַׂמֵּחַ Bring great joy to these loving friends,
as You gave joy to Your creations in the Garden of Eden.
Blessed are You, LORD,
who gives joy to the bridegroom and bride.

בָּרוּךְ Blessed are You, LORD our God, King of the Universe,
who created joy and gladness, bridegroom and bride,
happiness and jubilation, cheer and delight,
love, fellowship, peace and friendship.
Soon, LORD our God, may there be heard in the cities of Judah,
and in the streets of Jerusalem, the sounds of joy and gladness,
the sounds of the bridegroom and bride,
the joyous sounds of bridegrooms from their wedding canopy
and of young people at their feasts of song.
Blessed are You, LORD,
who makes the bridegroom rejoice with the bride.

בָּרוּךְ Blessed are You, LORD our God, King of the Universe,
who creates the fruit of the vine.

שבע ברכות הנשואין

בָּרוּךְ אַתָּה יהוה אֱלֹהֵינוּ מֶלֶךְ הָעוֹלָם
שֶׁהַכֹּל בָּרָא לִכְבוֹדוֹ.

בָּרוּךְ אַתָּה יהוה אֱלֹהֵינוּ מֶלֶךְ הָעוֹלָם
יוֹצֵר הָאָדָם.

בָּרוּךְ אַתָּה יהוה אֱלֹהֵינוּ מֶלֶךְ הָעוֹלָם
אֲשֶׁר יָצַר אֶת הָאָדָם בְּצַלְמוֹ, בְּצֶלֶם דְּמוּת תַּבְנִיתוֹ
וְהִתְקִין לוֹ מִמֶּנּוּ בִּנְיַן עֲדֵי עַד.
בָּרוּךְ אַתָּה יהוה, יוֹצֵר הָאָדָם.

שׂוֹשׂ תָּשִׂישׂ וְתָגֵל הָעֲקָרָה בְּקִבּוּץ בָּנֶיהָ לְתוֹכָהּ בְּשִׂמְחָה.
בָּרוּךְ אַתָּה יהוה, מְשַׂמֵּחַ צִיּוֹן בְּבָנֶיהָ.

שַׂמֵּחַ תְּשַׂמַּח רֵעִים הָאֲהוּבִים כְּשַׂמֵּחֲךָ יְצִירְךָ בְּגַן עֵדֶן מִקֶּדֶם.
בָּרוּךְ אַתָּה יהוה, מְשַׂמֵּחַ חָתָן וְכַלָּה.

בָּרוּךְ אַתָּה יהוה אֱלֹהֵינוּ מֶלֶךְ הָעוֹלָם
אֲשֶׁר בָּרָא שָׂשׂוֹן וְשִׂמְחָה, חָתָן וְכַלָּה
גִּילָה, רִנָּה, דִּיצָה וְחֶדְוָה, אַהֲבָה וְאַחֲוָה וְשָׁלוֹם וְרֵעוּת.
מְהֵרָה יהוה אֱלֹהֵינוּ
יִשָּׁמַע בְּעָרֵי יְהוּדָה וּבְחוּצוֹת יְרוּשָׁלָיִם
קוֹל שָׂשׂוֹן וְקוֹל שִׂמְחָה, קוֹל חָתָן וְקוֹל כַּלָּה
קוֹל מִצְהֲלוֹת חֲתָנִים מֵחֻפָּתָם וּנְעָרִים מִמִּשְׁתֵּה נְגִינָתָם.
בָּרוּךְ אַתָּה יהוה, מְשַׂמֵּחַ הֶחָתָן עִם הַכַּלָּה.

בָּרוּךְ אַתָּה יהוה אֱלֹהֵינוּ מֶלֶךְ הָעוֹלָם
בּוֹרֵא פְּרִי הַגָּפֶן.

קריאת התורה לשבת מנחה

THE READING OF THE TORAH FOR SHABBAT MINHA

BERESHIT בראשית

בראשית א: א–כג

FIRST ALIYA: 1:1–5
The first day of creation: Light and darkness, day and night.

בְּרֵאשִׁית בָּרָא אֱלֹהִים אֵת הַשָּׁמַיִם וְאֵת הָאָרֶץ: וְהָאָרֶץ
הָיְתָה תֹהוּ וָבֹהוּ וְחֹשֶׁךְ עַל־פְּנֵי תְהוֹם וְרוּחַ אֱלֹהִים מְרַחֶפֶת
עַל־פְּנֵי הַמָּיִם: וַיֹּאמֶר אֱלֹהִים יְהִי־אוֹר וַיְהִי־אוֹר: וַיַּרְא
אֱלֹהִים אֶת־הָאוֹר כִּי־טוֹב וַיַּבְדֵּל אֱלֹהִים בֵּין הָאוֹר וּבֵין
הַחֹשֶׁךְ: וַיִּקְרָא אֱלֹהִים ׀ לָאוֹר יוֹם וְלַחֹשֶׁךְ קָרָא לָיְלָה
וַיְהִי־עֶרֶב וַיְהִי־בֹקֶר יוֹם אֶחָד:

לוי

SECOND ALIYA: 1:6–8
The second day of creation: Heaven.

וַיֹּאמֶר אֱלֹהִים יְהִי רָקִיעַ בְּתוֹךְ הַמָּיִם וִיהִי מַבְדִּיל בֵּין
מַיִם לָמָיִם: וַיַּעַשׂ אֱלֹהִים אֶת־הָרָקִיעַ וַיַּבְדֵּל בֵּין הַמַּיִם
אֲשֶׁר מִתַּחַת לָרָקִיעַ וּבֵין הַמַּיִם אֲשֶׁר מֵעַל לָרָקִיעַ וַיְהִי־
כֵן: וַיִּקְרָא אֱלֹהִים לָרָקִיעַ שָׁמָיִם וַיְהִי־עֶרֶב וַיְהִי־בֹקֶר יוֹם
שֵׁנִי:

ישראל

THIRD ALIYA: 1:9–13
The third day of creation: Land and sea; vegetation.

וַיֹּאמֶר אֱלֹהִים יִקָּווּ הַמַּיִם מִתַּחַת הַשָּׁמַיִם אֶל־מָקוֹם אֶחָד
וְתֵרָאֶה הַיַּבָּשָׁה וַיְהִי־כֵן: וַיִּקְרָא אֱלֹהִים ׀ לַיַּבָּשָׁה אֶרֶץ
וּלְמִקְוֵה הַמַּיִם קָרָא יַמִּים וַיַּרְא אֱלֹהִים כִּי־טוֹב: וַיֹּאמֶר
אֱלֹהִים תַּדְשֵׁא הָאָרֶץ דֶּשֶׁא עֵשֶׂב מַזְרִיעַ זֶרַע עֵץ פְּרִי
עֹשֶׂה פְּרִי לְמִינוֹ אֲשֶׁר זַרְעוֹ־בוֹ עַל־הָאָרֶץ וַיְהִי־כֵן: וַתּוֹצֵא
הָאָרֶץ דֶּשֶׁא עֵשֶׂב מַזְרִיעַ זֶרַע לְמִינֵהוּ וְעֵץ עֹשֶׂה־פְּרִי אֲשֶׁר
זַרְעוֹ־בוֹ לְמִינֵהוּ וַיַּרְא אֱלֹהִים כִּי־טוֹב: וַיְהִי־עֶרֶב וַיְהִי־בֹקֶר
יוֹם שְׁלִישִׁי:

Some extend the ישראל portion on the Thursday reading:

וַיֹּאמֶר אֱלֹהִים יְהִי מְאֹרֹת בִּרְקִיעַ הַשָּׁמַיִם לְהַבְדִּיל בֵּין
הַיּוֹם וּבֵין הַלָּיְלָה וְהָיוּ לְאֹתֹת וּלְמוֹעֲדִים וּלְיָמִים וְשָׁנִים:

וְהָי֤וּ לִמְאוֹרֹת֙ בִּרְקִ֣יעַ הַשָּׁמַ֔יִם לְהָאִ֖יר עַל־הָאָ֑רֶץ וַֽיְהִי־כֵֽן׃
וַיַּ֣עַשׂ אֱלֹהִ֔ים אֶת־שְׁנֵ֥י הַמְּאֹרֹ֖ת הַגְּדֹלִ֑ים אֶת־הַמָּא֤וֹר הַגָּדֹל֙
לְמֶמְשֶׁ֣לֶת הַיּ֔וֹם וְאֶת־הַמָּא֤וֹר הַקָּטֹן֙ לְמֶמְשֶׁ֣לֶת הַלַּ֔יְלָה
וְאֵ֖ת הַכּוֹכָבִֽים׃ וַיִּתֵּ֥ן אֹתָ֛ם אֱלֹהִ֖ים בִּרְקִ֣יעַ הַשָּׁמָ֑יִם לְהָאִ֖יר
עַל־הָאָֽרֶץ׃ וְלִמְשֹׁל֙ בַּיּ֣וֹם וּבַלַּ֔יְלָה וּֽלֲהַבְדִּ֔יל בֵּ֥ין הָא֖וֹר וּבֵ֣ין
הַחֹ֑שֶׁךְ וַיַּ֥רְא אֱלֹהִ֖ים כִּי־טֽוֹב׃ וַֽיְהִי־עֶ֥רֶב וַֽיְהִי־בֹ֖קֶר י֥וֹם
רְבִיעִֽי׃

וַיֹּ֣אמֶר אֱלֹהִ֔ים יִשְׁרְצ֣וּ הַמַּ֔יִם שֶׁ֖רֶץ נֶ֣פֶשׁ חַיָּ֑ה וְעוֹף֙ יְעוֹפֵ֣ף עַל־
הָאָ֔רֶץ עַל־פְּנֵ֖י רְקִ֥יעַ הַשָּׁמָֽיִם׃ וַיִּבְרָ֣א אֱלֹהִ֔ים אֶת־הַתַּנִּינִ֖ם
הַגְּדֹלִ֑ים וְאֵ֣ת כָּל־נֶ֣פֶשׁ הַֽחַיָּ֣ה ׀ הָֽרֹמֶ֡שֶׂת אֲשֶׁר֩ שָׁרְצ֨וּ הַמַּ֜יִם
לְמִֽינֵהֶ֗ם וְאֵ֨ת כָּל־ע֤וֹף כָּנָף֙ לְמִינֵ֔הוּ וַיַּ֥רְא אֱלֹהִ֖ים כִּי־טֽוֹב׃
וַיְבָ֧רֶךְ אֹתָ֛ם אֱלֹהִ֖ים לֵאמֹ֑ר פְּר֣וּ וּרְב֗וּ וּמִלְא֤וּ אֶת־הַמַּ֙יִם֙ בַּיַּמִּ֔ים
וְהָע֖וֹף יִ֥רֶב בָּאָֽרֶץ׃ וַֽיְהִי־עֶ֥רֶב וַֽיְהִי־בֹ֖קֶר י֥וֹם חֲמִישִֽׁי׃

NOAH נח

בראשית ו: ט–כב

FIRST ALIYA: 6:9–16
Noah was righteous and walked with God. The population of the world had become corrupt and violent. God decrees He will destroy the world with a flood, and commands Noah to build an ark.

SECOND ALIYA: 6:17–19
God enacts a covenant with Noah to save him and his family and two of each species, male and female, in order to repopulate the world.

אֵ֚לֶּה תּוֹלְדֹ֣ת נֹ֔חַ נֹ֗חַ אִ֥ישׁ צַדִּ֛יק תָּמִ֥ים הָיָ֖ה בְּדֹרֹתָ֑יו אֶת־
הָֽאֱלֹהִ֖ים הִֽתְהַלֶּךְ־נֹֽחַ׃ וַיּ֥וֹלֶד נֹ֖חַ שְׁלֹשָׁ֣ה בָנִ֑ים אֶת־שֵׁ֖ם אֶת־
חָ֥ם וְאֶת־יָֽפֶת׃ וַתִּשָּׁחֵ֥ת הָאָ֖רֶץ לִפְנֵ֣י הָֽאֱלֹהִ֑ים וַתִּמָּלֵ֥א הָאָ֖רֶץ
חָמָֽס׃ וַיַּ֧רְא אֱלֹהִ֛ים אֶת־הָאָ֖רֶץ וְהִנֵּ֣ה נִשְׁחָ֑תָה כִּֽי־הִשְׁחִ֧ית
כָּל־בָּשָׂ֛ר אֶת־דַּרְכּ֖וֹ עַל־הָאָֽרֶץ׃ וַיֹּ֨אמֶר אֱלֹהִ֜ים
לְנֹ֗חַ קֵ֤ץ כָּל־בָּשָׂר֙ בָּ֣א לְפָנַ֔י כִּֽי־מָלְאָ֥ה הָאָ֛רֶץ חָמָ֖ס מִפְּנֵיהֶ֑ם
וְהִנְנִ֥י מַשְׁחִיתָ֖ם אֶת־הָאָֽרֶץ׃ עֲשֵׂ֤ה לְךָ֙ תֵּבַ֣ת עֲצֵי־גֹ֔פֶר קִנִּ֖ים
תַּעֲשֶׂ֣ה אֶת־הַתֵּבָ֑ה וְכָֽפַרְתָּ֥ אֹתָ֛הּ מִבַּ֥יִת וּמִח֖וּץ בַּכֹּֽפֶר׃ וְזֶ֕ה
אֲשֶׁ֥ר תַּעֲשֶׂ֖ה אֹתָ֑הּ שְׁלֹ֨שׁ מֵא֤וֹת אַמָּה֙ אֹ֣רֶךְ הַתֵּבָ֔ה חֲמִשִּׁ֤ים
אַמָּה֙ רָחְבָּ֔הּ וּשְׁלֹשִׁ֥ים אַמָּ֖ה קוֹמָתָֽהּ׃ צֹ֣הַר ׀ תַּעֲשֶׂ֣ה לַתֵּבָ֗ה
וְאֶל־אַמָּה֙ תְּכַלֶּ֣נָּה מִלְמַ֔עְלָה וּפֶ֥תַח הַתֵּבָ֖ה בְּצִדָּ֣הּ תָּשִׂ֑ים
תַּחְתִּיִּ֛ם שְׁנִיִּ֥ם וּשְׁלִשִׁ֖ים תַּעֲשֶֽׂהָ׃ *וַאֲנִ֗י הִנְנִי֩ מֵבִ֨יא אֶת־הַמַּבּ֥וּל לוי
מַ֙יִם֙ עַל־הָאָ֔רֶץ לְשַׁחֵ֣ת כָּל־בָּשָׂ֗ר אֲשֶׁר־בּוֹ֙ ר֣וּחַ חַיִּ֔ים מִתַּ֖חַת

הַשָּׁמָיִם כֹּל אֲשֶׁר־בָּאָרֶץ יִגְוָע: וַהֲקִמֹתִי אֶת־בְּרִיתִי אִתָּךְ
וּבָאתָ אֶל־הַתֵּבָה אַתָּה וּבָנֶיךָ וְאִשְׁתְּךָ וּנְשֵׁי־בָנֶיךָ אִתָּךְ:
וּמִכָּל־הָחַי מִכָּל־בָּשָׂר שְׁנַיִם מִכֹּל תָּבִיא אֶל־הַתֵּבָה לְהַחֲיֹת
ישראל אִתָּךְ זָכָר וּנְקֵבָה יִהְיוּ: *מֵהָעוֹף לְמִינֵהוּ וּמִן־הַבְּהֵמָה לְמִינָהּ
מִכֹּל רֶמֶשׂ הָאֲדָמָה לְמִינֵהוּ שְׁנַיִם מִכֹּל יָבֹאוּ אֵלֶיךָ לְהַחֲיוֹת:
וְאַתָּה קַח־לְךָ מִכָּל־מַאֲכָל אֲשֶׁר יֵאָכֵל וְאָסַפְתָּ אֵלֶיךָ וְהָיָה
לְךָ וְלָהֶם לְאָכְלָה: וַיַּעַשׂ נֹחַ כְּכֹל אֲשֶׁר צִוָּה אֹתוֹ אֱלֹהִים
כֵּן עָשָׂה:

THIRD ALIYA: 6:20–22
Noah did as he had been commanded by God.

LEKH LEKHA
לך לך

בראשית יב: א–יג
וַיֹּאמֶר יהוה אֶל־אַבְרָם לֶךְ־לְךָ מֵאַרְצְךָ וּמִמּוֹלַדְתְּךָ וּמִבֵּית
אָבִיךָ אֶל־הָאָרֶץ אֲשֶׁר אַרְאֶךָּ: וְאֶעֶשְׂךָ לְגוֹי גָּדוֹל וַאֲבָרֶכְךָ
וַאֲגַדְּלָה שְׁמֶךָ וֶהְיֵה בְּרָכָה: וַאֲבָרְכָה מְבָרְכֶיךָ וּמְקַלֶּלְךָ אָאֹר
לוי וְנִבְרְכוּ בְךָ כֹּל מִשְׁפְּחֹת הָאֲדָמָה: *וַיֵּלֶךְ אַבְרָם כַּאֲשֶׁר דִּבֶּר
אֵלָיו יהוה וַיֵּלֶךְ אִתּוֹ לוֹט וְאַבְרָם בֶּן־חָמֵשׁ שָׁנִים וְשִׁבְעִים
שָׁנָה בְּצֵאתוֹ מֵחָרָן: וַיִּקַּח אַבְרָם אֶת־שָׂרַי אִשְׁתּוֹ וְאֶת־
לוֹט בֶּן־אָחִיו וְאֶת־כָּל־רְכוּשָׁם אֲשֶׁר רָכָשׁוּ וְאֶת־הַנֶּפֶשׁ
אֲשֶׁר־עָשׂוּ בְחָרָן וַיֵּצְאוּ לָלֶכֶת אַרְצָה כְּנַעַן וַיָּבֹאוּ אַרְצָה
כְּנָעַן: וַיַּעֲבֹר אַבְרָם בָּאָרֶץ עַד מְקוֹם שְׁכֶם עַד אֵלוֹן מוֹרֶה
וְהַכְּנַעֲנִי אָז בָּאָרֶץ: וַיֵּרָא יהוה אֶל־אַבְרָם וַיֹּאמֶר לְזַרְעֲךָ
אֶתֵּן אֶת־הָאָרֶץ הַזֹּאת וַיִּבֶן שָׁם מִזְבֵּחַ לַיהוה הַנִּרְאֶה אֵלָיו:
וַיַּעְתֵּק מִשָּׁם הָהָרָה מִקֶּדֶם לְבֵית־אֵל וַיֵּט אָהֳלֹה בֵּית־אֵל
מִיָּם וְהָעַי מִקֶּדֶם וַיִּבֶן־שָׁם מִזְבֵּחַ לַיהוה וַיִּקְרָא בְּשֵׁם יהוה:
וַיִּסַּע אַבְרָם הָלוֹךְ וְנָסוֹעַ הַנֶּגְבָּה:

FIRST ALIYA: 12:1–3
God's call to Avram to migrate to Eretz Yisrael; God promises Avram blessings and progeny.

SECOND ALIYA: 12:4–9
Avram and his entourage make the journey to Eretz Yisrael. God appears to Avram and promises this land to his progeny.

ישראל וַיְהִי רָעָב בָּאָרֶץ וַיֵּרֶד אַבְרָם מִצְרַיְמָה לָגוּר שָׁם כִּי־כָבֵד
הָרָעָב בָּאָרֶץ: וַיְהִי כַּאֲשֶׁר הִקְרִיב לָבוֹא מִצְרָיְמָה וַיֹּאמֶר
אֶל־שָׂרַי אִשְׁתּוֹ הִנֵּה־נָא יָדַעְתִּי כִּי אִשָּׁה יְפַת־מַרְאֶה אָתְּ:
וְהָיָה כִּי־יִרְאוּ אֹתָךְ הַמִּצְרִים וְאָמְרוּ אִשְׁתּוֹ זֹאת וְהָרְגוּ אֹתִי
וְאֹתָךְ יְחַיּוּ: אִמְרִי־נָא אֲחֹתִי אָתְּ לְמַעַן יִיטַב־לִי בַעֲבוּרֵךְ
וְחָיְתָה נַפְשִׁי בִּגְלָלֵךְ:

THIRD ALIYA: 12:10–13
Avram and Sarai are forced to leave Eretz Yisrael for Egypt due to famine in the land.

וירא
VAYERA

בראשית יח: א–יד

FIRST ALIYA: 18:1–5
Avraham is visited by three strangers, who unbeknown to him are angels.

וירא אליו יהוה באלני ממרא והוא ישב פתח־האהל
כחם היום: וישא עיניו וירא והנה שלשה אנשים נצבים
עליו וירא וירץ לקראתם מפתח האהל וישתחו ארצה:
ויאמר אדני אם־נא מצאתי חן בעיניך אל־נא תעבר מעל
עבדך: יקח־נא מעט־מים ורחצו רגליכם והשענו תחת
העץ: ואקחה פת־לחם וסעדו לבכם אחר תעברו כי־על־
כן עברתם על־עבדכם ויאמרו כן תעשה כאשר דברת:

לוי

SECOND ALIYA: 18:6–8
Avraham shows the angels hospitality in his home.

*וימהר אברהם האהלה אל־שרה ויאמר מהרי שלש
סאים קמח סלת לושי ועשי עגות: ואל־הבקר רץ אברהם
ויקח בן־בקר רך וטוב ויתן אל־הנער וימהר לעשות אתו:
ויקח חמאה וחלב ובן־הבקר אשר עשה ויתן לפניהם
והוא עמד עליהם תחת העץ ויאכלו: *ויאמרו אליו איה

ישראל

THIRD ALIYA: 18:9–14
The angels deliver God's promise that Sarah will have a son. Sarah is disbelieving due to her advanced age, and laughs to herself.

שרה אשתך ויאמר הנה באהל: ויאמר שוב אשוב אליך
כעת חיה והנה־בן לשרה אשתך ושרה שמעת פתח
האהל והוא אחריו: ואברהם ושרה זקנים באים בימים
חדל להיות לשרה ארח כנשים: ותצחק שרה בקרבה
לאמר אחרי בלתי היתה־לי עדנה ואדני זקן: ויאמר יהוה
אל־אברהם למה זה צחקה שרה לאמר האף אמנם אלד
ואני זקנתי: היפלא מיהוה דבר למועד אשוב אליך כעת
חיה ולשרה בן:

חיי שרה
HAYYEI SARA

בראשית כג: א–טו

FIRST ALIYA: 23:1–7
Sarah dies. Avraham negotiates to buy her a burial plot in Ḥevron.

ויהיו חיי שרה מאה שנה ועשרים שנה ושבע שנים שני
חיי שרה: ותמת שרה בקרית ארבע הוא חברון בארץ
כנען ויבא אברהם לספד לשרה ולבכתה: ויקם אברהם
מעל פני מתו וידבר אל־בני־חת לאמר: גר־ותושב אנכי
עמכם תנו לי אחזת־קבר עמכם ואקברה מתי מלפני:
ויענו בני־חת את־אברהם לאמר לו: שמענו ׀ אדני נשיא
אלהים אתה בתוכנו במבחר קברינו קבר את־מתך איש

ממנו את־קברו לא־יכלה ממך מקבר מתך: ויקם אברהם
לוי וישתחו לעם־הארץ לבני־חת: *וידבר אתם לאמר אם־
יש את־נפשכם לקבר את־מתי מלפני שמעוני ופגעו־לי
בעפרון בן־צחר: ויתן־לי את־מערת המכפלה אשר־לו
אשר בקצה שדהו בכסף מלא יתננה לי בתוככם לאחזת־
קבר: ועפרון ישב בתוך בני־חת ויען עפרון החתי את־
אברהם באזני בני־חת לכל באי שער־עירו לאמר: לא־
אדני שמעני השדה נתתי לך והמערה אשר־בו לך נתתיה
לעיני בני־עמי נתתיה לך קבר מתך: וישתחו אברהם לפני
ישראל עם־הארץ: *וידבר אל־עפרון באזני עם־הארץ לאמר אך
אם־אתה לו שמעני נתתי כסף השדה קח ממני ואקברה
את־מתי שמה: ויען עפרון את־אברהם לאמר לו: אדני
שמעני ארץ ארבע מאת שקל־כסף ביני ובינך מה־הוא
ואת־מתך קבר: וישמע אברהם אל־עפרון וישקל אברהם
לעפרן את־הכסף אשר דבר באזני בני־חת ארבע מאות
שקל כסף עבר לסחר:

SECOND ALIYA: 23:8–12
The negotiations continue between Avraham and Ephron, the owner of the field.

THIRD ALIYA: 23:13–16
Negotiations are concluded successfully and Avraham purchases the field for the inflated price of four hundred silver shekels.

TOLEDOT תולדות

בראשית כה:יט–כו:ה

ואלה תולדת יצחק בן־אברהם אברהם הוליד את־יצחק:
ויהי יצחק בן־ארבעים שנה בקחתו את־רבקה בת־בתואל
הארמי מפדן ארם אחות לבן הארמי לו לאשה: ויעתר
יצחק ליהוה לנכח אשתו כי עקרה הוא ויעתר לו יהוה
ותהר רבקה אשתו: ויתרצצו הבנים בקרבה ותאמר אם־
לוי כן למה זה אנכי ותלך לדרש את־יהוה: *ויאמר יהוה לה
גוים שני גיים בבטנך ושני לאמים ממעיך יפרדו ולאם מלאם
יאמץ ורב יעבד צעיר: וימלאו ימיה ללדת והנה תומם
בבטנה: ויצא הראשון אדמוני כלו כאדרת שער ויקראו
שמו עשו: ואחרי־כן יצא אחיו וידו אחזת בעקב עשו
ויקרא שמו יעקב ויצחק בן־ששים שנה בלדת אתם:

FIRST ALIYA: 25:19–22
Yitzhak marries Rivka, who cannot have children. He prays to God and she becomes pregnant with twins.

SECOND ALIYA: 25:23–26
The twin boys are born, first Eisav, then Yaakov.

THIRD ALIYA: 25:27–26:5
Eisav becomes a hunter and Yaakov a wholesome man. After an exhausting day hunting, Yaakov gives Eisav a stew he was making, in exchange for his birthright.

*וַיִּגְדְּלוּ הַנְּעָרִים וַיְהִי עֵשָׂו אִישׁ יֹדֵעַ צַיִד אִישׁ שָׂדֶה וְיַעֲקֹב ישראל
אִישׁ תָּם יֹשֵׁב אֹהָלִים: וַיֶּאֱהַב יִצְחָק אֶת־עֵשָׂו כִּי־צַיִד בְּפִיו
וְרִבְקָה אֹהֶבֶת אֶת־יַעֲקֹב: וַיָּזֶד יַעֲקֹב נָזִיד וַיָּבֹא עֵשָׂו מִן־
הַשָּׂדֶה וְהוּא עָיֵף: וַיֹּאמֶר עֵשָׂו אֶל־יַעֲקֹב הַלְעִיטֵנִי נָא מִן־
הָאָדֹם הָאָדֹם הַזֶּה כִּי עָיֵף אָנֹכִי עַל־כֵּן קָרָא־שְׁמוֹ אֱדוֹם:
וַיֹּאמֶר יַעֲקֹב מִכְרָה כַיּוֹם אֶת־בְּכֹרָתְךָ לִי: וַיֹּאמֶר עֵשָׂו הִנֵּה
אָנֹכִי הוֹלֵךְ לָמוּת וְלָמָּה־זֶּה לִי בְּכֹרָה: וַיֹּאמֶר יַעֲקֹב הִשָּׁבְעָה
לִּי כַּיּוֹם וַיִּשָּׁבַע לוֹ וַיִּמְכֹּר אֶת־בְּכֹרָתוֹ לְיַעֲקֹב: וְיַעֲקֹב נָתַן
לְעֵשָׂו לֶחֶם וּנְזִיד עֲדָשִׁים וַיֹּאכַל וַיֵּשְׁתְּ וַיָּקָם וַיֵּלַךְ וַיִּבֶז עֵשָׂו
אֶת־הַבְּכֹרָה:

וַיְהִי רָעָב בָּאָרֶץ מִלְּבַד הָרָעָב הָרִאשׁוֹן אֲשֶׁר הָיָה בִּימֵי
אַבְרָהָם וַיֵּלֶךְ יִצְחָק אֶל־אֲבִימֶלֶךְ מֶלֶךְ־פְּלִשְׁתִּים גְּרָרָה:
וַיֵּרָא אֵלָיו יהוה וַיֹּאמֶר אַל־תֵּרֵד מִצְרָיְמָה שְׁכֹן בָּאָרֶץ אֲשֶׁר
אֹמַר אֵלֶיךָ: גּוּר בָּאָרֶץ הַזֹּאת וְאֶהְיֶה עִמְּךָ וַאֲבָרְכֶךָּ כִּי־לְךָ
וּלְזַרְעֲךָ אֶתֵּן אֶת־כָּל־הָאֲרָצֹת הָאֵל וַהֲקִמֹתִי אֶת־הַשְּׁבֻעָה
אֲשֶׁר נִשְׁבַּעְתִּי לְאַבְרָהָם אָבִיךָ: וְהִרְבֵּיתִי אֶת־זַרְעֲךָ כְּכוֹכְבֵי
הַשָּׁמַיִם וְנָתַתִּי לְזַרְעֲךָ אֵת כָּל־הָאֲרָצֹת הָאֵל וְהִתְבָּרְכוּ
בְזַרְעֲךָ כֹּל גּוֹיֵי הָאָרֶץ: עֵקֶב אֲשֶׁר־שָׁמַע אַבְרָהָם בְּקֹלִי
וַיִּשְׁמֹר מִשְׁמַרְתִּי מִצְוֺתַי חֻקּוֹתַי וְתוֹרֹתָי:

VAYETZEH ויצא

FIRST ALIYA: 28:10–12
Yaakov flees Eisav, and on his way dreams of a ladder with angels ascending and descending.

בראשית כח:י–כב

וַיֵּצֵא יַעֲקֹב מִבְּאֵר שָׁבַע וַיֵּלֶךְ חָרָנָה: וַיִּפְגַּע בַּמָּקוֹם וַיָּלֶן שָׁם
כִּי־בָא הַשֶּׁמֶשׁ וַיִּקַּח מֵאַבְנֵי הַמָּקוֹם וַיָּשֶׂם מְרַאֲשֹׁתָיו וַיִּשְׁכַּב
בַּמָּקוֹם הַהוּא: וַיַּחֲלֹם וְהִנֵּה סֻלָּם מֻצָּב אַרְצָה וְרֹאשׁוֹ מַגִּיעַ
הַשָּׁמָיְמָה וְהִנֵּה מַלְאֲכֵי אֱלֹהִים עֹלִים וְיֹרְדִים בּוֹ: *וְהִנֵּה לוי
יהוה נִצָּב עָלָיו וַיֹּאמַר אֲנִי יהוה אֱלֹהֵי אַבְרָהָם אָבִיךָ וֵאלֹהֵי
יִצְחָק הָאָרֶץ אֲשֶׁר אַתָּה שֹׁכֵב עָלֶיהָ לְךָ אֶתְּנֶנָּה וּלְזַרְעֶךָ:
וְהָיָה זַרְעֲךָ כַּעֲפַר הָאָרֶץ וּפָרַצְתָּ יָמָּה וָקֵדְמָה וְצָפֹנָה וָנֶגְבָּה
וְנִבְרְכוּ בְךָ כָּל־מִשְׁפְּחֹת הָאֲדָמָה וּבְזַרְעֶךָ: וְהִנֵּה אָנֹכִי עִמָּךְ

SECOND ALIYA: 28:13–17
God appears to him in this dream and promises him that the land will be inherited by his descendants.

וּשְׁמַרְתִּיךָ בְּכֹל אֲשֶׁר־תֵּלֵךְ וַהֲשִׁבֹתִיךָ אֶל־הָאֲדָמָה הַזֹּאת
כִּי לֹא אֶעֱזָבְךָ עַד אֲשֶׁר אִם־עָשִׂיתִי אֵת אֲשֶׁר־דִּבַּרְתִּי לָךְ:
וַיִּיקַץ יַעֲקֹב מִשְּׁנָתוֹ וַיֹּאמֶר אָכֵן יֵשׁ יְהוָה בַּמָּקוֹם הַזֶּה
וְאָנֹכִי לֹא יָדָעְתִּי: וַיִּירָא וַיֹּאמַר מַה־נּוֹרָא הַמָּקוֹם הַזֶּה אֵין
ישראל זֶה כִּי אִם־בֵּית אֱלֹהִים וְזֶה שַׁעַר הַשָּׁמָיִם: *וַיַּשְׁכֵּם יַעֲקֹב
בַּבֹּקֶר וַיִּקַּח אֶת־הָאֶבֶן אֲשֶׁר־שָׂם מְרַאֲשֹׁתָיו וַיָּשֶׂם אֹתָהּ
מַצֵּבָה וַיִּצֹק שֶׁמֶן עַל־רֹאשָׁהּ: וַיִּקְרָא אֶת־שֵׁם־הַמָּקוֹם
הַהוּא בֵּית־אֵל וְאוּלָם לוּז שֵׁם־הָעִיר לָרִאשֹׁנָה: וַיִּדַּר יַעֲקֹב
נֶדֶר לֵאמֹר אִם־יִהְיֶה אֱלֹהִים עִמָּדִי וּשְׁמָרַנִי בַּדֶּרֶךְ הַזֶּה
אֲשֶׁר אָנֹכִי הוֹלֵךְ וְנָתַן־לִי לֶחֶם לֶאֱכֹל וּבֶגֶד לִלְבֹּשׁ: וְשַׁבְתִּי
בְשָׁלוֹם אֶל־בֵּית אָבִי וְהָיָה יְהוָה לִי לֵאלֹהִים: וְהָאֶבֶן הַזֹּאת
אֲשֶׁר־שַׂמְתִּי מַצֵּבָה יִהְיֶה בֵּית אֱלֹהִים וְכֹל אֲשֶׁר תִּתֶּן־לִי
עַשֵּׂר אֲעַשְּׂרֶנּוּ לָךְ:

THIRD ALIYA: 28:18–22
In the morning, Yaakov builds a stone monument, and names the place Bet-El.

VAYISHLAH וישלח

בראשית לב:ג-יב וַיִּשְׁלַח יַעֲקֹב מַלְאָכִים לְפָנָיו אֶל־עֵשָׂו אָחִיו אַרְצָה שֵׂעִיר
שְׂדֵה אֱדוֹם: וַיְצַו אֹתָם לֵאמֹר כֹּה תֹאמְרוּן לַאדֹנִי לְעֵשָׂו
כֹּה אָמַר עַבְדְּךָ יַעֲקֹב עִם־לָבָן גַּרְתִּי וָאֵחַר עַד־עָתָּה: וַיְהִי־
לִי שׁוֹר וַחֲמוֹר צֹאן וְעֶבֶד וְשִׁפְחָה וָאֶשְׁלְחָה לְהַגִּיד לַאדֹנִי
לוי לִמְצֹא־חֵן בְּעֵינֶיךָ: *וַיָּשֻׁבוּ הַמַּלְאָכִים אֶל־יַעֲקֹב לֵאמֹר
בָּאנוּ אֶל־אָחִיךָ אֶל־עֵשָׂו וְגַם הֹלֵךְ לִקְרָאתְךָ וְאַרְבַּע־
מֵאוֹת אִישׁ עִמּוֹ: וַיִּירָא יַעֲקֹב מְאֹד וַיֵּצֶר לוֹ וַיַּחַץ אֶת־
הָעָם אֲשֶׁר־אִתּוֹ וְאֶת־הַצֹּאן וְאֶת־הַבָּקָר וְהַגְּמַלִּים לִשְׁנֵי
מַחֲנוֹת: וַיֹּאמֶר אִם־יָבוֹא עֵשָׂו אֶל־הַמַּחֲנֶה הָאַחַת וְהִכָּהוּ
ישראל וְהָיָה הַמַּחֲנֶה הַנִּשְׁאָר לִפְלֵיטָה: *וַיֹּאמֶר יַעֲקֹב אֱלֹהֵי אָבִי
אַבְרָהָם וֵאלֹהֵי אָבִי יִצְחָק יְהוָה הָאֹמֵר אֵלַי שׁוּב לְאַרְצְךָ
וּלְמוֹלַדְתְּךָ וְאֵיטִיבָה עִמָּךְ: קָטֹנְתִּי מִכֹּל הַחֲסָדִים וּמִכָּל־
הָאֱמֶת אֲשֶׁר עָשִׂיתָ אֶת־עַבְדֶּךָ כִּי בְמַקְלִי עָבַרְתִּי אֶת־
הַיַּרְדֵּן הַזֶּה וְעַתָּה הָיִיתִי לִשְׁנֵי מַחֲנוֹת: הַצִּילֵנִי נָא מִיַּד אָחִי

FIRST ALIYA: 32:4–6
Yaakov sends an advance party ahead to Eisav to prepare for their meeting.

SECOND ALIYA: 32:7–9
They returned with news that Eisav is approaching with four hundred men by his side. Yaakov divides his camp into two in a defensive formation.

THIRD ALIYA: 32:10–13
Yaakov prays to Hashem to save him in the impending confrontation.

מיד עשו כי־ירא אנכי אתו פן־יבוא והכני אם על־בנים:
ואתה אמרת היטב איטיב עמך ושמתי את־זרעך כחול
הים אשר לא־יספר מרב:

VAYESHEV וישב

בראשית לז:א–יא

FIRST ALIYA: 37:1–3
Yaakov loved Yosef more than his other children and made for him a colorful woolen tunic.

וישב יעקב בארץ מגורי אביו בארץ כנען: אלה ׀ תלדות
יעקב יוסף בן־שבע־עשרה שנה היה רעה את־אחיו בצאן
והוא נער את־בני בלהה ואת־בני זלפה נשי אביו ויבא יוסף
את־דבתם רעה אל־אביהם: וישראל אהב את־יוסף מכל־
בניו כי־בן־זקנים הוא לו ועשה לו כתנת פסים: *ויראו לוי

SECOND ALIYA: 37:4–7
Yosef's brothers were jealous of him. Their jealousy increased when he related his first dream, where their sheaves of wheat bowed down to his sheaf.

אחיו כי־אתו אהב אביהם מכל־אחיו וישנאו אתו ולא
יכלו דברו לשלם: ויחלם יוסף חלום ויגד לאחיו ויוספו
עוד שנא אתו: ויאמר אליהם שמעו־נא החלום הזה
אשר חלמתי: והנה אנחנו מאלמים אלמים בתוך השדה
והנה קמה אלמתי וגם־נצבה והנה תסבינה אלמתיכם
ותשתחוין לאלמתי: *ויאמרו לו אחיו המלך תמלך עלינו ישראל

THIRD ALIYA: 37:8–11
In Yosef's second dream, the sun and the moon and eleven stars (representing his father, mother and brothers) bow down to Yosef.

אם־משול תמשל בנו ויוספו עוד שנא אתו על־חלמתיו
ועל־דבריו: ויחלם עוד חלום אחר ויספר אתו לאחיו
ויאמר הנה חלמתי חלום עוד והנה השמש והירח ואחד
עשר כוכבים משתחוים לי: ויספר אל־אביו ואל־אחיו
ויגער־בו אביו ויאמר לו מה החלום הזה אשר חלמת
הבוא נבוא אני ואמך ואחיך להשתחות לך ארצה:
ויקנאו־בו אחיו ואביו שמר את־הדבר:

MIKETZ מקץ

FIRST ALIYA: 41:1–4
Pharaoh has a dream seven healthy cows ascend from the River Nile, followed by seven starved cows.

בראשית מא:א–יד

ויהי מקץ שנתים ימים ופרעה חלם והנה עמד על־היאר:
והנה מן־היאר עלת שבע פרות יפות מראה ובריאת
בשר ותרעינה באחו: והנה שבע פרות אחרות עלות
אחריהן מן־היאר רעות מראה ודקות בשר ותעמדנה

אצל הפרות על־שפת היאר: ותאכלנה הפרות רעות
המראה ודקת הבשר את שבע הפרות יפת המראה
לוי והבריאת וייקץ פרעה: *ויישן ויחלם שנית והנה ׀ שבע
שבלים עלות בקנה אחד בריאות וטבות: והנה שבע
שבלים דקות ושדופת קדים צמחות אחריהן: ותבלענה
השבלים הדקות את שבע השבלים הבריאות והמלאות
ישראל וייקץ פרעה והנה חלום: *ויהי בבקר ותפעם רוחו וישלח
ויקרא את־כל־חרטמי מצרים ואת־כל־חכמיה ויספר
פרעה להם את־חלמו ואין־פותר אותם לפרעה: וידבר
שר המשקים את־פרעה לאמר את־חטאי אני מזכיר
היום: פרעה קצף על־עבדיו ויתן אתי במשמר בית שר
הטבחים אתי ואת שר האפים: ונחלמה חלום בלילה
אחד אני והוא איש כפתרון חלמו חלמנו: ושם אתנו
נער עברי עבד לשר הטבחים ונספר־לו ויפתר־לנו את־
חלמתינו איש כחלמו פתר: ויהי כאשר פתר־לנו כן היה
אתי השיב על־כני ואתו תלה: וישלח פרעה ויקרא את־
יוסף ויריצהו מן־הבור ויגלח ויחלף שמלתיו ויבא אל־
פרעה:

SECOND ALIYA: 41:5–7
In Pharaoh's second dream a stalk of wheat had seven ears of healthy grain, and following them seven dry grains.

THIRD ALIYA: 41:8–14
Pharaoh asked from his ministers to find an interpretation, but none could. His head butler recalled Yosef and his ability to interpret dreams.

VAYIGASH ויגש

בראשית מד:יח–ל

ויגש אליו יהודה ויאמר בי אדני ידבר־נא עבדך דבר
באזני אדני ואל־יחר אפך בעבדך כי כמוך כפרעה: אדני
שאל את־עבדיו לאמר היש־לכם אב או־אח: ונאמר אל־
אדני יש־לנו אב זקן וילד זקנים קטן ואחיו מת ויותר הוא
לוי לבדו לאמו ואביו אהבו: *ותאמר אל־עבדיך הורדהו אלי
ואשימה עיני עליו: ונאמר אל־אדני לא־יוכל הנער לעזב
את־אביו ועזב את־אביו ומת: ותאמר אל־עבדיך אם־לא
ירד אחיכם הקטן אתכם לא תספון לראות פני: ויהי כי

FIRST ALIYA: 44:18–20
Yehuda steps forward to try to convince Yosef to let Binyamin go free and take him in his stead.

SECOND ALIYA: 44:21–24
Yehuda explains to Yosef the impact Binyamin's incarceration will have on his father Yaakov.

ישראל

THIRD ALIYA: 44:25–30
Yehuda explains that the situation is made worse for his father because he has already lost a son (Yosef who is lost to him).

עָלִינוּ אֶל־עַבְדְּךָ אָבִי וַנַּגֶּד־לוֹ אֵת דִּבְרֵי אֲדֹנִי: *וַיֹּאמֶר
אָבִינוּ שֻׁבוּ שִׁבְרוּ־לָנוּ מְעַט־אֹכֶל: וַנֹּאמֶר לֹא נוּכַל לָרֶדֶת
אִם־יֵשׁ אָחִינוּ הַקָּטֹן אִתָּנוּ וְיָרַדְנוּ כִּי־לֹא נוּכַל לִרְאוֹת פְּנֵי
הָאִישׁ וְאָחִינוּ הַקָּטֹן אֵינֶנּוּ אִתָּנוּ: וַיֹּאמֶר עַבְדְּךָ אָבִי אֵלֵינוּ
אַתֶּם יְדַעְתֶּם כִּי שְׁנַיִם יָלְדָה־לִּי אִשְׁתִּי: וַיֵּצֵא הָאֶחָד מֵאִתִּי
וָאֹמַר אַךְ טָרֹף טֹרָף וְלֹא רְאִיתִיו עַד־הֵנָּה: וּלְקַחְתֶּם גַּם־
אֶת־זֶה מֵעִם פָּנַי וְקָרָהוּ אָסוֹן וְהוֹרַדְתֶּם אֶת־שֵׂיבָתִי בְּרָעָה
שְׁאֹלָה: וְעַתָּה כְּבֹאִי אֶל־עַבְדְּךָ אָבִי וְהַנַּעַר אֵינֶנּוּ אִתָּנוּ
וְנַפְשׁוֹ קְשׁוּרָה בְנַפְשׁוֹ:

VAYHI

ויחי

בראשית
מז:כח–מח:ט

FIRST ALIYA: 47:28–31
Yaakov nears the end of his life. He makes Yosef promise to bury him in Eretz Yisrael and not in Egypt.

וַיְחִי יַעֲקֹב בְּאֶרֶץ מִצְרַיִם שְׁבַע עֶשְׂרֵה שָׁנָה וַיְהִי יְמֵי־
יַעֲקֹב שְׁנֵי חַיָּיו שֶׁבַע שָׁנִים וְאַרְבָּעִים וּמְאַת שָׁנָה: וַיִּקְרְבוּ
יְמֵי־יִשְׂרָאֵל לָמוּת וַיִּקְרָא ׀ לִבְנוֹ לְיוֹסֵף וַיֹּאמֶר לוֹ אִם־נָא
מָצָאתִי חֵן בְּעֵינֶיךָ שִׂים־נָא יָדְךָ תַּחַת יְרֵכִי וְעָשִׂיתָ עִמָּדִי
חֶסֶד וֶאֱמֶת אַל־נָא תִקְבְּרֵנִי בְּמִצְרָיִם: וְשָׁכַבְתִּי עִם־אֲבֹתַי
וּנְשָׂאתַנִי מִמִּצְרַיִם וּקְבַרְתַּנִי בִּקְבֻרָתָם וַיֹּאמַר אָנֹכִי אֶעֱשֶׂה
כִדְבָרֶךָ: וַיֹּאמֶר הִשָּׁבְעָה לִי וַיִּשָּׁבַע לוֹ וַיִּשְׁתַּחוּ יִשְׂרָאֵל
עַל־רֹאשׁ הַמִּטָּה:

לוי

SECOND ALIYA: 48:1–3
Yosef brings his sons Ephraim and Menashe to receive a blessing from Yaakov before he dies.

וַיְהִי אַחֲרֵי הַדְּבָרִים הָאֵלֶּה וַיֹּאמֶר לְיוֹסֵף הִנֵּה אָבִיךָ חֹלֶה
וַיִּקַּח אֶת־שְׁנֵי בָנָיו עִמּוֹ אֶת־מְנַשֶּׁה וְאֶת־אֶפְרָיִם: וַיַּגֵּד
לְיַעֲקֹב וַיֹּאמֶר הִנֵּה בִּנְךָ יוֹסֵף בָּא אֵלֶיךָ וַיִּתְחַזֵּק יִשְׂרָאֵל
וַיֵּשֶׁב עַל־הַמִּטָּה: וַיֹּאמֶר יַעֲקֹב אֶל־יוֹסֵף אֵל שַׁדַּי נִרְאָה־
אֵלַי בְּלוּז בְּאֶרֶץ כְּנָעַן וַיְבָרֶךְ אֹתִי: *וַיֹּאמֶר אֵלַי הִנְנִי מַפְרְךָ

ישראל

THIRD ALIYA: 48:4–9
Yaakov informs Yosef that Ephraim and Menashe will be considered his sons, and will each have a tribe in their own right.

וְהִרְבִּיתִךָ וּנְתַתִּיךָ לִקְהַל עַמִּים וְנָתַתִּי אֶת־הָאָרֶץ הַזֹּאת
לְזַרְעֲךָ אַחֲרֶיךָ אֲחֻזַּת עוֹלָם: וְעַתָּה שְׁנֵי־בָנֶיךָ הַנּוֹלָדִים
לְךָ בְּאֶרֶץ מִצְרַיִם עַד־בֹּאִי אֵלֶיךָ מִצְרַיְמָה לִי־הֵם אֶפְרַיִם
וּמְנַשֶּׁה כִּרְאוּבֵן וְשִׁמְעוֹן יִהְיוּ־לִי: וּמוֹלַדְתְּךָ אֲשֶׁר־הוֹלַדְתָּ

אַחֲרֵיהֶם לְךָ יִהְיוּ עַל שֵׁם אֲחֵיהֶם יִקָּרְאוּ בְּנַחֲלָתָם׃ וַאֲנִי ׀
בְּבֹאִי מִפַּדָּן מֵתָה עָלַי רָחֵל בְּאֶרֶץ כְּנַעַן בַּדֶּרֶךְ בְּעוֹד כִּבְרַת־
אֶרֶץ לָבֹא אֶפְרָתָה וָאֶקְבְּרֶהָ שָּׁם בְּדֶרֶךְ אֶפְרָת הִוא בֵּית
לָחֶם׃ וַיַּרְא יִשְׂרָאֵל אֶת־בְּנֵי יוֹסֵף וַיֹּאמֶר מִי־אֵלֶּה׃ וַיֹּאמֶר
יוֹסֵף אֶל־אָבִיו בָּנַי הֵם אֲשֶׁר־נָתַן־לִי אֱלֹהִים בָּזֶה וַיֹּאמַר
קָחֶם־נָא אֵלַי וַאֲבָרְכֵם׃

SHEMOT — שמות

וְאֵלֶּה שְׁמוֹת בְּנֵי יִשְׂרָאֵל הַבָּאִים מִצְרָיְמָה אֵת יַעֲקֹב אִישׁ שמות א:א-יז
וּבֵיתוֹ בָּאוּ׃ רְאוּבֵן שִׁמְעוֹן לֵוִי וִיהוּדָה׃ יִשָּׂשכָר זְבוּלֻן
וּבִנְיָמִן׃ דָּן וְנַפְתָּלִי גָּד וְאָשֵׁר׃ וַיְהִי כׇּל־נֶפֶשׁ יֹצְאֵי יֶרֶךְ־יַעֲקֹב
שִׁבְעִים נָפֶשׁ וְיוֹסֵף הָיָה בְמִצְרָיִם׃ וַיָּמׇת יוֹסֵף וְכׇל־אֶחָיו וְכֹל
הַדּוֹר הַהוּא׃ וּבְנֵי יִשְׂרָאֵל פָּרוּ וַיִּשְׁרְצוּ וַיִּרְבּוּ וַיַּעַצְמוּ בִּמְאֹד
מְאֹד וַתִּמָּלֵא הָאָרֶץ אֹתָם׃

FIRST ALIYA: 1:1–7 Transition from the seventy souls descended from Yaakov who settled in Egypt, to a populous and mighty Jewish people living amongst the Egyptians.

וַיָּקׇם מֶלֶךְ־חָדָשׁ עַל־מִצְרָיִם אֲשֶׁר לֹא־יָדַע אֶת־יוֹסֵף׃ לוי
וַיֹּאמֶר אֶל־עַמּוֹ הִנֵּה עַם בְּנֵי יִשְׂרָאֵל רַב וְעָצוּם מִמֶּנּוּ׃
הָבָה נִתְחַכְּמָה לוֹ פֶּן־יִרְבֶּה וְהָיָה כִּי־תִקְרֶאנָה מִלְחָמָה
וְנוֹסַף גַּם־הוּא עַל־שֹׂנְאֵינוּ וְנִלְחַם־בָּנוּ וְעָלָה מִן־הָאָרֶץ׃
וַיָּשִׂימוּ עָלָיו שָׂרֵי מִסִּים לְמַעַן עַנֹּתוֹ בְּסִבְלֹתָם וַיִּבֶן עָרֵי
מִסְכְּנוֹת לְפַרְעֹה אֶת־פִּתֹם וְאֶת־רַעַמְסֵס׃ וְכַאֲשֶׁר יְעַנּוּ

SECOND ALIYA: 1:8–12 A new Pharaoh comes to power who does not feel indebted to Yosef and his people, and feels threatened by their number and strength. The enslavement begins.

אֹתוֹ כֵּן יִרְבֶּה וְכֵן יִפְרֹץ וַיָּקֻצוּ מִפְּנֵי בְּנֵי יִשְׂרָאֵל׃ *וַיַּעֲבִדוּ ישראל
מִצְרַיִם אֶת־בְּנֵי יִשְׂרָאֵל בְּפָרֶךְ׃ וַיְמָרְרוּ אֶת־חַיֵּיהֶם בַּעֲבֹדָה
קָשָׁה בְּחֹמֶר וּבִלְבֵנִים וּבְכׇל־עֲבֹדָה בַּשָּׂדֶה אֵת כׇּל־עֲבֹדָתָם
אֲשֶׁר־עָבְדוּ בָהֶם בְּפָרֶךְ׃ וַיֹּאמֶר מֶלֶךְ מִצְרַיִם לַמְיַלְּדֹת
הָעִבְרִיֹּת אֲשֶׁר שֵׁם הָאַחַת שִׁפְרָה וְשֵׁם הַשֵּׁנִית פּוּעָה׃
וַיֹּאמֶר בְּיַלֶּדְכֶן אֶת־הָעִבְרִיּוֹת וּרְאִיתֶן עַל־הָאׇבְנָיִם אִם־
בֵּן הוּא וַהֲמִתֶּן אֹתוֹ וְאִם־בַּת הִוא וָחָיָה׃ וַתִּירֶאןָ הַמְיַלְּדֹת

THIRD ALIYA: 1:13–17 A system is established of crushing national enslavement, and male infanticide. The midwives of Egypt refuse to implement the policy.

אֶת־הָאֱלֹהִים וְלֹא עָשׂוּ כַּאֲשֶׁר דִּבֶּר אֲלֵיהֶן מֶלֶךְ מִצְרָיִם
וַתְּחַיֶּיןָ אֶת־הַיְלָדִים׃

VA'ERA — וארא

FIRST ALIYA: 6:2–5
God reassures Moshe that He has heard the Israelites suffering, and remembered His covenant to bring them out of Egypt to the Land of Israel.

SECOND ALIYA: 6:6–9
God asks Moshe to deliver this message to the Israelites, in the form of four expressions of redemption.

וַיְדַבֵּר אֱלֹהִים אֶל־מֹשֶׁה וַיֹּאמֶר אֵלָיו אֲנִי יְהוָה׃ וָאֵרָא שמות ו:ב–יג
אֶל־אַבְרָהָם אֶל־יִצְחָק וְאֶל־יַעֲקֹב בְּאֵל שַׁדָּי וּשְׁמִי יְהוָה
לֹא נוֹדַעְתִּי לָהֶם׃ וְגַם הֲקִמֹתִי אֶת־בְּרִיתִי אִתָּם לָתֵת לָהֶם
אֶת־אֶרֶץ כְּנָעַן אֵת אֶרֶץ מְגֻרֵיהֶם אֲשֶׁר־גָּרוּ בָהּ׃ וְגַם ׀ אֲנִי
שָׁמַעְתִּי אֶת־נַאֲקַת בְּנֵי יִשְׂרָאֵל אֲשֶׁר מִצְרַיִם מַעֲבִדִים
אֹתָם וָאֶזְכֹּר אֶת־בְּרִיתִי׃ *לָכֵן אֱמֹר לִבְנֵי־יִשְׂרָאֵל אֲנִי יְהוָה לוי
וְהוֹצֵאתִי אֶתְכֶם מִתַּחַת סִבְלֹת מִצְרַיִם וְהִצַּלְתִּי אֶתְכֶם
מֵעֲבֹדָתָם וְגָאַלְתִּי אֶתְכֶם בִּזְרוֹעַ נְטוּיָה וּבִשְׁפָטִים גְּדֹלִים׃
וְלָקַחְתִּי אֶתְכֶם לִי לְעָם וְהָיִיתִי לָכֶם לֵאלֹהִים וִידַעְתֶּם כִּי
אֲנִי יְהוָה אֱלֹהֵיכֶם הַמּוֹצִיא אֶתְכֶם מִתַּחַת סִבְלוֹת מִצְרָיִם׃
וְהֵבֵאתִי אֶתְכֶם אֶל־הָאָרֶץ אֲשֶׁר נָשָׂאתִי אֶת־יָדִי לָתֵת
אֹתָהּ לְאַבְרָהָם לְיִצְחָק וּלְיַעֲקֹב וְנָתַתִּי אֹתָהּ לָכֶם מוֹרָשָׁה
אֲנִי יְהוָה׃ וַיְדַבֵּר מֹשֶׁה כֵּן אֶל־בְּנֵי יִשְׂרָאֵל וְלֹא שָׁמְעוּ אֶל־
מֹשֶׁה מִקֹּצֶר רוּחַ וּמֵעֲבֹדָה קָשָׁה׃

THIRD ALIYA: 6:10–13
Moshe is concerned about his ability to deliver the message to Pharaoh.

וַיְדַבֵּר יְהוָה אֶל־מֹשֶׁה לֵּאמֹר׃ בֹּא דַבֵּר אֶל־פַּרְעֹה מֶלֶךְ ישראל
מִצְרָיִם וִישַׁלַּח אֶת־בְּנֵי־יִשְׂרָאֵל מֵאַרְצוֹ׃ וַיְדַבֵּר מֹשֶׁה לִפְנֵי
יְהוָה לֵאמֹר הֵן בְּנֵי־יִשְׂרָאֵל לֹא־שָׁמְעוּ אֵלַי וְאֵיךְ יִשְׁמָעֵנִי
פַרְעֹה וַאֲנִי עֲרַל שְׂפָתָיִם׃
וַיְדַבֵּר יְהוָה אֶל־מֹשֶׁה וְאֶל־אַהֲרֹן וַיְצַוֵּם אֶל־בְּנֵי יִשְׂרָאֵל
וְאֶל־פַּרְעֹה מֶלֶךְ מִצְרָיִם לְהוֹצִיא אֶת־בְּנֵי־יִשְׂרָאֵל מֵאֶרֶץ
מִצְרָיִם׃

FIRST ALIYA: 10:1–3
Prologue to the eighth plague: God sends Moshe and Aharon back to Pharaoh.

BO — בא

וַיֹּאמֶר יְהוָה אֶל־מֹשֶׁה בֹּא אֶל־פַּרְעֹה כִּי־אֲנִי הִכְבַּדְתִּי אֶת־ שמות י:א–יא
לִבּוֹ וְאֶת־לֵב עֲבָדָיו לְמַעַן שִׁתִי אֹתֹתַי אֵלֶּה בְּקִרְבּוֹ׃ וּלְמַעַן

תספר באזני בנך ובן־בנך את אשר התעללתי במצרים
ואת־אתתי אשר־שמתי בם וידעתם כי־אני יהוה: ויבא
משה ואהרן אל־פרעה ויאמרו אליו כה־אמר יהוה אלהי
העברים עד־מתי מאנת לענת מפני שלח עמי ויעבדני:
לוי *כי אם־מאן אתה לשלח את־עמי הנני מביא מחר ארבה
בגבלך: וכסה את־עין הארץ ולא יוכל לראת את־הארץ
ואכל | את־יתר הפלטה הנשארת לכם מן־הברד ואכל
את־כל־העץ הצמח לכם מן־השדה: ומלאו בתיך ובתי
כל־עבדיך ובתי כל־מצרים אשר לא־ראו אבתיך ואבות
אבתיך מיום היותם על־האדמה עד היום הזה ויפן ויצא
ישראל מעם פרעה: *ויאמרו עבדי פרעה אליו עד־מתי יהיה זה
לנו למוקש שלח את־האנשים ויעבדו את־יהוה אלהיהם
הטרם תדע כי אבדה מצרים: ויושב את־משה ואת־אהרן
אל־פרעה ויאמר אלהם לכו עבדו את־יהוה אלהיכם מי
ומי ההלכים: ויאמר משה בנערינו ובזקנינו נלך בבנינו
ובבנותנו בצאננו ובבקרנו נלך כי חג־יהוה לנו: ויאמר
אלהם יהי כן יהוה עמכם כאשר אשלח אתכם ואת־טפכם
ראו כי רעה נגד פניכם: לא כן לכו־נא הגברים ועבדו את־
יהוה כי אתה אתם מבקשים ויגרש אתם מאת פני פרעה:

SECOND ALIYA: 10:4–6
Moshe and Aharon warn Pharaoh of the impending eighth plague: locusts.

THIRD ALIYA: 10:7–11
Pharaoh refuses to let the entire people go.

BESHALLAH בשלח

שמות יג:יז–יד:ח

ויהי בשלח פרעה את־העם ולא־נחם אלהים דרך ארץ
פלשתים כי קרוב הוא כי | אמר אלהים פן־ינחם העם
בראתם מלחמה ושבו מצרימה: ויסב אלהים | את־העם
דרך המדבר ים־סוף וחמשים עלו בני־ישראל מארץ
מצרים: ויקח משה את־עצמות יוסף עמו כי השבע
השביע את־בני ישראל לאמר פקד יפקד אלהים אתכם
והעליתם את־עצמתי מזה אתכם: ויסעו מסכת ויחנו
באתם בקצה המדבר: ויהוה הלך לפניהם יומם בעמוד

FIRST ALIYA: 13:17–22
God led the Israelites on a longer route to the Land of Israel, in order to avoid the land of the Philistines.

ענן לנחתם הדרך ולילה בעמוד אש להאיר להם ללכת
יומם ולילה: לא־ימיש עמוד הענן יומם ועמוד האש
לילה לפני העם:

SECOND ALIYA: 14:1–4
God strengthens Pharaoh's heart and he changes his mind.

לוי וידבר יהוה אל־משה לאמר: דבר אל־בני ישראל וישבו
ויחנו לפני פי החירת בין מגדל ובין הים לפני בעל צפן
נכחו תחנו על־הים: ואמר פרעה לבני ישראל נבכים
הם בארץ סגר עליהם המדבר: וחזקתי את־לב־פרעה
ורדף אחריהם ואכבדה בפרעה ובכל־חילו וידעו מצרים
ישראל כי־אני יהוה ויעשו־כן: *ויגד למלך מצרים כי ברח העם

THIRD ALIYA: 14:5–8
Pharaoh orders his forces to pursue the Israelites.

ויהפך לבב פרעה ועבדיו אל־העם ויאמרו מה־זאת
עשינו כי־שלחנו את־ישראל מעבדנו: ויאסר את־רכבו
ואת־עמו לקח עמו: ויקח שש־מאות רכב בחור וכל
רכב מצרים ושלשם על־כלו: ויחזק יהוה את־לב פרעה
מלך מצרים וירדף אחרי בני ישראל ובני ישראל יצאים
ביד רמה:

YITRO יתרו

שמות יח:א־יב

FIRST ALIYA: 18:1–4
Yitro, the father in law of Moshe, heard all that God did for the Israelites in Egypt.

וישמע יתרו כהן מדין חתן משה את כל־אשר עשה
אלהים למשה ולישראל עמו כי־הוציא יהוה את־ישראל
ממצרים: ויקח יתרו חתן משה את־צפרה אשת משה
אחר שלוחיה: ואת שני בניה אשר שם האחד גרשם
כי אמר גר הייתי בארץ נכריה: ושם האחד אליעזר כי־

SECOND ALIYA: 18:5–8
Yitro takes his daughter Tzippora (Moshe's wife) and her two sons, and joins Moshe and the Israelites.

לוי אלהי אבי בעזרי ויצלני מחרב פרעה: *ויבא יתרו חתן
משה ובניו ואשתו אל־משה אל־המדבר אשר־הוא חנה
שם הר האלהים: ויאמר אל־משה אני חתנך יתרו בא
אליך ואשתך ושני בניה עמה: ויצא משה לקראת חתנו
וישתחו וישק־לו וישאלו איש־לרעהו לשלום ויבאו
האהלה: ויספר משה לחתנו את כל־אשר עשה יהוה
לפרעה ולמצרים על אודת ישראל את כל־התלאה אשר

ישראל מצאתם בדרך ויצלם יהוה: *ויחד יתרו על כל־הטובה
אשר־עשה יהוה לישראל אשר הצילו מיד מצרים: ויאמר
יתרו ברוך יהוה אשר הציל אתכם מיד מצרים ומיד
פרעה אשר הציל את־העם מתחת יד־מצרים: עתה
ידעתי כי־גדול יהוה מכל־האלהים כי בדבר אשר זדו
עליהם: ויקח יתרו חתן משה עלה וזבחים לאלהים ויבא
אהרן וכל ׀ זקני ישראל לאכל־לחם עם־חתן משה לפני
האלהים:

THIRD ALIYA: 18:9–12
Yitro rejoiced in everything that God had done in Egypt, and offered sacrifices to Him in thanks.

MISHPATIM משפטים

שמות כא: א–יט
ואלה המשפטים אשר תשים לפניהם: כי תקנה עבד עברי
שש שנים יעבד ובשבעת יצא לחפשי חנם: אם־בגפו יבא
בגפו יצא אם־בעל אשה הוא ויצאה אשתו עמו: אם־אדניו
יתן־לו אשה וילדה־לו בנים או בנות האשה וילדיה תהיה
לאדניה והוא יצא בגפו: ואם־אמר יאמר העבד אהבתי
את־אדני את־אשתי ואת־בני לא אצא חפשי: והגישו
אדניו אל־האלהים והגישו אל־הדלת או אל־המזוזה ורצע
לוי אדניו את־אזנו במרצע ועבדו לעלם: *וכי־
ימכר איש את־בתו לאמה לא תצא כצאת העבדים:
לו אם־רעה בעיני אדניה אשר־לא יעדה והפדה לעם נכרי
לא־ימשל למכרה בבגדו־בה: ואם־לבנו ייעדנה כמשפט
הבנות יעשה־לה: אם־אחרת יקח־לו שארה כסותה
וענתה לא יגרע: ואם־שלש־אלה לא יעשה לה ויצאה
ישראל חנם אין כסף: *מכה איש ומת מות יומת:
ואשר לא צדה והאלהים אנה לידו ושמתי לך מקום
אשר ינוס שמה: וכי־יזד איש על־רעהו
להרגו בערמה מעם מזבחי תקחנו למות: ומכה
אביו ואמו מות יומת: וגנב איש ומכרו ונמצא
בידו מות יומת: ומקלל אביו ואמו מות

FIRST ALIYA: 21:1–6
The laws of Jewish slaves.

SECOND ALIYA: 21:7–11
The father's rights and responsibilities to his daughter when she is sold as a slave.

THIRD ALIYA: 21:12–19
The laws of murder and manslaughter.

יוּמָֽת׃ וְכִֽי־יְרִיבֻ֣ן אֲנָשִׁ֔ים וְהִכָּה־אִישׁ֙ אֶת־
רֵעֵ֔הוּ בְּאֶ֖בֶן א֣וֹ בְאֶגְרֹ֑ף וְלֹ֥א יָמ֖וּת וְנָפַ֥ל לְמִשְׁכָּֽב׃ אִם־יָק֞וּם
וְהִתְהַלֵּ֥ךְ בַּח֛וּץ עַל־מִשְׁעַנְתּ֖וֹ וְנִקָּ֣ה הַמַּכֶּ֑ה רַ֥ק שִׁבְתּ֛וֹ יִתֵּ֖ן
וְרַפֹּ֥א יְרַפֵּֽא׃

TERUMA תרומה

FIRST ALIYA: 25:1–5
The funding of the Tabernacle.

שמות כה:א–טז וַיְדַבֵּ֥ר יְהֹוָ֖ה אֶל־מֹשֶׁ֥ה לֵּאמֹֽר׃ דַּבֵּר֙ אֶל־בְּנֵ֣י יִשְׂרָאֵ֔ל וְיִקְחוּ־
לִ֖י תְּרוּמָ֑ה מֵאֵ֤ת כׇּל־אִישׁ֙ אֲשֶׁ֣ר יִדְּבֶ֣נּוּ לִבּ֔וֹ תִּקְח֖וּ אֶת־
תְּרוּמָתִֽי׃ וְזֹאת֙ הַתְּרוּמָ֔ה אֲשֶׁ֥ר תִּקְח֖וּ מֵאִתָּ֑ם זָהָ֥ב וָכֶ֖סֶף
וּנְחֹֽשֶׁת׃ וּתְכֵ֧לֶת וְאַרְגָּמָ֛ן וְתוֹלַ֥עַת שָׁנִ֖י וְשֵׁ֥שׁ וְעִזִּֽים׃ וְעֹרֹ֨ת
לוי אֵילִ֧ם מְאׇדָּמִ֛ים וְעֹרֹ֥ת תְּחָשִׁ֖ים וַעֲצֵ֥י שִׁטִּֽים׃ *שֶׁ֖מֶן לַמָּאֹ֑ר

SECOND ALIYA: 25:6–9
God commands the building of the Tabernacle.

בְּשָׂמִים֙ לְשֶׁ֣מֶן הַמִּשְׁחָ֔ה וְלִקְטֹ֖רֶת הַסַּמִּֽים׃ אַבְנֵי־שֹׁ֕הַם
וְאַבְנֵ֖י מִלֻּאִ֑ים לָאֵפֹ֖ד וְלַחֹֽשֶׁן׃ וְעָ֥שׂוּ לִ֖י מִקְדָּ֑שׁ וְשָׁכַנְתִּ֖י
בְּתוֹכָֽם׃ כְּכֹ֗ל אֲשֶׁ֤ר אֲנִי֙ מַרְאֶ֣ה אוֹתְךָ֔ אֵ֚ת תַּבְנִ֣ית הַמִּשְׁכָּ֔ן
ישראל וְאֵ֖ת תַּבְנִ֣ית כׇּל־כֵּלָ֑יו וְכֵ֖ן תַּעֲשֽׂוּ׃ *וְעָשׂ֥וּ אֲר֖וֹן

THIRD ALIYA: 25:10–16
Instructions of how to make the Ark.

עֲצֵ֣י שִׁטִּ֑ים אַמָּתַ֨יִם וָחֵ֜צִי אׇרְכּ֗וֹ וְאַמָּ֤ה וָחֵ֨צִי֙ רׇחְבּ֔וֹ וְאַמָּ֥ה וָחֵ֖צִי
קֹמָתֽוֹ׃ וְצִפִּיתָ֤ אֹתוֹ֙ זָהָ֣ב טָה֔וֹר מִבַּ֥יִת וּמִח֖וּץ תְּצַפֶּ֑נּוּ וְעָשִׂ֧יתָ
עָלָ֛יו זֵ֥ר זָהָ֖ב סָבִֽיב׃ וְיָצַ֣קְתָּ לּ֗וֹ אַרְבַּע֙ טַבְּעֹ֣ת זָהָ֔ב וְנָ֣תַתָּ֔ה
עַ֖ל אַרְבַּ֣ע פַּעֲמֹתָ֑יו וּשְׁתֵּ֣י טַבָּעֹ֗ת עַל־צַלְעוֹ֙ הָֽאֶחָ֔ת וּשְׁתֵּי֙
טַבָּעֹ֔ת עַל־צַלְע֖וֹ הַשֵּׁנִֽית׃ וְעָשִׂ֥יתָ בַדֵּ֖י עֲצֵ֣י שִׁטִּ֑ים וְצִפִּיתָ֥
אֹתָ֖ם זָהָֽב׃ וְהֵבֵאתָ֤ אֶת־הַבַּדִּים֙ בַּטַּבָּעֹ֔ת עַ֖ל צַלְעֹ֣ת הָאָרֹ֑ן
לָשֵׂ֥את אֶת־הָאָרֹ֖ן בָּהֶֽם׃ בְּטַבְּעֹת֙ הָאָרֹ֔ן יִהְי֖וּ הַבַּדִּ֑ים לֹ֥א
יָסֻ֖רוּ מִמֶּֽנּוּ׃ וְנָתַתָּ֖ אֶל־הָאָרֹ֑ן אֵ֚ת הָעֵדֻ֔ת אֲשֶׁ֥ר אֶתֵּ֖ן אֵלֶֽיךָ׃

TETZAVEH תצוה

FIRST ALIYA: 27:20–28:5
Instruction on how to make the oil for the menorah in the Tabernacle, and the priestly garments.

שמות כז:כ–כח:יב וְאַתָּ֞ה תְּצַוֶּ֣ה ׀ אֶת־בְּנֵ֣י יִשְׂרָאֵ֗ל וְיִקְח֨וּ אֵלֶ֜יךָ שֶׁ֣מֶן זַ֥יִת זָ֛ךְ כָּתִ֖ית
לַמָּא֑וֹר לְהַעֲלֹ֥ת נֵ֖ר תָּמִֽיד׃ בְּאֹ֣הֶל מוֹעֵ֡ד מִחוּץ֩ לַפָּרֹ֨כֶת אֲשֶׁ֜ר
עַל־הָעֵדֻ֗ת יַעֲרֹךְ֩ אֹת֨וֹ אַהֲרֹ֧ן וּבָנָ֛יו מֵעֶ֥רֶב עַד־בֹּ֖קֶר לִפְנֵ֣י יְהֹוָ֑ה
חֻקַּ֤ת עוֹלָם֙ לְדֹ֣רֹתָ֔ם מֵאֵ֖ת בְּנֵ֥י יִשְׂרָאֵֽל׃ וְאַתָּ֗ה

הַקְרֵב אֵלֶיךָ אֶת־אַהֲרֹן אָחִיךָ וְאֶת־בָּנָיו אִתּוֹ מִתּוֹךְ בְּנֵי
יִשְׂרָאֵל לְכַהֲנוֹ־לִי אַהֲרֹן נָדָב וַאֲבִיהוּא אֶלְעָזָר וְאִיתָמָר בְּנֵי
אַהֲרֹן: וְעָשִׂיתָ בִגְדֵי־קֹדֶשׁ לְאַהֲרֹן אָחִיךָ לְכָבוֹד וּלְתִפְאָרֶת:
וְאַתָּה תְּדַבֵּר אֶל־כָּל־חַכְמֵי־לֵב אֲשֶׁר מִלֵּאתִיו רוּחַ חָכְמָה
וְעָשׂוּ אֶת־בִּגְדֵי אַהֲרֹן לְקַדְּשׁוֹ לְכַהֲנוֹ־לִי: וְאֵלֶּה הַבְּגָדִים
אֲשֶׁר יַעֲשׂוּ חֹשֶׁן וְאֵפוֹד וּמְעִיל וּכְתֹנֶת תַּשְׁבֵּץ מִצְנֶפֶת
וְאַבְנֵט וְעָשׂוּ בִגְדֵי־קֹדֶשׁ לְאַהֲרֹן אָחִיךָ וּלְבָנָיו לְכַהֲנוֹ־לִי:
וְהֵם יִקְחוּ אֶת־הַזָּהָב וְאֶת־הַתְּכֵלֶת וְאֶת־הָאַרְגָּמָן וְאֶת־
תּוֹלַעַת הַשָּׁנִי וְאֶת־הַשֵּׁשׁ:
לוי וְעָשׂוּ אֶת־הָאֵפֹד זָהָב תְּכֵלֶת וְאַרְגָּמָן תּוֹלַעַת שָׁנִי וְשֵׁשׁ
מָשְׁזָר מַעֲשֵׂה חֹשֵׁב: שְׁתֵּי כְתֵפֹת חֹבְרֹת יִהְיֶה־לּוֹ אֶל־
שְׁנֵי קְצוֹתָיו וְחֻבָּר: וְחֵשֶׁב אֲפֻדָּתוֹ אֲשֶׁר עָלָיו כְּמַעֲשֵׂהוּ
מִמֶּנּוּ יִהְיֶה זָהָב תְּכֵלֶת וְאַרְגָּמָן וְתוֹלַעַת שָׁנִי וְשֵׁשׁ מָשְׁזָר:
וְלָקַחְתָּ אֶת־שְׁתֵּי אַבְנֵי־שֹׁהַם וּפִתַּחְתָּ עֲלֵיהֶם שְׁמוֹת בְּנֵי
ישראל יִשְׂרָאֵל: *שִׁשָּׁה מִשְּׁמֹתָם עַל הָאֶבֶן הָאֶחָת וְאֶת־שְׁמוֹת
הַשִּׁשָּׁה הַנּוֹתָרִים עַל־הָאֶבֶן הַשֵּׁנִית כְּתוֹלְדֹתָם: מַעֲשֵׂה
חָרַשׁ אֶבֶן פִּתּוּחֵי חֹתָם תְּפַתַּח אֶת־שְׁתֵּי הָאֲבָנִים עַל־שְׁמֹת
בְּנֵי יִשְׂרָאֵל מֻסַבֹּת מִשְׁבְּצוֹת זָהָב תַּעֲשֶׂה אֹתָם: וְשַׂמְתָּ
אֶת־שְׁתֵּי הָאֲבָנִים עַל כִּתְפֹת הָאֵפֹד אַבְנֵי זִכָּרֹן לִבְנֵי יִשְׂרָאֵל
וְנָשָׂא אַהֲרֹן אֶת־שְׁמוֹתָם לִפְנֵי יְהוָה עַל־שְׁתֵּי כְתֵפָיו לְזִכָּרֹן:

SECOND ALIYA: 28:6–9
Instructions on the making of the High Priest's garments and breastplate.

THIRD ALIYA: 28:10–12
The details of the twelve precious stones in the High Priest's breastplate.

KI TISSA כי תשא

שמות ל:יא–כא וַיְדַבֵּר יְהוָה אֶל־מֹשֶׁה לֵּאמֹר: כִּי תִשָּׂא אֶת־רֹאשׁ בְּנֵי־
יִשְׂרָאֵל לִפְקֻדֵיהֶם וְנָתְנוּ אִישׁ כֹּפֶר נַפְשׁוֹ לַיהוָה בִּפְקֹד
אֹתָם וְלֹא־יִהְיֶה בָהֶם נֶגֶף בִּפְקֹד אֹתָם: זֶה ׀ יִתְּנוּ כָּל־הָעֹבֵר
עַל־הַפְּקֻדִים מַחֲצִית הַשֶּׁקֶל בְּשֶׁקֶל הַקֹּדֶשׁ עֶשְׂרִים גֵּרָה
לוי הַשֶּׁקֶל מַחֲצִית הַשֶּׁקֶל תְּרוּמָה לַיהוָה: *כֹּל הָעֹבֵר עַל־
הַפְּקֻדִים מִבֶּן עֶשְׂרִים שָׁנָה וָמָעְלָה יִתֵּן תְּרוּמַת יְהוָה:
הֶעָשִׁיר לֹא־יַרְבֶּה וְהַדַּל לֹא יַמְעִיט מִמַּחֲצִית הַשֶּׁקֶל לָתֵת

FIRST ALIYA: 30:11–13
The census of the Jewish people will be carried out through the giving of a half shekel.

SECOND ALIYA: 30:14–16
All men above the age of twenty will be counted in the census.

אֶת־תְּרוּמַת יְהוָה לְכַפֵּר עַל־נַפְשֹׁתֵיכֶם׃ וְלָקַחְתָּ אֶת־כֶּסֶף
הַכִּפֻּרִים מֵאֵת בְּנֵי יִשְׂרָאֵל וְנָתַתָּ אֹתוֹ עַל־עֲבֹדַת אֹהֶל
מוֹעֵד וְהָיָה לִבְנֵי יִשְׂרָאֵל לְזִכָּרוֹן לִפְנֵי יְהוָה לְכַפֵּר עַל־
נַפְשֹׁתֵיכֶם׃

ישראל

THIRD ALIYA: 30:17–21
Instructions of the making of the copper basin for the priests to wash in the Tabernacle.

וַיְדַבֵּר יְהוָה אֶל־מֹשֶׁה לֵּאמֹר׃ וְעָשִׂיתָ כִּיּוֹר נְחֹשֶׁת וְכַנּוֹ
נְחֹשֶׁת לְרָחְצָה וְנָתַתָּ אֹתוֹ בֵּין־אֹהֶל מוֹעֵד וּבֵין הַמִּזְבֵּחַ
וְנָתַתָּ שָׁמָּה מָיִם׃ וְרָחֲצוּ אַהֲרֹן וּבָנָיו מִמֶּנּוּ אֶת־יְדֵיהֶם וְאֶת־
רַגְלֵיהֶם׃ בְּבֹאָם אֶל־אֹהֶל מוֹעֵד יִרְחֲצוּ־מַיִם וְלֹא יָמֻתוּ
אוֹ בְגִשְׁתָּם אֶל־הַמִּזְבֵּחַ לְשָׁרֵת לְהַקְטִיר אִשֶּׁה לַיהוָה׃
וְרָחֲצוּ יְדֵיהֶם וְרַגְלֵיהֶם וְלֹא יָמֻתוּ וְהָיְתָה לָהֶם חָק־עוֹלָם
לוֹ וּלְזַרְעוֹ לְדֹרֹתָם׃

VAYAK-HEL ויקהל

שמות לה:א–כ

FIRST ALIYA: 35:1–3
Shabbat: you may work for six days and must rest on the seventh which is a holy day.

וַיַּקְהֵל מֹשֶׁה אֶת־כָּל־עֲדַת בְּנֵי יִשְׂרָאֵל וַיֹּאמֶר אֲלֵהֶם אֵלֶּה
הַדְּבָרִים אֲשֶׁר־צִוָּה יְהוָה לַעֲשֹׂת אֹתָם׃ שֵׁשֶׁת יָמִים תֵּעָשֶׂה
מְלָאכָה וּבַיּוֹם הַשְּׁבִיעִי יִהְיֶה לָכֶם קֹדֶשׁ שַׁבַּת שַׁבָּתוֹן
לַיהוָה כָּל־הָעֹשֶׂה בוֹ מְלָאכָה יוּמָת׃ לֹא־תְבַעֲרוּ אֵשׁ בְּכֹל
מֹשְׁבֹתֵיכֶם בְּיוֹם הַשַּׁבָּת׃

לוי

SECOND ALIYA: 35:4–10
Donations to the Tabernacle.

וַיֹּאמֶר מֹשֶׁה אֶל־כָּל־עֲדַת בְּנֵי־יִשְׂרָאֵל לֵאמֹר זֶה הַדָּבָר
אֲשֶׁר־צִוָּה יְהוָה לֵאמֹר׃ קְחוּ מֵאִתְּכֶם תְּרוּמָה לַיהוָה כֹּל
נְדִיב לִבּוֹ יְבִיאֶהָ אֵת תְּרוּמַת יְהוָה זָהָב וָכֶסֶף וּנְחֹשֶׁת׃
וּתְכֵלֶת וְאַרְגָּמָן וְתוֹלַעַת שָׁנִי וְשֵׁשׁ וְעִזִּים׃ וְעֹרֹת אֵילִם
מְאָדָּמִים וְעֹרֹת תְּחָשִׁים וַעֲצֵי שִׁטִּים׃ וְשֶׁמֶן לַמָּאוֹר וּבְשָׂמִים
לְשֶׁמֶן הַמִּשְׁחָה וְלִקְטֹרֶת הַסַּמִּים׃ וְאַבְנֵי־שֹׁהַם וְאַבְנֵי
מִלֻּאִים לָאֵפוֹד וְלַחֹשֶׁן׃ וְכָל־חֲכַם־לֵב בָּכֶם יָבֹאוּ וְיַעֲשׂוּ

ישראל

THIRD ALIYA: 35:11–20
The construction of the Tabernacle.

אֵת כָּל־אֲשֶׁר צִוָּה יְהוָה׃ *אֶת־הַמִּשְׁכָּן אֶת־אָהֳלוֹ וְאֶת־
מִכְסֵהוּ אֶת־קְרָסָיו וְאֶת־קְרָשָׁיו אֶת־בְּרִיחָו אֶת־עַמֻּדָיו
וְאֶת־אֲדָנָיו׃ אֶת־הָאָרֹן וְאֶת־בַּדָּיו אֶת־הַכַּפֹּרֶת וְאֵת פָּרֹכֶת
הַמָּסָךְ׃ אֶת־הַשֻּׁלְחָן וְאֶת־בַּדָּיו וְאֶת־כָּל־כֵּלָיו וְאֵת לֶחֶם

הַפָּנִים: וְאֶת־מְנֹרַת הַמָּאוֹר וְאֶת־כֵּלֶיהָ וְאֶת־נֵרֹתֶיהָ וְאֵת
שֶׁמֶן הַמָּאוֹר: וְאֶת־מִזְבַּח הַקְּטֹרֶת וְאֶת־בַּדָּיו וְאֵת שֶׁמֶן
הַמִּשְׁחָה וְאֵת קְטֹרֶת הַסַּמִּים וְאֶת־מָסַךְ הַפֶּתַח לְפֶתַח
הַמִּשְׁכָּן: אֵת ׀ מִזְבַּח הָעֹלָה וְאֶת־מִכְבַּר הַנְּחֹשֶׁת אֲשֶׁר־
לוֹ אֶת־בַּדָּיו וְאֶת־כׇּל־כֵּלָיו אֶת־הַכִּיֹּר וְאֶת־כַּנּוֹ: אֵת קַלְעֵי
הֶחָצֵר אֶת־עַמֻּדָיו וְאֶת־אֲדָנֶיהָ וְאֵת מָסַךְ שַׁעַר הֶחָצֵר:
אֶת־יִתְדֹת הַמִּשְׁכָּן וְאֶת־יִתְדֹת הֶחָצֵר וְאֶת־מֵיתְרֵיהֶם:
אֶת־בִּגְדֵי הַשְּׂרָד לְשָׁרֵת בַּקֹּדֶשׁ אֶת־בִּגְדֵי הַקֹּדֶשׁ לְאַהֲרֹן
הַכֹּהֵן וְאֶת־בִּגְדֵי בָנָיו לְכַהֵן: וַיֵּצְאוּ כׇּל־עֲדַת בְּנֵי־יִשְׂרָאֵל
מִלִּפְנֵי מֹשֶׁה:

PEKUDEI פקודי

שמות לח:כא–לט:א אֵלֶּה פְקוּדֵי הַמִּשְׁכָּן מִשְׁכַּן הָעֵדֻת אֲשֶׁר פֻּקַּד עַל־פִּי מֹשֶׁה
עֲבֹדַת הַלְוִיִּם בְּיַד אִיתָמָר בֶּן־אַהֲרֹן הַכֹּהֵן: וּבְצַלְאֵל בֶּן־
אוּרִי בֶן־חוּר לְמַטֵּה יְהוּדָה עָשָׂה אֵת כׇּל־אֲשֶׁר־צִוָּה
יְהֹוָה אֶת־מֹשֶׁה: וְאִתּוֹ אׇהֳלִיאָב בֶּן־אֲחִיסָמָךְ לְמַטֵּה־
דָן חָרָשׁ וְחֹשֵׁב וְרֹקֵם בַּתְּכֵלֶת וּבָאַרְגָּמָן וּבְתוֹלַעַת הַשָּׁנִי
לוי וּבַשֵּׁשׁ: *כׇּל־הַזָּהָב הֶעָשׂוּי לַמְּלָאכָה בְּכֹל
מְלֶאכֶת הַקֹּדֶשׁ וַיְהִי ׀ זְהַב הַתְּנוּפָה תֵּשַׁע וְעֶשְׂרִים כִּכָּר
וּשְׁבַע מֵאוֹת וּשְׁלֹשִׁים שֶׁקֶל בְּשֶׁקֶל הַקֹּדֶשׁ: וְכֶסֶף פְּקוּדֵי
הָעֵדָה מְאַת כִּכָּר וְאֶלֶף וּשְׁבַע מֵאוֹת וַחֲמִשָּׁה וְשִׁבְעִים
שֶׁקֶל בְּשֶׁקֶל הַקֹּדֶשׁ: בֶּקַע לַגֻּלְגֹּלֶת מַחֲצִית הַשֶּׁקֶל בְּשֶׁקֶל
הַקֹּדֶשׁ לְכֹל הָעֹבֵר עַל־הַפְּקֻדִים מִבֶּן עֶשְׂרִים שָׁנָה וָמַעְלָה
לְשֵׁשׁ־מֵאוֹת אֶלֶף וּשְׁלֹשֶׁת אֲלָפִים וַחֲמֵשׁ מֵאוֹת וַחֲמִשִּׁים:
וַיְהִי מְאַת כִּכַּר הַכֶּסֶף לָצֶקֶת אֵת אַדְנֵי הַקֹּדֶשׁ וְאֵת אַדְנֵי
ישראל הַפָּרֹכֶת מְאַת אֲדָנִים לִמְאַת הַכִּכָּר כִּכָּר לָאָדֶן: *וְאֶת־
הָאֶלֶף וּשְׁבַע הַמֵּאוֹת וַחֲמִשָּׁה וְשִׁבְעִים עָשָׂה וָוִים לָעַמּוּדִים
וְצִפָּה רָאשֵׁיהֶם וְחִשַּׁק אֹתָם: וּנְחֹשֶׁת הַתְּנוּפָה שִׁבְעִים כִּכָּר
וְאַלְפַּיִם וְאַרְבַּע־מֵאוֹת שָׁקֶל: וַיַּעַשׂ בָּהּ אֶת־אַדְנֵי פֶּתַח

FIRST ALIYA: 38:21–23
An introduction to the accounts of the donations to the Tabernacle.

SECOND ALIYA: 38:24–27
Summary of the materials used in the construction of the Tabernacle.

THIRD ALIYA: 38:28–39:1
Continuation of the summary of the materials used in the construction of the Tabernacle.

אֹהֶל מוֹעֵד וְאֵת מִזְבַּח הַנְּחֹשֶׁת וְאֶת־מִכְבַּר הַנְּחֹשֶׁת אֲשֶׁר־
לוֹ וְאֵת כׇּל־כְּלֵי הַמִּזְבֵּחַ׃ וְאֶת־אַדְנֵי הֶחָצֵר סָבִיב וְאֶת־אַדְנֵי
שַׁעַר הֶחָצֵר וְאֵת כׇּל־יִתְדֹת הַמִּשְׁכָּן וְאֶת־כׇּל־יִתְדֹת הֶחָצֵר
סָבִיב׃ וּמִן־הַתְּכֵלֶת וְהָאַרְגָּמָן וְתוֹלַעַת הַשָּׁנִי עָשׂוּ בִגְדֵי־
שְׂרָד לְשָׁרֵת בַּקֹּדֶשׁ וַיַּעֲשׂוּ אֶת־בִּגְדֵי הַקֹּדֶשׁ אֲשֶׁר לְאַהֲרֹן
כַּאֲשֶׁר צִוָּה יהוה אֶת־מֹשֶׁה׃

VAYIKRA ויקרא

ויקרא א:א–יג וַיִּקְרָא אֶל־מֹשֶׁה וַיְדַבֵּר יהוה אֵלָיו מֵאֹהֶל מוֹעֵד לֵאמֹר׃
דַּבֵּר אֶל־בְּנֵי יִשְׂרָאֵל וְאָמַרְתָּ אֲלֵהֶם אָדָם כִּי־יַקְרִיב מִכֶּם
קׇרְבָּן לַיהוה מִן־הַבְּהֵמָה מִן־הַבָּקָר וּמִן־הַצֹּאן תַּקְרִיבוּ אֶת־
קׇרְבַּנְכֶם׃ אִם־עֹלָה קׇרְבָּנוֹ מִן־הַבָּקָר זָכָר תָּמִים יַקְרִיבֶנּוּ
אֶל־פֶּתַח אֹהֶל מוֹעֵד יַקְרִיב אֹתוֹ לִרְצֹנוֹ לִפְנֵי יהוה׃ וְסָמַךְ
לוי יָדוֹ עַל רֹאשׁ הָעֹלָה וְנִרְצָה לוֹ לְכַפֵּר עָלָיו׃ *וְשָׁחַט אֶת־בֶּן
הַבָּקָר לִפְנֵי יהוה וְהִקְרִיבוּ בְּנֵי אַהֲרֹן הַכֹּהֲנִים אֶת־הַדָּם
וְזָרְקוּ אֶת־הַדָּם עַל־הַמִּזְבֵּחַ סָבִיב אֲשֶׁר־פֶּתַח אֹהֶל מוֹעֵד׃
וְהִפְשִׁיט אֶת־הָעֹלָה וְנִתַּח אֹתָהּ לִנְתָחֶיהָ׃ וְנָתְנוּ בְּנֵי אַהֲרֹן
הַכֹּהֵן אֵשׁ עַל־הַמִּזְבֵּחַ וְעָרְכוּ עֵצִים עַל־הָאֵשׁ׃ וְעָרְכוּ בְּנֵי
אַהֲרֹן הַכֹּהֲנִים אֵת הַנְּתָחִים אֶת־הָרֹאשׁ וְאֶת־הַפָּדֶר עַל־
הָעֵצִים אֲשֶׁר עַל־הָאֵשׁ אֲשֶׁר עַל־הַמִּזְבֵּחַ׃ וְקִרְבּוֹ וּכְרָעָיו
יִרְחַץ בַּמָּיִם וְהִקְטִיר הַכֹּהֵן אֶת־הַכֹּל הַמִּזְבֵּחָה עֹלָה אִשֵּׁה
ישראל רֵיחַ־נִיחוֹחַ לַיהוה׃ *וְאִם־מִן־הַצֹּאן קׇרְבָּנוֹ מִן־
הַכְּשָׂבִים אוֹ מִן־הָעִזִּים לְעֹלָה זָכָר תָּמִים יַקְרִיבֶנּוּ׃ וְשָׁחַט
אֹתוֹ עַל יֶרֶךְ הַמִּזְבֵּחַ צָפֹנָה לִפְנֵי יהוה וְזָרְקוּ בְּנֵי אַהֲרֹן
הַכֹּהֲנִים אֶת־דָּמוֹ עַל־הַמִּזְבֵּחַ סָבִיב׃ וְנִתַּח אֹתוֹ לִנְתָחָיו
וְאֶת־רֹאשׁוֹ וְאֶת־פִּדְרוֹ וְעָרַךְ הַכֹּהֵן אֹתָם עַל־הָעֵצִים אֲשֶׁר
עַל־הָאֵשׁ אֲשֶׁר עַל־הַמִּזְבֵּחַ׃ וְהַקֶּרֶב וְהַכְּרָעַיִם יִרְחַץ בַּמָּיִם
וְהִקְרִיב הַכֹּהֵן אֶת־הַכֹּל וְהִקְטִיר הַמִּזְבֵּחָה עֹלָה הוּא אִשֵּׁה
רֵיחַ נִיחֹחַ לַיהוה׃

FIRST ALIYA: 1:1–4
The laws of an elevation offering.

SECOND ALIYA: 1:5–9
Continuation of the laws of an elevation offering.

THIRD ALIYA: 1:10–13
Elevation offerings from sheep and goats.

TZAV צו

ויקרא ו:א–יא וַיְדַבֵּר יְהוָה אֶל־מֹשֶׁה לֵּאמֹר: צַו אֶת־אַהֲרֹן וְאֶת־בָּנָיו לֵאמֹר
זֹאת תּוֹרַת הָעֹלָה הִוא הָעֹלָה עַל מוֹקְדָה עַל־הַמִּזְבֵּחַ כָּל־
הַלַּיְלָה עַד־הַבֹּקֶר וְאֵשׁ הַמִּזְבֵּחַ תּוּקַד בּוֹ: וְלָבַשׁ הַכֹּהֵן מִדּוֹ
בַד וּמִכְנְסֵי־בַד יִלְבַּשׁ עַל־בְּשָׂרוֹ וְהֵרִים אֶת־הַדֶּשֶׁן אֲשֶׁר
תֹּאכַל הָאֵשׁ אֶת־הָעֹלָה עַל־הַמִּזְבֵּחַ וְשָׂמוֹ אֵצֶל הַמִּזְבֵּחַ:
לוי ★וּפָשַׁט אֶת־בְּגָדָיו וְלָבַשׁ בְּגָדִים אֲחֵרִים וְהוֹצִיא אֶת־הַדֶּשֶׁן
אֶל־מִחוּץ לַמַּחֲנֶה אֶל־מָקוֹם טָהוֹר: וְהָאֵשׁ עַל־הַמִּזְבֵּחַ
תּוּקַד־בּוֹ לֹא תִכְבֶּה וּבִעֵר עָלֶיהָ הַכֹּהֵן עֵצִים בַּבֹּקֶר בַּבֹּקֶר
וְעָרַךְ עָלֶיהָ הָעֹלָה וְהִקְטִיר עָלֶיהָ חֶלְבֵי הַשְּׁלָמִים: אֵשׁ
ישראל תָּמִיד תּוּקַד עַל־הַמִּזְבֵּחַ לֹא תִכְבֶּה: ★וְזֹאת
תּוֹרַת הַמִּנְחָה הַקְרֵב אֹתָהּ בְּנֵי־אַהֲרֹן לִפְנֵי יְהוָה אֶל־פְּנֵי
הַמִּזְבֵּחַ: וְהֵרִים מִמֶּנּוּ בְּקֻמְצוֹ מִסֹּלֶת הַמִּנְחָה וּמִשַּׁמְנָהּ
וְאֵת כָּל־הַלְּבֹנָה אֲשֶׁר עַל־הַמִּנְחָה וְהִקְטִיר הַמִּזְבֵּחַ רֵיחַ
נִיחֹחַ אַזְכָּרָתָהּ לַיהוָה: וְהַנּוֹתֶרֶת מִמֶּנָּה יֹאכְלוּ אַהֲרֹן וּבָנָיו
מַצּוֹת תֵּאָכֵל בְּמָקוֹם קָדֹשׁ בַּחֲצַר אֹהֶל־מוֹעֵד יֹאכְלוּהָ: לֹא
תֵאָפֶה חָמֵץ חֶלְקָם נָתַתִּי אֹתָהּ מֵאִשָּׁי קֹדֶשׁ קָדָשִׁים הִוא
כַּחַטָּאת וְכָאָשָׁם: כָּל־זָכָר בִּבְנֵי אַהֲרֹן יֹאכְלֶנָּה חָק־עוֹלָם
לְדֹרֹתֵיכֶם מֵאִשֵּׁי יְהוָה כֹּל אֲשֶׁר־יִגַּע בָּהֶם יִקְדָּשׁ:

FIRST ALIYA: 6:1–3
Elevation offerings should burn all night.

SECOND ALIYA: 6:4–6
The ash must be removed to outside the camp.

THIRD ALIYA: 6:7–11
The laws of the meal offering.

SHEMINI שמיני

ויקרא ט:א–טז וַיְהִי בַּיּוֹם הַשְּׁמִינִי קָרָא מֹשֶׁה לְאַהֲרֹן וּלְבָנָיו וּלְזִקְנֵי יִשְׂרָאֵל:
וַיֹּאמֶר אֶל־אַהֲרֹן קַח־לְךָ עֵגֶל בֶּן־בָּקָר לְחַטָּאת וְאַיִל לְעֹלָה
תְּמִימִם וְהַקְרֵב לִפְנֵי יְהוָה: וְאֶל־בְּנֵי יִשְׂרָאֵל תְּדַבֵּר לֵאמֹר
קְחוּ שְׂעִיר־עִזִּים לְחַטָּאת וְעֵגֶל וָכֶבֶשׂ בְּנֵי־שָׁנָה תְּמִימִם
לְעֹלָה: וְשׁוֹר וָאַיִל לִשְׁלָמִים לִזְבֹּחַ לִפְנֵי יְהוָה וּמִנְחָה
בְּלוּלָה בַשָּׁמֶן כִּי הַיּוֹם יְהוָה נִרְאָה אֲלֵיכֶם: וַיִּקְחוּ אֵת
אֲשֶׁר צִוָּה מֹשֶׁה אֶל־פְּנֵי אֹהֶל מוֹעֵד וַיִּקְרְבוּ כָּל־הָעֵדָה
וַיַּעַמְדוּ לִפְנֵי יְהוָה: וַיֹּאמֶר מֹשֶׁה זֶה הַדָּבָר אֲשֶׁר־צִוָּה יְהוָה

FIRST ALIYA: 9:1–5
Moshe gives instructions about the inauguration of the priestly service in the Tabernacle.

SECOND ALIYA: 9:6–10
The priestly service is inaugurated in the Tabernacle.

לוי תַּעֲשׂוּ וְיֵרָא אֲלֵיכֶם כְּבוֹד יהוה׃ *וַיֹּאמֶר מֹשֶׁה אֶל־אַהֲרֹן קְרַב אֶל־הַמִּזְבֵּחַ וַעֲשֵׂה אֶת־חַטָּאתְךָ וְאֶת־עֹלָתֶךָ וְכַפֵּר בַּעַדְךָ וּבְעַד הָעָם וַעֲשֵׂה אֶת־קָרְבַּן הָעָם וְכַפֵּר בַּעֲדָם כַּאֲשֶׁר צִוָּה יהוה׃ וַיִּקְרַב אַהֲרֹן אֶל־הַמִּזְבֵּחַ וַיִּשְׁחַט אֶת־עֵגֶל הַחַטָּאת אֲשֶׁר־לוֹ׃ וַיַּקְרִבוּ בְּנֵי אַהֲרֹן אֶת־הַדָּם אֵלָיו וַיִּטְבֹּל אֶצְבָּעוֹ בַּדָּם וַיִּתֵּן עַל־קַרְנוֹת הַמִּזְבֵּחַ וְאֶת־הַדָּם יָצַק אֶל־יְסוֹד הַמִּזְבֵּחַ׃ וְאֶת־הַחֵלֶב וְאֶת־הַכְּלָיֹת וְאֶת־הַיֹּתֶרֶת מִן־הַכָּבֵד מִן־הַחַטָּאת הִקְטִיר הַמִּזְבֵּחָה כַּאֲשֶׁר

THIRD ALIYA: 9:11–16
Aharon conducts the priestly service in the Tabernacle.

ישראל צִוָּה יהוה אֶת־מֹשֶׁה׃ *וְאֶת־הַבָּשָׂר וְאֶת־הָעוֹר שָׂרַף בָּאֵשׁ מִחוּץ לַמַּחֲנֶה׃ וַיִּשְׁחַט אֶת־הָעֹלָה וַיַּמְצִאוּ בְּנֵי אַהֲרֹן אֵלָיו אֶת־הַדָּם וַיִּזְרְקֵהוּ עַל־הַמִּזְבֵּחַ סָבִיב׃ וְאֶת־הָעֹלָה הִמְצִיאוּ אֵלָיו לִנְתָחֶיהָ וְאֶת־הָרֹאשׁ וַיַּקְטֵר עַל־הַמִּזְבֵּחַ׃ וַיִּרְחַץ אֶת־הַקֶּרֶב וְאֶת־הַכְּרָעָיִם וַיַּקְטֵר עַל־הָעֹלָה הַמִּזְבֵּחָה׃ וַיַּקְרֵב אֵת קָרְבַּן הָעָם וַיִּקַּח אֶת־שְׂעִיר הַחַטָּאת אֲשֶׁר לָעָם וַיִּשְׁחָטֵהוּ וַיְחַטְּאֵהוּ כָּרִאשׁוֹן׃ וַיַּקְרֵב אֶת־הָעֹלָה וַיַּעֲשֶׂהָ כַּמִּשְׁפָּט׃

TAZRIA תזריע

ויקרא יב:א–יג:ה

FIRST ALIYA: 12:1–4
The laws concerning post-childbirth.

וַיְדַבֵּר יהוה אֶל־מֹשֶׁה לֵּאמֹר׃ דַּבֵּר אֶל־בְּנֵי יִשְׂרָאֵל לֵאמֹר אִשָּׁה כִּי תַזְרִיעַ וְיָלְדָה זָכָר וְטָמְאָה שִׁבְעַת יָמִים כִּימֵי נִדַּת דְּוֺתָהּ תִּטְמָא׃ וּבַיּוֹם הַשְּׁמִינִי יִמּוֹל בְּשַׂר עָרְלָתוֹ׃ וּשְׁלֹשִׁים יוֹם וּשְׁלֹשֶׁת יָמִים תֵּשֵׁב בִּדְמֵי טָהֳרָה בְּכָל־קֹדֶשׁ לֹא־תִגָּע

SECOND ALIYA: 12:5–8
Post-childbirth offerings.

לוי וְאֶל־הַמִּקְדָּשׁ לֹא תָבֹא עַד־מְלֹאת יְמֵי טָהֳרָהּ׃ *וְאִם־נְקֵבָה תֵלֵד וְטָמְאָה שְׁבֻעַיִם כְּנִדָּתָהּ וְשִׁשִּׁים יוֹם וְשֵׁשֶׁת יָמִים תֵּשֵׁב עַל־דְּמֵי טָהֳרָה׃ וּבִמְלֹאת ׀ יְמֵי טָהֳרָהּ לְבֵן אוֹ לְבַת תָּבִיא כֶּבֶשׂ בֶּן־שְׁנָתוֹ לְעֹלָה וּבֶן־יוֹנָה אוֹ־תֹר לְחַטָּאת אֶל־פֶּתַח אֹהֶל־מוֹעֵד אֶל־הַכֹּהֵן׃ וְהִקְרִיבוֹ לִפְנֵי יהוה וְכִפֶּר עָלֶיהָ וְטָהֲרָה מִמְּקֹר דָּמֶיהָ זֹאת תּוֹרַת הַיֹּלֶדֶת לַזָּכָר אוֹ לַנְּקֵבָה׃ וְאִם־לֹא תִמְצָא יָדָהּ דֵּי שֶׂה וְלָקְחָה שְׁתֵּי־תֹרִים

אוֹ שְׁנֵי בְּנֵי יוֹנָה אֶחָד לְעֹלָה וְאֶחָד לְחַטָּאת וְכִפֶּר עָלֶיהָ
הַכֹּהֵן וְטָהֵרָה׃
וַיְדַבֵּר יהוה אֶל־מֹשֶׁה וְאֶל־אַהֲרֹן לֵאמֹר׃ אָדָם כִּי־יִהְיֶה ישראל
בְעוֹר־בְּשָׂרוֹ שְׂאֵת אוֹ־סַפַּחַת אוֹ בַהֶרֶת וְהָיָה בְעוֹר־בְּשָׂרוֹ
לְנֶגַע צָרָעַת וְהוּבָא אֶל־אַהֲרֹן הַכֹּהֵן אוֹ אֶל־אַחַד מִבָּנָיו
הַכֹּהֲנִים׃ וְרָאָה הַכֹּהֵן אֶת־הַנֶּגַע בְּעוֹר־הַבָּשָׂר וְשֵׂעָר בַּנֶּגַע
הָפַךְ ׀ לָבָן וּמַרְאֵה הַנֶּגַע עָמֹק מֵעוֹר בְּשָׂרוֹ נֶגַע צָרַעַת הוּא
וְרָאָהוּ הַכֹּהֵן וְטִמֵּא אֹתוֹ׃ וְאִם־בַּהֶרֶת לְבָנָה הִוא בְּעוֹר
בְּשָׂרוֹ וְעָמֹק אֵין־מַרְאֶהָ מִן־הָעוֹר וּשְׂעָרָה לֹא־הָפַךְ לָבָן
וְהִסְגִּיר הַכֹּהֵן אֶת־הַנֶּגַע שִׁבְעַת יָמִים׃ וְרָאָהוּ הַכֹּהֵן בַּיּוֹם
הַשְּׁבִיעִי וְהִנֵּה הַנֶּגַע עָמַד בְּעֵינָיו לֹא־פָשָׂה הַנֶּגַע בָּעוֹר
וְהִסְגִּירוֹ הַכֹּהֵן שִׁבְעַת יָמִים שֵׁנִית׃

THIRD ALIYA: 13:1–5
The laws of *Tzara'at*.

METZORA מצורע

וַיְדַבֵּר יהוה אֶל־מֹשֶׁה לֵּאמֹר׃ זֹאת תִּהְיֶה תּוֹרַת הַמְּצֹרָע ויקרא
בְּיוֹם טָהֳרָתוֹ וְהוּבָא אֶל־הַכֹּהֵן׃ וְיָצָא הַכֹּהֵן אֶל־מִחוּץ יד:א-יב
לַמַּחֲנֶה וְרָאָה הַכֹּהֵן וְהִנֵּה נִרְפָּא נֶגַע־הַצָּרַעַת מִן־הַצָּרוּעַ׃
וְצִוָּה הַכֹּהֵן וְלָקַח לַמִּטַּהֵר שְׁתֵּי־צִפֳּרִים חַיּוֹת טְהֹרוֹת
וְעֵץ אֶרֶז וּשְׁנִי תוֹלַעַת וְאֵזֹב׃ וְצִוָּה הַכֹּהֵן וְשָׁחַט אֶת־הַצִּפּוֹר
הָאֶחָת אֶל־כְּלִי־חֶרֶשׂ עַל־מַיִם חַיִּים׃ *אֶת־הַצִּפֹּר הַחַיָּה לוי
יִקַּח אֹתָהּ וְאֶת־עֵץ הָאֶרֶז וְאֶת־שְׁנִי הַתּוֹלַעַת וְאֶת־הָאֵזֹב
וְטָבַל אוֹתָם וְאֵת ׀ הַצִּפֹּר הַחַיָּה בְּדַם הַצִּפֹּר הַשְּׁחֻטָה
עַל הַמַּיִם הַחַיִּים׃ וְהִזָּה עַל הַמִּטַּהֵר מִן־הַצָּרַעַת שֶׁבַע
פְּעָמִים וְטִהֲרוֹ וְשִׁלַּח אֶת־הַצִּפֹּר הַחַיָּה עַל־פְּנֵי הַשָּׂדֶה׃
וְכִבֶּס הַמִּטַּהֵר אֶת־בְּגָדָיו וְגִלַּח אֶת־כָּל־שְׂעָרוֹ וְרָחַץ בַּמַּיִם
וְטָהֵר וְאַחַר יָבוֹא אֶל־הַמַּחֲנֶה וְיָשַׁב מִחוּץ לְאָהֳלוֹ שִׁבְעַת
יָמִים׃ וְהָיָה בַיּוֹם הַשְּׁבִיעִי יְגַלַּח אֶת־כָּל־שְׂעָרוֹ אֶת־רֹאשׁוֹ
וְאֶת־זְקָנוֹ וְאֵת גַּבֹּת עֵינָיו וְאֶת־כָּל־שְׂעָרוֹ יְגַלֵּחַ וְכִבֶּס אֶת־
בְּגָדָיו וְרָחַץ אֶת־בְּשָׂרוֹ בַּמַּיִם וְטָהֵר׃ *וּבַיּוֹם הַשְּׁמִינִי יִקַּח ישראל

FIRST ALIYA: 14:1–5
The first stage of purification from *Tzara'at*.

SECOND ALIYA: 14:6–9
The second stage of purification from *Tzara'at*.

THIRD ALIYA: 14:10–12
The final stage of purification from *Tzara'at*.

שְׁנֵי־כְבָשִׂים תְּמִימִם וְכַבְשָׂה אַחַת בַּת־שְׁנָתָהּ תְּמִימָה
וּשְׁלֹשָׁה עֶשְׂרֹנִים סֹלֶת מִנְחָה בְּלוּלָה בַשֶּׁמֶן וְלֹג אֶחָד שָׁמֶן:
וְהֶעֱמִיד הַכֹּהֵן הַמְטַהֵר אֵת הָאִישׁ הַמִּטַּהֵר וְאֹתָם לִפְנֵי
יְהוָה פֶּתַח אֹהֶל מוֹעֵד: וְלָקַח הַכֹּהֵן אֶת־הַכֶּבֶשׂ הָאֶחָד
וְהִקְרִיב אֹתוֹ לְאָשָׁם וְאֶת־לֹג הַשָּׁמֶן וְהֵנִיף אֹתָם תְּנוּפָה
לִפְנֵי יְהוָה:

AHAREI MOT — אחרי מות

FIRST ALIYA: 16:1–6
The High Priest's preparation for the Yom Kippur service.

וַיְדַבֵּר יְהוָה אֶל־מֹשֶׁה אַחֲרֵי מוֹת שְׁנֵי בְּנֵי אַהֲרֹן בְּקָרְבָתָם ויקרא טז:א–יז
לִפְנֵי־יְהוָה וַיָּמֻתוּ: וַיֹּאמֶר יְהוָה אֶל־מֹשֶׁה דַּבֵּר אֶל־אַהֲרֹן
אָחִיךָ וְאַל־יָבֹא בְכָל־עֵת אֶל־הַקֹּדֶשׁ מִבֵּית לַפָּרֹכֶת אֶל־
פְּנֵי הַכַּפֹּרֶת אֲשֶׁר עַל־הָאָרֹן וְלֹא יָמוּת כִּי בֶּעָנָן אֵרָאֶה
עַל־הַכַּפֹּרֶת: בְּזֹאת יָבֹא אַהֲרֹן אֶל־הַקֹּדֶשׁ בְּפַר בֶּן־בָּקָר
לְחַטָּאת וְאַיִל לְעֹלָה: כְּתֹנֶת־בַּד קֹדֶשׁ יִלְבָּשׁ וּמִכְנְסֵי־בַד
יִהְיוּ עַל־בְּשָׂרוֹ וּבְאַבְנֵט בַּד יַחְגֹּר וּבְמִצְנֶפֶת בַּד יִצְנֹף בִּגְדֵי־
קֹדֶשׁ הֵם וְרָחַץ בַּמַּיִם אֶת־בְּשָׂרוֹ וּלְבֵשָׁם: וּמֵאֵת עֲדַת בְּנֵי
יִשְׂרָאֵל יִקַּח שְׁנֵי־שְׂעִירֵי עִזִּים לְחַטָּאת וְאַיִל אֶחָד לְעֹלָה:
וְהִקְרִיב אַהֲרֹן אֶת־פַּר הַחַטָּאת אֲשֶׁר־לוֹ וְכִפֶּר בַּעֲדוֹ וּבְעַד

SECOND ALIYA: 16:7–11
The Yom Kippur service: The lots and the goat for Azazel.

בֵּיתוֹ: *וְלָקַח אֶת־שְׁנֵי הַשְּׂעִירִם וְהֶעֱמִיד אֹתָם לִפְנֵי יְהוָה לוי
פֶּתַח אֹהֶל מוֹעֵד: וְנָתַן אַהֲרֹן עַל־שְׁנֵי הַשְּׂעִירִם גֹּרָלוֹת
גּוֹרָל אֶחָד לַיהוָה וְגוֹרָל אֶחָד לַעֲזָאזֵל: וְהִקְרִיב אַהֲרֹן
אֶת־הַשָּׂעִיר אֲשֶׁר עָלָה עָלָיו הַגּוֹרָל לַיהוָה וְעָשָׂהוּ חַטָּאת:
וְהַשָּׂעִיר אֲשֶׁר עָלָה עָלָיו הַגּוֹרָל לַעֲזָאזֵל יָעֳמַד־חַי לִפְנֵי
יְהוָה לְכַפֵּר עָלָיו לְשַׁלַּח אֹתוֹ לַעֲזָאזֵל הַמִּדְבָּרָה: וְהִקְרִיב
אַהֲרֹן אֶת־פַּר הַחַטָּאת אֲשֶׁר־לוֹ וְכִפֶּר בַּעֲדוֹ וּבְעַד בֵּיתוֹ

THIRD ALIYA: 16:12–17
The Yom Kippur service: The incense service.

וְשָׁחַט אֶת־פַּר הַחַטָּאת אֲשֶׁר־לוֹ: *וְלָקַח מְלֹא־הַמַּחְתָּה ישראל
גַחֲלֵי־אֵשׁ מֵעַל הַמִּזְבֵּחַ מִלִּפְנֵי יְהוָה וּמְלֹא חָפְנָיו קְטֹרֶת
סַמִּים דַּקָּה וְהֵבִיא מִבֵּית לַפָּרֹכֶת: וְנָתַן אֶת־הַקְּטֹרֶת עַל־
הָאֵשׁ לִפְנֵי יְהוָה וְכִסָּה ׀ עֲנַן הַקְּטֹרֶת אֶת־הַכַּפֹּרֶת אֲשֶׁר

על־העדות ולא ימות: ולקח מדם הפר והזה באצבעו
על־פני הכפרת קדמה ולפני הכפרת יזה שבע־פעמים
מן־הדם באצבעו: ושחט את־שעיר החטאת אשר לעם
והביא את־דמו אל־מבית לפרכת ועשה את־דמו כאשר
עשה לדם הפר והזה אתו על־הכפרת ולפני הכפרת:
וכפר על־הקדש מטמאת בני ישראל ומפשעיהם לכל־
חטאתם וכן יעשה לאהל מועד השכן אתם בתוך
טמאתם: וכל־אדם לא־יהיה | באהל מועד בבאו לכפר
בקדש עד־צאתו וכפר בעדו ובעד ביתו ובעד כל־קהל
ישראל:

KEDOSHIM קדושים

ויקרא יט:א־יד

וידבר יהוה אל־משה לאמר: דבר אל־כל־עדת בני־
ישראל ואמרת אלהם קדשים תהיו כי קדוש אני יהוה
אלהיכם: איש אמו ואביו תיראו ואת־שבתתי תשמרו אני
יהוה אלהיכם: אל־תפנו אל־האלילם ואלהי מסכה לא
לוי תעשו לכם אני יהוה אלהיכם: ★וכי תזבחו זבח שלמים
ליהוה לרצנכם תזבחהו: ביום זבחכם יאכל וממחרת
והנותר עד־יום השלישי באש ישרף: ואם האכל יאכל
ביום השלישי פגול הוא לא ירצה: ואכליו עונו ישא
כי־את־קדש יהוה חלל ונכרתה הנפש ההוא מעמיה:
ובקצרכם את־קציר ארצכם לא תכלה פאת שדך לקצר
ולקט קצירך לא תלקט: וכרמך לא תעולל ופרט כרמך
לא תלקט לעני ולגר תעזב אתם אני יהוה אלהיכם:
ישראל ★לא תגנבו ולא־תכחשו ולא־תשקרו איש בעמיתו: ולא־
תשבעו בשמי לשקר וחללת את־שם אלהיך אני יהוה:
לא־תעשק את־רעך ולא תגזל לא־תלין פעלת שכיר
אתך עד־בקר: לא־תקלל חרש ולפני עור לא תתן מכשל
ויראת מאלהיך אני יהוה:

FIRST ALIYA: 19:1–4
The mitzvot of respecting one's parents, keeping Shabbat, and the prohibition of idolatry.

SECOND ALIYA: 19:5–11
Rejected offerings, agricultural laws that protect the poor, and the prohibitions against stealing and lying.

THIRD ALIYA: 19:12–14
The prohibition against swearing falsely in God's name, the laws of honest business practice, and laws that protect the deaf and blind.

EMOR אמור

וַיֹּאמֶר יהוה אֶל־מֹשֶׁה אֱמֹר אֶל־הַכֹּהֲנִים בְּנֵי אַהֲרֹן וְאָמַרְתָּ ויקרא כא:א–טו

FIRST ALIYA: 21:1–6
The laws of being a priest: laws ensuring priestly holiness is maintained.

אֲלֵהֶם לְנֶפֶשׁ לֹא־יִטַּמָּא בְּעַמָּיו: כִּי אִם־לִשְׁאֵרוֹ הַקָּרֹב אֵלָיו
לְאִמּוֹ וּלְאָבִיו וְלִבְנוֹ וּלְבִתּוֹ וּלְאָחִיו: וְלַאֲחֹתוֹ הַבְּתוּלָה
הַקְּרוֹבָה אֵלָיו אֲשֶׁר לֹא־הָיְתָה לְאִישׁ לָהּ יִטַּמָּא: לֹא יִטַּמָּא
בַּעַל בְּעַמָּיו לְהֵחַלּוֹ: לֹא־יקרחה קָרְחָה בְּרֹאשָׁם וּפְאַת יִקְרְחוּ
זְקָנָם לֹא יְגַלֵּחוּ וּבִבְשָׂרָם לֹא יִשְׂרְטוּ שָׂרָטֶת: קְדֹשִׁים יִהְיוּ
לֵאלֹהֵיהֶם וְלֹא יְחַלְּלוּ שֵׁם אֱלֹהֵיהֶם כִּי אֶת־אִשֵּׁי יהוה לֶחֶם
אֱלֹהֵיהֶם הֵם מַקְרִיבִם וְהָיוּ קֹדֶשׁ: *אִשָּׁה זֹנָה וַחֲלָלָה לֹא לוי

SECOND ALIYA: 21:7–12
Priestly marital laws and the laws of the High Priest.

יִקָּחוּ וְאִשָּׁה גְּרוּשָׁה מֵאִישָׁהּ לֹא יִקָּחוּ כִּי־קָדֹשׁ הוּא לֵאלֹהָיו:
וְקִדַּשְׁתּוֹ כִּי־אֶת־לֶחֶם אֱלֹהֶיךָ הוּא מַקְרִיב קָדֹשׁ יִהְיֶה־לָּךְ
כִּי קָדוֹשׁ אֲנִי יהוה מְקַדִּשְׁכֶם: וּבַת אִישׁ כֹּהֵן כִּי תֵחֵל לִזְנוֹת
אֶת־אָבִיהָ הִיא מְחַלֶּלֶת בָּאֵשׁ תִּשָּׂרֵף: וְהַכֹּהֵן
הַגָּדוֹל מֵאֶחָיו אֲשֶׁר־יוּצַק עַל־רֹאשׁוֹ ׀ שֶׁמֶן הַמִּשְׁחָה וּמִלֵּא
אֶת־יָדוֹ לִלְבֹּשׁ אֶת־הַבְּגָדִים אֶת־רֹאשׁוֹ לֹא יִפְרָע וּבְגָדָיו
לֹא יִפְרֹם: וְעַל כָּל־נַפְשֹׁת מֵת לֹא יָבֹא לְאָבִיו וּלְאִמּוֹ לֹא
יִטַּמָּא: וּמִן־הַמִּקְדָּשׁ לֹא יֵצֵא וְלֹא יְחַלֵּל אֵת מִקְדַּשׁ אֱלֹהָיו
כִּי נֵזֶר שֶׁמֶן מִשְׁחַת אֱלֹהָיו עָלָיו אֲנִי יהוה: *וְהוּא אִשָּׁה ישראל

THIRD ALIYA: 21:13–15
Marital laws concerning the High Priest.

בִבְתוּלֶיהָ יִקָּח: אַלְמָנָה וּגְרוּשָׁה וַחֲלָלָה זֹנָה אֶת־אֵלֶּה לֹא
יִקָּח כִּי אִם־בְּתוּלָה מֵעַמָּיו יִקַּח אִשָּׁה: וְלֹא־יְחַלֵּל זַרְעוֹ
בְּעַמָּיו כִּי אֲנִי יהוה מְקַדְּשׁוֹ:

FIRST ALIYA: 25:1–3
During the *shemitta* year, which is the seventh year in the cycle, the land will rest.

BEHAR בהר

וַיְדַבֵּר יהוה אֶל־מֹשֶׁה בְּהַר סִינַי לֵאמֹר: דַּבֵּר אֶל־בְּנֵי ויקרא כה:א–יג
יִשְׂרָאֵל וְאָמַרְתָּ אֲלֵהֶם כִּי תָבֹאוּ אֶל־הָאָרֶץ אֲשֶׁר אֲנִי נֹתֵן
לָכֶם וְשָׁבְתָה הָאָרֶץ שַׁבָּת לַיהוה: שֵׁשׁ שָׁנִים תִּזְרַע שָׂדֶךָ
וְשֵׁשׁ שָׁנִים תִּזְמֹר כַּרְמֶךָ וְאָסַפְתָּ אֶת־תְּבוּאָתָהּ: *וּבַשָּׁנָה לוי

SECOND ALIYA: 25:4–7
During this year the land must not be farmed, and produce must not be sold.

הַשְּׁבִיעִת שַׁבַּת שַׁבָּתוֹן יִהְיֶה לָאָרֶץ שַׁבָּת לַיהוה שָׂדְךָ
לֹא תִזְרָע וְכַרְמְךָ לֹא תִזְמֹר: אֵת סְפִיחַ קְצִירְךָ לֹא תִקְצוֹר

ואת־ענבי נזירך לא תבצר שנת שבתון יהיה לארץ:
והיתה שבת הארץ לכם לאכלה לך ולעבדך ולאמתך
ולשכירך ולתושבך הגרים עמך: ולבהמתך ולחיה אשר
ישראל בארצך תהיה כל־תבואתה לאכל: ★וספרת
לך שבע שבתת שנים שבע שנים שבע פעמים והיו לך
ימי שבע שבתת השנים תשע וארבעים שנה: והעברת
שופר תרועה בחדש השבעי בעשור לחדש ביום הכפרים
תעבירו שופר בכל־ארצכם: וקדשתם את שנת החמשים
שנה וקראתם דרור בארץ לכל־ישביה יובל הוא תהיה
לכם ושבתם איש אל־אחזתו ואיש אל־משפחתו תשבו:
יובל הוא שנת החמשים שנה תהיה לכם לא תזרעו
ולא תקצרו את־ספיחיה ולא תבצרו את־נזריה: כי יובל
הוא קדש תהיה לכם מן־השדה תאכלו את־תבואתה:
בשנת היובל הזאת תשבו איש אל־אחזתו:

THIRD ALIYA: 25:8–13
The 50th *Yovel* year, after seven cycles of seven *shemitta* years, will be another year of rest for the land, and ancestral land will return to original owners.

BEHUKKOTAI בחוקותי

ויקרא כו:ג–יג אם־בחקתי תלכו ואת־מצותי תשמרו ועשיתם אתם:
ונתתי גשמיכם בעתם ונתנה הארץ יבולה ועץ השדה
יתן פריו: והשיג לכם דיש את־בציר ובציר ישיג את־
זרע ואכלתם לחמכם לשבע וישבתם לבטח בארצכם:
לוי ★ונתתי שלום בארץ ושכבתם ואין מחריד והשבתי חיה
רעה מן־הארץ וחרב לא־תעבר בארצכם: ורדפתם את־
איביכם ונפלו לפניכם לחרב: ורדפו מכם חמשה מאה
ומאה מכם רבבה ירדפו ונפלו איביכם לפניכם לחרב:
ופניתי אליכם והפריתי אתכם והרביתי אתכם והקימתי
ישראל את־בריתי אתכם: ★ואכלתם ישן נושן וישן מפני חדש
תוציאו: ונתתי משכני בתוככם ולא־תגעל נפשי אתכם:
והתהלכתי בתוככם והייתי לכם לאלהים ואתם תהיו־
לי לעם: אני יהוה אלהיכם אשר הוצאתי אתכם מארץ

FIRST ALIYA: 26:3–5
Blessing: If the Jewish people obey God's commands, then they will be blessed with rain and prosperity.

SECOND ALIYA: 26:6–10
Blessing continued: You will live in tranquility on the land.

THIRD ALIYA: 26:11–13
Blessing: God's presence will be felt among the people in the land.

מִצְרַיִם מִהְיֹת לָהֶם עֲבָדִים וָאֶשְׁבֹּר מֹטֹת עֻלְּכֶם וָאוֹלֵךְ
אֶתְכֶם קוֹמְמִיּוּת׃

BEMIDBAR — במדבר

במדבר א:א–יט

FIRST ALIYA: 1:1–4
The census: every family will be counted according to the men of military age (from twenty years and above).

SECOND ALIYA: 1:5–16
The tribal leaders, one from each tribe, will assist Moshe and Aharon in this task.

THIRD ALIYA: 1:17–19
The entire populace gathered together arranged according to their genealogy for this purpose.

וַיְדַבֵּר יְהוָה אֶל־מֹשֶׁה בְּמִדְבַּר סִינַי בְּאֹהֶל מוֹעֵד בְּאֶחָד
לַחֹדֶשׁ הַשֵּׁנִי בַּשָּׁנָה הַשֵּׁנִית לְצֵאתָם מֵאֶרֶץ מִצְרַיִם לֵאמֹר׃
שְׂאוּ אֶת־רֹאשׁ כָּל־עֲדַת בְּנֵי־יִשְׂרָאֵל לְמִשְׁפְּחֹתָם לְבֵית
אֲבֹתָם בְּמִסְפַּר שֵׁמוֹת כָּל־זָכָר לְגֻלְגְּלֹתָם׃ מִבֶּן עֶשְׂרִים שָׁנָה
וָמַעְלָה כָּל־יֹצֵא צָבָא בְּיִשְׂרָאֵל תִּפְקְדוּ אֹתָם לְצִבְאֹתָם
אַתָּה וְאַהֲרֹן׃ וְאִתְּכֶם יִהְיוּ אִישׁ אִישׁ לַמַּטֶּה אִישׁ רֹאשׁ
לוי לְבֵית־אֲבֹתָיו הוּא׃ *וְאֵלֶּה שְׁמוֹת הָאֲנָשִׁים אֲשֶׁר יַעַמְדוּ
אִתְּכֶם לִרְאוּבֵן אֱלִיצוּר בֶּן־שְׁדֵיאוּר׃ לְשִׁמְעוֹן שְׁלֻמִיאֵל
בֶּן־צוּרִישַׁדָּי׃ לִיהוּדָה נַחְשׁוֹן בֶּן־עַמִּינָדָב׃ לְיִשָּׂשכָר נְתַנְאֵל
בֶּן־צוּעָר׃ לִזְבוּלֻן אֱלִיאָב בֶּן־חֵלֹן׃ לִבְנֵי יוֹסֵף לְאֶפְרַיִם
אֱלִישָׁמָע בֶּן־עַמִּיהוּד לִמְנַשֶּׁה גַּמְלִיאֵל בֶּן־פְּדָהצוּר׃ לְבִנְיָמִן
אֲבִידָן בֶּן־גִּדְעֹנִי׃ לְדָן אֲחִיעֶזֶר בֶּן־עַמִּישַׁדָּי׃ לְאָשֵׁר פַּגְעִיאֵל
בֶּן־עָכְרָן׃ לְגָד אֶלְיָסָף בֶּן־דְּעוּאֵל׃ לְנַפְתָּלִי אֲחִירַע בֶּן־עֵינָן׃
קְרוּאֵי אֵלֶּה קריאי הָעֵדָה נְשִׂיאֵי מַטּוֹת אֲבוֹתָם רָאשֵׁי אַלְפֵי
ישראל יִשְׂרָאֵל הֵם׃ *וַיִּקַּח מֹשֶׁה וְאַהֲרֹן אֵת הָאֲנָשִׁים הָאֵלֶּה אֲשֶׁר
נִקְּבוּ בְּשֵׁמוֹת׃ וְאֵת כָּל־הָעֵדָה הִקְהִילוּ בְּאֶחָד לַחֹדֶשׁ הַשֵּׁנִי
וַיִּתְיַלְדוּ עַל־מִשְׁפְּחֹתָם לְבֵית אֲבֹתָם בְּמִסְפַּר שֵׁמוֹת מִבֶּן
עֶשְׂרִים שָׁנָה וָמַעְלָה לְגֻלְגְּלֹתָם׃ כַּאֲשֶׁר צִוָּה יְהוָה אֶת־מֹשֶׁה
וַיִּפְקְדֵם בְּמִדְבַּר סִינָי׃

NASO — נשא

במדבר ד:כא–לז

FIRST ALIYA: 4:21–24
Census of the priestly family of Gershon.

וַיְדַבֵּר יְהוָה אֶל־מֹשֶׁה לֵּאמֹר׃ נָשֹׂא אֶת־רֹאשׁ בְּנֵי גֵרְשׁוֹן גַּם־
הֵם לְבֵית אֲבֹתָם לְמִשְׁפְּחֹתָם׃ מִבֶּן שְׁלֹשִׁים שָׁנָה וָמַעְלָה
עַד בֶּן־חֲמִשִּׁים שָׁנָה תִּפְקֹד אוֹתָם כָּל־הַבָּא לִצְבֹא צָבָא
לַעֲבֹד עֲבֹדָה בְּאֹהֶל מוֹעֵד׃ זֹאת עֲבֹדַת מִשְׁפְּחֹת הַגֵּרְשֻׁנִּי

לוי לַעֲבֹד וּלְמַשָּׂא: *וְנָשְׂאוּ אֶת־יְרִיעֹת הַמִּשְׁכָּן וְאֶת־אֹהֶל
מוֹעֵד מִכְסֵהוּ וּמִכְסֵה הַתַּחַשׁ אֲשֶׁר־עָלָיו מִלְמָעְלָה וְאֶת־
מָסַךְ פֶּתַח אֹהֶל מוֹעֵד: וְאֵת קַלְעֵי הֶחָצֵר וְאֶת־מָסַךְ ׀
פֶּתַח ׀ שַׁעַר הֶחָצֵר אֲשֶׁר עַל־הַמִּשְׁכָּן וְעַל־הַמִּזְבֵּחַ סָבִיב
וְאֵת מֵיתְרֵיהֶם וְאֶת־כָּל־כְּלֵי עֲבֹדָתָם וְאֵת כָּל־אֲשֶׁר
יֵעָשֶׂה לָהֶם וְעָבָדוּ: עַל־פִּי אַהֲרֹן וּבָנָיו תִּהְיֶה כָּל־עֲבֹדַת
בְּנֵי הַגֵּרְשֻׁנִּי לְכָל־מַשָּׂאָם וּלְכֹל עֲבֹדָתָם וּפְקַדְתֶּם עֲלֵהֶם
בְּמִשְׁמֶרֶת אֵת כָּל־מַשָּׂאָם: זֹאת עֲבֹדַת מִשְׁפְּחֹת בְּנֵי
הַגֵּרְשֻׁנִּי בְּאֹהֶל מוֹעֵד וּמִשְׁמַרְתָּם בְּיַד אִיתָמָר בֶּן־אַהֲרֹן
ישראל הַכֹּהֵן: *בְּנֵי מְרָרִי לְמִשְׁפְּחֹתָם לְבֵית־אֲבֹתָם
תִּפְקֹד אֹתָם: מִבֶּן שְׁלֹשִׁים שָׁנָה וָמַעְלָה וְעַד בֶּן־חֲמִשִּׁים
שָׁנָה תִּפְקְדֵם כָּל־הַבָּא לַצָּבָא לַעֲבֹד אֶת־עֲבֹדַת אֹהֶל
מוֹעֵד: וְזֹאת מִשְׁמֶרֶת מַשָּׂאָם לְכָל־עֲבֹדָתָם בְּאֹהֶל מוֹעֵד
קַרְשֵׁי הַמִּשְׁכָּן וּבְרִיחָיו וְעַמּוּדָיו וַאֲדָנָיו: וְעַמּוּדֵי הֶחָצֵר
סָבִיב וְאַדְנֵיהֶם וִיתֵדֹתָם וּמֵיתְרֵיהֶם לְכָל־כְּלֵיהֶם וּלְכֹל
עֲבֹדָתָם וּבְשֵׁמֹת תִּפְקְדוּ אֶת־כְּלֵי מִשְׁמֶרֶת מַשָּׂאָם: זֹאת
עֲבֹדַת מִשְׁפְּחֹת בְּנֵי מְרָרִי לְכָל־עֲבֹדָתָם בְּאֹהֶל מוֹעֵד בְּיַד
אִיתָמָר בֶּן־אַהֲרֹן הַכֹּהֵן:

SECOND ALIYA: 4:25–28
The responsibilities of the family of Gershon during the process of dismantling and transporting of the Tabernacle.

THIRD ALIYA: 4:29–37
The census and responsibilities of the family of Marari during the process of dismantling and transporting of the Tabernacle.

Some extend the ישראל portion:

וַיִּפְקֹד מֹשֶׁה וְאַהֲרֹן וּנְשִׂיאֵי הָעֵדָה אֶת־בְּנֵי הַקְּהָתִי
לְמִשְׁפְּחֹתָם וּלְבֵית אֲבֹתָם: מִבֶּן שְׁלֹשִׁים שָׁנָה וָמַעְלָה וְעַד
בֶּן־חֲמִשִּׁים שָׁנָה כָּל־הַבָּא לַצָּבָא לַעֲבֹדָה בְּאֹהֶל מוֹעֵד:
וַיִּהְיוּ פְקֻדֵיהֶם לְמִשְׁפְּחֹתָם אַלְפַּיִם שְׁבַע מֵאוֹת וַחֲמִשִּׁים:
אֵלֶּה פְקוּדֵי מִשְׁפְּחֹת הַקְּהָתִי כָּל־הָעֹבֵד בְּאֹהֶל מוֹעֵד אֲשֶׁר
פָּקַד מֹשֶׁה וְאַהֲרֹן עַל־פִּי יְהוָה בְּיַד־מֹשֶׁה:

BEHA'ALOTEKHA בהעלותך

FIRST ALIYA: 8:1–4
The Menora in the Tabernacle lit by Aharon.

במדבר ח:א-יד
וַיְדַבֵּר יְהוָה אֶל־מֹשֶׁה לֵּאמֹר: דַּבֵּר אֶל־אַהֲרֹן וְאָמַרְתָּ אֵלָיו
בְּהַעֲלֹתְךָ אֶת־הַנֵּרֹת אֶל־מוּל פְּנֵי הַמְּנוֹרָה יָאִירוּ שִׁבְעַת

הַנֵּרוֹת: וַיַּעַשׂ כֵּן אַהֲרֹן אֶל־מוּל פְּנֵי הַמְּנוֹרָה הֶעֱלָה נֵרֹתֶיהָ
כַּאֲשֶׁר צִוָּה יהוה אֶת־מֹשֶׁה: וְזֶה מַעֲשֵׂה הַמְּנֹרָה מִקְשָׁה
זָהָב עַד־יְרֵכָהּ עַד־פִּרְחָהּ מִקְשָׁה הִוא כַּמַּרְאֶה אֲשֶׁר הֶרְאָה
יהוה אֶת־מֹשֶׁה כֵּן עָשָׂה אֶת־הַמְּנֹרָה:
לוי וַיְדַבֵּר יהוה אֶל־מֹשֶׁה לֵּאמֹר: קַח אֶת־הַלְוִיִּם מִתּוֹךְ בְּנֵי
יִשְׂרָאֵל וְטִהַרְתָּ אֹתָם: וְכֹה־תַעֲשֶׂה לָהֶם לְטַהֲרָם הַזֵּה
עֲלֵיהֶם מֵי חַטָּאת וְהֶעֱבִירוּ תַעַר עַל־כָּל־בְּשָׂרָם וְכִבְּסוּ
בִגְדֵיהֶם וְהִטֶּהָרוּ: וְלָקְחוּ פַּר בֶּן־בָּקָר וּמִנְחָתוֹ סֹלֶת
בְּלוּלָה בַשָּׁמֶן וּפַר־שֵׁנִי בֶן־בָּקָר תִּקַּח לְחַטָּאת: וְהִקְרַבְתָּ
אֶת־הַלְוִיִּם לִפְנֵי אֹהֶל מוֹעֵד וְהִקְהַלְתָּ אֶת־כָּל־עֲדַת בְּנֵי
ישראל יִשְׂרָאֵל: *וְהִקְרַבְתָּ אֶת־הַלְוִיִּם לִפְנֵי יהוה וְסָמְכוּ בְנֵי־
יִשְׂרָאֵל אֶת־יְדֵיהֶם עַל־הַלְוִיִּם: וְהֵנִיף אַהֲרֹן אֶת־הַלְוִיִּם
תְּנוּפָה לִפְנֵי יהוה מֵאֵת בְּנֵי יִשְׂרָאֵל וְהָיוּ לַעֲבֹד אֶת־
עֲבֹדַת יהוה: וְהַלְוִיִּם יִסְמְכוּ אֶת־יְדֵיהֶם עַל רֹאשׁ הַפָּרִים
וַעֲשֵׂה אֶת־הָאֶחָד חַטָּאת וְאֶת־הָאֶחָד עֹלָה לַיהוה לְכַפֵּר
עַל־הַלְוִיִּם: וְהַעֲמַדְתָּ אֶת־הַלְוִיִּם לִפְנֵי אַהֲרֹן וְלִפְנֵי בָנָיו
וְהֵנַפְתָּ אֹתָם תְּנוּפָה לַיהוה: וְהִבְדַּלְתָּ אֶת־הַלְוִיִּם מִתּוֹךְ בְּנֵי
יִשְׂרָאֵל וְהָיוּ לִי הַלְוִיִּם:

SECOND ALIYA: 8:5–9
The consecration of the Levites.

THIRD ALIYA: 8:10–14
The offerings given as part of the service of consecrating the Levites.

שלח SHELAH

במדבר יג:א–כ וַיְדַבֵּר יהוה אֶל־מֹשֶׁה לֵּאמֹר: שְׁלַח־לְךָ אֲנָשִׁים וְיָתֻרוּ
אֶת־אֶרֶץ כְּנַעַן אֲשֶׁר־אֲנִי נֹתֵן לִבְנֵי יִשְׂרָאֵל אִישׁ אֶחָד
אִישׁ אֶחָד לְמַטֵּה אֲבֹתָיו תִּשְׁלָחוּ כֹּל נָשִׂיא בָהֶם: וַיִּשְׁלַח
אֹתָם מֹשֶׁה מִמִּדְבַּר פָּארָן עַל־פִּי יהוה כֻּלָּם אֲנָשִׁים רָאשֵׁי
לוי בְנֵי־יִשְׂרָאֵל הֵמָּה: *וְאֵלֶּה שְׁמוֹתָם לְמַטֵּה רְאוּבֵן שַׁמּוּעַ
בֶּן־זַכּוּר: לְמַטֵּה שִׁמְעוֹן שָׁפָט בֶּן־חוֹרִי: לְמַטֵּה יְהוּדָה כָּלֵב
בֶּן־יְפֻנֶּה: לְמַטֵּה יִשָּׂשכָר יִגְאָל בֶּן־יוֹסֵף: לְמַטֵּה אֶפְרָיִם
הוֹשֵׁעַ בִּן־נוּן: לְמַטֵּה בִנְיָמִן פַּלְטִי בֶּן־רָפוּא: לְמַטֵּה זְבוּלֻן
גַּדִּיאֵל בֶּן־סוֹדִי: לְמַטֵּה יוֹסֵף לְמַטֵּה מְנַשֶּׁה גַּדִּי בֶּן־סוּסִי:

FIRST ALIYA: 13:1–3
God commands Moshe to send spies to gather information on the Land of Israel.

SECOND ALIYA: 13:4–16
The names of the spies, each a distinguished man of his tribe.

לְמַטֵּה דָן עַמִּיאֵל בֶּן־גְּמַלִּי׃ לְמַטֵּה אָשֵׁר סְתוּר בֶּן־מִיכָאֵל׃
לְמַטֵּה נַפְתָּלִי נַחְבִּי בֶּן־וָפְסִי׃ לְמַטֵּה גָד גְּאוּאֵל בֶּן־מָכִי׃
אֵלֶּה שְׁמוֹת הָאֲנָשִׁים אֲשֶׁר־שָׁלַח מֹשֶׁה לָתוּר אֶת־הָאָרֶץ
ישראל וַיִּקְרָא מֹשֶׁה לְהוֹשֵׁעַ בִּן־נוּן יְהוֹשֻׁעַ׃ *וַיִּשְׁלַח אֹתָם מֹשֶׁה
לָתוּר אֶת־אֶרֶץ כְּנָעַן וַיֹּאמֶר אֲלֵהֶם עֲלוּ זֶה בַּנֶּגֶב וַעֲלִיתֶם
אֶת־הָהָר׃ וּרְאִיתֶם אֶת־הָאָרֶץ מַה־הִוא וְאֶת־הָעָם
הַיֹּשֵׁב עָלֶיהָ הֶחָזָק הוּא הֲרָפֶה הַמְעַט הוּא אִם־רָב׃ וּמָה
הָאָרֶץ אֲשֶׁר־הוּא יֹשֵׁב בָּהּ הֲטוֹבָה הִוא אִם־רָעָה וּמָה
הֶעָרִים אֲשֶׁר־הוּא יוֹשֵׁב בָּהֵנָּה הַבְּמַחֲנִים אִם בְּמִבְצָרִים׃
וּמָה הָאָרֶץ הַשְּׁמֵנָה הִוא אִם־רָזָה הֲיֵשׁ־בָּהּ עֵץ אִם־אַיִן
וְהִתְחַזַּקְתֶּם וּלְקַחְתֶּם מִפְּרִי הָאָרֶץ וְהַיָּמִים יְמֵי בִּכּוּרֵי
עֲנָבִים׃

THIRD ALIYA: 13:17–20
Moshe delivers the mission to the spies.

KORAH קורח

במדבר טז:א–יג

וַיִּקַּח קֹרַח בֶּן־יִצְהָר בֶּן־קְהָת בֶּן־לֵוִי וְדָתָן וַאֲבִירָם בְּנֵי
אֱלִיאָב וְאוֹן בֶּן־פֶּלֶת בְּנֵי רְאוּבֵן׃ וַיָּקֻמוּ לִפְנֵי מֹשֶׁה וַאֲנָשִׁים
מִבְּנֵי־יִשְׂרָאֵל חֲמִשִּׁים וּמָאתָיִם נְשִׂיאֵי עֵדָה קְרִאֵי מוֹעֵד
אַנְשֵׁי־שֵׁם׃ וַיִּקָּהֲלוּ עַל־מֹשֶׁה וְעַל־אַהֲרֹן וַיֹּאמְרוּ אֲלֵהֶם
רַב־לָכֶם כִּי כָל־הָעֵדָה כֻּלָּם קְדֹשִׁים וּבְתוֹכָם יהוה וּמַדּוּעַ
לוי תִּתְנַשְּׂאוּ עַל־קְהַל יהוה׃ *וַיִּשְׁמַע מֹשֶׁה וַיִּפֹּל עַל־פָּנָיו׃
וַיְדַבֵּר אֶל־קֹרַח וְאֶל־כָּל־עֲדָתוֹ לֵאמֹר בֹּקֶר וְיֹדַע יהוה אֶת־
אֲשֶׁר־לוֹ וְאֶת־הַקָּדוֹשׁ וְהִקְרִיב אֵלָיו וְאֵת אֲשֶׁר יִבְחַר־בּוֹ
יַקְרִיב אֵלָיו׃ זֹאת עֲשׂוּ קְחוּ־לָכֶם מַחְתּוֹת קֹרַח וְכָל־עֲדָתוֹ׃
וּתְנוּ־בָהֵן ׀ אֵשׁ וְשִׂימוּ עֲלֵיהֶן ׀ קְטֹרֶת לִפְנֵי יהוה מָחָר וְהָיָה
הָאִישׁ אֲשֶׁר־יִבְחַר יהוה הוּא הַקָּדוֹשׁ רַב־לָכֶם בְּנֵי לֵוִי׃
ישראל *וַיֹּאמֶר מֹשֶׁה אֶל־קֹרַח שִׁמְעוּ־נָא בְּנֵי לֵוִי׃ הַמְעַט מִכֶּם
כִּי־הִבְדִּיל אֱלֹהֵי יִשְׂרָאֵל אֶתְכֶם מֵעֲדַת יִשְׂרָאֵל לְהַקְרִיב
אֶתְכֶם אֵלָיו לַעֲבֹד אֶת־עֲבֹדַת מִשְׁכַּן יהוה וְלַעֲמֹד לִפְנֵי
הָעֵדָה לְשָׁרְתָם׃ וַיַּקְרֵב אֹתְךָ וְאֶת־כָּל־אַחֶיךָ בְנֵי־לֵוִי אִתָּךְ

FIRST ALIYA: 16:1–3
Koraḥ, Datan, and Aviram, together with 250 men, rebel against Moshe and Aharon.

SECOND ALIYA: 16:4–7
Moshe sets up the stand-off, invoking God to prove who has the legitimate claim.

THIRD ALIYA: 16:8–13
Moshe tries to deescalate the situation, but to no avail.

ובקשתם גם־כהנה: לכן אתה וכל־עדתך הנעדים על־
יהוה ואהרן מה־הוא כי תלונו עליו: וישלח משה לקרא תלינו
לדתן ולאבירם בני אליאב ויאמרו לא נעלה: המעט כי
העליתנו מארץ זבת חלב ודבש להמיתנו במדבר כי־
תשתרר עלינו גם־השתרר:

HUKAT חוקת

במדבר יט:א–יז

FIRST ALIYA: 19:1–6
The laws of the Red Heifer.

וידבר יהוה אל־משה ואל־אהרן לאמר: זאת חקת התורה
אשר־צוה יהוה לאמר דבר | אל־בני ישראל ויקחו אליך
פרה אדמה תמימה אשר אין־בה מום אשר לא־עלה
עליה על: ונתתם אתה אל־אלעזר הכהן והוציא אתה
אל־מחוץ למחנה ושחט אתה לפניו: ולקח אלעזר הכהן
מדמה באצבעו והזה אל־נכח פני אהל־מועד מדמה שבע
פעמים: ושרף את־הפרה לעיניו את־ערה ואת־בשרה
ואת־דמה על־פרשה ישרף: ולקח הכהן עץ ארז ואזוב
ושני תולעת והשליך אל־תוך שרפת הפרה: *וכבס בגדיו לוי

SECOND ALIYA: 19:7–10
The post ritual purification of the serving priest.

הכהן ורחץ בשרו במים ואחר יבא אל־המחנה וטמא
הכהן עד־הערב: והשרף אתה יכבס בגדיו במים ורחץ
בשרו במים וטמא עד־הערב: ואסף | איש טהור את
אפר הפרה והניח מחוץ למחנה במקום טהור והיתה
לעדת בני־ישראל למשמרת למי נדה חטאת הוא:
*וכבס האסף את־אפר הפרה את־בגדיו וטמא עד־הערב ישראל

THIRD ALIYA: 19:11–17
The laws of ritual contamination from a corpse.

והיתה לבני ישראל ולגר הגר בתוכם לחקת עולם: הנגע
במת לכל־נפש אדם וטמא שבעת ימים: הוא יתחטא־
בו ביום השלישי וביום השביעי יטהר ואם־לא יתחטא
ביום השלישי וביום השביעי לא יטהר: כל־הנגע במת
בנפש האדם אשר־ימות ולא יתחטא את־משכן יהוה
טמא ונכרתה הנפש ההוא מישראל כי מי נדה לא־זרק
עליו טמא יהיה עוד טמאתו בו: זאת התורה אדם כי־

ימות באהל כל־הבא אל־האהל וכל־אשר באהל יטמא
שבעת ימים: וכל כלי פתוח אשר אין־צמיד פתיל עליו
טמא הוא: וכל אשר־יגע על־פני השדה בחלל־חרב
או במת או־בעצם אדם או בקבר יטמא שבעת ימים:
ולקחו לטמא מעפר שרפת החטאת ונתן עליו מים חיים
אל־כלי:

BALAK בלק

במדבר כב:ב–יב וירא בלק בן־צפור את כל־אשר־עשה ישראל לאמרי:
ויגר מואב מפני העם מאד כי רב־הוא ויקץ מואב מפני
בני ישראל: ויאמר מואב אל־זקני מדין עתה ילחכו הקהל
את־כל־סביבתינו כלחך השור את ירק השדה ובלק
לוי בן־צפור מלך למואב בעת ההוא: *וישלח מלאכים
אל־בלעם בן־בעור פתורה אשר על־הנהר ארץ בני־
עמו לקרא־לו לאמר הנה עם יצא ממצרים הנה כסה
את־עין הארץ והוא ישב ממלי: ועתה לכה־נא ארה־לי
את־העם הזה כי־עצום הוא ממני אולי אוכל נכה־בו
ואגרשנו מן־הארץ כי ידעתי את אשר־תברך מברך
ואשר תאר יואר: וילכו זקני מואב וזקני מדין וקסמים
ישראל בידם ויבאו אל־בלעם וידברו אליו דברי בלק: *ויאמר
אליהם לינו פה הלילה והשבתי אתכם דבר כאשר ידבר
יהוה אלי וישבו שרי־מואב עם־בלעם: ויבא אלהים אל־
בלעם ויאמר מי האנשים האלה עמך: ויאמר בלעם
אל־האלהים בלק בן־צפר מלך מואב שלח אלי: הנה
העם היצא ממצרים ויכס את־עין הארץ עתה לכה
קבה־לי אתו אולי אוכל להלחם בו וגרשתיו: ויאמר
אלהים אל־בלעם לא תלך עמהם לא תאר את־העם כי
ברוך הוא:

FIRST ALIYA: 22:2–4
Balak, the king of Moav, becomes intimidated and fearful of the powerful numerous Israelites.

SECOND ALIYA: 22:5–7
He sends messengers to Balaam the prophet to attempt to employ him in pronouncing a curse on the Jewish people.

THIRD ALIYA: 22:8–12
Balaam enquires of God as to whether he can perform this role, and is denied.

FIRST ALIYA: 25:10–12
Pineḥas receives from God eternal priesthood for his descendants, and a "Covenant of Peace" as a reward for his zealousness.

SECOND ALIYA: 25:13–18
God commands Moshe to initiate a military campaign against Midyan in response to their attempt to corrupt the Israelites.

THIRD ALIYA: 26:1–4
After the plague that punished those Israelites that were corrupted by Midyan, a census was carried out.

PINEḤAS פינחס

במדבר כה:י–כו:ד וַיְדַבֵּר יְהוָה אֶל־מֹשֶׁה לֵּאמֹר: פִּינְחָס בֶּן־אֶלְעָזָר בֶּן־אַהֲרֹן
הַכֹּהֵן הֵשִׁיב אֶת־חֲמָתִי מֵעַל בְּנֵי־יִשְׂרָאֵל בְּקַנְאוֹ אֶת־
קִנְאָתִי בְּתוֹכָם וְלֹא־כִלִּיתִי אֶת־בְּנֵי־יִשְׂרָאֵל בְּקִנְאָתִי: לָכֵן
לוי אֱמֹר הִנְנִי נֹתֵן לוֹ אֶת־בְּרִיתִי שָׁלוֹם: *וְהָיְתָה לּוֹ וּלְזַרְעוֹ
אַחֲרָיו בְּרִית כְּהֻנַּת עוֹלָם תַּחַת אֲשֶׁר קִנֵּא לֵאלֹהָיו וַיְכַפֵּר
עַל־בְּנֵי יִשְׂרָאֵל: וְשֵׁם אִישׁ יִשְׂרָאֵל הַמֻּכֶּה אֲשֶׁר הֻכָּה אֶת־
הַמִּדְיָנִית זִמְרִי בֶּן־סָלוּא נְשִׂיא בֵית־אָב לַשִּׁמְעֹנִי: וְשֵׁם
הָאִשָּׁה הַמֻּכָּה הַמִּדְיָנִית כָּזְבִּי בַת־צוּר רֹאשׁ אֻמּוֹת בֵּית־
אָב בְּמִדְיָן הוּא:

ישראל וַיְדַבֵּר יְהוָה אֶל־מֹשֶׁה לֵּאמֹר: צָרוֹר אֶת־הַמִּדְיָנִים וְהִכִּיתֶם
אוֹתָם: כִּי־צֹרְרִים הֵם לָכֶם בְּנִכְלֵיהֶם אֲשֶׁר־נִכְּלוּ לָכֶם עַל־
דְּבַר פְּעוֹר וְעַל־דְּבַר כָּזְבִּי בַת־נְשִׂיא מִדְיָן אֲחֹתָם הַמֻּכָּה
בְיוֹם־הַמַּגֵּפָה עַל־דְּבַר פְּעוֹר: וַיְהִי אַחֲרֵי הַמַּגֵּפָה
וַיֹּאמֶר יְהוָה אֶל־מֹשֶׁה וְאֶל אֶלְעָזָר בֶּן־אַהֲרֹן הַכֹּהֵן לֵאמֹר:
שְׂאוּ אֶת־רֹאשׁ ׀ כָּל־עֲדַת בְּנֵי־יִשְׂרָאֵל מִבֶּן עֶשְׂרִים שָׁנָה
וָמַעְלָה לְבֵית אֲבֹתָם כָּל־יֹצֵא צָבָא בְּיִשְׂרָאֵל: וַיְדַבֵּר מֹשֶׁה
וְאֶלְעָזָר הַכֹּהֵן אֹתָם בְּעַרְבֹת מוֹאָב עַל־יַרְדֵּן יְרֵחוֹ לֵאמֹר:
מִבֶּן עֶשְׂרִים שָׁנָה וָמָעְלָה כַּאֲשֶׁר צִוָּה יְהוָה אֶת־מֹשֶׁה וּבְנֵי
יִשְׂרָאֵל הַיֹּצְאִים מֵאֶרֶץ מִצְרָיִם:

FIRST ALIYA: 30:2–9
The laws of vows and oaths.

MATOT מטות

במדבר ל:ב–יז וַיְדַבֵּר מֹשֶׁה אֶל־רָאשֵׁי הַמַּטּוֹת לִבְנֵי יִשְׂרָאֵל לֵאמֹר זֶה
הַדָּבָר אֲשֶׁר צִוָּה יְהוָה: אִישׁ כִּי־יִדֹּר נֶדֶר לַיהוָה אוֹ־הִשָּׁבַע
שְׁבֻעָה לֶאְסֹר אִסָּר עַל־נַפְשׁוֹ לֹא יַחֵל דְּבָרוֹ כְּכָל־הַיֹּצֵא
מִפִּיו יַעֲשֶׂה: וְאִשָּׁה כִּי־תִדֹּר נֶדֶר לַיהוָה וְאָסְרָה אִסָּר
בְּבֵית אָבִיהָ בִּנְעֻרֶיהָ: וְשָׁמַע אָבִיהָ אֶת־נִדְרָהּ וֶאֱסָרָהּ
אֲשֶׁר אָסְרָה עַל־נַפְשָׁהּ וְהֶחֱרִישׁ לָהּ אָבִיהָ וְקָמוּ כָּל־נְדָרֶיהָ

וְכָל־אִסָּר אֲשֶׁר־אָסְרָה עַל־נַפְשָׁהּ יָקוּם׃ וְאִם־הֵנִיא אָבִיהָ
אֹתָהּ בְּיוֹם שָׁמְעוֹ כָּל־נְדָרֶיהָ וֶאֱסָרֶיהָ אֲשֶׁר־אָסְרָה עַל־
נַפְשָׁהּ לֹא יָקוּם וַיהוָה יִסְלַח־לָהּ כִּי־הֵנִיא אָבִיהָ אֹתָהּ׃
וְאִם־הָיוֹ תִהְיֶה לְאִישׁ וּנְדָרֶיהָ עָלֶיהָ אוֹ מִבְטָא שְׂפָתֶיהָ
אֲשֶׁר אָסְרָה עַל־נַפְשָׁהּ׃ וְשָׁמַע אִישָׁהּ בְּיוֹם שָׁמְעוֹ וְהֶחֱרִישׁ
לָהּ וְקָמוּ נְדָרֶיהָ וֶאֱסָרֶהָ אֲשֶׁר־אָסְרָה עַל־נַפְשָׁהּ יָקֻמוּ׃
וְאִם בְּיוֹם שְׁמֹעַ אִישָׁהּ יָנִיא אוֹתָהּ וְהֵפֵר אֶת־נִדְרָהּ אֲשֶׁר
עָלֶיהָ וְאֵת מִבְטָא שְׂפָתֶיהָ אֲשֶׁר אָסְרָה עַל־נַפְשָׁהּ וַיהוָה
לוי יִסְלַח־לָהּ׃ *וְנֵדֶר אַלְמָנָה וּגְרוּשָׁה כֹּל אֲשֶׁר־אָסְרָה עַל־
נַפְשָׁהּ יָקוּם עָלֶיהָ׃ וְאִם־בֵּית אִישָׁהּ נָדָרָה אוֹ־אָסְרָה
אִסָּר עַל־נַפְשָׁהּ בִּשְׁבֻעָה׃ וְשָׁמַע אִישָׁהּ וְהֶחֱרִשׁ לָהּ לֹא
הֵנִיא אֹתָהּ וְקָמוּ כָּל־נְדָרֶיהָ וְכָל־אִסָּר אֲשֶׁר־אָסְרָה עַל־
נַפְשָׁהּ יָקוּם׃ וְאִם־הָפֵר יָפֵר אֹתָם ׀ אִישָׁהּ בְּיוֹם שָׁמְעוֹ
כָּל־מוֹצָא שְׂפָתֶיהָ לִנְדָרֶיהָ וּלְאִסַּר נַפְשָׁהּ לֹא יָקוּם אִישָׁהּ
ישראל הֲפֵרָם וַיהוָה יִסְלַח־לָהּ׃ *כָּל־נֵדֶר וְכָל־שְׁבֻעַת אִסָּר לְעַנֹּת
נָפֶשׁ אִישָׁהּ יְקִימֶנּוּ וְאִישָׁהּ יְפֵרֶנּוּ׃ וְאִם־הַחֲרֵשׁ יַחֲרִישׁ
לָהּ אִישָׁהּ מִיּוֹם אֶל־יוֹם וְהֵקִים אֶת־כָּל־נְדָרֶיהָ אוֹ אֶת־
כָּל־אֱסָרֶיהָ אֲשֶׁר עָלֶיהָ הֵקִים אֹתָם כִּי־הֶחֱרִשׁ לָהּ בְּיוֹם
שָׁמְעוֹ׃ וְאִם־הָפֵר יָפֵר אֹתָם אַחֲרֵי שָׁמְעוֹ וְנָשָׂא אֶת־עֲוֺנָהּ׃
אֵלֶּה הַחֻקִּים אֲשֶׁר צִוָּה יהוה אֶת־מֹשֶׁה בֵּין אִישׁ לְאִשְׁתּוֹ
בֵּין־אָב לְבִתּוֹ בִּנְעֻרֶיהָ בֵּית אָבִיהָ׃

SECOND ALIYA: 30:10–13
The laws of vows made by a widow or divorcee.

THIRD ALIYA: 30:14–17
The laws of oaths and vows made by a wife.

MASEI מסעי

במדבר לג:א–נג
אֵלֶּה מַסְעֵי בְנֵי־יִשְׂרָאֵל אֲשֶׁר יָצְאוּ מֵאֶרֶץ מִצְרַיִם לְצִבְאֹתָם
בְּיַד־מֹשֶׁה וְאַהֲרֹן׃ וַיִּכְתֹּב מֹשֶׁה אֶת־מוֹצָאֵיהֶם לְמַסְעֵיהֶם
עַל־פִּי יהוה וְאֵלֶּה מַסְעֵיהֶם לְמוֹצָאֵיהֶם׃ וַיִּסְעוּ מֵרַעְמְסֵס
בַּחֹדֶשׁ הָרִאשׁוֹן בַּחֲמִשָּׁה עָשָׂר יוֹם לַחֹדֶשׁ הָרִאשׁוֹן
מִמָּחֳרַת הַפֶּסַח יָצְאוּ בְנֵי־יִשְׂרָאֵל בְּיָד רָמָה לְעֵינֵי כָּל־
לוי מִצְרָיִם׃ *וּמִצְרַיִם מְקַבְּרִים אֵת אֲשֶׁר הִכָּה יהוה בָּהֶם כָּל־

FIRST ALIYA: 33:1–3
A summary of the journeys of the Israelites when they left Egypt.

SECOND ALIYA: 33:4–6
The journeys from Ramses to Eitam.

THIRD ALIYA: 33:7–10
The journeys from Eitam to the Reed Sea.

בְּכ֑וֹר וּבֵאלֹ֣הֵיהֶ֔ם עָשָׂ֥ה יְהוָ֖ה שְׁפָטִֽים׃ וַיִּסְע֥וּ בְנֵֽי־יִשְׂרָאֵ֖ל
מֵרַעְמְסֵ֑ס וַֽיַּחֲנ֖וּ בְּסֻכֹּֽת׃ וַיִּסְע֖וּ מִסֻּכֹּ֑ת וַיַּחֲנ֣וּ בְאֵתָ֔ם אֲשֶׁ֖ר
ישראל בִּקְצֵ֥ה הַמִּדְבָּֽר׃ *וַיִּסְעוּ֙ מֵאֵתָ֔ם וַיָּ֙שָׁב֙ עַל־פִּ֣י הַחִירֹ֔ת אֲשֶׁ֥ר
עַל־פְּנֵ֖י בַּ֣עַל צְפ֑וֹן וַֽיַּחֲנ֖וּ לִפְנֵ֥י מִגְדֹּֽל׃ וַיִּסְעוּ֙ מִפְּנֵ֣י הַחִירֹ֔ת
וַיַּֽעַבְר֥וּ בְתוֹךְ־הַיָּ֖ם הַמִּדְבָּ֑רָה וַיֵּ֨לְכ֜וּ דֶּ֣רֶךְ שְׁלֹ֤שֶׁת יָמִים֙
בְּמִדְבַּ֣ר אֵתָ֔ם וַֽיַּחֲנ֖וּ בְּמָרָֽה׃ וַיִּסְעוּ֙ מִמָּרָ֔ה וַיָּבֹ֖אוּ אֵילִ֑מָה
וּ֠בְאֵילִם שְׁתֵּ֨ים עֶשְׂרֵ֜ה עֵינֹ֥ת מַ֛יִם וְשִׁבְעִ֥ים תְּמָרִ֖ים וַיַּחֲנוּ־
שָֽׁם׃ וַיִּסְע֖וּ מֵאֵילִ֑ם וַֽיַּחֲנ֖וּ עַל־יַם־סֽוּף׃

Some extend the לוי *portion:*

וַיִּסְע֖וּ מִיַּם־ס֑וּף וַֽיַּחֲנ֖וּ בְּמִדְבַּר־סִֽין׃ וַיִּסְע֖וּ מִמִּדְבַּר־סִ֑ין וַֽיַּחֲנ֖וּ
בְּדָפְקָֽה׃ וַיִּסְע֖וּ מִדָּפְקָ֑ה וַֽיַּחֲנ֖וּ בְּאָלֽוּשׁ׃ וַיִּסְע֖וּ מֵאָל֑וּשׁ וַֽיַּחֲנוּ֙
בִּרְפִידִ֔ם וְלֹא־הָ֨יָה שָׁ֥ם מַ֛יִם לָעָ֖ם לִשְׁתּֽוֹת׃ וַיִּסְע֖וּ מֵרְפִידִ֑ם
וַֽיַּחֲנ֖וּ בְּמִדְבַּ֥ר סִינָֽי׃ וַיִּסְע֖וּ מִמִּדְבַּ֣ר סִינָ֑י וַֽיַּחֲנ֖וּ בְּקִבְרֹ֥ת
הַֽתַּאֲוָֽה׃ וַיִּסְע֖וּ מִקִּבְרֹ֣ת הַתַּאֲוָ֑ה וַֽיַּחֲנ֖וּ בַּחֲצֵרֹֽת׃ וַיִּסְע֖וּ
מֵחֲצֵרֹ֑ת וַֽיַּחֲנ֖וּ בְּרִתְמָֽה׃ וַיִּסְע֖וּ מֵרִתְמָ֑ה וַֽיַּחֲנ֖וּ בְּרִמֹּ֥ן פָּֽרֶץ׃
וַיִּסְע֖וּ מֵרִמֹּ֣ן פָּ֑רֶץ וַֽיַּחֲנ֖וּ בְּלִבְנָֽה׃ וַיִּסְע֖וּ מִלִּבְנָ֑ה וַֽיַּחֲנ֖וּ בְּרִסָּֽה׃
וַיִּסְע֖וּ מֵרִסָּ֑ה וַֽיַּחֲנ֖וּ בִּקְהֵלָֽתָה׃ וַיִּסְע֖וּ מִקְּהֵלָ֑תָה וַֽיַּחֲנ֖וּ בְּהַר־
שָֽׁפֶר׃ וַיִּסְע֖וּ מֵהַר־שָׁ֑פֶר וַֽיַּחֲנ֖וּ בַּחֲרָדָֽה׃ וַיִּסְע֖וּ מֵחֲרָדָ֑ה וַֽיַּחֲנ֖וּ
בְּמַקְהֵלֹֽת׃ וַיִּסְע֖וּ מִמַּקְהֵלֹ֑ת וַֽיַּחֲנ֖וּ בְּתָֽחַת׃ וַיִּסְע֖וּ מִתָּ֑חַת
וַֽיַּחֲנ֖וּ בְּתָֽרַח׃ וַיִּסְע֖וּ מִתָּ֑רַח וַֽיַּחֲנ֖וּ בְּמִתְקָֽה׃ וַיִּסְע֖וּ מִמִּתְקָ֑ה
וַֽיַּחֲנ֖וּ בְּחַשְׁמֹנָֽה׃ וַיִּסְע֖וּ מֵחַשְׁמֹנָ֑ה וַֽיַּחֲנ֖וּ בְּמֹסֵרֽוֹת׃ וַיִּסְע֖וּ
מִמֹּסֵר֑וֹת וַֽיַּחֲנ֖וּ בִּבְנֵ֥י יַעֲקָֽן׃ וַיִּסְע֖וּ מִבְּנֵ֣י יַעֲקָ֑ן וַֽיַּחֲנ֖וּ בְּחֹ֥ר
הַגִּדְגָּֽד׃ וַיִּסְע֖וּ מֵחֹ֣ר הַגִּדְגָּ֑ד וַֽיַּחֲנ֖וּ בְּיָטְבָֽתָה׃ וַיִּסְע֖וּ מִיָּטְבָ֑תָה
וַֽיַּחֲנ֖וּ בְּעַבְרֹנָֽה׃ וַיִּסְע֖וּ מֵעַבְרֹנָ֑ה וַֽיַּחֲנ֖וּ בְּעֶצְיֹ֥ן גָּֽבֶר׃ וַיִּסְע֖וּ
מֵעֶצְיֹ֣ן גָּ֑בֶר וַיַּחֲנ֥וּ בְמִדְבַּר־צִ֖ן ה֥וּא קָדֵֽשׁ׃ וַיִּסְע֖וּ מִקָּדֵ֑שׁ
וַֽיַּחֲנוּ֙ בְּהֹ֣ר הָהָ֔ר בִּקְצֵ֖ה אֶ֥רֶץ אֱדֽוֹם׃ וַיַּ֩עַל֩ אַהֲרֹ֨ן הַכֹּהֵ֜ן
אֶל־הֹ֥ר הָהָ֛ר עַל־פִּ֥י יְהוָ֖ה וַיָּ֣מָת שָׁ֑ם בִּשְׁנַ֣ת הָֽאַרְבָּעִ֗ים
לְצֵ֤את בְּנֵֽי־יִשְׂרָאֵל֙ מֵאֶ֣רֶץ מִצְרַ֔יִם בַּחֹ֥דֶשׁ הַחֲמִישִׁ֖י בְּאֶחָ֥ד
לַחֹֽדֶשׁ׃ וְאַהֲרֹ֕ן בֶּן־שָׁלֹ֧שׁ וְעֶשְׂרִ֛ים וּמְאַ֖ת שָׁנָ֑ה בְּמֹת֖וֹ בְּהֹ֥ר

הָהָר׃ וַיִּשְׁמַע הַכְּנַעֲנִי מֶלֶךְ עֲרָד וְהוּא־יֹשֵׁב
בַּנֶּגֶב בְּאֶרֶץ כְּנָעַן בְּבֹא בְּנֵי יִשְׂרָאֵל׃ וַיִּסְעוּ מֵהֹר הָהָר
וַיַּחֲנוּ בְּצַלְמֹנָה׃ וַיִּסְעוּ מִצַּלְמֹנָה וַיַּחֲנוּ בְּפוּנֹן׃ וַיִּסְעוּ מִפּוּנֹן
וַיַּחֲנוּ בְּאֹבֹת׃ וַיִּסְעוּ מֵאֹבֹת וַיַּחֲנוּ בְּעִיֵּי הָעֲבָרִים בִּגְבוּל
מוֹאָב׃ וַיִּסְעוּ מֵעִיִּים וַיַּחֲנוּ בְּדִיבֹן גָּד׃ וַיִּסְעוּ מִדִּיבֹן גָּד וַיַּחֲנוּ
בְּעַלְמֹן דִּבְלָתָיְמָה׃ וַיִּסְעוּ מֵעַלְמֹן דִּבְלָתָיְמָה וַיַּחֲנוּ בְּהָרֵי
הָעֲבָרִים לִפְנֵי נְבוֹ׃ וַיִּסְעוּ מֵהָרֵי הָעֲבָרִים וַיַּחֲנוּ בְּעַרְבֹת
מוֹאָב עַל יַרְדֵּן יְרֵחוֹ׃ וַיַּחֲנוּ עַל־הַיַּרְדֵּן מִבֵּית הַיְשִׁמֹת
עַד אָבֵל הַשִּׁטִּים בְּעַרְבֹת מוֹאָב׃ *וַיְדַבֵּר ישראל
יהוה אֶל־מֹשֶׁה בְּעַרְבֹת מוֹאָב עַל־יַרְדֵּן יְרֵחוֹ לֵאמֹר׃ דַּבֵּר
אֶל־בְּנֵי יִשְׂרָאֵל וְאָמַרְתָּ אֲלֵהֶם כִּי אַתֶּם עֹבְרִים אֶת־הַיַּרְדֵּן
אֶל־אֶרֶץ כְּנָעַן׃ וְהוֹרַשְׁתֶּם אֶת־כָּל־יֹשְׁבֵי הָאָרֶץ מִפְּנֵיכֶם
וְאִבַּדְתֶּם אֵת כָּל־מַשְׂכִּיֹּתָם וְאֵת כָּל־צַלְמֵי מַסֵּכֹתָם תְּאַבֵּדוּ
וְאֵת כָּל־בָּמוֹתָם תַּשְׁמִידוּ׃ וְהוֹרַשְׁתֶּם אֶת־הָאָרֶץ וִישַׁבְתֶּם־
בָּהּ כִּי לָכֶם נָתַתִּי אֶת־הָאָרֶץ לָרֶשֶׁת אֹתָהּ׃

DEVARIM דברים

דברים
א:א–יא

אֵלֶּה הַדְּבָרִים אֲשֶׁר דִּבֶּר מֹשֶׁה אֶל־כָּל־יִשְׂרָאֵל בְּעֵבֶר
הַיַּרְדֵּן בַּמִּדְבָּר בָּעֲרָבָה מוֹל סוּף בֵּין־פָּארָן וּבֵין־תֹּפֶל וְלָבָן
וַחֲצֵרֹת וְדִי זָהָב׃ אַחַד עָשָׂר יוֹם מֵחֹרֵב דֶּרֶךְ הַר־שֵׂעִיר
עַד קָדֵשׁ בַּרְנֵעַ׃ וַיְהִי בְּאַרְבָּעִים שָׁנָה בְּעַשְׁתֵּי־עָשָׂר חֹדֶשׁ
בְּאֶחָד לַחֹדֶשׁ דִּבֶּר מֹשֶׁה אֶל־בְּנֵי יִשְׂרָאֵל כְּכֹל אֲשֶׁר צִוָּה
יהוה אֹתוֹ אֲלֵהֶם׃ *אַחֲרֵי הַכֹּתוֹ אֵת סִיחֹן מֶלֶךְ הָאֱמֹרִי לוי
אֲשֶׁר יוֹשֵׁב בְּחֶשְׁבּוֹן וְאֵת עוֹג מֶלֶךְ הַבָּשָׁן אֲשֶׁר־יוֹשֵׁב
בְּעַשְׁתָּרֹת בְּאֶדְרֶעִי׃ בְּעֵבֶר הַיַּרְדֵּן בְּאֶרֶץ מוֹאָב הוֹאִיל
מֹשֶׁה בֵּאֵר אֶת־הַתּוֹרָה הַזֹּאת לֵאמֹר׃ יהוה אֱלֹהֵינוּ דִּבֶּר
אֵלֵינוּ בְּחֹרֵב לֵאמֹר רַב־לָכֶם שֶׁבֶת בָּהָר הַזֶּה׃ פְּנוּ ׀ וּסְעוּ
לָכֶם וּבֹאוּ הַר הָאֱמֹרִי וְאֶל־כָּל־שְׁכֵנָיו בָּעֲרָבָה בָהָר וּבַשְּׁפֵלָה
וּבַנֶּגֶב וּבְחוֹף הַיָּם אֶרֶץ הַכְּנַעֲנִי וְהַלְּבָנוֹן עַד־הַנָּהָר הַגָּדֹל

FIRST ALIYA: 1:1–3
Moshe begins his farewell speech to his people.

SECOND ALIYA: 1:4–7
Moshe reiterates the promise of the Land of Israel as the premise of the covenant between the Jewish people and God.

נְהַר־פְּרָת: *רְאֵה נָתַתִּי לִפְנֵיכֶם אֶת־הָאָרֶץ בֹּאוּ וּרְשׁוּ ישראל
אֶת־הָאָרֶץ אֲשֶׁר נִשְׁבַּע יְהוָה לַאֲבֹתֵיכֶם לְאַבְרָהָם לְיִצְחָק
וּלְיַעֲקֹב לָתֵת לָהֶם וּלְזַרְעָם אַחֲרֵיהֶם: וָאֹמַר אֲלֵכֶם בָּעֵת
הַהִוא לֵאמֹר לֹא־אוּכַל לְבַדִּי שְׂאֵת אֶתְכֶם: יְהוָה אֱלֹהֵיכֶם
הִרְבָּה אֶתְכֶם וְהִנְּכֶם הַיּוֹם כְּכוֹכְבֵי הַשָּׁמַיִם לָרֹב: יְהוָה
אֱלֹהֵי אֲבוֹתֵכֶם יֹסֵף עֲלֵיכֶם כָּכֶם אֶלֶף פְּעָמִים וִיבָרֵךְ אֶתְכֶם
כַּאֲשֶׁר דִּבֶּר לָכֶם:

THIRD ALIYA: 1:8–11
Moshe describes the multitude that is the Jewish nation.

VA'ET-ḤANAN ואתחנן

דברים ג:כג–ד:ח

וָאֶתְחַנַּן אֶל־יְהוָה בָּעֵת הַהִוא לֵאמֹר: אֲדֹנָי יֱהוִה אַתָּה
הַחִלּוֹתָ לְהַרְאוֹת אֶת־עַבְדְּךָ אֶת־גָּדְלְךָ וְאֶת־יָדְךָ הַחֲזָקָה
אֲשֶׁר מִי־אֵל בַּשָּׁמַיִם וּבָאָרֶץ אֲשֶׁר־יַעֲשֶׂה כְמַעֲשֶׂיךָ
וְכִגְבוּרֹתֶךָ: אֶעְבְּרָה־נָּא וְאֶרְאֶה אֶת־הָאָרֶץ הַטּוֹבָה אֲשֶׁר
בְּעֵבֶר הַיַּרְדֵּן הָהָר הַטּוֹב הַזֶּה וְהַלְּבָנֹן: *וַיִּתְעַבֵּר יְהוָה בִּי לוי
לְמַעַנְכֶם וְלֹא שָׁמַע אֵלָי וַיֹּאמֶר יְהוָה אֵלַי רַב־לָךְ אַל־תּוֹסֶף
דַּבֵּר אֵלַי עוֹד בַּדָּבָר הַזֶּה: עֲלֵה ׀ רֹאשׁ הַפִּסְגָּה וְשָׂא עֵינֶיךָ
יָמָּה וְצָפֹנָה וְתֵימָנָה וּמִזְרָחָה וּרְאֵה בְעֵינֶיךָ כִּי־לֹא תַעֲבֹר
אֶת־הַיַּרְדֵּן הַזֶּה: וְצַו אֶת־יְהוֹשֻׁעַ וְחַזְּקֵהוּ וְאַמְּצֵהוּ כִּי־הוּא
יַעֲבֹר לִפְנֵי הָעָם הַזֶּה וְהוּא יַנְחִיל אוֹתָם אֶת־הָאָרֶץ אֲשֶׁר
תִּרְאֶה: וַנֵּשֶׁב בַּגָּיְא מוּל בֵּית פְּעוֹר:

וְעַתָּה יִשְׂרָאֵל שְׁמַע אֶל־הַחֻקִּים וְאֶל־הַמִּשְׁפָּטִים אֲשֶׁר
אָנֹכִי מְלַמֵּד אֶתְכֶם לַעֲשׂוֹת לְמַעַן תִּחְיוּ וּבָאתֶם וִירִשְׁתֶּם
אֶת־הָאָרֶץ אֲשֶׁר יְהוָה אֱלֹהֵי אֲבֹתֵיכֶם נֹתֵן לָכֶם: לֹא
תֹסִפוּ עַל־הַדָּבָר אֲשֶׁר אָנֹכִי מְצַוֶּה אֶתְכֶם וְלֹא תִגְרְעוּ
מִמֶּנּוּ לִשְׁמֹר אֶת־מִצְוֹת יְהוָה אֱלֹהֵיכֶם אֲשֶׁר אָנֹכִי מְצַוֶּה
אֶתְכֶם: עֵינֵיכֶם הָרֹאוֹת אֵת אֲשֶׁר־עָשָׂה יְהוָה בְּבַעַל פְּעוֹר
כִּי כָל־הָאִישׁ אֲשֶׁר הָלַךְ אַחֲרֵי בַעַל־פְּעוֹר הִשְׁמִידוֹ יְהוָה
אֱלֹהֶיךָ מִקִּרְבֶּךָ: וְאַתֶּם הַדְּבֵקִים בַּיהוָה אֱלֹהֵיכֶם חַיִּים
כֻּלְּכֶם הַיּוֹם: *רְאֵה ׀ לִמַּדְתִּי אֶתְכֶם חֻקִּים וּמִשְׁפָּטִים ישראל

FIRST ALIYA: 3:23–29
Moshe narrates the succession of leadership to Yehoshua.

SECOND ALIYA: 4:1–4
Moshe motivates the people to commit to following God, citing the comeuppance received by those who strayed to worship Ba'al Peor.

THIRD ALIYA: 4:5–8
Moshe urges the people to maintain observance of God's commands.

כַּאֲשֶׁר צִוַּנִי יְהוָה אֱלֹהָי לַעֲשׂוֹת כֵּן בְּקֶרֶב הָאָרֶץ אֲשֶׁר
אַתֶּם בָּאִים שָׁמָּה לְרִשְׁתָּהּ: וּשְׁמַרְתֶּם וַעֲשִׂיתֶם כִּי הִוא
חָכְמַתְכֶם וּבִינַתְכֶם לְעֵינֵי הָעַמִּים אֲשֶׁר יִשְׁמְעוּן אֵת כָּל־
הַחֻקִּים הָאֵלֶּה וְאָמְרוּ רַק עַם־חָכָם וְנָבוֹן הַגּוֹי הַגָּדוֹל הַזֶּה:
כִּי מִי־גוֹי גָּדוֹל אֲשֶׁר־לוֹ אֱלֹהִים קְרֹבִים אֵלָיו כַּיהוָה אֱלֹהֵינוּ
בְּכָל־קָרְאֵנוּ אֵלָיו: וּמִי גּוֹי גָּדוֹל אֲשֶׁר־לוֹ חֻקִּים וּמִשְׁפָּטִים
צַדִּיקִם כְּכֹל הַתּוֹרָה הַזֹּאת אֲשֶׁר אָנֹכִי נֹתֵן לִפְנֵיכֶם
הַיּוֹם:

EKEV עקב

FIRST ALIYA: 7:12–21
The promised rewards for the observance of the covenant with God.

דברים ז:יב–ח:י
וְהָיָה ׀ עֵקֶב תִּשְׁמְעוּן אֵת הַמִּשְׁפָּטִים הָאֵלֶּה וּשְׁמַרְתֶּם
וַעֲשִׂיתֶם אֹתָם וְשָׁמַר יְהוָה אֱלֹהֶיךָ לְךָ אֶת־הַבְּרִית וְאֶת־
הַחֶסֶד אֲשֶׁר נִשְׁבַּע לַאֲבֹתֶיךָ: וַאֲהֵבְךָ וּבֵרַכְךָ וְהִרְבֶּךָ וּבֵרַךְ
פְּרִי־בִטְנְךָ וּפְרִי־אַדְמָתֶךָ דְּגָנְךָ וְתִירֹשְׁךָ וְיִצְהָרֶךָ שְׁגַר־
אֲלָפֶיךָ וְעַשְׁתְּרֹת צֹאנֶךָ עַל הָאֲדָמָה אֲשֶׁר־נִשְׁבַּע לַאֲבֹתֶיךָ
לָתֶת לָךְ: בָּרוּךְ תִּהְיֶה מִכָּל־הָעַמִּים לֹא־יִהְיֶה בְךָ עָקָר
וַעֲקָרָה וּבִבְהֶמְתֶּךָ: וְהֵסִיר יְהוָה מִמְּךָ כָּל־חֹלִי וְכָל־מַדְוֵי
מִצְרַיִם הָרָעִים אֲשֶׁר יָדַעְתָּ לֹא יְשִׂימָם בָּךְ וּנְתָנָם בְּכָל־
שֹׂנְאֶיךָ: וְאָכַלְתָּ אֶת־כָּל־הָעַמִּים אֲשֶׁר יְהוָה אֱלֹהֶיךָ נֹתֵן
לָךְ לֹא־תָחֹס עֵינְךָ עֲלֵיהֶם וְלֹא תַעֲבֹד אֶת־אֱלֹהֵיהֶם כִּי־
מוֹקֵשׁ הוּא לָךְ: כִּי תֹאמַר בִּלְבָבְךָ רַבִּים הַגּוֹיִם
הָאֵלֶּה מִמֶּנִּי אֵיכָה אוּכַל לְהוֹרִישָׁם: לֹא תִירָא מֵהֶם זָכֹר
תִּזְכֹּר אֵת אֲשֶׁר־עָשָׂה יְהוָה אֱלֹהֶיךָ לְפַרְעֹה וּלְכָל־מִצְרָיִם:
הַמַּסֹּת הַגְּדֹלֹת אֲשֶׁר־רָאוּ עֵינֶיךָ וְהָאֹתֹת וְהַמֹּפְתִים וְהַיָּד
הַחֲזָקָה וְהַזְּרֹעַ הַנְּטוּיָה אֲשֶׁר הוֹצִאֲךָ יְהוָה אֱלֹהֶיךָ כֵּן־
יַעֲשֶׂה יְהוָה אֱלֹהֶיךָ לְכָל־הָעַמִּים אֲשֶׁר־אַתָּה יָרֵא
מִפְּנֵיהֶם: וְגַם אֶת־הַצִּרְעָה יְשַׁלַּח יְהוָה אֱלֹהֶיךָ בָּם עַד־
אֲבֹד הַנִּשְׁאָרִים וְהַנִּסְתָּרִים מִפָּנֶיךָ: לֹא תַעֲרֹץ מִפְּנֵיהֶם

SECOND ALIYA: 7:22–8:3
The promise of enemies delivered, and a historical recap of the journey from Egypt.

כִּי־יְהוָה אֱלֹהֶיךָ בְּקִרְבֶּךָ אֵל גָּדוֹל וְנוֹרָא: *וְנָשַׁל יְהוָה לוי
אֱלֹהֶיךָ אֶת־הַגּוֹיִם הָאֵל מִפָּנֶיךָ מְעַט מְעָט לֹא תוּכַל כַּלֹּתָם
מַהֵר פֶּן־תִּרְבֶּה עָלֶיךָ חַיַּת הַשָּׂדֶה: וּנְתָנָם יְהוָה אֱלֹהֶיךָ
לְפָנֶיךָ וְהָמָם מְהוּמָה גְדֹלָה עַד הִשָּׁמְדָם: וְנָתַן מַלְכֵיהֶם
בְּיָדֶךָ וְהַאֲבַדְתָּ אֶת־שְׁמָם מִתַּחַת הַשָּׁמָיִם לֹא־יִתְיַצֵּב אִישׁ
בְּפָנֶיךָ עַד הִשְׁמִדְךָ אֹתָם: פְּסִילֵי אֱלֹהֵיהֶם תִּשְׂרְפוּן בָּאֵשׁ
לֹא־תַחְמֹד כֶּסֶף וְזָהָב עֲלֵיהֶם וְלָקַחְתָּ לָךְ פֶּן תִּוָּקֵשׁ בּוֹ כִּי
תוֹעֲבַת יְהוָה אֱלֹהֶיךָ הוּא: וְלֹא־תָבִיא תוֹעֵבָה אֶל־בֵּיתֶךָ
וְהָיִיתָ חֵרֶם כָּמֹהוּ שַׁקֵּץ | תְּשַׁקְּצֶנּוּ וְתַעֵב | תְּתַעֲבֶנּוּ כִּי־חֵרֶם
הוּא:
כָּל־הַמִּצְוָה אֲשֶׁר אָנֹכִי מְצַוְּךָ הַיּוֹם תִּשְׁמְרוּן לַעֲשׂוֹת לְמַעַן
תִּחְיוּן וּרְבִיתֶם וּבָאתֶם וִירִשְׁתֶּם אֶת־הָאָרֶץ אֲשֶׁר־נִשְׁבַּע
יְהוָה לַאֲבֹתֵיכֶם: וְזָכַרְתָּ אֶת־כָּל־הַדֶּרֶךְ אֲשֶׁר הוֹלִיכְךָ
יְהוָה אֱלֹהֶיךָ זֶה אַרְבָּעִים שָׁנָה בַּמִּדְבָּר לְמַעַן עַנֹּתְךָ
לְנַסֹּתְךָ לָדַעַת אֶת־אֲשֶׁר בִּלְבָבְךָ הֲתִשְׁמֹר מִצְוֹתָו אִם־
לֹא: וַיְעַנְּךָ וַיַּרְעִבֶךָ וַיַּאֲכִלְךָ אֶת־הַמָּן אֲשֶׁר לֹא־יָדַעְתָּ וְלֹא
יָדְעוּן אֲבֹתֶיךָ לְמַעַן הוֹדִיעֲךָ כִּי לֹא עַל־הַלֶּחֶם לְבַדּוֹ יִחְיֶה
ישראל הָאָדָם כִּי עַל־כָּל־מוֹצָא פִי־יְהוָה יִחְיֶה הָאָדָם: *שִׂמְלָתְךָ

THIRD ALIYA: 8:4–10
The promise of inheriting a wonderful land.

לֹא בָלְתָה מֵעָלֶיךָ וְרַגְלְךָ לֹא בָצֵקָה זֶה אַרְבָּעִים שָׁנָה:
וְיָדַעְתָּ עִם־לְבָבֶךָ כִּי כַּאֲשֶׁר יְיַסֵּר אִישׁ אֶת־בְּנוֹ יְהוָה אֱלֹהֶיךָ
מְיַסְּרֶךָּ: וְשָׁמַרְתָּ אֶת־מִצְוֹת יְהוָה אֱלֹהֶיךָ לָלֶכֶת בִּדְרָכָיו
וּלְיִרְאָה אֹתוֹ: כִּי יְהוָה אֱלֹהֶיךָ מְבִיאֲךָ אֶל־אֶרֶץ טוֹבָה
אֶרֶץ נַחֲלֵי מָיִם עֲיָנֹת וּתְהֹמֹת יֹצְאִים בַּבִּקְעָה וּבָהָר: אֶרֶץ
חִטָּה וּשְׂעֹרָה וְגֶפֶן וּתְאֵנָה וְרִמּוֹן אֶרֶץ־זֵית שֶׁמֶן וּדְבָשׁ:
אֶרֶץ אֲשֶׁר לֹא בְמִסְכֵּנֻת תֹּאכַל־בָּהּ לֶחֶם לֹא־תֶחְסַר כֹּל
בָּהּ אֶרֶץ אֲשֶׁר אֲבָנֶיהָ בַרְזֶל וּמֵהֲרָרֶיהָ תַּחְצֹב נְחֹשֶׁת:
וְאָכַלְתָּ וְשָׂבָעְתָּ וּבֵרַכְתָּ אֶת־יְהוָה אֱלֹהֶיךָ עַל־הָאָרֶץ הַטֹּבָה
אֲשֶׁר נָתַן־לָךְ:

RE'EH ראה

FIRST ALIYA: 11:26–31
The ceremony of the blessings and the curses on Mount Gerizim.

רְאֵה אָנֹכִי נֹתֵן לִפְנֵיכֶם הַיּוֹם בְּרָכָה וּקְלָלָה: אֶת־ דברים
הַבְּרָכָה אֲשֶׁר תִּשְׁמְעוּ אֶל־מִצְוֺת יהוה אֱלֹהֵיכֶם אֲשֶׁר יא:כו–יב:י
אָנֹכִי מְצַוֶּה אֶתְכֶם הַיּוֹם: וְהַקְּלָלָה אִם־לֹא תִשְׁמְעוּ
אֶל־מִצְוֺת יהוה אֱלֹהֵיכֶם וְסַרְתֶּם מִן־הַדֶּרֶךְ אֲשֶׁר אָנֹכִי
מְצַוֶּה אֶתְכֶם הַיּוֹם לָלֶכֶת אַחֲרֵי אֱלֹהִים אֲחֵרִים אֲשֶׁר
לֹא־יְדַעְתֶּם: וְהָיָה כִּי יְבִיאֲךָ יהוה אֱלֹהֶיךָ אֶל־
הָאָרֶץ אֲשֶׁר־אַתָּה בָא־שָׁמָּה לְרִשְׁתָּהּ וְנָתַתָּה אֶת־הַבְּרָכָה
עַל־הַר גְּרִזִים וְאֶת־הַקְּלָלָה עַל־הַר עֵיבָל: הֲלֹא־הֵמָּה
בְּעֵבֶר הַיַּרְדֵּן אַחֲרֵי דֶּרֶךְ מְבוֹא הַשֶּׁמֶשׁ בְּאֶרֶץ הַכְּנַעֲנִי
הַיֹּשֵׁב בָּעֲרָבָה מוּל הַגִּלְגָּל אֵצֶל אֵלוֹנֵי מֹרֶה: כִּי אַתֶּם
עֹבְרִים אֶת־הַיַּרְדֵּן לָבֹא לָרֶשֶׁת אֶת־הָאָרֶץ אֲשֶׁר־יהוה
אֱלֹהֵיכֶם נֹתֵן לָכֶם וִירִשְׁתֶּם אֹתָהּ וִישַׁבְתֶּם־בָּהּ: *וּשְׁמַרְתֶּם לוי
לַעֲשׂוֹת אֵת כָּל־הַחֻקִּים וְאֶת־הַמִּשְׁפָּטִים אֲשֶׁר אָנֹכִי נֹתֵן
לִפְנֵיכֶם הַיּוֹם: אֵלֶּה הַחֻקִּים וְהַמִּשְׁפָּטִים אֲשֶׁר תִּשְׁמְרוּן
לַעֲשׂוֹת בָּאָרֶץ אֲשֶׁר נָתַן יהוה אֱלֹהֵי אֲבֹתֶיךָ לְךָ לְרִשְׁתָּהּ
כָּל־הַיָּמִים אֲשֶׁר־אַתֶּם חַיִּים עַל־הָאֲדָמָה: אַבֵּד תְּאַבְּדוּן
אֶת־כָּל־הַמְּקֹמוֹת אֲשֶׁר עָבְדוּ־שָׁם הַגּוֹיִם אֲשֶׁר אַתֶּם
יֹרְשִׁים אֹתָם אֶת־אֱלֹהֵיהֶם עַל־הֶהָרִים הָרָמִים וְעַל־
הַגְּבָעוֹת וְתַחַת כָּל־עֵץ רַעֲנָן: וְנִתַּצְתֶּם אֶת־מִזְבְּחֹתָם
וְשִׁבַּרְתֶּם אֶת־מַצֵּבֹתָם וַאֲשֵׁרֵיהֶם תִּשְׂרְפוּן בָּאֵשׁ וּפְסִילֵי
אֱלֹהֵיהֶם תְּגַדֵּעוּן וְאִבַּדְתֶּם אֶת־שְׁמָם מִן־הַמָּקוֹם הַהוּא:
לֹא־תַעֲשׂוּן כֵּן לַיהוה אֱלֹהֵיכֶם: כִּי אִם־אֶל־הַמָּקוֹם אֲשֶׁר־
יִבְחַר יהוה אֱלֹהֵיכֶם מִכָּל־שִׁבְטֵיכֶם לָשׂוּם אֶת־שְׁמוֹ שָׁם
לְשִׁכְנוֹ תִדְרְשׁוּ וּבָאתָ שָּׁמָּה: *וַהֲבֵאתֶם שָׁמָּה עֹלֹתֵיכֶם ישראל
וְזִבְחֵיכֶם וְאֵת מַעְשְׂרֹתֵיכֶם וְאֵת תְּרוּמַת יֶדְכֶם וְנִדְרֵיכֶם
וְנִדְבֹתֵיכֶם וּבְכֹרֹת בְּקַרְכֶם וְצֹאנְכֶם: וַאֲכַלְתֶּם־שָׁם לִפְנֵי
יהוה אֱלֹהֵיכֶם וּשְׂמַחְתֶּם בְּכֹל מִשְׁלַח יֶדְכֶם אַתֶּם וּבָתֵּיכֶם
אֲשֶׁר בֵּרַכְךָ יהוה אֱלֹהֶיךָ: לֹא תַעֲשׂוּן כְּכֹל אֲשֶׁר אֲנַחְנוּ

SECOND ALIYA: vv. 11:32–12:5
The command to rid the land of idolatrous alters.

THIRD ALIYA: 12:6–10
Offerings to be given upon entering the land.

עֹשִׂים פֹּה הַיּוֹם אִישׁ כָּל־הַיָּשָׁר בְּעֵינָיו׃ כִּי לֹא־בָאתֶם
עַד־עָתָּה אֶל־הַמְּנוּחָה וְאֶל־הַנַּחֲלָה אֲשֶׁר־יְהוָה אֱלֹהֶיךָ
נֹתֵן לָךְ׃ וַעֲבַרְתֶּם אֶת־הַיַּרְדֵּן וִישַׁבְתֶּם בָּאָרֶץ אֲשֶׁר־יְהוָה
אֱלֹהֵיכֶם מַנְחִיל אֶתְכֶם וְהֵנִיחַ לָכֶם מִכָּל־אֹיְבֵיכֶם מִסָּבִיב
וִישַׁבְתֶּם־בֶּטַח׃

SHOFETIM
שופטים

דברים טז:יח–יז:יג

FIRST ALIYA: 16:18–20
The establishment of the justice system.

SECOND ALIYA: 16:21–17:10
The laws of blemished sacrifices, and the punishment for idolatry.

שֹׁפְטִים וְשֹׁטְרִים תִּתֶּן־לְךָ בְּכָל־שְׁעָרֶיךָ אֲשֶׁר יְהוָה אֱלֹהֶיךָ
נֹתֵן לְךָ לִשְׁבָטֶיךָ וְשָׁפְטוּ אֶת־הָעָם מִשְׁפַּט־צֶדֶק׃ לֹא־
תַטֶּה מִשְׁפָּט לֹא תַכִּיר פָּנִים וְלֹא־תִקַּח שֹׁחַד כִּי הַשֹּׁחַד
יְעַוֵּר עֵינֵי חֲכָמִים וִיסַלֵּף דִּבְרֵי צַדִּיקִם׃ צֶדֶק צֶדֶק תִּרְדֹּף
לְמַעַן תִּחְיֶה וְיָרַשְׁתָּ אֶת־הָאָרֶץ אֲשֶׁר־יְהוָה אֱלֹהֶיךָ נֹתֵן
לָךְ׃ *לֹא־תִטַּע לְךָ אֲשֵׁרָה כָּל־עֵץ אֵצֶל מִזְבַּח לוי
יְהוָה אֱלֹהֶיךָ אֲשֶׁר תַּעֲשֶׂה־לָּךְ׃ וְלֹא־תָקִים לְךָ מַצֵּבָה אֲשֶׁר
שָׂנֵא יְהוָה אֱלֹהֶיךָ׃ לֹא־תִזְבַּח לַיהוָה אֱלֹהֶיךָ
שׁוֹר וָשֶׂה אֲשֶׁר יִהְיֶה בוֹ מוּם כֹּל דָּבָר רָע כִּי תוֹעֲבַת יְהוָה
אֱלֹהֶיךָ הוּא׃ כִּי־יִמָּצֵא בְקִרְבְּךָ בְּאַחַד שְׁעָרֶיךָ
אֲשֶׁר־יְהוָה אֱלֹהֶיךָ נֹתֵן לָךְ אִישׁ אוֹ־אִשָּׁה אֲשֶׁר יַעֲשֶׂה
אֶת־הָרַע בְּעֵינֵי יְהוָה־אֱלֹהֶיךָ לַעֲבֹר בְּרִיתוֹ׃ וַיֵּלֶךְ וַיַּעֲבֹד
אֱלֹהִים אֲחֵרִים וַיִּשְׁתַּחוּ לָהֶם וְלַשֶּׁמֶשׁ ׀ אוֹ לַיָּרֵחַ אוֹ לְכָל־
צְבָא הַשָּׁמַיִם אֲשֶׁר לֹא־צִוִּיתִי׃ וְהֻגַּד־לְךָ וְשָׁמָעְתָּ וְדָרַשְׁתָּ
הֵיטֵב וְהִנֵּה אֱמֶת נָכוֹן הַדָּבָר נֶעֶשְׂתָה הַתּוֹעֵבָה הַזֹּאת
בְּיִשְׂרָאֵל׃ וְהוֹצֵאתָ אֶת־הָאִישׁ הַהוּא אוֹ אֶת־הָאִשָּׁה הַהִוא
אֲשֶׁר עָשׂוּ אֶת־הַדָּבָר הָרָע הַזֶּה אֶל־שְׁעָרֶיךָ אֶת־הָאִישׁ אוֹ
אֶת־הָאִשָּׁה וּסְקַלְתָּם בָּאֲבָנִים וָמֵתוּ׃ עַל־פִּי ׀ שְׁנַיִם עֵדִים
אוֹ שְׁלֹשָׁה עֵדִים יוּמַת הַמֵּת לֹא יוּמַת עַל־פִּי עֵד אֶחָד׃ יַד
הָעֵדִים תִּהְיֶה־בּוֹ בָרִאשֹׁנָה לַהֲמִיתוֹ וְיַד כָּל־הָעָם בָּאַחֲרֹנָה
וּבִעַרְתָּ הָרָע מִקִּרְבֶּךָ׃

כִּי יִפָּלֵא מִמְּךָ דָבָר לַמִּשְׁפָּט בֵּין־דָּם ׀ לְדָם בֵּין־דִּין לְדִין וּבֵין
נֶגַע לָנֶגַע דִּבְרֵי רִיבֹת בִּשְׁעָרֶיךָ וְקַמְתָּ וְעָלִיתָ אֶל־הַמָּקוֹם
אֲשֶׁר יִבְחַר יהוה אֱלֹהֶיךָ בּוֹ: וּבָאתָ אֶל־הַכֹּהֲנִים הַלְוִיִּם
וְאֶל־הַשֹּׁפֵט אֲשֶׁר יִהְיֶה בַּיָּמִים הָהֵם וְדָרַשְׁתָּ וְהִגִּידוּ לְךָ
אֵת דְּבַר הַמִּשְׁפָּט: וְעָשִׂיתָ עַל־פִּי הַדָּבָר אֲשֶׁר יַגִּידוּ לְךָ
מִן־הַמָּקוֹם הַהוּא אֲשֶׁר יִבְחַר יהוה וְשָׁמַרְתָּ לַעֲשׂוֹת כְּכֹל
ישראל אֲשֶׁר יוֹרוּךָ: *עַל־פִּי הַתּוֹרָה אֲשֶׁר יוֹרוּךָ וְעַל־הַמִּשְׁפָּט
אֲשֶׁר־יֹאמְרוּ לְךָ תַּעֲשֶׂה לֹא תָסוּר מִן־הַדָּבָר אֲשֶׁר־יַגִּידוּ
לְךָ יָמִין וּשְׂמֹאל: וְהָאִישׁ אֲשֶׁר־יַעֲשֶׂה בְזָדוֹן לְבִלְתִּי שְׁמֹעַ
אֶל־הַכֹּהֵן הָעֹמֵד לְשָׁרֶת שָׁם אֶת־יהוה אֱלֹהֶיךָ אוֹ אֶל־
הַשֹּׁפֵט וּמֵת הָאִישׁ הַהוּא וּבִעַרְתָּ הָרָע מִיִּשְׂרָאֵל: וְכָל־הָעָם
יִשְׁמְעוּ וְיִרָאוּ וְלֹא יְזִידוּן עוֹד:

THIRD ALIYA: 17:11–13
The laws of the rebellious elder.

כי תצא KI TETZEH

דברים כא:י–כא

כִּי־תֵצֵא לַמִּלְחָמָה עַל־אֹיְבֶיךָ וּנְתָנוֹ יהוה אֱלֹהֶיךָ בְּיָדֶךָ
וְשָׁבִיתָ שִׁבְיוֹ: וְרָאִיתָ בַּשִּׁבְיָה אֵשֶׁת יְפַת־תֹּאַר וְחָשַׁקְתָּ
בָהּ וְלָקַחְתָּ לְךָ לְאִשָּׁה: וַהֲבֵאתָהּ אֶל־תּוֹךְ בֵּיתֶךָ וְגִלְּחָה
אֶת־רֹאשָׁהּ וְעָשְׂתָה אֶת־צִפָּרְנֶיהָ: וְהֵסִירָה אֶת־שִׂמְלַת
שִׁבְיָהּ מֵעָלֶיהָ וְיָשְׁבָה בְּבֵיתֶךָ וּבָכְתָה אֶת־אָבִיהָ וְאֶת־
אִמָּהּ יֶרַח יָמִים וְאַחַר כֵּן תָּבוֹא אֵלֶיהָ וּבְעַלְתָּהּ וְהָיְתָה
לְךָ לְאִשָּׁה: וְהָיָה אִם־לֹא חָפַצְתָּ בָּהּ וְשִׁלַּחְתָּהּ לְנַפְשָׁהּ
וּמָכֹר לֹא־תִמְכְּרֶנָּה בַּכָּסֶף לֹא־תִתְעַמֵּר בָּהּ תַּחַת אֲשֶׁר
לוי עִנִּיתָהּ: *כִּי־תִהְיֶיןָ לְאִישׁ שְׁתֵּי נָשִׁים הָאַחַת
אֲהוּבָה וְהָאַחַת שְׂנוּאָה וְיָלְדוּ־לוֹ בָנִים הָאֲהוּבָה וְהַשְּׂנוּאָה
וְהָיָה הַבֵּן הַבְּכֹר לַשְּׂנִיאָה: וְהָיָה בְּיוֹם הַנְחִילוֹ אֶת־בָּנָיו אֵת
אֲשֶׁר־יִהְיֶה לוֹ לֹא יוּכַל לְבַכֵּר אֶת־בֶּן־הָאֲהוּבָה עַל־פְּנֵי בֶן־
הַשְּׂנוּאָה הַבְּכֹר: כִּי אֶת־הַבְּכֹר בֶּן־הַשְּׂנוּאָה יַכִּיר לָתֶת לוֹ פִּי
שְׁנַיִם בְּכֹל אֲשֶׁר־יִמָּצֵא לוֹ כִּי־הוּא רֵאשִׁית אֹנוֹ לוֹ מִשְׁפַּט
ישראל הַבְּכֹרָה: *כִּי־יִהְיֶה לְאִישׁ בֵּן סוֹרֵר וּמוֹרֶה אֵינֶנּוּ

FIRST ALIYA: 21:10–14
The laws of the captive woman in times of war.

SECOND ALIYA: 21:15–17
The rights of the firstborn son.

THIRD ALIYA: 21:18–21
The laws of the rebellious son.

שְׁמֵעַ בְּקוֹל אָבִיו וּבְקוֹל אִמּוֹ וְיִסְּרוּ אֹתוֹ וְלֹא יִשְׁמַע אֲלֵיהֶם׃
וְתָפְשׂוּ בוֹ אָבִיו וְאִמּוֹ וְהוֹצִיאוּ אֹתוֹ אֶל־זִקְנֵי עִירוֹ וְאֶל־שַׁעַר
מְקֹמוֹ׃ וְאָמְרוּ אֶל־זִקְנֵי עִירוֹ בְּנֵנוּ זֶה סוֹרֵר וּמֹרֶה אֵינֶנּוּ שֹׁמֵעַ
בְּקֹלֵנוּ זוֹלֵל וְסֹבֵא׃ וּרְגָמֻהוּ כָּל־אַנְשֵׁי עִירוֹ בָאֲבָנִים וָמֵת
וּבִעַרְתָּ הָרָע מִקִּרְבֶּךָ וְכָל־יִשְׂרָאֵל יִשְׁמְעוּ וְיִרָאוּ׃

KI TAVO כי תבוא

FIRST ALIYA: 26:1–3
The taking of the first fruits to Jerusalem.

וְהָיָה כִּי־תָבוֹא אֶל־הָאָרֶץ אֲשֶׁר יְהוָה אֱלֹהֶיךָ נֹתֵן לְךָ נַחֲלָה דברים כו:א–טו
וִירִשְׁתָּהּ וְיָשַׁבְתָּ בָּהּ׃ וְלָקַחְתָּ מֵרֵאשִׁית ׀ כָּל־פְּרִי הָאֲדָמָה
אֲשֶׁר תָּבִיא מֵאַרְצְךָ אֲשֶׁר יְהוָה אֱלֹהֶיךָ נֹתֵן לָךְ וְשַׂמְתָּ
בַטֶּנֶא וְהָלַכְתָּ אֶל־הַמָּקוֹם אֲשֶׁר יִבְחַר יְהוָה אֱלֹהֶיךָ לְשַׁכֵּן
שְׁמוֹ שָׁם׃ וּבָאתָ אֶל־הַכֹּהֵן אֲשֶׁר יִהְיֶה בַּיָּמִים הָהֵם וְאָמַרְתָּ
אֵלָיו הִגַּדְתִּי הַיּוֹם לַיהוָה אֱלֹהֶיךָ כִּי־בָאתִי אֶל־הָאָרֶץ אֲשֶׁר
נִשְׁבַּע יְהוָה לַאֲבֹתֵינוּ לָתֶת לָנוּ׃ *וְלָקַח הַכֹּהֵן הַטֶּנֶא מִיָּדֶךָ לוי

SECOND ALIYA: 26:4–11
The ceremony of the bringing of the first fruits.

וְהִנִּיחוֹ לִפְנֵי מִזְבַּח יְהוָה אֱלֹהֶיךָ׃ וְעָנִיתָ וְאָמַרְתָּ לִפְנֵי ׀ יְהוָה
אֱלֹהֶיךָ אֲרַמִּי אֹבֵד אָבִי וַיֵּרֶד מִצְרַיְמָה וַיָּגָר שָׁם בִּמְתֵי מְעָט
וַיְהִי־שָׁם לְגוֹי גָּדוֹל עָצוּם וָרָב׃ וַיָּרֵעוּ אֹתָנוּ הַמִּצְרִים וַיְעַנּוּנוּ
וַיִּתְּנוּ עָלֵינוּ עֲבֹדָה קָשָׁה׃ וַנִּצְעַק אֶל־יְהוָה אֱלֹהֵי אֲבֹתֵינוּ
וַיִּשְׁמַע יְהוָה אֶת־קֹלֵנוּ וַיַּרְא אֶת־עָנְיֵנוּ וְאֶת־עֲמָלֵנוּ וְאֶת־
לַחֲצֵנוּ׃ וַיּוֹצִאֵנוּ יְהוָה מִמִּצְרַיִם בְּיָד חֲזָקָה וּבִזְרֹעַ נְטוּיָה
וּבְמֹרָא גָּדֹל וּבְאֹתוֹת וּבְמֹפְתִים׃ וַיְבִאֵנוּ אֶל־הַמָּקוֹם הַזֶּה
וַיִּתֶּן־לָנוּ אֶת־הָאָרֶץ הַזֹּאת אֶרֶץ זָבַת חָלָב וּדְבָשׁ׃ וְעַתָּה
הִנֵּה הֵבֵאתִי אֶת־רֵאשִׁית פְּרִי הָאֲדָמָה אֲשֶׁר־נָתַתָּה לִּי
יְהוָה וְהִנַּחְתּוֹ לִפְנֵי יְהוָה אֱלֹהֶיךָ וְהִשְׁתַּחֲוִיתָ לִפְנֵי יְהוָה
אֱלֹהֶיךָ׃ וְשָׂמַחְתָּ בְכָל־הַטּוֹב אֲשֶׁר נָתַן־לְךָ יְהוָה אֱלֹהֶיךָ
וּלְבֵיתֶךָ אַתָּה וְהַלֵּוִי וְהַגֵּר אֲשֶׁר בְּקִרְבֶּךָ׃ *כִּי ישראל

THIRD ALIYA: 26:12–15
The confession said over the bringing of agricultural tithes.

תְכַלֶּה לַעְשֵׂר אֶת־כָּל־מַעְשַׂר תְּבוּאָתְךָ בַּשָּׁנָה הַשְּׁלִישִׁת
שְׁנַת הַמַּעֲשֵׂר וְנָתַתָּה לַלֵּוִי לַגֵּר לַיָּתוֹם וְלָאַלְמָנָה וְאָכְלוּ
בִשְׁעָרֶיךָ וְשָׂבֵעוּ׃ וְאָמַרְתָּ לִפְנֵי יְהוָה אֱלֹהֶיךָ בִּעַרְתִּי הַקֹּדֶשׁ

מן־הבית וגם נתתיו ללוי ולגר ליתום ולאלמנה ככל־
מצותך אשר צויתני לא־עברתי ממצותיך ולא שכחתי:
לא־אכלתי באני ממנו ולא־בערתי ממנו בטמא ולא־
נתתי ממנו למת שמעתי בקול יהוה אלהי עשיתי ככל
אשר צויתני: השקיפה ממעון קדשך מן־השמים וברך
את־עמך את־ישראל ואת האדמה אשר נתתה לנו כאשר
נשבעת לאבתינו ארץ זבת חלב ודבש:

NITZAVIM נצבים

דברים כט:ט-כח אתם נצבים היום כלכם לפני יהוה אלהיכם ראשיכם
שבטיכם זקניכם ושטריכם כל איש ישראל: טפכם נשיכם
וגרך אשר בקרב מחניך מחטב עציך עד שאב מימיך:
לעברך בברית יהוה אלהיך ובאלתו אשר יהוה אלהיך
לוי כרת עמך היום: *למען הקים־אתך היום | לו לעם והוא
יהיה־לך לאלהים כאשר דבר־לך וכאשר נשבע לאבתיך
לאברהם ליצחק וליעקב: ולא אתכם לבדכם אנכי כרת
את־הברית הזאת ואת־האלה הזאת: כי את־אשר ישנו
פה עמנו עמד היום לפני יהוה אלהינו ואת אשר איננו
ישראל פה עמנו היום: *כי־אתם ידעתם את אשר־ישבנו בארץ
מצרים ואת אשר־עברנו בקרב הגוים אשר עברתם:
ותראו את־שקוציהם ואת גלליהם עץ ואבן כסף וזהב
אשר עמהם: פן־יש בכם איש או־אשה או משפחה או־
שבט אשר לבבו פנה היום מעם יהוה אלהינו ללכת
לעבד את־אלהי הגוים ההם פן־יש בכם שרש פרה ראש
ולענה: והיה בשמעו את־דברי האלה הזאת והתברך
בלבבו לאמר שלום יהיה־לי כי בשררות לבי אלך למען
ספות הרוה את־הצמאה: לא־יאבה יהוה סלח לו כי אז
יעשן אף־יהוה וקנאתו באיש ההוא ורבצה בו כל־האלה
הכתובה בספר הזה ומחה יהוה את־שמו מתחת השמים:

FIRST ALIYA: 29:9–11
Renewing the covenant between the people and God.

SECOND ALIYA: 29:12–14
The eternal nature of the covenant, with those present at that time as well as future generations.

THIRD ALIYA: 29:15–28
Warnings against idolatrous practices.

וְהִבְדִּילוֹ יְהוָה לְרָעָה מִכֹּל שִׁבְטֵי יִשְׂרָאֵל כְּכֹל אָלוֹת הַבְּרִית
הַכְּתוּבָה בְּסֵפֶר הַתּוֹרָה הַזֶּה: וְאָמַר הַדּוֹר הָאַחֲרוֹן בְּנֵיכֶם
אֲשֶׁר יָקוּמוּ מֵאַחֲרֵיכֶם וְהַנָּכְרִי אֲשֶׁר יָבֹא מֵאֶרֶץ רְחוֹקָה
וְרָאוּ אֶת־מַכּוֹת הָאָרֶץ הַהִוא וְאֶת־תַּחֲלֻאֶיהָ אֲשֶׁר־חִלָּה
יְהוָה בָּהּ: גָּפְרִית וָמֶלַח שְׂרֵפָה כָל־אַרְצָהּ לֹא תִזָּרַע וְלֹא
תַצְמִחַ וְלֹא־יַעֲלֶה בָהּ כָּל־עֵשֶׂב כְּמַהְפֵּכַת סְדֹם וַעֲמֹרָה
אַדְמָה וצביים אֲשֶׁר הָפַךְ יְהוָה בְּאַפּוֹ וּבַחֲמָתוֹ: וְאָמְרוּ כָּל־ וּצְבוֹיִם
הַגּוֹיִם עַל־מֶה עָשָׂה יְהוָה כָּכָה לָאָרֶץ הַזֹּאת מֶה חֳרִי הָאַף
הַגָּדוֹל הַזֶּה: וְאָמְרוּ עַל אֲשֶׁר עָזְבוּ אֶת־בְּרִית יְהוָה אֱלֹהֵי
אֲבֹתָם אֲשֶׁר כָּרַת עִמָּם בְּהוֹצִיאוֹ אֹתָם מֵאֶרֶץ מִצְרָיִם:
וַיֵּלְכוּ וַיַּעַבְדוּ אֱלֹהִים אֲחֵרִים וַיִּשְׁתַּחֲווּ לָהֶם אֱלֹהִים אֲשֶׁר
לֹא־יְדָעוּם וְלֹא חָלַק לָהֶם: וַיִּחַר־אַף יְהוָה בָּאָרֶץ הַהִוא
לְהָבִיא עָלֶיהָ אֶת־כָּל־הַקְּלָלָה הַכְּתוּבָה בַּסֵּפֶר הַזֶּה:
וַיִּתְּשֵׁם יְהוָה מֵעַל אַדְמָתָם בְּאַף וּבְחֵמָה וּבְקֶצֶף גָּדוֹל
וַיַּשְׁלִכֵם אֶל־אֶרֶץ אַחֶרֶת כַּיּוֹם הַזֶּה: הַנִּסְתָּרֹת לַיהוָה
אֱלֹהֵינוּ וְהַנִּגְלֹת לָנוּ וּלְבָנֵינוּ עַד־עוֹלָם לַעֲשׂוֹת אֶת־כָּל־
דִּבְרֵי הַתּוֹרָה הַזֹּאת:

וילך VAYELEKH

דברים לא:א–יג
וַיֵּלֶךְ מֹשֶׁה וַיְדַבֵּר אֶת־הַדְּבָרִים הָאֵלֶּה אֶל־כָּל־יִשְׂרָאֵל:
וַיֹּאמֶר אֲלֵהֶם בֶּן־מֵאָה וְעֶשְׂרִים שָׁנָה אָנֹכִי הַיּוֹם לֹא־אוּכַל
עוֹד לָצֵאת וְלָבוֹא וַיהוָה אָמַר אֵלַי לֹא תַעֲבֹר אֶת־הַיַּרְדֵּן
הַזֶּה: יְהוָה אֱלֹהֶיךָ הוּא ׀ עֹבֵר לְפָנֶיךָ הוּא־יַשְׁמִיד אֶת־הַגּוֹיִם
הָאֵלֶּה מִלְּפָנֶיךָ וִירִשְׁתָּם יְהוֹשֻׁעַ הוּא עֹבֵר לְפָנֶיךָ כַּאֲשֶׁר דִּבֶּר
יְהוָה: *וְעָשָׂה יְהוָה לָהֶם כַּאֲשֶׁר עָשָׂה לְסִיחוֹן וּלְעוֹג מַלְכֵי לוי
הָאֱמֹרִי וּלְאַרְצָם אֲשֶׁר הִשְׁמִיד אֹתָם: וּנְתָנָם יְהוָה לִפְנֵיכֶם
וַעֲשִׂיתֶם לָהֶם כְּכָל־הַמִּצְוָה אֲשֶׁר צִוִּיתִי אֶתְכֶם: חִזְקוּ וְאִמְצוּ
אַל־תִּירְאוּ וְאַל־תַּעַרְצוּ מִפְּנֵיהֶם כִּי ׀ יְהוָה אֱלֹהֶיךָ הוּא
הַהֹלֵךְ עִמָּךְ לֹא יַרְפְּךָ וְלֹא יַעַזְבֶךָּ: *וַיִּקְרָא ישראל

FIRST ALIYA: 31:1–3
Moshe begins his final farewell.

SECOND ALIYA: 31:4–6
Moshe delivers words of comfort and inspiration for the coming military campaign to conquer the land.

מֹשֶׁה לִיהוֹשֻׁעַ וַיֹּאמֶר אֵלָיו לְעֵינֵי כָל־יִשְׂרָאֵל חֲזַק וֶאֱמָץ
כִּי אַתָּה תָּבוֹא אֶת־הָעָם הַזֶּה אֶל־הָאָרֶץ אֲשֶׁר נִשְׁבַּע
יהוה לַאֲבֹתָם לָתֵת לָהֶם וְאַתָּה תַּנְחִילֶנָּה אוֹתָם׃ וַיהוה
הוּא ׀ הַהֹלֵךְ לְפָנֶיךָ הוּא יִהְיֶה עִמָּךְ לֹא יַרְפְּךָ וְלֹא יַעַזְבֶךָּ
לֹא תִירָא וְלֹא תֵחָת׃ וַיִּכְתֹּב מֹשֶׁה אֶת־הַתּוֹרָה הַזֹּאת
וַיִּתְּנָהּ אֶל־הַכֹּהֲנִים בְּנֵי לֵוִי הַנֹּשְׂאִים אֶת־אֲרוֹן בְּרִית יהוה
וְאֶל־כָּל־זִקְנֵי יִשְׂרָאֵל׃ וַיְצַו מֹשֶׁה אוֹתָם לֵאמֹר מִקֵּץ ׀ שֶׁבַע
שָׁנִים בְּמֹעֵד שְׁנַת הַשְּׁמִטָּה בְּחַג הַסֻּכּוֹת׃ בְּבוֹא כָל־יִשְׂרָאֵל
לֵרָאוֹת אֶת־פְּנֵי יהוה אֱלֹהֶיךָ בַּמָּקוֹם אֲשֶׁר יִבְחָר תִּקְרָא
אֶת־הַתּוֹרָה הַזֹּאת נֶגֶד כָּל־יִשְׂרָאֵל בְּאָזְנֵיהֶם׃ הַקְהֵל אֶת־
הָעָם הָאֲנָשִׁים וְהַנָּשִׁים וְהַטַּף וְגֵרְךָ אֲשֶׁר בִּשְׁעָרֶיךָ לְמַעַן
יִשְׁמְעוּ וּלְמַעַן יִלְמְדוּ וְיָרְאוּ אֶת־יהוה אֱלֹהֵיכֶם וְשָׁמְרוּ
לַעֲשׂוֹת אֶת־כָּל־דִּבְרֵי הַתּוֹרָה הַזֹּאת׃ וּבְנֵיהֶם אֲשֶׁר לֹא־
יָדְעוּ יִשְׁמְעוּ וְלָמְדוּ לְיִרְאָה אֶת־יהוה אֱלֹהֵיכֶם כָּל־הַיָּמִים
אֲשֶׁר אַתֶּם חַיִּים עַל־הָאֲדָמָה אֲשֶׁר אַתֶּם עֹבְרִים אֶת־הַיַּרְדֵּן
שָׁמָּה לְרִשְׁתָּהּ׃

THIRD ALIYA: 31:7–13 Moshe delivers words of inspiration and strength to Yehoshua, and then gives the people the command of *Hak-hel*, the public reading of the Torah in front of the entire people every seven years.

האזינו
HA'AZINU

דברים לב:א–יח

FIRST ALIYA: 32:1–3 Moshe begins his song to inspire his people as he says farewell.

הַאֲזִינוּ הַשָּׁמַיִם וַאֲדַבֵּרָה — וְתִשְׁמַע הָאָרֶץ אִמְרֵי־פִי׃
יַעֲרֹף כַּמָּטָר לִקְחִי — תִּזַּל כַּטַּל אִמְרָתִי
כִּשְׂעִירִם עֲלֵי־דֶשֶׁא — וְכִרְבִיבִים עֲלֵי־עֵשֶׂב׃
כִּי שֵׁם יהוה אֶקְרָא — הָבוּ גֹדֶל לֵאלֹהֵינוּ׃

SECOND ALIYA: 32:4–6 Moshe's poetic description of God.

לוי *הַצּוּר תָּמִים פָּעֳלוֹ — כִּי כָל־דְּרָכָיו מִשְׁפָּט
אֵל אֱמוּנָה וְאֵין עָוֶל — צַדִּיק וְיָשָׁר הוּא׃
שִׁחֵת לוֹ לֹא בָּנָיו מוּמָם — דּוֹר עִקֵּשׁ וּפְתַלְתֹּל׃
הַ לְיהוה תִּגְמְלוּ־זֹאת — עַם נָבָל וְלֹא חָכָם
הֲלוֹא־הוּא אָבִיךָ קָּנֶךָ — הוּא עָשְׂךָ וַיְכֹנְנֶךָ׃

Some start the לוי *portion here:*

ישראל *זְכֹר יְמוֹת עוֹלָם — בִּינוּ שְׁנוֹת דֹּר־וָדֹר

THIRD ALIYA: 32:7–12 Moshe's poetic description of God's role in Jewish history.

שְׁאַל אָבִיךָ וְיַגֵּדְךָ   זְקֵנֶיךָ וְיֹאמְרוּ לָךְ׃
בְּהַנְחֵל עֶלְיוֹן גּוֹיִם   בְּהַפְרִידוֹ בְּנֵי אָדָם
יַצֵּב גְּבֻלֹת עַמִּים   לְמִסְפַּר בְּנֵי יִשְׂרָאֵל׃
כִּי חֵלֶק יְהוָה עַמּוֹ   יַעֲקֹב חֶבֶל נַחֲלָתוֹ׃
יִמְצָאֵהוּ בְּאֶרֶץ מִדְבָּר   וּבְתֹהוּ יְלֵל יְשִׁמֹן
יְסֹבְבֶנְהוּ יְבוֹנְנֵהוּ   יִצְּרֶנְהוּ כְּאִישׁוֹן עֵינוֹ׃
כְּנֶשֶׁר יָעִיר קִנּוֹ   עַל־גּוֹזָלָיו יְרַחֵף
יִפְרֹשׂ כְּנָפָיו יִקָּחֵהוּ   יִשָּׂאֵהוּ עַל־אֶבְרָתוֹ׃
יְהוָה בָּדָד יַנְחֶנּוּ   וְאֵין עִמּוֹ אֵל נֵכָר׃

Most finish here; some start the ישראל *portion here:*

*יַרְכִּבֵהוּ עַל־בָּמוֹתֵי אָרֶץ   וַיֹּאכַל תְּנוּבֹת שָׂדָי   בָּמֳתֵי
וַיֵּנִקֵהוּ דְבַשׁ מִסֶּלַע   וְשֶׁמֶן מֵחַלְמִישׁ צוּר׃
חֶמְאַת בָּקָר וַחֲלֵב צֹאן   עִם־חֵלֶב כָּרִים
וְאֵילִים בְּנֵי־בָשָׁן וְעַתּוּדִים   עִם־חֵלֶב כִּלְיוֹת חִטָּה
וְדַם־עֵנָב תִּשְׁתֶּה־חָמֶר׃   וַיִּשְׁמַן יְשֻׁרוּן וַיִּבְעָט
שָׁמַנְתָּ עָבִיתָ כָּשִׂיתָ   וַיִּטֹּשׁ אֱלוֹהַ עָשָׂהוּ
וַיְנַבֵּל צוּר יְשֻׁעָתוֹ׃   יַקְנִאֻהוּ בְּזָרִים
בְּתוֹעֵבֹת יַכְעִיסֻהוּ׃   יִזְבְּחוּ לַשֵּׁדִים לֹא אֱלֹהַּ
אֱלֹהִים לֹא יְדָעוּם   חֲדָשִׁים מִקָּרֹב בָּאוּ
לֹא שְׂעָרוּם אֲבֹתֵיכֶם׃   צוּר יְלָדְךָ תֶּשִׁי
וַתִּשְׁכַּח אֵל מְחֹלְלֶךָ׃

VEZOT HABERAKHA וזאת הברכה

FIRST ALIYA: 33:1–7 Moshe leaves the people with his blessings for each of the twelve tribes. This sections sees his blessings to Reuven and Yehuda.

דברים לג:א–ה
וְזֹאת הַבְּרָכָה אֲשֶׁר בֵּרַךְ מֹשֶׁה אִישׁ הָאֱלֹהִים אֶת־בְּנֵי
יִשְׂרָאֵל לִפְנֵי מוֹתוֹ׃ וַיֹּאמַר יְהוָה מִסִּינַי בָּא וְזָרַח מִשֵּׂעִיר
לָמוֹ הוֹפִיעַ מֵהַר פָּארָן וְאָתָה מֵרִבְבֹת קֹדֶשׁ מִימִינוֹ אשדת   אֵשׁ דָּת
לָמוֹ׃ אַף חֹבֵב עַמִּים כָּל־קְדֹשָׁיו בְּיָדֶךָ וְהֵם תֻּכּוּ לְרַגְלֶךָ יִשָּׂא
מִדַּבְּרֹתֶיךָ׃ תּוֹרָה צִוָּה־לָנוּ מֹשֶׁה מוֹרָשָׁה קְהִלַּת יַעֲקֹב׃
וַיְהִי בִישֻׁרוּן מֶלֶךְ בְּהִתְאַסֵּף רָאשֵׁי עָם יַחַד שִׁבְטֵי יִשְׂרָאֵל׃

יְחִי רְאוּבֵן וְאַל־יָמֹת וִיהִי מְתָיו מִסְפָּר: וְזֹאת
לִיהוּדָה וַיֹּאמַר שְׁמַע יהוה קוֹל יְהוּדָה וְאֶל־עַמּוֹ תְּבִיאֶנּוּ
יָדָיו רָב לוֹ וְעֵזֶר מִצָּרָיו תִּהְיֶה:
לוי וּלְלֵוִי אָמַר תֻּמֶּיךָ וְאוּרֶיךָ לְאִישׁ חֲסִידֶךָ אֲשֶׁר נִסִּיתוֹ בְּמַסָּה
תְּרִיבֵהוּ עַל־מֵי מְרִיבָה: הָאֹמֵר לְאָבִיו וּלְאִמּוֹ לֹא רְאִיתִיו
וְאֶת־אֶחָיו לֹא הִכִּיר וְאֶת־בָּנָו לֹא יָדָע כִּי שָׁמְרוּ אִמְרָתֶךָ
וּבְרִיתְךָ יִנְצֹרוּ: יוֹרוּ מִשְׁפָּטֶיךָ לְיַעֲקֹב וְתוֹרָתְךָ לְיִשְׂרָאֵל
יָשִׂימוּ קְטוֹרָה בְּאַפֶּךָ וְכָלִיל עַל־מִזְבְּחֶךָ: בָּרֵךְ יהוה
חֵילוֹ וּפֹעַל יָדָיו תִּרְצֶה מְחַץ מָתְנַיִם קָמָיו וּמְשַׂנְאָיו מִן־
יְקוּמוּן: לְבִנְיָמִן אָמַר יְדִיד יהוה יִשְׁכֹּן לָבֶטַח עָלָיו
ישראל חֹפֵף עָלָיו כָּל־הַיּוֹם וּבֵין כְּתֵפָיו שָׁכֵן: *וּלְיוֹסֵף
אָמַר מְבֹרֶכֶת יהוה אַרְצוֹ מִמֶּגֶד שָׁמַיִם מִטָּל וּמִתְּהוֹם
רֹבֶצֶת תָּחַת: וּמִמֶּגֶד תְּבוּאֹת שָׁמֶשׁ וּמִמֶּגֶד גֶּרֶשׁ יְרָחִים:
וּמֵרֹאשׁ הַרְרֵי־קֶדֶם וּמִמֶּגֶד גִּבְעוֹת עוֹלָם: וּמִמֶּגֶד אֶרֶץ
וּמְלֹאָהּ וּרְצוֹן שֹׁכְנִי סְנֶה תָּבוֹאתָה לְרֹאשׁ יוֹסֵף וּלְקָדְקֹד
נְזִיר אֶחָיו: בְּכוֹר שׁוֹרוֹ הָדָר לוֹ וְקַרְנֵי רְאֵם קַרְנָיו בָּהֶם
עַמִּים יְנַגַּח יַחְדָּו אַפְסֵי־אָרֶץ וְהֵם רִבְבוֹת אֶפְרַיִם וְהֵם
אַלְפֵי מְנַשֶּׁה:

SECOND ALIYA: 33:8–12
Moshe's blessings to Levi and Binyamin.

THIRD ALIYA: 33:13–17
Moshe's blessing to Yosef (Ephraim and Menashe).

שערי תפילה
GATES TO PRAYER

DAILY PRAYER

ON WAKING

1 The custom is to say מוֹדֶה אֲנִי immediately on waking, even before washing hands [משנ״ב או״ח, א:ח].

Laws of Washing Hands; בִּרְכַּת אֲשֶׁר יָצַר; אֱלֹהַי נְשָׁמָה

2 Upon waking, one is obligated to wash hands [שבת, קח:]. Some hold that one should not walk four *amot* (around six feet) prior to washing hands [משנ״ב או״ח, א:ב (בשם הזוהר)].

3 According to some authorities, there is a separate obligation to wash hands prior to prayer [ערוה״ש או״ח, ד:ה]. One who washes and says the blessing of עַל נְטִילַת יָדַיִם after waking, does not repeat the blessing when washing prior to prayer [רמ״א או״ח, ו:ב].

4 Hands should preferably be washed using a cup, but a cup is not required [שו״ע ורמ״א, או״ח: ד, ז]. The custom is to pour water from the cup onto the right hand, then the left, and repeat a total of three times [משנ״ב, שם: י]. Where water is unavailable, one may clean one's hands using any appropriate material; in that case, the blessing is changed to עַל נְקִיּוּת יָדַיִם [שו״ע או״ח, ד:כב].

5 The blessing of עַל נְטִילַת יָדַיִם may be said before drying one's hands or afterward [משנ״ב, ד:ב].

6 A number of reasons have been offered for washing hands upon waking. The Gemara states that, during the night, hands are enveloped by an "evil vapor," רוח רעה, which is removed by washing one's hands [שבת, קח:]. In addition, there is a concern that, while sleeping, one's hands may have touched an unclean part of

the body [רא״ש ברכות, פ״ט: כג]. Finally, it is noted that a person who wakes is like a newborn; therefore, one needs to sanctify oneself by washing [שו״ת רשב״א ח״א, קצא].

7 The blessing of אֲשֶׁר יָצַר should be said each time after relieving oneself. It is recommended that one should go to the bathroom immediately after washing hands, then say the blessings of עַל נְטִילַת יָדָיִם followed by אֲשֶׁר יָצַר. However, even if one does not relieve oneself, one is permitted to say אֲשֶׁר יָצַר after washing hands [רמ״א או״ח, ד: א]. One should not postpone going to the bathroom [שו״ע או״ח, ג: יז].

8 According to the Gemara, the blessing of אֱלֹהַי נְשָׁמָה should be said upon waking [ברכות, ס:]. The contemporary custom is to say אֱלֹהַי נְשָׁמָה immediately after אֲשֶׁר יָצַר [משנ״ב, שם: יב]. However, some rule that one who stays up all night should not say אֱלֹהַי נְשָׁמָה and the blessing הַמַּעֲבִיר שֵׁנָה מֵעֵינַי, and should instead hear them from others [משנ״ב, מו: כד].

9 The custom is to say the *Birkhot HaTorah* after אֲשֶׁר יָצַר, because one should not read or recite Torah verses before making the requisite blessings on Torah study [שו״ע ורמ״א, או״ח: מו, ט].

Laws of Tzitzit

10 Putting on a four-cornered garment with tzitzit attached fulfills an affirmative mitzva from the Torah. The obligation applies only during the daytime [מנחות, מג.]. Since wearing tzitzit is a time-bound mitzva, women are exempt [שו״ע או״ח, יז: ב].

11 The accepted practice is to wear a *tallit katan* all day long and to wear a *tallit gadol* during Shaḥarit [שו״ע או״ח, כד: א]. The dominant Ashkenazi custom is to begin wearing a *tallit gadol* when one marries [משנ״ב, יז: י], but Jews of German and Sephardi descent begin wearing the *tallit gadol* at an earlier age. Nevertheless, the custom is to wear a *tallit gadol* – even if unmarried – when acting as *Shaliaḥ Tzibbur,* reading from or being called up to the Torah, opening the Ark or performing *hagbaha* or *gelila.*

12 One should put on the *tallit katan* immediately upon dressing. One should first examine the strings of the tzitzit to ensure that they are not torn [שו״ע או״ח, ח: ט]. Then, while standing [שו״ע או״ח, ח: א], one should say the blessing of עַל מִצְוַת צִיצִית and immediately put on the garment [רמ״א או״ח, ח: ו]. One does not say the blessing if (a) one is about to put on a *tallit gadol,* and (b) one will have in mind the *tallit katan* when saying the blessing on the *tallit gadol.* On the other hand, if there is a substantial interruption between the time one puts on the *tallit katan* and one puts on the *tallit gadol,* one should say the separate blessing on the *tallit katan* [שו״ע או״ח, ח: יג].

13 The blessing on tzitzit may be said at daybreak, but not before [רמ״א או״ח, יח: ג].

14 Similarly with the *tallit gadol*, one should first examine the strings, then while standing, say the blessing לְהִתְעַטֵּף בַּצִּיצִית and put on the *tallit gadol*. The word לְהִתְעַטֵּף means to wrap oneself; one should initially wrap the *tallit gadol* around to cover one's head and face for a few moments, after which it is sufficient that it cover the torso [מג״א, ח: ב].

15 If one removes the *tallit gadol* for any reason, one should repeat the blessing when putting the tallit back on [שו״ע או״ח, ח: יד]. The blessing is not repeated if the *tallit gadol* is put back on soon after taking it off, and either (a) one was wearing a *tallit katan* all along, or (b) one's original intention was to put the tallit back on shortly [משנ״ב, שם: לז].

16 If one's head is otherwise covered, there is no requirement to cover one's head with the *tallit gadol* [ט״ז או״ח, ח: ג]. Some authorities nevertheless require married men to cover their heads with the *tallit gadol* throughout Shaḥarit, because it promotes reverence in prayer [בה״ט או״ח, ח: ג (בשם הרדב״ז)]. Others have the custom to cover their heads during the Amida only, or from *Barekhu* through the end of the Amida. Unmarried persons should not wear the *tallit gadol* over their heads [קידושין, כט:].

SERVICES

Laws of Birkhot HaShaḥar and Pesukei DeZimra

17 According to the Gemara [ברכות, ס:], *Birkhot HaShaḥar* (Morning Blessings) were originally said separately, in conjunction with the performance of the associated activity. Thus, upon dressing one would say the blessing of מַלְבִּישׁ עֲרֻמִּים, and upon standing up one would say the blessing of זוֹקֵף כְּפוּפִים. However, the custom now is to say all of the blessings together in the synagogue [שו״ע או״ח, מו: ב].

18 The insertion of the verse (or verses) of Shema after *Birkhot HaShaḥar* was not meant to satisfy the individual's obligation to say the Shema every morning [רמ״א, שם: ט]. However, as discussed in further detail in law 25, the three paragraphs of Shema must be said within the first half of the morning (measured as ¼ of the time from daybreak to nightfall). Since some congregations hold Shaḥarit services late, especially on Shabbat, and as such the communal recitation of the Shema in Shaḥarit may take place too late to fulfill the halakhic obligation,

under such circumstances it is recommended to say all three paragraphs of Shema after *Birkhot HaShaḥar* [משנ״ב, שם: לא].

19 One should say the biblical verses describing the קרבן תמיד (page 199), preferably with the congregation [רמ״א או״ח, מח]. Some authorities require one to stand [משנ״ב, שם: ב].

20 The fifth chapter of מסכת זבחים and the ברייתא דרבי ישמעאל were added after the biblical passages regarding sacrifices to institutionalize the daily study of Scripture, Mishna and Gemara [שו״ע או״ח, נ: א].

21 Saying Kaddish, *Barekhu* or *Kedusha* requires the presence of a *minyan* (ten adult males) [שו״ע או״ח, נה: א].

22 One should not utter idle speech from the beginning of the words בָּרוּךְ אַתָּה יהוה in *Barukh SheAmar* until one completes the Amida [שו״ע או״ח, נא: ד]. Certain responses are permitted, as detailed in the chart on pages 848–850.

23 If one comes late to the synagogue, one may skip all, or portions, of *Pesukei DeZimra*, as follows:

  a If there is sufficient time, say *Barukh SheAmar*, the weekday *Pesukai DeZimra*, *Nishmat*, and *Yishtabaḥ*.

  b If there is less time, say *Barukh SheAmar*, Psalms 145–150, *Nishmat* and *Yishtabaḥ*.

  c If there is less time, say *Barukh SheAmar*, Psalms 145, 148, 150, *Nishmat* and *Yishtabaḥ*.

  d If there is less time, say *Barukh SheAmar*, Psalm 145, and *Yishtabaḥ*.

  e If there is less time, omit *Pesukei DeZimra* altogether. Complete the rest of the service with the congregation, then say *Pesukei DeZimra* privately, omitting *Barukh SheAmar* and *Yishtabaḥ* [רמ״א ושו״ע או״ח, נב].

Morning Shema – קריאת שמע של שחרית

24 Saying the three paragraphs of the Shema each morning and each night fulfills an affirmative mitzva from the Torah. Since saying the Shema is a time-bound mitzva, women are exempt [שו״ע או״ח, ע: א]. Nevertheless, women are required to say the first verse to express their acceptance of עול מלכות שמים ("the yoke of the kingdom of Heaven") [ב״ח, שם]. Women are permitted to say the Shema and its preceding and following blessings [משנ״ב, שם: ב].

25 There is a set time period every morning during which the Shema may be said. The optimal time is immediately before sunrise, when there is assumed to be sufficient light to recognize an acquaintance from a distance of four *amot* (around 6 feet). If necessary, the Shema may be said from daybreak [שו״ע או״ח, נח: ג].

After sunrise, the earlier the Shema is said, the better [שם: ב]. At the latest, the Shema must be said during the first quarter of the day (in halakhic terminology, three halakhic "hours," where each hour represents 1/12 of the day; regarding the measure of a "day." There is a dispute between halakhic authorities whether the day is measured from daybreak to nightfall (Magen Avraham), or from sunrise to sunset (Vilna Gaon). One should follow local communal practice in this regard) [שם: א]. After that time, one is permitted to say the Shema with the blessings during the fourth halakhic "hour," that is, until the end of the first third of the day. After that, the Shema may be said without the blessings, but this does not fulfill the mitzva [שם: ו].

26 If one says the Shema without its preceding and following blessings, one has still fulfilled the mitzva. However, one should say the blessings afterward, preferably repeating the Shema as well [שו"ע או"ח, ס: ב].

27 The Shema must be said with concentration and awe [שו"ע או"ח, סא: א]. Each word and syllable should be pronounced correctly and carefully, without slurring consonants [שו"ע או"ח, סא: טו–כא].

28 Some authorities ruled that one should say the Shema with *Ta'amei HaMikra*. Today, however, most people do not do so [שו"ע ורמ"א, שם: כד].

29 The custom is to cover the eyes with the right hand while saying the first verse, so as not look at anything that might disturb one's concentration [שו"ע או"ח, סא: ה].

30 It is customary to draw out one's pronunciation of the letters ח and ד in the word אֶחָד to emphasize God's sovereignty over creation [שו"ע או"ח, סא: ו].

31 The sentence בָּרוּךְ שֵׁם כְּבוֹד מַלְכוּתוֹ לְעוֹלָם וָעֶד is said quietly, because it does not appear in the biblical text of the Shema [שו"ע שם: יג; משנ"ב, שם: ל].

32 If one enters the synagogue and hears the congregation about to begin saying the Shema, one is required to say the first verse of the Shema together with the congregation [שו"ע או"ח, סה: ב].

Laws of the Shaḥarit Amida

33 There is a set time period every morning during which the Amida may be said. In general, the Amida should be said at or after sunrise. At the latest, the Amida should be said during the first third of the day, (four halakhic "hours"; regarding the measure of a "day," see law 25). If the Amida was said between daybreak and sunrise, the mitzva has been fulfilled. If necessary, it is permissible to say the Amida after the first third of the day, but before midday [שו"ע או"ח, פט: א].

34 One should not eat or drink before saying the Amida, although drinking water is

permitted. Moreover, anyone who needs to eat or drink in order to concentrate on his prayers is permitted to do so [שו״ע או״ח, פט: ג–ד].

35 The Amida is said facing the site of the Temple in Jerusalem. Thus, outside Israel, one faces the land of Israel; inside Israel, one faces Jerusalem; and inside Jerusalem, one faces the Temple Mount [שו״ע או״ח, צד: א]. If one is praying in a synagogue, one should pray facing the Ark [משנ״ב, שם: ס״ק י].

36 The Amida is said standing with feet together in imitation of the angels who, according to tradition, present the appearance of having only one leg [ברכות, י:, רש״י, ד״ה ״ורגליהם״]. One should bow one's head and imagine one is standing in the Temple, like a servant before his master [שו״ע או״ח, צה: א–ב].

37 When saying the Shaḥarit Amida, one may not allow any interruption or disruption between the conclusion of the blessing גָּאַל יִשְׂרָאֵל and the introductory words to the Amida [שו״ע או״ח, סו: ח; שם, קיא: א]. This includes not responding to Kaddish, *Barekhu*, *Kedusha* or *Modim*, although on Shabbat one may do so [רמ״א, שם]. One may also answer "Amen" if one hears someone else concluding the blessing גָּאַל יִשְׂרָאֵל [רמ״א או״ח, סו: ז].

Laws of חזרת הש״ץ

38 During the Repetition of the Amida, the congregation is required to listen attentively to the blessings and respond "Amen" [שו״ע או״ח, קכד: ד].

39 In order to begin the Repetition of the Amida, at least nine men are required to be listening attentively [שם].

40 Some require the congregation to stand during the Repetition of the Amida [רמ״א, שם].

41 Under extenuating circumstances, the *Shaliaḥ Tzibbur* may begin saying the Amida aloud, while the congregation says the Amida quietly along with him. The *Kedusha* is said aloud in the customary fashion and, after the *Shaliaḥ Tzibbur* finishes the blessing הָאֵל הַקָּדוֹשׁ, he and the congregation continue saying the Amida quietly [רמ״א, שם: ב].

42 At the conclusion of the Repetition of the Amida, it is recommended that the *Shaliaḥ Tzibbur* say quietly the verse יִהְיוּ לְרָצוֹן אִמְרֵי־פִי, except when Full Kaddish immediately follows the Repetition of the Amida [משנ״ב קכג: כא]. Some also say this verse during the individual's silent Amida.

Laws of Kedusha

43 There are different customs regarding what the congregation says during the *Kedusha*: (1) The congregation says only the biblical verses (קָדוֹשׁ...; בָּרוּךְ...; יִמְלֹךְ...)

[שו״ע או״ח, קכה:א]; (2) The congregation says every word of the *Kedusha*, with the *Shaliaḥ Tzibbur* repeating each sentence [בה״ט, שם (בשם האר״י)]; (3) The congregation says נְקַדֵּשׁ and all the biblical verses [ערוה״ש, שם:ב].

Laws of Birkat Kohanim

44 The Kohen has an affirmative obligation from the Torah to bless the congregation, provided there are at least ten males aged 13 or over (including the Kohen himself) [שו״ע או״ח, קכח:א–ב].

45 In most congregations in Israel, *Birkat Kohanim* is said every day in Shaḥarit and, where applicable, in Musaf, as well as in *Ne'ila* on Yom Kippur. On those occasions and when no Kohen is present, the *Shaliaḥ Tzibbur* says אֱלֹהֵינוּ וֵאלֹהֵי אֲבוֹתֵינוּ (page 357).

46 The custom outside Israel and in certain northern Israeli congregations, is for the *Shaliaḥ Tzibbur* to say אֱלֹהֵינוּ וֵאלֹהֵי אֲבוֹתֵינוּ instead of the Kohanim saying *Birkat Kohanim*, except in Musaf of Yom Tov [רמ״א או״ח, קכח:מד].

47 The Kohen is required to wash his hands (without a blessing) before saying *Birkat Kohanim*. It is customary for a Levi to pour the water [שם, ו]. If there is no water, or if the Kohen did not have enough time to wash, he may say *Birkat Kohanim*, provided that: (a) he washed his hands before Shaḥarit, and (b) since washing for Shaḥarit he has not touched anything unclean, even his own shoes [משנ״ב, שם:כ].

48 Each Kohen removes his shoes before ascending to say *Birkat Kohanim* [שם, ה]. When the *Shaliaḥ Tzibbur* begins רְצֵה, the Kohanim ascend to the Ark and stand with their backs to the congregation [שם, ח:ו–י]. After the congregation answers "Amen" to the blessing הַטּוֹב שִׁמְךָ וּלְךָ נָאֶה לְהוֹדוֹת, if there is more than one Kohen, the *Shaliaḥ Tzibbur* calls out "Kohanim," and they turn around and say the blessing. If only one Kohen has ascended to the Ark, he starts the blessing without being prompted [שם:י–יא]. The *Shaliaḥ Tzibbur* does not answer "Amen" at the end of the blessing [משנ״ב, שם:עא].

49 The *Shaliaḥ Tzibbur* reads each word of *Birkat Kohanim* and the Kohanim repeat it in unison. At the end of each verse, the congregation answers "Amen" [שו״ע ורמ״א, שם:יג]. The *Shaliaḥ Tzibbur* does not answer "Amen" at the end of each verse [שו״ע, שם:יט].

50 If the *Shaliaḥ Tzibbur* is himself a Kohen, some rule that he should not say the blessing, unless no other Kohanim are in the synagogue [שו״ע, שם:יט]. However, the custom today is for the *Shaliaḥ Tzibbur* to participate in the blessing [משנ״ב, שם:עה].

1 During *Birkat Kohanim*, the congregation should stand silently with eyes lowered and concentrate on the words of the Kohanim. One should not look at the faces or hands of the Kohanim [שו״ע, שם: כג].

Laws of Torah Reading

2 To ensure that the Torah is read at least once every three days, Moses established the public reading of the Torah on Shabbat, Yom Tov, Ḥol HaMo'ed, Rosh Ḥodesh, and Monday and Thursday mornings. Ezra added the public reading in Shabbat Minḥa [רמב״ם הלכות תפילה פי״ב ה״א].

53 On weekdays and Shabbat Minḥa, three people are called up [שו״ע או״ח, קלה: א]. On Shabbat morning, seven are called up, though additional individuals (*hosafot*) may also be called [שו״ע או״ח, רפב: א]. On Yom Kippur morning, six are called up, five on Yom Tov, and four on Ḥol HaMo'ed and Rosh Ḥodesh.

54 If a Kohen is present, he is called up first. If a Levi is also present, he is called up second; for subsequent *aliyot*, one calls up a Yisrael [שו״ע או״ח, קלה: ג]. If a Kohen is present but a Levi is not, the same Kohen is called up for the first two *aliyot* [שם: ח]. If a Levi is present and a Kohen is not, the Levi need not be called up, but if the Levi is called up, he should be first [שו״ע ורמ״א או״ח, קלה: ו].

55 The custom is to avoid calling up a Kohen after a Yisrael, except for Maftir and, in some communities, for אחרון, provided it is a *hosafa* [רמ״א, שם: י].

56 Other individuals who are given priority for an *aliya* include: a bridegroom on his wedding day and the Shabbat preceding and following the wedding; a Bar Mitzva; the father of a newborn baby; one commemorating a parent's *yahrzeit*; and a person obligated to say *Birkat HaGomel* [בה״ל, קלו: ד״ה ״בשבת״].

57 It is considered bad luck to call up two brothers or a father and son one after the other [שו״ע או״ח, קמא: ו]. While the custom is to avoid the practice, if one is called up after one's brother or father, one should accept the *aliya*.

58 One who is called up to the Torah should take the shortest route to the *bima* [שו״ע, שם: ז]. He should open the scroll to locate where the *aliya* begins. Still holding the handle, he should say the blessing, taking care to look away from the Torah (or close the scroll or his eyes), so as not to appear to be reading the blessing from the scroll itself [שו״ע ורמ״א או״ח, קלט: ד].

59 If, after the blessing is said, the *ba'al koreh* discovers that the blessing was said over the wrong passage of the Torah, the scroll is rolled to the correct location and the *oleh* repeats the blessing. The blessing does not need to be repeated if the correct passage was visible when the blessing was said [שו״ע או״ח, קמ: ג; משנ״ב, שם: ט].

60 The Torah is read standing [שו״ע או״ח, קמא: א]. The *oleh* is also required to stand. The rest of the congregation is not obligated to stand, but it is proper to do so [ערוה״ש, שם: ב].

61 The *oleh* should read the words quietly along with the *ba'al koreh* [שו״ע או״ח, קמא: ב].

62 If the *ba'al koreh* makes an error that affects the meaning of the words, he needs to reread the Torah portion from the location of the error [שו״ע ורמ״א או״ח, קמב: א].

63 If an error is found in the Torah scroll, the reading is stopped, a new scroll is brought out, and the reading is continued from the location of the error [שו״ע או״ח, קמג: ד]. It is not required to call up all of the *aliyot* a second time to read from the new scroll, but if the remainder of the reading can be divided into the appropriate number of *aliyot* for that day, it is preferable to do so [משנ״ב, שם: טז].

64 It is customary to say a prayer for a sick person (מִי שֶׁבֵּרַךְ, page 377) at the conclusion of the Torah reading, or between *aliyot*.

65 On the Shabbat before a *yahrzeit*, it is customary to say a prayer for the deceased relative (אֵל מָלֵא רַחֲמִים, page 381), usually after the Shabbat Minḥa Torah reading.

66 After completing the reading from a Torah scroll, the open scroll is raised and displayed to the entire congregation. The congregation says וְזֹאת הַתּוֹרָה (page 383) [שו״ע ורמ״א או״ח, קלד: ב].

Laws of Birkat HaGomel

67 After being saved from mortal danger, one should say *Birkat HaGomel* [שו״ע או״ח, ריט: א, ו–ט; משנ״ב, שם: לב] (see page 377). The blessing should be said no later than three days after the event [שו״ע, שם: ו]. *Birkat HaGomel* is said only in the presence of a *minyan*; the custom is to say the blessing after the Torah reading [שם: ג]. If one will not be in the presence of *minyan* within three days, one is permitted to say the blessing without a *minyan* [משנ״ב, שם: ח].

68 A husband may say *Birkat HaGomel* for his wife, or a father for his children [משנ״ב, שם: יז]. But, according to most authorities, it is preferable that a woman say *Birkat HaGomel* for herself in the presence of a *minyan*.

Laws of Mourner's Kaddish

69 The Mourner's Kaddish is generally said after specific chapters of Psalms at the beginning and end of a service. It is said by one who is either (a) in mourning for a relative, or (b) commemorating the *yahrzeit* of a relative. When no such person is present, the Mourner's Kaddish is generally omitted, except after *Aleinu* at the end of Shaḥarit [רמ״א או״ח, קלב: ב], when it is said by one whose parents have died or whose parents do not object to their child saying the Mourner's Kaddish [שם].

70 Historically, the Mourner's Kaddish was said by one individual. A set of rules developed for allocating among different mourners the various opportunities for saying it [ביאור הלכה, שם; קונטרס מאמר קדישין, י]. Today, most congregations allow group recitation of the Mourner's Kaddish. In such cases, they should say the words in unison [סידור יעב"ץ].

Laws of the Minḥa Amida

71 There is a set time period every afternoon during which the Minḥa Amida may be said. At the earliest, one may say the Amida one half of a halakhic "hour" from midday (a halakhic hour is 1/12 of the day measured from daybreak to nightfall). At the latest, the Amida must be said before nightfall. It is preferable to say the Amida at least 3½ halakhic "hours" after midday [שו"ע או"ח, רלג:א].

72 One should wash hands before saying Minḥa, even if they are not dirty; but if no water is available, one need not wash [שו"ע או"ח, רלג:ב]. No blessing is said on the hand-washing.

Laws of the Evening Shema and Ma'ariv

73 There is a set time period every night during which the Shema may be said. At the earliest, one may say the Shema from nightfall [שו"ע או"ח, רלה:א]. It is preferable to say the Shema before midnight (measured from nightfall to daybreak), but one is permitted to say the Shema until daybreak [שם:ג].

74 Some congregations hold Ma'ariv services early, with the result that the communal recitation of the Shema in Ma'ariv may take place too early to fulfill the halakhic obligation. Under such circumstances, one should repeat all three paragraphs of Shema after nightfall [שו"ע, שם:א].

75 If one enters the synagogue and hears the congregation about to begin saying the Amida, one should say the Amida together with the congregation, then afterward say the Shema with its preceding and following blessings [שו"ע או"ח, רלו:ג].

76 After the blessings of the Shema, the congregation says בָּרוּךְ יהוה לְעוֹלָם (page 597), except in Israel. One who begins Ma'ariv late should omit בָּרוּךְ יהוה לְעוֹלָם in order to say the Amida with the congregation, then say בָּרוּךְ יהוה לְעוֹלָם after Ma'ariv, without the final blessing [משנ"ב, שם:יא].

Laws of Keri'at Shema al HaMita (the Shema Before Sleep at Night)

77 *Keri'at Shema al HaMita* should be said before retiring, when one is feeling sleepy [משנ"ב או"ח, רלט:ג], after which one should not eat, drink or speak [רמ"א, שם:א].

LAWS OF HAND-WASHING, HAMOTZI AND BIRKAT HAMAZON

78 Before eating bread, one is required to wash one's hands [שו"ע או"ח, קנח: א]. After washing but before drying the hands, one says the blessing עַל נְטִילַת יָדָיִם; however, if one forgot, one may say the blessing after one's hands are dry [רמ"א, שם: יא]. One should dry one's hands carefully before touching the bread [שו"ע, שם: יב].

79 Hands should be washed using a cup or other container that holds at least a *revi'it* (about 4.4 ounces) of liquid [שו"ע או"ח, קנט: א]. Holding one's hands under flowing water is not valid [שו"ע, שם: ז].

80 One should wash each hand up to the wrist, although the minimum requirement is to wash the fingers up to the knuckle furthest from the nail [שו"ע או"ח, קסא: ד]. Hands should be free of dirt or other material that one normally removes. In addition, rings should be removed before washing [שם: א–ג].

81 If the hands are clean, it is sufficient to pour water once on each hand [שו"ע או"ח, קסב: ב], but twice on each hand is preferable [מ"ב שם, כא].

82 After washing, one should take care not to allow one's wet hands to touch the unwashed hands of another. If they do so, one must dry them and wash them again [שו"ע שם, ד].

83 If one makes the blessing הַמּוֹצִיא לֶחֶם מִן הָאָרֶץ on bread, no blessing need be said on foods that are part of the meal. If one eats foods that are not eaten with bread or are not part of the meal, such as fruit eaten as dessert, they require a separate blessing [שו"ע, קעז: א].

84 If wine is served during the meal, the blessing בּוֹרֵא פְּרִי הַגָּפֶן must be said, as the blessing on bread does not cover wine [שו"ע או"ח, קעד: א]. But if wine is drunk before the meal (or as part of Kiddush), the blessing need not be repeated when drinking wine during the meal [שם: ד].

85 One should not remove bread from the table until after *Birkat HaMazon* is said [שו"ע או"ח, קפ: א].

86 Prior to saying *Birkat HaMazon*, one should wash the grime off one's fingers with *mayim aḥaronim* [שו"ע או"ח, קפא: א]. Some have the custom not to wash with *mayim aḥaronim*, because the original reasons for the practice no longer apply [שם, י; משנ"ב שם, כב], but a fastidious person who washes after a meal should wash with *mayim aḥaronim* before *Birkat HaMazon* [שו"ע: שם].

87 Women are obligated to say *Birkat HaMazon* [שו"ע או"ח, קפו: א].

88 *Birkat HaMazon* should be said where one ate. If one forgot to say *Birkat*

HaMazon and went elsewhere, one should return to the site of the meal to say *Birkat HaMazon*. If one cannot return to the site of the meal, one is permitted to say *Birkat HaMazon* as soon as one remembers to do so [שו"ע ורמ"א או"ח, קפד: א; משנ"ב, שם: ז].

89 If one forgets to say *Birkat HaMazon* at the end of the meal, it must be said afterward, so long as one does not feel hungry [שו"ע או"ח, קפד: ד]. If one wants to eat again, one may wash hands and say הַמּוֹצִיא again; the subsequent *Birkat HaMazon* then covers the first meal as well [רמ"א או"ח, קעח: ב].

90 On Ḥanukka or Shushan Purim in Jerusalem, one adds עַל הַנִּסִּים (page 741) to the second blessing. If one forgets עַל הַנִּסִּים, one is not required to repeat *Birkat HaMazon* [שו"ע או"ח, תרפב: א; שו"ע ורמ"א או"ח, תרצה: ג].

91 On Shabbat, one adds רְצֵה (page 745) to the third blessing. On Rosh Ḥodesh, and Ḥol HaMo'ed, one adds יַעֲלֶה וְיָבוֹא (page 745) to the third blessing; if it is also Shabbat, one says רְצֵה, then יַעֲלֶה וְיָבוֹא. If one forgets to say the required addition on Shabbat or Yom Tov, one repeats the entire *Birkat HaMazon*. Alternatively, if one remembers before beginning the fourth blessing, one may say a special blessing in honor of Shabbat [שו"ע או"ח, קפח: ה–ו]. If one forgets the required addition on Rosh Ḥodesh or Ḥol HaMo'ed, one is not required to repeat *Birkat HaMazon* [שם: ז].

92 If one started eating while it was Shabbat, Rosh Ḥodesh or other days on which additions to *Birkat HaMazon* are said, and continued the meal after sunset, one still says the additions to *Birkat HaMazon* [שם: י] (see laws 89–90 above).

93 If three adult males eat a meal together, they are required to preface *Birkat HaMazon* with *zimmun* (page 737). If women are present, they are required to join in the *zimmun* as well. Three adult females may also form a *zimmun*, but are not obligated to do so. If ten or more males are present, the word אֱלֹהֵינוּ is added to the formula [שו"ע או"ח, קצב: א].

94 *Zimmun* is required if all three participants ate bread. If only two participants ate bread, but a third person either eats a *kezayit* (about 1.5 ounces) of any food, or drinks a *revi'it* (about 4.4 ounces) of any beverage (other than water), the three should say *zimmun* [שו"ע או"ח, קצו: ג; משנ"ב, שם: כב].

95 Even if the participants are not sitting together, as long as some of the participants can see each other, they can join together in a *zimmun* [שו"ע או"ח, קצה: א].

96 If one of the three participants said *Birkat HaMazon* by himself, he may still join the other two to make a *zimmun*, but if two of them (or all three) said *Birkat HaMazon* by themselves, then no *zimmun* may be said [שו"ע או"ח, קצד: א].

97 At a *Sheva Berakhot* meal, a special addition is made to the *zimmun* (page 775) [שו״ע אבה״ע, סב: יג; ערוה״ש, שם: יח], and the *Sheva Berakhot* (page 777) are said after *Birkat HaMazon* [שו״ע, שם: ז].

98 At the meal after a Brit Mila, a special *zimmun* (page 765) is said, and a series of prayers (pages 767–769) is added before the end of *Birkat HaMazon*.

ROSH ḤODESH PRAYER

99 On Rosh Ḥodesh, יַעֲלֶה וְיָבוֹא is added to the blessing רְצֵה of the Amida in Ma'ariv, Shaḥarit and Minḥa [שו״ע או״ח, תכב: א], and to the third blessing of *Birkat HaMazon* (page 745) [שם, תכד: א].

100 If one forgets to say יַעֲלֶה וְיָבוֹא in its proper place in the Amida, but realizes before beginning the blessing הַמַּחֲזִיר שְׁכִינָתוֹ לְצִיּוֹן, one should immediately say יַעֲלֶה וְיָבוֹא and continue with the rest of the blessing. If one realizes the omission immediately after completing the blessing הַמַּחֲזִיר שְׁכִינָתוֹ לְצִיּוֹן, one should say יַעֲלֶה וְיָבוֹא and continue with the following blessing. If one realizes the omission after beginning the words מוֹדִים אֲנַחְנוּ לָךְ, one must repeat the Amida from the beginning of the seventeenth blessing (from the word רְצֵה). If one realizes the omission after completing the Amida, one must repeat the Amida from the beginning [שו״ע או״ח, תכב: א].

101 If one forgets to say יַעֲלֶה וְיָבוֹא in Ma'ariv, one does not repeat the Amida [שם].

102 One adds special verses for Rosh Ḥodesh in the *Korbanot* (page 207) [שו״ע או״ח, תכא: א]. יַעֲלֶה וְיָבוֹא is added to the Amida (see laws 99–100). After the Repetition of the Amida, the congregation says Half Hallel [שו״ע או״ח, תכב: ב], followed by Full Kaddish.

Laws of Hallel

103 Hallel is said standing [שו״ע או״ח, תכב: ז]. On Rosh Ḥodesh and Ḥol HaMo'ed Pesaḥ, the abridged form, Half Hallel, is said [שו״ע או״ח, תכב: ב; תצ, ד], omitting the first halves of Psalm 115 (לֹא לָנוּ) and Psalm 116 (אָהַבְתִּי, כִּי־יִשְׁמַע).

104 At the beginning of Psalm 118 (הוֹדוּ לַיהוה כִּי־טוֹב, page 689), it is customary for the *Shaliaḥ Tzibbur* to say each of the four verses out loud, and the congregation responds with הוֹדוּ לַיהוה כִּי־טוֹב, כִּי לְעוֹלָם חַסְדּוֹ [משנ״ב תכב, כ]. Some advise the congregation to quietly say each verse with the *Shaliaḥ Tzibbur*.

SHABBAT PRAYER

EREV SHABBAT

105 Minḥa: as for weekdays. *Taḥanun* is omitted [שו״ע או״ח, רסז: א].

SHABBAT EVE

106 Candle lighting: At least two candles are lit [שו״ע או״ח, רסג: א]. There is a custom to light one candle for each member of the household. After lighting, one says the blessing לְהַדְלִיק נֵר שֶׁל שַׁבָּת [שו״ע ורמ״א או״ח, רסג: ה]. It is customary to cover one's eyes when saying the blessing [רמ״א, שם].

107 The custom is to light Shabbat candles 18 minutes prior to sunset. In any case, the candles must be lit before sunset, at which time all labor must cease [שו״ע ורמ״א או״ח, רסא: א]. After lighting the candles, one may not perform any labor, even if one lit prior to sunset, unless one's intention to perform necessary labor before sunset is articulated explicitly prior to lighting [רמ״א או״ח, רסג: י; משנ״ב, שם: מב].

108 The candles must be lit in a location where one will benefit from the light before the candles burn out [שו״ע, שם: ט].

109 If one is not eating at home on Friday night, one should still light candles at home [שו״ע, שם: ו]. If one is not sleeping at home on Friday night, one should light where one sleeps or make a nominal payment to one's host, so as to participate in the host's candle lighting. This is not required if a family member is at home and lights candles with one in mind [שו״ע, שם: ז].

110 Kabbalat Shabbat: Many congregations sing *Yedid Nefesh* before Kabbalat Shabbat. Because Kabbalat Shabbat is not considered part of Ma'ariv, it is customary for the *Shaliaḥ Tzibbur* to stand at the *bima*, rather than at the front of the synagogue [אשי ישראל, לו: יד]. For the same reason, it is permissible for a male under the age of 13 to lead Kabbalat Shabbat.

111 When saying the last stanza of *Lekha Dodi*, the custom is to stand facing the door or the rear, which is usually the western side, of the synagogue [משנ״ב או״ח, רסב: י].

112 By custom, mourners who are sitting *shiva* remain outside the synagogue for Kabbalat Shabbat, entering when the congregation finishes *Lekha Dodi*. As they enter, the congregation calls out in unison הַמָּקוֹם יְנַחֵם אֶתְכֶם בְּתוֹךְ שְׁאָר אֲבֵלֵי צִיּוֹן וִירוּשָׁלָיִם (page 67) [ערוה״ש יו״ד, ת: ה].

113 The congregation says the last two psalms of Kabbalat Shabbat, מִזְמוֹר שִׁיר לְיוֹם הַשַּׁבָּת (Ps. 92) and יהוה מָלָךְ (Ps. 93). This is followed by the Mourner's Kaddish and the second chapter of Mishna *Shabbat* (בַּמֶּה מַדְלִיקִין) [שו״ע או״ח, ער: א]. Some congregations outside Israel say בַּמֶּה מַדְלִיקִין after Full Kaddish at the end of Ma'ariv instead [משנ״ב, שם: ב].

114 Ma'ariv for Shabbat and Yom Tov: וְהוּא רַחוּם is omitted [טור או״ח, רסז]. The *Shaliaḥ Tzibbur* moves to the front of the synagogue to say *Barekhu*. It is preferable for Ma'ariv to begin after nightfall. If it does not, the congregation needs to repeat the Shema after nightfall [משנ״ב או״ח, רסז: ג]. The conclusion of הַשְׁכִּיבֵנוּ is different from the weekday formula, and בָּרוּךְ יהוה לְעוֹלָם is omitted [שו״ע שם, ג]. If one erroneously concludes הַשְׁכִּיבֵנוּ with the weekday blessing, one should say the correct blessing, provided one remembers immediately. If not, one does not repeat the blessing [משנ״ב, שם: ט]. It is customary to say וְשָׁמְרוּ (page 99) before the Amida [משנ״ב, שם].

115 The Shabbat Ma'ariv Amida is said (page 103). On Rosh Ḥodesh, יַעֲלֶה וְיָבוֹא is added in the fifth blessing (page 111). On Ḥanukka or Shushan Purim in Jerusalem, עַל הַנִּסִּים is added in the sixth blessing (page 113).

116 If one begins to say the Amida for weekdays on Shabbat and remembers in the middle of the Amida, one should complete the blessing already started, then begin the fourth blessing for the appropriate Shabbat Amida [שו״ע או״ח, רסח: ב]. If one remembers after completing the Amida, the correct Amida should be said from the beginning [שם: ד].

117 One who says the Amida for the wrong Shabbat service (e.g., saying the Amida for Shaharit during Minḥa), does not repeat the Amida. The exception is one who says the wrong Amida during Musaf, or the Musaf Amida during a different service, in which case the Amida must be repeated [שם: ו]. If, however, one remembers during the Amida, one goes back to the beginning of the fourth blessing of the correct Amida [משנ"ב, שם: טו].

18 After the Amida, the *Shaliaḥ Tzibbur* and congregation say וַיְכֻלּוּ (page 121) [שו"ע או"ח, רסח: ז]. The *Shaliaḥ Tzibbur* says the abbreviated Repetition of the Amida, unless prayers are said in a location where (a) services are not held in a regular fashion, or (b) there is no Torah scroll [משנ"ב, שם: כד]. The *Shaliaḥ Tzibbur* says the Full Kaddish. Some congregations say בַּמֶּה מַדְלִיקִין (page 75) at this point. From Shabbat Ḥol HaMo'ed Pesaḥ until Shavuot, the Omer is counted (page 661). The congregation says *Aleinu*, followed by the Mourner's Kaddish. From the 1st of Elul through Shemini Atzeret, Psalm 27 (page 133) is said. It is customary to conclude with the singing of Yigdal or Adon Olam.

19 Some congregations have the custom to say Kiddush in the synagogue prior to *Aleinu*. However, since Kiddush should generally be said where the Shabbat meal is eaten, where possible, the Kiddush wine should be drunk by a child (or children) under the age of bar/bat mitzva. If this is not possible, the person making Kiddush may drink the wine [שו"ע או"ח, רסט: א].

20 Upon returning home, the custom is to say (or sing) a number of traditional songs and prayers. Some have the custom to bless their children. The Kiddush for Shabbat is an affirmative mitzva from the Torah. By custom, one person says Kiddush and the others listen attentively, fulfilling their obligation by proxy (based on the principle of שומע כעונה – "one who hears is as one who says"). Women are obligated in this mitzva, and a woman is permitted to say Kiddush for herself and others [שו"ע או"ח, רעא: ב]. It is customary to punctuate the meal with *Zemirot*. After the meal, one adds רְצֵה to the third blessing of *Birkat HaMazon* (page 745). On Rosh Ḥodesh, יַעֲלֶה וְיָבוֹא (page 745) is added after רְצֵה [שו"ע או"ח, קפח: ה].

SHABBAT DAY

121 One does not put on tefillin. Prayers begin as on weekdays, although one adds special verses for Shabbat in the section of *Korbanot* (page 207) [שו"ע ורמ"א או"ח, מח: א]. *Pesukei DeZimra*: as for Shabbat and Yom Tov (page 221) [שו"ע או"ח, נא: ט]. After אָז יָשִׁיר, the congregation says *Nishmat*. The *Shaliaḥ Tzibbur* for Shaḥarit begins from the words שׁוֹכֵן עַד.

122 Shaḥarit: as for Shabbat and Yom Tov. After *Barekhu*, the congregation says הַכֹּל יוֹדְוּךָ (page 299). The Shabbat Amida is said. On Rosh Ḥodesh, יַעֲלֶה וְיָבוֹא is added in the fifth blessing (page 351). On Ḥanukka or Shushan Purim in Jerusalem, עַל הַנִּסִּים is added in the sixth blessing (page 355). After the Repetition of the Amida, on Rosh Ḥodesh, the congregation says Half Hallel [שו"ע או"ח, תכב:ב]. The *Shaliaḥ Tzibbur* then says Full Kaddish. Some congregations follow the Sephardi custom of saying at this point the Daily Psalm (Ps. 92) and, if applicable, Ps. 104 or 27 (see law 125), followed by the Mourner's Kaddish.

123 Torah Reading: see laws 52–66. Seven are called up, though additional individuals may also be called up [שו"ע או"ח, רפב:א]. After completing the final *aliya*, the *Ba'al Koreh* says Half Kaddish. The Maftir is called up, and the appropriate portion is read, followed by the Haftara. After the Haftara and its blessings, the congregation says *Yekum Purkan* and the blessing for the congregation (page 385) [רמ"א או"ח, רפד:ז]. This is followed by the prayers for the government and the State of Israel. On a Shabbat immediately preceding Rosh Ḥodesh, *Birkat HaḤodesh* is said (page 399), except on the Shabbat preceding Tishrei.

124 The congregation says אַב הָרַחֲמִים, except (a) on days when *Taḥanun* is omitted, (b) when *Birkat HaḤodesh* is said (except for the months of Iyar and Sivan), and (c) on *Shabbat Shekalim, Zakhor, Para* and *HaḤodesh* [רמ"א או"ח, רפד:ז]. *Ashrei* is said, the Torah is returned to the Ark, and the *Shaliaḥ Tzibbur* says Half Kaddish.

125 Musaf for Shabbat: On Rosh Ḥodesh, the entire fourth blessing follows a special formula (אַתָּה יָצַרְתָּ, page 421); on Ḥanukka or Shushan Purim in Jerusalem, עַל הַנִּסִּים (page 435) is added in the sixth blessing. The *Shaliaḥ Tzibbur* repeats the Amida. This is followed by Full Kaddish, *Ein Keloheinu*, the Rabbis' Kaddish, *Aleinu*, Mourner's Kaddish, and the Daily Psalm (Ps. 92). On Rosh Ḥodesh, Psalm 104, *Barekhi Nafshi* (page 537), is added; from the 1st of Elul to Shemini Azeret, Psalm 27 is added (page 459). Mourner's Kaddish, *Anim Zemirot* (page 463), Mourner's Kaddish, and Adon Olam.

126 The time for saying Musaf is immediately after Shaḥarit. Musaf should be said no later than the seventh halakhic "hour" of the day, which is 7⁄12 of the period from daybreak to nightfall. However, if one said Musaf at any time before sunset, one has fulfilled the obligation [שו"ע או"ח, רפו:א].

127 Shabbat Morning Kiddush should be said where one eats the Shabbat meal [שו"ע או"ח, רפט:א]. If no wine or grape juice is available, one may say Kiddush over a cup of liquor or other beverage, but not over water or bread [שם:ב].

128 Minḥa: After *Ashrei* and וּבָא לְצִיּוֹן, the *Shaliaḥ Tzibbur* says Half Kaddish, the congregation says וַאֲנִי תְפִלָּתִי־לְךָ (page 501), and the Torah is taken from the Ark [שו"ע ורמ"א או"ח, רצב:א]. Three are called up, and the beginning of the following week's Torah portion is read. Half Kaddish is not said. After the Torah is returned to the Ark, the *Shaliaḥ Tzibbur* says Half Kaddish, and the congregation says the Shabbat Minḥa Amida. On Rosh Ḥodesh, יַעֲלֶה וְיָבוֹא is added in the fifth blessing (page 519). On Ḥanukka or Shushan Purim in Jerusalem, עַל הַנִּסִּים is added in the sixth blessing (page 523). After the Repetition of the Amida, the congregation says צִדְקָתְךָ, except on a day when *Taḥanun* is omitted [שם: ב]. This is followed by Full Kaddish, *Aleinu* and Mourner's Kaddish.

129 Some congregations say Psalm 104 (בָּרְכִי נַפְשִׁי) and the fifteen psalms beginning שִׁיר הַמַּעֲלוֹת, Ps. 120–34 (pages 537–543) after Shabbat Minḥa, from *Shabbat Bereshit* until *Shabbat HaGadol* [רמ"א, שם].

130 It is customary to read a chapter of the Ethics of the Fathers (*Pirkei Avot*, page 545) after Shabbat Minḥa, from the Shabbat after Pesaḥ to the Shabbat before Rosh HaShana [שם].

131 One should have a third meal (*Seuda Shelishit*) on Shabbat [שו"ע או"ח, רצא: א]. Women are also obligated to eat *Seuda Shelishit* [שם: ו]. The meal should begin with bread, unless one is too full to eat bread [שם: ה]. After the meal, one adds רְצֵה (page 745) to *Birkat HaMazon*, even if the meal extends past nightfall.

MOTZA'EI SHABBAT

132 In some congregations, Psalms 144 and 67 (page 587) are sung before Ma'ariv.

133 Ma'ariv: as for weekdays (page 589). In the fourth blessing of the Amida, אַתָּה חוֹנַנְתָּנוּ (page 605) is added [שו"ע או"ח, רצד: א]. On Rosh Ḥodesh, יַעֲלֶה וְיָבוֹא (page 615) is added in the seventeenth blessing. If one forgets either of these additions, one does not repeat the Amida [שם]. After the silent Amida, unless Yom Tov falls in the following week, the *Shaliaḥ Tzibbur* says Half Kaddish and the congregation says וִיהִי נֹעַם and וְאַתָּה קָדוֹשׁ (pages 623–625) [רמ"א או"ח, רצה: א]. The *Shaliaḥ Tzibbur* then says Full Kaddish. From the second day of Pesaḥ until Shavuot, the Omer is counted (page 661). Some have the custom to say וְיִתֶּן לְךָ (page 631) [שם]. In most congregations, the *Shaliaḥ Tzibbur* says Havdala [שו"ע, שם]. The congregation says *Aleinu*, followed by Mourner's Kaddish. From the 1st of Elul to Shemini Azeret, Psalm 27 is said (page 643).

134 After nightfall, one may not perform labor until one says Havdala or hears it said. If one says אַתָּה חוֹנַנְתָּנוּ in Ma'ariv (page 605), one may perform labor after nightfall prior to Havdala [רמ"א או"ח, רצט: י].

135 Each month, one says Kiddush Levana (page 645) on seeing the New Moon

at night. Kiddush Levana may be said from the eve of the fourth day of the new month until the middle day of the month. By custom, it is said on the first Motza'ei Shabbat that falls within the time span, preferably outdoors with a *minyan*. [שו״ע ורמ״א או״ח, תכו].

136 Havdala is said at home if (a) one did not say אַתָּה חוֹנַנְתָּנוּ or hear Havdala in the synagogue; (b) one said אַתָּה חוֹנַנְתָּנוּ or heard Havdala, but intended not to fulfill one's obligation; or (c) someone at home did not yet hear Havdala [שו״ע או״ח, רצו:ז; משנ״ב, שם:לב]. Women may say Havdala for themselves [משנ״ב, שם:לה–לו]. If one forgets to say Havdala on Motza'ei Shabbat, one may say it as late as Tuesday night.

137 After Shabbat, one should eat a meal, the *Melaveh Malka*, as a way of marking the end of Shabbat [שו״ע או״ח, ש:א].

TABLE OF PERMITTED RESPONSES

	Pesukei DeZimra (from Barukh SheAmar to Yishtabaḥ)	*Within a paragraph of the Shema or the preceding blessings*[1]	*Between the paragraphs of the Shema or the preceding blessings*	*Between concluding the blessing* גָּאַל יִשְׂרָאֵל *and beginning the Amida*[2]
אָמֵן יְהֵא שְׁמֵהּ רַבָּא; אָמֵן following דַּאֲמִירָן בְּעָלְמָא[3]	Permissible	Permissible	Permissible	Forbidden [שו"ע או"ח סו, ט; משנ"ב נא, ח]
אָמֵן following any blessing	Permissible	Forbidden	Permissible	Forbidden[4]
בָּרוּךְ הוּא וּבָרוּךְ שְׁמוֹ; בְּרִיךְ הוּא	Forbidden[5]	Forbidden	Forbidden	Forbidden
Tallit	Put on the tallit, but say the blessing between paragraphs [משנ"ב נג, ה]	Put on the tallit, but say the blessing after the Amida [שו"ע ורמ"א או"ח סו, ב]	Put on the tallit, but say the blessing after the Amida	Forbidden [שו"ע או"ח סו, ח]
Barekhu[6]	Permissible	Permissible	Permissible	Forbidden

1. The paragraphs are as follows: from the blessing יוֹצֵר אוֹר to יוֹצֵר הַמְּאוֹרוֹת; from אַהֲבָה רַבָּה or אַהֲבַת עוֹלָם to Shema; from Shema to וּבִשְׁעָרֶיךָ; from וְהָיָה אִם שָׁמֹעַ to עַל־הָאָרֶץ; from וַיֹּאמֶר to גָּאַל יִשְׂרָאֵל [שו"ע או"ח סו, ה]. Responses permitted within a paragraph are also permissible within a verse, though it is preferable to respond only at the end of a thought.
2. Some rule that on Shabbat one may respond to Kaddish, *Barekhu*, *Kedusha* or *Modim* [רמ"א או"ח קיא, א]. See law 37.
3. Only these are required responses; the other responses of אָמֵן in Kaddish are only a custom [משנ"ב סו, יז].
4. One may answer אָמֵן if one hears another concluding the blessing גָּאַל יִשְׂרָאֵל [רמ"א או"ח סו, ז].
5. These responses are only a custom, as they are not mentioned in the Gemara [משנ"ב נא, ח].

	Pesukei DeZimra (from Barukh SheAmar to Yishtabaḥ)	*Within a paragraph of the Shema or the preceding blessings*[1]	*Between the paragraphs of the Shema or the preceding blessings*	*Between concluding the blessing* גָּאַל יִשְׂרָאֵל *and beginning the Amida*[2]
Shema	Say the first verse with the congregation [משנ"ב סה, יא]	Forbidden, except to close one's eyes and sing the melody of the Shema	Forbidden, except to close one's eyes and sing the melody of the Shema[7] [שו"ע או"ח סה, ב]	Forbidden
Kedusha	Permissible[8] [משנ"ב נא, ח]	Say only the verses beginning קָדוֹשׁ and בָּרוּךְ	Say only the verses beginning קָדוֹשׁ and בָּרוּךְ	Forbidden [משנ"ב סו, יז]
אָמֵן after הָאֵל הַקָּדוֹשׁ and שׁוֹמֵעַ תְּפִלָּה	Permissible	Permissible	Permissible	Forbidden [רמ"א או"ח סו, ג]
Modim DeRabanan	Permissible	Say only the words מוֹדִים אֲנַחְנוּ לָךְ	Say only the words מוֹדִים אֲנַחְנוּ לָךְ	Forbidden [משנ"ב סו, כ]
Being called up to the Torah[9]	Permissible	Permissible – but not in the middle of the first verse of the Shema or בָּרוּךְ שֵׁם כְּבוֹד מַלְכוּתוֹ לְעוֹלָם וָעֶד	Permissible	Forbidden [משנ"ב סו, כו]

6. Whether before the blessings of the Shema or before the Reading of the Torah. The blessings said by the עוֹלֶה are like any other blessing [משנ"ב סו, יח].
7. If the congregation is saying *Aleinu*, one should stand and bow with them [ערוה"ש או"ח סה, ו].
8. Say only the biblical verses [אשי ישראל פט"ז, לא; see law 43].
9. The Gabba'im should not call up to the Torah one who is in the middle of prayer; however, if only one Kohen is present, he may be called up. Likewise, if only one person knows how to read the Torah, he may interrupt his prayers in order to be the *ba'al koreh* [משנ"ב סו, כו].

	Pesukei DeZimra (from Barukh SheAmar to Yishtabaḥ)	*Within a paragraph of the Shema or the preceding blessings*[1]	*Between the paragraphs of the Shema or the preceding blessings*	*Between concluding the blessing* גָּאַל יִשְׂרָאֵל *and beginning the Amida*[2]
אֲשֶׁר יָצַר	Say the blessing between paragraphs [בה״ל, נא ד״ה צריך]	Wash one's hands, but say the blessing after the Amida	Wash one's hands, but say the blessing after the Amida	Wash one's hands, but say the blessing after the Amida [משנ״ב סו, כג]
Blessing on thunder or lightning	Permissible	Forbidden	Permissible, if the opportunity may not recur	Forbidden [משנ״ב סו, יט]

GENERAL RULES

MA'ARIV

The rules regarding responses are identical to those of Shaḥarit. After the blessing שׁוֹמֵר עַמּוֹ יִשְׂרָאֵל לָעַד until Half Kaddish, is considered to be between paragraphs, even in the middle of בָּרוּךְ יהוה לְעוֹלָם אָמֵן וְאָמֵן [ביאור הלכה סו ד״ה ואלו].

HALLEL

The laws regarding responses during Hallel are identical to those of the Shema [שו״ע או״ח תפח, א].

REMOVING A CRYING CHILD

One should remove a crying child from the synagogue even while saying the Amida, in order to avoid disturbing others who are praying [אשי ישראל פל״ב, יג (בשם החזון אי״ש)].

KADDISH DURING PESUKEI DEZIMRA

A mourner is permitted to say Kaddish during *Pesukei DeZimra,* if he will be unable to say it afterwards [אשי ישראל פט״ו הערה קט].

THE CONCEPTS OF KEVOD SHABBAT AND ONEG SHABBAT

One of the biggest challenges of beginning a life filled with ritual is figuring out what you are supposed to do. Judaism in general and Shabbat in particular have so many rules that are so foreign that one can feel as if one has come upon another planet. There is so much to remember, there are so many questions that one has, there can be so much internal or external pressure to fit in, that it is extremely difficult to maintain focus on the message, the meaning, the excitement of the ritual and the way that it is supposed to transform or shape our perspective and our lives.

One of the biggest challenges of a life filled with rituals is to make sure that they maintain their meaning and significance in our lives. It's hard. Like any behavior that becomes a habit, we have a tendency to go through the motions without thinking about them a lot. It just becomes a part of who we are and how we identify ourselves; all the more so if we live in a community where everyone else is doing the same thing. It is in the nature of our being to take things for granted. The danger is that in so doing we can lose sight of the message, the meaning, the excitement of the ritual and the way that it is supposed to transform or shape our perspective and our lives.

One of the biggest mistakes that one can make, then, is to just walk into an experience like Shabbat and expect that its power will be felt; either the newness or the sameness of it all can get in the way. This is especially so given the numerous prohibitions that there are, the so called 39 Categories of Forbidden Labor which translate into scores of rules which are designed to prevent the Shabbat from dissolving into yet another day of the week like any other. If one loses sight of that goal, if one loses sight of the "island in time" that Shabbat is supposed to represent, then all of the rules can begin to feel restrictive and inhibiting rather than liberating and enthralling. The same danger can exist for the prayer services on

Shabbat. They can be especially long primarily because we finally have the opportunity to be spiritually uplifted and inspired. Without the right frame of mind, however, they can seem interminable and burdensome. It all depends upon us, on our attitude toward the day and what we seek from it, how we hope to draw from its energy and power.

One needs to work at this frame of mind, however. Not completely unlike playing an instrument or a sport, one needs to stretch and train one's spiritual muscles. Not completely unlike an important relationship, one needs to attend to and nurture it, lest it be taken for granted and grow stale. Toward that end, there are two major *halakhic* (legal) categories which can be used to infuse one's Shabbat with meaning and to help maintain the excitement, the passion and the spirituality of the Shabbat experience, week in and week out.

Kevod Shabbat – Honoring the day

An event tends to take on greater significance when we prepare for it. Our sense of anticipation adds to our excitement and to our ultimate enjoyment. Imagine if we heard one day that we were going to get a visit in our home by the president of the United States. Most of us would not simply "show up"; we would get the house ready, think about what we are going to say, what we would be going to wear, who else we might invite. In short, we would prepare but the preparations themselves are either a manifestation of or a catalyst for our excitement about the visit.

That's what Shabbat is like. It's an opportunity to have the King of the world come to visit our home. It's a rendezvous with the Divine Presence and, as such, it is worthy of our attention long before it happens. In fact, perhaps because of the sublime and intangible nature of the holiness of this encounter, Rabbi Joseph B. Soloveitchik is often quoted as saying that there can be no holiness without preparation. That is why the Israelites were required to prepare for three days before the giving of the Torah, because from a psychological perspective one cannot move from a "desert" experience to a "revelation on Sinai" experience without preparation. This is why we count the days from Pesaḥ to Shavuot in anticipation of the giving of the Torah. Similarly, the *Kohen Gadol* (High Priest) was sequestered for a week before his service on Yom Kippur and, in the same vein, during the month prior to Rosh HaShana and Yom Kippur our custom is to prepare ourselves for those days. One cannot go from a secular existence to a holy existence, from the everyday to the unusual, without preparation.[1]

That would seem to be the explanation for a group of laws which are referred to as *Kevod Shabbat,* literally "honor of the Shabbat," a series of practical acts that relate to how one prepares for the arrival of Shabbat before it actually arrives (Rambam, *Shabbat* 30:2-6; *Biur HaGra* 529:4). Herewith is a list of some aspects of that commandment.

Shop for Shabbat. The midrash (*Mekhilta* on *Shemot* 20:7, *Beitza* 16a) cites two different outlooks by two prominent sages. When Shammai would find some good food during the week, he would set it aside for Shabbat. If he subsequently found something better, he would replace the previous purchase. In this way, he always saved the best for last. Hillel, on the other hand, would say that one needs to have confidence in Hashem's ability to provide, and so there was no need to set the food aside; Hashem would take care of your Shabbat needs. Unlike in most other cases where these two sages disagree, in this case most authorities side with Shammai (with some claiming that Hillel really agrees when it applies to the average person) (*Mishna Berura* 250:2; res. *Ketav Sofer* OḤ 38). Even in this age of supermarkets and boutique markets where all delicacies are readily available, the psychological advice still holds true. Shop early if you can but make sure that you are shopping for the honor of Shabbat. Set aside that special treat not only for yourself but for Shabbat too.[2]

1 "The word *"shomer"* in the phrase *"shomer Shabbat"* meaning one who "keeps" the laws of Shabbat, is comparable to its use in the Torah (*Bereshit* 37:11), when after the telling of Yosef's dreams and his brothers hated him, we are told that Yaakov "kept the matter in mind" (*shamar et hadavar*) as if to say that he anticipated when that day of the fulfillment of the dream would actually arrive. So, too, a person must have a burning anticipation for the arrival of the holy Shabbat, a longing for this precious gift, the influence of its holiness and the great spiritual impact that it has on everyone, each according to his ability to perceive and receive. Obviously one needs six days of the week to be ready to be influenced this way. "And according to his preparation will be his attainment" (Rabbi Avraham Yehoshua Heschel of Apta, d. 1825).

2 One should begin one's preparations from early in the morning. The pious Rabbi

◂ *Think about*

Think about Shabbat every day. Recall that in the Hebrew language there were never really names for the days of the week other than Shabbat. Instead, each day of the week is referred to as a number relative to Shabbat, for example, today is the first day of the week relative to Shabbat, today is the second day of the week... (see also the first line of each of the Daily Psalms in the weekday siddur). Consider, too, that at the end of the Daily Psalm for Wednesday, the rabbis tacked on the first two lines from the Friday night service (*Lekhu neranena*), as if to say: "Hang in there, Shabbat is coming." In short, every day there is an opportunity to recall the centrality of Shabbat in our week and in our lives.

Plan around Shabbat. Knowing that on Shabbat you will not be able to do the things you normally do on a weekday inevitably means that you need to plan the rest of your week accordingly. Taking your car to the mechanic in such a way that ensures that he will not have to do the work on Shabbat, finishing your homework assignments or business deadlines without relying on having a Saturday to catch up, ordering something and making sure that delivery does not specifically take place on Shabbat, are just a few examples of what it means to preserve Shabbat as an island in time. To the uninitiated or to those for whom Shabbat may feel like more of a burden than a liberating existence, this mindset may seem disquieting or intrusive. But the more one consciously rearranges one's life so that Shabbat is at the center and, yes, the more one has to sacrifice to squeeze everything into six days of the week instead of seven, the more meaningful and welcome does the day become, and, ironically, the more fulfilling can the other six days become.

Do something yourself for Shabbat. Each person needs to prepare for this encounter themselves. It doesn't matter whether you have a

---

Avraham HaLevi ז"ל was a great guardian of Shabbat and early Friday morning, two hours before daylight, he would go around knocking on doors to wake women to tell them to start preparing for Shabbat and kneading the dough, and he warned them that there should be no food still cooking on the fire right before Shabbat. He would tell each of them: "Just know that if I find such food, I will take it and give it out to the poor." And the women were afraid of him and did everything they could to make sure that everything was ready on time. They say that he was a man of his word and he actually carried through on the threat, for he went from house to house, confiscated the food and gave it to the poor (*Siddur Or Zarua LaTzaddik*).

◂ room-mate

room-mate, a spouse, or servants who take care of most of the arrangements, you still need to make your own contribution.[3] The Talmud (*Shabbat* 119) relates that some of the most famous and wealthiest rabbis each contributed to Shabbat in their own way. Rav Safra would roast the head of an animal, Rava would salt a fish, Rav Huna would light the lamp, Rav Papa would twine wicks, Rav Ḥisda would cut beets, Rabba and Rav Yosef would chop wood, Rav Zeira would kindle the fire with twigs. These are people who could easily have gotten others to do the jobs for them. Nevertheless, each made a point weekly of doing something that they could connect to. The more you can do, the better, but don't discount the little things. Many men have a custom of lighting the candles that are to be used for Shabbat and then blow them out as a way of preparing the wicks so that they catch fire immediately and cleanly when eventually lit for Shabbat. Children should also be included in the preparations whether it involves cleaning their rooms or setting the table; everyone has something to offer, and to gain.

Bathe for Shabbat. Regardless of whether you are a shower-in-the morning or at-night person, regardless of the supposed benefits of one over the other, one bathes on Friday not so much for oneself but *for the Shabbat*, not for physical hygiene alone but for spiritual preparedness as well. Skip the morning shower if you can (and buy yourself some extra minutes of sleep) but, regardless, make sure that you enter into Shabbat feeling fresh.[4]

Dress for Shabbat. Using the analogy of preparing for a guest, then one can appreciate why Jewish law insists that one should dress appropriately for Shabbat. This does not mean that one needs to dress to impress, at least not other people, and as many an adolescent has protested, "why

3 One should always be involved in the preparation for Shabbat even if one has servants and especially when the days are short [in the winter when there is less time to prepare]. For I have seen many men of high standing, great Torah scholars who would prepare for Shabbat so that everything would be ready in time. And don't ever say: It's beneath my dignity and honor to do this, for your honor comes from honoring the Shabbat. (*Ḥayyei Adam* 1:3)

4 What is *kavod* [honor]? This is what the rabbis meant when they said it was a mitzva to wash one's face and hands and legs with hot water. (Rambam, *Hilkhot Shabbat* 30:2)

◂ should God

should God care what I wear?!" The answer is less about God than it is about ourselves. We feel different when we are dressed differently and if we are dressing for Shabbat and not for ourselves, then how we dress can potentially make all the difference in the world. That is why there are those who have a special suit or dress that they only wear on Shabbat, a special tie that they don't wear during the week or a special blouse; these are special because the only day of the week they are worn is on Shabbat itself. It's also the reason why some men have an additional *tallit* that they only wear on Shabbat. Recognizing that not everyone could afford a second set of clothes, *halakha* (Yerushalmi *Pe'a* 8:8) suggested that in such a case one could at least turn down the hem of one's weekday garment, just as royalty would, anything so that one's weekday clothes and Shabbat clothes are different.[5]

Give charity for Shabbat. Research has often shown that people who are religious tend to give more to charity than people who are not. Why should this be so? Shouldn't it be enough to believe in the need to reach out to one's fellow man on a humanitarian level without involving God in the process? Apparently not. Perhaps one reason is that religious people tend to have a heightened sense of *hakarat hatov*, gratitude for what they have and for what God gave to us in His own act of generosity, namely, giving us the world in which we live. As King David said: "The earth is the LORD's and all it contains." That said, what better way to get into the spirit of Shabbat than to get in touch with our own sense of indebtedness to Hashem by emulating His kindness and giving to others! One need not run out and find a poor person necessarily, though it is common to find communities that deliver food to those in need on Thursday nights or Fridays. Instead, one can write a weekly small check to the charity of your choice, or keep on hand a small *pushke* (a small charity box with a slit at the top) where you can readily deposit some loose change. If you have children, share the mitzva with them as a regular pre-Shabbat ritual. By

5 When I used to get dressed for Shabbat on Friday afternoon I would give enormous thanks to Hashem with great happiness and would say with all my heart: My Maker, my Creator, may Your name be blessed, I thank You for having given me these valuable clothes in honor of the holy Shabbat not because of my good deeds, but out of Your great mercy and loving-kindness. (Ethical will of Rabbi Alexander Ziskind of Horodno)

◂ giving to

giving to those in need, we acknowledge many things including what we have, our connectedness to others, and the fact that everything ultimately comes from Him.[6]

Clear your mind for Shabbat. This one is hard and the challenge is not new. There is a midrash which wonders how it is possible for a person to truly emulate God on this day in terms of work. For when the verse says, "And God completed all of His work on the seventh day" (*Bereshit* 2:2), surely man cannot do the same? Our work never ends. It will still be there when Shabbat is over. Indeed, perhaps the midrash was anticipating our own workaholic existence in which it can be very difficult to walk away from weekday responsibilities, not physically but in our own heads. The office/school/job follows me wherever I go. The answer the midrash gives is psychologically astute – you need to walk into Shabbat *as if* you completed all of your work, that is, you need to train yourself into shutting off your mind and leaving your work behind you. Easier said than done but a worthwhile challenge nevertheless. Mental-health professionals will tell you about the importance of taking time for you and turning off your mind so that you can truly rest and heal and breathe. That's what Shabbat can do. In a different context, the medieval commentator Avraham ibn Ezra suggests that a pauper can never imagine that he will one day marry the princess; you can dream occasionally but, for the most part, the unattainable is off your mental and emotional radar. There are just certain things in life that you don't contemplate, as if they don't exist at

6 "I heard from the elders of the city that long ago the practice in Frankfurt was not for the people responsible for collecting charity (*gabba'ei tzedaka*) to distribute funds to the city's poor every week. Rather, the poor themselves had to go from house to house every Friday before Shabbat [collecting what they could], until one time a poor woman who had died appeared in front of the courtyard of the synagogue. They told me her name but I have since forgotten it. When they asked her what she wanted, she said that she came to warn everyone that they should discontinue this practice of forcing the poor to embarrass themselves every *Erev Shabbat* by having to go door to door, and if the community would not desist from this practice then the entire city, God forbid, would be punished severely. It is for this reason that it was decreed that every month on Rosh Ḥodesh, until this very day, monies are collected for distribution to the poor from week to week so that they need not be humiliated by having to go from house to house. I heard this from a reliable source." (*Yosef Ometz*, Rabbi Yosef Hahn 1570–1637)

◂ all. That's

all. That's the mindset that many people have as they walk into Shabbat. Work and other such worries or responsibilities just do not exist. Yes, it's hard. But so is any mindful practice. It's like training a muscle. In the end, you will be stronger and healthier for it.[7]

Anticipate Shabbat. "'Well,' said Pooh, 'what I like best,' and then he had to stop and think. Because although Eating Honey was a very good thing to do, there was a moment just before you began to eat it which was better than when you were, but he didn't know what it was called" (*Winnie the Pooh*, by A.A. Milne). Unlike honey, Shabbat is even more enthralling when you first get excited about its arrival. Exactly what aspect of it will conjure this up the most within you is up to you. But consider the custom that there is to recite *Shir HaShirim*, the biblical book of the Song of Songs just before Shabbat arrives. The book is an allegorical love story taken as metaphor for the love between the Jewish people and Hashem or, in this case if you will, between the individual and Shabbat. It is referred to in the plural (Song of Songs), says the Slonimer Rebbe, because it actually comprises two songs – that of man for Hashem and that of Hashem for man. That relationship, that excitement, that anticipation is what *Erev Shabbat* is all about.[8]

---

7 "There are those who totally don't understand the holiness of Shabbat and think that it is only about not working on that day and so Shabbat is very difficult for them, and so they come late to Shabbat and leave early, exclaiming that they already see the three stars in the sky that mark the end of Shabbat. Of them the prophet said (*Yeshayahu* 54:7), 'In a single minute I abandoned you,' for had you waited one more minute I would have redeemed you. And this too is what is meant by the verse (*Yeshayahu* 5:20), 'Woe to those who speak of bad as good and of good as bad, who make darkness into light and light into darkness.' The evil, which are the days of the week, they refer to as good because it is good for business and prosperity; and the good, which is Shabbat, they call bad because it is bad for business. Therefore they turn darkness to light, because on Friday night, when it is already dark, they still do business because they say it is still light, and light into darkness, for on Saturday night when it is yet light, they claim that Shabbat is already over." (Rabbi Ḥayyim Aryeh of Jedwabne)

8 "Allow me, please, to make a "private confession" concerning a matter that has caused me much loss of sleep. I am not so very old, yet I remember a time when 90 percent of world Jewry were observant and the secularists were a small minority at the fringes of the camp. I still remember – it was not so long ago – when Jews were

◂ *Light candles*

Light candles for Shabbat. Creating a flame to light candles is one of the last "weekday" acts one does before the onset of Shabbat itself. It thus qualifies as *Kevod Shabbat* (Honoring the Shabbat) because it is preparation one does beforehand (*Shabbat* 24b; Rashi 25b). In this context, the purpose of having candles is not so much for their symbolic value but for the actual light which they provide. As we shall see, there is a mitzva to have lights on in the house, especially Shabbat night. In our own age, electric lights serve this purpose as well, even better than candles, and so there are those who specifically require that one extinguish the electric light, then put them back on, then say the blessing over the candles and have in mind the electric lighting as well (based on *Tosafot, Shabbat* 25b). Traditionally, emphasis was placed on having light in the place where one eats but, in our more spacious living arrangements, having lights on in multiple places can enhance one's enjoyment. Even so, making sure there are no lights on in bedrooms, even attached to a timer, can ensure that everyone ends up spending more time together than they might during the week when everyone retreats to their rooms.

Oneg Shabbat – Enjoying and spiritualizing the day

The prophet *Yeshayahu* (58:13–14) called upon the Jewish people to proclaim the Shabbat day a delight (*oneg*) and by doing so they would then delight in Hashem. There are those who suggest that he was just giving expression to a commandment already mandated by the Torah that one delight in the Shabbat (res. *Rashba* 1:127). But what exactly does this mean in practical terms? Minimally it is understood to incorporate the pleasures of Shabbat – a festive meal replete with wine and meat and foods made especially for the occasion.

still close to God and lived in an atmosphere pervaded with holiness… [I]t is not for the Sabbath that my heart aches, it is for the forgotten 'eve of the Sabbath.' There are Sabbath-observing Jews in America, but there are no 'eve-of-the-Sabbath' Jews who go out to greet the Sabbath with beating hearts and pulsating souls. There are many who observe the precepts with their hands, with their feet and/or with their mouths – but there are few, indeed, who truly know the meaning of service of the heart!" (Rabbi J. B. Soloveitchik in *On Repentance*)

◂ *Eat for Shabbat*

Eat for Shabbat. Make the meal special. This need not mean multiple lavish courses and haute cuisine. It simply means doing something different than you would do the rest of the week. I am always reminded of the mother who once wrote to me that her daughter was unexcited about Shabbat meals until the mom finally decided to make her daughter a salami sandwich, the child's favorite, which made all of the difference in her excitement about coming to the table. Treat yourself and your guests, always keeping in mind that the true guest at the table is Shabbat.[9]

Sing for Shabbat. William James is often quoted as saying "I don't sing because I'm happy; I'm happy because I sing." Our slightly different emphasis might come from the words of the fourteenth-century *Sefer HaḤinukh*: "our hearts are affected by our actions." Singing can help us get to a place where thoughts or words alone may not bring us. No wonder, then, that there is such an esteemed history, especially in the last few centuries, to singing at the Shabbat table. These songs (*zemirot*) are built around themes related to Shabbat and thereby help provoke and evoke an appreciation of the day. If you don't know the tunes, ask someone to teach them to you or go online to find some examples.

Table talk for Shabbat. In *Pirkei Avot* (3:4) we are taught: "Rabbi Shimon said: Three people who ate at the same table and did not speak words of Torah are as if they had eaten from sacrifices to dead [idols]... But three who ate at the same table and did speak words of Torah are as if they had eaten from Hashem's table, as it states, 'And he [the angel] said to me: This [altar] is the table that is before Hashem (*Yeḥezkel* 41:22).'" Perhaps a true test of whether a meal is for the sake of self-indulgence or for the sake of some loftier value is the table-talk that accompanies it. Minimally, food is about survival. On Shabbat, it is especially about enjoyment, and while we inject it with spiritual significance via the blessings

9 "The Rabbis, may their memory be blessed, said 'whoever delights the Shabbat' not 'whoever delights oneself on Shabbat,' for the intent is not to indulge in oneself but rather to delight in honor of Shabbat itself. This is what the verse means when it says 'and you shall call Shabbat a delight,' that you should call the Shabbat a delight... Therefore, those who stuff themselves unbelievably like a horse or a mule and afterwards, because of their excess eating, fall asleep, are people who do not delight the Shabbat but rather they are simply delighting themselves on Shabbat... and they thereby separate themselves from the possibility of feeling closer to God." (*Shela*)

◂ recited before

recited before and after, sharing words of Torah during the meal lends a different aura and flavor to the festivities. At the very least, it reminds us that the cause for this celebration is ultimately for a higher purpose; our table is thereby turned into an altar. Besides, how often during the week does one get to spend time with family or friends talking about ideas? If there are children present, make sure that they are included in conversation and that they are encouraged to contribute in their own way. There are hundreds of resources available for finding *divrei Torah* online or in bookstores (or just try wrapping your head around the weekly reading). Alternatively, think in advance of conversations worth having about any issues that would make your eating place "the table that is before Hashem."

Invite guests for Shabbat. There is a very venerable tradition in Jewish life to share one's Shabbat table with others.[10] This isn't just an attempt to reach out to those in need but to anyone at all. It speaks to our closeness as a community and our bond as a people. Shabbat meals are just one of the many ways that we can instantly become part of any Jewish community in the world.

And, in keeping with the mitzva of *oneg*, the day is enjoyed all the more in the company of others. While everyone wants their private time, meals are generally an opportunity to come out of the shell that is sometimes imposed upon us during the week. Recall a Jewish custom from medieval Provence which was to ultimately use the wood from one's table for the construction of one's coffin, for how one used one's table was considered a measure of how one had lived one's life (Rabbeinu Beḥaye, *Shemot* 25:23).[11]

---

10 The heads of the community in Horodno would send notes to the townspeople to insist that they invite poor guests to their table for Shabbat. In the great synagogue on one of the pillars at the front there hung a black wooden sign on which was written in white: "So and so refused to invite any guests to his table." In this way they embarrassed people who were too stingy to invite anyone.

11 "The table is a symbol for the altar of atonement and the bread upon it is like the sacrifice. For the verse says (*Yeḥezkel* 41:22 'The altar was of wood... He said to me, This is the Table that is before Hashem.' The verse began with a description of the altar but concluded as if it were talking about the table. From here one learns that in the times of the *Beit HaMikdash*, the altar was the place for atonement. Once it was destroyed, a person's table becomes his place of atonement." (*Berakhot* 55a)

◂ If you

If you have children, make sure you invite company for them as well and don't ask them to sit at the table unnecessarily longer.

Sleep. We are a sleep-deprived civilization and Shabbat is certainly a day for catching up. As one of the *zemirot* declares "sleep on Shabbat is a pleasure" (*ta'anug,* from the same root as *oneg*) and some even went so far as to find a biblical justification for doing so![12] Nevertheless, sleeping more is different from oversleeping (instead of going to services) or sleeping through meals or sleeping the entire day away. One may be part of *oneg Shabbat*; the other is part of simple self-indulgence. You will no doubt wake up with your body refreshed if you sleep a lot but your soul will still need rejuvenation.

Learn Torah. Set some time aside every Shabbat for learning something new about Judaism. If not on Shabbat, then when will you do it?[13] How will you grow in your knowledge and understanding of Judaism if you don't invest time in it? There is a very old custom to learn the week's Torah reading twice together with a commentary (*shenayim mikra ve'eḥad targum*) but in this day of translations, there is no end to the possibilities of learning original sources that were once closed to the uninitiated. You can learn whatever your heart desires. Indeed, let your heart be drawn in as well as your brain, for learning Torah in its broadest sense expands the heart and feeds the soul.

Talk Shabbat. How we express ourselves is an important element in who we are, how we view others, and how others view us. Language is

12 "During the week, people get up early in the morning to go to the synagogue to pray or to learn, but on Shabbat they sleep in longer. The reason for this is because in the verse about the daily *Tamid* sacrifice (*Bemidbar* 28:4) it says "in the morning in the morning" whereas in the verse about the *Tamid* of Shabbat (*Bemidbar* 28:9) it says "on Shabbat day" implying that it is later in the day than the morning. This reason was heard by Rav Yose bar Rav Yehuda in the city of Rome, and retold by Rav Hai Gaon" (Mordekhai, thirteenth century).

13 The midrash gives voice to this tension. At the time the Torah was given in the desert, the Torah said to God, "When the people enter the Land they will all run off to their vineyards or their fields, and what then will happen to me?!" He said to her, "I have a mate for you, and its name is Shabbat. On that day they will abandon their work and be able to embrace you" (see *Tur* and *Arukh HaShulḥan* 290:2).
And lest you say that there isn't enough time in the day, "whoever does not waste time, has time for everything" (*Ḥida, Avodat Kodesh*).

◂ the primary

the primary medium for not only conveying our knowledge but also our values and it can help set the tone for our interactions. Words help create our reality; even the smallest things can make a difference. That is perhaps one reason why on Shabbat we greet one another differently by saying "*Shabbat Shalom*" (or its Yiddish equivalent "*Gut Shabbos*"). That greeting can take the place of "hello," "good morning," "good night," or even "goodbye." That's because there is no greater blessing on this day than to wish someone the peace (*shalom*) and fulfillment (*shleimut*) that Shabbat can bring. We need only speak to it.[14]

Treat every Shabbat like it's the first. As we mentioned elsewhere, Shabbat is not about recreation; rather, it's about re-creation. If on this day we mark the creation of the world, then every Shabbat is like the world was created anew. Every Shabbat is a new experience, a new chance to start all over again. If last Shabbat was not what you wanted it to be, then this Shabbat can be different – because you too are different.

14 "Arriving on *Erev Shabbat* we were grieved to learn that an elderly relative had experienced renal failure and was in critical condition… I was informed that the doctors were unanimous in their opinion that the patient was terminal… The doctor could see no point in prolonging life… As a matter of Halakha I had no choice but to insist upon the administration of therapeutically indicated medication… Late Shabbat afternoon I returned from *Minḥa* and although the patient had been totally unresponsive for over thirty-six hours, I walked into the hospital room and said *"Gut Shabbos"* in a loud voice. I was greeted in response by the flickering of an eyelid and, in a weak but clear voice the words *"Gut Shabbos"* in return. At that moment there flashed across my mind the comments of Rav Akiva Eiger (*Oraḥ Ḥayyim* 271:1) who declares that even the simple, standard Shabbat greeting expressed by one Jew to another constitutes a fulfillment of the mitzva: "Remember the Sabbath day to keep it holy." At that moment, I realized not only intellectually, but also emotionally, that every moment of life is of inestimable value. Here was a dramatic unfolding of the lesson that every moment of life carries with the opportunity for the performance of yet one more mitzva." (Rabbi J. David Bleich)

IN CONCLUSION: A THOUGHT ON SHABBAT

Friday afternoon, during these rehearsals, inevitably seems to come when the project is tottering on the edge of ruin. I have sometimes felt guilty of treason, holding to the Sabbath in such a desperate situation. But then, experience has taught me that a theater enterprise almost always is in such a case. Sometimes it does totter to ruin, and sometimes it totters to great prosperity, but tottering is its normal gait, and cries of anguish are its normal tone of voice. So I have reluctantly taken leave of my colleagues on Friday afternoon and rejoined them on Saturday night. The play has never yet collapsed in the meantime. When I return I find it tottering as before, and the anguished cries as normally despairing as ever. My plays have encountered in the end both success and failure, but I cannot honestly ascribe either result to my observing the Sabbath.

Leaving the gloomy theater, the littered coffee cups, the jumbled scarred-up scripts, the haggard actors, the shouting stagehands, the bedeviled director, the knuckle-gnawing producer, the clattering typewriter, and the dense tobacco smoke and backstage dust, I have come home. It has been a startling change, very like a brief return from the wars. My wife and my boys, whose existence I have almost forgotten in the anxious shoring up of the tottering ruin, are waiting for me, gay, dressed in holiday clothes, and looking to me marvelously attractive. We have sat down to a splendid dinner at a table graced with flowers and the old Sabbath symbols: the burning candles, the twisted loaves, the stuffed fish, and my grandfather's silver goblet brimming with wine. I have blessed my boys with the ancient blessing; we have sung the pleasantly syncopated Sabbath table hymns. The talk has had little to do with tottering ruins. My wife and I have caught up with our week's conversation. The boys, knowing that the

Sabbath is the occasion for asking questions, have asked them. The Bible, the encyclopedia, the atlas have piled up on the table. We talk of Judaism. and there are the usual impossible boys' queries about God, which my wife and I field clumsily but as well as we can. For me it is a retreat into restorative magic.

Saturday has passed in much the same manner. The boys are at home in the synagogue, and they like it. They like even more the assured presence of their parents. In the weekday press of schooling, household chores, and work – and especially in a play-producing time – it often happens that they see little of us. On the Sabbath we are always there, and they know it. They know too that I am not working and that my wife is at her ease. It is their day.

It is my day too. The telephone is silent. I can think, read, study, walk or do nothing. It is an oasis of quiet. When night falls, I go back to the wonderful nerve-racking Broadway game. Often I make my best contribution of the week then and there to the grisly literary surgery that goes on and on until opening night. My producer one Saturday night said to me, "I don't envy you your religion, but I envy you your Sabbath."

Herman Wouk,
Pulitzer Prize-winning author and playwright
This Is My God

GLOSSARY OF NAMES AND TERMS

Aharon – Aaron the High Priest, brother of Moshe.

Alef-Beit – the Hebrew alphabet.

Aliya LaTorah – Literally, ascent to the Torah. When there is public Torah reading, three people are called to make the *berakhot* on the Torah reading on weekdays, five on Yom Tov, and seven on Shabbat.

Amida – the central prayer of each service; often referred to as *Shemoneh Esreh.*

Amoraim – scholars of the Talmud who lived in Babylonia or Israel from approximately 200–500 CE.

Aramaic – A Semitic language that was the spoken language of Jews in Talmudic times. Many ancient Jewish texts are written in Aramaic, most famously the Talmud, but also some biblical texts, such as the book of Daniel. Several prayers are also written in Aramaic, including *Kaddish.*

Ashkenazi/Ashkenazim – a reference to those Jews whose origins are generally in Europe.

Avot – The Patriarchs. A reference, too, to the first blessing of the *Amida,* which has the Patriarchs as its theme.

Avraham – Abraham of the Bible.

Barekhu – A call to prayer (literally Bless the Lord) signifying the beginning of the *berakhot* before the *Shema,* in the *Shaḥarit* and *Ma'ariv* services. *Barekhu* is considered a *davar shebikedusha* and can only be said with a *minyan.*

Beit HaMikdash – The Temple in Jerusalem. The term is applied equally to the First Temple which was destroyed in 586 BCE and the Second Temple which was destroyed in 70 AD.

◂ *Birkat HaMazon*

Birkat HaMazon – Grace after meals. Recited after a meal in which bread has been eaten.

Davar Shebikedusha – Literally "something that is holy." These are the sections of the prayer service that can only be said in the presence of a *minyan* due to their holiness. These include the Repetition of the *Amida*.

Gemara – The portion of the Talmud (the Babylonian Talmud unless otherwise specified) which deals with commentary and discussions about the Mishna.

HaKadosh Barukh Hu – A reference to God: The Holy One blessed be He.

Halakha – Jewish law.

Hallel – A prayer service of praise to God (the meaning of the Hebrew word *Hallel* is praise) said after *Shaḥarit* on special days in the Jewish calendar, including Rosh Ḥodesh and various festivals. *Hallel* is comprised of chapters 113–118 of *Tehillim*.

HaMotzi – the blessing made on bread, but this can also be a reference to the ritual part of the Shabbat meal where this *berakha* is made over two loaves of bread (*Ḥallot*).

Hashem – God. Literally means "The Name," and specifically refers to the four-letter name of God that one is forbidden to pronounce although Hashem can be used any time to refer to God in general as opposed to that Name in particular.

Ḥasidut/Hasidism – A system of Jewish philosophical thought and practice developed by the followers of the Ba'al Shem Tov. Followers of *Ḥasidut* are called Hasidim (singular – Hasid).

Ḥazal – An acronym for the Hebrew words "חכמינו זיכרונם לברכה" ("Our sages, may their memory be blessed") which generally refers to the sages of Talmudic times.

Ḥazan – The prayer leader in a synagogue service. Also called the *Shaliaḥ Tzibbur*, or emissary of the congregation.

Ḥesed – The mitzva of performing acts of loving-kindness.

Hilkhot – The Jewish laws of...

◂ *Ḥol HaMo'ed*

Ḥol HaMo'ed – The intermediate days of a long festival such as Sukkot or Pesaḥ. These holy days last for seven or eight days, with one or two days on either end (one day in Israel, two days in the Diaspora) marked as a *yom tov* akin in many ways to Shabbat. The intermediate days are the days in between which have the character of both a weekday (*ḥol*) and a holy day (*mo'ed*).

Ḥuppa – The canopy under which a Jewish wedding takes place. The *Ḥuppa* symbolizes the home that the couple will build together.

Kabbalat Shabbat – Literally "accepting Shabbat," the prayer service that precedes the evening service on a Friday night, inaugurating Shabbat.

Kabbala/kabbalists – Literally "receiving/tradition," the mystical system of Jewish thought, that draws on biblical and Talmudic primary sources. Kabbalists are scholars and practitioners of this system of thought.

Kaddish – A prayer that magnifies and sanctifies God, said by the prayer leader and mourners in the community.

Kavana – The act of praying with "directed consciousness" (Rabbi Aryeh Kaplan), the root of the word *k-v-n* means to aim or direct, but the word is often translated in the context of prayer as feeling, emotion, concentration, or devotion.

Kedusha – Literally "holiness," a responsive addition to the third *berakha* of every *Amida*, said by the *Ḥazan* only in the presence of a *minyan* of ten men during the Repetition of the *Amida*.

Keriat HaTorah – The public reading of the Torah that takes place on Shabbat and Yom Tov morning, Shabbat afternoon, and the weekday services on Monday and Thursday, as well as other festivals.

Kiddush – Literally, sanctification. Refers to the blessing of the sanctification of the day, said over wine on holy days and Shabbat at night and in the morning.

King Shaul – The biblical king Saul.

Korbanot – Sacrifices or offerings. Referring to the offerings that were part of the sacrificial service in the Temple, now no longer in existence since the destruction of the Temple in 70 CE. The root of the Hebrew word is *k-r-b* which means closeness. The sacrificial act is aimed to bring one closer to God.

Ma'ariv – The evening prayer service. Derives from the word *erev* meaning evening.

Maḥzor – The festival prayer book. The word *Maḥzor* literally means cycle, referring to the annual cycle of Jewish festivals.

Minḥa – The afternoon prayer service. Derives from the word "gift," alluding to the meal offering which accompanied sacrifices in the Temple.

Mishkan – Literally, "dwelling place," a reference to the Tabernacle in the desert during the exodus and the settlement of the land of Israel.

Mishna – The collection of oral laws and traditions redacted in approximately 200 CE which is the basis for discussions in the Gemara.

Mitzva – Literally, "a commandment." It usually refers to a commandment in the Torah but can also be a commandment enacted by the Rabbis and can sometimes be used to refer to a meritorious deed that does not have the same force of law.

Moshe – The biblical Moses.

Musaf – The additional prayer service that takes place on Shabbat and holy days.

Oral Law – An expression used to describe the oral laws and instructions that were passed along by Moshe when he received the written Torah on Sinai. Those laws were eventually written down in the Talmud and *midrashim* and in sum represent a commentary and complement to the written law that is the Torah.

Pesaḥ – The Hebrew name for the holiday of Passover.

Pesukei DeZimra – The passages of the *Shaḥarit* service that are comprised of a collection of psalms and prayers whose focus is on praise.

Rabbis – A general term that usually refers to the rabbinic authorities of the Talmudic period.

Rosh Ḥodesh – The day(s) designated for the beginning of the new lunar month in the Hebrew calendar.

Sefaradi/Sephardic – A general term used to describe Jews of Iberian descent and the areas of North Africa and the Middle East.

Seuda Shelishit – The third meal. There is a halakhic requirement to have three meals over the course of Shabbat. One at night, one in the morning, and this, the third meal, in the afternoon.

Shema – A group of three texts that are biblically ordained to be said twice daily – the mitzva of *Keriat Shema*. The *Shema* is said as part of the morning and evening services. The *Shema* consists of *Devarim* 6:4–9; *Devarim* 11:13–21; and *Bemidbar* 15:37–41. The first of those paragraphs is also said as a separate mitzva in bed before sleep. This is called *Keriat Shema al Hamita*.

Shaḥarit – The name of the morning prayer service. Derives from the word *shaḥar* or morning.

Shekhina – The Divine Presence of God. A feminine form that derives from the word for "dwelling."

Shemoneh Esreh – Literally, eighteen. The name of the *Amida* prayer that is recited during the week, so called because it originally had eighteen blessings.

Tallit – Four-cornered garment with *tzitzit* on each corner. A *tallit katan* (small *tallit*) is usually worn underneath one's clothes, while a *tallit gadol* is a four-cornered prayer shawl with *tzitzit* on each corner worn during prayers services, normally *Shaḥarit*.

Talmud – The compendium of the Oral Law completed in sixth-century Babylonia and in the land of Israel; it includes the Mishna and the Gemara.

Tanakh – The twenty-four books of the canon of the Hebrew Bible: the Five Books of Moses, the books of the prophets and the other holy books known as "Writings," such as Proverbs, Psalms, etc.

Tefillin – Leather boxes containing scrolls of parchment with sections from the Torah (*Shemot* 13:1–10; *Shemot* 13:11–16; *Devarim* 6:4–9; and *Devarim* 11:13–21). These are worn on the arm and head, during the weekday morning prayer service.

Tehillim – The biblical book of Psalms.

◂ Tetragrammaton

Tetragrammaton – The four-letter name of God whose real pronunciation is never uttered and is read as *Adonai* instead.

Torah – Specifically the Five Books of Moses but is also often used more broadly to incorporate the entire corpus of religious writing, thought and practice. For example, living a life of Torah.

Tzitzit – Ritual tassels tied around each corner of a four-cornered garment, known as a *tallit* or *tallit katan*. These are worn in fulfillment of the biblical command to "make tassels on the corners of your garments" (*Bemidbar* 15:37).

Written Law – A reference in particular to the laws of the Torah incorporating the Five Books of Moses that were revealed at Sinai but can include laws found in the rest of the biblical canon as well.

Yaakov – The biblical Patriarch Jacob.

Yehoshua – The biblical leader Joshua.

Yeshivot – Academies of religious learning. Singular is *yeshiva*.

Yitzḥak – The biblical Patriarch Isaac.

Yom HaAtzma'ut – Israel Independence Day.

Yom Tov – Literally, good day. The name given to any of the biblical holy days such as Sukkot, Pesaḥ, and the like.

z"l (ז"ל) – Abbreviation for *zikhro livrakha,* may his memory be for a blessing, added to the name of someone who is deceased.

BOOKS AND AUTHORS REFERENCED

Aaron, Rabbi David, b. 1957, Jerusalem. Founder of Isralight and the post-high-school Yeshivat Orayta, Rabbi Aaron writes extensively on issues related to Jewish spirituality, including a book about prayer called *Tefillah Training.*

Aboab, Rabbi Isaac (*Menorat HaMaor*), fourteenth century, Spain. The name comes from the title of his very influential and popular work on the beauty of Jewish life and ethics. He also wrote a commentary on the Siddur.

Abudarham, Rabbi David, c. 1340, Spain. He wrote an important commentary on the siddur (*Abudarham HaShalem*) which includes comments and laws gathered from the Geonim, the Jerusalem and Babylonian Talmuds in addition to including customs and laws prevalent in his native Spain.

Aḥad HaAm – Asher Zvi Hirsch Ginsberg (1856–1927), Russia. Hebrew essayist known by his pen name *Aḥad Ha'am* (lit. *one of the people, Bereshit* 26:10). He was one of the foremost Zionist thinkers and considered the founder of cultural Zionism.

Albo, Rabbi Yosef, 1380–1444, Spain. Jewish philosopher most known for his work on the fundamentals of Jewish belief, *Sefer HaIkarim.*

Alsheikh – Rav Moshe Alsheikh HaKadosh, c. 1508–1600, Safed. He was a student of Rav Yosef Karo and is best known for his popular homiletic commentaries on Tanakh, some of which have been translated.

Angel, Rabbi Marc, b. 1945. Rabbi and communal leader in the U.S.A. Author of more than a dozen books, especially about Sephardic life,

◂ and the

and the founder of the Institute for Jewish Ideas and Ideals. He is the author of an article called "Thoughts on Prayer," which appears in *Seeking Good, Speaking Peace,* Angel, H. ed. Ktav Publishing House, Hoboken, 1994.

Arama, Rabbi Yitzḥak, 1420–1494, Spain. He is especially known for his philosophical commentary on the Torah, *Akeidat Yitzḥak,* parts of which have been translated.

Ari *z"l* – Rabbi Isaac ben Solomon Luria, 1534–1572, Tzefat. Known simply as the Ari (the Lion) or the Arizal (a contraction of Ari *z"l*), he was a teacher and mystic who founded the school known as the Lurianic Kabbala. He had a profound influence through his disciples on much of Jewish life including the siddur.

Arukh HaShulḥan – An influential halakhic work composed by Rabbi Yeḥiel Michel Epstein, 1829–1908, Lithuania.

Asevilli, Rabbi Yom Tov ben Avraham (Ritva), 1250–1330, Spain. His last name is a derivation of the town he came from, Seville. A leading student of Rashba and Ra'ah, he wrote a concise but oft-cited commentary on the Torah.

Aviner, Rav Shlomo Ḥayyim HaKohen, b. 1943. French-born Israeli rabbi who is one of the leaders of the Religious Zionist community. He has written numerous works on a wide variety of subjects including a three-volume commentary on the Siddur.

Avoda Zara – A tractate of the Talmud.

Ba'al Shem Tov – Rabbi Yisrael ben Eliezer, 1698–1760, Ukraine. The founder of Hasidism.

Baḥ – A contraction of the name of a commentary on the *Tur* called *Bayit Ḥadash* by Rabbi Joel Sirkes, 1561–1640, Eastern Europe.

Barukh SheAmar – Commentary on the siddur by Barukh HaLevi Epstein, 1860–1941, Lithuania, son of the *Arukh HaShulḥan.*

Bava Batra – Tractate of the Talmud.

Beit Yosef – See *Shulḥan Arukh.*

◂ *Beitza*

Beitza – Tractate of the Talmud.

Bemidbar – The biblical book of Numbers.

Benet, Rabbi Mordekhai ben Avraham, 1753–1829, scholar and Chief Rabbi of Moravia.

Berakhot – Tractate of the Talmud.

Bereshit – The biblical book of Genesis.

Bereshit Raba – A collection of *midrashim* or homiletic teachings on the book of *Bereshit* compiled around the sixth century CE from the Amoraic period.

Da'at Mikra – A multivolume contemporary commentary on the entire Bible that combines a traditional outlook with modern research.

Da'at Soferim – See Rabbi Ḥayyim Dov Rabinowitz.

Danzig, Rabbi Avraham (Ḥayyei Adam), 1748–1820, Poland. A digest of the *Oraḥ Ḥayyim* section of the *Shulḥan Arukh* intended for the informed layman as opposed to the scholar. Often cited by the *Mishna Berura,* it became popular for its conciseness and scholarship.

Devarim – The biblical book of Deuteronomy.

Divrei HaYamim – The biblical book of Chronicles.

Divrei Kehillot – An eighteenth-century collection of customs regarding prayer in Frankfurt am Main by Solomon Zalman Geiger.

Dover Shalom – Printed in 1910, a collection of the teachings of Rabbi Shalom Roke'aḥ (1779–1855), the founder of the dynasty of Belz Hasidim.

Eidels, Rabbi Shmuel (Maharsha), 1555–1631, Poland. Communal rabbi who wrote an important commentary on the Talmud, Rashi and Tosafot, including a commentary on the aggadic portions of the Talmud.

Elimelekh of Lizhensk – See Weisblum, Rabbi Elimelekh of Lizhensk.

Etz Yosef – Rabbi Ḥanokh Zundel ben Yosef, d. 1859, Poland. Wrote this commentary on the Siddur, in addition to numerous other commentaries on collections of Midrash and Aggada. Found in the collection *Otzar HaTefillot.*

Gombiner, Rabbi Avraham (Magen Avraham), c. 1635–1682, Poland. He is known by the name of his indispensable commentary to the *Shulḥan Arukh.*

Gra – See Vilna Gaon.

Greenberg, Blu, b. 1936, U.S.A. A writer and speaker about modern Judaism especially relating to women's issues.

Ḥafetz Ḥayyim – See Rabbi Yisrael Meir HaKohen Kagan.

Hagahot Maimoniyot – Commentary on the Rambam's *Mishna Torah* by Rabbi Meir ben Yekutiel HaKohen, who died in a massacre in 1298 in Germany.

Ḥagiga – Tractate of the Talmud.

HaManhig – A halakhic work from the twelfth century written by Rabbi Avraham ben Natan HaYarḥi of Provence.

Ḥarlap, Rabbi Yaakov, 1882–1951, Jerusalem. A student of Rav Avraham Yitzḥak Kook who assumed leadership of Rav Kook's yeshiva upon the latter's death. Among his many writings is a collection called *Mei Marom* which includes a commentary on the siddur.

Ḥatam Sofer – Rabbi Moshe Sofer, 1762–1839, Germany. Known by his main work, the *Ḥatam Sofer,* he was leader of European Orthodoxy, and its opposition to the Reform movement.

Hertz, Rabbi Joseph, 1872–1946, England. Chief Rabbi of the United Hebrew Congregations of the British Empire. Wrote a commentary on the Siddur called *The Authorised Daily Prayer Book.*

Ḥida – Acronym for Rabbi Ḥayyim Yosef David Azulai, 1724–1806. Born in Jerusalem he traveled extensively across Europe as an emissary of the small community in Israel. He was a most prolific writer, writing tens of volumes covering numerous areas of Jewish law and life including a siddur which he edited and arranged.

Ḥinukh – See *Sefer HaḤinukh.*

Hirsch, Rabbi Shimshon Raphael, 1808–1888, Germany. Leader of Orthodox German Jewry, best known for his philosophy of *Torah im*

◂ *Derekh Eretz*

Derekh Eretz. He wrote numerous works including commentaries on the Torah, *Tehillim* and the Siddur.

Hoshea – The biblical book of Hosea.

Ḥovot HaLevavot – (*Duties of the Heart*) is a book of Jewish philosophy written by Baḥya ibn Pakuda, 1050–1120, Spain.

Ibn Ezra – Rabbi Avraham ibn Ezra, 1089–1164, Spain. A poet, astronomer, and philosopher best known for his commentaries on Tanakh including *Tehillim*.

Isserles, Rabbi Moshe (Rema), 1520–1572, Poland. Leading rabbi, Talmudist and philosopher, known especially as the authoritative Ashkenazic halakhic commentator on the *Shulḥan Arukh*.

Jacobson, Rabbi Yissakhar, 1901–1972, Israel. A prominent teacher, lecturer and academic he is known primarily for a multi-volume work on the siddur which contains a collection of commentaries and notes on the history and content of the prayers. Two of the volumes have been translated into English.

Kagan, Rabbi Yisrael Meir HaKohen (Ḥafetz Ḥayyim), 1838–1933, Lithuania. One of the leading Ashkenazic halakhic authorities of modern times and an ethicist known for his gossip-censuring work called the *Ḥafetz Ḥayyim*. His halakhic magnum opus is the *Mishna Berura* on that part of the *Shulḥan Arukh* dealing with everyday life including *tefilla*.

Kaminetzky, Rabbi Yaakov, 1891–1986, U.S.A. A European-born rabbinic scholar who went on to become the head of the Brooklyn yeshiva Torah Vadaat and a communal leader.

Kedushat Levi – A book of biblical commentary and homilies by Rabbi Levi Yitzḥak of Berditchev, 1740–1809, Ukraine, one of the early leaders of Hasidism.

Kiddushin – A tractate of the Talmud.

Kimḥi, Rabbi David (Radak), 1160–1235, Provence. Rabbinic authority, biblical commentator, philosopher and grammarian.

◂ *Kli Yakar*

Kli Yakar – Commentary on the Torah by Rabbi Shlomo Ephraim ben Aaron Luntschitz, 1550–1619, Eastern Europe.

Kol Bo – (*Everything Is In It*). A book of halakha from about the thirteenth or fourteenth century of disputed authorship.

Kook, Rabbi Avraham Yitzḥak HaKohen, 1865–1935. First Ashkenazic Chief Rabbi of British Mandatory Palestine. In addition to being a halakhic authority and communal leader, he was a profound thinker whose influence on the Religious Zionist community continues today through his writings. He wrote a commentary on the Siddur called *Olat Re'iya*.

Kotzker – See Morgensztern.

Lamm, Rabbi Norman, b. 1927, New York. A renowned rabbinic and communal leader and scholar who also served as president of Yeshiva University.

Leibowitz, Nechama, 1905–1997, Jerusalem. Nechama, as she was called by her students, revolutionized the way that Tanakh was studied. Her weekly study pages and her books on studies of the weekly *parasha* earned her an international reputation. In her classes, she frequently would point to the meaning of words and phrases in the Siddur.

Levush – Known also as *Levush Malkhut* (*Robes of Royalty*). A halakhic work emphasizing the customs of Eastern Europe by Rabbi Mordekhai ben Avraham Joffe (1530–1612, Posen) who was a student of the Rema.

Magen Avraham – See Rabbi Avraham Gombiner.

Maggid of Mezeritch – Rabbi Dov Ber of Mezeritch, d. 1772. One of the leading disciples of the Ba'al Shem Tov.

Maharal – Rabbi Yehuda Loew ben Betzalel, c. 1520–1609. Known as the Maharal (Moreinu HaRav Loew) of Prague. Leading communal rabbi, scholar and mystic. Author of over a dozen works.

Maharam of Rothenburg – Rabbi Meir of Rothenburg (Germany), 1215–1305. One of the *Tosafot*, a medieval halakhist and poet.

Mahari Bruna – Rabbi Israel Bruna (Mahari is an acronym for "our teacher, Rabbi Israel"), 1400–1480, Germany. A major rabbinic authority of his time who is often cited by the Rema.

Maharsha – See Rabbi Shmuel Eidels.

Maḥzor Vitry – An important collection of religious practices and response compiled by Simḥa ben Shmuel of Vitry, d. 1105, France.

Maimonides – see Rambam

Malbim – See Meir Leibush ben Yeḥiel Mikhel Wisser.

Mateh Efraim – Halakhic work on the laws from Rosh HaShana to Yom Kippur by Rabbi Zalman Efraim Margulies, 1762–1828, Galicia.

Me'am Loez – A commentary on the Torah in Ladino begun by Rabbi Yaakov Khuli in 1730; others subsequently adopted his style and completed the work on all of Tanakh. The commentary draws heavily from Midrash and Talmud and went through periods of being immensely popular. The sections on Torah have been translated.

Mecklenburg, Rabbi Yaakov Tzvi, 1785–1865, Prussia. A communal leader, he wrote a commentary on the Siddur in addition to a famous commentary on the Torah, *HaKtav VeHaKabbala*.

Meiri, Rabbi Menaḥem, 1249–1315, Provence. In addition to his interest in philosophy, he is known especially for his monumental work on the Talmud which was only revived in modern times. He also wrote commentaries on *Mishlei* and *Tehillim*.

Mekhilta – Also known as the *Mekhilta* of Rabbi Yishmael. A compilation of *midrashim*, mostly but not exclusively on the halakhic portions of the book of *Shemot*. It is one of the earliest collections from the Tannaitic period, commonly assumed to be dated around the third century.

Melakhim – The biblical book of Kings.

Melakhim Beit – The second book of the biblical book of Kings.

Menaḥem Tziyon – (*Comforter of Zion* – a play on the author's name). A commentary on Torah, *Tehillim*, and holy days written by Rabbi Menachem Ben-Zion Zaks a prominent rabbinic figure in Chicago in the twentieth century.

◂ *Menorat*

Menorat HaMaor – See Rabbi Isaac Aboab.

Metzudot – A popular commentary on *Nevi'im* and *Ketuvim* begun by Rabbi David Altschuler (1687–1769, Galicia) and completed by his son Yeḥiel. His son divided the commentary into two parts called *Metzudat David* and *Metzudat Tziyon*. His father sought to write a commentary that would be more accessible to the masses who had a more difficult time understanding Rashi and Biblical Hebrew.

Midrash Shoḥer Tov – A collection of *midrashim* on *Tehillim*, compiled in Israel around the tenth and eleventh centuries.

Mishna – The collection of oral laws and traditions redacted in approximately 200 CE, which is the basis for discussions in the Gemara.

Mishna Berura – see Ḥafetz Ḥayyim.

Modena, Rabbi Leon, or Yehuda Aryeh MiModena, 1571–1648, Italy. A controversial personality, he wrote numerous works including responsa, anti-Christian polemics, a work on ethics and a collection of poetry.

Morgensztern, Rabbi Menaḥem Mendel (Kotzker Rebbe), 1787–1859, Poland. Better known as the Kotzker Rebbe, he was a student of Rav Simḥa Bunim and is considered a spiritual founder of Ger Hasidism.

Moshe Leib of Sassov, 1745–1807, Eastern Europe. A disciple of the Maggid of Mezeritch who went on to establish his own Ḥassidic dynasty.

Munk, Rabbi Elie, 1900–1981, Paris and Germany. Communal rabbi and author who wrote a popular two-volume commentary on the Siddur called *The World of Prayer*. See Bibliography.

Nahmanides – see Ramban

Noheg KeTzon Yosef – Laws and customs especially of the Jewish community of Frankfurt am Main, by Rabbi Yosef Yospe Kosman, d. 1758.

Ohel Yaakov – Collection of homilies on the Torah by Rabbi Yaakov ben Wolf Kranz, commonly known as the Maggid of Dubno, a famous preacher (*maggid*), 1741–1804, Eastern Europe.

◂ *Or Zarua*

Or Zarua – A halakhic work written by Rabbi Yitzḥak ben Moshe of Vienna, 1180–1250.

Pesaḥim – A tractate of the Talmud.

Petura DeAbba – A work on the customs of the Ari *z"l* by Rabbi Uri Stralisker, based on the *Shemona She'arim* of Rabbi Ḥayyim Vital (1905).

Pirkei DeRabbi Eliezer – A collection of *midrashim* on the Torah compiled sometime around the middle of the eighth century.

Rabbeinu Baḥye – Rabbi Baḥye ben Asher ibn Halawa, 1255–1340, author of an extensive commentary on the Torah.

Rabbeinu Tam – Yaakov ben Meir, 1100–1171, France. A grandson of Rashi, Rabbeinu Tam was one of the leading Tosafists and halakhists of his day.

Rabbeinu Yona – See Yona ben Avraham Gerondi.

Rabbi Yehuda HeḤasid (the Pious) – Rabbi Yehuda ben Shmuel of Regensburg, 1140–1217, Germany. Was the head *Ḥasidei Ashkenaz*, a movement of German mystics who emphasized specific moral and pious conduct many of which are described in his *Sefer Ḥasidim* (*The Book of the Pious*).

Rabinowitz, Rabbi Ḥayyim Dov (Da'at Soferim), 1909–2001, Lithuania, Tel Aviv. The *Da'at Soferim* is a multivolume commentary on all of Tanakh that distinguishes itself for the way in which it addresses difficult issues from a very traditionalist perspective as well as emphasizing the hand of God in human history.

Rabinowitz, Rav Tzaddok HaKohen of Lublin, 1823–1900, Poland. A famous child prodigy who went on to become a leading Hasidic thinker in halakha, Hasidism, Kabbala, and ethics.

Radak – See Rabbi David Kimḥi.

Rambam – Rabbi Moshe ben Maimon, also known as Maimonides, 1135–1204, Spain and Egypt. One of the pivotal figures in Jewish intellectual history. His halakhic code, *Mishneh Torah*, remains a foundation for Jewish law today.

Ramban – Rabbi Moshe ben Naḥman, also known as Nahmanides, 1194–1270, Spain, Israel. A leading scholar, philosopher, doctor, kabbalist who is best known for his commentaries on the Torah and Talmud.

Rashba – Rabbi Shlomo ben Aderet, 1235–1310, Spain. Known for his thousands of halakhic responsa and a commentary on the Talmud.

Rashi – Rabbi Shlomo Yitzḥaki, 1040–1104, France. One of the most influential intellectual giants in Jewish life. Among his works in addition to his extensive commentaries on almost all of Tanakh and Talmud there is a *Siddur Rashi* compiled by one of his students.

Rav Natronai Gaon – Head of the academy in Sura Babylonia in the second half of the ninth century.

Rav Tzaddok – See Rabinowitz, Rav Tzaddok HaKohen of Lublin.

Rema – See Isserles, Rabbi Moshe.

Rif – Acronym for Rabbi Yitzḥak Alfasi, 1013–1103, Morocco. He is best known as the author of the first basic work in halakhic literature which extracts the legal rulings from the Talmud.

Rinat Ḥayyim – A commentary on the siddur by Rabbi Chaim Friedlander, 1923–1986, *mashgiaḥ* (spiritual adviser) of the Ponevezh Yeshiva in Benei Berak, Israel.

Riskin, Rabbi Shlomo, b. 1940, Israel. A prominent activist rabbi in New York City who made *aliya* to Israel with many of his congregants and became founding Chief Rabbi of Efrat as well as founder and chancellor of Ohr Torah Institutions, a series of schools, as well as advanced yeshivot and seminaries.

Ritva – See Asevilli, Rabbi Yom Tov ben Avraham.

Roke'aḥ – Rabbi Elazar of Worms, 1176–1238, Germany. Wrote a number of works but best known for his book *HaRoke'aḥ,* on Jewish ethics and halakha.

Rosh HaShana – A tractate of the Talmud.

Sa'adia Gaon, Rav, c. 882–942, Egypt. Rabbi, philosopher and biblical commentator. One of the first rabbinic figures to write in Arabic and to integrate elements of Greek philosophy with Judaism. Also wrote a copy of the text of the Siddur including his own poetry called *Siddur Rav Sa'adia Gaon.*

Sacks, Rabbi Lord Jonathan, b. 1948. Former Chief Rabbi of the United Hebrew Congregations of the Commonwealth. A renowned author of philosophical and popular writings including a commentary on the Siddur published by Koren Publishers, Jerusalem.

Salanter, Rabbi Yisrael, also known as Yisroel ben Ze'ev Wolf Lipkin, 1810–1883, Lithuania. He was the father of the Musar (ethics) movement and a famed Rosh Yeshiva and Talmudist.

Sanhedrin – A tractate of the Talmud.

Schwab, Rabbi Shimon, 1908–1995. A German-born rabbi who became the communal leader of the German community in Washington Heights in New York City. In addition to numerous books and articles published in his lifetime, a collection of his lectures on prayer were published posthumously, called *Rav Schwab on Prayer.*

Seder Rav Amram Gaon – Liturgical work by Rav Amram Gaon who was the head of the Talmudic academy in Sura Babylonia in the ninth century. The work is essentially a siddur which was written as a responsum to the Jewish community of Spain and left an indelible mark on liturgical tradition.

Sefat Emet – Yehuda Aryeh Leib Alter, 1847–1905, Poland. He was the second rebbe of the dynasty of Gerer Hasidim. He composed commentaries on a number of tractates on the Talmud but is known more widely for his homilies on the Torah, collectively called the *Sefat Emet.*

Sefer HaḤinukh – (*Book of Education*) was written anonymously in the fourteenth century. It is a systematic discussion of the 613 commandments in the Torah based on Maimonides' enumeration and includes a rationale for each commandment as well as a description of its basic laws.

Sefer HaItim – A book by Rav Yehuda ben Barzilai of Barcelona, eleventh to twelfth century, Spain. He is best known for this halakhic work,

◂ much of

much of which is on the laws of Shabbat, but much of which was also lost.

Sefer Ḥaredim – A book by Rabbi Elazar ben Moshe Azikri, 1533–1600, Safed. A leading kabbalist and poet, known both for his work on ethics as well being the author of the famous poem *Yedid Nefesh*.

Sefer Ḥasidim – See Rabbi Yehuda HeḤasid.

Seforno – Rabbi Ovadia ben Yaakov, 1475–1550, Italy. A rabbi, philosopher, and medical doctor best known for his biblical commentaries.

Shabbat – A tractate of the Talmud.

Sharansky, Natan, b. 1948. He was known for years as a Soviet refusenik who spent more than nine years in a Soviet prison for his advocacy for human rights and for his desire to make *aliya*. He was subsequently released and has gone on to become a politician, cabinet member, and human rights activist in Israel. His book, *Fear No Evil,* describes his experiences in prison.

Shemot – The biblical book Exodus.

Shevuot – A tractate of the Talmud.

Shibbolei HaLeket (*Ears of Gleaning*) – A systematic compilation of halakhic rules primarily governing prayer and holy days by Zedekiah ben Abraham Anaw, 1210–ca. 1280, Rome.

Shir HaShirim – The biblical book Song of Songs.

Shela – Acronym for Rabbi Yeshayahu HaLevi Horowitz, also known as the *Shela HaKodesh* (The Holy Shela), 1565–1630, Europe and Israel. He was Rabbi of Prague and Frankfurt but is especially known for his writings regarding ritual, ethics and mysticism through which he had a strong influence on the early Hasidic movement.

Shmuel (Shmelke HaLevi) of Nikolsburg – See Horowitz, Rabbi Shmuel (Shmelke HaLevi) of Nikolsburg.

Shmuel I, II – The biblical book Samuel I and II.

Shneur Zalman of Liadi, 1745–1812. The first Lubavitcher rebbe. He is called the Ba'al HaTanya after the name of his famous work on Hasidic philosophy titled *Tanya* which has been translated.

Shoḥer Tov – See *Midrash Shoḥer Tov*.

Shulḥan Arukh – The authoritative code of law written by Rabbi Yosef Karo, 1488–1575, Safed. He first wrote an extensive commentary on the *Tur* called the *Beit Yosef*, and he also authored a commentary on Rambam's *Mishneh Torah* entitled the *Kesef Mishneh*. The core of his rulings are accepted by all, while the work also includes traditions and customs unique to Sephardic communities.

Simḥa Bunim of Peshischa, Rabbi, 1765–1827, Poland. A businessman and pharmacist but most especially a major Hasidic rebbe who was a student of the Ḥozeh of Lublin and the Yid HaKadosh. Among his students were some of the leaders of Hasidism of the next generation including the Kotzker, the Gerer and the Alexander rebbes.

Soloveitchik, Rabbi Joseph B., 1903–1993. A descendant of the famous Lithuanian Soloveitchik dynasty, he was the leading figure in modern Orthodox Jewish life in America in the twentieth century. His interpretations of *tefilla* are found throughout his writings and a representative compendium was published by Koren Publishers, Jerusalem.

Sota – A tractate of the Talmud.

Steinsaltz, Rabbi Adin, b. 1937, Jerusalem. One of the leading Jewish personalities in modern times known especially for his Hebrew translation and commentary on the Talmud which is now published in English by Koren Publishers, Jerusalem.

Ta'anit – A tractate of the Talmud.

Tamid – A tractate of the Talmud. Also the name of a daily sacrifice offered in the Temple.

Tanḥuma – A collection of *midrashim* on the Torah dating back to fifth-century Israel but consisting of later additions as well.

Tanna Devei Eliyahu – A collection of unique *midrashim* on Tanakh whose time of redaction is not precisely known, although it is mentioned in the Talmud.

◂ *Tehillot*

Tehillot HaShem – Rabbi Eliyahu ben Avraham Shlomo HaKohen HaItamari, 1659–c. 1729, Turkey. This is a commentary on *Tehillim* that the author wrote in addition to tens of other books, including a popular work on *musar* called *Shevet Musar.*

Tikkunei Zohar – Part of the *Zohar* literature, the foundational text of the mystical Kabbala.

Torah Temima – A commentary on the Torah which seeks to reconcile the Oral and Written Law. See *Barukh SheAmar.*

Tosafot. Not a single author but a collection of commentaries written primarily on the Talmud during the twelfth and thirteenth centuries in Western Europe. Some of these comments or glosses have been incorporated into the standard page of Talmud opposite Rashi's commentary, while others exist as independent collections.

Tur – See Rabbi Yaakov ben Asher.

Twerski, Rabbi Abraham Joshua, b. 1930. An American scion of the Chernobyl Hasidic dynasty, and a psychiatrist specializing in substance abuse. Has written dozens of books, a number of which focus on *tefilla.*

Vayikra – The biblical book Leviticus.

Vidal, Rabbi Ḥayyim, Israel. Author of *Sefatai Tiftaḥ,* a book about the *Shemoneh Esreh* published in 2011.

Vilna Gaon – Rabbi Eliyahu ben Shlomo, 1720–1797, Lithuania. One of the foremost leaders of non-Hasidic Jewry who wrote numerous commentaries especially on *Shulḥan Arukh* and the Talmud. A siddur reflecting his views was also published and known as *Siddur HaGra.* Also sometimes referred to as the Gra, an acronym for the Gaon Rabbi Eliyahu.

Weisblum, Rabbi Elimelekh of Lizhensk, 1717–1787, Galicia. One of the founders of the Hasidic movement. He was a student of the Maggid of Mezeritch and thus became a leader of the third generation of Hasidic dynasties together with his brother Rabbi Zushya.

Wiesel, Elie, b. 1928 in Romania. Nobel Prize winner and renowned writer on the Holocaust. He delivered a paper called "Prayer and Modern Man" published in *Prayer in Judaism: Continuity and Change* (Cohn, G.H. and Fish, H. eds., NJ: Jason Aronson, 1996).

Wisser, Meir Leibush ben Yeḥiel Mikhel (Malbim), 1809–1879, Russia. A communal rabbinic leader, he is best known for his unique commentary on Tanakh, some of which has been translated.

Wohlgemuth, Rabbi Isaiah, 1915–2008. European-born beloved teacher at the Maimonides High School in Boston where he taught a course on *Biur Tefilla*. His notes were subsequently published in a volume called *A Guide to Jewish Prayer*.

Ya'arot Devash – See Eybeschutz, Rabbi Yonatan.

Ya'avetz – See Emden, Rabbi Yaakov.

Yaakov ben Asher, Rabbi, c. 1269–1343, Germany and Spain. Known by the title of his work on Jewish law called the *Arba'a Turim* or simply the *Tur*, a predecessor and basis for the *Shulḥan Arukh* as well as a commentary on the Torah called the *Ba'al Turim*.

Yalkut Shimoni – A collection of *midrashim* on all of *Tanakh*, compiled by Rabbi Shimon HaDarshan of Frankfurt in the thirteenth century, containing many older *midrashim* which are not found in other collections.

Yeḥezkel – The biblical book Ezekiel.

Yerushalmi – The shortened name of the Talmud Yerushalmi or the Jerusalem Talmud which is a parallel but different text to the Babylonian Talmud, compiled in Israel during the fourth and fifth centuries. Also known as the Palestinian Talmud.

Yesod Shoresh VaAvoda (*The Foundation and Root of [Divine] Service*) – A work by Rabbi Alexander Ziskind, d. 1794, Lithuania, heavily influenced by Kabbala and the writings of the Ari. A manual for increasing one's devotion in the service of God in prayer, in one's interpersonal relations and in one's relationship with God.

Yevamot – A tractate of the Talmud.

Yeshayahu – The biblical book Isaiah.

◂ *Yismaḥ*

Yismaḥ Moshe – A commentary on the *Tanakh* by Rabbi Moshe Teitelbaum, 1758–1841, who was instrumental in bringing Hasidism to Hungary.

Yoma – A tractate of the Talmud.

Zevaḥim – A tractate of the Talmud.

Zohar – The foundational text of Kabbala, the Jewish mystical tradition.

Koren Tanakh Alef-Beit Chart © NJOP

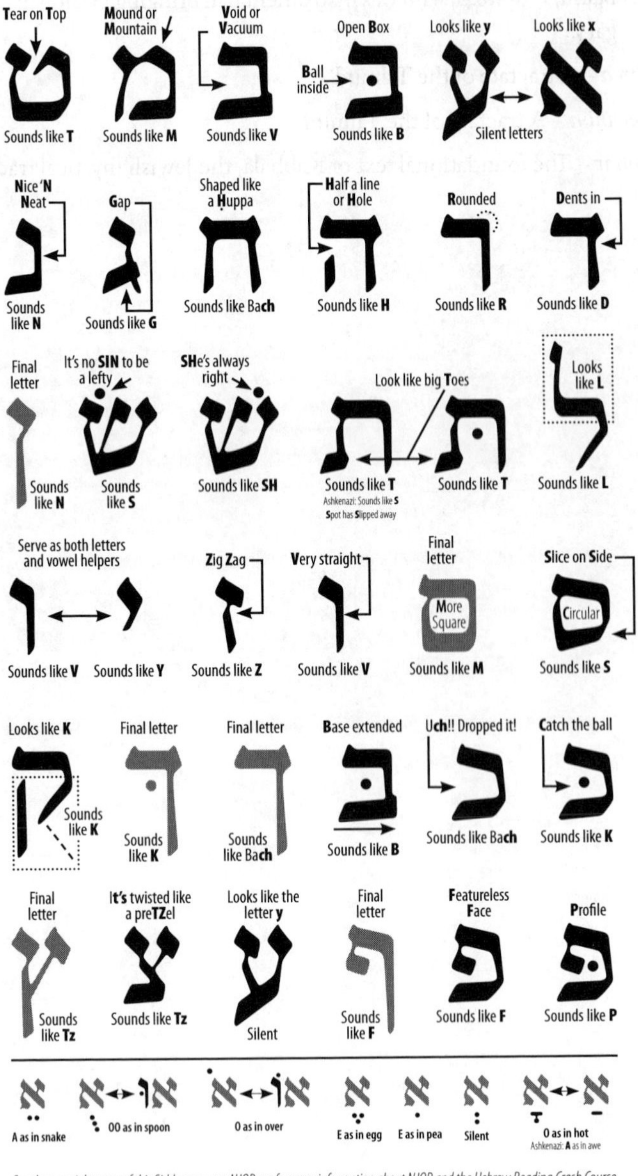

See the copyright page of this Siddur or www.NJOP.org for more information about NJOP and the Hebrew Reading Crash Course.

Koren Siddur Alef-Beit Chart © NJOP

See the copyright page of this Siddur or www.NJOP.org for more information about NJOP and the Hebrew Reading Crash Course.

SHEMA

The following verse should be said aloud, while covering the eyes with the right hand:

Shema Yisrael, Adonai Eloheinu, Adonai Eḥad.

Quietly: Barukh shem kevod malkhuto le-olam va-ed.

Ve-ahavta et Adonai Elohekha, bekhol levavekha uvekhol nafshekha uvekhol me-odekha. Vehayu hadevarim ha-eleh, asher anokhi metzavekha hayom, al levavekha. Veshinantam levanekha, vedibarta bam, beshivtekha beveitekha, uv-lekhtekha vaderekh, uv-shokhbekha uvkumekha. Uk-shartam le-ot al yadekha, vehayu letotafot bein einekha. Ukh-tavtam, al mezuzot beitekha uvisharekha.

Vehaya im shamo-a tishme-u el mitzvotai asher anokhi metzaveh etkhem hayom, le-ahava et Adonai Eloheikhem ul-ovdo, bekhol levavkhem uvekhol nafshekhem. Venatati metar artzekhem be-ito, yoreh umalkosh, veasafta deganekha, vetiroshekha veyitzharekha. Venatati eisev besadekha livhemtekha, ve-akhalta vesavaata. Hishameru lakhem pen yifteh levavkhem, vesartem va-avadetem elohim aḥeirim, vehishtaḥavitem lahem. Veḥara af Adonai bakhem, ve-atzar et hashamayim, velo yiheyeh matar, veha-adama lo titein et yevula, va-avadetem meheira me-al ha-aretz hatova asher Adonai noten lakhem. Vesamtem et devarai eleh al levavkhem ve-al nafshekhem, uk-shartem otam le-ot al yedkhem, vehayu letotafot bein eineikhem. Velimadetem otam et beneikhem ledaber bam, beshivtekha beveitekha, uvelekhtekha vaderekh uv-shokhbekha uv-kumekha. Ukhtavtam, al mezuzot beitekha uvisharekha. Lema-an yirbu yemeikhem vimei veneikhem al ha-adama asher nishba Adonai la-avoteikhem latet lahem, kimei hashamayim al ha-aretz.

Vayomer Adonai el Mosheh leimor. Daber el Benei Yisrael ve-amarta aleihem, ve-asu lahem tzitzit al kanfei vigdeihem ledorotam, venatenu al tzitzit hakanaf petil tekhelet. Vehaya lakhem letzitzit, ur-item oto uzkhartem et kol mitzvot Adonai va-asitem otam, velo taturu akharei levavkhem, ve-akharei eineikhem, asher atem zonim akhareihem. Lema-an tizkeru va-asitem et kol mitzvotai, vihyitem kedoshim leloheikhem. Ani Adonai Eloheikhem, asher hotzeiti etkhem me-eretz Mitzrayim, lihyot lakhem l'Elohim, Ani Adonai Eloheikhem.

Emet

RABBIS' KADDISH

Mourner: Yitgadal ve-yitkadash shemeh raba. (*Cong:* Amen)
Be-alema di vera khir'uteh, ve-yamlikh malkhuteh,
be-ḥayyeikhon, uv-yomeikhon,
uv-ḥayyei de-khol beit Yisrael,
ba-agala uvi-zman kariv,
ve-imru Amen. (*Cong:* Amen)

All: Yeheh shemeh raba mevarakh le'alam ul-alemei alemaya.

Mourner: Yitbarakh ve-yishtabaḥ ve-yitpa'ar ve-yitromam ve-yitnaseh
ve-yit-hadar ve-yit'aleh ve-yit-hallal
shemeh dekudsha, berikh hu. (*Cong:* Berikh hu)
Le-ela min kol birkhata
/*Between Rosh HaShana & Yom Kippur:* Le-ela le-ela mi-kol birkhata/
ve-shirata, tushbeḥata ve-neḥemata,
da-amiran be-alema,
ve-imru, Amen. (*Cong:* Amen)

Al Yisrael, ve-al rabanan,
ve-al talmideihon, ve-al kol talmidei talmideihon,
ve-al kol man de-asekin be-oraita
di be-atra (*In Israel:* kadisha) ha-dein ve-di be-khol atar
va-atar, yeheh lehon ul-khon shelama raba,
ḥina ve-ḥisda, ve-raḥamei,
ve-ḥayyei arikhei, um-zonei re-viḥei,
u-furkana min kodam avuhon di vish-maya,
ve-imru Amen. (*Cong:* Amen)

Yeheh shelama raba min shemaya
ve-ḥayyim (tovim) aleinu ve-al kol Yisrael,
ve-imru Amen. (*Cong:* Amen)

Bow, take three steps back, as if taking leave of the Divine Presence, then bow, first left, then right, then center, while saying:
Oseh shalom/*Between Rosh HaShana & Yom Kippur:* ha-shalom/
bim-romav,
hu ya'aseh ve-raḥamav shalom aleinu, ve-al kol Yisrael,
ve-imru Amen. (*Cong:* Amen)

FULL KADDISH

Leader: יִתְגַּדַּל Magnified and sanctified
may His great name be,
in the world He created by His will.
May He establish His kingdom
in your lifetime and in your days,
and in the lifetime of all the house of Israel,
swiftly and soon –
and say: Amen.

All: May His great name be blessed for ever and all time.

Leader: Blessed and praised, glorified and exalted,
raised and honored, uplifted and lauded be
the name of the Holy One, blessed be He,
beyond any blessing,
song, praise and consolation
uttered in the world –
and say: Amen.

(*All:* In compassion and favor accept our prayer.)

May the prayers and pleas of all Israel
be accepted by their Father in heaven –
and say: Amen.

(*All:* May the name of the Lord be blessed from now and for ever.) *Ps. 113*

May there be great peace from heaven,
and life for us and all Israel –
and say: Amen.

(*All:* My help comes from the Lord, Maker of heaven and earth.) *Ps. 113*

Bow, take three steps back, as if taking leave of the Divine Presence, then bow, first left, then right, then center, while saying:

May He who makes peace in His high places,
make peace for us and all Israel –
and say: Amen.

קדיש שלם

ש״ץ: יִתְגַּדַּל וְיִתְקַדַּשׁ שְׁמֵהּ רַבָּא (קהל: אָמֵן)
בְּעָלְמָא דִּי בְרָא כִרְעוּתֵהּ
וְיַמְלִיךְ מַלְכוּתֵהּ
בְּחַיֵּיכוֹן וּבְיוֹמֵיכוֹן וּבְחַיֵּי דְכָל בֵּית יִשְׂרָאֵל
בַּעֲגָלָא וּבִזְמַן קָרִיב, וְאִמְרוּ אָמֵן. (קהל: אָמֵן)

קהל וש״ץ: יְהֵא שְׁמֵהּ רַבָּא מְבָרַךְ לְעָלַם וּלְעָלְמֵי עָלְמַיָּא.

ש״ץ: יִתְבָּרַךְ וְיִשְׁתַּבַּח וְיִתְפָּאַר וְיִתְרוֹמַם וְיִתְנַשֵּׂא
וְיִתְהַדָּר וְיִתְעַלֶּה וְיִתְהַלָּל
שְׁמֵהּ דְּקֻדְשָׁא בְּרִיךְ הוּא (קהל: בְּרִיךְ הוּא)
לְעֵלָּא מִן כָּל בִּרְכָתָא וְשִׁירָתָא, תֻּשְׁבְּחָתָא וְנֶחֱמָתָא
דַּאֲמִירָן בְּעָלְמָא, וְאִמְרוּ אָמֵן. (קהל: אָמֵן)
(קהל: קַבֵּל בְּרַחֲמִים וּבְרָצוֹן אֶת תְּפִלָּתֵנוּ)

תִּתְקַבַּל צְלוֹתְהוֹן וּבָעוּתְהוֹן דְּכָל יִשְׂרָאֵל
קֳדָם אֲבוּהוֹן דִּי בִשְׁמַיָּא, וְאִמְרוּ אָמֵן. (קהל: אָמֵן)
(קהל: יְהִי שֵׁם יהוה מְבֹרָךְ מֵעַתָּה וְעַד־עוֹלָם:) תהלים קיג

יְהֵא שְׁלָמָא רַבָּא מִן שְׁמַיָּא
וְחַיִּים, עָלֵינוּ וְעַל כָּל יִשְׂרָאֵל, וְאִמְרוּ אָמֵן. (קהל: אָמֵן)
(קהל: עֶזְרִי מֵעִם יהוה, עֹשֵׂה שָׁמַיִם וָאָרֶץ:) תהלים קיג

Bow, take three steps back, as if taking leave of the Divine Presence, then bow, first left, then right, then center, while saying:

עֹשֶׂה שָׁלוֹם בִּמְרוֹמָיו
הוּא יַעֲשֶׂה שָׁלוֹם
עָלֵינוּ וְעַל כָּל יִשְׂרָאֵל, וְאִמְרוּ אָמֵן. (קהל: אָמֵן)

MOURNER'S KADDISH

Mourner: Yitgadal ve-yitkadash shemeh raba. (*Cong:* Amen)
Be-alema di vera khir'uteh, ve-yamlikh malkhuteh,
be-ḥayyeikhon, uv-yomeikhon,
uv-ḥayyei de-khol beit Yisrael,
ba-agala uvi-zman kariv,
ve-imru Amen. (*Cong:* Amen)

All: Yeheh shemeh raba mevarakh le'alam ul-alemei alemaya.

Mourner: Yitbarakh ve-yishtabaḥ ve-yitpa'ar ve-yitromam ve-yitnaseh
ve-yit-hadar ve-yit'aleh ve-yit-hallal
shemeh dekudsha, berikh hu. (*Cong:* Berikh hu)
Le-ela min kol birkhata
/*Between Rosh HaShana & Yom Kippur:* Le-ela le-ela mi-kol birkhata/
ve-shirata, tushbeḥata ve-neḥemata,
da-amiran be-alema,
ve-imru, Amen. (*Cong:* Amen)

Yeheh shelama raba min shemaya
ve-ḥayyim aleinu ve-al kol Yisrael,
ve-imru Amen. (*Cong:* Amen)

Bow, take three steps back, as if taking leave of the Divine Presence, then bow, first left, then right, then center, while saying:

Oseh shalom/*Between Rosh HaShana & Yom Kippur:* ha-shalom/
bim-romav,
hu ya'aseh shalom aleinu, ve-al kol Yisrael,
ve-imru Amen. (*Cong:* Amen)

קורן ירושלים